Sociology

Sociology

Concepts and Applications in a Diverse World

Eighth Edition

Thomas J. Sullivan

New York   San Francisco   Boston   Upper Saddle River
London   Toronto   Sydney   Tokyo   Singapore   Madrid
Mexico City   Munich   Paris   Cape Town   Hong Kong   Montreal

CIP data on file at the Library of Congress

Editor-in-Chief: Karen Hanson
Series Editorial Assistant: Courtney Shea
Marketing Manager: Kelly May
Production Editor: Patrick Cash-Peterson
Editorial Production Service: Pre-Press PMG
Manufacturing Buyer: Debbie Rossi
Electronic Composition: Pre-Press PMG
Photo Researcher: Corey Kahn
Cover Administrator: Joel Gendron

For related titles and support materials, visit our online catalog at www.pearsonhighered.com.

Pearson Education LTD   Pearson Education Singapore, Pte. Ltd
Pearson Education Canada, Inc.   Pearson Education–Japan
Pearson Education Australia PTY, Limited   Pearson Education North Asia, Ltd., Hong Kong
Pearson Educación de Mexico, S.A. de C.V.   Pearson Education Malaysia, Pte. Ltd
Pearson Education Upper Saddle River, New Jersey

Allyn & Bacon
is an imprint of

10 9 8 7 6 5 4 3 2 1   RRD-OH 12 11 10 09 08

ISBN 13:   978-0-205-62806-3
ISBN 10:   0-205-62806-0

FOR NANCY

BRIEF CONTENTS

PART I   THE SOCIOLOGICAL PERSPECTIVE   1

Chapter 1   What Is Sociology?   2
Chapter 2   Culture, Society, and Diversity   33

PART II   THE INDIVIDUAL IN SOCIETY   62

Chapter 3   Socialization   63
Chapter 4   Groups and Organizations   88
Chapter 5   Deviance, Crime, and Social Control   117

PART III   STRATIFICATION AND SOCIAL INEQUALITY   145

Chapter 6   Social Stratification and Social Inequality   146
Chapter 7   Social Inequality: Race and Ethnicity   176
Chapter 8   Social Inequality: Gender   208

PART IV   SOCIAL INSTITUTIONS   237

Chapter 9   Family and Human Sexuality   238
Chapter 10   Health and Health-Care Institutions   272
Chapter 11   Religion   305
Chapter 12   Education and the Mass Media   331
Chapter 13   Political and Economic Institutions   359

PART V   HUMAN ECOLOGY AND SOCIAL CHANGE   391

Chapter 14   Human Ecology: Population, Community, and Environment   392
Chapter 15   Collective Behavior, Social Change, and Modernization 424

CONTENTS

Preface   xv
About the Author   xx

PART I The Sociological Perspective   1

CHAPTER 1

What Is Sociology?   2
   MYTHS & FACTS: About the Social World   3
What Is Sociology?   5
   The Sociological Perspective   5
   Sociology as a Science   8
   APPLYING SOCIOLOGY: Untangling Myths and Facts:
   Sociology and Common Sense   9
   The Social Sciences   10
Theoretical Perspectives in Sociology   10
   Theories and Hypotheses   11
   The Functionalist Perspective   12
   The Conflict Perspective   13
   The Interactionist Perspective   14
   Using the Theoretical Perspectives   15
Conducting Sociological Research   16
   Research Methods   16
   SOCIOLOGY OF MEDIA AND TECHNOLOGY: Applying
   the Sociological Perspectives: Mass Media, Global
   Communications and the Online World   17
   Steps in Conducting Research   21
   Issues in Conducting Sociological Research   22
   OTHER WORLDS, OTHER WAYS: South Africa:
   Sociological Research in Diverse Cultures   24
Putting Sociology to Use   25
   The Development of Sociology   25
   Basic and Applied Sociology   26
   Sociological Practice   26
   SOCIOLOGY ON THE INTERNET   27
   Using Sociology in Everyday Life   27
Study & Review   27
For Further Reading   31

CHAPTER 2

Culture, Society, and Diversity   33
   MYTHS & FACTS: About Culture and Society   34
What Is Culture?   36
   Material Culture and Nonmaterial Culture   36
The Components of Culture   36
   Beliefs and Values   37
   Norms   39
   OTHER WORLDS, OTHER WAYS: The Amish of
   Pennsylvania: Diverse Values within a Culture   40
   Language   42

Cultural Consensus and Diversity   43
   Cultural Integration   43
   Cultural Change   44
   Ideal Culture versus Real Culture   44
   Ethnocentrism and Cultural Relativity   45
   Subcultures   46
   APPLYING SOCIOLOGY: Argot: The Special Language
   of Subcultures   46
Social Structure   48
   Status   48
   Roles   49
   SOCIOLOGY OF MEDIA AND TECHNOLOGY:
   Mass Media, the Electronic World, and the Production
   and Transmission of Culture   52
   Groups and Social Institutions   54
A Comparative View of Societies   54
   Preindustrial Societies   54
   Industrial Societies   55
   A Global Perspective: Postindustrialism
   and Global Interdependence   56
   SOCIOLOGY ON THE INTERNET   57
Study & Review   57
For Further Reading   61

PART II The Individual in Society   62

CHAPTER 3

Socialization   63
   MYTHS & FACTS: About Socialization   64
Heredity and the Environment   66
   Biology and Human Behavior   66
   Children Raised in Isolation   67
The Process of Socialization   68
   The Development of Self: The Interactionist Perspective   68
   Agencies of Socialization   72
   APPLYING SOCIOLOGY: Day Care: Problem or Solution?   74
   SOCIOLOGY OF MEDIA AND TECHNOLOGY:
   Who Socializes the Young in an Electronic World?   76
   Types of Socialization   77
   OTHER WORLDS, OTHER WAYS: Japan:
   Learning Cultural Values Through Primary Socialization   78
   Socialization through the Life Span   79
Additional Perspectives on Socialization   81
   The Functionalist Perspective   82
   The Conflict Perspective   82
   SOCIOLOGY ON THE INTERNET   83
Study & Review   84
For Further Reading   87

CHAPTER 4

Groups and Organizations 88
  MYTHS & FACTS: About Groups and Organizations 89
Types of Groups 90
  Primary Groups 90
  Secondary Groups 91
  In-Groups and Out-Groups 92
  Reference Groups 93
  Social Collectivities 93
Group Structure and Process 93
  Status and Role 94
  Leadership 95
  Decision Making in Groups 96
  Group Cohesion 97
  Group Conformity 97
  Organizations 99
  Bureaucracy 99
  The Human Relations Approach 102
  The Informal Structure 103
  Gender in Organizations 104
  APPLYING SOCIOLOGY: Diagnosing Organizational
  Culture: Helping Organizations to Function Better 105
Sociological Perspectives on Organizations 106
  The Functionalist Perspective 106
  The Conflict Perspective 106
  OTHER WORLDS, OTHER WAYS: China:
  Cultural Values and Group Behavior—Social Loafing in
  Organizations 107
  The Interactionist Perspective 108
The Future of Bureaucracy 108
  Bureaucracy and Oligarchy 108
  Limits to Bureaucracy 109
  SOCIOLOGY OF MEDIA AND TECHNOLOGY:
  Community and Group Life in the Cyberworld 110
  SOCIOLOGY ON THE INTERNET 112
Study & Review 112
For Further Reading 116

CHAPTER 5

Deviance, Crime, and Social Control 117
  MYTHS & FACTS: About Deviance and Crime 118
The Relativity of Deviance 119
Explanations of Deviance 120
  Nonsociological Approaches 120
  The Functionalist Perspective 121
  The Conflict Perspective 122
  The Interactionist Perspective 123
  SOCIOLOGY OF MEDIA AND TECHNOLOGY: Mass
  Media and the Social Construction of Crime and Justice 125
Extent of Deviance and Crime 126
  Sexual Deviance 126
  Drug and Alcohol Abuse 127

  APPLYING SOCIOLOGY: Influencing Policy on
  Youth Gangs and Juvenile Crime 128
  Mental Illness 128
  Violent Crimes 129
  Organized Crime and Globalized Crime 130
  Cybercrime 130
  White-Collar Crime 131
Deviance: Its Consequences for Society 132
  The Dysfunctions of Deviance 132
  The Functions of Deviance 133
Deviance and Social Control 134
  Internal Sources of Social Control 134
  External Sources of Social Control 134
Crime in the United States 135
  The High Crime Rate 135
  Reducing Crime 136
  OTHER WORLDS, OTHER WAYS: Japan:
  Social and Cultural Underpinnings of Crime 139
  SOCIOLOGY ON THE INTERNET 140
Study & Review 140
For Further Reading 144

PART III Stratification and Social Inequality 145

CHAPTER 6

Social Stratification and Social Inequality 146
  MYTHS & FACTS: About Social Stratification 148
Dimensions of Stratification 148
  Weber's Analysis 148
  Socioeconomic Status 150
  Types of Stratification Systems 150
Theories of Stratification 152
  The Functionalist Perspective 152
  The Conflict Perspective 153
  Synthesis: An Evolutionary View 153
  A Global Perspective on Stratification 155
  OTHER WORLDS, OTHER WAYS: Brazil and Venezuela:
  The Third-World Poor in the Global Stratification System 157
Social Class in the United States 158
  Measuring Socioeconomic Status 158
  Class Structure in the United States 159
  Inequality and Poverty 159
  APPLYING SOCIOLOGY: Creating and Evaluating
  Programs That Assist the Poor 165
Social Mobility 166
  Extent of Social Mobility 166
  Sources of Social Mobility 167
Consequences of Stratification 168
  Educational Achievement 168
  Health 168
  SOCIOLOGY OF MEDIA AND TECHNOLOGY: Impact of
  Technology on Stratification Systems 169

Status Inconsistency 170
Self-Esteem 170
SOCIOLOGY ON THE INTERNET 171
Study & Review 171
For Further Reading 175

CHAPTER 7

Social Inequality: Race and Ethnicity 176
MYTHS & FACTS: About Race and Ethnicity 177
Minority Groups 178
Race and Ethnicity 179
Racism 179
Sources of Prejudice and Discrimination 180
Social Sources 180
Social Psychological Sources 182
Consequences of Discrimination 182
Patterns of Intergroup Relations 183
Forms of Domination 183
OTHER WORLDS, OTHER WAYS: Britain, Germany, Yugoslavia: The Social and Economic Sources of Racial Hatred and Conflict 184
Minority Reaction to Domination 186
Switzerland: Cooperation in a Multiethnic Society 186
Racial and Ethnic Minorities in the United States 187
African Americans 187
Hispanic Americans 189
American Indians 191
Asian Americans 192
Arab Americans 193
Today's Immigrants 194
Achievement and Assimilation among Immigrant Groups 195
Current Issues in the United States 196
SOCIOLOGY OF MEDIA AND TECHNOLOGY: Image and Access: Race/Ethnicity and Communications Technologies 197
Assimilation or Pluralism? 196
Race Relations Today: Race or Class? 198
Advances, Setbacks, and Controversial Policies 200
APPLYING SOCIOLOGY: Combating Prejudice, Discrimination, and Racial Polarization 201
SOCIOLOGY ON THE INTERNET 203
Study & Review 203
For Further Reading 207

CHAPTER 8

Social Inequality: Gender 208
MYTHS & FACTS: About Gender Inequality 209
Men and Women in Society 211
The Biological Perspective 211
The Functionalist Perspective 212
The Conflict Perspective 213
The Interactionist Perspective 214

The Socialization of Men and Women 214
The Family 215
The Schools 215
SOCIOLOGY OF MEDIA AND TECHNOLOGY: Shaping Gender Identity 216
The Media and the Electronic World 217
The Extent of Gender Inequality in the United States 217
Economic Discrimination 217
Discrimination in the Military 222
Other Types of Discrimination 223
Gender Inequality Involving Males 223
Gender Stratification in Global Perspective 224
Toward Gender Equality 224
Collective Action and the Feminist Movement: A Global Struggle 224
OTHER WORLDS, OTHER WAYS: Mexico: Poor Women and the World Economy 225
Current Trends in the United States 227
APPLYING SOCIOLOGY: Sexual Assault, Sexual Harassment, and the Empowerment of Women 229
Masculine, Feminine, or Human? 231
SOCIOLOGY ON THE INTERNET 231
Study & Review 231
For Further Reading 237

PART IV   Social Institutions 237

CHAPTER 9

Family and Human Sexuality 238
MYTHS & FACTS: About the Family and Human Sexuality 240
Family and Kinship in Cross-Cultural Perspective 240
Rules of Descent 240
Rules of Marriage 241
Rules of Authority 241
Size of Family Unit 242
Mate Selection and Marriage Transactions 242
The Family in Society 243
The Functionalist Perspective 243
The Conflict Perspective 245
Marriage and Divorce in the United States 246
Choosing a Mate and Attitudes toward Marriage 246
Divorce 246
The Minority Family Experience 251
OTHER WORLDS, OTHER WAYS: Vietnam: Family and Religion among Immigrants to the United States 253
Diversity and Change in Sexual Behavior 254
Premarital Sex 254
Extramarital Sex 254
Homosexuality 255
Diverse Family Lifestyles in Modern Societies 256
Dual-Earner Families 256
Singlehood 257

Cohabitation 258
Single Parenthood 258
Gay Families 260
A Global Perspective 262
Violence in the Family 262
APPLYING SOCIOLOGY: Creating and Evaluating
Programs to Fight Domestic Violence 263
The Future of the Family 264
SOCIOLOGY OF MEDIA AND TECHNOLOGY:
Family in the Electronic Age 265
SOCIOLOGY ON THE INTERNET 266
Study & Review 267
For Further Reading 271

CHAPTER 10

Health and Health-Care Institutions 272
MYTHS & FACTS: About Health and Health-
Care Institutions 273
Sociological Perspectives on Health, Illness,
and Health Care 274
The Functionalist Perspective 274
The Conflict Perspective 275
The Interactionist Perspective 275
Politics, Stigma, and the AIDS Epidemic 277
APPLYING SOCIOLOGY: Combating the Spread of AIDS 278
Health, Illness, and Society 278
Health and Societal Development 279
Health and Social Position 282
OTHER WORLDS, OTHER WAYS: Congo:
The Spread of AIDS in a Developing Nation 284
Health-Care Systems in Cross-Cultural Perspective 285
Personalistic Health-Care Systems 285
Naturalistic Health-Care Systems 285
Scientific Health-Care Systems 286
Chinese Medicine 286
Holistic Medicine 286
The Social Structure of Health Care 287
Seeking Health Care 287
The Medical Profession 288
SOCIOLOGY OF MEDIA AND TECHNOLOGY:
Globalized Medicine in Cyberspace 289
The Nursing Profession 290
New Health-Care Practitioners 290
Hospitals and the Corporatization of Health Care 290
Issues in Health Care in the United States 292
Rising Health-Care Costs 292
Access to Medical Services 292
Quality of Medical Services 294
Gender Inequality in Health Care 294
Financing Health Care in the United States 296
Publicly Funded Health Insurance 296
Employer-Financed Health Insurance 297
Health Maintenance Organizations and Managed Care 297
Health Care: A Privilege or a Right? 298

Paying for Health Care in Other Nations: Canada
and Sweden 298
SOCIOLOGY ON THE INTERNET 299
Study & Review 299
For Further Reading 303

CHAPTER 11

Religion 305
MYTHS & FACTS: About Religion 308
What Is Religion? 307
A Global Perspective: Religions of the World 307
Judaism 308
Christianity 309
Islam 309
Hinduism 310
Buddhism 310
Confucianism 310
Diffusion of Religion 311
Sociological Approaches to the Study of Religion 312
Durkheim: A Functionalist Perspective 312
Marx: A Conflict Perspective 312
Weber: Religion and Social Change 313
The Organization of Religion 314
OTHER WORLDS, OTHER WAYS: China, Iran, and
Afghanistan: Religion and Political Change 315
Religion in the United States 317
Extent of Religiosity 317
Socioeconomic Status and Politics 318
Secularization 319
Religious Pluralism 321
SOCIOLOGY OF MEDIA AND TECHNOLOGY:
Communication Technologies and Religious Experience 322
APPLYING SOCIOLOGY: Identifying Extremism in
Religious Cults 325
SOCIOLOGY ON THE INTERNET 326
Study & Review 327
For Further Reading 330

CHAPTER 12

Education and the Mass Media 331
A Global Perspective on Education 332
Informal Education 332
MYTHS & FACTS: About Education and the Mass Media 333
Colonization and Education 333
Modernization and Education 334
Sociological Perspectives on Education 335
The Functionalist Perspective 335
The Conflict Perspective 337
The Interactionist Perspective 338
Education in the United States 339
A Historical View 339
Schools as Bureaucracies 339

Effectiveness of the Educational System 341
Reforms and Trends 342
APPLYING SOCIOLOGY: Evaluating Educational Innovations 344
Higher Education 346

Education, Communication, and the Mass Media 347
OTHER WORLDS, OTHER WAYS: Japan:
Variations in Educational Institutions in Industrial Societies 348
Emergence of the Mass Media 349
Effects of the Mass Media 350
SOCIOLOGY OF MEDIA AND TECHNOLOGY:
Education in the Electronic World 351
Control of the Mass Media 352
The Global Mass Media: Neocolonization? 353
SOCIOLOGY ON THE INTERNET 354

Study & Review 354
For Further Reading 358

CHAPTER 13

Political and Economic Institutions 359
MYTHS & FACTS: About Political and Economic Institutions 360
Politics, Power, and Authority 362
Types of Authority 363
State and Government 363
Sociological Perspectives on Political and Economic Institutions 364
The Functionalist Perspective 364
The Conflict Perspective 364
Types of Government 365
Oligarchy and Totalitarianism 365
Democracy 365
Types of Economic Systems 368
Capitalism 368
Socialism 369
Mixed Economies 370
Who Rules in the United States? 370
The Power Elite Model 370
The Pluralist Model 370
Assessment of the Models 371
The U.S. Economy: Concentration and Change 372
The Corporate Economy 372
The Changing Labor Force 373
Global Competition: Worker Dislocation and Unemployment 375
The Global Political and Economic System 377
Concentration and Inequality 377
The Structure of Globalization 378
Unemployment, Dislocation, and Resistance 379
OTHER WORLDS, OTHER WAYS: Nicaragua:
Political and Economic Change in a Peripheral Nation 380
APPLYING SOCIOLOGY: Intervening in the Process of Economic Globalization 382

Politics, the Economy, the Media, and the Cyberworld 382
Politics, Persuasion, and Propaganda 383
SOCIOLOGY OF MEDIA AND TECHNOLOGY:
The Media and the Military in Wars 384
Advertising 385
SOCIOLOGY ON THE INTERNET 385
Study & Review 386
For Further Reading 390

PART V Human Ecology and Social Change 391

CHAPTER 14

Human Ecology: Population, Community, and Environment 392
MYTHS & FACTS: About Population, Community, and Environment 394
The Study of Human Populations 395
Elements of Demographic Change 395
Population Composition: Age and Sex Structure 397
World Population Growth 397
The Demographic Transition 398
The Extent of Overpopulation 399
The Consequences of Overpopulation 401
Controlling Population Growth 402
Communities and Urbanization 403
The Emergence of Cities 403
Suburbanization 404
The Postindustrial City 406
SOCIOLOGY OF MEDIA AND TECHNOLOGY:
Technology and the Growth of Cities 406
A Global Perspective on Urbanization 406
OTHER WORLDS, OTHER WAYS: Mexico:
The Social Organization of Slums in Poor Communities 408
Urbanism as a Way of Life 408
Urban Consciousness 408
Urban Communities 409
Urban Subcultures 409
Urban Life: An Assessment 410
Urban Ecology 410
Urban Processes 410
Urban Structures 411
The Future of Cities in the United States 412
Economic Decline 412
Government Programs and Urban Renewal 413
Private Investment 414
Gentrification 414
APPLYING SOCIOLOGY: Fear of Crime: Working to Improve the Quality of Urban Life 415
Population and the Environment 416
Social Sources of Environmental Problems 416
Extent of Environmental Problems 417
Solving Environmental Problems 418

SOCIOLOGY ON THE INTERNET 419
Study & Review 419
For Further Reading 423

CHAPTER 15

Collective Behavior, Social Change, and Modernization 424

MYTHS & FACTS: About Collective Behavior and Social Change 425
The Nature of Collective Behavior 426
The Preconditions of Collective Behavior 427
APPLYING SOCIOLOGY: Preventing Urban Riots: The Los Angeles Riot in Retrospect 428
Rumors 429
Mass Behavior 430
Crowds 431
Social Movements 434
The Development of Social Movements 434

OTHER WORLDS, OTHER WAYS: Afghanistan: The Social Roots of Terrorist Violence 436
Social Change 437
Theories of Change 438
The Future: Global Modernization? 440
Modernization in the Less Developed Nations 440
SOCIOLOGY OF MEDIA AND TECHNOLOGY: Social Movements and Resistance to Globalization 440
The United States: A Postindustrial Future? 442
The Globalization of Labor 443
SOCIOLOGY ON THE INTERNET 444
Study & Review 444
For Further Reading 447

Glossary 449
Bibliography 456
Answers to Cumulative Practice Tests 482
Name Index 485
Subject Index 495

The world has changed in some dramatic ways in recent decades. Not long ago, the Soviet Union collapsed, the Berlin Wall fell, and Germany was reunited, thus ending decades of the Cold War. Communications satellites and computer technology have transformed to include the Internet, cell phones, and iPods, which make possible continual and instantaneous communication around the globe. At the same time, not all the developments of recent decades have been positive. A decade after the Cold War ended, the murderous terrorist attacks on New York and Washington on September 11, 2001, reminded those who may have forgotten that human social life sometimes involves horror and destruction. Ethnic antagonisms have raged with tragic consequences in such places as Bosnia and Herzegovina, Kosovo, Rwanda, and Burundi. The nations of the world exhibit growing levels of interdependence, but well-paying manufacturing jobs in the United States disappear as employers seek cheaper labor in Mexico, Thailand, and other developing nations. The scourge of cocaine, alcohol, methamphetamine, and other drugs continues to increase health and crime problems in the United States.

Sociology emerged as a field of study in the nineteenth century because people found that the sociological perspective offered *empowerment:* It provided insight into the problems societies faced as they industrialized, and it helped them find ways to improve society. Against the backdrop of the progress and problems alluded to in the preceding paragraph, many people, including myself, find that empowerment continues to be one of the most enthralling attractions of the discipline of sociology: It offers not only knowledge and understanding but also a set of tools that helps us work on improving the world around us.

In the last few decades, the discipline of sociology has continued to expand our understanding of how societies work and how cultural, structural, and institutional forces shape human behavior. In addition, sociology in the early twenty-first century continues its focus on applying sociological knowledge to make positive changes in social institutions, social structures, and people's everyday lives. This application goes beyond the goal of understanding how societies operate or what determines human behavior. Using the well-developed foundation of basic sociological theory and research, many contemporary sociologists focus their work on suggesting and evaluating solutions to social problems or helping people to improve their lives. In fact, I believe that these efforts to apply sociology have been as exciting, innovative, and important as the more

basic research that is still being done by many sociologists.

This eighth edition of *Sociology: Concepts and Applications in a Diverse World,* then, is designed for people who envision themselves as actively engaged in their world. It is for people who want the empowerment that sociology has to offer so that they can be activists in the world and strive to make it a better place. It retains the features from earlier editions and adds some significant new content that assists in achieving these goals. This edition provides a solid introduction to the discipline of sociology while developing these themes:

- The excitement and contribution of **applied sociology.**
- The value of taking a **global perspective** that recognizes the growing interconnectedness of cultures and societies in today's world and the trends toward unification across cultures.
- The growing importance of **diversity and difference** in the United States and the world.
- The central role that **technology,** and especially the modern **technologies of communication, computer-mediated communications, and the electronic world** have in shaping society and people's daily lives.

Organizing Themes and Features

The major features of the earlier editions of this text were effective in developing the themes of this book and assisting students in exploring the world as sociologists. These features have been retained for this edition:

1. *Theoretical Perspectives*   The presentation of the discipline of sociology continues to be organized around the three core theoretical perspectives: functionalism, conflict theory, and interactionism. These perspectives, which serve as a foundation on which to build a framework of understanding of the sociological approach, are introduced in the first chapter and then used throughout the book. This approach provides students with a sound understanding of the perspectives by the end of the semester, and the perspectives can then be used to analyze any sociological issue.

2. *Applied Sociology*   Throughout the book, sociology is applied to the understanding, evaluation, and solution of problems in the United States and the world. In addition, each chapter contains one

boxed section titled *Applying Sociology* that addresses issues of applied research, social policy development, clinical sociology, and personal applications of sociological principles in the student's life and work. This feature addresses the discipline's growing focus on applied sociology and shows how sociological theory and research can guide the search for solutions to societal and personal problems. In addition, Chapter 1 includes a major section describing the field of applied sociology.

3. *Globalization, Cross-Culturalism, and Diversity*   An important theme running through this book is globalization: the trend toward increasing interconnectedness, interdependence, and uniformity among the nations and peoples of the world. Nations can no longer be studied as independent entities because the political, economic, and social forces that shape people's lives now operate on a global level. This makes a global perspective essential to preparing students to live and work in the modern world. A part of this global view is a *cross-cultural perspective* that helps students to understand the social and cultural nature of human societies and to see how cultures and peoples are similar to and different from one another. In addition, an emphasis on *diversity* is important because diversities of race, ethnicity, gender, cultural heritage, or lifestyle are often at the core of discrimination, differential opportunities, and social conflict. Issues of globalization, cross-culturalism, and diversity are addressed in this book in four ways:

A. The book begins with an extensive discussion of the importance of diversity, a global perspective, and the sociological imagination in Chapter 1.

B. Practically every chapter has a section that explores a global perspective on the topic of that chapter. This assists the student in exploring issues of, for example, gender inequality or changes in family structure not only in the United States but also in societies around the world.

C. Boxed sections called *Other Worlds, Other Ways* illustrate sociological concepts and issues in the context of societies and cultures around the world. One such section is included in each chapter.

D. Each chapter opens with an in-depth discussion of the issues in that chapter as they apply to a culture different from the contemporary, mainstream culture of the United States.

All these features discuss cultures and nations from all parts of the world, although they take a repeated look at some nations that are especially important to the United States or the world, such as China, Mexico, and Japan. In addition to these specific features, issues of globalization, cross-culturalism, and diversity are incorporated throughout the book.

4. *Sociology of Media and Technology*   In the high-tech, global environment of the twenty-first century, the mass media and computer-mediated communications technologies are far more pervasive and important than many people imagined thirty or fifty years ago. They influence values, norms, and behavior as well as help to shape social institutions and contribute to patterns of dominance and inequality. In addition, a significant part of social interaction has now moved online, so the study of society must now include a study of this electronic world. A separate insert titled *Sociology of Media and Technology* is included in each chapter to give this content emphasis and prominence. In addition, one-quarter of Chapter 12 is devoted to discussing the media as a social institution.

5. *Myths & Facts Feature*   This feature encourages students to recognize that social reality is complex and that our commonsense knowledge of the world can be either wrong or so overly simplified that it seriously distorts our understanding of the social world. This feature encourages students to distinguish beliefs that have no scientific foundation from sociological facts that have been substantiated through systematic research. It highlights the central role of research in understanding social issues. This feature is introduced in Chapter 1 in the Myths & Facts section and the Applying Sociology section; thereafter, it appears as a boxed section at the beginning of each chapter.

6. *Study & Review*   At the end of each chapter, a *Study & Review* section gives students an opportunity to test how well they have grasped the material in the chapter. The section begins with a summary that is organized around the learning objectives that are identified for each major heading in the chapter. Each learning objective is repeated in the summary and is followed by the summary of that section. Following the Summary is the Chronological Practice Test, which is also organized by major heading. The Chronological Practice Test has numerous testing formats: Key Concepts, True/False Questions, Concept Completion Statements, Graphics Review, and Critical Thinking questions. The answers to the True/False questions and the Concept Completion Statements are at the end of the Chronological Practice Test. This is followed by a Cumulative Practice Test that contains twenty multiple-choice questions. These questions cover material from throughout each chapter. The answers to these questions are at the

end of the book. This Study & Review section should be of great utility to students who wish to assess how well they have learned the material in each chapter. The various testing formats offer an assessment of the different kinds of information found in each chapter and assist students in organizing their study. They also serve as a comprehensive review of the content in the chapter, as well as help in preparing for exams.

7. *For Further Readings*   Each chapter concludes with a short list of books relevant to topics in that chapter. These books should be available in college or community libraries or bookstores. They include books that further the themes of cross-culturalism, diversity, and applied sociology that are central to this textbook. Students whose imaginations have been stimulated by this introduction to sociology can continue to sharpen their sociological eye by looking at some of these suggested readings.

8. *Sociology on the Internet*   Extending the focus on modern communications technologies, exercises on how to explore the Internet for sociologically relevant material are included as a boxed section in each chapter. The exercises are designed to encourage the students to gain insight into the sociological significance of what they find on the Internet and to use it as a vehicle for deepening their understanding of the sociological imagination. The results obtained from these exercises can be used by the student as a part of a term paper project or by the instructor as a focus for classroom discussions.

9. *Pedagogical Aids*   A number of elements are integrated into the text to assist the student in learning the material. The *Study & Review* section, which includes a summary, at the end of each chapter gives the student the opportunity to review the material in a variety of different ways. A *Learning Objective* has been placed, in bold, below every major heading in the text; this cues students to the broad points to learn and remember as they read each section.

Changes in the Eighth Edition

A new edition of a textbook must be approached on the basis of new developments in the field, as well as feedback from students and faculty who have used the previous edition. These sources of information suggested that a new edition could benefit from some new content, as well as the updating of some current content. The major changes in the eighth edition focus on three realms.

1. While previous editions did take a global perspective, I have expanded on this focus considerably by providing a **more extensively developed presentation of globalization and its impact on society and culture**. The eighth edition recognizes the fact that globalization may be as important a transition in human social organization as was agriculturalism and industrialism. New conceptual material is introduced and presented to the student as new bold-faced terms, including "globalization" (Chapter 1), "cultural globalization" (Chapter 2), "political globalization" (Chapter 13), and "economic globalization" (Chapter 13). There is also new material on global crime (Chapter 5), the structure of globalization (Chapter 13), and global social movements among indigenous peoples that represent resistance to political and economic globalization around the world (Chapter 15). Overall, this edition presents a more extensive and integrated presentation of globalization as a feature of modern social life.

2. While previous editions of the book have had a theme of the Sociology of Media and Technology, this has focused on the more traditional media of television, movies, and print. The eighth edition retains this but also expands the focus to the **newer technologies of the Internet and the online, electronic world**. Because more of social, economic, political, and cultural life has moved online, it is essential to incorporate sociological research and analysis on the ramifications of this for culture, group life, social interaction, identity, social cohesion, alienation, and so on. Sufficient sociological research on the Internet and the electronic world has now accummulated that we can begin to draw some solid conclusions. This new material has been introduced by, for example, a substantial or complete revision of 10 of the 15 Sociology of Media and Technology inserts. In addition, there is a new discussion of cybercrime (Chapter 5), along with the use of the new electronic world for purposes of persuasion and propaganda (Chapter 13). Also, the Sociology of Media and Technology insert in Chapter 15 now discusses three perspectives on technology (utopian, dystopian, and realist) as a way to tie technology clearly into the topic of social change and discuss the issue of collective resistance to technological change.

3. A major **new section on environmental issues, and especially global warming and climate change**, has been added to Chapter 14. Previous editions had almost no discussion of environmental topics. With substantial research now showing the possibly dire consequences of these developments, it is a topic that should be addressed—it is not possible today to present the student with an introduction to human ecology without addressing the impact of human populations and communities on the physical environment. So, the new material discusses the sources of environmental

problems, their extent in the world today, and what might be done about it.

Beyond these major changes, all the data in the text, tables, and figures have been updated wherever it is possible to do so. In addition, many parts of the text have been significantly updated and changed based on new theories, research, or other developments. These are the major updates:

- New data on the effects of day care on children is presented in the Applying Sociology insert of Chapter 3.
- Some of the tables and figures in Chapter 7 now include data on Asian Americans/Pacific Islanders (in addition to data on Anglo Americans, African Americans, and Hispanics); this provides a more complete view of the racial and ethnic picture in the United States.
- The discussion of affirmative action in Chapter 7 now includes an analysis of the implications of the most recent Supreme Court decisions on this topic.
- The section on the effectiveness of the educational system in the United States has been updated with the most recent research results.
- The section on the changing labor force in Chapter 13 adds to the reasons for the decline in unions in the United States by discussing the efforts made by corporations to fight unionization.

A detailed list of the changes and updates in each chapter (including the page number where the changes are found in the text) can be found in the *Instructor's Manual* that accompanies this book. This makes it simple for the instructor to review the changes and updates.

Organization

The sequence of chapters remains the same as in the previous edition. The chapters are grouped according to sociological themes. Consequently, the book is organized into five parts. Part I has two chapters that introduce the student to the *sociological perspective,* including a discussion of theoretical perspectives, research methods, and the concepts of culture, society, and social structure. Part II contains three chapters that focus on the major links between the *individual and society,* including socialization, groups and organizations, and deviance and social control. Part III consists of three chapters whose focus is *social stratification and social inequality,* including analyses of class, race, ethnicity, and gender. Part IV includes five chapters that cover the major *social institutions:* the family, health care, religion, education, and politics and the economy. Part V contains two chapters whose themes are *human ecology and social change,* including

population issues, urbanization, environmental issues, collective behavior, social change, and modernization.

Ancillary Materials

A number of materials have been prepared to assist the instructor and the student in using this textbook. More information about these materials can be obtained from your Pearson sales representative or from the Web page for this book at the Pearson Web site: www.pearsonhighered.com.

Web site. Visit VangoBooks.com to take your understanding of the material to the next level. The site provides Multiple Choice, True-False, Fill in the Blank and Essay questions to test knowledge of the material. The site also includes to additional resources such as Flash Cards and supplemental articles.

Instructor's Manual and Test Bank. I have prepared a combined Instructor's Manual and Test Bank to accompany this book. The Instructor's Manual section contains, for each chapter, a number of materials to assist the instructor in teaching the course: an outline of the chapter, a list of the learning objectives for the chapter, a list of changes in the new edition, a series of suggestions for teaching and discussion, and a list of films that can accompany the chapter. The test bank section contains 10 essay questions, 70 multiple-choice questions, and 15 true-false questions for each chapter.

Computerized Test Bank. The printed Test Bank is also available through Pearson's online test generating system, MyTest. The user-friendly interface allows you to view, edit, and add questions; transfer questions to tests; and print tests. Search and sort features allow you to locate questions quickly and arrange them in whatever order you prefer.

PowerPoint Presentation. PowerPoint presentations are available by download and provide lecture outlines for the course.

Acknowledgments

Many people have contributed to the completion of this new edition. At Allyn and Bacon, Karen Hanson provided valuable support for the project, and the book has benefited immensely from her support. I also received some excellent advice and assistance from a number of colleagues at one point or another in the development of this book: Lisa A. Barnett, Coe College; Donna C. Bird, University of Southern Maine; Lynda Ann Ewen, West Virginia Institute of Technology; William R. Garrett, Saint Michael's College; Tonya Hilligoss, Sacramento City College; Mara Kent-Skruch, Anne Arundel Community College;

Roger W. Little, University of Illinois at Chicago Circle; Duane A. Matcha, Siena College; Juanita Nada, San Antonio College; David Neal, Texas Women's University; Alton M. Okinawa, University of Hawaii at Hilo; Ann Lencyk Pawliczko, Fordham University; Brenda Phillips, Texas Women's University; Jim Phillips, Kings River Community College; Kathleen H. Powell, Frostburg State University; William F. Powers, Suffolk County Community College; Christine Rodriguez, East Los Angeles College; Steven Schada, Oakton Community College; J. Carroll Sims, Virginia State University at Petersburg; William L. Smith, Georgia Southern University; Shirley Strom, Henry Ford Community College; Joseph Ventimiglia, University of Memphis; Theodore C. Wagenaar, Miami University; and Renxin Yang, Northern Michigan University. I am grateful also to the following reviewers of this edition: Richard Ball, Ferris State University; Melba Green, The Community College of Baltimore County; Margaret E. Preble, Thomas Nelson Community College; and Kenrick Thompson, Arkansas State University.

For me, sociology continues to be one of the most exciting, fast-paced, and demanding disciplines because it presents a continual challenge to traditional and established ways of thinking about the world. Over the years that I have been a sociologist, I have engaged in sociological research and practice in many diverse settings. I have evaluated programs to help school children in need and programs for services targeted at pregnant teenagers; I have advised administrators who run programs for homeless teens as well as those providing services to women recovering from drug addictions; I have conducted research on people's responses to life-threatening illnesses. Through all of this, my passion for the sociological enterprise has grown stronger. Sociology engenders an openness, an eagerness, and an intense desire to learn more about all aspects of the human condition. By knowing other people, their lives, and their society, we can better understand ourselves. My hope is that this book will generate the same passion in the students who read it; as a result, a few may start down the exciting road to becoming the next generation of sociologists.

Thomas J. Sullivan
Marquette, Michigan

THOMAS J. SULLIVAN recently retired from his position as Professor of Sociology at Northern Michigan University, a position he held for many years. He specializes in social psychology, research methods, applied sociology, and medical sociology. He earned his undergraduate degree in sociology from San Francisco State University and his M.A. and Ph.D. in sociology from the University of California at Santa Barbara. He is the author of *Introduction to Social Problems,* 8th ed. (Allyn and Bacon, 2009), *Methods of Social Research* (Wadsworth, 2001), and *Applied Sociology: Research and Critical Thinking* (Allyn and Bacon, 1992); he is the coauthor of *Applied Social Research: Tool for the Human Services,* 7th ed. (Thomson Brooks/Cole, 2008). He has published articles in *Social Science and Medicine* and *Humboldt Journal of Social Relations.* His applied work has focused on evaluation research of social service delivery in elementary schools and of teen pregnancy prevention and intervention services. He has served in various elected and appointed positions for the American Sociological Association, the Society for Applied Sociology, and the Midwest Sociological Society.

THE SOCIOLOGICAL PERSPECTIVE

CHAPTER ONE
What Is Sociology?

CHAPTER TWO
Culture, Society, and Diversity

Part I introduces the sociological perspective and includes a discussion of the three theoretical perspectives in sociology, the scientific method as used in sociology, and the specific research methods that are used for making observations. It also explores two basic components that help us understand human societies: culture and social structure.

CHAPTER 1

What Is Sociology?

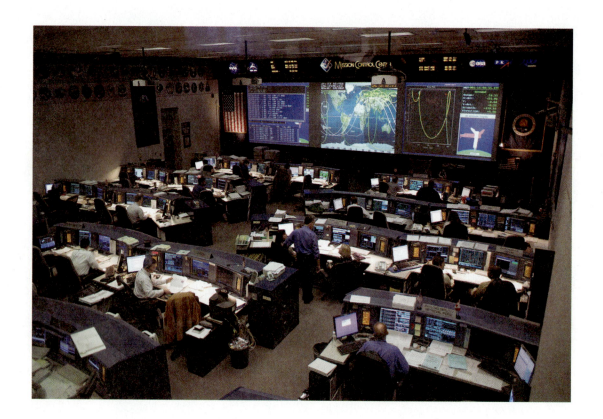

MYTHS & FACTS: About the Social World

What Is Sociology?
    The Sociological Perspective
        The Diversity of Social Reality
        Cross-Cultural Perspectives
        Globalization
    Sociology as a Science
        APPLYING SOCIOLOGY: Untangling Myths and Facts:
        Sociology and Common Sense
    The Social Sciences

Theoretical Perspectives in Sociology
    Theories and Hypotheses
    The Functionalist Perspective
    The Conflict Perspective

The Interactionist Perspective
Using the Theoretical Perspectives

Conducting Sociological Research
    Research Methods
        SOCIOLOGY OF MEDIA AND TECHNOLOGY: Applying the
        Sociological Perspectives: Mass Media, Global
        Communications, and the Online World
        Observational Techniques
        Surveys
        Experiments
    Steps in Conducting Research
    Issues in Conducting Sociological Research
        Reactivity
        Values and Objectivity
        Ethics

OTHER WORLDS, OTHER WAYS: South Africa:
Sociological Research in Diverse Cultures

Putting Sociology to Use
The Development of Sociology
Basic and Applied Sociology

Sociological Practice
Using Sociology in Everyday Life
SOCIOLOGY ON THE INTERNET

Study & Review

Myths & Facts

About the Social World

Everyone has considerable experience with the social world, which is the topic of sociology as a scientific discipline. Yet people often believe they know more about the social world than they actually do. Some of what people believe is accurate, of course, but some of those beliefs are wrong, others are misleading, and still others are far too simple to help us understand a complex social reality. One of the themes that I want to stress in this book is that the science of sociology is a tool for separating the myths from the facts—distinguishing beliefs that are wrong or misleading from those that have been shown to be true through scientific observation. I return to this issue later in this chapter, but for now consider the following:

Myth:

Poor and uneducated people commit many more crimes than do middle-class, better-educated people.

Fact:

Social reality is complicated on this issue. If we look at arrest statistics, then this statement is true, but most people who commit crimes are not arrested. A growing body of evidence based on self-reports of criminal activity suggests that what distinguishes the social classes is not the amount of crime but rather the types of crimes and the likelihood of being arrested. The poor are more likely to commit highly visible crimes, such as homicide or assault, which are likely to be reported to the police and result in arrests. Middle-class people commit crimes such as embezzlement, fraud, and tax evasion that often go unreported (see Chapter 5).

Myth:

Divorce was relatively unheard of in societies before the twentieth century, but it has been increasing dramatically in the United States in recent years.

Fact:

This statement is partly true and partly false. In many premodern societies, married couples had the option of dissolving their union. In some hunting and gathering bands, in fact, divorce was easier to accomplish and much more common than it is in the United States today:

Marriage ended when a couple decided to stop living together. It is true, however, that the divorce rate in the United States has increased, from 8.8 per thousand married women in 1940 to almost 18 per thousand today. However, the divorce rate may not continue to increase in the future; it has held fairly steady or declined slightly over the past three decades (see Chapter 9).

Myth:

Because of the civil rights movement and affirmative action legislation, the gap in income between African Americans and white Americans has narrowed substantially in the past three decades.

Fact:

Unfortunately, research shows that the gap has not narrowed at all. Although many African Americans have benefited from such developments, the poverty of some blacks has been especially intransigent to change. Overall, average black income was 61 percent of average white income in 1970; it is about the same today (see Chapter 7).

Myth:

Teenagers are too young to be mature and responsible, and this is why societies encourage them to stay in school until they are eighteen years old rather than work for a living or begin raising a family.

Fact:

This, again, is a myth. Teenagers are quite capable of mature, responsible behavior. In fact, in preindustrial societies, most people have joined the adult world of work by their teen years and may have even begun raising a family. Industrial societies, by contrast, have created a new stage in the life cycle called adolescence, consisting of people who are biologically mature but considered by society to be dependent and immature. Having such a stage in the life cycle fulfills certain needs for industrial societies: It makes possible an extended period of education during which young people learn what they need to know in order to become contributing adults. Society expects teens to be immature and irresponsible because this expectation makes it easier to keep them in a dependent status (see Chapter 3).

Bonerate is one of the many islands that make up the nation of Indonesia (Broch, 1990). Located a few hundred miles north of Australia, near Java, it has about 5,000 inhabitants, many of whom live in small villages of a few hundred people. Residents of Bonerate survive by gathering naturally growing foods, engaging in limited agriculture, fishing, and taking part in the copra and spice trade between the Moluccas and Java. Bonerate does not, however, provide an easy or plentiful existence. The soil is poor, and many of the fields have coral limestones in them that cannot be removed and make working the fields difficult. Water is scarce on the island, especially during the dry season, when the island becomes arid. This scarcity means that the growing season for various fruits and vegetables is short. Agriculture is also difficult because of the lack of irrigation and fertilizers, and both agriculture and fishing are hampered by the rather primitive level of technology used on the island.

Life is hard on Bonerate, and the people would be considered poor by the standards of many around the world. The islanders must work hard to earn a living. In common with other Indonesian peasants, they see life as difficult and to an extent bad, fraught with adversities and dangers (Koentjaraningrat, 1988). Consequently, they focus their attention on the present, not the future, and feel compelled to do their best. If they work hard, they believe, difficulties caused by fate, accidents, or disasters can be overcome. Despite this worldview, however, they are not necessarily unhappy with their situation. An anthropologist described one small village on Bonerate this way:

> Miang Tuu is a small village where all of the residents know each other well. It is a dense community where few secrets can be kept from fellow villagers. This setting provides a good feeling of unity, but also at times "a feeling of being watched and having to conform," the villagers say. Most Miang Tuuans express love for their home village. (Broch, 1990, p. 10)

Basically the islanders' sense of security in the face of adversity arises from the existence of the *gotong royong,* or mutual self-help system. If they have difficulties, family members and fellow villagers will come to their aid. In other words, a community network of support helps the residents of Bonerate get through life. People will provide food if someone's crops are attacked by insects and help rebuild a house if it is destroyed by bad weather. And it is assumed that people will help their neighbors in turn when they confront adversity. The people of Bonerate are very aware that their lives depend on others, and they work hard at maintaining good relationships with one another. Bonerate culture emphasizes the importance of getting along with others and maintaining cooperative and agreeable relationships. To this end the islanders are adept at controlling their emotions and not angering or alienating others. The purpose of such behavior is to maintain the community, which is the ultimate support for the people on Bonerate.

If we shift our attention from Bonerate to the United States, we see a remarkable contrast. Compared to Bonerate, the United States is a much more individualistic—some would say self-centered—culture. In fact, the sociologist Robert Bellah and his colleagues, concluding an in-depth investigation of cultural values in the United States, stated that individualism "lies at the very core of American culture" (1985, p. 142). Individualism places personal desires and achievements ahead of collective accomplishments and goals. Bellah and colleagues argue that individualism in the United States goes to such an extreme that "anything that would violate our right to think for ourselves, judge for ourselves, make our own decisions, live our lives as we see fit, is not only morally wrong, it is sacrilegious" (1985, p. 142). In the United States, people say things like "Watch out for Number One" and "What's in it for me." They assume that others recognize, if not agree with, the sentiment implied, namely, that individual desires are as important as, if not more important than, collective or community needs. In the United States in the twenty-first century, enjoyment and personal pleasure seem to challenge duty or obligation to the group as preeminent forces in life. People divorce their spouse, leave their family, move across the country to find a job or a place in the sun—all in search of the elusive goal of *self*-fulfillment.

How different from the people of Bonerate and their practice of *gotong royong!* They make efforts to get along with one another. Although people in the United States certainly cooperate at times, they are much more likely than the islanders to compete openly and display overt disdain, anger, or hostility toward others. In fact, Bellah and his colleagues identified this tendency as a serious problem in the United States: "We have committed what to the republican founders of our nation was the cardinal sin: we have put our own good, as individuals . . . ahead of the common good" (1985, pp. 284–285).

A principle that is so supportive and sustaining in Bonerate—community—seems disturbingly absent in the United States. But what has been said so far should not be taken as an indictment of culture or community in the United States or as an affirmation of Bonerate life. What is being emphasized, first of all, is the importance of *community* in the many forms that it can take. Bellah expresses a theme that is central to the discipline of sociology: that human beings are social creatures both shaped and sustained by community. Not all sociologists will agree with Bellah's critical assessment of the condition of community in the United States. In fact, evidence of community in the United States can be found in the impressive assistance that people often give their neighbors during floods, fires, earthquakes, and other natural disasters. But all sociologists would agree that community in the United States is different from community on Bonerate and that some type of community is vital to human social life and constitutive of human nature.

The second point this comparison is intended to emphasize is the cultural diversity found among human groups, as illustrated by the contrast between Bonerate and the United States. Only by observing and comprehending that diversity can we fully grasp what it means to be human and social. The approach this book will take is to look at many different cultures and societies. If we limit our vision to the United States, we will see only part of the picture. Only the broadest cultural reach will provide us with the most accurate assessment of how societies work and how human behavior is shaped. This book will encourage you, as it reviews the values and social practices in many cultures, to assess critically what works and why and then to apply that knowledge to your own culture.

Sociology is a scientific discipline that strives to understand human beings and human social behavior. This chapter introduces the subject matter of sociology, including its unique perspective. It also describes how sociology uses the scientific method to gain systematic knowledge about human behavior.

What Is Sociology?

You should be able to discuss the sociological perspective and describe the main characteristics of the other social sciences and science in general.

Sociology is *the scientific study of societies and human social behavior.* The basic premise of sociology is that human behavior is largely determined by the groups to which people belong and by the societies in which they live. Human groups can range from small collections of friends to larger configurations such as football teams or concert audiences. Among the things that interest sociologists regarding such groups are the following: How do they develop? How are new members incorporated into groups? How does face-to-face contact between group members affect each person's behavior? How does the group respond when confronted by another, possibly hostile, group?

When a number of groups coordinate their actions, another level of social activity emerges in the form of organizations such as corporations, hospitals, or schools, and sociologists also study these types of human affiliations. Finally, groups and organizations combine to form societies, the most encompassing of human social forms. Societies can range from small

bands of fifty people who survive by hunting game and gathering fruits and berries to enormous industrial societies with millions of people. Sociologists are interested in how these societies function and also how they differ from one another on such matters as the distribution of resources and the role of family and kinship in people's lives. At the core of all sociological investigations is a particular perspective that sets sociology apart from other approaches to human behavior.

The Sociological Perspective

A perspective is a point of view or a distinctive way of viewing something. Sociology offers a unique perspective on human beings, recognizing that human behavior consists of far more than individuals acting independently of one another. The sociological perspective emphasizes *the powerful role that group membership and social forces play in shaping behavior.* Sociologists focus on social interaction and social relationships rather than on individuals. Each person is born into a particular group in a given society, and life becomes a progression from one set of groups to another. Most of us begin our lives in a family, which provides us with social standing in a community and makes available certain fundamental opportunities in life—to learn, mature, and become independent. As we grow older, we develop friendships and enter school. Aspirations and desires that will shape our choices later in life are nurtured by each of these very important groups. As adults, we may develop our own families or establish intimate ties with other adults. In a sense, we are never really alone because we constantly remember, reflect on, and imagine how others have responded to us. The sociological perspective, then, concentrates on human groups and their multiple influences on human behavior.

THE DIVERSITY OF SOCIAL REALITY   A key insight of the sociological perspective is that beliefs, values, and behaviors are *relative* to particular groups or societies and can be understood only in the context of those affiliations. The members of a group or society share a view of reality that determines what they believe to be right and wrong, proper or reprehensible. This means that tremendous diversity exists in human behavior from one society to another. Among the Tuareg in Saharan Africa, for example, it is customary for men to wear veils over their faces at virtually all times. They do so despite the fact that the practice is physically uncomfortable and inconvenient when eating or smoking (Murphy, 1968). Basuto women in southern Africa, as evidence of their undying love, rub their beloved's sweat, blood, or hair into open wounds on their bodies. The resulting scars are symbols of their affection (Ashton, 1967). Many people in the United States might view these social

The sociological perspective is based in the insight that human beliefs, values and behaviors are relative to particular groups and societies and that this results in tremendous diversity in behavior from one society to another. The colorful outfits of these Mexican dancers, in comparison to what would be seen in other cultures, are symptomatic of this diversity.

practices as silly, degrading, or repulsive. Yet the Tuareg and the Basuto would think it stupid for a man or woman in the United States to confine his or her feet in uncomfortable and smelly shoes on a hot day and would laugh at U.S. men and women who have their earlobes, noses, lips, and even tongues pierced to accommodate shiny baubles they think are attractive. The point is that none of these social practices can be completely understood unless it is viewed in the context of the shared view of reality found in a particular culture.

Within any society, there is also considerable variation in beliefs, values, and behaviors from one group to another. Marijuana and cocaine, for instance, are accepted among some rock musicians, entertainers, affluent singles, and college students in the United States. Many others, by contrast, disdain these drugs but consume alcohol freely. At the other extreme, Baptists are strongly opposed to the use of any alcohol or drugs, and Mormons reject the use of tea or coffee containing caffeine, which they consider a drug. This tremendous diversity, both within U.S. society and across cultures, has led sociologists to realize that beliefs, values, and behaviors can be fully understood only within the social context in which they occur.

CROSS-CULTURAL PERSPECTIVES   In the twenty-first century, one can easily overlook diversity. After all,

people drive cars and drink Coke in Caracas and Bangkok and eat at McDonald's restaurants in Moscow and Beijing; at the same time, movies, music, and MTV from the United States are a hit with young people in more and more nations. It seems that everyone is grasping for what is characteristic of the United States in aspirations, lifestyle, and economic relations. There is a danger, however, of overemphasizing superficial realities and ignoring more fundamental differences between peoples. Eating at McDonald's or drinking Coke does not mean that a person has adopted U.S. culture. Culture is much more pervasive than these food preferences, involving many complex and subtle beliefs, values, and aspirations. Much of the convergence we see in the world today involves material technology rather than beliefs, values, and aspirations. The United States, Saudi Arabia, and Japan are much alike in technological development but worlds apart in terms of religious beliefs or the value placed on the individual. If we overemphasize what people share in common, we miss something very significant: the extent of cultural diversity and an understanding of the substantial impact that culture has on our perceptions, values, desires, and behaviors. People of different cultures do truly live in a different world. Recognizing and understanding the importance of this diversity is one of the keys to developing a true sociological perspective.

Consider something familiar: misunderstandings between generations. For example, parents may not understand why certain clothing styles or hairstyles are in vogue or out among their teenage offspring, and adolescents may feel that their parents do not understand what is important to them. Two things are sociologically significant for understanding this parent–adolescent misunderstanding. The first is that adolescents and their parents are at different stages in their lives. Adolescents are very much concerned with proving their self-worth among their peers and establishing their sexual identity. One of the ways they do these things is by being in style or hip (or whatever it is called at a given time). Adults in their thirties or forties, on the other hand, may be more concerned with paying a home mortgage or saving for their children's college tuition than being "cool" or in style. For both groups, their location in the life span influences what they value and what takes on importance for them.

The second thing that is sociologically significant is that adolescents and their adult parents grew up at different points in history. Research shows that people's experiences in their teens and early twenties, while they are coming of age, have a powerful impact on their overall viewpoint and what they value and perceive as important (Alwin, Cohen, & Newcomb, 1991). So, adolescents and their adult parents have different viewpoints because they came of age at different points in history.

Based on these ideas, the sociologist C. Wright Mills (1959) argued that the sociological perspective offers the ability to understand that our own behavior and viewpoints are shaped by the intersection of biography and history: the point we are at in our own lives (biography) and the point in history in which we live. The adolescent and adult who have just been mentioned differ from each other in both biography and history. Yet, they are also very similar: Because they are parent and child, they may share the same racial or ethnic character, social class setting, neighborhood, and gender. Despite these similarities, they have difficulty understanding each other. This difficulty demonstrates the impact that small differences in biography and history can produce.

Now imagine much vaster differences. Compare a wealthy white European with a poor Haitian of African descent. Or imagine how biography and history would shape the viewpoint of a Comanche Indian of the seventeenth century when encountering white Europeans, who would call themselves "settlers" but would likely be seen as "invaders" by the Comanche. To go further afield, would the biographical and historical experiences of an Australian Aborigine of 500 years ago produce behavior, values, or viewpoints that twenty-first century Anglo Americans could comprehend? This is the challenge of sociology: to understand the role of this diversity in shaping our own and others' lives and societies. The sociological task is not to assess which values, viewpoints, or behaviors are "correct" or proper but rather to achieve the insight that every set of values, viewpoints, and behaviors is a product of a particular social situation, an intersection of biography and history.

Every chapter of this book includes many illustrations of this diversity, within both modern U.S. society and societies around the world and through history. In some examples, the discussion of diversity is incorporated in the text; in others, special sections titled *Other Worlds, Other Ways* highlight some especially important issues.

The issue of diversity is important because it is central to grasping the sociological perspective. It is also important because diversity often produces, or is the justification for, social inequality, discrimination, mistreatment, differential opportunities, and social conflict. Efforts to reform society and change these conditions require an accurate understanding of the nature, extent, and importance of diversity. Sociology offers this understanding. In fact, from sociology's inception in the nineteenth century, many sociologists have viewed their discipline as a key tool for accomplishing such reform.

GLOBALIZATION   Having just talked about the extent and importance of diversity in human social life, we also need to address contemporary trends that may be pushing social life in the opposite direction—toward greater uniformity across societies and cultures. Globalization refers to *trends toward increasing interconnectedness between different peoples around the world and the growing unification of social and cultural life.* Fueled in part by technological developments that have made possible rapid transportation over long distances and fast communication, societies around the world are now increasingly intertwined in their daily lives. For example, in economic life, products are now sold in locations that are far removed from where they were produced and often take the form of "information" (such as computer code or digital X-ray images) that can be sent instantaneously to any point on the globe. In addition, various cultural values and ways of life are now available to anyone around the world through the media or on the Internet, often reducing the centrality or attraction of local or traditional ways of doing things.

It is beginning to look like this process of globalization will take its place alongside the discovery of agriculture and industrialization as a major development that has profound effects on human social and cultural life. A very significant part of human social life is now moving online. The Internet, especially, is a technological development that causes distance and boundaries to have considerably less significance in social life, if not to vanish altogether. Any understanding of the modern world must take this new development into account. We don't yet know, of course, how far these tendencies toward uniformity will extend, but this trend and its impacts will be analyzed throughout this text. Some issues related to globalization are discussed in the regular text, but in other cases they are part of special sections titled *Sociology of Media and Technology* and *Other Worlds, Other Ways.* Where appropriate, a major section of the chapter is devoted to a global view of the chapter topic.

While some may believe that interdependence among peoples is something new since the twentieth century, in fact, trade and wars between peoples are as old as history. For example, during the Crusades, legions of soldiers from Europe went to the Middle East centuries before the Iraq War. The movement of slaves from Africa to the Western hemisphere in the sixteenth and seventeenth centuries was an ancient counterpart to the modern-day movement of labor around the globe. The plight of seventeenth-century farmers in New England was affected by the decisions of merchants and politicians in London and Paris, just as the livelihood of modern-day autoworkers in the United States is affected by decisions made in Tokyo or Seoul. There is, however, a difference today in the intensity, complexity, pervasiveness, and immediacy of global interdependence. Although some people might have ignored it or been unaware of it in earlier eras, such ignorance is impossible today. What is also different today is that we have sciences such as sociology and anthropology to help guide us through the thicket of cross-cultural misunderstanding that can arise when people from very different cultures come together at work, in school, or in other settings.

To summarize, the sociological perspective is a unique and remarkable view; it is a form of consciousness that recognizes that human behavior consists of far more than individuals acting independently of one another. Group memberships, social interaction, and social relationships are at the center of sociologists' attention. The sociological perspective offers a special awareness of the world that enables people to approach their own lives with introspection and insight. Peter Berger (1963) referred to the sociological perspective as an "emancipated vista" that can free people from blind submission to social forces that they do not understand. C. Wright Mills (1959) coined the term sociological imagination in referring to *the ability to understand the relationship between what is happening in people's personal lives and the social forces that surround them.* For both Berger and Mills, the more people learn about society and social processes, the better equipped they will be to understand their own lives and the impact of society on them. To be emancipated, of course, is not always pleasant because we often learn that social forces hinder us from achieving sought-after

goals. A poverty-stricken mother, for example, may not like the realization that her children will be penalized by the inequities in the U.S. educational system, which have adverse effects on the poor. Nevertheless, it is precisely a better understanding of the role of such inequities that can lead to improvements in the educational process. In providing this insight, sociology offers not only emancipation but also *empowerment:* It assists people in taking control of their own circumstances and lives.

Sociology as a Science

Traditional and religious sources of knowledge rest on untested or unquestioned assumptions. Sociology, by contrast, uses a scientific approach to studying people, which distinguishes it from other means of understanding human behavior. Some people are leery of studying human beings scientifically because they believe human behavior is so spontaneous and unpredictable that objective procedures are of little use. Other people maintain that a scientific approach reduces people to "statistics," human emotions to numerical equivalents, and in so doing ignores that undefinable kernel that makes us "human." In reality, people are quite predictable, as will be shown throughout this book. Where hesitation to study people scientifically exists, it usually rests on a misunderstanding of science—its possibilities as well as its limitations.

Science is *a method of obtaining objective and systematic knowledge through observation.* Science has certain characteristics that distinguish it from nonscientific sources of knowledge (Sullivan, 2001).

First, science is *empirical,* which means that it is based on observation. Scientists must be able to demonstrate that what they claim to be true can actually be observed in reality. Commonsense reasoning and traditional or intuitive knowledge cannot take the place of this observation.

Second, science is *systematic;* it follows methodical and generally accepted procedures. Consequently, scientific research is always open to critical review and assessment by other scientists in order to determine whether errors or biases have influenced the conclusions. As part of this assessment, scientific investigations are often repeated, a process that scientists term *replication.* Replication helps prevent unreliable or selective interpretations by determining whether other scientists reach the same conclusions using the same procedures. Replication provides further verification for scientific findings.

Third, science focuses on *causation.* Scientists assume that all events are caused, or determined, by something else. A major feature of scientific research is the search for these causes. For two or more phenomena to be causally related, there must be an association between them. For example, when water is heated to 212 degrees Fahrenheit (100 degrees Celsius) at an air pressure of one atmosphere, it will change from a liquid to a gas. As far as we know, there are no exceptions to this association. In other cases, the association between two or more phenomena is probabilistic. This means that the occurrence of one event increases the likelihood, or probability, that the other will occur, but the relationship does not necessarily occur in every case. As you learn about sociology in this book, you will see that most associations involving social phenomena are probabilistic.

Fourth, science is *provisional*. The results of scientific investigations are considered tentative, and they are always open to question and possible repudiation. There are no ultimate, sacred, or unchangeable truths in science. In the early part of the twentieth century, for example, many social scientists accepted the findings of the Italian criminologist Cesare Lombroso (1911) that some people are "born criminals," genetically inferior human beings who are throwbacks to a more primitive human type. Lombroso had empirical data, although not very systematically collected, to prove his point. But acceptance by scientists is always provisional and never unquestioned, so continued testing of Lombroso's ideas showed them to be false. Today, social scientists recognize that crime is a product mostly of learning and social conditions rather than genetics.

Finally, science is *objective*. Scientists strive to prevent their personal values from affecting their investigations. This impersonality does not mean that scientists have no values or emotional passions. Many are intensely concerned about social issues such as crime, divorce, environmental pollution, nuclear power, strategic arms control, and equal rights. At the same time, scientists realize that personal values can, and probably will, bias their findings. They have therefore introduced checks such as replication and provisionality to guard against the influence of personal bias on the body of scientific knowledge.

Science is not foolproof, but it is the most effective means of acquiring systematic, verifiable knowledge about the world. Science, of course, has its limitations, and it is crucial to understand which issues it cannot resolve. Science is the preferred source of knowledge on issues that can be resolved *through observation*. Some issues are not amenable to such resolution. For example, science cannot verify the existence of a supreme deity or say which religious beliefs are correct, because these are not issues that can be settled through observation. They are matters of faith, choice, or revelation, not of science. Likewise, science cannot tell us which personal values are right or preferable because these are again matters of personal judgment. Science may help show us how to live up to our values or the consequences of following particular values, but it cannot tell us which values we should live by. This choice may best be served by religious teachings, traditional knowledge, or ethical principles. The Applying Sociology section provides some further comparisons of the scientific approach of sociology with the commonsense approach on which people often rely.

Applying Sociology   Untangling Myths and Facts: Sociology and Common Sense

Sociologists take the position that scientific research provides the most accurate and useful knowledge with which to understand human social behavior. Science, of course, is not the only way to gain an understanding of the world. For example, people often use tradition as a source of guidance. Tradition might take the form of religious teachings about sex and marriage or proverbs such as "Birds of a feather flock together" and "Two heads are better than one." People also turn to their own personal experience for direction. If we visit a prison and see that most inmates are nonwhite, this experience can lead us to believe that most crimes are committed by nonwhites. Knowledge based on tradition and experience often accumulates and blends together to form what people call common sense: practical wisdom that people believe is sound but with no special training or expertise to support it. Every generation adds to the store of commonsense knowledge, and we routinely rely on it in our everyday lives when assessing situations or making decisions.

In fact, sociology has been called "the science of common sense" by critics who assume that it merely "proves" what everybody else already knows. Of course, sociology sometimes does confirm what many people already accept. We should not be surprised that scientific research shows that some commonsense beliefs are true, because people need some accurate commonsense knowledge of human behavior to interact with others and function effectively in society. However, sociological research also shows that many commonsense beliefs about human behavior are false or at least vastly oversimplified, as we saw in the opening Myth–Fact section of this chapter.

What is wrong with common sense as a source of knowledge? Basically, common sense does not normally involve an empirical and systematic effort to distinguish fact from fiction. Rather, it tends to accept untested and unquestioned assumptions because "everyone knows" they are true, and to reject contradictory information. In other words, some commonsense knowledge is a myth

(continued)

in that there is little evidence of its truth, although some people still accept it as true. Commonsense knowledge is also very slow to change—even when change seems called for—because the change may threaten cherished values or social patterns. In addition, common sense often explains everything, even when those explanations contradict one another. When we see two people with similar personalities become friends, we say, "Birds of a feather flock together." Yet when we see an athletic woman dating a bookish, cerebral man, we say, "Opposites attract." But which assertion is true?

Scientific research does far more than merely document what we already know. Sometimes it does just that, but at other times it directly contradicts common sense. Most of the time, however, the truth is vastly more complicated than common sense suggests. Sociological research incorporates procedures that advance our knowledge by establishing facts through observation and by using procedures that reduce bias. Common sense is important and should not be ignored, but an unthinking and unverified acceptance of commonsense beliefs can blind people to social realities. This fact has important implications for social policy. The realization, for example, that the income gap between African Americans and white Americans has changed relatively little over the past four decades suggests that the struggle to overcome racial inequities and achieve true equal opportunity is far from won. It is only through the development of an accurate, scientifically verified understanding of such social problems that we can hope to overcome them—even if it means relinquishing some of our most cherished commonsense preconceptions.

Each chapter of this book includes two features that emphasize these points. At the beginning of each chapter, a "Myths & Facts" section contrasts some inaccurate or misleading commonsense beliefs about the topics in that chapter with the facts as they have been established through research. This comparison encourages students to distinguish beliefs that have no empirical foundation and may in fact be myths from facts that have been substantiated through observation. Each chapter also includes an "Applying Sociology" section, which illustrates the use of sociological research in solving problems or evaluating how effective solutions are. This section emphasizes the theme of applying sociological research to solve human problems and instills an awareness that solutions to problems should rest, at least in part, on research and testing to see what works. ▪

The Social Sciences

There are many scientific disciplines, each investigating a particular sphere of the world. The *natural sciences* study nature and the physical universe. They include the physical sciences, such as chemistry and geology, and the biological sciences, such as biology and zoology. The *social sciences* are the disciplines that use the scientific method to study human behavior, groups, and society. Sociology is one of the major social sciences; there are a number of others.

Anthropology, the social science most similar to sociology, is the study of the cultures, customs, origins, evolution, and physical characteristics of human beings. Sociology places more emphasis on group structures, processes within cultures, and the impact of face-to-face social interaction than does anthropology.

Psychology focuses on the mental processes of individuals, dealing with phenomena such as memory, perception, motivation, and emotions. Although sociologists are also interested in explaining the behavior of individuals, they do so by studying the social environment that surrounds people. Sociology and psychology overlap in the subdiscipline of *social psychology*, which is the study of how people's thoughts, feelings, and behaviors are influenced by their interactions with others.

Economics, one of the oldest of the social sciences, is concerned with the production, distribution, and consumption of goods and services and with people's behavior as economic consumers. Sociology is concerned with economics as a form of social behavior, and economists draw heavily on the findings of sociologists in explaining economic behavior.

Political science has traditionally been most involved with political philosophy and the study of governmental forms. In the twentieth century, however, there was a shift toward a more systematic study of political processes. This shift has been influenced in part by the development of *political sociology,* which is the study of social behavior and social processes in political or governmental contexts.

Although the other social sciences narrow their focus to a particular realm of human social behavior, sociology is more general and encompassing. Sociologists deal with *all* forms of human social behavior, whether they occur in an economic, a political, a religious, or some other context.

Theoretical Perspectives in Sociology

You should be able to explain the roles of theories and hypotheses in sociological research and to discuss the major theoretical perspectives in sociology and explain how they are used.

To this point, sociology has been defined in terms of its unique perspective and its use of the scientific method.

The practice of sociology actually involves the continual interplay of two key elements: *theories,* which embody the sociological perspective, and *research,* which is based on the scientific method. The goal of a science like sociology is to shape our knowledge into theories. Theories provide ideas that can be investigated through research, whereas the research, in turn, provides evidence on the accuracy or veracity of the theories. First, theories and their role in the scientific process are discussed; then an outline of the major theories in contemporary sociology is presented; finally, there is a brief overview of how sociologists conduct research.

Theories and Hypotheses

A theory is *a set of statements that explains the relationship among phenomena.* Students occasionally approach theories as if they were mysterious, unusual, or possibly superfluous. In fact, people use theories frequently in their daily lives. Law enforcement officials investigating crimes, for example, rely on them heavily.

> The stereotype of the detective who asks for "just the facts" is inaccurate, for detectives are always working with and testing theory. . . . For instance, in homicide cases, the first people generally contacted by detectives are friends, relatives, or acquaintances of the victim. Behind such investigative procedures is the theory that most homicides are committed by people who are socially close to the victim. (Sanders, 1974, p. 3)

The theories used by detectives and other laypeople are less systematic than those used by scientists, but they serve the same purpose: to relate phenomena in a causal framework and thereby explain and predict behavior. One sociological theory, for example, explains the relationship between family life and juvenile delinquency (Agnew, 1991; Hirschi, 1969). Referred to as *control theory,* this explanation maintains that juvenile delinquency increases when the attachment of young people to their families decreases. *Attachment* refers to such things as maintaining open channels of communication with parents, along with love, respect, and affection for them. According to control theory, communication reduces delinquency because it affords youth the chance to express their problems to parents before these difficulties explode into delinquency. Love and respect for parents play an important role because young people who have these feelings are more likely to avoid actions that might bring disapproval from their parents.

An important ingredient of theories is variables. A variable is *a property or characteristic of something that can take on different values.* Age, for example, is an important sociological variable, and its value ranges over all of those ages that people can possibly be. Ethnicity is another sociological variable, with its values being the various ethnicities people can have, such as Hispanic, Jewish, Italian, and Polish. Juvenile delinquency and family attachment are two of the variables that make up control theory. In terms of delinquency, a youngster may have engaged in no delinquent acts at all, a few such actions, or many of them. Family attachment, likewise, could range from virtually no attachment whatsoever to intimate involvement.

In the investigation of causal relationships, theories contain two different types of variables. Independent variables are *those that bring about changes in other variables.* Dependent variables are *those that are changed.* In control theory, family attachment is the independent variable that brings about the changes in delinquency, which is the dependent variable in this case. Of course, a dependent variable in one situation may serve as an independent variable in another, or vice versa. In a different setting, for example, juvenile delinquency could be the independent variable that affects how well a person does in school or the likelihood of a person's becoming an adult criminal. The important point here is that independent and dependent variables both play unique roles in the causal process.

Scientific theories are linked to scientific research through hypotheses, which are *tentative statements that can be tested regarding relationships between two or more variables.* The following hypothesis, for example, could be derived from control theory: Children who engage in delinquent acts such as vandalism will be less likely than nondelinquents to feel that they can confide in their parents. This is a statement whose accuracy can be assessed through observation. In cases such as this, a hypothesis is deduced from an existing theory; if the hypothesis is confirmed through research, it provides further support for that theory. In other cases, where no theory exists relating to a particular phenomenon, hypotheses are developed from intuition or "hunches" that often derive from earlier research. If these are confirmed, then a start can be made in building a theory to explain the findings. In this fashion, all scientific theories are subject to *verification:* Continued investigations determine whether the relationships specified by hypotheses derived from a theory do, in fact, exist. Confidence in any theory rests on this verification process. If hypotheses derived from a theory are verified, then we have greater confidence in the theory; if they are not, our confidence is reduced (Figure 1.1).

Some sociological theories focus on specific arenas of social life, such as learning the causes of juvenile delinquency or the sources of marital satisfaction. Quite a few of these theories are discussed throughout this

Figure 1.1
The Process of Theory Verification

book. In addition to these specialized theories, however, there are a number of broader explanations of social reality called theoretical perspectives. These perspectives *provide some fundamental assumptions about the nature and operation of society and commonly serve as sources of the more specific theories.* In the 150 years since sociology was established as a scientific discipline, a heated debate has continued about the nature of the fundamental processes that underlie the operation of society. In approaching this question, most sociologists today are guided by one or more of the following theoretical perspectives: functionalism, conflict theory, or interactionism. The functionalist and conflict approaches are frequently referred to as *macrosociology* because they focus on large groups and social institutions and on society as a whole. The interactionist perspective falls under the category of *microsociology* because it concentrates on the intimate level of everyday interactions between people. This section first summarizes the perspectives and then suggests how to use them in analyzing social behavior.

The Functionalist Perspective

The functionalist perspective grew out of the similarities early sociologists observed between society and biological organisms. The human body, for example, is composed of many different parts—the heart, the eyes, and the kidneys, to name but three—each of which performs a particular function. The heart pumps blood to the other organs of the body, the eyes transmit information about the external world to the brain, and the kidneys remove waste materials from the blood. These parts of the body do not exist in isolation, however, but are interrelated and interdependent. If one of them ceases to perform its function—if the heart stops, the eyes go blind, or the kidneys fail—the effective operation of the whole body is threatened, and survival itself may be in doubt.

Society, functionalists argue, operates in a way somewhat analogous to that of a biological organism. According to the functionalist perspective, *society is a system made up of a number of interrelated and interdependent elements, each performing a function that contributes to the operation of the whole* (Merton, 1968; Turner & Maryanski, 1979). The elements of society include, for example, institutions such as the family, education, and the economy. The family provides for the bearing and rearing of children until they can live on their own. Educational institutions provide training in the various skills needed to fill jobs in society. The economy is responsible for producing food, clothing, and other necessities needed by families to survive as well as providing the books and other supplies needed for education. The family and the schools could not survive without the goods provided by the economy, and economic organizations need workers who have been socialized by the family and trained by the schools to work industriously. In addition to institutions, society is also made up of many social roles, social groups, and subcultures, and all these parts fit together into a reasonably well-integrated whole. For functionalists, then, all parts of society are interdependent and function together to provide the things that are essential to maintain society. In addition, there needs to be considerable agreement among the members of society regarding the content of important values and norms.

In a system with all the parts so tightly interdependent, a change in one element of society will probably lead to changes in other parts. For example, the establishment of compulsory education in the United States caused significant alterations in the economic sphere by removing children and eventually adolescents from the labor force, which made more jobs available for adults. Compulsory education also affected the family—with young people no longer working, the financial burden on parents was increased. When children could no longer help support the family financially, a gradual shift to smaller families began. Thus, changes in the educational sphere had important ramifications for the family and economic structures. Small changes can usually be absorbed with relative ease, but large or sudden changes can cause major social disruption. Therefore, functionalists argue, social systems are characterized by stability and a tendency toward *equilibrium*—a state of balance in which the relationships among the various parts of the system remain the same.

A central concern of the functionalist approach is the determination of just what functions each element in society performs. Such determination is not always easy because some functions are not as obvious as those in the preceding example. In fact, the sociologist Robert K.

Merton (1968) suggests that there are two different types of functions: manifest and latent. *Manifest functions* are intended consequences of some action or social process and refer to what most people expect to result. *Latent functions* are consequences that are unexpected or unintended. For example, one of the manifest functions of colleges and universities is to provide people with specialized training. However, institutions of higher learning perform a number of latent functions. For instance, they serve as a marriage market, and they reduce unemployment by keeping some adults out of the job market. These latent functions are just as much a part of the system of higher education as its manifest purposes. In addition, some social practices may be *dysfunctional;* that is, they may disrupt social equilibrium rather than contribute to it. For example, encouraging large families in a society that is already overpopulated would be dysfunctional.

One major criticism of the functionalist perspective is that it overemphasizes the extent of stability and order in society. Because of this emphasis, it is argued, functionalism is a conservative approach that supports existing social conditions, even though these may be inequitable or oppressive. Functionalism tends to downplay the fact that social practices that are beneficial to one group in society may be dysfunctional to another. The functionalist perspective also ignores the fact that conflict and disharmony may be inherent features of society. The conflict perspective provides an alternative approach with respect to these shortcomings.

The Conflict Perspective

Conflict theorists emphasize the inevitability of coercion, domination, conflict, and change in society. The conflict perspective is based on *the idea that society consists of different groups who struggle with one another to attain the scarce societal resources that are considered valuable, be they money, power, prestige, or the authority to impose one's values on society.* In the nineteenth century Karl Marx provided the foundation for the conflict perspective when he viewed society as consisting of different social classes (1867–1895/1967). The two key social classes of his era were the workers and those who owned businesses and factories. Marx saw these classes as being in constant struggle with each other to improve their respective positions in society. The workers tried to gain more income and control over their work; the owners tried to make more profits by lowering labor costs and getting workers to work harder. For Marx, this conflict was irreconcilable because what benefits one group necessarily works to the disadvantage of the other. Furthermore, if one group can gain an advantage in this struggle, it will dominate and oppress the other group and enhance its

own position. It might, for example, gain control of the government and pass legislation that limits the ways the subordinate groups could otherwise compete. In the nineteenth-century United States, for example, it was illegal for workers to organize for the purpose of collective bargaining. This law benefited factory owners because workers were unable to use their strength of numbers to gain higher wages or better working conditions.

Although Marx limited his focus to class struggle, modern versions of conflict theory in sociology hold that domination, coercion, and the exercise of power occur to some degree in all groups and societies because they are the basic social mechanisms for regulating behavior and allocating resources (Collins, 1975; Duke, 1976). In any society, there are dominant groups whose members will exert power over others to ensure that their interests are served. For example, because lucrative and rewarding occupational positions tend to be in short supply, dominant groups will try to preserve them for their own members. Whites might bar nonwhites from such jobs, or affluent groups might ensure that only their members have access to the education needed for certain jobs. In fact, Chapter 12 shows that controlling access to education is an important mechanism in modern societies for allocating desirable resources.

In the conflict view, groups exert what power they possess over others when it serves their interests, and society consists of a wide array of interest groups struggling to acquire a share of societal resources. An *interest group* is a group whose members share distinct and common concerns. Members of an interest group all tend to benefit from the same policies, practices, or distribution of resources, and those policies and practices probably work to the disadvantage of other interest groups. Some interest groups are formal organizations, such as the National Rifle Association, the Sierra Club, the National Manufacturers Association, or the American Civil Liberties Union. Others are informal, and people may not fully recognize that they are members of them. For example, college students constitute an informal interest group because all college students benefit from such things as lower tuition and increased government funding for student loans. Taxpayers without children of college age are another interest group, and they might oppose such policies because the policies would raise their taxes.

In the conflict view, social change involves redistributing scarce resources among various interest groups. The inevitable clash of interests ensures that any existing social arrangements will eventually be rearranged. Out of the resulting struggle, new winners will emerge and uneasy truces will be established. These truces, however, will be temporary, because new conflicts will develop that will lead to further struggle and change.

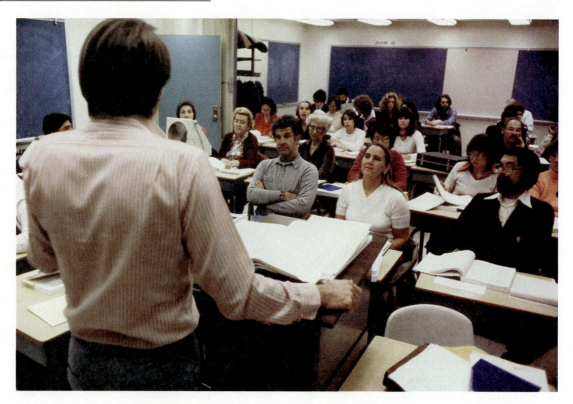

The functionalist perspective makes us aware that all the parts of a social system need to make a contribution to the operation of the whole. In some cases, people learn how to make a contribution by going through training in an educational context such as the one pictured.

The conflict perspective can be criticized for overemphasizing the importance of conflict and disregarding the prevalence of stability. In addition, whereas functionalists are often accused of being too conservative, some conflict theorists can be criticized for having a radical view that places too much emphasis on changing society rather than trying to understand how order and stability can be maintained. Nevertheless, the conflict perspective helps us to understand the many ways in which conflict and the exercise of power are critical elements in social life.

The Interactionist Perspective

Although the functionalist and conflict perspectives offer competing views of social life, the interactionist perspective strikes out in a different direction by showing how the social processes described in those perspectives enter into people's daily lives and shape their behavior. The *interactionist perspective* *focuses on everyday social interaction among individuals rather than on large societal structures such as politics and education* (Hewitt, 2007; Stryker, 1990). For interactionists, society consists of people interacting with one another; to understand society we must understand social interaction. It is through such interactions that groups, organizations, and society as a whole are created, maintained, and changed. The operation of educational institutions can be observed, for example, through students interacting with teachers and school administrators making decisions. It is these day-to-day interactions that lend education its shape and substance.

A central assumption of the interactionist perspective can be summarized by a paraphrase of a statement by the sociologists William and Dorothy Thomas (1928): If people define situations as real, the situations are real in their consequences. In other words, human action involves a period of examination and deliberation before people decide to act, and then they act on the basis of their beliefs and perceptions about situations. The term *definition of the situation* refers to *people's perceptions and interpretations of what is important in a situation and what actions are possible or appropriate*. A central part of social interaction is people's interpretations or definitions of others' behavior.

This process of definition or interpretation rests on the ability of human beings to use symbols. It is our symbol-using capabilities that enable us to attach complex social meanings to objects, events, or people. A *symbol* is something that stands for, represents, or takes the place of something else. Anything—any object, event, or word—can serve as a symbol. A crucifix, for example, symbolizes Roman Catholicism whether it is made from wood, metal, or plastic; the Star of David likewise symbolizes Judaism. The meaning attached to a symbol is derived from social consensus. We simply agree that a particular object will represent something. Figure 1.2 illustrates some gestures that have symbolic meanings and suggests how important it is in a global world to be aware of how the meanings of symbols and gestures can change from one setting to another.

Because of our ability to use symbols, we live in a world that we create ourselves, through the meanings we attach to phenomena. In other words, we respond to symbolic or social meanings rather than to actual physical objects or actions, and what we do is the result of how we define and interpret those meanings. If someone shoves you at a football game, for example, you will probably assess or "interpret" the situation before responding. What was the person's intent and what did she mean by shoving me? Was it a hostile action or an accident, or was she trying to avoid being crushed by the crowd? On the basis of this interpretation, you will decide what response is appropriate.

SYMBOL:

MEANINGS:
1. Victory in battle (England, 1940s)
2. Peace (United States, 1960s)
3. Up yours (England, 1980s, with palm facing inward and upward jerk of hand)

SYMBOL:

MEANINGS:
1. A-OK or all right (United States, 1990s)
2. A scatological insult (Latin America, 1950s)
3. Zero or worthless (south of France, 1990s)
4. Money (Japan, 1990s)

Figure 1.2

Some Symbols and the Various Meanings That Have Been Attached to Them

Another example of how humans attach social meanings to objects or phenomena is through the use of labels that we give to people. When we label someone as a mother, a politician, or a bureaucrat, certain meanings that we have learned go along with the label. For some, *mother* is seen as virtuous, *politician* as untrustworthy, and *bureaucrat* as rigid and unthinking. Labels of deviants, such as *whore, crook,* or *nutcase,* typically carry some stigma and influence how we relate to these people. Moreover, when people have been labeled, we come to expect them to behave in certain ways. A central tenet of the interactionist perspective is that such social expectations, or norms, tend to influence the behavior of people who have been labeled, especially when the people themselves accept the meaning of the label attached to them. The prostitute, for example, who internalizes the social meaning implied by the label *cheap whore* may not aspire toward any other way of life. Her world and behavior are shaped by the fact that she accepts the stigmatizing label, whether it is true or not. This fact points to another important assertion of the interactionist perspective: What is important is not whether a particular definition of the situation is actually true but rather whether people believe the definition to be true.

For interactionists, social life rests on the development of consensus about expected behavior. Such shared expectations guide our activities and make cooperative actions possible. If this consensus breaks down, some sort of change must occur. Thus, for interactionists, social change involves developing some new consensus with different meanings and expectations.

The individual looms larger in the interactionist perspective than in the first two approaches. The interactionist perspective, however, also has its limitations. Because of the emphasis on face-to-face interaction in shaping social reality, there is a tendency to ignore the part that social institutions, such as the family, religion, and the economy, play in molding human behavior. Interactionism also tends to ignore large-scale social forces, such as industrialization, that are beyond the face-to-face setting but that greatly influence both the amount of stability and the extent of change in society.

Using the Theoretical Perspectives

The preceding discussion of the sociological perspectives is brief and simplified, and there will be more detail in the remaining chapters. The major elements of each perspective are outlined in Table 1.1. A special feature of this book, titled "Sociology of Media and Technology," enables you to explore the insight that sociology offers regarding modern mass media and communications technologies. In this chapter, the insert also explores in more detail how the three theoretical perspectives can be applied to gain greater understanding of social

Table 1.1

AN OUTLINE OF THE SOCIOLOGICAL PERSPECTIVES

	Functionalism	Conflict Theory	Interactionism
View of society	A system of interrelated and interdependent parts	Made up of groups struggling with one another over scarce resources	Individuals in face-to-face interaction create social consensus
View of the individual	Little concern with personality; people are shaped by society to perform important functions for society	Little concern with personality; people are shaped by social institutions and the position of their groups in society	People are symbol manipulators; the self (personality) arises from communication and social interaction
View of social change	The social system tends to resist change as disruptive	Change is inevitable and continuous	Change occurs when there is no shared consensus about expected behavior; change involves developing a newly found consensus
Key concepts	Integration, interdependence, stability, equilibrium	Interest, power, dominance, conflict, coercion	Interpretation, consensus, symbols, shared expectations, socially created reality

phenomena. The three perspectives should not be viewed as either right or wrong, nor should one select a favorite and ignore the others. Instead, the perspectives should be seen as three different tools, each of which is useful in analyzing particular social phenomena. The three perspectives are not equally useful for examining every social topic, nor can any single perspective explain all aspects of human behavior and society. Furthermore, to gain a full understanding of any particular topic, the use of more than one approach may be required.

Conducting Sociological Research

You should be able to describe the three most commonly used research methods in sociology and discuss the problems of reactivity, objectivity, and ethics that all researchers confront.

It was pointed out earlier that science rests on systematic observation to determine how the world works. This section gives a brief introduction to how this observation is made in sociology so that you can better appreciate the contribution sociology makes to our understanding of the world.

Sociological research can have three distinct goals. Some research focuses on *description*, the search for factual information about some event, condition, or behavior. Descriptive research is typically used with a new topic about which we know little. Although

description is an important part of research, most sociologists would also hope to explain and predict what they observe. *Explanation* is the goal of telling why or how something happened, whereas *prediction* refers to using known facts and explanations to forecast what will happen in the future or in different settings. In actuality, a single research project might involve description, explanation, and prediction.

Research Methods

Once hypotheses have been constructed, sociologists develop *a detailed plan that specifies how observations will be made in order to test the hypotheses.* Such plans are called research methods. The three methods most commonly used by sociologists are observational techniques, surveys, and experiments.

OBSERVATIONAL TECHNIQUES   One of the fundamental research techniques used by sociologists involves looking, listening, and recording what they have observed. Observational techniques refer to *the direct observation of behavior by sociologists, either by seeing or hearing what people do.* These techniques can be used in many different settings. Observations are sometimes made in the artificial setting of a laboratory, where people are observed through a one-way window or their behavior is videotaped. In one study, for example, people were asked to report to a room in order to participate in a study of group activity. When they

Sociology of Media and Technology

Applying the Sociological Perspectives: Mass Media, Global Communications, and the Online World

The twentieth century was, without question, remarkable in terms of the impact of technology on social life. At the beginning of the century, such devices as telephones, televisions, airplanes, and, of course, computers were essentially nonexistent. By the end of the century, personal computers, cell phones, global positioning satellites, supersonic airplanes, and the Internet had tied people together into a massive communications network that has shrunk the globe in ways unimaginable a few centuries ago. And these remarkable changes have continued into the twenty-first century as communication and commerce have moved online in unprecedented ways (National Telecommunications and Information Administration, 2008). In 1900, most people who communicated around the globe did so by letter, which could take weeks or even months; today, people communicate instantaneously around the globe through e-mail, text message, and other forms of electronic communication. Increasingly large numbers of people access the Internet on a regular basis; the number of providers offering high-speed Internet access has increased more than ten-fold since this new century began, and the number of subscribers and users of broadband Internet access has grown by 1,100 percent (see Figure 1.3).

These technological changes have been truly stunning in terms of the capabilities they afford people, but what do they portend for social life? How do they impact on society and human social behavior? In this book, I want to devote special attention to this question by focusing in each chapter on a field known as "the sociology of media and technology." The major focus is on the modern mass media, communications technologies, and the online world; but I use this discussion as a platform from which to explore the impact of technology in general.

The **mass media** are *the channels of communication in modern societies that can reach large numbers of people, sometimes instantaneously*. They consist of print media, such as books, magazines, and newspapers, as well as electronic media in the form of television, radio, and the Internet. Given the technological advances of the past two decades, social scientists now speak of **computer-mediated communication**, *the various forms of communication made possible by modern computer technology*, including the Internet, e-mail, chat rooms, and the like (Croteau & Hoynes, 2002; Howard & Jones, 2004). This communications network, now global in nature, has become a central element of modern social life. In this chapter, the media and modern communications technologies are used as a way of applying the three sociological perspectives to a particular realm of social life, and each remaining chapter contains a special discussion of the mass media, global communications, and the online world.

Recall that a central question for the *functionalist perspective* is what functions are performed by a particular part of society. If something exists, it must be performing some social functions. In the case of the mass media, a number of functions are being performed—some quite obvious, others less so. Most clearly, the mass media are one of the major mechanisms of communicating and exchanging information and ideas in the modern world. We learn about what products are for sale, what our political leaders have to say, and who is being traded by the New York Yankees or the Chicago Cubs by seeing it

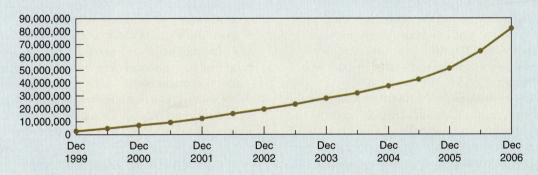

Figure 1.3

Total High-Speed Lines Available for Internet Access in the United States, 1999–2006

Source: Federal Communications Commission, *High-Speed Services for Internet Access: Status as of December 31,* 2006. Washington, D.C.: U.S. Government Printing Office, October 2007.

(continued)

on television or online or by reading it in newspapers or magazines. Certainly, we could learn about these things in other ways; earlier societies relied largely on word of mouth to communicate most such information. But word of mouth is considerably slower and less efficient and unnecessary now that technology makes possible rapid, almost instantaneous, and global information exchanges.

A less obvious function of the mass media is that the media makes possible higher levels of social integration and social uniformity than are possible without this "connective tissue." This occurs because, with the media and the online world, vast numbers of people—whole nations or even the global population—can be exposed to major beliefs, values, and guidelines for behavior. Role models in the media and online encourage people to accept certain language or clothing styles or particular moral guidelines. This modeling has always occurred, of course, but on a much narrower scale. Because of the instantaneous and global reach of communications today, the media and the online world have the potential to reduce regional variations in language, clothing styles, moral standards, and other social forms. In Chapter 2, we will consider whether this is bringing about a *cultural globalization:* an interconnectedness and uniformity of cultural values, norms, and ways of life among all people around the world.

From the *conflict perspective,* the modern mass media are instruments of social control that can assist one group in the domination of other groups. Those who control the media have an advantage over other groups in that the controllers can shape what information and ideas are available to others. The more powerful groups who monopolize the media are in a position to influence others to purchase their products or accept their ideas and values. Modern media technologies are especially effective at this because they have such an alluring and irresistible appeal. Advertising, for example, can be so colorful and engaging that it influences people even though they are unaware of the influence. Political leaders can also use the media to propagate some ideas and suppress others. This selective presentation of information gives a significant advantage to those who control the media.

From the conflict perspective, the mass media are also big business. Considerable profits are to be made by convincing the public to watch the television programs, rent the movies, and buy the monogrammed shirts that will make the media elite wealthy. This represents a shift in resources from the less-well-off to the well-to-do. From the conflict perspective, there is a tendency for the mass media, and the wealth it produces, to become concentrated in the hands of a smaller and smaller group of people at the top of society. Yet, modern electronic communications technologies represent a change in the power dynamic: Because the online world is accessible to so many people and so interactive, it may offer a channel for relatively powerless individuals and groups to communicate, organize, and possibly exert more influence than such groups in the past may have had. Irrespective of the ultimate outcome, the conflict perspective makes us aware that the electronic world will be contested territory among various groups seeking to pursue their own advantages.

From the *interactionist perspective,* the key characteristic of the mass media is the power to shape definitions of a given situation through the ability to create, manipulate, and distribute symbols. By selecting what is presented and how it is presented, the media shape what people see as important and the meanings that are attached to people and events. As is seen in Chapters 8 and 9, for example, people's definitions of what is proper behavior for men and women are influenced by how certain behaviors are portrayed in the media. In the 1950s, television shows such as *Father Knows Best,* or *Leave It to Beaver* portrayed men as the intelligent, strong workers who earned money to support their families while the women stayed at home and did housework and raised children. Although this portrayal was a reflection of reality to an extent, it was also a distortion of reality because many women with children worked, and single mothers were not uncommon (although less common than today). Even though distorted, however, this portrayal of family life on television influenced the social meanings that people attached to the institution of the family: People tended to see the normal or desired family as consisting of a working father, a stay-at-home mother, and two children. The media rendition of the family became the symbol against which people tended to compare and assess their own personal circumstances. Today, with the explosion of media outlets in the electronic world, people are exposed to a much wider variety of images, models, and social definitions. One consequence is that traditional sources of such social definitions and guidance, such as parents or religious leaders, may become considerably less influential in people's lives.

arrived, however, there was no one in the room and no hints were provided about what they should do. The investigator, Sandra Ball-Rokeach (1973), then observed through a one-way mirror how the people dealt with this very ambiguous situation. Her findings provided valuable information about how people react to confusing or ambiguous experiences, such as earthquakes or the bewildering aftermath of a war.

However, observation in such artificial settings is less common for sociologists than is observation done in natural settings. This observational technique is called participant observation, in which *the investigators take part in the activities of the people being studied*. Participant observation gives sociologists access to the everyday routines of people in a natural setting. Proponents of participant observation maintain that it is the most effective way to understand behavior from the perspective of the people under investigation and to learn about their beliefs, values, and views of their lives (Berg, 2007; Lofland et al., 2006).

A good illustration of participant observation research is a study by the sociologist Ruth Horowitz (1987) of a Latino gang. She lived in the community where the gang members lived and went to their dances, parties, and homes. From this vantage point, Horowitz was able to learn how gang members and community members viewed the violence the gangs occasionally engaged in. Community residents disapproved of gang violence, but they also recognized that such violence was the youths' response to a distortion of the value of "honor" common in Latin American communities. Honor includes the idea that a man should command respect in his contacts with others. For the youths, toughness and violence (often alluded to as *machismo*) become a prime way of maintaining honor. Another good participant observation study was done by sociologist Terry Williams (1989) among teenage cocaine dealers in New York City. He spent two hours a day, three days a week, hanging out with these teens in the bars, discos, restaurants, parties, crack houses, and street corners where they spent their days. Through this exposure, he was able to see why they couldn't get jobs—good entry-level jobs were disappearing—and why they dealt cocaine—the opportunity was there and they could make a lot of money. He also learned that these kids were shrewd businesspeople, worked very hard, and most of all sought the same kind of respect and reward that motivates people pursuing more conventional careers. Sociologist Philippe Bourgois and his colleagues conducted participant observation research on homeless heroin addicts in San Francisco (Bourgois, Lettiere, & Quesada, 1997). Bourgois and colleagues observed the addicts for extended periods over a two-year span to gather direct observational evidence of their risky behaviors in regard to drug use and HIV infection, especially sharing of needles and other drug paraphernalia. Their research, which is discussed in more detail in Chapter 10, helped sociologists to better understand the social factors that lead to such risky behaviors.

By using participant observation, Horowitz, Williams, and Bourgois were able to observe processes and grasp levels of meaning that other methods, such as surveys, would not have been able to uncover. These participant observations provide us with rich insight into the complexity that underlies social behavior.

Other research methods could not have provided this intimate view of the workings of youth gangs, drug businesses, and homeless communities.

Observational studies are valuable in that they focus on behavior in real-life situations where people are neither coaxed nor coached by the investigator. People behave much as they would if they were not being studied. Observational techniques also have certain drawbacks, however. The data gathered are often difficult to analyze, and the investigator's interpretation of the data often cannot be evaluated effectively by someone who was not at the scene. Thus, it is difficult to detect whether the investigator may have overemphasized some events and ignored others. In addition, participant observers sometimes find themselves under considerable pressure to join in the ways of those they are studying, so there is the danger that they may "go native" and become so identified with the group being studied that they lose objectivity (Shupe & Bromley, 1980).

SURVEYS Surveys involve *the collection of data by asking people questions about their behavior or attitudes*. Surveys can take the form of interviews or questionnaires.

In *interviews,* the investigator or an assistant asks questions and records answers. Some interviews are highly structured, with an interviewer asking the same questions of each person in the same order. Less-structured interviews allow the investigator to deviate from a specified list of questions in order to make the inquiry more clear or to pursue some novel issue that may arise.

A *questionnaire* is a survey based on printed questions that people answer directly on a prepared form without the aid of an interviewer. Some questionnaires are administered directly to people, and others are conducted through the mail, over the phone, or over the Internet.

An interesting example of an ongoing survey is one conducted on first-year college students every year by the Higher Education Research Institute (2004) at the University of California at Los Angeles. The survey is given each fall to a nationally representative sample of 700 two-year and four-year colleges and universities. The surveys ask, among other things, about the students' values and goals in life. One question is the following:

Indicate the importance to you personally of each of the following:
a. helping others who are in difficulty
b. raising a family
c. being very well-off financially
d. developing a meaningful philosophy of life

For each alternative, the students can choose from these response choices: essential, very important, somewhat important, and not important. Between 1966 and today, there has been a dramatic increase in materialistic values, with many more students today saying that "being financially well-off" is "essential" or "very important" to them; there has also been a dramatic decline in students who place value in "developing a meaningful philosophy of life." During the same period, family issues seem to have grown in importance.

When doing surveys, sociologists are often interested in the responses of a large group of people, such as all college students, all Roman Catholics, or all Democrats. Obviously, it would be very expensive to survey such large groups, so instead researchers select a *sample,* a portion of the large group of interest, and the survey is then given to the sample. A critical consideration is to ensure that the sample is representative of the whole group. A *representative sample* is one that accurately reflects the characteristics of the population under study. The problems created when samples are not representative were illustrated in early investigations of homosexuality. During the 1940s and 1950s, studies of gay men by psychologists and psychiatrists using samples of people who had received psychological counseling led to the conclusion that homosexuality was the result of a personality disturbance that stemmed from disordered relationships with parents during childhood (Bieber et al., 1962). Virtually all of the homosexuals in the samples had such relationships with their parents—a strong association, indeed. The problem in the sampling technique employed is fairly obvious, however. Gay men who seek psychological or psychiatric counseling *are not representative* of all gay men. People who seek therapy, whether they be homosexual or heterosexual, do so because they *already* have personal problems. Gay men who did not have problems did not seek counseling in the first place, so they were not in the population from which the samples were chosen. Thus, these early studies contained a built-in bias toward the finding that gay men were psychologically disturbed. More recent surveys that included gays who were not receiving counseling have concluded that gay men and lesbians are no more likely than heterosexuals to have

personality disturbances (Cabaj & Stein, 1996; Ross, Paulsen, & Stalstrom, 1988).

Surveys permit scientists to gather data inexpensively from a large number of people. They also enable sociologists to gather data about events that occurred in the past, such as how people voted in the last presidential election. In addition, surveys are used in tracing changes in behavior over time by replicating the survey at suitable intervals. But like all research techniques, surveys have their shortcomings. Because surveys are based on people's reports of their attitudes and behaviors, the resulting data may be inaccurate if people forget or misrepresent their views. In addition, surveys do not afford the rich data that are often obtained through other, more "natural" research designs, such as participant observation.

EXPERIMENTS An *experiment* is *a controlled method of observation in which independent variables are manipulated in order to assess their effects on a dependent variable.* In a common type of experiment, an *experimental group* is exposed to some factor, the independent variable, while a *control group*, which is like the experimental group in all other respects, is not exposed to that factor (Figure 1.4). If a change occurs in the dependent variable within the experimental group but not the control group, then the change can be attributed to the independent variable. The key to an experiment is to make sure that the experimental and control groups are as similar as possible (in terms, for example, of age, gender, education, or social class background) so that variations in these factors can be ruled out as causes of differences between the two groups on the dependent variable.

An example of a sociological experiment was a study of how to reduce *recidivism,* or crimes committed by people after their release from prison (Rossi, Berk, & Lenihan, 1980). On the assumption that ex-prisoners commit crimes because they cannot support themselves, these sociologists hypothesized that ex-prisoners would be less likely to commit future crimes if their financial situation was improved upon release from prison.

Figure 1.4

A Basic Experimental Design

The focus of the Baltimore LIFE (Living Insurance For Ex-prisoners) Project was inmates in Maryland state prisons who, on the basis of prior studies of released prisoners, were judged likely to commit another felony after release. These "high-risk" inmates were young males with multiple convictions, little financial security, and at least one property-related arrest. Two independent variables were used in this study: the provision of financial aid and job-placement services to these men upon release from prison. There were three experimental groups. One received financial aid and job-placement services; a second received financial aid but no job-placement services; and the third received job-placement services but no financial aid. The fourth group, a control group, received neither job-placement services nor financial aid. Inmates were randomly assigned to one of these four groups. The dependent variables were whether the ex-prisoners committed crimes after release and whether they were returned to prison.

The results of the study suggested that financial aid helped to reduce recidivism. The two groups who received financial aid had considerably lower rates of property-related crimes after being released than the other groups, a longer period of time passed before they were arrested again, and they were less likely ever to return to prison. However, financial aid did not affect the likelihood of these ex-prisoners committing *non-property* crimes. Job-placement counseling did not appear to help reduce recidivism: The two groups receiving financial aid had lower rates of recidivism whether or not they received job-placement counseling.

The Baltimore LIFE Project exemplifies *field experiments,* which are conducted in natural settings as people go about their everyday affairs. In *laboratory experiments,* artificial environments are constructed in which selected elements of the natural environment can be simulated and features of the investigation can be controlled. In one classic laboratory experiment, for example, authority relationships were simulated through an experimenter issuing orders to those participating in the study to administer strong electrical shocks to others. Although no one actually received electrical shocks, those who participated thought they were giving shocks and were surprisingly willing to obey the orders (Milgram, 1973). Through such simulations, we can learn about other authority relationships, such as soldiers obeying the commands of their superiors.

The major advantage of experiments is the ability to control extraneous variables and to determine whether changes in independent variables are the cause of changes in the dependent variable. Experiments can have drawbacks, however. The artificial setting of laboratory experiments, for example, may lead people to behave differently from the way they would if exposed to similar influences in a natural setting. In addition, in both field and laboratory experiments, the experiment and the experimenter may influence people's behavior in ways that cannot be predicted. This possibility is sometimes called the *experimenter effect*. The subjects in experiments may consciously or unconsciously pick up cues from the researcher about how they should respond. If they do, then changes in the dependent variable may be due to these influences rather than to the effects of the independent variable. Finally, many experiments, especially those conducted in laboratory settings, are limited to rather small samples, which makes generalizations to larger groups somewhat hazardous.

Steps in Conducting Research

Whether a sociologist conducts observational, survey, or experimental research, six common steps are followed (Figure 1.5). The first step is *problem*

Figure 1.5
Steps in Conducting Social Research

formulation: clearly identifying exactly what issue or problem will be researched. This is a critical step because some problems about which we might desire answers are not scientific questions at all, and no amount of research will answer them. Other problems, though possibly interesting and intriguing, might prove impractical from a methodological, ethical, or financial standpoint. Another element of problem formulation is to shape a concern into a specific researchable question. A problem such as "understanding crime" or "stopping drug addiction" is far too broad to be considered a research problem. Concerns need to be narrowed down to specific problems for which empirical data can be gathered, such as: How does social class standing influence the amount or types of crimes people commit? Or, Do drug education programs in the elementary schools reduce drug experimentation among teenagers?

Having successfully established a researchable problem, the second step is to *develop a research design,* a detailed plan outlining how observations will be made. The plan is followed by the researcher as the project is carried out. Research designs always address certain key issues, such as who will be studied, how these people will be selected, and what information will be gathered from or about them. In fact, the research design spells out in considerable detail what will occur in the following stages of the research process.

The third step in research is *data collection,* which might be based on direct observation, surveys, experiments, or some other, less commonly used research methods. The data collected at this stage constitute the basic observations from which conclusions will be drawn, so great care must be exercised over exactly how the data are collected. Errors or inadequacies that occur at this point, such as survey forms that are not completely filled out, may permanently and seriously compromise the ultimate conclusions that can be drawn from the research.

The fourth step in research, *data analysis,* is what unlocks the information hidden in the raw data and transforms it into something useful and meaningful. During data analysis, you learn whether your ideas are confirmed or refuted by empirical reality. During the course of data analysis, researchers often make use of statistical tools that can range from simple percentages to very complex statistical tests that require much training to understand and master.

The fifth step in conducting social research is to *draw conclusions* from the data analysis. The form this takes depends in part on the goals of the research project. A descriptive study, for example, would simply present what was found, possibly in a summarized form to make it more easily understood. Predictive and explanatory research, on the other hand, usually have hypotheses, or statements of what the researchers expect to find, stated before the data are collected. In this case, a major element of drawing conclusions is to

assess how much support exists for the hypotheses and how much verification is provided for the theories from which the hypotheses were derived.

Research findings are of little value if they remain the private property of the researchers who produce them. Therefore, the sixth step of *public dissemination of findings* by publishing them in a book or professional journal or presenting them to a professional organization is a crucial stage of social research. This disseminates the newly created knowledge to those who can put that knowledge to use or who can build on it in future research. In fact, public dissemination of knowledge is a major mechanism for scientific advancement. Public dissemination also makes it possible for others to identify whether any errors or biases influenced the research conclusions.

As Figure 1.5 implies, these steps in research are not always followed in the exact order described, nor does one step necessarily end before the next begins. While research will always begin with some degree of problem formulation, after that the steps may overlap and the order may in some cases be rearranged. In some kinds of research, for example, the results of data analysis may lead to changes in problem formulation, research design development, or the kind of data collected. However, in all social research, these six steps can be readily identified.

Issues in Conducting Sociological Research

Scientists studying human social behavior face some difficulties that are quite different from those that confront natural scientists. People, after all, are self-aware; they have opinions, emotions, and personalities that can make the sociologist's task more difficult, and in some cases very frustrating.

REACTIVITY   The term *reactivity* refers to the fact that people react to being studied and may behave differently from the way they do when they don't think they are being studied. Suppose you are a parent and a sociologist enters your home to observe your relationships with your children. Videotaping equipment is set up to record your every word and move. Would you behave in the same way you would if the observer were not present? You might, but most people would feel strong pressures to be on their toes and present themselves as good parents. You might be tempted to be more permissive with and tolerant of your child than usual, giving fewer negative sanctions and being more forgiving. In other words, people *react* to being observed, and sociologists must take this tendency into account when conducting their research.

The effects of reactivity on sociological research were well illustrated in a study of worker productivity conducted at the Hawthorne Plant of the Western Electric Company near Chicago several decades ago

(Jones, 1990; Roethlisberger & Dickson, 1939). The investigators began by introducing a number of improvements in the working environment, such as better lighting, more rest periods, and shorter workdays. Following each of these changes, worker productivity increased, which was what the investigators expected to happen. Had they stopped at this point, however, their conclusions would have been inaccurate, as the next phase in the investigation demonstrated. The experimenters then *reversed* the improvements by dimming the lighting, shortening the rest periods, and lengthening the workday. To the investigators' surprise, productivity continued to increase! After careful assessment, it became clear what had happened. The attention that the workers received as a consequence of being subjects in the study, rather than the specific changes in working conditions, led to the observed alterations in their performance. The workers viewed themselves as a special group who had been "chosen" to receive personal treatment by the company, and they responded by working harder. This type of reactivity is now referred to as the *Hawthorne effect:* The attention that people receive because they are involved in a scientific inquiry may alter their behavior. The experimenter effects discussed under the topic of experimental research designs are another form of reactivity.

VALUES AND OBJECTIVITY   An issue that is especially important and quite controversial regarding research in sociology is that of scientific objectivity, or the attempt by scientists to prevent their personal values from affecting the outcome of their research. This effort does not mean that scientists are without values or passions. Many are intensely concerned about social problems such as crime, divorce, family violence, and nuclear war. At the same time, scientists realize that their personal values can, and probably will, bias their research. Early in the twentieth century, the sociologist Max Weber laid out one position on this issue when he argued that sociology should remain as *value-free* as possible because human values can distort sound scientific investigation (1919/1958). Weber thought that sociologists should suspend their personal and political values when engaging in scientific research. Present-day advocates of Weber's position would concede that such suspension is difficult to accomplish but that abandoning the effort would be disastrous: There would be no means of acquiring an accurate body of knowledge about human social behavior (Gordon, 1988).

Karl Marx (1848/1964) eloquently stated a position opposite to that of Weber's on this controversy. Marx was a strong champion of the cause of the poor and the downtrodden, and he wanted to use science to improve their plight. He thought that social scientists should bring strong moral commitments to their work and use science to change

inequitable or immoral social conditions. Likewise, some sociologists today believe that social research should be guided by personal and political values and directed toward alleviating social ills (Fay, 1987; Shostak, 2001).

The sociologist Alvin Gouldner (1976) has suggested a reasonable middle ground between these two positions. He agreed that scientists have values and that the influence of those values on research, which is often very subtle, can never be totally eliminated. But he proposed that we should deny neither our values nor the negative impact they can have on research. He urged that scientists should be explicit about what their values are. In this way, other scientists are forewarned and are thus better able to spot ways in which research findings may be influenced by personal bias.

Of course, science has built-in checks against the influence of personal bias. For example, because science is provisional and studies are often repeated, a particular area of inquiry is likely to be investigated by many scientists holding different values. If these diverse scientists reach similar conclusions, we can be reasonably confident that the conclusions are not biased by personal values. Checks such as these, although they are not foolproof, do enable the scientific method to advance toward establishing an objective body of knowledge about human social behavior.

ETHICS   Sociological research is not an abstract affair carried out in the confines of musty academic halls. Quite the contrary, research brings sociologists in direct contact with people in all realms of their lives, and research can change those people's lives. Therefore, sociologists must consider whether research they conduct is ethical. Ethics has to do with what is proper or improper behavior, with moral duty and obligation. Basically, ethical research avoids violating the rights of the people being studied or harming them in any fashion. One ethical standard that sociologists follow is to protect people's right to *privacy,* or their ability to control when and under what conditions researchers will have access to their beliefs, thoughts, or behaviors. A related ethical standard is *confidentiality,* or ensuring that information or responses that people give a sociologist are not made public in a way that others could identify whose responses they are.

Problems of violating these ethical standards were dramatically raised in a very controversial research project conducted by Laud Humphreys (1970). Humphreys made observations of men having quick and impersonal sex in public restrooms. This research was participant observation, in which Humphreys acted as the "watch-queen," who warned of the approach of the police or of straight males while two other men had sex. Humphreys did not tell the other participants that he was a researcher making scientific

Other Worlds, Other Ways

SOUTH AFRICA: SOCIOLOGICAL RESEARCH IN DIVERSE CULTURES

SOUTH AFRICA
0   miles   2000

Conducting sound sociological research can be a challenge in a culturally diverse world because the social and cultural context in which research is carried out can influence what kind of research can be done, how it can be done, and the validity of the results. In other words, sociologists need to know a lot about the culture in which they will be conducting research.

Certain political and social values are widely held in the United States. For example, most Americans believe that people should have autonomy and a right to self-determination—a right to control their life and what happens to them. Another widely held value is individualism, the belief that the individual's desires and achievements are more important than society's advancement or goals. Congruent with these values, the United States incorporates into its legal system many protections for individuals against the arbitrary exercise of power by the state or by powerful groups over the less powerful. In the realm of sociological research, these values imply that participation in such research should be voluntary and considered; people should never be tricked or coerced into participating. In line with these values, as has been shown, sociologists are expected to obtain informed consent in which the people participating in the research are told what the research is about; what they will be expected to do as participants; any discomfort, harm, or stress they might experience; and who will benefit from the research. This expectation works well in most situations in the United States where most people are well educated and tend to be knowledgeable about the rights and protections that are available to them. In this cultural context, the ASA Code of Ethics can be implemented in a straightforward fashion: People are asked to sign a consent form on which is written all they need to know in deciding whether they will agree to participate.

If the research project is shifted from North America to black South Africa during the period of apartheid, when black South Africans were rigidly oppressed and had few social, political, or economic rights or opportunities, the situation is entirely different. For example, the sociologist Ivy Goduka conducted research on black schoolchildren in South Africa in the 1980s, before the end of apartheid. As Goduka put it at that time:

> South Africa is an authoritarian society that gives little or no state protection of individual rights, particularly for blacks. . . . [The apartheid laws] deny blacks in South Africa the right to vote and serve to keep them landless, powerless, and lacking in all the basic resources necessary for survival. Because they lack basic resources, blacks are not only illiterate and poverty-stricken, but also ignorant, vulnerable, and powerless to make decisions and choices directly affecting their own lives. (1990, pp. 329–330)

At that time, black South Africans could be told where to live, moved arbitrarily by the government, and even have their homes demolished if the government deemed it necessary. In all these circumstances, individuals had little say. The implications for informed consent in research are straightforward, according to Goduka: "Informed consent has no meaning to subjects who cannot even choose where they are to live, much less consent through elections to the government that makes those decisions for them" (1990, p. 333). The parents of the children Goduka studied lacked the education to read and understand the consent form. Established institutions such as school or government were so authoritarian that these black South Africans did not feel they had any choice in signing a consent form their child brought home from school. They agreed to participate in Goduka's research, but for most it was not a free and considered decision. Rather, they agreed so that no troubles would come to their children or as a submissive response to what were seen as all-powerful institutions. Some probably consented because they looked up to well-educated black South Africans (such as Goduka) who, they hoped, might be able to bring some positive change to their lives.

So, the world looked very different to these South Africans, and the informed consent form had a meaning for them that was very different from the meaning it had for most people in North America or Europe. In fact, Goduka approached families in Michigan with the same consent form and encountered substantial resistance from both teachers and parents to the use of their students and children in research. People in the United States may not have understood the intricacies of sociological research, but they could read and understand the consent form, and more importantly, they accepted the belief that they could refuse participation even if that meant challenging institutional sources of power such as schools or the government. However, the South African experience cautions sociologists to recognize that some people in the United States may not be in a position to give truly informed consent either. Any subordinate group—prison inmates, the poor, racial minorities, in some cases even women—may feel strong pressures to agree to participate in research, especially when those requesting consent are the people or organizations that exercise some control over them. Once again, diversity both between and within societies provides some insight into social life. ■

observations. He also noted the license plate numbers of the men's cars and was able to learn their addresses through public motor vehicle records. He then interviewed the men in their homes, gathering details about their personal lives but never letting on that he was doing research on their sexual behavior.

Many sociologists heavily criticized Humphreys's procedures on the grounds that he violated the subjects' right to privacy. Even though the men were clearly trying to hide their behavior from prying eyes, Humphreys made his observations without seeking their approval. One way of protecting privacy is through *informed consent*: telling research participants of all aspects of the research that might reasonably be expected to influence their decision about whether to participate. Issues of privacy, confidentiality, and informed consent are especially important in Humphreys's research because the men observed were engaging in highly stigmatized behavior. If the behavior became public knowledge, it might have changed their lives, since many of the men were married and had children. Many sociologists fault Humphreys for violating the men's privacy and failing to obtain informed consent.

Humphreys and his defenders argue that no ethical violations occurred because the men were in a public place and thus their behavior was legitimately accessible to Humphreys or anyone else who had a right to be in that place. In addition, Humphreys went to great lengths to protect the confidentiality of the information he collected. He took steps to ensure that the men's identities could not be discovered by anyone other than himself, and he destroyed anything that could identify them once he was done with his research project. In fact, none of the men's identities ever did become known to anyone but Humphreys.

Humphreys's research illustrates how ethical problems can be controversial and difficult to resolve. They can also require as much attention from the sociologist as does the actual conduct of the research itself. Humphreys spent much of his career debating and justifying his research. In recent years, some sociologists have actually spent time in jail in order to protect the privacy or confidentiality of their research subjects. For example, the sociologist Rik Scarce (1994) conducted research on activists in the animal liberation movement in the early 1990s. A federal grand jury was investigating break-ins by such activists at university laboratories, and some of the activists the grand jury was interested in had been interviewed by Scarce as part of his research. He refused to answer certain questions about these activists put to him by the grand jury because he thought that it would violate the confidentiality he had extended to the people he interviewed. He was jailed for four months on contempt-of-court charges, suggesting how important the ethical issue of confidentiality was to Scarce. Generally, the courts have held that confidential communication between a researcher and research participant is not privileged, that is, protected from intrusion by the courts.

So, the consequences of research can be profound, and sociologists are very careful about what research they do and how they do it in order to avoid making ethical breaches. In fact, the American Sociological Association (ASA), the Society for Applied Sociology (SAS), and the Sociological Practice Association (SPA) all publish a Code of Ethics that assists sociologists in dealing with these issues. However, these issues are inherently complicated, and they are made more complex when sociologists do research in cultures different from their own, as the Other Worlds, Other Ways section (p. 24) illustrates.

Putting Sociology to Use

You should be able to distinguish between basic and applied sociology, describe the different types of sociological practice, and show how sociology can be used in your everyday life.

The Development of Sociology

Sociology emerged in the 1800s and early 1900s as an instrument of both understanding and social reform (Lazarsfeld & Reitz, 1989). The nineteenth-century French philosopher Auguste Comte is considered the father of sociology because he was the first to use the term *sociology*. He argued strongly that society should be studied according to the same scientific methods that were used to understand the natural world. At about the same time, Harriet Martineau set the tone for a reformist sociology with her sociological work in England. She did research and writing on issues of slavery, colonialism, and the impact of industrialization on women (Hoecker-Drysdale, 1992). Early sociologists in the United States were also strongly motivated by a desire to reform society and make life better for people. In the early 1900s, for example, Albion Small focused his sociological analysis on problems of corruption and poverty in the United States, while Jane Addams concentrated her sociological work on the problems of poor women in the slums of Chicago. W.E.B. Du Bois, an African American sociologist, used sociological insight to attack the racism and exploitation that African Americans experienced at the hands of whites in the United States and elsewhere. Another African American sociologist, E. Franklin Frazier, conducted a groundbreaking study of a race riot in Harlem in 1935 that was a considerable advance over the understanding of such riots at the time (Deegan, 1988; Platt, 1991).

While this reform tradition has continued in sociology, another important trend emerged by the 1930s: the attempt to establish sociology as a legitimate and respected field of study in the eyes of laypeople, especially influential people who had money and other resources that the new discipline needed to support its research and develop new theoretical and methodological tools. For many sociologists, the discipline could best gain legitimacy and respectability by emphasizing the scientific, quantitative, and objective nature of the discipline. The best way to carve a societal niche, many thought, was to emphasize sociology's objective quest for knowledge and stress its independence from any special interests in society. To achieve this objectivity, many sociologists downplayed the reform emphasis of the discipline, and the pursuit of knowledge for the sake of knowledge rather than social change became the overriding thrust of many sociologists' work for a number of decades.

By the 1960s and 1970s, sociology had secured its position in society, and many sociologists were ready to give renewed emphasis to issues of reform and the practical uses of sociology. Today the discipline exhibits more of a balance between what have come to be called basic and applied sociology. In addition, sociologists remain as diverse a group as they were in earlier years in terms of racial or ethnic background and gender. Small, Martineau, and Du Bois have been replaced by black, Asian, and Hispanic male and female sociologists in the United States and around the world. As pointed out in Other Worlds, Other Ways: South Africa, this diversity is important to the ability of the discipline to understand diverse ways of life.

Basic and Applied Sociology

All sciences, including sociology, make a distinction between basic (or pure) science and applied science. The primary focus of basic science is to advance our understanding of some phenomenon, whereas applied science focuses on solving some real-world problem. Both basic and applied sociology are based on observation, but what they do with these observations is quite different. Basic sociology refers to *sociological research whose purpose is to advance our knowledge about human social behavior with little concern for any immediate practical benefits that might result.* Basic sociology is an attempt to develop theories that explain how societies work and why people behave the way they do; the goal of basic sociology is to subject theories to the process of hypothesis testing and theory verification described earlier in this chapter.

Applied sociology consists of *research and other activities designed to focus sociological knowledge or research tools on a particular problem identified by some client with some practical outcome in mind* (Larson, 1995; Sullivan, 2001). The primary focus of applied sociology is on policy or changes in behavior: making

recommendations about social programs or policies that might be implemented or about how to change behaviors. Applied sociology uses sociological theories and research tools to tackle some particular problem that somebody wants solved. It addresses questions like these: How well does some program or practice work? Does it achieve its goals? What consequences does it have? The overall focus is to direct existing knowledge and research tools toward the end of social intervention. We may learn something new about human behavior along the way, but that is not the main point.

Sociologists who do basic research are typically employed at colleges or universities where their professional duties include doing research as well as teaching. Some applied sociologists are employed by universities, but many work for federal, state, or local government, private industry, or nonprofit organizations.

Sociological Practice

Applied sociologists do a number of specific kinds of jobs (Bruhn & Rebach, 1996; Straus, 2002). Some are *applied researchers* who collect and analyze data in order to recommend solutions to a particular problem faced by a client or organization. Some applied researchers, for example, have collected and analyzed data for the government to assess how well welfare reform policies achieve their goals. Others work for private corporations analyzing the best markets for new products.

A second type of applied sociologist is *sociological consultants*, sometimes called *social engineers*. They make recommendations to clients for changes in policies, programs, or practices based on the existing body of sociological knowledge about human groups and human social behavior. Unlike applied researchers, consultants do not collect and analyze data themselves but rather rely on the sociological knowledge distilled from the research, both basic and applied, of others. For example, a sociological consultant might use past research on the link between socioeconomic status and attitudes toward crime to help a lawyer pick a jury that would be most fair in its treatment of the lawyer's client.

A third category of applied sociologist is *clinical sociologists,* who attempt a sociological diagnosis of group problems and the behavior of people in groups and develop a planned program of change. Some clinical sociologists, for example, conduct family counseling directed toward helping families overcome problems, whereas others help people change undesired behaviors such as overeating or alcohol abuse (Fritz, 1991; Roberts, 1991). As with sociological consultants, sociological clinicians use existing sociological knowledge without conducting research themselves.

Sometimes the terms *applied sociology* or *sociological practice* are used to refer to these three

Sociology on the Internet

Each chapter of this text offers suggestions for useful explorations of the Internet relevant to the topics in this course. One good way to begin is to look for Web sites relevant to the discipline of sociology and the study of social problems. For example, go to the search engine called Yahoo! (www.yahoo.com) and begin by selecting the "Directory" search category and entering the terms "Social Science," "Sociology," and "organization." This will offer you choices of going to the home pages of many sociological organizations in the United States, Canada, New Zealand, and other countries. Start by choosing "American Sociological Association" (www.asanet.org), which is the main U. S. organization for the discipline of sociology. At its Web site, you can learn more about sociology and about the way in which the national professional organization supports the work of sociologists. Look at some of the other sociology organizations whose links are in the Yahoo! search. What information do you find there relevant to your study of sociology?

To learn more about the focus of sociology on the understanding and solution of social problems, go to the Web site of the Society for the Study of Social Problems (www.sssp1.org). This is an interdisciplinary organization of researchers engaged in the scientific study of social problems. There, you can read the organization's newsletter, learn about its annual meeting, and find links to other relevant Web sites. Another excellent Web site is Sociosite: Social Science Information System at the University of Amsterdam (www.sociosite.net). It contains an enormous number of links to other Web sites about particular sociologists, organizations in sociology, newsletters, and journals, as well as information about how sociologists investigate and attempt to find solutions to social problems.

Also, Allyn & Bacon, which publishes this book, maintains a Web site called the Social Problems Supersite, for the use of students in sociology (wps.ablongman.com/ab_socialprob_sprsite_1). At that site, you will find a variety of materials to assist you in the study of sociology and social problems. One set of materials is a list of Problem Areas in the study of social problems. For materials relevant to this chapter, click on "Problem Area: General Sociology." Later chapters identify parts of this Web site relevant to the chapter. ■

spheres taken together (applied research, sociological consulting, and clinical sociology).

Using Sociology in Everyday Life

Most people who work as professional sociologists have either a master's degree or a doctorate in sociology. However, it is not necessary to achieve this level of education in order to put sociology to use. People with a bachelor's degree in sociology work in corrections, social service agencies, private business, journalism, urban planning, and many other job settings. In these jobs, sociological training is valuable because it informs the workers about the social sources of crime, poverty, and worker motivation, as well as about how cities work and organizations function. In fact, because virtually all jobs involve working with people and their social behaviors at some level, training in sociology can provide valuable knowledge for many jobs. In addition to teaching about social behavior, sociological training also imparts specific skills that employers are looking for: skills in research (including statistical and computer analysis training), critical thinking and problem solving, and interpersonal communication.

Beyond its utility in the workplace, sociology also has applications to our everyday lives as we make our way as social creatures through a world filled with other social creatures. The understanding of human behavior that sociology imparts can provide insight into the daily actions and choices of ourselves and others around us. Sociology tells us about why people marry and divorce, what functions religion performs, and how racism and sexism can affect the self-esteem and accomplishments of those against whom they are directed. Because practically all of us have some experience with these issues in our lives, sociology can provide us with the insight to make more informed choices. It also offers a valuable perspective, the sociological imagination, which makes us aware of how much our lives and behavior are shaped by social factors (biography and history) as much as by biological or psychological ones.

Study & Review
SUMMARY OF LEARNING OBJECTIVES

You should be able to discuss the sociological perspective and describe the main characteristics of the other social sciences and science in general.

Sociology is the scientific study of societies and human social behavior. The sociological perspective emphasizes the powerful role that group membership and social forces play in shaping human behavior. A key element of the sociological perspective is the recognition that beliefs, values, and behaviors can be understood only in the context of the view of reality shared by a particular group or society. Sociology is a science, which means that it is based on objective and systematic knowledge gained through empirical observation. Science, as a source of knowledge, is empirical, systematic, focused on causation, provisional, and objective. Other social sciences include anthropology, psychology, economics, and political science.

You should be able to explain the roles of theories and hypotheses in sociological research and to discuss the major theoretical perspectives in sociology and explain how they are used.

In order to explain social phenomena, sociologists develop theories, which are linked to sociological research through hypotheses. Three theoretical perspectives guide most sociological research. The functionalist perspective views society as a system made up of interrelated and interdependent parts, each performing a function that contributes to the operation of the whole. The conflict perspective views society as consisting of numerous interest groups that struggle with one another in order to obtain scarce resources. The interactionist perspective focuses on everyday social interaction that is shaped by social meanings and shared expectations.

You should be able to describe the three most commonly used research methods in sociology and discuss the problems of reactivity, objectivity, and ethics that all researchers confront.

Research methods are the detailed plans that sociologists develop regarding how they will make observations to test hypotheses. The three most-used research methods are observational techniques, surveys, and experiments. Six common steps are usually followed in conducting research. In studying human behavior, sociologists confront some special difficulties, including reactivity, values and objectivity, and ethical concerns.

You should be able to distinguish between basic and applied sociology, describe the different types of sociological practice, and show how sociology can be used in your everyday life.

The primary goal of basic sociology is to test theories and advance our knowledge of human social behavior; applied sociology focuses on social intervention,

solving problems, and practical outcomes. Sociological practice can involve applied research, sociological consulting, and clinical sociology.

CHRONOLOGICAL PRACTICE TEST

For answers to Key Concepts, see the page number in parentheses; for other answers see page 30.

What Is Sociology?
Key Concepts

1. Sociology (5)
2. Sociological perspective (5)
3. Globalization (7)
4. Sociological imagination (8)
5. Science (8)

True/False

6. T F In comparing the contrasting viewpoints of adolescents and adults, the key task that a sociological analysis would focus on is to determine which viewpoint is correct.
7. T F Sociologists do not conduct research on commonsense beliefs because they mostly turn out to be true.
8. T F Sociology, economics, and anthropology are all considered to be social sciences.

Concept Completion

9. In discussing social life on Bonerate, an Indonesian island, the beginning of the chapter was stressing the importance of _____.
10. The ability to understand the relationship between what is happening in people's personal lives and the social forces that surround them is what C. Wright Mills called _____.
11. When we say that science is *empirical*, we mean that science is based on _____.

Critical Thinking

12. Define sociology and the sociological perspective. What is the sociological view of diversity, and why is a cross-cultural perspective so important for sociology? Use the chapter-opening discussion of Bonerate to provide specific examples.
13. List and describe the characteristics of science.
14. What is commonsense knowledge? What are its weaknesses? How does scientific knowledge differ from common sense? How does science overcome the weaknesses associated with commonsense knowledge?

Theoretical Perspectives in Sociology
Key Concepts

15. Theory (1)
16. Variable (11)
17. Independent variables (11)
18. Dependent variables (11)
19. Hypotheses (11)

20. Theoretical perspectives (12)
21. Functionalist perspective (12)
22. Conflict perspective (13)
23. Interactionist perspective (14)
24. Definition of the situation (14)
25. Mass media (17)
26. Computer-mediated communication (17)

True/False

27. T F Independent variables are variables that are presumed to bring about changes in other variables.
28. T F One of the main criticisms of the conflict perspective is that it overemphasizes the extent of social stability in society.
29. T F One of the core ideas of the interactionist perspective is that society consists of parts that are interrelated and interdependent.

Concept Completion

30. Scientific theories are linked to scientific research through _____, which are tentative statements that can be tested regarding relationships between factors.
31. According to the functionalist perspective, social practices that disrupt social equilibrium rather than contribute to it are called _____.
32. Two key concepts of the conflict perspective are _____ and _____.
33. The concept of _____, attributed to sociologists William and Dorothy Thomas, is a key concept of the interactionist perspective.

Graphics Review

34. Describe why Figure 1.2 on page 15 is a good illustration of some of the social processes described by the interactionist perspective in sociology.

Critical Thinking

35. Define the terms *theory*, *variable*, and *hypothesis*. What different kinds of variables are used in scientific work? How do all of these work together in the process of science?
36. What are the basic assumptions of the functionalist perspective regarding the nature and operation of society?
37. Describe the conflict and interactionist theories in sociology and show how they differ from one another.

Conducting Sociological Research

Key Concepts

38. Research methods (16)
39. Observational techniques (16)
40. Participant observation (19)
41. Surveys (19)
42. Experiment (20)

True/False

43. T F The major advantage of surveys is that, compared to other research methods, they best enable researchers to determine if changes in an independent variable are the cause of changes in a dependent variable.
44. T F Max Weber is the sociologist who argued that sociology should remain as value-free as possible.
45. T F One of the ethical standards that sociologists attempt to adhere to in conducting research is reactivity.

Concept Completion

46. When research is conducted by making direct observations in natural settings where the investigator takes part in the activities of the people being studied, the research method being used is called _____.
47. When sociologists conduct experiments in natural settings where people are going about their everyday affairs, these experiments are called _____.

Graphics Review

48. Use Figure 1.4 on page 20 to explain how experiments enable us to establish what factors have caused changes in a dependent variable.

Critical Thinking

49. Define the three research methods described in the chapter, and give examples. What are the advantages and drawbacks of each?
50. Describe the various positions that sociologists have taken on the issue of scientific objectivity. Include in your answer a discussion of the role of values in the scientific process.
51. With what kind of ethical issues do sociologists grapple? How do sociologists attempt to resolve these issues? Illustrate your answer with a discussion of how this point related to research done in South Africa.

Putting Sociology to Use

Key Concepts

52. Basic sociology (26)
53. Applied sociology (26)

True/False

54. T F Sociological consulting is one of the forms of applied sociology.

Concept Completion

55. _____ are applied sociologists who are sometimes called social engineers.

Critical Thinking

56. Define and clearly distinguish between basic sociology and applied sociology. What are the different forms in which sociological practice can be carried out?

ANSWERS TO CHRONOLOGICAL PRACTICE TEST

6. F; 7. F; 8. T; 27. T; 28. F; 29. F; 43. F; 44. T; 45. F; 54. T
9. community
10. sociological imagination
11. observation
30. hypotheses
31. dysfunctions
32. interest, power, dominance, conflict, coercion
33. definition of the situation
46. participant observation
47. field experiments
55. Sociological consultants

CUMULATIVE PRACTICE TEST

See page 482 for answers.

1. Which of the following statements would *not* be considered a part of the definition of the discipline of sociology?
   a. It is a scientific study.
   b. It studies societies.
   c. It studies human social behavior.
   d. It studies human genetic predispositions.
   e. All of the above are part of the definition.
2. The basic premise of sociology is that human behavior
   a. is largely determined by our biological heritage.
   b. is largely determined by the groups to which people belong and by the societies in which they live.
   c. is largely determined by our personalities, which are fully formed early in life.
   d. is a product of many unrelated decisions, making human life largely unpredictable.
   e. is unrelated to the kind of society in which a person lives.
3. Which sociologist coined the term "sociological imagination"?
   a. Robert K. Merton.
   b. C. Wright Mills.
   c. Karl Marx.
   d. Laud Humphreys.
   e. Max Weber.
4. The "sociological imagination" is best described as
   a. the creative use of sociological perspectives by sociologists.
   b. the creative use of sociological perspectives by nonsociologists.
   c. the ability of people to understand the relationship between what is happening in their personal lives and the social forces that surround them.
   d. the imagination required of sociologists to develop accurate theories of human social behavior.
   e. both a and b.
5. To say that science is *objective* means that
   a. scientists have no personal values.
   b. scientists can set aside their personal values in order to discover the truth.
   c. replication is no longer necessary in science.
   d. science is a foolproof way to achieve knowledge.
   e. scientists strive to prevent their personal values from affecting their investigations.

6. Which of the following is *not* one of the distinguishing characteristics of science?
   a. Causation.
   b. Provisional.
   c. Objective.
   d. All of the above are distinguishing characteristics.
   e. Only a and c are distinguishing characteristics.
7. According to the chapter, commonsense knowledge
   a. is often superior to scientific knowledge.
   b. is based on systematic observation.
   c. usually involves representative samples.
   d. tends to accept untested and unquestioned assumptions.
   e. is what derives from observational research.
8. According to the text, sociology involves a continual interplay between
   a. reactivity and research.
   b. the functionalist and conflict perspectives.
   c. participant observation and surveys.
   d. theories and common sense.
   e. research and theory.
9. If we say that engaging in delinquent actions will produce a decline in school performance, then "decline in school performance" is a(an)
   a. independent variable.
   b. dependent variable.
   c. control variable.
   d. hypothesis.
   e. theory.
10. The term *macrosociology* refers to theoretical perspectives in sociology that
    a. derive from the functionalist perspective.
    b. focus on the intimate level of everyday interactions between people.
    c. focus on people's ability to use symbols and to interpret social meanings in social interaction.
    d. are used mostly in the field of applied sociology.
    e. focus on large groups and social institutions and on society as a whole.
11. Which sociological perspective grew out of the similarities that early sociologists observed between society and biological organisms?
    a. The conflict perspective.
    b. The commonsense perspective.
    c. The interactionist perspective.
    d. The sociological imagination.
    e. The functionalist perspective.
12. Which of the following statements would most likely be associated with the functionalist perspective?
    a. Change involves the redistribution of scarce resources among various interest groups.
    b. Change occurs when social consensus about shared expectations breaks down.
    c. People use strategies to create a sense that shared meanings exist and govern social interaction.
    d. Because the parts of society are interdependent, a change in one part will probably lead to changes in other parts.
    e. Change occurs out of a failure of the sociological imagination.
13. Which sociological perspective has at its core the idea that coercion and the exercise of power are basic social

mechanisms for regulating behavior and allocating resources?
a. The functionalist perspective.
b. The sociological imagination.
c. The interactionist perspective.
d. The conflict perspective.
e. The verification perspective.

14. A group whose members share distinctive and common concerns and whose members benefit from similarities in policies and social practices is called
a. a conflict group.
b. a shared consensus.
c. a social system.
d. a control group.
e. an interest group.

15. Which of the following statements would be most consistent with the interactionist perspective?
a. Society is made up of groups struggling with one another over scarce resources.
b. Social problems arise when some element in society becomes dysfunctional.
c. Society is a system made up of interrelated and interdependent parts.
d. Both manifest and latent functions are important to understanding society.
e. People are symbol manipulators who create their own world.

16. All of the following are described in the text as social functions performed by the modern mass media, as identified by the functionalist perspective, *except*
a. the mass media assist the exchange of information.
b. the mass media serve as a "connective tissue" that enhances social uniformity.
c. the mass media are a major mechanism for communicating ideas.
d. the mass media help promote social integration and social uniformity.
e. the mass media enable the powerful to concentrate more resources in their own hands.

17. In conducting her observational research on Latino gangs, sociologist Ruth Horowitz
a. lived in the community where the gang members lived.
b. engaged in participant observation research.
c. discovered that for Latino youths, toughness and violence are a prime way of maintaining honor.
d. All of the above.
e. a and c above.

18. Which sociological research method involves the collection of data by asking people questions about their behavior or attitudes?
a. Observational techniques.
b. Experiments.
c. Surveys.
d. Reactivity.
e. Participant observation.

19. In an experiment, which of the following groups is exposed to the independent variable?
a. The sample group.
b. The control group.
c. The reactive group.
d. The experimental group.
e. The sampled group.

20. Which of the following statements best characterizes basic and applied sociology today?
a. Basic sociology has been dispensed with, and applied sociology now dominates.
b. There is a balance between basic and applied sociology.
c. Applied sociology has been dispensed with, and basic sociology now dominates.
d. Both basic and applied sociology have been dispensed with in favor of scientific sociology.
e. Basic and applied sociology have been combined into theoretical sociology.

FOR FURTHER READING

Berger, Bennett M. (1990). *Authors of their own lives: Intellectual autobiographies by twenty American sociologists.* Berkeley: University of California Press. This book gives an inside peek at what led twenty well-known sociologists to choose that field of study. It conveys some of the excitement and promise of the field.

Bruhn, John G., & Rebach, Howard M. (1996). *Clinical sociology: An agenda for action.* New York: Plenum. This book offers an overview of the field of consulting and clinical sociology. It gives many examples of the work of applied sociologists and focuses on "action sociology" with which practitioners actively intervene to improve social conditions.

Collins, Randall. (1992). *Sociological insight* (2d ed.). New York: Oxford University Press. This book, in the vein of Mills's sociological imagination, tries to impart the power and insight of the general perspective of sociology.

Heiner, Robert. (2005). *Social problems: An introduction to critical constructionism* (2d ed.). New York: Oxford University Press. This book combines the conflict and the interactionist perspectives in sociology into an approach called "critical constructionism," which sees social issues and problems as constructed in such a way that they reflect the interests of elites in society to the detriment of those with the least power.

Mills, C. Wright. (1959). *The sociological imagination.* New York: Oxford University Press. An excellent book by an irreverent iconoclast who takes critical aim at his fellow sociologists. This is the work in which Mills develops the notion that each person's behavior is produced by the intersection of biography and history.

Nathan, Richard P. (1988). *Social science in government: Uses and misuses*. New York: Basic Books. Nathan, a political scientist, discusses some major applied research projects that have been sponsored by the government and points out the benefits as well as the drawbacks. He discusses research on welfare reform, job-training programs, revenue-sharing programs, and others.

Straus, Roger A., ed. (2002). *Using sociology: An introduction from the applied and clinical perspectives* (3d ed.). Lanham, MD: Rowman & Littlefield. This book offers an overview of the field of applied and clinical sociology, including many examples of the work of applied sociologists in such settings as health care, the workplace, and the criminal justice field. It describes sociological practitioners actively intervening to improve social conditions.

Sullivan, Thomas J. (1992). *Applied sociology: Research and critical thinking*. New York: Macmillan. This book provides a brief introduction, easily understandable by the undergraduate, to applied sociological research. It describes the many ways in which sociological research is used to shape social policy and alleviate social problems.

Culture, Society, and Diversity

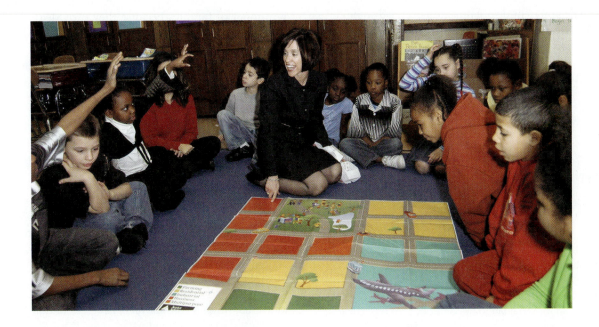

MYTHS & FACTS: About Culture and Society

What Is Culture?

Material Culture and Nonmaterial Culture

The Components of Culture

Beliefs and Values
U.S. Values
Japanese Values
Diversity and Change in Value Systems
Norms
OTHER WORLDS, OTHER WAYS: The Amish of Pennsylvania: Diverse Values within a Culture
Language
Linguistic Relativity
Language Reproduces Society

Cultural Consensus and Diversity

Cultural Integration
Cultural Change
Ideal Culture versus Real Culture
Ethnocentrism and Cultural Relativity

Subcultures
APPLYING SOCIOLOGY: Argot: The Special Language of Subcultures

Social Structure

Status
Roles
Social Roles and Social Interaction
Role Strain and Role Conflict
Alleviating Role Strain
SOCIOLOGY OF MEDIA AND TECHNOLOGY: Mass Media, the Electronic World, and the Production and Transmission of Culture
Groups and Social Institutions

A Comparative View of Societies

Preindustrial Societies
Industrial Societies
A Global Perspective: Postindustrialism and Global Interdependence
SOCIOLOGY ON THE INTERNET

Study & Review

The Comanche people roamed the southern Great Plains in the 1700s and 1800s, hunting buffalo from Wyoming and Nebraska south to Texas (Foster, 1991; Thurman, 1982; Wallace & Hoebel, 1952). The Comanches had a reputation among the early European settlers in the Great Plains as a fierce, combative people. In fact, the Comanches were a puzzle to the Euro-American traders and soldiers who began to fill the Great Plains in the 1800s because they seemed both disorganized and dishonest. The soldiers found it difficult to determine who led the Comanches, and deals made with a chief would not be adhered to by other Comanches. One Comanche might promise safe passage to merchants only to have another Comanche attack and plunder the group. The apparent disorganization even led some Euro-Americans to question whether the Comanches were a single people at all.

The confusion of these early settlers was due to the fact that they expected Comanche social life to be organized much like other societies they were familiar with, where a clearly identifiable leader (a president or king) existed and all other people and social units were subordinate to that person. Comanche social organization was quite different from this pattern; it consisted of five levels to which each Comanche belonged. The first was the *family*, which comprised all relatives who lived in the same camp together year-round and shared in game and agricultural surplus. The second level was the *residence band*, which was a number of families that were linked with a particular leader or headman. Sometimes a residence band contained only one family and might be as small as twenty people, but usually it contained a number of families because they provided a larger and more productive economic unit that was less threatened by variations in the food supply.

The third level of Comanche social organization was the *division*, which consisted of a group of residence

Myths & Facts

About Culture and Society

Myth:

Slang language is more commonly used among the less educated.

Fact:

Slang is an informal language or argot that is peculiar to a particular group. All subcultures show some development of argot because this special language performs important functions for groups.

Myth:

The role of working women with young children is a stressful one, and these women experience high levels of psychological distress because of all the demands on their time.

Fact:

This statement is true if the women do not have assistance in carrying out their competing roles. If society provides some help, however, in the form of a husband who helps with the children or easy availability of child care, the stress and depression levels of working mothers are as low as those of working women with no children.

Myth:

The individualism found in advanced industrial societies such as the United States in the early twenty-first

century is unique. Few other industrial societies and no preindustrial societies give such free rein to individual actions.

Fact:

Individualism as a cultural value can be found in other societies, including preindustrial ones. The Comanche Indians of the southern Great Plains, for example, valued individualism, especially for males. In fact, European settlers were confused by this individualism because they could not fathom that the actions of individual Comanches were not controlled by their chief.

Myth:

People naturally seek to better themselves, a tendency that makes it impossible for human societies to avoid disparities in wealth, prestige, and power.

Fact:

Disparities in wealth and power are the product of certain kinds of societies. Small hunting-and-gathering bands have little surplus of food or material goods, so people are mostly equal in terms of wealth, prestige, and power.

bands that farmed, traded, and hunted in the same geographic territory. A popular leader or brave warrior might exercise some control over a division, but this domination was more evanescent and temporary than leadership that Euro-Americans were used to. Such leaders might or might not exist for a particular division, and they might change rapidly. In addition, their leadership was incomplete, applying to some realms of social life but not others. In Comanche divisions, there was neither the organization nor the institutionalization of authority and leadership that the Euro-Americans were used to in terms of permanent leadership and ongoing structures, such as elections, to replace leaders. Also, the division performed largely ceremonial functions rather than served as a focus for food gathering or other practical tasks. Divisional gatherings, which might draw more than a thousand Comanches together, were a time to perform rituals, renew relationships, and possibly recruit others for a raiding party. When the divisional gathering was over, Comanche families and residence bands went their own ways.

The fourth level of Comanche social organization was the *focused-activity group,* which formed for a particular purpose and dissolved once the objective had been achieved. So, for example, a few male warriors who wished to raid a settlers' camp would form a focused-activity group (the Comanches didn't use that name for it, of course) to do so. The group was not organized or sanctioned by a chief or leader and was not under the control of the head of a family, residence band, or division. Such unsanctioned activity was perfectly acceptable for Comanches, and most males engaged in it periodically. These focused-activity groups might be organized to seize more horses, exact revenge for an insult, or enhance a warrior's reputation. They were not a part of family or residence-band life but rather emerged from more personal goals or interpersonal conflicts.

These focused-activity groups point to the highly individualistic nature of Comanche society. Comanches acted more as individuals than as representatives of a family, residence band, or division. A raiding party, for example, might be formed by men from a number of different divisions who saw the raid as a vehicle for them to enhance their own personal reputation as warriors. Euro-Americans found this individualism hard to understand, even though individualism was important in their own culture. Anyone who understood what it meant to "be Comanche" could comprehend the motivation of these warriors.

"Being Comanche" brings us to the most expansive, and at the same time most amorphous, fifth level of Comanche social organization—the *Comanche community.* The community was a sense of common heritage and ancestry shared by all Comanches, and it was based on a shared sense of what it meant to "be Comanche." Being Comanche was more than just speaking the Comanche language; it also meant valuing the things other Comanches valued and seeing the world the way they did. Being Comanche meant understanding that men should display bravery as well as generosity in public and that kinship compelled a person to support other Comanches, no matter which residence band or division they belonged to. The divisional gatherings provided the periodic context in which Comanche values and personal relationships could be publicly enacted and reaffirmed. The Comanche community was important because it provided a common identity for the different Comanche divisions and residence bands that might never all gather together at one time. However, the Comanche community had no single, identifiable leader, a fact that many Euro-Americans failed to comprehend. They searched for a clear-cut leader or an identifiable institutional structure that would tie all Comanches together, without realizing that it did not exist.

You can begin to see the difficulty the Euro-American settlers confronted in dealing with the Comanches. Comanche "leaders" represented, at best, divisions and in some cases only residence bands. Even at the divisional level, their authority was limited to specific issues, and they were considered intermediaries who should report back to the residence band or division before concluding any negotiations. Comanche leaders might call themselves chiefs, but they were not paramount leaders in the way the Euro-Americans understood leadership. Add to that the individualism and the focused-activity undertakings of Comanches, and the Euro-Americans' conclusions about the disorganized nature of Comanche social life become more understandable.

Chapter 1 pointed out that sociology is the scientific study of societies and human social behavior. One reason for discussing Comanche society at some length is to illustrate the great diversity that exists in how societies are organized and what social behaviors are considered appropriate. Another reason for focusing on the Comanches is to reiterate the point that it can be a challenge to comprehend societies that are very different from one's own because of the natural tendency to see others through one's own lenses. Sociologists approach this diversity by discovering and analyzing the social elements that are common to *all* societies. Sociologists define society as *a group of people who are relatively self-sufficient and who share a common territory and culture.*

The fundamental elements that can be found in all societies fall under the headings of *culture* and *social structure.* These two terms are keys to understanding the sociological perspective because the basic components of culture and social structure are the building blocks of the sociological analysis of society. This chapter introduces these basic elements, which will then serve as the foundation for the sociological analysis in the rest of this book.

What Is Culture?

You should be able to define *culture* and differentiate material and nonmaterial culture.

The term *culture* has a number of different meanings, all of them valid for some uses. To examine the idea scientifically, however, requires distinguishing these meanings. People often use the term to refer to rather high-toned pastimes such as reading great literature, listening to classical music, or dining on gourmet foods. This meaning is implied when we speak of someone as being "cultured," and it has something of a judgmental air about it. It intimates that some people have culture and some people don't.

Sociologists take a much broader view of the term. For them, culture refers to *the total lifestyle of a people, including all of the ideas, values, knowledge, behaviors, and material objects that they share* (Geertz, 1973; Kroeber & Kluckhohn, 1952). This meaning seems to be what the anthropologist Sir E. B. Tylor had in mind more than a century ago when he defined culture as "that complex whole which includes knowledge, belief, art, morals, law, custom and any other capabilities and habits acquired by man as a member of society" (1871/1958, p. 1). According to the sociological view, then, all people have culture, for it is the learned social heritage that people accumulate through time and pass on from generation to generation. Moreover, it provides people with a blueprint for how to lead their lives. It is from their culture that people learn what is good or bad, what is right or wrong, what they should or should not do, and even what they desire and what they dislike.

Often the terms *culture* and *society* are used interchangeably. This practice, although common, is somewhat imprecise sociologically. In the strictest sense, *society* refers to a *group of people* who are relatively self-sufficient and who share a common territory and culture; *culture* refers to that people's *traditions, customs,* and *behaviors.*

Material Culture and Nonmaterial Culture

The various elements of culture fall into two general categories: material culture and nonmaterial culture. Material culture consists of *all the physical objects,* or *artifacts, made or used by people, such as canoes, stone clubs, jet airplanes, and skyscrapers.* Nonmaterial culture consists of *those things that have no physical existence, such as language, ideas, knowledge, and behaviors.*

Material and nonmaterial culture are closely interrelated. Consider, for example, the many modern appliances, such as telephones, refrigerators, and televisions, that are found in most homes in the United States. These products are part of the material culture. They are things that only a society with advanced technological knowledge could produce, a point underlined when we consider that none of them existed, at least as we know them today, as recently as one hundred years ago. Moreover, these products have themselves shaped the nonmaterial culture. Television and the Internet, for instance, deliver vast amounts of information to previously unheard-of numbers of people. In fact, in the relatively short time they have been around, television and the Internet have become the major means for the transmission of nonmaterial culture in modern societies.

Sociologists and anthropologists rely heavily on the interrelations between material and nonmaterial culture in studying societies that no longer exist. Many earlier peoples left behind no written records, but from such artifacts as cave paintings, pottery, arrowheads, and burial mounds, investigators have been able to piece together some conception of the nonmaterial cultures of many of these societies.

The Components of Culture

You should be able to discuss the different elements of culture, including beliefs, values, norms, and language.

Culture is a complex phenomenon that can be expressed in an infinite number of ways. Consider, for instance, the foods people from different cultures eat. Common foods in the United States are such things as hamburgers, hot dogs, and french fries. Somewhere in the world there are people who consider octopus, locusts, and ants to be delicacies. The BaMbuti Pygmies in the Ituri rain forest in Zaire consider termites to be a delicacy (Turnbull, 1961). In some parts of Asia, the hot dog that is served is, in fact, canine. These foods would probably nauseate many people in the United States.

Attitudes toward parenthood are another example of the variety in human cultures. Western societies find it natural for children to come from the union of husband and wife. In fact, some groups in the United States consider birth under any other circumstances to be immoral. The Banaro of New Guinea, however, would be horrified to learn that firstborn children in the United States are normally fathered by the husband. Their traditions hold that a married couple's first child should be the offspring of a close friend selected by the wife's father (Goodman, 1967).

Obviously, it would be impossible to describe all of the variation that exists among cultures or, for that matter, all the facets of any single culture. It is possible, however, to isolate certain components that are common to all cultures, and understanding these components is an important first step in grasping how cultures and societies work. These components include beliefs, values, norms, and language.

Beliefs and Values

The most basic component of culture is beliefs, which are *the conceptions people have about what is true in the world.* Beliefs include ideas about what things exist in the world, how they work, and how they are related to one another. Some beliefs can be verified by observation. For example, we can measure how long it takes a plane to fly from Boston to San Francisco or how far it is from the Earth to the moon. Other beliefs, however, cannot be proven or disproven. For example, people around the world believe in any number of deities and devils. Many hold that there is some form of life after death, whereas others disagree.

These cultural beliefs help people understand the world and their place in it. However, people are seldom content simply to believe in something. They also tend to imbue their beliefs with moral significance. When that happens, beliefs become values, which are *people's ideas about what is good or bad, right or wrong.* People then use these values as guidelines for choosing goals and judging behaviors. Values, however, tend to be general and abstract rather than specific. For example, many people in the United States place considerable value on individualism, but individualism can be expressed in many different ways. A hard-driving executive may work so much that she has little personal life, whereas a political activist might organize demonstrations against nuclear power and an artist might spend long, solitary months creating a painting that departs from current artistic standards. In spite of their different pursuits, each of these people is expressing a version of the value of individualism.

U.S. VALUES   Because values serve as guidelines for choosing goals and judging behaviors, the cultural values of a society must be considered in any study of that society. To begin, what can we say about values in the United States? A little thought will reveal that the development of a definitive list of U.S. values would be an impossible task. U.S. society is characterized by diversity. There are, for instance, many different racial, ethnic, and religious

groups, and each has its own distinctive set of values. Certain mainstream values have a long tradition in the United States, however. They have played a significant role in shaping U.S. society, and they are still widely held by powerful groups (Bellah et al., 1985; Parsons, 1971; Williams, 1970). Some of the more prominent of these values are discussed here, keeping in mind that the coverage is by no means exhaustive.

One of the key cultural values in the United States is the importance placed on *success.* Most often defined in terms of career achievement, success is taken as a sign that a person is worthy. In fact, stories of people who maximize their abilities and, in spite of almost overwhelming odds, make their mark on the world provide a theme that runs through much of our literature. Political candidates from humble backgrounds are quick to take advantage of our reverence for success by pointing out how hard they had to struggle to make it on their own. The emphasis on the value of success seems to be growing, at least among college students. In the 1960s, as noted in Chapter 1, fewer than 45 percent of first-year college students believed that being well-off financially was "very important" or "essential" to them. By 2004, this figure had grown to over 70 percent (Higher Education Research Institute, 2004). Also, college women have become much more like college men in the emphasis they place on success as being essential to one's life and happiness.

Work and *activity* are also highly valued by many people in the United States. Indeed, some people place so much emphasis on work that they often define their own self-worth in terms of their jobs, and they tend to judge others in terms of the work they do. One of the first things people in the United States usually want to know about people they meet is what those people do for a living. Even in their leisure, they tend to view inactivity as undesirable, if not downright immoral. As a result, people in the United States always seem to be doing something—taking a trip, improving their tennis game, or pursuing a hobby like carpentry or needlepoint.

Another cluster of mainstream values in the United States consists of *progress, efficiency,* and *practicality.* People in the United States value striving to make things better, to improve the future in comparison to the present, and to do so in the most practical and efficient way. This value brings with it an acceptance of change, at least in material things and technology. Furthermore, people think developments and changes should be effected as quickly and as economically as possible so that nothing is wasted. One embodiment of this cluster of values is the emergence of the assembly line as a rapid and inexpensive mode of production that made mass quantities of consumer goods available. However, it also changed the work experience for many workers. Taking pride in work and investing personal meaning in what is produced became more difficult for assembly-line workers. Goods were produced quickly and cheaply, but workers were less involved in their work and more alienated from it.

A value that some sociologists say "lies at the very core of American culture" is *individualism* (Bellah et al., 1985, p. 142). This is the belief that individual desires, achievements, and self-worth are more important than collective accomplishments and goals. Individual rights should not be interfered with by other needs of society, such as political, economic, or family needs. In other words, people should be free to pursue whatever they like without undue hindrance. The Bill of Rights of the U.S. Constitution spells out these individual rights, and the courts have generally striven to protect them. This individualism is expressed in many ways: the mythical cowboy/hero/loner portrayed in fiction; the mobility of people who leave home and family to find a job, get an education, or just travel; and the adulation some people in the United States give to individual sports stars. A corollary of this value of individualism is *freedom:* to be free from demands by society, family, friends, or strangers that a person conform to their desired mode of conduct.

People in the United States also tend to place high value on *materialism* and *material comfort.* They expect to have nice cars, big houses, fine clothes, televisions, compact disc players, and the like. A high standard of living and the possession of numerous material goods have become almost synonymous with the U.S. way of life for many people, both in the United States and abroad. In a sense, people define their self-worth in terms of their ownership of such things. They feel proud to own a fine, new car rather than a battered car fifteen years old—even if both run well. In fact, the automobile may be the epitome of this materialism in the sense that much of the culture revolves around the automobile in the same way the culture of the Plains Indians revolved around the buffalo. Many people in the United States spend a good portion of their income supporting their cars; they wash them and ride around in them; they go to auto shows and races; they even went to war in the Middle East in part to protect the flow of oil that fuels their cars.

The final mainstream value to be mentioned is *equality.* Many people in the United States believe that everyone should be treated with dignity and respect and should not be denied opportunities because he or she belongs to a particular gender or religious or racial or ethnic group. Furthermore, people in the United States tend to be antielitist, believing that there are few inherent differences between people and that a person's birthright does not bestow any special qualities or privileges.

These mainstream U.S. values are not, of course, exclusive to the United States. You read in the opening to this chapter, for example, that the Comanche

Indians also valued individualism. There can be much variation, however, in the way cultures act on these values. Based on the same general value, a person in the United States might leave his family and climb the corporate career ladder, whereas the Comanche might join a focused-activity group to raid a settler's abode.

JAPANESE VALUES We can gain a better comprehension of U.S. cultural values and their importance in people's lives by comparing them to a different set of values. Japan is like the United States in some ways: It is a modern, industrial nation, highly urbanized, with a fairly affluent standard of living. Its history and traditions, however, have produced a set of cultural values very different from those found in the United States. In reviewing Japanese cultural values, it is important not to see them as simply the reverse of U.S. values; they need to be understood on their own terms, as a unique blend of history and tradition (Burks, 1984; Kerbo & McKinstry, 1995; Reischauer, 1988).

Japanese culture stresses the importance of the *collectivity,* or community, and places high value on the group or the family. Individual Japanese feel a strong obligation to their family, their work group, and their nation, and groups feel a strong sense of responsibility for their members. Each group member bears a share of the responsibility for preserving and protecting the group and avoiding bringing disgrace to it. People try to do well in business or education in part because success brings honor to the group. This point of view is very different from the emphasis on individualism in the United States. Of course, Japanese have a sense of their own individuality and self-worth, but it derives much more directly and completely from belonging to a group. A person expresses himself or herself by working for and supporting the collectivity and is rewarded with social approval.

The Japanese also value *harmony,* or getting along with people—what they call *wa.* They avoid contention and confrontation, and they are taught to help others and control the expression of their own desires. People are supposed to act politely and recognize and understand the feelings of others. Japan is racially and ethnically much more homogeneous than many other nations, certainly more so than the United States, and its people have achieved a high degree of cultural homogeneity. These conditions make harmony easier to achieve. Much more so than the United States, Japan exhibits a high degree of consensus regarding basic values. To say that the Japanese value harmony is not to say that aggression and competition are absent. They are also important elements of Japanese culture, but they are directed into arenas that are supportive of cooperation and the achievement of group goals.

The Japanese also value *tradition* and *authority.* They exhibit a strong respect for laws, rules, and customs. This attitude undoubtedly derives in part from Confucian teachings about uprightness, duty, and obligation (see Chapter 11). People obey the law and follow rules not solely out of fear of punishment but because it is a citizen's obligation. This does not mean that the Japanese never adopt new ways; they certainly do. The new ways, however, are incorporated into preexisting traditions, including the importance of community and harmony.

The differing value systems of Japan and the United States derive from profoundly different historical and societal developments. Japanese religious history involves Shintoism, Buddhism, and Confucianism; the United States is heavily Judeo-Christian. The Japanese have historically lived on a small, crowded island where cooperation and harmony were essential to social stability, whereas the United States had a huge continent that was sparsely populated for much of its development. The cultivation of rice in Japan, the major crop, required cooperation among people because of the irrigation and other requirements of that subsistence system; farmers and ranchers in the United States could cultivate large plots of land with less need for the assistance of others.

DIVERSITY AND CHANGE IN VALUE SYSTEMS   Although the values just described are important influences in the United States and Japan, diverse groups in both societies hold strongly to values that are quite different from these mainstream values. Other Worlds, Other Ways: The Amish (pp. 40–41) describes one such value system in the United States. All these different, and sometimes conflicting, values contribute to the pluralistic mosaic that is the United States at the beginning of the twenty-first century.

Values also change over time in response to new societal developments. For example, in the United States since the 1970s, the traditional materialism may have taken a turn toward *private materialism,* including a decline in interest in public goals and service to community. In other words, the weakness of community, bemoaned by Robert Bellah in the beginning of Chapter 1, seems even more severe in the 2000s. This trend is especially noticeable among high school and college students, who have placed increasing emphasis on making money as a major goal in life. Reflecting this trend, these students express growing interest in jobs in business, and especially large corporations, and less desire for public interest or social service jobs. Young people have also retreated from the ideas of political activism and government involvement in social change (Higher Education Research Institute, 2004).

Some people would argue that the traditional emphasis placed on materialism in the United States has also been changing toward *consumerism* and *commodification.* People seem to have become obsessed with things, or commodities, and how much

people can purchase has become a defining aspect of their worth. Some have called this trend the *mallification* of society, referring to the central importance that shopping malls now play in social life, as shopping and consumerism become primary leisure-time activities. This trend is the product of the emerging subsistence pattern of advanced industrial capitalism, which is based on continued economic growth. Large corporations survive by producing goods and expanding markets. They need a mass of consumers to purchase these goods, and advertising encourages people to desire the products produced. These two trends—toward private life and consumerism—illustrate how cultural values are dynamic rather than static; they change as social conditions evolve.

Norms

A people's culture is such an ingrained part of their lives that most take it for granted. Furthermore, its effects are frequently so subtle that people are rarely aware of how strongly or in how many areas it influences them. For example, the distance at which people feel comfortable when talking to one another is strongly influenced by culture (Hall, 1966). Most people in the United States regard the area from six to eighteen inches around them as an intimate zone. The only people they normally allow within this zone are very close friends or lovers. Should a stranger invade it, they are likely to feel uncomfortable and anxious. Among Arabs, however, practically all social interaction takes place within this zone. In fact, Arabs may be insulted if someone tries to converse with them from outside it.

The example of personal distance brings us to *norms,* the third component of culture. Norms are *rules of conduct that guide people's behavior in particular situations.* They are the expectations that people in a society share about how they ought to behave. Unlike values, which involve general preferences, norms are specific guidelines for behavior. In the United States, for instance, people usually dress appropriately for wherever they are going, they avoid spitting in public places, they acknowledge people they know when they meet them, and they try to show up on time for appointments. Norms, then, are an integral part of day-to-day lives. They provide a script for personal behavior, and they allow people, to some extent, to predict the behavior of others. By so doing, they provide the order and stability necessary for a society to exist.

A society teaches its members the types of behavior that are expected through sanctions, which are *rewards or punishments for conforming to or violating norms.* Sanctions can take many forms, depending on the type

THE AMISH OF PENNSYLVANIA: DIVERSE VALUES WITHIN A CULTURE

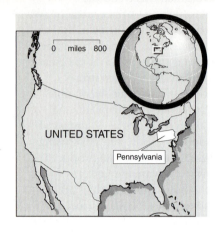

The Old Order Amish descend from sixteenth-century Swiss Anabaptists, sometimes called Mennonites because of Menno Simons, an early leader of the group (Hostetler, 1993; Schaefer & Zellner, 2007). Simons was originally a Roman Catholic priest in the Netherlands, but he formed his own denomination in the 1500s because of some deeply held differences with the Roman Catholic church. For example, he believed in the separation of church and state and the right to refuse to bear arms or take oaths—positions strongly opposed by the church of that era. The Amish broke with the Mennonites in 1693 over a theological dispute, and some Amish began migrating to the New World in the early eighteenth century, originally settling in Pennsylvania.

The Old Order Amish have prospered in the United States. They have maintained their own separate existence and their distinct lifestyle over almost three centuries of rapid cultural and technological change. Most people are familiar with images of the Amish people's small, horse-drawn carriages; their wide-brimmed hats; and their dark, simple coats and dresses. They seem to have achieved an almost impossible resistance to the booming culture around them. Indeed, their value system is as distinct as their clothing and their carriages. Some values they share with the larger, mainstream culture, such as their belief in the importance of hard work. For the Amish, however, work has a deeply religious meaning, whereas for many other people in the United States work is considered a secular, although still important, activity. Other Amish values are quite different from mainstream U.S. values. For example, the Amish reject the materialism that surrounds them. Their main concern is what God, not their fellow humans, thinks of them, and God, they believe, focuses on inner qualities, not outward appearances. The austerity in their clothing and general lifestyle is a product of this belief. Instead of materialism, the Amish value *humility* and *self-denial.* Pride and self-aggrandizement are considered sins, and one should never set oneself above one's fellows. So traits that are common in many societies—such as bragging or boasting—are rarely encountered among the Amish. In fact, cameras are forbidden, and it is considered wrong to have one's picture taken because that

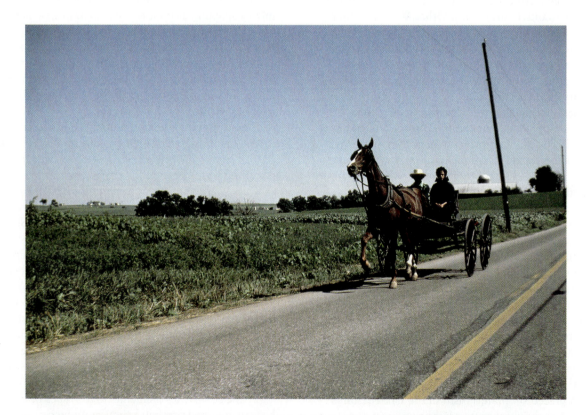

As the simple clothing and travel conveyance of this Amish family show, the Amish culture places great value on austerity, humility, and self-denial because their religion tells them that God only cares about inner qualities, not outer appearances.

(*continued*)

implies that there is something special about one's looks. Each person is important not as an individual but as a hard worker for the community.

This view leads to another important Amish value: *group solidarity.* The Amish believe that family and community (and a faith in God) will give people all the support they need to get through life. The Amish take care of one another; they do not accept welfare or Medicare or most Social Security benefits. If a person needs a barn raised, hundreds of neighbors will show up to do it; if someone is aged and infirm, the family will look after him or her. The community takes care of individuals and thus is more important than individuals—a direct contradiction to the individualism of the mainstream culture.

The final set of Amish values is *obedience* and *submission.* Each individual submits to and obeys family, community, and God, an attitude that is alien to individualism. The freedom that characterizes the larger culture is severely truncated among the Amish. They have the freedom to vote for the politician of their choice, but they are not free when it comes to matters of obeying the community or the church. People who exercise their freedom in these realms suffer severe disapproval and possibly even ostracism.

The Amish lifestyle seems to many in the United States to be uncompromisingly severe and restricted. Yet it is probably the unrelieved rejection of non-Amish ways— along with rural isolation—that has enabled the Amish to survive and thrive. They have problems, of course. Government regulation sometimes threatens to interfere with their way of life; young people are sometimes attracted by the materialism around them; and some Amish communities have left the fold in pursuit of a less severe lifestyle. Yet, overall, they have maintained a thriving existence, and they represent one of the many sets of diverse cultural values that give direction to the lives of various groups in the United States. With a society as large and complex as that of the United States, this diversity in value systems will undoubtedly continue. ▪

---

of behavior and the type of norm involved. They can be weak or strong, formal or informal, and positive or negative. The smile and "thank you" that a person receives for opening a door for another is a weak, informal, positive sanction. The frown the person gets for not opening it is a weak, informal, negative sanction. Chapter 5 analyzes this process of social control at greater length.

Norms that are customary, popular, and widely performed, but not required, are called folkways (Sumner, 1906). Examples of folkways in the United States include shaking hands, bathing frequently, and being quiet in church. There is some pressure to conform to folkways; violating them usually results in weak, informal, negative sanctions. Such violations occur frequently, however, and they are normally not taken very seriously, although a person who repeatedly ignores folkways may be viewed as strange or eccentric. Still, when we observe the social scene around us, we see that most people comply with most folkways most of the time.

Mores are *norms that are associated with strong feelings of right and wrong, the violation of which usually results in sanctions.* They are the social rules that deal with such things as murder, incest, theft, and public nudity, and they are taken very seriously. People who violate folkways are usually tolerated, but people who violate mores are usually punished. The sanctions applied tend to be strong, formal, and negative. Violators may be ostracized, banished, flogged, put in prison, or put to death. These strong reactions are one reason people adhere to mores. More important, however, is the fact that people are taught to adhere to their cultural mores almost from the time they are born. As a result, people incorporate the mores into their own personal codes of conduct. This process, called

internalization, *causes people to view the violation of most mores with antipathy such that they would not even consider committing such a violation. As a result, they control their own behavior.* Most people, for example, are so horrified at the thought of incest that they never even consider it. This example illustrates an important point about culture: Much of it is so ingrained that we are unaware that we have learned it and don't feel that the beliefs, values, and norms are an imposition. We learn to *want* what our culture *demands* of us. Chapter 3 analyzes this learning process in more detail.

Laws are *norms that have been formally codified by political authority.* Many laws are based on mores, for people usually strive to give legal status to norms they believe in strongly. Familiar examples would include laws against murder, incest, and theft. Not all laws, however, are based on mores. Some, such as "blue laws" that prohibit stores from selling alcohol on Sunday morning, are based on folkways. Others, such as parking restrictions, are basically administrative and reflect no norms at all. Some laws even run counter to generally accepted norms. The prohibition of alcohol during the 1920s in the United States, for example, was followed one decade later by its repeal because many people ignored the law and continued to use alcohol. Similarly, 40 percent of teens and adults in the United States have used marijuana and 14 percent have used cocaine—both against the law (U.S. Bureau of the Census, 2007, p. 129). So, the generally accepted norms in some groups make the use of marijuana, cocaine, and other drugs acceptable, even though use of them violates the law. These examples illustrate that laws can be established that go against strongly held custom, but there is also pressure in such cases to change or repeal the laws.

Language

The final component of culture that is discussed here is language. *Language* is a set of written or verbal symbols that people use in an agreed-upon way to communicate with one another (Miller, 1963; Strauss, Denzin, & Lindesmith, 1999). As discussed in Chapter 1, *symbols* are things that stand for and convey the meaning of other things. Language is a particularly important component of culture because it is through language that the other components—beliefs, values, and norms—are stored, communicated, and absorbed.

Our ability to use language lets us do many things that other animals cannot. We are not limited, as they are, by our physical environment or by barriers of time and space. Language permitted our primitive ancestors to store knowledge and transmit it to new generations. The invention of the written word vastly expanded this ability by freeing us from the limitations of human memory. Today, the mushrooming technologies of computerization, miniaturization, and microprocessing promise a virtual explosion in the amount of information that is available to us and the ways in which it can be disseminated. Symbols and language also let us contemplate and use abstract ideas like *justice, equality,* and the *perfect person.* Our social and legal machinery is based on our notions of justice and equality, and our personal behavior is often guided by our ideal of what it is to be "perfect."

LINGUISTIC RELATIVITY   To understand fully the role of language in our lives, it is important to recognize that language is not solely a mechanism for communication. It can also shape our perceptions of the world. This insight originated with the anthropologist Edward Sapir (1929) and the linguist Benjamin Whorf (1956). After studying many different languages, they developed what has come to be called the *Sapir-Whorf hypothesis* or the *linguistic-relativity hypothesis.* Simply stated, this hypothesis proposes that the language we speak shapes how we think about and perceive the world. Far from being a passive means of communication, language actually influences what that world is like for each of us. Using language is like looking at the world through tinted glasses—we see what the filter presents to us.

One way that language filters reality is through the categories that it provides. Inuit (Eskimos), for example, have more than twenty different words for snow. Obviously, Inuit culture has developed and passed on this elaborate category system because making fine distinctions between types of snow is important to survival in the environment in which Inuit live. Sapir and Whorf's point is, though, that when Inuit children learn their language, they also learn to perceive and identify aspects of snow that would be imperceptible to speakers of a language such as

English. (At the other extreme, the Aztecs of pre-Columbian Mexico, for whom snow was a rare event, used a single word for "ice," "snow," and "cold.") As another example, the Zuni, a Pueblo people of the American Southwest, had one word to indicate the colors orange and yellow—colors that speakers of English clearly distinguish. When confronted with an array of colors, speakers of Zuni are considerably less likely than speakers of English to separate the oranges and yellows as distinct colors. Other research shows that remembering colors is enhanced if a person's language has a name for the color (Kelling, 1975; Lucy & Shweder, 1979).

Language may also influence our understanding of nature. For example, the Hopi language of the Southwest made no distinctions among past, present, and future. The Hopi had no verb tenses and no nouns indicating times, days, or years. The Hopi language classified nature in terms of duration and considered time to be a continuous process, without breaks or stops. English, by contrast, has tenses and an elaborate set of words for dividing up time periods (*day, week, year,* etc.). In addition, English has a bipolar view of the world: It divides nature into nouns (people, objects, or events) and verbs (activities). In English, *lightning* and *eddy* are nouns; in Hopi, however, they are verbs because of their short duration. So, speakers of these two languages will perceive the world somewhat differently. Certainly, time will have a much more precise, measured, and quantifiable meaning for speakers of English than it will for speakers of Hopi, who have difficulty distinguishing, in language, past from future and precisely measuring time periods.

Sapir and Whorf have been criticized for arguing that language is all-powerful. Research done in linguistics, anthropology, and cognitive psychology since the Sapir-Whorf hypothesis was first proposed has established universals in languages: cognitive processes and tendencies in language that are found in all cultures. Sapir and Whorf, however, were aware of the limits of language's impact: They recognized that reality shapes languages in the sense that each language is an adaptation to a particular physical and cultural environment. Once language exists, however, it takes on a life of its own and shapes and reinforces the culture from which it arose. Language and culture, then, are mutually reinforcing (Gumperz & Levinson, 1996; Hoffman, Lau, & Johnson, 1986).

LANGUAGE REPRODUCES SOCIETY   Language not only reflects the social practices of a culture; it also helps to maintain and reinforce them by reproducing the structure of society. This fact is strikingly illustrated by the use of language in Java (Hoebel, 1972).

In Javanese, there are four forms of speech. Which form is used in a particular situation depends on the relationship between the people involved. Individuals low on the social ladder address those higher up in one form and are themselves addressed in a second form. The socially elite have a third distinct form exclusive to their group, and the more common people have yet a fourth form. Thus the people of Java are constantly reminded of their relative positions in society when they conform to the proper language form. Furthermore, by following these language conventions, the Javanese continually reaffirm their acceptance of the existing social hierarchy.

The way people speak also has important social implications in the United States. *Standard English* or *European American English* is the form of English that is taught in the schools, and it is the form used in this textbook. However, some groups in the United States do not automatically learn Standard English. In many African-American communities, for instance, people speak a dialect called *Black English, African American Vernacular English,* or *Ebonics* (Craig, Thompson, Washington, & Potter, 2003; Edwards & Winford, 1991; Rickford, 1999). Black English is a variant of Standard English that developed from the languages of the west coast of Africa and the pidgin languages that served the maritime trade of the eighteenth and nineteenth centuries. The isolation of blacks in the United States, first on plantations and later in ghettos, along with centuries of servitude, slavery, and oppression, provided fertile ground for the development of a distinct dialect among blacks in the United States (Mufwene, Rickford, Bailey, & Baugh, 1998). Some of the reasons why dialects emerge under these conditions are discussed later in this chapter in Applying Sociology: Argot.

Black English is a distinct dialect having its own phonology, grammar, and syntax. For instance, consider the following phrases:

> It be kind of complicated.
> They be doing.
> If you be talking.
> We do be out.

In these examples, the word *be* is used in a way that is not found in Standard English. *They be doing* does not mean *they are doing* or *they were doing* or *they will be doing*. Rather, it is a tenseless use of the verb *be* that refers to doing something intermittently over a period of time without any particular reference to past, present, or future.

Neither Black English nor Standard English is inherently correct. Languages are, after all, merely systems for combining words that users have agreed on. Both languages can be used to communicate quite effectively by those who understand the rules of the language. Yet the dominant groups in the United States speak Standard English and assume that it is a superior language. These people presume that those who speak Black English, or any other version of English, do not know how to speak the language "correctly." This assumption can make it more difficult for speakers of Black English in school or on the job. Students, for example, may receive a lower grade for speaking or writing English "incorrectly," and workers may not be hired if they do not speak "proper" English. So, success can hinge on the ability to speak Standard English, and those who speak another dialect may be at a distinct disadvantage in terms of educational and occupational opportunities. This fact illustrates the powerful contribution of language in reproducing and reinforcing existing social hierarchies in society.

This section has reviewed the four basic components of culture. These concepts will be at the center of the analysis of society throughout this book. You need to recognize at this point, however, that these components are linked with one another in intricate ways. The next section considers these components in operation in society, as they combine to coordinate social behavior and to promote as well as resist cultural change.

Cultural Consensus and Diversity

> You should be able to describe cultural integration as well as the various types of cultural change, including the sources from which change may arise.

People are seldom aware of the dynamic nature of culture. In fact, the components of culture just discussed are often taken as givens, as conditions that are imposed on people and over which they have virtually no control. But in reality, beliefs, values, norms, and language are changing constantly in response to developments that arise either inside or outside society. Change takes place because the elements of culture are actually mechanisms that enable societies to adapt to their environment and survive. The purpose of this section is to offer a better appreciation of the dynamic nature of culture by looking at some of the forces that promote cultural changes as well as some of those that resist them.

Cultural Integration

Any culture includes countless beliefs, values, norms, and artifacts. Consider, for instance, some of the cultural elements that exist in the twenty-first-century United States. It has schools, televisions, polluted rivers, cell phones, communications satellites, pornographic movies, football games, automobiles, the gay liberation movement, personal computers, iPods, and handguns. Such a list could obviously go on and on. Indeed, listing all the elements of any culture would be an impossible task. There are simply too many of them.

The elements of a culture, in spite of their wide diversity, are linked together in many intricate and sometimes subtle ways. Frequently, various elements are in conflict. The massive quantities of consumer goods that people in the United States desire and have become used to, for example, are in many instances at odds with their desire for a pollution-free environment. More often, however, the different elements of a culture complement one another. They are more or less integrated into reasonably well organized patterns.

The extent to which cultures are integrated can sometimes be more easily seen in societies other than one's own. The Kapauku Papuans, a group of people who live in New Guinea and who were studied by the anthropologist Leopold Pospisil (1963), provide an especially vivid illustration. Among the Kapauku, pigs are the major source of wealth and power. The pigs are fed on sweet potatoes, which makes agriculture an important part of Kapaukun culture. Custom, however, dictates that only women can cultivate sweet potatoes and raise pigs, making women vital to the production of wealth. This fact is reflected in the Kapaukun family structure. The Kapauku are polygynous, which means that a man can have more than one wife. Needless to say, the more wives a man has, the more wealth they can produce for him. To ensure that there are enough wives to go around, there must be more women than men. This necessity has, in turn, affected the Kapauku view of warfare and the war-related roles of men and women. Intertribal wars are a regular occurrence, but killing women in these wars is considered highly immoral, simply because they are so valuable. A number of males, though, are killed off in war regularly, which guarantees that the necessary surplus of females is maintained.

Cultural Change

Cultural integration has a major impact on the changes that occur in cultures. As noted in Chapter 1, any system made up of interrelated parts tends to develop a state of equilibrium. As a result, change in one part of the system causes changes in other parts. This process is particularly evident in cultures, which makes cultural change a very important topic in sociology. This chapter looks at some of the sources of cultural change. Chapter 15 investigates this topic more fully.

Changes in a society's culture can come from the outside or can develop internally. A major external source of change is *diffusion*, which is the spread of cultural elements from one culture to another. Diffusion is likely whenever two cultures come into contact. For example, the first people to smoke tobacco were American Indians. In the 1500s, however, English and Spanish explorers of the New World carried tobacco with them when they returned home, and its use soon spread throughout Europe, northern Africa, and the Middle East. With modern communications technologies and the global mass media, the process of cultural diffusion around the world has become rapid, extensive, and continuous. Cultural beliefs, values, and other items are spread (for example, through the Internet) such that the traditional boundaries between cultures have become much more vague. In fact, a global cyberculture may be emerging from this process of cultural diffusion.

An important internal source of change is *innovation,* which is the development of new ideas, behaviors, or material products. Although innovations have occurred throughout human history, the twentieth century witnessed unbelievably rapid innovations with far-reaching effects on people's lives. Automobiles, computers, nuclear bombs, airplanes, television, and fiber-optic cables have made people's lives in the twenty-first century very different from life at any other time in human history. Today, people live longer and more comfortable lives with more and better food and housing. These discoveries and inventions demand that workers have more knowledge and skills than in the past, a requirement that has transformed educational structures from informal learning into a highly formal, lengthy, and complex educational process (see Chapter 12). The result has been a highly literate and educated workforce and populace. These technological discoveries and inventions have also brought about a more elaborate occupational structure, with thousands upon thousands of different jobs for people to fill.

Discoveries and inventions can also produce negative outcomes. Technological change has created weapons of mass destruction that are capable of killing millions of people in a short period of time. Airplanes and missiles can rain death from the sky. One nuclear bomb exploding over a major city would probably kill 3 million people almost instantaneously. So, cultural change has become pervasive and constant, with both positive and negative outcomes.

Ideal Culture versus Real Culture

Another important internal source of change for many societies is the difference between ideal culture and real culture (Schusky & Culbert, 1967). Ideal culture refers to *the beliefs, values, and norms that people claim to follow.* Real culture refers to their *actual behavior in relation to these professed beliefs, values, and norms.* In the United States, for example, people place value on such ideals as equality, honesty, and obeying the law.

Despite the ideal of equality, however, there has always been considerable discrimination, particularly against minority groups and women. Moreover, even though most people in the United States consider themselves to be honest and law-abiding, lying, cheating, and stealing are common occurrences.

That there is a gap between what people claim is proper and the way they actually behave does not mean that people are by nature two-faced. Rather, it indicates that many factors influence people's behavior. Honesty, for example, is a praiseworthy ideal, but some individuals may feel that cutting a few corners is necessary just to make a decent living. They see themselves as honest people confronted with situations that prevent them from behaving honestly. Furthermore, there is inconsistency in the ideal culture itself. For instance, though honesty is highly valued in the United States, so is success. Often, then, people are faced with choosing which aspects of the ideal culture should come first.

As the gap between the ideal culture and the real culture widens, the contradictions in people's lives begin to create tensions. If the gaps become sufficiently large, pressures to reduce them often lead to cultural change. This is well illustrated by recent changes in the economy and culture of Mexico (Fowler-Salamini & Vaughan, 1994; LeVine, 1993; Riding, 1989). As is true in many developing nations, the ideal culture in Mexico emphasizes the value of the extended family, which has combined financial resources and an elaborate network of support for people who do not have much of their own. Traditionally, the ideal Mexican family has also been patriarchal, with males having most of the power and decision-making authority. This emphasis on family has been supported by the high value placed on *machismo* in Mexican culture. *Machismo* refers to dominant manliness as personified by the Spanish conquistador—the aggressive, action-oriented, virile man.

These ideals, however, are being challenged by recent changes in the structure of the Mexican economy: the automation of agriculture, which means fewer jobs in rural areas; the growth of low-paying jobs in the industrial sector, fueled by economic demand in other nations; and a weak labor-union movement, the development of which has been discouraged by both business people and politicians in Mexico. The result has been pervasive unemployment and low wage levels for many workers, including men. This forces many Mexicans, mostly men, to migrate in search of jobs, and this population dispersal puts substantial pressure on both the value of the family and male dominance in the family (Brydon & Chant, 1989; Massey, 1987). Migration removes the men from their families for long periods, sometimes permanently. Their absence seriously erodes the control and authority they

can exercise in the family. When they are away, women run the household and raise the children, and the essential nature of male support for the family is called into question. In addition, the low wages that poor Mexican men can command are often not enough to support a family. For these reasons, poor Mexican women often work to support their families (Fernandez-Kelly, 1983a). Often, they move from a rural area to a large city where jobs can be found working as domestics or laborers in factories. This may entail leaving their extended families and their husbands, who may not be able to find work in the same city or may have gone to the United States looking for work. The women set up their own households with their children. Although they maintain ties with their families, the bonds inevitably grow weaker as time and distance separate family.

So, whether Mexicans like it or not, these women gain more independence and autonomy from both males and their families. The consequence is increasing difficulty in maintaining the ideal culture of extended family and male dominance. As more Mexicans face these same dilemmas, the ideal culture is likely to change to take into account the realities of modern life.

Ethnocentrism and Cultural Relativity

Many people in the United States find it difficult to imagine living in another culture, and people from other cultures feel much the same way about living in the United States. Indeed, just about everyone thinks that his or her way of life is the one "right" way. *This tendency to view one's own culture as the best and to judge other cultures in comparison to it* is called ethnocentrism.

Ethnocentrism is a natural result of the fact that a society creates its own beliefs, values, and norms. It also promotes the sense of "we-ness" that holds societies together. Ethnocentrism, however, can get out of control and become destructive. Especially when one group feels threatened by another, those under threat tend to become more ethnocentric, developing increasing dislike for the threatening group and establishing more social distance from them (Grant, 1991). Too often, a group's belief in its own superiority leads to racism, persecution, exploitation, and even genocide. The Nazi treatment of Jews and the treatment of American Indians by European colonists of the New World are but two haunting examples.

Ethnocentrism can also undermine our efforts to understand ways of life different from our own. Being too quick to judge a social practice or belief of another culture as wrong or absurd can blind us to the meaning it has for the people involved and the way it fits into their lives. Social scientists therefore promote the idea of cultural relativity, which holds that *the lifestyles of various peoples should be viewed in terms of their own culture rather than that of the observer.* Basically, it involves suspending judgment and realizing that each culture reflects a particular society's adaptation to its environment. This objectivity in no way means that we should unquestioningly accept the beliefs and social practices of other cultures. For example, few people in the United States today would accept the Trobriand Islanders' belief that pregnancy is caused by the spirit of a dead ancestor entering a woman's body (Malinowski, 1954). However, by applying the idea of cultural relativity, we can understand that this belief is central to the Trobriand Islanders' view of the world and is therefore a valid part of their lives.

Subcultures

Although it is possible to describe some of the aspects of U.S. culture and list a few of its mainstream values, it is not possible to develop a truly comprehensive picture of culture in the United States. The society is simply too diverse. The norms of the ghetto are light years away from those of the middle-class suburb, the values of the young have little meaning for the elderly, and the beliefs of the well-to-do are largely foreign to the poor. One result of all this diversity is the formation of subcultures. A subculture is *a group within a culture that shares some of the beliefs, values, and norms of the*

larger culture but also has some that are distinctly its own. As is true of most large societies, particularly those that have industrialized, the United States has a large number of subcultures. There are, for example, the Amish in Pennsylvania, the Cubans in Miami, the gays in most large cities, the Hip-Hop culture, and the drug set. There are even a few hippies left over from the 1960s.

Actually, everyone in the United States could belong to a wide array of subcultures based on such characteristics as age, gender, social standing, job, religion, or leisure pastimes. However, membership in a subculture is not simply a matter of fitting into a particular category. Instead, it is based on accepting the beliefs, values, and norms of the subculture and identifying with other members of it (Fine & Kleinman, 1979; Widdicombe & Wooffit, 1995). A person can, for instance, be a prison inmate without belonging to the prison subculture or a sports fan without belonging to a sports subculture if that person does not identify with the subculture and share its ideas.

Subcultures tend to develop when members of a segment of society become aware of the fact that they share interests—beliefs, practices, or characteristics—that differ from those of the larger culture. This tendency is especially strong when the people in that segment of society are denied participation in some dimensions of the larger culture. By seeking out their

---

Applying Sociology   Argot: The Special Language of Subcultures

There are thousands of subcultures in the United States, and everyone belongs to some. People often take for granted their participation in subcultures without realizing the important social functions subcultures perform. Even the way members of a subculture speak contributes to achieving these functions (Widdicombe & Wooffit, 1995). As you review language usage in a few subcultures in the United States, you should think about the subcultures to which you belong and their special languages.

The specialized language of a subculture is known as an *argot*. There are almost as many argots as there are subcultures. Reports have been published on the argots of musicians, teenagers, prostitutes, beauticians, lumberjacks, convicts, furniture salespeople, miners, sailors, undertakers, and sugar-beet workers, to mention just a few. That the use of argot is so widespread suggests that it serves important social functions, but in understanding argot several factors should be kept in mind. First, the groups that develop argots are almost endlessly diverse, and in many cases the terms they devise are unique to their situations. The term *gun,* for example, would be

used to mean "syringe" only in a drug subculture. Second, argot changes constantly. Some of the terms cited here will almost certainly have gone out-of-date by the time you read this. Indeed, an argot may die out altogether if the subculture that uses it disappears, as happened with the vaudeville and hobo subcultures of the early twentieth century. Nevertheless, it is possible to identify some of argot's general social functions.

Probably the most important function is that it separates group members from nonmembers. A group's argot may function in much the same way as a password. Those who know it are the "ins"; those who do not are the "outs." In a way, argot serves this purpose even better than a password—you could bribe someone to tell you a password, but an argot can be learned only by intimate association with the group that uses it. Among teenage drug gang members in Michigan, for example, a *skeezer* is a woman of low status, *def* means "first rate" or "desirable," and *diss* means "to show disrespect for" (Taylor, 1993). Some of the argot used by teenagers in chat rooms, instant messages, and e-mails (see Table 2.1) would be incompre-

Table 2.1

SUBCULTURAL ARGOT

Argot of Michigan Prison Inmates, 1986		Argot of Teens in Online World	
Blood	Young inmate	brb	be right back or bathroom break
Break bad	Your wife or girlfriend leaves you	lol	laughing out loud
Do whopper	A young, loud inmate	r u	are you
Doing all day	Serving a life sentence	rents	parents
Hang it up	Commit suicide	gurlz	girls
Ride out	Transfer to another prison	peeps	people, friends
Short	Cigarette butt	P911	parents are in the room (P = parents, 911 = emergency, drop subject, watch language)
Sweat hogs	White female correctional officers		
What it be?	How's it going with you?	POS, POTS	parents over the shoulder, can't really talk
Kite	An inmate's letter to a prison official about an official matter	phat	awesome, cool
Skating	Being in an unauthorized place	stammin	very nice, Cool
Works	Needle and syringe used for injecting drugs	ttyl	talk to you later
Be cool pills	Authorized psychtropic medication	Kewl	cool
Bogart	Flush drugs down toilet.		

hensible to people not familiar with that subculture. Anyone ill-advised enough to try to learn the gang or teen argot from a book would be bound to make mistakes, and there are few things more embarrassing than using a term incorrectly when you are trying to show that you are one of the "ins."

A related function of argot is that of reinforcing group solidarity and identity. One of the ways groups define themselves is by excluding those who lack certain characteristics. By signifying that some do not belong, the use of argot draws together those who do. Indeed, some words in the argots of certain subcultures may be used precisely because they are unintelligible to others. Teenagers, for example, might use the words *kewl, phat,* and *brb* in chat rooms and instant messages (see Table 2.1) in part because such words set them apart from their parents, teachers, and others of a different generation. What better way to develop a separate identity than to devise a language that the uninitiated have trouble understanding?

In the same way, argot can reflect and reinforce a subculture's own values, goals, and priorities. In the teen online argot, for example, the use of words like P911 and POTS suggests how important it is to these teens to maintain a social world into which their parents find it difficult to enter. A key element of teen development is establishing an identity independent of parents, and this goal is reflected in their argot.

Argot also often contains special words to describe those who belong and those who don't, as a further way of separating insiders from outsiders. Prison inmates in Michigan, for example, call white female correctional officers *sweat hogs,* whereas young prisoners are *bloods* (see Table 2.1). Female drug gang members in Michigan call the police *the hook.*

Finally, an argot may offer concise ways to refer to roles and statuses not generally found in the mainstream of society. A survey of terms used in Michigan prisons uncovered these terms in the inmate subculture (Kalinich & Pitcher, 1987): *jocker* for an aggressive partner in a homosexual relationship; *daddy* for one who controls a homosexual, similar to a pimp; and *kid* for a young, passive homosexual. Although many prison inmates do not participate in homosexual activities, it is clear that homosexuality is a salient element of the inmate subculture, and virtually all inmates need to be familiar with the associated argot.

Argot often serves these functions without the speaker or listener being aware of it. Applying sociology in this fashion to your own life can offer insight into some of the functions of the argots you speak at work, in school, in church, or among your friends and family. Without your being aware of it, the language you speak every day helps maintain and reinforce group boundaries and impart a sense of belonging and identity. ■

own kind and banding together, they are able to create their own support system. Often it allows them to develop sufficient strength not only to preserve their own interests but also to improve their social lot. Consider, for example, the recent increases in the subcultural consciousness of African Americans and many other racial and ethnic minorities, as well as gay men and lesbians. Applying Sociology: Argot (pp. 46–47) adds further insight into these ideas by showing how the special languages used in subcultures can enhance their solidarity and make them more effective support systems.

Social Structure

You should be able to describe the functions of statuses, roles, groups, and institutions in maintaining social structure.

Now that some of the more important aspects of culture have been examined, it is time to look at the other general category of characteristics common to all societies—social structure. Social structure refers to *the organized patterns of social interaction and social relationships that exist in a group or society.* Although we may not be aware of it, we deal with such patterns almost constantly, at school, at work, even at home with friends or family. Without these organized patterns of behavior, social life as we know it would be impossible, for social structure provides the order and stability necessary for any group or society to function. An understanding of social structure is therefore a fundamental building block of the science of sociology. Indeed, much of this book is a detailed examination of concepts and ideas introduced in this section.

The section begins by examining *status* and *role*, two concepts that underlie any type of interaction among people. Then it looks at *groups* and *social institutions*, two of the most important manifestations of social structure.

Status

Status, like *culture*, is a term that has more than one meaning, even among sociologists. People often talk about high-status jobs such as doctor, lawyer, or government official and low-status jobs such as janitor, stripper, or prostitute. They also talk about status symbols—

For most of human history, culture was produced and transmitted largely through personal, face-to-face contacts between people. This media control room symbolizes how, today, the modern technologies of communication have become central in this process, making it possible to distribute cultural products around the world and possibly contribute to cultural globalization.

expensive foreign cars, designer clothes, or memberships in exclusive clubs—which are things people buy to show how well off they are. Used in these ways, status equates with prestige and implies judgments that rank people in comparison to one another. Although this meaning is somewhat similar to the way sociologists use the term, it is defined here without referring to rankings or value judgments because differences in status do not always imply that one person is higher or lower in prestige than another person. Here, then, status will refer to *a designated position in a group or society.*

Virtually any identifiable aspect of a person, such as gender, age, job, race, religion, or social class, can be a status. Each status is imbedded in a network of statuses, and every individual has many statuses. People using this book, for instance, probably have some of the following social positions: student, young person, adult, middle-aged person, male, female, black, Latino, Baptist, Roman Catholic, Buddhist, agnostic, American, or Canadian. These positions locate them in relation to other people who have specific statuses. If one is female, for example, one has a somewhat different relationship with other males and females than if one is male.

Statuses can be either ascribed or achieved. Ascribed statuses *are assigned to people and represent social positions over which people have little say about occupying.* For example, each of us is born either male or female and as a member of some race. In addition, we may become cancer sufferers or crime victims, also ascribed statuses. Achieved statuses, by contrast, *are based on people's accomplishments or activities and reflect social positions people gain through their own efforts.* Someone who earns a college degree, for example, achieves the status of college graduate. Other achieved statuses are occupation, marital state, parenthood, check forger, and bank robber.

Sometimes, *a particular status becomes central to the way people view themselves or are viewed by others.* Such a social position is called a master status. In the United States, as in many other societies, gender, race, and age are frequently master statuses. For example, people often react differently to male rather than female secretaries or to older rather than younger entertainers. Many times, however, the way people see others differs from the way others see themselves. For instance, employees may see their supervisor in the master status of *boss,* but the supervisor may see herself as *low person on the executive totem pole.*

Whether a particular social position is a master status depends in part on the situation. For example, at work the master status of a female college professor is most likely to be *professor.* The fact that she is also *female* will probably be less relevant. By contrast, a woman who works as a stevedore, as a jockey, or in some other job where women are still relatively uncommon may be viewed by her coworkers in the master status of *woman.*

Master statuses can also play a part in prejudice and discrimination. Frequently, people judge others according to characteristics they automatically associate with a particular master status without ever looking at the individuals themselves. Women as well as blacks and members of other minority groups run into this often, but it can happen to anyone. The English, for instance, often view red-haired people with suspicion.

Roles

Roles are, in a sense, *clusters of norms; they are the behaviors expected of a person who occupies a certain status.* Every status has a number of roles associated with it. For example, a person with a status of soldier is expected to be neat, appear patriotic, follow the orders of superiors, and serve as a good example for subordinates. Similarly, a college professor is expected to teach, write, give and grade tests, and counsel students. *All the roles associated with a particular status* are called the role set (Merton, 1968). A schematic diagram indicating roles and role sets for the statuses of university professor, police officer, and mother is presented in Figure 2.1. Because the terms are so closely related, people sometimes have a tendency to confuse *status* and *role.* Keeping them separate is easy, however, if one simply remembers that a person occupies a status and performs a role.

SOCIAL ROLES AND SOCIAL INTERACTION   In playing various roles, people are guided by *role expectations,* which are norms based on custom and tradition that outline how a particular role should be performed. Role expectations are a major source of order and stability in society and make cooperative activities possible. People are usually aware of the expectations associated with their own roles, as well as those of people with whom they are likely to interact. Thus they can anticipate how others will probably behave toward them and can coordinate their own behavior accordingly. Social interaction thereby can become reasonably predictable.

For instance, consider the common interchange that occurs between a customer and a cashier in a grocery store. Both are usually aware of what each expects. Customers are supposed to select the items they want, take them to the cashier, and pay the amount rung up. The cashier, in turn, is supposed to check the items, charge the proper amount, give the correct change, and provide a sales receipt. If these expectations are not met, some sort of trouble may ensue. For example, if customers try to leave a store without paying, they run the risk of being arrested. Or, if the cashier tries to charge too much, a heated argument is likely to occur.

Of course, people do not always behave according to role expectations. We see violations every day.

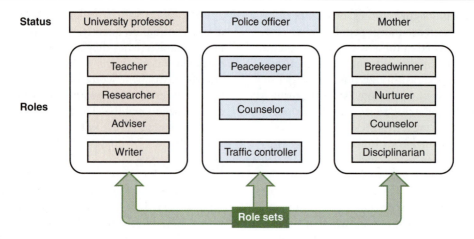

Figure 2.1

A Schematic Presentation of the Relationship among Status, Role, and Role Set

If these violations become too widespread, however, the fabric of social order would be seriously threatened.

The expectations of a particular role are influenced by the statuses of the people with whom one interacts. For example, students are normally expected to be respectful and somewhat deferential when dealing with professors. With other students, however, they are expected to behave as equals. Furthermore, role expectations are colored by the situation. Students, for instance, would normally be more casual with their professors at a student–faculty ball game than they would be in the classroom.

Although role expectations provide general guidelines for how a role should be played, we should not assume that they are rigid. In fact, *role performance,* the actual behavior of people in particular roles, can vary tremendously. Unmarried college students, for example, may be expected to date, but dating can take many forms. Students may go out with one person or with many. They may prefer quiet strolls through museums or crowded parties. They may go out almost every night or only on weekends. And some, in the interest of their studies, may rarely date at all.

One of the most obvious reasons for differences in role performance is personality. Some people are outgoing, some are reserved, some tend to dominate, and some tend to be submissive. Personal characteristics such as these play a big part in the way people behave. So do the other statuses they occupy. For instance, the behavior of a married college student who is also a mother or father will probably be quite different from that of a student who is still dating. Similarly, the concerns of students who are middle aged or older will differ from those of students just out of high school, and these concerns will normally affect the ways they perform their student roles.

The variation in the way people behave means that social interaction is a creative process. To help explain how it occurs, the sociologist Erving Goffman (1959) developed a "dramaturgical" analogy. People, said Goffman, can be viewed as similar to actors in a play. They begin with a basic script in the form of role expectations. Then, using their imagination and ingenuity, they create their own special performance of their roles. An important part of this process is impression management, which is *an individual's effort to control the meanings that others attach to his or her performance.*

One example of impression management is the clothing and hairstyles people select for themselves. Businesspeople in many settings wear neat suits and ties in order to communicate respectability and conservatism to other business people and customers. College students, by contrast, may wear jeans, slacks, or sweatpants, depending on what they want to communicate to those around them. These same students may raise their hand and ask many questions in class in order to convince the professor and other students that they are bright and interested. Or some students may never raise their hand in class because they believe that such an expression of interest in academic or intellectual matters will make them appear "uncool." This flexibility makes for interesting and versatile role performances, but it also makes predicting people's behavior more difficult and complex. *Predicting how others will behave, or how they think and feel,* is a process that sociologists call role-taking, and it is central to social interaction. When role-taking, we try to imagine how others perceive a situation. We imaginatively put ourselves in their place and try to figure out what meanings they attach to people or events. Role-taking occurs in everyday situations, such as when someone tries to imagine how another will react to a request for a date, and it occurs in momentous situations, such as when President Bush and his advisers tried to imagine how the Taliban in Afghanistan would react to the bombing campaign that began in 2001. This process of role-taking, then, shapes people's behavior as they use these predictions of others' likely actions in deciding how to behave. (People don't ask for dates because they predict rejection, whereas President Bush proceeded with the bombing after predicting that it would bring about the collapse of the Taliban regime.)

ROLE STRAIN AND ROLE CONFLICT   Most of the time, role expectations make life more manageable. As has been noted, they help to create social order and stability by providing us with a general idea of what will happen in interactions with others. However, role expectations can also create problems. In certain instances, they can lead to role strain and role conflict. Role strain *develops when people have difficulty performing a role* (Goode, 1960). Sometimes a person does not have the skills or qualities required to perform a particular role. For example, a promotion may place a person who has inadequate business training and is not very adept at handling people in the role of manager. Similarly, students may enter medical or law school only to find that they do not have the desire or dedication necessary to bear the tremendous workload. Role strain can also occur when a person simply does not like some aspects of a role. College professors, for instance, are often expected to write articles or books in their fields of professional expertise. In fact, being published is sometimes a criterion for receiving tenure. Some professors, however, love teaching but find writing difficult. Many students run into similar problems when they take courses that require term papers.

Another form of role strain is called role conflict. Role conflict occurs *when two or more roles a person must play are incompatible or inconsistent.* Sometimes the conflict involves roles associated with different statuses. Consider the problem faced by a police officer who goes to a party thrown by a college friend who offers his guests marijuana. As a police officer, the person is expected to enforce the law. As a friend, however, she is expected to bring no harm to her friend. Thus, no matter what she does, she will violate the expectations of at least one of her roles.

Roles associated with the same status can also be in conflict. Nurses, for example, are expected to care about their patients. At the same time, they are expected to maintain objectivity and a degree of professional distance. Similarly, mothers and fathers are expected to provide their children with affection, but they are also expected to discipline them when they misbehave.

ALLEVIATING ROLE STRAIN   Unfortunately, role conflict and role strain are inevitable, particularly in a society as complex as that of the United States where individuals occupy many different statuses that require them to perform many different roles. As a result, role conflicts are problems everyone must face. One major application of sociological research over the years has been to assess precisely what the consequences of role strain are for people and organizations, and how the social structure might be changed to alleviate role strain and its negative impact.

Role strain can have a detrimental impact on people's health, being linked to heart disease and many other physical and mental ailments (Krantz, Grunberg, & Baum, 1985). People react to role strain with feelings of anxiety, depression, or unhappiness. They feel overworked and unfulfilled. For example, the sociologists Catherine Ross and John Mirowsky (1988) found that mothers who work have higher levels of depression than female workers who do not have child-rearing responsibilities. In addition, they found that two factors in the social structure had a major impact on working women's psychological well-being: the easy availability of child care and a husband who shares in the child-care responsibilities. Women who had these two advantages had relatively low levels of depression because these arrangements reduced the extent of role strain the women experienced.

Studies of nurses have also found high levels of role strain resulting in part from heavy work schedules that do not permit nurses to give the kind of personal care to patients that they were trained to give, and shift work that disrupts nurses' personal lives (Stamps & Piedmonte, 1986). The same thing has been found among correctional officers in prisons. George Gross and his colleagues (1991) found that certain structural conditions produce stress among correctional officers: having too few officers to provide adequate security, having unclear departmental policies about what correctional officers can do, and having unclear policies regarding what is appropriate behavior in dealing with inmates. Nurses and correctional officers who work under such conditions of role strain suffer high levels of physical and emotional distress as well as interpersonal problems. When professionals such as these experience role strain, it sometimes results in *burnout*: an emotional disengagement from clients, dissatisfaction on the job, feelings of worthlessness, and physical and interpersonal problems. Because of these problems, burnout creates high levels of employee turnover as people quit their jobs in response to this role strain. Turnover is costly for organizations including hospitals and prisons because skilled workers leave and new workers must be trained.

Sometimes, people simply accept the fact that some of the expectations of their roles will create conflict or strain. Nurses and parents, for example, may feel that the pleasure and satisfaction they receive from their roles outweigh the difficulties. Applied sociological research, however, can point to ways to alleviate some role strain. Such research also illustrates the point made in Chapter 1: that sociologists identify personal problems, such as depression or burnout, as *structural* problems—arising out of characteristics of the social structure such as role expectations and role strain. As for alleviating role strain at the structural level, sociolo-gists advise organizations to change the workplace to give nurses or correctional officers a lighter workload or more control over the flow of their work. In other cases, sociologists suggest social policies, such as more widely available day-care services, which would allevi-ate the stress of women who work and have children. When changing the social structure is not possible or

Sociology of Media and Technology

Mass Media, the Electronic World, and the Production and Transmission of Culture

For most of human history, culture was produced and transmitted largely through personal, face-to-face contacts between people. By watching the behaviors and hearing the words of relatives or neighbors with whom they were familiar, people learned what values were most desired, what norms were acceptable, and which social role performances would be received posi-tively. With the emergence of the modern mass media and technologies of communication over the past few centuries, all of this has changed dramatically. One aspect of this change is that the new technologies made it possible for culture to be produced and distributed by centralized, impersonal, powerful groups and institutions. This is probably best exemplified by the tra-ditional mass media that became pervasive during the twentieth century: television, movies, the print media, music videos, and so on. People now learn about cultural values, norms, and social roles through these media, which means that family, friends, and neighbors become less influential in the production and transmission of cul-ture (Howard and Jones, 2004). This media presentation of culture is impersonal; it is directed at a large and heterogeneous audience rather than shaped and focused for consumption by particular individuals. Mass-media culture is also carefully crafted and orchestrated rather than spontaneous. Finally, mass-media culture in most cases involves a one-way transmission of information rather than an interaction between the source and the recipient. Because of these characteristics, the culture transmitted through the mass media tends to be less spontaneous and more standardized and simplified. It tends to encourage reaction and acceptance on the part of the recipient rather than reflection, choice, and involvement in the production of culture.

Since the elites in society tend to control the media, the cultural images that the mass media present tend to reflect and support the mainstream values of those elites. In the United States, for example, the media stress the value of material consumption, reflecting one of the cen-tral mainstream values discussed earlier in this chapter. Through advertising and other images, people are told that the way to fulfillment is through owning shiny new cars, handsome (and expensive) clothing, and an endless array of other material products.

Another common theme in the media in the United States is the importance of youth and physical beauty. A study of magazines devoted to teenagers (mostly females), for example, found that about half the space in these magazines is devoted to advertising (Evans, Rutberg, Sather, & Turner, 1991). In addition, the articles and advertisements in magazines such as *Seventeen, Young Miss,* and *Sassy* overwhelmingly stressed the importance of fashion and physical beauty. One-half of the advertisements in these magazines were for clothing, beauty products, fashion products, and other appearance-enhancing items. The message communicated is that self-improvement through proper use of makeup and hairstyles is the road to success, especially for young women.

Contemporary music and music videos also stress the importance of youth, physical beauty, and physical strength. MTV, for example, portrays youth and physical beauty in an appealing way. It also portrays violence as a common, if not integral, part of sexuality and gender relationships. In fact, heavy viewers of MTV are more likely to accept sexual violence as a part of relationships and to believe that women cannot or should not defend themselves from aggression on the part of males (Basow, 1992; Lindsey, 2005).

The stress on physical beauty is also a manifestation of the value of individualism in U.S. culture: The road to success is through individual, rather than collective, actions. The mythical lone hero is pervasive in the media, whether it be Clint Eastwood in the *Dirty Harry* movie series, Arnold Schwarzenegger as the Terminator, or Superman. The theme presented is that real, positive heroes act alone, often against the resistance of others. Collective involvement and cooperative actions are not given nearly the same stress.

With recent technological developments, modern communication technologies have created an electronic world that has another impact on the production and distribution of culture: It has opened up vast possibilities for communication between individuals that did not

The earliest human societies, especially the hunters and gatherers, had much simpler social structures than are found in industrial and postindustrial societies. In these earlier societies, such as these Seneca hunters, there were far fewer statuses and roles for people to choose among and fewer separate social institutions to fulfill the needs of society.

exist in the past. This personal communication is, of course, one of the ways in which values, norms, and other aspects of culture are produced, communicated, and reinforced. These technological developments began with the invention of the printing presses many centuries ago, but escalated with the development of telephones in the last century and the Internet and electronic communications of this century. Now, cell phones, iPods, Blackberries, text messaging, and so on, make it possible for individuals to be in instant communication with one another and to control whom they communicate with and when. Children and teenagers, for example, can circumvent the influence of their parents by text messaging with their friends or creating a set of friends on social networking Web sites such as Facebook. Children can text-message with their friends while in the same room or car with their parents, thus introducing a source of influence regarding values, norms, and what is important that the parents may be totally unaware of. Unlike the traditional mass media, communication in this electronic world is personal and decentralized; it is also spontaneous and interactive, in that individuals respond directly to one another with personal and intimate messages. But unlike the traditional, pre-technological world, communication in this electronic world is less under the influence of powerful elites or traditional sources of authority such as parents or other kin members, and is, as a consequence, less dominated by them.

Some modern technologies tend to homogenize culture—that is, to spread a common culture over widely diverse groups. Other technologies, however, make it possible for a variety of distinct subcultures to emerge and maintain themselves through magazines, music, and the electronic world of the Internet. And it makes it possible for individuals to communicate in ways that may at times support conventional and mainstream values but at other times encourage the development of less conventional values, norms, and ways of life. So, the modern technologies of communication play an important, but complex, part in producing and transmitting culture, with tendencies toward both homogenizing and diversifying a culture.

does not entirely alleviate the problem, clinical sociologists, psychologists, and other counselors develop stress-reduction programs or suggest alternate occupational goals that make it possible to avoid stressful situations (Church, 1991). Gross and his colleagues (1991), for example, recommended the establishment of support groups that would enable the families of correctional officers to help relieve their stress. Some clinical sociologists work with families to rearrange the norms of family life in situations in which mothers work so that a more equitable distribution of responsibilities can be achieved. Sometimes, however, people simply cannot handle certain role expectations and therefore abandon the role. The police officer mentioned earlier, for instance, might stop seeing her buddy, and some medical and law students decide to drop out of school.

The modern mass media and communications technologies play a critical role in shaping and transmitting the components of culture and social structure discussed in this chapter. The Sociology of Media and Technology insert explores this issue.

Groups and Social Institutions

Although status and role are concepts that apply to individuals, they actually come into operation only when two or more people interact. A mother, for instance, can only play the role of nurturer when she has a child to take care of, and a college professor must have students in order to play the role of teacher. Furthermore, interaction among people usually takes place in some sort of group context—a family, a class, a clique, and so on. Indeed, sociology could be considered the study of groups, for virtually all the areas of interest normally investigated by sociologists pertain to groups either directly or indirectly. Because groups are so important, Chapter 4 discusses this subject in detail. For now, groups may be defined as *collections of people who interact with one another on the basis of interrelated statuses and roles and who feel some awareness that they share something in common.*

Social institutions are *relatively stable clusters of statuses, roles, and groups that work together to fulfill some need that all societies must satisfy.* For instance, societies must ensure the physical survival of their members by providing food, clothing, shelter, and health care. They must maintain social order and provide for defense. They must replenish their population through reproduction or recruitment and then train these new members so that these individuals fit into the society productively. Finally, they must develop some sort of belief system to provide meanings and goals that can be shared by most, if not all, of their members. These needs, though few in number, are vital and are filled by political, economic,

educational, family, health-care, and religious institutions. Indeed, no society can hope to survive unless it develops enduring ways of meeting these needs effectively. Chapters 9 through 13 examine, in considerable depth, the major institutions found in all societies.

A Comparative View of Societies

You should be able to describe the five basic subsistence patterns and explain how societies change as they make the transition to industrialism, postindustrialism, and global interdependence.

Our comprehension of the world today is strongly shaped by the prevalence of industrial societies. To be sure, there are still a few scattered primitive groups such as the Indians of the western Amazon forests of Brazil. There are also some countries that are still largely agricultural, particularly in Africa. All these societies, however, are rapidly giving way to industrial technologies and lifestyles. Nevertheless, one of the best ways to understand one's own society is to view it in comparison to other types of societies. By looking at the variety of means people have used in adapting to their particular environments and technologies, people can better appreciate the forces influential in their own society, both now and in the past. Therefore, this chapter takes a brief look at the social structure of several different types of societies.

These societies may be classified by their subsistence patterns, or how they solve the problem of securing the basic necessities of food, clothing, and shelter. Five subsistence patterns emerge—hunting and gathering, pastoralism, horticulturalism, agriculturalism, and industrialism (see Gregg, 1991; Johnson & Earle, 1987; Nolan & Lenski, 2006).

Preindustrial Societies

The oldest and simplest social structure is that found in *hunting-and-gathering societies,* which are most often nomadic groups that number no more than sixty or so individuals. In these societies, everyone who is able must participate in the search for food. Furthermore, there is seldom a surplus of food, so no one is able to amass any wealth. Thus, hunting-and-gathering societies are essentially egalitarian. The only statuses are normally those based on gender and age. The men usually hunt, fish, and make or repair weapons. The women gather nuts and berries, make clothes, and tend to the cooking. Children take on adult tasks as soon as they are physically able. There are no specialized leadership roles, and decisions about such things as where to hunt or whether it is time to move to a new territory are usually made by common consensus. Similarly, whatever social control is needed is administered by the entire group through gossip and ridicule or, in cases of serious infractions, through ostracism. The family is a key institution in hunting-and-gathering societies, and most societal needs are accomplished in the family. Thus, economic, political, and even religious tasks are performed by family members, and there are no separate institutions that fulfill these needs. Families are usually loosely organized, and the responsibility for raising children is frequently shared by all the adults.

Social structure becomes somewhat more complex in pastoral and horticultural societies, both of which first emerged some twelve thousand years ago. *Pastoralism* involves raising herds of domesticated animals, and *horticulturalism* is based on cultivating plants such as wheat, rice, and other grains using a few simple tools. These patterns of subsistence are far more productive than hunting and gathering. As a result, pastoral and horticultural societies not only are assured of a steady supply of food, but also can manage surpluses in the form of food or livestock. As a result, they tend to be much larger than hunting-and-gathering societies, numbering in the hundreds and in some cases the thousands. The food surplus also frees some people from the necessity of food production, and more specialized statuses emerge. Such activities as providing political and economic leadership, performing religious rituals, and healing the sick become special statuses that are distinct from people's positions in the family. In addition, the increased size and complexity of these societies make specialized statuses essential. Furthermore, some individuals or families manage to accumulate more wealth and, as a result, more power than others. This power often becomes hereditary (i.e., passed on through generations), which leads to the development of some social class distinctions. For the most part, however, statuses and roles are still determined by gender and age. The men usually farm, herd livestock, collect fuel for fires, and prepare leather for clothes. The women tend small gardens, prepare food, and make clothing and utensils.

Some six thousand years ago, the invention of the plow led to the development of *agricultural societies*. The plow, which brings nutrients to the surface of the soil, greatly increases the productivity of the land and allows it to be farmed almost continuously. This development, in turn, gave rise to much larger societies with much greater food surpluses and significantly reduced the number of people needed in the actual production of food.

Agricultural societies have very complex social structures, mainly because they need so much coordination, management, and support. For instance, they require centralized political and economic organizations to coordinate the production and distribution of food, set up trade relations with other societies, and maintain social order. One consequence of this centralization is the appearance of cities. Another is a tremendous increase in the number and variety of statuses, which include merchants, artists, metalworkers, physicians, traders, religious figures, and bureaucrats. Furthermore, wealth and power tend to become concentrated in the hands of a few people. Economic differences among people become more pronounced, and a fairly rigid class structure emerges. In fact, extensive inequality is an inherent feature of virtually all agricultural societies. Thus, although age and gender are still important statuses, people's social positions become increasingly determined by other statuses such as occupation, ethnicity, family background, and wealth.

Industrial Societies

The most complex social structure is found in industrial societies, which, as mentioned at the beginning of this section, have become the most pervasive type of society in the world today. Industrialism is an extremely productive subsistence pattern in which machines and power tools, run by new sources of energy such as fossil fuels, accomplish tasks that were previously done by hand. As a result, a relatively small number of people can feed the rest of the population.

There is a virtual explosion in the number and variety of economic activities in industrial societies. In addition, most tasks are broken down into small, specialized segments, each of which is performed by a different person. Consequently, industrial societies have an elaborate system of statuses and roles. Although gender and age are still important in some contexts, occupation is the chief determinant of a person's social position. Moreover, extreme wealth and power become harder to hold onto in industrial societies, so there is a decrease in the overall amount of social inequality. Thus achievement replaces ascription, and such statuses as race and family background begin to decline in importance.

The most dramatic shift in societal evolution has been between the four preindustrial societies and industrial society (Table 2.2). Industrial societies have social structures that stand in stark contrast to all the others. The German sociologist Ferdinand Tönnies described the difference in terms of *gemeinschaft* versus *gesellschaft* types of societies (1887/1963).

Gemeinschaft, which translates roughly as *"community," refers to social life that is governed by personal, informal considerations, with tradition and custom prevailing.* People place the welfare of the community before personal interest, are strongly bound to the other members of their community, and value these community ties very highly. In the gemeinschaft, people relate to one another because of liking, sympathy, or enjoyment—because the relationship itself provides

Table 2.2

THE TRANSITION FROM PREINDUSTRIAL TO INDUSTRIAL SOCIETIES

	Preindustrial	Industrial
Social relations	More personal and intimate	Very impersonal
Social structure	Few statuses and roles; ascription is important	Complex array of statuses and roles; achievement overshadows ascription
Institutions	May be some specialized institutions, but family tends to be most important	Specialized institutions emerge in political, educational, and other realms; family overshadowed by other institutions
Social control	Largely informal	Formal means, such as the police, become ever more important
Division of labor	Simple, based most often on age and sex	Complex, based on many characteristics, but occupation is especially important; age and gender are secondary
Culture	Homogeneous, with value consensus and few subcultures	Diverse, with many subcultures and numerous conflicting values

many positive feelings and personal fulfillments. Gemeinschaft-like social relationships tend to predominate in preindustrial societies.

Gesellschaft, meaning *"society" or "association,"* *refers to social relations characterized by specialization, individualism, and rationality.* Specialization emerges in the form of separate social roles and social institutions that are developed to accomplish specific tasks and to achieve certain goals. Individualism and a concern with personal interest predominate and come to replace loyalty to a group or society. The ends or goals that people seek in social relationships are more specific and limited, such as making money or exchanging products. Calculation, impersonality, and formality come to dominate social relationships. Increasingly, relationships become contractual rather than personal. Gesellschaft-like social relationships tend to predominate in industrial societies.

A Global Perspective: Postindustrialism and Global Interdependence

As industrial societies have continued to develop, what emerged first were postindustrial societies, which are *dominated by a highly technological form of production and devote more attention to service industries, information production, and economic consumption than they do to industrial production and manufacturing* (Bell, 1973; Esping-Andersen, 1999). Fewer people work in factories producing goods. Subsistence shifts its focus to producing information, organizing people, and providing services. The key resources are no longer physical skills and strength;

instead, education, intellectual skills, the ability to manipulate information, and skills at organizing people become important. The positions in the social structure that receive high rewards are those of writers, teachers, scientists, managers, and the designers of products. As information and knowledge become more important, the result is further innovations—robotics, computers, cybernetics, fiber optics—that lead to a further shift toward an information-based, service-oriented economy. Today, 76 percent of the jobs in the United States are white-collar or service jobs (see Chapter 13).

This postindustrialism is a part of the trend toward *globalization*, introduced in Chapter 1: the increasing interconnectedness between different peoples around the world and the growing unification of social and cultural life. Societies today, much more so than in the past, live in an interdependent global community. The global societies that are emerging are now integrated into a worldwide network of communication and economic exchange that has the potential for tying them together into a single social, economic, and cultural entity. This situation has wide ramifications for the social structure in the United States in terms of the jobs and opportunities that are available. Increasingly, assembly-line and production jobs are going to less developed nations while the design and information jobs remain in the advanced industrial nations. Beyond this, we can speak of a cultural globalization: *the spread of a set of beliefs, values, norms, language, and meaning systems that are shared by people who participate in this global community.* This global culture transcends the many individual cultures that are the unique heritage of particular peoples or nations. It reflects the fact that modern electronic communications technologies

Sociology on the Internet

One of the wondrous things about the Internet is that it offers an opportunity to explore the cultures of the world with a few keystrokes. Chapter 2 discusses cultural diversity in the United States and around the world, and this exercise moves you toward exploring this diversity on the Internet. There are almost an infinite number of routes that can be taken; I will describe one route to illustrate how this can be done. Log on to the AltaVista search engine. In the search box, type "culture and Asia." This will produce many results, including a list of nations and regions. Selecting one of these can serve as a gateway to learning a great deal about religion in Asian culture, and especially about Islam, which most Westerners identify as a religion of the Middle East rather than

Asia. Using this search and others like it, locate information that relates to Asian cultural values, norms, roles, and social institutions, as discussed in Chapter 2. How does what you find here point to differences from mainstream U.S. culture?

If you choose a search engine other than AltaVista, you will get somewhat different results, but you can still make the same kind of exploration, searching for different cultural ways and trying to describe and understand them. Each student in your class should try going down a different cultural path. You can do the same sort of search for subcultures in the United States. Locate as many subcultures as you can and identify the elements of their culture and social structure.

---

make it possible for peoples around to globe to share some of the same material culture (computers, iPods, Blackberries, and so on) as well as some of the same nonmaterial culture (values that praise the worth of individualism or economic efficiency and are expressed through the global distribution of movies or music). This cultural globalization will likely reduce the diversity in human cultures around the globe, as some cultures change and others disappear in response to this onslaught. To use language as a cultural element to illustrate this trend: It is debatable whether the outcome will be a single world language, but it seems likely that many languages will disappear as a few become dominant (possibly English, Spanish, or some kind of electronic-speak).

Yet, this global culture, as important as it is likely to become, will not necessarily supplant all of the other distinct cultures. Rather, global culture is an adaptation to the growing contact and interdependence among the world's peoples that is a product of the modern technologies of communication. Certainly many local cultural variations will persist, possibly eventually being seen as subcultures within the context of the larger global culture.

Study & Review
SUMMARY OF LEARNING OBJECTIVES

You should be able to define culture and differentiate material and nonmaterial culture.

Societies vary greatly in development, size, and social practices. To study them effectively, sociologists look at a few fundamental characteristics common to all societies. These characteristics pertain to culture and social structure. Culture refers to the total lifestyle of a

people. Cultural elements can be divided into material culture and nonmaterial culture. Material and nonmaterial culture are closely interrelated, and each greatly affects the other.

You should be able to discuss the different elements of culture, including beliefs, values, norms, and language.

Beliefs, values, norms, and language are components that are common to all cultures. Beliefs are people's conceptions about what is true in the world. Values are very general guidelines for behavior. Whereas mainstream values can be found in all cultures, there is also a diversity of values, and values change over time as social conditions change. Norms are more specific guidelines for behavior. Some norms are internalized, while others are codified into laws. Language not only makes possible communication but also shapes our view of reality and reinforces social practices.

You should be able to describe cultural integration as well as the various types of cultural change, including the sources from which change may arise.

There are forces in cultures that both promote and resist change. Because the elements of a culture are usually fairly well integrated, change in one aspect usually results in change in another. Change can come either from outside or from within a culture. A major source of external change is diffusion. Sources of internal change include innovation and the gap between ideal culture and real culture. Ethnocentrism promotes a feeling of "we-ness," but it can undermine our efforts to understand other cultures. Social scientists therefore promote the idea of cultural relativity, which holds that the lifestyles of various peoples can be understood only in terms of their own culture rather than that of the observer. The United States and most other advanced nations are too diverse to have one common culture. They have a number of subcultures. Membership in a subculture requires sharing its values and identifying with its members.

You should be able to describe the functions of statuses, roles, groups, and institutions in maintaining social structure.

Social structure helps to make social interaction orderly and predictable. The foundation of social structure lies in the concepts of status and role. Role expectations, which are based on custom and tradition, provide general guidelines for people to use in devising their performance of their roles. Most of the time, they help to make life more manageable, but they sometimes cause people trouble in the form of role strain and role conflict. Two important manifestations of social structure are groups and institutions. Most social interaction occurs in some sort of group context. Institutions are relatively stable clusters of statuses, roles, and groups that work together to meet the basic needs of a society.

You should be able to describe the five basic subsistence patterns and explain how societies change as they make the transition to industrialism, postindustrialism, and global interdependence.

Five different types of subsistence patterns have been identified among human societies, and they involve movement toward more extensive and more elaborate social structures. This is generally characterized as a shift from a *gemeinschaft* type of society to a *gesellschaft* type. Societies are also distinguished in terms of whether they are preindustrial, industrial, or postindustrial in nature. *Cultural globalization* is an emerging response to the changes made possible by modern technologies of communication.

CHRONOLOGICAL PRACTICE TEST

For answers to Key Concepts see the page number in parentheses; for other answers see page 59.

What Is Culture?
Key Concepts

1. Society (36)
2. Culture (36)
3. Material culture (36)
4. Nonmaterial culture (36)

True/False

5. T F The Comanche Indian society of the nineteenth century stressed individualism, as did the Euro-American culture of the time.

Concept Completion

6. The term _____ refers to the total lifestyle of a people, including all of the ideas, values, knowledge, behaviors, and material objects that they share.
7. The various elements of culture fall into two general categories: _____ and _____.

Critical Thinking

8. Describe the kind of social organization found among the Comanche people of the Great Plains. Why did it confuse the early Euro-Americans settlers in the plains?

The Components of Culture
Key Concepts

9. Beliefs (37)
10. Values (37)
11. Norms (39)
12. Sanctions (39)
13. Folkways (41)
14. Mores (41)
15. Internalization (41)
16. Laws (41)

True/False

17. T F One of the mainstream cultural values in the United States, according to this chapter, is tradition.
18. T F Cultural norms are more specific guidelines for behavior than are cultural values.
19. T F Based on the linguistic-relativity hypothesis, the chapter concludes that language is a powerful force-shaping culture while culture has little impact on language.

Concept Completion

20. The fact that people in the United States strive to make things better and to improve the future in comparison to the present reflects the cultural value of _____.
21. _____ refers to the process by which people incorporate social norms into their own personal codes of conduct.

Graphics Review

22. What does the photo on page 40 illustrate about the Amish values and way of life?

Critical Thinking

23. Define the four components of culture discussed in the text. Give two examples of each: one example from the United States and one from another culture.
24. Compare and contrast mainstream cultural values in the United States with those in Japan.

25. Who are the Amish? Describe their beliefs and values.
26. What is the linguistic relativity hypothesis? What is the evidence for and against it?

Cultural Consensus and Diversity
Key Concepts
27. Ideal culture (44)
28. Real culture (44)
29. Ethnocentrism (45)
30. Cultural relativity (45)
31. Subculture (47)

True/False
32. T F *Diffusion* refers to a source of cultural change that is internal to a society rather than external.
33. T F In the study of other cultures, social scientists promote ethnocentrism, rather than cultural relativism, as the more useful way to understand a culture.

Concept Completion
34. When two cultures come into contact, cultural change is likely to occur through a process of _____.
35. Argot is the specialized language of a _____.

Critical Thinking
36. Discuss the notions of cultural integration and cultural change. Why are these important? How do they help us understand how cultures work?
37. What functions does a specialized argot perform for a subculture?

Social Structure
Key Concepts
38. Social structure (48)
39. Status (49)
40. Ascribed statuses (49)
41. Achieved statuses (49)
42. Master status (49)
43. Roles (49)
44. Role set (49)
45. Impression management (50)
46. Role-taking (50)
47. Role strain (51)
48. Role conflict (51)
49. Groups (54)
50. Social institutions (54)

True/False
51. T F What is important about a master status is that it is central to the way in which people view themselves or are viewed by others.
52. T F Role conflict is one form of role strain.

Concept Completion
53. What distinguishes the concepts *status* and *role* is that a person _____ a status and _____ a role.

54. _____ refers to imaginatively putting yourself in another's place and trying to figure out what meanings that person attaches to situations and what behaviors he or she will engage in.

Critical Thinking
55. What part do roles play in the process of social interaction? Include in your answer the various concepts, such as role-taking and impression management, that were discussed in this chapter in relation to roles.
56. What problems can role strain create for people and society? Give some examples. What can be done about these problems?

A Comparative View of Societies
Key Concepts
57. Gemeinschaft (55)
58. Gesellschaft (56)
59. Postindustrial society (56)
60. Cultural globalization (56)

True/False
61. T F Industrial societies place more stress on *gemeinschaft* than do preindustrial societies.
62. T F The text argues that the emerging global culture will result in the disappearance of virtually all subcultures.

Concept Completion
63. The oldest and simplest types of social structure is found in _____ societies.
64. Societies that stress service industries and information production rather than industrial production and manufacturing are called _____.

Critical Thinking
65. Compare and contrast social life in preindustrial and industrial societies in terms of culture, social structure, social institutions, and social control.

ANSWERS TO CHRONOLOGICAL PRACTICE TEST
5. T; **17.** F; **18.** T; **19.** F; **32.** F; **33.** F; **51.** T; **52.** T; **61.** F; **62.** F
6. culture
7. material culture, nonmaterial culture
20. progress, efficiency, practicality
21. Internalization
34. diffusion
35. subculture
53. occupies, performs
54. role-taking
63. hunting-and-gathering
64. postindustrial societies

CUMULATIVE PRACTICE TEST

See page 482 for answers.

1. The total lifestyle of a people, including all of the ideas, knowledge, behaviors, and material objects that they share, is termed a
   a. society.
   b. social structure.
   c. culture.
   d. belief system.
   e. heritage.

2. All of the following would be considered a part of material culture *except*
   a. physical objects.
   b. language.
   c. physical artifacts.
   d. televisions.
   e. home appliances.

3. "Conceptions that people have about what is true in the world" is known as which component of culture?
   a. Values.
   b. Language.
   c. Ideal culture.
   d. Real culture.
   e. Beliefs.

4. Success and achievement are examples of _____ in the United States.
   a. values
   b. beliefs
   c. norms
   d. mores
   e. folkways

5. All of the following were listed as Japanese cultural values *except*
   a. harmony.
   b. collectivism.
   c. authority.
   d. tradition.
   e. material success.

6. Which of the following exemplifies "sanctions"?
   a. A person is rewarded for conforming to a norm.
   b. People are given rules of conduct to guide their behavior.
   c. People control their own behavior.
   d. Language shapes people's perceptions of reality.
   e. All of the above.

7. The austere clothing of the Amish of Pennsylvania is a reflection of which of their cultural values?
   a. Individualism.
   b. Collectivism.
   c. Equality.
   d. Humility.
   e. Harmony.

8. In most societies, the prohibitions against murder and incest would be considered to be
   a. folkways.
   b. material culture.
   c. social roles.
   d. mores.
   e. role strain.

9. Which of the following statements about laws is/are true?
   a. All laws are based on mores.
   b. Many laws are based on mores.
   c. Practically all laws are based on folkways.
   d. Laws seldom reflect norms.
   e. All of the above are true statements.

10. Which of the following is the most accurate statement of the linguistic relativity hypothesis?
    a. Language reflects the world in which we live.
    b. The language we speak shapes how we think about and perceive the world.
    c. Our perceptions of the world shape the kind of language that we speak.
    d. Language is a passive and neutral means of communicating what we perceive in the world.
    e. Language does not serve as a filter for reality.

11. The spread of cultural elements from one culture to another is referred to as
    a. innovation.
    b. invention.
    c. diffusion.
    d. discovery.
    e. sanctions.

12. The ideal culture in Mexico would be best characterized as
    a. matriarchal.
    b. patriarchal.
    c. individualistic.
    d. socialistic.
    e. postindustrial.

13. The tendency to view one's own culture as the best and to judge other cultures in comparison to it is called
    a. innovation.
    b. cultural relativity.
    c. diffusion.
    d. racism.
    e. ethnocentrism.

14. Which of the following are functions that can be served by an argot?
    a. It separates group members from nonmembers.
    b. It reinforces group identity.
    c. It offers concise ways to refer to roles and statuses not generally found in the mainstream of society.
    d. It reinforces a subculture's values and priorities.
    e. All of the above.

15. Which of the following would be the best example of an ascribed status?
    a. Being born male.
    b. Graduating from college.
    c. Getting married.
    d. Selling drugs.
    e. Joining a religion.

16. Occupation, marital status, parenthood, and bank robber are all examples of
    a. ascribed statuses.
    b. norms.
    c. achieved statuses.
    d. role sets.
    e. role strain.

17. Which of the following is the best definition of a "master status"?
    a. A status that is based on a person's accomplishments or activities.
    b. A status that is central to the way people view themselves or are viewed by others.
    c. A status that is assigned to people and over which they have little say about occupying.
    d. All of the roles associated with a particular status.
    e. A status that has important expectations associated with it.
18. Which sociologist was responsible for developing a dramaturgical analogy in studying social interaction?
    a. Talcott Parsons.
    b. Robert K. Merton.
    c. Karl Marx.
    d. Edward Sapir.
    e. Erving Goffman.
19. The subsistence pattern that involves raising herds of domestic animals is known as
    a. hunting and gathering.
    b. pastoralism.
    c. horticulturalism.
    d. agriculture.
    e. industrialism.
20. Which of the following characteristics applies to preindustrial societies more than to industrial ones?
    a. Social relations are personal and intimate.
    b. Specialized institutions emerge in institutional realms.
    c. Formal means of social control develop.
    d. Achievement overshadows ascription.
    e. None of the above are more characteristic of preindustrial societies.

FOR FURTHER READING

Berger, Arthur Asa. (2002). *Video games: A popular culture phenomenon*. New Brunswick, NJ: Transaction Publishers. This is a thought-provoking book that analyzes the video game phenomenon from the perspective of the concepts to understand culture discussed in this chapter.

Callaghan, Karen A. (Ed.). (1994). *Ideals of feminine beauty*. Westport, CT: Greenwood. This book explores the extent to which standards of feminine beauty involve values and norms that are an integral part of a cultural heritage. It provides some excellent cross-cultural comparisons regarding ideals of feminine beauty.

Coakley, Jay. (2007). *Sport in society: Issues and controversies* (9th ed.). New York: McGraw-Hill. Sports is a key institution in cultures and societies, and this book explores the many aspects of the impact of sports: how it affects and is affected by race, ethnicity, politics, the economy, gender, religion, the media, and so on.

DeVita, Philip R., & Armstrong, James D. (2002). *Distant mirrors: America as a foreign culture* (3rd ed.). Belmont, CA: Wadsworth. This is an intriguing view of U.S. culture from the perspective of foreigners who have settled in the United States. It gives a glimpse of what the country looks like to others.

Goffman, Erving. (1959). *The presentation of self in everyday life*. New York: Doubleday. This is still the classic statement on role expectations and role performance from a dramaturgical perspective. Goffman, now deceased, was a master at unveiling some of the hidden ways we shape our social world.

Harris, Marvin. (1974). *Cows, pigs, wars, and witches: The riddles of culture*. New York: Vintage. A noted anthropologist takes a fascinating look at unique and often bizarre social practices in other cultures. He offers interesting ideas regarding their origin and meaning, suggesting that what seems puzzling to us is usually explicable in the context of its own culture.

Wolf, Daniel R. (1991). *The rebels: A brotherhood of outlaw bikers*. Toronto: University of Toronto Press. This is an ethnography of a motorcycle gang illustrating many of the points made in the chapter regarding subcultures.

Zellner, William W. (1995). *Countercultures: A sociological analysis*. New York: St. Martin's Press. This author provides an excellent sociological analysis of a number of subcultures in the United States, such as satanist, survivalists, and a number of other religious and nonreligious groups. Calling them countercultures implies that they are, at least in part, deviant from mainstream cultural values.

THE INDIVIDUAL IN SOCIETY

CHAPTER THREE
Socialization

CHAPTER FOUR
Groups and Organizations

CHAPTER FIVE
Deviance, Crime, and Social Control

Part II covers the basic ways in which individuals are linked to society by learning shared meanings and patterns of behavior that make cooperative involvement with others possible. The chapters cover such topics as socialization, groups and organizations, deviance, and social control.

Socialization

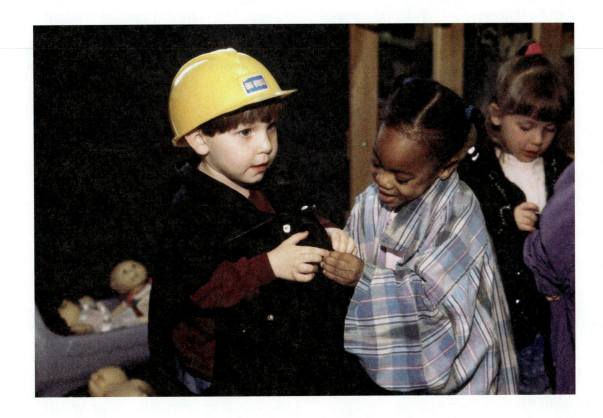

MYTHS & FACTS: About Socialization

Heredity and the Environment

Biology and Human Behavior
Children Raised in Isolation

The Process of Socialization

The Development of Self: The Interactionist Perspective
Cooley
Mead
Erikson
Agencies of Socialization
The Family
The Peer Group
The School
The Mass Media
APPLYING SOCIOLOGY: Day Care: Problem or Solution?
Types of Socialization
Primary Socialization

SOCIOLOGY OF MEDIA AND TECHNOLOGY: Who Socializes the Young in an Electronic World?
OTHER WORLDS, OTHER WAYS: Japan: Learning Cultural Values through Primary Socialization
Anticipatory Socialization
Resocialization
Socialization through the Life Span
Gaining Independence
Work and Family
Relationships

Additional Perspectives on Socialization

The Functionalist Perspective
The Conflict Perspective
SOCIOLOGY ON THE INTERNET

Study & Review

The Samoan Islands include more than 1,200 Pacific islands between Hawaii and Australia. They were originally settled, possibly as long as 3,000 years ago, by voyagers in canoes coming from the west. Traditionally, Samoans survived by gathering wild food such as coconuts as well as by fishing and raising pigs and chickens. The basic social unit was the *aiga*, or extended family group, and Samoan cultural values emphasized deference and respect for those older than oneself. Samoan social structure was hierarchical, with some *aiga* having more status and prestige than others. Whereas the Samoan culture has been heavily influenced by the intrusion of industrialism and a market economy in the past century, many traditional values and practices persist, including the central role of the *aiga* and respect for age.

Early in the twentieth century, leading anthropologists, including Margaret Mead, observed Samoan and other traditional cultures around the world and interpreted what they saw as support for a position called cultural determinism, which posits that *cultural influences determine the behaviors and personalities of people*. In other words, human beings are infinitely malleable and are molded by the culture in which they are raised. Mead (1961) described the Samoans as a gentle and harmonious people who were respectful to others, especially their elders. They were moderate in their behavior and controlled in the expression of their feelings. They were also compassionate and considerate and showed generosity to others. For Mead, these characteristics were the Samoan personality, stamped in by the socialization experiences of Samoans as children.

Myths & Facts

About Socialization

Myth:

The most positive psychological and social development of children occurs when they are raised in families by their mothers and fathers.

Fact:

There has been much research on this issue, and so far the conclusion is that removal from the family, at least for a time, may not be detrimental to children. For example, children who are sent to day-care settings seem to develop as well as children raised totally within their families. Day care may have a more negative impact on very young children, and poor-quality day care is certainly undesirable. However, children seem to be able to adapt to many different settings for socialization.

Myth:

Entertaining television shows and movies that contain some violence, such as *NYPD Blue, The Sopranos,* or *The Patriot,* do not harm young people who watch them as long as the shows are clearly fictional and fanciful.

Fact:

Television can be a powerful socializing agent, teaching the young norms for acceptable behavior. Most research evidence concludes that young people who watch violent shows on television are more likely to behave aggressively or violently themselves, especially in situations that are conducive to violence. This likelihood is especially true for boys between the ages of eight and twelve and for those who are more aggressive to begin with.

Myth:

Socialization and development occur while people are growing to biological maturity and are accomplished by the time people reach adulthood. By the 1990s, adulthood for men and women had become quite similar.

Fact:

Socialization and development continue throughout people's lives, and adulthood is a time of periodic changes in life tasks and goals for most people. Adulthood for many women is still quite different from adulthood for many men because society places different demands on women. For example, the decision to have children has more serious implications for the possibilities and accomplishments of adult women than it does for men.

Myth:

The stages of the life cycle, such as infancy, adolescence, and adulthood, are shaped largely by biological considerations, particularly by what people are capable of doing at a given chronological age.

Fact:

Actually, the reality of the life cycle is far more complicated than this. Although biological limitations play a part in what society allows us to do, particularly among the very young and very old, the social structure is more important than biology in shaping the life cycle from childhood through adulthood. In fact, one stage in the life span—adolescence—does not even exist in most preindustrial societies. Adolescence is a social creation to meet the unique demands of industrial societies and has virtually nothing to do with biological maturation or capabilities.

More recent research, however, describes a more complicated socialization process in which Samoans are molded by their culture but also resist some of the pressures and demands that are put on them. The result is more variation in personality and behavior than Mead and other early anthropologists believed existed (Freeman, 1983; Mageo, 1991; Ritchie & Ritchie, 1989). For example, Samoan culture does discourage open displays of strong emotion and affection between people, as Mead suggested. In old Samoa, husbands and wives never touched or showed affection toward each other in public. In fact, there is no Samoan equivalent of the English phrase *being in love* with someone. Children begin to learn this emotional distancing at a young age. Early in life, parents begin to distance themselves emotionally from their children. For example, by the time children are about six months old, parents stop picking them up and attending to their crying. This behavior is to discourage children from focusing on their own needs and to encourage them to take their proper place in the family or larger communal group. Further parental distancing is achieved by shifting most child-rearing tasks from parents to older children.

Both parents and children, however, resist this cultural pressure toward emotional distance: When children are sick, parents become very emotional and hold and attend to their children constantly. Children for their part throw tantrums when parents distance themselves. And Samoan culture makes adaptations by providing a substitute or compensation: the ethos of *alofa,* or a love for all people. This love imparts a general warmth to Samoan social life and is reflected in the exchange of goods in traditional ceremonies. It focuses attention away from the individual relationship and directs it toward the communal. What is important is not the bond between individuals but the linkage of the individual to the whole group. In addition, despite the cultural socialization, some people are expressively emotional. In fact, Samoans call people with a tendency toward excessive emotional displays *lotovaivai,* or having a weakness as far as emotions go. Such emotional outbursts are especially common when someone dies or departs on a journey. So, *alofa* and *lotovaivai* are, in a sense, cultural concessions that recognize that socialization is not perfect; not everyone will at all times display the moderate and controlled emotions that are the Samoan ideal.

Respect for and deference to one's elders are also taught to Samoan children at a young age. For example, one elder will tell a child to take an object to another elder some distance away, and the latter will thank the child for the object. This procedure will be repeated many times until the obedience becomes habitual, at which point the "thank you" is omitted. Then the child is expected to respond automatically to the orders of an older person. Evidence shows that these socialization practices do instill a tendency toward deference among Samoans that can be detected even in adulthood. Yet, some children resist this pressure to obey elders and become *failoto,* or stubborn, rather than deferential. In addition, though it is frowned on, some Samoans will negotiate status deference by refusing to respond to an elder. Other Samoans will refuse to demand the deference that is rightfully theirs because of age or family position or will deemphasize status issues when interacting with others.

Socialization is *the process by which people develop personal identities and learn the ways of a particular group or society.* The Samoan experience illustrates the power of the socialization process: It produces a Samoan personality that is, on the whole, clearly different from the personalities of people in the United States or people from many other cultures. Samoans do tend to be more gentle, considerate, and respectful of their elders. However, the Samoan experience also shows that cultures are not perfect in imparting attitudes, personalities, or behaviors. Situational differences as well as variations in individual temperament lead some Samoans to be less gentle, considerate, and respectful than other Samoans. Culture is important in socialization, but it is not the only influence. The Samoan personality that Mead described is more the ideal or model behavior and attitude among Samoans. As with all ideals, people approach it to varying degrees, and some people diverge significantly from it. The rigid cultural determinism of Mead and other early anthropologists is too simplified to describe a socialization process that is actually a two-way street: Culture pressures and demands while individuals react and resist. The outcome, in terms of identities and behaviors, is a product of both forces.

So, through the socialization process, society exerts considerable power over its members by teaching them what they should be like and how they ought to behave. As the sociologist Peter Berger (1963) points out, however, this power is not usually seen as harsh or domineering.

> For most of us the yoke of society seems easy to bear . . . because most of the time we ourselves desire just that which society expects of us. We want to obey the rules. We want the parts that society has assigned to us. (p. 93)

In other words, many of the beliefs, values, and norms of a culture become so internalized by its members that adherence to them seems self-directed. This chapter analyzes how the socialization process achieves this end and which social groups play a part in it.

Heredity and the Environment

You should be able to assess the different approaches to the roles of heredity and the environment in the socialization process and compare the contributions of each.

Before looking at the socialization process, this chapter considers the relative importance of heredity and the environment in shaping human behavior. The question of which has more influence, usually referred to as the *nature versus nurture* issue, has been, and still is, the source of much debate.

On the one hand, the *nature* position holds that human behavior is the product of a person's heredity, which is determined at birth and is thus beyond human control. According to this view, many of our characteristics, abilities, and personality traits are dictated by our biological equipment, innate intelligence, and hormonal makeup.

On the other hand, the *nurture* position argues that human beings are flexible and adaptable and that human behavior is determined by the learning and social contact that people experience as they mature. The philosopher John Locke, for example, argued that human beings are born *tabula rasa,* which means "with a clean slate." He believed that people have few biologically imposed limitations and that their behaviors and abilities are largely the result of learning during the socialization process.

Biology and Human Behavior

To assess the nature versus nurture debate, we must first look at the role of biology in human behavior. Biological determinism, in contrast to Mead's cultural determinism, posits that *human behavior and many elements of social structure are a product of the genetic and physiological characteristics of people.* Certainly, our biological makeup does have implications for our social behavior. For one thing, human beings have *biological reflexes,* such as sucking or coughing. But these reflexes are relatively simple physiological responses, and they operate only briefly in terms of our whole life span. Moreover, they can be shaped by learning. For example, human infants are born with an automatic reflex to suck when objects are placed in the mouth. However, this reflex is quickly replaced through learning as children begin to choose what they will suck on.

Human beings also have certain *biological drives,* such as hunger, thirst, and the desire for sex. These are generalized urges that can motivate behavior. There are no biologically based cues, however, that tell people how to act on these drives. We must therefore learn how to satisfy them. With regard to hunger, for instance, we learn what to eat (fruits and vegetables rather than insect larvae), when to eat (three times a day rather than one or five), and how to eat (usually with a knife and fork rather than with our hands).

Finally, human beings have certain *biological characteristics* that shape both our abilities and our behavior. For example, children with Down syndrome, a genetic disorder that is sometimes called *mongolism,* are severely limited in their capacity for learning. In addition, some people have greater manual dexterity, more athletic prowess, a more active disposition, or a more cheerful temperament than do others. But these things are also influenced by learning and social experience. The person with great athletic prowess will become an athlete only if given certain opportunities, and the naturally cheerful person can become morose if negative events happen in her life.

So, human behavior is a result of both biological and social forces. But do human beings have *instincts,* meaning complex patterns of behavior that are inborn and largely beyond their control? After all, the behavior of many other animals is controlled by instincts. For instance, if we isolate a male rat at birth and place it, as an adult, in the company of a sexually receptive female rat, the completely inexperienced rat will be able to perform sexually with an expertise equal to that of far more experienced male rats.

Most scientists today conclude that human behavior is not under such rigid biological control. Yet, evidence can be found for a strong, if less rigid, biological control over complex social behavior in humans and many other animals. Recent applications of these ideas have been labeled sociobiology, *a field based on the idea that the genetic makeup of humans and other animals plays a powerful role in shaping their social behavior* (Nielson, 1994; van der Dennen & Falger, 1990). Sociobiologists maintain that there are many parallels between human and animal behavior. A male stickleback fish, for example, will protect against all intruders a nest containing fertilized eggs deposited by the female stickleback. Anything approaching the nest that resembles another stickleback will be viciously attacked (Tinbergen, 1955). Such protection of territory can be found in many species, and it is clearly a biologically produced behavior in these species rather than a product of learning. Robert Ardrey (1967) popularized such behavior as the *territorial imperative,* suggesting that such protection is necessary for some species to survive. Human parallels of such territoriality would include such things as protecting territory from other human groups through warfare or other means.

As another example, animals of a number of species exhibit *altruism,* which refers to doing things that benefit others of one's species even though it may be dangerous or deadly to oneself. Kamikaze bees will die defending their hive, soldier termites will end their lives in order to spray a deadly liquid at their enemies, and human beings will place their own lives in danger to protect their children. Other behavioral tendencies that are common in both humans and animals include aggressiveness, selfishness, and the formation of dominance hierarchies.

Sociobiologists argue that these tendencies are common in species because they are inborn traits determined by genes. These various traits exist because they enhance the chances of survival for the species. The stronger, more powerful, and more aggressive members of a species are more likely to survive, mate, and pass on their genes to the next generation. A mother who dies to save her children enhances the likelihood that her genes will survive in the gene pool even though she herself dies. Sociobiologists reason that aggressiveness and altruism are a part of our genetic makeup because people who behave aggressively or altruistically increase the chances for the survival of their genes. Over many eons, those aggressive and altruistic genes come to predominate in the gene pool of the species. This happens, sociobiologists argue, in humans as well as in other animals.

These biological explanations of human behavior have been controversial because they can be interpreted to mean that people have little control over their actions and that society has little influence over people's behavior in these realms. In fact, the biological explanations are currently being used by some to explain such complex social behaviors as crime, warfare, and homosexuality. Are these social behaviors programmed into our genes as sociobiologists suggest? For a number of reasons, both sociologists and sociobiologists recognize that reality is more complex than this biological determinism (Maryanski & Turner, 1992; Wolfe, 1993).

First, few human traits or behaviors are universal among human beings. The prevalence of behaviors such as altruism or aggressiveness varies widely from person to person, situation to situation, and culture to culture. Although every kamikaze bee will die protecting its hive, some human beings protect their children whereas others abuse, abandon, or even kill them. In fact, infanticide has at times been an accepted social practice among some human groups. If altruism and aggressiveness were completely instinctive, this variation would not occur.

Second, a vast body of evidence from social science research, some of it presented throughout this book, documents the extent to which people's behavior is a function of learning and social influence. The further up the evolutionary chain we look toward human beings with a highly developed cerebral cortex, the more powerful a role learning and culture play in shaping behavior.

Finally, sociobiologists recognize that genetically determined behavioral tendencies create only general tendencies to behave in certain ways. Whether people actually behave aggressively or altruistically depends on numerous social and cultural influences. In fact, sociobiologists recognize that these genetic tendencies in human beings can be altered or in some cases even overcome by learning and other social forces.

Most experts today agree that both biological determinism and cultural determinism are incomplete answers to the nature versus nurture debate. Both biological and sociocultural factors are important parts of the explanation of human social behavior. Whereas Locke's *tabula rasa* notion may not be entirely accurate, the images on the slate at birth are vague and undeveloped and are given shape and form through learning and experiences after birth.

Children Raised in Isolation

Whatever the influences of heredity may be, contact with others is important throughout our lives, and it is especially vital during our early years. Infants are incapable of taking care of themselves, so they are totally dependent on others for survival. Furthermore, social interaction is essential during this period if biological, psychological, and social development is to proceed normally. This point is poignantly illustrated by studies of children who have been raised in isolation from human contact.

In 1938, a six-year-old girl named Anna was discovered in the attic of a farmhouse (Davis, 1940). She had been strapped to a chair, with her hands tied above her head. Anna was born to an unmarried woman, and her grandfather, being ashamed of this, insisted that she be kept out of sight. As a result, she spent her first six years in isolated, dreary surroundings, receiving only the minimal attention necessary to keep her alive. When finally discovered, Anna was unable to walk, talk, feed herself, or keep herself clean. She was apathetic, expressionless, and indifferent to other people.

At about the same time, a young girl named Isabelle, whose history was remarkably like Anna's, was also found (Davis, 1947). Isabelle, too, had been hidden away because she was born out of wedlock. She spent most of her first six years in a dark room with her mother, who was a deaf mute. When she was discovered, Isabelle had developed intellectually only to about the level of a six-month-old infant. Although she made strange croaking sounds, she could not speak. She was able to communicate with her mother through gestures, however. Isabelle was also afraid of strangers, especially men, and acted something like a wild animal around them.

In 1970, yet another girl, Genie, was discovered living in isolation (Curtiss, 1977). Genie had spent almost all of her first thirteen years locked in a room by herself. When she was found, Genie could not speak. She was also disruptive and disgusting. For instance, she would blow her nose onto anything available and, when excited, would urinate wherever she happened to be.

What was the fate of these three unfortunate youngsters? When Anna died four years after being found, she had made some progress, but her level of development was still far from appropriate for her age. She could speak some words and phrases, but she could not construct sentences. She was able to follow the directions of her caretakers, however, and she could call them by name.

Isabelle was placed in an institution where she received expert training. She quickly learned to speak, to walk and run without difficulty, and even to sing in musical harmony. In fact, by the time she was eight and a half, her level of development appeared to be comparable to that expected of others in her age group. Isabelle's good fortune probably stems from the skill of her trainers and the fact that she had intimate contact with her deaf-mute mother during her isolation. This interaction, limited though it was, was something that Anna did not experience, and it probably accounts for some of the differences in the subsequent development of the two girls.

Genie, who had also had virtually no contact with other humans when she was isolated, did not fare as well as Isabelle, either. After five years of training, she had developed some language skills and was able to form relationships with people, but she still lagged behind her age group in these areas.

These three tragic cases demonstrate the critical importance of human contact and affection in infancy. Without them, a child cannot learn even the basic rudiments of human behavior. Personality and social behavior do not arise from biological maturation alone; they also require social contact and social experience. Furthermore, if social deprivation is extensive and prolonged, as was true for Anna and Genie, development may be permanently stunted. Recognizing the importance of social interaction to human development, this chapter now considers how the process of socialization occurs.

The Process of Socialization

You should be able to describe the contributions made by Cooley, Mead, and Erikson to our understanding of the socialization process and discuss the functioning of the agencies of socialization and the different types of socialization.

Socialization is a complex process. It begins at birth and continues throughout people's lives as they learn the ways of their society and of the various groups to which they belong. This section looks at some of the more important aspects of the socialization process. It begins with a discussion of the development of personality and self-concept, which provide the foundation for all later socialization. It then examines the groups and institutions through which socialization is accomplished as well as the different types of socialization. It closes with a discussion of socialization as a lifelong experience.

The Development of Self: The Interactionist Perspective

Human beings are unique among animals in part because we can say "I." We have, in other words, an awareness of ourselves as individuals. We can also think about ourselves in various circumstances. We can imagine, for instance, what it would be like to be somebody else, or how another person might view us. We are not born with this ability, however. Human infants have no sense of themselves as something separate from their surroundings. According to the interactionist perspective, we develop this awareness of self, this sense of our own identity, through interaction with other people.

An important aspect of our identity is our **personality**, which is *a constellation of attitudes, needs, traits, feelings, and ways of behaving.* Our personality develops over time, but once formed it usually remains fairly constant throughout our life. Another important aspect of our identity is our **self-concept**, which is *the conception that we all have about who we are—our unique characteristics and attributes—as well as about our nature and worth as human beings.* Personality and self-concept are closely interrelated, but self-concept is less constant than personality. It tends to change periodically throughout people's lives, especially when their position in the social structure changes.

The initial development of personality and self-concept occurs during infancy and childhood. Indeed, these two aspects of self form the foundation of the socialization process and strongly influence the nature and success of other aspects of socialization. Thus, infancy and childhood are critical times for all of us in the socialization process. People who do not develop an adequate self as children will have difficulty fitting well into society. For these reasons, any examination of the socialization process must begin with a look at how personality and self-concept emerge.

COOLEY   Charles Horton Cooley was one of the founders of the interactionist perspective. In Cooley's view (1902), we are not born with a self, nor does the self emerge merely because we mature biologically. Instead, the self is a social product. It develops through our interactions with other people. According to Cooley, an important ingredient of these interactions is people's ideas of how others view them or their behavior. He coined the term **looking-glass self** to refer to *the process through which we develop our sense of self based on the reactions of other people to us or to our actions*. There are, Cooley maintained, three basic steps in the *looking-glass* process. First, we imagine how we, or our behavior, appear to other people. For example, we may think that someone sees our appearance as neat and attractive or as disheveled and ugly. Second, we imagine how these people evaluate us or our behavior. We decide, for instance, that they judge our appearance as good or bad. Third, we experience some feeling because of this judgment. We may feel pride if we imagine a good evaluation or shame if we think that it is bad. We engage in this process continuously. Thus, every time we are aware of someone reacting to us in any way—as smart or dumb, nice or mean—that person either reinforces or contradicts our concept of ourselves. In this way, our self-concepts are developed and then maintained or changed.

To see better how the looking-glass self operates, consider your own gender identity, the sense you have of yourself as male or female. Of critical importance in the development of gender identity are other people's reactions to us. Normally, others treat us consistently as having a particular gender. In fact, these reactions are what initially form our sense of who we are sexually, and they reinforce it all the time. Try to imagine, though, how you might feel if everyone suddenly began to treat you as a member of the opposite sex. Surprise and amusement might quickly turn into anger and then, possibly, into confusion and doubt. Although such an occurrence is highly unlikely, thinking about it should illustrate the extent to which we all depend on the reactions of others for a sense of who we are.

Other people's reactions also influence our behavior because we normally strive to behave in ways that are consistent with our conceptions of ourselves. If, for instance, you view yourself as a friendly person, you will usually behave toward others in a fashion consistent with that self-concept; that is, you will probably be friendly. Similarly, if you think of yourself as intelligent, you will probably do things, such as read, study hard, and pay attention in class, that are consistent with that self-concept. Furthermore, by doing these things, you are likely to improve your performance in school and thereby reinforce your conception of yourself as intelligent. Thus, the looking-glass process can be self-reinforcing. The looking-glass process is diagrammed in Figure 3.1. It shows that a person's behavior is influenced by his or her self-concept, although other factors also shape behavior. Then, others around the person assess and react to that person's behavior. The person, in turn, perceives and interprets those reactions, and this interpretation influences the person's self-concept.

Cooley reasoned that some elements of our self-concepts, such as our identity and our sense of self-worth, are formed during childhood and remain fairly stable throughout life. For such elements, the development of self is more important in childhood than at other times in our lives. Nevertheless, Cooley and other interactionists emphasize that the looking-glass process functions throughout the life span. Every time we enter a new social situation, develop new social relationships, or take on new statuses, the reactions of others influence our self-concepts.

MEAD George Herbert Mead is generally credited with having expanded on Cooley's ideas and with having provided the theoretical basis for the interactionist approach to sociology. Mead (1934) viewed society as an arena of interaction in which people relate to each other and exchange information, attitudes, reactions, and meanings. Like Cooley, Mead stressed that people not only react to each other, but also interpret each other's actions. Integral to this interpretation is the use of symbols, which are things that represent other things

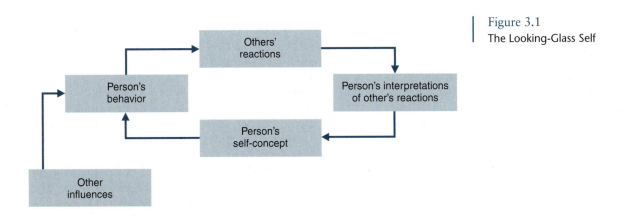

Figure 3.1
The Looking-Glass Self

(see Chapter 1). Mead used the term significant symbols to refer to *those symbols that many people recognize and understand in the same way.* For example, the traffic signal is a significant symbol in modern societies. All drivers attach the same meaning to the colors red (stop), yellow (caution), and green (go). From the time of our birth, we begin to acquire an array of significant symbols. One of the most important sets of significant symbols we acquire is language (see Chapter 2).

Mead viewed the socialization process as a sequence of stages through which people develop the social skills that enable them to coordinate their behavior with that of others (Strauss, Denzin, & Lindesmith, 1999). Early in the socialization process, human infants are capable only of simple *imitation.* They mimic other people because doing so brings rewards such as food or attention. For example, one-year-olds are often coaxed by their parents to wave when someone leaves the house. Although the infant may learn to wave at the appropriate time, waving is not a significant symbol for the infant because it does not have the same meaning for the infant as it does for the parents.

As the child matures, imitation gives way to pretending. During the *play stage,* children begin to act out the roles of other people. For example, they move toy trucks around a "construction site," play at being cowboys or police officers, or use dirt and water to make mud "pies." According to Mead, this pretend behavior is critical to human development. When they take the roles of other people, even if only pretending, children behave as though they were that other person and thereby learn how to view the world from different perspectives. At this point in the socialization process, according to Mead, children take the roles of significant others: *specific people, such as a parent or sibling, whose opinions the children care about.*

During the play stage, role-taking is compartmentalized. Children usually play only one role at a time. In addition, because it is a pretend situation, they need not take the actual reactions of other people into account. In Mead's next stage, the *game stage,* children perform roles that require them to coordinate their actions with those of real people. This requirement calls for them to assess situations from different perspectives. Role-taking becomes more complex because children must ask themselves how others will react to what they do and how they should react to what others do. Through this role-taking and coordination of behavior, what Mead called the *generalized other* begins to emerge. The generalized other refers to *the organized attitudes, rules, and judgments of an entire group.* This general viewpoint becomes internalized, providing guidelines for behavior and criteria for assessing self-worth. Mead used baseball as an analogy in explaining the game stage.

In a baseball game, each player must assess the actions of all the other players and coordinate his or her behaviors accordingly. In other words, each person's behavior is contingent on everyone else's behavior. The rules of baseball are analogous to Mead's generalized other, in that both provide explicit guides for behavior.

Mead viewed the self as consisting of two interrelated parts: the *me* and the *I.* The *me* is the part of the self that reflects our perceptions of what other people think of us. It is the part that permits evaluation and enables us to control our behavior. But if the *me* were the only aspect of the self, human behavior would be mechanical, repetitive, and frankly, quite boring. Mead was not content with the idea that human beings are merely social puppets, however. Human interaction is both symbolic and interpretive. Although we respond to others, we also manipulate symbols ourselves and interpret different situations according to what we have learned through our own socialization. Hence, Mead proposed another part of the self, the *I.* The *I* is the independent, spontaneous, and unpredictable side of the self. Thus our behavior is shaped not by the *me* alone but by the ongoing interaction between the *me* and the *I.* The *I* is the subjective, internal part of the self; the *me* is more external and objective. Imagine yourself interacting with a friend. The *I* is more spontaneous: "I want to tell this person what I'm thinking." The *me* is more controlled: "She will probably get angry, and I don't want her mad at me, so I won't say it."

ERIKSON Cooley and Mead focus on describing and analyzing the general process of social interaction that occurs throughout childhood and shapes personality and self-concept. Socialization does not end with childhood, however, or even with adolescence, and the psychologist Erik Erikson (1950, 1982) developed a theory of socialization that recognized this fact. His theory describes eight distinct stages of development and provides more detail on how social interaction at each stage can affect a person's self-concept. The general interactional processes described by Cooley and Mead are the mechanisms by which many of the developments Erikson proposes actually occur. Each of Erikson's stages involves a challenge or crisis that must be confronted regarding how one views oneself and one's relationships with others. How the conflict is resolved determines how the person thinks about himself or herself and whether he or she develops a stable, positive personal identity and social maturity. Furthermore, Erikson viewed the stages as sequential: positive resolution of one stage cannot be achieved until the challenges of the previous stages have been satisfactorily resolved.

Infancy is Erikson's first stage of development, and the challenge of this stage is *trust versus mistrust.* The infant is thoroughly dependent on others for care, affection, and even survival. If the support is there, and if it is provided in a loving and stable fashion, then the infant develops a sense of security and trust about the world in general and other people in particular. If neglected or treated poorly, the infant learns to mistrust others. These feelings of trust or mistrust then extend into later life and influence the resolution of later stages and the development of social relationships.

In the stage of *early childhood,* children two and three years old face the crisis of *autonomy versus shame or doubt.* They begin to explore their environment, and the challenge they confront is to develop a sense that they can deal effectively with their surroundings. When children are encouraged to try new things and are supported in doing so, they can become self-confident and develop feelings of autonomy, responsibility, and independence. If they are overprotected, criticized, or rejected, then shame and self-doubt are likely to emerge.

Children in *late childhood,* ages four and five, are confronted with *initiative versus guilt.* They begin to do more exploration independent of their parents, such as developing new friends to play with, and their social worlds expand considerably. This stage includes Mead's play stage, and playing with peers is a way of trying out different roles. If they are supported in this activity by their parents and are accepted by peers, they develop a sense of initiative, purpose, and direction. If they are discouraged or rejected, a sense of guilt develops because they have done something on which both adults and peers frown.

Children of *school age,* between six and twelve years old, confront the crisis of *industry versus inferiority.* School challenges them with the impersonal world of adult social institutions and expectations. Children are expected to develop new skills and compete with others. If successful, they develop a sense of industry, or mastery, because they have accomplished tasks that are viewed as important by society and that transcend the world of children. A sense of inferiority and failure results if the child has difficulty at these tasks or is constantly criticized for each misstep along the way.

The challenge of *adolescence* is *identity versus role confusion.* Adolescents are coming close to taking their place in the adult world, and they need to develop a sense of who they are, what their capabilities are, and how they will relate to other people. Especially important at this stage is the development of close intimacy with peers of both sexes. Erikson recognized that adolescents' preoccupation with what others think of them reflects the basic challenge of the adolescent stage. Even fleeting adolescent infatuations are a reflection of this struggle for identity—finding out who one is by seeing oneself reflected in peers' reactions. If adolescents have supportive adults and positive relationships with peers, they come through this stage with a clear and positive

personal identity. Without such supports, they can develop low self-regard and confusion as to who they are and what they might become.

The challenge of *young adulthood* is *intimacy versus isolation.* The major life task at this stage is to establish an enduring intimate relationship and pursue a career or adult vocation. For many people, the intimacy takes the form of marriage and family, but other forms of intimacy, such as close companionship, are also possible. When such intimacy does not develop, feelings of isolation appear.

The challenge of *adulthood into middle age* is *generativity versus stagnation.* As people move through adulthood, they attempt to avoid stagnation and self-absorption by making renewed efforts to contribute to community welfare and future generations. The opposite is stagnation into undemanding, unrewarding, unexciting routines.

The final stage is *old age,* where the challenge is one of *integrity versus despair.* As they confront the end of their lives, people review and reflect on the past. If this assessment brings a sense of accomplishment, completeness, and fulfillment, then people can feel a sense of integrity, or acceptance of their life as positive and significant. If the reflection is heavy with failure and lost opportunities, then the result is despair and the feeling that one's life has been wasted or unimportant.

Erikson's developmental theory has been very influential because it captures important challenges that people confront at different stages in the life span. Furthermore, research supports Erikson's contention that there is a definite sequencing to the stages and that resolution of the challenges at one stage is important to positive resolution of challenges at later stages (Whitbourne, Zuschlag, Elliot, & Waterman, 1992). This sequencing, however, is not rigid, in the sense, for example, that identity is an issue only during adolescence. The identity issue can arise at numerous points in the life span as people move into new jobs, marry, or make other role transitions. These later identity crises, however, tend to be of less magnitude and less centrality than identity issues during adolescence. Identity crises in adulthood occur against a backdrop of already having resolved identity issues in adolescence. The person who has successfully resolved the challenge of adolescence and emerged with a positive and coherent sense of identity will be better equipped to handle identity crises in adulthood than the person who experienced role confusion in adolescence.

Although Erikson was a psychologist, his theory of socialization was thoroughly sociological and consistent with the interactionist perspective. After all, the center of his attention was the development of people's self-concepts through social interaction. He recognized that the self consists of social meanings

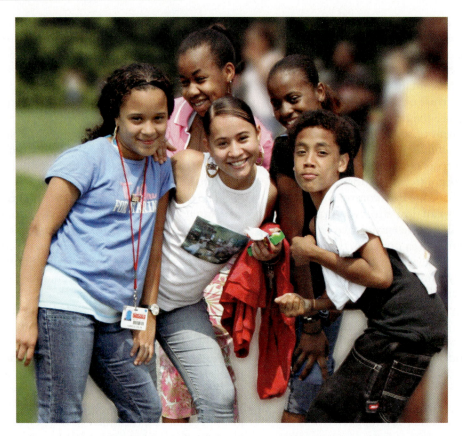

One of the key agencies of socialization for the young is the peer group, which consists of people of approximately the same age. It is among peers, that young people learn how to develop egalitarian relationships with other people and an identity that supports some independence from their families.

communicated during social interaction and that the self develops as a result of challenges from the social environment and changes in the person's role structure. Going into school (school age), gaining independence from the family (adolescence), and developing a career (young adulthood) are all changes in status that require some reorganization of roles and selves. So, it is ultimately social challenges that precipitate the development of the self.

Agencies of Socialization

Socialization occurs in various settings in which a variety of individuals and groups leave their imprints on children as they mature and on adults as they move through life. In some cases, this process involves direct, face-to-face contact, as when a parent scolds a child or friends congratulate a person for landing a new job. In other cases, it occurs indirectly, as when educators shape school policies that determine what children will learn in the classroom. Agencies of socialization are *the people, groups, and institutions that play a part in the socialization process.* Here four of the most important agencies of socialization—the family, peer groups, schools, and the media—are discussed.

THE FAMILY   The most important agency of socialization for most human beings is undoubtedly the family. The sensitive and malleable early years of life, when we are defenseless and dependent, have traditionally been spent almost exclusively within the family context. It is there that we first learn about intimacy, emotions, power, and other elements of human relationships as we experience our initial interactions with other human beings. It is there, also, that we begin to learn the components of culture and social structure, including language, norms, and values. In short, it is in the family that we learn to be human. The learning that occurs during this period is effective and influential because the family usually protects us and provides us with nourishment and affection. This dependence makes us especially receptive to the influence, both formal and informal, of family members.

Another reason for the pervasive influence of family in the socialization process is that it provides us with our social positions in society. The family determines such ascribed statuses as racial and ethnic background and influences other statuses, such as religion and social class. These statuses strongly shape our contacts with others and our opportunities in the world. They also determine how we are brought up.

For instance, parents from different backgrounds raise their children in different ways and expect different things from them. Working-class parents tend to encourage obedience, conformity, respect, cleanliness, and neatness. Middle-class parents are more likely to encourage curiosity, self-direction, and expressiveness and to place more emphasis on egalitarian relationships (Ellis & Petersen, 1992; Kohn & Slomczynski, 1990).

Although the impact of later experiences is very important, the first few years of life in the family context provide people with a crucial foundation in terms of the development of personality, self-concept, and a distinct system of values. Subsequent experiences tend to build on this foundation rather than replace it. There has been considerable debate over the centrality of parents and the family in this early socialization or whether such socialization tasks can be taken over effectively by people outside the family. The Israeli kibbutzim, or communal communities, for example, have taken an approach of removing some responsibility for child rearing from the family and giving it to the whole community (Aviezer, van Ijzendoorn, Sagi, & Schuengel, 1994; Blasi, 1986; Bornstein, Maital, and Tal, 1997). In the kibbutz, specially trained child-care workers called *metaplot* (singular *metapelet*) are assigned to raise a group of children and may continue to work with the same children as they develop. The *metapelet* supervises the children in toilet training and in learning to eat and dress, as well as other routine activities. The kibbutz devotes considerable resources to raising children and ensuring that the *metaplot* are well trained and attuned to the needs of children at different stages of development. The *metapelet* is not, however, a surrogate parent but rather acts as a child-care professional. The kibbutz and the *metapelet* are seen as supports to the parents in their efforts to be both parents and workers in the commune. Parents visit their children often and do many things with them. The kibbutz tries to assist the parents in having relaxed and pleasurable time to spend with their children and to avoid situations where the children must compete with the parents' work for attention and affection. Through all this training, individualism is deemphasized while working for the good of the community is held in high regard. In this way, the kibbutz passes on to the new generation the communal values that serve as the community's foundation.

If we look at societies throughout history, something resembling the communal child rearing of the kibbutz is far more common than the isolation of child rearing in the nuclear family in the United States. Studies of the effectiveness of child rearing show that kibbutz child-rearing practices are probably no less effective and no more detrimental than familial child rearing (Rabin & Beit-Hallahmi, 1982). Applying Sociology: Day Care extends this discussion of the role of the family in childhood socialization by exploring the issue of whether children raised in day care in the United States suffer any difficulties in comparison to children raised at home by their families.

THE PEER GROUP The agency of socialization that is probably second in importance to the family is the peer group, which is a group of friends who are approximately the same age and have similar social positions. The family is a hierarchal group, with parents in a position of authority and dominance over the children. In a peer group, however, children find more egalitarian relationships because no one child in the group is normally dominant in all respects. There is therefore more give-and-take, which gives children the opportunity to learn how to relate to others in a cooperative framework (Kohlberg, 1981; Youniss, 1985).

Eventually, the family is supplanted by the peer group as the main social relationship for young people. Especially after entering school, young people begin to spend more time with their peers than with members of their families, with the possible exception of siblings who are very close to each other in age. Furthermore, virtually all children have to live apart from their families sooner or later, and in a world that is somewhat different from that of their parents. Children usually confront different values and technologies and have different experiences. The peer group helps substantially in the transition that is required. It provides young people with a subculture that gives them a set of norms, values, and beliefs that offers an alternative to those of their parents.

Peer groups offer young people an identity that supports some independence from their families. This offer is especially important in industrial societies where young people are typically isolated from the statuses and rewards of the adult world. The peer group offers an alternative status and reward system. It might take the form of familiarity with contemporary music, proficiency in athletics, or outstanding academic achievement. Chapter 2 noted that a distinctive language, or argot, can play an important role for teenagers by encapsulating the values of their subculture. In their many forms, then, peer group subcultures offer young people ways to feel important and worthwhile. Moreover, they give young people a sense of contributing to society or, at least, to their peer group.

THE SCHOOL In the family and in peer groups, children are involved in intimate personal relationships that are normally based on love or some other type of attachment. When they enter school, however, they

Applying Sociology   Day Care: Problem or Solution?

In 1970, one-quarter of women with children under the age of six were working; by the end of the twentieth century, this figure had grown to over 60 percent (U.S. Bureau of the Census, 2007, p. 380). Single-parent and two-earner families have to make arrangements for taking care of their children, and day-care centers have arisen to meet this need (Figure 3.2). However, the emergence of day care has been controversial. On the one hand, many working parents feel they must work to support their families but do not have friends or relatives available who can assist with child care. On the other hand, some critics of day care argue that only parents can give children the love, attention, and intimate involvement that they need to develop into emotionally healthy and socially competent adults. In fact, for some, day care seems to violate the traditional notion that children should be raised by their parents, and critics see the spread of day care as another symptom of the erosion of the family in modern societies. It is in controversies like this—in which traditional values and ethnocentric beliefs might lead to biased conclusions—that it is important to

turn to research by applied sociologists and other social scientists to see what the actual impact of day care on child socialization is.

Decades of such research have now accumulated, comparing children who attended various types of day-care centers with children raised in the home by parents, relatives, or others. Virtually all this research shows that children exposed to day care do at least as well as, and often better than, children raised exclusively in the home by their parents (Belsky, 2006; Burchinal, 1999; Campbell et al., 2001; Loeb et al., 2004; Loeb et al., 2007). Day-care children do as well in verbal and cognitive abilities, creativity, cooperation, and social competence as do home-raised children. Children placed in day care do at least as well as children raised at home in intelligence and psychosocial development and in sociability and academic achievement. Further, economically disadvantaged children in day care show significant benefits over those not in day care. Day-care children are also as attached to their parents as are children cared for in the home.

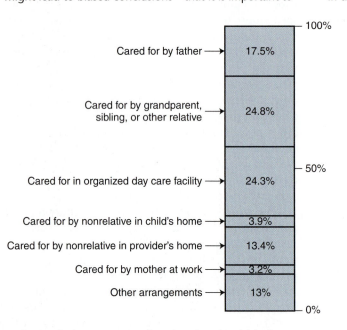

Figure 3.2

Child-Care Arrangements Used by Employed Mothers of Children under Five Years of Age in the United States, 2002

Note: From Current Population Reports Series P-70-101. Who's Minding the Kids? Child Care Arrangements: Winter 2002, "Survey of Income and Program Participation" (www.census.gov/population/www/socdemo/childcare.html) by U.S. Bureau of the Census, 2005, p. 9.

Cared for by father → 17.5%
Cared for by grandparent, sibling, or other relative → 24.8%
Cared for in organized day care facility → 24.3%
Cared for by nonrelative in child's home → 3.9%
Cared for by nonrelative in provider's home → 13.4%
Cared for by mother at work → 3.2%
Other arrangements → 13%

Research does suggest a few situations in which day care may not be best for children (Burchinal, 1999; Loeb et al., 2007; National Institute of Child Health and Human Development Early Child Care Research Network, 2003; Stolberg, 2001). For example, while day care generally does not increase levels of aggression, children enrolled in day care for extended periods or at a very young age may become more aggressive and less cooperative, may develop more behavior problems, and may experience more stress; but the effects of day care on these behaviors is small. In addition, economically disadvantaged children are often sent to poor-quality day-care

centers, which may adversely affect their emotional development. But this mass of research leaves us fairly confident that high-quality day care can do at least as well in raising children as the parents can. Actually, this conclusion should not be surprising, because day-care centers have the resources to offer children much more—in terms of people to interact with, adults trained in child development and education, and such physical resources as games and educational materials—than does the average home. The typical nuclear family offers a child a much more limited range of social contacts and educational experiences. ◼

begin to experience the impersonality of the world, usually for the first time. Parents tend to accept and respect their children regardless of their performance in reading, writing, or other tasks. But teachers, who replace the parents as authority figures in schools, are more demanding. They judge performance on the basis of impersonal criteria, and poor performance brings low grades, rebukes, and possibly the failure to advance to the next grade. In school, then, children begin to learn the value placed on performance in an industrial society, and they become acquainted with the costs that accompany failure.

Schools teach children the basic literacy skills, particularly reading and writing, that are necessary in an industrial society, and they provide training in the more complicated skills that will be used later in the adult world of work. In addition, schools supplement the family in transmitting the components of culture and social structure. For example, U.S. schools teach children patriotic values through such subjects as history and such rituals as reciting the Pledge of Allegiance. They also communicate to students values of the larger society. Furthermore, children in schools learn about new statuses and roles that do not exist in the family. For instance, they learn about the school hierarchy, which consists of the assistant principals and principals above the teachers and the janitors and kitchen staff below the teachers. Young people become aware that they too occupy a position—as students—in the school hierarchy. They also learn that the school has a rhythm of its own. They must be on time even though they might wish to be late, and they must switch from one subject to another, say, from art to math, as directed by the clock rather than personal whim. In short, children in school learn that there are pressures and demands in the real world over which they have little control but to which they must adapt.

Finally, school brings some independence from the family. In fact, school may be the child's first major contact with the world outside the family. In school, children are largely isolated from adults, which encourages the formation of peer group associations. Moreover, schools offer children a wide range of peers with whom they can become involved. Thus, schools enhance the socializing impact of peer groups and further reduce the influence of the family.

These elementary school students watch a broadcast of CNN in the classroom. Modern communications technologies have complicated effects on the socialization of the young. Overall, however, they have probably produced more erosion of the influence of family in children's lives rather than enhancement of it.

THE MASS MEDIA   Although socialization is not a manifest function of the media and communications technologies, it has become one of its latent functions (see Chapter 1). Television, in particular, has become a pervasive socializer, especially for young children. In the process, it has further diluted the role of the family and the schools by competing with both for children's time and attention. The Sociology of Media and Technology insert explores some of the ways that modern media technology socializes the young.

Sociology of Media and Technology

Who Socializes the Young in an Electronic World?

Modern communications technologies—from television to video games to text messaging to iPods—provide children and teenagers with an "eye on the world" which enables them to learn a great deal. And they offer a perspective that is largely independent of the supervision and control from parents or other kin who are traditionally very influential in the socialization of the young. For example, children can learn verbal and mathematical skills from public television programs such as *Sesame Street.* Similarly, they are encouraged in their self-development by such programs as *Mr. Rogers' Neighborhood* and *Barney,* which teach them to view themselves positively and to value their own and others' individuality. In addition, the media enable children to view a wide array of role models such as sports figures, movie stars, police officers, or cartoon characters. Modern communication technologies are one of the major sources of information for the young about culture and social structure in the United States. In addition, these technologies compete with parental and familial influences in the effort to socialize children, and the impact of the media may not always be what the parents might wish.

In 1950, only 9 percent of households in the United States had a television set. Today virtually all have at least one (Figure 3.3). We saw in Chapter 1 that high-speed access to the Internet is growing at a rapid rate. As the media have become more pervasive over the decades, social science research on the impact of the media has also been accumulating. For example, one area that has been studied extensively is the relationship between viewing violence on TV or other media and violent or aggressive behavior. This research mostly concludes that watching violence on television and in the movies does increase the likelihood that children and youth will act aggressively or violently themselves, especially in situations that are conducive to violence (see the extended discussion of this subject in Chapter 12). But it is a complex relationship: The impact is greater on males

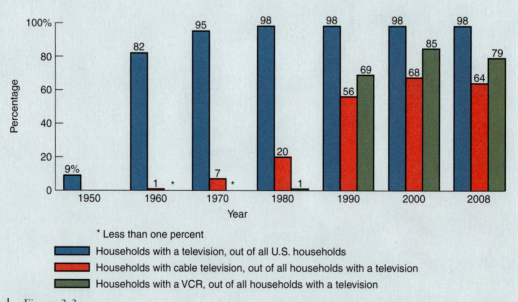

* Less than one percent

■ Households with a television, out of all U.S. households
■ Households with cable television, out of all households with a television
■ Households with a VCR, out of all households with a television

Figure 3.3

Use of the Mass Media in the United States, 1950–2008

Note: From Television Bureau of Advertising, Inc., *Trends in Television,* www.tvb.org and Nielsen Media Research. Accessed May 24, 2008.

than on females, and on children between the ages of eight and twelve. There is also growing evidence that playing violent video games has the same effect: They lead children to become more aggressive, at least in the short term (Emes, 1997; Schor, 2004).

Music and music videos are another force for socializing the young, and music's ability to reach and influence large numbers of young people is dramatically enhanced by modern communications technologies. Sometimes, of course, the content and style of music is controlled by mainstream elites, as is often the case with religious music. When this is true, the musical messages the young hear will be consistent with mainstream cultural values. However, increasingly, modern communications technologies make it possible for musical styles to emerge among the young themselves, sometimes promoted by a commercialized music industry guided primarily by what is marketable to the young. The messages expressed by such a commercial music industry may not be supportive of—may even be resistive to—mainstream cultural values. This was true of rock and roll when it emerged in the 1950s and 1960s, with positive images of a more free and open stance toward sexuality that were quite at variance with mainstream values of the time. This is also true today of many music videos and such musical innovations as rap and hip-hop (Martinez, 1997; Schor, 2004; Smitherman, 1997). For example, music videos often portray violence, usually in a positive light and perpetrated by attractive role models. Rap and hip-hop portray positively an aggressive image of masculinity and a rhetoric of hostility toward and resistance to the dominant, white, Eurocentric culture—messages that resonate positively among some African American, Latino, and Indian as well as white youth.

Going beyond the traditional media, modern communications technologies provide ways for children and teenagers to maintain identity and social interactions that are separate from, and in some cases hidden from, the world of their parents and other adults. Cell phones and text messaging, for example, enable youth to maintain supportive and largely secretive social worlds in which they can interact with one another and provide mutual support and identity-building at almost any place or time. These technologies break down the barriers of distance, geography, and architecture that inhibited communication for earlier generations. And it can be done mostly out of the surveillance of adults. For example, a teen in the front seat on a car ride can text message with a friend or sibling in the back seat while the parent who is driving has no idea what is going on. Again, the impact of the technology is complex because it can also enhance the opportunities for parents to communicate with, and thus exercise some control over, their children. Some families find that cell phones and even text messaging enhance parent-child contact because offspring can be expected to report their whereabouts frequently, and parents can insist that children have their cell phones on at all times and answer when called. Even with regard to music, the technology to produce music and music videos and to upload them to the Internet is now so widespread and inexpensive that almost anyone can become a producer and distributor of music. As a consequence, the influence of music on the young is now much more decentralized than in the past and much more in the control of young people themselves rather than traditional authorities, such as parents or corporations.

Overall, however, the modern communications technologies, especially in comparison to more traditional ones, have probably produced more erosion of the influence of family in children's lives rather than enhancement of it.

Types of Socialization

Socialization can take a number of forms. Three of the most important forms are primary socialization, anticipatory socialization, and resocialization.

PRIMARY SOCIALIZATION Primary socialization occurs in childhood. It is *the process that transforms infants into truly social human beings by teaching them basic values, skills, and language.* It also accounts for the initial development of personality and self-concept. A major debate among social scientists involves the extent to which primary socialization influences other socialization experiences occurring in later stages of the life span. Sigmund Freud and some present-day psychologists have argued that early life experiences largely, though not exclusively, determine people's personalities and behaviors throughout their lives. These scholars maintain that the resolution of early childhood conflicts, such as those between societal demands and a child's impulses, establishes personality tendencies that are fairly impervious to change.

Sociologists view self-concept and personal identity as more malleable than this deterministic view, with people going through periodic transitions throughout their lives during which their self-concept must adapt. People can even change radically in later life. Nonetheless, sociologists recognize that primary socialization in early childhood certainly influences the development of

Other Worlds, Other Ways

JAPAN: LEARNING CULTURAL VALUES THROUGH PRIMARY SOCIALIZATION

Chapter 2 presents terms such as *cultural values* and *social structure,* which can seem abstract and removed from people's everyday lives. According to the interactionist perspective, socialization is one of the key vehicles for translating these elements of society into daily thoughts and behavior. As children interact with parents and others, they learn what things are valued and how to perform roles properly. Some of this information is communicated by the way parents talk to their children. To understand more fully how this communication occurs, sociologists study the routine interactions between parents and children to see what in language varies from one culture to another.

Some aspects of parents' talk with their children are found in all cultures. For example, parents everywhere speak to their young children in shorter and more simplified speech than they use with adults because parents recognize that young children are not capable of the sophisticated communications of adults. Beyond these basics, however, culture plays a powerful role in shaping parent–infant talk. In Japan, for example, mothers make more extensive use of baby talk, or nonsense words, with their children and use it for a longer period of time than do mothers in the United States (Fernald & Morikawa, 1993). Japanese mothers also use a more simplified speech with their children—fewer words and less complex sentences. In addition, they use more frequent backchannel vocalizations with their children (White, 1989). *Backchannel* is a term used by linguists to refer to verbal and nonverbal communications that send information to a speaker without claiming the floor. For example, head nods and utterances like *uh-huh* and *yeah* tell a person who is speaking that the silent person is listening but without actually interrupting and taking over as the main speaker.

These differences reflect and support some important cultural values in Japan. One such value is *omoiyari,* or maintaining harmony in the relationships between people. Another value is *amae,* or mutual dependence, especially between mother and infant. When Japanese mothers use baby talk and simple speech, they are treating their child gently and emphasizing the supportiveness of the

relationship between mother and child; they are trying to make it easy for the child to speak to the mother. In other words, Japanese mothers place importance on establishing a positive emotional bond with their children. When mothers in the United States speak to their children, they emphasize teaching to increase the child's linguistic competence and to encourage independence. The use of backchannel communication indicates harmony in social interaction and also places the other person, the speaker, rather than oneself, the listener, at the center of attention. So, even in the ways that mothers talk to their children, the children are learning not only language but also cultural values. In Japan, they learn of the importance of mutual dependence between people and harmony in social relations.

Examples of this process can be seen when mothers play with toys with their children. Mothers in the United States tend repeatedly to tell the child the name of the toy ("That's a car. See the car?"), whereas Japanese mothers talk about exchanging the toy with the child ("I give it to you. Now give this to me. Yes! Thank you.") and actually name the toy much less frequently. In the Japanese approach, the emphasis is on giving as a way of maintaining a relationship. The point of playing with the toy with a child is not to teach the child the name of it but to communicate the value of polite exchanges between people. Other research shows that Japanese mothers place more stress on showing empathy and positive feelings for toys that children are playing with or for other people (Clancy, 1986). They also more explicitly teach their children the cultural norms for polite speech and rehearse them in the social routines that will be expected of them as adults. They teach their children to be polite to others and to consider the thoughts and feelings of others. They expect their children to master polite expressions at a younger age. All of this socialization places great emphasis on the child's role as a member of the social group and community.

Parents may not be consciously aware of all that goes on as they talk with their children. Nevertheless, language learning during primary socialization plays a part in introducing the child to basic cultural values and norms. ◾

---

adult self-esteem and personal identity. For example, what children learn from their parents about racial identity influences their adult behavior. Studies of African Americans show that when parents teach their children racial pride and the value of their African heritage, as adults those children are more committed to African culture and identify more closely with the African American community (Demo & Hughes, 1990). In addition, black children who are raised to keep their distance from whites and to be cautious or fearful of them have less contact with whites as adults. So,

primary socialization has a continuing effect on people's lives, with important implications for the way people feel about themselves as adults and the way they relate to other people. Other Worlds, Other Ways: Japan documents how primary socialization contributes to the learning of basic cultural values and norms.

ANTICIPATORY SOCIALIZATION **Anticipatory socialization** *involves learning the values, beliefs, and behaviors of a group that a person does not presently belong to but plans to join in the future.* It allows people to begin to make the changes in their attitudes and actions that will be necessary once they enter the new group. For example, students in medical, nursing, or law school experience anticipatory socialization when they are encouraged to think like doctors, nurses, and lawyers although they do not yet occupy those statuses. Similarly, a pregnant woman may read all she can about raising children and may even begin to plan how she will treat her own child before she actually becomes a mother.

The primary purpose of anticipatory socialization is to ease the transition into a new status or group. Research on army recruits, for example, shows that soldiers who adopt the beliefs and values of army officers, which are quite distinct from the beliefs and values of enlisted personnel, are more likely than other soldiers to be promoted, are more readily accepted by the new group, and make more rapid adjustments to their new status (Merton, 1968). Other research shows that expectant parents can benefit from anticipatory socialization to the parental role. Socialization experiences such as babysitting someone else's child or attending parenting classes make for better adjustment to the parental role with less stress (Gage & Christensen, 1991).

Although anticipatory socialization is beneficial in helping people make the transition to a new status or group, it is not always functional for the group that a person plans to leave. For example, an office worker who hopes to move into a supervisory position may begin adopting the values and attitudes of his supervisors. He may begin to frown on fellow workers who do things supervisors dislike, such as take coffee breaks that are longer than allowed, pilfer small quantities of office supplies, or refuse to work as hard as they might. Because his attitudes go against the interests of the other office workers, tension, difficulties with cooperation, and even a reduction in productivity may result.

RESOCIALIZATION   When infants begin to learn about the world, they have a clean slate with little to "unlearn." When a twenty-seven-year-old woman becomes a mother, however, she has had twenty-seven years of learning experience. Some of this experience may help her make the transition to motherhood, but other parts of it may hinder her adaptation. In any event, this new mother will have to undergo resocialization, which refers to *learning new sets of values, beliefs, and behaviors that are different from those previously held*. A person experiencing resocialization must unlearn the old as well as learn the new.

All of us experience resocialization throughout our lives as we move from one status to another and one group to another. In some situations, this process is rather mild, as when we take a new job or become parents. In other situations, it requires dramatic changes, as when a person enters prison. One example of resocialization is the transition from a high school to a college or university environment. Expectations in high school are quite different from those that confront a college student. Those who begin or return to college after engaging in other life experiences, such as working or raising children, also undergo resocialization, if only in having to learn how to relate to younger adults.

Socialization through the Life Span

The concepts of anticipatory socialization and resocialization make us aware that socialization is a lifelong process. It continues throughout our lives as we take on new roles and make role transitions that take us from infancy through adulthood to old age. Children give up their dependency on parents and devote more attention to peers, young adults leave their families to establish their own relationships, and older adults must confront the certainty of their mortality. Society, however, does not leave people alone to struggle with these transitions. Through socialization, people are provided with new roles and relationships to replace the old.

Societies carve out people's lives into a series of stages. These stages constitute the life span or life cycle, which is *a succession of statuses and roles that people in a particular society experience in a fairly predictable pattern as they grow older* (Atchley & Barusch, 2004). Biology plays an important role in the life cycle, particularly at the beginning and the end. In infancy, each of us is dependent on others for our survival, and thus the statuses open to us are limited. In old age, physiological degeneration may limit our capabilities and again make us dependent on others. Society cannot rely on any of us during these periods to the extent that it can during the other stages of the life cycle. Between infancy and old age, however, the social structure of a society is more important than biology in shaping our lives. Thus, although biology does play a role, we should be cautious about viewing the life cycle as a biologically created sequence. Rather, it is a socially approved sequence of stages, adjusted for certain biological limitations, that guides people's behavior as they live their lives.

In some societies, the stages of the life cycle are based strictly on age considerations, and all people of a particular age group have similar statuses and roles (Foner & Kertzer, 1978). Among the Latuka of Sudan, for example, the life cycle has five stages: children, youths, rulers of the village, retired elders, and the very old. People in a particular stage are viewed as a single body in terms of their rights and obligations, and they make the transition to the next stage as a group. In industrial societies, chronological age is only one determinant of the rights and privileges of individuals. Many other factors, such as social class, ethnicity, and personal achievement, also play important roles. Early research on the adult life cycle in industrial societies such as the United States was done mostly on affluent white males. The conclusion drawn from this research was that a single sequence of stages existed that most or all adults were presumed to experience (Hudson, 1991; Levinson, 1978). Erikson's theory of socialization, for example, included three stages during the adult years. More recent research on populations that are diverse in terms of race, ethnicity, gender, social class, and other factors suggests that the adult life span in industrial societies is more complex and varied and cannot be very accurately described by a single set of sequenced stages. Certain issues or conflicts commonly arise for most or all adults, but when these issues arise and how they are resolved are highly variable. Among the issues that people confront during adulthood are gaining independence from one's parents, finding fulfilling work or career, establishing a family, developing intimate relationships, and confronting midlife crises. However, instead of each issue arising and being resolved at a particular point in adulthood, each challenge may arise at a number of points or may even be a continuous crisis that an individual has to deal with (Blumstein & Schwartz, 1983; Levinson, 1996; Schlossberg, 1985). The following sections look at some of these issues and the various forms they can take.

GAINING INDEPENDENCE   The first major transition in adulthood for most people involves gaining independence from one's family, which usually occurs in the late teens or early twenties. Sometimes the transition is abrupt, as when a teenage couple marries and sets up their own household. Other times, the transition is gradual, as when a person be-

The U. S. Air Force Academy is a total institution in which members are isolated from the rest of society, have their behavior tightly controlled, and experience a coercive form of socialization. Such socialization is necessary if the organization is going to train its members to make great sacrifices.

gins college but comes home for vacations or gets a job and becomes financially independent while still living at home. Eventually, most adults establish living arrangements independent from their families. Yet, there are exceptions: A young couple with children or a single mother may continue to live with a parent because they need the financial and social supports that this arrangement affords. At the other end of the adult life span, elderly persons may see their independence dissipate as physical or financial difficulties force them to move in with their children. So, gaining independence is a shifting phenomenon for many people.

WORK AND FAMILY   Finding fulfilling work and establishing a family tend to be closely interrelated issues for many people. A part of this issue is the decision about whether to go to college, which is closely related to social class, race, and gender. Obviously, those unable to attend college will have fewer opportunities in terms of finding fulfilling careers (see Chapter 12). In earlier decades, college attendance normally occurred in the later teens or early twenties, but this close link between age and college attendance has weakened substantially. In 1980, only 10 percent of college students were thirty-five years old or older; this figure has now increased to 17 percent (U.S. Bureau of the Census, 2007, p. 177). Many of these older students are attending college for the first time, after having spent years working at another job or raising a family. Others of these students are returning to college to get additional training to advance them in a career. Today, higher education is perceived not as something that is accomplished in early adulthood but as something that may occur at any point in the adult life span.

Earlier characterizations of the adult life span described people in their thirties and forties as settling down and solidifying occupational gains. This happens for some, but others find themselves switching careers during this period, and some women in their thirties and forties are just entering the occupational realm after spending one or two decades devoted to child rearing. Women, especially in recent decades, experience a significant tension between following the traditional mother/homemaker role and the nontraditional career role. A choice between these two roles is a decision that men, for the most part, do not have to make. Some women resolve the dilemma by choosing the homemaker role, but this choice often creates midlife anxieties over whether their lives have been unnecessarily limited and they have become too dependent on others.

The women who choose the career path also confront tension because most do not abandon the mother/homemaker role and must decide the relative weight to give to each. This can create anxieties over whether they are performing satisfactorily in either role (an example of role strain, discussed in Chapter 2). In addition, pursuing these dual roles can actually make it more difficult for women to do as well as men in their careers. After all, in families where women work and pursue a career, they also often do most of the cooking, shopping, babysitting, and cleaning. These dual responsibilities can interfere with the ability of women to achieve occupational goals. In their twenties and thirties, when men are establishing themselves in the world of work, women spend precious energy on these homemaking and child-rearing duties. If they take time off work to raise their children, their career advancement may be set back. Even women who pursue a career are more constrained in their career choices by family considerations than are men. For example, women who receive doctoral degrees and seek university teaching positions often choose their teaching jobs on the basis of where their husbands can find work (Gallagher, Johnson, Van Valey, & Malaret, 1992). Men, by contrast, are more free to choose jobs on the basis of what will most advance their career. As a consequence, women tend to teach at lower-status universities than do men and are more likely to experience downward mobility in their careers. Thus, even career women experience more demands to accommodate their career to family needs and to the husbands' career advancement. Women who enter the career world after bearing and rearing children must do in their late thirties and forties what men did in their twenties and early thirties. These women will be competing against younger and more recently educated workers, and their potential career span and earning time are shorter by ten to twenty years in comparison to that of men. This difference can put women at a considerable competitive disadvantage. It can also mean disrupting established family patterns in order to accommodate the mother's new career. Because of these difficulties and anxieties associated with adult development in women, women often express more uncertainty and ambivalence about their lives. In many ways, women's adult lives are more difficult than men's, and they are less happy with what they have done (Hudson, 1991; Kaufman & Richardson, 1982; Levinson, 1996).

RELATIONSHIPS   Another challenge that adults confront is establishing intimate relationships. In this realm, men may confront greater challenges than do women. Research suggests that, during the socialization process in childhood, men and women learn fundamentally different ways of relating to the world and to other people and that this difference has implications for adult development. Men learn to be separate, autonomous, self-reliant, independent, self-sufficient, and aggressive. Women learn to be connected, caring, nurturant of others, attached, and interdependent. This difference influences adult development because the characteristics of

men seem more associated with advancement and success in the work world, whereas the characteristics of women give them more advantage in developing intimate relationships and performing family and nurturant roles. In fact, the psychologist Carol Gilligan (1983) points out that the description of adult development has "focused on the progress of the solitary self—wandering through stages with a focus on achievement and work." Whereas the male model has people marching predictably through a sequence of stages, Gilligan argues that women are confronted with a series of "renegotiations" of interdependence and caring about other people during their life cycles. So, when women enter the work world, they experience some degree of tension because it reduces their ability to maintain their nurturant and caring roles with family and others. Men do not experience the same tension because their socialization equips them to accept more readily independence and separateness from others. However, with men living longer than in the past and often today sharing the breadwinner role with their spouses, work and career can sometimes become less of a lifelong focus for men. In fact, Gail Sheehy (1998) calls the years after the forties the "second adulthood" for men: a time for men to focus more on relationships with spouses, children, and others. Connectedness and relationships can become more important than work and achievement as a life focus.

Gay men and lesbians confront some unique twists on these issues of family and relationships. Because of court reluctance to allow gays and lesbians to adopt children or gain custody of their children, establishing family and nurturant relationships with children may be difficult or impossible. In addition, society has remained reluctant to recognize gay relationships as being the equivalent of marriages, so establishing intimate relationships may have a different trajectory for gay men and lesbians.

This assessment of the conflicts and challenges that people face in adulthood illustrates the point that any single sequence of adult life stages is unlikely to capture the complexity and diversity of stages that actually exist in people's lives. Role transitions and the accompanying socialization continue throughout the adult years, but it is impossible to specify one sequence of stages that can be considered "normal" for all, or even most, adults.

Additional Perspectives on Socialization

You should be able to explain and contrast the functionalist and conflict perspectives on socialization.

This chapter imparts a sense of what socialization is all about. Future chapters cover a lot more about this process as they examine more closely the groups, institutions, and social forces that interact to make society what it is. We must remember, however, that not only is the topic of socialization incredibly vast, but also there are a number of ways of looking at it. The interactionist view of socialization has already been discussed through the work of Cooley, Mead, and Erikson. Therefore, this chapter closes with a brief consideration of some of the concerns of the two other major theoretical approaches to socialization.

The Functionalist Perspective

From the functionalist perspective, socialization is the essential mechanism for integrating human beings into society. It therefore plays a critical role in maintaining societal equilibrium and in enabling society to achieve its goals:

> Socialization is . . . training . . . for participation in society, a participation that is seen as occurring on terms set "by society" rather than on the individual's own terms. The emphasis is on the social purpose of socialization, a process conceived of as designed to achieve conformity of individuals to social norms and rules. (LeVine, 1969, p. 507)

The process of molding human beings into individuals who are able to function coherently and productively within society begins during infancy. It continues as people move into new social positions and new social relationships. Throughout their lives, then, people must become acquainted with new values, attitudes, and skills. Most develop the personal qualities that enable them to function in society. However, if people are not appropriately socialized at each stage in the life span, the equilibrium and stability of society are threatened.

One important element in lifelong socialization, according to the functionalist perspective, is the *rite of passage*, a ceremony that marks and celebrates a person's transition from one status to another (Brown, 1969; Van Gennep, 1960). Rites of passage symbolize and publicly proclaim the adoption of new statuses. Furthermore, these rites encourage people to identify with their new statuses and to internalize the values and norms that go with them. Puberty rites, which mark the transition from childhood to a more adult status, are common in many societies, for instance. Often, youngsters must fast, wear different kinds of clothing, or kill particular animals as a part of the puberty rites. Some societies call for circumcision of males to mark their ascent to manhood and clitoridectomy, or removal of the clitoris, to mark the sexual maturity of females (Bodley, 1994). Examples of puberty rites in the United States include religious ceremonies such as the Jewish bar mitzvah and the Roman Catholic confirmation. For

functionalists, clear and dramatic rites of passage are important because they demonstrate the acceptance of people occupying new positions in society.

Functionalists also argue that the stages of the life span are intimately related to the needs of particular societies. For this reason, the stages that occur in industrial societies differ substantially from those in preindustrial societies (Ariès, 1962; Flacks, 1971). In preindustrial societies, people usually learn how to fill adult positions fairly early in life. The technology is relatively simple, so little training or education is required. In addition, most people need not be literate in order to be productive. Therefore, the transition from childhood to adulthood generally takes place by the midteens, and sometimes it occurs as early as age eight. Only among select groups in society, such as a ruling elite or priesthood, are inactivity and nonproductivity prolonged.

In industrial societies, by contrast, the complex technology and elaborate division of labor demand a highly educated and literate populace. Thus training and education must be more extensive than in preindustrial societies. Furthermore, the abundance of goods and services provided by industrial technology makes it possible for a small number of people to supply everything that society needs. As a consequence, it is not necessary for all physically mature people to participate in the workforce.

These two factors contribute to two major differences between life stages in preindustrial and industrial societies. First, the age at which people in industrial societies are allowed to enter the adult world is postponed (Côté & Allahar, 1996; Kett, 1977). Childhood continues into the early teens and is followed by a new stage, adolescence, which runs from roughly thirteen to eighteen years of age. Adolescence is viewed as a time of preparation for adulthood, in terms of both education and psychological maturation. People in this age category are not considered adults. They are not expected to assume adult obligations such as supporting a family, and they are not accorded certain adult privileges, such as being able to vote or to drink alcohol.

The second difference between the life stages in preindustrial and industrial societies involves old age. In preindustrial societies, people normally work until they die. In industrial societies, however, many men and women retire from work long before death. This difference exists because industrial societies require fewer workers and because people tend to live longer in industrial societies.

The Conflict Perspective

Most approaches to socialization have a distinctly functionalist emphasis. However, socialization can also be seen from the conflict perspective. From this point of view, socialization seems to be a coercive process that advances the interest of one group while working to the disadvantage of others. It reflects and supports the existing social structure of a society, including the predominant power relationships. In hunting-and-gathering societies, where there are few distinctions made on the basis of wealth and power, there are also few groups with competing interests. Thus the socialization process is usually not terribly coercive. In more complex societies, however, there are great disparities in wealth and power, and many competing groups exist. In these societies, socialization becomes a tool that the more powerful use to maintain their upper hand.

The coercive dimension of socialization may be most dramatically illustrated in *total institutions*, which are *organizations isolated from the rest of society in which the behavior of the members is tightly controlled and regimented* (Goffman, 1961). Mental institutions and prisons are examples of total institutions. Some other organizations, such as the military and primary and secondary schools, have some of the characteristics of total institutions. Total institutions can be seen as microcosms of society. They therefore face many of the same problems as a society, including the need to integrate new members in a nondisruptive fashion. Entrance into prison, for example, is marked by a jarring resocialization process during which the prior values, roles, and identities of the inmates are stripped away and replaced with new ones that are compatible with their place in the prison hierarchy. Prisoners are forced to accept a thoroughly powerless and dependent position. Even such mundane personal matters as eating, sleeping, and bathing occur at a pace and in a manner dictated by organizational rhythms rather than individual needs. Through these procedures, inmates learn their position in the prison social structure, which is a degrading and humiliating one, and their identity in the organization, which is based primarily on dependence and ineffectuality.

The socialization process in the larger society can also frustrate human needs and desires. For example, some conflict theorists argue that children born into lower-class families are "socialized to fail." It is in the family that children acquire their aspirations for the future, their psychological orientation toward those in authority, and their assessment of the characteristics of their own social group. Lower-class youngsters, however, are less likely than more affluent youngsters to be taught to aspire to desirable and powerful occupations, to see authority figures as equals who can be manipulated, or to view themselves as powerful and positive individuals who can gain mastery over their environment. Instead, they are more likely to learn to be content with low-prestige jobs; to take a submissive and, indeed, almost fearful posture toward people in authority; and to view themselves as shackled by social forces beyond their control. Lower-class children who develop these characteristics are unlikely, as adults, to strive for desirable or rewarding positions; as a result, the amount of competition that those in the middle class must face is reduced (Knottnerus, 1987; MacLeod, 2008).

From the conflict perspective, then, the socialization process is not a mechanism for fitting human cogs into the wheels of society. Instead, it is a means of ensuring that the unequal division of the social pie will continue and that the large share that the dominant groups receive will not be threatened. Ultimately, it is a coercive and divisive process that places groups in opposition to one another.

Study & Review
SUMMARY OF LEARNING OBJECTIVES

You should be able to assess the different approaches to the roles of heredity and the environment in the socialization process and compare the contributions of each.

Culture and social structure are transmitted through socialization. Socialization begins during infancy and continues throughout life. Both heredity and the environment play a necessary role in shaping human behavior. Instincts control much of the behavior of lower animals, but most scientists today agree that human behavior is not dictated by instincts.

You should be able to describe the contributions made by Cooley, Mead, and Erikson to our understanding of the socialization process and discuss the functioning of the agencies of socialization and the different types of socialization.

Through social interaction, people develop a self, or identity, which includes a personality and a self-concept. The interactionist approach to personality and self-concept places more importance on the role of face-to-face social interaction and downplays the importance of biological drives and the assumption that the individual and society are in conflict. Charles Horton Cooley coined the phrase the *looking-glass self* to refer to the process by which we develop our sense of self through the reactions of other people to ourselves or our behavior. George Herbert Mead saw human interaction as a process of reacting to each other and interpreting each other's actions through the use of symbols. The socialization process, according to Mead, begins with imitation. It then moves through the play stage to the game stage. In this process, each of us learns to take the roles of other people, which ultimately allows us to see ourselves playing a variety of roles in society. Mead also saw the self as having two parts: the I and the me.

Erik Erikson identified eight stages in the socialization process, from infancy to old age. Socialization occurs in various settings as individuals move through their lives. Agencies of socialization are the people, groups, and institutions that play a part in socialization. Four of the most important are the family, peer groups, schools, and the media. There are three major types of socialization: primary socialization, anticipatory socialization, and resocialization. Societies tend to divide people's lives into a series of stages. These stages constitute the life span or life cycle, which is a succession of statuses and roles that people in a particular society experience in a fairly predictable pattern as they age.

You should be able to explain and contrast the functionalist and conflict perspectives on socialization.

For functionalists, socialization plays a critical role in maintaining societal equilibrium and in enabling society to achieve its goals. It is the essential mechanism for integrating human beings into society. From the conflict perspective, socialization can be seen as a coercive process that advances the interests of one group while working to the disadvantage of others. The coercive dimension of socialization is most dramatically illustrated in total institutions.

CHRONOLOGICAL PRACTICE TEST

For answers to Key Concepts see the page number in parentheses; for other answers see page 85.

Heredity and the Environment
Key Concepts

1. Cultural determinism (64)
2. Socialization (65)
3. Biological determinism (66)
4. Sociobiology (66)

True/False

5. T F This chapter concludes that the biological makeup of human beings does have implications for human social behavior.
6. T F The experiences of the young girls Anna and Genie demonstrate that, even in the absence of human contact during infancy and young childhood, human beings readily learn language and other social skills.

Concept Completion

7. When the philosopher John Locke argued that human beings are born *tabula rasa,* he meant that they are born with _____.
8. _____ is a field based on the idea that the genetic makeup of humans and other animals plays a powerful role in shaping their social behavior.

Critical Thinking

9. Make arguments both for and against the position of biological determinism. Include in your answer an assessment of sociobiology.
10. Describe the experiences of the three children described in this chapter who had been raised in some degree of isolation from human contact. What do their experiences teach us about learning and socialization?

The Process of Socialization
Key Concepts

11. Personality (68)
12. Self-concept (68)
13. Looking-glass self (69)
14. Significant symbols (70)
15. Significant others (70)
16. Generalized other (70)
17. Agencies of socialization (72)
18. Primary socialization (77)
19. Anticipatory socialization (79)
20. Resocialization (79)
21. Life span (79)
22. Life cycle (79)

True/False

23. T F Personality tends to be less constant during a person's life than does self-concept.
24. T F During the game stage, according to George Herbert Mead, children develop social skills by simply mimicking or imitating what other people do.
25. T F Erik Erikson views the stages in his theory of socialization as sequential.
26. T F One reason that the family is such an important influence in socializing young children is that the children are dependent on the family.
27. T F Seeing violence in the mass media increases the likelihood that children will act aggressively or violently themselves.
28. T F Biology plays a more important role in shaping behavior in the middle of the life span than it does at the beginning or the end.
29. T F Current research on the adult life span suggests that the middle-class, male model of life-span development should be the norm for all men and women.

Concept Completion

30. Two stages in the socialization process described by George Herbert Mead were the _____ and the _____.
31. According to Mead, the two interrelated parts of the self are the _____ and the _____.
32. According to Erik Erikson, the challenge that infants confront during the first stage of development is _____.
33. The agency of socialization that is probably second in importance to the family is _____.
34. One of the important impacts of the media in the socialization of children is enabling them to _____.

35. Two important cultural values that Japanese children learn during the socialization process are _____ and _____.
36. Learning new sets of values, beliefs, and behaviors that are different from those previously held is called _____.

Critical Thinking

37. According to Cooley and Mead, how does socialization during childhood occur?
38. Describe how Erikson's theory of socialization is different from Cooley's and Mead's.
39. Describe the stages in Erikson's theory.
40. Assess the issue of whether children sent to day care are reared as effectively as children raised in the home. Summarize the research on both sides of the issue.
41. Describe the four agencies of socialization discussed in the chapter in terms of the special contributions that each makes to the socialization of the young.
42. Describe the three most important forms that socialization can take. State what each accomplishes, and give an example of each.
43. How does the primary socialization of children in Japan and the United States differ?
44. Summarize the research on the issue of whether adults go through a single, common sequence of development. How does the adult development of women and men differ?

Additional Perspectives on Socialization
Key Concept

45. Total institutions (83)

True/False

46. T F The point at which people are allowed to enter the adult world generally occurs at an older age in industrial societies than it does in preindustrial societies.

Concept Completion

47. _____ is a ceremony that marks and celebrates a person's transition from one status to another.

Critical Thinking

48. Compare and contrast the functionalist and conflict perspectives on the process of socialization.

ANSWERS TO CHRONOLOGICAL PRACTICE TEST

5. T; 6. F; 23. F; 24. F; 25. T; 26. T; 27. T; 28. F; 29. F; 46. T
7. a clean slate
8. Sociobiology
30. imitation, play stage, game stage
31. I, me
32. trust versus mistrust
33. peer group
34. view role models
35. harmony, mutual dependence
36. resocialization
47. A rite of passage

CUMULATIVE PRACTICE TEST

See page 482 for answers.

1. Margaret Mead's analysis of socialization among the Samoans, discussed in the beginning of the chapter, would be most consistent with which position?
   a. Biological determinism.
   b. Sociobiology.
   c. The conflict perspective.
   d. Cultural determinism.
   e. Both a and c.

2. Philosopher John Locke argued that human beings are born *tabula rasa*. This view would be most supportive of which of the following positions?
   a. The nature position.
   b. Erikson's theory of development.
   c. Cooley's looking-glass self.
   d. The nurture position.
   e. Sociobiology.

3. Which of these positions would be most consistent with that of sociobiology?
   a. Cultural determinism.
   b. Biological determinism.
   c. The nurture position on human behavior.
   d. The *tabula rasa* position on human behavior.
   e. The looking-glass self.

4. Which of the following is most consistent with this book's position on the relationship between biology and human social behavior?
   a. Specific genes that cause particular forms of human behavior have been identified.
   b. Sociologists have concluded that biology plays little, if any, role in human behavior.
   c. Learning and other social forces can alter inborn genetic tendencies.
   d. Altruism and aggression have been shown to result mostly from biological factors.
   e. We just don't know yet whether or not biology plays a part in human social behavior.

5. Studies of children who have been raised in isolation from human contact illustrate that
   a. heredity is more important to socialization than is social interaction.
   b. nature is more crucial than nurture in socialization.
   c. personality develops before self-concept does.
   d. social interaction is essential during infancy if human development is to proceed normally.
   e. All of the above.

6. With respect to personality and self-concept, the text points out that
   a. the two characteristics are closely interrelated.
   b. self-concept is more constant than personality.
   c. the initial development of both characteristics occurs during adolescence.
   d. All of the above.
   e. None of the above.

7. The sociologist responsible for coining the term "looking-glass self" and one of the founders of the inter-actionist perspective was
   a. George Herbert Mead.
   b. Robert K. Merton.
   c. Emile Durkheim.
   d. Charles Horton Cooley.
   e. Erving Goffman.

8. The looking-glass-self process most clearly derives from which sociological perspective?
   a. The functionalist perspective.
   b. The conflict perspective.
   c. The biological-determinism perspective.
   d. The significant-other perspective.
   e. The interactionist perspective.

9. Specific persons whose opinions children care about, such as parents or siblings, are referred to by sociologists as
   a. generalized others.
   b. specified others.
   c. realistic others.
   d. anticipatory others.
   e. significant others.

10. According to Erik Erikson, the key challenge that people confront during adolescence is
    a. trust.
    b. industry.
    c. generativity.
    d. identity.
    e. integrity.

11. Which of the following statements is true regarding the peer group as an agency of socialization?
    a. It is more important than the family during infancy.
    b. It provides children with their first exposure to self-concept development.
    c. It offers young people an identity that supports some independence from the family.
    d. It exposes children to more hierarchical relationships than does the family.
    e. It teaches children basic literacy skills.

12. Which of the following is *not* a conclusion of the research regarding the impact of day care cited in this chapter? In comparison to children raised at home,
    a. day-care children are as attached to their parents.
    b. day-care children do as well in intelligence and psychosocial development.
    c. day-care children are less sociable.
    d. children enrolled in day care for extended periods may become more aggressive.
    e. All of the above were conclusions cited.

13. Child rearing in the Israeli kibbutz is different from child rearing in most other industrial societies in that in the kibbutz child rearing is seen as the responsibility of
    a. the nuclear family.
    b. the government.
    c. the grandparents.
    d. the extended family.
    e. the whole community.

14. Which of the following statements is *not* asserted in the text regarding the role of the mass media and modern communications technologies in the socialization of the young?
    a. They transmit the components of culture and social structure to the young.
    b. They offer a perspective that is largely independent of the supervision and control of parents.

c. They have probably produced more erosion of the influence of family in children's lives than enhancement of it.

d. They enable children to view various role models.

e. Parents control most of the messages distributed by these technologies.

15. The process that transforms infants into truly social human beings by teaching them basic values, skills, and language is referred to as
a. primary socialization.
b. anticipatory socialization.
c. resocialization.
d. reactive socialization.
e. cultural determinism.

16. Students in medical school would be most clearly going through
a. primary socialization.
b. sociobiology.
c. biological determinism.
d. total institutionalization.
e. anticipatory socialization.

17. An expectant mother playing with her sister's small child exemplifies
a. anticipatory socialization.
b. resocialization.
c. secondary socialization.
d. primary socialization.
e. biological determinism.

18. "Resocialization" is best defined as
a. the process that transforms infants into truly social human beings by teaching them basic values and skills.
b. learning the values, beliefs, and behaviors of a group that one plans to join in the future.
c. learning new sets of values, beliefs, and behaviors that are different from those previously held.
d. unlearning much of what has been previously learned.
e. the initial development of personality and self-concept during infancy.

19. The first major transition in the life cycle in adulthood for most people is
a. negotiating primary socialization.
b. establishing a career.
c. developing a self-concept.
d. having children.
e. gaining independence from one's family.

20. From the conflict perspective, the socialization process could be best characterized as
a. playing a critical role in maintaining the equilibrium of society.
b. a mechanism for integrating people into productive positions in society.
c. serving the needs of the whole society rather than some special interest group.

d. involving little coercion in industrial societies.

e. a coercive and divisive process that places groups in opposition to one another.

FOR FURTHER READING

Adler, Patricia A., & Adler, Peter. (1998). *Peer power: Preadolescent culture and identity.* New Brunswick, NJ: Rutgers University Press. This very engaging book describes what socialization and identity are like for young children. It especially focuses on the influence of peers in these arenas.

Ariès, Philippe. (1965). *Centuries of childhood: A social history of family life.* New York: Vintage. The book is an eye-opening look at what childhood was like and how children were viewed in some preindustrial European societies.

Duncan, Greg J., & Brooks-Gunn, Jeanne (Eds.). (2000). *Consequences of growing up poor.* New York: Russell Sage. This compilation of research documents how the socialization experiences of children have very important impacts on their intellectual development and their adolescent behavior.

Lewontin, R. C. (1984). *Not in our genes.* New York: Pantheon. This book is about biological and sociobiological explanations of socialization and human development. As the title suggests, the author is a critic of such approaches, but his analysis is complete and fair.

Mead, Margaret. (1961). *Coming of age in Samoa.* New York: Dell. (Original work published 1928.) Although Mead's work has been unfavorably criticized, it is still a classic analysis of the adolescent period in a society quite different from American society.

Quart, Alissa. (2002). *Branded: The buying and selling of teenagers.* New York: Perseus. This book, written by a journalist, shows the extent to which the socialization of children and teens today is accomplished in part through a comprehensive and sophisticated marketing campaign to get them to buy products. Quart explores the many disturbing implications of this.

Rymer, Russ. (1993). *Genie: An abused child's flight from silence.* New York: HarperCollins. This is a truly fascinating book about Genie, the girl discussed in the chapter who suffered severe isolation in childhood. The author discusses controversies regarding language socialization and describes how the scientific community treated Genie and the abilities she developed in early adulthood.

Turkle, Sherry. (1995). *Life on the screen: Identity in the age of the Internet.* New York: Simon & Schuster. Children today grow up using computers, and this sociologist argues that computers and how we use them play a part in shaping our self-concepts during the process of socialization.

CHAPTER 4

Groups and Organizations

MYTHS & FACTS: About Groups and Organizations

Types of Groups

Primary Groups
Characteristics
Cultural Variation
Secondary Groups
In-Groups and Out-Groups
Reference Groups
Social Collectivities

Group Structure and Process

Status and Role
Leadership
Decision Making in Groups
Group Cohesion
Group Conformity

Organizations

Bureaucracy
Characteristics of Bureaucracies
A Critique of Bureaucratic Organization

The Human Relations Approach
The Informal Structure
Gender in Organizations
APPLYING SOCIOLOGY: Diagnosing Organizational Culture: Helping Organizations to Function Better

Sociological Perspectives on Organizations

The Functionalist Perspective
The Conflict Perspective
OTHER WORLDS, OTHER WAYS: China: Cultural Values and Group Behavior—Social Loafing in Organizations
The Interactionist Perspective

The Future of Bureaucracy

Bureaucracy and Oligarchy
Limits to Bureaucracy
SOCIOLOGY OF MEDIA AND TECHNOLOGY: Community and Group Life in the Cyber World
SOCIOLOGY ON THE INTERNET

Study & Review

Myths & Facts
About Groups and Organizations

Myth:
Individual decision making is clearly superior to group decision making: "If you want something fouled up, just depend on a committee to decide what to do."

Fact:
Research has demonstrated that group decisions are more reasoned and reliable than individual decisions. In this case, the old commonsense saying, "Two heads are better than one," is supported by empirical evidence.

Myth:
Groups are cautious and reserved in making decisions. That explains why it takes so long for groups to reach a decision.

Fact:
Group decisions tend to be more extreme—sometimes more daring, other times more cautious—than those made by individuals. This tendency has been referred to as the *risky shift* phenomenon and described as *group polarization.*

Myth:
Bureaucracies are slow and inefficient.

Fact:
Although bureaucracies can be legitimately criticized for being inflexible and rigid, they are extremely efficient in accomplishing well-structured and straightforward tasks that involve a uniform sequence of events.

Myth:
Computer technology is decentralizing the workplace by allowing more people to be their own boss and run their business from their home.

Fact:
The impact of computers on the workplace is more complicated than this. Although some workers benefit, others who work at home are isolated employees with little power to influence the conditions of their work or to bargain for health benefits or other advantages.

It has been six hundred years since European explorers first made landfall in the Western Hemisphere. For most of those years, it made little difference to the Yanomamo Indians, as the Europeans gradually transformed the Americas. However, the good fortune of the Yanomamo (also called Yanomama) in avoiding the encroachment of the newcomers could not last forever.

The Yanomamo people live in remote portions of southern Venezuela and northern Brazil, scattered in 125 villages that contain between 40 and 250 people each (Chagnon, 1992; Smole, 1976). Their territory is so remote that most of these villages had little or no contact with outsiders until the 1970s. The Yanomamo territory is heavily forested, its rolling hills covered with palm, hardwood trees, scrub brush, and vines. The Indians live in huts made from the poles, vines, and leaves of the tropical rain forest. They subsist by hunting monkeys, pigs, and wild turkeys and gathering wild fruits, nuts, and tubers. They also have gardens, where they cultivate plantain, banana, sweet manioc, and maize. Although rain forests seem lush to those unfamiliar with them, wild game and flora are sparse and the soil is shallow. Therefore, the Yanomamo must periodically find new hunting areas and move their gardens as the topsoil is depleted. In the terms used in Chapter 2, the Yanomamo have a

mixed hunting-and-gathering and horticultural subsistence pattern.

Yanomamo daily life in these small villages is casual and personal. Everyone knows everyone else. Some people wake before dawn to build up the fire, and then they visit others to make plans for the day or maybe go back to sleep. When it is light, men or women prepare breakfast, and the men who will hunt that day leave the village. Other men go out to work in their garden, transplanting banana cuttings or felling trees and clearing brush. Women collect firewood and help with planting and weeding. By midmorning, it is too hot and humid to continue working, so everyone retires to bathe in a stream, eat a meal, and rest in their hammocks. Children play close to the adults all day and learn what they need to know to be good Yanomamo by watching the adults hunt, cultivate, or rest. In late afternoon, as the weather cools, some men and women go back to working in the gardens or gathering firewood, while others relax in the shadows and take hallucinogenic drugs. The large evening meal is a time to relax and socialize with others. Successful hunters show their solidarity with others in the group by giving away much of the meat they caught that day. Both men and women participate in food preparation, although women do the larger share. After dusk, fires are prepared for the night; if a person's fire has gone out, he or she simply borrows a few glowing sticks from a neighbor to restart it. Daily routines in one Yanomamo village are described thus:

> Life is public both within and without the village-house. People know how one another's children behave and how a man treats his wife. They know what food others eat, what game a hunter captures, and what game was not successfully retrieved. Yanomama may respond to the activity of others with indifference, vocal anger, casual interest, or laughter. (Early & Peters, 1990, p. 5)

In Yanomamo society, no one would have to fend for himself or herself; the community ties discussed in Chapter 1 are elaborate and comprehensive. The daily routines just described are repeated from one season to the next, and there are not great variations in wealth and poverty. There are distinctions: Men have higher status than women. Someone not born in a particular village is considered an "outsider" and discouraged from participating in some Yanomamo activities. A headman in a village has some privileges that others do not have. Yet, for the most part, life for the Yanomamo is highly egalitarian and personal.

Lest this picture seem idealized, the Yanomamo are also known as "the fierce people" because they can be aggressive and violent. Men settle disputes by battling one another with clubs, and elders proudly flaunt their scars as signs of their bravery over the years. Women can be cruelly beaten by their husbands or kidnapped by raiders from another Yanomamo village. Yet, the Yanomamo social structure, as with all social structures at their level of subsistence, is relatively small, simple, and personal. Everyone knows everyone else and his or her place in the social order.

As the Europeanization and bureaucratization of the Western Hemisphere proceeded, it finally affected Yanomamo life and social structure. In the 1950s, missionaries made contact with some Yanomamo villages, bringing them the Bible and "civilized" life. Over the following two decades, farmers in Brazil and Venezuela gradually encroached on Yanomamo lands, clearing forests for cropland. In the 1980s, gold was discovered in Yanomamo territory, bringing prospectors and miners looking for wealth. In 1993, Brazilian gold miners were blamed for the massacre of forty Yanomamo men, women, and children and the burning of their village. The mining companies have also been accused of wreaking havoc on the Yanomamo's environment and introducing deadly diseases such as tuberculosis and malaria. After centuries of isolation, the Yanomamo are being unwillingly drawn into a very different type of social organization, characterized by large, impersonal, formal organizations quite alien to their traditional way of life. Impersonal organizations and decisions made by people they are unfamiliar with change their lives in ways over which they have little control; corporations and bureaucracies, often located in foreign lands, now shape their fate.

Traditional Yanomamo life and the new world they now confront represent the extremes of the types of groups that humans create in order to survive. As described in Chapter 2, social structure is one of the fundamental elements that is found in all societies, and groups and organizations are two important manifestations of social structure. A *social group* was defined as a collection of people who are aware of their membership, have common goals and interests, share statuses and roles, and interact with one another. People live out their lives in a vast network of such groups. A Yanomamo male is born into and socialized by a family, goes out to hunt with a small group of other men, and sits around the fire in a casual group in the evening to exchange stories. In modern industrial societies, similar small groups can be found, but large and impersonal groups such as business, educational, and government organizations—unknown in traditional Yanomamo society—have become much more prominent. In an almost infinite variety of ways, groups and organizations shape our relationships with others and guide our behavior. This chapter analyzes the most important types of groups and organizations in terms of their structures and how they function to influence behavior.

Types of Groups

> You should be able to describe the major types of social groups and discuss their functions.

There are many different types of social groups, and each plays a different part in our lives. The study of groups and group processes begins by distinguishing among the groups that perform different functions for people and for society. One central distinction between groups is that between those in which we have close personal ties with people and those in which we do not. Along these lines, sociological analysis makes an important distinction between primary and secondary groups.

Primary Groups

CHARACTERISTICS Primary groups are *small in size and characterized by personal, intimate, and nonspecialized relationships between their members.* A family, a friendship group, an athletic team, and a pair of lovers are examples of primary groups. Primary groups usually involve face-to-face contact; generate strong feelings of group loyalty and identification; and provide warm, supportive, and emotionally gratifying ties with others. In fact, one of the major functions of primary groups in society is to provide people with a relatively secure refuge in which they can be themselves without fear of rejection or ridicule. In addition, primary groups function as mediators between the individual and other parts of society (Dunphy, 1972). The family, for example, provides socialization in the values and norms of society. Likewise, peer groups serve as buffers that help us cope with the impersonal or alienating elements of school or work. We can tolerate some degree of such impersonality because of the support that we receive in primary groups. Finally, primary groups play a central role in shaping our personalities and self-concepts. It is typically from family and friends that we gain a sense of who we are and of our value and worth. However, even when primary groups perform the same function in two different cultures, cultural values and traditions still stamp some distinct patterns and meanings on how people in primary groups relate to one another.

CULTURAL VARIATION   Friendships are primary groups that fulfill many of the functions of primary groups mentioned, and they perform some similar functions in all cultures. Yet, there are some significant differences, especially in the social meanings attached to friendships and how friends relate to one another (Barnlund, 1989). In Japan, for example, friendship is surrounded by obligation and responsibility. To take on a friend means to take seriously the obligation to assist that person in any difficulties he or she might have. In fact, this obligation is taken so seriously that Japanese are more reluctant than people in the United States to take on new friendships. They seem more aware of and sensitive to the burden that friendship creates, while in the United States people tend to think in terms of "the more friends the better." As a part of the burden of friendship, Japanese see friendships as more permanent than do people in the United States, as lifelong connections and responsibilities. The ending of a friendship is seen very negatively in Japan, whereas in the United States it is viewed as common and sometimes necessary—not good, but something that happens because people move, change, or become interested in new things. Even when separated by some geographic distance, Japanese friends are reluctant to say their friendship has ended. Such reluctance is also found, to an extent, in the United States, but friends are usually more willing to let friendships go in the United States.

Friends in Japan avoid arguments, disagreements, and other sorts of conflict as much as possible (Halloran, 1969; Ozaki, 1978). Japanese are surprised at the amount of explicit conflict that can occur between friends in the United States. With the strong emphasis placed on individualism in the United States, people consider open conflict to be an honest display of one's feelings and may feel that Japanese are being dishonest or insincere when they don't tell friends what they truly think. The Japanese approach, however, is not a matter of dishonesty but of maintaining harmonious social relations (see the discussion of Japanese cultural values in Chapter 2). For the Japanese, harmony is more important than what they might consider a selfish display of emotion. In addition, the Japanese identity is more firmly grounded in social relationships, like friendships, whereas people in the United States tend to idealize the isolated self. In the United States, people will break off friendships over some conflict or other and then become reconciled and resume the friendship at a later date. Japanese avoid letting conflict build to the point that it threatens a relationship. There is conflict in Japan and friendships do break up; reconciliations, however, are rare.

Thus, although the status of "friend" can be found in all cultures, the social meaning of the primary group of "friends" is quite variable and shaped by cultural values. This variability illustrates the emphasis of the interactionist perspective on the emergence of social meanings through social interaction. In preindustrial societies, much of life revolved around primary groups. As noted in Chapter 2, family and kinship played an important role in hunting-and-gathering, horticultural, and agricultural societies. However, the German sociologist Ferdinand Tönnies (1887/1963) observed how this changes with the coming of industrialization, and he distinguished between gemeinschaft and gesellschaft types of societies (see Chapter 2). The type of group that dominates in gesellschaft (industrial) societies is the secondary group.

Secondary Groups

Secondary groups are based on task-oriented, impersonal, and specialized ties with people; they may be small but are often large. Business organizations, universities, the U.S. Army, and hospitals are all examples of secondary groups. Consider the last time that you dealt with people who work in the registrar's office or other unit in your school. Unless these people were close friends, your relationship with them was probably secondary in nature. In your role as a student, for example, the people who work in the registrar's office interact with you in a contractual way, rather than a personal, primary fashion. Despite their impersonality, secondary groups are very important in an industrial society because they enable us to achieve specified goals. By treating you in an impersonal way, the registrar's office at your school can process hundreds of students each day. Were the relationship unspecialized—if you decided to chat with the clerk about football because you were both interested in the topic—the major goal of the registrar's office, to register students in classes, would not be achieved as quickly or completely, or perhaps at all.

Figure 4.1
The Continuum of Primary and Secondary Groups

Pure Primary Groups

Family

College hockey team

College sociology class

Corporate business office

Criminal trial in court

Pure Secondary Groups

The distinction between primary and secondary groups is one of degree. Some primary relationships may involve certain secondary elements, and some of the interchanges in a secondary group may be warm and personal (Figure 4.1). Likewise, over time, one type of group can change into the other. The important point is to understand the extent to which a particular group has primary or secondary characteristics and thus serves different functions in social life.

In-Groups and Out-Groups

In addition to noting the distinction between primary and secondary groups, sociologists also call attention to how people view their own and other groups. William Graham Sumner (1906) coined the terms *in-group* and *out-group* to distinguish between groups that generate quite different feelings. An in-group is *one that we feel positively toward and identify with, and that produces a sense of loyalty or "we" feeling.* Out-groups are *those to which we do not belong and that we view in a neutral or possibly hostile fashion.* We view out-groups as "they," as different from and less desirable than ourselves. In-groups might include your family, your friends, the church you attend, or the bowling team to which you belong. Out-groups might include bowling teams that compete with yours, those who hold different religious beliefs, your supervisors at

work, or the administrators and faculty at your university. In-groups and out-groups depend on a person's perspective: One person's in-group is another's out-group. In addition, in-groups and out-groups may be primary or secondary, large or small. Your baseball team, which may be a primary group, may be an in-group for you but an out-group for opposing teams. Likewise, a high school, which is a secondary group, can serve as an in-group for its members but an out-group for people attending other high schools.

All groups have boundaries to distinguish those who belong from those who do not, and boundaries help to distinguish in-groups from out-groups. In some groups, the boundaries are clearly demarcated by formal entrance rituals. People join a religion by undergoing a formal ritual such as baptism; one becomes a physician by graduating from medical school and passing the required examinations; a person enters a fraternity by successfully enduring "hell" week or other hazing ceremonies. In other groups, boundaries are defined by certain visible signs: wedding rings may define a married pair; clothing styles can signify one's allegiance to particular groups; skin color identifies one as a member of a particular racial group. For many groups, however, there are no rituals or visible signs to demarcate boundaries. For these groups, identification and we-feelings are important elements in defining boundaries and maintaining membership. Among friends, for example, membership is defined by one's loyalty to the group as measured by how much time is spent with them or what one is willing to do for them. Although we-feelings are important in many groups, they are especially important in groups that possess few other mechanisms for defining group boundaries. (Chapter 2 discussed the role of argot, or a group's special language, in helping identify group boundaries.)

In-groups and out-groups are important because of the roles they play in social life. The loyalty generated among members of an in-group, for example, can motivate people to endure many hardships together. People will give, sacrifice, or suffer a great deal to help members of their families, whereas the needs of an acquaintance or stranger would be ignored. In addition, we often stereotype members of an out-group, and those stereotypes influence the way we treat the members of that group. The elderly, for example, are often stereotyped as being frail and senile, and younger people's treatment of them often reflects this view—sometimes to the point of being condescending and insulting. As is discussed in Chapters 7 and 8, discrimination against a group can arise from such stereotypes. Finally, threats from an out-group can increase loyalty and cohesion among in-group members. The most obvious example is warfare, in which nations view each other as threatening and people on both sides rally together to overcome the foe.

Reference Groups

A reference group is *a group that people use as a standard in evaluating or understanding themselves, their attitudes, and their behavior.* A person in college, for example, may adopt the attitudes, clothing styles, and leisure interests of other college students. One need not be enrolled in college, however, to use college students as a reference group. Some high school students may identify with their college counterparts, attend college athletic events, and adopt the clothing styles of college students as a standard of fashion. Thus people are not necessarily *members* of the reference groups they use as standards.

Reference groups can be very powerful and pervasive elements in our lives, serving as sources of values, attitudes, and standards of conduct. Because we regard membership in or acceptance by these groups as important, we adopt their perspective on many things, often without being aware that we have done so. This process is illustrated by a classic study of political attitudes among college students. Theodore Newcomb (1943, 1958) initiated his study in the 1930s at Bennington College, an exclusive women's college in Vermont. At the time, Bennington had a young and very liberal faculty, whereas the students came from families that were generally conservative. When students first enrolled at Bennington, they tended to hold the conservative views of their parents. That tendency did not last, however. Newcomb found that there was a strong likelihood that the students' political attitudes would become more liberal the longer they attended Bennington. The reason was that the prestige of a student at Bennington depended in part on her political stance. To be accepted by other students, to gain entrance to sororities, to be elected to student office—all were easier if one had liberal political attitudes. Many of the students adjusted their attitudes accordingly. In short, the reference group for the students in relationship to political and social attitudes gradually changed from their parents to the faculty and other students. A restudy of the original Bennington women in the 1980s offers yet further support for the importance of reference groups in shaping attitudes (Alwin, Cohen, & Newcomb, 1991). Throughout their lives, the impact of college experiences on the political attitudes of these women persisted. Of course, some of their attitudes did change over time, but change was most likely to occur because of the impact of other reference groups, especially their spouses, their friends, and their children. When change occurred, it was typically to bring their attitudes closer into alignment with postcollege reference groups to which they were exposed.

A few Bennington students maintained their conservative views, retaining their parents as a reference group for their political attitudes. Newcomb found that these students maintained closer contacts with their families, telephoned their parents more frequently, and made numerous trips back to their home community. They were also less likely to participate in campus politics or the major sororities and clubs. Instead, they joined groups on campus that were isolated from the mainstream of campus events. It was easier to maintain their parents as a reference group if they kept closer ties with them and reduced ties with liberal students and other similar groups.

Reference groups, then, serve as standards against which we assess ourselves and the validity of our beliefs and values. They also serve as sources of aspiration. When people attend college, for example, they learn the goals other college students aspire to and may come to value those goals themselves. As we move from one group to another, such situations can create difficulties, of course. Friends who do not attend college, for example, may not understand why your attitudes are changing as you attend college because they do not use college as a reference group as you do. They may view your pulling away from them as insensitivity, but you are actually beginning to assess yourself by the standards of a different group.

Social Collectivities

Some collections of people that are commonly called groups do not qualify as such under the restricted way that sociologists use the term. The term *social category* refers to people who share some characteristic in common, such as Italians, Muslims, rock fans, golfers, or racquetball players. The term *aggregate* refers to people who happen to be in the same place at the same time, even though they may not interact with one another. Examples would include people riding the same bus or people in an elevator together. Such collectivities do not qualify as a social group in the sociological sense because they do not have interrelated statuses and roles or an awareness of sharing something in common. Such social collectivities are important, however, because social categories, and especially aggregates, can transform themselves into a group if the members begin interacting and other group characteristics develop.

Group Structure and Process

You should be able to describe the social structure of groups and explain the processes involved in group leadership, group decision making, and ensuring group conformity.

In the previous section, groups were distinguished in terms of the functions they perform. Sociologists also distinguish between groups in terms of their size, ranging from small groups, where people engage in face-to-face interaction, to large, impersonal organizations. Much social life is lived out in small groups. Even in large organizations, much social activity occurs in small groups, as when, for example, people in a corporation meet to make business decisions or teachers in schools counsel students. These small-group settings are sufficiently important to understanding social life that sociology devotes considerable attention to studying their structure and the process of social interaction that takes place within them (Hare, Blumberg, & Davies, 1996).

Status and Role

As indicated in Chapter 2, statuses and roles are two central elements of social structure, and they can be found in all groups—large or small, primary or secondary—because all groups have a social structure. These statuses and roles organize and coordinate the behavior of group members in relation to one another and indicate what behaviors are appropriate for each group member. In this fashion, they contribute to stable and orderly social interaction in groups. This phenomenon can be illustrated by examining the group structure of youth gangs.

Sociologists have studied youth gangs since early in the twentieth century, often using participant observation research as described in Chapter 1 (Decker & Van Winkle, 1996; Jankowski, 1991; Whyte, 1965). These gangs tend to be informally structured, and their membership can shift from week to week. Nonetheless, by spending a good deal of time with these gangs, sociologists have been able to identify the statuses and roles that constitute a part of their social structure. These statuses and roles define the rights and obligations of each member of the gang. Chapter 2 discusses how differences in status do not always imply differences in ranking or prestige. In most youth gangs, however, some statuses are ranked in terms of prestige or importance. Usually one or a few members of the gang can be identified as the leader, and these people are accorded more respect or deference. A person might become a leader because the person is big and tough and can best others in a physical confrontation. Or the person may be especially smart or crafty, be willing to commit serious crimes or deal drugs, or be willing to risk arrest. The leader is also often an older member of the gang, who has had many opportunities to develop skills and display prowess and toughness. Irrespective of how they become leaders, inhabiting that status means that those individuals have more control and influence over others and may have some privileges that others don't have (as in an extra share of the take from drug proceeds). In some gangs, leaders are expected to lend money to other gang members but not to borrow from them. Leaders also often have additional responsibilities for deciding what activities or crimes the gang will take on and for settling disputes among gang members.

The status structure of a gang can also influence the expectations for conformity to group norms and roles. Leaders and other high-status people, for example, are often under greater pressure to conform than are other members of the group. While all gang members are expected to help one another—this is a general expectation for anyone in the role of "gang member"—leaders and other high-status people are expected to offer more extensive and continuous assistance. When a gang member is in serious trouble—say, with the police—it is the leaders who are most expected to provide help, even if it might be costly to, or bring police attention to, the leader.

Beyond the leader role, the specialized roles that emerge in gangs depend on the specific circumstances of each gang. Some members might be especially adept at dealing drugs, others at acquiring and using guns. Some gang members may be especially skilled at finding entertaining social activities for the gang to participate in. Gang members, of course, do not talk about "statuses," "roles," and "social structure" and may not even have labels for all of the statuses in their group. Nonetheless, sociologists, by observing what gang members say and do, can identify the various features of the gang's social structure and how they influence members' behavior.

As mentioned, membership in youth gangs shifts over time; this drifting into and out of such groups is common. Sociologists have studied the group dynamics involved in joining and leaving such groups. One influential factor is how many social connections a person has in the group (McPherson, Popielarz, & Drobnic, 1992). The more connections, such as friendships or obligations to individuals in the group, people have, the less likely they are to leave the group. This fact is especially true when those connections involve people who are similar to one another in terms of gender, race, or some other important characteristic. Generally, high-status individuals in a group have a greater network of connections than those of less status, partly because they are likely to have been in the group longer. Knowledge of such group dynamics is helpful to group leaders, who can work to increase the connections of new members in the group as a way of reducing the likelihood they will drift away.

So, studies of youth gangs by sociologists illustrate how group structure—statuses and roles—shapes behavior by defining which behaviors are appropriate for each position in the group. You probably belong to at least one informal group of friends that has some parallels to these youth gangs. Certainly the status and role structure of your group will not mirror exactly those of youth gangs, but you should be sensitive to the statuses and roles that do exist. Which people have higher status? Who has influence over whom? Who initiates activities, makes decisions, or settles disputes?

Who can get away with nonconformity? Who has the greatest impact in determining whether a new person will be permitted to join the group? The precise form of a particular group's social structure depends on many factors. One such factor is leadership, which is used to illustrate some further dimensions of group structure and process.

Leadership

One of the most important, and more thoroughly investigated, statuses in groups is that of leader. Leadership refers to *the exercise of influence over a group such that group behavior is directed toward particular outcomes or goals* (Hall & Tolbert, 2005). In some groups, leadership is a formal position, as with a teacher in the classroom. In other settings, leadership is informal, shifting, and sometimes difficult to determine clearly. In peer groups, athletic teams, or a crowd at a homecoming party, it is often difficult to predict who will guide the actions of the group, and leadership may shift from one person to another over time.

Two important roles that leaders perform and that need to be performed in all groups are *task* and *socioemotional roles* (Bales, 1953; Fiedler, 1981). Task roles (also called instrumental roles) are *the actions of leaders that move the group toward achieving its goals.* Examples of task leadership would include a teacher directing students, a manager overseeing the activities of a group of employees, or a mother working to support her family. Socioemotional roles (also known as expressive or relationship-oriented roles) are those in which *leaders work to produce harmony, enjoyment, relaxation, or high morale among group members.* A surgeon who jokes to ease tension, an employer who hosts a party for his or her employees, or a friend who listens to the complaints of a buddy—all would be performing socioemotional roles.

These two leadership roles can be performed by the same person or by different people. It is sometimes difficult for the same person to accomplish both because they are, to a degree, inconsistent with each other. In a family, for example, a mother who works outside the home may have to insist that her children mow the lawn while she is away when they would prefer to play. Her exercise of authority and her absence—both called for by her position as instrumental leader—may, in fact, increase tension or disharmony in the family. Socioemotional leadership, by contrast, would call for listening, understanding, and sympathy—all of which may make it more difficult to get the lawn mowed. Furthermore, the two roles sometimes call for different skills. The task role may require skills in coordination and command, whereas the socioemotional role may require patience and understanding. Although some people possess all these skills, many do not.

In addition to variations in how they perform their task and socioemotional roles, leaders differ in their degree of *directiveness.* Different levels of directiveness can influence the attitudes and behaviors of group members (Lewin, Lippitt, & White, 1939; White & Lippitt, 1960). *Autocratic leaders* are thoroughly directive, dictating all actions and techniques to be used in achieving group goals. *Democratic leaders* allow group members to take part in shaping the policies of the group and choosing procedures for accomplishing group goals. Group members are allowed more freedom in deciding what their own actions will be. *Laissez-faire leaders* withdraw from participation in the group and give group members almost complete freedom to make decisions and choose alternative actions.

Higher levels of tension and conflict are found in groups with directive leaders than with less-directive types. In autocratic groups, for example, more hostility and aggression are generated and scapegoating is common, with a single individual often serving as the target of the group's hostility. In addition, group members are more positive toward groups with nondirective leaders, and less-directive leadership creates more satisfaction among group members, greater interest in the group, and more friendly and enjoyable relationships among group members. Directive leaders, however, appear to encourage more productivity. Although some studies find no differences in productivity as a result of leadership, few studies conclude that nondirective leadership is more productive (Fiedler, 1967; Shaw, 1976; Whitcomb & Williams, 1978).

With an understanding of the impact of leader directiveness on group behavior, it can be seen that having a directive leader is sometimes beneficial and sometimes not. In battle or in surgery, for example, there is neither the time nor the luxury for debate, freedom, or choice. In a work group, directive leadership may be less satisfying to group members but still preferable because it enhances productivity. Evidence shows, however, that democratic rather than authoritarian directiveness in leaders is more influential and results in higher employee productivity and commitment (Tjosvold, Andrews, & Struthers, 1992). In groups where membership and participation depend on people's satisfaction and interest, however, nondirective leadership may be necessary to hold the group together. Among friends or in charity drives where participation is voluntary, nondirective leaders may be essential to avoid the disintegration of the group. In other words, the best style of leadership depends on the type of group involved and the goals of the group (Fiedler, 1981). It also depends on the environment in which the group carries out its work. In a stressful environment where the group experiences hindrances to its work, a less-structured group without clear-cut leadership seems to do better; in a quiet, stable, positive environment, groups with structured leadership outperform less-structured groups at the same tasks (Worchel & Shackelford, 1991). It can be seen, therefore, that many factors come into play to influence leadership in groups, and sociologists need a lot of information (about group goals, environment, membership characteristics, and so on) before making recommendations about the most effective leadership for a particular group.

Finally, in regard to leadership, considerable research and controversy over the years have been generated over the role of gender. Over the years, much popular wisdom, supported by some early social science research, suggested that men are more natural leaders and women more natural followers. This view is certainly consistent with the traditional sex-role stereotype of women as the weaker and more passive of the two sexes. Research of the last two decades, however, paints a more complicated picture from which it is more difficult to conclude that the members of one sex are more effective leaders (Eagly & Johannesen-Schmidt, 2001; Ridgeway, 2001; Schein, 2001). Research shows that, because of gender stereotyping and gender discrimination, men are more likely to be chosen for leadership positions and women are still discriminated against when it comes time to select a leader in a variety of settings. As a result, men have more opportunities to hold leadership positions and gain experience at doing so. So it becomes a self-fulfilling prophecy: The cultural stereotype of men as leaders results in men being pressured to take such positions, and the experience they gain in those positions imparts more leadership abilities to them than to women. As women gain the same opportunities for leadership, they tend to develop equivalent leadership skills. Research also shows that more than one style of leadership exists and can be effective and that leadership style is affected by gender. Men's leadership style tends to be more task focused, involving movement toward specified goals; women's style tends to be more socioemotionally focused, involving a concern with interpersonal relations and maintaining morale. Each leadership style can be effective in some contexts, and thus persons belonging to either gender can be more effective leaders in the contexts appropriate to their leadership style.

Decision Making in Groups

This discussion of the social structure of groups has considered issues related to social interaction among group members, such as the degree of directiveness in the interaction between leaders and members. Another area of social interaction among group members that has been extensively studied is decision making in groups.

Some people believe that "two heads are better than one"—that group decisions are superior to those made by individuals. Others believe that decision making by groups is inherently inefficient and faulty. What is the reality behind these contradictory commonsense notions? Actually, it depends on whether the group is solving a problem or exercising judgment and making choices. Research has demonstrated that groups are clearly superior to individuals in everything except speed when it comes to solving problems. Groups come up with a wider range of solutions to problems, and the solutions are better and more accurate (Shaw & Costanzo, 1982). There are a number of probable reasons for the superiority of group performance in problem solving: More individual effort and creativity are brought to bear in a group; groups are more likely to recognize and reject errors; the ablest and most confident group members strongly influence the group decision; and greater interest in the problem is aroused in a group and people are more highly motivated to seek a solution (Phillips & Wood, 1984; Watson, Michaelsen, & Sharp, 1991).

Many decisions that groups make are not related to problem solving but rather involve judgment, assessment, and choice among a number of alternatives. And no alternative is necessarily correct. For example, deciding how to spend a weekend has this judgmental character. Group decisions on judgmental issues are characterized by a phenomenon known as group polarization: *The decisions tend to be more extreme than those made by individuals* (Friedkin, 1999; Myers & Lamm, 1976). This phenomenon was originally identified as a *risky shift*: People in groups tend to make more daring and bold choices than they would if acting individually. To some extent, this tendency contradicts the commonsense notion that groups are cautious and reserved. Continuing research has shown, however, that although group discussion *does* bring about a shift in the decisions of individuals, the shift *need not* be in the direction of more risk. If the group's position is cautious and conservative, then individuals tend to shift their decisions in that direction. In short, group decisions tend to be more extreme—either more daring *or* more cautious—than decisions made individually by the same people. This phenomenon has been found to occur in many diverse settings, including people making business decisions as well as burglars deciding whether a location is an appropriate target (Cromwell, Marks, Olson, & Avary, 1991; Williams & Taormina, 1992).

There are several possible reasons for the group polarization phenomenon (Hong, 1978; Mackie & Cooper, 1984). First, it may be that during group discussions, people shift their decisions in directions that appear to be more highly valued by the group. In other words, people tend to adopt the values of the group in making decisions. Another reason for group polarization may be that people shift their opinions because they have been persuaded by the information and arguments emerging from group discussion. Group members who hold extreme positions may feel more strongly about their positions, argue more persuasively, and thus have greater influence on the group's decisions. Finally, especially in groups exhibiting a risky shift, people in groups probably feel less responsibility for the decisions and thus less inhibited in making risky ones.

Group Cohesion

One of the more important group characteristics is group cohesion, or *the degree to which groups stick together and members feel committed to one another and attracted to the group.* In other words, cohesive groups tend to stick together, even under adversity, whereas less-cohesive groups more easily disintegrate under pressure or competing demands. More-cohesive groups have higher levels of morale and less difficulty retaining members and are often more persistent and effective in achieving their goals.

One example of how cohesion affects group performance can be found in studies of behavior in combat. For the military to be effective, soldiers must continue to fight as a cohesive group even under the most adverse conditions—combat, where deprivation, injury, and death are routine. Applied sociologists have been conducting research and helping the military services establish policies that will result in the most cohesive fighting force. The focus of much of this research has been on the role of primary groups in motivating soldiers to fight. Beginning with studies of the German army during World War II, sociologists showed that many German units continued to fight well even when they were badly outnumbered and had probably lost the war (Shils & Janowitz, 1948; Stouffer et al., 1949). It was not a belief in the Nazi cause that produced this tenacity in battle, because many German soldiers showed little commitment to the Nazi ideology. Instead, sociologists discovered that it was the solidarity and loyalty that soldiers felt toward others in their squad or platoon that motivated their effective combat performance under adverse conditions. They did not want to let their buddies down or feel their buddies' wrath should they not pull their weight. All the research done by sociologists during World War II and since shows the same thing: Group solidarity is one of the most effective factors in keeping soldiers going in combat.

A number of group characteristics can increase a group's cohesiveness: small size, frequent opportunities for group members to interact with one another, being together for a long period of time, similar characteristics among group members, and strong distinctions between those who belong to the group and those who do not (Hechter, 1987). Building on these findings, sociologists have experimented with having teams of soldiers train together and be transferred to new units together as a way of enhancing primary-group ties and group cohesion. In comparison to training and transferring soldiers individually, this approach does produce higher levels of both morale and performance (Moskos, 1970; Segal, Schubert, & Li, 1991). Findings on group cohesion have also been used to support arguments against permitting women to serve in combat. Since more cohesive groups are those whose members are similar to one another, the argument is that combat units with gender differences in them will be less cohesive than those that are all male (or, presumably, all female). To this point, no research exists on this presumed effect of gender, so it is still an open question. However, these examples point to ways in which knowledge about group cohesion is used to design more effective groups.

Group Conformity

Although groups can provide support and security, they can also be controlling and coercive. They can be powerful instruments for getting people to conform to group norms. An early experiment by the social psychologist Muzafer Sherif (1936) documented that in ambiguous situations people tend to conform to the expectations of those around them. When we find it difficult to judge on our own what are proper actions to take, we turn to others to help us make the judgment. And, Sherif found, people denied that the group had influenced their behavior. A particularly nightmarish illustration of such conformity occurred in March 1968 in the Vietnamese village of My Lai. On orders from their superiors, American soldiers shot and killed hundreds of Vietnamese men, women, and children, even though they offered no resistance and may not have been Vietcong soldiers or supporters (Hersch, 1970). Why was there such conformity, with a horrendous outcome, at My Lai? Although any such incident is extremely complicated, we can identify a few factors that contributed to its occurrence.

One element, obviously, that influenced the soldiers' behavior was fear. As one reporter who was in Vietnam put it: "You're scared to death out there. We just wanted to go home" (quoted in Hersch, 1970, p. 48). Fear alone, however, is an insufficient explanation, because some people react to fear with bravery, some by withdrawal, and others by committing inhumane acts. There was another important dimension at My Lai that day: The soldiers were a part of a group in the army with an established authority structure and leadership. Military officers were in command, and their authority over enlisted men was understood and recognized by all. Some of the soldiers probably assumed that officers in positions of authority had good reason for giving the order to shoot. For other soldiers, their reluctance to defy authority was probably more overpowering than the atrocities they were ordered to commit. Few things are more deeply ingrained in a soldier's awareness than the necessity to obey the commands of superior officers. In battle, prompt obedience to orders can save lives, and the punishment for disobedience can be severe. Confronted with the dilemma of either conforming or perhaps being severely disciplined for refusal, some of the soldiers—with little time to think over the issues—chose to conform because it probably seemed to be the less risky path in the long run.

There was yet another factor in operation at My Lai: The ambiguity of clearly defining who the enemy was and where battle lines were drawn. Vietnam was a guerrilla war, and "the enemy"—the Vietcong—was elusive. They wore no uniforms to distinguish them from civilians; they often lived in areas where they fought and thus could melt back into the population after battle; and civilians—young and old, men and women—were often used to carry weapons and supplies and to participate in battles or in terrorist activities. In just such ambiguous situations, Sherif has shown us, there is a strong tendency to conform to the expectations and actions of others around you. For many of the soldiers at My Lai on that day, conformity meant joining in the shooting.

Irving Janis (1982) has found that when groups make decisions, there are pressures to avoid controversy that might cast doubt on the wisdom of the group's decision. This process, which Janis dubbed *groupthink*, *involves pressuring group members to make decisions unanimously, sometimes at the expense of critical thinking and the realistic appraisal of alternatives.* The pressure is especially strong in highly cohesive groups (Schafer & Crichlow, 1996; Street, 1997). Dissenters might be ridiculed or ignored, or group members might withhold their doubts about a decision rather than threaten the camaraderie that accompanies group consensus. Janis even concludes from his research that some historical fiascoes resulted in part from groupthink. He attributes the lack of preparedness at Pearl Harbor in 1941, for example, to the unwillingness of high government officials to challenge the existing consensus that the Japanese would not attack. More recent researchers have suggested that groupthink influenced the decision to launch the space shuttle *Challenger* in 1986, which exploded a minute after launch, killing all seven astronauts on board. After analyzing events leading up to the disaster, researchers concluded that problems with the shuttle might not have been ignored had groupthink not played a part (Moorhead, Ference, & Neck, 1991).

Bureaucratic organization does sometimes have its shortcomings. For example, bureaucracies can be rigid and inflexible, which at times can lead to difficulties and delays in conducting business with them, as these people waiting to conduct business with an organization illustrate.

This discussion has barely touched on the myriad ways in which small groups influence human behavior. This topic is discussed again at numerous points in the remainder of this book. For now, however, we need to recognize that the small groups that we belong to are frequently parts of larger organizations. It is to these organizations that we now direct our attention.

Organizations

> You should be able to compare Weber's analysis of bureaucracies with the human relations approach and explain the functioning of informal structures in organizations.

As pointed out earlier, primary groups play a central role in our lives. Today, however, we spend much of our time in secondary groups such as schools, factories, government offices, or banks. Sociologists refer to these types of secondary groups as formal organizations: *large, special-purpose groups that are explicitly designed to achieve specific goals* (Hall & Tolbert, 2005). Like other groups, formal organizations are characterized by sets of interrelated statuses, roles, and norms, although these features are more complex in organizations than in smaller groups. Formal organizations also involve clearly established rules, regulations, and standards of conduct that are designed to coordinate people's behavior to achieve specific organizational goals. There are many different types of formal organizations (Table 4.1).

There has been considerable debate among sociologists over the central features of formal organizations. This chapter presents two major models of formal organizations—the bureaucratic and the human relations models—and then assesses them using the theoretical perspectives. As it does so, try to evaluate the models from your own experiences in formal organizations—the schools you have attended, the places you have worked, and the religious groups to which you have belonged.

Bureaucracy

The sociologist Max Weber (1925/1947) characterized those formal organizations that dominate modern societies as bureaucracies: *rationally created formal organizations that are based on hierarchical authority and explicit rules of procedure.* Weber recognized that bureaucracies existed in preindustrial societies as well, such as ancient Egypt and China and in the Roman and Byzantine empires. Not until the past few centuries, however, with the emergence of large societies based on complex technologies, have bureaucracies come to permeate people's daily lives. The

Table 4.1

TYPES OF FORMAL ORGANIZATIONS

Type	Membership	Benefits	Examples
Voluntary	People join of their own volition and receive no financial compensation	Members gain some personal gratification from pursuing a hobby or goal	New York Road Runners Association, the United Way, U.S. Olympic Committee
Coercive	People are required to join for either their own benefit or societal good	Society or some groups benefit from the membership of some in these organizations	Schools with compulsory education, prisons, the military when there is a compulsory draft
Utilitarian	People are not forced to join a particular organization but feel compelled to join some organization	People join because it would otherwise be difficult or impossible to achieve personal goals	Organizations from which we make a living
Mutual benefit	Membership could be either voluntary or coercive	Members of the organization are the main recipients of its benefits	Schools, churches, labor unions
Service	Membership could be either voluntary or coercive	Clients of the organization are the main beneficiaries	Stores, social service agencies, community mental health centers, auto repair shops
Common-weal	Membership could be either voluntary or coercive	It provides a service to the general public rather than to specific clients	Environmental Protection Agency, the Rockefeller Foundation

Note: From *Formal Organizations: A Comparative Approach* by Peter M. Blau and W. Richard Scott, 1962 (San Francisco. Chandler); *A Comparative Analysis of Complex Organizations* by Amitai Etzioni, 1975 (Glencoe, IL: Free Press).

reason is simple. Spontaneous, casual, and personal relationships—such as those found in primary groups—are inefficient when it comes to coordinating the activities of many people working toward specific goals. Imagine trying to build a library with no hierarchical authority among the workers or explicit rules of procedure. If no workers felt like mixing cement, the walls could not be built. If the electricians decided to spend the day at the beach, the drywallers could not construct the walls. To cope with these problems, the trend in modern societies has been toward *rationalization*—the replacement of spontaneous, shifting, and ambiguous rules of procedure with explicit rules that are based on the most efficient means to achieve practical goals. This growing rationalization has resulted in the development of bureaucracies.

CHARACTERISTICS OF BUREAUCRACIES   Weber's analysis of bureaucracy was based on an *ideal type,* which is an abstract description based on many observations of actual bureaucracies. An ideal type highlights the essential features of such organizations. Although no single bureaucracy fits this ideal type exactly, Weber identified six characteristics that make bureaucracies distinctive.

First, bureaucracies are characterized by a *division of labor*—each person is responsible for a specific, specialized set of tasks at which that person is to become proficient. In a university, for example, we turn to the campus police rather than the physics department

for traffic control and to the food service rather than the registrar to prepare a luncheon.

Second, bureaucracies also have a *hierarchy of authority* that specifies the chain of command—who must answer to whom (Figure 4.2). This hierarchy is typically pyramidal, with each person responsible to a particular person above and responsible for the activities of particular people below. Without a hierarchy of authority, there would be little centralized control. In most universities, faculty members have authority over students in that they can require the students to write papers and take examinations to pass a course. In turn, the faculty are accountable to the chairpersons of their departments and the deans of their college or school.

Third, people's conduct and job responsibilities in a bureaucracy are governed by *formal rules and procedures* that typically appear in written form. In a university, for example, the university bulletin is a set of rules that specifies what each student must do to earn a degree. One university bulletin, for example, specifies that a sociology major must complete 124 course credits, including 38 credits in sociology course work, in order to receive his or her college degree.

Fourth, *specialized skills and knowledge* are established as criteria for occupying a position in the bureaucracy. In a university, faculty positions require a certain educational background and research experience, usually including a Ph.D. The steam plant engineer, responsible for maintaining the heating system, may have been trained through

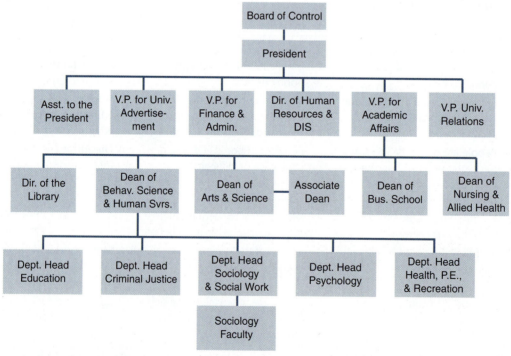

Figure 4.2
Bureaucratic Organization of the Academic Division of a University

experience and promoted from apprentice positions in the university.

Fifth, many positions in the bureaucracy are full-time occupations, with *career ladders and advancement* occurring within the organization. This aspect of bureaucracies enhances their stability over time and the commitment of people to the organization. Advancement is usually determined by merit, seniority, or both. Other criteria, such as friendship or family ties, are generally not considered, at least not openly, because they might result in positions being filled by unqualified people.

Finally, relationships in bureaucracies are ideally characterized by *impartiality and impersonality.* People relate to one another as positions in the bureaucracy rather than as individuals with special needs and qualities, because personal considerations might interfere with efficiency and fairness. College professors assign grades on the basis of students' performance, not on the basis of how friendly, interested, or enthusiastic they appear to be. To do otherwise might result in unqualified people receiving college degrees.

A CRITIQUE OF BUREAUCRATIC ORGANIZATION With these characteristics, bureaucracies clearly have certain advantages, at least with respect to some tasks (Gross & Etzioni, 1985; Handel, 2002). Bureaucracies are orderly and stable, and the people in them know who can do what and when they will do it. They are also speedy and efficient organizations for accomplishing certain kinds of things, especially well-structured and straightforward tasks that involve a uniform sequence of events. Automobile or breakfast cereal factories, for example, benefit from bureaucratic organization, as do military organizations and prisons. College students, however, who are no strangers to bureaucracy because virtually all institutions of higher education today are bureaucratic, may disagree that bureaucracies are speedy and efficient. You are undoubtedly familiar with the laments—sometimes cynical, sometimes resigned—that are directed at bureaucracies: "You can't beat the system," "We're drowning in red tape," or "It's the old (name your institution here) shuffle." These comments point to the fact that, despite their advantages, bureaucracies have shortcomings.

One of the major shortcomings of bureaucracies is that their strong emphasis on following established rules and regulations can lead to rigidity and inflexibility. The rules become ends in themselves rather than means of achieving organizational goals. Early in the twentieth century, Thorsten B. Veblen (1912) coined the term *trained incapacity* to refer to a situation in which people have been trained so completely to follow the rules that they are unable to act independently or innovatively. They develop bureaucratic "tunnel vision." Such behavior arises when participants forget the overall goal of the organization and become totally preoccupied with the means of obtaining that goal.

The normal operation of bureaucracies, then, can have the effect of stifling creativity. Bureaucratic rules and regulations are designed to apply to standard situations; they become inefficient and sometimes useless when applied to the novel or unusual. Bureaucracies tend to reward obedience to rules rather than the creation of new ways to achieve goals. The sociologist Robert Merton (1968) has even argued that a *bureaucratic personality* develops, which emphasizes conformity, rigidity, and timidity. Along similar lines, C. Wright Mills (1959, p. 171) feared "the ascendency of the cheerful robot"—the person who willingly accepts and obeys authority in bureaucratic settings rather than questioning, challenging, and innovating.

Another shortcoming of bureaucratic organization is widely known as the Peter Principle. It can be stated succinctly: In a hierarchy, employees tend to rise to their level of incompetence (Peter & Hull, 1969). To illustrate, a person may be hired or promoted into a position for which she is competent, let's say as an ad designer in a marketing division of a corporation. Good performance at that level may lead to further promotions. At some point, says the Peter Principle, there is a good chance that the person will be promoted to a position for which she is not competent. Suppose she is promoted to a management position but her strengths are not in managing people but in designing creative advertising. Once she is in this new position, mechanisms operate to retain her there: Those who promoted her do not want to admit a mistake, and she may work to protect her position, concealing her incompetence by relying on competent secretaries and subordinates in the bureaucracy. She has risen to her level of incompetence.

One critic pointed to a final shortcoming of bureaucracies by arguing that bureaucrats are like crabgrass in that both proliferate rapidly and resist efforts to cut back their number (Joyner, 1978). That critic might have been thinking of Parkinson's Law, which states that work in a bureaucracy tends to occupy the number of workers assigned to it and fill the time available for its completion, regardless of the actual amount of work involved (Parkinson, 1962). Bureaucrats must *appear* to be busy or they may be considered expendable. If a task can be finished in less than the time available for it, they may actually create work to fill the remaining time. Eventually, they come to regard this "make-work" as very important, and they feel burdened under the load. Thus, according to Parkinson, bureaucracies tend to grow even when the work they do does not. Parkinson's Law may be behind the tendency of governments at every level to expand.

Although this list of the shortcomings of bureaucracies may paint a rather grim picture of incompetence and inertia, reality in most organizations is not quite that bleak. Most bureaucracies perform reasonably well, and most bureaucrats are conscientious and reasonably competent. Nevertheless, bureaucratic organizations do have the tendencies described here, and efforts must be made to structure them in ways that reduce the negative impacts.

The Human Relations Approach

Anyone who has experienced bureaucratic life can recognize that Weber's characterization of bureaucracies ignores several important considerations. In particular, Weber's view says little about *people* and their hopes and needs. To incorporate these elements into the operation of organizations, the human relations model of organizations has emerged. The *human relations approach* is based on the assumption that the social, psychological, and physical needs of people who work in organizations must be considered if the organizations are to be productive and efficient (Hall & Tolbert, 2005). The human relations model rose to

prominence in the 1920s and 1930s following investigations in a number of industrial settings. Elton Mayo (1933), for example, was called in to a textile mill near Philadelphia to find reasons for an astonishingly high turnover rate of 250 percent a year among employees. Various incentive schemes had failed to resolve this problem, and Mayo experimented with a number of changes. He gave the workers a rest period, let workers on each group of machines decide when they would stop, and made a nurse available to them for injuries. Following these changes, a sense of group cohesion and unity emerged, and productivity increased while turnovers declined. In part to extend Mayo's work, a series of investigations was conducted between 1927 and 1932 in the Hawthorne plant of the Western Electric Company near Chicago, where telephone equipment was assembled (Roethlisberger & Dickson, 1939). Various improvements were made in the work conditions, such as the provision of rest breaks and a shorter workday. As a consequence, the productivity of the workers improved. Today we recognize that the link between these environmental factors and work performance is complicated, but these early investigations laid the

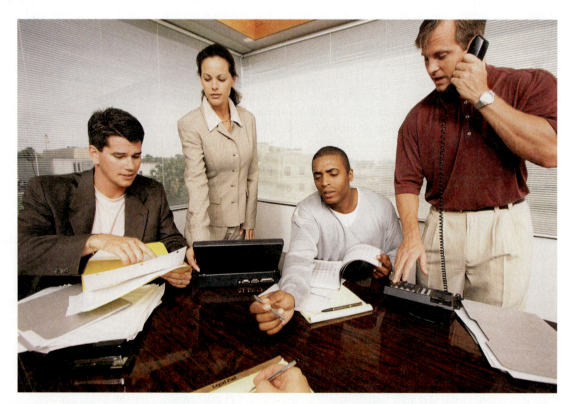

In an ideal bureaucracy, people would be treated on the basis of the skills and expertise they bring to the organization. However, characteristics such as gender can lead people to be treated differently, especially when relatively few people in the organization possess that characteristic.

foundation for the human relations approach to formal organizations.

Proponents of the human relations approach argue that the feelings, desires, and aspirations of workers must be satisfied, at least to a degree, if organizations are to be efficient (Argyris, 1964; Likert, 1967). The desire for companionship or creativity, for example, cannot be "turned off" once employees cross the factory gate or the office door. Rather, these personal elements—an anathema to Weber's bureaucratic model—should be considered in the structure of a formal organization. For example, satisfying social contacts in the work environment could be provided by organizing the work flow and rest breaks so that people have opportunities for relaxed conversation with other workers. Alternatively, work groups can be made smaller so that primary-group relations and cohesiveness are more likely to develop.

Proponents of the human relations approach to organizations argue against a rigid hierarchy or authority structure. Within the framework of this approach, supervision should be supportive and personal rather than dictatorial or exploitive. In addition, workers should play a role in the decision-making process whenever possible, and supervisors should be accountable to the people under them. Although supervisors have greater authority than their subordinates, the former should be attentive to the latter's concerns or complaints, especially if identifiable grounds exist for the dissatisfaction. In fact, the relationship between supervisors and their subordinates can be viewed as having many of the qualities of a primary group. The bond between supervisor and worker should not be solely utilitarian—it should be a broader tie that involves many more personal elements.

The major elements of the bureaucratic and human relations models are presented in Figure 4.3. The human relations approach does not reject every element of Weber's bureaucratic model. Clearly, a division of labor, a hierarchy of authority, rules and procedures, and special qualifications to hold positions are necessary. The impersonality of Weber's approach is explicitly rejected, however, and adherence to rules is viewed flexibly rather than rigidly. In addition, whereas Weber conceived of authority flowing down the hierarchy, the human relations model offers employees some input into the decisions made by those above them. This approach seems most suitable for organizations in which extreme discipline is not necessary, tasks are not rigidly uniform, or employee motivation or morale is important. Thus a university, a hospital, or an advertising firm might benefit from this type of organization (Hall & Tolbert, 2005; Scott, 2003).

The Informal Structure

All organizations develop some type of informal structure. This structure involves personal relationships guided by norms and rituals that emerge separately from the formal rules and regulations of the organization. Informal structures perform a number of functions. First, they provide people with personal ties

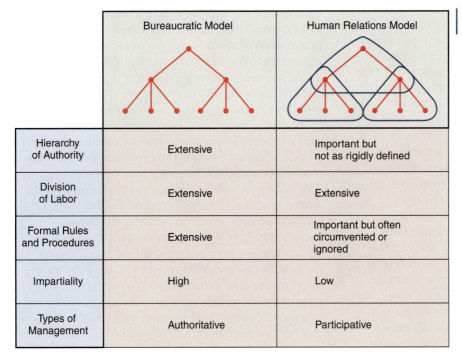

Figure 4.3
Approaches to Formal Organizations

	Bureaucratic Model	Human Relations Model
Hierarchy of Authority	Extensive	Important but not as rigidly defined
Division of Labor	Extensive	Extensive
Formal Rules and Procedures	Extensive	Important but often circumvented or ignored
Impartiality	High	Low
Types of Management	Authoritative	Participative

that the formal structure lacks. We all enjoy being with people who like and respect us, whether at work or at play, and organizational rules severely restricting or eliminating such ties are likely to be ineffective. Even in organizations modeled on the human relations approach, concern about the personal needs of the organization's members is to a degree utilitarian: The purpose is to increase productivity. People seek primary relationships, as has been noted, because such relationships are pleasurable and help reduce stress. So people in organizations become friends, fall in love, and develop close ties with one another—all largely independently of organizational dictates.

The informal structure does more, however, than simply provide for personal relationships. It also helps people protect themselves against what they perceive as unreasonable or dangerous demands of the organization. The workers at the Hawthorne plant mentioned earlier, for example, informally regulated the speed at which they worked so that they did not have to work too fast. Sarcasm and ridicule were used to control those who were inclined to work harder. They were castigated as *rate busters* and singled out for a *binging,* being hit on the arm. These actions, although mild, expressed the displeasure of the group and encouraged conformity to informal group norms.

In addition, the informal structure permits adaptations to situations or demands that are not provided for in the formal structure. In some cases, adaptation may involve violating official rules to help achieve organizational goals. During the Korean War, for example, the sociologist Roger Little (1970) lived with an army rifle company in Korea and observed an informal practice called *scrounging,* which involved collecting all the supplies abandoned by other companies upon leaving an area. Officially, discarded supplies must be turned in to a central supply depot, but the supply sergeants usually kept the equipment as a barter bank. If their company developed a supply shortage because of carelessness or a slowdown in official supply channels, items in the barter bank could be traded for the scarce supplies. Although officially illegal, scrounging was tolerated and sometimes encouraged by company commanders because it was an efficient way to keep their units fully supplied. In fact, supply sergeants who were highly skilled at scrounging were in great demand among the units.

Finally, the informal structure in organizations makes it possible to adjust to individual variations in skills, resources, and characteristics. We are not, after all, mindless, emotionless automatons, waiting to do the bureaucracy's bidding. Some people are faster than others, some more intelligent, some more outgoing. Although bureaucratic rules may consider all people in a given position to be the same, people take these differences into account informally.

Gender in Organizations

Gender is one difference that often shapes how people are treated by the informal structure of organizations. Sociologist Rosabeth Moss Kanter (1993) found this in one large corporation that she has studied at length. One characteristic of organizations that she found to be important is *relative numbers,* or the ratio of people with a particular characteristic in an organization to those who do not have that characteristic. In the case of gender, men substantially outnumber women in the upper-management ranks. Or to put it more colloquially, women in management are often "tokens." Kanter found that this characteristic of corporations substantially influenced the opportunities for women and their behavior. For one thing, it made these women highly visible; they became symbols for "what women can accomplish." As a result, they felt tremendous pressures to work harder, to avoid making mistakes, and to perform better than the men. They also sometimes felt lonely because they were different from other members of the work group; when a group has token status, it is easy for the majority group to exaggerate the differences between tokens and the others, and this may lead to feelings of isolation and exclusion on the part of the token.

Of course, the visibility of token women in corporations has positive benefits for some; for example, it can lead to getting more attention and this can sometimes enhance possibilities for advancement in the corporation. However, Kanter's point is to show how a person's position in the structure of an organization—in this case, a group's relative numbers—shapes opportunities and behavior. Presumably, any tokens in an organization, such as men in a largely female corporation, would have similar experiences. Kanter argued that women's experiences in corporations would change when their numbers grew and they were no longer tokens. However, as Chapter 8 shows, that may not be happening. As the number of women in corporations grows, it appears that male managers feel their positions threatened and sometimes respond by discrimination in wages or promotions—women get paid less and are less likely to be promoted to the top ranks (DeLaat, 2007; Glass Ceiling Commission, 1995). There is often a "glass ceiling" beyond which women find it difficult to be promoted. So, even though corporations may claim that gender is irrelevant to how they operate, Kanter's and others' research on the informal structure of organizations documents that gender is very influential in terms of opportunities and behavior.

Applied sociologists have played an important part in understanding how organizations work and designing them to operate more effectively and with fewer negative consequences. Applying Sociology: Diagnosing Organizational Culture describes some of this work.

Applying Sociology   Diagnosing Organizational Culture: Helping Organizations to Function Better

The concept of *culture* is introduced in Chapter 2 as a characteristic of a society or a whole group of people. Organizations and bureaucracies can also possess a culture. Organizational culture refers to *the ideas, values, knowledge, behaviors, and material objects that are shared by members of a particular organization* (Schein, 1992). Like other cultures, organizational cultures are shared; they are passed on from one generation in the organization to the next; they contain beliefs, values, norms, and languages; and they are powerful influences on peoples' behavior, often in ways that people are not aware of. One of the ways that applied sociologists assist organizations is by providing organizational diagnoses: *using the theories, methods, and research findings from sociology and other social sciences to assess the cultures of particular organizations and how those cultures affect organizational operation* (Harrison, 1991). When organizations believe they have problems with people, groups, or interpersonal relationships, they turn to sociologists and organizational diagnoses as a way of understanding and solving these problems. These problems, after all, can make an organization less competitive or less effective at achieving its goals. Let's look at some examples.

As we have seen in this chapter, groupthink is a problem organizations can face. An organization's culture might promote ways of making decisions that encourage groupthink rather than a more careful and critical assessment of all alternatives. In conducting an organizational diagnosis related to groupthink, sociologists rely on past research that shows what social conditions are conducive to groupthink and how groups can be changed to reduce it. They may also collect data on how the organization operates, possibly through direct observation or with surveys. Armed with this information, the sociologist recommends changes that would reduce the likelihood of groupthink. Depending on the particular organization, the following might be included among the recommendations:

1. Organizational managers should encourage the open airing of doubts and objections to any decision.
2. Outsiders should participate in the decision-making process to challenge the positions of group members.
3. Several independent groups should be set up to study the issues.
4. Other groups should be brought into the decision-making process to avoid being isolated from competing viewpoints.
5. Conflict should be built into the decision-making process. This can be done either by assigning each

group member to be a devil's advocate and criticize the group decision or by structuring the decision making into a debate where both sides of the issue are fully aired.

These sociological recommendations focus on the group process by which a decision is made rather than on telling the business which decision to make.

Organizational culture can also influence the opportunities and treatment of women in organizations. When women, for example, are treated in a particular way by an organization over a long period of time, that mode of treatment can become normative, or seen as the only appropriate way of treating women. In other words, it becomes a part of the organizational culture (DeLaat, 2007). People follow these patterned ways of doing things without questioning them. It may be, for example, that women have never been placed into certain positions, so the organizational culture defines these positions as "men's" positions, although this may not be explicitly stated. Or it may be that a request for child-care leave or part-time work is seen as disloyalty or a lack of strong commitment to the organization. The hidden assumption, or norm, in such an organizational culture is that loyalty and commitment can be demonstrated only by full-time commitment and always choosing organizational involvement over family involvement. As we saw in Chapter 2, elements of culture, such as these assumptions, are often implicit and unstated. In doing an organizational diagnosis, applied sociologists try to make those cultural elements explicit so that their impact can be evaluated and alternatives considered.

Cultures are meaning systems that provide social definitions of reality. When the meaning systems in organizational cultures encourage definitions of reality that are male-centered, these can create difficulties for women working in the organizations. For example, considerable research shows that women are more inclined than men to share their problems with others (Tannen, 1994b). Women do so, in part, as a way of seeking empathy and support but also as a way of establishing connections and developing intimacy with others. However, in an organizational culture where the meaning system is male-oriented, such sharing of problems might be misinterpreted to mean that women have more problems than men or that they are incapable of solving problems on their own. Men who keep their problems to themselves may appear to be more competent. Once again, an organizational diagnosis would try to discover these implicit meanings so that their consequences can be considered.

Sociological Perspectives on Organizations

You should be able to compare and contrast the functionalist, conflict, and interactionist perspectives on formal organizations.

The sociological approaches to the study of formal organizations just presented are either explicitly or implicitly functionalist in orientation. To round out an understanding of organizations, it is useful to make this functionalist emphasis explicit and then contrast it with the conflict and interactionist approaches to organizations.

The Functionalist Perspective

Functionalists view organizations as systems of interrelated parts that are organized to achieve goals in a way that enhances efficiency and productivity (Parsons, 1956; Scott, 2003). An elaborate division of labor, for example, is viewed as beneficial because each worker becomes highly proficient at a small task that can be learned quickly. Efficiency is enhanced as the work process is broken into units that can be rapidly accomplished by individual workers. Consensus regarding the overall goal of the organization, whether it involves assembling a product or providing a service, is assumed to be widespread. The nature of the tasks necessary to accomplish goals is important in determining whether the organization takes a bureaucratic or human relations form. Some organizations combine elements of more than one of these models, having some divisions organized according to one model and some based on the other. A pharmaceutical company might organize its production and distribution divisions on the basis of bureaucratic organization and its marketing departments on the basis of the human relations approach. The different tasks of each division dictate the structure most suited to it.

Conflict is recognized as an element of organizational life, arising as individuals adapt to organizational demands or as the organization responds to internal or external events. Functionalists, however, view this conflict as either an unwanted organizational element that needs to be kept within reasonable limits or as a catalyst for organizational changes that will result in greater efficiency and productivity.

The functionalist perspective also views organizations as one of many parts of larger social and cultural systems. As in all systems, these parts must be reasonably well integrated, and this connectedness means that the workings of one part of the system may be affected by elements of other parts of the broader social and cultural system. Other Worlds, Other Ways: China illustrates this fact by showing how cultural values can affect how well people in organizations work and thus how well organizations achieve their goals.

The Conflict Perspective

Despite the overwhelming functionalist bent of sociologists studying organizations, there have been efforts to assess organizations and bureaucracies from the conflict perspective (Heydebrand, 1977; Scott, 2003; Zey-Ferrell, 1981). From this perspective, organizations are viewed as mechanisms of social control within the context of a struggle between interest groups. Power relations and a class struggle exist *before* an organization develops, and organizational properties reflect those underlying power and class relations. The goals of the organization, the technology used, the division of labor—all reflect the interests of dominant groups and support their interests, giving them an advantage over subordinate groups. The division of labor, for example, places the worker at a substantial disadvantage in relationship to the owners. When the work process is broken down into simple units, individual workers become expendable because others can quickly learn their jobs, which involve few skills. This procedure is highly coercive because workers who can be replaced easily are likely to make few demands on management. This is not to say that these organizations are not also efficient and productive. It has been shown, however, that bureaucracies have weaknesses that reduce their efficiency but that these inefficiencies are insufficient motivation for organizational change. Inefficiencies are tolerated because bureaucratic organization still coerces and controls subordinates effectively, and these coercive purposes are as important in determining organizational structure as the productivity that the structure offers.

Although the human relations model diverges in many ways from the bureaucratic model, organizations of this sort are nonetheless mechanisms of domination. From the conflict perspective, the human relations approach simply offers management new ways of controlling through subtle manipulation (Carey, 1967; Rice, 1982). It points to ways of inducing workers to increase their productivity voluntarily, irrespective of increases in economic return to workers. In other words, subtle manipulation of a worker's environment replaces direct coercion through a hierarchy of authority, but the goal is still the same: to further the interests of management by getting more productivity from workers.

In the 1980s and 1990s, many corporations in the United States tried to introduce elements of the human relations model into work settings (Waldman, 1987). They hired consultants to run programs to provide attitudinal training and changes in values among their employees. The idea was to change the corporate culture from a highly bureaucratic one to one that emphasized partnership between management and employee, cooperation, teamwork, and company

Other Worlds, Other Ways

CHINA: CULTURAL VALUES AND GROUP BEHAVIOR— SOCIAL LOAFING IN ORGANIZATIONS

The value system of China has traditionally emphasized a collectivist orientation, which still persists today (Hofstede, 1980; Li, 1978). Collectivism is a set of values that places more emphasis on the group and group goals than on the individual. It discourages individual achievement and the advancement of self-interest, especially when these come in conflict with group needs. Chinese society focuses on collective action and social interests rather than personal goals. Although the coming of communism to China in 1949 may have given additional emphasis to this value orientation, collectivism predates the Communist Revolution and finds expression in Confucian beliefs about uprightness, duty, and obligation that go back thousands of years. It leads people to act on the basis of what best serves their in-group and to condemn those who pursue their own personal interests. In a collectivist environment, a major force is cooperation rather than competition.

This collectivist orientation in China is quite at odds with the individualistic, competitive values of the United States, where people emphasize self-sufficiency, control, and pursuit of personal goals that may clash with group goals. With these widely varying cultural orientations, it should not be surprising that people in China and the United States respond quite differently to some of the group and organizational processes discussed in this chapter. One impact these values have is on how well people work in groups— whether they work hard to achieve the goals of the group or take it easy and let others do the work. The term *social loafing* refers to the tendency for people in groups to put out less effort to achieve goals than when working alone (Comer, 1995; Latane, Williams, & Harkins, 1979). When in a group, the social-loafing attitude is: "I can coast and others will take up the slack and do the work."

Social loafing is more likely to occur in large groups, in groups that are low in group cohesion, and in situations where people are not held accountable for their individual

tasks (Comer, 1995; Karau & Hart, 1998). In addition, cultural orientation affects social loafing. A study was done of the work of managerial trainees in a variety of manufacturing and service organizations in Guangzhou, China, and in the United States (Earley, 1989). Social loafing was found among the workers in the United States but not among the Chinese workers. In the United States, workers put out more effort when working alone toward a goal than when working in a group. In China, it was the reverse. The collective ethic in China leads workers to place group goals ahead of their own personal interests. They value the group goals and are at least as willing to work toward the group goals as toward their own personal goals. They seem to gain satisfaction from group accomplishments. In addition, Chinese workers expect other workers to make contributions rather than to loaf, and they are willing to work without worrying that others will take advantage of them by loafing. By contrast, workers in the United States place more value on individual accomplishments and rewards. When placed in a group, they loaf when someone else will take up the slack and work to achieve the group goals. And workers in the United States, unlike those in China, assume that other workers will loaf, and thus they will be taken advantage of if they do not loaf.

The collective orientation in Chinese culture has other implications for group processes. There is evidence, for example, that Chinese internalize stronger conformist values than do people in the United States and that they are socialized to place greater value on unity and cooperation in groups and to avoid anger and hostility toward group members. The Chinese also seem to place more value on strong leadership in groups and to see that leadership as legitimate and essential to group accomplishments (Hofstede, 1980; Wilson, 1977).

These cultural differences have important implications for the policies of organizations and agencies. For example, work groups that depend on cooperation and that do not provide rewards for individual accomplishments may enhance performance in collectivist cultures such as China and Japan. The same programs, however, may reduce productivity because of social loafing if implemented unchanged in the United States. The way people respond to the same group structures, such as leadership, and the same group processes, such as work groups, depends on the cultural orientation of the people involved. ■

---

loyalty. This *transformation work* presumably represented a new ideology of management. However, Harley Shaiken, a professor of work and technology, is skeptical that anything substantially new has developed: "Unfortunately, most of the so-called transformation work today is really just a substitute for giving workers real autonomy and responsibility"

(quoted in Waldman, 1987, p. 1). At one insurance company, a training program was followed by a 20 percent increase in work quotas, and employees who objected were fired. From the conflict perspective, the goal of most of these programs is simple: to increase corporate productivity by changing worker apathy into complaisance or corporate loyalty.

The Interactionist Perspective

Interactionists tend to shift the focus from formal structure and hierarchy in organizations to informal structure (Day & Day, 1977; Fine, 1984; Strauss, Fagerhaugh, Suczek, & Wiener, 1985). From this perspective, formal organizations are not rigid, static structures emphasizing only rationality and efficiency. Rather, they constitute a *negotiated order,* which is created out of the formal structure through the social interaction prescribed by the informal structure. The formal structure is important, but it comes to life only as people interact with one another. People with varying amounts of power and resources and with various characteristics "negotiate" with one another regarding what is acceptable and appropriate organizational behavior. Models of formal organizations would include this informal structure because it is an essential element in understanding how effectively an organization achieves its goals.

The Future of Bureaucracy

You should be able to explain the potential dangers of the bureaucratic tendency toward oligarchy and discuss possible future trends in bureaucracy.

Bureaucracy and Oligarchy

What lies in store for the future? It seems reasonable to assume that large bureaucratic organizations are here to stay and will continue to flood our lives with secondary relationships. Industrial societies are sufficiently large and technologically complex that such organizations appear to be inevitable. Need we be concerned about this trend? There appear to be some potential dangers associated with bureaucracies that are especially chilling in democratic societies. In 1915, Robert Michels pointed out that bureaucracies display a tendency toward oligarchy: *Power tends to become concentrated in the hands of a few people at the top of organizations.* Michels referred to this tendency as the *iron law of oligarchy.* As Michels put it: "Who says organization, says oligarchy" (Michels, 1915/1966, p. 256). As such organizations become more powerful, people are in danger of losing more and more control over events in their daily lives, of finding themselves powerless and dominated by a few individuals they do not even know.

For Michels, the iron law of oligarchy derives from three elements of organizations. First, to operate effectively, any large organization must develop mechanisms for coping with administrative and decision-making problems, and it is more efficient if only a few people are responsible for this function. Spreading authority over a large number of people can cause uncertainties about who is empowered to do what and conflicts over incompatible decisions. Second, those who emerge as leaders in organizations tend to be adept at influencing and controlling members, and they can use the resources of the organization to maintain their position. They can, for example, place loyal followers into strategic positions in organizational administration. Finally, in many organizations, most rank-and-file members do not have the time, energy, resources, or desire to contest the power of the leadership.

In many ways, Michels's argument is persuasive. We can plainly see that, in many large U.S. organizations, such as Wal-Mart or IBM, control and decision making are concentrated among a few people at the top. In addition, political decisions are concentrated in the hands of a relatively few powerful politicians at the state and national levels. Because democracy presumably rests on the consent of the governed, and because individual freedom and autonomy are basic values in the United States, oligarchical organizations and governments pose a potential threat. Yet, the conflict perspective informs us that there are social mechanisms that can counter the tendency toward oligarchy. Namely, people can form interest groups and join organizations that can serve as countervailing forces to the leaders of political or organizational hierarchies. Such civic engagement involves average citizens being active in groups that connect people with the social and political life of their communities and that help shape the economic, political, and legal structures of those communities. This has been done effectively by the civil rights movement a few decades ago and by the environmental movement today. Both groups have been able to change the direction of some of the policies of oligarchical organizations in dramatic ways.

Finally, bureaucratic organizations can be designed to reduce oligarchical tendencies. Power and control can be dispersed among a number of semiautonomous groups to keep one from gaining total dominance over the others (Olsen, 1978). This *balancing of power* can be seen in the structure of many colleges and universities. Although the administration has a great deal of decision-making authority, this power is balanced by a board of trustees or board of control (which is typically composed of community members) and faculty groups (such as an academic senate) that maintain some control over curriculum-related decisions.

Predictably, there is no ultimate solution to the problem of oligarchy. Bureaucracies present a formidable test of democratic principles, most of which were formed in an era of small communities and town hall meetings, long before the appearance of the huge organizations so common today. At the same time, as Michels pointed out, bureaucracies are beneficial in structuring an enormous social organization, and modern societies would be hard-pressed to maintain their current lifestyle without them. The challenge, then, is to ensure that the balance of power does not slip too far toward oligarchy. In this quest, sociological knowledge of groups and organizations can be extremely helpful in seeking and achieving the proper balance. These issues are explored in more depth in Chapter 13.

Limits to Bureaucracy

Although large organizational and bureaucratic structures are likely to be central features of modern life in the future, are there limits to how far their reach will extend? Are there trends in the opposite direction? Answers to these questions are both controversial and speculative, but some thoughts can be offered (Bartos, 1996). First of all, the U.S. economy is shifting from an industrial economy based on the production of goods to an economy that emphasizes service, information, and consumption. (See Chapter 2 and Chapter 15.) Along with this change has come a shift from manual labor jobs that require little more than muscle power to more professional occupations that require intellectual skills and high levels of education. Such occupations, including those of doctors, teachers, scientists, lawyers, and social workers, are less likely to involve complete dependence on highly bureaucratic organization. These professionals do at least some of their work in what are called *professional organizations* or *postentrepreneurial organizations,* which are smaller, are less hierarchical, and have fewer rules and procedures (Handel, 2002; Kanter, 1989). Professionals have more autonomy in when, where, and how they do their work and are more likely to treat coworkers as equals. In professional organizations, supervisors are more likely to serve as

coordinators who make materials and resources available for other professionals to do their work. Organizations in a service economy are still bureaucratic to a degree, but the nature of the work being done by some of them benefits from a more professional, less hierarchical emphasis. That is not true of all of them, however. Even in the service and educational industries, workers who are doing manual labor still tend to be in highly bureaucratic environments. So, the shift to a service and information economy may produce changes in some employees' lives, but those whose jobs involve well-structured and repetitive tasks that can be rationalized will likely continue to work in highly bureaucratic settings.

Another development that may have implications for bureaucratization and centralization is the revolution in computer technology and communications. The growing availability of personal computers, fiber-optic cable, instantaneous data transmission, and communications satellites points to the possibility of decentralizing the workplace and removing people from some of the bureaucratic structures. In 1980, the futurist Alvin Toffler coined the phrase *electronic cottage* to describe the workplace that such technologies would make possible (Toffler, 1980). People could work in their homes, linked to other people and work settings through fiber-optic cables and radio signals. Professors' lectures could be projected to many distant settings, and secretaries could work at home and send their products instantaneously around the globe as e-mail attachments. Today, business executives in many locations hold meetings through televised conference calls. Toffler believed that technology would enable many more people to become self-employed and allow others to work much more independently of bureaucratic organizations.

With modern technologies of communication, a significant amount of social life and social interaction now occurs on line. Sociologists are still exploring whether social interaction online is the equivalent of face-to-face interaction and whether social life online can attain the status of a full-fledged community.

Sociology of Media and Technology

Community and Group Life in the CyberWorld

The modern technologies of media and communication have pervasive and profound impacts on community and group life, and sociologists have grappled with identifying how group life and social interaction will be different in a world where a good part of life transpires online. People today do spend an increasing amount of time online and often interact with groups and organizations online rather than face-to-face (see Figure 4.4). We bank online, take college courses online, trade stocks and bonds online, and search for a job online. A standard part of sociologists' definition of a community is that people share a common territory where they interact for a period of time and where tradition and custom develop and prevail (see Chapters 2 and 14). Furthermore, community involves interactions that are, at least in part, personal, intimate, and nonspecialized (Driskell & Lyon, 2002). Many of the online transactions that people engage in would be classified as involving secondary groups. Banking and trading stocks, for example, are task-oriented, impersonal, and specialized, and they seem sociologically equivalent to such transactions occurring in a face-to-face format.

Yet, full-fledged community is more than this: It also involves what we would call primary group ties. The sociological concept of a primary group implies that people share a social place where they have common goals, interests, and statuses and interact with one another. For most of the human experience, this social space has involved a territorial component: Some of people's interactions with one another played out over time in a common physical location. Can electronic space provide the same experience that geographical space did in the past? For example, social network sites, such as Facebook, presumably offer the opportunity to establish and maintain friendships, which are normally considered primary groups by sociologists. But are such online encounters truly personal, intimate, and nonspecialized, which is what constitute primary groups? Or are they necessarily more limited and less intimate because the interaction is mediated through a medium that inherently limits access to the other person. Online, people's interactions are often specialized and narrowly focused, revolving around particular hobbies, personal interests, or job-related needs on various blogs, lists, or chat rooms (Spears, Postmes, Lea, & Wolbert, 2002;

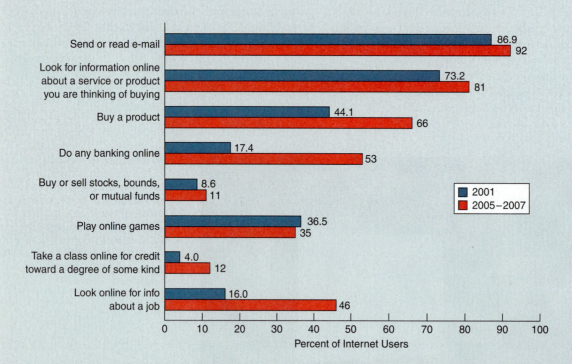

Figure 4.4
Change in online activities, 2001–2007

[a] For 2001, the percent is based on people age 15 and over; for 2005-2007, the percent is based on people age 18 and over.
Note: 2001 data from U. S. Department of Commerce, National Telecommunications and Information Administration, *A National Online: Entering the Broadband Age* (Washington, DC: U. S. Government Printing Office, 2004) p. 8; 2005–2007 data from Pew Internet & American Life Project, *Internet Activities*, accessed March 3, 2008, www.pewinternet.org/trends.asp

Wellman, 2001). In addition, interaction on the Internet involves less "social presence" than does face-to-face social interaction: Many of the social cues that guide our interactions with others, such as facial expressions, vocal intonations, or body postures, are missing or less prominent. There is research suggesting that this can lead people to feel more anonymous and to be less sensitive to assessments of them by others (Amichai-Hamburger, 2005). When communicating online, it can be easier to disagree with others, to make negative or even aggressive comments about others, and to take more extreme positions on issues. All of this means that online communication, because of the nature of the medium, can take on a more aggressive or confrontational, even destructive, character. This is true even when audio and video is uploaded to the Internet since people can control (and even shut off) these inputs in ways that are more difficult or impossible to do when people are physically present. As a result, it may be more difficult for people to develop full primary relationships until they have a face-to-face meeting (which, of course, does sometimes follow the development of a relationship online).

This is not to say, of course, that people don't engage in social interaction in the cyberworld. They clearly do. The debate is about the nature of the social interaction. Many of the interactions online are equivalent to secondary groups. But these interactions may rarely, if ever, be equivalent to the face-to-face interactions people engage in when they share a geographic social space. They may never achieve the true qualities of primary groups because they remain less intimate, less personal, and less encompassing. They may provide weak primary group ties (possibly the equivalent of the hockey team or the sociology class in Figure 4.1).

To look at this issue from another angle, modern technologies may have negative consequences for community by encouraging people to withdraw from some groups and organizations into more private realms. For example, as television availability has grown over the past fifty years (see Figure 3.3, p. 76), research has shown

that the amounts of time people spend visiting neighbors and engaging in informal socializing has declined significantly (Putnam, 2000). In addition, memberships in clubs and voluntary organizations, such as the PTA, the League of Women Voters, or a labor union, have dropped by one-half, and leisure time has become primarily private. Today, one need not go outside or be with others in order to be entertained. Involvement in the cyberworld may also have negative consequences for community: Recent research shows that Internet use reduces the amount of contact that people have with family members, friends, and fellow workers (Nie et al., 2004). Such privatization of social life, whether because of television or the Internet, comes at the expense of nearly every other type of group activity outside the home.

One disturbing element of this trend is that it is through "joining"—coming together with others in various groups and organizations—that people can resist the dominance of bureaucracies and oligarchies. When people withdraw from civic life, formal organizations and bureaucracies may become even more powerful and controlling. Yet, because the Web is so accessible and interactive, some commentators see it as an empowering technology, possibly overcoming the privatizing and oligarchical tendencies of technology (Mukerji & Simon, 1998). Individuals can come into contact with a wide array of groups and organizations, or they can use the technology to form new organizations and attract and communicate directly with a large audience of people with similar interests. If such things occur, then the technology of the Internet may erode the bureaucratic monopoly of communications that previously existed. In the past, most people depended on television, newspapers, and magazines for information about events and opinions, and those same people had limited opportunities to communicate their opinions and positions with others. Computer-mediated communications technology means that thousands of sources of information and opinion are instantaneously available, and each recipient of messages can also create and send messages to those thousands of people.

Some of Toffler's projections have come true, with over 20 million people working at home in the United States (U.S. Bureau of the Census, 2007, p. 383). Electronic technology has been a boon, especially for people who can do their work alone (for example, writers or other creative people) and for those who are independently employed and do not need a large office in which to meet and work with clients. Of those who work at home, 30 percent are self-employed. One-half are people who take work home from the office after hours, while 17 percent are *telecommuters*, employees

whose bosses allow them to work at home instead of the office for at least part of the week. The occupations where people are most likely to work at home are in managerial, professional, construction, and sales fields. Most of those who work at home use computers, the Internet, and e-mail as a part of their work.

These numbers, along with other research, tell us a couple of things about Toffler's vision of the impact of computer and telecommunications technology on work (Volti, 2006; Wellman et al., 1996). First, although many people do work at home, a good number of them

Sociology on the Internet

Begin by going to the Dead Sociologists Index described in Chapter 3. Review what Max Weber had to say about bureaucracy. What do you learn here that was not covered in the text discussion of bureaucracy?

The textbook discusses a number of different types of formal organizations, such as coercive and commonweal (see Table 4.1). You can search online to find examples of these types of organizations and learn about their structure and membership. Describe these organizations in terms of what goals they pursue, how they get their members, and how large and bureaucratic they are. You can also search for some of the other concepts discussed in this chapter, such as primary group or groupthink. Also look for

research on how social interaction and personal identities are different in the cyber world (see, for example, www.rider.edu/users/suler/psycyber/psycyber.html).

Another useful search is for "community networks" which are based in part on computer-mediated communications technologies. One of these is the Blacksburg (Virginia) Electronic Village (**www.bev.net**). These communities use modern communications technologies to link their citizens together. Describe these community networks and discuss ways in which they might empower citizens and serve as a counterforce to the oligarchical power of bureaucracies and large formal organizations.

are still part of a bureaucratic organization. Although physically separated from others in the bureaucracy, these home workers must still interact with office people and are constrained by the rules of the bureaucracy. Second, the people who benefit most from this trend are professionals and creative people because their tasks can best be done in nonbureaucratic settings. These workers are least likely to be in highly bureaucratic settings anyway. Third, some home workers gain little advantage, other than convenience, from working at home: They still do low-paying, boring, repetitive work for large corporations. Some such workers, for example, input information from insurance policies and claims reports into computer files for insurance companies. Many such workers are women with young children at home. They often work on a piece-rate basis and are deprived of the opportunity for unionization and company-supplied health and retirement benefits. The irony in their situation is that such home-based work was banned in many industries, such as textiles, early in the twentieth century because it promoted the exploitation of workers. Computer technology seems to be expanding such exploitive workplace environments again. In fact, many labor unions have pushed for extending bans on such work. As one union spokesperson put it: "If history is any guide, we can say with certainty that abuse of electronic homeworkers is inevitable. . . . An early ban would try to prevent a repeat of past experiences in a new guise" (quoted in Volti, 1995, p. 168).

As with so many things, the impact of these new technologies will be complicated. Some groups will benefit while others will definitely be hurt. Groups that benefit will be those with the educational credentials or other resources that will enable them to take advantage of changing conditions. Groups without significant resources could find themselves worse off. Furthermore, these changes may not produce a significant overall lim-

itation on bureaucracies in modern societies as a whole, although they will have an impact on which people will be affected by bureaucracies and in what form these people will be affected. How will the modern technologies of media and communication affect formal organizations and bureaucracies? The Sociology of Media and Technology insert explores this issue.

Study & Review
SUMMARY OF LEARNING OBJECTIVES

You should be able to describe the major types of social groups and discuss their functions.

Five types of groups are identified as important by sociologists: primary groups, secondary groups, in-groups, out-groups, and reference groups. Social groups are distinct from collectivities, such as social categories and aggregates.

You should be able to describe the social structure of groups and explain the processes involved in group leadership, group decision making, and ensuring group conformity.

Statuses and roles provide the basis for the social structure and help coordinate the behavior of group members. Structure and coordination contribute to the stability of social interaction in groups. One of the most important statuses in groups is that of leader. Group decisions on judgmental issues are characterized by group polarization—originally identified as a *risky shift*. Group cohesion is an important factor in producing enduring and effective groups. The term *groupthink* refers to tendencies in highly cohesive groups toward encouraging unanimity of opinion and consensus at the expense of critical abilities and the realistic appraisal of alternatives.

You should be able to compare Weber's analysis of bureaucracies with the human relations approach and explain the functioning of informal structures in organizations.

Certain types of secondary groups are known as *formal organizations*, which are large, special-purpose groups that are explicitly designed to achieve specific goals. The formal organizations that dominate modern societies are called *bureaucracies*. Bureaucracies have been criticized for their impersonality, and out of this critique has emerged the human relations approach, which is based on the assumption that the social, psychological, and physical needs of people who work in organizations must be considered in order for organizations to be productive and efficient. All organizations develop some type of informal structure, referring to personal relationships that are guided by norms and rituals that develop separately from the formal rules and regulations of the organization.

You should be able to compare and contrast the functionalist, conflict, and interactionist perspectives on formal organizations.

Each sociological perspective offers some special insight into organizations and how they operate. Functionalists stress how organizations operate to coordinate people's behavior and help them achieve complex and difficult goals efficiently. The conflict perspective sees organizations as mechanisms of social control and coercion. Interactionists stress the importance of the informal structure and a negotiated order in organizations.

You should be able to explain the potential dangers of the bureaucratic tendency toward oligarchy and discuss possible future trends in bureaucracy.

Bureaucracies display a tendency toward oligarchy. Yet there are also forces in modern societies that counter this tendency and work toward democratization and the decentralization of power in societies and organizations. The mass media and technologies of modern communication also have wide ramifications for groups and organizations, displaying tendencies toward the concentration of control but also toward decentralization and the empowerment of the average citizen.

CHRONOLOGICAL PRACTICE TEST

For answers to Key Concepts see the page number in parentheses; for other answers see page 114.

Types of Groups
Key Concepts

1. Primary groups (90)
2. Secondary group (91)
3. In-group (92)
4. Out-groups (92)
5. Reference group (93)

True/False

6. T F People in the United States see friendships as being more permanent than do people in Japan.
7. T F A corporate business office would be more likely to be a secondary group than would a college hockey team.
8. T F Sociologists would consider all Japanese Americans to constitute a social category.

Concept Completion

9. Groups that focus on task-oriented, impersonal, and specialized ties between people are called _____ groups.
10. Sociologists would call all of the people riding on the same subway train one morning _____.

Critical Thinking

11. This chapter discusses five different types of social groups. Define each one and describe the functions that it performs. Give an example of each.
12. What are social collectivities, and how do they differ from social groups? Define two types of social collectivities, and give an example of each.
13. Describe the social meanings associated with friendship in the United States and Japan. How are they similar and how do they differ?

Group Structure and Process
Key Concepts

14. Leadership (95)
15. Task roles (95)
16. Instrumental roles (95)
17. Socioemotional roles (95)
18. Expressive roles (95)
19. Relationship-oriented roles (95)
20. Group polarization (96)
21. Group cohesion (97)
22. Groupthink (98)

True/False

23. T F A professor lecturing on U.S. history to a class of students would be performing an instrumental role rather than an expressive role.

24. T F Research has found that, on the whole, people in groups tend to make less risky and daring choices than they would if acting individually.

Concept Completion

25. A store manager who throws a party for her employees so that they can relax and enjoy themselves is performing a(n) _____ role.
26. Leaders who are thoroughly directive, dictating all actions and techniques to be used in achieving group goals, are called_____ leaders.

Critical Thinking

27. Describe the social structure of groups, including in your answer a discussion of status and role.
28. What is groupthink? When is it likely to occur? What are its consequences?

Organizations
Key Concepts

29. Formal organizations (99)
30. Bureaucracies (99)
31. Organizational culture (105)
32. Organizational diagnoses (105)

True/False

33. T F Bureaucracies first emerged in the industrial societies of the nineteenth century.
34. T F Parkinson's Law refers to the fact that groupthink tends to occur in cohesive groups.
35. T F The informal structure of organizations helps people protect themselves against what they perceive as unreasonable demands of the organization.
36. T F The collective orientation in China results in less social loafing than in the United States.

Concept Completion

37. _____ refers to a situation in which people have been trained so completely to follow bureaucratic rules that they are unable to act independently or innovatively.
38. The _____ states that, in a bureaucracy, people tend to rise to their level of incompetence.
39. In a(n) _____, sociologists use their theories and methods to assess how well an organization operates and how its performance can be improved.

Critical Thinking

40. What are the characteristics of the bureaucratic model of organizations as described by Max Weber?
41. What are the advantages and disadvantages of a bureaucratic form of organization?
42. Describe the human relations approach to formal organizations. How does it differ from the bureaucratic approach?

Sociological Perspectives on Organizations
True/False

43. T F From the interactionist perspective, formal organizations can be considered a negotiated order.

Concept Completion

44. The _____ perspective argues that organizations are systems of interrelated parts designed to achieve goals efficiently and productively.
45. _____ refers to a tendency for people in groups to put out less effort to achieve goals than when working alone.

Critical Thinking

46. Discuss the functionalist, conflict, and interactionist perspectives on organizations. Show how they differ from one another.

The Future of Bureaucracy
Key Concept

47. Oligarchy (108)

Concept Completion

48. Robert Michels is quoted as saying, "Who says organization, says _____."

Critical Thinking

49. Will there be more bureaucracy in our lives in the future or less? Describe the trends that point in each direction.

ANSWERS TO CHRONOLOGICAL PRACTICE TEST

6. F; 7. T; 8. T; 23. T; 24. F; 33. F; 34. F; 35. T; 36. T; 43. T
9. secondary
10. an aggregate
25. socioemotional, expressive, relationship-oriented
26. autocratic
37. Trained incapacity
38. Peter Principle
39. organizational diagnosis
44. functionalist
45. Social loafing
48. oligarchy

CUMULATIVE PRACTICE TEST

See page 482 for answers.
1. Which of the following types of groups has a major function of providing people with a secure refuge in which they can act without fear of ridicule or rejection?
   a. Secondary groups.
   b. Reference groups.
   c. Primary groups.

  d. Social categories.
  e. In-groups.
2. In comparison with the United States, friendships in Japan tend to
  a. involve less obligation and responsibility.
  b. be temporary rather than lifelong commitments.
  c. be more permanent.
  d. involve more overt conflict between the friends.
  e. be more secondary than primary in nature.
3. Which of the following groups would be *least* like a primary group?
  a. A business organization.
  b. A family.
  c. An athletic team.
  d. A friendship group.
  e. All of the above are considered primary.
4. Out-groups
  a. are always primary groups.
  b. may be primary or secondary groups.
  c. are always secondary groups.
  d. are always large.
  e. are always small.
5. Reference groups most clearly do which of the following?
  a. Serve as standards for people to evaluate their own attitudes and behaviors.
  b. Produce a sense of loyalty or "we" feeling.
  c. Make for task-oriented, impersonal exchanges between people.
  d. Involve personal, intimate, and nonspecialized relationships between people.
  e. Generate strong feelings of group loyalty and identification.
6. Which of the following defines the groupings of people that sociologists identify as a social aggregate but not a social group?
  a. They share some characteristic in common.
  b. They have interrelated statuses and roles.
  c. They are aware of themselves as a social aggregate.
  d. They are in the same place at the same time.
  e. Both a and c would be true of social aggregates.
7. The purpose of the social structure of small groups is to
  a. serve as a standard against which to assess our beliefs and values.
  b. provide people with a secure refuge where they can be themselves without fear of rejection.
  c. encourage conflict between group members so that problems can be resolved.
  d. organize and coordinate the behavior of group members in relation to one another.
  e. provide for the development of self-concept and personality.
8. A manager overseeing the activities of a group of employees is most clearly an example of which type of leadership role?
  a. Expressive.
  b. Task.
  c. Autocratic.
  d. Socioemotional.
  e. Both a and d.
9. Which of the following statements is true about leadership in groups?
  a. Nondirective leaders produce more tension in the group than do directive leaders.
  b. Nondirective leaders encourage higher group productivity than do directive leaders.
  c. Laissez-faire leaders are more directive than are autocratic leaders.
  d. Women are more autocratic leaders than are men.
  e. Nondirective leaders produce more positive feelings toward the group among group members than do directive leaders.
10. Groups are superior to individuals in making decisions in all of the following ways *except*
  a. Groups come up with a wider range of solutions to problems.
  b. Groups make speedier decisions.
  c. Groups come up with better solutions to problems.
  d. Groups come up with more accurate solutions to problems.
  e. Groups are superior in all of these ways.
11. When making judgments, groups have a tendency toward *group polarization*, which means that
  a. they tend to split into two polarized factions.
  b. they tend to make the wrong judgments.
  c. they pressure group members to make the decision unanimous.
  d. they tend to lose cohesiveness after making a judgment.
  e. they tend to make decisions that are more extreme than those made by individuals.
12. Research by sociologists during World War II has concluded that German soldiers fought well under adverse conditions because
  a. the Germans had superior equipment.
  b. the Germans were strongly committed to the Nazi ideology.
  c. the Germans had strong ties to their families.
  d. the Germans felt loyalty toward others in their military unit.
  e. the Germans were superior in numbers.
13. The process of pressuring group members to make decisions unanimously, sometimes at the expense of critical thinking, is called
  a. group polarization.
  b. task leadership.
  c. groupthink.
  d. oligarchy.
  e. organizational culture.
14. According to research, the pressure toward groupthink is especially strong in
  a. social collectivities.
  b. out-groups.
  c. groups with laissez-faire leaders.
  d. groups during group polarization.
  e. highly cohesive groups.
15. According to Max Weber, _____ has been the major trend in modern societies that has contributed to the development of bureaucracies.
  a. gemeinschaft

b. oligarchy

c. rationalization

d. socialism

e. groupthink

16. Which of the following is true of bureaucratic organizations?

a. They are highly flexible and adaptive.

b. They tend to encourage creativity and innovation.

c. They are efficient at doing well-structured tasks.

d. They are unstable organizations.

e. They tend to be slow and inefficient for all tasks.

17. As applied to bureaucracies, the term "trained incapacity" refers to

a. a person without the standardized skills and training to fill a position.

b. the oligarchical tendencies that arise in all organizations.

c. the inability of the formal structure of organizations to meet the personal needs of organizational members.

d. the inability to prevent groupthink in organizations.

e. people who have been trained so completely to follow the rules that they are unable to act innovatively.

18. In contrast with organizations based on the bureaucratic model, organizations based on the human relations model tend to

a. place more stress on impartiality.

b. have a more rigid and extensive hierarchy of authority.

c. stress authoritative management.

d. give more emphasis to formal rules and procedures.

e. stress more participative management.

19. "Social loafing" in organizations occurs more frequently

a. when workers have a collectivist rather than individualist cultural orientation.

b. in large groups rather than small ones.

c. when people are not held accountable for their individual tasks.

d. All of the above.

e. Only b and c.

20. Which of the following perspectives would be most likely to view conflict as an unwanted element in an organization?

a. The conflict perspective.

b. The functionalist perspective.

c. The interactionist perspective.

d. The negotiated order perspective.

e. The bureaucratic perspective.

FOR FURTHER READING

Berger, Peter, Berger, Brigitte, & Kellner, Hansfried. (1979). *The homeless mind: Modernization and consciousness.* New York: Vintage. This enjoyable little book describes how living in a bureaucratic society affects our consciousness and our way of thinking—often in ways we would not imagine.

Goffman, Erving. (1961). *Asylums.* Garden City, NY: Anchor/Doubleday. Although four decades old, this book remains one of the seminal investigations of the impact of formal organizations on behavior and identity. Goffman, now deceased, was probably one of the most sensitive sociological observers of the human scene.

Jankowski, Martin Sanchez. (1991). *Islands in the street: Gangs and American urban society.* Berkeley: University of California Press. This book is an interesting study of gangs, but it also involves an analysis of the organizational aspects of gang life.

Johnson, David W., & Johnson, Frank P. (2009). *Joining together* (10th ed.). Boston: Allyn & Bacon. This book is a good summary of the theory and research on how groups work effectively. It is a good review of group structure and process.

Kane, Joe. (1996). *Savages.* New York: Knopf. This book provides a detailed account of what happened to one South American tribe when Western oil companies wanted to develop its land. A repeat of the Yanomamo experience as described in the beginning of this chapter.

Martin, Joanne. (1992). *Cultures in organizations: Three perspectives.* New York: Oxford University Press. This book recognizes that culture—in the form of values, norms, ritual, language, and the like—exists in organizations. The author shows how to do a cultural analysis of organizations and what some of the implications of such analysis are.

Rawlins, William K. (1992). *Friendship matters: Communication, dialectics, and the life course.* New York: Aldine de Gruyter. This fascinating book summarizes research on how friendships—a key primary group in most people's lives—develop and change from childhood into old age. Gender differences are discussed throughout.

Ritzer, George. (2008). *The McDonaldization of society* (5th ed.). Thousand Oaks, CA: Pine Forge Press. This sociologist puts forth the intriguing proposition that formal organizations, as well as modern society as a whole, are increasingly organized in a fashion similar to fast-food restaurants. The implications of this are fascinating to consider.

Wilson, Gerald L. (2005). *Groups in context: Leadership and participation in small groups* (7th ed.). New York: McGraw-Hill. This book is designed to teach people the practical aspects of how to organize and lead groups and how groups work. It covers and goes beyond the principles discussed in this chapter.

CHAPTER 5

Deviance, Crime, and Social Control

MYTHS & FACTS: About Deviance and Crime

The Relativity of Deviance

Explanations of Deviance

Nonsociological Approaches
The Functionalist Perspective
The Conflict Perspective
The Interactionist Perspective

SOCIOLOGY OF MEDIA AND TECHNOLOGY: Mass Media and the Social Construction of Crime and Justice

Extent of Deviance and Crime

Sexual Deviance
Drug and Alcohol Abuse

APPLYING SOCIOLOGY: Influencing Policy on Youth Gangs and Juvenile Crime

Mental Illness
Violent Crimes
Organized Crime and Globalized Crime

Cybercrime
White-Collar Crime

Deviance: Its Consequences for Society

The Dysfunctions of Deviance
The Functions of Deviance

Deviance and Social Control

Internal Sources of Social Control
External Sources of Social Control

Crime in the United States

The High Crime Rate
Reducing Crime

OTHER WORLDS, OTHER WAYS: Japan: Social and Cultural Underpinnings of Crime

SOCIOLOGY ON THE INTERNET

Study & Review

Singapore is a tiny nation of about three million people at the southern tip of the Malay Peninsula (Milne & Mauzy, 1990). It is a former British colony that gained full independence in 1965. Most of its citizens are ethnic Chinese, but 15 percent are Malay and 7 percent are Indian. It is capitalist, urban, industrialized, and quite affluent, with a per capita annual income about equal to that in the United States. Although Singapore is economically similar to the United States, it is socially and politically quite different. In fact, socially and politically, it has been referred to as a soft authoritarianism because of the extensive efforts its leaders make to control people's personal and political behavior (Branegan, 1993; Perry, Kong, & Yeoh, 1997).

Singaporean officials would like to see their people become more courteous, industrious, and healthier as well as more patriotic (Wilkinson, 1988). They hope to achieve this improvement through a combination of education, suggestion, and encouragement along with the iron fist of the law when necessary. For example, the government has strong powers to stifle political dissent, including a law that enables authorities to detain people without trial. Before they are released, political dissenters must make a public confession. The government also sharply restricts statements that might cause religious or racial tension and allows only token political opposition, with the government owning television stations and indirectly controlling the press. Radio, television, and newspapers are considered propaganda outlets for the government, and censorship of and outright bans on some magazines are common.

The government also has some ideas about how proper breeding can create a superior people in Singapore, so they encourage well-educated and successful people to have many children. Such people receive tax credits if they have more than three children, and some people receive a tax cut if they acquire more education. Through such policies, the Singaporean government actively encourages achievement and initiative in its citizens. The government also sponsors many educational programs focused on encouraging cohesiveness among different social and ethnic groups and discouraging antisocial behaviors, such as littering or spitting on the street.

The social-control efforts extend into realms that leave many people shaking their heads and wondering about the reasonableness of it all. There are stiff penalties for "antisocial" behaviors such as littering ($625 fine), failing to flush a public toilet ($94), and eating on a subway ($312). Chewing gum has been outlawed, and smoking in many public places is illegal.

How do Singaporeans react to the "soft" authoritarianism of their rulers? Many think that a lot of it

Myths & Facts

About Deviance and Crime

Myth:

There is a clear line between the "criminal element" in society and the law-abiding and respectable people. If we could put that criminal element behind bars, the crime problem would be solved.

Fact:

Once again, social reality is far more complex than many commonsense beliefs would have it. It turns out that many crimes are committed by people who are otherwise considered quite respectable. For example, who commits vandalism? Teenage punks? Hostile and alienated losers? The social psychologist Philip Zimbardo conducted an intriguing study of people who vandalize automobiles in New York (Zimbardo, 1973). After seeing many stripped and battered automobiles on his way to work, he decided to observe who the vandals were. He bought an old car, left it on a street near New York University, and watched from a hidden location. Within ten minutes, the first vandals appeared: a father, mother, and their eight-year-old son! The mother served as lookout while the father and son removed the battery and radiator. Later, another vandal was pushing an infant in a baby carriage. There followed a virtual parade of people who removed everything of value from the car and then began battering what was left. These vandals were often well dressed and chatted amiably with passersby as they toiled. Zimbardo's research leads to the conclusion that many criminals not only appear quite respectable but also probably consider themselves quite law-abiding.

Myth:

The most serious drug problem that confronts the United States is the flow of heroin, cocaine, and marijuana across its borders and into its cities.

Fact:

In terms of the number of people affected and the economic costs to society, most specialists on drug problems consider alcohol abuse to be the most severe drug problem in the United States.

is silly or heavy-handed, but most acquiesce and many believe it to be beneficial. Their view becomes more understandable when we look more closely at Singaporean society and culture. Singapore is a nation of immigrants coming mostly from poor and unstable countries. With this history, the residents place great value on stability and affluence. There may be too many controls in Singapore, but people also have a comfortable life without political and social chaos. In light of this immigrant background, some of the social-control efforts are focused on engendering a sense of common nationhood among Singaporeans. Officials are concerned that some immigrants are mostly devoted to seeking their fortune in Singapore rather than to the nation itself. Officials blame a lot of what they perceive as problems on what they call "Western values," such as individualism, permissiveness, and decadence. They wish to encourage "Asian values," which center on honesty, respect for elders and authority, and devotion to family and nation. These Asian values derive from traditional Chinese values, especially the Confucian teachings regarding obedience to established authority.

This description of Singapore centers around the core issues of this chapter: deviance, crime, and social control. Sociologists define deviance as *behaviors or characteristics that violate important group norms and as a consequence are reacted to with social disapproval.* Much of the focus in earlier chapters was on the degree to which people conform to cultural values and group norms that are approved by a particular group. Sociologists also recognize, however, that deviance, or socially *disapproved* behavior, is common in society. Sociology tries to understand and explain deviant behavior as well as conforming behavior. Sociology also investigates the mechanisms of social control that groups and society use to bring deviants into line. A key element of the sociological approach to deviance is that deviance is a function of the judgments of particular groups. Behaviors are deviant *because they are so defined by a particular group.* Authorities in Singapore defined having long hair or failing to flush a toilet as deviant, whereas the same actions in another society might be socially acceptable. This difference points once again to the diversity in human societies and to the relative nature of deviance.

The Relativity of Deviance

You should be able to describe the sociological perspective on deviance and explain how it differs from the absolute and statistical views.

Some people approach deviance in an *absolute* way, judging certain behaviors and characteristics to be good or bad and right or wrong by comparing them to some fixed standards. Religious views of deviance, for example, often reflect this approach, with some divinely revealed truths representing the standard. Others adopt a *statistical* view of deviance: Deviance involves a departure from an established average. Thus, a man who is seven feet tall could be considered deviant from this perspective, because the average height of most males is closer to five feet ten inches. Likewise, a heroin addict would be deviant because most people are not heroin addicts.

Sociologists, however, find neither the absolute nor the statistical views to be very useful because they cannot explain the enormous variety in people's definitions of deviance. In part, what is considered deviant depends on the culture in which it occurs. For example, in societies such as the Inuit (Eskimo) in the Arctic or the Murngin in Australia, a form of geronticide, or killing the elderly, was once practiced. If food was scarce and the band needed to move quickly to a new territory, the group would abandon older people to starvation, especially if they were sick and a burden on the others in the group (Harris, 1977). Although acceptable to the Inuit or Murngin, such practices would be considered highly deviant in most modern cultures.

Even within a single culture, there is considerable variation from one group to another in what is considered deviant. Some people in the United States, for example, view homosexuality as an acceptable form of sexual expression, whereas others are repelled by it. In addition to differences between cultures and subcultures, definitions of deviance also vary from one situation to another. It is acceptable, for example, to remove one's clothing in a physician's examination room, but the same action in a college classroom would be considered highly deviant.

To explain this variety, sociologists maintain that deviance is *relative*, or based on the social definitions of some group. Behaviors or characteristics can be considered deviant only within the context of the norms and values of a particular culture, subculture, or group. In fact, deviance is not inherent in *any* behavior or characteristic; rather, it arises from the relationship between a behavior and the social definition of that behavior by some group. As one sociologist put it, "Deviance, like beauty, is in the eyes of the beholder" (Simmons, 1969, p. 4). Most human actions have been defined as deviant by some group at some time, and most of us have engaged in some of these deviant actions, although we may not have defined them as deviant ourselves. But deviance refers not only to violating some rules or norms; in addition, there must be some *stigma,* or mark of disgrace, attached to the violation that sets the deviant apart from others (Goffman, 1963; Jones et al., 1984).

The following section briefly reviews some nonsociological explanations of deviance and then presents the major sociological approaches to deviance. Underlying these sociological explanations is the idea that deviance is relative.

Explanations of Deviance

> You should be able to discuss the major explanations of deviance, including biological and psychological perspectives, as well as the three sociological perspectives on deviance.

Like all behavior, deviance is complex, and many people find it hard to understand. In fact, because deviance is often viewed as threatening or repugnant, it may be one of the more difficult forms of human behavior for people to comprehend, and people are often tempted to settle for overly simple explanations. To appreciate the complexity of deviance and crime, familiarity with nonsociological as well as sociological approaches to the issue is essential.

Nonsociological Approaches

Over the years, a variety of *biological approaches* to deviance have both gained and lost popularity, and most have proven of little value in explaining deviance. Biological approaches view deviance as arising, at least in part, from people's physical or biological makeup (Fishbein, 1990). For example, Cesare Lombroso (1911), an Italian army doctor and criminologist, argued that some people are born criminals, throwbacks to a more primitive stage of human evolution. Using male prison inmates as subjects, Lombroso defined and measured physical characteristics such as abnormally large jaws, high cheekbones, good eyesight, and an insensibility to pain. These people were, he claimed, more like apes than men, and their primitive development made it difficult for them to conform to conventional norms. Although popular in the early 1900s, Lombroso's biological explanation of crime has now been thoroughly rejected. Subsequent research has failed to establish any link between Lombroso's physical characteristics and criminality (Sykes & Cullen, 1992).

Since Lombroso's time, there have been numerous efforts to link such diverse forms of deviance as mental illness, alcoholism, and crime to solely biological causes. Most of these efforts have failed. One major criticism of these studies is that they typically are based on unrepresentative samples of people, such as criminals in prison. Recall the discussion in Chapter 1 about the importance of representative samples. Furthermore, in studies suggesting that biology does play a role, it appears to be but one contributing factor rather than the sole cause of deviance. For example, biological factors may play a part in a particularly severe form of mental illness known as schizophrenia (Cockerham, 2006). Some schizophrenics, although certainly not all, appear to inherit a tendency to develop this mental disorder. However, this inherited tendency alone often does not bring about schizophrenic behavior. In these cases, such behavior emerges when personal and social stress factors are also present. In addition, with some schizophrenics, there appears to be no genetic element involved. Purely biological theories of deviance, then, have been discredited, and sociologists have concluded that much deviance has nothing to do with biology (Chambliss, 1991; Gottfredson & Hirschi, 1990).

Psychological approaches to deviance, however, still receive considerable support (Adler, Mueller, & Laufer, 2004). From this perspective, deviance is believed to result from some personality disorder or maladjustment that develops, often during childhood. For example, alcoholism has been explained in terms of excessive dependency needs and aggressiveness that can result from faulty childhood socialization. If children receive contradictory treatment from parents—loving indulgence some of the time, but threat and rejection at other times—they may grow up with a compulsive need for love and strong feelings of dependence on other people. The anxiety created when their disproportionate needs are not met, it is maintained, can lead to the excessive use of alcohol as a way of relieving these tensions.

Although sociologists recognize the importance of personality and psychological processes in people's lives, such explanations offer only a partial understanding of deviance. In many cases, people who manifest various forms of deviance are free from the personality problems and psychological disorders that presumably cause them, and people with those disorders often do not exhibit particular patterns of deviant behavior. Many alcoholics, for example, are not excessively dependent on others. Even when psychological disturbances are associated with deviance, the causal direction is unclear: Do personality factors cause deviance, or does engaging in deviance, along with the stigma that often results, lead people to develop unique personality characteristics?

Sociologists have emphasized the role of culture, social structure, and social interaction in bringing about deviance. This chapter will discuss the major sociological approaches to deviance and crime: the functional, conflict, and interactionist perspectives.

The Functionalist Perspective

An early functionalist, Emile Durkheim, provided one of the explanations for high levels of deviance and crime in industrial societies. One of the key features of industrial societies, he argued, is the weakening of many of the social bonds important in preindustrial societies. Ties to family, community, and church become less important in industrial societies as families become smaller and workers more mobile and independent of their families (see Chapter 9). People are more free to pursue their own needs and fulfill their own desires; they are less constrained by the need to please relatives or account to a priest or minister. But this freedom has its costs. The reduction in social constraints also results in a degree of social disorganization as people pursue needs and goals that may be detrimental to the overall good of society. After all, bonds to family and church were one of the key mechanisms constraining people from committing crimes or engaging in other socially disapproved activities. When those bonds are weakened or removed, a certain amount of crime and social disorder will result. For Durkheim, then, deviance is one of the costs that we must pay to live in the type of society that we do, and recent research comparing many different societies supports his theory (Leavitt, 1992). More recently, Durkheim's views have been applied to juvenile delinquency in the form of a *social-control* theory of delinquency. The basic idea is that the chances of delinquency occurring can be reduced if youngsters maintain attachments and commitments to the conventional world of their parents, schools, and peers (Agnew, 1991; Hirschi, 1969).

Another influential functionalist approach to deviance and crime is Robert K. Merton's anomie theory (1968), which *posits that inconsistencies and contradictions in the social system precipitate many forms of deviance and crime.* Merton observed that *people in the United States are taught to strive for certain goals but are not always provided with the culturally approved means necessary to attain these goals.* Merton referred to *such inconsistencies and the confusion they can cause in people* as anomie. In the United States, for example, an important cultural goal is success, which is defined largely in material terms. One culturally approved way to become successful is to gain an education and work in some legitimate occupation. Some people, however, are prevented from succeeding in this fashion because of poverty, discrimination, or some other social condition. When people are thus hindered from achieving desired goals, deviance in one of its many forms may result. Deviance is the person's *mode of adaptation* to the anomie, although the person

Table 5.1

MODES OF INDIVIDUAL ADAPTATION TO ANOMIE

Modes of Adaptation	Accepts Culturally Approved Goals	Accepts Culturally Approved Means
I. Conformity	+	+
II. Innovation	+	−
III. Ritualism	−	+
IV. Retreatism	−	−
V. Rebellion	±	±

+ Signifies acceptance
− Signifies rejection
± Signifies rejection of prevailing goals and means and the substitution of new goals and means

Note: Reprinted with the permission of The Free Press, a Division of Simon & Schuster Adult Publishing Group, from *Social Theory and Social Structure*, by Robert K. Merton. Copyright © 1967, 1968 by Robert K. Merton. Copyright © 1957 by The Free Press; copyright renewed 1985 by Robert K. Merton. All rights reserved.

may not think of it this way (Table 5.1). Most people, of course, accept the culturally approved goals and use the culturally approved means of achieving them. According to Merton, this *conformity* provides stability for society. Most college students fall into this category, because they are using educational paths, which are socially approved means toward respectable and legitimate occupations.

The four modes of adaptation other than conformity may involve some deviant or criminal behaviors. The most common of these Merton called *innovation,* in which people pursue the cultural goals through illegal or other socially disapproved means. Innovation is likely to occur when people feel that legitimate routes to success are closed and that their only option is to turn to illegitimate ones. People who are unemployed or underemployed, for example, can provide for their families and themselves through robbery or burglary. Likewise, a person running a marginal business concern can survive by cheating on taxes or using deceptive advertising practices.

Another response to anomie is *ritualism,* which occurs when an individual almost compulsively accepts the culturally approved means but does not use them to achieve cultural goals. Merton uses as an example of a ritualist the minor bureaucrat who has no hopes of improving his or her position yet follows closely all the rules and routines of the bureaucracy. Except in extreme cases, such ritualism would not be considered deviant by most groups.

People can also respond to anomie through *retreatism,* rejecting both the culturally approved goals and the legitimate means for achieving them. Unlike innovators, who feel that they lack access to the means, retreatists have often attempted to obtain these goals through legitimate means but have failed. Their adaptation to anomie, as illustrated by drug addicts or alcoholics, is to drop out and "escape."

Finally, *rebellion* occurs when people reject both the socially approved goals and the socially approved means and then seek to replace them with alternative goals and means. In many communes, for example, the conventional U.S. value of material success is rejected, as are the traditional means of achieving this success. Yet instead of simply dropping out, communards work to establish their own social order based on new cultural goals, such as the common ownership of goods, and new means, such as cooperative rather than competitive social relationships. A more radical example of rebellion is found in revolutionary groups such as the Zapatistas in the Chiapas region of Mexico or the Islamic rebels in Chechnya, the republic of Russia. Both rebel groups reject the authority of their central governments (in Mexico City and Moscow, respectively) and have made concerted efforts to replace the existing social order in their regions with new economic and political structures.

Research on crime supports anomie theory. For example, crime rates, especially for property crimes, are higher in communities with greater economic inequality or with a larger disparity between incomes among groups. In such cities, the less fortunate can readily see the affluence around them, and some turn to crime to improve their own circumstances (Simons & Gray, 1989). Crime also goes up when there is an economic recession (Devine, Sheley, & Smith, 1988). Crime rates are high among the unemployed and low among the employed (Allan & Steffensmeier, 1989; Lafree, Drass, & O'Day, 1992).

The importance of anomie theory for understanding crime as a form of deviant behavior should be clear: A portion of criminal activity derives from the social and economic conditions of U.S. society, especially such conditions as unemployment, limited opportunities, and large economic disparities between groups. In fact, the criminologist Elliott Currie (1985) has argued that the low crime rate in industrial societies such as Japan results in part from their programs promoting high employment and the fact that income disparities are much smaller than in the United States.

The functionalist perspective also emphasizes the interrelatedness of the various parts of the social system. Changes in one part bring about changes in other seemingly unrelated parts. Certain social trends and changes in the U.S. lifestyle over the past few decades have increased the opportunities for committing certain kinds of crime, particularly burglary, larceny, and theft (Cohen & Felson, 1979; Cohen, Felson, & Land, 1980; Miller & Ohlin, 1985). For example, the number of women working has increased dramatically since the 1960s; there has been an increase in the number of households with only one adult member; and people take more vacations now than in the past. The result of these three trends is that homes are much more likely to be left unattended for a part of the day and therefore become tempting targets for burglars. There has also been tremendous growth in consumer spending for items such as televisions and automobiles that are likely objects for theft. In short, the rise in crime results in part from the increasing opportunities to commit crimes made available by trends that many people in the United States view as desirable.

Merton's theory of deviance has some shortcomings (Adler, Mueller, & Laufer, 2004; Thio, 2007). Some sociologists question whether different groups within a society aspire toward the same cultural goals. Given the heterogeneous nature of industrial societies, for example, striving for success is highly valued by some people but certainly not by all. In addition, Merton's theory does not tell us why people adopt one response to anomie rather than another. Why do some people respond by becoming criminals whereas others become retreatists and still others rebel? Despite these criticisms, Merton's theory has been very influential and has helped explain many forms of deviance. Other approaches to deviance can help us in the areas where Merton's theory is weak.

The Conflict Perspective

In reviewing the functionalist argument, conflict theorists observe that the analysis of the "crime and deviance problem" tends to focus heavily on behavior that is more likely to occur among the less-powerful groups in society: the young, the poor, and the nonwhite. In fact, the Federal Bureau of Investigation's Crime Index, the most widely publicized statistic on the amount of crime, emphasizes crimes such as assault, which the less well-to-do are more likely to commit, rather than embezzlement, gambling, or tax evasion, which are committed more by middle-class and "respectable" people. The so-called deviance and crime problem, then, as it is defined by the police, the courts, and the public, results from the activities of the less fortunate in society.

From the conflict perspective, the legal and criminal justice systems are geared to benefit the dominant groups in society (Kennedy, 1990; Quinney & Shelden, 2001). Laws, after all, are mechanisms whereby some groups exercise control over the activities of other groups. Generally, it is the powerful who establish legislation defining what activities will be considered criminal and who decide what the penalties will be for those crimes. Thus, removing a television from a store is regarded as criminal, whereas polluting a stream may not be. Armed robbery can bring a fifteen-year prison sentence, whereas price-fixing that costs the public millions of dollars in excess expenditures may be punished with a light prison sentence or a fine.

It is also the powerful who can get the police to enforce the laws against some crimes while ignoring other infractions of the law. There are, for example, periodic and highly publicized drives against robbery, prostitution, and drug offenses. For the past 20 years, for example, the U.S. government has declared "war" on illegal drugs, proclaiming that this problem is the United States' number-one crime issue. One is less likely to see, however, a politician launch such a campaign against corporate crime. From the conflict perspective, then, the social problem of deviance and crime is not simply a matter of social disorganization; it is also influenced by the preferences, predilections, and interests of various groups in society.

Conflict theorists who have been influenced by the writings of Karl Marx view the causes of crime very differently from the way functionalists do. These conflict theorists blame certain characteristics of capitalism as an economic system (Headley, 1991). Capitalism is characterized by a constant search for greater profits, or at least a struggle against falling profits. This process can be especially fierce in a global economy such as we have today where countries at many different levels of development compete with one another. In the process, capitalists search for ways to enhance profits by reducing costs through mechanization or automation of work or through relocation to areas where resources and labor are cheaper. Both mechanization and relocation put people out of work or force people into competition for lower-wage jobs. Because this process is a continual one, capitalism inevitably contains recurring cycles in which people are thrown out of work and communities are decimated by the loss of jobs. These inherent features of capitalism, then, mean that certain levels of poverty and the crime associated with it will always be with us, although which groups or communities are affected may shift over time.

In addition, capitalists need to sell their goods to make a profit, so they must instill in people a desire for the many products that capitalism can produce. At the same time, capitalists attempt to keep wages low to reduce the costs of production. A mass of unemployed people also benefits a capitalist economy by serving as a cheap labor force when new workers are needed. The unemployed also serve as a lesson to employed workers: Do not demand too high a salary or you, too, may be among the unemployed. The result, according to William Chambliss (1975), is a contradiction: "Capitalism creates both the desire to consume and—for a large mass of people—an inability to earn the money necessary to purchase the items they have been taught to want" (p. 151). For these people, crime is one way of resolving this dilemma. Unlike anomie theory, however, Marxian conflict theory does not assume that the problem can be alleviated through full employment; rather, it sees these contradictions as inherent in a capitalist economy.

The Interactionist Perspective

Interactionist approaches see the functionalist and conflict views as incomplete because they do not explain how a person becomes deviant or why one person responds to anomie through crime or drug use and another does not. To find answers to these questions, we need to look at the socialization and interaction processes that influence people's daily lives.

Cultural transmission theories posit that *deviance is a learned behavior that is culturally transmitted through socialization.* The most influential of these theories is the differential association theory, developed by the criminologist Edwin Sutherland during the 1920s and the 1930s, which draws on the interactionist concern with social meaning arising from social interaction. According to Sutherland, *deviant behavior is learned in interaction with other people, for the most part within intimate primary groups such as families and peer groups* (Sutherland & Cressey, 1978). There are two elements of this learning process. First, people learn the specific techniques for engaging in deviance. For example, to use illicit drugs, a person needs to know how to obtain and take drugs such as heroin or cocaine. Second, one must learn to value deviant behavior more than nondeviant behavior. By associating with other deviants, people are more likely to learn to value their deviant activities and learn a rationale for why deviance is preferable to a more conventional way of life. Some people who use cocaine or other drugs, for example, claim that drugs make them feel more relaxed, sociable, and perceptive than they feel when not using drugs. Whether people become deviant depends on the extent and intensity of contact with groups that value a particular form of deviance and can train them in deviant techniques. It also depends on whether a person identifies with and takes the role of those deviants. Association with deviants without such identification is not likely to result in deviance.

According to cultural transmission theories, then, learning to be deviant involves mechanisms of socialization similar to those associated with learning any social status (see Chapter 3). If people have primary-group ties with nondeviants, then they are likely to learn to value that lifestyle. Others who associate with deviants are more likely to become deviant.

Another interactionist approach to deviance is *labeling theory,* which shifts attention away from the individual deviant and toward the ways that others react to the deviant (Cavender, 1991). It also shifts attention from isolated or sporadic occurrences of deviance and toward deviance that is engaged in repeatedly and becomes a part of a person's lifestyle. Labeling theory suggests that *whether other people define or label a person as deviant is a critical determinant in the development of a pattern of deviant behavior*. According to this theory, many people engage in activities that could be defined as deviant, at least occasionally. In all likelihood, you have engaged in actions that have been so defined. Few of us, however, are caught and labeled—either by our friends or by official agencies—as deviants or criminals. Labeling theorists refer to this *violation of social norms in which a person is not caught or is excused rather than labeled deviant* as primary deviance. But labeling theory does not attempt to explain this type of deviance. Labeling theory concentrates on secondary or career deviance—*the deviant behavior that a person adopts in response to the reaction of others to his or her primary deviance*. Consider how such a response could happen (Matsueda, 1992).

We know that shoplifting among teenagers, at least of small items, is not uncommon. Imagine that a teenager, possibly out of curiosity or on a dare from peers, engages in a single act of shoplifting. This act would constitute primary deviance, because there has been no labeling and no change in the teenager's or the community's image of him or her. If, however, the young person's shoplifting is brought to the attention of the police, they may begin the labeling process by notifying the offender's parents. If this label becomes "public," it is quite likely that some stigma will attach to this teenager's reputation—perhaps a criminal record.

One key consequence of this labeling process is its effect on a person's self-concept. Because the teenage years are formative ones in terms of personal identity, the person may respond to others' reactions, at least in part, by accepting their judgment. After all, the stigma associated with deviant labels such as "criminal" and "delinquent" implies something negative about people who behave in that fashion. The terms *murderer, thug, robber*, and *thief* suggest the strong emotions that underlie these labels of deviants, and such labels can affect the way people view themselves. To the extent that labeling produces changes in a person's self-concept, this is an example of the looking-glass-self process discussed in Chapter 3.

A second key consequence of labeling involves the effect that labeling has on people's social relationships. After all, labels of deviants typically denote *master statuses* that powerfully shape how others define and relate to the deviant (see Chapter 2). If the criminal activity becomes publicly known, some of the person's conventional friends may shun him or her out of fear

for their own reputations. The person may also find it difficult to develop new friends, at least among conventional peers, finding acceptance, instead, among youngsters who are already engaging in delinquent or criminal actions on a large scale.

As a result of these changes in self-concept and social contacts, labeling theorists argue, the likelihood of a deviant career developing is increased. Thus, labeling can perpetuate deviance and crime because, once people have been labeled, they have fewer alternatives, and the deviance becomes a part of their social identity. This situation represents secondary deviance because it results from a person's efforts to cope with the responses of others to primary deviation. It also represents, in a sense, a *self-fulfilling prophecy* in that the label of deviant helps to bring about the pattern of career deviance that people thought they were merely identifying when they first attached the label (Heimer & Matsueda, 1994).

One must be cautious in being overly deterministic about the influence of labeling. Labeling can and does have the effects that have been described, but such outcomes are not inevitable. People with strong and stable self-concepts may be able to avoid the negative influence of pejorative labels. They may also choose to associate with others who are unaware of the label, as when someone does not reveal to a new circle of friends that he is an "ex-con." Furthermore, labeling theory fails to account for the existence of primary deviance. A few early labeling theorists claimed that labeling could cause people to become deviant in the first place, but there is little evidence for this statement. The effects of the label usually arise *after* a person commits a deviant act and has been recognized and labeled.

Now that the major sociological theories of deviance have been described, you should understand better why sociologists take the position that deviance is *relative*. According to anomie theory, what is defined as deviant depends on what are considered socially approved means and goals in a particular society. Conflict theory sees deviance within a framework of definitions and judgments that are formulated and enforced by those in positions of power. For cultural transmission theory, deviance is a result of socialization, and people are capable of learning a wide variety of things. Finally, labeling theory makes us aware that being identified as a deviant depends, among other things, on the resources a person possesses and on his or her ability to avoid the negative aspects of being labeled. You should keep in mind in reviewing some different types of deviance that the line between deviance and nondeviance is shifting and vague rather than clear and obvious. This notion is elaborated on in the Sociology of Media and Technology insert, which explores the way in which modern communications technologies play a part in the social construction of issues surrounding crime and justice.

Sociology of Media and Technology

Mass Media and the Social Construction of Crime and Justice

The sociological perspectives help us understand not only why people might engage in deviant behavior or criminal activity but also how deviance and crime come to be defined by people as important public issues toward which individuals and policymakers should direct their attention. The interactionist perspective, in particular, suggests that the mass media play an important role in this process of defining the situation or reality construction, because many people gain much of their information on and attitudes about crime by what they read in newspapers or magazines or watch on television (Cuklanz, 1996; Kooistra, Mahoney, & Westervelt, 1998; Sacco, 1995).

In terms of shaping the public's definition of reality, the picture of crime portrayed in the media is in some ways a significant distortion of reality. Comparing the media portrayals with the statistics and research on crime that social scientists have accumulated, the media give the distinct impression that the volume of crime is much higher than it actually is. Furthermore, the media reports suggest that violent crime is more common than nonviolent crime, whereas crime statistics clearly indicate the reverse is true. The vast majority of crimes reported in the media are crimes committed by individuals, such as homicide or robbery, rather than crimes committed by organizations or corporations, such as price-fixing, securities violations, or the violation of environmental regulations.

In regard to the criminal justice system, the media present the police as more effective in solving crimes and apprehending criminals than the statistics suggest they actually are. The media also tend to feature the police quite prominently in news reports, but other facets of the criminal justice system (the courts, prisons, probation officers, and so on) are given less attention than their role in controlling crime would seem to warrant. Finally, the media often present a distorted image of crime victims, portraying all citizens as equally likely to be affected. In reality, poor minorities in inner-city communities are most likely to be victims. The chance that an affluent suburbanite will become a victim of, say, drug violence is actually quite small. Yet portraying victimization as randomly spread through the community is more likely to generate general concern about crime and lead people to see it as an important public issue.

The reasons the media present this image of crime and criminal justice have a lot to do with the organizational processes of news production and the position of the media in the political and economic institutions of society. First of all, the media are mostly private companies motivated by profit, and they devote attention to crimes they see as profitable—crimes that increase the sales of newspapers and magazines and the audience of television shows. To attract large numbers of readers or viewers, they prefer stories that are short, simple, and personal. Crimes committed by individuals, especially street crimes like homicide or drug dealing, tend to be much simpler and can be focused on individuals such as the victim and the offender. Organizational and corporate crimes tend to be more complex and harder to explain to an audience unfamiliar with the complicated legalities of antitrust laws or securities violations. Uncomplicated crime stories are also easier for news organizations to write and produce, and this is important when shows or stories must be produced under rigid, daily deadlines.

Another aspect of news organizations that influences the reporting of crime is that journalists and newsmakers sometimes try to organize individual stories around a broader news "theme" in order to legitimize the presentation of particular stories. After all, one reason for reporting about a particular crime, which may seem of little significance by itself, is that it is a part of a "crime wave." That is, this crime is symptomatic of a broader news issue that the public needs to be aware of. One study in New York, for example, found journalists reporting increasing numbers of crimes against the elderly as a part of a growing crime wave in the city (Fishman, 1978). Yet reviews of actual crime statistics and criminal victimization of the elderly could detect no actual increases in these types of crimes. The process of competitive journalism also contributes to this trend. Once one news source reports such a crime wave, other newspapers or television news organizations feel some pressure to follow suit in the competition for audiences (Orcutt & Turner, 1993).

Technological developments have expanded the opportunities to show crime and police activities on television. Video-recording equipment is now small, inexpensive, and mobile; it is in the hands of many police and civilians; some police cars are now permanently equipped with video cameras. As a result, many crimes and police activities get recorded, and a spate of reality-based crime shows has emerged on television, such as *Cops*, *America's Most Wanted*, and *NYPD 24/7*. Some of these shows use actors to reenact actual crimes, but all use as much live video footage as they can locate. The result is that television viewers can be repeatedly exposed to live criminal activities, sometimes in a very dramatic and frightening portrayal. And these shows affect people's attitudes: People who watch reality-based police programs make higher estimates of how prevalent crime is (Oliver & Armstrong, 1998). Many of these shows also contain a preponderance of images of African Americans as the criminals, and this affects attitudes: People who watch

(continued)

these shows make higher estimates of the prevalence of crime among African Americans. So, these programs are shaping people's definitions of reality, even when those definitions are not consistent with the facts.

Given all of these considerations, it is not surprising that the media present a distorted view of crime. This view, once presented, is a powerful force in shaping the public's definition of the "crime problem." The police and other criminal justice authorities play an important part in creating this definition, because the media are heavily dependent on the police for access to news about crime.

The police are typically the people who have most information about crimes and access to offenders, victims, and crime scenes; the police are also credible sources of information, which is important for the media. In giving information to the media, the police tend to portray themselves in the most positive light, by dwelling on cases they have successfully solved. One social scientist concluded that "the police role as the dominant gatekeeper means that crime news is often police news and that the advancement of a police perspective on crime and its solution is facilitated" (Sacco, 1995, p. 146).

Extent of Deviance and Crime

You should be able to describe the major forms of deviance and crime found in the United States and explain why they occur.

It is important to distinguish between crime and deviance. A crime is *an act that violates a criminal code that has been enacted by an officially constituted political authority*. Some crimes are commonly perceived as deviant (Figure 5.1); acts of this sort may be referred to as *mala in se*, or "bad in and of themselves." Rape, homicide, robbery, assault, and burglary are all acts that fall into this category because they represent violations of important group norms. Some behaviors, however, are criminal but not necessarily viewed as deviant. These acts fall under the category *mala prohibita*, or "bad because they are prohibited." Parking violations and minor tax evasion, for example, are not considered deviant by most people, and little stigma usually attaches to them even though they are violations of a criminal code. In addition, some behaviors and characteristics may be perceived as deviant but not classified as criminal. Extreme obesity and some forms of mental illness, for example, would, by the judgments of some groups, fall

into this category. This chapter reviews some types of deviance that are crimes and others that are not.

Sexual Deviance

The varieties of human sexual expression are almost endless, and most of them have been condemned, at one time or another, as deviant. Many people believe that there is a "natural" or "instinctive" expression of sexuality that people are aware of largely or completely without learning. Reflecting this belief, some people refer to variant sexual acts as "violations of nature." So for many people in the United States, "natural" sex is sex between men and women who are married. Some would even extend this "naturalness" to the sexual position assumed: genital contact in the "missionary" position (face-to-face with the male on top). Yet studies of other cultures indicate that socially acceptable sex takes far more forms than this. Consider one such culture:

> Sex—sex for pleasure and sex for procreation—is a principal concern of the Polynesian people on tiny Mangaia . . . . They demonstrate that concern in the startling number of children born to

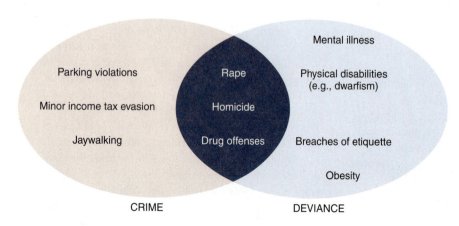

Figure 5.1
The Relationship between Crime and Deviance

unmarried parents, and in the statistics on frequency of orgasm and numbers of sexual partners. But that concern is simple fact-of-life—not morbid preoccupation . . . . There is great directness about sex, but the approach to sex is correspondingly indirect . . . . A flick of the eye, a raised eyebrow in a crowd, can lead to copulation—without a word. (Marshall, 1974, pp. 26–27)

Thus Mangaians have what people in the United States would call an extremely permissive attitude toward sexual behavior. Although sexual intercourse among unmarried persons is accepted by many people in the United States, multiple partners and casual sex tend to be frowned on, especially for women. If there is a natural or instinctive form of sexual expression, what are we to make of the Mangaians?

Consider some examples from other cultures (Bullough, 1976; Davenport, 1977). In Tahiti, young people are encouraged to masturbate. In the Truk Islands of the Pacific, sexual gratification is associated with pain and frustration, and sexual foreplay involves lovers inflicting pain on each other. Kissing is a part of sexual expression in most human societies, but there are people among whom sexual intercourse occurs completely without kissing. The Siriono of Bolivia find kissing to be a disgusting act.

Sexual norms, then, are like other societal rules: They vary widely from one context to another, and people learn to accept what is socially approved in their group or culture. For many in the United States, prostitution is considered a deviant form of sexual behavior, even though it is widespread there and is considered acceptable in many other societies. Prostitution has been called the "world's oldest profession," for it has been present throughout recorded history. Estimates place the number of prostitutes in the United States at between 100,000 and 500,000 and the money generated each year at between $1 billion and $10 billion (Thio, 2007). The trade is clearly thriving, and the explanation is primarily economic: There are people willing to pay for the services and others who are willing to supply them for a price. Although prostitution is usually associated with women, almost one-third of those arrested for prostitution in the United States are males.

Drug and Alcohol Abuse

The use of drugs is another realm of human behavior where there is much disagreement about where normality leaves off and deviance begins. Some drugs, such as alcohol, are legal; others, such as heroin and marijuana, are not. Still other drugs are "controlled." For example, cocaine is illegal on the street, but it is used regularly in the practice of medicine. During the twentieth century, attitudes in the United States have changed considerably

about whether certain drugs should be legal or illegal. Between 1920 and 1933, alcohol was illegal but marijuana was legal in most states. Today the reverse is true. When it comes to deviance, most of the attention surrounding drugs involves their abuse.

The abuse of alcohol, or *alcoholism*, is defined as a dependence on the substance by people who drink more than is socially acceptable in their group, or whose drinking has damaged their health, social relationships, or job performance. People in the United States are simultaneously enamored with the use of alcohol and concerned about its abuse. It is by far the most widely used, and abused, mood-altering drug in the United States. Estimates of the number of alcoholics in the United States vary, but most authorities agree that there are at least 10 million problem drinkers, or approximately 4 percent of the population.

Following alcohol, marijuana is probably the most widely used drug. Although it is still illegal in most places, many people have come to view the use of marijuana as the equivalent of the use of alcohol: For some, its occasional use is accepted, although excessive use is frowned on. It is estimated that about one-half of young adults between eighteen and twenty-five and about one-third of those older than twenty-five have used marijuana. Among high school seniors, 20 percent used marijuana at least once during a thirty-day period. However, rates of use of marijuana have declined considerably in the past twenty-five years (Johnston et al., 2007; Substance Abuse and Mental Health Services Administration, 2007; U.S. Bureau of the Census, 2007, p. 129).

Cocaine, a stimulant derived from coca leaves, has become a popular psychoactive drug. Today, 15 percent of all adults aged twenty-six and older in the United States have tried cocaine, compared with about 1 percent in the mid-1970s. Among young people aged eighteen to twenty-five years old, 10 percent have tried it compared with 12 percent in 1974. The number of current users seems to be declining, however: Today, fewer than 2 percent of eighteen- to twenty-five-year-olds reported that they had used cocaine in the last month compared with 10 percent in 1979. In fact, cocaine use seems to have peaked between 1980 and 1985 and has shown a substantial decline since then.

Gangs tend to be involved in the drug trade, as with many other types of crime. However, there is a lot of misinformation about gangs in the United States. Applying Sociology: Influencing Policy on Youth Gangs and Juvenile Crime clears up some of the misunderstanding as well as discusses some of the contributions that sociological practitioners have made to dealing with the gang and drug problem in the United States.

Applying Sociology   Influencing Policy on Youth Gangs and Juvenile Crime

Youth gangs have been a concern of sociologists since the 1920s when Frederic Thrasher did an extensive study of 1,313 gangs in Chicago. In the course of these decades of study, we have learned a lot about gangs (Dukes, Martinez, & Stein, 1997; Monti, 1993). For example, we know that youth typically join these gangs for a sense of identity and community. We have learned that youth join gangs, at least in part, because they are only weakly integrated into conventional groups and lack conventional opportunities to make money. We also know that much gang activity is social rather than criminal in nature. This means that much of gang life involves hanging out with friends, cruising the neighborhood or parks, and engaging in routine activities such as eating or working on cars. Of course, gangs do engage in crimes and violence; however, crime and violence often consume a relatively small part of gang life, and some of what is labeled "gang violence" really involves individuals acting on their own rather than under gang direction and organization.

The gangs that exist today are different in some significant ways from the gangs of earlier decades (Klein, 1995). One difference is that today's gangs are involved in more violent crimes, are more likely to use guns, are more likely to injure or kill themselves or nongang members, and are more likely to be involved in dealing or using drugs. A second difference is that today's gangs tend to have both youth and adults as members whereas earlier gangs were more likely to contain just a cohort of youth. While there are wide variations on what gangs do, and while some gangs are relatively benign, all of these differences mean that today's gangs on the whole tend to be more socially disruptive than the gangs of the past.

The sociologist Daniel J. Monti (1991) became interested in gangs through his work on urban redevelopment in St. Louis. He learned of gangs in some of the neighborhoods he had studied and wanted to learn more of their impact on the neighborhoods undergoing redevelopment. He interviewed many gang members, but his findings were not well received because many police and city officials did not want to admit to the existence of an extensive gang problem. Later, Monti was appointed to the Missouri State Advisory Committee to the U.S. Commission on Civil Rights. In this position, he was able to use his sociological analysis of gangs to organize testimony regarding the impact of proposed legislation on the problem of gangs and drugs. The testimony showed how school desegregation had an impact on gangs by helping to move gang activity to new areas. It also showed that some white gangs emerged in response to what they saw as a threat of minority students, and possibly gangs, moving into previously white schools. Through his sociological research, then, Monti was able to demonstrate links between educational policies and gang activities. He was also able to show that legislation proposed to control the gang and drug problems would be both discriminatory and ineffective because it would tag some minority youth as gang members who were not and fail to detect gang members among white youth.

The work of Monti and other sociologists has resulted in the development of a variety of social programs and projects to reduce the involvement of children and youth in gangs and the drug world (Godley & Velasquez, 1998; Pattillo, 1998). These programs involve educational efforts and comprehensive substance abuse services as well as efforts to enhance the informal social networks in neighborhoods so that community residents can divert youth from both gangs and drugs. Research on these programs demonstrates that they work well: They reduce involvement in both gangs and drugs and increase academic performance among youth. This work illustrates how sociological research becomes a significant part of the social-policy process and helps to develop programs to attack important social problems. ■

Mental Illness

Mental illness is stigmatized in many societies, even though millions of people are considered to have serious mental disorders, such as schizophrenia, that severely impair their ability to function (Cockerham, 2006). Far more people suffer from milder mental disorders, such as anxieties and obsessions, but most are able to function in their daily lives. The stigma associated with mental illness probably arises from the belief that mentally disturbed people are prone to be disruptive or violent.

Many people, including some psychologists and psychiatrists, view mental illness as much like physical illness in that there is some malfunction in the person that, when corrected, will cure the mental disorder. Sociologists recognize that some of the symptoms of mental disorders are caused by problems or stresses in people's social lives. In some cases, mental disorders arise, or are made worse, because a person is labeled as mentally ill and then responds to that label. Thomas Scheff (1999), for example, argues that mental illness is a social role with certain

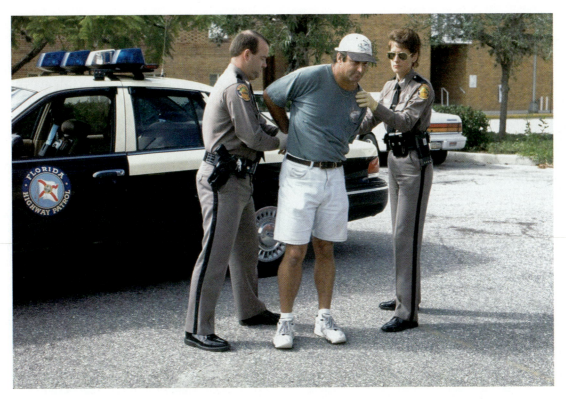

Violent crimes, such as homicide and assault, are the crimes that most frighten some people and seem most disruptive to social stability, but white collar crimes and cybercrimes are often more economically costly to society.

expectations associated with it. Once we label a person as mentally ill, the person's behavior is shaped by the expectations associated with the label. As discussed earlier under labeling theory, the tag *mental illness* can become a self-fulfilling prophecy. In other words, secondary deviance arises as the person begins to behave in a way that he or she thinks a mentally ill person should. In fact, some have gone so far as to argue that who is labeled mentally ill is to a degree arbitrary. In a disturbing and now classic study, the psychologist D. L. Rosenhan (1973) managed to have himself and seven other people admitted to mental institutions as schizophrenics by saying that they were hearing voices that said things like "thud" and "hollow." All these people performed normally on various psychological tests and acted perfectly normal once admitted to the institutions. Yet all hospital personnel, including psychiatrists and nurses, accepted the label *schizophrenia* and treated them accordingly. In fact, the staff tended to interpret the patients' normal behavior as symptomatic of their mental illness. Note-taking, for example, or questions regarding when they would be released were considered abnormal.

The positions of people like Scheff and Rosenhan do not mean that there are not people with psychologi-

cal disturbances that can have agonizing effects on their lives. The point is that mental illness is a complex type of deviance and involves social behaviors that require interpretation. What is normal behavior in one setting may be viewed as quite abnormal in another. Sociologists don't view mental illness as something inside a person's head but rather as a social role whose content can vary from one setting to another or one culture to another.

Violent Crimes

Violent crimes such as murder, assault, robbery, and rape are clear violations of group norms and the law. More than 16,000 murders were committed in 2006, along with 900,000 aggravated assaults (Federal Bureau of Investigation, 2007). Many murders are situational, in that they occur as a result of some dispute, frequently trivial, over money or some element of personal demeanor; they are only rarely planned in advance. The victim is often a relative, friend, or acquaintance of the assailant. One-quarter of all homicides arise from an argument, whereas only 16 percent occur during the commission of a felony. However, the reasons for and circumstances surrounding homicide have changed some over the past few decades; today, homicide is more often related to the drug trade, juvenile gang killing, and robbery or debt settlement among strangers rather than growing out of a dispute among people known to one another (Lattimore et al., 1997). Assaults are much more likely to involve strangers than were murders. In addition to these offenses, there are more than a half million robberies every year, some of which involve personal injury to the victims.

Forcible rape, another violent criminal offense, occurs when an assailant sexually assaults another person. In 2006, there were almost 100,000 rapes known to the police in the United States, but many estimates place the actual number much higher because victims may be reluctant to report the crime. According to survey results, rape is the crime that women, especially those under thirty-five years of age, fear the most. Especially in urban areas, this fear affects their daily lives as they avoid going out alone, refuse to enter certain neighborhoods, and install deadbolt locks in their homes (Stanko, 1995). In addition to the physical danger and degradation experienced by rape victims, the act also has a political element in that it symbolizes and reinforces the power and domination of the assailant over the victim. As one social scientist put it regarding female rape victims: "Rape is to women as lynching was to blacks: the ultimate physical threat" (Brownmiller, 1975, p. 254). As discussed in Chapter 8, only in recent decades, because of pressure from women's groups, have states made raping one's wife a crime (Bergen, 1999).

Organized Crime and Globalized Crime

Some forms of criminal activity benefit from large-scale organization. For example, the drug trade, gambling, and prostitution can be highly profitable to those who organize them, especially if that organization is national or global in scope. This led, in the twentieth century, to organized crime, or *syndicates*: criminal operations in which several criminal groups coordinate their illegal activities (Abadinsky, 2007; Kleinknecht, 1996). The Mafia, or La Cosa Nostra, in the United States, for example, consisted of nationwide alliances of families, based on kinship and ethnic solidarity, that coordinated their criminal actions and controlled large areas of criminal activity. Organized crime today includes many other racially or ethnically based criminal gangs, including Asian organized crime, Colombian drug-trafficking organizations, and Hispanic street gangs. Many of these gangs operate in local or regional criminal markets, although some gain a national reach.

By the twenty-first century, some organized crime had become globalized, with vast and integrated worldwide networks run by the Mafia, the Yakusa in Japan (see p. 139), and other syndicates. They are like any other global business, seeking investments, market share, and profits. Some of their activities involve legal business enterprises, but a significant part of their activities is illegal. Their global reach means that the markets for such crime are huge and the potential rewards enormous. This, of course, attracts many people to organized crime and produces intense, often violent, competition to control different parts of these enterprises. Many other kinds of crime, such as assaults or homicides, are a byproduct of this intense competition. Globalized organized crime is so vast and profitable that criminal syndicates have access to astonishing amounts of resources to engage in criminal activities, to hide their activities, and to fight against efforts to stop them. Drug "lords" in some countries, for example, have become so powerful that they rival the central government. Modern transportation and communication technologies have been important in the globalization of crime because they make possible the rapid movement of prostitutes and drugs and the other materials of crime. Instantaneous global communication also makes possible the efficient coordination of criminal activities over vast distances.

Cybercrime

As soon as the electronic world came into existence, crime took advantage of it. *Cybercrime* refers to crime that is committed with the aid of networked communications devices, such as computers, and it has become very costly and disruptive to normal social life (McQuade, 2006; Wall, 2007). In some cases, cybercrime involves crimes that are facilitated by computer technology but may have been committed without it. For example, prostitution is now often conducted partially online through Web pages, the Internet, and text messaging. This enables prostitutes and their customers to communicate without drawing the attention of law enforcement. In other cases, cybercrime involves offenses that require use of the networked communications technology. For one example, hackers who break into computer networks and steal data or who perpetrate computer viruses that destroy hardware and software are committing crimes that did not exist before such computer networks. A second example is the copyright law violations that involve peer-to-peer file-sharing technology.

Globalized crime and cybercrime call for new ways of thinking about crime fighting and law enforcement. Firstly, police and detectives must be highly educated and technologically sophisticated in order for them to understand the crimes they confront and how to catch the criminals. Secondly, our understanding of crime fighting must encompass a global view of law enforcement. Increasingly, nations agree to international treaties and agreements that coordinate national laws on crime, encourage transnational cooperation in criminal investigations, and facilitate the cooperation and sharing of information about crime across national boundaries. The Convention on Cybercrime of 2004, for example, did this for cybercrime and Internet crime.

White-Collar Crime

White-collar crimes are offenses committed by people in positions of respect and responsibility during the ordinary course of their business (Coleman, 2006). One such offense is antitrust violations, or attempts by businesses to monopolize a segment of the economy. White-collar crime can also take the form of price-fixing, in which competitors agree to sell their products for a price higher than they would be able to in a truly competitive market. In the mid-1970s, for example, a price-fixing scheme involving the four major breakfast cereal makers in the United States is estimated to have cost the public some $128 million. Another type of white-collar crime is the fraudulent

use of funds. A number of offenses of this sort came to light in 2002 when the top executives of a number of large corporations were accused of using their corporations to make illegal, off-the-balance-sheet loans to themselves of millions of dollars. The same year, a number of Enron Corporation executives were accused of using Enron to engage in sham business with companies in which the executives had invested. This sham business made the companies look like they were growing and thus increased the companies' stock price and the value of the companies' stock, in which the executives had invested. Because of these and other illegal or shady practices, Enron collapsed into bankruptcy, with the result that thousands of people lost their jobs and saw their retirement savings dwindle significantly.

As these illustrations should make clear, white-collar crime can be very costly to society and damaging to many people. In fact, white-collar crime may actually hurt more people than does street crime (Reiman, 2007). Despite this cost, the Federal Bureau of Investigation classifies most white-collar crimes as less serious offenses. The public in both the United States and Canada also seems to view most white-collar crimes as less serious than other crimes (Cullen, Link, & Polanzi,

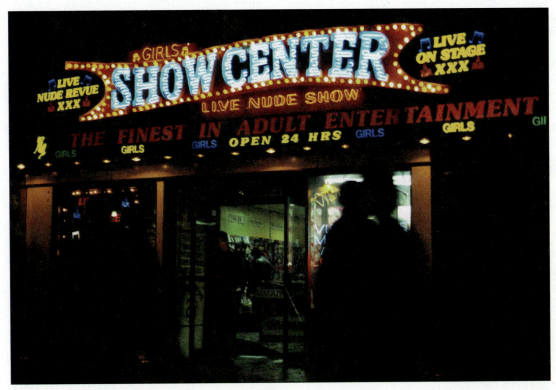

Many people in the United States would consider the sex shows illustrated in this photo to be unacceptable and deviant. Yet, sociologists have learned that sexual norms are like other social rules: What is considered acceptable varies widely from one context to another.

1982; Goff & Nason-Clark, 1989). Occasionally, corporate criminals go to jail, as have some corporate executives involved in the corporate scandals mentioned in the previous paragraph. But critics argue that these tend to be the exception rather than the rule and that the law is lenient on white-collar criminals, especially influential ones. Some of this leniency may come from the fact that white-collar criminals often cooperate with prosecutors in exposing other participants in illegal activities.

It should be clear that deviance is widespread and varied, especially in heterogeneous industrial societies. In all likelihood, you have engaged in actions that have been defined by some groups as deviant. Table 5.2 lists some activities that are illegal in the state of Michigan and likely to be considered deviant by some groups. Few college students can honestly claim to have never committed some of these offenses. I personally asked students in my college classes whether they had committed one or more of these offenses, and most said they had. Yet the students did not regard themselves as either criminals or deviants.

Deviance: Its Consequences for Society

You should be able to explain the functional and dysfunctional consequences of deviance for society.

Deviance is widespread, and its consequences are also broadly felt, ultimately affecting all parts of society. However, although many people tend to view deviance as "bad," sociologists recognize that deviance can be functional as well as dysfunctional.

The Dysfunctions of Deviance

One of the negative consequences of deviance is its cost. In sheer economic terms, crime costs U.S. society billions of dollars every year, through the maintenance of police forces, court systems, and prisons to house offenders. It costs $74,000 yearly to keep one offender in a maximum-security prison. Other forms of deviance, such as alcoholism, also result in financial

Table 5.2

CRIMINAL ACTIVITIES UNDER THE STATE OF MICHIGAN PENAL CODE

1. You attempt to strike another person physically, but do not succeed.
(Sec. 750–81/750.92: Attempted Assault and Battery)
2. During a fight, you break your opponent's nose.
(Sec. 750.81a: Assault and Battery with Bodily Harm)
3. You set a fire in a wastebasket located in a public rest room.
(Sec. 750.73–81: Arson)
4. You intentionally damage somebody else's property.
(Sec. 750.377a: Malicious Destruction of Property)
5. You knowingly trespass on another person's property.
(Sec. 750.552: Trespass)
6. You write a check, knowing that it exceeds the amount you have in your account.
(Sec. 750.218: False Pretenses)
7. You shoplift minor articles (candy bar, cigarettes, magazines).
(Sec. 750.356: Larceny)
8. You purchase a compact disc player that you know or believe is stolen.
(Sec. 750.535: Receiving Stolen Property)
9. You hide in the trunk of a friend's car in order to gain entrance to a drive-in movie without paying the admission fee.
(Sec. 750.292–93: Failure to Pay)
10. You participate in sexual activity with an animal.

(Sec. 750.158: Crime Against Nature)
11. You are married, and you have voluntary sexual intercourse with a person other than your spouse.
(Sec. 750.29: Felonious Adultery)
12. You engage in an act of sexual intercourse for money.
(Sec. 750.44: Soliciting and Accosting)
13. You participate in procuring a prostitute for another person or direct that person to a place of prostitution.
(Sec. 750.450: Aiders and Abettors)
14. You engage in sexual intercourse with any female under the age of 16 years.
(Sec. 750.13: Enticing Away Female Under Age 16)
15. You are involved in a fight involving two or more persons in a public establishment.
(Sec. 750.167: Disorderly Conduct)
16. You use obscene, profane language in the presence of women and children.
(Sec. 750.337: Improper Language)
17. You throw an empty can of soda out the window of your car.
(Sec. 752.901: Littering)
18. You play poker for money at a friend's home.
(Sec. 750.301: Accepting Money or Valuable Thing Contingent on an Uncertain Event)
19. You hide a firearm or knife with a blade exceeding three inches on your person while outside of your home.

Note: From *Michigan Compiled Laws* (vols. 38–39), 1987, St. Paul, MN: West.

This execution chamber in a prison in Ohio is designed to use lethal injection. Many states use the death penalty as a formal mechanism of social control to punish and hopefully deter serious crimes.

losses in the form of absenteeism from work, shoddy work from people who go to work while under the influence of alcohol, and the deterioration of personal relationships. These costs affect not only employers and employees but also the taxpayer, who is eventually touched by these behaviors.

Deviance has a number of other personal costs. One of these is the fear of crime felt by many urban residents, who barricade themselves in their homes each night and use double-bolt locks, burglar alarms, and watchdogs to put their minds at ease. Another personal cost of deviance is the tension created when people with conflicting lifestyles live side by side. For example, people who insist on "respectability" in their neighborhood may feel personally threatened if prostitutes begin to move in.

Another dysfunction of deviance is that some people may become disillusioned with conformity and choose to become deviant themselves. For example, when others are not penalized for cheating in business or selling illegal drugs, those who have previously conformed in these realms may begin to question the wisdom of their conformity. In addition, widespread deviance can lead people to lose faith and trust in societal institutions.

In addition to the previous dysfunctions, there are usually negative consequences for the people who are regarded as deviant. For one thing, people who are defined as deviant may be denied opportunities in society. Former prison inmates, the mentally ill, or the obese, for example, may be denied job opportunities that would probably be available to them had they not acquired a deviant status. Furthermore, the stigma associated with many forms of deviance can impair a person's self-concept, leading him or her to ignore opportunities or abandon efforts toward achieving socially valued goals, such as a respected occupation. A prostitute, for example, may internalize the social reaction that she is just a "cheap whore" and never aspire toward another way of making a living.

The Functions of Deviance

Deviance can have destructive consequences, but some forms of deviance can actually contribute to the maintenance of society. As one sociologist put it, a deviant "is not a bit of debris spun out by faulty social machinery, but a relevant figure in the community's overall division of labor" (Erikson, 1966, p. 19).

How is this figure "relevant" to the community? In other words, what part does deviance play in the functioning of society? First, the identification and sanctioning of deviants provides a lesson in what behaviors and characteristics society will tolerate. When people deride alcoholics as "drunks" or "winos," they are warning others about the denigration and ostracism they would suffer should they behave in a similar fashion. Emile Durkheim argued that deviance is actually a normal and quite necessary part of society because it helps identify the boundaries of acceptability.

Second, the punishment of deviance is a collective reaffirmation of those values that the deviant has violated, and this reaffirmation enhances group solidarity. When Germans stoned Jews in the streets in the 1930s, Germans were reinforcing their perception that they were a superior racial group and promoting a strong in-group feeling (see Chapter 4).

Third, deviance can act as a warning signal that there is a serious inconsistency or defect in society. High rates of drug abuse, for example, suggest that the social structure has failed to provide meaningful or satisfying positions for some in society.

Fourth, deviance can serve as a safety valve to prevent social discontent from being directed at basic societal values and institutions. The poor and the unemployed, for example, may turn to alcohol or drugs rather than supporting radical political groups advocating changes in the economic system and a redistribution of wealth. In this way, deviance contributes to the stability of society.

Finally, deviance can contribute to social change. In the 1950s, for example, cohabitation among young adults was highly stigmatized and rather uncommon, being limited largely to marginal groups such as "beatniks" or the poor. Since the 1960s, cohabitation has grown in acceptability and now provides an acceptable alternative for some adults who wish to carry on a sexual and emotional relationship openly but prefer not to marry. In short, what is deviant and stigmatized in one era may become normal in another era.

Deviance and Social Control

> You should be able to explain the functioning of internal and external social controls and differentiate formal and informal social controls.

Despite the many types and causes of deviance, social order predominates, and society is surprisingly stable and predictable. We have little fear that the bureaucrat will appear at his desk in the nude, that the bank teller will assault us, or that a college professor will exhibit schizophrenic behavior. We are highly dependent on this social stability in our daily lives. It is achieved through various means of social control. Social control refers to *the set of mechanisms societies use to encourage people to conform to the norms of society* (Black, 1993).

Internal Sources of Social Control

There are many forms of deviant behavior—from prostitution to armed robbery to striptease dancing—but most would probably have no particular appeal for you even if there were no possibility of detection and punishment. These feelings on your part are largely the result of socialization, through which each of us internalizes sets of norms that guide our behavior. Conformity to internalized norms is an *internal* source of social control. The norms internalized are those of society or of some group to which we belong, and they can be so powerful that the very thought of violating them generates anxiety and guilt. As noted in Chapter 3, "most of the time we ourselves desire just that which society expects of us. We *want* to obey the rules. We *want* the parts that society has assigned to us" (Berger, 1963, p. 93). Most of us, for example, are so horrified at the thought of eating human flesh that the possibility would not even enter our minds unless faced with imminent starvation. Even then, many people have refused to do so and have died. Through socialization, then, *social* control can become *self*-control. From society's point of view, self-control is the most effective means of social control because it requires little surveillance and few active efforts to punish wrongdoers. People conform because they want to, not because they fear punishment.

External Sources of Social Control

The socialization process is pervasive but not completely effective. There are a host of psychological, sociological, biological, and situational influences that can channel people's behavior in socially disapproved directions. In addition, some deviance is inherently pleasurable and enticing. Thus socialization is not, by itself, sufficient to ensure conformity, and all societies develop external techniques of social control. These external techniques can be either informal or formal in nature.

Informal social controls are the various types of social pressures exerted by people in face-to-face settings to ensure the general observance of norms. Through these techniques, people express disapproval and thereby exert pressure on others to modify their behavior. There are many forms of informal social control. Criticism and ridicule, for example, can be effective means of exerting social pressure. Wearing a bathing suit to church or the opera, for instance, may draw a raised eyebrow, a hostile stare, or possibly a verbal reprimand. If the opinion of the congregation or the opera crowd is important to that person, such criticism will probably lead him or her to think twice about his or her dress.

Among the Kapauku Papuans of New Guinea, the public reprimand was one of the most important techniques of social control (Pospisil, 1958). For violations of important norms, members of the tribe would subject the offender to angry reproaches, sometimes continuing intermittently for many days. This experience was considered deeply humiliating for the offender, because people in such small societies must be concerned about everyone's opinion of them. This sanction caused so much shame among the Kapaukans that it was considered second only to death in its severity.

Gossip can also be an effective informal mechanism of social control. People tend to pass on accounts about the social "misbehavior" of others. Because most people are concerned about their reputations, gossip, or the threat of it, might motivate a person to forgo an adulterous affair or to conduct it in such a way that detection is less likely.

Social pressure can also be exerted through shunning or ostracism. Among the Mzab of southern Algeria, for example, a woman who has violated community rules, especially sexual mores, can be ostracized, a condition known as *tebreya*, for up to two years. During this period, other women are forbidden to have any conversations with her, and she is excluded from public ceremonies and religious rituals (Farrag, 1971). Such experiences can be painful and even terrifying. Because our self-concepts and sense of self-worth are largely derived from membership in groups, terminating or curtailing those memberships can affect our perceptions of our worth.

Formal social controls are the techniques that have been codified by a society and are applied by specifically designated agents, such as law enforcement bodies or the courts. In heterogeneous, industrial societies, formal social control becomes especially important because informal means are often inadequate. Informal social control through shunning or gossip is effective only if the people affected care about the opinions of others, and in modern societies where secondary relationships abound, that is frequently not the case. Ostracism can be exercised only if the deviant belongs to a group from which he or she can be isolated. Many deviants are strangers over whom we do not have such control, however. Thus we use formal agents of social control, such as the police and the courts, that have the power to control behavior through levying fines or imprisoning people. In the United States, these formal agents of social control tend to focus on deviance that is dangerous, such as crime. Other forms of deviance, which may be repugnant to some but not threatening to person or property, are less likely to come under the purview of formal agents of control. In some societies, however, such as Singapore and China, many different types of deviance are the focus of formal social-control efforts.

Crime in the United States

You should be able to describe and explain the high crime rate in the United States and explain proposals for reducing crime.

Crime rates have risen rapidly in the United States in the past few decades. Many prisons house far more inmates than they can handle, and the public and politicians clamor for funds to build yet more prisons. Unlike noncriminal deviance, there is considerable consensus that something needs to be done about crime. But what? This chapter closes with an assessment of the crime problem, focusing especially on the role of recent social developments in changes in the crime rate.

The High Crime Rate

The Federal Bureau of Investigation (FBI) publishes an annual document called the Uniform Crime Reports (UCR). The report summarizes crime statistics collected by the FBI each month from law enforcement authorities in more than 12,000 cities and towns. In the UCR, the FBI distinguishes between what are called Part I, or more serious, criminal offenses, and Part II, or less serious offenses (Table 5.3). Part I offenses are considered more serious because many believe they pose the greatest and most direct threat to personal safety and property. The FBI also presents a Crime Index, which is the official crime rate typically reported in the media. The Crime Index comprises the number of Part I offenses known to the police for every 100,000 people.

Between 1970 and 1980, according to the FBI, the rate of Crime Index offenses rose by a startling 49 percent. The 1980s, however, were another story: Crime Index offenses actually dropped by 2 percent between 1980 and 1990. Most of this drop was accounted for by the drop in property crimes. During the 1980s, violent crimes rose by 22 percent, but this was less of an increase than the 64 percent rise in the 1970s (Figure 5.2). Since 1990, the crime rate has shown a steady and significant decline: about a one-third decline in both violent and property crimes. Despite these declines, the crime rate is still far higher than in earlier decades. If crimes were evenly spaced throughout the day, there would have been one serious crime about every three seconds of each day and one violent crime approximately every twenty-two seconds (Federal Bureau of Investigation, 2007).

Some of these increases, however, need to be placed in perspective. They may in part reflect changes in the

Table 5.3

CLASSIFICATION OF CRIMINAL OFFENSES BY THE FEDERAL BUREAU OF INVESTIGATION

Part I Offenses		Part II Offenses	
Murder and nonnegligent manslaughter Forcible rape Robbery Aggravated assault	Violent crimes	Other assaults Forgery and counterfeiting Fraud Stolen property; buying, receiving, possessing Vandalism	Driving under the influence Liquor laws Drunkenness Disorderly conduct Vagrancy
Burglary Larceny-theft Motor vehicle theft Arson	Property crimes	Weapons; carrying, possessing, etc. Prostitution and commercialized vice Sex offenses (except forcible rape and prostitution) Drug abuse violations Gambling Offenses against family and children	All other offenses (except traffic) Suspicion Curfew and loitering law violations

likelihood of reporting crimes rather than actual increases in crime. Rape, for example, has traditionally been a vastly underreported crime. With more public discussion of rape in recent decades, and strong pressure from feminist groups, both the police and the public have become more sensitive to the problems of rape victims. Many hospitals provide counseling for rape victims, and many states have rules that limit the use of information about a victim's previous sexual activities as evidence in court. These changes have encouraged more women to report rapes, and this encouragement undoubtedly accounts for some, although not all, of the increase in reported rapes compared to earlier decades.

Another reason for caution about UCR crime statistics is that they are based on crimes known to the police, and considerable crime is not brought to the attention of the police. Such unreported crime is not reflected in these statistics, which are conservative indicators of the nation's crime problem. It is estimated, for example, that only half of all violent crimes are reported to the police and as few as 30 percent of the thefts (Maguire & Pastore, 2004, p. 210).

Not only are crime rates in the United States higher than in earlier decades, but the United States also appears as a disturbingly crime-ridden society when compared to other nations around the world. Figure 5.3 compares the homicide rate in the United States with the rate in various other nations. The U.S. rate is far higher than the rate in all European nations except for the Russian federation—a nation in considerable economic, social, and cultural collapse. The U.S. homicide rate is also much higher than in most Asian and Middle Eastern nations, even though many of these nations are relatively poor. Some struggling nations in Latin America have higher homicide rates, but other poor nations in that region, such as Nicaragua, have homicide rates that are lower than that of the United States. The homicide rate in the United States is eleven times higher than the rate in Japan.

Reducing Crime

The question of how to reduce crime is highly controversial. However, the analysis of the sociological sources of deviance and crime earlier in the chapter points to a number of promising reforms. Given the role of poverty and economic inequities in fostering crime, it is plausible that reducing poverty and the economic disparity between the affluent and the poor would help reduce some forms of crime and delinquency. Especially important along these lines would be to provide equal educational and occupational opportunities for all people. Given Elliott Currie's (1985) analysis of crime in Japan discussed earlier, it may be possible to reduce poverty and economic disparity through programs that encourage fuller employment—government and private-sector programs to create new jobs and to provide job training to those without adequate job skills. In addition, the jobs people get must pay a living wage so that people can support their families. Furthermore, the sociologist Mark Colvin (1991) recommends that we fight crime by investing in the institutions that prepare people for productive roles in society: families and schools (see Chapters 9 and 12). Failures in the educational institutions and families have contributed to the inability of many young people to find and make use of legitimate avenues to opportunity. These calls for social reform are an attempt to attack the social and structural conditions that have created much, although

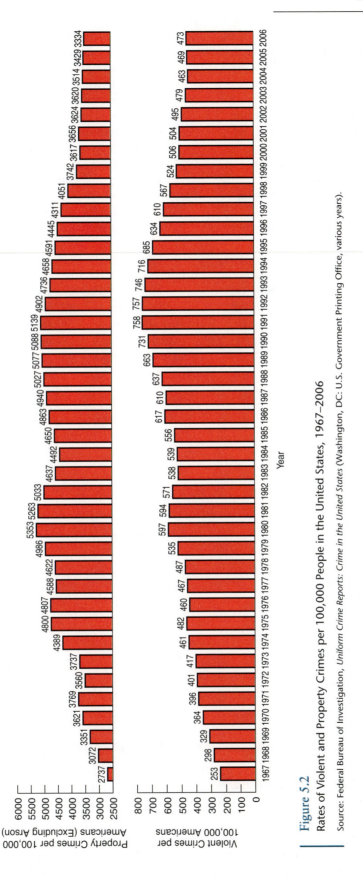

Figure 5.2

Rates of Violent and Property Crimes per 100,000 People in the United States, 1967–2006

Source: Federal Bureau of Investigation, *Uniform Crime Reports: Crime in the United States* (Washington, DC: U.S. Government Printing Office, various years).

not all, of the crime problem. Other Worlds, Other Ways: Japan explores in more depth the differences between Japan and the United States in this regard.

Beyond this social reform, a number of measures could be taken to reduce crime in the United States.

1. Legalize many victimless crimes, such as gambling, prostitution, and some drug violations. This would reduce the secondary crime associated with victimless offenses and free the criminal justice system to work with more serious crimes.

2. Focus judicial reform on providing swift, certain, and fair punishment rather than overly long and counterproductive prison terms.

3. Make punishment equitable, whether the crime occurs on a slum street or in a corporate boardroom. Disparities in punishment resulting from the racial, sexual, or socioeconomic characteristics of the offender should be carefully monitored and controlled.

4. Narrow the discretionary options of police officers, prosecutors, and judges and develop procedures to hold them accountable to the public for the fairness and reasonableness of their decisions and actions.

5. Provide all criminal defendants with truly equal legal counsel in order to reduce the inequities in convictions and sentences.

6. Develop correctional programs that promote rather than undermine personal responsibility and that provide offenders with real opportunities to succeed in legitimate occupations. These might include increased occupational training and counseling while imprisoned and work release and other alternatives to incarceration.

7. Make efforts to reduce the environmental opportunities for committing crime. These can take the form of better physical security, such as burglar-proof locks; better detection of crime through such mechanisms as burglar alarms and antishoplifting tags in stores; and improved surveillance, such as better street lighting.

Certainly other reforms can be considered. Which reforms will have a beneficial effect on the crime problem and on inadequacies in the criminal justice system can be determined only after programs have been initiated and evaluated. What should be clear is that only a broad-based and coordinated attack is likely to have a significant impact.

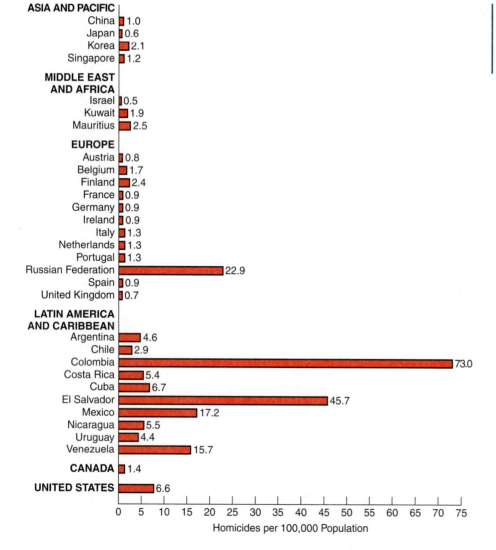

Figure 5.3

Homicide Rates in Various Nations

Note: From *Demographic Yearbook*, 1999 (pp. 479–506) by the United Nations, 2001, New York: United Nations.

Other Worlds, Other Ways

JAPAN: SOCIAL AND CULTURAL UNDERPINNINGS OF CRIME

Figure 5.3 demonstrates that the United States has an astonishingly high crime rate in comparison to Japan. The United States has eighteen times more rapes, eleven times more homicides, six times more burglaries, and nine times more drug-related offenses (Currie, 1985; Hendry, 1995; Thornton & Endo, 1992).

What accounts for this dramatic contrast with Japan? The unavailability of handguns in Japan plays a part, as does the much narrower gap between the affluent and the poor, as mentioned earlier in this chapter. Chapter 2 also noted that Japan and the United States have some dramatically contrasting cultural values, which undoubtedly play a part. One widely recognized difference is that Japanese society places much higher value on the group and family, whereas the United States emphasizes individualism and personal autonomy. Individual Japanese feel a strong obligation to their family and society, and families feel a strong sense of responsibility for the behavior of their members. Each family member bears a share of the responsibility for preserving the reputation of the family and avoiding bringing disgrace to it by doing something that might be socially disapproved such as committing a crime. Consequently, informal mechanisms of social control, such as threatened exclusion from the group, can control crime more effectively in Japan than in the United States.

Another difference is that Japanese culture instills a strong sense of respect for laws, rules, and customs. Such respect is seen as part of a citizen's social obligation, probably deriving from Confucian teachings about uprightness, duty, and obligation. In Japan, people obey the law because of this obligation, not just out of fear of authority or punishment; in the United States, people are more inclined toward cynical violation of the law if they think they can get away with it.

A third difference is that Japan is a much more racially and culturally homogeneous society where there is considerable consensus regarding desirable values and appropriate behaviors. Homogeneity removes one important source of misunderstanding, tension, and conflict that exists in the United States. Without these social fault lines, Japan offers its citizens a much more cohesive and supportive neighborhood and community environment.

A final difference is that Japanese society is much more *supportive* of individuals and their families than is U.S. society. Through economic and social policies, Japan strives toward full employment of its workers and tries to create a stable connection of workers to the workplace. As a consequence, the income distribution in Japan is much more equitable than in the United States, and no severely deprived and permanently disadvantaged underclass exists. These supportive policies create the foundation for the emergence of strong and stable family and neighborhood ties, which in turn exert strong social controls over misbehavior. In addition, Japan, along with many Western European industrial nations, has social policies that cushion the disruptions and hardships that can accompany the loss of work. These nations, for example, allow more generous unemployment benefits and give them to more unemployed workers than does the United States. Because of this generosity, less disruption of family and communal roles accompanies unemployment. This continuity is important because it is not just economic circumstances that motivate crime; the destruction of family and communal supports that can accompany unemployment also reduces controls over misbehavior (Currie, 1985).

Thus, different cultural values account for some of the differences in crime between the two societies. Reality, however, is still more complicated. Many other factors contribute to Japan's low crime rate, but just one will be mentioned here (Kersten, 1993). Japan has very active and extensive criminal organizations, called *yakuza*, with hierarchies of bosses and an extensive corporate structure. They engage in illegal and semilegal as well as legal enterprises, and they have links to important politicians. They have extensive networks going into many Japanese neighborhoods, and their activities may actually serve to reduce crime overall. For example, they settle civil disputes, such as those arising over traffic accidents, and collect overdue loans. They also have tight control over Japan's illegal drug market, which helps to prevent a lot of the crime and violence that surround the wide-open market in illegal drugs in the United States. In addition, the *yakuza* probably deter small-scale robbery and theft in the neighborhoods where they have a considerable presence.

When considered separately, each of these elements of Japanese culture may make only a small contribution to the low Japanese crime rate; in combination, however, they advance a good way toward understanding the yawning gulf between crime in the United States and crime in Japan. They also emphasize the sociological perspective on crime, namely, that crime emerges from particular social and cultural conditions and can be reduced by changing these conditions. ■

Sociology on the Internet

Government agencies now make a lot of data about crime, crime victims, and criminal justice issues available at their Internet Web sites. Take a look at the Web sites of the FBI (**www.fbi.gov**), the Bureau of Justice Statistics at the Department of Justice (**www.ojp.usdoj.gov/bjs/**), and the Bureau of Prisons (**www.bop.gov.**) Many of the documents and data sets at these sites can be down-loaded to your own computer (some require special software, such as Acrobat Reader). For example, the FBI's *Uniform Crime Report* is available at its Web site, and the Bureau of Justice Statistics' *Sourcebook of Criminal Justice Statistics* can be found at this Web site: **www.albany. edu/sourcebook/**. Gather data at these various sites to update and supplement the information in this chapter. Share the data with your class.

You can also explore the Internet for information about white-collar and corporate crime. Use the search engines to locate Web sites on these topics. One of Ralph Nader's public interest groups maintains a Web site on recent episodes of corporate crime: **www.citizenworks. org/enron/corp-scandal.php**

For further information and discussion, go to Allyn & Bacon's Social Problems Supersite and explore Problem Area: Crime, Violence, Drugs, and the Criminal Justice System.

Study & Review
SUMMARY OF LEARNING OBJECTIVES

You should be able to describe the sociological perspective on deviance and explain how it differs from the absolute and statistical views.

Deviance consists of behaviors or characteristics that violate important group norms and that as a consequence are reacted to with disapproval. Behaviors and characteristics are deviant because they are so defined by a particular group. Sociologists view deviance as relative to the norms and values of a particular culture, subculture, or group. Deviance is not inherent in any behavior or characteristic but rather arises from the relationship between a behavior and the social definition of the behavior by some group.

You should be able to discuss the major explanations of deviance, including biological and psychological perspectives, as well as the three sociological perspectives on deviance.

Two prominent nonsociological explanations of deviance are those resting on biological and psychological grounds. Purely biological theories of deviance have been discredited. In a few cases, biology may play a limited role in bringing about deviance, but most deviance has nothing to do with biology. Although psychological approaches to deviance may shed some light on some forms of deviance, the role of psychological disturbances is limited, and it is often the deviance, and the public's reaction to it, that results in changes in personality. Sociologists have emphasized the role of culture, social structure, and social interaction in bringing about deviant behavior. Functionalist theories of deviance focus on such things as social bonds, anomie, and opportunities for deviance or crime created by changes in the social system. The conflict perspective emphasizes the point that powerful groups have the resources to define what will be considered crime or deviance and to decide which behaviors social control will be exercised against. This perspective also emphasizes that the structure of some economic systems may force some groups into criminal or deviant patterns of behavior. The interactionist perspective explains deviance and crime through processes of cultural transmission, differential association, and labeling.

You should be able to describe the major forms of deviance and crime found in the United States and explain why they occur.

Crime and deviance overlap, but they are not the same thing. Some crimes are considered deviance and others are not. Likewise, some forms of deviance are not crimes. There are many types of deviance, both criminal and noncriminal. In fact, deviance can take such a variety of forms that virtually everyone has engaged in activities that some groups have defined as deviant. The types of deviance or crime discussed in this chapter are sexual deviance, drug and alcohol abuse, mental illness, violent crimes, organized crime, globalized crime, cybercrime, and white-collar crime.

You should be able to explain the functional and dysfunctional consequences of deviance for society.

Deviance can be dysfunctional for society in a number of ways: It creates personal and economic costs, leads to disillusionment among conventional people, and results in reduced opportunities and possibly negative self-concepts for those who are stigmatized as deviant. However, deviance can also be functional: Punishing deviants helps clarify the limits of acceptable behavior and reaffirms important values. Deviance also points to defects in society, can serve as a safety valve for easing discontent, and can contribute to social change.

You should be able to explain the functioning of internal and external social controls and differentiate between formal and informal social controls.

Social control refers to societal mechanisms for encouraging people to conform. Some norms are internalized sufficiently that social control becomes self-control. There are also external mechanisms of social control, some of which are informal, such as gossip or ostracism, and others of which are formal, such as the police or the courts.

You should be able to describe and explain the high crime rate in the United States and explain proposals for reducing crime.

The crime rate in the United States is at a high level compared to the past, although it has dropped some in the past decade. The U.S. crime rate is also high compared to other nations. Proposals to reduce crime derive from the sociological perspectives and point to such factors as reducing poverty and economic inequality, providing educational and occupational opportunities, and investing in the institutions that prepare people for productive roles in society.

CHRONOLOGICAL PRACTICE TEST

For answers to Key Concepts see the page number in parentheses; for other answers see page 142.

The Relativity of Deviance
Key Concept

1. Deviance (119)

True/False

2. T F For sociologists, a behavior can be inherently deviant, without regard to people's interpretation or judgment of the behavior.

Critical Thinking

3. Define the term *deviance,* as sociologists use it. How is deviance handled in Singapore? How is it different from the treatment of deviance in the United States?

Explanations of Deviance
Key Concepts

4. Anomie theory (121)
5. Anomie (121)
6. Cultural transmission theories (123)
7. Differential association theory (123)
8. Labeling theory (124)
9. Primary deviance (124)
10. Secondary deviance (124)
11. Career deviance (124)

True/False

12. T F Anomie theory can lead to the conclusion that large disparities between income groups can cause crime.
13. T F According to anomie theory, most deviant behavior is produced by the mode of adaptation called ritualism.
14. T F Cultural transmission theories posit that crime can be blamed on certain characteristics of capitalism as an economic system.
15. T F Reality-based police shows on television tend to lead their viewers to believe that less crime occurs than is actually the case.

Concept Completion

16. According to _____ approaches to deviance, deviance is linked to personality disorders or maladjustments.
17. Inconsistencies and contradictions in the social system and the confusion they can cause in people are referred to as _____.
18. The most important mode of adaptation, according to Robert Merton, and the one that might take the form of deviant or criminal behavior, is called _____.
19. The differential association theory of crime is one example of a _____ theory.
20. If a drug user is discovered and responds to the discovery by becoming more closely involved with other drug users, this would be an example of _____ deviance.

Critical Thinking

21. Describe the psychological approaches to deviance. How do sociologists assess them as explanations of deviance?
22. Describe the functionalist explanation of deviance and crime. Include in your answer a discussion of all of the modes of adaptation to anomie.
23. Explain deviance and crime from the conflict perspective. Show how it differs from the functionalist approach.
24. According to the differential association theory, what is the explanation for why some people commit crimes or engage in deviance while others do not?

Extent of Deviance and Crime
Key Concept

25. Crime (126)

True/False

26. T F Instances of minor income tax evasion would be considered both crime and deviance by most people.

27. T F Sexual norms are like other societal rules: They vary widely from one social context to another.
28. T F People in the United States view most white-collar crimes as less serious than other crimes.

Concept Completion

29. Syndicates are associated with _____ crime.
30. Antitrust violations are one type of _____ crime.

Graphics Review

31. Looking at Figure 5.1, what is the point that it makes about the relationship between crime and deviant behavior.

Deviance: Its Consequences for Society
Critical Thinking

32. Describe the functions that deviant behavior performs for society.
33. Describe how deviance is dysfunctional for society.

Deviance and Social Control
Key Concept

34. Social control (134)

Concept Completion

35. _____ are the techniques for ensuring conformity to norms that are codified by society and applied by specifically designated agents.

Critical Thinking

36. Define social control. Describe the forms it can take and give an example of each form.

Crime in the United States
True/False

37. T F Even though handguns are largely unavailable in Japan, crime rates in Japan are at the same level as in the United States.
38. T F The text recommends making punishments swift and certain rather than overly lengthy.

Concept Completion

39. Japanese citizens' sense of respect for law and social obligation probably derives from _____ teachings.
40. The text recommends that the United States fight crime by investing in the social institutions primarily responsible for preparing people for productive roles in society: _____ and _____.

Critical Thinking

41. Why is the crime rate in Japan so much lower than it is in the United States?
42. What policies are suggested in the text to help reduce the crime rate in the United States?

ANSWERS TO CHRONOLOGICAL PRACTICE TEST

2. F; 12. T; 13. F; 14. F; 15. F; 26. F; 27. T; 28. T; 37. F; 38. T
16. psychological
17. anomie
18. innovation
19. cultural transmission
20. secondary, career
29. organized
30. white-collar
35. Formal social controls
39. Confucian
40. families, schools

CUMULATIVE PRACTICE TEST

See page 482 for answers.

1. Judging certain behaviors and characteristics to be good or bad and right or wrong by comparing them to some fixed standards exemplifies _____ approach to deviance.
   a. a relative
   b. a statistical
   c. an unrealistic
   d. a sociological
   e. an absolute
2. A key element of the sociological approach to deviance is that
   a. deviance is viewed as a function of the judgments of particular groups of people.
   b. deviance is regarded primarily as a statistical phenomenon.
   c. there are frequently situations when deviance must be viewed in an absolute way.
   d. All of the above.
   e. None of the above.
3. Which of the following figures developed an influential biological approach to deviance?
   a. Robert K. Merton.
   b. Cesare Lombroso.
   c. Max Weber.
   d. Edwin Lemert.
   e. Elliott Currie.
4. According to _____ approaches to deviance, deviance is believed to result from some personality disorder or maladjustment that typically develops during childhood.
   a. psychological
   b. sociological
   c. criminological
   d. biological
   e. labeling
5. As for biological explanation of deviance, sociologists have concluded that
   a. biology explains a substantial amount of deviance.
   b. biology plays no role in causing deviance.
   c. biological explanations are more important than psychological ones in understanding deviance.

d. they should be given more weight than cultural transmission theories.

e. when biology does play a role, it is but one contributing factor rather than the sole cause of deviance.

6. In an early application of functionalist theory to deviance, French sociologist Emile Durkheim argued that
   a. deviance is dysfunctional to social organization.
   b. deviance results in part from weak social bonds and the resulting social disorganization.
   c. deviance should be judged by absolute standards.
   d. All of the above.
   e. Only a and c.

7. The concept of "anomie" is linked with which theoretical perspective in sociology?
   a. The conflict perspective.
   b. The interactionist perspective.
   c. The biological perspective.
   d. The functionalist perspective.
   e. The psychological perspective.

8. Ritualism, as a mode of adaptation to anomie, is defined as
   a. strong acceptance of cultural goals and values.
   b. compulsively accepting the culturally approved means but not using them to achieve cultural goals.
   c. pursuing societal goals through culturally approved means.
   d. rejecting both the socially approved goals and the culturally approved means of achieving them.
   e. pursuing both innovation and rebellion at the same time.

9. Conflict theorists argue that the causes of crime and deviance can be found in
   a. the labeling process.
   b. biological inadequacies of individuals.
   c. weakened social bonds in industrial societies.
   d. the learning that occurs through primary group ties.
   e. certain characteristics of capitalism.

10. According to _____ theory, deviant behavior is learned in interaction with other people, for the most part within intimate primary groups such as families and peer groups.
    a. conflict
    b. anomie
    c. functional
    d. social control
    e. differential association

11. Violations of social norms in which a person is not caught, or is excused rather than labeled deviant, are referred to as
    a. relative deviance.
    b. secondary deviance.
    c. tertiary deviance.
    d. career deviance.
    e. primary deviance.

12. Which of the following is an accurate representation of how, according to the text, the media distort the view of crime presented to the public?
    a. They present less crime than there actually is.
    b. They present the police as more effective than they actually are.
    c. They present mostly corporate and organizational crime rather than individual crime.

d. They present nonviolent crime as more common than violent crime.

e. Both b and d are correct.

13. According to the text, a *crime* is
    a. an act that is bad in and of itself.
    b. an act that is bad because it is prohibited.
    c. an act that is stigmatized by some powerful group.
    d. an act that violates a criminal code that has been enacted by an officially constituted political authority.
    e. none of the above.

14. The most widely used mood-altering drug in the United States is
    a. marijuana.
    b. alcohol.
    c. cocaine.
    d. heroin.
    e. nicotine.

15. Which of the following statements would be most consistent with the labeling theory approach to understanding mental illness?
    a. Mental illness is much like physical illness.
    b. Mental illness is the result of childhood traumas that produce maladjustment.
    c. Mental illness is caused by a shift from secondary deviance to primary deviance.
    d. Mental illness is a mode of adaptation to anomie.
    e. The symptoms of mental illness arise when people conform to the expectations of how they think a mentally ill person should behave.

16. Which of the following is true of homicides?
    a. They are rarely planned in advance.
    b. The majority occur during the commission of a felony.
    c. The majority of homicide victims are strangers to their assailants.
    d. The majority are committed as a part of organized crime activities.
    e. They are less likely to be related to the drug trade today than in the past.

17. "Syndicates" are associated with which type of crime?
    a. White-collar crime.
    b. Organized crime.
    c. Sexual crime.
    d. Drug offenses.
    e. Property crime.

18. When the techniques for encouraging conformity have been codified by a society and are applied by specifically designated agents, such as law enforcement bodies or the courts, they are called
    a. formal social controls.
    b. informal social controls.
    c. internal sources of social control.
    d. diffused social controls.
    e. dysfunctional social controls.

19. Which of the following is true regarding the crime rate in the United States, as reported by the FBI?
    a. It has doubled since 1980.
    b. Since 1980, the rate of property crimes has risen while the rate of violent crimes has dropped.
    c. Pre-1980 rates are not comparable to post-1980 rates.
    d. It is lower today than it was in the 1960s.
    e. It has declined significantly since 1990.

20. The text recommends all of the following to help in the fight against crime and delinquency *except*
    a. reduce poverty.
    b. legalize some victimless crimes.
    c. promote personal responsibility among prison inmates.
    d. encourage fuller employment.
    e. give longer prison sentences for most crimes.

FOR FURTHER READING

Abadinsky, Howard. (2008). *Drug use and abuse: A comprehensive introduction* (6th ed.). Belmont, CA: Wadsworth/Cengage Learning. This book provides an excellent overview of the drug problem in modern societies, covering history, causes, treatment, and social policy.

Cole, David. (1999). *No equal justice: Race and class in the American criminal justice system*. New York: New Press. This author, a law professor, reviews the abysmal treatment of racial minorities and people of low economic standing by the U.S. criminal justice system. He proposes various remedies, especially suggesting that the system move away from the punitive and toward the rehabilitative.

Dyer, Joel. (2000). *The perpetual prisoner machine: How America profits from crime*. Boulder, CO: Westview Press. The book identifies the groups that benefit from high incarceration rates in the United States and suggests how fears of crime can be manipulated to maintain and enhance the interests of this "prison industrial complex."

Erikson, Kai T. (1966). *Wayward Puritans*. New York: Wiley and Sons. This classic sociological work on deviant behavior uses the experiences of the Puritans to demonstrate that deviance is relative and performs important functions in society.

Mokhiber, Russell. (1988). *Corporate crime and violence: Big business power and the abuse of public trust*. San Francisco: Sierra Club Books. A muckraker's view of white-collar and corporate crime: Thirty-six cases are described in which corporate misconduct killed people or significantly harmed the environment.

Pattillo, Mary, Weiman, David, & Western, Bruce (Eds.). (2004). *Imprisoning America: The social effects of mass incarceration*. New York: Russell Sage Foundation. The readings in this book explore the many negative consequences of incarcerating people—to families, communities, and others—and argue for policies that promote less incarceration of criminals and incarcerate only when the benefits clearly outweigh the costs.

Reinarman, Craig, & Levine, Harry G. (Eds.). (1997). *Crack in America: Demon drugs and social justice*. Berkeley: University of California Press. This book of readings offers an excellent overview of the social, political, and legal issues involved in the policy decision of whether to prohibit, decriminalize, or legalize crack cocaine.

Sikes, Gini. (1997). *8 ball chicks: A year in the violent world of girl gangsters*. New York: Anchor. This fascinating account, which debunks the notion that females don't engage in dangerous and violent activities, is based on the author's years of association with female gangs.

Simon, David R. (2008). *Elite deviance* (9th ed.). Boston: Allyn & Bacon. An excellent antidote to the myth that deviance occurs mostly among poor and disreputable people, this book chronicles the deviant activities of the rich and powerful.

Spradley, James P. (1970). *You owe yourself a drunk: An ethnography of urban nomads*. Boston: Little, Brown. Spradley uses an anthropological approach to deviant subcultures in a heterogeneous society—in this case, focusing on hoboes and street people who some might consider deviant.

STRATIFICATION AND SOCIAL INEQUALITY

CHAPTER SIX
Social Stratification and Social Inequality

CHAPTER SEVEN
Social Inequality: Race and Ethnicity

CHAPTER EIGHT
Social Inequality: Gender

The chapters in Part III analyze the hierarchical nature of human societies, discussing the tendency for social stratification and social inequality to characterize societies. In particular, the chapters assess inequality that is based on social class, race, ethnicity, and gender.

CHAPTER 6

Social Stratification and Social Inequality

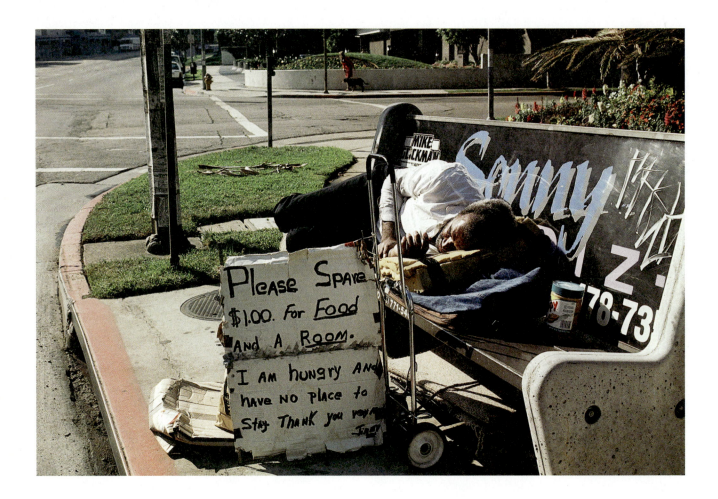

MYTHS & FACTS: About Social Stratification

Dimensions of Stratification

Weber's Analysis
Socioeconomic Status
Types of Stratification Systems
Caste Systems
Estate Systems
Class Systems

Theories of Stratification

The Functionalist Perspective
The Conflict Perspective

Synthesis: An Evolutionary View
A Global Perspective on Stratification
OTHER WORLDS, OTHER WAYS: Brazil and Venezuela: The Third-World Poor in the Global Stratification System

Social Class in the United States

Measuring Socioeconomic Status
Class Structure in the United States
The Upper Class
The Upper-Middle Class
The Lower-Middle Class
The Working Class
The Lower Class

Inequality and Poverty
Extent of Inequality
A Global View of Poverty
Causes of Poverty
APPLYING SOCIOLOGY: Creating and Evaluating Programs That Assist the Poor

Social Mobility
Extent of Social Mobility
Sources of Social Mobility

Consequences of Stratification
Educational Achievement
Health
SOCIOLOGY OF MEDIA AND TECHNOLOGY: Impact of Technology on Stratification Systems
Status Inconsistency
Self-Esteem
SOCIOLOGY ON THE INTERNET

Study & Review

In small hunting-and-gathering bands, there is little differentiation between or ranking of people. As described in Chapter 2, however, when societies become larger and a surplus of food and other resources accumulates, distinctions between people in terms of their social worth become common. The Natchez (pronounced "nachay") Indians developed an elaborate, rigid, and somewhat unusual ranking system (Swanton, 1911; White, Murdock, & Scaglion, 1971). At the time of first contact with Europeans in the mid-1500s, the Natchez were a tribe of about four thousand in the territory that is today the border between the states of Louisiana and Mississippi. They lived a sedentary village life that revolved around food production, mostly of maize. The Natchez worshiped the sun, and they were ruled by a group of nobles called Suns, with the chief being called the Great Sun. The Suns were treated with great deference and respect by other Natchez. The Great Sun was carried from one place to another on a litter lifted by eight men, and he had the authority to distribute food and other resources as well as to tell people when to work in the fields or when to hunt or fish. When the Great Sun died, his wives, guards, and retainers were also expected to die, and it is said that they considered such death a great honor.

Below the Suns in Natchez ranking were two more noble groups, called the Nobles and the Honored People; at the bottom were the lowly Stinkards. The Natchez reckoned descent through the mother's line, so at birth people were placed in the group of their mother. In most highly differentiated societies, people tend to marry those of approximately the same rank as themselves; the Natchez were unusual in that every member of the three noble classes was required to marry a Stinkard. Since social position is determined through the woman's lineage, this rule meant that a Stinkard male who married a Sun or a Noble experienced a rise in social status to the noble rank of his wife, or what sociologists call upward mobility. It also meant that a male Sun who married a Stinkard woman was downwardly mobile, although only by one step in the hierarchy. In other words, the Natchez ranking system and marriage customs were such that they forced a certain amount of circulation of people among the different ranks in society (Farb, 1978). Such circulation, or social mobility, is found as well in modern industrial societies such as the United States. As will be shown, however, it occurs in those societies not because of custom, as among the Natchez, but because of other aspects of the social structure.

There were other routes to social mobility among the Natchez. One common method was through warfare. If a Stinkard performed great deeds in war, he might become one of the Honored People, and his wife and children would move into the new position with him. They would even be given a new name to symbolize their new social position. So, even though heredity played an important part in determining people's social position among the Natchez, their ranking system was complicated, and there was more movement among the ranks than is found in many other societies. Another thing of note about the Natchez ranking system is that, although differences in prestige and resources existed among the different groups, the vast disparity between the wealthy and the poor that is found in many societies today did not exist. With control over the distribution of resources, the Great Sun could make sure that everyone was provided for. And since all in the noble classes would marry a Stinkard, they had some interest in the well-being of those people.

Unlike the Natchez, modern societies exhibit vast differences in wealth and poverty, even in the United States. In most societies around the world today, some people live in poverty while a privileged few have considerable wealth. The purpose of this chapter is to explain this ranking and differentiation in human societies, whether it be among the Natchez Indians or in the modern United States. Sociologists use the term social stratification to refer to *the ranking of people into a hierarchy in which the resources considered valuable by society are unequally distributed.*

This chapter and the next two will focus on the origins and dimensions of stratification systems and how they regulate inequalities in the distribution of resources. In addition, they will consider the extent of inequality in the United States, especially as it is influenced by such factors as race, ethnicity, and gender.

Myths & Facts

About Social Stratification

Myth:

The United States is moving toward an egalitarian society in which social classes will be largely eliminated and there will be no poverty.

Fact:

Looking at the historical and cross-cultural record, most sociologists argue that some stratification and inequality are probably inevitable in society because they perform positive functions for the social order. There is controversy over this view, however, in that inequality may not be inevitable but rather benefits those with wealth and power. Stratification might exist without poverty if the well-to-do were willing to share a larger part of their wealth with the poor.

Myth:

The United States is the only society in the world with a truly open class system where people's positions in the stratification hierarchy are determined largely by their own accomplishments.

Fact:

Characteristics that are unrelated to one's accomplishments—race, sex, and family background come to mind—exert a strong influence on what a person can achieve in the United States, so the U.S. stratification system is by no means completely open. Furthermore, there is only slightly greater opportunity for upward mobility in the United States when compared to other industrial nations.

Myth:

The poor are a drain on the public treasury that affluent citizens have to support out of their hard-earned dollars.

Fact:

Both the poor and the affluent in the United States are a drain on the public treasury, and both pay to support it. The affluent receive government handouts such as loans for college students, price-support payments to farmers, tax deductions for meals and entertainment expenses connected with business, and tax deductions for home mortgage interest. So, the similarity is that both the affluent and the poor receive public assistance in the United States; the difference is that the poor are labeled disreputable and stigmatized for doing so.

Myth:

The impoverished nations of the Third World can be blamed for the plight of their own people because of their political instability and their failure to inculcate an ethic of industriousness and hard work in their citizens.

Fact:

Although the nations themselves are not blameless, reality is more complicated. Over the centuries, and continuing today, some of these nations have suffered through invasions by Western colonial powers as well as Western economic interests. The exploitation they experienced as a result—in terms of the export of goods, natural resources, and profits—has contributed to the difficulties they confront today in building viable economies and reducing poverty.

Dimensions of Stratification

You should be able to discuss Weber's interpretation of the stratification system, define socioeconomic status, and list the major characteristics of the caste, estate, and class stratification systems.

Weber's Analysis

Like most people, you have probably compared your own social position with that of others around you—students, laborers, lawyers, millionaire baseball players, or the unemployed. What criteria do you use to locate yourself in relation to these people? The sociologist Max Weber argued that there are three major dimensions of stratification systems: wealth, prestige, and power (Weber, 1919/1958).

Wealth refers to *people's economic assets*, and it exists in many forms, depending on the characteristics of a particular society. Among the Swazi of South Africa, for example, a person's wealth is determined by the number of cows possessed (Kuper, 1963). In medieval Europe, wealth depended on the hereditary possession of land, without which it was difficult to gain a respected position in society. In the United States, wealth is often equated with *income:* the wages and salaries people earn for the work they do. For most people in the United States, income is the primary economic resource. There are many other sources of wealth, however, including property, equity in a home, stocks, bonds, trusts, and other resources that can be converted into money. According to Weber, *differences due to wealth or economic position create social strata,* which he called social classes. People in a given class *share similar life chances or opportunities to accumulate wealth* and material possessions. For example, you probably regard yourself as similar to certain other people economically, such as friends who appear to have about the same amount of economic resources. In contrast, those who have far more material things than you do may be seen as being in a different "class."

Chapter 2 defines a social status as a location or position in a group or society and says that everyone occupies many different statuses. Some statuses are hierarchical in nature, such that people who occupy particular positions are regarded as more deserving or honorable than others. Weber called this kind of regard *status honor*. It is now more commonly termed prestige, which means *the social esteem or honor that is accorded to particular people by others*; for Weber it was the second key dimension of stratification systems. As with wealth, sources of prestige vary from one society to another. Among the Plains Indians of North America, for example, warriors on horseback were accorded great prestige. They were critical to the survival of the tribe because there was considerable raiding and warfare among the various groups of Plains Indians (Oliver, 1968). One major determinant of prestige in the United States today is a person's occupation. Table 6.1 shows the results of a study that assessed how much prestige people in the United States accord to a variety of occupations. It can readily be seen that people give a higher prestige score to occupations that require more educational preparation, receive higher incomes, and involve more responsibility or supervision over people. A person's prestige in society does not, however, derive from occupation alone; it can also stem from the neighborhood in which one lives, the car one drives, or the club to which one belongs. According to

Table 6.1

OCCUPATIONAL PRESTIGE IN THE UNITED STATES

Occupation Title	Prestige Score	Occupation Title	Prestige Score
Physician	86	Funeral director	49
Lawyer	75	Enlisted person, army	49
College professor	74	Trained machinist	47
Architect	73	Stenographer	47
Chemist	73	Plumber	45
Aerospace engineer	72	Insurance agent	45
Dentist	72	Keypunch operator	41
Judge	71	Locomotive engineer	41
Chief executive and general administrator public administration	70	Farm operator or manager	40
Member of the clergy	69	Automobile mechanic	40
Pharmacist	68	Carpenter	39
High school teacher	66	TV repair person	38
Athlete	65	Automobile dealer	34
Public grade school teacher	64	Hand-working occupations	32
Veterinarian	62	Cook in restaurant	31
Computer programmer	61	Precision worker	30
Physician's assistant	61	Trailer truck driver	30
Pilot	61	Cashier	29
Police officer	60	Coal miner	29
Reporter	60	Shoe salesperson	28
Announcer	55	Waitress	28
Construction foreman	54	Garbage collector	28
Personnel and labor relations manager	54	Bartender	25
Firefighter	53	Laborer	24
Social worker	52	Farm worker	23
Electrician	51	Maid	20
Manager and administrator, business	51	News vendor	19
Computer operator	50	Food prep, restaurant	17

Note: From *General Social Surveys, 1972–2000*, Chicago: National Opinion Research Center, producer; Storrs, CT: The Roper Center for Public Opinion Research, University of Connecticut, distributor, 2001.

All societies exhibit some degree of social stratification, or the hierarchical ranking of people. Those on the bottom, such as these homeless families in India, often have considerably fewer social and economic resources than do others.

Weber, *people who occupy similar prestige levels and share a common lifestyle* form **status groups**.

Weber argued that *power* is a third dimension of the stratification system, along with wealth and prestige. **Power** refers to *a social relationship in which people are able to realize their will, even against the resistance of others.* Power, of course, can arise from wealth or status, but it also has other sources. In some situations, power can emerge through the exertion of pure physical force, as when a large person coerces a smaller one. In other situations, *power becomes legitimized,* and we refer to it as **authority**. Professors, for example, have a form of power with respect to a student's college career, because they possess the authority to determine the grades the student receives. Weber used the term **parties** to refer to *the social strata resulting from differences in power.* Parties can take the form of political parties or any kind of political blocs or factions that attempt to influence the power structure of a group or society.

Socioeconomic Status

Weber recognized that the three dimensions of stratification are frequently interrelated, but they can also be independent of one another. Sometimes, for example, people possess considerable prestige but have very little power or influence. A well-known artist may be accorded esteem based on her work but have little opportunity to affect the actions of others. In other cases, people with immense and unquestionable power, such as organized crime leaders, are accorded little prestige. It is also possible to have wealth but possess little power or prestige. A few prostitutes, for example, can earn considerably more than the average citizen, but their lifestyle is viewed with disdain by most people and they are unlikely to possess any real power.

Sociologists use the term **socioeconomic status (SES)** *to describe a person's social location based on all three dimensions of the stratification system.* SES is one of the critical factors shaping our lives. Consider why you attend college, socialize with one group of friends rather than another, read certain magazines, or enjoy particular leisure-time activities. Although many factors influence such behaviors, SES is one of the most important. In fact, two sociologists summed up the results of decades of research on stratification by concluding that "the best single predictor of lifestyle is SES" (Zablocki & Kanter, 1976, p. 272). Later this chapter assesses the dimensions of stratification in the United States and their consequences for people's lives, but first it is helpful to examine some of the different types of stratification systems that can be found in societies.

Types of Stratification Systems

Stratification systems differ in the degree to which the movement of people from one level to another is permitted or encouraged. At one extreme are **closed stratification systems**, *which have well-defined ranks and rather rigid boundaries that are difficult or impossible for people to cross.* Ascribed statuses, such as those based on race or ancestry, play important roles in determining people's social position in closed stratification systems, and people usually remain in the same social position throughout their lives. At the other extreme are **open stratification systems**, *having ranks with less well-defined boundaries that may be crossed more readily.* There are fewer barriers to advancement, and social position is determined more by individual achievement and merit. Achieved statuses that are based on factors like educational attainment are important in open systems. Stratification systems are never fully closed or fully open but vary widely between these two extremes. A sense of the variation possible in different stratification systems can be gained by looking at three types of systems: the relatively closed caste and estate systems and the more open class system.

CASTE SYSTEMS   A caste system is *a stratification system in which membership in social ranks is hereditary, people in different ranks are rigidly segregated from one another, and marriage between ranks is strictly forbidden* (Berreman, 1987). The stratification system in India is an illustration of a caste system. Although no longer sanctioned by India's government, the caste system is justified by the Hindu religion and still has important influences on people's lives. At the foundation of this caste system is the Hindu belief in reincarnation, the notion that a person's soul is reborn, time and time again, in either human or non-human form. Furthermore, the quality of future reincarnations is determined by how well people live their present lives. The caste into which one is born is, in a sense, one's assignment for this incarnation. If a person fails to live according to the prescriptions and proscriptions of his or her caste, that person may be reincarnated in a lower caste position or in some non-human form. Thus the caste system in India is based on powerful religious beliefs that are backed by custom and ritual. By restricting marriage to members of the same caste, the homogeneity of each group is maintained and the possibilities for social interaction across caste boundaries are limited. Also, members of different castes are not permitted to eat in the company of one another, and other forms of social interchange are limited. Through such restrictions, the likelihood that caste barriers will be informally breached is reduced.

Some sociologists argue that there is a caste-like quality to parts of the stratification system in the United States in that certain racial, ethnic, and gender characteristics powerfully influence people's opportunities and social patterns (Hurst, 1992). White males, for example, find it much easier to achieve wealth, status, and power. They experience less discrimination in areas such as employment and housing than do females and some nonwhites (see Chapters 7 and 8). Some of the customs and rituals governing caste behavior in India also seem to have parallels in the United States, albeit with less force and rigidity. Marriage across racial lines, for example, is still somewhat uncommon in the United States. Less than 1 percent of all marriages involve a black-white couple (U.S. Bureau of the Census, 2007, p. 52). In addition, segregated residential patterns and schools mean that social contact between people of different races is also limited. So, although the United States is not a true caste stratification system, it contains social barriers to movement and interaction that have some similarities to castes.

ESTATE SYSTEMS   In an estate system of social stratification, *social position is still strongly influenced by heredity, but unlike in the caste system, land ownership and political or military power can also be important*. In estate systems, people's rights and duties are spelled out in laws rather than authorized solely by religious or social custom. Estate systems are still rigidly stratified societies, but one's hereditary characteristics are not the exclusive determinants of one's position in society. The feudal societies of medieval Europe were examples of estate stratification systems.

Developing in a time of weak or nonexistent central government, the feudal system was characterized by a lord–vassal relationship in which the lord exercised authority over some land by virtue of his birth or by conquest and allotted use of some land to vassals or serfs in exchange for loyalty and military service. Lords depended on the labor of serfs. Traditionally the serfs had a right to work a particular parcel of land because generations of them had worked it. They were "bound" to the land. They had obligations to the lord of the manor in the form of working part of the time in his fields or kitchens or stables and paying him some of their produce. The lord, in turn, provided them with military and civil protection, settled disputes, and gave assistance during floods or other difficulties. So there was a reciprocal relationship between lord and serf.

One major difference between caste and estate systems is that the former relies more on acceptance of the underlying value system that supports the prestige rankings. In the Indian caste system, for example, if people accept the religious beliefs that justify it, then they are likely to accept the legitimacy of the stratification system and their place in it. Estate systems rely more on the authority of monarchs or the exercise of military power to enforce acceptance of the system.

Another major difference is that estate systems permit more mobility than do caste systems. In some estate systems, for example, military or religious service stands as one institutionalized route to changing one's position in society. A serf in medieval Europe could gain some power, prestige, and possibly even ownership of land by loyal service to a lord in a military capacity, although such advancement was uncommon. He would thus rise out of his inherited estate. This change would be especially likely if the person showed extraordinary loyalty and talent and the lord wished to reward him. Military strength would be another way to gain land. A person who could get together a warring party and wrest some territory from others could, over time, claim a legal, hereditary right to the land. So, although heredity is important, it is not the sole way of placing people in the stratification hierarchy in estate systems. During the 1700s and 1800s the estate system of Europe evolved into a class stratification system, which will be discussed next. Estate systems, however, have persisted until more recent times in some parts of the world.

CLASS SYSTEMS In *class systems*, *the boundaries between classes are more permeable, a person's socioeconomic position depends more on achievement, and there are fairly frequent opportunities to change social positions.* There are few legal or formally sanctioned inequalities between people, and social mobility is based on accomplishments and achieved characteristics, but inequalities still exist. Social contact and marriage are not officially restricted, although there may be considerable informal restrictions, such as a parent's admonition to a son or daughter: "I can't *stop* you from seeing that person, but I would *prefer* that you didn't." The informal mechanisms of social control described in Chapter 5 can be effective deterrents to contact and socializing between people at different levels of a class system. Because there is no single criterion for determining one's position in an open stratification system and because movement between ranks does occur, class systems do not exhibit clear and distinct boundaries between different social strata. Class lines tend to blur and considerable overlap exists.

Although the United States has many elements of a class system, it is not completely open because numerous ascribed characteristics still influence a person's social position. Some people, for example, are born to families with considerable wealth, which affords them an educational background that increases their likelihood of success. Having upper-middle-class parents and attending elite schools expose a person to social contacts that make advancement more likely. Likewise, people who live in a neighborhood with a superior educational system have an advantage that is unavailable to those residing in poor communities or in rural areas where the schools are likely to be of lower quality. In short, hereditary and other ascribed differences among people in U.S. society play important roles in the stratification system.

Theories of Stratification

You should be able to describe the functionalist, conflict, and evolutionary theories of stratification as well as discuss the global dimensions of stratification.

The controversy regarding the origins and persistence of social stratification has been ongoing and frequently emotional. This controversy is understandable, because the issue of "haves" versus "have nots" has always elicited passionate debate. The central debate in sociology has been whether stratification exists because it is necessary for society or because its existence benefits powerful groups.

The Functionalist Perspective

Functionalists argue that stratification exists because it makes some contribution to the ongoing maintenance of society. According to Kingsley Davis and Wilbert Moore (1945), for instance, all societies must ensure that people fill essential positions and perform important tasks. Somebody must produce food, build shelter, heal the sick, and bury the dead. Otherwise, society cannot survive. Some of these positions, however, are considered more important than others. For example, physicians are more crucial than janitors. Some positions are inherently more pleasant to perform. Most people would rather be a teacher than a garbage collector. Further, some positions call for natural abilities possessed by only a few. Not many among us, for example, could play professional tennis or football. Finally, some positions require extensive and difficult training for their proper performance.

According to Davis and Moore, the major problem that confronts any society concerns *motivation*: How can people be persuaded to occupy important positions and to perform the tasks associated with them adequately? Their answer is that rewards must be distributed such that people will want to fill the positions that need to be occupied, however difficult or unpleasant they may be. Higher rewards should go to the positions that are judged more important or less pleasant. Likewise, positions for which there is a scarcity of talent or that require extensive training should receive higher rewards. Social stratification, then, is a mechanism for allocating those differential rewards and motivating people to fill key positions in society.

Talcott Parsons (1951), also taking a functionalist view toward stratification, pointed out that the values of society tend to be integrated with, and supportive of, the stratification system. It is in part through the value system that tasks and positions are defined as important and useful to society. In the United States, for example, people place considerable value on economic achievement and material success (see Chapter 2), and those who succeed in those realms are usually accorded high positions on the three dimensions of the stratification system. People in the United States also value youth and physical beauty, and those who possess these characteristics, such as movie stars or athletes, are also awarded top positions in the stratification system.

Davis and Moore's functional approach has led to an ongoing debate concerning the degree to which rewards are actually related to the importance of a position or the scarcity of qualified personnel to fill it. One study found that the importance of positions was unrelated to rewards (Wanner & Lewis, 1978). In addition, a study of public school teachers over a forty-year span showed little support for the functionalist prediction that incomes would be higher when the supply of teachers was scarce (Betz, Davis, & Miller, 1978). At the same time, other research has provided support for Davis and Moore's basic propositions (Cullen & Novick, 1979). Thus there is still considerable controversy among sociologists regarding the extent to which stratification systems in modern societies perform the functions suggested by Davis and Moore. In fact, some have viewed the functionalist theory of stratification as merely a rationalization for the status quo (Tumin, 1953).

The Conflict Perspective

Karl Marx's (1867–1895/1967) conflict approach to stratification contrasts sharply with the functionalist view. Marx believed that economic forces are the central factors shaping both society and individual consciousness. Economic systems, he argued, influence the beliefs, values, norms, and social institutions of a society. In contrast to Weber, Marx maintained that prestige and power flow from one's economic position rather than being independent dimensions of stratification. For Marx, *a social class* consists of all those people who share a common economic position. In nineteenth-century England, Marx considered two social classes to be especially important. The *bourgeoisie,* or middle class, were those who owned the means of economic production such as the factories, the trading companies, and the banks. The *proletariat* were the working people, who owned little and sold their labor to the bourgeoisie in return for wages.

Marx viewed society as involving a constant struggle between social classes over scarce resources, with some managing to capture more of these resources than others. Thus stratification systems involve the unequal distribution of resources, which has little to do with rewarding talent or filling important positions. People gain desirable positions in the stratification system through coercion, exploitation, or possibly inheritance, and then they work toward protecting their resources against inroads by less-fortunate groups. One way for powerful groups to protect their positions is to convince subordinate groups that the existing distribution of resources is "natural" or preferable. Through schools and the media, for example, people may be convinced to believe that everyone will be successful if he or she works sufficiently hard. The implication, of course, is that a lack of success is due to one's not having worked hard enough. One blames oneself rather than recognizing the role of coercion by powerful groups in limiting the opportunities of the less power-ful. Marx called this failure to recognize what is in one's best interests *false class consciousness.* Eventually, Marx believed, the proletariat would develop *class consciousness,* or an awareness that their interests would be served by struggling with the bourgeoisie in order to change existing social arrangements. This struggle, said Marx, would culminate in a revolution that would replace capitalism with communism. These economic systems are discussed in more detail in Chapter 13, but at this point, it should be recognized that under communism, according to Marx, scarcity would be eliminated; there would be no social classes and thus

no inequality. Unlike most sociologists, then, Marx did not believe that social stratification is inevitable.

Many of Marx's predictions did not materialize. His forecast, for example, about the demise of capitalism, the emergence of communism, and the withering away of stratification and inequality has not proven accurate. Many of his observations are insightful, however, and modern conflict theorists have worked to modify and broaden his approach. C. Wright Mills (1956), for example, argued that Marx's emphasis on the ownership of economic resources as the basis for stratification oversimplifies today's class system. In reality, ownership in a corporate economy is spread over a large number of stockholders, most of whom have little actual control over the corporations. In the United States today, for example, power and authority rest with those who hold high-level positions in business, industry, or government where important decisions are made. Mills also viewed stratification as inevitable because huge economic institutions, whether capitalist or not, are controlled by people at the top of a society's hierarchy who possess considerable power.

Ralf Dahrendorf (1959) has broadened Marx's approach to stratification by shifting the focus of attention from economic relationships to authority relationships. In order to ensure conformity to role expectations in any group, argues Dahrendorf, someone must impose sanctions for nonconformity, and that person must have the power to do so. When the powerful are given the legitimate right to dominate others, then their power is transformed into authority. In Dahrendorf's view, then, stratification is a coercive system in which power and authority are used to control behavior, and some degree of stratification is probably inevitable in order to maintain social order in any group and in society as a whole.

Synthesis: An Evolutionary View

The controversy between functionalist and conflict views of stratification has raged for decades. To help resolve the debate, Gerhard Lenski (1966) has proposed a synthesis of the two views. Lenski begins by recognizing that people are basically selfish and interested in their own survival and that of those who are close to them. Socialization may dampen these tendencies in some people, but self-centeredness is still a part of human life. How, then, are goods and resources distributed? Do people simply hoard all that they can acquire? Such actions would be counterproductive as a sole distribution mechanism because we often need help from others. Lenski suggests that people share their resources with others in order to receive needed goods in return. In societies with little material surplus, such as hunting-and-gathering groups or some horticultural and pastoral societies, this type of sharing is essential for people to survive. When people share what they produce, there is little inequality. *Need,* rather than *power,* determines the distribution of resources in such societies.

As societies become more advanced, however, surpluses of food and material resources begin to accumulate, and the means for distributing them change radically. According to Lenski, "power will determine the distribution of nearly all of the *surplus* of goods" (Lenski, 1966, p. 44, italics added). In the power struggle for surplus resources, some people will be more competitive, some stronger, some faster, and some more crafty. The outcome, as suggested by the conflict approach, is the inequitable distribution of resources, with the inequities being substantial in agricultural and early industrial societies. Lenski recognizes that some inequalities may be functional for society, but he also argues that most societies are far more stratified than they need to be in order to survive. When power comes into play in distributing goods, those who have power accumulate all that they can. Furthermore, once inequities have been

established, they tend to persist long after they serve any useful purpose. So, although functionalism might explain the necessity of some inequalities, it cannot explain *all* the inequity in stratification systems.

Lenski's approach is sometimes referred to as *evolutionary* because it assumes that societies move through a sequence of development that influences their stratification systems. As the type of economic production changes, so does the amount of inequality found in society (Figure 6.1). Unlike Marx, however, Lenski is not an economic determinist. He recognizes that many factors, such as the natural resources available, the characteristics of leaders, and external military threats, play a role in generating inequalities. He also disputes Marx's contention that inequality would be greatest in industrial societies. In fact, Lenski argues that the level of inequality will decline in advanced industrial societies such as the United States and Western Europe because the new jobs created will

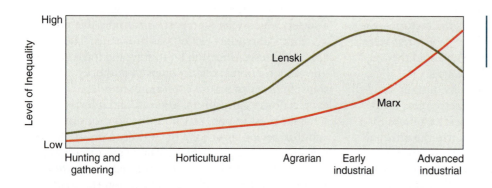

Figure 6.1

Marx's and Lenski's Views on the Relationship between Industrialization and Inequality

Table 6.2

A SUMMARY OF THE MAJOR SOCIOLOGICAL APPROACHES TO SOCIAL STRATIFICATION

	Conflict			Functionalist		Synthesis
	Marx	Dahrendorf	Mills	Parsons	Davis/Moore	Lenski
Basis of stratification	Economic relations resulting from *ownership* of resources	Authority relations	Economic relations resulting from *control* of resources	Evaluation of tasks as useful and important to society	Motivation to perform essential tasks	Distributive relations
Key processes	Scarcity and the division of labor	Role differentiation and the imposition of sanctions	Control of key decision-making positions	Ranking of positions a reflection of commonly held values	Unequal distribution of rewards to positions that are more important, etc.	With no surplus, *need* the determinant of distribution of resources, with surplus, *power* the determinant of distribution of resources
Is stratification inevitable?	No	Yes	Yes	Yes	Yes	Yes

make it possible for people to improve their lives, and the great wealth that industrialism provides will make more resources available to people. This situation is accompanied by income redistribution policies such as welfare and unemployment benefits and progressive income taxes. Table 6.2 is a summary of the major theoretical approaches to social stratification.

A Global Perspective on Stratification

The perspectives on social stratification discussed thus far view stratification systems as a property of one society that can be analyzed separately from stratification systems in other societies. In today's world, however, we need to go beyond this position, because an interdependent world system seems to be emerging. World-system theory, pioneered by the sociologist Immanuel Wallerstein (1979, 1984), *posits that the world's nations have become increasingly interdependent, both economically and politically, and are now linked in a worldwide stratification system, with some nations having more power and resources than others.* The major force in this world system is capitalism and its emphasis on market forces, profit making, and surplus accumulation. This world system is described in more detail in Chapter 13, but it is relevant here because capitalism's drive to expand and find new markets creates a pressure to seek out new territories in which to invest. In fact, one of the unique characteristics of capitalism is its commitment to economic growth and expansion. The world expansion of capitalism began in the fifteenth century with the European voyages to the New World to find natural resources and trade that would be profitable for the European colonial nations, and it continues today as corporations seek new markets in a global economy.

The key to this world system is trade, with some nations being exporters of goods while others serve primarily as a labor pool and provider of natural resources. Whereas Marx saw the owners and the workers as the significant classes in the stratification of industrial societies, world-system theory views nations as the significant actors in a worldwide stratification system. One consequence of this world system is its impact on the stratification systems in the nations that are affected, often precipitating a transition from an estate to a class stratification system. A second consequence is that an international stratification system emerges, with a hierarchy of nations ranging from *core nations* at the top (capitalist, technologically advanced nations searching for opportunities to expand investment) to *peripheral nations* at the bottom (less developed nations that provide cheap labor and produce food and raw materials). There are also *semiperipheral nations* in between that are large

or have some special resources; they are therefore less dependent on the core nations and sometimes act as core nations themselves (Apter, 1986; Chase-Dunn & Grimes, 1995; Chirot, 1986).

In this international stratification system, the core nations dominate and exploit the peripheral nations. In fact, some world-system theorists argue that the nature of capitalism is such that it creates social inequalities through its tendency to distribute resources unequally. Such inequalities occur within nations, which have both rich and poor people, and at the international level, where the policies of core nations help keep peripheral nations less developed. The core nations extract natural resources from the peripheral nations and use these countries as cheap labor pools to produce agricultural and industrial goods that are then exported for profit. Through political, economic, and sometimes military intervention, the core nations encourage the emergence of political and economic elites in the peripheral nations that will support and assist in economic expansion of the core. This elite group in the peripheral nations benefits from the world system and supports policies that will maintain its role in the world capitalist system. For example, the political elites in some less developed nations in Latin America have discouraged labor unions that would work to increase the pay and improve the working conditions of citizens of those nations, because unions might discourage investment by corporations from core nations that are looking for a cheap and passive labor force. Whereas elites in the peripheral nations may benefit from this policy, it tends overall to result in a shift of wealth from the periphery to the core as the corporations of the core nations drain profits from the periphery.

At the height of European imperial expansion, from the 1600s to the 1900s, the core nations often dominated through military conquest and occupation. Today, domination is more often through free markets, trade agreements with elites in peripheral nations, and loans and investments that create a dependent relationship. In fact, world-system theory is sometimes called *dependency theory* because of the dependence of the peripheral nations on economic assistance, and sometimes military assistance, from the core nations. The international stratification system, then, rests on economic superiority within a worldwide division of labor. Figure 6.2 shows the nations of the world based on their wealth as measured by their gross national income (GNI) per person. The GNI is the total of all the goods and services produced by a nation. In general, the high-income nations can be considered the core nations, the middle-income nations the semiperipheral nations, and the low-income nations the peripheral nations. However, a nation may shift from one category to another over time and because of special circumstances (Bornschier and Trezzini, 1997). In addition, as with

Figure 6.2

Global Stratification System: Nations Classified by Gross National Income (GNI) per Capita

Note: From World Development Report 2008: Agriculture for Development. Copyright © 2007 by The International Bank for Reconstruction and Development/The World Bank. Reprinted by permission of the World Bank.

GNI per capita in 2006

- **Low** $905 or less
- **Lower middle** $906 to $3,595
- **Upper middle** $3,596 to $11,115
- **High** $11,116 or more
- **No data**

Other Worlds, Other Ways

BRAZIL AND VENEZUELA: THE THIRD-WORLD POOR IN THE GLOBAL STRATIFICATION SYSTEM

Brazil is a nation of 160 million people on territory about the same size as the United States. Brazil was colonized by Portugal, which makes it unique in Latin America in having Portuguese, rather than Spanish, as its national language. Brazil today gives some appearances of doing quite well. The United Nations Conference for Trade and Development (UNCTAD) classifies Brazil as a developing country that is a major exporter of manufactured goods; the World Bank calls Brazil a developing country with an economy that is in the upper range of the middle-income economies. Rich Brazilians live in high-rise condominiums along the beach in Rio de Janeiro; shiny glass office buildings tower over the downtowns of Rio, São Paulo, and other Brazilian cities; well-dressed office workers eat in posh restaurants and talk over cell phones in their cars.

Yet there is another side to Brazil that shows the vast inequities of its stratification system (Rizzini, 1996; Scheper-Hughes, 1993). Thousands of Brazilian children live in the streets, supporting themselves however they can, legally or illegally. Their plight came to light in a gruesome way in 1993 when about a dozen were shot to death as they slept in the middle of the night in alleys and doorways. Such killings of street children are not rare events in Brazil. No one is sure who killed them, although some suspect it may have been off-duty police hired by businesspeople to clean up the streets and sidewalks of commercial areas. Such shootings have happened in the past, and there is even a name in Brazil for these assassins of children: *justicieros,* or "people who do justice." The children are considered a nuisance by many merchants when the children shine shoes, clean windshields, sell gum, or beg around stores and shopping areas. Some of the children also steal merchandise, rob tourists, and sell drugs. In the mean streets in which they live, they must do these things to survive.

Brazil had a strong economy in the 1970s and 1980s, but it seems to have benefited the few at the expense of the many (Maddison et al., 1992). The wealthiest 10 percent of Brazilians possessed 45 percent of the nation's wealth in 1980, and this disparity had grown to 53 percent by 1990. (For a contrast, the equivalent figure in the United States is 48 percent [Oliver & Shapiro, 1990]). The poorest 20 percent of all Brazilians receive only 2 percent of national income while the wealthiest 20 percent receive 64 percent of national income (World Bank, 2004). For many Brazilians, this disparity produces grinding poverty with little hope of improvement in the teeming *favelas,* or "slums," that surround the sparkling business centers and affluent residential areas of Brazil's cities.

Venezuela is classified as a semiperipheral nation by some world-system theorists (Bornschier & Trezzini, 1997). The UNCTAD calls it a major petroleum exporter among the developing countries, and it has a per capita income almost twice that of Brazil. Yet, in 1989, four days of bloody rioting occurred, with people protesting government policies and looting supermarkets and stores (Silverstein, 1993). Called the *27-F riots* because they began on February 27, they were put down brutally by police and security forces. Demonstrators and looters were slaughtered in the streets. People found in their homes with goods thought by police to have been looted were shot to death, and others died when security forces opened fire into slum shanty towns. In the end, the government reluctantly admitted that hundreds of people, mostly poor, had been killed. The military conceded that 2,500 victims may have been killed; human-rights activists put the figure at 4,000 or more. Like Brazil, Venezuela also exhibits a vast chasm between the well-to-do and the poor. Because of its oil wealth, Caracas is a modern, sophisticated city with many skyscrapers, theaters, and trendy restaurants. At the same time, one-third of Venezuela's people live below the poverty line (World Bank, 2007).

World-system theorists argue that both Brazil and Venezuela reflect the current conditions in the world capitalist system (Braun, 1997). Land is owned by a small elite, and the masses of people are dispossessed. Those who cannot find work in the agricultural sector flock to teeming cities because there is nowhere else to go. Foreign corporations invest in agriculture and manufacturing in ways that emphasize maximization of profits. This policy often results in capital-intensive ventures that employ relatively few people and focus on export to affluent countries. Many people benefit from this arrangement: the multinational corporations, the political and economic elites in Brazil and Venezuela who invest in those corporations, and the limited number of workers who can find jobs in these enterprises. The core nations encourage these developments on the periphery by providing billions of dollars in loans directly or through such organizations as the International Monetary Fund and the World Bank. These loans are typically for capital-intensive, export-oriented, high-profit economic developments. Such developments certainly benefit multinational corporations in the core nations, but world-system theorists question whether the poor in peripheral nations see much benefit. And these loans become burdensome during economic downturns. In bad times, both Brazil and Venezuela have slashed programs for the poor, often at the demand of the core-nation lending institutions, in order to keep up payments on the loans.

So, some social classes in Brazil and Venezuela benefit from these policies, especially the agricultural and industrial

(continued)

elites, merchants, and some skilled workers. For the lower social classes, however, which constitute a good percentage of both nations, they have meant abject poverty interspersed with brief periods of slight improvement.

World-system theorists thus argue that the international stratification system based on world capitalism is a powerful influence on the distribution of socioeconomic resources in these two nations. ■

any stratification system, the world system is complicated and influenced by special traditions, historical circumstances, and geographic considerations. Other Worlds, Other Ways: Brazil and Venezuela (pp. 157–158) looks at some of the implications of the world system for people living in peripheral nations.

It should be clear by now that social stratification is a complex phenomenon that can be understood only by analyzing it from a number of different perspectives. You should now have a number of possible answers to the question of why hierarchies, rankings, stratification, superiority, and subordination exist in societies. With this basic knowledge in hand, we can now shift our attention to a discussion of stratification in the United States.

Social Class in the United States

You should be able to explain how socioeconomic status is measured, describe the major social classes found in the United States, and discuss the extent and causes of inequality in societies.

Relying on Weber's three-dimensional model of stratification systems, this chapter analyzes the class structure in the United States in terms of wealth, prestige, and power. It reviews the distribution of wealth and prestige, particularly the prestige associated with occupations. Chapters 7 and 8 assess how such ascribed statuses as race, ethnicity, and gender shape the stratification system. Then, Chapter 13 analyzes the distribution of power in the United States while discussing political and economic institutions. First, however, the way sociologists measure stratification must be discussed, because people often mean different things when they use the terms *class* or *socioeconomic status*.

Measuring Socioeconomic Status

A common approach to measuring SES a few decades ago was the *reputational approach,* in which class structure was determined by the assessments of community "judges" of their fellow citizens. In other words, a person's reputation in the community was assessed by other community members who were familiar with large numbers of people. The reputational approach has

fallen into disuse, however, because it cannot be used in large communities or at the national level, where "judges" could not be expected to make accurate assessments of the class position of many individuals. Another approach to measuring SES, still used sometimes today, is the *subjective approach,* also called the *self-placement approach*. With this technique, people are asked where they believe they fit into the class hierarchy. A 2006 survey, for example, found people in the United States placing themselves in the following way: upper class, 3 percent; middle class, 46 percent; working class, 45 percent; and lower class, 5 percent (Davis & Smith, 2007). One of the major disadvantages of the subjective approach is that it assumes that people can accurately place themselves in the stratification hierarchy. People, for example, may place themselves where they wish to be rather than where they are actually located.

Because of the limitations of these two approaches, sociologists today rely heavily on an *objective approach* to measuring SES. In the objective approach, people are placed in the class hierarchy through the use of "objective" criteria that the investigator determines are relevant to class placement and that do not depend on the judgments of members of the community under study. The following objective criteria have been used individually and in various combinations in studies of social class: occupation, income, source of income, educational attainment, racial or ethnic background, and lifestyle. The most widely used objective criterion of social class is occupation, because it combines in some fashion Weber's three dimensions of stratification. It reflects social prestige, it is related to one's income or wealth, and it is associated with the amount of power or authority possessed. Occupation has been used in two major ways. One approach is for the sociologist to rank occupations into a specified number of classes. The second approach has been to establish a prestige score for each occupation, based on the judgments of a sample of people from the community (see Table 6.1). These prestige rankings differ significantly from the reputational approach because occupations rather than individuals are being judged. One major weakness of the objective approach is that it simplifies a complex social reality by reducing many dimensions of stratification to a few. For example, occupations that are quite different in terms of income and educational requirements may be placed into the same social class, based largely on prestige. Nevertheless, the objective approach is subject to the least error and provides the investigator with the most information.

Class Structure in the United States

Because of the complexity of class structure in the United States, there are many ways to describe it. One useful approach is to consider five major classes: upper, upper-middle, lower-middle, working, and lower (Beeghley, 2008; Gilbert, 1998; Rossides, 1990).

THE UPPER CLASS   The upper class, which constitutes less than 4 percent of the population, consists of those people with great wealth who play a large part in the political and economic institutions in the United States. Actually, there are a number of different groups in the upper class. For some, their positions are based on "old" wealth that has been passed on through a number of generations. Some of the more familiar names are Rockefeller, duPont, and Vanderbilt. Another group in the upper class is the *nouveau riche,* people, such as Bill Gates, who have recently amassed large fortunes through investments in oil, computers, telecommunications, real estate, or other money-making endeavors. Although most people would not notice the difference, members of the old wealth tend to view the nouveau riche as "upstarts" who lack the proper cultivation and sophistication to be fully accepted into the highest circles. A third group in the upper class—actually just on the doorstep—consists of those at the top of the federal bureaucracy and in elite managerial positions in large corporations. Because of their positions, they have considerable power over political and economic decisions, although their wealth may not be nearly as substantial as that of others in the upper class. Former Presidents Ronald Reagan and Bill Clinton and some of their key advisers could be classified in this group. Their hold on an upper-class position is more tenuous than it is in the other two groups because it rests on their political position, which can be lost.

THE UPPER-MIDDLE CLASS   The upper-middle class, constituting between 10 and 15 percent of the populace, consists of the business, professional, and managerial people who have relatively high incomes and a limited amount of wealth accumulated, primarily in the form of property and savings. Members of this class commonly have a college education, which is often supplemented by graduate training. Some self-employed people without college degrees, however, have gained entrance into this class through success in business. In addition, some upper-middle-class people,

such as college professors, gain entrance to this class through the prestige of their occupations rather than large incomes.

THE LOWER-MIDDLE CLASS   About one-third of the U.S. population would be considered lower-middle class. This class is made up of people with modest incomes and comfortable lifestyles who must work hard to maintain their standard of living. Because they accumulate little wealth beyond small savings, their existence is somewhat more precarious than that of those above them in the stratification hierarchy. Examples of the lower-middle class are people who run small businesses, teachers, insurance agents, police officers, salespeople, lower-level management personnel, and clerical workers. This class, along with the upper-middle class, dominates U.S. society in terms of values, attitudes, and lifestyles.

THE WORKING CLASS   The working class, about 45 percent of the population, consists of skilled and unskilled blue-collar workers whose jobs generally involve manual labor. This category includes factory workers, construction workers, repair people, and so on. Working-class people may earn modest but comfortable incomes; sometimes their salaries are considerably greater than those of certain lower-middle class groups of people, such as public school teachers. However, their jobs are accorded less prestige by most people in the United States. They nonetheless consider themselves to be respectable and hardworking, the "solid core" that supports society.

THE LOWER CLASS   At the bottom of the stratification hierarchy are people with poverty-level incomes or with no jobs, and those receiving welfare and other public assistance. The lower class includes the "working poor": 60 percent of the families that live below the poverty level have at least one member who earns wages for work. The lower class also includes people such as welfare recipients, migrant farm workers, derelicts, and many mentally ill and mentally retarded people who have been released from institutions into the community. One major question regarding the lower class is what societal mechanisms, if any, should be established to assist them in coping with their meager financial resources. Another major question that has been raised regarding the lower class is whether poverty is inevitable in a society like the United States. Is it possible to have stratification without poverty?

Inequality and Poverty

EXTENT OF INEQUALITY   How unequal is the distribution of income and wealth in the United States? Two beliefs regarding U.S. economic inequality are widely held but demonstrably untrue. The first is that economic resources were widely distributed prior to industrialization, with few rich people and few poor. One estimate of the wealth in the country prior to the American Revolution, however, places about 45 percent of the total wealth in the hands of about 10 percent of the populace (Pessen, 1971). This figure has remained true up to today, with 10 percent of the people in the United States possessing close to 50 percent of the wealth. The second fallacious belief regarding economic inequality in the United States is that, since the Great Depression of the 1930s, government programs have reduced inequality by redistributing the existing wealth among larger numbers of people. In 1928, just prior to the Depression, 1 percent of the population possessed 36 percent of the total wealth. This figure declined to about 20 percent in 1949—the lowest amount ever in U.S. history—and since then has fluctuated between 20 and 30 percent.

Figure 6.3 shows the extent of inequality in the past forty years. Today, the poorest 20 percent of the population receives less than 4 percent of the total income in the United States while the wealthiest 20 percent receives 50 percent. Furthermore, these differences have increased over the past four decades. In fact, the percentage of total income going to the poorest families is less today than it was in 1967 or 1980; the only group who saw their share of the total income increase since 1967 is the wealthiest 20 percent of families.

The maldistribution of resources in the United States is even greater when one looks at wealth (earned income, stocks, savings, equity in a home, and other economic resources) rather than just income. The top 20 percent of U.S. households possess 80 percent of the total wealth, whereas the bottom 20 percent have a negative net worth because they have more debts than assets (Wolff, 1995). This topic has been hotly debated, but most analysts agree with what Figure 6.3 suggests: In the last 40 years in the United States, the rich have gotten richer and the poor have gotten poorer (Alperovitz, 2004; Mishel, Bernstein, & Schmitt, 2001). Also, poverty seems to have become more chronic, with people who fall into poverty today remaining poor for longer periods of time than was true in the 1960s and 1970s.

The official poverty level in the United States is established by the Social Security Administration (Ruggles, 1990). The level is based on how much it costs to purchase a nutritionally adequate diet. Once the amount of money necessary for that purpose has been established, this amount is multiplied by three to arrive at the poverty income, based on the fact that the average family spends one-third of its income on food. Thus, three times the cost of food is assumed to provide adequate income for food, housing, medical care, and the other necessities of life. The poverty income cutoff is adjusted for family size, and it changes each year to take inflation into account. Using this fixed-dollar cutoff point to define poverty is an *absolute* approach because it assumes that we can define poverty without making reference to the standard of living of other people in society.

According to this absolute definition of poverty, then, a family of four people with an annual income of approximately $20,400 is considered by the government to be poor (Table 6.3), which means that 36 million people in the United States—one out of every nine— were living in poverty in 2006. Throughout the 1980s, the poverty rate remained considerably higher than

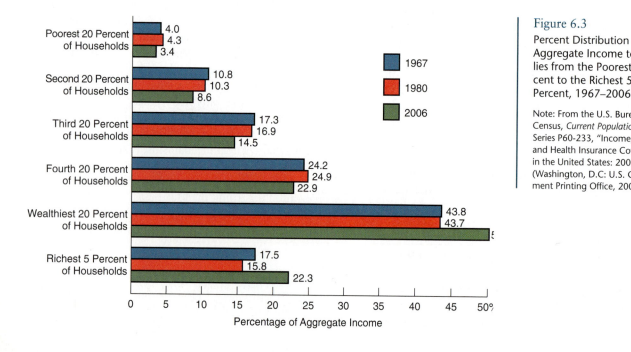

Figure 6.3

Percent Distribution of Aggregate Income to Families from the Poorest 20 Percent to the Richest 5 Percent, 1967–2006

Note: From the U.S. Bureau of the Census, *Current Population Reports*, Series P60-233, "Income, Poverty, and Health Insurance Coverage in the United States: 2006" (Washington, D.C.: U.S. Government Printing Office, 2007).

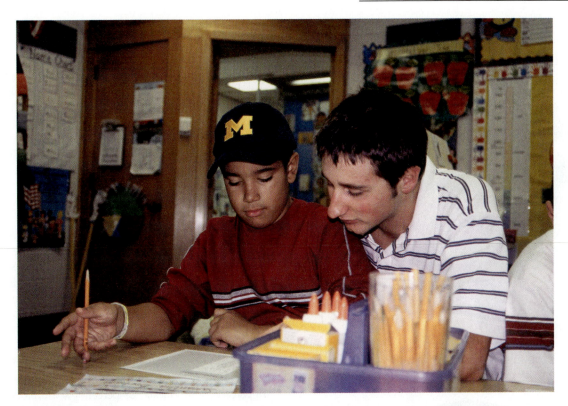

Social programs such as Head Start provide early educational experiences for disadvantaged children. Evaluations of these programs conducted by sociologists have documented that the programs help such children do better in school and increase their ability to find and keep good jobs as adults.

Table 6.3

PEOPLE IN POVERTY IN THE UNITED STATES AND POVERTY INCOME, 1960–2006

Year	Number of People below Poverty Level (Millions)	Percentage of Total Population	Poverty Income Cutoff for a Family of Four	Median Family Income of All Families
1960	39.9	22.2	$3,022	$5,620
1970	25.4	12.6	3,968	9,867
1980	29.3	13.0	8,414	21,023
1990	33.6	13.5	13,359	35,353
2000	31.1	11.3	17,463	49,350
2006	36.4	12.3	20,444	59,894

Sources: U.S. Bureau of the Census, *Current Population Reports*, Series P60–221, *Money Income in the United States: 2002* (Washington, DC: U.S Government Printing Office, 2003): Series P60–233, "Income, Poverty and Health Insurance Coverage in the United States: 2006" (Washington, DC: U.S. Government Printing Office, 2007).

it had been in the 1970s. In 2006, the poverty rate was 12.3 percent—one of the lower rates since the 1960s—but more people were poor in 2006 than in 1970. Furthermore, the gap between the nonpoor and the poor has been growing as the median family income has increased at a faster rate than has the poverty income cutoff.

Certain groups in the United States are far more likely to be poor than are others (Figures 6.4 and 6.5). Contrary to what many believe, two-thirds of the poor are white. Nonwhites are poor, however, at levels disproportionate to their numbers in the population. African Americans, for example, make up 25 percent of those below the poverty line. Thirty-five percent of the nation's poor are children under eighteen, and 9 percent of the impoverished are elderly. These figures, which show that many of the nation's poor are very young or very old, suggest how misleading it is to say that most people are poor because they refuse to work. Finally, many poor people are working poor in that

RACE

AGE

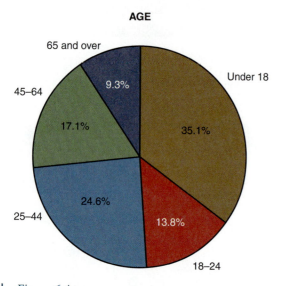

Figure 6.4

People Living below the Poverty Level by Race or Ethnicity and Age, as a Percentage of All Poor People, 2006

Note: From the U.S. Bureau of the Census, *Current Population Survey, 2007: Annual Social and Economic Supplement* (Washington, DC: U.S. Government Printing Office, 2007), www.census.gov/hhes/www/povery/poverty.html

[1]The Census survey permits people to choose more than one race to identify themselves; people who do so are includes in this category.

they do work, although for very low wages, or would work if jobs were available (Shipler, 2004). In fact, less than 2 percent of the families in poverty have male heads of household who are simultaneously able to work, unemployed, and not looking for work.

A development that has been viewed with some alarm in recent years is the "feminization" of poverty. Despite increasing pressures toward eliminating

inequities due to gender, some women—especially female heads of households—seem to be losing ground. For example, 9 percent of all families in the United States live below the poverty level, but the rate among female-headed families is 29 percent. And things may actually be getting worse. In 1959, 23 percent of all families living in poverty were headed by women; this figure has grown to 50 percent (U.S. Bureau of the Census, 2007). As Figure 6.5 shows, children living in single-parent, female-headed families are especially likely to be living in poverty. (Issues of gender inequality are discussed in more detail in Chapter 8.)

A GLOBAL VIEW OF POVERTY By the standards of many nations around the world, many poor people in the United States would be considered reasonably well-off. Some people in other nations live in absolute poverty that is so stark and dehumanizing that it is difficult for people in the United States to imagine. For these people, survival itself is a struggle. Few, if any, of the poor in the United States would fall into this category. In nations such as Haiti, Colombia, and Zambia, as many as 65 percent of the people may live in poverty; in El Salvador, the figure is 48 percent; in Indonesia, 27 percent (World Bank, 2007). Compared to these nations, the United States is well-off. However, as Figure 6.6 demonstrates, it is not so well-off when compared to other industrial nations. In that comparison, U.S. poverty rates tend to be significantly higher, especially among children.

Figure 6.3 shows a lopsided distribution of wealth in the United States. Are we out of line in this regard in comparison to other nations? It depends on whom we compare ourselves to (Wolff, 1995; World Bank, 2007). In many less developed countries around the world—such as Paraguay, Pakistan, Brazil, and South Africa—the wealthiest 20 percent of the families earn 60 percent or more of the family income. In Brazil and Paraguay, the poorest 20 percent of the families receive only 2 percent of annual income—a small share indeed! So, the United States has a more equitable distribution of wealth than do these nations. In comparison to other wealthy nations in the world, however, the U.S. income distribution is lopsided. In only three of the twenty wealthiest nations do the top 20 percent of the families receive as large a share of income as in the United States; in none of these twenty nations does the bottom fifth receive as small a share as in the United States. For example, the wealthiest 1 percent of households in the United States possess nearly 40 percent of the nation's wealth. By contrast, the wealthiest 1 percent of households in Britain possess only 18 percent of that nation's wealth. In addition, trends of the past century have produced higher levels of inequality in the United States while the trend in Britain has been toward reducing levels of inequality (Smeeding, 1997).

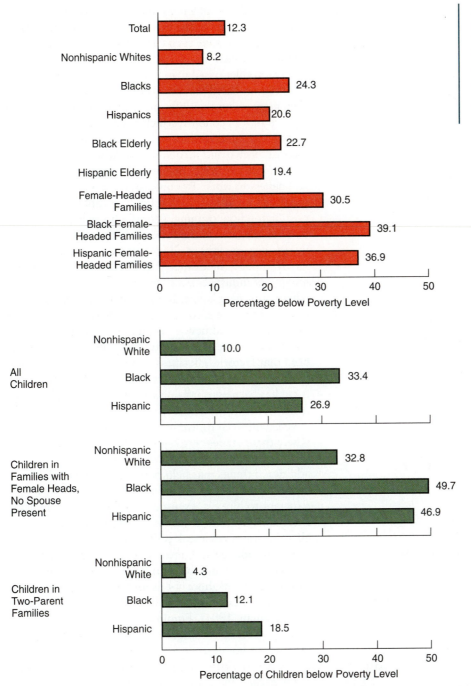

Figure 6.5

Percentage of People in Various Groups below the Poverty Level in the United States, 2006

Note: From U.S. Bureau of the Census, *Current Population Survey,* "2006 Poverty Table of Contents," *Annual Social and Economic Supplement,* www.census.gov/hhes/www/poverty/poverty.html.

CAUSES OF POVERTY Why is there so much poverty in the United States? Many people believe it is because poor people are too lazy to work. People in the United States believe strongly in the work ethic and in the notion that their country is a land of opportunity where those who are willing to work can get ahead (Scott & Leonhardt, 2005). Sociological research, however, shows that reality is more complicated than this picture. Research finds, for example, that poor people, especially the youth, want to work and are willing to work. It is not desire or ambition that they lack, but rather the opportunity to find jobs that pay enough to enable them to support their families in a respectable fashion (Freeman & Holzer, 1986; Newman, 1999). Also, as has been noted, many poor do work, and many of those who do not work are children, the elderly, the disabled, and mothers with young children.

So, the reason for high rates of poverty in the United States lies elsewhere than failed ambition. Part of the explanation is that there are many single-parent and female-headed families, which are at greater risk of falling into poverty. In addition, there are too few low-skill but adequately paying jobs that will enable people to support themselves and their families (Levy, 1998;

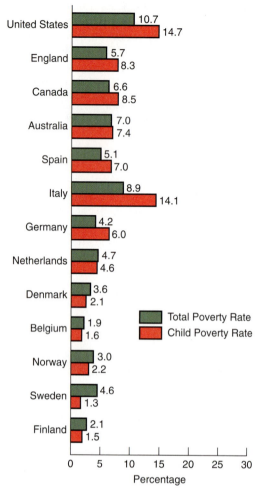

Figure 6.6

Poverty Rates in Selected Industrial Nations (Data from the Mid-1990s)

Source: Timothy M. Smeeding, Lee Rainwater, and Gary Burtless, "U.S. Poverty in a Cross-National Context." In Sheldon H. Danziger and Robert H. Haveman (eds.), Understanding Poverty (New York: Russell Sage Foundation and Harvard University Press, 2001), p. 173. Reprinted with permission of Timothy Smeeding and the Harvard University Press.

Phelps, 1997). The proportion of jobs that pay poverty-level wages has been increasing for the past three decades, and the new jobs created since the 1990s have tended to be at the low end of the pay scale. People without access to education or job-training programs are likely to be stuck with these low-paying jobs, if they can find a job at all.

Much concern about poverty in the United States has focused on the entrenched poor, sometimes called the *truly disadvantaged* or the *underclass,* who are isolated from the mainstream of society and remain poor for a long period of time (Devine & Wright, 1993; Marks, 1991). Both the functionalist and conflict perspectives point to some economic and political structures that contribute to the circumstances of this desperate group. William Wilson (1987, 1996) attributes the

emergence of the underclass to some fundamental structural changes in the U.S. economy over the past several decades. One such change is the evolving labor market in modern industrial societies that are shifting from a product-based manufacturing economy to an information-based service economy. People in the underclass are without the skills and work experience useful in the latter-type economy, which places more emphasis on verbal talent and educational qualifications than on physical brawn and manual labor. At one time, there were ample jobs for people with strong backs and a willingness to work. By contrast, most well-paying jobs today call for at least high school education and often post-high-school training. People who lack these credentials are relegated to the lowest-paying jobs or, increasingly, no jobs at all (Perrucci & Wysong, 2002).

Another basic change in the economy has been the moving of industries away from the communities where poor people live. Relocation has occurred for a number of reasons, such as government policies providing funds to build new housing in the suburbs and freeways to get there (see Chapter 14). The outcome has been that factories, businesses, and jobs have fled poor neighborhoods and relocated in nonpoor areas. This trend has been especially disastrous for African Americans, who, because of discrimination in housing, have been forced to live in segregated neighborhoods where there are few good jobs (Massey, 1990).

Christopher Jencks (1992) points to some additional things that help perpetuate the underclass: because of stereotyping and racism, employers are reluctant to hire blacks, especially young black males. After all, even though jobs have left a community, ghetto residents can seek jobs outside their neighborhood, even in the suburbs. But Jencks points to research showing that employers direct hiring efforts toward white neighborhoods and prefer not to recruit inner-city blacks, especially males (Neckerman & Kirschenman, 1991). Employers may perceive young black males as less skilled, educated, or trustworthy than white workers.

Is poverty inevitable? This is not the same question as the earlier one about whether social stratification is inevitable, because society could have stratification, or a hierarchical ranking of people with an inequitable distribution of resources, without poverty. Many functionalists would argue that some level of poverty is probably inevitable because it performs important functions, especially motivating people to seek and perform well at the jobs that society needs done. Functionalists would also argue, however, that poverty can be reduced through programs to provide people with the education and skills necessary to find jobs in an advanced industrial economy. These programs should teach people basic literacy skills and enable them to earn a high school diploma or other

Applying Sociology   Creating and Evaluating Programs That Assist the Poor

Chapter 1 noted that sociology has a significant history of interest in social reform, and one focus of that interest has been the plight of the poor. Although sociologists do not necessarily believe that poverty can be eliminated, they do believe that many poor people suffer unfair disadvantages because of the structural conditions that limit their opportunities. To change these conditions, much sociological work has focused on discovering the causes of poverty in order to develop social policies that will assist the poor. One important barrier that the poor confront is that their school and home lives do not give them adequate preparation for finding and keeping good jobs. This sociological wisdom was translated into social policy in the 1960s in the form of the Head Start program, which provides preschool children with enrichment and early learning experiences that middle-class children are more likely to receive at home (Zigler & Muenchow, 1992). These experiences are intended to instill in the children a desire for achievement, useful reading and writing skills, and a more positive self-concept that will help them in school and in life.

Sociological practitioners have played a part in the ongoing evaluation of Head Start. In a type of research called *program evaluation,* sociologists collect data to assess whether a program or policy is actually achieving the goals that have been set for it. This evaluation begins by translating the general objectives of a program into measurable goals. In the case of Head Start, the program's immediate goals are such measurable achievements as better grades in school, reduced need for remedial education, and lower rates of being held back a grade in school. More long-range goals might be higher rates of graduation from high school or entrance into college. This evaluation has involved

comparing youngsters who have been through Head Start with equally poor youngsters who have not in order to see which group has higher grades in school or is more likely to graduate from high school. Such comparison provides objective, observable, and measurable information with which to evaluate social policy programs.

The results of this sociological and other social scientific research have provided strong evidence that Head Start gives poor children some significant advantages (Love et al., 2002; Ramey & Ramey, 2000; Reynolds, Temple, Robertson, & Mann, 2001). For example, research has shown that Head Start children, when compared to other poor children, are less likely to be assigned to special education classes or to be kept back a grade in school, and they do better on mathematics achievement tests and show more improvement in IQ scores. Head Start children are also less likely to get in trouble with the law or become teenage mothers. In addition, they have a better family life and a more positive self-concept. Finally, as young adults, Head Start children are more likely to go to college and hold a steady job requiring a skill. With benefits such as these, Head Start children should be better equipped to support themselves and their families as adults.

When social programs were being cut in the last two decades, Head Start retained considerable support from politicians and protection from cuts, in part because research demonstrated the clear benefits that derive from the program. Head Start is thus a good example of the role that sociologists play in the policy-making process, as they provide objective and accurate information with which to evaluate various policy alternatives. ◼

credentials they need to gain entry into the modern, service-based economy.

Conflict theorists, especially non-Marxians, would agree that stratification is inevitable but not poverty. Rather poverty results from the greed of elites who pursue a massively unbalanced distribution of resources. In this view, poverty could be ended by a redistribution of wealth, although that would not eliminate stratification; a more just distribution of wealth would leave some quite a bit better off than others but without the extremes of wealth and poverty that are found in many nations today. Economic forces, however, may make such a redistribution of wealth unlikely. Since the United States is part of the world capitalist system, companies with high-paying jobs in this country may continue to seek low-priced laborers in other countries, leaving U.S. workers with fewer

good jobs. As has been shown, stratification systems are now international in nature, and it is helpful to think of the various social classes as transcending national boundaries. So the corporate elites in the United States, Brazil, and Venezuela all benefit from certain practices, such as the movement of jobs around the globe to find the cheapest labor. Likewise, the poor in these three nations are relatively powerless and at the mercy of the decisions these elites make.

The question of poverty and its alleviation is important because, as Brazil and Venezuela demonstrate, extreme maldistributions of wealth tend to produce hopelessness and despair among the poor, lead to drug trafficking and other crimes, and are fertile grounds for social and political unrest. It should be recalled, however, that in class stratification systems, people can and do change their positions in the hierarchy. The next section will analyze how much of this social mobility occurs and why. Applying Sociology: Creating and Evaluating Programs That Assist the Poor describes the role that sociologists have played in increasing the chances for upward mobility among the poor in the United States.

Social Mobility

You should be able to describe the nature and extent of social mobility in industrial societies.

Ronald Reagan was born in a small town in Illinois and lived in a small apartment above a store as a child. He went on to gain considerable wealth as an actor and spokesman for corporations, and, of course, was elected to the highest public office in the United States. His life, along with the lives of people such as Abraham Lincoln, John D. Rockefeller, Andrew Carnegie, and H. L. Hunt, supports the belief that opportunity awaits those who are willing to work and persevere. Yet, how true is this belief?

Social mobility refers to *the movement of people from one social position to another in the stratification hierarchy.* There are two types of social mobility: horizontal and vertical. *Horizontal mobility* refers to a change in position that does not involve a corresponding change in social status. The son of a physician who

becomes a lawyer or the store clerk who becomes a restaurant cook are examples of horizontal mobility, which is quite widespread in most societies. *Vertical mobility* refers to a change in position that involves an upward or downward shift in social status. The clerk who obtains a business degree in night school, a coal miner's daughter who becomes a physician, and a business executive who becomes an alcoholic and loses his job are all examples of vertical mobility.

Extent of Social Mobility

There are two primary types of vertical mobility. *Intergenerational mobility,* also called *generational mobility,* involves a change between the parents' position in the occupational hierarchy and that of their offspring. *Intragenerational mobility,* also called *career mobility,* is a change from an individual's first job and the occupation that becomes his or her major career position. Intergenerational mobility is especially important because it enables us to assess the extent to which inequities are built into society. If one's social position at birth determines later chances for achievement, then there will be little intergenerational mobility. Because of this fact, sociologists have been most interested in this type of mobility.

Social mobility is widespread in the United States and has increased since World War II. In 1945 less than

Social mobility, or movement up or down the stratification hierarchy, occurs to some degree in most societies. The delighted college graduates in this photo illustrate that, today, access to a college education is a key factor in achieving upward mobility.

one-third of males in the United States experienced intergenerational upward mobility; by the 1970s, this figure was about 50 percent (Featherman & Hauser, 1978). However, most of this mobility is short-range—the offspring of a blue-collar employee advances to a somewhat more prestigious blue-collar job, while that of a white-collar worker attains a slightly improved white-collar position. Thus, the stratification system in the United States is characterized by considerable stability with a high degree of occupational inheritance. That is, most children tend to take jobs that are quite similar in SES to those of their parents. Long-distance social mobility, such as from a low blue-collar to a high white-collar position, is relatively rare, although it does occur (Scott & Leonhardt, 2005).

There are racial and regional variations in mobility rates (Horton et al., 2000; Matras, 1984). African Americans have considerably lower rates of upward mobility and higher rates of downward mobility than do whites, even when their family backgrounds and parents' educational levels are similar. However, these racial disparities are not as large as they once were. Southerners have lower rates of mobility than do people from other regions. In addition, family disruptions, such as one's parents' divorce, experienced during childhood, reduce a person's likelihood of experiencing upward social mobility (Biblarz & Raftery, 1993). It seems that single-parent families and stepparent families, among other things, do less supervision and monitoring of schoolwork and provide fewer influential role models. These differences mean that children in families with both biological parents present have a better platform from which to compete in school and in the occupational world.

There also appear to be slightly more opportunities for upward mobility in the United States than in other industrialized countries, but the differences are not great (Fox & Miller, 1965; Lipset & Bendix, 1959; Wong, 1990). Working-class people in the United States have a better chance of moving into professional occupations than do their counterparts in other countries. Their chances for upward mobility, however, are still rather small, and there is a tendency for elite positions in the United States and other industrial nations to be inherited. What comes through most strongly in this cross-national research are the basic similarities of the stratification systems in industrialized societies.

Sources of Social Mobility

Some traditional beliefs in the United States posit that high rates of social mobility are due to the antielitist and antiaristocratic ideology that pervades U.S. culture. According to this view, advantages of birth or accident are less important in determining a person's position in society than are individual skills and initiative. However, such individual characteristics would not result in mobility unless there were opportunities in society for mobility. After all, the idea that people can improve their social position through individual accomplishments can be traced back many centuries, long before today's high levels of mobility existed. Furthermore, other industrial nations, including those with a historical aristocracy such as Britain and France, also have high rates of mobility. It would appear, then, that the critical factor associated with high rates of social mobility today is not a grass-roots belief about equality and achievement, but rather industrialization.

In fact, much of the social mobility that occurred in the twentieth century is referred to as *structural social mobility*, indicating that it is the result of basic changes in the occupational and social structures of societies as they industrialize (Blau & Duncan, 1967; Hauser & Featherman, 1973). As societies industrialize, the number of low-status jobs declines, and the number of high-status jobs increases (DiPrete, 1993; Wright & Martin, 1987). Agricultural occupations, for example, have declined from about 37 percent of the workforce in 1900 to less than 3 percent today (see Chapter 13). In addition, there has been a decline in the number of unskilled manual-labor jobs with a consequent increase in the number of skilled-labor jobs. Finally, there are fewer blue-collar occupations and more white-collar managerial positions. The two occupational designations that have shown the largest increase since 1940 are salaried professionals and managers. As a consequence of these changes, a surplus of workers develops in lower-status jobs and a scarcity of people in the higher-status ones. Social mobility occurs as workers move up the occupational scale to fill the positions for which there is a scarcity of workers.

A related development involves the different fertility rates found in families at various occupational levels. Families in occupations at the lower end of the scale, such as farmworkers and unskilled laborers, generally have larger numbers of children, whereas those at the higher end, such as professionals and managers, tend to have fewer offspring. Consequently, families in occupational categories where there are fewer jobs are having more children, and families in expanding occupational categories are producing an insufficient number of children to fill those jobs. The result is a "push" on people at the lower end of the scale to move up in the occupational hierarchy in order to secure jobs. This push brings about social mobility, although we have seen that it mostly tends to be short-range.

For most of the twentieth century, then, and especially between World War II and the 1970s, there was considerable upward mobility in the United States, largely accounted for by opportunities created by these structural changes in the economy. There are reasons to believe, however, that significantly less upward mobility will be possible in the future

(Levy, 1998). First of all, as the economy approaches a mature industrial phase, the occupational structure is stabilizing, with little growth in the higher-status or better-paying jobs (Hout, 1988; Krymkowski & Krauze, 1992). The Bureau of Labor Statistics projects a considerable slowdown in the growth of executive, administrative, and managerial jobs in the United States in the coming years, while low-status jobs, such as service workers, will not decline nearly as much. In addition, corporations today use more "contingent" workers—part-time, temporary, or contract workers who are paid less, receive fewer benefits, and can be released more easily. The result will probably be fewer opportunities for mobility in the future, or at least stiffer competition for the good jobs.

Second, the United States now competes in a world economy, and many better-paying jobs from the United States have moved overseas where labor costs are lower. As this worldwide economic competition grows, the United States, with its high standard of living in comparison to most of the world, may lose more good jobs, and U.S. workers may face reduced opportunities for upward mobility because of it.

Third, social mobility may also decrease if people do not leave the workforce at a pace sufficiently rapid to create openings for all those entering it. As the U.S. population becomes older, top positions will be held longer by older men and women, and young people entering the workforce will find it more difficult to locate jobs and achieve upward mobility.

A lower overall mobility rate could create problems if people from various levels of the occupational hierarchy find themselves competing for the same desirable jobs. There could be tensions including increased discrimination and unrest. For example, families in desirable social positions might try to increase the likelihood that their own children, rather than young people from lower occupational rankings, would replace them in their desirable jobs.

Consequences of Stratification

You should be able to explain how people's positions in the stratification system affect various aspects of their lives.

Max Weber argued that economic differences between people translate into differences in *life chances*, or what people can accomplish during their lives. In addition, status differences lead to variations in lifestyles among people. In other words, a person's SES correlates with that individual's beliefs, choices, and behaviors. This chapter concludes with a review of some of the consequences of stratification for society. The Sociology of Media and Technology insert explores the implications of media and other technologies for social stratification and inequality.

Educational Achievement

The belief in equality in the United States rests heavily on the assumption that all people have equal access to an education, which they believe serves as a stepping-stone toward improving one's lot in life. Although the doors of schools in the United States are generally open to people irrespective of social background, the chances of advancing in the educational world are powerfully affected by SES (McClendon, 1976; Treiman & Terrell, 1975). In 1957, William Sewell (1971) began an ambitious study of the career plans of nine thousand high school seniors in Wisconsin. Dividing them into four socioeconomic groups, he followed their educational experiences for fourteen years. The differences among the groups were dramatic. Those with the highest SES were four times more likely than those with the lowest status to attend college. They were nine times more likely to receive some graduate or professional training. In other words, the higher the educational attainment, the greater the divergence between the achievement of people at different levels in the stratification system. Furthermore, these differences were not entirely a function of ability. Among high-income students with high abilities, only 10 percent chose not to attend college, whereas 25 percent of the low-income students of similar ability failed to go to college (Jencks et al., 1972). Some of these differences are undoubtedly due to economic opportunities, with low-income people less able to afford college. Yet in many cases, parents and teachers fail to develop the desire for higher education in students of low SES. Furthermore, inequalities in educational experience affect people throughout their lives, because those with better educations tend to have more desirable jobs and higher lifetime earnings. Although this link between SES and educational achievement still exists, recent investigations have concluded that it is weaker today than it was forty years ago, primarily because of the wider availability of college educations to people at all levels of the socioeconomic scale (Baker & Vélez, 1996).

Health

Although physical and mental illnesses can be found at all class levels, socioeconomic position strongly influences an individual's health status (Cockerham, 2007). For example, infants born to families of lower SES are more likely to die during the first year of life than are those born into more affluent families. People of lower status are also more likely to contract a wide range of illnesses, including arthritis, high blood pressure, visual problems, heart disease, diabetes, and cancer. In addition, lower-class people are more likely to suffer from severe mental disorders than are more affluent people (Cockerham, 2006).

Sociology of Media and Technology

Impact of Technology on Stratification Systems

One impact of technology, certainly, is that it makes people better off, at least in some ways. But this chapter is not about whether people are better off; it is about social inequality: the differences among people that emerge as a part of systems of stratification. While everyone in a high-technology environment might be, on average, better off than everyone in a low-technology environment, is there more or less social inequality in the former than in the latter? We saw earlier in the chapter that industrial societies exhibit more social inequality than do the much simpler hunting-and-gathering societies. In general, industrialization, modernization, and technological development tend to be associated with fairly high levels of social inequality. While industrialization and high technology are very good at producing goods and services, they do not necessarily produce a just and equitable distribution of those resources. What role do the mass media and computer-mediated communications technologies play in this? Let's look at the United States first and then the global picture.

As with other resources, it is the well-to-do who tend to have access to technological resources, and this access can help to perpetuate and enhance the differences among people. Almost everyone today has access to television, but access to the new, computer-mediated communication technologies tends to be concentrated among the wealthier, the better educated, and whites. Figure 6.7 shows how those with more education are dramatically more likely to have access to the Internet, and Figure 7.5 (on p. 197) shows a similar impact on Internet access by ethnicity and race. Such access, we have seen in other chapters, is virtually essential to fully participating in the modern world. With less access to the online world, the poor and the less educated are also handicapped as far as achieving social mobility and financial or occupational success.

Another role of the media is that it can present images that perpetuate myths about social inequality in the United States. Portrayals on television, in the movies, and in most magazines generally give the impression that average people are much more affluent than they actually are and that wealth is rather easily obtained. Most media portrayals show people living in quite sumptuous homes in luxurious neighborhoods. It tends not to show the much more modest living arrangements of most people and the stark housing of the inner-city and rural poor. When some modest amount of wealth is accumulated by people, this wealth is typically the product of many years of work and

savings. Most people are in their fifties and sixties when this accumulation occurs.

The portrayal of people at the other end of the spectrum—the poor—also tends to be distorted (Bullock, Wyche, & Williams, 2001; Gilens, 1996). Studies show that television news shows and newsmagazines tend to portray the poor as disproportionately made up of the unemployed, working-age adults, and African Americans and Latinos. As we saw earlier in this chapter, this image is not a very accurate portrayal of reality, but it does help to perpetuate some myths—in particular, myths that suggest that poverty is due to personal failings rather than a lack of opportunities and access to resources. When television news shows, for example, stress that some sizeable percentage of the homeless have mental disorders or use drugs or alcohol, this emphasis suggests that personal weaknesses or inadequacies cause homelessness. Just as with the portrayal of crime in Chapter 5, these images of individuals are much easier and more dramatic to produce in a short segment for a news show. Some of the elements of the social structure discussed in this chapter do not lend themselves so readily to a visually appealing video segment.

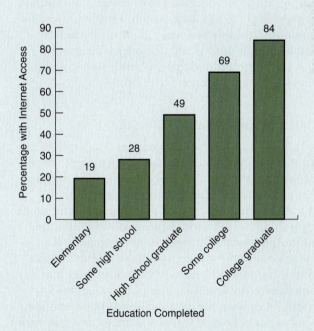

Figure 6.7

Percentage of Households with Internet Access, by Educational Level of Head of Household, 2007

Note: From U.S. Bureau of the Census, *Current Population Survey*, October 2007, www.nitia.doc.gov/reports/2008/Networked Nation.html

(continued)

If we shift attention to the global stratification system, technology and media have also come to play a critical part. The modern media and computer-mediated communications technologies have become global and highly concentrated businesses. These issues are discussed in more detail in Chapters 12 and 13, but basically a few megacorporations headquartered in a few advanced industrial nations now control most of worldwide media and communications. This situation represents an enormous concentration of power and wealth in the hands of a relatively small group. It also concentrates resources in the hands of the core nations of the world, and enables them to exercise a disproportionate amount of control over the images, ideas, and ideologies that are available to people through the media. With these resources, the core, industrial nations can exercise cultural domination by spreading capitalist and consumerist values through the media. This can help perpetuate the existing distribution of resources in the world system by encouraging people in many cultures to accept as natural social relations that tend to benefit the dominant nations of the world.

There are a number of reasons for these differences. First, the poor cannot afford the level of health care available to more affluent people and are therefore more likely to let their health deteriorate before seeking care. Although the United States has made considerable strides in seeing that health care is available to all citizens, there are still costs, such as transportation or time lost at work, that can hinder one's ability to obtain medical care. Second, the poor often live in unsanitary conditions and have a nutritionally poor diet, and these increase one's susceptibility to disease. Third, the poor are less likely to recognize that they are ill and are more inclined to delay seeking medical care. This delay greatly increases the chances that an illness will become more severe or incapacitating. The affluent, by contrast, are more likely to seek care quickly. Finally, lower-class people are less likely to engage in preventive health care. They visit dentists and doctors less frequently, especially if there is nothing apparently wrong with them (Andersen & Anderson, 1979).

Status Inconsistency

Stratification can result in a situation that sociologists call *status inconsistency,* especially when people experience social mobility related to one dimension of stratification, such as wealth, but not to others, such as education or prestige. Status inconsistency occurs when *a person ranks high on one dimension of stratification but low on another.* The self-made millionaire, for example, can have substantial wealth and an affluent lifestyle but may not receive the social prestige that comes from high levels of education or from "old wealth." Likewise, the highly educated member of a racial minority holds statuses that are inconsistent with each other.

Status inconsistency can create difficulties for people because it is often unclear which status is relevant in a particular setting. People normally expect others to relate to them on the basis of their higher status, but that may not always happen. This condition can also lead people to become disenchanted with the status quo, because it does not provide them with the rewards they feel they deserve. As a result, status inconsistency can lead to tension and unhappiness that might have a number of outlets. For example, people whose income level is low and whose educational and occupational statuses are higher are more supportive of making changes in society than are those whose statuses are consistent (Wilson & Zurcher, 1976). In addition, men who have an occupational status that is inconsistently low for their level of education are at greater risk of abusing their wives than are men who are free of such status inconsistency (Hornung, McCullough, & Sugimoto, 1981). These examples illustrate the complexity of modern stratification systems.

Self-Esteem

Those who occupy high positions in the stratification system are accorded substantial honor and privilege, whereas people below them receive less, in some cases very little. This differential distribution of honor and privilege would seem to imply a judgment about people's worth. Chapters 2 and 3 emphasize that people are shaped by the positions they hold in the social structure. Societal beliefs say that the successful, intelligent, hard-working, worthy people rise to the top. What does that say about those on the bottom of the hierarchy? Placement in the lower reaches of the hierarchy seems to imply a collective societal judgment that a person is less worthy. In other words, placement in the stratification system may influence people's self-concepts.

Self-esteem refers to the judgment that people make regarding their own overall worth; it is anchored in social circumstances and social relationships. Children born into families of low SES are likely to have lower self-esteem than do children in well-to-do families (Rosenberg & Pearlin, 1978; Wiltfang & Scarbecz, 1990). Furthermore, low self-esteem can have detrimental effects in many areas of people's lives. It can discourage children from applying themselves in school and deter adults from seeking higher-paying and

Sociology on the Internet

The U.S. Census Bureau provides enormous amounts of information about stratification and economic inequality in the United States. Start by going to the Bureau's home page: **www.census.gov/**. Click on "People: Poverty" or "People: Income," and you will have numerous links to explore. Exploring these sites provides you with much detailed data on income distribution and inequality in the United States, in some cases going back fifty years. Another useful site is the Office of the Assistant Secretary for Planning and Evaluation of the Department of Health and Human Services (**aspe.hhs.gov/index.shtml**). From these various sites, try to answer these questions: How much income inequality is there? Are the disparities getting wider? How does this information supplement (and support or contradict) the data presented in the text? Explore the overall Census Bureau site. Can you find information on poverty, unemployment, or homelessness that will provide additional insight into the U.S. stratification system? Share what you find with the class.

Explore the issues of stratification and inequality in other cultures. Select one of the search engines and enter some key words that include a particular nation or region that you are interested in, such as "stratification and Russia," "class and Africa," or "inequality and Brazil." Report what you find to the class. The United Nations Development Programme maintains a Web site (**www.undp.org**) on which it publishes much data, including its annual publication *Human Development Report*. Also, look for Web sites maintained by the World Bank, the International Monetary Fund, and Amnesty International. At all these sites, explore issues of income, wealth, and poverty in nations around the world.

For further information and discussion, go to Allyn & Bacon's Social Problems Supersite (see Chapter 1) and explore Problem Area: Problems of Poverty and Work.

---

more prestigious jobs. However, the link between stratification and self-esteem, although measurable, is not that strong. One reason for this weak linkage is that many social conditions and social relationships influence one's self-concept, as was discussed in Chapter 3, and these can dilute the impact of the stratification system. A second reason for the weak relationship has to do with the *reference groups* discussed in Chapter 4. Reference groups are groups that we use as standards in evaluating ourselves. The reference groups that are chosen in making such comparisons depend in part on one's class position. If poor people compare themselves with the wealthy, they will not fare well in the comparison. But people can choose other standards or criteria than wealth in assessing their self-worth. People might claim that decency, morality, or religiosity are more important than wealth, education, or fame. So, through choosing reference groups with which one compares favorably, the threat of degradation that can accompany low social standing may be eased.

Study & Review
SUMMARY OF LEARNING OBJECTIVES

You should be able to discuss Weber's interpretation of the stratification system, define socioeconomic status, and list the major characteristics of the caste, estate, and class stratification systems.

Social stratification is the ranking of people into a hierarchy in which the resources considered valuable by society are unequally distributed. Max Weber argued that there are three interrelated dimensions of stratification systems: wealth, prestige, and power. Caste systems of stratification are those in which membership in social classes is hereditary, with people in different ranks being rigidly separated from one another. Estate stratification systems are those in which inheritance still strongly influences social position but landownership and political or military power are also determinants. In class systems, the boundaries between classes are more permeable, a person's socioeconomic position depends more on achievement, and there are fairly frequent opportunities to change social positions.

You should be able to describe the functionalist, conflict, and evolutionary theories of stratification as well as discuss the global dimensions of stratification.

Four different theories of stratification are prominent in sociology. Functionalists argue that stratification exists because it makes some contribution to the ongoing maintenance of society. Conflict theorists argue that society involves a constant struggle between social classes over scarce resources. Gerhard Lenski has tried to synthesize these two views using an evolutionary approach, in which it is assumed that, as the type of economic production changes, so does the amount of inequality found in society. World-system theory recognizes that stratification systems are now global in scope.

You should be able to explain how socioeconomic status is measured, describe the major social classes found in the United States, and discuss the extent and causes of inequality in societies.

Social scientists have employed numerous techniques in measuring socioeconomic status (SES). In the past, these included the reputational approach and the subjective, or self-placement, approach. Because of weaknesses in these approaches and changes in society, sociologists today rely heavily on the objective approach. Most sociologists view the class structure of the United States today in terms of five levels: upper, upper-middle, lower-middle, working, and lower class. Poverty exists in the United States, and it is fairly extensive. It results primarily from the lack of sufficient jobs that pay a good wage.

You should be able to describe the nature and extent of social mobility in industrial societies.

Social mobility refers to the movement of people from one position to another in the stratification hierarchy. There are two types of mobility: horizontal and vertical. A critical factor associated with mobility is industrialization, and much of the upward social mobility that occurred in the twentieth century is referred to as *structural*, indicating that it was due to basic changes in the occupational and social structures as societies industrialize.

You should be able to explain how people's positions in the stratification system affect various aspects of their lives.

Stratification systems have multiple consequences for people, and economic differences among people translate into differences in life chances, or what people can accomplish during their lives. Among the things affected by stratification are educational achievement, health, status inconsistency, and self-esteem.

CHRONOLOGICAL PRACTICE TEST

For answers to Key Concepts see the page number in parentheses; for other answers see page 173.

Dimensions of Stratification

Key Concepts

1. Social stratification (147)
2. Wealth (148)
3. Social classes (148)
4. Prestige (149)
5. Status groups (150)
6. Power (150)
7. Authority (150)
8. Parties (150)
9. Socioeconomic status (SES) (150)
10. Closed stratification systems (150)
11. Open stratification systems (150)
12. Caste system (151)
13. Estate system (151)
14. Class system (152)

True/False

15. T F According to Max Weber, differences due to wealth or economic position create social strata that he called *parties*.
16. T F In the United States, people give higher prestige rankings to occupations that require more educational preparation as compared to those requiring less education.

Concept Completion

17. The social strata that are produced by differences due to wealth or economic position are called _____.
18. _____ refers to a person's social location-based wealth, prestige, and power.

Critical Thinking

19. Describe the nature of stratification systems as analyzed by Max Weber. Include in your answer an assessment of the three major dimensions of stratification systems.
20. Describe the different kinds of stratification systems that are found in societies based on the degree to which people are permitted to move from one level of the stratification hierarchy to another.

Theories of Stratification

Key Concept

21. World-system theory (155)

True/False

22. T F Because some of Karl Marx's predictions have not come true, modern sociologists have rejected his approach to social stratification.
23. T F Gerhard Lenski's evolutionary theory of stratification posits that societies move through a sequence of development that influences the type of stratification system they have.
24. T F World-system theory is also sometimes called *dependency theory*.

Concept Completion

25. According to the functionalist perspective, social stratification is a mechanism for _____ people to fill key positions in society.
26. Karl Marx argued that some people have _____, which means that they fail to recognize what is in their own best interests.

27. According to world-system theory, the key to the operation of the world system is _____.

Critical Thinking

28. Describe the stratification systems of Brazil and Venezuela. In your answer, use the sociological concepts that were used to describe them in the text.
29. Compare and contrast the functionalist, conflict, and evolutionary theories of stratification. Show clearly how they differ from one another.
30. What is world-system theory as it relates to social stratification? How does it differ from the other theories of stratification?

Social Class in the United States
True/False

31. T F Taken together, the upper class and the upper-middle class in the United States constitute about one-half of the total population.
32. T F Rates of poverty in the United States are significantly lower than they are in other industrial nations.
33. T F Program evaluations conducted on the Head Start program have concluded that the program gives poor children a significant advantage over comparably poor children not in Head Start.

Concept Completion

34. The _____ approach to measuring socioeconomic status asks people to state where they believe they fit into the class hierarchy.
35. The term _____ refers to the entrenched poor in the United States who are isolated from the mainstream of society and remain poor for a long period of time.
36. _____ is a type of research in which sociologists collect data to assess whether a program or policy is actually achieving the goals that have been set for it.

Critical Thinking

37. Describe the class structure in the United States as it was presented in the text. Describe how large each class is and who is a member of it.
38. How does the text answer the question of why there is so much poverty in the United States?

Social Mobility
Key Concept

39. Social mobility (166)

True/False

40. T F African Americans have higher rates of both upward mobility and downward mobility than do white Americans.

Concept Completion

41. _____ is social mobility that is due to basic changes in the occupational and social structures of societies as they industrialize.

Critical Thinking

42. How extensive has social mobility been in the United States during the past century? What have been the sources of this social mobility?

Consequences of Stratification
Key Concept

43. Status inconsistency (170)

True/False

44. T F The link between a person's position in the stratification system and that person's level of self-esteem is weak because many other social conditions influence self-esteem.

Concept Completion

45. When a person ranks high on one dimension of the stratification system but low on another, the person is experiencing _____.

Critical Thinking

46. What consequences do people's positions in the stratification system have for their educational achievement and their health?
47. What consequences do people's positions in the stratification system have for their self-esteem? What are the consequences of status inconsistency?

ANSWERS TO CHRONOLOGICAL PRACTICE TEST

15. F; 16. T; 22. F; 23. T; 24. T; 31. F; 32. F; 33. T; 40. F; 44. T
17. social classes
18. Socioeconomic status (SES)
25. motivating
26. false class consciousness
27. trade
34. subjective, self-placement
35. truly disadvantaged, underclass
36. Program evaluation
41. Structural social mobility
45. status inconsistency

CUMULATIVE PRACTICE TEST

See page 482 for answers.
1. Social stratification is best defined as
    a. the beliefs, values, and material products that constitute the way of life of a group of people.
    b. the ranking of people into a hierarchy in which the resources considered valuable by society are unequally distributed.
    c. the organized pattern of social interaction that exists in a group or society.
    d. differences in life chances due to differences in wealth or economic position.
    e. the ranking of people where ranks are hereditary and people in different ranks are rigidly segregated from one another.

2. An important politician would rank above many other people in the stratification system of the United States. The factor that accords him or her this position, according to Max Weber's categories, would likely be his or her position in which social strata?
   a. Social class.
   b. Party.
   c. Status group.
   d. Wealth.
   e. Estate.

3. According to Max Weber, people who occupy similar prestige levels and share a common lifestyle form
   a. social classes.
   b. parties.
   c. open strata.
   d. status groups.
   e. estates.

4. A closed stratification system is one in which
   a. people from other cultures are not allowed to enter.
   b. only members of one racial or ethnic group are allowed entrance.
   c. ranks have ill-defined boundaries that make it difficult for people to cross them.
   d. well-defined ranks serve as rather rigid boundaries that are difficult or impossible for people to cross.
   e. social classes, status groups, and parties are kept separate from one another.

5. The stratification system in the United States today could be best characterized as a/an _____ system.
   a. caste
   b. estate
   c. closed
   d. structured
   e. class

6. The central debate in sociology regarding social stratification has been
   a. how to devise a social structure in which stratification is no longer necessary.
   b. how to move societies from a class to a caste stratification system.
   c. how to reduce the amount of social mobility that occurs.
   d. whether social inequality is due to changes in the social structure or to biological factors that affect different social classes.
   e. whether it exists because it is necessary for society or because it benefits some groups.

7. Estate stratification systems differ from caste stratification systems in that estate systems
   a. permit more social mobility.
   b. rely more on religious values to enforce acceptance of the system.
   c. rely less on military power to enforce acceptance of the system.
   d. permit no social mobility between ranks in the system.
   e. rely more heavily on heredity to determine social placement.

8. Which of the following theorists argued that stratification systems are not inevitable in societies?
   a. Karl Marx.
   b. C. Wright Mills.
   c. Gerhard Lenski.
   d. Talcott Parsons.
   e. Kingsley Davis and Wilbert Moore.

9. Which of the following would be true regarding Lenski's evolutionary view of stratification?
   a. It is based on economic determinism.
   b. It argues that inequality will continue to increase in advanced industrial societies.
   c. It assumes that stratification is based on the ownership of economic resources.
   d. It argues that the functional view cannot account for all of the inequities found in stratification systems.
   e. It argues that estate stratification systems will replace class stratification systems.

10. "People gain desirable positions in the stratification system through exploitation or inheritance and then work to protect their resources against inroads by less fortunate groups." This statement reflects the
    a. functionalist perspective.
    b. interactionist perspective.
    c. conflict perspective.
    d. evolutionary perspective.
    e. world-system perspective.

11. World-system theory views _____ as the significant actors in a worldwide stratification system.
    a. owners and workers
    b. nations
    c. politicians
    d. proletariat
    e. armies

12. According to the text, which of the following groups tends to benefit most from the dependency of Brazil and Venezuela on export trade with core nations?
    a. The poor.
    b. Agricultural and industrial elites.
    c. Racial minorities.
    d. Peasants.
    e. The lower classes.

13. The most widely used objective criterion used to measure socioeconomic status is
    a. education.
    b. reputation.
    c. income.
    d. subjective position.
    e. occupation.

14. One of the weaknesses of the objective approach to measuring socioeconomic status is that
    a. it cannot be used in large communities.
    b. people may place themselves where they wish to be in the stratification hierarchy rather than where they are.
    c. it simplifies a very complex social reality.
    d. it is based on the subjective assessment of community judges.
    e. it is accurate with estate stratification systems but not class stratification systems.

15. Business and professional people who have relatively high incomes and have accumulated a limited amount of wealth would be considered in the
    a. upper class.
    b. middle class.
    c. working class.
    d. upper-middle class.
    e. lower-middle class.

16. Which of the following statements is true about poverty and wealth in the United States?
    a. In the past thirty years, the rich have gotten richer and the poor have gotten poorer.
    b. Prior to industrialization, economic resources were equitably distributed, with few rich and few poor people.
    c. The poverty rate is higher now than it was in the 1960s.
    d. Two-thirds of the poor are nonwhites.
    e. One-third of all people in the United States live below the poverty level.

17. Which of the following is true of the "underclass" of poor people in the United States today?
    a. They do not have the education and skills that are essential to landing a good job.
    b. They tend to remain poor for only short periods of time.
    c. They have better chances for social mobility than did the poor of 50 years ago.
    d. All of the above are true.
    e. Only a and b are true.

18. When applied sociologists collect data to assess whether a social program or policy is achieving the goals that have been set for it, they are engaging in _____ research?
    a. participant observation
    b. experimental
    c. survey
    d. program evaluation
    e. replication

19. Which of the following is true regarding educational achievement and socioeconomic status in the United States?
    a. The link between the two is stronger today than forty years ago.
    b. The link between the two is about the same today as forty years ago.
    c. There is no longer any link between the two.
    d. The link between the two is weaker today than forty years ago.
    e. People from low-income backgrounds do better at educational achievement than do people from high-income backgrounds.

20. If a person experiences upward social mobility related to one dimension of the stratification system, such as wealth, but not the others, such as education or prestige, what can result is called
    a. generational mobility.
    b. structured mobility.
    c. status inconsistency.
    d. horizontal mobility.
    e. estate conflict.

FOR FURTHER READING

DeMott, Benjamin. (1990). *The imperial middle: Why Americans can't think straight about class*. New York: William Morrow. This is a very readable book about the myth that many accept in the United States that social class is unimportant or irrelevant. The author describes many ways in which this belief leads us astray and can be destructive.

DeParle, Jason. (2004). *American dream: Three women, ten kids, and a nation's drive to end welfare*. New York: Viking. This is an intriguing, personal, and detailed look at how welfare and welfare reform impact the lives of three women and their children. It shows how complex the impacts of poverty and social policies are on people's lives.

Ehrenreich, Barbara. (2001). *Nickel and dimed: On (not) getting by in America*. New York: Metropolitan Books. This book offers an intriguing, firsthand account of the difficult life of the working poor in the United States. The author, a writer and social commentator, worked the minimum-wage jobs and lived off these earnings in order to gain an understanding of this lifestyle.

Gans, Herbert J. (1995). *The war against the poor: The underclass and antipoverty policy*. New York: Basic Books. This book on social policy relating to poverty in the United States focuses on the tendency to stereotype and stigmatize the poor and to treat them as moral inferiors who are at least partially responsible for their circumstances. The author documents the many ways in which this tendency is highly negative and destructive as well as quite inaccurate.

Kerbo, H. R. (2006). *Social stratification and inequality: Class conflict in historical and comparative perspective* (6th ed.). New York: McGraw-Hill. This thorough textbook on social stratification provides more coverage than is possible in this chapter and also offers some important cross-cultural and international comparisons.

Kotlowitz, Alex. (1991). *There are no children here: The story of two boys growing up in the other America*. New York: Doubleday. This realistic and wrenching description of what it is like to grow up poor and black in Chicago helps the reader see what poverty is like through the eyes of the poor.

Liebow, Elliott. (1993). *Tell them who I am: The lives of homeless women*. New York: Free Press. This enlightening and compassionate look at the lives of women who are homeless tells how they got that way and how they cope with it. Liebow is an anthropologist who did participant observation research to uncover this aspect of life in the United States.

Newman, Katherine. (1993). *Declining fortunes: The withering of the American dream*. New York: Basic Books. In class stratification systems where social mobility occurs, some of that mobility is downward rather than upward. This anthropologist explores the nature, extent, and experience of downward mobility among middle-class, suburban families in the United States.

Phillips, Kevin. (2002). *Wealth and democracy: A political history of the American rich*. New York: Broadway Books. This political analyst discusses the growing gap between the rich and the less well-to-do in the United States, looks at it throughout history, and discusses the corrosive negative consequences such a gap can produce.

Social Inequality: Race and Ethnicity

MYTHS & FACTS: About Race and Ethnicity

Minority Groups

Race and Ethnicity
Racism

Sources of Prejudice and Discrimination

Social Sources
Ethnocentrism
Competition
Socialization and Conformity
Institutionalized Discrimination
Social Psychological Sources
Consequences of Discrimination

OTHER WORLDS, OTHER WAYS: Britain, Germany,
Yugoslavia: The Social and Economic Sources of Racial Hatred
and Conflict

Patterns of Intergroup Relations

Forms of Domination
Minority Reaction to Domination
Switzerland: Cooperation in a Multiethnic Society

Racial and Ethnic Minorities in the United States

African Americans
Hispanic Americans
American Indians
Asian Americans
Arab Americans
Today's Immigrants
Achievement and Assimilation among Immigrant Groups

SOCIOLOGY OF MEDIA AND TECHNOLOGY: Image and
Access: Race/Ethnicity and Communications Technologies

Current Issues in the United States
  Assimilation or Pluralism?
  Race Relations Today: Race or Class?
  Advances, Setbacks, and Controversial Policies

APPLYING SOCIOLOGY: Combating Prejudice, Discrimination, and Racial Polarization
SOCIOLOGY ON THE INTERNET

Study & Review

Portuguese explorers heading for passage to India through the Cape of Good Hope in April 1500 were blown off course to the west and made the first European sighting of what would later become Brazil. Their ship anchored offshore, a few hundred miles north of modern-day Rio de Janeiro, and a small party of twenty or so Indians, completely naked and carrying bows and arrows, quickly gathered on the beach. The Portuguese sailors landed for the first meeting between Europeans and this new race of people in the Western Hemisphere. The contact was entirely peaceful, and the Indians were fascinated with the sailors' iron tools and their celebration of the Christian mass on the beach. The Portuguese, in turn, were fascinated by the unembarrassed nakedness of the Indians, both men and women. In these early contacts, the Portuguese found the Indians to be generous and innocent and to exhibit an extraordinary sense of freedom. Enchantment and fascination quickly turned to a sense of offense, however, because the Portuguese had been taught that nudity was immoral. Before this first contact was over, the Portuguese were giving the Indians clothing and trying to convince them to wear their new possessions (Hemming, 1978).

Myths & Facts
About Race and Ethnicity

Myth:

The Civil Rights Act, affirmative action, and other social policies have eliminated racism in the United States.

Fact:

Although the amount of overt prejudice and discrimination against racial minorities has declined in the past few decades, research still finds considerable racism and discriminatory practices. Recent studies, for example, document discrimination against African Americans still occurring in housing and employment (see p. 196).

Myth:

If people insist on retaining a strong racial or ethnic identity, then ethnocentric tendencies make conflict, and sometimes violence, an inevitable development in such multiracial or multiethnic societies.

Fact:

Although such conflict and violence are all too common, political and social structures can be created that minimize the likelihood of it. Switzerland, for example, is made up of three distinct ethnic groups. Yet, they have overcome conflicts and worked together peacefully and cooperatively because of a political system that ensures the participation and influence of minorities.

Myth:

American Indians live comfortably with the benefits they receive from the government for being Indian and with the proceeds from the gambling casinos that are now permitted on some reservation land.

Fact:

Of all U.S. minorities, American Indians remain among the poorest. As a group, they suffer very high unemployment rates and have a median income that is only two-thirds of the national average. More than one-third of all Indians live below the official poverty level. American Indians living on reservations tend to be worse off than their nonreservation counterparts.

Myth:

Nonwhites in the United States continue to lag behind whites in education, income, and occupational status in the twenty-first century.

Fact:

Contemporary reality is more complicated than this statement. African Americans, for example, have made considerable improvement, and their educational levels are coming very close to those of whites. Cuban Americans, Chinese Americans, and Japanese Americans are among the best educated groups in the United States. Some inequities persist, however. For example, African Americans and Hispanic Americans still lag considerably behind whites in average family income.

Some Europeans were much impressed with the newly discovered peoples of Brazil, seeing them as "noble savages." Roman Catholic missionaries saw them as innocents in the forest who needed to be protected and, of course, converted to Christianity. Thus began a horrendous episode of conquest, displacement, and enslavement for Brazilian Indians. In 1511 the Portuguese ship *Bertoa* made landfall near where Rio de Janeiro would later rise; she departed for Portugal a short time later with a cargo of brazilwood, parrots, jaguar skins—and thirty-five Indian slaves. Thus, a decade after discovery, the Indians were seen by some Europeans as an inferior race who could be treated like property, their human dignity and rights ignored. Some Indians went willingly to Europe, believing that they and their children were being taken to a promised land; many others were simply enslaved and forced to do the bidding of their European masters.

Gradually, many Europeans came to believe that the Indians—because of culture, temperament, and physical constitution—were not suited to slave labor. This change of heart, however, did not make things better for the Indians. Since the European colonizers and their heirs in the new land were driven by the dual engines of conquest and exploitation, the Indians came to be seen as worthless—or, worse yet, as obstacles to progress. As the colonizers and their descendants expanded away from the coast, they drove these "obstacles" from their lands and massacred the Indians when they resisted. Some Europeans protested the decimation of the Indians, but Brazil was far away and very large, and it seemed to many that there should be room for all. Also the colonial expansion enriched many in the Old World as well as the New. So, the pressures and the horrors continued unrelentingly over the centuries.

There was resistance to the displacement, enslavement, and slaughter of the Brazilian Indians. Jesuit missionaries, for example, organized some Indians into quasi-military missions that were independent of colonial government control and offered some protection against attacks by slavers. But the Jesuits were expelled from Brazil in 1760 (Hemming, 1987). Some Indians retreated into the impenetrable forests of interior Brazil and fought ferociously to protect their lands, killing anyone who intruded. But each of these forest strongholds was breached eventually by the Europeans. The Europeans who were on the front lines of this assault against the Indians were the *bandeirantes,* or "frontiersmen," and they are portrayed as mythic heroes by some present-day Brazilians—like the cowboys of the American West—but the Indians see them as slavers and killers of their ancestors. Some Indian tribes, such as the Botocudos, the Kayapos, and the Kaingangs, defended themselves admirably and effectively for some time, but their success only resulted in the mounting of major military expeditions to defeat

them. In 1835, there was even a massive revolt on the part of the Indians and *mestizos* (people of mixed Indian and European ancestry) that spread along much of the Amazon River, but it was violently suppressed after four years. In the end, the Europeans proved too well organized and powerful, with their centralized authority that could coordinate and direct massive resources around the globe. The small, nomadic, unorganized, Stone Age tribes were simply no match for them. (The Yanomamo, discussed in the beginning of Chapter 4, are an example of a group continuing this battle today.)

This remarkable story of the Indians of Brazil contains within it many of the themes that sociologists find when people of different racial and ethnic groups come together: Racial or ethnic identity becomes the context for discrimination, exploitation, violence, and resistance. The United States, of course, has its own history of displacing Indian peoples and enslaving those of a different, nonwhite race. In a diverse world, these are important issues to understand if we are to comprehend how societies persist, develop, and change. Much of our attention on this topic is directed toward issues of social inequality—the extent to which opportunities and access to resources are differentially allocated on the basis of race or ethnicity. Such inequality is a central concern in the United States today, since the populace is becoming increasingly diverse in racial and ethnic composition and since the country is far from eliminating hostility, prejudice, and discrimination based on racial and ethnic identity.

The preceding chapter discussed social stratification in societies in general. This chapter and the following one continue that analysis by discussing how characteristics such as race, ethnicity, and gender shape the system of stratification in society. Characteristics such as race and ethnicity are *ascribed statuses* because they are assigned to people and represent social positions that people have little or no say about occupying. Such statuses can serve as the basis for unequal treatment of groups, functioning as criteria for allocating resources and determining life chances and lifestyles. Sociologists refer to such groups as *minority groups,* and a discussion of what constitutes a minority group is the first topic in this chapter.

Minority Groups

You should be able to define *minority group* and *racism* and identify what constitutes a racial and an ethnic group.

A **minority group** is *a group whose members share distinct physical and cultural characteristics, who are* *denied access to power and resources available to other groups, and who are accorded fewer rights, privileges, and opportunities* (Marden, Meyer, & Engel, 1992). In the United States, black, Hispanic, Vietnamese, and some white ethnic groups such as rural Appalachians are considered minority groups because each has lower levels of educational and occupational attainment than other groups, and each has fewer opportunities. Chapter 8 shows that despite the numerical majority of women in the population, women are also considered a minority group because they have been denied equal access to education, jobs, and important positions that men have controlled for some time. This chapter, however, focuses only on minorities whose disadvantaged status arises from their racial or ethnic group membership.

The term *minority group,* then, refers not to numerical size but to a position in the stratification system of society. A rather extreme case of a numerically large group of people being dominated by a much smaller group can be found in South Africa's traditional system of *apartheid,* which persisted until it was dismantled in the early 1990s (Adam & Moodley, 1986). About 85 percent of South Africa's population was made up of black Africans who were oppressed by a small group of white Afrikaaners. Under apartheid, black South Africans had virtually no power, and a system of legal segregation maintained a rigid separation between the social worlds of blacks and whites. Blacks could not vote, they received limited educations, they were restricted to certain occupations, their travel in their own country was rigidly controlled, and they could live only in certain designated areas. These arrangements made South Africa one of the most rigidly stratified societies in the world. As explained in Chapter 6, *social stratification* refers to the ranking of people into a hierarchy in which the resources considered valuable by society are unequally distributed. Ascribed characteristics such as race and ethnicity often determine a person's position in the stratification system. But the terms *race* and *ethnicity* can be easily misunderstood.

Race and Ethnicity

Scientists use the term *race* as a biological concept to identify a population that differs from others in terms of certain key genetic, hereditary traits. There is much controversy among anthropologists and biologists, however, over whether any traits are unique to particular races in the world today. Certainly some traits are more common in some races than others. But with extensive interbreeding among racial groups throughout human history, genetic traits and characteristics have tended to spread around the world. Indeed, if we were to take a representative group of people from two different racial groups in the United States, it would be difficult to determine, based on visible physical characteristics, where one group left off and the other began. However, although the biological reality of race may be hazy, its social reality is not. In fact, sociologists' definition of race is based on people's *belief* in racial differences: A race is *a group of people who are believed to be a biological group sharing genetically transmitted traits that are defined as important.* Thus, race is a social category because in U.S. society, as in others, people make important distinctions between people on the basis of such presumed biological differences, even when these variations are actually vague or nonexistent (Montagu, 1998).

An ethnic group is *a people who share a common historical and cultural heritage and sense of group identity and belongingness.* Groups that share distinctive cultural traits such as a common language, national origin, religion, or a sense of historical heritage have been a major source of diversity that has enriched life in many societies. Hispanic Americans, Polish Americans, Gypsies, the Amish, and the Jews are but a few of the many ethnic groups in the United States that have made significant contributions to this nation's way of life. Nevertheless, a fair amount of the tension, conflict, and violence that have been part and parcel of U.S. history and still characterize social life today have focused on ethnic differences.

Racism

The subordination and oppression of minority groups is commonly supported by an ideology that assumes that members of the minority are innately inferior and thus deserving of their subordinate status. Racism is *the view that certain racial or ethnic groups are biologically inferior and that practices involving their domination and exploitation are therefore justified.* Racist ideologies in Nazi Germany justified genocidal attacks on the Jews, just as racism in the United States has been at the core of discrimination against African Americans, Asians, and other racial groups. For example, assaults on and murders of African Americans have been periodically carried out by skinheads, Nazis, and Ku Klux Klan members, motivated in part by racist beliefs.

Clearly, some degree of racism persists in some parts of the United States. At this point in the discussion, it is helpful to understand how this kind of ideology arises and, in particular, how prejudice and discrimination develop and affect minority groups.

Sources of Prejudice and Discrimination

| You should be able to explain the social and social psychological sources of prejudice and discrimination and describe the consequences that discrimination has for individuals and society.

Prejudice and discrimination are closely intertwined, so much so that people are likely to view them as the same thing. In reality, they are quite distinct. A prejudice is *an irrational attitude toward certain people based solely on their membership in a particular group* (Levin & Levin, 1994). Individuals are prejudged on the basis of whatever undesirable characteristics the whole group is presumed to possess. Prejudices can be positive, but they are often negative.

Discrimination, by contrast, refers to *behavior, particularly unequal treatment of people because they are members of a particular group*. The type of discrimination with which this chapter is most concerned is the denial of equal access to resources, privileges, or opportunities, practices that are often based on illogical and irrational grounds.

The relationship between prejudice and discrimination is complex. Although they are likely to go together, Robert K. Merton (1949) has demonstrated that sometimes they do not. In fact, people may combine prejudice and discrimination in four different ways. The most desirable combination, from the point of view of political and social values in the United States, is the *unprejudiced nondiscriminator,* who accepts other racial or ethnic groups in both belief and practice. The *prejudiced discriminator* has negative feelings toward a particular group and translates these sentiments into unequal treatment of people in that group. Members of the Ku Klux Klan, for example, have a strong prejudice against blacks and members of other racial groups; they advocate segregated schools and neighborhoods. These first two possibilities involve a consistency between belief and practice, but there are other possibilities. The *prejudiced nondiscriminator* is a kind of "closet bigot" who is prejudiced against members of some groups but does not translate these attitudes into discriminatory practices. A landlord, for example, may be prejudiced against Asian Americans yet still rent apartments to them because of laws forbidding housing discrimination. Because there are now many laws against discrimination that are strictly enforced, the incidence of this kind of relationship between prejudice and discrimination is probably more common than in the past. The *unprejudiced discriminator* treats the members of some groups unequally because it is convenient or advantageous to do so rather than out of personal antipathy toward them. Salespeople in a real estate agency, for example, may have no personal prejudices but still decline to show houses in certain neighborhoods to African Americans because of the prejudices of people who already live in those neighborhoods.

Social Sources

Prejudice and discrimination can be understood in part through the theoretical explanations of social stratification presented in Chapter 6: the functionalist, conflict, and evolutionary perspectives. That discussion will not be repeated here. Instead the text will discuss some additional elements of the perspectives that apply especially well to problems of prejudice and discrimination.

ETHNOCENTRISM   Chapters 2 and 4 discuss how important it is that people feel positive about their society and the groups to which they belong. Ethnocentrism is *the tendency to view one's own group or culture as an in-group that follows the best and the only proper way to live.* Feeling positive about one's own group, of course, is good because it gives one a sense of belonging and self-worth. For functionalists, ethnocentrism is functional because it produces loyalty, cohesiveness, and strong group ties. All these characteristics help groups stick together and achieve their goals. Ethnocentrism can, however, lead one to believe that other groups—especially those that are very different—have unfavorable characteristics. If one's own way of life is the only proper way to live, an individual may conclude that other lifestyles are improper. This conclusion can be used to justify unfair, hostile, and even genocidal attacks on other groups. Under Adolf Hitler, for example, the Nazis were so thoroughly convinced of the superiority of the alleged Aryan race that the Jews became a despised out-group. Likewise, many Europeans who came to the Americas as colonists believed that their heritage contained all that was wise and desirable, and these racist beliefs fueled their treatment of Indians in the New World. Thus, if ethnocentrism gets out of hand, it can become dysfunctional and create social disorganization in the form of hostility, conflict, and discrimination, which can threaten the social order. Although ethnocentrism can have these negative consequences, according to functionalists, such outcomes are not inevitable if people are aware of and guard against them.

COMPETITION   According to the conflict perspective, prejudice and discrimination arise when two groups find themselves in competition. This competition is often economic, for jobs or land, but it can also be based on noneconomic valued resources, such as access to attractive marriage partners or the right to practice a preferred religion. The more intensely groups compete, the more threatening each group becomes to the other and the more likely negative and hostile views are to emerge. When there are obvious differences between the groups, such as in skin color or religious practices, these differences can become the focus of prejudice. Discriminatory practices may emerge, sanctioned by law or custom, as a way to limit the access of the less powerful group to the scarce resources. Prejudice and discrimination can arise from competitive situations in a number of specific ways (Olzak, 1992).

Sociologist Edna Bonacich (1972) called one type of competitive situation a split labor market. A split labor market is *one in which two groups of workers are willing to do the same work, but for different wages.* In a split labor market, lower-priced laborers have a competitive advantage because employers prefer to hire them. Higher-priced workers find their position threatened by those willing to work more cheaply. In such a situation, the higher-priced workers will be inclined to discriminate against the inexpensive laborers in an effort to exclude them from certain occupations. Bonacich argues that this discrimination is a key factor in much racial, ethnic, and sexual antagonism because the presumed biological differences between the two groups can serve as the focus of discrimination that can be justified on racist grounds. For example, the impact of the split labor market has been documented in Israel where Jews have functioned as the higher-priced laborers who have responded to the lower-priced labor of Arabs by discriminating against them in various occupational sectors (Bernstein, 1996, 1998).

If people believe that members of a particular racial group are lazy or untrustworthy, then this belief is a rationale for excluding that group from jobs that demand hard work and trustworthiness. Likewise, if people believe that women are best suited for clerical and secretarial positions, then this belief can be used to discriminate against women when they try to obtain more lucrative jobs in construction or other professions.

Another type of economic competition is one in which a powerful group exploits a weaker one for its own gain. A clear example would be the relationship between the slaveholder and the slave in which the former gains substantially from the relationship, to the detriment of the latter. Slavery in the United States was clearly a form of economic exploitation supported by racist beliefs about the inferiority of blacks. Many of the poor today suffer a similar kind of exploitation because their work at low-paying and demeaning jobs benefits the more affluent in society (see Chapter 6). A variant of this type of exploitation is internal colonialism, in which *a subordinate group provides cheap labor that benefits the dominant group and is then further exploited by having to purchase expensive goods and services from the dominant group* (Doob, 1999). For example, the poor in the United States not only provide cheap labor but also purchase health care, televisions, food, and other products that provide substantial profit to dominant groups.

SOCIALIZATION AND CONFORMITY   Once patterns of prejudice and discrimination arise, they become incorporated into the values and norms of the group. Prejudice and discrimination toward particular groups then become legitimated, transmitted to new members through the socialization process, and frequently internalized (Blalock, 1982). A study of regional differences in prejudice toward African Americans during the 1960s, for example, found, not surprisingly, that there was greater prejudice in the South, especially within the states of the old Confederacy (Middleton, 1976). It also found, however, that people who lived in the South as children and then moved to other regions were less prejudiced than those who remained in the South. In the same way, people who grew up outside the South and then moved there were more prejudiced than those who remained outside the South. In other words, people tend to conform to the prejudiced beliefs, values, and norms that are considered appropriate in the groups to which they belong.

INSTITUTIONALIZED DISCRIMINATION   Prejudice and discrimination sometimes become incorporated into social policies and practices, which can result in the perpetuation of prejudice and discrimination through institutionalized discrimination or institutionalized racism: *the inequitable treatment of a group resulting from practices or policies that are incorporated into social, political, or economic institutions and that operate independently from the prejudices of individuals.* One form of institutionalized discrimination is the use of physical size requirements as qualifications for certain jobs. Many police departments, for example, set minimum height requirements for police officers. Asian Americans have protested against this requirement because Asians are, on the average, shorter than whites and many therefore cannot qualify for police work. Discrimination in this form may not be direct; people may not be excluded from jobs because of their racial group. Rather, it is the minimum entrance requirements that effectively bar most members of a particular minority group from the jobs while serving as a barrier to only a few people in the dominant group. Through institutionalized discrimination, social inequality can persist long after prejudicial attitudes may have changed. In fact, much of the civil rights effort in the

United States over the past fifty years has concentrated on eliminating this kind of discrimination.

Social Psychological Sources

A number of social psychological factors can play a part in the emergence of prejudice and discrimination. One involves the human tendency to categorize. The physical and social world is sufficiently complex that we need to simplify it by thinking in terms of general categories or by lumping together the elements that have something in common. Categories, however, can become *stereotypes*—rigid and oversimplified images in which each element or person in a category is assumed to possess all the characteristics associated with that category. Because some Jews work in banking, for example, some people might assume that all Jews are proficient in financial matters. Thus, stereotyping can contribute to prejudice and discrimination.

Prejudice and discrimination can arise when people become frustrated by their inability to achieve sought-after goals. Social psychologists have shown that frustration can lead to aggression in both overt and covert forms (Baron & Richardson, 1994; Berkowitz, 1971). Aggression can be expressed by direct physical assaults or through prejudice or discrimination. One form this aggression can take is *scapegoating,* or placing the blame for one's troubles on an individual or group incapable of offering effective resistance. This happened, for example, in the southern United States between 1880 and 1930 when thousands of blacks were lynched by angry mobs of whites, many of whom were unemployed or experiencing other economic problems. People experiencing severe difficulties or frustrations in their own lives sometimes lash out with racial hatred against others because such actions deflect their attention from their own disappointments or failings. Blame for the difficulties is diverted toward the out-group (Olzak, 1992).

The sources of prejudice and discrimination are complex, resulting from the intertwining of numerous sociological and social psychological factors. Most sociological research concludes that social factors such as ethnocentrism, competition, socialization, and institutionalized discrimination play the most important roles in that they set the stage for the operation of social psychological mechanisms. Without this social underpinning, prejudice and discrimination resulting from the social psychological mechanisms alone would likely be sporadic and unorganized. This finding is exemplified in the just-mentioned example of the lynchings of blacks by whites. Research makes clear that the frustration that helped create such horrid aggression was produced in part by the economic competition that existed in some communities in the South between whites and blacks. In locales where there was less such competition, lynchings were substantially less common,

although they did occur (Soule, 1992). Unfortunately, the social sources of prejudice and discrimination are all too often present, and the consequences can be devastating to both society and individuals.

Consequences of Discrimination

Prejudice by itself can be relatively harmless, but it can become destructive when it fuels discrimination. Discrimination marks the spot where the social problems surrounding race and ethnic relations begin. In modern societies, discrimination against minorities has had a detrimental impact, although some groups benefit in the short run. First and most important, discrimination forces some groups into a disadvantageous position in the stratification system and adversely affects their life chances. Chapter 10 shows that discrimination results in higher rates of illness, injury, and death for minorities. This chapter discusses the fact that many minorities in the United States enjoy fewer socioeconomic resources and opportunities than do members of dominant white groups. Because the society's ideology holds out the promise that all can share in the American dream, being deprived of these opportunities can produce simmering resentments that periodically erupt in destructive violence.

A second consequence of discrimination is its effects on people's views of themselves. Those who feel the brunt of discrimination may come to accept the devalued and stigmatized view of themselves that is implied by their being powerless and on the bottom of society. Minority youth, for example, often have more negative self-concepts and a poorer sense of self-worth than do nonminority youth. Such negativity does not always occur, and the negative consequences can be overcome by supportive families, high-quality schools, and a minority culture that insulates people from the negativism implied by low social standing. Yet the research is clear that racism can and does result in lower self-esteem among minorities in some contexts (Martinez & Dukes, 1991; Pallas, Entwisle, Alexander, & Weinstein, 1990). And people with negative views of themselves and their worth may contribute less to society and may exacerbate existing social problems through criminal behavior, long-term poverty, domestic violence, child neglect, and the like.

A third consequence of discrimination is that it creates tense, hostile, and sometimes violent encounters between dominant and minority group members, thus destroying trust, communication, and cooperation. In settings such as school or the workplace where members of different groups interact, discrimination makes it difficult for people to work together (Wilson, 1999). For example, racial clashes have at times plagued the U.S. military, and these conflicts make it more difficult to develop a cohesive, coordinated, and effective military organization. Other Worlds, Other Ways: Britain, Germany, Yugoslavia explores the all too common hostility and violence at many points around the globe and suggests some of the social conditions that produce it.

A final consequence of discrimination is that it can undermine social and political values and institutions. Because the United States professes to value equality and human dignity, the violation of these values because of racism and discrimination can generate cynicism regarding U.S. political and economic institutions. It can also threaten the legitimacy of those institutions if people see them merely as tools to benefit those fortunate enough to have acquired some power in society. From the functionalist perspective, such undermining may represent the most serious of trends to combat—when people begin to lose faith in the system's core values and foundation, that system's survival may be in jeopardy.

Patterns of Intergroup Relations

You should be able to describe the patterns of intergroup relations that emerge between dominant and minority groups and the minority reactions to such domination as well as discuss the possibilities for cooperation in a multiracial or multiethnic society.

When different racial and ethnic groups live together in one society, racial and ethnic differences are sometimes ignored and play no part in how people relate to one another. In many situations, however, prejudice and discrimination produce some specific patterns of intergroup relations based on dominance and subordination. The sociologists George Simpson and J. Milton Yinger (1985) have identified six distinct relationships, each founded in the subordination of one group by another.

Forms of Domination

At one extreme, a dominant group might engage in genocide, or *the attempt to exterminate an entire minority group*. Genocide is, unfortunately, all too common in history. The Nazis attempted to exterminate the Jews and other groups during World War II, and the Serbs in the former Yugoslavia in the early 1990s were accused of the wholesale slaughter of Muslims in an attempt at "ethnic cleansing." The policies and practices of the European immigrants to the New World during and

This photo depicts the experiences of Jews in Poland who were held in concentration camps by Germans during World War II. Their treatment is grim testimony to the tragic consequences that can result from ethnic differences and hatreds.

Other Worlds, Other Ways

BRITAIN, GERMANY, YUGOSLAVIA: THE SOCIAL AND ECONOMIC SOURCES OF RACIAL HATRED AND CONFLICT

In too many places around the globe, we can see the social sources of prejudice and discrimination producing intense racial hatred and conflict. The details change, in terms of the racial or ethnic identity of the antagonists and the epithets hurled, but the underlying conditions that produce them are distressingly similar and familiar.

In London in 1993, for example, an avowed racist from a neo-Nazi political party was elected to Parliament on a platform calling for deportation of all nonwhites from Britain (Stevenson, 1993). His supporters at a victory rally chanted "We hate Pakis" and "There ain't no black in the Union Jack." In this case, the hatred was directed against immigrants from former British colonies of Pakistan, India, and some islands in the Caribbean. Racially motivated attacks on Asians and blacks by whites were on the increase in Britain in the late 1980s and 1990s. Often, they consisted of a small group of attackers descending on one individual, but there were also extensive street brawls. Large groups of minority youth have attacked the police, whom the youth often view as highly racist themselves rather than as the defenders of minorities. Mobs of neo-Nazi skinheads have rampaged through minority neighborhoods breaking shop windows, stealing from stores, and menacing local residents. In some cases, the police do little to stop them. Fueling this hostility are high levels of unemployment in Britain—the neo-Nazi elected to Parliament was himself unemployed.

In recent years, Germany has also experienced one of the largest waves of racial violence since World War II (Levin & McDevitt, 1993). Neo-Nazi and skinhead youth have openly attacked Vietnamese, Mozambicans, and Turks on the street, in one case killing an African by pushing him off a train. They have firebombed homes, hotels, and apartment buildings where immigrant foreigners live. In some cases, these attacks have involved mobs of hundreds of youths in terrifying descents on relatively helpless immigrants and their families. In Germany, as in Britain, the violence is attributed to a relatively small number of neo-Nazis and racist skinheads, but public opinion polls point to substantial support for the attitudes these youth espouse, especially for "racial purity" in Germany and the removal of foreign workers.

In Germany, these episodes have been influenced by the end of the Cold War, the collapse of the Soviet Union, and the resulting reunification of Germany. Germany has had to absorb the devastated economy of the former East Germany. This problem has meant dealing with highly inefficient factories, undertrained workers, and environmental disasters. The result for Germany has been soaring unemployment and growing expenditures for social services such as welfare and health care. Germany also faces a shortage of housing and fairly deplorable living conditions for some of its citizens. Apparently, neo-Nazi activism is proving to be a persuasive and attractive force as a source of authority for young Germans attempting to navigate the largely uncharted waters of their new post–Cold War world. The irony in this situation is that immigrant workers—the source of the young Germans' fury—may play a big role in repairing the German economy because they provide a source of cheap labor to rebuild competitive industries and attract investment. In addition, Germany is an aging society with a fairly low birthrate and may not be able to supply an adequate labor force from indigenous sources. Nonetheless, the immigrants offer a ready scapegoat for the anger of the youth.

The collapse of the Soviet Union also unleashed intense ethnic and religious hostilities in the former Yugoslavia (Kressel, 1996; Neier, 1998). Centuries-old hostilities among Orthodox Christian Serbs, Roman Catholic Croats, and Muslims have led to a horrific struggle in which each group has tried to grab a piece of territory for itself. This intense and protracted war has produced tens of thousands of deaths, concentration camps where inmates were starved and brutalized, rapes of thousands of women and girls, and masses of refugees without homes. Most recently in the Kosovo region of Yugoslavia, thousands of Albanian Kosovars were killed and hundreds of thousands driven into exile by the Serbs (Mertus, 1999). The authoritarian rule of communism was able to stifle these hostilities in Yugoslavia for many decades, although it obviously did not eliminate them. Once the central government was weakened and the struggle for the control of postcommunist Yugoslavia began, these ethnic and religious connections became the organizational focus for those who wished to gain power. Some groups attempted to organize a multiethnic, multireligious Yugoslavia that would accept and tolerate differences, but they have been overwhelmed by more powerful forces seeking "ethnically cleansed" territories for their people.

These and other examples of racial and ethnic conflict around the world point to the role of social forces in bringing them about or in making them much more extensive than they might otherwise be. Ethnocentrism by itself can produce some mix of racism and xenophobia. That is certainly true in the former Yugoslavia, where ethnic and religious traditions go back hundreds of years and are an important source of identity and community authority. Likewise, whites in Germany and Britain trace their ancestry to what they understand as white forefathers, and some find the imposition of foreign ways on their heritage to be offensive. Beyond ethnocentrism, competition has also been an important fuel to these hatreds. In Germany and Britain, for example, people are clearly responding to economic difficulties and unemployment by trying to drive out those they feel are unfairly competing for what they see as rightfully their jobs. To this extent, they are part of the capitalist world system described in Chapter 6. The movement of immigrants from one part of the globe to another makes available a supply of cheap labor that can be used by capitalists to develop new markets and industries. Such movement is not a new phenomenon—the transportation of slaves from Africa to the Western Hemisphere in the 1600s was part of the global movement of labor fueled by the needs of capitalism. The immigrants in Germany and Britain are an extension of that same process. The global fluidity of labor helps to keep costs down and profits up, but it also produces conflict and hatred when those immigrants are perceived to threaten the opportunities of indigenous labor. ■

---

after the 1500s came very close to genocide of the native peoples. For instance, the Portuguese decimated the Brazilian Indians discussed in the beginning of this chapter. The Natchez people discussed in the beginning of Chapter 6 were almost completely wiped out by the French after the Natchez, upset with French encroachment on their territory, attacked a trading post. The few Natchez remaining after the brutal massacre were sold into slavery in the West Indies (Farb, 1978). Estimates are that at least two-thirds of the Indian population in the United States was annihilated by the direct and indirect actions of the white Europeans.

A more common relationship between dominant and minority groups is segregation, *an arrangement in which the social lives of the two groups are kept separate.* In many nations, members of dominant and minority groups go to different schools and churches and live in different neighborhoods. South Africa's apartheid was a very rigid form of segregation, and the separation of African Americans and whites in the United States was almost as rigid until a few decades ago. Even today, continuing discrimination, along with social norms and informal pressures, have produced a high level of residential segregation and a minimal level of social contact between blacks and whites in the United States (Massey, 2001; Massey & Denton, 1992; Sigelman, Bledsoe, Welch, & Combs, 1996). In Chicago, for example, 71 percent of African Americans live on a block where 90 percent of the residents are also African American. Among Asian Americans, Vietnamese are the most highly segregated group, and Asian Americans as a whole live in communities that are highly segregated from African Americans. All this segregation persists despite the fact that the Civil Rights Act of 1964 outlawed racial discrimination in housing.

Most minorities experience some degree of continued subjugation, in which *the dominant group uses a variety of practices to maintain subordination and exploitation.* Subjugation can be achieved through laws that prohibit minorities from holding certain occupations or going to certain schools. These practices of subjugation are designed to protect the position of the dominant group from any possible inroads by the minority. In most cases where racial or ethnic identity is relevant to intergroup relations, continued subjugation is pervasive.

In some situations, dominant groups control minorities through population transfer, *the voluntary or involuntary movement of minorities to particular geographic areas.* South Africa forcibly moved many black South Africans to new residential communities. White European settlers in the United States used the strategy to gain control of native lands: They relocated Indians to reservations. In such population transfers, the dominant group usually reserves the most desirable, productive, and profitable lands for itself while relegating the minority to lands that are limited or marginal. Population transfer also occurred recently in the former Yugoslavia as Serbs forced Muslims out of Serb-dominated communities.

Assimilation is *the process by which a racial or ethnic minority loses its distinctive identity and way of life and becomes absorbed into the dominant group* (Alba, 1995). In some situations, especially when a minority group is small and powerless, assimilation occurs with few changes in the lifestyle of the dominant group. The Inuit in Alaska, for example, have had little impact on the dominant society of white European immigrants to the United States. The Inuit, however, have had to adapt by forgoing their traditional subsistence activities of fishing and hunting and by taking jobs in the cash economy that the Europeans brought to the Western Hemisphere. By contrast, when minorities are large or cohesive, or have some power, their members may change the dominant culture in the process of assimilating. Italian Americans, for instance, have become largely assimilated yet have left their distinctive mark on U.S. culture in the form of such foods as pizza and spaghetti.

Assimilation is neither a rapid nor a simple process, and people can assimilate in some realms and not others. People are reluctant to change deeply held values or practices, but they will more readily change things they see as less important or more practical. In addition, dominant groups may permit particular racial or ethnic groups to assimilate in some realms but discourage it in others. As a consequence, sociologists identify a number of different ways in which people can assimilate (M. M. Gordon, 1978). *Cultural assimilation* refers to adopting the cultural patterns of dominant groups, such as their religious beliefs or their social values. It is often the first, and sometimes the only, type of assimilation to occur. *Structural assimilation* refers to joining the important social groups and organizations of the dominant group, such as their schools, churches, or clubs. Jewish Americans, for example, have achieved cultural assimilation along with some structural assimilation, but they are still excluded from some groups and organizations of non-Jewish Anglos.

Pluralism, the sixth pattern of intergroup relations, is one in which *a number of racial and ethnic groups live side by side, each retaining a distinct identity and lifestyle while also sharing in some aspects of the larger culture* (Simpson, 1995). In other words, to use a term introduced in Chapter 2, pluralism involves the persistence of a variety of subcultures. One type of pluralism is *cultural pluralism*, in which a group retains values, norms, beliefs, and maybe a language that is somewhat distinct from that of the dominant culture. In both Canada and the United States, for example, many Indian and Inuit peoples retain their traditional language and religious beliefs and values in a society whose dominant group speaks English and practices either Protestantism or Roman Catholicism. *Structural pluralism* exists when minorities maintain groups, organizations, and institutions separate from those of the dominant culture. African Americans, for example, have created their own churches largely because they were not welcome in the churches of the dominant group.

Minority Reaction to Domination

How minority groups respond to domination depends on their numbers and on the power and other resources they have available. Groups without much power may have little choice but *submission*, where they accept their subordinate status, even if grudgingly, and cooperate or at least acquiesce to the demands placed on them. Slaves in ancient Rome and nineteenth-century Brazil and the United States had little choice but to go along and appear reasonably accepting of their place. To do anything else could have been dangerous because of the enormous disparity in power between slave and slaveowner.

When minorities have more resources, and especially when they have some support and sympathy among significant factions of the dominant group, *social protest* becomes feasible: actions that express disapproval of and attempt to change conventional patterns of dominance and subordination. Such protest could take the form of marches, demonstrations, or civil disobedience that attempts to force authorities to change some policy or practice. The civil rights movement of the 1960s was such a social protest movement in which African Americans and many Anglo supporters attacked entrenched forms of discrimination in the United States.

Separatism is like segregation but with the minority group taking the initiative for creating a separation of dominant and minority groups. It is a common reaction among minorities who have some resources but little support in the dominant group. The nation of Pakistan was created in 1947 by a separatist movement of Muslims who were a small minority in India, which was dominated by a Hindu majority. The Muslim minority had the numbers and the political and military resources to fight successfully for a separate political existence.

Infrequently, a minority will go to the point of *rebellion*, attempting to overthrow the political authority of the dominant group. During the 1970s and 1980s, the Irish Republican Army attempted to reunite Northern Ireland, which was under British control, with the rest of Ireland (Rose, 1990). Irish Catholics were in the minority in Northern Ireland and felt oppressed by the Protestant majority. The Irish Catholics believed that British control of Northern Ireland was a colonial relic that prevented the achievement of the Irish destiny of complete control of the island of Ireland. Bombings and deaths in this long-lasting rebellion continued into the 1990s.

Switzerland: Cooperation in a Multiethnic Society

Switzerland is often pointed to as a model of effective pluralism because it is made up of three distinct ethnic groups—German, French, and Italian—that work together peacefully and cooperatively. Prior to the nineteenth century, ethnic conflict in Switzerland was constant and often violent (Schmid, 1981; Steiner, 1990). Then, interethnic relations, dominated by German-speaking Swiss, at times verged on civil war. Religious conflict between Catholics and Protestants, often intense and bitter, also contributed to the strife. Ethnic and linguistic equality was imposed on Switzerland by the French, who conquered the country in 1798. Finally, a brief civil war in the 1840s ended with the adoption of a constitution in 1848, which continued the protection of linguistic minorities and created a system of power sharing among ethnic groups that has enabled the Swiss to live in harmony for the last 150 years.

The basic assumption of this power-sharing system is that all three language groups are assured of representation in the government. The Swiss Federal Council, the executive body, includes members from all three ethnic groups, in rough proportions to their numbers in the population. The chairmanship of the council (equivalent to the U.S. presidency) is rotated to a different ethnic group each year, assuring each group a turn. The parliament is elected by proportional representation, with each ethnic group being represented in approximate proportions to its size in the population. Civil service positions and military appointments are also made on the basis of proportional representation. All three languages are considered the national languages of Switzerland. The political system is one of decentralized federalism, with the governments of each canton, or district, having autonomy in the conduct of many of its affairs. Thus, each canton, dominated by a particular ethnic group, controls its own schools and police.

The pluralist Swiss system amounts to what would be called a quota system in the United States. In contrast to Swiss power sharing, the United States and many other nations tend more toward power competition, a system in which each group strives to concentrate as much power in its own hands as it can. Such competition can lead to instability and chaos and often leaves minorities largely disenfranchised and dissatisfied.

Swiss pluralism works for a number of reasons. First, since the three ethnic groups are of European heritage, they share a lot of history and culture in common, despite their differences. Second, the three groups have been settled in the region for centuries, and compromises and accommodations have been worked out over the years. Third, the Swiss state has been stable for a number of years, without the political instability that can serve as fertile ground for ethnic conflict. Finally, the Swiss ethnic minorities did not have to go through a protracted or bitter struggle for their rights that could have left simmering antagonisms. In the light of these reasons, some observers have argued that the Swiss are an exception: The Swiss experience is unique and cannot serve as a model for other societies where conditions make solutions to racial and ethnic conflicts much more difficult. Nevertheless, Jurg Steiner (1990), who has studied the Swiss, says they are not a different or "naturally peaceful" people. Rather, from experience over a long period of time, they have created a system that reduces conflict between groups and produces greater cooperation, stability, and prosperity. As another expert put it, the lesson to learn from Switzerland is that "successful democratic pluralism depends on minorities' being continually accommodated within the political system" (Schmid, 1981, p. 155).

Racial and Ethnic Minorities in the United States

> You should be able to describe the major racial and ethnic minorities in the United States, discuss their current circumstances and opportunities, explain the variation in achievement found among them, and show how the mass media influence the position of minorities in society.

The picture of prejudice, discrimination, and intergroup relations in the United States is not always a pretty one or one to be proud of. There is not space to focus on all racial and ethnic minorities in the country, so this section will discuss only those that are the largest numerically or that more effectively illustrate sociological approaches to intergroup relations.

The United States is, of course, a land of immigrants. The only difference between groups in this regard is the time of their arrival. Even the group with the deepest roots in American soil, who have called themselves Native Americans or American Indians, are descendants of immigrants who traversed the Bering Straits land bridge from Asia to the Americas tens of thousands of years ago. Beyond immigrant status, however, there is considerable variation in the positions of racial and ethnic groups in the United States, and we need to keep in mind that people may belong to more than one of these groups. The treatment of these groups today and in the past illustrates how prejudice and discrimination have functioned in U.S. history and illuminates some of the consequences of social stratification discussed in Chapter 6.

African Americans

African Americans comprise the largest nonwhite minority group in the United States, numbering approximately 38 million, or about 12.8 percent of the total population (U.S. Bureau of the Census, 2007, p. 11). In addition, they are one of the oldest minority groups, with the first Africans arriving in 1619, not long after the first permanent European settlers in the New World. They are also the only minority group in the United States that was held as slaves. When the British colonized the New World, they followed the practices of the Spanish and Portuguese in bringing black African slaves to work the land (Phillips, 1963; Westermann, 1955). Black Africans were particularly vulnerable to slavery because many of them lived in small, isolated tribes and were unable to protect themselves against more formidable foes. In fact, some of the larger African tribes, such as the Ashanti, actually sold other Africans into slavery (Sowell, 1981).

Technically, all slaves in the United States gained their freedom with the end of the Civil War. However, after a short period during which African Americans exercised a degree of freedom and political control, white Southerners began to reassert their dominance when federal troops left the South in 1877. In 1896 the Supreme Court ruled in *Plessy v. Fergusson* that it was constitutional to provide "separate but equal" public facilities for members of different races, and the era of widespread legal segregation began. For six decades, the *Plessy* case served as the foundation for discrimination against African Americans in schools, housing, and other areas. During this period, a split labor market in black–white relations prevailed (Marks, 1981). Because of deteriorating race relations after the *Plessy* decision and economic distress in the South, a massive migration of young southern blacks to eastern and midwestern cities began. That was the beginning of large black ghettos in cities such as New York, Detroit, Boston, and Chicago. These concentrations of blacks in cities would later serve as an important mobilizing element in the efforts of African Americans to gain equality.

The 1950s and 1960s were a period of considerable change in the lives of African Americans (J. Bloom, 1987). In the *Brown v. The Board of Education* decision of 1954, the U.S. Supreme Court ruled that the separate-but-equal doctrine was unconstitutional. The southern states were ordered to integrate their schools "with all deliberate speed," but this process turned out to be rather slow. The civil rights movement emerged, however, and, along with more militant black groups, initiated a drive for more economic and social opportunities for African Americans. Out of the demonstrations, protests, and rioting came the Civil Rights Act of 1964 and the Voting Rights Act of 1965. Later, affirmative-action programs and school busing would be used to provide greater opportunities for blacks in the United States.

The position of African Americans has improved substantially since the 1960s. For example, the number of blacks enrolled in college has increased fourteen times since 1960, whereas enrollment of whites has increased only by a factor of five; African Americans now constitute 13 percent of all college students, compared to 6 percent in 1960 (U.S. Bureau of the Census, 2007, p. 177). The number of blacks in professional occupations has also increased at a much faster rate than among whites. The percentage of blacks registered to vote has doubled, and the number of blacks holding elected political office has increased by five times.

The current picture, however, is by no means one of unblemished progress, because African Americans still lag behind many other groups by some measures of socioeconomic status (Table 7.1 and Figure 7.1). For example, although the average income of African Americans has climbed in the past forty years, so has the income of whites, and their relative positions have changed only a little. The ratio of black income to white income has increased only modestly in the past forty years. Although channels of mobility are open to some African Americans, other blacks are trapped in poverty or in occupations that offer little prestige or hope for advancement. At the beginning of the twenty-first century, for example, the number of

Table 7.1

INCOME OF WHITE, BLACK, HISPANIC, AND ASIAN/PACIFIC ISLANDER FAMILIES, 1960–2005

Year	Median Income				Ratio of Black to White Income	Ration of Hispanic to White Income
	White	Black	Hispanic	Asian/Pacific Islander		
1960	$5,835	$3,230	NA*	NA*	.55	
1965	7,251	3,993	NA*	NA*	.55	
1970	10,236	6,279	NA*	NA*	.61	
1975	14,268	8,779	$9,551	NA*	.61	.67
1980	21,904	12,674	14,716	NA*	.58	.67
1985	29,152	16,786	19,027	NA*	.58	.65
1990	36,915	21,423	23,431	$42,246	.58	.63
1995	42,646	25,970	24,570	46,356	.61	.58
2000	53,029	33,676	34,442	62,617	.64	.65
2005	59,317	35,464	37,867	68,957	.60	.64

* Data not available

Source: U.S. Bureau of the Census, *Statistical Abstract of the United States*, 1985 (Washington, DC: U.S. Government Printing Office, 1984), p. 446; U.S. Bureau of the Census, *Statistical Abstract of the United States*, 2008 (Washington, DC: U.S. Government Printing Office, 2005), p. 449.

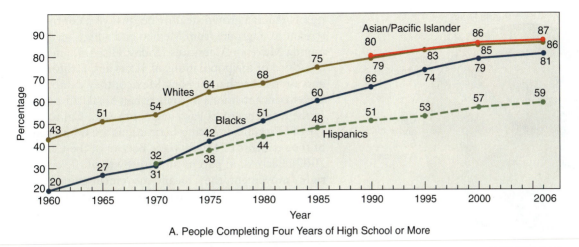

A. People Completing Four Years of High School or More

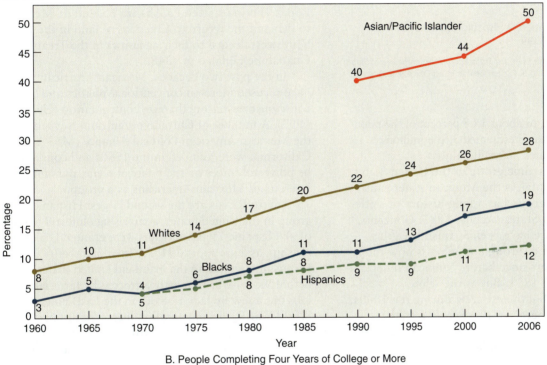

B. People Completing Four Years of College or More

Figure 7.1

Educational Attainment, by Race or Ethnicity, Among People Twenty-Five Years Old and Older, 1960–2006

Sources: U.S. Bureau of the Census, *Statistical Abstract of the United States,* 2008 (Washington, DC: U.S. Government Printing Office, 2007), p.145.

blacks in poverty was actually higher than it had been in 1970, with the poverty rate being three times higher among blacks than among nonhispanic whites (see Chapter 6). This lagging achievement is not due to a lack of aspirations, however, since research shows that African American youth actually have higher educational and occupational aspirations than do white youth (Solorzano, 1991). Somewhere along the way, those high aspirations get sidetracked before becoming reality. The end of this section will explore some reasons for the variations in achievement among racial and ethnic minorities in the United States.

Hispanic Americans

Hispanic Americans, or Latinos, are Americans whose ancestral home is Mexico, Central America, South America, or the Caribbean. They include Mexican Americans (Chicanos), Cubans, and Puerto Ricans. (Some members of this group prefer to be called Hispanic and others Latino; there is no consensus about a proper designation. This text uses Hispanic as the primary designation because it is the term used by the Census Bureau from which much of the data in this chapter was obtained.) There are 44 million Hispanic Americans

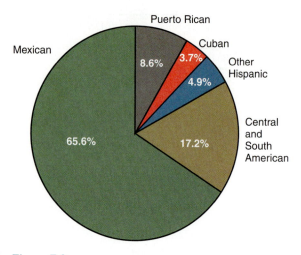

Figure 7.2

Percentage Distribution of Hispanic Americans by Type of Spanish Origin, 2006

Source: U.S. Bureau of the Census, *Statistical Abstract of the United States: 2008* (Washington, DC: U.S. Government Printing Office, 2007), p. 41.

in the United States, or about 14.8 percent of the population. There are also an estimated 3 to 6 million Hispanics in the United States illegally.

The largest Hispanic group in the United States, two-thirds of the total, is the Mexican Americans (Figure 7.2). This group has a long history of settlement in the United States (Acuna, 1987; Gonzalez, 2000). In fact, there have been Spanish-speaking communities located throughout what is now the American Southwest since before Mexican independence from Spain in 1821. But as the white population in the Southwest grew during the 1800s, the economic prospects for these early settlers declined. Light-skinned, pure Spanish settlers who had adopted the white lifestyle were accepted into the white world, but the darker-skinned settlers who maintained their heritage, especially those with some Indian heritage, were viewed as inferiors and bore the brunt of prejudice and discrimination. Following the Mexican Revolution in 1909, hundreds of thousands of Mexican peasants migrated to the Southwest, where there was much demand for inexpensive labor because of expanding agriculture and railroads. The status of these more recent migrants to the United States, however, was low, although perhaps slightly higher than it had been in Mexico. The Depression of the 1930s resulted in a decline in farmwork, driving many Mexican Americans into the cities to seek employment or public relief. The first urban barrios, or Spanish-speaking neighborhoods, began to spring up in such cities as Denver, Phoenix, and Los Angeles.

Since World War II, the position of Mexican Americans has changed substantially. First, their

numbers have grown steadily because of a continuing stream of migrants from Mexico and a high birthrate among Mexican Americans. Today, Hispanics make up one-third of the populations of Texas and California and almost one-half of New Mexico; they exhibit even larger concentrations in some urban areas: 75 percent of the residents of El Paso and Santa Ana, California, are of Hispanic or Latino heritage, as are 65 percent of the residents of Miami (U.S. Bureau of the Census, 2007). Second, in part as an outgrowth of the civil rights movement, the Chicano movement gained support in the 1960s in championing the rights of all Hispanics. Cesar Chavez organized the United Farm Workers to fight for better pay and working conditions for Chicano farmworkers, and Reyes Lopez Tijerina started La Alianza Federal de Mercedes to demand the return to Chicanos of land in the Southwest deeded to their ancestors in the Treaty of Guadalupe Hidalgo in 1848.

In the past two decades, Mexican American efforts have focused more on conventional politics and consciousness-raising than on confrontation (Hero, 1992). A number of Chicano organizations, such as the Mexican American Political Alliance (MAPA) in California, were founded in the 1960s and continue to be powerful forces on the political scene, pursuing the interests of Mexican Americans as a group.

Puerto Ricans are the second largest Hispanic group in the United States, comprising almost 9 percent of all Hispanics. Puerto Ricans were granted U.S. citizenship, as a group, in 1917. A small number of Puerto Ricans immigrated to the mainland United States before World War II, mostly attracted by farm-labor jobs but a few by factory work in the East. Following World War II, this immigration increased dramatically, in large part because of the chronically depressed economy of Puerto Rico. Puerto Ricans have tended to settle in New York City and Chicago (Fitzpatrick, 1987).

Mexican Americans and Puerto Rican Americans today face much the same problems as African Americans: poverty, low educational levels, and poor health in comparison to Anglos (see Table 7.1 and Figures 7.1 and 7.3). For example, two out of five Puerto Rican families in the United States live in poverty, and just 59 percent of Hispanic Americans have completed four years of high school or more, whereas 86 percent of whites have done so. As with African Americans, the incomes of Hispanic families have persistently lagged behind those of white families, remaining at 64 percent of white incomes today.

Hispanics in the United States today are a diverse group (Gonzalez, 2000; Suro, 1998). In addition to the variation among Hispanic groups already mentioned, for example, Cuban Americans have generally been different from other Hispanics in that they come from more middle-class and affluent origins. Despite their

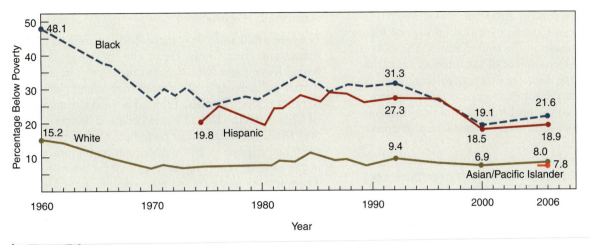

Figure 7.3

Percentage of Families in the United States with Incomes Below the Poverty Level by Race, 1960–2006

Sources: U. S. Bureau of the Census, *Current Population Reports, Series P-60*, "Poverty in United States." (Washington, DC: U.S. Government Printing Office), various years; U. S. Bureau of the Census, *Current Population Survey*, "2006 Poverty Table of Contents," Annual Social and Economic Supplement, www.census.gov/hhes/www/poverty/poverty.html.

diversity, some Hispanic groups may be moving toward a more common ethnic identity and consciousness (Totti, 1987). Being of a different color, having a common origin in the "south," speaking related languages, many sharing the experience of discrimination and outsider status—all these characteristics may be forging an ethnic awareness that spans the diversity found in such groups as Mexican Americans and Puerto Ricans. In fact, the term *Latinismo* has been coined to describe a sentimental and ideological identification and loyalty that transcend individual Latino ethnic groups in the United States (Padilla, 1985). This emerging Latino consciousness may be in part political, that is, a realization that advantage can be gained in the struggle for equality and fair treatment by combining forces behind a common symbol. However, Latinismo also represents an identification with and devotion to the collective concerns of peoples in the United States speaking related languages. Groups such as the League of United Latin American Citizens and the National Council of La Raza have emerged to represent all Latin ethnic groups, whereas groups such as MAPA and the Puerto Rican Organization for Political Action devote some attention to the concerns of particular nationalities. All these groups recognize that Hispanics—who, by the time this book is published, will be the largest ethnic minority in the United States—can become an effective force for political and social change if they can get beyond their differences and combine their forces.

American Indians

During the fifteenth and sixteenth centuries, there were probably between one million and ten million people living on tribal lands in North America (Snipp, 1989). By the late 1800s, there were only about 250,000. After the founding of the United States, the U.S. Constitution required the federal government to negotiate treaties with these American Indians, but treaties did not prevent whites from robbing Indians of their lands. (Again, there is disagreement about what to call this group. Some members prefer *Native American* to *American Indian*; others insist that only tribal names, such as Comanche, Cree, and Apache, be used because there was much diversity among the native peoples. This text will use American Indian because it is the term used by the Census Bureau from which much of the data in this chapter was obtained.)

In 1824, Congress created the Bureau of Indian Affairs (BIA) as a division of the War Department to seek a military solution to what many in Congress referred to as the "Indian problem." By 1830, Congress succumbed to pressures for opening up more Indian lands to white settlement and ordered the BIA to relocate all American Indians west of the Mississippi River. It was not until 1924 that Congress passed the Indian Citizenship Act, granting U.S. citizenship to all American Indians. In 1968, Congress enacted the Indian Civil Rights Act, which extended the basic human rights guaranteed by the Bill of Rights to people living on tribal lands. Although this act undoubtedly had many positive benefits, it may have had the negative effect of undermining tribal control and unity among groups that possessed their own judicial systems based on tribal customs (Schaefer, 2008).

There are 3 million American Indians in the United States (U.S. Bureau of the Census, 2007, p. 12, 40; U.S. Bureau of Indian Affairs, 2008). Two percent of U.S. land (56 million acres) is still managed by the BIA "on behalf of" the Indians. In 2000, there were about 500,000 American Indians, Inuit (Eskimos), and Aleuts living on reservations in the United States. The BIA, now part of the Department of the Interior, has conservation as its prime directive rather than economic development. This deemphasis on economic matters has contributed to the problems of American Indians by making it more difficult for them to improve their economic position.

American Indians suffer significant social, economic, and health disadvantages in comparison to other ethnic and racial groups (Snipp, 1989; U.S. Bureau of the Census, 2007; Young, 1994). Nonreservation Indians are somewhat better off than their reservation counterparts, but half of all American Indians live on reservations that are in rural areas. They suffer high levels of unemployment, low levels of income, and poverty rates disproportionate to their numbers in the population. They are also less likely to graduate from high school than people in most other groups.

The 1960s were years when many minority groups began to resist oppression, and American Indians were among them. In 1969 a group of Indians seized Alcatraz Island to call attention to their exploitation. In 1973 members of the American Indian Movement (AIM) staged an armed takeover of Wounded Knee, South Dakota, where whites had killed hundreds of American Indians in the late nineteenth century. These protests may be in part responsible for some recent court decisions ruling that Indian tribes should receive payment for land taken from their ancestors during the nineteenth century. Still, there is a lingering feeling among many American Indians that exploitation continues, albeit in more subtle ways than before (Prucha, 1985).

Today, the American Indian community in the United States is growing in number and showing renewed pride in its history and culture. Although many serious problems persist, a college-educated middle class of American Indians has emerged, and the number of businesses owned by Indians is increasing significantly. Tribes on reservations have been able to exploit gambling and tourism to create jobs, and some have built successful manufacturing businesses. With the economic resources made available by these endeavors, American Indians have hired lawyers and lobbyists who go to state capitals and Washington, DC, to fight for their interests. Some tribes are even struggling to establish tribal sovereignty, which in their view would make tribal lands the equivalent of independent nations. All these developments together suggest that a cohesive and powerful American Indian community is emerging in the United States that will improve the circumstances of American Indians both on and off tribal lands.

Asian Americans

Between 1820 and 1969, more than one million legal immigrants from China, Japan, the Philippines, Hong Kong, Korea, and India came to the United States—a mere 3.7 percent of all immigration taking place during that period (Daniels, 1988). The heaviest migration of Chinese to the United States occurred between 1849 and 1882. Although racial prejudices existed toward the Chinese prior to 1849, once their immigration began in large numbers, these sentiments intensified. There was a feeling among many people in the United States that the Chinese would deprive whites of jobs in mining and railroading, another illustration of the split labor market discussed earlier. These feelings culminated in the Chinese Exclusion Act of 1882, which prohibited the entrance of Chinese laborers into the United States for ten years.

Between 1882 and World War II, racist attitudes in the United States characterized the Chinese as a "yellow peril." Many Chinese returned to their own country because of this hostility. Those who remained were forced to move to ghettos called *Chinatowns*. Chinese people were often referred to by the pejorative term *coolies*, and the racism toward Chinese often implied biological differences between Chinese and Anglos. An anthropological study in 1877, for example, concluded, "It is true that ethnologists declare that a brain capacity of less than 85 cubic inches is unfit for free government, which is considerably above that of the coolie as it is below that of the Caucasian" (quoted in Miller, 1969, p. 145).

These anti-Chinese attitudes persisted in the United States until the 1940s. Following Japan's attack on Pearl Harbor, hostilities shifted toward the Japanese, and the Chinese came to be regarded in a more positive way. In 1943, the Chinese remaining in the United States were granted citizenship. Between 1950 and 1970, Chinese Americans became upwardly mobile, with children of the original immigrants attending colleges and universities and moving into professional and technical positions. Today, the socioeconomic status of Chinese Americans, especially those who have been in the United States for some years, is considerably above the average for Americans as a whole (Barringer, Takeuchi, & Xenos, 1990; Hirschman & Wong, 1986).

The peak period of Japanese immigration to the United States began after the Chinese Exclusion Act, between 1880 and 1924. Unlike the Chinese, Japanese immigrants were permitted to bring their wives with them, which aided in the formation of stable Japanese families, and early relations between white Americans and the Japanese were positive. After Pearl Harbor, Japanese Americans were the object of considerable discrimination, being forced to sell their property and being interned in concentration camps (Kitano, 1976; O'Brien & Fugita, 1991). Along with the enslavement of African Americans and the genocidal attacks on American Indians, the imprisonment of Japanese Americans—none of whom had been proven disloyal to the United States—stands as one of the darkest examples of racism in U.S. history.

After their release from the concentration camps after the war, Japanese Americans led successful lives, exceeding many whites in occupational achievements, and most Americans appear to have a high regard for Japanese Americans today (Barringer, Takeuchi, & Xenos, 1990; Ima, 1982). Still, there are occasional flare-ups of the racism that was so prevalent during World War II.

Significant immigration from Asia to the United States has continued in recent decades (Min, 1994). For example, in the 1970s and 1980s, tens of thousands of refugees entered the United States from Vietnam, Laos, and Cambodia as well as from other parts of Asia. These recent immigrants have mostly followed the route of their predecessors as far as integrating themselves into the United States, taking undesirable jobs that most workers tend to reject, or opening small businesses to make a living. Although there is little widespread discrimination against Asian immigrants, violence does occur. In the 1992 riot in south central Los Angeles, for example, Korean American businesses were apparently targeted for looting and burning by African American and Hispanic American rioters who were angry over what they perceived as mistreatment of blacks and Hispanics by Korean store owners (Lee, 2002). This riot reflects the economic sources of racial discrimination and conflict discussed earlier. African Americans and Hispanic Americans find themselves in a position of economic subordination to Korean store owners. This subordination has led to stereotyping on both sides, with Koreans accusing blacks and Hispanics of stealing and blacks and Hispanics accusing Koreans of selling poor products at high prices and refusing to hire black or Hispanic employees. Exacerbating this situation is the fact that Koreans have little contact with African Americans and Hispanics outside of this economic (merchant–customer) context.

Arab Americans

People are classified as Arab Americans by the U.S. Bureau of the Census if they claim an ancestry from one of the predominantly Arab-speaking countries

These American children of Indian heritage celebrate their heritage with a parade in New York. They symbolize the extent to which immigration to the United States has changed in the past 150 years. Today, immigrants are largely from Asia and Central and South America rather than from Europe.

(such as Lebanon or Iraq) or regions of the world (such as the Middle East) or if they make a general ancestry claim of Arabic. Using this definition, about one-half of 1 percent of the U.S. population would be considered at least part Arabic (U.S. Bureau of the Census, 2005). Although a relatively small ethnic group, Arab Americans give us some additional perspectives on race and ethnic relations in the United States. One wave of Arab immigration to the United States occurred between 1870 and World War I and involved mostly people seeking better economic opportunities for their families (Read, 2004). This group was predominantly Christian and tended to assimilate into the mainstream after arrival. The second wave of Arab immigration began after World War II and continues today. For this group, immigration has been motivated more by an effort to escape the political turmoil in their native land. This group is predominantly Muslim, better educated, and retains a stronger attachment to their native culture. Despite the diversity in religion and national background of the Arab immigrants, they mostly share a common language and set of cultural values.

Arab Americans as a group are well integrated into life in the United States and have done quite well for themselves (U.S. Bureau of the Census, 2005). As a group, they are considerably better educated than other Americans, have higher incomes, are more likely to be working in management jobs rather than service or blue-collar jobs, and over half of them are Christians. They are a group of ethnic immigrants who have mostly succeeded in the United States.

However, the Arab American experience has not been all positive. For one thing, they have higher rates of poverty than other Americans, probably reflecting the fact that some in this group are recent immigrants. In addition, Arab Americans have experienced significant prejudice and discrimination since the September 11,

2001, terrorist attacks. Since the war on terrorism has focused substantially on Islamic extremists, many Arabic, Muslim, and Arab-appearing peoples feel that they have been unfairly and unnecessarily targeted with arrest and harassment as a part of the war on terrorism. In other words, they feel that one particular ethnic group has become the scapegoat as the United States deals with a very frustrating and amorphous problem. Many Arab Americans feel that their success in the United States is the embodiment of many American cultural values and ideals, and yet many also feel that their treatment since 9/11 unveils the prejudices of some Americans against Arabs, Muslims, and people from the Middle East.

Today's Immigrants

In 1965, a totally revamped immigration act removed all racial and ethnic quotas for immigrants to the United States. As a consequence of this act and other trends, today's immigrants are quite unlike those of the past (see Figure 7.4). For most of U.S. history, more than three-quarters of the immigrants have been from Europe, with very small proportions coming from Asia or Central and South America. Today, only 13 percent come from Europe, 33 percent come from Asia, and another 44 percent come from Central and South America.

The data in Figure 7.4 include only people who are legal immigrants to the United States. They do not include tourists, those visiting relatives, and those here on business. Also excluded from those figures are people who enter the United States illegally. It is difficult to know for sure how many undocumented immigrants there are in the United States, but the U.S. Department of Homeland Security (2007) located over one million deportable aliens in 2006. Most are from Central and South America, with over one-half crossing into the United States from Mexico. Most of these

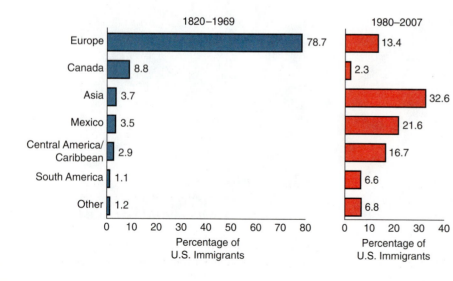

Figure 7.4

Immigrants to the United States, by Country of Last Permanent Residence, 1820–2007

Source: U.S. Department of Homeland Security, *Yearbook of Immigration Statistics,* 2007 (Washington, DC: U.S. Government Printing Office, 2008), www.dhs.gov/ximgtn/statistics/publications/yearbook.shtm

undocumented immigrants are economic refugees, fleeing squalor and poverty in their homelands. Some are hoping to remain permanently in the United States, although most plan to stay only for a short period and then return to their homelands.

The impact of these undocumented immigrants on the United States is complex. On the one hand, they accept jobs that many workers in the United States seem disinclined to do: low-paying, back-breaking farmwork, for example. On the other hand, there is some concern that undocumented immigrants also take some jobs that U.S. citizens may be willing to hold. To protect against this eventuality, hiring undocumented immigrants is now against the law, and employers who do so can be subjected to economic penalties and even imprisonment (Schaefer, 2008). It is hoped that such penalties will help keep undocumented immigrants out of jobs that citizens would like to have.

Achievement and Assimilation among Immigrant Groups

A report by the Census Bureau concludes that immigrants to the United States in recent years have been a varied lot (U.S. Bureau of the Census, 2001). One-third of recent immigrant families live below the poverty line, but one-quarter of immigrants have a college degree when they arrive here. Many immigrant groups see their incomes rise significantly above poverty level within a decade of coming to the United States. This variety of experience is documented in the picture just painted of various racial and ethnic minorities in the United States: Some, such as Japanese and Chinese Americans, have become quite successful, whereas others, such as African Americans and Puerto Ricans, still lag behind on most indicators of socioeconomic status. Why the different experiences? The answer is complex. Part of the reason has to do with the cultural background and histories of each group (Sowell, 1996).

The upward mobility of Japanese Americans has a lot to do with their own cultural heritage (Kitano, 1976). First, the work ethic in Japanese culture is congruent with the values regarding work found in dominant groups in the United States. Japanese culture imbues Japanese Americans with cultural orientations that increase their likelihood of gaining an education or making money in the United States. Second, the Japanese family is highly valued, and family reputation and goals are regarded as more important than individual ones. Individuals gain a sense of self-worth from family membership, and they work hard to avoid bringing shame or disrepute to their family by their own failings. Individual success reflects positively on the family. Third, the Japanese who came to the United States never identified with the lower

classes, even when living in poverty. They perceived themselves as successful and respectable, and they passed on middle-class expectations and aspirations to their children. With a cultural heritage like this, young Japanese Americans are fairly well equipped to compete in various economic arenas if given the opportunity to do so.

The Japanese experience suggests, therefore, that "cultural legacy" is the key factor: The values, skills, and traditions that people bring with them play a big part in their success. This cultural heritage has certainly also played a part in the experiences of some recent immigrant groups, such as Koreans, Vietnamese, Arabs, and Cubans. These immigrants often were part of the business and professional classes in their native lands, and this background endowed them with an entrepreneurial spirit, an educational background, or business experience that made it easier for them to do well in the United States. Yet cultural legacy does not always carry the day. For example, in Ireland and other European countries in earlier centuries, Protestants were generally more prosperous than Catholics. Yet Irish Catholic immigrants to the United States have done better than Irish Protestant immigrants (Jencks, 1992).

Although cultural legacy can play an important part, we need to look at other factors as well, some of which may be unique to particular groups. One is the mutual aid organizations that spring up to provide support for some immigrants. They played a role in the success of Irish Catholics as well as some recent immigrants. Koreans, and some other immigrants, for instance, have been able to raise venture capital among friends and family within the ethnic community and sometimes from relatives in their native lands. In some cases, organized "investment clubs" emerge among an ethnic group to provide low-interest loans to start businesses. In other cases, immigrants have ties to the business community in their native lands, which provide them with information and support in starting a new business (Katz & Ryan, 1992). In the case of Cuban immigrants to south Florida in the 1960s and 1970s, some early immigrants were well educated and experienced in business, and they were able to find important positions in banking and commerce. In the name of ethnic solidarity, they then assisted later Cuban immigrants who had less education and fewer resources with which to get a start in business in the United States (Portes & Stepick, 1993).

Some differences between the experience of African Americans and that of other immigrant groups help explain why the black struggle for success has been so difficult (Jencks, 1992). One difference is that, unlike most other immigrants, blacks came involuntarily. European and Asian immigrants saw migration as a new opportunity to be seized and planned to adapt and make the new country their home; those who did not like it or did not do well could return whence they came. Not so for African Americans. Many Africans were forcibly torn from their native lands with little regard for their culture or their heritage and were given no freedom to achieve or develop in the land to which they were brought. Slaves from many different cultural backgrounds were forced together. Slaves were strongly disciplined for showing initiative or independence, and there was often little regard for the integrity of the black family. Whatever entrepreneurial spirit existed in their native cultures was largely destroyed during the slave experience.

A second difference is that African immigrants had, at best, an ambivalence regarding the legitimacy of the social and legal institutions that enslaved them. For many it was outright hostility and resentment. As a consequence, the African American culture that emerged incorporated this resentment and tolerated if not admired resistance to what some perceived as illegitimate social institutions. A variation on this analysis is described in some research as an "oppositional peer culture" among some African American students that is characterized by low expectations—that is, by a belief that effort and achievement in school are not likely to produce economic or occupational advances. These low expectations are produced by experiences of discrimination in jobs and education and result in peer pressures that discourage African American students from making academic efforts (Farkas, Lleras, & Maczuga, 2002). A third difference is that European immigrant groups, if they shed their ethnic heritage, could become "just plain Americans" and participate in the American success story. Because of visible differences, blacks were never allowed to participate, and so there was less incentive to adopt mainstream culture. Fourth, the mutual supports that some ethnic groups could offer their members have been almost nonexistent among African Americans. Living in poverty in the United States with no link to their native lands meant that there was nowhere to turn for investment loans or other supports.

A final reason for the relatively slow improvement in the circumstances of African Americans is that they still suffer persistent social and economic discrimination (Brown et al., 2003; Feagin, Vera, & Batur-VanderLippe, 2000). This fact has been further corroborated by a series of reports published recently showing persisting discrimination against black and Hispanic Americans in jobs and in the rental or purchase of housing (Munnell, Tootell, Browne, & McEneaney, 1996; Turner et al., 2002–2003; Yinger, 1995). When blacks, Hispanics, and whites, all with the same income and educational levels, inquire about renting or buying a house, blacks and Hispanics

experience discrimination by being told the house is already rented or sold, being steered to housing in predominantly minority neighborhoods, or being refused a home mortgage loan. This and other research document that African Americans and Hispanic Americans are still not treated equally, nor are their opportunities the same as for white Americans.

So, the factors that lead to success among immigrant groups in the United States are complicated. We cannot assume that, because one group has made it, all have the same opportunities. Their historical experiences and current opportunities are so varied that the outcomes for each group must be considered separately. For African Americans, it has only been in the past few decades that the structures of racial discrimination and oppression have begun to be dismantled, and, as we have seen, discrimination still persists in many forms. As these structures are further dismantled, and a supportive cultural environment emerges, the achievements of African Americans will likely improve. It will take time, however, to overcome the ghastly legacy of the treatment of African Americans in the United States.

The Sociology of Media and Technology section discusses the role of modern mass media in shaping the position of racial and ethnic minorities in society.

Current Issues in the United States

You should be able to describe the various issues and controversies related to race and ethnic relations in the United States and assess programs intended to improve relations.

At the beginning of the twenty-first century, significant issues remain regarding the relationships between various racial and ethnic groups in the United States. This chapter closes by reviewing a few of them.

Assimilation or Pluralism?

What pattern of minority–majority relations is most desirable in the United States—assimilation, pluralism, or some other pattern? People's response to this question is often colored by a misconception about what has happened historically. The United States is often referred to as a *melting pot* in which the beliefs, values, and lifestyles of many different racial and ethnic groups have been blended together into a unique mix that is called *American*. If this blending had occurred, it would be a form of assimilation in which all groups have changed to some degree in creating an American identity. Actually, the experience of most immigrants has come closer to what Milton Gordon (1964) has called *Anglo conformity*: To share fully in the American dream, immigrants have been required to

Sociology of Media and Technology

Image and Access: Race/Ethnicity and Communications Technologies

The mass media play an important, although complicated, role in the relationship between majority and minority groups in the United States. The images that the media present of people of various races and ethnic groups can paint a particular group in a positive or negative light. Furthermore, these images, as the interactionist perspective suggests, help to shape people's perceptions and expectations regarding particular groups. After all, the portrayal of an African American or American Indian on television or in a movie is a cultural image that has some societal legitimacy by virtue of having been given space in the mainstream media. So, from the conflict perspective, the media are *contested territory* that groups attempt to influence and control as a part of the struggle over resources in society.

The media are controlled mostly by the dominant racial and ethnic groups in any society, and thus it is their stereotypes of races and ethnic groups that are most likely to find space in the media (Biagi & Kern-Foxworth, 1997; Wilson, Gutiérrez, & Chao, 2004). As a result, in the United States, whites tend to be disproportionately portrayed in the media and to be placed in the more positive roles—as the good person, the success, the hero, the winner. In fact, until the 1960s at least, movies and television were pretty much a white landscape: Nonwhites appeared only in minor roles, in menial positions, or as criminals or villains.

The media images of minorities in the past three decades have certainly improved. As opportunities for minorities in all areas of society have gotten better, more minorities have begun to work in the media industries that produce culture; there are more minority actors, producers, directors, and newscasters. Media stars such as Spike Lee, Geraldo Rivera, Jennifer Lopez, Oprah Winfrey, and Bill Cosby have become influential in shaping the presentation of culture through the media.

Yet, despite these changes, minorities in general are still underrepresented in the media, and Latinos, considering their numbers in the population, may be one of the most underrepresented ethnic groups in the media (National Council of La Raza, 1997; Children Now, 2004). In addition, the image of minorities presented is still often a distorted and negative one. For example, recent studies of local television news stories and reality-based police shows demonstrate the distorted images of race that are presented. African Americans, for example, appear in the local news as violent criminals and in very few other roles (Entman, 1997; Gilliam, Iyengar, Simon, & Wright, 1997). Furthermore, African Americans are presented as criminals in these news shows in numbers that are far disproportionate to their actual contribution to the crime problem. African Americans are also portrayed in more dangerous images than whites, in glowering mug shots or being led around in handcuffs. The overall impression presented in these television shows is that the crime problem is due to blacks and that whites are the victims.

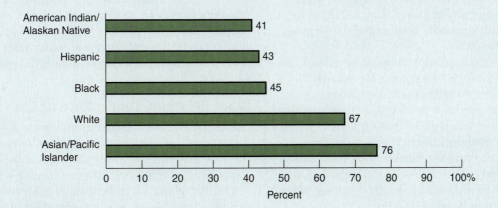

Figure 7.5

Percentage of Households With Internet Access in the Home, by Race/Hispanic Origin, 2007

Source: U. S. Department of Commerce, National Telecommunications and Information Administration, data from the Current Population Survey (October 2007), U.S. Census Bureau, www.ntia.doc.gov/reports/2008/NetworkedNation.html

(continued)

As the twentieth century came to a close, the explosion in media, computers, and telecommunications may have actually created more opportunities for expression on the part of minorities as more media outlets called for the production of more media products. Since some of these new outlets will be targeted at minority audiences, this expansion will likely create a demand for minority-produced media materials. This will make it more possible for minorities to find media work, contribute to the portrayal of minorities in the media, and make positive minority role models available. In fact, some of the television networks that have emerged with the explosion of cable television in the past two decades, such as UPN, WB, and Fox, have targeted programming at minority audiences as a way to gain a foothold in a very competitive industry.

As we saw in Chapter 6, access to modern communications technologies have important implications for the stratification system in society by influencing opportunities for financial and occupational success. Race and ethnicity play an important role in this, especially in terms of having access to the Internet, as Figure 7.5 suggests. In addition to the other disadvantages experienced by black and Hispanic Americans documented in this chapter, these two groups are also considerably less likely to have access to the Internet, especially those in the lower income groups. A few other things are notable. One is that socioeconomic status, as measured by income, has a powerful effect here: The financially well-off are much more likely to have Internet access. A second thing of note is that Asian Americans have high rates of access in all income groups but especially in the lower income levels. This differential access to the technologies of modern life is one of the mechanisms through which stratification systems tend to reproduce themselves from one generation to the next: Those born into lower positions in the stratification system often lack access to the technologies that would assist them in achieving social mobility.

renounce their ancestral culture in favor of the beliefs, values, and lifestyle of the dominant white Anglo-Saxon Protestants, WASPs. These WASPs were among the earliest European immigrants to North America. They came from the British Isles and Germany, and they dominated political, economic, and social life in the United States from the sixteenth through the nineteenth centuries. The WASPs were sufficiently fearful of people who immigrated after them—from places such as Ireland, Italy, and Eastern Europe—that they attempted to "Americanize" them rather than let them build their own social institutions and way of life. Many people today still insist on a version of Anglo conformity by arguing that groups such as Hispanics and Asians should learn only English and not be given a bilingual education.

Although Anglo conformity worked for quite a while, it has not persisted. Over time, the original WASP group became such a small minority that it became more difficult for it to force its lifestyle onto others. The outcome, at least to this point, is that the United States remains a highly pluralistic society with many distinct racial and ethnic subcultures. Furthermore, some minorities, especially groups such as blacks and Hispanics, who were never allowed to assimilate by the dominant white groups, prefer it that way.

Whether pluralism is desirable is a matter of considerable controversy (Pettigrew, 1988; Triandis, 1988). Many people argue that extensive pluralism will promote tensions that could flare into conflict in the future, even going so far as separatist movements. They point to the efforts of French Canadians in Quebec to secede from Canada as the kind of discord that pluralism can generate. In fact, the Census Bureau reports that Spanish rather than English is spoken at home by 14 percent of the population of the United States (U.S. Bureau of the Census, 2007, p. 48). Concern over this possibility has become so strong in some groups that 30 states have now passed laws making English the official language (Figure 7.6).

Proponents of pluralism, by contrast, contend that racial and ethnic diversity contributes to the richness of U.S. culture and symbolizes the country's roots as a nation open to the oppressed of all lands. Furthermore, ethnic identity can be a source of pride and positive self-regard for individuals, and speaking in one's native tongue can play an important part in this. Among Latinos, for example, speaking Spanish and having a large and powerful Spanish-language media in the United States are sources of cultural pride and ethnic identity.

Race Relations Today: Race or Class?

As discussed earlier, some minority groups, such as blacks, still lag significantly behind other groups on various indicators of socioeconomic status. There is considerable debate over whether this lag is because of racial discrimination or because of the class position held by many blacks, which places them in a weak situation from which to compete for jobs and income.

Sociologist William J. Wilson (1987, 1996) argues that class, rather than race, is the more important factor in determining the social positions of African Americans today. Wilson does not deny that racial antagonism is still with us, or that substantial discrimination against and oppression of blacks not only has

The collective protest of the civil rights movement, illustrated by this march on Washington of hundreds of thousands of people in 1963, forced the United States to confront the racial and ethnic prejudices and discrimination that existed and to adopt policies that would improve these conditions.

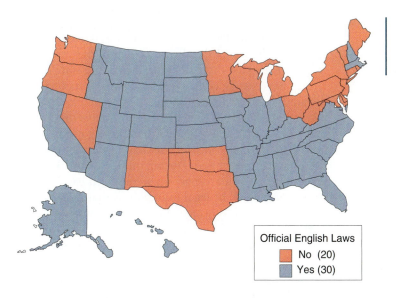

Official English Laws
▨ No (20)
▨ Yes (30)

Figure 7.6
States With Official English-Language Laws, 2008

Note: From U.S. English, Inc., Washington, D.C., www.us/english.org/. Copyright © U.S. English, Inc.

clouded U.S. history but also lingers today. But he points out that the real problem lies in the continuing existence of an underclass of poor, marginally skilled blacks who have little opportunity to obtain the education and skills necessary to succeed in a modern industrial society (see the discussion of poverty in Chapter 6).

Such an underclass can also be found among poor whites and among Puerto Ricans and other Hispanic groups (Alex-Assensoh, 1995; Tienda, 1989). Wilson attributes the persistence of this underclass to basic changes in the structure of the U.S. economy, including the relocation of industries away from the communities where many poor people live and a labor market in which people with few job skills or little education are limited to low-paying work with little opportunity for advancement. The primary barrier that this underclass faces, argues Wilson, is the lack of appropriate job-related skills, not racial discrimination. Blacks or Hispanics with job skills or a college education, he argues, will enjoy opportunities and privileges similar to those of their white counterparts in the class hierarchy and will probably not face significant discrimination even if economic conditions deteriorate.

On the other side of this argument are sociologists Joe Feagin and Melvin Sykes (1994), who argue that racial oppression is still a key factor influencing race relations in the United States. They argue that blacks are still oppressed and discriminated against because of their race, although the forms and mechanisms of racial oppression may have changed since the 1950s and 1960s. One difference today is that the overt individual racism of the past has declined considerably, but there is still widespread, institutionalized racism in which such things as residential and school segregation place barriers before the advancement of many blacks but few whites. In addition, many whites find the black urban culture of today alien and threatening (Jencks, 1992). Consequently, they are less likely to hire blacks, particularly young males. In addition, employers have other motivations for discriminating against blacks in hiring. For example, an employer might believe that a black employee will not attract white customers. In professional sports for many years, owners and managers believed that white fans would not pay to see black players. Today some companies still refuse to hire blacks for highly visible positions, such as receptionist or salesperson, when customers are white.

Feagin and Sykes (1994) interviewed hundreds of middle-class African Americans, who are presumably the ones least affected by race, according to Wilson's argument. Based on these interviews, Feagin and Sykes concluded that "few middle-class African Americans interviewed . . . see the significance of racism in their lives declining" (p. 12). For all these reasons, Feagin and Sykes argue that race still very much determines the position of African Americans as a group.

So, controversy continues over whether the continuing chasm between the achievements of blacks and whites is due predominately to class or to race. Although it may be difficult to resolve the proportionate role of each, it is certain that each plays some part. The issues involved are important, because the contrasting positions on this controversy point to very different policy recommendations for their solutions. The chapter now considers some of the policies put forth in the past few decades to improve the quality of race relations in the United States.

Advances, Setbacks, and Controversial Policies

Most people would agree that the United States has achieved much over the past few decades in terms of racial and ethnic relations. The collective protest of the civil rights movement forced the nation to confront inequities in the 1950s and 1960s, and a foundation of legislation was established to prevent or punish discrimination on the basis of racial or ethnic identity and to reduce inequities in the stratification system. Surveys by sociologists since the 1960s indicate that people in the United States now show less racial prejudice and are more tolerant of racial diversity than ever before (Steeh & Schuman, 1992). In addition, racial and ethnic minorities are more organized, confident, and optimistic than in the past. Applying Sociology: Combating Prejudice describes some of the contributions sociologists have made to this improving picture.

Some of the policies that have resulted in advances have been controversial (Swain, 2001). Affirmative-action legislation, for example, was intended to force schools and employers to aggressively seek out minorities when they have vacancies. That policy probably has made it possible for some minorities to overcome persisting discrimination and obtain jobs or entrance into schools that they probably would not have obtained otherwise. Some argue, however, that it has produced reverse discrimination, in which whites lose jobs or positions in school to nonwhites, and the less qualified people are hired over those who are more qualified. What is certainly true is that the policy has produced feelings of frustration, resentment, anger, and cynicism among some whites who feel they are being passed over and are losing out (Bunzel, 1991; Lynch & Beer, 1990).

Over the past three decades, courts and state legislatures have struggled to satisfy the two competing demands in the realms of hiring, promotion, and admission: that all people be treated equally, on the one hand, and that the goal of maintaining racial and ethnic diversity in the civil life of society be encouraged, on the other hand. During the 1980s and 1990s, programs of affirmative action were scaled back; the courts weakened the legal foundations that minorities successfully used to bring affirmative-action lawsuits against employers or schools; and some states banned the use of racial preferences in college admissions, state hiring, and the awarding of state contracts (Bowen & Bok, 1998). In 2003, the U.S. Supreme Court ruled on the constitutionality of affirmative action in a way that gave some support to both sides of the issue. The court supported the position that promoting diversity in student bodies and in workforces was a compelling societal interest because everyone benefited from such diversity. Furthermore, the court ruled that an applicant's race could be used as one of a number of

Applying Sociology   Combating Prejudice, Discrimination, and Racial Polarization

During and following World War II, many people, including many sociologists and other social scientists, were horrified by the genocidal attacks on Jews and other groups by Nazis in France, Poland, and other European nations. In part in response to this outrage, applied sociologists have devoted much attention to locating the sources of prejudice and discrimination as well as to developing and evaluating programs to combat them. This applied sociological work has played a key role in developing policies to deal with these problems.

For example, community leaders and citizens in St. Louis wanted to attack problems of racial isolation and polarization, as well as the lack of educational and occupational opportunities among African Americans in their community (Farley, 1991). They called in sociologists to identify the extent of housing segregation in the community and locate its causes. The sociologists found that one source of segregation was the tendency for some realty companies to steer customers to particular neighborhoods based on the customers' racial identity. This finding was highly controversial because the real estate agents in St. Louis, who were among the community leaders supporting programs to attack racial polarization, felt that they were being unfairly singled out as the source of community segregation. That was not true, since the sociologists involved also identified many other sources of segregation. Despite the debate, the sociological data proved to be convincing because they clearly showed that racial steering did occur. This knowledge translated directly into policies to establish educational and sensitivity programs for real estate agents on multiculturalism and racial diversity.

Sociological research has also been used to document the consequences of racial isolation. In the project in St. Louis, applied sociologists showed that segregation in housing dramatically reduced the occupational opportunities for African Americans, increasing their poverty and other social problems in the St. Louis area. This and other sociological research has also shown that racial isolation produces negative stereotyping, prejudice, and hostility, whereas contact between different racial groups can reduce prejudice (Brewer & Miller, 1996; Pettigrew, 1998). This knowledge about the effects of intergroup contact can then be used to develop programs that will encourage people to view members of another racial or ethnic group more positively. One such program was run at a summer camp for children (Clore, Bray, Itkin, & Murphy, 1978). The camp included equal numbers of black and white children, and they came from all levels of the socioeconomic hierarchy. In the camp, all children had the same rights and the same work duties. There was also an equal mix of blacks and whites among the administrators and counselors in the camp, so that the authority structure was not racially biased. In other words, blacks were as likely to exercise power over the children as were whites. During their one-week stay at the camp, children were required to work on cooperative tasks involving group rather than individual goals. By the end of the week, the children who came to the camp with negative attitudes toward members of the other racial group had shifted toward more positive views, suggesting that such intergroup contact can reduce prejudice.

Similar programs have been established in many schools to enhance learning, reduce feelings of prejudice, and promote a sense of we-feeling among students of diverse racial and ethnic backgrounds (Aronson & Gonzalez, 1988; Slavin, 1985; Stevens & Slavin, 1995). The basic idea is to create a classroom environment that encourages cooperation and interdependence in learning rather than competition. Classes are kept small and ethnically diverse, and the students teach one another. Evaluations of cooperative classroom settings indicate that they promote a sense of positive regard among the students, they reduce racial and ethnic prejudice, and they increase the amount of social interaction among students from diverse racial and ethnic backgrounds.

Research findings from studies like the children's camp and the classroom studies have accumulated over the decades and have provided applied sociologists with a solid foundation from which to make recommendations on how to design contact so that levels of prejudice and intergroup hostility are reduced rather than increased. To be effective, the contact should have the following characteristics:

1. The contact should have high acquaintance potential, which means that people have the time and opportunity to get to know one another and to have some personal and intimate associations.
2. The contact should be between people of equal status, rather than between a low-status minority and a higher-status member of the dominant group.
3. The behavior of the minority-group person in the contact should contradict the usual stereotype of members of that group.
4. As a part of the contact, people should work toward cooperative and interdependent goals rather than competitive ones; that is, no one in the group can achieve his or her individual goals unless all the participants work together.
5. The contact situation should have the support of legitimate authorities, such as a school or church, and should involve social norms that dictate friendliness and respect between people.

(continued)

Many of these features were built into the programs at the children's camp and the classroom environments just described. Clearly, though, many of our everyday contacts with members of different races violate these principles, as, for example, when an African American or Hispanic American interacts with an Anglo teacher or social worker. Nonetheless, sociological research and practice have given us the knowledge and the tools to point us in the direction of how to structure situations to reduce racial prejudice and polarization.

When such social programs are established, they should be evaluated to see if they achieve their goals; this evaluation is another common task of applied sociologists (Farley, 1991). In the St. Louis program, for example, sociologists devised a plan for assessing whether different parts of the program achieved their intended goals. Evaluation is a difficult but important task, because it tells whether a particular community-wide effort is just spinning its wheels or maybe making things worse. Sociologists are trained in the research methods and statistical procedures necessary to do such evaluation effectively (Sullivan, 2001).

---

factors in admissions and hiring decisions. However, the court also ruled that using race as a collective criterion that applied to every case or using strict racial quotas would be unconstitutional. Then in 2007, the Supreme Court ruled that it was unconstitutional for schools to explicitly use race as a criterion for assigning students to schools for purposes of achieving racial integration. Such court rulings will make it more difficult to integrate schools and will probably lead policy makers and educators to search for other ways to achieve some degree of school integration.

Despite affirmative action, the evidence is clear that some discrimination against minorities in jobs and education still persists. In situations where affirmative-action policies have been eliminated, the result has been a decline in the numbers of African Americans, Hispanic Americans, and American Indians admitted to the schools. In addition, research shows that plans that ignore or significantly downplay race as a criterion for admission are not nearly as effective at promoting diversity in colleges as are affirmative-action and other more race-conscious efforts (Horn & Flores, 2003).

Another controversial program has been school busing, which is discussed at greater length in Chapter 12. School busing began in the 1960s, when sociologists published reports documenting the extensive segregation that existed in schools and arguing that the segregation was part of the reason for the poor performance of many African American students. A number of programs were established to provide academic assistance to poor and minority children, including the Head Start program discussed in Chapters 6 and 12. School busing was also initiated to achieve some racial balance in the schools and improve the educational environment for all students. In addition, it was believed that the resulting school integration would bring about reductions in prejudice and discrimination as students of different racial identities met and worked together in school. School busing does seem to have provided modest educational advantages to minority students, and minorities in desegregated schools do show more educational and occupational achievement (Armor, 1995; Entwisle & Alexander, 1994; Longshore & Prager, 1985). It has also reduced levels of racial isolation, which will probably result in less racial tension and stereotyping in the future (Hawley et al., 1983).

Despite its advantages, busing has remained highly controversial and has produced some conflict itself. For example, some argue that busing has caused *white flight,* or whites leaving the cities for the suburbs in order to avoid integrated schools. White flight has occurred, although it cannot be blamed solely on busing. Yet, busing probably played a part, and white flight has tended to increase segregation in cities and schools (Rivkin, 1994; Smock & Wilson, 1991).

Although there is much in U.S. history to be lamented, people can be proud of the advances in race relations since the 1960s. Yet there are reasons for uncertainty about the future. As noted, some minorities still lag significantly behind Anglos on various indicators of achievement, and sociologists can document blatant discrimination against many minorities, but especially Hispanic Americans and African Americans, in finding jobs or housing. In addition, although racial violence has been limited of late, periodic outbursts indicate that such conflict is just below the surface. The riot in south central Los Angeles in 1992 was the most recent manifestation of the anger and resentment that can trigger such violence. (The reasons for this outburst are analyzed in detail in Chapter 15.) The same thing happened in Miami in 1989, when a police officer shot and killed a black man on a motorcycle. These violent riots express the anger that many minority youths feel about their position and opportunities today. They illustrate the potential for racial conflict that simmers despite the improvements that have been made. The potential for prejudice, discrimination, and racial violence remains strong and can be rekindled if the proper social conditions arise.

Sociology on the Internet

The Internet is an excellent place to search for materials on minority groups and on issues of prejudice and discrimination. However, be forewarned that some material you come across may be offensive to you. A good way to begin is by logging on to the Yahoo! search engine. Type "Society and Culture" in the Directory Search and then choose "Cultures and Groups." Now you have various alternatives, such as "People of Color" and "White Pride and Racialism." As you can begin to see, some of these sites may contain material that is disturbing to some, but the reality is that racism and racial hatred are a part of the social reality of race and ethnic relations and need to be understood.

There is also a box where you can type in various keywords for Yahoo! to search on. You should try to locate materials on minority groups that are not covered in this book or are only briefly covered. You could also search under key words, such as "racism," "hate groups," "multiculturalism," "American Indian Movement," or "La Raza." You could also search for particular individuals, such as

"Leonard Peltier" or "Russell Means." Don't know who they are? Look them up and report back to the class.

Another approach is to look for organizations that fight against discrimination and for social justice for minorities. One of the largest in the United States is the National Association for the Advancement of Colored People (NAACP) at www.naacp.org. At that site, you can find updates on state and national legislation relevant to minorities and social justice as well as current news events relating to minorities. How many other such organizations can you find on the Internet?

In all this searching, find information that addresses two additional issues: (1) race and ethnic relations in places other than the United States, and (2) viewpoints on issues of race and ethnic relations that are often not found expressed in the mainstream media.

For further information and discussion, go to Allyn & Bacon's Social Problems Supersite (see Chapter 1) and explore Problem Area: Problems of Racial and Ethnic Inequality.

Study & Review
SUMMARY OF LEARNING OBJECTIVES

You should be able to define minority group and racism and identify what constitutes a racial and an ethnic group.

A minority group is a group whose members share distinct physical and cultural characteristics, have less access to power and resources than do members of other groups, and are accorded fewer rights, privileges, and opportunities. The term *minority,* as used by sociologists, relates to a group's position in the stratification system rather than to numerical size. The term *race* refers to people who are believed to share certain biological characteristics, whereas *ethnicity* has to do with a common historical and cultural heritage.

You should be able to explain the social and social psychological sources of prejudice and discrimination and describe the consequences that discrimination has for individuals and society.

Among the social causes of prejudice and discrimination are ethnocentrism, competition, socialization, and institutionalized discrimination. Social psychological causes include stereotyping, frustration and aggression, and the authoritarian personality. Discrimination has a number

of consequences, including an adverse effect on people's life chances and an increase in tension and hostility in society.

You should be able to describe the patterns of intergroup relations that emerge between dominant and minority groups and the minority reactions to such domination as well as discuss the possibilities for cooperation in a multiracial or multiethnic society.

The patterns of intergroup relations most commonly found are genocide, segregation, continued subjugation, population transfer, assimilation, and pluralism. The most typical reactions of minorities to domination are submission, social protest, separatism, and rebellion. Switzerland provides a system of power sharing whereby various ethnic groups are guaranteed input into political decisions.

You should be able to describe the major racial and ethnic minorities in the United States, discuss their current circumstances and opportunities, explain the variation in achievement found among them, and

show how the mass media influence the position of minorities in society.

Among racial and ethnic groups, African Americans and Hispanic Americans are the largest minorities, and they lag considerably behind other groups in access to education, power, and economically rewarding jobs. One of the most important reasons for this lag is the long history of discrimination and oppression suffered by both groups, making it difficult for them to improve their position in U.S. society. American Indians experience some of the worst conditions of all minority groups in the United States. Some Asian Americans, by contrast, have been able to attain a degree of affluence despite the substantial prejudice and discrimination they have experienced. Arab Americans have also done well but have experienced prejudice and discrimination because of the war on terrorism. The achievements of immigrant groups in the United States have been highly varied and affected by the group's cultural legacy as well as the severity of the oppression and discrimination they experience at the hands of dominant groups. The mass media influence people's perceptions of minority groups, as well as serve as a contested territory of cultural resources.

You should be able to describe the various issues and controversies related to race and ethnic relations in the United States and assess programs intended to improve relations.

Currently in the United States, there is considerable controversy over whether minorities should assimilate or whether a high degree of pluralism is acceptable. There is also controversy over whether the continuing gap between black and white achievements is the result of racism or class position. There have been advances and setbacks in race relations in recent decades, and some policies aimed at reducing prejudice and discrimination, such as affirmative action and school busing, have been controversial.

CHRONOLOGICAL PRACTICE TEST

For answers to Key Concepts see the page numbers in parentheses; for other answers see page 205.

Minority Groups
Key Concepts

1. Minority group (178)
2. Race (179)
3. Ethnic group (179)
4. Racism (179)

True/False

5. T F Race and ethnicity are ascribed statuses.

Concept Completion

6. _____ is the view that certain racial or ethnic groups are biologically inferior and can be discriminated against because of this.

Sources of Prejudice and Discrimination
Key Concepts

7. Prejudice (180)
8. Discrimination (180)
9. Ethnocentrism (180)
10. Split labor market (181)
11. Internal colonialism (181)
12. Institutionalized discrimination (181)
13. Institutionalized racism (181)

True/False

14. T F From the functionalist perspective, ethnocentrism is always considered to have negative consequences for members of an in-group.
15. T F According to the conflict perspective, prejudice and discrimination arise when two groups find themselves in competition with one another.
16. T F The text concludes that racism does lower the self-esteem of minorities in some contexts.

Concept Completion

17. Fred and Mary believe that their high school is superior to all the other high schools in their district. This is an example of the tendency toward _____.
18. In a split labor market, the group that receives the brunt of the discrimination is the _____.
19. In terms of contributing to prejudice and discrimination, categorization becomes a problem when the categories become _____.

Critical Thinking

20. What is ethnocentrism? What role does it play in prejudice and discrimination?
21. How do competition and socialization influence prejudice and discrimination?
22. According to the text, what detrimental consequences does discrimination have for society?

Patterns of Intergroup Relations
Key Concepts

23. Genocide (183)
24. Segregation (185)
25. Continued subjugation (185)
26. Population transfer (185)
27. Assimilation (185)
28. Pluralism (186)

Concept Completion

29. _____ occurs when a dominant group moves the members of a minority group, either voluntarily or involuntarily, to a particular geographic area.

30. In contrast to the Swiss political system in which power is shared among various ethnic groups, the United States tends more toward power _____.

Critical Thinking

31. Describe the forms that domination of a minority group by a majority group can take. Give an example of each. How do minority groups respond to this domination?
32. Describe the pattern of intergroup relations that has emerged among the three major ethnic groups in Switzerland. How well does it work? Why?

Racial and Ethnic Minorities in the United States
True/False

33. T F African Americans were the only minority group to be enslaved in the United States.
34. T F Because of casino gambling and other economic enterprises on American Indian reservations, income and educational levels on reservations now approach those for society as a whole.
35. T F Today, more than one-half of all the immigrants to the United States come from Mexico.
36. T F The text argues that cultural legacy probably has little to do with how well immigrants to the United States do economically.

Concept Completion

37. The ruling in which the U.S. Supreme Court declared the "separate but equal" doctrine to be unconstitutional was _____.
38. U.S. citizenship was granted to all American Indians in the decade of the _____.
39. In recent decades, the largest percentage of immigrants to the United States has come from the geographical region of _____.

Graphics Review

40. Review Table 7.1 and Figures 7.1 to 7.3. Summarize the conclusions that can be drawn from this table and these figures regarding the position of various racial and ethnic minorities in the United States and how that position has changed over time.

Critical Thinking

41. Describe the prejudice and discrimination that Japanese Americans and Chinese Americans experienced after immigrating to the United States.
42. In what ways has the experience of African Americans been different from that of other immigrant groups to the United States?

Current Issues in the United States
True/False

43. T F Contact between different racial and ethnic groups can reduce prejudice if the contact has high acquaintance potential.

44. T F The text concludes that "race" is more important than "class" in determining the social position of African Americans in the United States today.

Concept Completion

45. _____ occurs when white students leave a school district for suburban or private schools in order to avoid school busing or school integration.

Critical Thinking

46. What are the characteristics of the contact between racial groups that are most likely to reduce prejudice between the groups?
47. Is the situation of African Americans in the United States today mostly a function of "race" or "class"? Make the arguments for both sides of this issue.
48. What does the text conclude regarding what school busing has achieved in the United States?

ANSWERS TO CHRONOLOGICAL PRACTICE TEST

5. T; 14. F; 15. T; 16. T; 33. T; 34. F; 35. F; 36. F; 43. T; 44. F
6. Racism
17. ethnocentrism
18. lower-priced labor
19. stereotypes
29. Population transfer
30. competition
37. *Brown v. The Board of Education*
38. 1920s
39. Asia
45. White flight

CUMULATIVE PRACTICE TEST

See page 482 for answers.

1. Characteristics like race and ethnicity are called
   a. ascribed statuses.
   b. achieved statuses.
   c. minority statuses.
   d. status roles.
   e. None of the above.
2. Jewish Americans would most clearly be
   a. a racial group.
   b. an authoritarian group.
   c. an example of internal colonialism.
   d. an ethnic group.
   e. a split-labor group.
3. Mary has a negative stereotype toward and dislikes all people from the Middle East, but she does not discriminate against them in hiring for her store because of the laws against it. In Robert Merton's classification, she would be called
   a. an unprejudiced nondiscriminator.
   b. a prejudiced discriminator.
   c. a racist discriminator.
   d. an unprejudiced discriminator.
   e. a prejudiced nondiscriminator.

4. A negative attitude toward certain people based solely on their membership in a particular group is called
   a. prejudice.
   b. discrimination.
   c. a minority group.
   d. pluralism.
   e. segregation.

5. The tendency to view one's own group or culture as an in-group that follows the best and only proper way to live is termed
   a. discrimination.
   b. prejudice.
   c. ethnocentrism.
   d. institutionalized discrimination.
   e. assimilation.

6. Which of the following terms refers to a type of economic exploitation between a dominant group and a minority group?
   a. Ethnocentrism.
   b. Assimilation.
   c. Institutionalized discrimination.
   d. Internal colonialism.
   e. Genocide.

7. The split labor market could be best characterized as
   a. a situation in which a dominant group exploits a subordinate group for the benefit of the dominant group.
   b. an unprejudiced person who is a discriminator.
   c. two groups of workers willing to do the same work but for different wages.
   d. institutionalized discrimination by a dominant group against a minority group.
   e. an arrangement in which the social lives of two groups are kept separate.

8. Which of the following are among the social sources of prejudice and discrimination discussed in the text?
   a. Ethnocentrism.
   b. Assimilation.
   c. Socialization and conformity.
   d. All of the above.
   e. Only a and c.

9. Women who fail to qualify for employment in a fire department because they do not have sufficient upper-body strength to carry a heavy weight a long distance have encountered
   a. racism.
   b. apartheid.
   c. prejudiced nondiscrimination.
   d. institutionalized discrimination.
   e. internal colonialism.

10. According to the text, the lynchings of African Americans in the United States between 1880 and 1930 were due in part to
    a. the split labor market.
    b. economic competition.
    c. institutionalized discrimination.
    d. discrimination in housing.
    e. All of the above played a part.

11. According to the text, which of the following is a key factor in the racial hatred and violence found in both Britain and Germany in recent years?
    a. A rise in neo-communism.
    b. An increase in the number of jobs available.

c. High unemployment.
d. A mass exodus of workers from these nations.
e. Terrorist actions by Al Qaeda.

12. The Serbs forced Muslims to move out of certain territories in the former Yugoslavia. This pattern of intergroup relations is most clearly referred to as
    a. continued subjugation.
    b. genocide.
    c. population transfer.
    d. pluralism.
    e. separatism.

13. Of the minority reactions to domination discussed in the text, minority groups with little power would probably respond with
    a. separatism.
    b. rebellion.
    c. submission.
    d. social protest.
    e. population transfer.

14. All of the following are true about Hispanic Americans *except*
    a. the largest group among Hispanics is Mexican Americans.
    b. they are the third largest minority group discussed in the text.
    c. they suffer from low educational levels in comparison to whites.
    d. the gap between Hispanic and white income has widened slightly in the past thirty years.
    e. All of the above are true.

15. Which of the following is true, according to the discussion of Asian Americans in the text?
    a. Racial prejudices existed toward the Chinese prior to 1849, but once their immigration began in large numbers, these sentiments decreased.
    b. Asian Americans are considerably lower than white Americans in occupational achievements.
    c. The immigration experiences of Chinese and Japanese Americans were remarkably similar.
    d. The peak period of Japanese immigration to the United States began prior to the Chinese Exclusion Act of 1882.
    e. Between 1882 and World War II, racist attitudes in the U.S. characterized the Chinese as a "yellow peril."

16. Regarding factors that contribute to the success of minorities in the United States, the text concludes that
    a. cultural legacy explains most of the differences between groups.
    b. cultural legacy is relatively unimportant.
    c. if a group is willing to work hard, they can get ahead in the United States.
    d. cultural legacy can be important, but other factors also play a part.
    e. discrimination has not been a factor affecting the success of minorities in the United States.

17. The _____ perspective characterizes the mass media as "contested territory" that groups compete over.
    a. conflict
    b. functionalist
    c. interactionist
    d. assimilationist
    e. evolutionary

18. Over the history of the United States, the experience of most immigrants comes closest to
    a. a melting pot.
    b. Anglo conformity.
    c. continued subjugation.
    d. genocide.
    e. both a and b.
19. The text concludes which of the following regarding the impact of school busing programs on the performance of minority students?
    a. The amount of "white flight" from cities is reduced.
    b. Minorities show modest improvement in school performance.
    c. Minorities show dramatic improvements in school performance.
    d. Hostility between minorities and whites increases.
    e. Minorities show declines in school performance.
20. According to the Applying Sociology section on combating prejudice and discrimination, intergroup contact can reduce prejudice if the contact has which of the following characteristics?
    a. High "acquaintance potential."
    b. The contact is between people of equal status.
    c. The people involved in the contact work toward cooperative rather than competitive goals.
    d. The contact situation has the support of legitimate authorities.
    e. All of the above.

FOR FURTHER READING

Conley, Dalton. (1999). *Being black, living in the red: Race, wealth, and social policy in America.* Berkeley: University of California Press. This sociologist provides an in-depth analysis of the role of both race and class in determining the social and economic position of whites and blacks in the United States today.

Feagin, Joe R., and McKinney, Karyn D. (2003). *The many costs of racism.* Lanham, MD: Rowman & Littlefield. This book provides an excellent overview of how racism has substantial negative impacts on people and communities.

Marks, Paula Mitchell. (1998). *In a barren land: American Indian dispossession and survival.* New York: William Morrow. This is an excellent and readable history of Indians in the New World. It comes all the way to the present and suggests the complexity of factors that have shaped the status of Indians in the United States.

Robinson, Randall. (1998). *Defending the spirit: A black life in America.* New York: Dutton. This is an eye-opening memoir by a Harvard-educated African American lawyer about what it is like to grow up black in the United States. Robinson describes the insult and humiliation that he has suffered and the rage that can result.

Shorris, Earl. (1992). *Latinos: A biography of the people.* New York: W. W. Norton. This excellent book explores the lives and history of the fastest-growing minority group in the United States, the descendants of the Spanish conquest of the American Indian peoples. Through wonderfully insightful biographical sketches, the author communicates the complex diversity today in the group that is given the single designation of *Latino.*

Tobin, Gary A. (1988). *Jewish perceptions of antisemitism.* New York: Plenum. This book summarizes research on how much anti-Semitism exists in the United States and on Jews' perceptions of their status. It is an excellent analysis of the problems of prejudice and discrimination affecting one of the more successful ethnic groups in the United States.

Van Ausdale, Debra, & Feagin, Joe R. (2001). *The first R: How children learn race and racism.* Lanham, MD: Rowman & Littlefield. Based on direct observations of children interacting with one another, these sociologists explain how children learn and use racial identities in their lives.

Wilson, William Julius, & Taub, Richard P. (2006). *There goes the neighborhood: Racial, ethnic, and class tensions in four Chicago neighborhoods and their meaning for America.* New York: Knopf. Using Chicago as a case study, these sociologists explore the complexity of race and ethnic relations in the United States today, looking at sources of tension and conflict between various groups and proposing ways of bringing these diverse communities together.

Social Inequality: Gender

MYTHS & FACTS: About Gender Inequality

Men and Women in Society

The Biological Perspective
The Functionalist Perspective
The Conflict Perspective
The Interactionist Perspective

The Socialization of Men and Women

The Family
The Schools
The Media and the Electronic World

SOCIOLOGY OF MEDIA AND TECHNOLOGY: Shaping Gender Identity

The Extent of Gender Inequality in the United States

Economic Discrimination
Education
Work and the Workplace
Income
Discrimination in the Military
Other Types of Discrimination
Gender Inequality Involving Males

Gender Stratification in Global Perspective

OTHER WORLDS, OTHER WAYS: Mexico: Poor Women and the World Economy

Toward Gender Equality

Collective Action and the Feminist Movement: A Global Struggle
Current Trends in the United States

Changes in the Law
Changes in the Workplace
APPLYING SOCIOLOGY: Sexual Assault, Sexual Harassment, and the Empowerment of Women
The Changing Face of Politics
Masculine, Feminine, or Human?
SOCIOLOGY ON THE INTERNET

Study & Review

In the early 1600s, the Huron Indians lived in part of what the French explorers of the time called New France—on Georgian Bay north of present-day Toronto in Ontario, Canada (Grant, 1984). Approximately 20,000 in number spread throughout twenty-five villages, the Hurons engaged in slash-and-burn horticulture and were semisedentary. They also traded with various surrounding tribes for subsistence goods as well as luxuries and delicacies. The Hurons were a matrilineal society, meaning that they reckoned kinship and descent through the mother's line (see Chapter 9). The basic social unit for the Hurons was the household, but a number of matrilineally related households formed a longhouse, which was the key unit of production and consumption. Residence in the longhouse was matrilocal, meaning that a married couple lived in the longhouse of the wife's family. Children received their clan membership through their mother, not their father. The members of a longhouse cooperated in horticulture, hunting, and fishing, and

Myths & Facts

About Gender Inequality

Myth:
Women have taken their place in the workforce with men, holding more varied jobs and earning higher pay relative to men than ever before.

Fact:
More women work, but their pay still lags significantly behind that of men doing the same work. This lag is true in virtually all industrial nations, with women in Japan earning about one half of what men do. Also, many low-paying, low-prestige jobs are still female ghettos in the United States; 97 percent of secretaries, 93 percent of receptionists, and 99 percent of dental hygienists are women.

Myth:
More women are seeking political office than ever before.

Fact:
Women, who make up 51 percent of the U.S. population, held about 16 percent of the seats in the Senate and 17 percent of those in the House of Representatives in 2007. Women do well in Cuba and Finland, where they hold one-third of the parliamentary seats, but in some African and Arab nations, there are no women in the legislature.

Myth:
Modernized divorce laws enable women to leave bad marriages and receive alimony and child support from their ex-husbands.

Fact:
In the United States, women who have children and who divorce suffer a serious decline in their standard of living, whereas men who divorce actually experience an improvement in their standard of living.

Myth:
By the 1990s, the United States was solidly supportive of equal rights for women.

Fact:
The Equal Rights Amendment to the Constitution, which would prohibit discrimination on the basis of gender, has yet to be approved.

Myth:
The courts have ruled that barring women from service and community organizations such as Rotary and the Kiwanis violates antidiscrimination laws. Thus, women now have the same access as men to community and business arenas.

Fact:
Women have the same access in communities that have antidiscrimination laws. In the thousands of communities where there are no such laws, however, women can be and are excluded from such organizations.

the product of their labors was distributed to all members of the longhouse according to certain norms.

By today's standards, Huron women were fairly powerful and independent, and their experience suggests how gender relations are shaped by the social structure, in this case by the matrilineal organization of kinship (Anderson, 1991). Clan leaders were male, but they were appointed by the women in the clan and held their position only as long as clan members thought they were doing an adequate job. The Hurons viewed marriage as a working partnership between a man and a woman rather than as the domination of one person by the other. If anything, given the matrilineal nature of Huron society, men were especially susceptible to the influence of their wife and their mother-in-law, who was the power in the longhouse.

Women held power, in part, because they could expel men from their longhouse. Although marriage was an important institution for the Hurons, they took on partners and divorced them much more casually than people do in the United States, especially before having children. One reason was that, although both men and women made important contributions to subsistence, the kinship structure was such that neither husband nor wife was dependent on the other for necessary foodstuffs. For example, although the men had responsibility for hunting and trading, women were not dependent on their husbands for meat and trade goods because norms called for other men in the women's clan to provide them. Also, since the Hurons were matrilocal, most men lived in their wife's longhouse and were dependent on the wife's family for some food and other daily needs. Actually, men often went back to their mother's longhouse, especially before the couple had a child. This custom gave Huron marriages a seemingly casual air to European explorers. Women's position in Huron society was also strengthened by the fact that men were absent hunting during the summer months, and the women in a longhouse, all of whom were kin and in the same clan, produced almost all the food.

The Hurons had rather open attitudes toward sexuality; premarital sex was widespread. In fact, unmarried couples often set up households, and the woman in such a relationship was called *asqua,* or "companion," rather than *atenoha,* or "wife." While in these relationships, each partner might take on other lovers, and these new relationships did not necessarily end if the couple married. The Hurons were also relatively free in expressing their feelings for others and acting on those feelings, a custom that included women reacting against men. Women often disagreed with and disputed the demands of men.

The early 1600s brought French explorers to the New World as a part of the capitalist expansion discussed in Chapters 6 and 7. Responding to growing merchant pressures for new markets and new sources of wealth, the French exploited the Western Hemisphere for fur, fish, agricultural products, and other natural resources. The Hurons came into direct contact with French explorers in 1609 and with French Jesuit missionaries in 1632 (Leacock, 1980). The Jesuits considered the Indians to be pagans who consorted with the devil, and they began what they believed was an apocalyptic battle of good against evil. Because they thought the Hurons' souls were at stake, the Jesuits would go to any lengths to convert the Hurons to Christianity. The Hurons were about to be irrevocably changed.

At the time, many Europeans held the widespread Christian conception that women were bad—evil temptresses, allies of the devil, harbingers of chaos—if they were not controlled. Holding this view, the Jesuits were horrified by what they saw among the Hurons. There was simply too much personal and sexual freedom. The Jesuits viewed the Huron women as wild, ill-mannered, and dangerously lewd because they refused to obey their husbands and fathers and to engage only in discrete, marital sexuality as the Jesuits knew was proper and holy. Some Huron married women even refused to convert to Christianity because it required lifetime fidelity to their husband, which they didn't feel they could promise. All this freedom and independence clashed with the seventeenth-century French view that social order could be based only on power, loyalty, submission, and fear. In the Jesuit idea of society, people submitted to the authority of God, and women submitted to the authority of their husbands—and the Jesuits set about to reproduce this version of reality among the Hurons.

To this end, they preached to the Hurons and coerced them into accepting the Christian view that sexuality outside marriage was evil. They frightened the women into viewing their sexuality as dangerous, something to be controlled. They also encouraged women to accept a subordinate position and submit to the authority of both the church and their husbands. Warfare with the Iroquois and epidemic diseases brought in by the Europeans decimated the Huron population, dropping their numbers by more than half in a few decades. This decline made them much more dependent on the Jesuits and the French. As the Hurons settled around French communities, the longhouse declined as the center of Huron life. Matrilineal control of the longhouse had been the foundation of women's authority and independence among the Hurons, and as the longhouse disappeared, women lost this institutional support. In a relatively short period of time, the French Jesuits, warfare, and disease combined to change the egalitarian gender relations of the Huron into relations of male dominance and female subordination.

This brief look at the Hurons suggests some of the variations in gender relations across societies—from relative equality among the Hurons to the substantial inequality among Europeans at the time. It also shows how sociologists look at social and institutional structures, such as family and kinship, to explain gender relations. For sociologists, gender inequality is another dimension of the system of social stratification analyzed in Chapters 6 and 7. Like race and ethnic identity, gender is an ascribed status that can serve as a basis for allocating valued resources and creating social inequality. In fact, in some societies, sexual stratification is so entrenched and irrevocable that it can be considered a form of caste stratification. Gender inequalities are typically justified by sexism, *an ideology based on the belief that one sex is inherently superior to and should dominate the other sex.* This chapter discusses the reasons why gender inequality occurs, its extent in the United States and around the world, and ways in which it may be changing.

Men and Women in Society

You should be able to describe the extent to which gender differences in behavior are due to biological factors and analyze why gender differences exist according to the three sociological perspectives.

Unlike achieved statuses (such as one's educational level or occupation), there is little, if anything, that people can do to alter their ascribed statuses, such as gender. Gender is also a *master status* because it has considerable social significance in all societies. It is a central determinant of how people view themselves and how others respond to them, and it frequently serves as a basis for social differentiation. In some societies discrimination based on gender is so irrevocable that women have virtually no chance to improve their status. To understand how and why gender shapes the structure of society, it is helpful to understand why gender is an element of social differentiation in societies at all. This chapter examines four different views on this issue.

The Biological Perspective

One perspective on the role of gender in determining one's position in society is that innate biological differences between men and women shape the contributions each can make to society. One question this raises, of

course, is, What precisely are the differences between the sexes? Modern research has documented some distinctions and shown that allegations of other differences are not supported by the available evidence. For example, evidence exists that men are more aggressive and violent and have greater upper-body strength than women. Men also seem to excel in visual-spatial abilities, whereas women do particularly well in verbal skills and creativity. As far as personality characteristics such as sociability, emotionality, dependence, or self-esteem, there is no consistent evidence that the genders differ. Are the differences found in research caused by biology? In only a few realms is there any evidence that they are (Fausto-Sterling, 1992; McCoy, 1985). Higher levels of aggressiveness in males, for example, are common in other species, such as rhesus monkeys, and the trait is almost universal in human cultures. Levels of aggressiveness can also be affected by changes in sex hormones. Thus, there is the suggestion, but by no means conclusive proof, that higher levels of aggressiveness in males are in part biological. In terms of the differences in verbal and spatial-visual ability, some evidence suggests that the brains of males and females are organized differently in this regard. In men, verbal skills are focused on one side of the brain and the spatial-visual skills on the other. In women, each skill can be found on both sides of the brain. This difference in the organization of the brain may account for why women tend to have more verbal skills and men are more adept at spatial-visual tasks. The greater upper-body strength of men is probably attributable to the higher levels of the hormone testosterone among males.

So there undoubtedly are some biological differences between men and women that have implications for social behavior. However, the differences are far fewer and much smaller than was once thought to be the case. Furthermore, the differences appear to relate to general tendencies, such as aggressiveness, rather than to specific social behaviors, such as fighting or playing football. In addition, despite any biological differences, men and women are highly flexible and extremely malleable in terms of what they are capable of doing. Most of our behavior is learned rather than biologically programmed, which means that men can learn to behave in a stereotypically female fashion, and women can learn to behave in ways that we would expect men to behave (Tavris, 1992). A final point is that the differences between men and women refer to average levels of performance, which ignores the significant overlap between the genders. Many women, for example, are more aggressive than some men, and some men are less aggressive than many women. Because of this overlap, gender status alone is a rather poor basis for establishing social policy or allocating social tasks and rewards.

The Functionalist Perspective

Functionalists argue that some tasks were allocated to men and others to women in preindustrial societies because such arrangements were more convenient and practical (Ford, 1970; Giele, 1978). On the whole, males are physically stronger than women and free of the responsibility of bearing and nursing children. Women, by contrast, were expected to spend much of their adult life either pregnant or rearing their children. In addition, women were a more valuable reproductive resource in that the loss of a woman, as in war, would reduce the reproductive potential of society. The loss of a man, by contrast, could easily be made up for through increased sexual activity on the part of other men. There would be no loss in the over-all reproductive potential of society. Given these considerations, functionalists argue, it was more practical in preindustrial societies to assign to men tasks, such as hunting or felling trees, that were physically demanding and might draw them away from home for long periods of time. Men were also assigned the dangerous tasks, such as protecting the group against attack from enemies. Women, who were limited by pregnancy and the need to nurse their young, were considered better suited to such tasks as gathering roots or berries, cooking food, and making pottery. Once these gender-role distinctions had become firmly established as a part of a group's tradition, they were then supported by strong group norms that made these differences independent of their origins. They came to be seen as the natural ways for men and women to behave rather than as practical means of accomplishing societal tasks (Brown, 1970; O'Kelly & Carney, 1986).

Industrialization ushered in a number of significant social changes: the separation of work from family life, smaller families, and a longer life expectancy. As a consequence, women tended to be isolated in the family and given prime responsibility for homemaking and child-rearing duties, whereas men went out and worked. Gender roles became divided on the basis of instrumental and expressive roles (see Chapter 4). *Instrumental tasks* such as hunting, building, or managing a work team were seen as male tasks, whereas *expressive tasks* such as maintaining harmony and emotional stability were seen as primarily a woman's responsibility. In fact, for men, it became a status symbol to have a wife who did not

Women were allowed to hold many traditionally male jobs during World War II when the men were unavailable, but the women were forced out of the jobs when the men returned after the war—a clear reflection of gender dominance and inequality, according to the conflict perspective.

work—an indication of how capable the man was at producing economically and supporting his family. To justify this division of tasks, sexist beliefs emerged that a woman's place was in the home and that women were not biologically equipped for most forms of male work. However, in most preindustrial societies, women were not removed from economically productive roles. Much of what they did, such as gathering roots, tending crops, or herding flocks, contributed significantly to the economic support of the group. They were by no means limited to child rearing or expressive tasks. Likewise, men were by no means limited to instrumental tasks in preindustrial societies (Murdock, 1934).

From the functionalist perspective, a gender-role division of labor that is no longer consistent with the needs of a particular society could be dysfunctional. To confine women to child rearing or to expressive activities would waste a valuable resource. In industrial societies, families have few children, and they have many supports, such as day care, to help in raising them. So it is no longer necessary for adults—either male or female—to devote their lives to such tasks. It would be better if they used their intellectual, creative, and productive abilities to make additional contributions to society. Because the birthrate is low and most jobs in industrial societies are not dangerous, there is no need to protect women as a reproductive resource, as was done in the past. In addition, great physical strength is no longer necessary for most jobs in a highly automated, technological society. For all of these reasons, functionalists argue, it is not particularly useful to use gender as a criterion for allocating jobs today. It would be more functional to assign tasks based on individual abilities.

The Conflict Perspective

Many sociologists have questioned whether the fact of a woman having children is the central element in shaping gender roles in society and especially whether it explains the continued existence of gender stratification. For example, the sociologist Randall Collins (1971) has argued that there is an inherent conflict of interest between men and women and that gender roles can serve as a mechanism by which one group dominates the other. In part, this domination results because males in general are physically stronger than women, which better equips them to use power to their own advantage and gain dominance. But the situation is more complex than this. Through the socialization process, a subtler form of power is exerted and control achieved: People learn to want those things that are in the interests of the dominant group in society. In most societies, women have learned to accept the dominance of males and their

own subordinate positions because they believe such dominance is appropriate and even desirable or because they feel they have no other choice.

The economic competition discussed in Chapter 7 also contributes to gender inequality. In simple hunting-and-gathering societies, there is a division of labor based on gender, as we have seen, but there is also considerable equality between men and women. The reason is that women produce as much as and sometimes more than men. Gathering nuts, roots, and berries produces a steady and dependable food supply, whereas the results of hunting can be sporadic. It might be days or weeks before men can fell some game. In the interim, women provide food for the group. In agricultural societies, men tend to dominate economic productivity, in part because their physical strength and freedom from childbearing duties enable them to engage in extensive, heavy labor that might take them away from home for hours or days at a time. This situation leaves women economically subordinate and unequal. As functionalists point out, this inequality continues into early industrial societies as men work and women stay home. This arrangement benefits men, of course, because they have a corner on the prestigious and powerful positions in society, and most men wish to continue those social practices.

The dominance of men continued well into the twentieth century in the United States. During World War II, for example, large numbers of women joined the workforce, replacing men serving in the military and showing that women were capable of performing many traditionally male jobs (Van Horn, 1988). Most people assumed that these women were housewives who had no financial need to work but who were doing their part for the war effort and who wanted to return to their traditional roles after the war. In fact, government and industry mounted a propaganda effort to encourage the public to accept this view. Reality for many of these working women, individually dubbed "Rosie the Riveter," was quite different: Many of them were married and needed those well-paying, previously all-male jobs to support their families. Some were single parents or single women for whom these jobs were their sole source of economic support. Despite the fact that these women had shown themselves to be capable of performing well in traditionally male jobs, there was a backlash against them when the war ended and returning servicemen competed with the women for jobs. Many people felt that the women had done their duty and now should return to their homes and families ("where they belonged") and make jobs available for returning servicemen. Public pressure and job discrimination resulted in most of these women leaving the traditionally male jobs (Honey, 1984). From the conflict perspective, then, gender differentiation becomes the battleground for a struggle over scarce resources—in this case, for jobs and prestige. However, this economic competition for jobs—a form of the split labor market discussed in Chapter 7 because women are typically paid less than men—was translated into the sexist ideology that women were incapable of performing the jobs as well as the men.

The Interactionist Perspective

According to the interactionist perspective, human beings relate to one another on the basis of symbols that have social meaning within a given culture or society. Those social meanings are created, communicated, and reinforced as people interact with one another on a daily basis. So we can understand a lot about the creation and maintenance of gender inequality if we watch how men and women interact in various settings. It is through those interactions that the place of men and women in society is defined. Probably the most important symbol system for human beings is language. Interactionists point out that many values, beliefs, and social meanings find expression in different language forms, and an analysis of some of these forms suggests a continuing gender bias in many languages, including English. For example, the gender-specific pronouns *he* and *his* can be used when referring to both men and women, and this convention in English may be a veiled way of maintaining male dominance. Research suggests that such sexist language is still very much with us and shows conclusively that use of the generic *he* does create predominantly male images in people's minds, especially for men (Gastil, 1990; Switzer, 1990). When people read or hear *he,* instead of *she* or *they,* they think of men, and this tendency can serve as symbolic reinforcement of the exclusion of women from many aspects of society. This linguistic usage, then, may reinforce and help perpetuate sexist thought and action, especially among men, by encouraging a predominantly male imagery when thinking about activities or realms of which both men and women might be a part.

The conversational styles of men and women can also reflect and reinforce gender patterns of dominance and subordination (Spencer & Drass, 1989; Tannen, 1994a). Such styles, for example, can have direct implications for gaining and keeping positions of leadership in groups. One investigation focused on the order in which people speak in mixed-sex groups (Aries, 1996). In general, men initiate more conversation and receive more interaction than women. People who initiate the most interaction in groups take up the most time and are considered by others in the group to be leaders. So if women are taught to be submissive or timid around men, they may be less likely or less able to assume

leadership in groups. As another example of the effect of conversational style, it is widely believed in the United States that women talk more than men (the stereotype has it that women "chatter on" about frivolous subjects). Yet, many investigations of conversational behavior in mixed groups show that men talk more than women and interrupt while others are talking more than women do. Men also answer questions not addressed to them and continue talking when there is an overlap in conversation. The impact of these different patterns of conversation on gender inequality is quite direct:

> The beliefs that women talk too much and talk about insignificant subjects function to keep women quieter than they might be and to allow men to monopolize social conversations and work groups. The expectation that whatever a woman says is trivial and unimportant creates insecurity, timidity in presenting ideas, and lower feelings of self esteem . . . . The lack of authority attached to female speech patterns lowers a woman's chances for success in many fields. (Kirsh, 1983, pp. 74–75)

So it is through interaction patterns such as these that beliefs and practices regarding gender inequality are maintained and reinforced in everyday life. Although the sociological perspectives differ on a number of issues relating to gender stratification, they would all concur with Lenski's view (see Chapter 6) that most societies could function well with much less stratification based on gender than there is, especially industrial societies.

The Socialization of Men and Women

You should be able to describe the role of the family, the schools, and the media and the electronic world in teaching people about gender.

Scientific research has demonstrated that much of our behavior as males and females is not a function of biology but rather of learning. This finding leads to the distinction that sociologists make between *sex* and *gender*. *Male* and *female* are used as sex-related terms—the innate, biological feature of sexual identity. Sex refers to *the biological role that each of us plays, such as in reproduction. Masculine* and *feminine,* by contrast, are used as gender-specific terms. Gender refers to *learned behavior involving how we are expected to act as males and females in society.* One of the key issues in analyzing gender inequality is how we learn to be masculine and feminine and how this learning contributes to gender differentiation and inequality. This learning occurs in good part through the socialization process, with three major agencies of socialization in industrial societies involved: the family, the schools, and the media and the electronic world.

The Family

Infancy represents the most crucial period for human development because patterns of personality and behavior are established during these years. These early years are also extremely important in the establishment of beliefs about appropriate masculine and feminine behavior. There is a growing body of literature that clearly demonstrates how parents are likely to treat male and female infants and young children in ways consistent with how they view masculinity and femininity. For example, fathers are typically "rougher" with boys and more gentle with girls, and both mothers and fathers tend to speak more softly to girls than to boys (MacDonald & Parke, 1986; Rossi, 1984).

By the age of three, children have acquired a gender identity, which means that they can correctly label themselves as male or female. But at this point, their identity is oversimplified and highly stereotyped. It is also based more on such things as hairstyle or dress than on an accurate awareness of genital differences between the sexes. Once the child's gender identity has been established, he or she then attempts to master the behaviors that are associated with that gender. Behaving "like a boy" or "like a girl" becomes rewarding because it brings approval from adults and peers. Parents still today tend to encourage boys to engage in instrumental play, such as building something, whereas girls are encouraged toward expressive play, such as "dressing up."

Even in childhood, it appears that male activities are valued more than female ones. For example, girls often display a fondness for the higher prestige of the masculine role by becoming tomboys (Burn, O'Neil, & Nederend, 1996; Martin, 1990). Tomboyism is acceptable to a much greater extent than a little boy's being a "sissy." In fact, girls are more prominent in boys' games than boys are in girls' games—testimony to the less-negative reactions to tomboys than to "sissies." Other investigators have discovered that boys play more competitive games than girls and that girls typically do not learn how to deal with direct competition (Berliner, 1988; Best, 1983). Children learn from their family experiences what it means to be male and female, and these experiences are extremely strong influences.

Research shows that parents today interact with their children differently from parents of a few decades ago. Parents today are more aware of the negative consequences of gender stereotyping, and they make greater efforts to treat all their offspring alike, regardless of gender. Yet, gender and traditional cultural ways of relating to males and females are powerful forces, and parents still relate to their male and female offspring differently. This statement is true even of parents who consider themselves egalitarian in terms of gender relations (Weisner, Garnier, & Loucky, 1994).

The Schools

A significant part of the socialization process occurs in the schools. School systems are characteristically staffed in such a way that children's perceptions of masculinity and femininity are reinforced. For example, although most elementary schoolteachers are female, most elementary school principals are male. Thus, from the beginning of school, children see men in positions of authority and dominance over women (Benokraitis & Feagin, 1995; Richmond-Abbott, 1992). In addition, schools and teachers treat children very differently based on their gender, with significant consequences for what children learn about gender (Best, 1983; Thorne, 1993). Investigations have shown that female teachers are more likely to encourage independence and assertion in boys than in girls. Teachers also tend to view girls as less creative than boys, to provide less attention to girls, and to reward female students for conforming and male students for being aggressive. The way teachers do so is quite subtle. Dependence in girls, for example, is encouraged by not sending them off to work on their own, although boys often work alone. As for aggressiveness, boys often have to misbehave to gain their teacher's attention, whereas girls who are quiet and demure are more likely to receive attention from the teacher. So teachers, often without realizing it, reward their students for behaving in a fashion consistent with their own gender-role stereotypes.

Two or more decades ago, the images of males and females presented in school textbooks typically reinforced traditional stereotypes: Males were pictured far more often than females, males were pictured in many occupations and women in few, and female pronouns such as *her* were uncommon. But have there not been changes in this situation in the past twenty years? Not as much as one might think. Things have improved, especially when efforts are made to produce materials that are nonsexist in their presentation. However, some stereotyping still persists. Studies of children's picture books, for example, find that women are portrayed more frequently than in the past but still less often than men, women are less likely to be portrayed as working outside the home, women are still shown in fewer occupations than men, and women are portrayed as less brave and adventurous and more helpless (Clark, Lennon, & Morris, 1993; Crabb & Bielawski, 1994; Peterson & Lach, 1990; Purcell & Stewart, 1990). Furthermore, although men are sometimes portrayed as expressing their emotions, denying one's feelings is still characterized in these books as a normal aspect of maleness.

Even college textbooks are not immune to these influences. Studies of the pictorial content of textbooks for college-level psychology and sociology courses found that women are shown less often than men and are portrayed more passively and negatively (Ferree & Hall, 1990; Peterson & Kroner, 1992). For example,

Sociology of Media and Technology

Shaping Gender Identity

Modern media and communications technologies have become extremely important in socialization and in shaping gender identities. The traditional media of television, movies, and music enable children and youth to view role models such as sports figures, movie stars, or cartoon characters. Television, in particular, allows children to observe a wide range of occupations, such as those of waitress, taxi driver, or police officer, and to gain some sense of what tasks and duties are associated with them. In spite of the fact that much of what children see on television and in the movies is distorted and unrealistic, it is one of their major sources of information about culture and social structure in the United States, and this observation is true in regard to gender as well as in other realms. Research has shown these media to be powerful influences on how young people view themselves. Despite changes over the years, these media still often portray stereotyped gender roles. Investigations reveal that television programs present a grossly distorted view of family life, with the majority of male roles portrayed in prime time reflecting the images of unmarried men who are "tough" and "cool." Over the last three decades, only 20 percent of the characters on prime time television shows were female, and most of the women shown were young, unemployed, family-bound, or in comic roles (Richmond-Abbott, 1992). Despite improvements, studies continue to document that only one out of three roles in prime time are played by women, and that anchors, newsmakers, and authorities on television news shows are overwhelmingly white men (Howard, 2002; Smith, 1997). Women are more likely to be shown as preoccupied with romance, dating, and personal appearance rather than with work or education. The portrayal of women in children's shows was even more lopsided, according to the reports.

So, some of the old stereotypes linger, and evidence shows that they affect youngsters' attitudes: Children tend to model what they see on television, and they identify with same-sex characters (Lindsey, 2005). The boys are attending to the strong and virile male characters while girls respond to the beautiful female portrayals. In addition, the teenagers most strongly affected by gender-role portrayals on television are those with the least sexist attitudes to begin with: fairly intelligent girls; they show the most change toward sexist attitudes.

Music is also a powerful medium for communicating about gender, and much of what has been said about portrayals of gender in other media formats is true for music (Lindsey, 2005). While one can find practically any message—including strongly egalitarian and feminist ones—in some musical formats, the predominant portrayals tend to be of men who are dominant, strong, and aggressive and women who are young, physically attractive, and sexually alluring. The images that predominate are those of the sexual temptress, the virginal girl-next-door, and the subordinate woman whose fulfillment is dependent on the actions of a man. Portrayals of the assertive, independent woman are far less common. Heavy metal, rap, hip-hop, and rock videos also often combine sexual images with images of male aggression and violence, sometimes perpetrated against women (Barongan & Hall, 1995; Smitherman, 1997; Sommers-Flanagan, Sommers-Flanagan, & Davis, 1993). Similar images predominate in video games: male conquest and males protecting fragile and dependent women (Gilmore & Crissman, 1997). The little research there is on the impact of exposure to such images suggests that it does reinforce traditional sex-role stereotypes, promote attitudes of indifference toward violence against women, and might actually promote such violence.

The Internet and the cyberworld have vastly expanded the possibilities for young people in the realm of gender identity. The technology creates the opportunity for young people to search for and come in contact with a vast array of groups and subcultures that can provide information and support for various kinds of gender identities. The easy searching capabilities of the Internet make it easy to find, and even join, groups that support traditional versions of gender identity or that promote more egalitarian gender relations. And, of course, one can find groups that promote male dominance, female dominance, gay and lesbian identities, transgender identities, and others. Social networking sites, such as MySpace and Facebook, also promote such online explorations. This technology is much more interactive than the traditional media technologies of television, movies, and music. Young people are freer to pick and choose that which they find acceptable—and to shape the gender images available in this medium by what they upload to a social networking site or by creating their own Web site. Sociologically, these possibilities are important because they put young people in more control over the whole process of shaping gender identity. Conversely, it means that traditional sources of such identity shaping, such as parents or schools or religious leaders, have less control over the process. Of course, such freedom and exploration does not necessarily promote positive outcomes since some young people will inevitably become immersed in online subcultures that promote negative and degrading identities.

the psychology books portray women as the victims of mental disorders and the clients in therapy, whereas men are pictured as the therapists. All these portrayals help to perpetuate the cultural stereotype that men tend to be stronger, more active, and working in the world to solve problems, whereas women are more likely to be weaker, more passive, and focusing their interests around home and family.

Because young schoolchildren are at a formative and impressionable stage in life, the impact that these school experiences have on them is substantial and long-lasting. Evidence shows that sexist treatment in the schools results in lower self-esteem for female grade school and high school students (Martinez & Dukes, 1991; Sadker & Sadker, 1994).

The Media and the Electronic World

Although socialization is not a manifest function of the media and modern communications technologies, Chapter 3 describes how socialization has become one of their important latent functions. Television, movies, music, and the electronic world have become pervasive socializers, especially for young children. In the process, they have diluted the role of the family and the schools by competing with both for children's time and attention. The Sociology of Media and Technology insert explores some of the ways in which modern media technology performs this function.

The Extent of Gender Inequality in the United States

You should be able to describe the extent to which women and men suffer discrimination in economic and other realms because of their gender.

Although women are a numerical majority in U.S. society, they comprise a minority group, and there are a number of important similarities between women and other minorities (see Chapter 7). Like African Americans, women still have unequal access to valued resources and suffer discrimination on many fronts. Although this chapter focuses primarily on the way in which women suffer from gender inequality, it also looks at some ways in which men have been discriminated against by unreasonable differentiation based on gender.

Economic Discrimination

Women occupy a subordinate position in comparison to men on virtually every dimension of socioeconomic status (SES). The three main dimensions of SES are education, occupation, and income.

EDUCATION   Today, a college education is especially important in gaining prestigious and powerful positions in society, but higher education has never been equally available to all. Until about 1850, women were almost completely excluded from colleges. It was assumed that women needed less education because their careers would be as homemakers and mothers. In fact, in 1873, the U.S. Supreme Court ruled that an Illinois woman could be denied a license to practice law on the grounds that she was female. One Supreme Court justice of the era defended this stance by saying that "the paramount mission and destiny of women are to fill the noble and benign offices of wife and mother. This is the law of the Creator" ("The Brethren's First Sister," 1981, p. 17).

Since 1950, the number of people in the United States twenty-five years of age or older with some college training has quadrupled, and there have been dramatic increases in the proportion of women who pursue some form of advanced education. The percentage of doctoral degrees going to women has grown from 14 percent in 1971 to 49 percent today, and 49 percent of law degrees go to women today, compared with only 5 percent in 1970 (U.S. Bureau of the Census, 2007, pp. 185, 188). Still, more men attain these degrees than do women, and as Figure 8.1 illustrates, the percentage of men who complete college still exceeds that of women, at least among Asian Americans and whites. Although women have gained on men in college graduation rates in the past forty years, a gap still exists.

Furthermore, a very substantial gender gap persists in particular educational fields, such as science, mathematics, computers, and engineering (U.S. Department of Education, 1997). Although young boys and girls have similar math and science proficiencies, differences begin to emerge in the early teen years: Girls show less interest in careers in these fields, less enjoyment in doing math, and by college age considerably less likelihood of majoring in math, science, engineering, and computer science. For example, only one out of five bachelor's degrees in engineering are awarded to women.

WORK AND THE WORKPLACE   While women constitute about 46 percent of the labor force in the United States, they are concentrated at the lower end of the status hierarchy. Table 8.1 illustrates that women tend to hold jobs such as secretary or receptionist, which provide relatively low income and prestige. The higher income and prestige occupations, such as physician or engineer, are held primarily by men. Evidence suggests that some of this difference, even today, is the result of

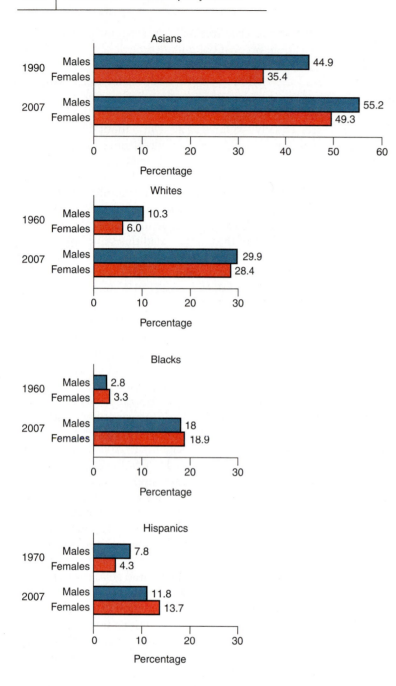

Figure 8.1

Percentage of People, Twenty-five Years Old or Older, Completing Four Years or More of College, by Gender and Race, 1960 and 2007

Note: From *Statistical Abstract of the United States, 2008* (p. 145) and Current Population Survey, *Educational Attainment in the United States: 2007,* www.census.gov/population/www/socdemo/ education/cps2007.html, both by the U.S. Bureau of the Census (Washington, DC: U.S. Government Printing Office).

discrimination in hiring practices. Some employers still prefer to hire men for jobs requiring technical or managerial skills based on the gender-role stereotype that men are more competent at such tasks. This is especially true when there is no evidence to suggest superior job performance on the part of either the male or female applicant for a job (DeLaat, 2007; Zebrowitz, Tenenbaum, & Goldstein, 1991). Table 8.1 illustrates that job opportunities for women have improved since the 1970s, with considerably more women moving into such lucrative jobs as lawyer, physician, or engineer. But the dark side of the issue is that many of the low-paying and low-prestige jobs are still almost exclusively filled by women. In addition, research shows that women who take traditionally male, blue-collar jobs encounter a hostile climate in terms of how they are treated by their male coworkers and supervisors. These women, as a result, are less satisfied with their jobs and experience more stress at work than do women in traditionally female jobs (Mansfield et al., 1991).

Even when educational opportunities are available to women, their chances for success in an occupation are often blocked by obstacles that men usually do not face, such as both overt and subtle forms of discrimination in hiring or promotion

Table 8-1

EMPLOYMENT POSITIONS HELD BY WOMEN, 1976–2007

Some Jobs Show Changes			Some Jobs Show Little Change		
	Percentage of Jobs Held by Women			Percentage of Jobs Held by Women	
Employment Positions	1976	2007	Employment Positions	1976	2007
Cashiers	87.7%	75.6%	Secretaries	99.0%	96.7%
Food counter clerks	85.5	64.5	Receptionists	96.2	93.0
Food service workers	68.7	56.4	Child-care workers	98.2	99.6
Real estate sales	41.2	55.4	Word processors and typists	96.7	89.6
Accountants and auditors	26.9	61.9	Bank tellers	91.9	87.5
Cleaning service workers	33.5	40.5	Bookkeepers	90.0	90.3
Financial managers	24.7	54.6	Health-service workers	86.2	89.3
College and university teachers	31.3	46.2	Hairdressers, cosmetologists	88.0	92.9
Lawyers and judges	9.2	32.6	Librarians	82.4	83.2
Physicians	12.8	30.0	File clerks	85.5	82.0
Police and detectives	3.7	13.7	Secondary schoolteachers	51.2	56.9
Civil engineers	1.8	11.5	Construction trades	1.6	2.7
Firefighters	0.0	5.3	Registered nurses	96.7	91.7

Note: From *Employment and Earnings*, 24(1), pp. 8–9, by U.S. Department of Labor, Bureau of Labor Statistics, 1977; *Employment and Earnings*, 55(1), pp. 212–219, by U.S. Department of Labor, Bureau of Labor Statistics, 2008.

practices (Raudenbush & Kasim, 1998). A number of government studies, for example, have found evidence that women are less likely to be promoted to management positions in industry (Glass Ceiling Commission, 1995; U.S. General Accounting Office, 2001). Although women make up 46 percent of the workforce, they constitute less than 5 percent of senior managers. In addition, the reports find evidence that the disparity is due to discrimination: Male senior managers refused to promote women and other minorities because they viewed such promotions as a direct threat to their own advancement.

Women in the legal profession also experience discrimination. Access to jobs in large law firms is one of the major routes to success in law. Yet, for many years, such firms closed their doors to women. While there has been an upsurge in the number of women lawyers since 1968—from less than 3 percent of the profession then to 32 percent today—women still make up only about 5 percent of the managing partners in large law firms, and recent research shows that female lawyers in the United States get paid less than male lawyers at every level of legal practice, are discriminated against in promotions in large law firms, find it much harder to become partners in large law firms than do men, and are less likely to become law professors than are men (Kay & Hagan, 1998; Rhode, 2001).

Another obstacle that women face in the occupational realm is that they tend to be saddled, more so than men, with familial obligations (Ferree, 1991; Lewin, 1998). Even when both spouses work, and even though men have taken on more responsibilities for these tasks in recent decades, women are still expected to take on more responsibility for raising the children, keeping up the home, and taking care of sick relatives. In fact, research shows that the cost of child care is an important reason why women sometimes quit the jobs they do get (Maume, 1991). Even among college-educated people, it is the rare couple who has a truly symmetrical relationship in which both partners share equally in household and work responsibilities.

INCOME Classical economic theory claims that wages are determined by the competitive forces of supply and demand. Employers are rational and pay workers what they are worth in terms of the employer's ability to produce goods and services for a price that consumers are willing to pay. In this view, discrimination in pay based on gender or other characteristics is irrational and thus will not persist in the long run. Many economists and much sociological research suggest that this is a simplistic view of the factors that influence the setting of wages (Blau, Ferber, & Winkler, 1998; Peterson, 1990). In addition to being affected by market forces,

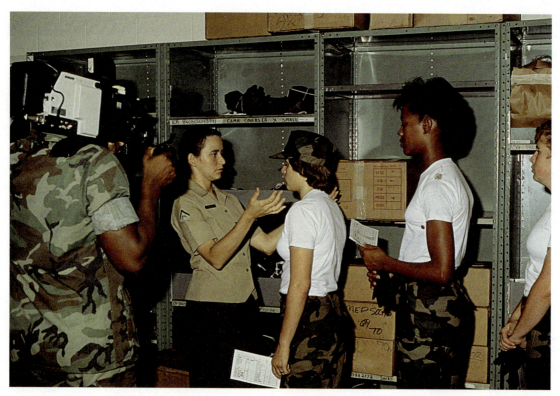

These women in training in the U.S. military illustrate the extent to which occupational opportunities for women in the military are now greater then ever, although still not identical with the opportunities for men.

income levels are also influenced by how much power different groups of workers possess and by cultural stereotypes of what different workers are worth as well as by the traditional levels of pay for different jobs. The effect of these "irrational" factors on women has been that they are paid considerably less than men.

In 2006, the median income for U.S. males working year-round and full-time was about $42,000; for females, it was only $32,000 (Figure 8.2). So, women's income is now about 77 percent of men's income among people who worked full time for the whole year. This shows some improvement—up from about 60 percent forty years ago. However, much of the improvement in this earnings ratio is due to declines in men's earnings rather than increases in women's earnings: Since the early 1970s, the median income of men has either stagnated or fallen. This gender inequality in income is found in virtually all industrial nations, with women in Sweden earning 81 percent of what men make and in Japan earning 44 percent of men's incomes (United Nations, 2006). This is a substantial difference. Even if we look at income levels of male and female workers in the same occupational categories who work year-round and full-time, women earn substantially less than men in every job category (Table 8.2). Some of these differences in income result

from the fact that some men have been working longer than women and thus have gained seniority and salary increases that have boosted their income. However, studies that have taken this factor into account still conclude that women have tended to earn less than men for doing the same job. A study by the U.S. Department of Education, for example, looked at the experiences of men and women who graduated from high school in 1972 and thus would be in the middle of their careers at the time of the study (Adelman, 1991). The study found that women on the whole did better in high school and college than men did, they finished college faster, and they had more positive attitudes toward their educational experience. However, by the midpoint in their careers, the women earned less than the men and were more likely to be unemployed. The study looked at comparable men and women, such as those who had no children and had been working equal lengths of time, but still found pay inequities: In only seven of the thirty-three occupations studied did pay equity between men and women occur. The other twenty-six occupations showed men making significantly more than women. No occupation showed women making more than men. Even among men and women in the same age brackets, income differences persist.

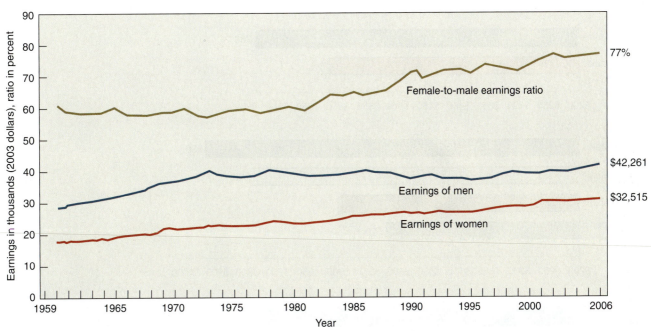

Figure 8.2

Median Earnings of Year-Round, Full-Time Workers by Sex, and Ratio of Female-to-Male Earnings, 1960–2006

Source: U.S. Bureau of the Census, *Current Population Reports*, Series P60-233, *Income, Poverty, and Health Insurance Coverage in States: 2006* (Washington, DC: U.S. Goverment Printing Office, 2007), p. 8.

Table 8.2

MEDIAN WEEKLY INCOME FOR YEAR-ROUND FULL-TIME WORKERS, BY GENDER AND OCCUPATIONAL CATEGORY, 2007

Occupational Group	Female Income	Male Income	Ratio Women/Men
Professional and related occupations	$835	$1148	0.73
Management and professional and related occupations	858	1187	0.72
Sales and related occupations	493	791	0.62
Service occupations	406	515	0.79
Office and administrative support occupations	570	619	0.92
Transportation and material moving	424	596	0.71
Construction and extraction occupations	573	648	0.88
Protective service occupations	588	754	0.78
Farming, forestry, and fishing	348	382	0.91

Source: Department of Labor, Bureau of Labor Statistics, *Employment and Earnings*, 55, no. 1 (January 2008), pp. 254–261.

Chapter 6 discussed the issues of the *feminization of poverty*, pointing to the fact that some women are especially vulnerable to falling below the poverty level. For example, 9 percent of all families in the United States live below the poverty level, but the rate among female-headed families is 29 percent. And things may actually be getting worse. In 1959, 23 percent of all families living in poverty were headed by women; this figure has grown to 50 percent (U.S. Bureau of the Census, 2004). As Figure 6.5 shows, children living in single-parent, female-headed families are especially likely to be living in poverty. About one out of six women over the age of 65 live below the poverty level—one out of four of those who live alone.

Chapter 7 discusses social inequality based on race and ethnicity. People in whom a subordinate

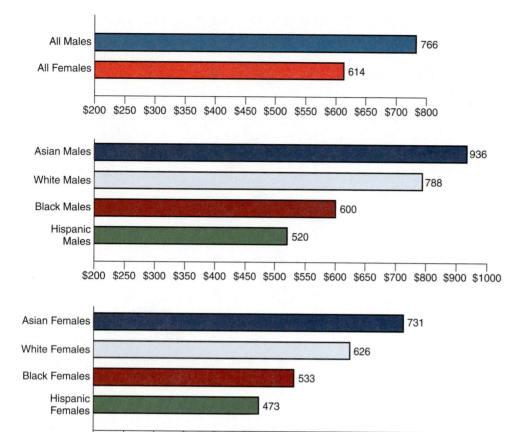

Figure 8.3

Median Weekly Earnings of Full-Time Workers, by Gender and Race, 2007

Note: From *Employment and Earnings, 55*(1), p. 252 by U.S. Department of Labor, Bureau of Labor Statistics, 2008.

racial or ethnic status is combined with a subordinate sexual status are even worse off than women in general (Figure 8.3). Sixty percent of elderly black women who live alone are living in poverty, and minority females who work earn less than do their male counterparts or white females, even among those working in management positions. Clearly, minority women in the United States are in a weak and vulnerable position when it comes to competing for economic resources.

Discrimination in the Military

Even women who choose the military as a career do not have the same opportunities as men. Although they constitute 14 percent of the armed services, they are currently barred from serving in many combat positions. In 1993, the Clinton administration opened some, but not all, combat positions to

women. This limitation is important because serving in combat positions is one of the best ways to advance one's career in the military. The limitations continue to exist despite the fact that, during the Gulf War of 1991 and the Iraq War of 2003, female soldiers found themselves in combat, performed well by all standards, and were killed in action and taken prisoner by enemy troops. In fact, in a poll taken in 2005, 72 percent of the U. S. public favors women serving with support troops in combat zones and 44 percent favor women serving with ground troops doing most of the fighting (Carlson, 2005). The major arguments against women in combat positions, especially ground infantry units, is that they do not have the physical strength or aggressive nature needed for the job, that they would disrupt the cohesiveness and bonding that occurs among men in combat and is important to combat success, and that it violates deep-seated cultural values regarding manhood and womanhood in Western civilization. Supporters of equal opportunities for women argue that women can be trained for the strength and aggressiveness and that they proved themselves in recent wars. Furthermore, there is no reason to believe that women could not bond in a military unit as well as men. The major stumbling block, according to this view, is that fighting and military combat are one of the last bastions where men can maintain a separate world into which women are not allowed. Of course, a major factor fueling the movement of women into the military over the past thirty years has been the needs of the military itself, which is ultimately concerned with finding a sufficient number of educated and motivated recruits. Along these lines, three factors are propelling the greater use of women: The all-volunteer military; the increasingly high-tech workplace, which calls for brains and dexterity more than brawn; and the increasing feminization of the workforce. Given these trends, the military may see that it is in its own interests to expand opportunities for women, maybe by opening up more combat positions to them in the future.

Other Types of Discrimination

Discrimination on the basis of gender is not confined to education, occupation, and income. There are various other ways in which women are placed at a disadvantage in the United States. For example, the legal system has built into it a great deal of discrimination against women. Until recently, many states did not consider it a crime for husbands to rape their wives. While all states today prohibit marital rape, 33 states still provide husbands with some loopholes to avoid prosecution for raping their wives (Bergen, 1999). Depending on the state, for example, a man cannot be charged with raping his wife if the wife is unable to consent to having sex because she is physically impaired, asleep, or unconscious. Only seventeen states accord wives the same protection as other women by treating marital rape like any other rape.

Women have also experienced discrimination in the realm of retirement income. Retirement plans have traditionally paid women a smaller monthly income than they pay to men with the same accumulated retirement assets. This inequality has been based on the fact that women live longer, on the average, than men. The rationale has been that women will draw the same total assets from their retirement plan as men, but they will draw it out in smaller amounts over a longer period. Women, of course, have complained that this penalizes them for being healthy. They have also argued that

there are many other criteria than gender that could be used to determine retirement income, such as genetic susceptibility to heart disease or behavioral factors such as smoking.

Gender Inequality Involving Males

Most discussions of gender inequality focus on women, but men also suffer from unreasonable gender differentiation. Some have even spoken of a *masculine mystique* and the *myth of masculinity*: a set of stereotypes about men, such as their being strong, dominant, tough, unemotional, and so forth (Kimmel, 1996). Socially imposed expectations concerning male behavior can be as limiting for men as the stereotypes involving females have been for women. In terms of professional careers, for example, male secretaries were often regarded as social oddities not long ago. Men who entered such unconventional male roles had to be prepared for incredulous and sometimes even abusive reactions from others. At that time, most men probably did not even consider a profession such as nurse or secretary, even at times when jobs for college graduates in nursing were plentiful and other jobs were scarce. Still, today, very few men go into nursing (see Chapter 10).

The stereotypical male role also limits the opportunities open to men in terms of domestic activities, emotional expression, and relationships with children. Not that many years ago, if a male executive were to ask his employer for paternity leave, his boss would probably have laughed. Today, leaves of absence for new fathers are becoming more common. At the same time, a form of institutionalized discrimination is still involved, because the man who takes such a leave often loses ground in the competition for advancement and seniority. Although few males identify themselves occupationally as *house husbands*, it is more common than it once was for men to accept equal responsibility with their partners for domestic tasks (Lewis, 1984; McCall, 1988). In fact, despite the cultural assumption that work is the chief activity for men, one investigation found that 90 percent of the male respondents to a survey expressed strong attachments to their roles as husbands and fathers and defined their marital and parental roles as the most important (Cohen, 1987).

Other forms of discrimination against men can be found. For example, some states have laws that make it a punishable offense for men (and presumably other women) to use obscene language in the presence of females. Many insurance companies charge higher automobile insurance premiums to young males because of the higher rate of automobile accidents among that group. Thus, a young man who is a careful driver is penalized by virtue of his gender. Finally, men but not women are required to register for the military draft, and only men could be inducted into the military should the draft itself be reinstated. Women are not required to make any equivalent contribution to national public service.

Gender Stratification in Global Perspective

You should be able to describe the patterns of gender inequality that are found in various nations around the world.

The general patterns of gender inequality found in the United States are reproduced in other societies around the globe, but there are important differences that help us understand some of the intricacies of gender stratification. The overall conclusion, as stated by the Secretary General of the United Nations, is that "the majority [of women] still lag far behind men in power, wealth and opportunity" (United Nations, 1991, p. v). Over the past few decades, a growing number of women have entered the workforce, but in some areas their share of the labor force is still quite small: In Saudi Arabia, Oman, and the United Arab Emirates, only one in seven workers is female (United Nations, 2006; World Bank, 2003). In some areas, like Thailand and Turkey, women actually lost a little ground since 1970, seeing their share of the labor force decline. Women are also the most affected by economic recession: They are hired later when jobs are expanding and are let go quicker when jobs contract. The women who work generally have the less prestigious and lowest-paying jobs, a situation that cuts across levels of development. In industrialized nations such as Japan and South Korea, women earn about one-half what men do, but this is also true in a less developed nation such as Malaysia. In Sweden, women earn 89 percent of what men do, compared to 77 percent in the United States.

In all parts of the world, the rate of illiteracy is higher among women than men, almost twice as high in Asia. Also, in most places women lag behind men in enrollment in high school and college, although in thirty-three countries more women enroll in higher education than men (including the United States and many nations in Asia, Latin America, and the Caribbean). In addition, around the world, women in educational occupations tend to be in the lower levels teaching primary school rather than the more prestigious and higher-paying postsecondary education.

Worldwide, women are poorly represented in political positions where important decisions are made (United Nations, 2006). Women make up fewer than 10 percent of all members of parliaments or congresses in the world. Women do fairly well in some countries: Finland, Norway, Costa Rica, and Cuba have one-third of their parliamentary seats filled by women; and Sweden's parliament is 45 percent female. Some African and Arab nations have no women in parliament, and Japan's Diet has less than 10 percent women. The United States does a little better with 16 percent, but it still lags significantly behind most advanced nations.

Increasingly, women have fewer supports to help them take care of their families. In the past few decades, the proportion of births to unmarried women has increased in many nations around the world, and in some cases the increase is dramatic. The proportion has doubled in the United States to 38 percent, but in nations as diverse as Denmark, Norway, and Guam it has increased three or four times. In the Seychelles, French Guiana, and Martinique, two out of every three births are to unmarried women. In addition, many households are headed by women: almost half in nations such as Botswana and Barbados. In the United States 30 percent of households are headed by women, but in Kuwait, Iran, Pakistan, and Burkina Faso it is 7 percent or less. Other Worlds, Other Ways: Mexico explores in detail the circumstances of poor women in less developed countries and the institutional forces that shape their lives.

Toward Gender Equality

You should be able to describe the movement for gender equality in the United States and around the world, including what advances and setbacks there have been.

Gender inequality is more widely recognized as unacceptable today than in the past. One of the reasons for this change has been the efforts made by women and men around the world to draw attention to the inequities and to change the social practices that support them. An assessment of the future of gender inequality can begin with a look at the worldwide feminist movement.

Collective Action and the Feminist Movement: A Global Struggle

The feminist movement, or women's movement, refers to *the collective activities of individuals, groups, and organizations whose goal is the fair and equal treatment of women and men around the world* (Tobias, 1997). This movement has not been limited to the United States or even to Western democracies. Certainly, the democratic, egalitarian, and individualist ideologies that emerged in Europe and the United States in the seventeenth and eighteenth centuries have been influential

Other Worlds, Other Ways

MEXICO: POOR WOMEN AND THE WORLD ECONOMY

The intersection of a number of forces brought many poor Mexican women into the world export economy in the past half century. One force was the so-called Green Revolution of the 1950s and 1960s, which was an effort to increase agricultural production through the use of higher-yielding plant varieties and improved crop management. For many crops in Mexico, it succeeded. The resulting greater potential for profits on the export markets attracted multinational agribusinesses, which expanded production and concentrated land in their hands. This development undermined the traditional peasant economy that had been based on small plots of land farmed by families. It turned many men into day laborers or migratory workers, mostly to the United States where they could earn much more than was possible in the local Mexican economy.

A second force affecting poor Mexican women was the traditional, patriarchal family culture in Mexico (Moghadam, 1996). This culture, especially prominent in rural areas, strictly emphasizes subservience and obedience to the father before marriage and the husband after marriage. Marriage, homemaking, and child rearing are the major aspirations and obligations for women. They are not expected or encouraged to achieve high levels of education nor to pursue well-paying or prestigious jobs that men normally hold.

The collision of the forces of world capitalism and traditional gender relations has resulted in the exploitation of poor women in Mexico by multinational corporations. Because of the scarcity of jobs, especially in rural areas, families consent to sending young, unmarried women out to work. Many of these women are still very much under the control of their fathers, who can pressure them to work and support the family. Especially in rural areas, young women are not completely free to leave their family against the dictates of their father because that would reflect negatively on their reputation and might reduce their opportunities to find an acceptable man to marry. So, patriarchy and gender conspire to make these women prisoners of the local economy. To help their families, they look for work as domestics or preferably in the fields or packing plants, which pay better (Arizpe & Aranda, 1981). The women work for very low wages; the work is often insecure because the plants may be closed for months at a time; and they receive few, if any, fringe benefits. The women are willing to work under these conditions because they hope to marry and thus view the work as a temporary interlude. In addition, little other work is available, and they need work desperately to support their families. The multinational corporations even send female recruiters into the community to convince the women that the work is desirable and to assure their families that the women will be safe and protected in the work environment.

Unions have found this female workforce difficult to organize. Part of the reason is that the Mexican government has historically been hostile to unions because multinationals threaten to go elsewhere if they perceive workers to be at all assertive in demanding better wages or working conditions. Some industries, such as growing strawberries, involve very little capital investment, so it is not much of a loss for such a business to close down in Mexico and move to another nation in response to demands for higher wages. However, the women conspire in ensuring their own weakness because their primary goal is marriage and they see the work as temporary and the unions as too much trouble or as costing them money.

Similar gender exploitation occurs in more urban areas, especially along the northern border with the United States (Cravey, 1998; Peña, 1997; Young, 1993). For at least thirty years, the Mexican government has made efforts to attract international export industries to this area. These factories, called *maquiladoras,* import unfinished products, which are then assembled into automobiles, washing machines, or other finished products for export. One of the major attractions for international corporations is a supply of cheap labor, mostly young unmarried women. The income and benefits in these plants vary, but generally they are not sufficient to support a family. Some *maquiladora* women are a part of households with multiple sources of income, and they survive by combining a number of income streams. Other women live in families where a male, such as a father or brother, is unemployed or underemployed, and these women may be the only source of income in the family. As in the agribusiness, women are sought for *maquiladora* work because, in the eyes of the business managers, they make better workers. These managers told one researcher that women are sought because they are more compliant and docile; they are also more willing to do monotonous, repetitive, and exhausting factory work; all these factors make them difficult for union leaders to organize. Men, by contrast, are seen by these factory managers as poor workers—restless and rebellious and less willing to work at monotonous or difficult jobs or under poor working conditions. This researcher spelled out the implications of this perception:

> The incorporation of women with acute economic needs into the *maquiladora* industry represents . . . the use of

the most vulnerable sector of the population to achieve greater productivity and larger profits. The employment of men to perform similar operations would imply higher wages, better working conditions, and more flexible work schedules, all of which would increase labor costs and reduce capitalist gains. (Fernandez-Kelly, 1983b, p. 219)

So, in both rural and urban settings in less developed nations, international corporations take advantage of patriarchy, traditional gender relations, and the dependency of women in order to maximize profits and exercise control over labor. ◼

in many parts of the world. Many nations, however, have used their own religious beliefs and traditions, combined with ideas from elsewhere, to justify gender equality. The Arab world, for example, was certainly influenced by European belief and example in the 1800s and early 1900s (Barakat, 1993; Hourani, 1991). Yet, there are many in the Arab world who argue that Islamic traditions themselves support the emancipation of women and that the substantial subordination of women in the Arab world is the result of a misinterpre-

tation of the Koran, the Islamic holy book. For instance, one of the pioneers of Arab feminism, Qassem Amin, published a book in 1899 titled *The Liberation of Women* that called for extending to women most of the same rights that men enjoyed. Anticolonialist movements in places such as Palestine, Egypt, and Iraq mobilized women in support of nationalist causes, and this effort produced a variety of women's organizations that have continued the struggle for gender equality (Najjar, 1992). In 1923, Arab feminists convened at a

Women continue to move into the workforce in large numbers, including into traditionally male jobs such as fire fighter, corrections officer, and police officer. As this happens, social mechanisms are emerging to overcome some of the barriers that women faced in the past.

women's conference in Rome, and in 1944 an Arab women's conference held in Cairo called for women to have the same marital rights as men, including the right to initiate divorce. Even such tradition-bound societies as China and Cuba have an active feminist movement, which has at times gained significant support from the Communist government (O'Kelly & Carney, 1986).

Stirrings of feminist activity could also be found in the United States in the 1800s when women such as Susan B. Anthony and Elizabeth Cady Stanton campaigned for women's right to vote. Finally, in 1920, the Nineteenth Amendment to the U.S. Constitution—the Women's Suffrage Amendment—was passed. In the late 1940s, fueled by women's work experience during World War II, women renewed the campaign for equal rights, but they were beaten back by the conservative champions of another movement: the "return to normalcy" (Deckhard, 1979). Women were pressured to quit jobs that they held while men had been at war and to return to the home so that the country could resume "normal" operation again.

In 1963, a well-known advocate of women's rights, Betty Friedan, wrote a book titled *The Feminine Mystique*. She took issue with the assumption that women belong in the home, and her argument became the classic indictment of the presumption that women function best as mothers and homemakers. In 1966, Friedan and other feminists organized the National Organization for Women (NOW). At the time, this body of activist women was regarded as radical in mission, but many observers feel that "its style was actually somewhat conservative, and it stressed working through established legislative channels to achieve rights for women" (Richmond-Abbott, 1992, p. 354).

NOW concentrated much effort on passage of the Equal Rights Amendment (ERA), a constitutional amendment that would have banned discrimination based on gender. The ERA stated very simply: "Equality of the rights under the law shall not be denied or abridged by the United States or by any State on account of sex." In 1982, the deadline for ratification passed on the ERA because an insufficient number of states were willing to endorse it. The ERA was viewed by many as the Emancipation Proclamation for women. Proponents of the ERA viewed its defeat as a significant setback for the women's rights movement, and it certainly suggests that sentiment still lingers in the United States against complete equality for women. But again, reality is probably more complex than this. Some people opposed the ERA because they believed that existing legislation protected women adequately and that the amendment was redundant, whereas others thought it would produce unisex bathrooms and sanction same-sex marriages. Some women opposed it because they did not want to give up special privileges that they do receive, such as preference in child custody and divorce award cases. So, people opposed the ERA for many reasons, some of them having little to do with resistance to equality for women (Richmond-Abbott, 1992).

In recent decades, feminists in the United States and around the world have created a global network to push for gender equality, often working through international organizations such as the United Nations (UN) or the independent nongovernmental organizations (NGOs) discussed in Chapter 13. The UN formed its Commission on the Status of Women in 1946 to monitor the treatment of women and promote women's rights in all nations (United Nations, 2001). There followed a series of steps to expand the arenas in which nations were to be encouraged to accord equal treatment to women. In 1952, for example, the Convention on the Political Rights of Women established the mandate that all women should have the right to vote, hold office, and exercise public functions. UN conventions or conferences on women's issues were held in Nairobi in 1985, Beijing in 1995, and New York in 2000. Each time, additional plans were established to encourage governments to extend more rights to women. Specifically targeted were efforts to encourage governments to ensure that women have equal rights in education, training, and employment; to attack negative stereotypes and perceptions of women; to encourage men and women to share domestic responsibilities; and to collect statistics to monitor the situation of women. Of course, not all member nations of the United Nations are strongly enthusiastic about the advancement of gender equality, but a host of women's NGOs have maintained pressure on the United Nations to encourage nations on these issues. The outcome of these pressures has been the achievement of important victories in the quest for gender equality in many nations, although much gender inequality still persists on a global scale.

Current Trends in the United States

In the United States, the push for gender equality has been fueled in part by the growing number of women in the workforce and the increasing number of single-parent, female-headed families. These women find gender discrimination to be an unacceptable barrier to their efforts to support their families and achieve other goals. This analysis of gender stratification closes with a brief assessment of prospects for gender equality in the United States in the near future.

CHANGES IN THE LAW   Over the past forty years, a significant amount of legislation has been approved that contributes to the reduction of gender inequality. Legislation prohibits discrimination in loan eligibility based on gender or marital status. Title VII of the 1964 Civil Rights Act makes illegal any gender discrimination in employment practices. Title IX of the Educational Amendments Act specifies that any educational institution discriminating on the basis of gender will be denied federal aid. Other examples of legislation that helps women are the Displaced Homemaker Act (which assists women who have divorced but have few skills with which to support themselves) and legal provisions for wives who have been abused by their husbands.

In the past few decades, a new idea for reducing the economic inequities suffered by women has emerged, called *comparable worth*. The basic idea is that people whose jobs make equivalent demands on them and that call for similar skills, education, or responsibility should receive roughly similar pay; in other words, "equal pay for comparable worth" (England, 1992; Levine, 2001). For example, a judge in Seattle ruled in 1983 that the state government was in violation of Title VII of the 1964 Civil Rights Act because it routinely paid jobs performed mostly by women less than those performed mostly by men. His ruling was based in part on a comparison of state jobs in terms of "worth points," with points given for such things as knowledge and skills required, mental demands, accountability, and working conditions. Since then, twenty-two states have begun to reassess their pay schedules with these ideas in mind. Similarly, in Ontario, which is one of Canada's largest provinces, the Ontario Pay Equity Act, covering 1.7 million workers in public and private settings, now demands adherence to the principle of comparable worth.

Comparable worth has been a highly controversial development, with opponents arguing that it is impossible really to compare the worth of different jobs and that the free market should determine what people are paid. These opponents argue that if women are dissatisfied with low pay in some jobs, they should compete for the higher-paying jobs. Some even suggest that such interference with market mechanisms would disrupt the whole economic system. Supporters argue that women face significant barriers in the competition for jobs and that comparable worth would help overcome generations of discrimination in the way salaries are set. So far, comparable worth has not substantially altered the position of women in the United States.

CHANGES IN THE WORKPLACE   Research has clearly documented that two factors have been, and will continue to be, vital to improving opportunities for women in the workplace. One factor is government regulations and programs of affirmative action that encourage employers to hire and promote women. The second factor is the increasing numbers of women in the workplace (Cohen, Broschak, & Haveman, 1998). As more women enter low-level jobs, they gain the skills and

get the opportunities to be promoted to higher-level positions; as more women enter higher-level positions where they participate in decisions about hiring and promotions, women's chances of being hired or promoted are substantially greater than when such decisions are made mostly by men.

However, the picture of women in the workplace is not one of unimpeded progress. In fact, as the number of women in the workforce has increased and as they have moved into more traditionally male occupations, some new issues have risen to prominence. For example, some research disputes the belief that sexism in the workplace has declined as more women are employed. Resistance to women declines at first, but as the proportion of women in the work setting passes 15 percent, renewed resistance emerges because men feel their opportunities are being reduced due to competition with women. Research has also found that when many women are employed in the same job, that job comes to be defined as a woman's job. Once this happens, the job tends to be devalued, with less pay and a smaller budget than when more men held that position (Baron & Newman, 1990; Maume, 1998).

Another emerging reality concerning women in executive management positions is that some who occupy these positions are "bailing out" of the managerial workforce because trying to combine full-time, demanding careers with being wives and mothers has proved too difficult. The rate of turnover in management positions is considerably higher among women than among men, and many women who take maternity leave do not return to work (Conlin, 2002). In addition, young women appear to be less drawn to high-powered business careers today than they were in the 1970s and 1980s. For example, female enrollment in university business programs is stuck at about 30 percent, despite substantial efforts to increase it. It seems that women today are less willing to make as many compromises in the family area as some young women did twenty years ago (Alsop, 2001; Stone, 2007).

To alleviate this tension between work and child rearing, many employers have established "family-friendly" policies, such as flextime or a "mommy" career track, that would enable men or women to pursue their careers as well as spend time with their families. One career track, for example, called career-primary, would involve the expectations traditionally placed on male employees: career comes first, no time out for personal reasons, and work on nights and weekends if corporate needs demand it. The second track, called career-and-family or the "mommy track," would allow employees to pursue careers while also devoting themselves to their families. For example, maternity leave would not be frowned on and excessive demands would not be placed on the worker's free time. Critics of such policies argue that those in the mommy track—whether women or men—are discriminated against in any event

Applying Sociology   Sexual Assault, Sexual Harassment, and the Empowerment of Women

One of the more recent exposés of the mistreatment of women in the military came out of the U.S. Air Force Academy in 2003. A few brave female cadets stepped forward with charges that female cadets at the academy routinely confront sexual harassment, sexual assault, and even rape at the hands of their fellow cadets. Applied sociologists work with these problems of harassment and assault in the workplace by conducting research to determine the extent and nature of the problem. For example, sociologist Melanie Martindale (1991) conducted such research for the secretary of defense. Her findings, showing disturbingly high levels of assault and rape, served as a foundation for policies to alleviate the problem.

Part of the difficulty with sexual harassment is achieving consensus about what behaviors constitute harassment. Applied sociologists recognize that this difficulty is in part a cultural conflict resting on the fact that men and women tend to attach different meanings to some behaviors. Most men and women agree that demanding sexual favors as a condition of employment or promotion is wrong. However, the Equal Employment Opportunity Commission also defines as harassment behaviors that create a "hostile" environment that makes it more difficult for people to do their job. Thus, repeated sexual advances by a coworker, even if not linked to employment or promotion, could constitute harassment because they are disturbing to the woman and create an environment in which it is difficult for her to work (Gregory, 2003).

This point is where men's and women's perceptions sometimes differ. Many men see such behaviors as relatively harmless and claim they would even be flattered if they were the recipients of such actions by coworkers. Most women, by contrast, find such behaviors insulting, offensive, and even frightening when an economically or socially vulnerable woman sees an implied threat in the advance. Therefore, such behaviors do create a hostile atmosphere in many women's minds. That is why we repeatedly hear women exclaim about men: they just don't get it. In other words, men fail to understand why women find such behaviors offensive, demeaning, and maybe even frightening.

With an understanding of social structure, social interaction, and cultural values and norms, applied sociologists can mediate conflicts of this sort, especially when a problem is created or aggravated by a lack of understanding on one side or the other (Miller, 1991). Mediation could be a lengthy process, but it basically involves exercises that give both men and women a better perspective on women's views of these issues. The exercises might be as simple as the following short test to help decide whether a remark or a behavior is appropriate (Petrocelli & Repa, 1992):

1. Would you say or do the same thing in front of your spouse?
2. How would you feel if the same remarks or behavior were directed at your mother, sister, wife, or daughter?
3. How would you feel if a man made the same remarks or took the same actions toward you?

If your reaction to any one of these questions is negative, then the remark or behavior might well be seen as inappropriate harassment by a female coworker.

Applied sociologists also recognize that gender socialization can make women vulnerable to assault and exploitation. As Janet Mancini Billson and Estelle Disch (1991, p. 327) put it:

> Women traditionally have been raised to value nurturance, kindness, patience, being "nice," not making waves, being attractive, supportive, caring, understanding, tolerant, and responsible to and for others. This socialization blueprint can make it difficult for women to be confrontive or demanding; to feel comfortable in choosing to take care of self first; or to be honest and forthright.

With this recognition in mind, sociological practitioners work toward the empowerment of women, assisting them in acquiring the personal and social resources that can make them more powerful and less vulnerable in their relations with others. Part of this process involves gaining the educational qualifications and occupational skills that make people less economically dependent on others. Women are less likely to be harassed if they are the boss rather than the subordinate. Another part of this empowerment is for women to learn to view themselves as autonomous, powerful, and directive. In other words, empowerment for women means breaking through the culture of dependency and taking control of their lives.

Finally, sociological consultants work with employers to change the structure of the work environment so that sexual harassment and assault are less likely. Among the structural changes that have proven effective are the following: having a written and publicized policy against such actions, vigorously enforcing the policy, educating employees about what constitutes harassment and how to file a complaint about it, and providing sincere and significant top-management support for the policy (Gregory, 2003). Such steps should make the workplace of the twenty-first century a much more hospitable one for women. However, as noted in Chapter 7, discrimination, as well as harassment, tends to rear its head when competition between groups grows fierce. As more women take jobs traditionally held by men, harassment may emerge as a response to threatened losses. So continued vigilance may be necessary to control this problem.

through smaller pay increases or reduced opportunity for promotion. In fact, research shows that women who interrupt their careers for family reasons never catch up, in terms of income or promotions, to their female counterparts who stay on the job (Dobrzynski, 1996; Jacobsen & Levin, 1992). Apparently, their employers think they are not as serious about or as committed to their jobs. So, the career-and-family track would likely produce the same old outcome: women who choose to have children would be discriminated against because they did not follow the male model of career development.

Despite this difficulty we can predict that women will continue to join the workforce in even larger numbers. Substantial improvement is already observable. One-quarter of all businesses in the United States today are owned by women, and some labor experts project that this figure may soon hit 40 percent (U.S. Department of Commerce, 2001). Keep in mind that these numbers do not include large corporations, where it is difficult to determine ownership, and that most women's businesses are small. Nonetheless, the growth has been impressive, and credit and capital are now more available to women who wish to start or expand a business. In addition, research shows that college-educated women are becoming much more like their male counterparts in terms of the emphasis they place on work as being essential to a person's life and happiness (Fiorentine, 1988).

As women become more integrated into the workforce, mechanisms are developing to overcome some of the barriers that women have faced in the past. For example, women are excluded from fewer of the social and business networks that can assist one in a career or business. Because of court challenges based on antidiscrimination legislation, women have gained access to some chapters of such organizations as Rotary, the Lions Club, and the Kiwanis where businesspeople often gather. And it makes a big difference to success in

business. As one businesswoman put it after she joined Rotary, "Suddenly I was having lunch every week with all the movers and shakers in town. Now they think of me when business opportunities come up" (quoted in Zane, 1991, p. 35). In addition, new networks have emerged to help women. For example, WomenVenture is a nationwide organization that offers seminars and workshops to women on how to start or expand a business, as well as financial backing to 2,500 businesswomen each year. Numerous Web sites on the Internet offer business advice and assistance to women. Such organizations and contacts can make the difference between advancement and stagnation in one's business or career. The opportunities for advancement for women in the 2000s will undoubtedly improve with the further availability of such supports for women. However, thousands of clubs and organizations still do not admit women because there are no state or local antidiscrimination laws to force them to do so.

Sexual harassment and assault are serious problems that women face in the workplace. As Applying Sociology: Sexual Assault, Sexual Harassment, and the Empowerment of Women (pp. 229) shows, some important strides have been made in overcoming this problem.

THE CHANGING FACE OF POLITICS   The stark reality is that, although women make up 51 percent of the populace, very few of them are among elected representatives at the national level. Of the 100 senators, the number of women among them fluctuated from a low of none to a high of 2 between 1970 and 1992, rising to 16 in the 2006 election (Figure 8.4). However, this rather modest change hides some dramatic gains that women have made in politics over the past few decades. In 1970 only 25 women ran for seats in the U.S. House of Representatives; by 2006, this number had increased almost six times, to 136 women. Although only 17 percent of the House of

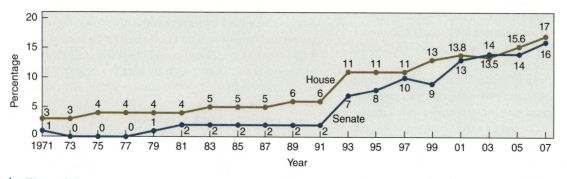

Figure 8.4

Women in the U.S. Senate and House of Representatives, as a Percentage of Each Body, 1971–2007

Note: From *Statistical Abstract of the United States, 1982–1983* (p. 485) by U.S. Bureau of the Census, 1982, Washington, DC: U.S. Government Printing Office; *Statistical Abstract of the United States, 2008* (p. 251) by U.S. Bureau of the Census, 2007, Washington, DC: U.S. Government Printing Office.

Sociology on the Internet

The Census Bureau Web site (**www.census.gov**) has much data available on women and their role in society. Use its alphabetical listing of subject categories to find the listings for women. From there, you can go to parts of the Census Web page that have information on women's education, women's income, businesses owned by women, and so on.

For a Web site that focuses primarily on women's issues in the United States, go to the site maintained by the National Organization for Women (**www.now.org**). This site is up to date on current social issues and legislation that have an impact on women. For a more global perspective, take a look at the Web site of the Feminist Majority Foundation Online (**www.feminist.org**). This has links to feminist issues and organizations around the world, including the Feminist Internet Gateway (lots of Web links), Feminist Research Centers, and Women and Girls in Sports. A different global perspective can be gained by going to the Web page of the United Nations' Department of Economic and Social Affairs (**www.un.org/esa/**) and then clicking on "Women."

This will enable you to find out what the United Nations is doing in relation to gender issues around the globe. Also look for nongovernmental organizations that address women's issues at this Web site.

A good way to learn about policies and practices related to sexual harassment is to do a Web search for "sexual harassment." Some of the most relevant sites to be found when doing this are SASH (Sociologists Against Sexual Harassment), a professional organization of sociologists whose research and social policy development focus on issues of sexual harassment, and the sexual harassment policies of a variety of universities and private companies. See if your university policy is displayed. What issues are commonly addressed in these policies? From all the sites you visit in this search, describe the social network of groups and organizations that have emerged to deal with the issue of sexual harassment.

For further information and discussion, go to Allyn & Bacon's Social Problems Supersite (see Chapter 1) and explore Problem Area: Problems of Gender Inequality.

Representatives in 2007 were women, that is 5 times greater than the 3 to 4 percent female representation of the 1970s. Gains have been especially impressive at the state and local levels. In 1971 women made up less than 5 percent of all state legislators, compared with 23 percent today (Center for American Women and Politics, 2008). (The best state for women running for the legislature in 2008: Vermont, with 37 percent of its legislature being women; South Carolina was on the bottom with a meager 9 percent.) Thirty years ago, a paltry 1 percent of mayors of large cities in the United States were women; today 16 percent are women. Although women are still far underrepresented in politics, they are beginning to move into more powerful and nationwide political positions. It takes time to get significant numbers of women entrenched in the political system to the point where they can make a run for a Senate seat. We will likely see more of women in politics in the future.

Masculine, Feminine, or Human?

Some of the problems surrounding gender inequality may arise in part because of the oversimplified view that people tend to have of gender, seeing things as either male or female, but not both. In reality, each individual can be seen as a combination of both feminine and masculine characteristics. In fact, masculinity and femininity may not be polar opposites but rather two independent sets of characteristics. So,

for example, some very feminine women may have few masculine characteristics, whereas other very feminine women might have many masculine traits. In fact, the word androgyny (from the Greek *andro*, "male," and *gyn*, "female") has been coined to describe *a condition where male and female characteristics are not rigidly assigned and there is a blending of the traits, attitudes, and roles of both sexes*. From this perspective, people explore a broad range of gender-role possibilities and choose emotions and behaviors without regard to gender stereotypes. This perspective does not mean that gender distinctions disappear but that one's biological sex becomes a less rigid determinant of which masculine and feminine traits a particular individual will exhibit. As a result, people can be more flexible in their role-playing and express themselves in a variety of ways other than the traditionally masculine or feminine ways. The trends toward gender equality discussed in this chapter may make more of this flexibility possible in the future.

Study & Review
SUMMARY OF LEARNING OBJECTIVES

You should be able to describe the extent to which gender differences in behavior are due to biological factors and analyze why gender differences

exist according to the three sociological perspectives.

Gender is an ascribed and a master status. Gender inequalities are typically justified by sexism. While some of the differences in behavior between men and women are due to biology, these differences are smaller than were once thought and relate to general tendencies rather than to specific social behaviors. In addition, men and women are highly malleable and can learn a wide range of different kinds of behaviors. The functionalist perspective sees the different behaviors of men and women as related to the needs of society; gender inequality becomes dysfunctional when it is no longer consistent with those needs. The conflict perspective sees gender differences as an outgrowth of the struggle for power and resources between men and women; gender inequality occurs when one gender can dominate in this conflict. For the interactionist perspective, gender differences emerge from the communication of symbols that have social meaning for people; it is through social interaction that the place of men and women in society is defined.

You should be able to describe the role of the family, the schools, and the media and electronic world in teaching people about gender.

Male and *female* are sex-related terms; *gender* refers to learned behavior involving how we are expected to act as males and females in society. One of the key issues in analyzing gender inequality is how we learn to be masculine and feminine and how this learning contributes to gender differentiation and inequality. This learning occurs through the socialization process, with three major agencies of socialization being primarily responsible: the family provides the basic foundation in personality and in appropriate masculine and feminine behavior; the schools contribute to gender socialization by exposing the child to other adults and to impersonal, bureaucratic organizations; the media and electronic world compete with the family and schools for children's attention, expose children to a wide range of role models from which to learn appropriate gender behavior, and offer opportunities to shape gender identities that are independent of traditional sources and more in the control of children and youth.

You should be able to describe the extent to which women and men suffer discrimination in economic and other realms because of their gender.

Gender inequality is widespread in the United States. Women occupy a subordinate position in comparison to men on virtually every dimension of socioeconomic status. Discrimination on the basis of gender is not confined to education, occupation, and income. Women also experience unequal treatment in the military and before the courts. Gender inequality also affects men when they are discouraged from pursuing certain kinds of jobs and can be drafted into the military when no equivalent service is asked of women.

You should be able to describe the patterns of gender inequality that are found in various nations around the world.

Women around the globe experience some of the same gender inequalities that women in the United States confront, in such areas as work, education, political participation, and family support. Women in some nations, however, are much better off than women in other nations.

You should be able to describe the movement for gender equality in the United States and around the world, including what advances and setbacks there have been.

Feminist movements can be found in many nations, including the United States, and they have been a significant force in expanding rights and opportunities for women. A global network of such feminist organizations now exists, often working through international organizations such as the United Nations. In the United States, there have been important changes in the law as it relates to gender equality and in the workplace, as more women join the labor force. The presence of women in politics has also increased and will likely continue to do so.

CHRONOLOGICAL PRACTICE TEST

For answers to Key Concepts see the page number in parentheses; for other answers see page 233.

Men and Women in Society
Key Concept

1. Sexism (211)

True/False

2. T F Gender is an ascribed status, but it is not a master status.
3. T F The text concludes that there are no biological differences between men and women that have any social significance.
4. T F The functionalist perspective argues that it is more functional in industrial societies to assign tasks to people on the basis of individual abilities rather than ascribed characteristics.

Concept Completion

5. _____ is an ideology based on the belief that one gender is superior to and should dominate the other gender.
6. Gender is a _____ because it is a central determinant of how people view themselves and how others respond to them.
7. Building a house or managing the activities of a work team are tasks that sociologists call _____ tasks.
8. The study of the conversational styles of men and women provides evidence for the _____ perspective.

Critical Thinking

9. What conclusions does the text draw regarding the impact of biological differences between men and women on social behavior?
10. According to the functionalist perspective, what factors shape the distribution of tasks and resources to men and women in preindustrial and industrial societies?
11. According to the conflict perspective, what are the reasons for sex stratification in society?
12. What does research show about the impact of gender on conversational styles? What is the importance of these gender differences? How do they relate to the interactionist perspective?

The Socialization of Men and Women
Key Concepts

13. Sex (214)
14. Gender (214)

True/False

15. T F Stereotyped views of gender roles have been largely eliminated in children's textbooks but can still be found in college-level textbooks.
16. T F The group of youngsters most affected by the portrayal of gender roles on television are teenage boys.

Concept Completion

17. The learned behavior involving how we are expected to act as males and females in society is referred to by sociologists as _____.

Critical Thinking

18. Describe the ways in which schools and the media contribute to the problem of gender inequality.

The Extent of Gender Inequality in the United States
True/False

19. T F There is a higher proportion of college graduates among women today than among men.
20. T F The percentage of secretaries who are men is virtually unchanged over the past twenty-five years.
21. T F One argument that is made for not allowing women into combat units in the military is that their presence would interfere with the male bonding that is important to combat success.

Concept Completion

22. The three main dimensions of socioeconomic status are education, _____, and _____.
23. The employment position that has the highest percentage of jobs held by women is _____.

Critical Thinking

24. Describe the impact of gender and race on people's educational opportunities and accomplishments in the United States?
25. What are the arguments for and against women serving in combat positions in the military?

Gender Stratification in Global Perspective
Concept Completion

26. Two of the forces affecting poor Mexican women, as mentioned in Other Worlds, Other Ways, are _____ and _____.

Critical Thinking

27. Describe the kinds of gender inequality that confront women in nations around the globe.

Toward Gender Equality
Key Concepts

28. Feminist movement (224)
29. Women's movement (224)
30. Androgyny (231)

True/False

31. T F The quest for gender equality today is a global movement rather than being limited to Western nations or industrial nations.
32. T F According to the text, androgyny is a thing of the past.

Concept Completion

33. The idea that people whose jobs make equivalent demands on them should receive roughly similar pay is called _____.
34. The two career tracks that some have proposed for women to choose between are _____ and _____.

Critical Thinking

35. What are some ways to reduce levels of sexual harassment in the workplace?
36. What changes have occurred in the workplace in the United States in the past thirty years as far as gender inequality is concerned?

ANSWERS TO CHRONOLOGICAL PRACTICE TEST

2. F; 3. F; 4. T; 15. F; 16. F; 19. F; 20. T; 21. T; 31. T; 32. F
5. Sexism
6. master status

7. instrumental
8. interactionist
17. gender
22. occupation, income
23. secretaries
26. Green Revolution, patriarchal family, traditional gender roles
33. comparable worth
34. career-primary, career-and-family or "mommy track"

CUMULATIVE PRACTICE TEST

See page 482 for answers.

1. Regarding biological differences between men and women, the text draws which of the following conclusions?
   a. The differences are actually larger than was once thought.
   b. The differences refer to averages that ignore the significant overlap between the sexes.
   c. Relatively little human behavior is learned through socialization.
   d. There has not been much research on the differences between the sexes.
   e. Most of our behavior is biologically programmed rather than learned.

2. The functionalist perspective is most clearly based on the notion that
   a. society benefits when the more powerful groups control the allocation of tasks and resources.
   b. male dominance arises from the superior physical strength of men.
   c. the allocation of resources by gender is shaped by the communication of symbols and social meanings.
   d. social meanings are created and reinforced through daily social interaction.
   e. tasks should be assigned to people on the basis of their individual abilities to perform the tasks.

3. The goal-oriented activities of the group, such as hunting, building something, or managing a work team are referred to as
   a. expressive tasks.
   b. leadership tasks.
   c. instrumental tasks.
   d. achievement tasks.
   e. none of the above.

4. Sociologist Randall Collins argues that
   a. there is an inherent conflict of interest between men and women.
   b. sex roles are functional in modern society.
   c. sex roles can serve as a mechanism by which one group dominates the other.
   d. All of the above.
   e. a and c above.

5. Which of these statements would be most consistent with the conflict perspective?
   a. The gender-role division of labor is most functional when it is consistent with the needs of society.
   b. Beliefs about gender inequality are maintained and reinforced through patterns of social interaction.
   c. Innate biological differences between men and women shape the contributions each can make to society.
   d. The allocation of resources by gender is shaped by the communication of symbols and social meanings.
   e. Gender differentiation is a battleground for the struggle over scarce resources.

6. According to the text, all three sociological perspectives would agree that
   a. some gender stratification is necessary for society.
   b. biology is as powerful a force as social factors in shaping gender behavior.
   c. the goal of social policy should be to eliminate stratification based on gender.
   d. most industrial societies could function well with less gender stratification than they have.
   e. the things denoted by the terms "sex" and "gender" are interchangeable.

7. According to the text, *gender* refers to
   a. learned behavior involving how we are expected to act as males and females in society.
   b. the biological role that each of us plays in reproduction.
   c. roles specific to sexual intercourse.
   d. All of the above.
   e. None of the above.

8. Regarding the socialization of children, the text concludes that
   a. boys are more prominent in girls' games than girls are in boys' games.
   b. most elementary school teachers treat boy students and girl students the same.
   c. socialization is a manifest function of the mass media.
   d. children's books have eliminated most stereotyped images of the sexes.
   e. in childhood, male activities tend to be more valued than female activities.

9. According to investigations of the content of school textbooks in the 1970s,
   a. boys were pictured in the books far more than girls.
   b. female gender-specific pronouns like "her" were commonplace in the books.
   c. stereotyped portrayals of adult men's and women's roles had become uncommon in school books.
   d. All of the above.
   e. a and c above.

10. Research shows which type of person was most affected by watching sexist portrayals on television?
    a. Fairly intelligent boys.
    b. Boys with sexist attitudes.
    c. Less intelligent girls.
    d. Fairly intelligent girls.
    e. Girls with sexist attitudes.

11. Among which of the following groups do a higher percentage of women graduate from college in the United States than the percentage among men?
    a. The elderly.
    b. Whites.
    c. Asian Americans.
    d. The poor.
    e. African Americans.

12. Classical economic theory claims that wages are determined by
    a. how much power different groups of workers possess.
    b. cultural stereotypes of what different groups of workers are worth.
    c. the competitive forces of supply and demand.
    d. Both a and b are consistent with classical economic theory.
    e. a, b, and c are consistent with classical economic theory.

13. Regarding the relationship between income and gender, recent research shows that
    a. women earn less than men because they do more poorly in high school and college.
    b. women earn less than men because they take longer to finish college.
    c. when women have no children and have worked as long as men have worked, they achieve pay equity with men in most occupations.
    d. in none of the occupations studied did women earn more than men.
    e. in all of the occupational groups studied, men earned more than women.

14. Which of the following is *not* presented in the text as an argument against women serving in combat positions?
    a. Women would disrupt the cohesiveness that occurs among men in combat.
    b. Women are not intelligent enough to handle the high-technology equipment.
    c. Women do not have the physical strength or aggressive nature needed to do the job.
    d. All of the above were given as arguments.
    e. Neither b nor c were given as arguments.

15. According to the text's discussion of discrimination on the basis of gender,
    a. the U.S. legal system has built into it a great deal of discrimination against women.
    b. all states have passed legislation treating marital rape like any other form of rape.
    c. recent legislation has eliminated discrimination in the realm of retirement income for women.
    d. All of the above.
    e. a and c above.

16. Which of the following is *not* true regarding the gender inequalities suffered by males in the United States today?
    a. Men but not women must register for the military draft.
    b. More women attend law school than do men.
    c. Men are sometimes charged more for automobile insurance than are women.
    d. Socially imposed expectations limit the freedom of men to choose stereotypically female occupations.
    e. All of the above are true.

17. Regarding the feminist movement, the text states that
    a. it is limited to Western democracies.
    b. many in the Arab world argue that Islamic traditions support the emancipation of women.
    c. communist governments have been very hostile to feminism.
    d. it is losing ground in the United States and around the world.
    e. the member states of the United Nations have not been supportive of it.

18. Which of the following is true regarding social policy relating to gender equality in the United States today?
    a. Comparable worth has been declared unconstitutional.
    b. The 1964 Civil Rights Act has been repealed.
    c. Laws against sexual harassment in the workplace have been declared unconstitutional.
    d. Men and women have identical opportunities in the military.
    e. The Equal Rights Amendment has not been approved.

19. Which of the following statements would be true of the U.S. Senate and the House of Representatives today?
    a. The percentages of women in both have declined in the past twenty years.
    b. Both contain at least one-third women.
    c. Women are better represented in the House than in the Senate.
    d. Women are better represented in the Senate than in the House.
    e. There are approximately equal percentages of women in both.

20. A situation where male and female characteristics are not rigidly assigned, but instead there is a blending of the traits of both sexes, is called
    a. androgyny.
    b. a master status.
    c. comparable worth.
    d. sexism.
    e. instrumental tasks.

FOR FURTHER READING

Billson, Janet Mancini. (1995). *Keepers of the culture: The power of tradition in women's lives.* New York: Lexington Books. This sociologist interviewed women of many cultures across Canada—Iroquois, Inuit, Jamaican, Ukrainian, and others—who are confronting social change. The book describes the entrenched and pervasive sexism and discrimination that these women face but also explores sources of empowerment for them.

Blum, Deborah. (1997). *Sex on the brain: The biological differences between men and women.* New York: Viking. This is a thorough and readable summary of the research on whether behavioral differences between men and women are due to biology or to cultural experiences.

Bonvillain, Nancy. (2001). *Women and men: Cultural constructs of gender* (3d ed.). Upper Saddle River, NJ: Prentice Hall. This book explores issues of gender and gender inequality in many cultures around the globe and in societies at many different levels of development, from hunters and gatherers to industrialists. It provides a complete and sophisticated view of the role of gender in society.

Kimmel, Michael S., & Messner, Michael A. (2004). *Men's Lives* (6th ed.). Boston: Allyn & Bacon. This book approaches issues of gender from the male perspective, focusing on inequality, discrimination, socialization, and masculinity in general.

MacKinnon, Catharine A. (2006). *Are women human? And other international dialogues.* Cambridge, MA: Boston University Press. This book, by a world-renowned feminist, focuses on issues of gender inequality and international law and particularly on the tendency for the international legal system to ignore the violence and intimidation that women experience worldwide.

Orenstein, Peggy. (1994). *Schoolgirls: Young women, self-esteem, and the confidence gap.* New York: Doubleday. By looking in depth at the lives of girls at two schools, this book documents the decline in self-esteem and self-confidence that many girls experience as they go through adolescence.

Reskin, Barbara, & Padavic, Irene. (2003). *Women and men at work* (2d ed.). Thousand Oaks, CA: Pine Forge Press. This book provides a detailed analysis of how men and women fare in the workplace. It is enlightening and includes some material from other cultures and from the minority experience.

Wolf, Naomi. (1991). *The beauty myth: How images of beauty are used against women.* New York: Morrow. This is an intriguing book about how Western culture encourages a conception of beauty that tends to coerce women into doing things that are not in their best interests. It is a thoughtful illustration of how cultures can exercise social control in subtle and often unrecognized ways.

Wood, Julia T. (2005). *Gendered lives: Communication, gender, and culture* (6th ed.). Belmont, CA: Wadsworth. This book provides a comprehensive overview of the multitude of ways that gender pervades our lives and profoundly shapes our thoughts, feelings, and behaviors—often in ways that we are totally unaware of.

SOCIAL INSTITUTIONS

CHAPTER NINE
Family and Human Sexuality

CHAPTER TEN
Health and Health-Care Institutions

CHAPTER ELEVEN
Religion

CHAPTER TWELVE
Education and the Mass Media

CHAPTER THIRTEEN
Political and Economic Institutions

The chapters in Part IV focus on social institutions—the clusters of statuses, roles, and groups that work together to meet certain needs of society. The particular institutions covered are the family, health care, religion, education, politics, and the economy.

CHAPTER 9

Family and Human Sexuality

MYTHS & FACTS: About the Family and Human Sexuality

Family and Kinship in Cross-Cultural Perspective

Rules of Descent
Rules of Marriage
Rules of Authority
Size of Family Unit
Mate Selection and Marriage Transactions

The Family in Society

The Functionalist Perspective
The Conflict Perspective

Marriage and Divorce in the United States

Choosing a Mate and Attitudes toward Marriage
Divorce
 The Divorce Rate
 Who Gets Divorced?
 The Effects of Divorce
The Minority Family Experience
OTHER WORLDS, OTHER WAYS: Vietnam: Family and Religion among Immigrants to the United States

Diversity and Change in Sexual Behavior

Premarital Sex
Extramarital Sex
Homosexuality

Diverse Family Lifestyles in Modern Societies

Dual-Earner Families
Singlehood
Cohabitation
Single Parenthood
Gay Families
A Global Perspective

Violence in the Family

APPLYING SOCIOLOGY: Creating and Evaluating Programs to Fight Domestic Violence

The Future of the Family

SOCIOLOGY OF MEDIA AND TECHNOLOGY: Family in the Electronic Age
SOCIOLOGY ON THE INTERNET

Study & Review

The Trobriand Islands are a part of Melanesia in the South Pacific, near New Guinea. The anthropologist Bronislaw Malinowski (1929) lived there in the early part of the twentieth century and found a family system that was quite different from that in the West. Trobrianders, for example, traced their inheritance through the mother's line rather than the father's (a matrilineal descent system), and a married couple lived with the wife's relatives rather than the husband's (a matrilocal system). Consequently, the role of the Trobriand father was quite different from what people in the United States are used to: The father was neither the primary authority over his children nor their major disciplinarian. Nor was he the major provider of food and other supports to his wife and children. In Trobriand society, the wife's brother performed both of these functions. This convention is very different from families in most Western societies in which paternal authority is usually dominant and the father is at the center of, or at least very important in, his own household. The Trobriand father was almost like a visitor—in some cases, almost a stranger—in his wife's household. The strongest kinship bond in this matrilineal society was that between sister and brother rather than that between husband and wife.

Trobriand sexual practices also were quite different from those in the United States. Premarital sexual intercourse was widely accepted and widely practiced, as is true of many tribal societies, especially in the Pacific. In fact, one anthropological estimate is that well over one-third of human cultures allowed unrestricted premarital sexual activity (Murdock, 1967). For unmarried Trobrianders, sex was common and without guilt. Nevertheless, despite this tolerance, bearing children outside marriage was strongly frowned on, and women who became pregnant were expected to marry. If a woman had a child without marrying, both she and the child were penalized and stigmatized. In fact, births outside marriage were rare among the Trobrianders.

Trobriand sexual and marital practices led Malinowski to argue that the key function of the family as a social institution is to provide children with a socially or legally approved father. In fact, Malinowski's theory was that the family's primary defining element is the legitimation of childbearing. In other words, the relationship between a parent and a child is not merely biological; it is also social and receives recognition or approbation from others depending on how the relationship is established. Marriage was not the social approval of sex between two Trobrianders, since premarital sexuality flourished; rather marriage was the official recognition of and control over childbearing.

Malinowski's theory has been a controversial one in anthropology and sociology. If it is true, what do we make of the many societies in which one-half or more of births are to unmarried mothers? Such birthrates outside marriage are found, for example, in some Caribbean nations as well as among some groups in the United States today. Clearly, issues of family and human sexuality are more complicated than Malinowski thought.

The example of the Trobriand Islanders, however, makes an important point: Human societies exhibit diverse family forms and sexual practices. In fact, there is some debate over exactly what constitutes a family. Does a family require children, as Malinowski suggests? Must two people be married in order to create a family? Do they even have to be of the opposite sex? Some employers today extend health and life insurance benefits to the unmarried domestic partners of their employees, including gay and lesbian couples. So, what had been defined as "family" benefits in the past are now sometimes extended to those in living arrangements that some would not consider families at all. This situation raises the question of what a family is, and many people have strong feelings about it. In fact, there is a great deal of ethnocentrism surrounding this question, as people claim that their version of the family is the only version possible or permissible. One of the goals of this chapter will be to describe and explain some of the diversity found in family forms.

Trobriand society also illustrates the intimate link between family and human sexuality. Sex and childbearing are related, and family institutions in all societies play a role in regulating both. That is why they are addressed in a single chapter.

Beginning with this chapter, the book returns to a topic introduced in Chapter 2, the importance of social institutions in understanding society. A *social institution* is a persistent and stable cluster of values, statuses, roles, groups, and organizations that function together to meet some basic needs of society that affect its survival. This chapter focuses on the institution of *family*. The following four chapters address *health-care* institutions (coping with problems of physical and mental health), *religion* (providing answers of ultimate meaning), *education* (learning necessary values and skills), and *politics and the economy* (the production and distribution of goods and services as well as collective power). This list of societal needs, of course, could be much longer, but it will serve as an adequate introduction to the role of social institutions and how they operate. The fact that this book devotes five chapters to the topic demonstrates the central importance of social institutions in the sociological analysis of societies.

Myths & Facts

About the Family and Human Sexuality

Myth:

Unhappy marriages should be maintained when children are involved—"for the sake of the children."

Fact:

Repeated investigations of divorce and its effects on children have failed to demonstrate the psychological benefits to children of maintaining an unhappy marriage. It may, in fact, be more damaging than divorce itself.

Myth:

Divorce is a modern phenomenon and was relatively unheard of in premodern societies.

Fact:

Not only did divorce exist in premodern societies, but it was sometimes easier to obtain and more common than in the United States today.

Myth:

Teenage pregnancies are on the rise in all modern societies because of the decline in traditional values and the rise in sexual promiscuity.

Fact:

The United States has many more teenage pregnancies than does any other industrial nation. In societies where effective sex education programs and contraceptives are available to teens, the rate of such pregnancies is two to three times lower than in the United States.

Myth:

Childbirth outside marriage and declining family sizes are unique to the wealthy industrial nations and come from the affluent lifestyle in those nations.

Fact:

These trends are found in many nations around the world, including less developed countries, and are the result of industrialization and modernization rather than affluence.

Family and Kinship in Cross-Cultural Perspective

You should be able to discuss the various social rules that govern practices related to descent, marriage, authority, family size, and mate selection.

The family is the oldest and most fundamental of all social institutions. In fact, the family was at one time the center of the political, economic, educational, and religious activities that will be discussed as separate social institutions in the next four chapters. However, the position of the family in society has changed considerably over time. Some people have even predicted the demise of the family as we know it, pointing to divorce, children born to unmarried women, and premarital sexual activity as evidence. Certainly many controversial issues surround the family in modern society, but before addressing these, we need to know what the family *is* and how it functions in society. The **family** is a *social institution based on kinship that functions to replace members of society and to nurture them*. This seemingly straightforward definition hides considerable complexity and controversy.

Every society has rules or norms that shape family and kin relationships, and the family can take many different forms depending on which particular combination of rules develops in a given society. Once the rules are established, people are socialized to accept their society's form of the family as "natural." In fact, the rules are usually embodied in central cultural values that are internalized, the violation of which is considered unthinkable. Some of the ways these rules can vary are described in this section.

Rules of Descent

All societies have rules of kinship and descent that define the rights of family members and their responsibilities toward one another. These standards establish who is obliged to help in emergencies, who will supervise ceremonies surrounding such events as marriage and death, and who will inherit authority when a powerful family member dies. The term **kin** refers to *people who are related to one another through common ancestry, marriage, or social agreement*. **Consanguineal kin** are *people who are biologically related to one another, such as brothers and sisters or parents and their children*. **Affinal kin** are *people who are related by virtue of a marriage bond, such as husband and wife or parents-in-law*. Many societies also recognize as kin some people who are related neither consanguineally nor affinally. For example, it is common in many societies for a person who is not related to a particular kin group to be placed in the role of guardian of a child and accorded some of the privileges of kinship. In Mexico and other Hispanic cultures, this guardianship takes the form of *compadrazgo,* or "co-parenthood." The co-parent develops close social ties with the family and is viewed as a kind of brother or sister to the parents of the child. He or she would assume child-rearing duties if anything happened to the parents (Slonim, 1991).

Societies differ from one another in terms of whether descent is reckoned through the male or female line. In patrilineal descent systems, which are the most common, *descent is determined by the male line, and children belong to the kin group of their father.* In patrilineal societies, a person would not inherit anything from his mother's parents or brothers and sisters because they would be affiliated with another kinship group. In a matrilineal descent system, *descent is determined through the female line, and children belong to the kin group of their mother.* In the United States, there is a bilateral descent system in which *descent is reckoned more or less equally through both male and female lines.* The boundaries of kin groups in the United States tend to be rather vague, depending on how close one feels to particular consanguineal or affinal kin. In most patrilineal and matrilineal systems, by contrast, membership in kin groups and the resulting social obligations are quite clearly defined.

Rules of Marriage

Every society also has rules that govern who can marry whom. Virtually all societies, for example, have an incest taboo that prohibits marriage or sexual contact between close relatives such as brothers and sisters or parents and their children (Middleton, 1962). In only a few rare instances, such as among the royal families of ancient Egypt and Hawaii, has incest ever been considered socially acceptable. Societies also regulate whom people are permitted to marry beyond their close kin. Some societies, for example, have *rules of* exogamy, *which require that people choose a mate outside of their own social group or community.* One benefit of exogamous rules is that alliances can be created between families or villages through intermarriage. At the opposite extreme are *rules of* endogamy, *which require marriage within a particular group or community.* In the United States, a form of endogamy has at times been practiced in which marriages across racial lines in particular are discouraged. During the 1950s, for example, more than thirty states prohibited marriage between whites and blacks.

In some jurisdictions, laws made it illegal for a white person to marry an American Indian, Chinese, Mexican, Hindu, Melanesian, or Japanese. It wasn't until 1967 that the U.S. Supreme Court ruled the last such miscegenation law unconstitutional (Coltrane & Collins, 2001).

Societies also regulate the number of spouses that a person may have. People in the United States tend to think of monogamy, or *marriage between one man and one woman at a time,* as the normal or "civilized" marriage. Yet only about one-quarter of human societies are strictly monogamous (Coult & Habenstein, 1965). In the other societies, polygamy is practiced, in which *people can have more than one spouse at a time.* One form of polygamy is polygyny, *in which a husband can have more than one wife.* It is a common form of marriage, being the preferred arrangement in parts of Africa, the Middle East, and Asia. Polygyny tends to arise in societies where women are regarded as social or economic assets. Among the Siwai of the South Pacific, for example, status is conferred on men by giving feasts at which roast pig is the main food. Because it is Siwai women who are responsible for cultivating the food to feed pigs, a man with many wives is better equipped to host large feasts (Oliver, 1955). Polygyny is also found in societies where many males are killed in warfare, creating an imbalance in the sex ratio. A second form of polygamy is polyandry, *in which a woman can marry more than one man at a time.* Among the Tibetans and the Toda of India, for example, a woman who marries a particular man is considered the wife of all that man's brothers—even brothers who have not yet been born at the time of the marriage (Goldstein, 1971). Among the Toda, fatherhood is not determined by biological paternity; it is conferred on one of the husbands during the wife's seventh month of pregnancy. Polyandry is much less common than polygyny. In societies where female infanticide is practiced, resulting in a shortage of females, polyandry makes it possible for all males to marry.

Rules of Authority

All societies have rules that determine who should wield power and authority in families. In patriarchal families, by far the most common, *males are dominant in regulating political and economic decision making.* There is a strong patriarchal trend in families throughout Western civilization, and religious teachings in the Bible and the Koran have been interpreted as strongly endorsing male dominance. Even today, there are strong patriarchal tendencies in many families in the United States, such as those in the upper classes. Families such as the Kennedys, the Hunts, and the Rockefellers are run largely by males. Matriarchal families, *in which women are dominant in power and authority,* are far less common. In fact, some anthropologists argue that no true matriarchies can be found, since even in societies where women gain considerable authority and power, it is shared with men. Among the Huron Indians discussed in the beginning of Chapter 8, and among the Iroquois, for instance, women had the sole authority to appoint men to leadership positions, such as clan leader, but the women could not hold those positions themselves (Farb, 1978).

Although patriarchal trends still exist in modern societies, an egalitarian family appears to be emerging *in which husbands and wives share more equally in power and authority.* Especially as women become more economically independent, it is likely that they will continue to gain a more equal say in family matters. Although this egalitarianism may become more common in the future, both patriarchal and matriarchal families will persist in the United States, in some cases because a spouse has left the family, in others because subcultural values dictate that one of these family forms is preferable.

Power and authority relations in families also determine residence patterns. Patriarchal families are also likely to be patrilocal, with *the married couple living with or near the husband's family.* Matriarchal families are likely to be matrilocal, that is, *living with or near the wife's family.* Although some matrilocal and patrilocal tendencies can be found in the United States, many couples form neolocal families, where *residence is separate from the families of either wife or husband.*

Size of Family Unit

Because kin groups can be quite extensive, involving hundreds of people, societies provide rules to regulate which of their members will live and work closely together as a cooperative unit. Thus the size of a typical family unit is normally quite a bit smaller than the kin group. An extended family consists of *three or more generations of people who live together or in close proximity and whose lives and livelihoods are closely intertwined* (Nimkoff, 1965). Extended families are often large and usually involve a strong sense of kinship obligation. Family members are expected to help other family members and to remain loyal to the family. Extended families are usually dominated by males, often the eldest male, and tasks are divided along age and sex lines. Extended families are more common in preindustrial than industrial societies for reasons that will be discussed shortly. A nuclear family consists of *parents and their offspring.* In contrast to extended families, nuclear families are small and less likely to be male dominated.

Families in modern societies are sufficiently complex that many of them cannot be easily classified as either extended or nuclear. Some, for example, can be considered modified extended families, *in which elaborate networks of visitation and support remain though each nuclear unit lives separately.* Another type is the reconstituted family, or blended family, which refers to *a family based on kinship ties that accumulate as a consequence of divorces and remarriages* (Cherlin & Furstenberg, 1994). These families involve relationships that are more complex than those of the standard nuclear family. For example, a child may live in a family with a full-blood sibling, a half-blood sibling, and an affinal sibling. The same child may have a "real" father and mother as well as stepfather or stepmother, and three sets of grandparents. Mothers and fathers may have both biological children and adopted children. Such arrangements, with their attendant complex kinship and legal linkages, can create complications and tensions that are less likely in traditional nuclear or extended-family arrangements (Johnson, Klee, & Schmidt, 1988). For example, in many blended families there is some degree of tension over whether the biological parents should retain the major allegiance of and authority over their children, or whether a stepparent, who has daily control over the child, should predominate.

Mate Selection and Marriage Transactions

Societies also have rules regarding the process of choosing a mate and getting married. For example, the mate selection process can vary from arranged marriages at one extreme to participant-run romances at the other.

In preindustrial societies, in which the extended family and kinship were core social institutions, parents played a key role in deciding when and to whom their children would marry. Because the family in these societies was the major institution performing important societal functions, it is not surprising that marital decisions were not left to whim or fancy. In many of these societies, *arranged marriages* occurred in which parents would select marriage partners for their children, sometimes shortly after their birth. The selection was based on what was considered best for the family, and the prospective marriage partners had little other choice. Such arranged marriages are still common in India and some other societies, and their members generally accept this practice as the wisest way to make marital choices.

A modified form of arranged marriage existed in the preindustrial United States, with young people having some choice in selecting a marriage partner but with parents still retaining substantial control over the ultimate decision. Courtship was common, but it occurred under the ever watchful eyes of parents and other elders in the community. It was a *parent-run* courtship process: Young men and women were allowed to choose from among a pool of partners who were considered acceptable by their parents but were strongly discouraged from going outside that pool (M. Gordon, 1978).

In modern industrial societies, the selection of marital partners is based primarily on the individual desires of the prospective mates. Parents can and do play a role in this process, but their influence is typically secondary and often no more important than the suggestions of a close friend. This courtship process, then, is more *participant run,* with romantic love as a primary factor drawing couples toward marriage. One reason for this declining role of parents over the years is that kinship is less important in modern societies, and one's kin, including one's parents, have considerably less stake in who marries whom. A second reason is that children have a greater degree of economic independence from their parents in industrial societies, and parents therefore have less leverage with which to demand a say in the choice of a marriage partner. In the past, parents could withhold economic support from a couple, which usually made it very difficult for them to establish a household. Today, young people are better able to get jobs independently of their families and to support themselves. As the position of the family in society has changed, then, people have gained more freedom of choice regarding a marriage partner.

Families do more than help their offspring choose an acceptable mate. They also sometimes transfer significant amounts of money, goods, or services between the two families involved (Schlegel & Eloul, 1988). The most common of these marriage transactions is called *bridewealth* by anthropologists and involves the bridegroom or his family giving gifts to the bride's family. This custom symbolizes the belief that the bride's family is losing a daughter and should be compensated by the bridegroom's family, which is gaining a daughter. It also demonstrates to the woman's family that the prospective husband has the resources to support a wife and children. Another common form of transfer is *brideservice,* in which the bridegroom offers labor rather than goods to the bride's family. He may work for the bride's father for a time as a means of "buying" the daughter, or in a matrilocal society the bridegroom may move in with and become a working member of his wife's family. Still another form of marriage transaction is the *dowry,* in which the bride's family gives her some money or goods that she and her husband can keep. In a sense, the bride's family "buys" the best husband for their daughter and also makes the dowry available for her economic support. The dowry custom is still practiced in some societies, such as India, today (Latha & Narendra, 1998).

The Family in Society

You should be able to analyze the role of the family in society from both the functionalist and conflict perspectives.

Considerable time has been spent discussing these variations of the family in order to emphasize the point that there is much diversity in the types of families found in human societies. To return to the earlier question of what a family is, we begin to realize that no single form of the family will serve all societies. Compared to other cultures, the family in the United States tends to be monogamous; somewhat patriarchal but leaning toward egalitarian and bilateral arrangements; mostly neolocal, but with pockets of matrilocalism and patrilocalism; and nuclear, but with a good mix of reconstituted and modified extended families. All the qualifications in the previous sentence are indicative of the diversity that exists, which will be elaborated on shortly. First, however, we can better understand why such variation in family types occurs from one culture to another, or from one time to another, if we explore what the sociological perspectives can tell us about the place of the family in society.

The Functionalist Perspective

Functionalists argue that some form of the family exists in all societies because the family performs certain basic functions that are essential to human survival and the maintenance of society (Eshleman & Bulcroft, 2006; Ogburn, 1938). Six major contributions that the family makes to society have been identified.

1. *Regulation of sexual behavior and reproduction.* All societies have rules governing who can engage in sexual activities with whom and under what conditions children should be conceived and born. In most societies, childbearing is limited to marriage and family contexts, which provide a stable setting for having and nurturing children. In this way, the family contributes to the process of replacing people from one generation to the next.

2. *Socialization and education.* All human beings must learn the values, norms, and language of their culture and develop the skills that are necessary to be useful in society. Parents and other family members usually have primary responsibility for ensuring that children are properly socialized. Thus, as was noted in Chapter 3, the family is the major agency of socialization.

3. *Status conferral.* Families confer on their children a place in society—a position or status relative to other people. By virtue of being born into a particular family, we have certain resources or opportunities available to us. Our racial or ethnic heritage, religion, and social class are determined by the family into which we are born, although some of these characteristics may change later in life.

4. *Economic activity.* The family often serves as the basic unit for economic production, with kinship ties defining who is obliged to work together in order to catch game, grow food, or build shelters. Family members work together to accomplish the economic tasks necessary for survival. Kinship ties also determine the distribution and consumption of economic goods by establishing who has a right to a share of the goods produced by a family.

5. *Protection.* Families in all societies provide various forms of care and protection to their members, helping them when they are too young, weak, sick, or old to help themselves.

6. *Affection and companionship.* All human beings need love, affection, and psychological support, and for many people these needs are fulfilled by family members. Such support enables us to develop a positive self-concept and sense of self-worth and to dispel loneliness.

All these functions taken together contribute to the continuity of society by ensuring that new members are born and properly socialized.

Although the family often performs these six functions, they can be accomplished in other ways. In fact, the family and society have been undergoing a major transformation over the past few centuries as a consequence of industrialization, and alternative ways of fulfilling many of these functions are emerging. For example, although most childbearing still occurs in marriages, a growing number of women are having children without marrying. Today, 1.5 million births to unmarried women occur in the United States each year, in comparison to about 400,000 in 1970 (U.S. Bureau of the Census, 2007, p. 66). This increase has occurred in part because women in industrial societies are better able to work and support their children without the assistance of a husband or other relatives. With regard to socialization and education, day-care centers, schools, and colleges are becoming increasingly important in transmitting culture and passing on skills and knowledge. Furthermore, people's positions in industrial societies are determined less by family position and more by their achievements than in the past, although family position does give a person a start in life. In terms of economic activity, most people work outside the

home, and the family no longer serves as the center of economic production. Finally, there are hospitals, nursing homes, retirement villages, and many other ways to offer the care and protection that people need.

In other words, the family has become less central in performing these functions as other institutional means of accomplishing them have arisen through industrialization. As a consequence, the traditional roles of family and kinship in society have changed, because they are simply not as important as they once were. In the process, the extended family that performed most of these functions in preindustrial societies has become less common. At the same time, the nuclear family has become more prominent because it is better suited to an urbanized industrial society. Industrialism calls for geographic mobility so that workers can go where the jobs are, and the nuclear families with weaker kinship ties make this mobility easier. Industrial societies also emphasize achievement rather than ascription, and these modified kinship relations make it easier for people to be upwardly mobile. Furthermore, large extended families are dysfunctional in urban settings where children are not economic assets. In preindustrial societies, children could work in agricultural settings and therefore contribute economically to the family. Small families are better suited to industrial societies; in fact, the size of the average family in the United States declined substantially throughout the twentieth century, and people are more likely to be living alone or in nonfamily households (Figure 9.1).

The part that families play in society, then, has changed with industrialization, and this change has contributed to such things as a rising divorce rate and the emergence of a number of alternatives to traditional family lifestyles. These social developments become a social problem when the changes in the family threaten society with disorganization or instability. One of the key debates regarding family problems centers on whether other institutions can adequately perform the traditional family functions. Can day care, for example, provide the same kind of socialization to cultural values and development of personality that occurs in the traditional family? This issue is analyzed in Applying Sociology: Day Care in Chapter 3. Do divorce and one-parent families result in less effective socialization and more behavior problems for youth when compared with two-parent families? This question is analyzed later in this chapter. The function of the family that has probably changed least during this process is the provision of affection and companionship, and nuclear families can probably perform this function as well as extended families did. But even this function might be fulfilled in other ways than by the traditional family.

A. Size, 1930–2006

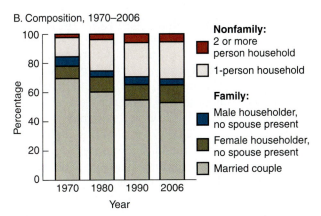

B. Composition, 1970–2006

Nonfamily:
- 2 or more person household
- 1-person household

Family:
- Male householder, no spouse present
- Female householder, no spouse present
- Married couple

Figure 9.1

The Average Size and Composition of Households in the United States, 1930–2006

Note: From *Statistical Abstract of the United States*, 1982–83 (p. 43) by U.S. Bureau of the Census, 1982, Washington, DC: U.S. Government Printing Office: *Statistical Abstract of the United States*, 2008 (p. 53) by U.S. Bureau of the Census, 2007. Washington, DC: U.S. Government Printing Office.

The Conflict Perspective

According to the conflict perspective, the family, along with other social institutions, serves the interests of the dominant groups in society, and there is no reason to assume that a single form of the family would benefit everyone. Rather, the version of the family that is most prominent in society is likely to be the one that is consistent with the values and benefits of the dominant groups. For example, patriarchy is the most common type of authority structure in families, and it serves the interests of men by enabling them to be dominant. In some societies, in fact, women have been so powerless in the family that they were virtual slaves (Chagnon, 1992). In industrial societies, male domination is not this extreme; fewer women today are willing to accept such a subordinate position. In general, women today

demand more egalitarian family roles. This change is occurring, however, because women have been accumulating resources that enable them to resist coercion by males. For example, male dominance can be expressed in the form of spouse abuse, which often involves husbands assaulting their wives. Research indicates that married women with greater economic, social, and educational resources are less likely to be abused and more likely to leave physically abusive husbands (Durfee & Rosenberg, 2004; Gelles, 1997).

The dominant form of the family in society also benefits particular economic interests. For example, the nuclear family serves the interests of capitalist economic institutions because it maximizes the number of consumption-oriented units in society. Each nuclear family buys many consumer items even though some are used only infrequently. Most families, for example, own their own television, stove, food processor, and automobile. A washing machine is used for only a few hours a week, yet most families purchase their own rather than share one with others. In extended or communal families, fewer such consumer goods would be needed because they would be shared, and thus the market for these goods would be smaller, which would hurt the interests of capitalists. Communal families, which are based on the belief in common ownership of at least some material goods, also threaten the basic value of private property on which a capitalist economy rests.

Conflict theorists would also argue that family systems can contribute to the perpetuation of social and economic inequality because inheritance in many societies, especially capitalist ones, is based on kinship. Inheritance makes it possible for a family to accumulate and perpetuate its wealth over generations. Such families as the Carnegies, the Rockefellers, the Bushes, the Kennedys, and the Gettys in the United States have amassed enormous fortunes. Anyone who can inherit wealth—of whatever amount—clearly has an advantage over those who come from modest or poor backgrounds. Thus, the family in such societies becomes a vehicle for perpetuating patterns of dominance and subordination.

Conflict theorists argue that the dominant groups protect themselves against threats to their position by teaching people through the schools, the media, and other means that monogamy, nuclear families, family inheritance, and private property are best. Through socialization and education, people internalize these beliefs, and they are unlikely, therefore, even to consider other forms of the family, such as communal arrangements. In addition, strong normative pressures motivate people to live in socially acceptable forms of the family. From the conflict perspective, family forms change when new groups acquire the power necessary to gain acceptance for a new form of family.

The organization of family life becomes a social problem when groups with the power to make their concerns heard believe that the existing family structure is not serving their interests and they act to change it. The dispute over the proper family form, however, is not couched in the language of personal interests but rather of conflicting values.

Marriage and Divorce in the United States

You should be able to describe the attitudes of people in the United States toward marriage, analyze the extent of divorce and its effects, and assess the family experiences of minorities.

Thus far this chapter has looked at the place of the family as a social institution by considering the many diverse forms of the family and reviewing what the sociological perspectives have to say on this subject. Now it is time to consider the subject in terms of what it means for the United States. First this section looks at mate selection practices and attitudes toward marriage; then it reviews the extent and consequences of divorce and explores some of the unique family experiences of minorities in the United States.

Choosing a Mate and Attitudes toward Marriage

It has been noted that the mate selection process in the United States today is participant run, with romantic love playing an important part. Nevertheless, the marriage decision is still strongly influenced by social pressures beyond romantic love. People assess a potential partner's intelligence, education, earning power, and other characteristics. People are likely, for example, to be drawn to each other if they are similar in terms of physical attractiveness. In other words, the marriage choice is in part an *exchange relationship* in which partners assess what they gain from a relationship in comparison to what they have to offer and the alternatives they forgo.

Marriages in the United States also tend to be *homogamous*—people tend to choose partners who have social characteristics similar to their own (Coltrane & Collins, 2001; Strong, DeVault, & Cohen, 2008). These characteristics are "social filters" that tend to narrow people's choices among eligible partners. *Age* is a significant filter, with husbands being an average of two and one-half years older than their wives; only 8 percent of married couples have an age difference of larger than ten years, and only 10 percent involve a wife older than her husband. *Religion* is

another filter, with Protestants having the highest rates of endogamy, followed by Jews and then Roman Catholics. *Race* is also a major filter, with less than 1 percent of all marriages involving black–white couples (U.S. Bureau of the Census, 2007, p. 52). A final filter is *socioeconomic status*, with people especially likely to choose partners at the same educational and occupational levels as themselves. When we see the effect of these filters narrowing people's choices of partners, we can see that mate selection is complex and influenced by many things other than romantic love.

Given the changes in the role of the family in industrial societies, are marriage and family living still popular today? It would seem so: More people in the United States marry than ever before, well over 90 percent. In 2006, 60 percent of all adult men were married, as were 57 percent of all adult women. These figures were about the same as in 1940 but somewhat lower than 1970 (Figure 9.2). Surveys over the past 20 years reveal that both young people and their parents have quite positive attitudes toward marriage and family (Axinn & Thornton, 2000; Moore & Stief, 1991; Popenoe & Whitehead, 2003). In a national sample of high school seniors, three-quarters reported that marriage and family life were "extremely important" to them, and a survey of young adults aged eighteen to twenty-two found that most of them plan to marry before the age of thirty. The vast majority of them also believed that when people marry, it should be "for life." Despite these positive views of marriage, however, the surveys detected some important changes: Compared with attitudes of the 1960s, today young men and women have fewer negative attitudes toward staying single, see fewer advantages in getting married over remaining single, and are not as certain that having children is the best way to go. In fact, the people interviewed seemed reluctant to choose either marriage or being single as the preferred alternative. In short, many view marriage quite positively in the United States today, but alternatives to marriage are also growing in popularity.

These changes in attitudes over the past thirty years suggest that the norms regarding family life in the United States are moving somewhat away from the more traditional and conventional demand that the family consist of a married couple and their children. For some, these changes are one indication that the family is in serious trouble. Some people also view the divorce rate in the United States as an indication of trouble.

Divorce

THE DIVORCE RATE   People usually view the widespread incidence and easy availability of divorce as having arisen only recently. In fact, the option for a married couple to

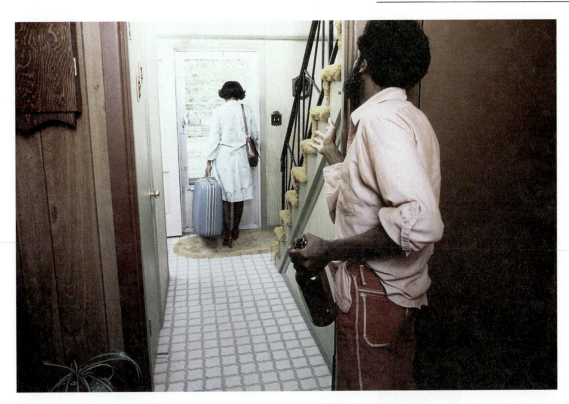

Marital disruptions, such as divorce, occur for many reasons, and they clearly produce difficulties for all involved. While the rate of divorce has increased in comparison to 50 years ago, it has actually declined slightly in the past few decades.

dissolve a marriage has existed in many premodern societies. In some hunting-and-gathering bands, for example, a marriage could be easily ended when a couple decided to stop living together, and in horticultural or pastoral societies where some gender equality had developed, divorce could be initiated by women as easily as by men (O'Kelly & Carney, 1986). Nevertheless, to those who believe that marriage should be a lifelong commitment involving a deep emotional sharing between the married couple, today's high divorce rate is viewed as a threat to the family as a social institution.

In calculating the incidence of divorce, most sociologists use a statistic called the refined divorce rate, *which is determined by dividing the number of divorces each year by the total number of existing marriages in that year.* This method provides a valid way of comparing the stability of marriages from one year to the next. As Figure 9.3 illustrates, the divorce rate has doubled since 1940. As a point of comparison, it has been estimated that there were only 1.2 divorces for every one thousand marriages in 1869—reflecting a seventeenfold increase over the following century (Saxton, 1980, p. 380). Although the trend in divorce rates over the past sixty years has been up, the divorce rate has actually declined a little since its high point around 1980.

The likelihood that a marriage would end in divorce in 1870 was 8 percent. Today, this figure has risen to between 40 and 50 percent (Strong, DeVault, & Cohen, 2008). So though it may be disturbing to many, the statistical likelihood of a marriage beginning today ending in divorce is about fifty-fifty. However, those people who divorce are apparently not totally disillusioned with marriage because 75 to 80 percent of them will eventually remarry. But a slightly greater number of these second marriages will end in divorce in comparison to first marriages (Coltrane & Collins, 2001).

The divorce rate is but one measure of marital dissolution. Approximately 3 percent of all marriages end in legal separation, where the partners decide to end their relationship but prefer, perhaps for religious reasons, not to divorce. Desertion is another way in which marriages are dissolved, although it is difficult to know the extent of this practice. In fact, given these marital practices, we might refer to the U.S. marriage system as one involving *serial* monogamy rather than monogamy or polygamy. Serial monogamy means that *a person is allowed to have more than one spouse, just not at the same time.*

People get divorces for many personal reasons— their spouse has become insensitive, they feel trapped

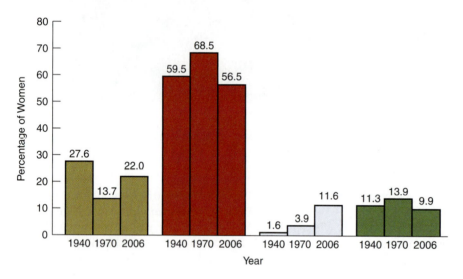

Figure 9.2

Marital Status of Adults in the United States, 1940–2006

Note: From *Statistical Abstract of the United States,* 1982–83 (p. 38) by U.S. Bureau of the Census, 1982, Washington, DC: U.S. Government Printing Office; *Statistical Abstract of the United States,* 2008 (p. 50) by U.S. Bureau of the Census, 2007. Washington, DC: U.S. Government Printing Office.

by limited career opportunities, or their sex lives are no longer exciting. Sociologists prefer to focus on the societal conditions that result in a high divorce rate rather than personal reasons for divorce. At least four such societal conditions account for the rising divorce rate over the past century.

First, we have seen that the family performs fewer functions today than in the past, which means there are fewer pressures on couples to stay together if they are unhappy. In the past, the same unhappy couple might have remained married because neither spouse felt he or she could raise the children alone or he or she needed the family for support in old age. Today, single parents are better prepared to raise a child, and most people are supported by government or private retirement plans in their old age. In fact, the high levels of affluence afforded by industrialization have made people less dependent on kinship ties for support, with consequent changes in the family as an institution.

Second, the increasing equality between men and women has created both opportunities and tensions that contribute to the divorce rate (Brehm, 1985). In terms of opportunities, many women today are part of the labor force and thus have the economic ability to support themselves and their children without a husband. This ability reduces the likelihood of women being willing to remain in unsatisfying relationships. In terms of tensions, gender equality has led to a redefining of the roles in the family, which can cause disagreements and stress that may precipitate divorce. A husband, for example, may feel that his wife should do most of the household chores, whereas she feels these tasks should be divided equally. Such conflicts are especially a problem for women who, after marrying, decide to pursue a career. This life change disrupts an established marital pattern and requires a renegotiation of male and female roles in the family, which is sometimes unsuccessful (Houseknecht, Vaughan, & Macke, 1984).

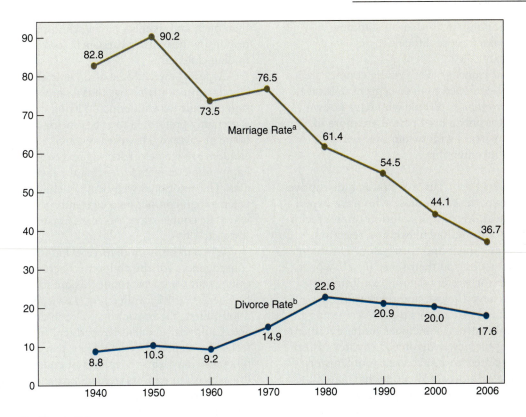

Figure 9.3

The Rate of Marriage and Divorce in the United States, 1940–2006

[a] Marriages per 1,000 unmarried women 15 years old and over.

[b] Divorces and annulments per 1,000 married women 15 years old and over.

Sources: National Center for Health Statistics, *National Vital Statistics Reports* (formerly *Monthly Vital Statistics Report*), various years; U.S. Bureau of the Census, *Statistical Abstract of the United States*, various years; and U.S. Bureau of the Census, *Current Population Survey*, various years.

A third reason for the rising divorce rate is that there is considerably less stigma attached to divorce today than in the past (Thornton, 1985). Divorce in the past was often viewed as a serious failing in a person's life, with divorced people frequently labeled as morally inferior. Females in particular bore the stigma of the divorcee as a "fallen" woman. Today, with twenty-three million divorced people in the United States, many view divorce as merely another lifestyle choice rather than a reflection of an allegedly weak character.

Finally, as negative attitudes toward divorce have eased, pressures have surfaced to simplify the legal process for obtaining a divorce. These developments have encouraged more people to seek dissolution when they encounter marital difficulties.

Taking all of these factors together, we can make an important overriding observation about the reasons for divorce in the United States: People expect a great deal from the marriage relationship. We allow people to form families partly on the basis of romantic love, which can be fickle and unpredictable. Then we expect those relationships to afford a lifetime of emotional fulfillment,

sexual gratification, companionship, and commitment. Is it so surprising, then, that many marriages fail to achieve these ideals? In the past, there were other, more pragmatic pressures for couples to stay together, such as economic constraints, reputation, religious ideals, and maintaining the marriage "for the sake of the children." Today, if the romantic ideal fails, other "barrier strengths" maintaining the marriage are less likely to prevent marital dissolution (Levinger & Moles, 1979).

WHO GETS DIVORCED? Some couples are at considerably greater risk of getting a divorce than are others (Strong, DeVault, & Cohen, 2008). Couples with an increased likelihood of divorcing have the following characteristics:

1. *Social differences between the couple, such as differences in religion, race, social class background, or values.* These differences can place substantial stress on a marriage.
2. *Low socioeconomic standing, such as low income or education.* Unemployment and other stresses

that often accompany low social standing probably make it more difficult to achieve a successful marriage.

3. *Young age at marriage.* Very young couples seem especially ill-equipped to make a go of marriage.

4. *Whirlwind romances.* People who have known each other for only a brief period are more likely to choose a partner with whom they will later prove to be incompatible.

THE EFFECTS OF DIVORCE Divorce can be a disruptive and troubling experience, as those who have experienced it will attest. Marital dissolution often precipitates feelings of failure, loneliness, and rejection, along with intense anger and frustration. For many, it represents an assault on their sense of self-worth. Even when a person prefers divorce, an intimate bond is severed nevertheless, and there is often nothing immediately to take its place. Symptoms of psychological distress, sometimes quite severe, are common among the newly divorced. Divorce is also sometimes associated with increased problems of physical health, with divorced people having more serious illnesses, more chronic disabling conditions, and a higher suicide rate than do single or married people (Kiccolt-Glaser et al., 1987; Verbrugge, 1979).

There has been considerable debate regarding whether the husband or the wife is treated more unfairly in divorce proceedings. Husbands complain about being gouged for alimony or child-support payments, whereas wives protest over allegedly meager or missing payments from husbands. Social scientists have done considerable research on this issue, comparing the experiences of divorced women with those of divorced men and also looking at people's circumstances before and after divorce. The conclusions are remarkably consistent: Women are much more likely than men to suffer economic decline after divorce, and even when men suffer, their economic slide is much less severe and much more short-lived than is that of women (Holden & Smock, 1991; McManus & DiPrete, 2001). One reason women end up worse off is that courts typically divide up only tangible property, such as a home, automobile, or belongings. Less tangible but often far more valuable property, such as a professional license that can translate into considerable income throughout a career, is usually not considered a part of the property settlement, and it is the man who is far more likely to possess these less tangible forms of property. There are other reasons for the postdivorce economic decline of women. It is typically the woman who takes custody of children after divorce, and child support awarded by the courts is usually meager compared to the father's income; only a minority of fathers comply fully with child-support awards; women earn substantially less

than men; and women, having child-rearing responsibilities, suffer barriers in looking for jobs and finding child care.

As far as the children of divorce are concerned, research consistently shows that divorce is without question difficult for children, and living in a loving home is certainly preferable to experiencing an unhappy home or divorce. However, research also shows that children are worse off staying in a conflict-ridden, unhappy home than experiencing the divorce of their parents. The emotional well-being of children is higher when a high-conflict marriage ends in divorce than when the couple stays together (Amato & Booth, 1997; Jekielek, 1998).

When parents do divorce, what are the consequences for the children? There are a number of things that we know about this question (Furstenberg & Cherlin, 1991; Wallerstein, Lewis, & Blakeslee, 2000). First, the impact on children depends on their age. Children between five and ten, for example, often feel some responsibility for their parents' divorce, and this sense may lead to feelings of guilt and failure. Preteens often express tremendous anger at their parents. Teenagers, by contrast, are often confronted with the matter of parental loyalty, feelings that they must take sides in the conflict and form a coalition with one or the other parent. Furthermore, although adolescents are better able to understand the reasons for divorce, they are often very worried about the effects of separation on their future. A second thing we know about the impact of divorce is that children in divorced homes seem more prone to delinquency (Wells & Rankin, 1991). Third, a common consequence of divorce for both boys and girls is a decline in school performance and a higher high-school dropout rate. Finally, research has shown that it is not the fact of the divorce itself that produces all of the negative consequences; the social and emotional conditions that often surround divorce are also a part of the problem (Amato, 1993; Amato & Rezac, 1994; Furstenberg & Teitler, 1994). The poor parenting, conflict between parents, and economic difficulties that often precede or follow divorce contribute to the negative consequences. In addition, divorce may reduce children's access to and ability to use various resources, such as the emotional support and role modeling of both parents.

The impact of divorce on children, however, is not all bad. Research shows that children living in one-parent families sometimes benefit from the experience (Amato, 1987; Dowd, 1997). For example, the single parent sometimes gives his or her teenage offspring more responsibility and a greater role in family decision making. In addition, the experience of divorce is less negative if a child continues to have contact with the parent he or she no longer lives with,

Social structural factors, such as race and ethnicity, affect family experiences in the United States, but the effect is complicated. In fact, all racial and ethnic groups have family lives that exhibit some significant strengths as well as weaknesses.

especially when the divorced parents have a low-conflict relationship.

In addition to all these impacts of divorce on children, divorce also changes children's attitudes toward family issues: Children whose parents have divorced have more positive attitudes toward premarital sex and cohabitation, express more acceptance of divorce, and have less positive attitudes toward marriage and childbearing (Axinn & Thornton, 1996). So, divorce has widespread and complicated consequences for children and society, and not all of the consequences can be clearly characterized as negative.

The Minority Family Experience

People's family experiences are affected by their position in the social structure. This fact is exemplified in the previous discussion by the analysis of how gender affects divorce outcome and how age and socioeconomic status affect the likelihood of divorce. Minority group status also affects family life, and an overview of the family experiences of a few minorities will round out this discussion of family in the United States.

The African American family today is actually much healthier than many people realize. Recent historical work shows that even during the period of slavery, many slaves lived in stable families and were a part of extensive kinship connections. Research on the black family early in the twentieth century comes to the same conclusion (Engerman, 1977; Gutman, 1976). Research also shows many black families in the past few decades doing well, with an upper class that is wealthy and privileged and very concerned about whom their children will marry (Billingsley, 1992; Zinn & Eitzen, 1990). Middle-class African American families are often dual-income families with good jobs and the resources to send their children to good colleges. In fact, these affluent black families often show more cohesiveness than comparable white families because of the adversity they face as a minority. This sense of adversity can translate into a feeling of embattlement that puts pressure on all family members to achieve—the mother to work and the children to succeed in college (Willie, 1981). Even poorer African American families exhibit significant strengths, such as more effective and extensive use of kinship networks than is found in white families (Jayakody, Chatters, & Taylor, 1993). For example, families headed by black women are more likely to get assistance from relatives, such as a sister or aunt living with them or nearby, than are families headed by white women. In fact, this reliance on a variety of kinship ties in an extended-family network is much closer to what "family" looks like in many other societies; defining the family largely or exclusively in terms of the husband–wife tie, as is done in most white families, is unusual.

Beyond these strengths, the marriage and family experience for African Americans is different in other ways (Patterson, 1999). There are far more black families headed by women—46 percent, compared to about 14 percent among white families. In addition, black women are far less likely to be married and living with a husband. Also, black families are much more likely to be poor, with all the problems poverty can present for a family. It has been popular to attribute the problems of the modern black family to the conditions imposed by slavery—the destruction of African tribal customs, the dispersal of tribal groups, and the disregard for institutions of marriage and family among the slaves. Although there is some truth in this argument, it is probably not a complete explanation of conditions that exist today. Whereas many slaves were treated cruelly, others were not, and there have been strong African families during slavery and since. In addition, the circumstances of the African American family have become noticeably worse since the 1960s (in 1960, only about 20 percent of black families were headed by women). As noted in Chapter 7, the shift in the U.S. economy to a service-oriented, information-based postindustrial economy has meant that people need high levels of skills and education to find good jobs. In addition, jobs have moved away from communities where poor people live. All this change has meant fewer good jobs that pay enough to support a family in black communities. Furthermore, there is ample evidence that racism and discrimination against African Americans in both employment and housing persist today. They are more likely to be denied good jobs, especially entry-level jobs, because of their race, and are often forced to live in segregated neighborhoods where there are few good jobs (see Chapter 7). As if all that were not enough, the criminal justice system devotes a good portion of its resources toward incarcerating young black males. The War on Drugs that began during the 1980s, for example, has put tens of thousands of young black and Hispanic men in jail. The result for the African American family has been fewer opportunities for black women to find men to marry and less chance for black men to get jobs that would enable them to support a family. Consequently many African American families have adapted to these elements in the social structure by deemphasizing the centrality

of the husband–wife tie and relying on a broader network of kin to fulfill the various functions of the family, such as child rearing. This adaptation is actually common among poor people in many societies.

Hispanic American families show some of the same variations found among African American families, in part because Hispanics also are more likely to be poor than are Anglos. So Hispanics have more female-headed families than Anglos but fewer than African Americans. However, Hispanic American families have some unique qualities (Slonim, 1991; Vega, 1990). Their strong belief in Roman Catholicism along with a strong family orientation in their culture produces a disapproval of divorce. As a consequence, Hispanics are more likely than either Anglos or blacks to be living in a family household and are as likely as Anglos to be in a married-couple household. Hispanics also receive more material and emotional support from an extended kin network than do Anglo and African Americans. However, this support is less a response to the single-parent problem facing black families than it is a part of a long tradition in Hispanic cultures of family solidarity, which places value on family ties over individual gratification. Nevertheless, there is much variation among Hispanic groups. For example, Cuban Americans are more affluent than many other Hispanic groups and they are more likely to have married-couple households.

Chinese and Japanese cultural values were described in Chapters 2, 3, and 5, and some of that discussion is relevant here because Asian American families bring some distinctive characteristics to U.S. society (Slonim, 1991; Suzuki, 1985). Chinese and Japanese Americans, for example, have retained some of their traditional cultural values such as the importance of the family or collectivity over the individual, self-discipline, social obligation, and respect for the elderly. These values are reflected in families with much stronger and more traditional kinship bonds than are found among other families in the United States. Although they have adopted the nuclear form of the family, there is more support for the elderly in Chinese and Japanese American families, and women are more likely to moderate their achievement aspirations in order to accommodate family demands. Among Asian immigrants from Vietnam and Cambodia in the past few decades, the extended family is often preserved, with many generations living in one home. The circumstances of these immigrants to the United States are explored in Other Worlds, Other Ways: Vietnam (pp. 253–254). This pattern may change as future generations assimilate into U.S. culture.

Given the rich racial and ethnic diversity that exists in the United States, this discussion could be extended to Arab Americans, Jewish Americans, and many others, but the point has been made that variations in cultural background and position in the social structure produce different family experiences.

Other Worlds, Other Ways

VIETNAM: FAMILY AND RELIGION AMONG IMMIGRANTS TO THE UNITED STATES

Vietnam is a small nation resting between two giants, China and India (Jamieson, 1993; Karnow, 1981). Over the centuries, Vietnam has been occupied and ruled, at various times, by the Chinese, the French, and the Japanese. The Vietnamese finally defeated the French at Dien Bien Phu in 1954, and Vietnam was divided into North Vietnam, ruled by the communists, and South Vietnam, supported by the United States. Twenty years later, the North Vietnamese and the Vietcong (communist guerrilla forces) defeated the United States and reunited the two parts of Vietnam.

Vietnam acquired its religious traditions from China—Buddhism, Confucianism, and Taoism (Henkin & Nguyen, 1981; Hickey, 1964). Buddhism and Taoism place great value on humility: They encourage detachment from the material world and view wealth and power as potentially corrupting forces. The way to peace is to reject worldliness and achieve reincarnation to a better life by doing good deeds in this life. This point of view can lead to an acceptance of things, both good and bad, that is difficult for Westerners to comprehend. For the Vietnamese, one endures. As noted in the discussion of cultural values in Japan and China, Confucianism places great importance on social obligation and duty to the group, whether it be society, community, or family. It requires each person to give obedience to those in authority over them, whether it be rulers over people, parents over children, or husband over wife. The good society, and the good family, is one in which subordinates faithfully and completely obey the emperor or father.

In the United States, people tend to belong to one religion or another, but the Vietnamese have no difficulty with combining many religious and philosophical systems, including some Western religions, into a coherent belief system that guides their lives. This eclecticism may be a reaction to their historical experience with colonial invaders over the centuries. These religious traditions shape the Vietnamese family, which is large, patriarchal, and extended. A household might contain young children, married sons and their wives, adult daughters who have yet to marry, and assorted other relatives who need support. The emphasis in the family is on collective obligation and decision making; the kind of individualism found in nuclear families in the United States is strongly discouraged. Gender, age, and birth order determine one's position in the family and the rights and obligations one has in relation to others in the family. For example, rights and duties such as supporting older family members, inheriting family property, and working to support the family are rigidly defined by kinship ties.

Primary responsibility for the support and moral guidance of the family rests on the oldest male. In traditional Vietnamese families, he will make the major decisions, such as choice of marriage partners or choice of occupations. He also controls family finances, and he decides how much money each family member needs and what

purchases to make with the whole family's interests in mind. Although the Vietnamese family is clearly patriarchal, an important tradition of female autonomy has evolved over time. Women play an important role in family finances, although men have the final say. In fact, many Vietnamese women translate their domestic roles into entrepreneurial activities outside the family, such as running a small restaurant. This practice enables them to maintain some independence and autonomy while still supporting a traditional family structure.

After the fall of Saigon and the withdrawal of U.S. forces in 1975, many South Vietnamese emigrated to the United States, large numbers of them settling in California. They brought their religious and family traditions with them, which they used to help them adapt to life in the United States (Gold, 1992; Haines, Rutherford, & Thomas, 1981). In particular, the family, with its emphasis on collective support and goals, has made it possible for them to overcome poverty and other sorts of adversity. The whole extended family might share one apartment or house, and they would have important links to other relatives who did not live with them. Even though other family members might be financially strapped themselves, they would give what assistance they could to others. One Vietnamese woman might employ some aunts or cousins in her restaurant, even though the business was only marginally profitable. Those aunts or cousins, in turn, would work long hours for low wages. Sometimes, they would keep these jobs, even when better ones came along, because of family obligation. The restaurant owner, in return, would give the workers food or clothing when it was available and let them work flexible hours. If the restaurant was successful, the owner would use some profits to help underwrite a relative's effort to start his or her own restaurant.

Familial obligations, then, are strong and extensive. The restaurant workers receive low wages, but they also know that the owner will do all she can to give family members work and certainly would never hire a nonrelative when kin were available to work. As one Vietnamese in the United States put it:

> We solve problems because the family institution is a bank. If I need money—and my brother and my two sisters are working—I tell them I need to buy a house. I need priority in this case. They say "okay," and they give money to me. And after only two years, I bought a house. . . . Now I help them. They live with me and have no rent. (quoted in Gold, 1992, p. 56)

If an elder in the family gets sick, everyone—sons, daughters, and their children—is available to help, and there is less need for expenditures on hospitals, nurses, or nursing homes.

As time has passed, of course, Vietnamese Americans have assimilated, or become more Americanized.

(continued)

Vietnamese American women, for example, have achieved very well in educational attainment, often surpassing their male counterparts. This trend would seem to reflect the adoption of Americanized norms of gender equality—and it does, to an extent—but Vietnamese American families still exercise substantial, patriarchal social control, even after generations in the United States. Vietnamese fathers encourage high levels of educational achievement among their daughters because the fathers believe that education will enable their daughters to attract high-status husbands, bring status to their families of origin, and enable them to support their families financially when they marry and have children. So, educational achievement is in part a response to continuing familial and patriarchal social control, although its long-term effect may be to reduce those influences and to encourage greater levels of gender equality (Bankston, 1995; Kibria, 1993). ■

Diversity and Change in Sexual Behavior

> You should be able to describe the extent of and changes in sexual behavior outside marriage and list some of the reasons for it.

Chapter 5 discussed sexual behavior in the context of deviance and concluded that there are no "natural" or "instinctive" expressions of human sexuality that people engage in largely or completely without learning. While sex is partly biological, it is also strongly shaped and regulated by cultural values and norms, the product of learning in a particular cultural environment. All societies regulate sexuality, although the nature and extent of regulation varies significantly across cultures. One important dimension of that regulation is the extent to which sexual expression is considered appropriate only in the family context. This section focuses on the sexual behaviors most relevant to the family: premarital, extramarital, and gay sexuality.

Premarital Sex

Many Western religions, such as Roman Catholicism, prohibit all sexual activity outside the marital bond. Such a complete prohibition on premarital sex is unusual in human societies. Anthropologists who have looked at many societies, both today and in the past, estimate that only about one-third of human societies require brides to be virgins. More than one-third allow almost completely unrestricted premarital sex (for example, the Trobriand Islanders mentioned in this chapter and the Huron Indians discussed in Chapter 8), and almost another third allow premarital sex with some restrictions, such as avoiding pregnancy (Murdock, 1967).

Today, people in the United States are more divided than in the past over premarital sexuality (Coltrane & Collins, 2001; Davis & Smith, 2007; Gallup, 2003). In the 1960s, only 20 percent believed that premarital sex was acceptable; today, about half of the public views it as permissible. Young people are much more likely to approve of premarital sex, as are those who are less religious and who have more egalitarian sex-role attitudes. As in so many other realms, however, attitudes and behavior are sometimes at variance; because people *approve* of a behavior does not mean that they *engage* in it themselves. Based on information from a variety of surveys and interviews, we can conclude that sex before marriage, which was once considered taboo in the United States, especially for women, has become routine. Today, 80 to 85 percent of women and 95 percent of men have had sex before marriage. This figure compares with about 50 percent of women and 66 percent of men in the 1920s. So, there has been a gradual increase since that time, but the change is less dramatic than many believe, since at least half of all men and women in the 1920s had premarital sexual experience. If there has been a sexual "revolution," it is among women.

Research shows that college-educated men have had an average of eight partners during their premarital years, with less educated men having slightly more. A majority of women seem to have no more than a few sexual partners before marriage (Tanfer & Cubbins, 1992; Tanfer & Schoorl, 1992). It also seems that Acquired Immune Deficiency Syndrome (AIDS) has changed sex for some people, with many claiming they abstain from sex more and have fewer partners than in the past (Hugick & Leonard, 1991; Roche & Ramsbey, 1993).

These changes in premarital sexual behavior are often misunderstood and exaggerated. There has been a dramatic change in how publicly people discuss sex and in how openly they recognize the reality of premarital sex. People are also less likely to insist that sex be limited to the marital context. Although changes in actual sexual behavior are real, they have not been as dramatic as many believe, especially when we consider the importance of cohabitation. Among some in the United States today, cohabitation has come to be viewed as a socially acceptable bonding between two people, including sexual exclusivity. In some cases, it even includes childbearing. Cohabitation looks a great deal like what Malinowski, when studying the

Trobriand Islanders, called the family. Many cohabitors gain social approval and legitimacy for their union from their friends and families. If we treat cohabitors like married couples and remove their sexual activity from the premarital category, the sexual "revolution" looks even less dramatic. In addition, some experts conclude that the most significant change has been the elimination of the double standard that permitted men to engage in premarital sex ("sow a few wild oats") without sanction but strongly discouraged the same behavior in women (Clement, 1989). Although there are still differences, women's sexual behavior has become much more similar to that of men in the past few decades.

What accounted for the changes in sexual behavior over the past century? One important factor, certainly, was the emergence of easy-to-use, unobtrusive, and reliable contraceptives. They have eased women's fears of pregnancy and widened their options for sexual behavior. A second major factor was the feminist movement, which emphasized that women should gain control of their lives and be able to make decisions for themselves. It also demanded that women's choices not be limited by sexist or stereotypical views of gender. Without question, many traditional views of women's sexuality were sexist, stereotyped, and wrong. A third factor producing changing sexual practices was technological developments, such as the automobile, that provide young people with more freedom and the means to escape surveillance by adults.

Extramarital Sex

In the United States, with its monogamous form of the family, marriage is defined in terms of sexual exclusivity: Husbands and wives are supposed to have sex only with each other, and there are strong legal and normative pressures toward this end. It is almost a property claim that one's spouse is off-limits sexually to anyone else. Reflecting this view, almost all people in the United States believe that extramarital sexual affairs are wrong (Davis & Smith, 2007). Despite this disapproval, such affairs are quite common, with about 12 percent of all married women and one-quarter of all married men having had at least one affair during their lives. These figures include, however, the many people who had only one affair during their life and were faithful the rest of the time. In fact, at any given moment, only a small percentage of married people are engaging in extramarital sex. These figures have increased over the past fifty years, but the increase has been larger for women than for men. About half of all women who have affairs have only one, and a lot of this activity occurs when a couple is separated but not legally divorced. So, part of the increase in extramarital affairs is due to the increase in the divorce rate over the past fifty years.

Whether extramarital sex occurs is in part a matter of opportunity. Working women have more such affairs than women who do not work, probably because they have the opportunity to meet more men. However, there is a double standard here, also, in that traditionally wives who have sex with someone other than their husband have met more disapproval than husbands who do the same. In addition, gender affects people's motivation for having an extramarital liaison: Women are more likely to have one for love and men for sex (Glass & Wright, 1992).

Homosexuality

When we look at other cultures, we find many that accept homosexuality as a normal sexual practice, at least for some people and at some points in their lives (Weinrich & Williams, 1990). In the United States, by contrast, almost half of the people believe that homosexual relations between consenting adults should be illegal (The Gallup Poll, 2007). Estimates of the number of adult males in the United States who are predominantly or exclusively gay range from 1 to 5 percent (Billy, Tanfer, Grady, & Keplinger, 1993; Strong, DeVault, & Cohen, 2008). Lesbians are probably about half as common. In addition, somewhere between 5 and 25 percent of all males have had at least one homosexual encounter. These figures should be viewed with caution, however, because many people undoubtedly refuse to admit to engaging in such behavior when interviewed.

The search for the causes of homosexuality has been very controversial (Hamer & Copeland, 1994; Rahman & Wilson, 2003). Research on twins has provided some evidence of a genetic influence on sexual orientation: Twins who share the same genetic material (monozygotic twins) are much more likely both to be gay than twins who do not share the exact same genetic material (dizygotic twins) or two adopted brothers who share no genetic material. However, to date, these research efforts have not been able to discover exactly what is inherited. It may be that what is inherited is not sexual orientation directly but rather behaviors that are more likely to be shaped into homosexuality in the proper environment. For example, people may inherit a tendency toward gender nonconformity, such as a tendency for young boys to behave in a stereotypically girlish fashion (be "sissies"). Then the reactions of others to that gender nonconformity may encourage ways of thinking and behaving that come to be defined as "homosexual." So a genetic predisposition may become shaped by social interaction during childhood and the teenage years.

Some psychologists have tried to explain homosexuality as arising from some psychological maladjustment, possibly stemming from a poor parent–child relationship. This explanation has been thoroughly studied over the years, yielding no evidence that homosexuality is linked with psychological problems. Heterosexuals have no fewer psychological problems than do gay men or lesbians, and the latter on the whole are as well adjusted, in both their lives and their sexual orientation, as are the former (Robinson, Skeen, Hobson, & Herrman, 1982; Ross, Paulsen, & Stalstrom, 1988).

Sociologists have recognized that the world does not divide simply into the gay and the straight. Some men and women combine both forms of sexuality in their lives, whereas others are exclusively one or the other. Some married people engage in homosexual affairs while also maintaining active heterosexual activities with their spouse (van der Geest, 1993). So human sexuality is complicated, and a number of social and situational factors shape sexual expression at a given time. In some cases, homosexuality is a matter of experimentation where people are looking for something new, different, or exciting. In others, it is a matter of opportunity, such as in prison when heterosexual partners may not be available. In these cases, the person may not define himself or herself as gay. For some people, however, the process of self-definition through the looking-glass self, as discussed in Chapter 3, comes into play (Troiden, 1989). If people label an individual as gay, such labeling increases the chances that the person will come to accept the label himself or herself. In addition, the labeling by self or others may lead to greater association with others who define themselves as gay. Such association can lead to more opportunities to explore homosexuality. So, the labeling and self-definition processes can precipitate gradual changes in a person's self-concept, along with a growing association with people in the gay community. These changes in turn may help solidify the person's gay self-definition and lifestyle.

There is still a lot that we do not know about sexual orientation. We have no idea whether all, or only some, of homosexuality is biologically linked. There may be many routes—some biological, some situational—to becoming straight or gay. In all likelihood, both biology and social forces will be found to play some part. Despite this uncertainty, we do know that homosexuality is a significant part of the sexuality that people express in society.

In conclusion, changes in attitude and behavior over the past fifty years in the United States have resulted in substantially more sexual activity outside the marriage bond. This activity has direct implications for what constitutes a family in the United States today, which is the next topic.

Diverse Family Lifestyles in Modern Societies

You should be able to describe the diverse family lifestyles that are found in modern societies and explain some of the reasons why they exist.

Earlier, this chapter discussed the diversity of families found around the world and the impact of industrialization on weakening the importance of kinship and encouraging the transition from extended to nuclear families. One consequence of these changes has been an increase in divorce; a second has been a growth in family lifestyles that diverge from the traditional extended or two-parent nuclear family. Some of these lifestyles have arisen as people adapt to the void left by divorce, whereas others are chosen because changes in modern society, including the changes in sexual behaviors just discussed, make them more attractive, or more necessary, options than in the past.

Dual-Earner Families

In most nuclear families in the United States in the past, women did not work. Today the norm is for women to work, even in families with young children; so, today, in almost two-thirds of two-parent families, both spouses work. In fact, as Figure 9.4 illustrates, it used to be that women with young children were much less likely to work, but that has changed. Now women are as likely to work in families with children under the age of six as they are in all families. In some families, the low wages of a spouse compel women to work in order to provide enough total income to support the family; in other cases, both spouses work because both wish to pursue a career. But when both spouses work, it can put stress on family relations. People who work have less time to spend with their spouses and their children. This limitation may stress the spousal relationship as well as contribute to difficulties that children have.

Dual-career families confront another stress: deciding whose career takes precedence. Such conflicts can arise, for example, if either husband or wife wants to move in order to advance a career, especially if such a transition would be detrimental to the spouse's career. On a routine basis, there may be disagreement over whose career must suffer in order to raise children or to accomplish household chores. Although these tensions suggest that dual-career marriages are more susceptible to divorce, there is little convincing evidence on this issue so far. Evidence does suggest that women who work out of choice are more satisfied with their marriages than women who

Figure 9.4
Percentage of Married Women with Spouse Present Who Are Employed, among All Such Women and among Women with Children under Six Years of Age, 1940–2005

Note: From *Statistical Abstract of the United States*, 1978 (p. 404) by U.S. Bureau of the Census, 1978, Washington, DC: U.S. Government Printing Office: *Statistical Abstract of the United States*, 2008 (p. 380) by U.S. Bureau of the Census, 2007. Washington, DC: U.S. Government Printing Office.

work out of a sense of financial obligation, and the men in dual-career families seem to be happy with their marriages (Barnett & Rivers, 1996; Vannoy-Hiller & Philliber, 1989). In addition, dual-career couples are more likely to remain childless, and childless couples tend to have higher levels of marital satisfaction than do couples with children (Houseknecht, 1987). One investigation of dual-career couples working in senior management positions described such marriages as "more equal than others" in that the couples share a more equal partnership, with a more egalitarian decision-making structure, than do couples in more traditional marriages. Furthermore, women in such marriages have greater opportunity to continue to pursue careers, as well as raise their children, in comparison to women in traditional families (Hertz, 1986).

Careers are attractive to both men and women because their work offers financial rewards, status, and excitement. However, the time and commitment devoted to careers compete with the energy people devote to family life, creating tensions in the family. Higher rates of childlessness among dual-career families may be an effort to avoid such competing demands. This solution might create other problems, however. If more people choose careers in the future, it is possible that many will resolve competing demands by choosing not to have children, possibly even choosing not to get married. This situation may well create a substantial difference in the standard of living between those who devote their energies to careers and those who feel family is important: Careerists will have a substantially more affluent lifestyle, which may make the decision to remain childless appealing to even more people. The

outcome, potentially, might be the birth of even fewer children in society. A low birthrate in turn could lead to a number of problems such as an increasingly aged and dependent population that would be difficult and expensive to support (see Chapter 14).

Singlehood

Today, 55 million adults in the United States have never been married. This figure includes slightly more males than females. Many of these people, of course, will eventually marry, but some will choose singlehood over marriage as a lifelong lifestyle. In addition, although the proportion of the population that is single declined between 1940 and 1970, it has increased considerably since then (see Figure 9.2). Added to these never-married people are the many widowed and divorced who, at least temporarily, are single.

Many people who remain single do so because they believe this lifestyle affords them distinct advantages: freedom from unnecessary commitments, economic independence, opportunities to meet new people and develop new relationships, room for personal growth, or the ability to have a more varied sex life that is free of guilt (Macklin, 1987). Remaining single does not mean, of course, that there is necessarily a lack of emotional involvement with a partner who is at least semipermanent. Many singles develop intimate relationships, but they choose not to allow these to become permanent bonds based on marital exclusivity. However, as with childlessness among dual-career couples, being single—especially if chosen permanently and in large numbers—may have a long-term effect of lowering the birthrate.

Cohabitation

Cohabitation, or what is commonly called "living together," refers to *relationships in which two people live in the same household and share sexual, emotional, and often economic ties without being legally married.* It is difficult to estimate the number of couples in cohabiting relationships because it is difficult to clearly define exactly who is cohabiting and such relationships can change rapidly. The Census Bureau determined that, in 2006, 5.4 million "unmarried couple" households existed in the United States, with two unrelated adults of the opposite sex sharing the same household (see Figure 9.5). Some of these were not cohabitants, of course, but merely roommates. In addition, 50 percent of women between the ages of 15 and 44 in one survey said they had cohabited at some point in their lives and 9 percent said they were currently in a cohabitation relationship (U.S. Department of Health and Human Services, 2005). These numbers give us some idea of the magnitude of the arrangement. Most of the couples involved are young, but about 5 percent of the Census's "unmarried couple" households involve at least one partner over age 65.

People cohabit for many reasons (Cherlin & Furstenberg, 1994; Loomis & Landale, 1994). For some, it is a trial marriage, a time for the couple to get to know each other and determine whether they are compatible before establishing the legal bond. Others view cohabitation as a replacement for marriage, which some women and men see as an unnecessary legal tie. In fact, one group among which cohabitation has increased considerably in the past thirty years is the divorced. People increasingly turn to cohabitation rather than remarriage as a vehicle for establishing an intimate relationship after a failed marriage. These people see cohabitation as being as acceptable as marriage as a context for family-related activities such as having children. Finally, for some elderly couples, for whom marriage means a reduction in Social Security income, cohabitation may be a matter of economic convenience or necessity.

As the number of cohabiting couples has grown, the stigma associated with this lifestyle has declined. Some employers, including some city and county governments, have established domestic partner provisions that accord cohabitants much the same benefits and rights as married couples. In addition, a number of courts have ruled that the relationship between cohabitants is not unlike that of married couples. For example, cohabitants can make legal arrangements to share their property, and one partner can sue the other for a share of the property and for support payments, or *palimony,* should the relationship dissolve. So, although some people continue to see marriage as the preferable route for organizing one's life, a growing number of people are choosing cohabitation, and the courts are establishing a legal framework that sees cohabitation as being very much like marriage.

Single Parenthood

A rapidly growing alternative to the conventional two-parent nuclear family is one in which there is only one parent. Today, 28 percent of all families with children under eighteen years of age are headed by only one parent, mostly by women (U.S. Bureau of the Census, 2007, p. 55). Furthermore, one out of every three children lives in a family in which one or both parents are absent (Figure 9.6), and half of all children may spend at least part of their childhood in a single-parent home. Although some families have only one parent because of the death of a spouse, most such situations are the result of divorce. Increasingly, however, children live with

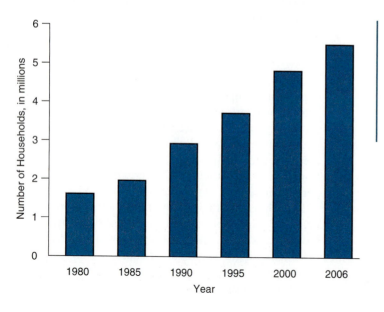

Figure 9.5

Number of Households with Unmarried, Heterosexual Couples, 1980–2006

Sources: U.S. Bureau of the Census, *Statistical Abstract of the United States,* 1998 (Washington, DC: U.S. Government Printing Office, 1998), p. 60; U.S. Bureau of the Census, Current Population Survey, *America's Families and Living Arrangements:* 2006 (Washington, DC: U.S. Government Printing Office, 2007), www.census.gov/population/www/socdemo/hh-fam.html

parents, usually mothers, who choose not to marry at all. The number of children living with a mother who has never married is now 10 percent. Currently, 38 percent of all births are to unmarried women, in comparison with 4 percent in 1950 (Figure 9.7). Given these

trends in divorce and single motherhood, the proportion of single-parent families is likely to grow considerably in the future. Needless to say, people who view marriage as the only acceptable context for raising children find such developments very disturbing.

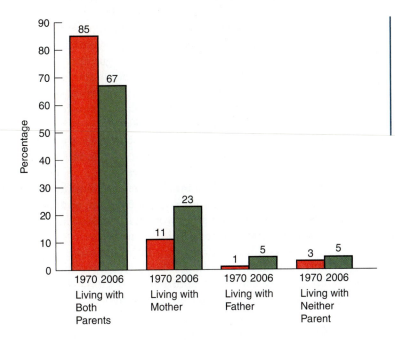

Figure 9.6

Living Arrangements of People in the United States under Eighteen Years of Age, 1970–2006

Note: From *Statistical Abstract of the United States,* 1995 (p. 66) by U.S. Bureau of the Census, 1995, Washington, DC: U.S. Government Printing Office; Current Population Survey, 2006, *Annual Social and Economic Supplement* by U.S. Bureau of the Census. September 2007, Washington, DC: U.S. Government Printing Office.

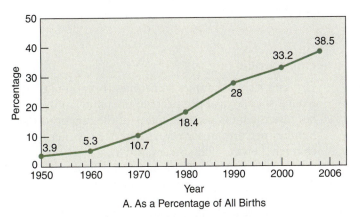

A. As a Percentage of All Births

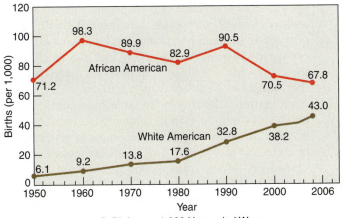

B. Births per 1,000 Unmarried Women Aged 15–44 Years, by Race

Figure 9.7

Births to Unmarried Women in the United States, by Race, 1950–2006

Note: U.S. Bureau of the Census, *Statistical Abstract of the United States,* various years; National Center for Health Statistics, *Vital Statistics Reports,* various years.

The issue of single parenthood has been controversial because suggestions that children raised by a single parent suffer more problems than children raised by both parents have been strongly attacked for implying that mothers are not adequate parents or that parents should not divorce. These suggestions have been interpreted as limiting women's choices in life, a stance that is not popular in this era of gender equality. Yet, the research does suggest, in a qualified way, that children are often worse off when raised by one parent rather than two, suffering consequences similar to those of children of divorce mentioned earlier (Cancian & Reed, 2001). A summary of this research concluded as follows:

> Growing up with only one biological parent frequently deprives children of important economic, parental, and community resources, and . . . these deprivations ultimately undermine their chances of future success . . . . While living with just one parent increases the risk of . . . negative outcomes, it is not the only, or even the major, cause of them. Growing up with a single parent is just one among many factors that put children at risk of failure. (McLanahan & Sandefur, 1994, pp. 2–3)

Not all children in single-parent families will suffer negative consequences, because many factors influence a child's development. Researchers attribute the difficulties of children in single-parent families to three factors: low income, inadequate parental guidance, and less access to community resources. If a single parent can overcome these difficulties, then the children can do quite well. For example, when the decision to have a child is well considered by a woman with the social and economic resources to raise the child adequately, the outcome does not raise serious problems for society, although it might clash with the personal or religious values of some groups.

So, the research does not lead necessarily to the conclusion that divorce or single parenthood is bad. However, single parenthood is especially widespread among groups who are more likely to lack the financial resources to support the child, such as minorities and teenagers (Kirby, 2001; Luker, 1996). For example, over half of all births to African American and Puerto Rican American women are to unmarried women, and both these groups have some of the highest rates of poverty in the United States (see Figure 9.7). Four out of every ten teenage girls get pregnant at least once before they are twenty years old (Kirby, 2001). Although the teen pregnancy rate in the United States has been falling somewhat recently, the rate is still far higher than in all comparable industrial nations; it is twice as high as in Great Britain and ten times higher than in the Netherlands or Japan. For teenagers, in particular,

becoming a mother is a difficult burden: They often lack the maturity and economic resources for good child rearing, and the burden often severely limits their educational and employment opportunities. This fact is especially true for teenagers from poor families and from families with a history of welfare use (Chase-Lansdale, Brooks-Gunn, & Paikoff, 1991).

The increase in single-parent families may be changing kinship in the United States toward a more *matrilineal* system. Anthropologists argue that the family in the United States has a somewhat matrilineal focus to begin with, in that mothers tend to be more prominent in kinship affairs and play a more central role in kinship matters (Johnson, Klee, & Schmidt, 1988). Men's role in the family system tends to be more peripheral and unstable. When the family is under stress, for example, it is more often the women who take control of the family. Men are considerably less likely to have custody of their children, and men are much more likely than women to be homeless or live in a nonfamily household. Furthermore, after divorce, children perceive their fathers as more socially and emotionally distant and less available to them. Postdivorce children also turn to their mothers for help much more than to their fathers. If divorce and single parenthood become more common, this matrilineal cast to kinship in the United States may become more prominent.

Gay Families

Gay and lesbian couples sometimes form units that, from a sociological perspective, resemble families because the units perform many of the functions that families perform in society, as described earlier in this chapter (Lewin, 1993; Stacey, 1998). These relationships are often monogamous, the norm for families in U.S. culture, with some degree of permanence and an emphasis on sexual exclusivity. In fact, lesbians value monogamy in a relationship and are about as possessive of their partners as are men and women in heterosexual marriages. A smaller percentage of gay men put as much value on sexual exclusivity in a relationship. Gay and lesbian couples sometimes have children from previous marriages or they adopt or conceive through artificial insemination. Children in gay or lesbian families are much less common than in heterosexual families because the courts have been reluctant to give custody to an openly gay parent, and adoption agencies have viewed gay homes as inappropriate for child placement. Estimates are that one-third of lesbians are mothers and between one-quarter and one-half of gay men are fathers, although many do not have custody of their offspring (Green & Bozett, 1991). Thus the

These police officers are dealing with an episode of family violence. Such violence is more widespread than many people believe, and it causes serious physical and psychological damage to those who are its victims.

socialization and education functions of the family are performed by some gay couples, and research gives no evidence that the children are compromised in any significant way by being raised by a gay parent (Golombok & Tasker, 1996; Johnson & O'Connor, 2002; Stacey & Biblarz, 2001).

Gay couples also often form an economic unit through the common ownership of property, such as a home, and the combining of financial resources. The courts have yet to give legal sanction to these economic ties, but some corporations are beginning to do so by extending benefits and rights to the unmarried domestic partners of their employees, whether they be a heterosexual couple or a gay couple. As evidence that the relationship is reasonably permanent, some employers look for signs of economic interdependence, such as joint bank accounts or co-owned property. Finally, many gay couples provide the protection and the personal gratification that are among the functions of the units typically called families.

So, many gay men and lesbians form relationships that have many of the sociological attributes normally associated with families. To be sure, gay couples face significant stressors, such as discrimination in both occupation and housing (Rodriguez Rust, 2004). They are also likely to be labeled deviant by many and cast into a marginal role. One way in which society marginalizes gays is by denying official legitimation to their bond in the form of marriage ceremonies or licenses that signify societal approval. Some gay couples have ceremonies, sometimes performed by ministers, to mark their commitment to each other; these rituals perform the same functions of public affirmation and legitimation that legally recognized marriage ceremonies do. As of this writing, the Netherlands and Belgium now provide for gay marriages; courts in Canada, California, and Massachusetts have ruled that the government must recognize gay marriage, and the state of Vermont and the Canadian province of Quebec have civil unions for gay couples, giving them much the same rights and obligations as married couples. In 2003, *Bride's* magazine published an article on same-sex weddings, discussing why gays and lesbians wanted a marriage option available and how guests should behave if invited to such a wedding. All these developments taken together suggest that a significant shift in attitudes and practices relating to gay families is underway. They are certainly testimony to the political clout of the gay community. Yet it is unclear what the future of these developments will be because strong opposition to them persists. So, there is substantial uncertainty at this point about whether gay and lesbian couples will make additional progress toward being considered married couples living in families.

A Global Perspective

Some of the trends in family life found in the United States are also occurring in other nations (United Nations, 2000; United Nations Development Fund for Women, 2002). In the past few decades, for example, the percentage of births to unmarried women has increased in most nations, in some cases dramatically. The proportion has doubled in the United States to 38 percent, but in nations as diverse as Denmark, Norway, and Guam it has increased 300 to 400 percent. In the Seychelles, French Guiana, and Martinique, two out of every three births are to unmarried women. In addition, many households are headed by women: almost 50 percent in nations like Botswana and Barbados, 31 percent in the United States. Household size has also been decreasing in every part of the world, suggesting that the family is becoming a smaller kinship unit. The birthrate in most societies around the world has been declining, and the divorce rate has been increasing. All these trends suggest the extent to which the form of the family is shaped by the needs of society. Earlier, this chapter pointed out that industrial societies generally tend to weaken kinship and family structures, in part because the family in such societies performs fewer functions and is thus less important. Industrial societies tend to encourage nuclear families and to be more permissive of divorce. Such societies also sometimes split families up as some members must migrate looking for work. In addition, greater gender equality and higher levels of education for women offer them more opportunities in terms of supporting their families. The result, in most nations, is that the family has declined in both size and significance, and women have fewer supports with which to take care of themselves and their families. It is a worldwide trend—a by-product of industrialization—although the pace and extent of the developments vary from one society to another.

Violence in the Family

You should be able to describe the nature and extent of violence in the family and the social conditions that produce it.

Intimate partner violence includes violence between spouses, former spouses, cohabiting partners, boyfriends or girlfriends, and dates. A recent survey by the National Institute of Justice and the Centers for Disease Control and Prevention found that one-quarter of all women and 8 percent of all men reported being the victim of violence by an intimate partner at some point during their life (Tjaden & Thoennes, 2000). Another study found that 20 percent of all nonfatal violence against women is perpetrated by an intimate partner and one-third of all women murder victims are killed by an intimate partner (Rennison, 2003). Possibly as many as one-quarter to one-third of gay men and lesbians have also been abused by an intimate partner (Durfee & Rosenberg, 2004). All these figures probably underestimate the amount of intimate partner violence that occurs because people are often reluctant to admit such goings-on in their own relationships. Even so, the numbers demonstrate that a serious problem exists.

How are we to explain this high level of intimate partner violence? One reason for it is that the use of violence to settle disputes is widely accepted in the United States, especially among males. Traditional norms in many U.S. subcultures support male domination in marriage. In fact, men with traditional, or nonegalitarian, views toward gender-role relationships are more likely to approve of using violence against a spouse and are more likely to have actually used severe violence against their spouse. A second reason is poverty: Serious violence within families is disproportionately a problem of the poor and economically disadvantaged. Families with low educational and occupational attainment are especially at risk of spouse abuse. A third reason contributing to intimate partner violence is gender inequality (Crossman, Stith, & Bender, 1990; Kalmuss & Straus, 1982; Straus, 1991). Wife beating is much more likely to occur in families where power over decision making is concentrated in the husband's hands—the rate is approximately twenty times that found in families where egalitarian decision making is accepted. When women have more social and economic resources, such as a job with which to support themselves, they are less likely to be abused and more likely to leave an abusive husband. A final reason contributing to intimate partner violence is social isolation: When a spouse has few contacts with people other than her husband, she is less likely to define the abuse as unjustified and to seek assistance (Stets, 1991).

Child abuse is also widespread in families in the United States, with 60 percent of couples acknowledging at least one violent act against a child. One investigation reported that more than twelve out of every one hundred children under the age of eighteen are the victims of serious abuse or neglect every year (U.S. Department of Health and Human Services, 2002). As with spouse abuse, child abuse is concentrated not only among low-income families but also among the extremely poor (Gelles, 1992). For these families, economic hardships interact with immediate situational stresses—disputes between parents, a burdensome number of children, a child who creates problems for parents—to bring about incidents of child abuse. Poor, young parents and poor, single mothers are especially at risk of using the most abusive forms of violence against their children. Child abuse is also a behavior pattern that is passed on from generation to generation in some families. For example, a review of studies on child abuse found that although around 3 percent of parents abuse their children, that rate is 30 percent or more among parents who were themselves abused as children (Gelles & Conte, 1990).

The elderly also experience abuse in families, with thirty-two out of every one thousand older people suffering some type of abuse, well over half of it physical violence (Flowers, 2000; Pillemer & Finkelhor, 1988). Older men are more likely to be victims of abuse than are older women, and women are more likely to abuse their elder husbands than men are to abuse their elder wives. However, women suffer more injuries and emotional distress when they are abused than do men. Also, those who live alone or who are not married are less likely to suffer abuse than those who are married or live with others, and those who live with a spouse and an offspring are especially at risk of suffering abuse. One conclusion from these findings is that abuse of the elderly is in part a matter of opportunity: Those who live alone or with fewer people are less likely to be abused because there are fewer people around to abuse them. This fact is probably part of the reason why men suffer more abuse than women: Because women live longer than men, older women are more likely to be living alone than are older men.

To some extent, abuse of the elderly reflects one of the weaknesses of the modern nuclear family: It lacks the extensive support network and additional helping hands that are available in the extended family or even the modified extended family. As has been noted, people often expect each person in the nuclear family to be a breadwinner, a companion, and so on. When society burdens one person with a wide range of difficult tasks, including taking care of a child or an impaired older parent, the stresses will sometimes accumulate to the point where abuse is likely. Recent research, however, points to a different relationship between dependency and abuse: Abuse is more likely to occur when the caregiver is dependent on the elderly person under his or her care. Such abuse is especially likely when the caregiver is financially dependent on the elderly person under his or her charge, is personally or emotionally troubled, or abuses alcohol or drugs (Greenberg, McKibben, & Raymond, 1990; Pillemer & Finkelhor, 1989). In these situations, caregivers may be responding to their feelings of powerlessness in the relationship and resorting to one of the few power resources they have available: force and violence.

Thus, research on abuse of the elderly provides further evidence for the part that inequitable distributions of power and resources play in family violence. Those who are dependent—whether they be children or frail elderly—are at risk of suffering violence at the hands of others. Those with access to economic and social resources, such as wives with careers or the elderly who can live on their own, are better equipped to avoid violence. And those who feel helpless and powerless—such as poor, single mothers or caregivers who are dependent on their elderly charges—may lash out in violence as a reaction to their circumstances. The Applying Sociology section describes some of the work that applied sociologists do to fight against domestic violence.

Applying Sociology   Creating and Evaluating Programs to Fight Domestic Violence

Domestic violence is a particularly tragic social problem, with its jarring intrusion of injury and cruelty into the intimacy of the family. It is also a difficult problem for police officers, who are often first on the scene of such violence and whose job it is to make complex and troubling decisions about how to handle the alleged perpetrator of the violence. Should they mediate the dispute between the couple, in an effort to resolve the conflict? Or should they aggressively pursue arrest? Or is there some other effective option, such as sending the abuser away in the hope that a period of separation will calm the passions that led to the violence?

In the past, this decision was left to the judgment of the individual officer at the scene. Those judgments were shaped in part by the experiences of the officers but also by each officer's personal feelings about spouse abuse and the relationship between men and women, and by many other social and cultural factors. Some officers had their favorite approach that they believed worked, but no one had any systematic knowledge about which strategy was really most likely to stop future outbreaks of domestic violence. In the early 1980s, the criminologist Lawrence Sherman and the sociologist Richard Berk (1984) developed an innovative program to collect systematic observations to begin resolving this problem. They based their approach on two competing theories of the effect of punishment in controlling crime. One theory, the specific deterrence doctrine, posits that punishment, such as an arrest, tends to stop people from committing future crimes because they fear further punishment. The opposite approach, labeling theory, argues that punishment by an official law enforcement agency increases the likelihood of future crimes because it starts the person down the path of becoming a career criminal.

(continued)

The police in Minneapolis cooperated with Sherman and Berk, who designed a field experiment to test their ideas (this type of research design was discussed in Chapter 1). They gave each officer a pad of police report forms that were in three different colors, each representing a type of intervention—separation, mediation, and arrest. The different-colored forms were ordered randomly in each officer's pad, and the officer took whatever action was called for by the color of the uppermost form. Thus each type of intervention was used an equal number of times and was chosen without the judgment of the officers coming into play. Sherman and Berk then looked to see which perpetrators of spouse abuse were most likely to be involved in repeat offenses over the next six months. (For ethical reasons, these procedures were followed only in cases of simple, or misdemeanor, assault where there was no severe injury or life-threatening situation.)

This was a complex piece of applied research, but basically Sherman and Berk discovered that arrest was the most effective form of intervention: Those who were arrested were less likely to be involved in another domestic assault over the next six months than were those who experienced mediation or separation. This fact was true even though those arrested were released quickly and thus were free to commit further abuse. And this research made a difference in the lives of many women and men because the findings were used as the justification for changing social policies. In the past, police in many cities would rarely arrest suspected abusers. As a result of Sherman and Berk's findings, police officers in many cities were ordered by their superiors to consider arrest the preferred intervention in dealing with domestic assault cases. In some states today, police are given authorization to arrest in such cases even if the victim does not make a complaint—a vast improvement over the past policy of neglect.

Because social behavior is complicated, sociologists recognize that one research study is not likely to tell us all we need to know. To see if the Sherman and Berk findings would hold up in other places and at other times, variations on their study have been done in a number of cities, including Milwaukee, Atlanta, Omaha, and Charlotte, North Carolina (Hirschel, Hutchison, & Dean, 1992; Maxwell, Garner, & Fagan, 2001; Pate & Hamilton, 1992). These replications have supported the efficacy of arrest, as did the Sherman and Berk study, but they also show that the efficacy of arrest is not nearly as strong or as consistent as earlier studies had suggested. It may be that Sherman and Berk inadvertently studied a select group of abusers for whom arrest was particularly effective. The later studies have included a broader sampling of abusers. In addition, research has been extended beyond the issue of arrest to explore such things as severity of sentencing, finding that more severe sentences (such as jail time rather than probation) tend to reduce future episodes of domestic violence (Thistlewaite, Wooldredge, & Gibbs, 1998). So, sociologists are now beginning to narrow down their understanding of which batterers of women are deterred by arrest or severe sentences. For example, they seem to deter domestic violence among people whose reputations would be affected by an arrest or jail time, such as the affluent and those with middle-class jobs. However, among those for whom conformity to conventional norms is less important to maintaining their lifestyle, such as those who are unemployed, arrest and jail time do not seem to have the desired effect. ■

The Future of the Family

You should be able to discuss what is in store for the family as a social institution in modern societies.

Most sociologists today are confident that the family as a social institution will survive in modern societies such as the United States. To be sure, the family is changing, and it confronts some serious problems, such as a high divorce rate and too much family violence. As noted, however, the family unit performs important functions for society, and some type of family will persist for that reason. The real issue is not whether the family will survive but what form it will take. What seems to be emerging in modern industrial societies is a pluralistic family system in which *a number of different types of family exist side by side, each having an attraction for some people.* So, in the United States today, some people live in extended families, some in blended families, and still others in same-sex families. Given the vast diversity in the culture and the changing role of the family, such pluralistic family arrangements are probably more adaptive. They permit people of many occupations, religions, ethnic groups, and lifestyles to find a form of the family that best fits their values and needs. Whereas some people are tolerant of this diversity, others find some alternatives to be morally unacceptable, and this conflict will probably persist in the future. Such conflict will be especially salient in the public policy arena where groups do battle to gain acceptability for their values or ways of life. For example, some have opposed public support for sex education for teenagers on the grounds that it promotes premarital sex and pregnancy outside marriage. Others have opposed treating gay couples as married couples, as some employers have done, for purposes of allocating employee benefits. The outcome of this conflict will determine which forms of the family are acceptable at any given moment, and that will likely change from time to time.

Some people have expressed alarm at the rise in the divorce rate during the twentieth century, predicting the demise of the family as we know it. Actually, the divorce rate has been fairly stable for a number of decades. It may have stopped increasing because the marriage rate has declined by almost one-half over the past thirty years (see Figure 9.3). It may also be, however, that the divorce rate has risen as high as it is likely to go in response to changing social conditions brought about by industrialization. Nevertheless, there is no reason to believe that the divorce rate will decline significantly in the future. The current divorce rate in the United States may well be one that is commensurate with social conditions and the position of the family in a mature industrial society. In fact, many of the trends we have observed in the United States—toward smaller families, more divorce, and less respect for elders—can be found occurring to a degree in more traditional societies such as China and Mexico as they industrialize and modernize (Kosberg, 1992).

Still, the state of the modern family has been the focus of intense debate among sociologists as well as lay people. The Sociology of Media and Technology section explores ways in which the mass media and modern music shape the image as well as the reality of the family in modern societies.

Sociology of Media and Technology

Family in the Electronic Age

This chapter explores a number of social forces that have produced dramatic changes in family life, especially the role of industrialization. The modern communications technologies, especially now that they are establishing a global reach, have been a significant and growing part of this impact since the middle of the twentieth century. As Chapter 3 points out, the media and the cyberworld are becoming more pervasive as agencies of socialization. In fact, they have probably come to rival the family as the most significant socializer of children. In most human societies through history, parents and families have been the dominant forces in children's lives and have largely controlled the transmission of values and norms having to do with religion, sexuality, and other matters. Today, advertisers, media corporate executives, and online communities have the attention of children–with limited interference from their parents. Some people have argued that this situation produces a further erosion of the importance of family and kinship in society.

Sociologists and other social scientists have attempted to assess scientifically the extent and consequences of these intrusions into traditional family realms. The research to date is equivocal in its condemnation of this new role for the media and communications technologies. Negative consequences can be found, of course. For example, Chapters 3 and 12 discuss the research showing that viewing violence in the media increases the likelihood that children will resort to violence in real life, and exposure to rap and hip-hop music may reduce some of the inhibitions to committing domestic violence in some people (Barongan & Hall, 1995; Johnson, Adams, Ashburn, & Reed, 1995). Other research documents that adolescents who watch music videos develop more permissive attitudes toward sex and more permissive sexual behaviors than their parents would prefer, especially among girls and when the family environment is not a positive one (Strouse, Buerkel-Rothfuss, & Long, 1995). In these realms, media and music exposure is probably socializing the young in ways the parents or society as a whole would not prefer. What is unclear, however, is whether, in the absence of these media influences, families would do a better job of socialization. In addition, Chapters 3, 8, and 12 also describe some positive socializing functions of the media and the electronic world, such as providing a wide range of role models and educational programs to the young.

In addition to its role as agent of socialization, the mass media also function to shape people's beliefs and values regarding what the family is like in society or what it should be like. Studies of the content of television shows over the decades document changing portrayals of the family. The portrayals mirror actual family forms in some respects but seriously distort them in others (Huston et al., 1992; Robinson & Skill, 2001). Through the 1950s, families on television always had two parents, and either they had two or three children or they were a recently married couple that had yet to begin having children. Needless to say, gays and gay couples were virtually never portrayed on television or in the movies during this era. Popular examples of the portrayal of families during this era were *Father Knows Best, Ozzie and Harriet,* and *I Love Lucy.* Although media

(continued)

executives claimed to be merely describing what most families then were like, this chapter has shown that at that time family violence was widespread, extramarital sex was not uncommon, and divorce did occur. Yet, television did not portray these social realities. Their absence from television helped to foster the belief that the happy, nuclear family with an average of two children was the norm. Television also tended to portray more middle-class and affluent families than existed in reality and to ignore working-class families or to portray them in a more negative light.

In the 1960s and 1970s, television began to portray more single-parent families; however, most of these families were headed by men even though in reality most single-parent families were headed by women. These early portrayals of single-parent families stood out in another regard: The family resulted from a parental death rather than divorce, even though divorce, then and now, is the far more common cause for a family to have only one parent. Despite the appearance of single-parent families on television during these decades, most family portrayals were still of traditional families, often presented in an almost idyllic version, such as on *The Waltons* and *Little House on the Prairie*.

In recent decades, the portrayal of families on television has become more realistically diverse, with more single-parent, female-headed families portrayed. However, the ratio of male to female single-parent families is still much more heavily skewed toward males than is the case among actual families. In addition, television still downplays some of the serious problems that confront modern families, such as poverty, access to child care, family conflict and violence, and unemployment.

There has also been a substantial growth in the portrayal of gay and lesbian characters in television and movies, to the point where it has become almost routine. However, gay couples or families are still rather scarce in these media, being portrayed in substantially smaller proportions than their real numbers would warrant if the media were attempting to reflect reality. Finally, music must be considered as part of the media technology that shapes images of the family, and some modern music presents a rather negative picture. Musical innovations such as rap and hip-hop, for example, sometimes portray positively an aggressive image of masculinity and an almost misogynistic view of women (Martinez, 1997). Such portrayals translate at times into a picture of violence between men and women as socially acceptable, or at least tolerable. And, in fact, some research suggests that exposure to rap and hip-hop music may reduce some of the inhibitions to committing domestic violence in some people (Barongan & Hall, 1995; Johnson, Adams, Ashburn, & Reed, 1995).

These portrayals of family and sexuality are important because research documents that young viewers' beliefs and values regarding family life and sexuality are affected by what they see and hear on television, in movies, and in music (Dorr, Kovaric, & Doubleday, 1990). They tend, for example, to see the traditional nuclear family as the norm, despite the enormous diversity that actually exists. To the extent that these images are a distortion of reality, young people's efforts to organize their own personal lives will be based on a distortion of what is possible. In addition, exposure to music can influence sexual attitudes and behaviors as well as propensities toward family violence, and these things also shape what people's family lives will look like.

Sociology on the Internet

One useful Web site that has numerous links to locations related to family issues the women's studies program at the University of Connecticut (www.womens.studies.uconn.edu/resources_&_links.html).

One of the issues discussed in this chapter is whether gay couples should be considered families. Using the Yahoo! search vehicle, go to the "More" choice and then "Directory" search category; then choose "Society and Culture" and then either "Lesbian," "Gay," or "Transgendered." You will then have many options to choose. Select "Organizations." Explore these various areas and identify all the issues and arguments that relate to the controversy over gay families.

The chapter also stresses the variety of families that can be found in the United States and in other cultures.

Search for Web sites that document and explore that diversity. Can you locate some types of families that were not discussed in this chapter? For an anthropological approach to these issues, try this Web site at the University of Manitoba: **www.umanitoba.ca/faculties/arts/anthropology/knititle.html**. It has a tutorial that looks at kinship as an aspect of social organization and is very informative.

For further information and discussion, go to Allyn & Bacon's Social Problems Supersite (see Chapter 1) and explore Problem Area: Problems of Families and Family Violence and Problem Area: Problems of Sexual Behavior and Sexual Orientation.

Study & Review
SUMMARY OF LEARNING OBJECTIVES

You should be able to discuss the various social rules that govern practices related to descent, marriage, authority, family size, and mate selection.

The family is a social institution based on kinship that functions to replace members of society and to nurture them. All societies have rules and norms that shape family and kin relations in terms of descent, marriage, authority, size of the family, mate selection, and marriage transactions.

You should be able to analyze the role of the family in society from both the functionalist and conflict perspectives.

In the United States today, the family tends to be monogamous, egalitarian, bilateral, neolocal, and nuclear. Many U.S. families, however, diverge from this pattern. The functionalist perspective posits that some form of the family has existed in all societies because the family performs certain basic functions that are essential to human survival and the maintenance of society. The conflict perspectives sees the family as serving the interests of the dominant groups in society.

You should be able to describe the attitudes of people in the United States toward marriage, analyze the extent of divorce and its effects, and assess the family experiences of minorities.

Mate selection in the United States is an exchange relationship and tends to be homogamous. Also, the attitudes of people in the United States toward marriage and family remain quite positive, although there have been changes in attitudes in the past thirty years toward less negative attitudes toward remaining single, seeing fewer advantages in getting married, and less certainty about whether having children is essential. The divorce rate has risen significantly over the past fifty years, although it has been fairly steady now for two decades. The rise may be attributed to the fact that people expect a great deal from the marriage relationship and to changing societal conditions, such as the fact that the family today performs fewer functions than in the past. Some couples are at considerably greater risk of divorcing than are others. Divorce has consequences in terms of people's health and the reactions of children. Minority families in the United States exhibit both strengths and weaknesses and display considerable variation in such things as rates of single-parent families, rates of divorce, strength of kinship ties, and so on.

You should be able to describe the extent of and changes in sexual behavior outside marriage and list some of the reasons for it.

The amount of sexual behavior occurring outside the family context—premarital and extramarital sex as well as homosexuality—has been increasing in the United States, a trend that has implications for what is considered to be a "family." Premarital sexual behavior has increased because of the availability of reliable contraceptives, changes in attitudes toward women, and technologies that make it more possible for the young to avoid surveillance by adults. Extramarital sex is in part a matter of opportunity. As for homosexuality, it is still unclear whether it is innate or learned, but for some people it involves a matter of self-definition through the looking-glass self.

You should be able to describe the diverse family lifestyles that are found in modern societies and explain some of the reasons why they exist.

Many different family lifestyles have increased in prominence in the past fifty years: dual-earner families, singlehood, cohabitation, single parenthood, and gay families. Many people consider the prominence of these lifestyles to be an indication of problems surrounding the family today. Many of these same developments can be found in nations around the world as a by-product of global industrialization.

You should be able to describe the nature and extent of violence in the family and the social conditions that produce it.

Violence among family members is common in the United States, occurring chiefly between intimate partners or directed at dependent children or the elderly.

You should be able to discuss what is in store for the family as a social institution in modern societies.

Most sociologists are confident that the family will survive as a social institution but that family relationships will be pluralistic in the future, with different forms of family existing side by side, each having an attraction for some segment of the population. The mass media and the electronic world have come to rival the family as a socializer of children. Portrayals in the mass media do not simply mirror what occurs in reality; they also function to shape people's beliefs and values regarding family and human sexuality.

CHRONOLOGICAL PRACTICE TEST

For answers to Key Concepts see the page number in parentheses; for other answers, see page 269.

Family and Kinship in Cross-Cultural Perspective

Key Concepts

1. Family (240)
2. Kin (240)
3. Consanguineal kin (240)
4. Affinal kin (240)
5. Patrilineal descent systems (241)
6. Matrilineal descent system (241)
7. Bilateral descent system (241)
8. Exogamy (241)
9. Endogamy (241)
10. Monogamy (241)
11. Polygamy (241)
12. Polygyny (241)
13. Polyandry (241)
14. Patriarchal families (241)
15. Matriarchal families (242)
16. Egalitarian family (242)
17. Patrilocal family (242)
18. Matrilocal family (242)
19. Neolocal families (242)
20. Extended family (242)
21. Nuclear family (242)
22. Modified extended families (242)
23. Reconstituted family (242)
24. Blended family (242)

True/False

25. T F The United States today has a bilateral descent system.

Concept Completion

26. In terms of residence patterns, patriarchal families are also likely to be _____ families.
27. The _____ family is one in which elaborate networks of visitation and support are found among extended relatives but each nuclear unit lives separately.
28. A(n) _____ family is one based on kinship ties that accumulate as a consequence of divorces and remarriages.
29. When marital partners are chosen primarily on the basis of the individual desires of the prospective mates, this is called a(n) _____ courtship process.
30. Marriage transactions involve an exchange of money, goods, or services between the families of the marrying couple; two forms of such marriage transactions are _____ and _____.

Critical Thinking

31. Describe the various rules of descent and rules of authority that are found in family systems in various cultures.

The Family in Society
True/False

32. T F The matriarchal family appears to be emerging in modern industrial nations.
33. T F Extended families are more functional in industrial societies than are nuclear families.

Critical Thinking

34. Compare and contrast the functionalist and conflict perspectives on the family. Be sure to address the functions that the family performs and how the two perspectives differ.

Marriage and Divorce in the United States
Key Concepts

35. Refined divorce rate (247)
36. Serial monogamy (247)

True/False

37. T F Young people in the United States today, when compared to their parents, have fewer negative attitudes toward staying single.
38. T F Even though it is difficult for parents to remain together in a conflict-ridden marriage, research shows that children are almost always better off when such parents stay together rather than divorce.
39. T F There is a higher divorce rate in Hispanic American families than in Anglo families.

Concept Completion

40. A homogamous marriage system is one in which people choose marriage partners who _____.
41. A marriage system that allows people to have more than one spouse, but not at the same time, is called _____.

Critical Thinking

42. How have attitudes toward marriage and having children changed over the past fifty years in the United States?
43. Describe the four social conditions discussed in the text that account for the rising divorce rate over the past century in the United States.
44. What are the social characteristics of couples who are at the greatest risk of experiencing a divorce?
45. Describe the family experiences of African Americans, Hispanic Americans, and Asian Americans. Show how their experiences are similar to and different from those of Anglo Americans.

Diversity and Change in Sexual Behavior
Concept Completion

46. Two factors that accounted for the increasing frequency of premarital sexual activity in the United States in the twentieth century are _____ and _____.

Critical Thinking

47. How and why have patterns of premarital sex and extra-marital sex changed in the United States during the twentieth century?

Diverse Family Lifestyles in Modern Societies

Key Concept

48. Cohabitation (258)

True/False

49. T F More adults are single (never married) today than was the case in 1940
50. T F Looking at the trends in divorce and single motherhood, the text predicts that the proportion of single-parent families will decline in the future.
51. T F While the proportion of births to unmarried women has been increasing in the United States, it has been declining in most nations around the world.

Concept Completion

52. The most common living arrangement for children and teenagers in the United States today is to be living with _____.

Critical Thinking

53. Describe the trends in cohabitation and single parenthood in the United States in the past few decades. What problems have these trends created?

Violence in the Family

True/False

54. T F Levels of child abuse are higher among the poor than they are among the affluent.

Critical Thinking

55. What are the social conditions that increase the likelihood of violence in a family?

The Future of the Family

Key Concept

56. Pluralistic family system (264)

Concept Completion

57. According to the text, the family organization that seems to be developing in modern industrial societies is the _____ family system.

Critical Thinking

58. According to the text, what is the likely future of the family in modern industrial societies?

ANSWERS TO CHRONOLOGICAL PRACTICE TEST

25. T; 32. F; 33. F; 37. T; 38. F; 39. F; 49. F; 50. F; 51. F; 54. T
26. patrilocal
27. modified extended
28. reconstituted, blended
29. participant-run
30. bridewealth, brideservice, dowry
40. have social characteristics similar to their own
41. serial monogamy
46. reliable contraceptives, feminist movement, technological developments that free the young
52. both parents
57. pluralistic

CUMULATIVE PRACTICE TEST

See page 482 for answers.

1. A matrilineal descent system is one in which
   a. descent is determined through the female line, and children belong to the kin group of their mother.
   b. descent is determined through the male line, and children belong to the kin group of their father.
   c. descent is determined through the female line, but children belong to the kin group of their father.
   d. descent is determined through the male line, but children belong to the kin group of their mother.
   e. descent is determined through both the male and female lines.

2. Rules of _____ require that people choose a mate outside of their own social group or community.
   a. endogamy
   b. homogamy
   c. monogamy
   d. polygamy
   e. exogamy

3. Which of the following perspectives would argue that family institutions exist in society because families make important contributions to human survival and the maintenance of society?
   a. The functionalist perspective.
   b. The conflict perspective.
   c. The interactionist perspective.
   d. The extended-family perspective.
   e. The pluralistic family perspective.

4. According to the text, which of the following is *not* a function that the family often performs in societies?
   a. Preparing people for specialized roles in an industrial society.
   b. Regulation of sexual behavior and reproduction.
   c. Socialization and education.
   d. Status conferral.
   e. Affection and companionship.

5. Today, the most common household in the United States has which of the following compositions?
   a. Male head of household, no spouse present.
   b. Female head of household, no spouse present.

c. A married couple.

d. A one-person household.

e. Two or more unrelated people.

6. Marriages in which people choose partners who have social characteristics similar to their own are called
   a. endogamous.
   b. exogamous.
   c. monogamous.
   d. polygamous.
   e. homogamous.

7. Which of the following statements is true regarding the marital status of people in the United States today as compared to 1940?
   a. A substantially smaller percentage of people are married today.
   b. A substantially larger percentage of people are divorced today.
   c. A substantially larger percentage of people are single today.
   d. A substantially larger percentage of people are widowed today.
   e. Both b and c are true.

8. Since 1940, the divorce rate in the United States has
   a. declined.
   b. increased by 10 percent.
   c. gone up over seventeenfold.
   d. doubled.
   e. stayed about the same.

9. The likelihood in the United States today that a marriage will end in divorce is closest to
   a. 30 percent.
   b. 45 percent.
   c. 70 percent.
   d. 85 percent.
   e. 95 percent.

10. All of the following were identified as placing a couple at a higher risk of divorce *except*
    a. social differences between the couple.
    b. high socioeconomic standing.
    c. young age at marriage.
    d. whirlwind romances.
    e. low socioeconomic standing.

11. Which of the following did *not* contribute to the changes in premarital sexual behavior in the United States during the twentieth century?
    a. The emergence of easy-to-use, reliable contraceptives.
    b. The feminist movement.
    c. Acceptance by all major religions of premarital sex.
    d. All of the above contributed.
    e. Neither b nor c contributed.

12. Which of the following statements is true regarding extramarital sexual affairs in the United States?
    a. Men are more likely to have such affairs than are women.
    b. Women are more likely to have such affairs than are men.
    c. Men and women are equally likely to have such affairs.
    d. The proportions of married people who have such affairs has declined over the past fifty years.
    e. Women who don't work are more likely to have such affairs than are women who work.

13. Over the past sixty years, the percentage of married women who work outside the home
    a. increased until 1970 and then declined.
    b. increased until 1970 and then leveled off.
    c. remained level until 1970 and then increased.
    d. declined steadily.
    e. increased steadily.

14. Which of the following is true of cohabitation in the United States today?
    a. It is on the decline.
    b. It is used by some people as a trial marriage.
    c. The stigma previously associated with it has declined.
    d. All of the above are true.
    e. Only b and c are true.

15. From a sociological perspective, gay and lesbian couples could be considered families because
    a. this would be a more fair and democratic stance to take.
    b. sexual orientation has been shown to be biologically caused rather than a choice people make.
    c. sexual self-definition is a result of the labeling process.
    d. those couples perform many of the functions that families perform in society.
    e. gay couples have become sufficiently common to be considered families.

16. Given the research findings on spouse abuse, which of the following women would most likely be at risk of being abused by a spouse?
    a. A woman who works and earns enough to support herself.
    b. A woman with high levels of education and other economic resources.
    c. A woman with an elaborate social network of friends and relatives.
    d. A woman who shares power over decision making equally with her husband.
    e. A woman whose spouse has traditional, nonegalitarian views toward gender-role relationships.

17. Which of the following elderly is at greatest risk of suffering abuse?
    a. Those who live alone.
    b. Those who are not married.
    c. Those who live with only one other person.
    d. Those who live with both a spouse and an offspring.
    e. Those who are still working.

18. A _____ family is one in which a number of different types of families exist side by side, each having an attraction for some segment of the populace.
    a. monolithic
    b. pluralistic
    c. reconstituted
    d. blended
    e. modern

19. Based on research on family violence, the text concludes that which of the following is a key element of the abuse of spouses, children, and the elderly?
    a. The high divorce rate.
    b. The growth in extended families.
    c. The inequitable distribution of power and resources in the family.
    d. A resurgence in patriarchy.
    e. The growth in the pluralistic family.

20. Which of the following is true of portrayals of families on television in the United States today?
    a. More male-headed single-parent families are portrayed than occur in the population.
    b. Fewer male-headed single-parent families are portrayed than occur in the population.
    c. More female-headed single-parent families are portrayed than occur in the population.
    d. The serious problems confronting families are overemphasized.
    e. The portrayal of families has become more looking at the lives and experiences of women who choose to have children although they are not married unrealistic and less diverse.

FOR FURTHER READING

Coontz, Stephanie. (1997). *The way we really are: Coming to terms with America's changing families*. New York: BasicBooks. This historian presents research on how well different types of families function and argues in support of the notion that effective families can come in many forms. She encourages people to identify and build on the strengths in their families rather than worrying about what is the "right" kind of family.

Hertz, Rosanna. (2006). *Single by chance, mothers by choice: How women are choosing parenthood without marriage and creating the new American family*. New York: Oxford University Press. This book challenges conventional conceptions of family by looking at the lives and experiences of women who choose to have children although they are not married. It present another view on what "the family" is.

Hill, Robert B. et al. (1993). *Research on the African-American family: A holistic approach*. Westport, CT: Auburn House. This is a comprehensive review of the current research on the strengths and weaknesses of the African American family in the United States today. It gives a thorough review of the social conditions in the African American community and society at large that have shaped the African American family.

Kitson, Gay C. (1992). *Portrait of divorce*. New York: Guilford Press. This book summarizes research on divorce and the divorce process. It looks at the reasons that people divorce, how divorce affects children, and ways that divorce might be prevented.

Loue, Sana. (2001). *Intimate partner violence: Societal, medical, legal, and individual responses*. New York: Kluwer Academic/Plenum Publishers. This book provides an excellent overview of social science theory and research on the causes of intimate partner violence, how people react to it, and what can be done about it.

Moen, Phyllis. (1989). *Working parents: Transformations in gender roles and public policies in Sweden*. Madison: University of Wisconsin Press. This book explores some innovative social policies in Sweden that encourage women to have children and continue working. Some of the policies might be useful to consider for the United States.

Stacey, Judith. (1996). *In the name of the family: Rethinking family values in the postmodern age*. Boston: Beacon Press. Based on interviews with single mothers and working-class families, this sociologist paints a positive picture of the family, documenting its strengths and its more egalitarian division of labor when compared to the past.

Waite, Linda, & Gallagher, Maggie. (2000). *The case for marriage: Why married people are happier, healthier, and better off financially*. New York: Doubleday. These sociologists present data on some of the benefits of marriage over divorce or singlehood. Their data suggest the wide array of impacts that marital status has on people's lives.

Wallerstein, Judith, Lewis, Julia, & Blakeslee, Sandra. (2000). *The unexpected legacy of divorce: A 25-year landmark study*. New York: Hyperion. Although this book has been criticized for using poor research methodology, the authors do document some of the ways in which divorce can negatively impact people both in childhood and adulthood.

CHAPTER 10

Health and Health-Care Institutions

MYTHS & FACTS: About Health and Health-Care Institutions

Sociological Perspectives on Health, Illness, and Health Care

The Functionalist Perspective
The Conflict Perspective
The Interactionist Perspective
Politics, Stigma, and the AIDS Epidemic
APPLYING SOCIOLOGY: Combating the Spread of AIDS

Health, Illness, and Society

Health and Societal Development
Health and Social Position
Socioeconomic Status
Gender
Race
Lifestyle

OTHER WORLDS, OTHER WAYS: Congo: The Spread of AIDS in a Developing Nation

Health-Care Systems in Cross-Cultural Perspective

Personalistic Health-Care Systems
Naturalistic Health-Care Systems
Scientific Health-Care Systems
Chinese Medicine
Holistic Medicine

The Social Structure of Health Care

Seeking Health Care
The Medical Profession
SOCIOLOGY OF MEDIA AND TECHNOLOGY: Globalized Medicine in Cyberspace
The Nursing Profession

New Health-Care Practitioners
Hospitals and the Corporatization of Health Care

Issues in Health Care in the United States

Rising Health-Care Costs
Access to Medical Services
Quality of Medical Services
Gender Inequality in Health Care

Financing Health Care in the United States

Publicly Funded Health Insurance
Employer-Financed Health Insurance
Health Maintenance Organizations and Managed Care
Health Care: A Privilege or a Right?
Paying for Health Care in Other Nations: Canada and Sweden
SOCIOLOGY ON THE INTERNET

Study & Review

In the late Middle Ages, around 1200 to 1400, Europe was still a largely feudal society where serfs worked the fields under the tutelage of the nobility. Most people lived in rural areas, but trade and commerce were expanding, both within Europe and with the Middle East and Far East. Much of this economic activity was centered in cities, where merchants from the surrounding countryside met with traders who had transported goods from a far distance. Medieval cities were small by today's standards but growing in size and becoming increasingly crowded and unsanitary. These conditions set the stage for a terrible pandemic that afflicted the Continent and England and illustrates the many social implications of health and illness.

In one of the earliest episodes of the pandemic, a trading ship from Genoa landed in Sicily with sailors dead and dying at their oars (Tuchman, 1978). They were foul-smelling and in great pain, with terrible black growths in their armpits and groins. From such beginnings the bubonic plague, or Black Death, swept through Europe in the mid-1300s. It was by far the worst epidemic experienced in human history. Estimates are that one-quarter of the population of Europe and the Middle East died in the decade

Myths & Facts

About Health and Health-Care Institutions

Myth:
The poor in the United States receive shoddy health care, finding it difficult to see a doctor or gain admission to a hospital.

Fact:
Some poor people are quite a bit more likely than the affluent to see a doctor or be hospitalized. Government health insurance for the poor has given some of them far more access to health care than ever before, although it may be of lower quality than the care available to more affluent people.

Myth:
Women are healthier than men (or vice versa).

Fact:
Reality is complicated on this question. Men have higher mortality rates, but women are more likely to have acute, non-life-threatening illnesses. Men, by contrast, tend to have higher rates of serious, chronic illnesses. So the conclusions on gender and health depend on how one measures health.

Myth:
Thanks to modern science, people today have a healthy diet and can look forward to a long life.

Fact:
People in most hunting-and-gathering societies probably had healthier diets than most people in the United States have today. They ate a wide range of fruits, nuts, grains, and other plant foods and relied less on meat. Hunters and gatherers could, if they survived infancy and childhood, look forward to a relatively long life. However, the hunters and gatherers still died at a younger age than most people today, and the quality of their life in terms of their health status was not nearly as good.

Myth:
By the early twenty-first century, modern medicine has triumphed by becoming so effective against disease that people around the world are coming to rely on it exclusively.

Fact:
Modern medicine has become effective, and most people do use it, but people are unwilling to put all their eggs in one basket when confronting something as frightening and unpredictable as disease or injury. People continue to rely on alternative healing practices in addition to modern medicine when they believe these approaches may be helpful.

beginning in 1348; England and Italy may have lost as much as one-half their populations. Possibly as many as nine out of ten Londoners died (Paul, 1966).

Bubonic plague is a bacterial disease that is normally found in field rodents, such as ground squirrels, chipmunks, and rats (Hirst, 1953). Fleas that bite these rodents can also contract the plague bacillus bacterium. Rat and flea bites spread the disease to humans. When humans are infected, they experience fever, pain, and swollen lymph nodes in the groin and armpit (called *buboes,* hence the name of the disease). If not treated with antibiotics, most infected people die within a few days as infection of the bloodstream produces heart failure. If the plague infects the lungs, the disease becomes highly communicable because the bacillus is spread to others through coughing.

The reason for this pandemic of bubonic plague had as much to do with social developments as with biological ones. After all, the plague bacillus is a constant presence in the rodent population, but social developments increased the chances of its transmission into human environments. One such development was the growing medieval cities, which concentrated more people together and also made an attractive environment for black rats. Most rodents avoid human contact as much as they can, but the black rat is an indoor animal. The thatch and wattle-and-daub houses of Europe in the 1300s offered easy entry and good hiding places for these rats. In addition, people stored food in their houses rather than in separate buildings, and the practice of the time was to throw garbage into the streets. The food in the houses and the streets filled with filth attracted more rats. All these social developments brought rats and fleas into closer contact with people. On top of that, medical knowledge was lacking in medieval Europe, and no one realized how the disease was spread. Pests and vermin were such a constant part of life of the times that no one suspected their role in disease.

Another social development was the growth in trade and commerce, which meant that more people were traveling around the Continent and over to England, as well as traveling overland and by ship from Russia and the Middle East. Infected rats, fleas, and humans spread the disease as they traveled. Medical researchers speculate that the plague entered Europe with travelers from southern Russia or China.

People responded to the plague with a variety of social behaviors that had implications for the spread of the disease and for other social institutions. Many fled the plague-ravaged cities for the countryside, not realizing that they often carried the disease with them. Social factors influenced who could take flight, since it was the rich who had country estates to flee to; meanwhile, as one historian put it, "the urban poor died in their burrows" (Tuchman, 1978, p. 98). Frightened

populations seized on outlandish explanations—that the plague was a punishment from God for sins, or that European Jews had poisoned the water and caused the plague. The latter rumor caused the persecution and slaughter of many Jews. The Roman Catholic Church lost influence and authority because it could do nothing to stop the terrible scourge. People took their religious fervor to one of the many new sects that emerged, and the plague may have helped set the stage for the Protestant Reformation a century and a half later when papal authority was effectively challenged. The plague may also have contributed to the disintegration of feudalism and the manorial system because it produced a labor shortage that drove up wages and made it easier for serfs to leave a lord's estate and find wage work in towns and cities.

Thus the bubonic plague illustrates how health and illness are not merely individual concerns or biological matters but have important social dimensions. Social factors influence whether people become ill, and cultural values and social structure influence how people respond to illness. Societies create health-care institutions to cope with illness and cultural beliefs about what causes disease and how to treat it. There is also a social structure of healing roles to assist people who are sick, and illnesses affect how other social institutions, such as religion or the family, operate. This chapter reviews these social dimensions of health, illness, and health-care institutions. Along the way, it also assesses the status of the health-care system in the United States.

Sociological Perspectives on Health, Illness, and Health Care

You should be able to analyze health, illness, and health-care institutions from the three theoretical perspectives and show how social and political factors influence what conditions are defined as illnesses.

The three theoretical perspectives—functionalist, conflict, and interactionist—provide an introduction to the sociological analysis of health, illness, and health-care institutions.

The Functionalist Perspective

From the functionalist perspective, illness has more to do with how well people can function in society than with their biological condition. Disease threatens the social order because those who are ill may be unable to make necessary contributions to society. Sick people may not be able to raise food, build houses, drive trucks, or rear children as they are expected to. This inability makes them burdensome and nonproductive; to use a concept from Chapter 5, it also makes them *deviant*, since they will not be behaving in ways society expects of them. In extreme cases, such deviance could threaten the survival of society if widespread disease produced social disorder. That happened among the Huron Indians, discussed at the beginning of Chapter 8, when French explorers brought diseases that devastated their populations.

Given these consequences, the sociologist Talcott Parsons (1951) argued that society needs mechanisms for returning people to their nondeviant roles. Ostracizing or imprisoning them, which are common responses to other deviant behaviors, is ineffective. Instead, society must help these deviants to become "normal" again. So, we call these people *ill* and place them in the sick role, which carries *a set of expectations intended to guide the behavior of people who are ill.* The normative expectations of the sick role are designed to facilitate people's return to health. For example, people occupying the sick role are excused from their normal role obligations to the extent that the illness calls for. This allowance provides people with rest that will facilitate the healing process. Sick people can also claim assistance and sympathy from others because such help can also advance the healing process. In addition, the sick role carries certain obligations: People are expected to seek competent care and cooperate with those trying to heal them. These obligations are also intended to speed people's return to health.

The function of health-care institutions, then, is to return people to normal social functioning. All the parts of the health-care system function to achieve that goal. Doctors, nurses, pharmaceutical companies, and hospitals each play a part in the process. To work effectively, the different parts of the health-care system need to be well integrated. Doctors diagnose illness, nurses assist doctors in bringing about a cure, and pharmaceutical companies provide the drugs that enable doctors and nurses to do their jobs. Each position in the social structure of health care has certain responsibilities. Doctors diagnose illness, but they don't manufacture drugs; likewise, nurses assist doctors in carrying out treatments, but they don't prescribe drugs. If the system works reasonably well, people will receive the help they need to regain health, if that is possible given the level of medical knowledge of the society. However, the system does not always work as smoothly as just described because social conditions can interfere.

For example, health care in the United States is operated largely as a profit-making institution, as is the rest of the economy (see Chapter 13). Because large sums of money can be made from medical services and products, there is considerable abuse in these areas, such as unnecessary surgeries and the overutilization of drugs. In addition, people who are unable to pay for services often do not receive adequate medical care.

The point is that, in some situations, the profit-making dimension of the health-care system is not well integrated with, and may work against, the goal of achieving the highest possible level of health.

The Conflict Perspective

Health and health care are highly valued in all societies, and they are also scarce resources. Interest groups compete with one another to gain what they feel is their fair share of those resources, as they do with other scarce resources. Staying healthy depends on having access to adequate food, satisfactory employment conditions, clean water, and good health care. Generally, as will be shown, people with higher social and economic standing in a society have greater access to these resources, and they are generally healthier than the less affluent. For example, high infant mortality among the poor is not surprising, from the conflict perspective, because the poor are less able to afford nutritious food, sanitary living conditions, access to prenatal care, and the other things that reduce infant mortality.

In addition to the issue of whether groups receive services is the problem of how much those services will cost—in both monetary and nonmonetary terms—and who benefits most from health-care treatment. In this context, the health-care system is an arena for competition among a variety of groups: health-care consumers, doctors, nurses, hospital administrators, medical technicians, pharmaceutical companies, and a host of others. People must pay, in some fashion, for health-care goods and services, and many people make a living through providing those goods and services. Naturally, what benefits one group, such as low health-care costs for the consumer, may work to the disadvantage of other groups, such as doctors and nurses. Beyond money, prestige and power are also involved in the health-care delivery process.

The inequitable distribution of money, prestige, and power in the health-care system may be viewed as a problem by those groups who feel they are receiving less than their fair share of resources. From the conflict perspective, however, there is no state of the system that is preferred or necessarily beneficial to all. If some group gains additional benefits, other groups must lose something. What determines who gains and who loses is the exercise of power. Groups have various power strategies available to them. Nurses and doctors, for example, can go on strike or in other ways withhold their services in order to force concessions from competing groups. Another power strategy is to influence Congress and state legislatures to approve legislation that benefits particular groups. In fact, many interest groups in the health field have formed political action committees to collect contributions and press their interests. The American Medical Association (AMA) and other physicians' groups have been very effective at lobbying over the years, partly because of the substantial economic resources of their constituents.

The Interactionist Perspective

The interactionist perspective emphasizes that health care is provided in a variety of medical encounters where people come together in face-to-face interaction (Waitzkin, 1991). In these encounters, doctors, nurses, and patients exchange symbols and social meanings as they perform their social roles. The symbols and meanings communicate information not only about disease and treatment but also about much more than that—about social standing, valued statuses, and a variety of other things. For example, the fact that many patients wait long periods of time to see doctors but doctors rarely wait for patients who are late communicates who has more power and importance in the relationship. When patients are fed or taken to the X-ray lab when the hospital wishes rather than when the patients would prefer, it is clear that patients have less control over events than does the hospital bureaucracy. When nurses address doctors with the honorific title *Doctor* and their surname while many doctors call nurses by their first names, the stratification hierarchy of the hospital is reproduced and reaffirmed. In all these ways, daily encounters in health settings communicate something about social standing, power, and worth, and tend to reflect those same elements in the larger society.

Illnesses themselves have social meaning and may imply something about the patient. Some illnesses such as cancer are frightening because of the pain and death that they imply. For a young man, a knee injury may be a badge of courage and prowess in athletic competition. Some health conditions may imply a socially devalued or stigmatized status, such as venereal disease for a prostitute or hepatitis for an intravenous drug user. In some societies, illness was considered to be retribution from God, and thus the sick were considered sinners. Some cultures considered the mentally ill to be possessed by the devil. In short, diseases are interpreted to mean something about the person who has them, and sometimes this meaning includes stigmatization and devaluation.

The three sociological perspectives identify social mechanisms that influence how people with illnesses are treated by others. This treatment can have

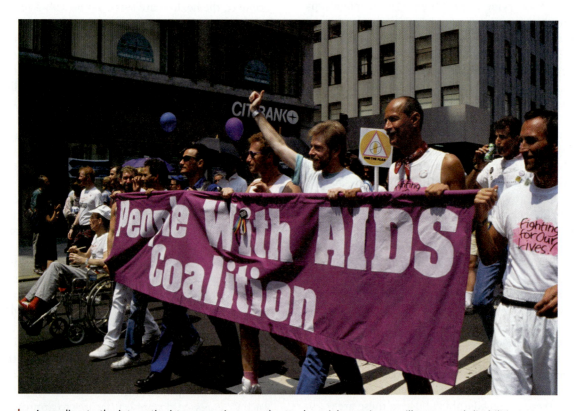

According to the interactionist perspective, people attach social meanings to illnesses and disabilities. When these meanings are negative, people may be stigmatized and discriminated against by others. People with AIDS have fought against this discrimination over the decades by, among other things, engaging in collective protest.

important—in some cases, life-and-death— consequences for people who become ill. Such was the case with Acquired Immune Deficiency Syndrome (AIDS), which emerged in the United States in the 1980s, and the sociological lessons to be learned from the history of this disease make it worth an extended analysis.

Politics, Stigma, and the AIDS Epidemic

Understanding diseases such as the bubonic plague and AIDS involves a complex intertwining of biology with political, social, and cultural considerations. As the interactionist perspective suggests, health, illness, and disease are given meaning by people in a particular social and cultural environment, and how we treat those who are ill is a function of these meanings. The impact of social and cultural forces on the treatment of the ill is especially evident in seriously threatening diseases (Sigerist, 1977). Among the ancient Babylonians, disease was viewed as punishment for sin and wickedness—it was believed that people who suffered pain and discomfort were paying for their sins. Because of the spiritually unclean nature of sick people, they were marked by the Babylonians with a stigma. They were not physically shunned, but they were socially isolated until they had made some atonement for their sins.

We might be tempted to think that by the beginning of the twenty-first century, our reactions to disease have become more rational and scientific than those of the ancient Babylonians. Yet social life is complex, and people's reactions to disease are no exception. In the case of AIDS, many social and cultural factors came together to produce a significant delay in the attack on the disease in the United States (Burkett, 1996; Shilts, 1987).

Despite the growing scientific evidence in the early 1980s about the mode of transmission of AIDS and the ominous realization about its potentially monstrous dimensions, tragedy was heaped on tragedy when research and policy development were delayed, as the disease spread. The reasons for this delay were complicated, but some of them are strikingly similar to the reactions to disease among the ancient Babylonians. First of all, stigmatization of the supposedly unclean or morally suspect patient clearly played a role: The disease was linked with male homosexuality and illegal injection-drug use. Many people in positions of political and economic power in the United States either thought that these were powerless groups whose problems need not be seriously attended to or that they were disreputable groups whose lifestyle ought to be discouraged if not eradicated. In fact, some fundamentalist religious leaders declared that AIDS was punishment for the sins of homosexuals—not a far cry from

the ancient Babylonian belief about disease (Shilts, 1987).

A second reason for the delayed response to AIDS was the Reagan administration policy of smaller government involvement and greater austerity in social and health programs. The first AIDS victim in the United States appeared in 1980, and the Reagan administration entered office in 1981. The competition for government funds in the early 1980s was fierce, and AIDS researchers typically lost out.

A third reason for the delay had to do with urban politics. New York City had the largest number of AIDS cases in the country, yet New York Mayor Edward Koch refused to do anything about it for a number of years, apparently because of the belief that support for "gay causes" would link him with the gay rights movement and hurt his chances for reelection.

The overall consequence of these political and social factors was that AIDS research and programs were delayed significantly and the disease gained a substantial foothold. Had the government acted quickly and aggressively, the spread of AIDS would have been much less substantial. Once the cause of the disease and the mode of transmission were established, steps were taken to control it. The gay community, in particular, has emphasized health education, the practice of safer sex, and a change in sexual lifestyles as ways of preventing the spread of the disease. And this effort has resulted in a dramatic decline in the rate of infection due to male-to-male sexual contact and injection drug use (Centers for Disease Control and Prevention, 2006).

Even if the disease were to stop spreading entirely, it is still a huge health problem. AIDS is now the leading cause of death among young adults. More than 300,000 people in the United States have AIDS, and 1 million are infected with the human immunodeficiency virus (HIV) that causes the disease; forty thousand new infections occur each year (Centers for Disease Control and Prevention, 2006). Currently in the United States, only 64 percent of new HIV infections involve male-to-male sexual contact or are due to intravenous drug use. Heterosexual transmission of AIDS is growing, with 36 percent of new infections resulting from heterosexual contact. Worldwide, however, 60 percent of HIV infections result from heterosexual intercourse.

The reaction to AIDS brings home to us how much people in the United States are like the Babylonians and all other human groups. Human response to disease is shaped not only by the biomedical nature of disease but also by the social meanings we impart to disease and its victims. Applying Sociology: Combating the Spread of AIDS describes some of the contributions that applied sociologists have made in discovering the causes and controlling the spread of AIDS.

Applying Sociology   Combating the Spread of AIDS

Over the past two decades, sociological research has played a critical role in attacking the AIDS epidemic. When AIDS first appeared in the United States in the early 1980s, scientists and doctors were puzzled by the new disease. The first indication of the epidemic was when healthy young men contracted diseases, such as rare forms of skin cancer, that are not normally found in healthy young people. A first step in understanding a new disease is often to focus on the social characteristics and lifestyles of people who contract it to see if some clues might be found regarding mode of transmission or potential causes. Scientists at the Centers for Disease Control and Prevention (CDC) in Atlanta did this with the early cases of the then still mysterious disease. They noticed something distinctive about the patients: They were either gay males or intravenous drug users. Participating in this study was William Darrow, a research sociologist at the CDC with expertise in sexually transmitted diseases and the gay community. Darrow, looking at the social characteristics and lifestyle patterns of the early victims, was alarmed and concluded: "It looks more like a sexually transmitted disease than syphilis" (Shilts, 1987, p. 87).

In the first half of the 1980s, Darrow and other CDC scientists attempted to gather evidence that AIDS was sexually transmitted. If they could show that it was, they could make some recommendations about curing, or at least controlling the spread of, AIDS. As an important step in establishing that the disease was sexually transmitted, they needed to compare the lifestyles and sexual activities of gay men with the disease to those of gay men without it (Jaffe et al., 1983). They asked health departments, private clinics, and private physicians to provide names of gay men who would be willing to participate in the study. They also asked each AIDS victim to provide the name of a gay male friend who had not been his sexual partner. All these men were interviewed extensively about their lives and sexual behavior. In this pioneering study, Darrow and his colleagues found a link between sexual activities and AIDS: people with AIDS, compared to those free of the disease, were more likely to engage in what is now called unsafe sex; they had many more sexual partners; and they were more likely to find sex partners in bathhouses. In a later study of AIDS among prostitutes, they used a similar sampling

procedure: recruiting prostitutes from among women in prison, from venereal disease clinics, and from methadone maintenance clinics. In these studies, they found that the prostitutes at greatest risk of contracting AIDS were those who were also intravenous drug users and who never used condoms (Darrow et al., 1987).

From research such as this, Darrow and other scientists fighting the AIDS battle were able to determine that AIDS was transmitted through contact with bodily fluid, such as blood or semen. Once this fact was established, they could make some critical public health recommendations aimed at controlling the spread of AIDS: test the blood supply for antibodies to the AIDS virus, educate people about safe sex, and close or closely regulate gay bathhouses and other settings conducive to multiple sex partners.

By the 1990s, the mosaic of AIDS had changed some, but applied research remained important in the battle against it. For example, sociologist Philippe Bourgois and his colleagues conducted research on homeless heroin addicts in San Francisco (Bourgois, Lettiere, & Quesada, 1997). Intravenous drug use had become one of the major risk factors for the spread of AIDS. Bourgois and colleagues observed the addicts for extended periods over a two-year span to gather direct observational evidence of the risky behaviors they engaged in, especially sharing of needles and other drug paraphernalia. Based on their observations, the researchers concluded that such risky behavior is much more common than other studies had shown and that existing public health efforts to reduce it are ineffective. They showed that the risky behaviors stem in part from the lifestyles of the addicts but also from the demeaning and stigmatized way in which public health workers relate to the addicts. Given this knowledge, they concluded, policies that focus on merely making clean needles available to addicts are not likely to reduce the risky behaviors a great deal.

So throughout the AIDS crisis, applied sociological research has been central to the development of social policies. In the early years, Darrow's interviews helped to locate causes of the disease and develop interventions, whereas in recent years observational data from Bourgois and others has enabled policymakers to evaluate how effectively interventions are working. ■

Health, Illness, and Society

You should be able to describe how levels of societal development and a person's social position influence health and illness.

Social epidemiology is *the branch of sociology that studies how social factors influence the distribution and spread of disease in a group.* Epidemiologists have learned that which diseases afflict people depends very much on the kind of society they live in and their position in the social structure.

Health and Societal Development

Most diseases can be classified as acute or chronic. Acute diseases are *those with a fairly quick, and sometimes dramatic and incapacitating, onset from which a person either dies or recovers.* They are often caused by an organism or parasite that infects or invades the body and disrupts its functioning, such as with influenza, tuberculosis, and gastroenteritis. Chronic diseases, such as heart disease and cancer, *progress over a long period of time and often exist long before they are detected.* Early symptoms of these diseases are often absent or easily ignored. They are usually caused by a mixture of biological, social, and environmental factors.

In preindustrial societies, infectious and parasitic diseases posed some of the more serious health threats (Black, 1978; Dunn, 1978). Diseases such as influenza, diphtheria, and typhoid could strike quickly and were highly contagious and often fatal, especially among infants, the weak, and the elderly. Accidents such as drowning and burns also took their toll, as did cannibalism, infanticide, and human sacrifice. All these threats added up to a life expectancy in preindustrial societies that was rather short by today's standards, probably around twenty-five to thirty-five years. However, this short life expectancy was the result in good part of high rates of infant and childhood mortality; if

one survived the illnesses of infancy and childhood, one had a reasonable chance to live much longer.

Anthropologists estimate that a hunter-gatherer who survived to age fifteen could anticipate an average life expectancy of fifty-five years (Antonovsky, 1972). In fact, the hunter-gatherer lifestyle was basically healthy, with a good diet including a wide variety of healthy foods. People had little contact with other groups, so the transmission of diseases was reduced. When agricultural societies emerged, people's lifestyles changed and so did the threats to their health. Agriculturalists typically depended on a smaller number of crops for most of their diet and were thus more vulnerable to failures in the food supply. So, starvation and malnutrition, which are infrequent among hunter-gatherers, became a more serious threat. In addition, agriculturalists usually engage in extensive trading with other groups, a practice that sets the stage for the spread of infectious and parasitic diseases.

With the emergence of industrial societies, there has been a dramatic increase in life expectancy, to around seventy-seven years in the United States today (see Table 14.1, p. 396). The death rate has also changed appreciably, dropping from 17 deaths per 1,000 people in the United States in 1900 to 8 deaths today (Figure 10.1). The declining death rate and increasing life expectancy can be attributed in good part to two related factors: declines in infant and childhood mortality and changes in lifestyle.

Infant mortality today is less than one-sixth of what it was a century ago. So a newborn infant today

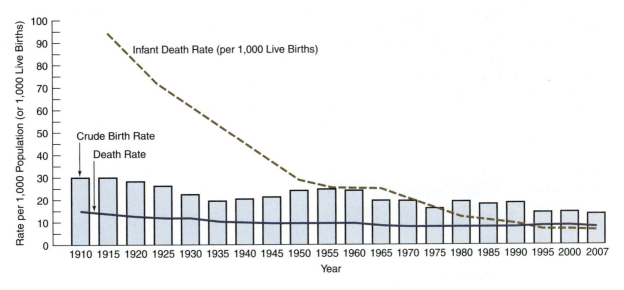

Figure 10.1
Birth and Death Rates in the United States, 1910–2007

Sources: U.S. Bureau of the Census, *Statistical Abstract of the United States,* 1982–83 (Washington, DC: U.S. Government Printing Office, 1982), p. 60; U.S. Bureau of the Census, *Statistical Abstract of the United States,* 1992 (Washington, DC: U.S. Government Printing Office, 1992), p. 64; National Center for Health Statistics, *National Vital Statistics Reports* (Hyattsville, MD: Public Health Service, various years).

has a far better chance of surviving than did infants in earlier times and consequently has a better chance of living into old age. For those who survive through childhood, however, industrialization has led to considerably smaller increases in longevity over that of their preindustrial counterparts. A study in Massachusetts, for example, revealed that the life expectancy of fifteen-year-olds in 1869 was only five years less than that of fifteen-year-olds a century later (Vinovskis, 1978). Furthermore, there was virtually no increase in the life expectancy of thirty-year-olds between 1869 and 1969. These figures illustrate that a major benefit of industrialization in terms of health and longevity is that we have a much greater chance of living through infancy and childhood. Industrialization provides less benefit in terms of longevity once we reach adulthood.

The second key factor in increasing longevity has been changes in people's lifestyles. In fact, such change has probably been at least as important as treatment offered by modern medicine (McKeown, Brown, & Record, 1972; McKeown, Record, & Turner, 1975). Industrialization has made available better diets, improved sanitation, better sewage disposal, and cleaner water. Consequently, people are exposed to fewer infectious and parasitic diseases and are better able to resist those to which they are exposed. The death rate for scarlet fever, for example, had dropped to practically zero by the 1940s, when effective medical treatment for it first became available (McKinlay & McKinlay, 1977).

Despite declining mortality rates and increasing longevity, we must all die someday, and the diseases we die of today are different from those of the past. In 1900 in the United States, the top three killers were acute infectious diseases, which accounted for more than twice the number of deaths that heart disease and cerebrovascular disease did (Figure 10.2). Today, four of the five leading causes of death are chronic diseases, the fifth being accidents. So acute infectious diseases have become relatively unimportant in terms of mortality, and chronic diseases confront society with a different set of problems than did the acute ones in an earlier era. Chronic diseases develop over a long period of time, may go unnoticed until extensive damage has occurred, and are often associated with people's lifestyles. Effective treatment of such diseases calls for continual rather than intermittent health care and may require that people change their lifestyles. Furthermore, the most effective and least expensive way of dealing with most chronic diseases is probably *preventive medicine, changes in lifestyle or other steps that help avoid the occurrence of disease* (McKinlay, 1986). Yet modern medicine is not organized around prevention but rather toward *curative* or *crisis medicine: treating people's*

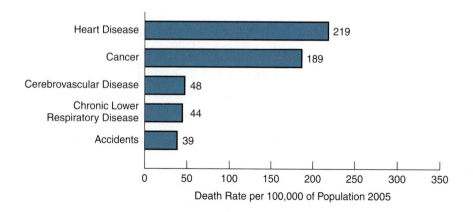

Figure 10.2

Leading Causes of Death in the United States, 1900 and 2005

Sources: U.S. Bureau of the Census, *Vital Statistics Rates in the United States,* 1900–1940 (Washington, DC: U.S. Government Printing Office, 1943), pp. 210–215; National Center for Health Statistics, Deaths: Preliminary Data for 2005. *Health E-State* (Hyattsville, MD: Public Health Service, Sept. 2007), www.cdc.gov/NCHS/deaths.htm

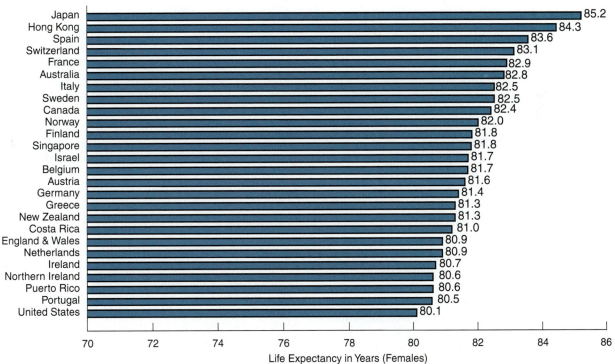

Figure 10.3
Life Expectancy at Birth, by Sex, 2003

Source: From National Center for Health Statistics, *Health, United States, 2007, with Chartbook on trends in the Health of Americans* (Hyattsville, MD: National Center for Health Statistics, (2007), p.173.

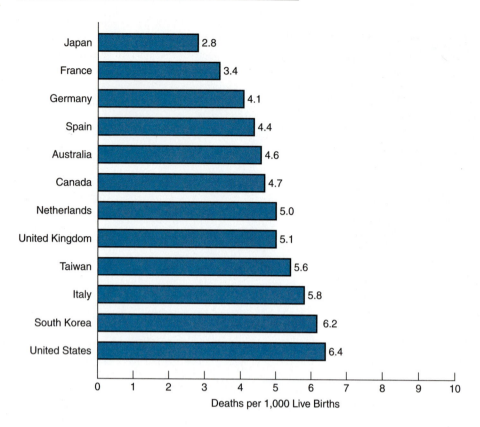

Figure 10.4
Infant Mortality Rates, Countries with Twelve Million or More Population, 2006

Note: From *Statistical Abstract of the United States,* 2008 (p. 831) by U.S. Bureau of the Census, 2007, Washington, DC: U.S. Government Printing Office.

illness after they become ill. Modern medicine arose early in the twentieth century when acute infectious diseases were the major health problems, and medical education trained doctors with a crisis orientation. This approach is effective with such infectious diseases as influenza, pneumonia, or diphtheria, in which medical measures introduced after a person becomes ill can often return the person to complete health. With chronic diseases, however, much damage has already been done—and often cannot be reversed—by the time symptoms manifest themselves and medical intervention occurs. A person who suffers a heart attack, for example, may already have severe blockage of coronary arteries, and the damage typically cannot be completely undone with such modern medical measures as angioplasty or coronary artery bypass surgery. To date in the United States, preventive medicine has had a considerably lower priority—in terms of research and program funding, the construction of medical facilities, and the allocation of health-care personnel—than has crisis-oriented medicine.

So one of the major problem areas in the health-care system in the United States today is that the health-care organization has not adapted to the changing nature of the diseases we face. Another problem is that, although death rates are down and life expectancy is up, people in the United States are not so well-off when compared with some other countries. For example, the life expectancy of women in twenty-six nations exceeds that of women in the United States, whereas

men in the United States have shorter life spans than their counterparts in twenty-five nations (Figure 10.3). Men and women in Spain, Greece, and Costa Rica live longer than men and women in the United States. Likewise, the United States has a higher infant mortality rate than at least eleven nations (Figure 10.4). In fact, infant mortality rates in the United States are *twice* as high as in Japan. Part of the reason the health status of the population is this low is that certain social and cultural factors have a detrimental impact on the health of many people.

Health and Social Position

Within any given society, social and cultural factors influence who is in greatest danger of becoming ill and dying. Four major sociocultural factors will be considered. Socioeconomic status, gender, and lifestyle have a similar impact on health in societies around the world. The fourth factor, race, is discussed because of the dramatic impact it has on morbidity and mortality in the United States.

SOCIOECONOMIC STATUS *Socioeconomic status* (SES) refers to people's position in society as measured by their income, educational attainment, and occupational status. The effect of SES on health is very clear: Those who are lower on such things as income, educational achievement, and occupational status generally have higher disease rates and death rates than do their more affluent counterparts (Lynch, Kaplan, & Shema, 1997; Williams & Collins, 1995). With few exceptions, the incidence of diseases such as cancer, heart disease, some types of diabetes, high blood pressure, and arthritis is higher among those in the lower SES ranges. Infant mortality is also substantially greater among children born into low SES families. One of the major reasons for the substandard health status of the poor is that they live in situations that substantially increase their general susceptibility to disease. They live under less sanitary conditions, have less nutritious diets, and are less likely to take preventive health actions such as obtaining routine physical examinations. Regarding infant mortality, poor women are less likely to have prenatal checkups and more likely to have poor diets that result in infants with low birth weights. These things contribute to infant mortality. Furthermore, despite the considerable advances brought about by Medicare and Medicaid, many poor people are not covered by these programs, and some health care still depends on out-of-pocket costs, which the poor usually cannot afford. Finally, the medical care that the poor do receive is likely to be of lower quality. They are more likely to be treated in a hospital outpatient clinic or emergency room where continuity of care, follow-up treatment, and patient education are less common than in a physician's office. And even when the poor have the same health insurance as the more affluent, such as Medicare, the poor do not receive the same level of health care: Poor people receive fewer preventive services, such as influenza immunizations, and less adequate care for chronic diseases (Gornick et al., 1996).

GENDER   Women appear to be healthier than men, especially if we consider longevity as the key measure of health. The life expectancy of women today is almost six years greater than that of men, compared with only three years more at the beginning of the twentieth century (see Figure 10.3; National Center for Health Statistics, 1997). Women also have lower rates of most serious chronic illnesses. What accounts for these differences? First, women may be biologically more capable of survival than are men (Bird & Rieker, 1999; Waldron, 1986). Males have higher death rates than females at every age, including deaths of fetuses. This fact suggests that women may have some sort of biological advantage in comparison with men, but the explanation is more complex than that. Higher mortality among males is also due to traditional gender-role definitions that encourage males to be aggressive and to seek more stressful and dangerous occupations where they might, for example, come into contact with industrial carcinogens. In addition, the lifestyles of men in the United States have traditionally been less healthy than those of women. For example, men drink more al-

cohol and smoke more tobacco (Waldron, 1986). Finally, cultural definitions of women as the "weaker sex" may lead women to respond more quickly to symptoms and to seek medical care earlier in an illness episode. If so, this treatment may enhance the likelihood of effective medical intervention for women.

RACE   Most studies of the relationship between health status and race have involved comparisons between African Americans and white Americans. All these studies reach distressingly similar conclusions: African Americans in the United States are at a serious disadvantage when it comes to health, having considerably higher death rates, shorter life expectancies, and more serious life-threatening health conditions such as hypertension and Type 2 diabetes than do whites (Smedley, Stith, & Nelson, 2002; Williams & Collins, 1995). One major reason for this difference, of course, is that race is associated with SES, with blacks being lower in SES on the average than whites. Yet even when researchers control for SES, some racial difference persists. This difference is probably accounted for by the unique social position of African Americans in the United States: The combination of years of racial oppression, poverty, and physically demanding occupations probably works to generate more stress in the lives of blacks than in other racial groups at the same SES level. This stress, in turn, produces greater susceptibility to disease. Minorities other than blacks also suffer substantial health problems. American Indians, especially those on reservations, have disproportionately high mortality rates from such things as accidents, alcoholism, and suicide, because of long-standing problems of poverty and unemployment (Young, 1994). Some of the impact of race on health has to do with discrimination: Research shows that, even when African Americans have the same level of health insurance as whites, they receive fewer and less adequate health-care services, and this fact undoubtedly contributes to their overall higher levels of illness and death (Smedley, Stith, & Nelson, 2002).

LIFESTYLE   Industrialization has unquestionably improved people's lives, but it has also created health hazards, largely unknown in preindustrial societies, that contribute to death and misery. For example, a substantial portion of all human cancers are caused in part by environmental conditions, such as air pollution or chemicals in the water and soil (Proctor, 1995). Occupational stress is linked to heart disease and hypertension (Schnall & Kern, 1986; Thoits, 1995). Unemployment, or even the threat of it, is associated with many physical and mental disorders (Kessler, House, & Turner, 1987). The use of alcohol, tobacco, and other drugs can also cause serious health

Other Worlds, Other Ways

CONGO: THE SPREAD OF AIDS IN A DEVELOPING NATION

The Democratic Republic of the Congo (formerly Zaire) is a nation of fifty million people in central Africa. Sixty-two percent of its population lives in rural areas (United Nations, 2004; U.S. Bureau of the Census, 2007). A relatively poor nation, Congo trails many Western nations in health statistics. The crude death rate stands at 15 per thousand, compared to 8.7 in the United States, and the infant mortality rate is 97 per thousand compared to 7 in the United States. The life expectancy in Congo is twenty-seven years shorter than in the United States. Congo also stands out in another respect—a very high rate of infection with the AIDS virus. Three percent of the population of Congo is infected with the AIDS virus; 7 percent of adults between the ages of fifteen and forty-nine are infected (United Nations, 2004). For comparison, worldwide infection rates are only about 1 percent, with the rate in the United States being 0.1 percent.

Congo's heavy burden of AIDS infection is reflected in many other nations in sub-Saharan Africa (Altman, 2002; United Nations, 2004). Overall estimates are that twenty-eight million adult Africans are infected with the virus and another one million children. Eleven million Africans have already died of AIDS. In the southern African countries of Botswana, Zimbabwe, and Lesotho, one out of every three adults is infected with the HIV virus or has AIDS. The AIDS epidemic in Africa is different from that in the United States in two important ways. First, almost all transmission of the virus is through heterosexual intercourse, with only a small fraction through homosexual contact. Second, women make up over half of the AIDS cases in Africa but only a small percentage in the United States.

The reasons for the pattern of the AIDS epidemic in Congo have to do with social and economic life in that nation and many other parts of Africa. In particular, political and economic conditions have produced very high levels of population migration (Packard & Epstein, 1992; World Health Organization, 1998). For example, especially in rural areas, impoverished families have few opportunities for earning money. Even small landholders find it difficult to survive on the land and must look for nonagricultural income. As a consequence, many African men migrate long distances from their family, for months at a time, to find work. Especially in rural areas, families send their members, both men and women, to seek employment in urban areas or on plantations and large agricultural projects. Other men make a living by driving long-haul truck routes. In addition

to these economic factors, political upheaval and ethnic conflicts drove many Africans from their homes in the 1990s in Congo, Rwanda, Sudan, and other nations.

This migratory lifestyle has made it difficult for African men and women affected by it to maintain stable family lives. It has, for example, created a class of men and women who work in urban and industrial settings but who cannot afford to support their families there and so are separated from them for long periods. For such men and women, this life encourages the use of multiple sexual partners. Women who cannot find other employment often turn to full-time or part-time prostitution. Some African men who work far from their families maintain a relationship, and may even set up households, with second wives. Other men engage prostitutes when they are away from home. These social practices result in multiple sexual partners, which increases the likelihood of transmission of the disease. It also produces a high prevalence of other sexually transmitted diseases, which cause lesions that make the transfer of the AIDS virus easier. The spread of AIDS in Congo and other parts of Africa, then, is assisted by the impoverishment and disruption of families.

Another factor contributing to the spread of AIDS is that many African men refuse to use condoms. Prostitutes are powerless to force such safer-sex practices on their customers because the easy availability of prostitutes puts the customer in a more advantageous position. Wives who are in a subordinate position and burdened with children also may not be in a position to make such demands.

The consequences of the AIDS epidemic in Africa could be dramatic. The World Health Organization (1998) estimates that the life expectancies in the hardest hit nations will be fifteen to thirty years lower than they would have reached in the absence of the AIDS epidemic. The economies of Congo and other nations could suffer a severe blow because of these high death tolls. In the cities of Congo and other central African countries, thousands in the professional elite groups have died in their prime. Some cash crops have remained unharvested because of the death toll among young agricultural workers. The same situation is occurring in mining, and Congo's share of world copper production may dwindle in the coming years. Pessimistic estimates are that one-quarter of the workers in Africa will fall ill with AIDS or die within the next fifteen years. The health-care systems in Congo and other African countries are not up to such a burden. They have far fewer doctors, nurses, and hospital beds than Western nations, and their fragile budgets cannot afford the costly medication that can ease the symptoms of AIDS but not cure the disease. In some cities, most of the hospital beds are already filled with patients with AIDS.

One way to limit the spread of AIDS in Africa is to reduce the migratory labor and prostitution that play such a key part. Such a change is unlikely in the near future, however, because there are not enough well-paying jobs near people's families so that they don't need to migrate. In addition, political and ethnic conflict has persisted, and in some cases gotten worse, in the past decade. As

long as these political and economic conditions exist, thousands of men will be migratory laborers and thousands of women will be forced into prostitution to support their families. Another approach is to encourage safer-sex practices, especially the use of condoms. ■

---

problems. There even appears to be an association between health and the quality of a person's family life: People who are married and have children are healthier than people who are single or have no children (Verbrugge, 1983).

Thus, in many complex ways people's position in the social structure affects their likelihood of becoming ill. Any overall solution to health problems must take into account the ways in which people's lives and social circumstances can be changed to improve their health. Other Worlds, Other Ways: Congo (pp. 284–285) explores how social position and lifestyle affected the spread of AIDS in an African nation.

Health-Care Systems in Cross-Cultural Perspective

You should be able to describe the health-care beliefs and practices of personalistic, naturalistic, and scientific health-care systems as well as those of Chinese and holistic medicine.

Human beings have come up with a variety of explanations for what causes disease and how to cure it. In fact, because disease is complicated, unpredictable, and frightening, societies often have a number of disease theories in order to increase their chance of finding a cure. This chapter reviews some of these beliefs and takes a look at some of the health-care systems in which they are found in order to gain a sense of the variety that exists.

Personalistic Health-Care Systems

Small hunting-and-gathering bands often had animistic religions, meaning that they believed souls or spirits lived in the world and did good or bad things to people (see Chapter 11). Hunters and gatherers applied this animistic conception to disease and concluded that disease was an unnatural condition sometimes caused by spirit intrusion, that is, invasion by an outside force such as a spirit, agent, or ancestor's soul that still roamed the world. These are called *personalistic* health-care systems because of the belief that disease is caused by the active, purposeful intervention of a sensate being (Foster & Anderson, 1978). In some cases,

the evil agent was believed to be directed by a human being, such as a witch or a sorcerer. In some societies, even accidents were viewed this way: Falling from a coconut palm could be caused by witchcraft performed on a person by someone else (Harley, 1941). Another cause of disease, in the view of hunter-gatherers, was improper behavior on the part of the patient, a breach of taboo, which displeased a spirit or ancestor.

Some personalistic beliefs can be found in folk medicine in many places today. For example, voodoo, which is practiced in some Caribbean countries and places that have many immigrants from the Caribbean, such as Florida, is founded on a belief in the supernatural and witchcraft. Voodoo *root doctors* are believed by their followers to be able to cast spells on people that can make them sick or cure them of illness. (Voodoo is discussed at greater length in Chapter 11.)

Healers in these personalistic systems are *shamans*, a combination of doctor and religious leader, or *diviners*, people knowledgeable about the spirit world. The healers address both the immediate physical problem, such as a broken leg or nausea, and the question of what has caused it. If they decide that the cause is spirit intrusion, then they might suggest a remedy to expel the spirit, such as inducing vomiting or bloodletting. If they decide the cause is breach of taboo, they might serve as a counselor, assisting the patient in making a confession and atoning for sins. The healers deal not only with all kinds of disease but also with misfortunes such as the loss of a relative or disappointment in love. In their healing capacity they can serve as agents of social control by defining illness as a sign that people have not been behaving properly. Their medical recommendation might be for people to behave according to the accepted moral code of their society in order to cure or prevent disease.

Naturalistic Health-Care Systems

In the preindustrial, agricultural societies of China, Greece, and India, health-care systems developed that relied much more heavily on natural forces as explanations of illness. Unlike personalistic medicine, *naturalistic* medicine considers disease as largely the result of the impersonal working of forces in nature or the body. Supernatural beings or spiritual forces can influence how or when these natural processes work, but disease is basically a natural process that human beings can understand and influence. In such belief systems, the body is seen as made up of a number of elements; health results when these elements are all in the proper balance, or equilibrium. Disease occurs when the elements fall out of balance. Depending on the health system, the elements in the body might be heat and cold, humors (fluids), or something else. The elements can fall out of balance because of excessive heat or cold in the person's environment, a poor diet, or excessive emotion. In Greek humoral pathology, for example, which can be traced back to the sixth century B.C., there were four humors: blood, phlegm, black bile, and yellow bile. The proper balance of these kept a person healthy.

The healers in naturalistic health-care systems are physicians or herbalists who are trained in the remedies that can restore the body's equilibrium. Unlike the personalistic systems in which the healers are also religious figures, in naturalistic systems they are skilled practitioners who learn their art through training and apprenticeship. The focus of treatment is to restore the proper balance through changes in diet or by bleeding and purgings. Surgery is not common, although occasionally it is resorted to as a way to restore equilibrium.

Scientific Health-Care Systems

Scientific health-care systems view disease as a natural process caused by specific biological factors responsible for each disease (Salmon, 1984). Medical knowledge is based on scientific research rather than religious tradition, as in personalistic systems. Unlike naturalistic medicine, scientific medicine admits of no spiritual or supernatural role in the disease process. Disease is caused by natural, biological forces, and social and emotional forces are seen as secondary or unimportant.

Healers in scientific medicine are extensively trained physicians with a thorough knowledge of anatomy, physiology, and biology. The physician has responsibility for diagnosis and cure, and the patient is in a relatively passive role. Physicians may use invasive, or heroic, drug and surgical interventions, such as chemotherapy or open heart surgery. Physicians also centralize their healing activities in hospitals or medical centers where patients come to them rather than the other way around. Scientific medicine has risen to its greatest prominence in Europe and the United States in the past two centuries, although it is found in all nations of the world today.

Chinese Medicine

Present-day Chinese medicine is a good example of a medical system that has incorporated a lot of scientific medicine while retaining many traditional Chinese be-

liefs about health and disease. Traditional Chinese medicine is a naturalistic system concerned with the balance of two basic elements or forces, the *yin* and the *yang*. In Chinese philosophy, the yin and the yang are the primordial elements from which the universe evolved, and these two forces lie behind all natural phenomena, including the human body (Ergil, 1996). They are seen as complementing dualities, such as right and left, heaven and earth, good and bad, male and female. Yang is heat and can cause fever, whereas yin is cold and causes chills. So, some diseases are yang diseases and others are yin diseases, but yin and yang constitute a single entity in an individual, and the proper balance of each is essential to health. Another important concept is the notion of *chi*, or vital energy, that flows through the body.

Healers in China have a number of procedures to influence the balance of the yin and the yang. One is acupuncture, in which fine needles are inserted into the body at key points to influence the flow of *chi* in the body. Another is acupressure, which uses fingertips on the same points to apply pressure. A third procedure is moxibustion, in which sticks made of rolled leaves are burned over points of the body for varying periods of time. The heat produced is thought to influence the flow of *chi*.

In modern China, scientific medicine and traditional Chinese medicine are used together to diagnose and treat disease. This combination is also favored by many Chinese Americans (and many others), who use acupuncture and herbal medicine alongside the medicines and surgeries offered by scientific medicine.

Holistic Medicine

Nonscientific healing systems treat the whole person in the sense that they focus on the psychological, social, and spiritual needs of the individual as well as the physical complaints. In naturalistic systems like the Chinese one, for example, it is assumed that a person's emotional state both affects and is affected by disease, so a healer might spend some time assessing the person's frame of mind and choose a remedy in part to produce a particular emotional outcome. Personalistic healers often come to a patient's home and include the whole family in healing rituals as a way of providing social support for the patient. Scientific medicine moved away from that practice by defining illness purely in biological terms. It assumes that emotions or spiritual condition is secondary or possibly irrelevant. Diagnosis and treatment can be accomplished by isolating the individual and treating the problem as purely biological.

In response to the impersonality of scientific medicine, many doctors, nurses, and patients have been drawn to *holistic medicine*, an effort to provide for the whole needs of sick people by using not only scientific medicine but also any other healing systems that devote attention to people's emotional, social, and spiritual needs (Gordon, 1984; Micozzi, 1996). Holistic healing assumes that a person constitutes a single biological, psychological, and social unit and that disease can be effectively treated only if all three aspects are considered. In holistic medicine, the unique needs of each individual are addressed, and there is an emphasis on educating the patient in order to encourage people to take care of themselves rather than become overly dependent on scientific healers. Holistic healing does not shy away from using healing techniques that have not been accepted by scientific medicine. It might use chiropractic, homeopathy, naturopathy, spiritual healing, herbal therapy, or a range of other interventions that from the scientific medical viewpoint have little therapeutic value. Many people use scientific medicine along with one or more of these other approaches when they become ill. One estimate is that one out of every three people in the United States uses healers in these alternative areas during a year, and it tends to be the better educated and those with higher incomes who go to them (Eisenberg et al., 1993). With something as unpredictable and potentially threatening as disease, people are inclined to use whatever is available rather than rely solely on one approach.

The Social Structure of Health Care

You should be able to describe the social factors influencing whether people seek health care, the various healing roles in the health-care system, and the consequences of the corporatization of health care.

In Chapter 2, *social structure* is defined as the organized patterns of interaction that exist in a group or society. Health-care institutions also have a social structure, involving identifiable and predictable ways that patients, nurses, doctors, and people in other healing roles interact with one another.

Seeking Health Care

One of the key roles in the social structure of health care is, of course, that of the person who is sick. The sick role has already been discussed along with some of the expectations associated with it. Recognizing that one is sick and seeking health care is a complicated process. The person must decide whether some physical or mental symptoms or distress is due to an illness and not just some temporary condition. If the person decides he or she has an illness that

needs attention, then the person must decide whether self-medication is appropriate or whether a professional healer is called for. If a professional is needed, then the question is whether to choose a doctor, chiropractor, herbalist, or some other kind of healer.

Sociologists have done much research on the factors involved in these decisions (Andersen, 1995; Kaplan, 1989). One of the major factors is, understandably, the severity of the symptoms. With severe symptoms, such as traumatic injury or a serious heart attack, virtually everyone defines himself or herself as ill and seeks treatment from professional healers. Most illness, however, involves less severe and more ambiguous symptoms, and even serious illness like heart disease often first appears with mild and ambiguous symptoms. It is in these circumstances that social and cultural factors play a greater role. One of the strongest social influences on how we seek health care is SES. People of higher SES are quicker to define symptoms as illness and to seek professional care. People of lower SES are more inclined to ignore minor symptoms or to define them as a part of the natural aging process. Part of the reason for this difference is financial: People of higher SES can better afford medical care. But more than finances are involved, since at each income level, people with more education tend to seek care more quickly than those with less education. Levels of knowledge also play a part; lower-class people tend to know less about the causes and meanings of various symptoms and to be more frightened of possible medical treatments.

Gender also influences whether one seeks help; women are more likely to seek medical attention than are men. The reason is partly that women have a higher rate of illness than men do. Also, because of gender-role socialization, women seem more inclined than men to seek assistance when they feel ill. Men are more inclined to ignore illness or attempt to take care of problems themselves.

Race and ethnicity also influence how people respond to symptoms (Cockerham, 2007). Mexican Americans and Asian Americans, especially recent immigrants, are more likely to rely on friends, relatives, or folk healers rather than go to a physician or a hospital. This preference is sometimes due to unfamiliarity with, or a distrust of, what seem like distant and impersonal medical institutions. It is also due to the greater availability of folk healers. In some Mexican American communities, for example, *curanderas* are available with many healing techniques familiar to people in the community.

The social structure of health care also includes the various healing roles. Some of the healing roles in other cultures were discussed earlier in the chapter, so this discussion focuses on the major healers in scientific health-care systems.

The Medical Profession

At the top of the hierarchy of healers in scientific medicine, of course, are physicians, scientifically trained practitioners who have primary responsibility for diagnosing and treating disease. Physicians have gained this position in part because of their effectiveness at curing disease and alleviating suffering. Equally important, however, is the fact that they have been politically active in seeking societal legitimation for their position as preeminent healers. In the United States, the establishment of the American Medical Association in 1847 marked the beginning of the effort to convince state legislatures to accord physicians a virtual legal monopoly over the practice of medicine.

Medicine today is considered a *profession*, an occupation that involves extensive training and in which members have exclusive control over a specified area of practice. Professionals also control entrance into the profession, set standards for performance, and exercise autonomy over the flow of their work (Freidson, 1970). As professionals, physicians receive considerably more income, prestige, and power than people in most other occupations. Chapter 6 noted that physicians rank high in the prestige hierarchy in the United States. In addition, they earn on the average approximately $205,000 a year, more than five times that of the average household income (U.S. Bureau of the Census, 2004, p. 109).

Along with a dominant position in society, physicians are also dominant in the social structure of health care. For example, they have much more control over the medical encounter than do patients. The discussion of the interactionist perspective noted that physicians can be late for appointments whereas most patients do not have that leeway. Doctors also have societal authority to decide who is sick by diagnosing and treating disease. They are given this authority because of their expert knowledge of disease and medicine. Yet, in this process, doctors are also influenced by cultural beliefs and the social characteristics of patients. For example, some physicians believe the cultural stereotype that women complain excessively and therefore may take the symptoms of women less seriously. Research shows that when women complain of chest pains, physicians are much more likely to dismiss the complaint as due to psychological distress than if male patients complain (Tobin et al., 1987; Waitzkin, 1991).

The practice of medicine has changed significantly in the past few decades (Hafferty & Light, 1995). Previously,

In the past, most health care services were delivered by physicians and nurses. Today the social structure of health care has been expanded so that many other healer roles exist, such a physicians assistants, nurse practitioners, paramedics (shown in picture), and others.

most physicians were solo practitioners who worked independently out of their own offices. Such practices are much less common today. Now, many physicians band together with other physicians into some kind of professional and financial association. A group of physicians may share office space and equipment, for example, thus

Sociology of Media and Technology

Globalized Medicine in Cyberspace

Globalization has spread modern, sophisticated knowledge and technology to many nations around the globe, including medical knowledge and technology. Globalization has also produced a global transportation system that enables people to travel long distances quickly and inexpensively. These technological developments, along with the skyrocketing costs of medical care in the United States, have provided incentives for Americans to travel to places like India or Indonesia for medical procedures that are much less expensive than in the United States, even when including the travel costs. In this sense, modern technology has enabled the medical marketplace to become a global one, with hospitals, doctors, and nurses in the United States competing with health care providers in countries around the globe. Some health-insurance policies now provide incentives for their policyholders to do so by, for example, waiving copays if procedures are obtained at low-cost facilities overseas.

Computer-mediated communications technologies have also contributed to globalizing health services by moving the provision of services into cyberspace. This is a part of the overall explosion of commerce in cyberspace (see Chapter 4). Historically, of course, the diagnosis and treatment of disease has rested fundamentally on the doctor–patient relationship and geographic proximity: Doctors meet with, talk to, and examine patients and make recommendations based on information gathered in such face-to-face encounters. Computer-mediated communications technologies substantially alter this playing field by eliminating the necessity for geographic proximity. Interaction between doctors and patients can now occur at great physical distance.

The first hints of these possibilities came with telephones and video equipment that made it possible for doctors to talk with and see patients in distant locations. This technology was used mostly for consultations in which a patient's physician could consult with other physicians about cases. These technologies produced only limited changes in the practice of medicine because the expense of the technology meant that its distribution was limited.

Today, this situation is changing dramatically. One of the major changes is that the computer-mediated communications technologies are now widely available, with most households having access to computers and the Internet. The first "cyberdocs" and electronic drugstores appeared toward the end of the twentieth century (Stolberg, 1999). People can now purchase some prescription drugs from a variety of Web sites. Some of these electronic drugstores employ physicians to review cases to determine if a drug is medically appropriate. The physicians review health histories filled out online by patients or faxed to the doctor, but in the not too distant future it may be feasible for large numbers of patients to send audio and video data to physicians over the Internet. In other words, while the physician would not be able to physically touch the patient, all other aspects of the medical interchange could occur online. Of course, some information that doctors need to make a diagnosis requires touching the patient, but many diagnoses can be made without this. In fact, this is what the cyber pharmacies claim: The drugs they sell online can be safely prescribed without physical contact between doctor and patient. As the technology becomes more available, the lower costs and increased convenience of cyber-diagnoses may provide an incentive for physicians to decide that the physical presence of the patient is less important to accurate diagnoses than they once thought.

These developments have been controversial because some powerful groups see their interests affected by them. For example, the American Medical Association and the National Association of Boards of Pharmacy oppose cyberdoctors and cyber pharmacies, claiming that good medical diagnoses and safe pharmaceutical prescriptions depend on a real, not virtual, doctor-patient relationship. In addition, of course, the professionals that these groups represent will confront vigorous economic competition from physicians and pharmacists around the globe as medical interchanges move to cyberspace. Furthermore, cyberspace may reduce the centralized control that professional organizations, such as the AMA, and state licensing authorities have exercised over the practice of medicine. For example, if the patient is in Texas, the doctor in California, and the Internet service provider in Colorado, in which state has the activity occurred? What if one of these parties is in Indonesia or Australia? Cyberspace seems to transcend the traditional ways that we think about and divide up physical space and control social and economic interchange. In the next few years, we will likely see a more intense struggle among competing interests in the health field over how far to extend medicine into cyberspace.

reducing costs and giving them more free time, since they can share the burden of work and cover for one another on nights and weekends. Another development is for physicians to become salaried employees, working for a group practice, a hospital, or a health maintenance organization. This opportunity is attractive, especially for young physicians, because it avoids the expense of setting up a practice. However, such arrangements mean a change in the practice of medicine because these employees, more than half of all physicians today, lose some of their autonomy. They are less able to decide which patients to see or how many to see, and they may lose some control over what diagnoses to make and treatments to recommend. The Sociology of Media and Technology section describes the impact of modern technologies on how doctors practice medicine.

The Nursing Profession

Nurses constitute the second most important group of healers in the social structure of scientific health care. During the nineteenth century, nurses had responsibility for hygiene and sanitation in hospitals and for maintaining discipline on wards. They were not considered to be assisting in the treatment process. With the proliferation of technology and specialization, nurses gradually came to be viewed as *ancillary* to medicine, with physicians assigning to them many routine chores, such as taking blood pressures. By the first few decades of the twentieth century, nurses had become defined as technical assistants to physicians, and the structure of domination among health-care providers had become solidified, with nurses subordinate to physicians (Bellaby & Oribabor, 1980).

This subordinate position of nursing in the health-care hierarchy has proved highly resistant to change, despite efforts by nursing leaders to emphasize the nurse–physician relationship as one of equals. Nurses have little control over their working conditions and little say in medical decision making. In addition, they are paid substantially less than physicians, with an average salary of $45,000 per year for a full-time registered nurse, and nurses share in little of doctors' prestige. Their subordinate position continues despite the fact that nurses today are highly trained and have considerable responsibility, dealing many times with life-and-death issues. In fact, much more of the health care of people who are hospitalized is provided by nurses than by doctors. One reason for the subordinate position of nursing is that many physicians have strongly opposed upgrading it because they view an autonomous nurse as a person practicing medicine and thus a threat to their monopoly. In addition, nursing is an overwhelmingly female occupation, and nurses face the same obstacles to change that other women have faced in a society that is male dominated.

New Health-Care Practitioners

Until recently, there has been a shortage of physicians in the United States, especially in rural and inner-city areas. To alleviate this problem, the government has supported the development of physician extenders, practitioners trained to perform some of the simple and routine health-care tasks traditionally accomplished by physicians. Nurse practitioners (NPs), for example, are registered nurses with advanced training that today usually includes a master's degree in nursing. Physician's assistants (PAs) have some medical training and can work only under the supervision of a physician. NPs and PAs do such things as conduct routine physical examinations or provide simple emergency and prenatal care. Health policymakers had hoped that alternative healers, such as PAs and NPs, would produce less reliance on traditionally trained physicians and thus make health care more accessible and less expensive. This substitution may not be happening, however, to the extent that it could. One reason is that some doctors are reluctant to accept these personnel, believing that only physicians are competent to provide key medical services. In addition, a surplus of physicians is now emerging, at least in some specialties. Consequently, physicians may come to see these other providers as competition for a shrinking health-care dollar. So the situation remains unsettled.

Hospitals and the Corporatization of Health Care

As a result of the development of modern medical knowledge and technologically sophisticated equipment over the past 150 years, hospitals have become modern medical centers for the effective practice of medicine. The social organization of these hospitals constitutes yet another dimension of the social structure of modern health-care systems.

Early in the twentieth century, most hospitals were nonprofit facilities run either by a religious order or charitable organization or by a city or county government. Their primary motivation was patient care, and they were highly accountable to their patients and the community they served. The people who ran the hospitals typically lived in the community they served, and the community had a variety of mechanisms for influencing hospital decisions and the allocation of resources. In the last few decades, a different type of hospital has become more significant: the *proprietary hospital,* an investor-owned, profit-making corporation. These hospitals are primarily motivated by maintaining and increasing profits, and as they become more widespread, the U.S. health-care system may change significantly.

In other words, health-care institutions are a part of the U.S. capitalist economic system described in

Chapter 13. This situation is not new. After all, physicians have been business entrepreneurs in the United States since the nation's founding, pharmaceutical companies have always tried to make a profit selling people drugs, and there have always been privately owned hospitals. What is different today are the size and scope of the privatization and corporatization of health care in the United States. One in six acute-care hospitals is now investor owned. In these corporate settings, control and authority over medical decisions and issues are gradually shifting from the hands of patients, physicians, and community leaders to corporate headquarters and medical industry entrepreneurs, and the primary motivation of these corporations is to increase corporate profits.

There are, of course, benefits to this privatization. Especially for those with good health insurance or the wealthy who can afford to pay on their own, medicine in the United States provides some excellent services. As is described in Chapter 13, capitalism is based on the assumption that competition and profit seeking will work in the interests of the consumer by providing the widest range of goods and services at the lowest price. These incentives should, in theory, encourage private health-care businesses to provide the highest-quality, least-expensive health care possible to their customers.

However, evidence suggests that it often doesn't work out that way. In areas where many hospitals compete with one another for patients, for example, both for-profit and nonprofit hospitals charge about the same for various procedures; when there is no competition, for-profits actually charge more for services than do the nonprofits (Lindorff, 1992). It seems that, in a noncompetitive environment, the temptation to raise charges, and thus increase profits, is too great for the for-profits to resist. The overall lower costs of nonprofit hospitals are especially surprising because they do not dump expensive services such as obstetrics in the way that the for-profits have. Also, research shows that investor-owned health insurance plans deliver a demonstrably lower quality of health care than do not-for-profit plans and that investor-owned nursing homes provide lower levels of care to their clients than do not-for-profit nursing homes (Harrington et al., 2001; Himmelstein, Woolhandler, & Hellander, 2001). In addition, there is ample research showing that government health insurance programs such as Medicare are less expensive—or at least, are no more expensive—than health insurance provided by private insurers (Boccuti & Moon, 2003; Gold, 2003). One of the reasons for this is that, surprising to some, the government programs have considerably lower administrative costs.

The privatization and corporatization of health care also mean that those who cannot afford health care—the poor who do not qualify for Medicaid and those who do not have health insurance on the job—do not have access to the health services they need. Even those with Medicaid find that they have limited access to the system because corporate hospitals and doctors prefer to serve those whose insurance will pay higher fees for services than will Medicaid. In addition, expensive medicine, such as obstetrics and emergency medicine, gets dumped onto publicly owned hospitals, which further taxes their ability to provide quality care to their patients. And some question whether profit seeking by doctors and hospitals always works in the best interests of the patient. As one health economist put it: "The real threat to health care is when the doctors' and the hospitals' interests become aligned against the interests of the patient. It's possible that the corporations could usurp the physicians' power" to act as an advocate for the patients (quoted in Lindorff, 1992, p. 86).

Dr. Arnold S. Relman (1980), editor of the prestigious *New England Journal of Medicine*, calls this a medical-industrial complex: *a coincidence of interests between physicians and other health-care providers and the industries producing health-care goods and services, with both parties profiting from the increased use of these commodities while the health-care consumer pays enormous costs for inadequate care.* This arrangement is analogous to the military-industrial complex discussed in Chapter 13. It can lead to a conflict of interest because many of the businesses are owned by doctors or employ doctors. Like other enterprises, these businesses stand to increase their profits by "selling" as much of their commodity as they can, just as a person who sells cars profits by increasing sales. This situation raises the question of whether health-care decisions are motivated by the health needs of the consumer or by the profit needs of the medical-industrial complex.

Many critics regard the free market and profit-making nature of the U.S. health-care system as a major factor leading people to pay more for lower-quality health care than they should. One problem is that the health-care field is not as subject to the laws of competition and the marketplace as are other economic realms. Health-care consumers, for example, cannot as readily shop for bargains and are heavily dependent on physicians, who benefit from high health-care expenditures, to tell them what health services they need. Another problem is that health corporations can be tempted to cut back on services, and possibly on necessary health care, in order to increase profits.

There is contentious debate about what, if anything, to do about all these problems. Relman has urged the AMA to discourage physicians from commercially exploiting health care by being financially involved in health-care businesses. Other

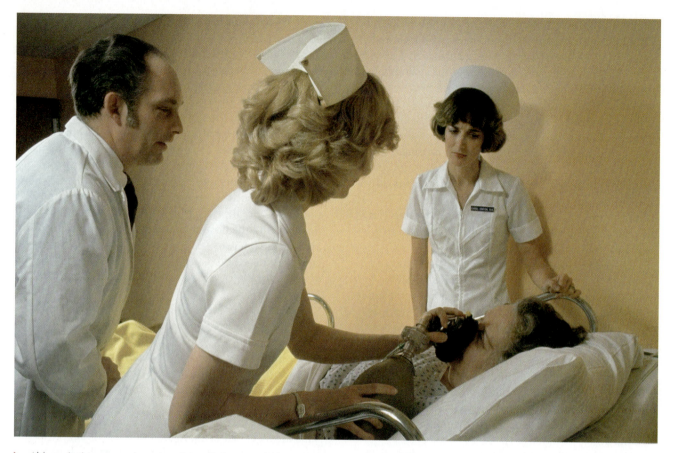

Although things are changing, it is still the case that men tend to hold the most powerful, authoritative, and well-paying positions in the health-care industry while women tend to hold more subordinate positions. This restricts women's access to good occupations as well as reducing the likelihood that the health-care system will work in the interests of women.

critics, such as Ivan Illich (1976) and Robert Sherrill (1995), believe that the capitalist nature of the health-care system is the fundamental problem. For these radical critics, only a complete restructuring of the system can prevent widespread abuses and exploitation. Some of these critics call for much more government involvement in protecting health-care consumers, controls over excess profit making in health care, and possibly even a socialized health-care system. Current social policy tends to support the profit-oriented nature of the system, but change could occur in the future.

Issues in Health Care in the United States

> You should be able to discuss and evaluate the issues of rising health-care costs, adequate access to health care, the quality of medical services, and gender inequality in health care.

The previous section noted that people who can obtain access to health care in the United States often receive very good treatment. Yet, some people do not have that access, and other problems exist in the health-care system. This section reviews some of the major problems that concern people today before turning to what might be done about solving them.

Rising Health-Care Costs

For most of the twentieth century, the rise in the cost of health care was remarkably rapid and consistent. In 1970 it cost about $74 to stay in a major hospital for one day. Today, the average cost of a one-day hospital stay has risen to $1,522 (U.S. Bureau of the Census, 2007, p. 116). Per capita expenditures for health care have increased over fifty times since 1950 (Table 10.1). People now pay approximately $6,697 each year for health-care goods and services for each man, woman, and child in the United States—over $26,000 a year for a family of four. Inflation accounts for some of this increase, but inflation during the same period increased overall prices only about seven times. A number of factors account for the sky-rocketing growth in health-care costs (McCue, 1989).

First and probably most important is the fact that there has been a growing demand for health-care services, and a basic economic principle is that increasing

Table 10.1

NATIONAL HEALTH EXPENDITURES IN THE UNITED STATES, 1940–2005

	1940	1950	1960	1970	1980	1990	2000	2005
Percentage of GNP	4.0%	4.6%	5.2%	7.2%	9.1%	12.2%	13.0%	16.0%
Per capita expenditures	$29	$78	$142	$334	$1,054	$2,690	$4,639	$6,697

Note: From "National Health Expenditures, Fiscal Year 1977" by Robert M. Gibson and Charles R. Fisher, 1978, *Social Security Bulletin*, 41, p. 15; National Center for Health Statistics, *Health, United States, 2007: With chartbook on trends in the Health of Americans* (Hyattsville, MD: National Center for Health Statistics, 2007), p. 375.

demand for something tends to push up prices. The U.S. population is larger, more affluent, and older, and these factors tend to increase the demand for a finite amount of health-care goods and services. Affluent people can afford more and better health care, and they are more knowledgeable about the services that are available. Older people have more health problems and require more health-care services. These services are also more widely available today because there are more physicians and more hospital services in suburbs and small towns.

Second, and probably equally important, is the availability of diagnostic and treatment procedures that were unheard of five, ten, or twenty years ago. These procedures can be very costly. Premature babies who would have died two decades ago are now saved in expensive, neonatal intensive care units (but at a high cost: from $200,000 to $1 million for an infant who weighs only one pound at birth). Laser surgery, CAT scanners, coronary bypass operations, angioplasty procedures, magnetic resonance imaging—these and many other procedures did not exist several decades ago. Some think that heart transplants will be routine in the not too distant future, and they now can cost more than $300,000 apiece.

Third, health care is a labor-intensive industry—it requires many people to act as providers—and the cost of health care rises quickly when health-care providers lobby for higher salaries. Also, savings through automation are not as easy to achieve in the health field as in other industries. Advances in health technology often involve completely new procedures, which call for new technicians, instead of replacing something that had been done less efficiently by older technology. Thus, improvements in health technology often result in the need for more, not fewer, workers.

Fourth, economic competition and the check on costs that it can afford are weaker in the health field than in other economic areas. Consequently, physicians and hospitals can raise costs with less concern about market considerations. As is discussed in Chapter 13, free competition is a key element in a capitalist economy, ensuring the lowest prices and the highest-

quality goods and services. The ways in which the health field diverges from the ideal of free competition were discussed in the preceding section.

Fifth, there is a tendency to overutilize health-care services and even to perform completely unnecessary diagnostic and treatment procedures (Brownlee, 2008). One reason for this is the way people pay for health care, which leaves both the physician and the patient with little reason to show restraint in the use of services. A very common mode of paying for health care, especially prior to the 1990s, has been through third-party medicine, in which *the patient pays premiums into a fund and the doctor or hospital is paid from this fund for each treatment provided the patient.* The first two parties in the transaction, of course, are the patient and the doctor or hospital. The third party might be a private health insurance company or a government program such as Medicare or Medicaid.

The basic flaw in such payment schemes is that the party paying the bill—the third-party source of funds—does not participate in the decision about how much or what kinds of services to provide. Patients have already paid their premiums and do not have to pay more as additional services are rendered, and physicians and hospitals benefit financially when more services are provided. The result is too many and sometimes completely unnecessary medical procedures being done.

Access to Medical Services

Many people in the United States do not have easy access to medical care when they need it (Quadagno, 2005). Because health care is a commodity sold in the marketplace, those who can afford to pay receive medical services, whereas those who cannot are left to fend for themselves. The high cost of health care means that only the wealthiest can afford to pay out of their own pockets for medical services. Most people rely on health insurance, either purchased by themselves or provided by an employer. The poor and less well-to-do, who cannot find a job or whose employer does not provide health insurance, are out in the cold (Seccombe & Amey,

1995). This situation has been eased somewhat with the introduction of programs of publicly financed health insurance such as Medicaid. Yet fewer than one-half of the poor are covered by Medicaid (U.S. Bureau of the Census, 2007, p. 104). As a consequence, one-third of the poorest people under the age of sixty-five have no health-insurance coverage; for them, access to medical care is quite limited. In addition to the poor, there are others who find themselves without health insurance: laid-off employees; people who retire before they are eligible for Medicare; young people who are too old for coverage under their parents' health-insurance plan; and widows, widowers, and divorced people who had depended on their spouses' health insurance. Altogether forty-seven million people, or 15 percent of the populace, are without health insurance (see Figure 10.5).

Quality of Medical Services

Rising costs and the intense competition among hospitals may be affecting the quality of health care in the United States. To keep costs down and profits up, hospitals are merging, cutting back on services to patients, and placing heavy workloads on nurses. As a result, many nurses have left nursing, making for a significant shortage in nurses (Stolberg, 2002). This trend has also led to the work of nurses being taken over by lower-paid and less highly trained nursing assistants and technicians. Registered nurses are also given responsibility for supervising these less trained workers, further taking away from nurses' direct contact with patients. These and other cutbacks are considered to be among the reasons for a decline in services to the point of increased injury and suffering to patients in some hospitals.

Cutbacks such as these, along with the highly bureaucratic organization of the health-care system, can result in highly impersonal and even dehumanizing health-care services. The standardization of health care can benefit the health-care system because it is less expensive. Yet it can lead patients to feel dissatisfied, lonely, and frightened.

Gender Inequality in Health Care

Gender inequality pervades the health-care system in the United States, with widespread ramifications. First, the health-care industry is male dominated, with men holding most of the prestigious, well-paying, and powerful positions (Figure 10.6). Men make up 70 percent of today's physicians, for example, whereas 92 percent of the registered nurses are women. Seventy-two percent of dentists are men, whereas practically all dental assistants and dental hygienists are women. Clearly, the health-care system involves men in positions of authority telling women what to do. This was not always the case. In the nineteenth century, women, working as midwives or other types of healers, provided much of the medical care for families. As more medical schools developed in the late 1800s, women were excluded from most of them. By the turn of the twentieth century, legislation banned the "practice of medicine" by anyone not trained in a state-approved medical school. The result: Women were effectively banned from the practice of medicine. It was not really until the late 1970s that medical and dental education began to open up to women. Today almost one-half of both medical and dental students nationwide are women (Figure 10.7). There has been

Figure 10.5
People without Health Insurance for the Entire Year, 1985–2006

Source: Carmen DeNavas-Walt, Bernadette D. Proctor, and Jessica Smith. *Current Population Reports*, P60-233. *Income, Poverty, and Health Insurance Coverage in the United States: 2006* (Washington, DC: U.S. Bureau of the Census, 2007), p.19.

Figure 10.6

Men and Women in Health Occupations in the United States, 2007

Note: From *Employment and Earnings: Vol. 55, no.1* (pp. 212–219) by U.S. Department of Labor, Bureau of Labor Statistics, 2008.

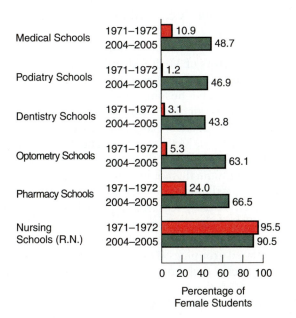

Figure 10.7

Enrollment of Women in Schools for Health Occupations, United States, Academic Years 1971–2005

Note: From *Health, United States,* by National Center for Health Statistics, (Hyattsville, MD: Public Health Service), various years.

less change, however, in the sparse numbers of men in nursing schools.

One reason for concern about male dominance in the health field is that it has severely restricted women's access to lucrative and prestigious occupations. These issues of economic discrimination are discussed in more detail in Chapter 8. Another reason for concern is that male dominance may have had a detrimental effect on the health and health care of women (Scully, 1994). Male physicians over the years held the same stereotypes about women that other men in the United States did, and these influenced what physicians defined as illness and what treatments they made available. For example, one stereotype viewed menstruation as unclean or abnormal, and physicians contributed to this view by "medicalizing" menstruation, defining it as a medical condition or weakness calling for some intervention. In the nineteenth century and well into the twentieth, menstruation was viewed as a pathological condition sometimes having serious consequences and influencing women's ability to think and make decisions. In fact, the reputed ill effects of women's reproductive biology have been an important staple in a sexist ideology justifying the inequitable treatment of women. From the late 1800s until recently, the process of childbirth has been viewed as a medical procedure rather than the profoundly natural and personal event that it really is. Women were routinely given powerful anesthetics that prevented them from experiencing the birth of their children. Then they might not even be permitted to see their infants for a few days after birth, a practice that interfered with the bonding that occurs between mothers and babies. More recently, the number of cesarean births has grown from 5 percent to 29 percent of all births, giving the United States the highest rate of such births (U.S. Bureau of the Census, 2007, p. 67). Some cesareans, of course, are medically justified, but there is much suspicion that some are performed for the convenience of medical personnel, to protect against malpractice suits, or because doctors and hospitals are reimbursed more for surgical births.

The medical procedure that is among those most likely to be performed unnecessarily— hysterectomy—affects only women. A conservative estimate is that one-third of all hysterectomies over the years were probably medically unjustified, and some studies find as many as 70 percent to be unnecessary (Broder et al., 2000). Some observers have questioned whether a medical profession dominated by women would have so routinely performed such surgeries. In addition, feminists argue that medical research has been dominated by the sexist assumption that it is the woman's responsibility to orchestrate birth-control efforts. Consequently, most birth-control research has been focused on female contraceptive devices rather than effective procedures for male contraception.

Financing Health Care in the United States

> You should be able to analyze the various alternative ways of financing health care in the United States and discuss whether health care is a privilege or a right.

One approach to alleviating some of the problems discussed in the preceding section is to find a better way of financing health care in the United States. Such financing has been a highly controversial issue, and this section reviews some of the major proposals for change.

Publicly Funded Health Insurance

One approach to increasing people's access to health care is through publicly funded health insurance. Two

government programs that have probably had the most profound effects on health-care delivery in the United States are Medicare and Medicaid, both established in 1965. These programs are based on the assumption that all citizens have a right to medical treatment irrespective of their financial circumstances. Medicare is *government health insurance for those over sixty-five years of age.* The program pays some of the costs for hospitalization, prescription drugs, nursing-home care, and some home health care. For a monthly fee, the elderly can also purchase medical insurance from Medicare that will cover other services such as doctors' fees and outpatient services. Medicaid is *a joint federal–state program to provide medical care for low-income people of any age.*

These two programs have gone a long way toward reducing the differences in the use of health care between the affluent and the poor. Unlike in the past, the poor today visit doctors and enter hospitals more frequently than the well-to-do. To that extent, these two programs have achieved one of their major goals, which was to make health care available to all citizens regardless of financial circumstances. But these plans are not without their problems. First, they are very expensive and growing more so. Both traditionally have involved third-party payment arrangements and suffered from the same cost problems of all such fee schemes. A second problem, especially with Medicaid, has been fraud, committed by both recipients and providers of health care. Some physicians have provided unneeded treatments, and some medical laboratories have routinely charged for tests never performed (Jesilow, Pontell, & Geis, 1993).

A number of efforts have been made to control the skyrocketing costs of Medicaid and Medicare. Some states have developed *preferred provider* programs for Medicaid in which a hospital or a group of doctors agrees to provide all health-care services to Medicaid recipients in a particular geographic area, receiving, in return, one annual, lump-sum payment. This arrangement encourages the providers to prevent costs from exceeding the annual amount that they are paid because they will not receive any additional payments and are contractually required to provide services. For Medicare, the federal government instituted a new payment mechanism in the early 1980s called diagnostically related groupings (DRGs). This strategy involves placing each hospitalization episode into one of about 450 diagnostic groupings. Then all treatments in a single grouping receive the same reimbursement, whether any particular case actually costs more or less. If a case costs more to treat, the hospital must make up the difference; if it costs less, the hospital keeps the surplus. The purpose is to offer doctors and hospitals a financial incentive for keeping an eye on lowering costs.

Medicare and Medicaid amount to government health insurance for the poor and the elderly. Some have proposed that these benefits be extended as a right to all citizens through national health insurance: *government health insurance covering all citizens.* Great Britain had such a program as early as 1911. In fact, the United States is alone among the industrial nations in not providing some form of national health insurance or health service (Lindorff, 1992). National health insurance would alleviate a number of problems. It would ensure health-insurance coverage to the many people who do not currently have any, such as low-income people ineligible for Medicaid and people who are between jobs. It would also give the government a more direct means of controlling health-care costs. Finally, it would reduce the likelihood of a two-tiered health-care system. However, national health insurance would still be a third-party payment system that could be costly if it did not include some cost-containment mechanisms, such as DRGs.

Employer-Financed Health Insurance

Some would prefer that the government not get involved in the actual provision of health insurance but rather just ensure that all citizens have access to some health insurance. Because many of the currently uninsured have jobs with no health-insurance benefits, one proposal is to have the government require that all employers provide comprehensive health insurance for their employees. For employers who are too small to afford such insurance, the government could pay the insurance premiums. The Clinton administration proposed such a program in 1994, called *managed competition,* but it gained insufficient support to win approval (Skocpol, 1996). Such a program would be expensive, of course, and it would put a burden on small businesses. In addition, the consumer would pay for it through higher prices for goods and services. Yet it would provide many more people with access to health care.

Health Maintenance Organizations and Managed Care

In discussing Medicaid, preferred provider programs were mentioned. When these kinds of arrangements emerged many decades ago, they were called *health maintenance organizations* (HMOs), and they represented an alternative to traditional health insurance for financing health care. A health maintenance organization is *an organization that agrees to provide for all of a person's health-care needs for a fixed premium.* Whereas health insurance is third-party medicine involving a separate payment for each

service rendered, HMOs receive a set fee and agree to take care of all of a person's health needs for that fee. In so doing, the HMO assumes a financial risk that the services they give patients might cost more than the premiums the HMO takes in. If this happens, the HMO loses money, so the HMO has an incentive to control costs that the physician or patient in third-party medicine does not have.

In the last decade, a number of trends discussed in this chapter—the corporatization of health care, increased competition in the health-care field, and rising costs—have led to the emergence of what is now called managed care: *a health-care system that focuses on controlling costs by monitoring and controlling the health-care decisions of doctors and patients* (Cockerham, 2007; Draper et al., 2002).

HMOs are a form of managed care. Some HMOs and managed-care systems own their own hospitals and employ health-care providers, including physicians. People in managed-care arrangements typically have a limited choice of doctors to select from, and the managed-care system exercises tight control over medical treatments and therefore costs. Two-thirds of the people who work at medium-sized and large companies in the United States today are enrolled in managed-care health systems rather than traditional health insurance. Whereas most HMOs used to be not-for-profit organizations, today most HMOs and managed-care systems are for-profit. Insurance companies, traditional HMOs, and hospitals have taken the lead in developing managed-care plans and offering them to employers, usually at a lower price than that of traditional health insurance. Many recipients of Medicare and Medicaid are now in managed-care systems.

One of the motivations for developing HMOs and managed-care systems has been cost containment, and studies of HMOs indicate that they are less expensive than traditional health insurance and provide equivalent levels and quality of services (Brown et al., 1993; Greenfield et al., 1995). They have lower hospitalization rates and do fewer unnecessary surgeries. These benefits may derive from the HMO's mode of financing, which gives the HMO an incentive to economize, or from their greater use of preventive health care. However, it may also be that, in the past when these studies were done, healthier people joined HMOs and this fact accounted for their lower costs. The managed-care systems of today have not yet been extensively studied in terms of these outcomes.

Despite the benefits, recent trends in managed care have been criticized on a number of grounds (Himmelstein, Woolhandler, & Hellander, 2001; Ware et al., 1996). First, managed care does nothing to help those without health insurance. Second, the oversight of medical decisions common in managed care threatens the independence and autonomy of medical practitioners. This is true in part because, in some communities, managed care enrolls so many people that insufficient business is left for physicians who are not part of the managed-care system. To make a living, doctors have little choice but to sign on with the managed-care system for whatever pay and working conditions it dictates. In fact, physicians' incomes have stopped rising and may even be falling because of the cost controls of managed care. A third criticism of managed-care systems is that they aggressively compete for contracts, offering employers low premiums and then pressuring doctors to limit medical procedures and hospitals to cut staff and procedures in order to come in under cost and make a profit. Patients may suffer from this practice if needed health-care services are not provided. This seems to be an especially likely outcome when HMOs are investor-owned: Research discussed earlier in this chapter shows for-profit health insurance plans, such as HMOs, deliver a lower quality of health care to patients than do not-for-profit plans.

A final criticism of managed care is that it represents a dramatic shift in control over medical decisions, from the hands of many dispersed doctors and local hospitals to the directors of these huge corporate empires. And these health empires have been merging at a rapid rate, with the result being that the system is moving toward an oligopoly (see Chapter 13). There is little evidence at this point that health-care consumers benefit from these mergers through better care or lower costs (Feldman, Wholey, & Christianson, 1996). So, the kind of health care that more and more people in the United States receive today is determined by a contract negotiated between their employer and a national (or global) corporate health-care giant. At this point, it is unclear what all the benefits and disadvantages of managed care are and whether the former outweigh the latter. For the moment, because of the stress on privatization in the United States, managed care is at the center of the social-policy stage, and other alternatives such as national health insurance are not much discussed.

Health Care: A Privilege or a Right?

The debate over how to finance health care has to do, in part, with whether people consider health care to be a privilege or a right. Some people see access to health care as a privilege of those who can afford to pay for it. This view is consistent with the capitalist and market foundations of the U.S. economy; health care is an economic service, and it can be most efficiently produced and distributed through competition in the marketplace. The opposite view is that society needs to ensure that people are healthy so that they can work and accomplish other tasks essential to the maintenance of society. Therefore, high-quality health care should be a fundamental right of all citizens. Most industrial nations today have taken the latter view, but there is still controversy regarding this issue in the United States, and many citizens have little or no access to health care. The chapter closes with a description of what health care looks like in nations that consider health care a right.

Paying for Health Care in Other Nations: Canada and Sweden

Earlier in this chapter, we saw that, in comparison to most other industrial nations, people in the United States live shorter lives, lose more infants to death, and pay more for health care. Why do consumers in these other nations pay less and receive more? Some critics attribute this difference to the largely unregulated, laissez-faire nature of the U.S. health-care system, which leaves many people with limited or no access to health care.

In Sweden, France, Australia, Germany, Canada, and many other nations, most health services are paid for with money collected by the government (Cockerham, 2007). This arrangement is similar to Medicare and Medicaid in the United States. Employers and employees pay taxes that are placed in a fund from which medical bills are paid. Canada, for example, provided hospital insurance for its citizens beginning in 1961 and physician's care insurance starting in 1971 (Bennett & Adams, 1993). The entire population is covered, and 95 percent of hospital and physician costs are paid by federal or provincial taxes. The system does not pay for some amenities, such as private hospital rooms or cosmetic surgery. Everything else is covered, and Canadians rarely even see a hospital bill. Patients can choose their own physicians, and physicians are private, self-employed practitioners, not government employees. Hospitals operate on a budget that is set largely by provincial governments. Thus Canada has an essentially private health-care system that is paid for almost entirely by public money.

One way in which the costs of such universal coverage can be paid for is by keeping the price of health care down. For example, in Canada, the government sets all doctor and hospital fees, and physicians cannot charge more for services than the insurance will pay. Canadian physicians do not earn the lucrative incomes that their U.S. counterparts do, although physicians are still among the highest-paid professional groups in Canada. However, Canadian doctors do not have to worry about billing patients, preparing insurance forms, or writing off bad debts.

Sociology on the Internet

There are innumerable sources of information about health issues worldwide available on the Internet. Begin by going to the Web page of the World Health Organization, a global organization that conducts research on and runs programs promoting world health: **www.who.int**. From the WHO home page, select "Publications," then "World Health Report" for the most current year. Explore this document with an eye toward identifying information about the rates of disease and death in various nations and regions and the impact of social and cultural factors on health and illness. Do the same thing for the United States at the Web sites of the Centers for Disease Control and Prevention (**www.cdc.gov**) and the American Public Health Association (**www.apha.org**).

The Internet also contains many resources regarding AIDS. The WHO, CDC, and APHA sites are very useful for this. At these sites, identify data on the extent and spread of AIDS currently in the United States and around the world. Are there any new developments since this text was published? In addition, locate organizations that are active in the fight against AIDS. What information can you find at these sites to illustrate issues discussed in this chapter? One of these organizations is the Gay Men's Health Crisis (**www.gmhc.org**).

For further information and discussion, go to Allyn & Bacon's Social Problems Supersite (see Chapter 1) and explore Problem Area: Problems of Health, Illness, and Health Care Delivery.

Of course, it is not possible to spend less on health care and cover more people, as the Canadians do, without some costs. One cost is that there are sometimes waits for hospital beds and some types of surgical procedures, especially nonemergency surgeries. In addition, some state-of-the-art technology, such as magnetic resonance imaging, is not as widely available as in the United States. Yet another cost is the higher taxes to pay for the universal, government-provided coverage.

One should look at health-care financing programs in terms of *who* bears the costs, since someone must bear the costs of any program. Currently, in the United States, those who benefit the most are the affluent; those fortunate enough to have good, employer-provided health insurance; and the elderly with Medicare. A shift to a Canadian-style system would mean redirecting some of the benefits from those groups to the poor, the unemployed, the underemployed, and other marginal groups. It comes down to *how* health care will be rationed, not whether it will be rationed. Will some poor and unemployed be denied basic health care, such as prenatal care or frequent doctor visits for sick people? Or will some of the affluent be denied rapid access to elective surgeries or exotic technologies, such as coronary bypass surgery for elderly patients?

Sweden has a truly socialized health-care system, with the government nationalizing most health-care facilities and employing health-care workers. Health services are free to any who need them, and little money changes hands between patient and health-care providers. Taxes support the health-care system, and Sweden does have high taxes, in part to support the health-care system. However, the Swedes are also among the healthiest people in the world. They live three years longer than people in the United States and have lower infant mortality. Sweden is an interesting contrast with both Canada and the United States in that it runs a generally effective, socialized system of health care in a capitalist country.

Study & Review
SUMMARY OF LEARNING OBJECTIVES

You should be able to analyze health, illness, and health-care institutions from the three theoretical perspectives and show how social and political factors influence what conditions are defined as illness.

From the functionalist perspective, illness threatens the survival of society because sick people cannot accomplish essential tasks. The health-care system becomes a problem when it fails to return sick people to normal social functioning. From the conflict perspective, health and health care are scarce resources over which interest groups compete. The inequitable distribution of these resources reflects the overall inequitable distribution of resources in society. This inequality becomes a problem when some group thinks that it is not receiving its fair share of these resources. The interactionist perspective recognizes that illnesses involve a network of social meanings and social expectations. In medical encounters, people exchange meanings about social standing, power, and worth in the medical setting as well as society as a whole. AIDS in the United States illustrates that cultures stigmatize some illnesses and that such stigmatization can influence how people who are sick are treated.

You should be able to describe how levels of societal development and a person's social position influence health and illness.

Social epidemiologists have researched how the kinds of diseases that affect us depend on the level of societal development and on our position in society. Diseases can be classified as acute or chronic, with the former contributing more to the death rate in preindustrial societies. In industrial societies, the death rate drops substantially and life expectancy increases, in large part as a result of declines in infant and childhood mortality and changes in lifestyle. The four sociocultural factors that have the most impact on health and illness are socioeconomic status, gender, race, and lifestyle.

You should be able to describe the health-care beliefs and practices of personalistic, naturalistic, and scientific health-care systems as well as those of Chinese and holistic medicine.

Personalistic health-care systems are found mostly among hunters and gatherers and are based on the belief that disease was caused by invasion of a force from outside the body, such as a spirit or agent. In agricultural societies, naturalistic health-care systems emerge that see disease largely as a result of the impersonal working of forces in nature or the human body. Scientific health-care systems view disease as a natural process caused by biological factors, and medical knowledge is based on systematic scientific research. Chinese medicine illustrates a system that uses modern scientific medicine along with more traditional beliefs about health and illness. Holistic medicine sees people as having psychological, social, cultural, and spiritual needs and focuses on treating disease at all those levels.

You should be able to describe the social factors influencing whether people seek health care, the various healing roles in the health-care system, and the consequences of the corporatization of health care.

Health-care institutions have a social structure that involves organized patterns of interaction between people who are sick and people in various healing roles. A variety of sociocultural factors influence whether people define themselves as sick, whether they seek care from a healer, and from which healer they seek care. Two key healer roles in scientific medicine are physicians and nurses, with the former having considerably more authority, status, and power than the latter. In modern societies, much of health-care delivery occurs in hospitals, which have become highly bureaucratic and are increasingly likely to be investor-owned corporations.

You should be able to discuss and evaluate the issues of rising health-care costs, adequate access to health care, the quality of medical services, and gender inequality in health care.

Health-care costs are rising because of growing demand for services, new medical procedures, labor costs, a lack of competition, and the overutilization of health care. Many people lack access to the health-care system because they are poor or unemployed or because their employer doesn't provide health insurance. The quality of health-care services is adversely affected by cutbacks in services and by health-care bureaucracies that become impersonal and dehumanizing. Health care has traditionally been dominated by men, although this domination is less extensive today than in the past. Male domination has meant fewer career opportunities for women in health care and a less woman-sensitive provision of health-care services.

You should be able to analyze the various alternative ways of financing health care in the United States and discuss whether health care is a privilege or a right.

A central issue in deciding how to attack problems in health care is whether access to health care should be every citizen's right or whether it is a privilege of those who can afford to pay for it. Problems have been attacked through publicly funded health insurance, employer-financed health insurance, and the emergence of health maintenance organizations and managed-care arrangements. Canada and Sweden provide two examples of how to organize and fund health care: the former is a private health-care system that is funded almost entirely through national health insurance provided by the government, whereas the latter is a socialized system of health care.

CHRONOLOGICAL PRACTICE TEST

For answers to Key Concepts see the page number in parentheses; for other answers see page 302.

Sociological Perspectives on Health, Illness, and Health Care
Key Concept
1. Sick role (275)

True/False

2. T F Worldwide, more than one-half of all new HIV infections result from male homosexual contact.

Concept Completion

3. The _____ refers to the set of expectations intended to guide the behavior of people who are ill.

Critical Thinking

4. Compare and contrast the functionalist, conflict, and interactionist perspectives on health and health care.
5. Using the examples of both the United States and Congo, what are the social, political, and economic factors that have contributed to the spread of AIDS in those two societies?

Health, Illness, and Society

Key Concepts

6. Social epidemiology (278)
7. Acute diseases (279)
8. Chronic diseases (279)
9. Preventive medicine (280)
10. Curative medicine (280)
11. Crisis medicine (280)

True/False

12. T F The transition from preindustrial to industrial societies has been associated with a shift from chronic diseases to acute diseases as the most serious health threat.
13. T F Because modern medicine arose when acute infectious diseases were the major health threats, medical education evolved to train doctors with a crisis orientation.
14. T F The United States has one of the lowest infant mortality rates in the world—only two nations have lower rates.

Concept Completion

15. The branch of sociology that studies how social factors influence the distribution and spread of disease is _____.
16. The kinds of diseases that pose the most serious health threats to preindustrial societies are _____.
17. Changes in lifestyle or other steps that help avoid the occurrence of disease are called _____ medicine.

Graphics Review

18. Summarize the information in Figures 10.1 through 10.4. What do they say about how the level of societal development affects people's health and illness?

Health-Care Systems in Cross-Cultural Perspective

True/False

19. T F Holistic medicine largely ignores scientific medicine and relies heavily on Chinese medicine.

Concept Completion

20. The healers in personalistic health-care systems are called _____ and _____.
21. Two procedures used in Chinese medicine to balance the yin and the yang are _____ and _____.

Critical Thinking

22. Compare and contrast personalistic, naturalistic, and scientific health-care systems in terms of their beliefs about disease and their healing practices.

The Social Structure of Health Care

Key Concept

23. Medical-industrial complex (291)

True/False

24. T F The trend in medicine today is for fewer physicians to be salaried employees and for more to go into solo practice.
25. T F The text takes the stance that no groups in the United States benefit from the corporatization of health care.

Concept Completion

26. In the United States, two relatively new healing roles that are classified as physician extenders are _____ and _____.
27. The _____ is the phenomenon in the health-care field that is analogous to the military-industrial complex.

Critical Thinking

28. Describe the social structure of health care in the United States, including a discussion of the social roles involved and social expectations for the behavior of people in those roles.
29. What is meant by the privatization and corporatization of health care in the United States? What are the benefits and disadvantages of this trend?

Issues in Health Care in the United States

Key Concept

30. Third-party medicine (293)

True/False

31. T F National health expenditures in the United States today constitute a larger percentage of the gross national product than was the case fifty years ago.
32. T F Third-party medicine, unless controlled, tends to lead to an overutilization of health-care services.
33. T F According to the text, the health-care system in Canada is an example of a truly socialized health-care system.

Critical Thinking

34. Explain why health-care costs have been rising in the United States over the past fifty years.
35. How much gender inequality exists in the health-care system in the United States? Why is it considered a problem?

Financing Health Care in the United States

Key Concepts

36. Medicare (296)
37. Medicaid (296)
38. National health insurance (297)
39. Health maintenance organization (297)
40. Managed care (297)

Concept Completion

41. When a patient pays premiums to a fund and then the hospital or doctor is paid from this fund for each treatment provided the patient, this is a system of _____ medicine.
42. Medicare and Medicaid amount to _____ for the elderly and the poor.

Critical Thinking

43. Describe the different methods for financing health care in the United States. What are their advantages and disadvantages?

ANSWERS TO CHRONOLOGICAL PRACTICE TEST

2. F; 12. F; 13. T; 14. F; 19. F; 24. F; 25. F; 31. T; 32. T; 33. F
3. sick role
15. social epidemiology
16. acute disease, infectious and parasitic disease
17. preventive
20. shamans, diviners
21. acupuncture, acupressure, moxibustion
26. nurse practitioners, physician's assistants
27. medical-industrial complex
41. third-party
42. government health insurance

CUMULATIVE PRACTICE TEST

See page 482 for answers.

1. The concept of the sick role is associated most clearly with the
   a. conflict perspective.
   b. functionalist perspective.
   c. managed-care perspective.
   d. deinstitutionalization perspective.
   e. interactionist perspective.

2. Which of the following statements would be most consistent with the conflict view on health care?
   a. Being healthy is the most desirable human condition.
   b. People who are ill should adopt the sick role.
   c. Sick people are "deviant," in that they can no longer fulfill their normal role obligations.
   d. The health-care system is an arena for competition among doctors, nurses, health-care consumers, and others.
   e. In health encounters, doctors, nurses, and patients exchange symbols and social meanings.

3. Which of the following statements would be most consistent with the interactionist perspective on health-care institutions?
   a. Health and health care are scarce resources, and interest groups compete with one another to gain a share of them.
   b. Disease is a threat to the social order because those who are ill are less able to make useful contributions to society.
   c. People attach social meanings to various illnesses, and the meanings may imply something about the worth of the person who is ill.
   d. The health-care system involves an inequitable distribution of money, prestige, power, and other resources.
   e. Sick people are "deviant," in that they can no longer fulfill their normal role obligations.

4. Around the world, the majority of HIV infections result from
   a. homosexual intercourse.
   b. heterosexual intercourse.
   c. use of dirty needles by intravenous drug users.
   d. contaminated food supplies.
   e. the spread of chronic disease.

5. The branch of sociology that deals with how social factors influence the distribution of disease within a population is
   a. social psychology.
   b. functionalist sociology.
   c. conflict sociology.
   d. social epidemiology.
   e. family practice.

6. Which of the following statements is true regarding the impact of social factors on health?
   a. Men live longer than women.
   b. The poor have higher death rates than do the affluent.
   c. Among African Americans and white Americans in the same social class, no differences in disease or death rates exist.
   d. All of the above are true.
   e. Both b and c are true.

7. The text points out that the major benefit of industrialization in terms of health and longevity is that
   a. people have a much greater chance of living through infancy.
   b. people over sixty-five have a much better chance of living into their nineties.
   c. people are exposed to a larger number of infectious and parasitic diseases.
   d. the major causes of death are acute diseases like cancer.
   e. None of the above.

8. The most common cause of death in the United States today is
   a. acute disease.
   b. cancer.
   c. pneumonia.
   d. cerebrovascular disease.
   e. heart disease.
9. Personalistic health-care systems are most likely to be found in which type of society?
   a. Hunting and gathering.
   b. Agricultural.
   c. Industrial.
   d. Postindustrial.
   e. *Gesellschaft.*
10. Which of the following is true of holistic medicine?
    a. It focuses on the psychological, social, and spiritual needs of people who are sick.
    b. It places emphasis on patient education.
    c. It avoids healing techniques that have not been accepted by scientific medicine.
    d. All of the above are true.
    e. Both a and b are true.
11. Which of the following statements is true regarding Chinese medicine today?
    a. It no longer uses acupuncture.
    b. It is an example of a personalistic health-care system.
    c. It has ignored scientific medicine.
    d. It incorporates both scientific medicine and traditional Chinese beliefs about disease.
    e. Both b and d are true.
12. Social and cultural factors have the most impact on how people seek health care when
    a. the sick person is a member of a minority group.
    b. symptoms are severe and incapacitating.
    c. the sick person is female rather than male.
    d. symptoms are mild and ambiguous.
    e. the sick person is male rather than female.
13. The social structure of health care would include all of the following *except*
    a. physicians.
    b. nurses.
    c. nurse practitioners.
    d. patients.
    e. All of the above groups are a part of the social structure of health care.
14. Which of the following are factors that have contributed to rising health-care costs in the United States?
    a. A growing demand for health-care services.
    b. The growth of new diagnostic and treatment procedures.
    c. Weak economic competition in the health-care field.
    d. All of the above are such factors.
    e. Both b and c.
15. A medical payment system in which the patient pays premiums into a fund and the doctor or hospital is paid from this fund for each treatment provided is called
    a. health maintenance organizations.
    b. Medicaid.
    c. the medical-industrial complex.
    d. curative medicine.
    e. third-party medicine.
16. Which of the following was *not* cited as a disadvantage in the Canadian health-care system in comparison with that of the United States?
    a. Canadians pay higher taxes.
    b. Canadian patients sometimes wait for hospital beds.
    c. Some advanced technology is not as widely available in Canada.
    d. Health-care costs are higher in Canada.
    e. All of the above were cited as disadvantages in Canada.
17. Which type of health-care financing arrangement pays for all of a person's health-care needs for a fixed premium each month or year?
    a. Medical-industrial complex.
    b. National health insurance.
    c. Third-party medicine.
    d. Socialized medicine.
    e. Health maintenance organizations.
18. Managed-care arrangements have been criticized on the grounds that
    a. they do not help people without health insurance.
    b. they will move the health-care system toward socialized medicine.
    c. they are more costly than third-party arrangements.
    d. they provide physicians with too much independence.
    e. they will shift control over medical decisions into the hands of individual physicians.
19. The program of "diagnostically related groupings," or DRGs, was instituted for the purpose of
    a. providing better health-care services to the poor.
    b. stemming the rising costs of Medicare.
    c. establishing national health insurance.
    d. encouraging the poor to join health maintenance organizations.
    e. promoting the spread of managed-care arrangements.
20. Concern over male dominance in the health field has been raised for all of the following reasons *except*
    a. it restricts women's access to lucrative occupations.
    b. it may have had a detrimental effect on the health care received by women.
    c. it contributes to the growth of the medical-industrial complex.
    d. it may lead to unnecessary treatments for women's health problems.
    e. All of the above were given as reasons for concern.

FOR FURTHER READING

Angell, Marcia. (2004). *The truth about the drug companies: How they deceive us and what to do about it.* New York: Random House. This is a well-researched and well-written argument for how pharmaceutical companies charge much more than they need to and provide less than people often think. It is a good description of the negative consequences of privatized health care and how one powerful group can influence the government to support them.

Budrys, Grace. (2003). *Unequal health: How inequality contributes to health and illness.* Blue Ridge Summit, PA: Rowman & Littlefield. This is an excellent overview of the research on how socioeconomic status and other social factors produce health disparities among people in the United States.

Callahan, Daniel. (1998). *False hopes: Why America's quest for perfect health is a recipe for failure*. New York: Simon and Schuster. The author makes a compelling argument for directing more of our resources toward preventive medicine rather than crisis medicine.

Gordon, Suzanne. (2005). *Nursing against the odds: How health care cost cutting, media stereotypes and medical hubris undermine nurses and patient care*. Ithaca, NY: Cornell University Press. This critical work points to how the position of nurses in the structure of health care impedes the ability of the health-care system to deliver top-notch care—and how the structure should be changed.

Lorber, Judith, & Moore, Lisa Jean. (2002). *Gender and the social construction of illness* (2d ed.). Walnut Creek, CA: Altamira Press. This book provides a valuable perspective on health and illness by showing how they are created and distributed as social problems based on such factors as gender.

Mirowsky, John, & Ross, Catherine E. (2003). *Social causes of psychological distress* (2d ed.). Hawthorne, NY: Aldine de Gruyter. These authors present convincing evidence to show that mental illness, especially depression and anxiety, is profoundly influenced by some very important social conditions.

Rushing, William A. (1995). *The AIDS epidemic: Social problems of an infectious disease*. Boulder, CO: Westview Press. This is a recent and comprehensive assessent of AIDS, including social factors in the spread of the disease as well as how society has reacted to it.

Starr, Paul. (1982). *The social transformation of American medicine*. New York: Basic Books. Starr gives an insightful analysis of the changes in the power and authority of the medical profession over the past two centuries. This is not an easy book, but it is one well worth spending time with.

Waitzkin, Howard. (2004). *At the front lines of medicine: How the health care system alienates doctors and mistreats patients . . . and what we can do about it*. Blue Ridge Summit, PA: Rowman & Littlefield. This is a very thought-provoking critique of our current organization of health care and includes some interesting suggestions for change.

CHAPTER 11

Religion

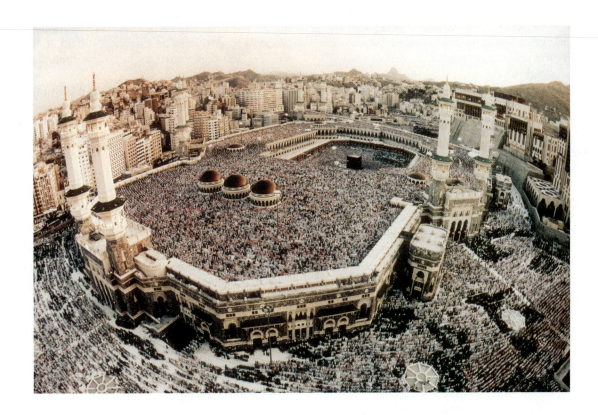

MYTHS & FACTS: About Religion

What Is Religion?

A Global Perspective: Religions of the World

Judaism
Christianity
Islam
Hinduism
Buddhism
Confucianism
Diffusion of Religion

Sociological Approaches to the Study of Religion

Durkheim: A Functionalist Perspective
Marx: A Conflict Perspective
Weber: Religion and Social Change
OTHER WORLDS, OTHER WAYS: China, Iran, and Afghanistan: Religion and Political Change

The Organization of Religion

Religion in the United States

Extent of Religiosity
Socioeconomic Status and Politics
Secularization
Religious Pluralism
The Ecumenical Movement
Fundamentalism and Evangelicalism
SOCIOLOGY OF MEDIA AND TECHNOLOGY: Communication Technologies and Religious Experience
Growth in Islam
New Religious Movements
Millenarian Religions
APPLYING SOCIOLOGY: Identifying Extremism in Religious Cults
SOCIOLOGY ON THE INTERNET

Study & Review

West Africa contains such present-day nations as Nigeria, Benin, and the Ivory Coast. In precolonial Africa, the religion of many peoples in this area was called *Vodu*, the Dahomean word for "deity" or "spirit." *Vodu* was a highly structured religious and magical system that was integrated into all parts of West African life (Mulira, 1990). It was based on the idea that a Supreme Being, or Creator, was at the top of a hierarchy of deities, and the lesser deities served as intermediaries between people and the Supreme Being. Families, clans, and villages had their own deities, who protected people and justified all aspects of social life. The deities legitimized who held power in a village, who headed a family, or who worked in a particular occupation. *Vodu* also included a host of priests, priestesses, apprentices, and others who served the deities and carried out sacred rituals.

Another powerful force in *Vodu* were witches, people who were feared because they were believed to have supernatural powers. They were considered highly destructive and had no positive role in society. Among many African groups, witches were postmenopausal women. They were believed to have the power to change people into animals and to gain control over people's actions and make them do as the witches pleased. All illnesses that could not be cured by herbalists, or root doctors, were believed to be the work of witches.

In the territory of the Yoruba tribe (present-day Nigeria), the people called their deities *orisha* (Brandon, 1990). In the Yoruba religion, each deity had a name and a personality. In ceremonies of spirit possession, it was believed that a deity would take control of a person and send him or her into a trance. The Yoruba also believed in reincarnation and, along with other West African tribes, used dance as a way to worship. Another form of worship was animal sacrifice.

Columbus first made landfall in the Western Hemisphere in 1492, and as noted in Chapter 7, the Portuguese made first contact in Brazil in 1500. These arrivals were the beginning of a massive expansion and colonization of the New World, fueled by capitalism's demand for economic growth. It was not long before African slaves were brought to the New World as a part of this colonization. The first African slaves arrived in the West Indies in 1504 and in the Jamestown colony (present-day Virginia) in 1619. Many of these slaves were from West Africa around present-day Benin and Nigeria, and they brought their native *Vodu* religion with them. In the New World, however, the religion changed some and so did the name. The religion now exists in two forms: *Voodoo* and *Santería* (Olmos & Paravisini-Gebert, 1997).

Voodoo first entered what is now the United States in the 1600s, probably in the New Orleans area, since many slaves there had come from Caribbean islands where voodoo was widely practiced. Voodoo today represents one clear survival of African culture in the New World. It adapted to its new surroundings. For example, the names of the *Vodu* deities were often changed to those of Roman Catholic saints, and the African concepts of good and evil were sometimes recast as the Christian heaven and hell. Slave owners sometimes suppressed voodoo because in the Caribbean and Brazil it had provided the organizational focus for slave revolts. Nevertheless, voodoo remains today a viable religious system with a pantheon of gods who are responsible for the physical and social order. It gives meaning and purpose to the lives of those who believe in it. Those unfamiliar with voodoo tend to see it as a magical system of spells and trances, but these practices, although important, are not its essence.

Santería is also an outgrowth of African tribal religion, and it combined elements of Roman Catholicism into a new folk religion among the slaves in the Caribbean (Vega, 2000). It emerged in Cuba during the period of slavery. *Santería* means "worship of the saints," and, like followers of voodoo, believers in *Santería* used the names of Roman Catholic saints for their deities. In fact, some followers used the Yoruba word for their deities (*orisha*) and the Spanish word for saint (*santos*) interchangeably. Today, there are an estimated one million followers of *Santería* in the United States and 75 million worldwide. Some U.S. cities outlawed animal sacrifice as a way of discouraging *Santería*, but the Supreme Court ruled unanimously in 1993 that the ordinance was unconstitutional and that First Amendment freedoms extend to Afro-Caribbean religious rituals just as they do to Judeo-Christian ones.

Santería and voodoo illustrate the importance and pervasiveness of religion, which archaeological and other evidence suggests is found in one form or another in all human societies. The earliest evidence of religious rituals can be found in the burial practices of early human groups who populated Europe and Southwest Asia more than thirty thousand years ago. These Paleolithic peoples buried their dead by laying them out carefully in pits dug into the floors of caves. They also placed tools, parts of animals, and other objects in the graves along with the bodies. Although no written record remains to confirm that these practices were religious, they strongly suggest that these early humans believed in a life after death or a spirit that would survive death.

As a scientific discipline, sociology does not assess the truth or falsity of religious beliefs. As pointed out in Chapter 1, such questions are matters of tradition, faith, or revelation. Some or all of the religious beliefs in the world may be true, but such verity cannot be settled through scientific observation. Sociology studies religion as a social institution that performs some

Myths & Facts

About Religion

Myth:

Religions appeared among human beings only with the rise of the great agricultural civilizations of the past ten thousand years. Earlier human groups were without religion.

Fact:

Evidence of religious rituals can be found among the artifacts of human groups at least thirty thousand years ago. In fact, historically, religion can be found in virtually all human societies.

Myth:

The European colonists who settled in North America in the 1500s and 1600s were escaping religious persecution. Therefore, they placed freedom of religion at the center of the new societies they created.

Fact:

Actually many of the colonies, even at the time of the Declaration of Independence in 1776, were intolerant of religious diversity and sometimes even established their own official state religions. However, complex social and historical forces (discussed in this chapter) led to the guarantee of religious freedom in the Constitution of the United States.

Myth:

New religious sects tend to come and go in the United States, with most of them lasting less than a decade and having little permanent impact on the religious scene.

Fact:

Although some new religions do not last long, most survive and become a continuing part of the religious environment in their communities.

Myth:

Until recent times, most nations were united behind one religion, such as Roman Catholicism in Spain, the Anglican Church in England, or Confucianism in China.

Fact:

Actually, religious history is much more complicated. Through trade and war, people have spread their religions around the globe for many centuries. So, Islam has been in China for more than one thousand years, and Roman Catholicism was spread around the globe beginning with the European colonial expansion five hundred years ago.

---

functions for society, is transmitted to the next generation through the socialization process, and is influenced by the social and cultural context in which it exists. These are some of the topics covered in this chapter.

What Is Religion?

You should be able to define religion and describe the major forms it can take.

When most people think about religion, they refer to their own spiritual preference, which for many people in the United States follows Judeo-Christian traditions. Yet there is tremendous variety in both religions and their expression. Sociologists have been careful to avoid a narrow definition of religion that could reflect ethnocentric biases about what religions *should* be like. Emile Durkheim (1915/1965), a pioneer in the sociological study of religion, argued that the distinctive feature of religion is that it views the world as divided into

things that are considered sacred and things that are regarded as profane. The sacred are *those things that are awesome, mysterious, extraordinary, or absolute and transcend everyday experience.* Such phenomena demand respect and reverence. The profane is *the world of the ordinary and routine,* which can be easily comprehended. Objects become sacred or profane when they are so defined by a particular group. Such definition is what makes possible a wide variety of religions: virtually anything can be defined as sacred.

Using Durkheim's distinction, then, we can define religion as *a collectively held set of symbols and rituals that express a basic understanding of the world, especially its sacred dimension, and address the ultimate concerns of the meaning of human existence* (Geertz, 1966). We can illustrate this definition by discussing several varieties of religion that can be found in the world.

Animism is *the belief that souls, spirits, or spiritual beings inhabit the world and play a significant role, for good or ill, in human affairs.* The people of Melanesia, for example, believed in *mana*—a power or spirit that could inhabit people, places, or things. Regardless of whether one had experienced extraordinarily good luck or calamitous misfortune, mana might be at work (Codrington, 1965).

A variant on animism is totemism, in which *a plant, animal, or object is considered to have some sacred power or spirit*. In totemistic religions, a family or village might believe that it has a special relationship with the totem object, which is considered both supernatural and ancestrally related to that family or village. Aboriginal groups in Australia, for example, had a complex totemistic religion in which each person had his or her own individual totem object as well as shared a different totem object with all others of the same gender and another based on the kinship group. Totems were believed to provide assistance in hunting and gathering and offer protection against disease. Totems could also punish people who had violated important social norms. Animism and totemism tend to be associated with simpler societies, such as those of hunter-gatherers and some horticulturalists, and some sociologists believe that totemism is one of the earliest forms of religion to emerge among human groups.

Theistic religions *posit the existence of one or more gods not of human origin that are believed to play a role in the creation and maintenance of the universe and take an interest in human affairs.* The Dahomeans of western Africa, for example, believed in a large number of gods, each being held responsible for the creation of a certain part of nature (Wallace, 1966). Dahomean gods went to war, participated in sexual activities, conducted business, and were prone to creating a degree of mischief. The Dahomean's religion was polytheistic, involving *a belief in many gods.* Monotheistic religions are based on *a belief in one supreme god that is ultimately responsible for the universe.* The three great religions that emerged in the Middle East—Judaism, Christianity, and Islam—are monotheistic, worshiping Yahweh, God, and Allah, respectively. In addition to the single supreme god, monotheistic religions often include supernatural beings or spirits, such as angels or devils, who are subordinate and possess considerably fewer powers.

Religions of the way are *religions that posit no deity, but rather center on immutable and life-guiding truths that reveal the proper way to achieve fulfillment.* Such religions as early Buddhism, early Confucianism, and philosophical Taoism, for example, do not have gods that are responsible for creating the world and telling people how to run their lives. Rather, these religions spell out an ethical way to live that provides ultimate personal harmony with the universe. Religions of the way consider their no-

ble truths and ideals to be sacred, transcending everyday experience and inspiring awe and reverence.

A Global Perspective: Religions of the World

You should be able to describe the basic beliefs, teachings, and holy figures of the six major religions in the world and discuss their similarities and differences.

This book emphasizes that the belief systems of human beings are highly diverse. This diversity is reflected in the religions of various cultures. Most people around the world claim adherence to a religion, of which there are literally thousands. There is no possible way to discuss all of them here, but it is useful to provide an overview of the religions with the most adherents and those that have been especially influential in the United States (H. Smith, 1991).

Judaism

The two religions that have played the greatest part in the development of Western Europe and the United States, of course, are Judaism and Christianity. The older of the two religions, Judaism, emerged in Mesopotamia, in the Middle East, about four thousand years ago. It is based on the Hebrew Bible, which is the Old Testament of the Christian Bible. The Torah, or first five books of the Hebrew Bible, is believed by Jews to contain God's will or law. Among other things, the Torah describes the lives of early Israelites, such as Abraham and Moses, as they migrated to Canaan (Palestine), were enslaved in Egypt, wandered the desert after gaining their freedom, and received the Ten Commandments from God at Mount Sinai. Additional aspects of the Jewish belief system are contained in the Talmud, a body of interpretation and scholarly teaching. Judaism was one of the first clearly monotheistic religions in the world, with the Hebrew Bible clearly stating that there is only one God. Judaism professes that ancient Israelites and modern Jews are a chosen people having a special relationship with God and a special obligation to bring God's word to other people through their example. Abraham is believed to have made a covenant with God that established the special position of Jews and also gave them a homeland that would be theirs and their descendants' forever. God leads the chosen people by speaking through the prophets. Jews believe that the Messiah will one day appear and bring redemption and God's rule to the world. Judaism emphasizes the importance of the family and of doing good deeds and that the human condition can be improved.

There is some diversity in present-day Judaism; there are three main branches in the United States. *Orthodox*

Judaism follows strictly the divine books and the laws as promulgated by Moses. Orthodox believers follow dietary laws (certain foods are designated *kosher*), observe the traditional Sabbath by abstaining from work and travel, and segregate men and women during religious services. *Reform Judaism* attempts to adjust to present-day conditions by allowing Jews to modify some rituals and practices to take into account new social and cultural developments. While retaining the basic ethical principles of Judaism, for example, Reform Judaism allows for the modification of the dietary rules or use of a language other than Hebrew in services. *Conservative Judaism* falls in between the two, with a strong emphasis on retaining Jewish traditions and following most of the observances provided for in the Torah but also allowing some compromise with modernity.

Christianity

The foundation of Christianity is the belief that Jesus was the Christ, meaning the anointed one or the Messiah looked for by the Jews. Christianity emerged about two thousand years ago as a result of a schism with Judaism over this belief. Christians follow Christ's teachings as found in the New Testament of the Bible. Like Jews, Christians are monotheistic, but they traditionally interpret monotheism as a Holy Trinity of three people who are three aspects of a unity: God the Father; Jesus—or God's Word made flesh; and the Holy Spirit, the universal presence of God.

Christianity has also diversified over the centuries. After Christ's death and believed resurrection in Jerusalem, Christianity spread through Europe and the Middle East as the Roman Empire expanded. After the Roman Empire collapsed in the West and was succeeded by the Byzantine Empire in the East in the fifth and sixth centuries, Christianity gradually split into two main bodies. The Latin church in the West was headed by the bishop of Rome, or Pope. The Byzantine church in the East—later called Orthodox—was under the authority of the emperor in Constantinople. In Europe in the sixteenth century, groups of Christian reformers in the West, who came to be known as Protestants, rejected papal authority, left the Church—the remains of which became the Roman Catholic Church—and established separate Christian denominations. Today, Roman Catholics are united under the authority of the Pope, there are many Protestant and other denominations, and there are many Orthodox churches and other Eastern churches associated with various national or ethnic groups. About 50 percent of the world's Christians are Roman Catholics, 21 percent are Protestant, and the remainder are Eastern Orthodox or belong to other small churches.

Islam

Islam, a more recent religion than Judaism or Christianity, was founded by the prophet Muhammad in the seventh century when he received the Koran (Islamic holy scriptures) from Allah (God). Islam is a monotheistic religion, whose followers (Muslims) believe that Muhammad is the final holy prophet in a line that traces back to Jesus, Moses, and Abraham. In fact, some Muslims believe that Muhammad was merely clarifying Abraham's teachings and correcting errors that Moses and Jesus had made.

Islam is Arabic for "submission" or "surrender," and it implies a total commitment in faith and obedience to the one God, Allah. Muslims surrender to the will of an awesome God whose righteousness and mercy permeate the universe. Muhammad, who was born in Mecca (in present-day Saudi Arabia) is considered a great prophet, but he is a man and is not worshiped as Christ is in Christianity; only Allah is worshiped. The Koran is a set of rules for conduct that relate to family and other realms of life. The family as characterized in the Koran is patriarchal, polygamous, and patrilineal (see Chapter 9), although most Muslims today do not practice polygamy. By most interpretations of the Koran, women are considered subordinate to men. However, some today argue that this view is a misinterpretation of the Koran, and as noted in Chapter 8, there are believers in gender equality and a feminist movement in Islamic nations. Muslims worship Allah through prayer five times a day while facing Mecca, by giving alms to the poor, and by making a pilgrimage to Mecca at least once during their lifetime. Islam prohibits eating pork, drinking alcohol, and engaging in usury (lending money at excessively high interest rates).

Islam has no central authority, such as the Pope in Roman Catholicism, so there are many variants on Islam around the world. The two main divisions in Islam are the Sunni and the Shi'ite. This schism occurred after Muhammad's death when a struggle ensued over who would be Muhammad's successor. The Sunni believed that the successor should be chosen by the elders in the Islamic community from among the men in Muhammad's tribe. They also believed that proper Islamic practice required a return to the original teachings of the Koran. So, the Sunni are more conservative in the sense of demanding a more strict adherence to the fundamentals of the Koran. Regarding successorship, the Shi'ites believe that there is a line of twelve pure and sinless *imams,* or religious leaders, who are the only proper inheritors of Muhammad's authority and of understanding of the Koran. The Shi'ites believe these *imams* receive divine inspiration when reading and interpreting the Koran so that new revelations are possible. Shi'ites also insist on a return to Islamic fundamentals, but they tend to choose more selectively from the teachings of the Koran.

Hinduism

Hinduism developed in India some 3,500 years ago. Its beliefs and practices are contained in its holy books, the Vedas and the Upanishads. Unlike the Bible and the Koran, which are considered to be the inspired words of God, these books consist of ritual hymns and the moral lessons of great teachers. Hinduism is really a large array of sects rather than a single religious organization with a clear-cut hierarchy. Over thousands of years, Hinduism evolved by incorporating many different Indian tribal beliefs and foreign beliefs, and much of this diversity still persists. On the popular level Hindus believe in many gods, a slightly different pantheon for each village or family, who act much like human beings, doing both good and evil in the world. Hindus worship these gods in order to have bountiful crops, ward off disease, or have sons. On a more sophisticated level, Hindus may devote themselves to worship of one supreme God or to meditating on the Absolute.

Central to Hinduism is a belief in an ideal way of life, embodied in the concepts of *dharma,* or order, and *karma,* or personal destiny. Hindus believe that there is a natural order to the cosmos that governs both nature and social life. The good person strives to understand that order and live according to its rules. *Karma* involves understanding one's personal place in this order and living in harmony with it. For Hindus, the key to life is to perform properly the duties of one's position as defined by caste, community, and gender. Thus, Hinduism is at the basis of the caste system in India, described in Chapter 6, because people should obey the rules of the caste into which they are born.

Another important concept in Hinduism is the transmigration of souls, according to which a person's soul is born again in another form after the earthly body dies. One is reincarnated as a higher or lower being depending on whether a person behaved in harmony with the cosmos in the previous life. So, for Hindus, it is important to live in accordance with one's position in life because doing so influences what happens in the next life. If the person continues to live in harmony with the cosmos, he or she will eventually be freed from earthly existence, never to be reincarnated again. Then the person will have achieved *nirvana.* In this life, people can work toward it by practicing the disciplines of Yoga, adhering to Vedic scriptures, or following a renowned guru, or teacher.

Buddhism

Buddhism was founded about 2,500 years ago in northern India by Siddhartha Gautama, who is known as the Buddha, or Enlightened One. The Buddha claimed to have attained enlightenment through meditation, and he attracted monks and nuns who carry on his teachings. Buddhism has many similarities with Hinduism, which should not be surprising since they developed in close proximity. In addition, Gautama was the son of an upper-caste Hindu ruling family in northern India, and Buddhism was a reaction against some Hindu traditions of the time. Like Hinduism, the Buddha preached that the goal of religious practice and moral behavior was nirvana, a state of enlightenment, and that people would go through a cycle of lives before achieving nirvana. In nirvana, people are released from the earthly cycle of suffering and rebirth. The basic principles of Buddhism are found in the Four Noble Truths: Earthly life involves suffering; suffering is caused by desire and self-centeredness; selfish desire can be overcome; it can be overcome through proper moral action supported by meditation. Thus, Buddhism is based on ethical practices as well as disciplined behavior.

Buddhism eventually spread through much of Asia, where it remains popular today. The Buddhist faithful consist of monks, nuns, and laypeople. Like Christianity, Buddhism developed a diversity of groups around the world. The majority recognize many Buddhist divinities. Most monks live in monastic communities supported by laypeople, where their days are filled with meditation, study, preaching, and going into the outside world to beg for food. Sometimes a Buddhist monk will develop a reputation for holiness so that his monastery becomes a holy shrine that attracts pilgrims who come to pray. Some monasteries have gathered a huge following in this fashion. Among laypeople, Buddhism is often practiced along with some other religion, such as Shinto in Japan. This plurality of religious practice is sometimes difficult for people in the West to understand because we think of people as belonging to only one religion. But it is not unusual in the East.

Confucianism

Confucianism was founded by Confucius, a Chinese teacher and scholar who lived about the same time as the Buddha. The followers of Confucius wrote down his teachings, and these writings, the *Analects,* form the basis of Confucianism. Confucius lived in a time of social upheaval and large-scale corruption that caused widespread oppression and misery in China. Unlike Buddha, who focused on withdrawal from the world to achieve personal salvation, Confucius gave practical advice aimed at achieving social harmony in the world. Confucianism is a moral system that stresses social

One function of religion is to provide sacred legitimation for social and political practices. So, politicians often associate themselves with revered religious figures, such as this Orthodox Bishop who delivered the benediction at a U.S. presidential inauguration. The hope is that such association will help enhance the legitimacy of the political authorities.

order, harmony, peace, and justice. These are to be achieved by changing individual behavior. Proper behavior includes the individual's duty to obey the elders in the family and the ruler of the state. The moral person strives for *jen,* or sympathy and respect for others, loyalty to others, and avoiding self-interestedness. The way family members treat one another, in terms of respect, support, and loyalty, should serve as the model for society.

At its inception, Confucianism was more a philosophy and ethical system than a religion because it had no conception of supernatural deities or a reality different from physical and social reality. Confucius did believe, however, that there was a moral force in the world that was like a divine order, and that morality was a form of spirituality. In addition, people incorporated local gods into Confucianism, and eventually some believers came to view Confucius himself as a deity. Confucianism has influenced not only China but also Korea, Vietnam, and Japan. Many people who are Taoists (Taoism is an ancient Chinese religion), Buddhists, or even Christians also abide by Confucian ideals, so the impact of Confucianism has been widespread.

Diffusion of Religion

Although each religion emerged in a particular geographic place and is most strongly identified with particular areas, the striking aspect of the major religions is their massive diffusion around the world. All the religions that have been discussed are practiced by at least a few people on all the world's continents. Islam was spread in Asia by traders and soldiers from its inception. Christianity and Judaism spread from the Middle East into Europe as the Roman Empire expanded and then were spread around the world beginning in the fifteenth century with the European colonial expansion. Chapters 7 and 8, for example, describe how the Spanish, French, and Portuguese brought Christianity to the tribal peoples of the Americas in the 1500s and 1600s. These instances illustrate how religion is often an important part of cultural conquest. Since cultural norms and values are embodied in and legitimated by native religions, the destruction of these religions or their adaptation to the ways of the dominant group is an important part of changing a people's way of life.

The twentieth century was witness to further diffusion of religion around the globe. Christian missionaries from the United States and Europe traveled to Asia, Africa, and South America looking for converts. Mormons mounted an especially extensive missionary effort. Following World War II, Western Europe opened its doors to foreign workers as a way of rebuilding its labor force, a policy that brought in Buddhists, Hindus, and Muslims from many nations. In the 1960s and then again in 1990, the United States changed its immigration laws so that more people from the Middle East and the Far East could enter. The result has been an influx of Buddhists, Hindus, and Muslims—and even some Taoists and Shintoists.

So, the world today is characterized by the diffusion of religions, which means that in most places people have many choices. Later, this chapter discusses some of the consequences of this diffusion in the United States.

Sociological Approaches to the Study of Religion

You should be able to describe the approaches of Durkheim, Marx, and Weber concerning the role of religion in society.

A major thrust of the sociological investigation of religion has been to decipher the part that religions play in society. This chapter will look at the work of the three sociologists—Durkheim, Marx, and Weber—who established the central issues in this area. Each man's work offers an insightful perspective, and each isolates important elements of the role of religion in society.

Durkheim: A Functionalist Perspective

Emile Durkheim's (1915/1965) perspective on religion is rather startling for many people. Durkheim concluded that when people worship deities or spirits, they are in reality worshiping their own society. He reached this conclusion by first assuming, as do all sociologists, that society has an enormous impact on people. During our relatively short lives, society provides us with many things that we had no part in creating: language, tools, norms, values, a name, kinship, and so on. It is these provisions made available by society that enable us to make our journey through life. Without society and the things it provides, we would not survive. Yet society is intangible and impossible to see. This truth, argued Durkheim, leads people to believe that invisible forces in the world provide for us, guide us, and, in some cases, hinder our progress. Not recognizing that society itself is this invisible force, people imagine a sacred world to which they accord the respect and awe that such powerful forces appear to warrant.

Durkheim's analysis of the origins of religion as being misplaced reverence for the powers of society is penetrating indeed, although many sociologists today question whether it is an accurate account of the origins of all religions (Mol, 1979). Nonetheless, Durkheim focused our concern on the functions that religion performs for society. Today we recognize that religion performs a number of social functions.

First, religion enhances social solidarity by establishing and reinforcing fundamental cultural values. Religious rituals are very important in this regard, because they provide a context for the public and communal expression of faith in values and traditions. By coming together periodically for public rituals, people can maintain a sense of common identity and shared purpose. The result is what Durkheim called a *moral community*: a group bound together by their religion-based values and identity.

Second, religion offers a sacred legitimation of values and social practices whose desirability may not be directly observable or verifiable. There is much that is unknown and unknowable in the world, and society must socialize people to behave in appropriate ways. Conformity to the social structure becomes not merely a practical matter but something required by powerful, awesome, and otherworldly forces.

Third, religion provides meaning for people's lives and purpose to their existence. Religion proposes answers to such questions as "Why am I here?" and "Why must I suffer and eventually die?" In answer to these questions, most religions posit some sort of afterlife as the ultimate goal of earthly existence, which offers consolation in the face of uncertainty, grief, and loss.

Finally, religion functions to support and interpret important life events and transitions. From birth to death, we experience many rites of passage that document our having moved into new positions in the social structure. Marriage ceremonies, bar and bat mitzvahs, and last rites—each places an event within a larger sacred context and provides guidance for how individuals should behave. In other words, when events are important to society, people are rarely left to experience and interpret them without careful guidance.

Marx: A Conflict Perspective

The conflict perspective on religion emerged in good part from the work of Karl Marx (1848/1964), who argued that religion can serve as a mechanism for perpetuating patterns of dominance and subordination. To understand how religion can play this role, it is helpful to use the concept of *alienation,* which refers to feelings of separation, isolation, and powerlessness. Marx insisted that people could become alienated from their religion just as they sometimes can from their work. People become alienated from religion by viewing it as something separate from and independent of human beings—they fail to recognize that religions are human creations. Instead, they come to believe that spirits, totems, or deities—rather than human beings—control the social world. It is the gods, people believe, that ordain what political, economic, and familial institutions should be like, and human beings are powerless to change these social arrangements.

Once this alienation occurs, it protects the status quo because people feel helpless in the face of the powerful spiritual forces that presumably have shaped society. In addition, Marx argued, it would seem arrogant for human beings to change what they believe some deity has ordained. In this fashion, groups benefiting from existing social arrangements find their positions protected by the force of religion. In India, for example, the Hindu religion justifies an elaborate caste system in which some people are born into high positions whereas others are relegated at birth to a highly stigmatized outcaste position (see Chapter 6). The Hindu belief in reincarnation encourages people to accept their fate rather than attempt to change society. Elements of Christianity and Judaism also persuade their followers to accept an inequitable distribution of resources. Christianity teaches, for example, that the meek shall inherit the earth and that important human rewards are to be found in the afterlife. These teachings suggest that people should concern themselves with spiritual issues and the afterlife rather than trying to acquire more political power and economic rewards in the here-and-now. Such an ideology can direct one's attention away from earthly oppression and inequality and encourage an acquiescence to the status quo. Gender inequalities have also been perpetuated by positing that male domination is in the divine order. In Roman Catholicism, for instance, only males can be priests, one of the more prestigious and powerful positions in the church. Orthodox Jewish men chant a prayer praising the virtues of manhood:

> Blessed art thou, O lord our God, King of the Universe that I was not born a gentile.
> Blessed art thou . . . that I was not born a slave.
> Blessed art thou . . . that I was not born a woman.

Given its role in society, Marx called religion *the opiate of the people* because, in his judgment, it dulled their discontents and misdirected their energies. He thought that religion encouraged *false class consciousness* by discouraging people from discovering those beliefs and practices that were in their own class interests, namely, for the oppressed to rise up and struggle for a greater share of societal resources.

Weber: Religion and Social Change

Although Durkheim's and Marx's views are quite different, they both characterized religion as a rather conservative force that perpetuates existing social arrangements. In contrast, Max Weber (1905/1958) suggested that religious beliefs could promote social change. Weber came to this conclusion because he observed a link between the emergence of capitalism in Europe and the beliefs of certain Protestant groups. He noticed that capitalism first arose in the West rather than the East and that it tended to emerge in Protestant European countries rather than in Roman Catholic ones. To explain this link, Weber focused on the development of some religious doctrines during the Protestant Reformation, a sixteenth-century religious movement that was an attempt to reform the Catholic Church. One such doctrine was Calvinism, based on the teachings of the sixteenth-century French theologian John Calvin. *Calvinism* is an extremely ascetic form of Protestantism that emphasizes self-denial, self-mortification, and austerity as means of salvation. Calvinists also believe that the sole reason people are alive is to glorify God through hard work and an ascetic life.

Another traditional element of Calvinism is *predestination,* the belief that a person's salvation has been determined by God before he or she is born, and nothing a person does on earth can change that outcome. This doctrine, needless to say, created enormous anxiety regarding whether a person is among the saved or the damned, and led people to search for some worldly sign of their fate. This worldly sign was tied to another important idea that emerged from the Protestant Reformation, a new version of "the calling." Prior to the sixteenth century, Christians had viewed a person's calling in a religious sense: People did God's work by becoming monks or nuns. Beginning with Martin Luther, however, a new concept of the calling emerged: People's duty on earth was to develop to their fullest whatever talents God gave them. Thus one could have a calling to be a merchant, a politician, or a laborer. According to Weber, this doctrine provided a moral justification for worldly pursuits, including economic activity. Calvinists came to believe that economic success meant that God looked favorably on a person, and it could be taken as a sign of salvation. Furthermore, hard work, an ascetic and strictly disciplined life, and deferred gratification increased a person's chances for economic success.

Weber used the term **Protestant ethic** to refer to *the belief that an ascetic life of strict discipline and hard work that results in economic success is a sign of one's worth or that one is among the elect who will go to heaven.* Weber's thesis was that this ascetic Protestantism played an important role in the emergence of capitalism. It encouraged such behavior as hard work, frugality, saving, and reinvestment of earnings, which represent the core of capitalism. These activities were consistent with the profit-seeking economic behavior encouraged by capitalists. The basic principles of the Protestant ethic are summarized in Figure 11.1.

Figure 11.1
The Relationship between the Protestant Ethic and Capitalism

Weber's hypothesis linking Protestantism and capitalism has caused great controversy (Cohen, 2002; Samuelsson, 1961). A major criticism of his conclusion is that economic change had begun in Europe prior to the Protestant Reformation and that this economic activity resulted in religious changes, rather than the reverse. Another criticism is that many Catholics were merchants and entrepreneurs in the early development of capitalism. However, Weber never claimed that Protestantism *caused* capitalism to come into being. Rather, he argued that the kernel of both the religious creed and the economic activity already existed, and there was an *elective affinity* between them. Because each was supportive of the other, people tended to link them in such a way that they became mutually reinforcing (Winter, 1977). Weber recognized that social change results from the confluence of many factors. His argument was that Calvinism was one among numerous forces in Europe following the Protestant Reformation that contributed to the emergence of capitalism. Other Worlds, Other Ways: China, Iran, and Afghanistan (pp. 315–316) suggests some other ways in which religion can be a part of the process of social change.

The Organization of Religion

You should be able to list the basic characteristics of churches, ecclesia, denominations, sects, and cults.

Just as religions vary greatly in terms of what their members define as sacred, so there is also great variation in the ways that religions are organized. The earliest religions, for example, had no formal religious organization, no church, and no specialized clergy (Bellah, 1964). Rather, ceremonies were informal, and each person might play many different roles in these rituals over time. More modern societies, however, have specialized religious organizations, and a priesthood emerges in the form of a full-time, professional religious class. In describing religion in modern societies, sociologists distinguish among a number of different levels of organization (Chalfant, Beckley, & Palmer, 1994; Stark & Bainbridge, 1979).

A church is *a religious organization that is recognized and socially accepted, tolerates other religions, and lives in harmony with the larger society.* In some societies, a church is what is called an ecclesia, *an official state religion.* Although other religions may not be forbidden, the ecclesia is given a special place in social life. It is believed to embody important cultural values, and the religious leaders may be consulted regarding political and economic decisions. The state often provides financial support for the ecclesia, which also supervises the education of the young. Prior to the Protestant Reformation, the Roman Catholic Church was an ecclesia in most European countries. The Anglican Church in England and the Islamic religion in Iran are other examples of ecclesia.

In the United States, there is no ecclesia. Rather, churches take the form of denominations: *organized churches that have no official sanction from the state.* Sociologists use the term *denomination* differently from its common everyday use, where it usually refers to one of the many denominations of Protestantism. For sociologists, *denomination* means any church that is established and socially accepted but is not a state-sanctioned church. As sociologists use the term, denominations in the United States today would include the various Protestant groups, such as Methodists and Presbyterians, as well as Roman Catholicism, Islam, and Judaism. The last three religions are well established but with no official state sanction, hence not *ecclesia.* (The terms *church* and *denomination* are sometimes used interchangeably when discussing religious organization in societies such as the United States that have no ecclesia.)

Sects are *smaller, less formally organized religious groups whose members reject some elements of the larger society and that exist in some degree of tension with society and the secular world.* In some cases, sects have broken away from an existing church. Calvary Chapel, for example, separated itself from mainline Protestant denominations in the 1970s and began with one church but now has hundreds of congregations

Other Worlds, Other Ways

CHINA, IRAN, AND AFGHANISTAN: RELIGION AND POLITICAL CHANGE

Kashgar is a city of more than 100,000 people in the Xinjiang autonomous region in the far west of China, bordering on Tibet, Pakistan, and nations that were part of the former Soviet Union. Much of the area is remote desert and mountains, and many people there are nomads who herd their flocks from horseback. In Kashgar, many men carry jeweled knives and the women wear veils; camels and donkeys are a common mode of transport seen on the streets.

Although Westerners associate China more with Confucianism or Buddhism, Islam has a long history in China (Gladney, 1991). Beginning in the seventh century, Arab, Persian, and Mongolian Muslim merchants, militia, and officials settled along the coasts of China. These Muslim settlers tended to live in tightly knit enclaves that zealously protected their culture and identity from defilement by the dominant ethnic group, the Han Chinese. Approximately twenty million Muslims live in China today, with heavy concentrations in the northwest and in the Xinjiang region.

Chinese troops crushed a small armed Muslim rebellion in Baren, Xinjiang, in 1990, allegedly precipitated by the efforts of the authorities to close mosques and stop the construction of new mosques and Islamic schools. In response, residents attacked the troops, and twenty-two people were killed before the rebellion was squashed. Since then, bombings and riots have broken out periodically, with many injuries and some deaths occurring. In 1993, a bomb destroyed much of the Oasis Hotel on the central square of Kashgar and killed three people. Although the bombers were never found, authorities assume that they were Islamic separatists intent on making Xinjiang an independent Muslim state (Eckholm, 2002; Tyler, 1997). The continuing presence of troops and roadblocks in the region attests to the authorities' belief that significant rebellious sentiment persists. Most Chinese in Xinjiang are Muslims, and many view the Chinese troops as an invading army. There are also ethnic differences, because most Xinjiang Muslims are Uighurs, Kazaks, and Uzbeks, whereas the majority ethnic group in China is Han. Some ethnic groups, such as the Uighurs, even speak their own language. The Islamic separatists in Xinjiang hope to establish an independent nation named Eastern Turkestan, suggesting the region's historical links with the Turkic peoples of central and western Asia rather than with the rest of China. After September 11, 2001, both China and the United States suggested that the Muslim separatist movement in western China was a part of

the worldwide Al Qaeda terrorist movement. While there may be some links, the Uighur movement is largely independent and focused on one goal, the creation of an Islamic state in the Xinjiang region.

The Islamic religion has been the focus of other important, and more successful, revolutionary efforts in recent decades (Kepel, 2002). The Islamic revolution in Iran in 1979 overthrew the Shah of Iran and ended centuries of monarchical rule. The Shah had been a strong ally of the United States, and the Iranian revolutionaries captured Americans working in the American embassy in Teheran and held them hostage for more than a year. The hostages were eventually released, but Islamic groups still control Iran. In the 1980s the Islamic mujahedeen took on Soviet troops in Afghanistan, triumphing in 1992 when the pro-Communist government in Afghanistan collapsed. After a few years of fighting among different factions, the Taliban, who promoted an extreme and oppressive version of Islam, took control of Afghanistan and imposed Islamic laws. The Taliban remained in power until the United States attacked Al Qaeda and the Taliban as part of its war on terrorism after the September 11 attacks in New York and Washington.

These revolutionary Islamic movements in China, Iran, Afghanistan, and a number of other countries are in part an outgrowth of the fact that Islam is, for many of its adherents, a broadly encompassing religious belief system that is meant to apply to all aspects of life and that denies any separation between personal life, religious life, and political life. In fact, a basic precept of Islamic faith is that "Islam is religion and state." This precept has made Islam into a powerful revolutionary force to overthrow non-Muslim rulers in many nations and establish *shari'a,* or "Islamic law," as the political and moral code of society. Some followers of these extreme versions of Islam believe that all Muslims have a religious obligation to fight against "heretical," or non-Islamic, governments and against nonbelievers in Islam, who are considered to be infidels. In an Islamic state, *shari'a* would prevail and apply to all people, non-Islamic as well as Islamic. So, these Islamic political revolutions are strongly religious crusades at the same time that they focus on political change in society.

Not all Muslims, of course, hold the extreme positions of these revolutionary groups. Nor is Islam the only religion that has produced such movements. A similar blending of religion with revolutionary political fervor can be found in some contemporary Christian religious movements in the United States. One such movement, called Christian Reconstructionism, believes that "Biblical Law," especially based in the Old Testament, should be used to reconstruct human societies (Goldberg, 2006). Presumably, a theocratic elite would control government and impose and oversee this rule. All people would be under this biblical law, and non-Christians would be marginalized, outcasts, or worse.

(continued)

As with Islam, Christianity can also be a broadly encompassing religious belief system that denies any separation between personal life, religious life, and political life. So, Muslims who would impose Islamic law and Christians who would impose biblical law illustrate how different religious theologies can be powerful tools in shaping society and promoting social change, just as Weber suggested with Protestantism and the rise of capitalism.   ■

(Miller, 1997). The Branch Davidians, of the Waco shoot-out fame of the 1990s, were in part an offshoot of the Seventh-Day Adventists. In other cases, a sect may be a totally new development, possibly imported from another society. The Heaven's Gate group believed that UFOs would visit the earth and transport all believers to a higher level of reality; the group ended in a mass suicide near San Diego in the mid-1990s. Joining sects can involve an intense conversion process, sometimes including withdrawal from previous commitments and relationships.

The distinction between churches and sects is one of degree. At one extreme are "pure" churches that possess all of the characteristics listed in Table 11.1, and at the other extreme are "pure" sects with all of the opposite characteristics. Many religious organizations fall somewhere in between. Some sects are referred to as cults: *small, loosely organized groups that are typically held together by a charismatic figure. Charisma* refers to that powerful, but often elusive, personal quality that provides one person with great influence over others. The Branch Davidians are an example of a cult. Their leader, David Koresh, exercised considerable charismatic influence over the members of the group until his death.

Sects and cults sometimes emerge when church members, dissatisfied with the traditionalism or lack of emotional involvement found in their church, break away and join or form a new religion that offers these characteristics. Over time, these sects may become more like churches as their members grow older and become more affluent and conservative. In addition, second-generation sect members are less likely to have the emotional commitment or to have experienced the dissatisfaction that the original sect followers had. Thus, a cycle can occur from church to sect and back again. Not all sects, however, can be traced to dissatisfied church members. Many sects, such as the Unification Church, are imported from another society and attract people because of their novelty. Furthermore, not all sects are destined to become churches. Some sects have existed for decades, and a few for centuries (Wilson, 1982).

The United States today provides a virtual supermarket of churches, sects, and cults—reflecting the same diversity that is found in the religions around the world. The remainder of this chapter investigates the diverse religious beliefs, practices, and organizations in the United States.

Table 11.1

CHARACTERISTICS OF CHURCHES AND SECTS

Churches Tend To	Sects Tend To
■ Be inclusive, in that their standards for membership are less rigorous	■ Be exclusive, in that they do not allow commitment to or membership in other religious groups
■ Accept and be willing to work with other religious groups	■ View themselves as a fellowship of the elect who alone hold the real truth
■ Tolerate some diversity of belief and controversy over principles	■ Emphasize purity of doctrine and traditional ethical principles
■ Have a professional, full-time clergy with educational credentials and formal ordination ceremonies	■ Emphasize lay participation in rituals and decision making, even though they may have some professionally trained clergy
■ Gain most new members because they are born to current members of the church	■ Gain many new members by conversion
■ Give more weight to rewards in this world	■ Emphasize otherworldly issues such as salvation and deliverance from hell
■ Emphasize formal religious expression with less congregational participation	■ Encourage spontaneous and emotional forms of religious expression
■ Tolerate other religious groups and endorse the existing social order	■ Be in protest against other religious groups or elements of the secular world

Religion in the United States

You should be able to discuss religiosity and its correlates, describe the effect of socioeconomic status and politics on religion, and analyze trends in secularization and religious pluralism in the United States.

In the past few decades, the debate over the extent and strength of religion in the United States has been intense and controversial. Are people in the United States less—or more—religious today than in the past? The answer depends in part on how one defines *religious*. Religiosity refers to *the degree of commitment to religion*. Sociologists measure religiosity by looking at people's religious preferences; their membership in churches, temples, or synagogues; and the actual religious practices in which they engage.

Extent of Religiosity

If we look at religious preferences, then people in the United States are quite religious, with 89 percent of adult Americans expressing a preference for some religious group (Figure 11.2). One-half choose a Protestant denomination and another one-quarter choose the Roman Catholic Church. If we look at church membership to assess religiosity, however, the picture changes a little, with only 61 percent of people in the United States claiming membership in a church, temple, or synagogue (The Gallup Poll, 2008). This figure suggests that many people express their religiosity in ways other than joining a church.

Church membership in the United States tends to be associated with certain characteristics (Chalfant, Beckley, & Palmer, 1994). For example, married people are more likely to be members than singles, and the elderly have considerably higher membership rates than the young. Furthermore, Jews have considerably lower membership rates than do Catholics or Protestants. These differences suggest that religious membership is more than simply an expression of faith in a particular set of beliefs. It is also a social act that entwines people in a network of relationships and serves a variety of functions. For example, for some married people, church membership serves as a means of providing religious training for children (Hoge & Carroll, 1978). For elderly people, the church may serve as a focal point for leisure activities and the development of friendships.

Although religious preferences are extensive in the United States, religious practice suggests that people have become *less* religious since the 1960s. In terms of church or synagogue attendance, there has been a noticeable decline from close to 50 percent attending once a week or more often in the 1950s to 30 percent today (The Gallup Poll, 2008). Since the mid-1970s, this decline has leveled off. Furthermore, levels of church attendance may actually be substantially lower than these, since these statistics are based on surveys that ask people to report whether they go to church or synagogue. There is strong evidence that many people tell surveyers that they attend church—probably because that seems like the socially acceptable thing to report—even when they do not attend as often as they claim (Hadaway, Marler, & Chaves, 1993).

However, compared to people in other countries, people in the United States are far more religious. When religiosity is measured by attendance at a church or synagogue at least two or three times a month, 39 percent in the United States do so, as compared to 17 percent in Britain and West Germany and 8 percent in Norway. People in the United States are also more likely to believe in God and in a life after death than

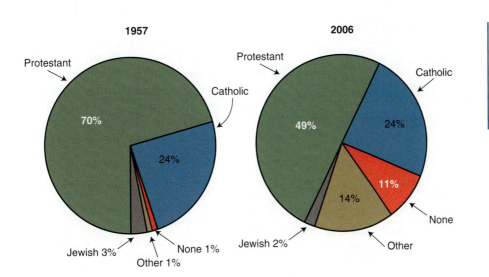

1957

Protestant

70%

Catholic

24%

Jewish 3%

Other 1%

None 1%

2006

Protestant

49%

Catholic

24%

None 11%

Other 14%

Jewish 2%

Figure 11.2

Religious Preference in the United States, 1957–2006

people in many other nations (Figure 11.3). If religiosity is measured by the importance attached to religion, religiosity in the United States is considerably above that of other industrial nations and is matched only by people living in Latin America, Africa, and Asia. Thus, although there have been important changes in religious behavior in the past few decades, the overall interest in religious practices is still quite high in the United States in comparison to that of other nations.

Socioeconomic Status and Politics

People's religiosity, especially church membership and religious practice, is linked to their social position. Consistent relationships exist between socioeconomic status (SES) and religion in the United States (Davis &

Smith, 2007; Greeley, 1989; Roof & McKinney, 1987). Figure 11.4 compares the income and educational achievements of many religious groups in the United States. Jews consistently rank among the highest of all religious groups on the three dimensions of SES—education, occupation, and income. Catholics stand at about the average in terms of educational achievement and occupational attainment. Episcopalians and Presbyterians rank high on education and occupation and are nearly equal to Jews. Methodists are lower on these dimensions but above Catholics. Lutherans and Baptists rank relatively low on most SES dimensions.

As has been noted, Marx viewed religion as a tool for appeasing the poor by convincing them to accept their disadvantaged plight. This view might lead us to expect that the poor would be more heavily involved in religious activity as they attempt to smooth the rough edges of their lives. In actuality, the reverse is true: people who are low in SES are less likely to be involved in religious activities (Gaede, 1977; Stark, 1972). Members of the middle and upper classes are more likely to participate in public religious rituals, join church organizations, and be knowledgeable about religious beliefs in general. These types of activities tend to confirm the respectability and success of the affluent. The poor, by contrast, are more likely to undergo intense religious experiences, to be strongly committed to their religious beliefs, and to feel that their own religion is the only means of salvation. These religious beliefs and activities may better meet the needs of the poor in terms of warding off feelings of failure, powerlessness, and isolation.

In addition to the links with SES, religion is also associated with politics. It is not clear whether religious people are more or less politically conservative than nonreligious people. What is clear, however, is that Jews are the most likely to be Democrats, followed closely by Catholics, and Protestants are more likely to be Republicans (Davis & Smith, 2007). These differences are even more marked if we look only at Protestant denominations without a large black membership. Such

Church Attendance Two or Three Times a Month or More

Religious Beliefs

Country	Church Attendance	Belief in God	Belief in life after death
USA	39.4	91.8	80.5
Northern Ireland	50.9	89.3	75.1
Ireland	73.3	93.6	77.3
Poland	61.8	95.1	77.8
Italy	43.6	87.5	72.6
Israel	*	81.3	62.6
Britain	16.9	68.3	59.4
New Zealand	21.2	69.2	62.5
West Germany	17.3	62.3	55.0
Hungary	18.9	66.2	39.2
Slovenia	23.0	63.4	42.1
Norway	8.7	58.4	52.5
Netherlands	18.1	58.5	59.8
East Germany	16.9	25.8	14.9

100 90 80 70 60 50 40 30 20 10 0
Percentage

0 10 20 30 40 50 60 70 80 90 100
Percentage

* Not available

■ Belief in God ■ Belief in life after death

Figure 11.3
Religiosity around the World, 1998

Note: From International Social Survey Program, National Opinion Research Center, University of Chicago, 1998.

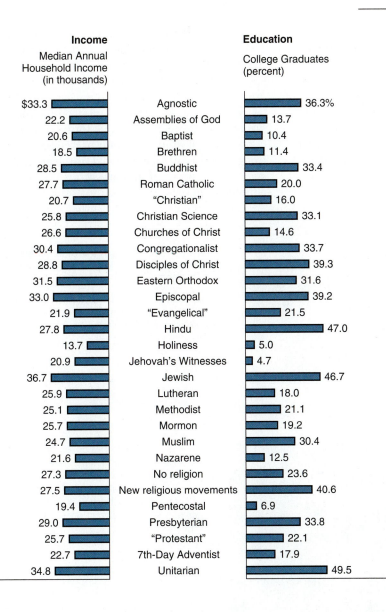

Income

Median Annual
Household Income
(in thousands)

Education

College Graduates
(percent)

	Income	Education
Agnostic	$33.3	36.3%
Assemblies of God	22.2	13.7
Baptist	20.6	10.4
Brethren	18.5	11.4
Buddhist	28.5	33.4
Roman Catholic	27.7	20.0
"Christian"	20.7	16.0
Christian Science	25.8	33.1
Churches of Christ	26.6	14.6
Congregationalist	30.4	33.7
Disciples of Christ	28.8	39.3
Eastern Orthodox	31.5	31.6
Episcopal	33.0	39.2
"Evangelical"	21.9	21.5
Hindu	27.8	47.0
Holiness	13.7	5.0
Jehovah's Witnesses	20.9	4.7
Jewish	36.7	46.7
Lutheran	25.9	18.0
Methodist	25.1	21.1
Mormon	25.7	19.2
Muslim	24.7	30.4
Nazarene	21.6	12.5
No religion	27.3	23.6
New religious movements	27.5	40.6
Pentecostal	19.4	6.9
Presbyterian	29.0	33.8
"Protestant"	25.7	22.1
7th-Day Adventist	22.7	17.9
Unitarian	34.8	49.5

Figure 11.4

Religion and Socioeconomic Status
in the United States

Note: From *One Nation Under God* by Barry A. Kosmin and Seymour P. Lachman. Copyright 1993 by Barry A. Kosmin and Seymour P. Lachman. Reprinted by permission of Harmony Books, a division of Crown Publishers, Inc.

findings are understandable when we recognize that historically, the Republicans have been the party of the privileged, and Protestants—at least the white congregations—are among the more privileged groups in the United States. Catholics and Jews have a more recent immigrant heritage and experienced prejudice and discrimination at the hands of the Protestant majority when they first arrived in the United States. Having neither wealth nor status, they tended to turn to the Democrats, who have historically been the party of working people and the underdog.

Secularization

Although many in the United States consider themselves religious, the trend over the past few centuries has been for people to relegate religion to a narrower sphere in their lives. These trends are broadly characterized as secularization: *the process through* *which the influence of religion is removed from many institutions in society and dispersed into private and personal realms* (Luckmann, 1967). One manifestation of this is shown in Figure 11.5: A substantially smaller percentage of people in the United States today would agree that religion is very important in their lives than was the case in the 1950s.

Secularization does not mean religion is disappearing but rather that it is practiced mostly at special times and places. At work, at play, or while shopping, for example, people's behavior is shaped mostly by nonreligious considerations, although religious beliefs may play a part in moral decisions or how people relate to others. The beginning of secularization can be traced back hundreds of years and can be attributed in good part to the emergence of highly differentiated societies with an elaborate division of labor. As this differentiation occurred, the various institutions in society came to serve special and limited functions.

Distinct political, economic, and religious institutions emerged, and the influence of religion was increasingly limited to narrower realms.

The growth of science and technology in the past few centuries has also played an important role in the declining influence of religion. One of the functions of religion is that it provides meaning to a mysterious world, but science uses reason and observation in order to understand the world, thus rendering it less mysterious. Instead of using religion to understand disease or to raise bountiful crops, we more frequently turn to

science and the technology that science has made available. Although science may not provide answers to questions of ultimate meaning, it does narrow the spheres of life where we may feel the need to turn to religion.

Despite the process of secularization, most sociologists agree that religion, in one form or another, will continue to play an important part in society. For one thing, people still face personal problems and seek answers to questions of ultimate meaning. Conventional churches will satisfy this need for some people, and

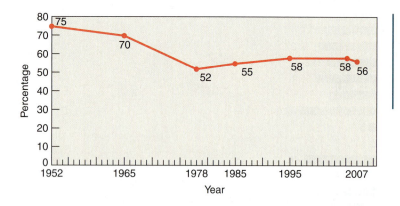

Figure 11.5

Percentage of People in the United States Who State That Religion Is Very Important in Their Lives, 1952–2007

Note: Copyright © 2007 Gallup, Inc. All rights reserved. Reprinted with permission. Gallup Poll News Service, www. gallup.com/poll/1690/religion.aspx. Accessed June 10, 2008.

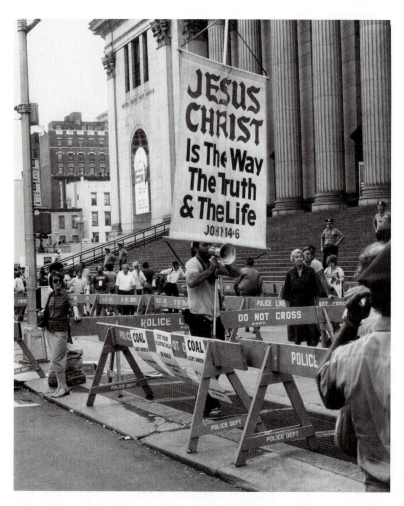

The United States has developed religious institutions that are characterized by pluralism and diversity, with many different religions competing for peoples' attention. Proselytizing, as this fundamentalist Christian is doing, is common as people try to attract others to their way of thinking.

others will turn to more personal and private practices or belief systems such as meditation, yoga, or Scientology. In addition, even in a secularized society, religion contributes to social solidarity and cohesion, which Durkheim argued is one of the central functions of religion in society. Robert Bellah (1988), for example, has argued that there is a *civil religion* in the United States that serves precisely this function. This civil religion is *a set of beliefs and rituals that exists outside any organized church and sanctifies a particular nation and its way of life.* It contains a set of symbols toward which people can express agreement and gain a sense of common heritage and unity. Civil religion in the United States rests on a set of general dogmas: beliefs in some deity, in a higher law, and in life after death. It also includes a belief in the sacredness of the United States and in the reward of virtue and the punishment of evil.

Religious Pluralism

Many of the European colonists who came to the New World were escaping religious persecution (Marty, 1984; Wuthnow, 2005). After arriving, they often re-created communities of religious intolerance. In some cases they maintained what was in effect an ecclesia or official state religion. The Puritans established a theocracy in Massachusetts that mixed religious law and secular law, and the Church of England became the official religion of the Virginia, Carolina, and Georgia colonies. At the time of the Declaration of Independence in 1776, nine of the thirteen colonies had officially established religions. Gradually, however, these religious monopolies began to break down under the weight of a number of social forces. One was the increasing religious diversity that resulted from wave after wave of new immigrants that arrived in the United States. The early immigrants came to constitute a small proportion of the population and found it difficult to maintain their monopoly over what was considered acceptable religious practice. Every colony had a growing number of religious dissenters. Because of this religious diversity, and because the values of the new nation emphasized freedom of choice and individual responsibility, the Constitution of the United States, ratified in 1789, was quickly amended to guarantee freedom of religion and the separation of church and state.

The result today in the United States is considerable religious pluralism (Eck, 2001; Wuthnow, 2005). Although Roman Catholicism, Protestantism, and Judaism are the three major religious groups and dominate in numbers, there is much diversity within each in terms of theology and social practice. In addition, there are many groups that fall outside these three. As Figure 11.2 shows, a smaller proportion of the U.S. population claims allegiance to one of the three major religious groups compared to forty years ago, while the percentage of the populace that claims a religious preference other than one of these has increased significantly. The major elements of this diversity and the constantly changing scene of religion in the United States are described in the rest of this chapter.

THE ECUMENICAL MOVEMENT   The term *ecumenism* refers to efforts at bringing harmony to the various religions and denominations by emphasizing the similarities of their doctrines and establishing cooperative interdenominational work. The ecumenical movement gained strength in the 1960s and 1970s in response to declining church memberships and contributions. Some religious leaders believed that a cooperative effort among religions would effectively stem the decline than would competition for new members. The ecumenical movement has resulted in many cooperative efforts, such as the integration of social services provided by different agencies, joint efforts at social activism, and occasionally the development of agreements about creeds and rituals and the sharing of clergy (McRoberts, 1999; Niebuhr, 1999). Much of this ecumenism, however, especially that involving church mergers and creedal agreements, has involved Protestant denominations whose doctrines are not too dissimilar and whose members have similar social backgrounds. In fact, this attempt to bring churches together sometimes creates further divisions between those churches who join the movement and those who do not. This ecumenical conflict also sometimes reflects a class conflict, with the ecumenical supporters consisting of mainline, more affluent Protestant denominations, and the opponents tending to be less-affluent, evangelical groups (Chalfant, Beckley, & Palmer, 1994). Ecumenism in the form of coordinated programs of social activism among a number of churches has remained fairly common. Many of these programs of social activism, such as those devoted to fighting poverty or promoting civil rights, are often associated with political liberalism and affluent churches, but theologically conservative churches in less-affluent urban communities also often participate in such ecumenical efforts (McRoberts, 1999).

FUNDAMENTALISM AND EVANGELICALISM   In the past few decades, there has been an upsurge in conservative Protestantism, including fundamentalism and evangelicalism (Miller, 1997). These terms are often misused and sometimes used interchangeably. *Fundamentalists* believe in a literal interpretation of the Bible and a return to the teachings of the Bible as a foundation for Christian faith. *Evangelicals* emphasize a personal commitment to Jesus Christ and the subjective experience of personal salvation, or being *born again*. Evangelicalism involves an intense commitment to one's church and beliefs and an effort to seek new converts through *testifying* to one's beliefs. Although some evangelicals are fundamentalists, not all of them are.

Some evangelicals and fundamentalists have become heavily involved in political and social issues, with many political candidates emphasizing their evangelical backgrounds and seeing politics as a way to pursue their religious agenda on issues such as divorce, school prayer, or gay rights. The term *New Christian Right* has been used to describe this loose but potent coalition of conservatives who would like to see the political and social life of the United States guided more by Christian principles. In fact, critics have charged that some actions of the New Christian Right threaten existing religious pluralism because it is attempting to legislate a particular set of religious beliefs, thus blurring the separation between church and state.

Along with the rise in fundamentalism and evangelicalism, there has also been a dramatic growth in what are called "megachurches" or "postdenominational churches": Christian congregations, often fundamentalist or evangelical, that are independent of the mainline Protestant denominations or the Roman Catholic Church (Miller, 1997). These churches are more informal and participatory; they downplay the role of clergy in religious ritual and experience and stress the centrality of individual involvement and Bible interpretation. The trappings of church buildings, clergy vestments, organs and hymnals, and religious symbols are not seen as important; the key to religiosity for these churches is the direct communication between an individual and the deity. These megachurches have been very successful at attracting people, especially those who have become dissatisfied with the more staid, elitist, and hierarchical traditional denominations; some megachurches have grown very large. As the Sociology of Media and Technology section describes, some of these new religious groups have used modern communication technologies to attract members.

Sociology of Media and Technology

Communication Technologies and Religious Experience

Traditionally, religious life occurred as a part of a physical community of people who shared beliefs and rituals. Modern communications technologies have the potential for changing this. Beginning almost a century ago, the Roman Catholic Bishop Fulton J. Sheen began broadcasting radio sermons in 1928 and later moved to television. In the past three decades, television evangelism has boomed with the emergence of *televangelists,* preachers who send their messages to millions of homes and raise millions of dollars to support their evangelical ministry (Frankl, 1998; Hadden, 1993). Pat Robertson, Jimmy Swaggart, Jim Bakker, and Joel Osteen, for example, became well known and at their height had celebrity status. The number of religious television stations continues to grow; the increasing number of channels on cable television has allowed for the expansion of religious programming; and television ministries will likely remain a fairly secure feature of religious life in the United States.

So, without ever stepping into a church building or meeting face-to-face with a minister, people join a church and "attend" religious services. People who watch televangelists tend to be female, older, with lower income and education, and from southern or midwestern states (Clymer, 1987; Horsfield, 1984). These characteristics point to one source of support for televangelists: part of their appeal is to people experiencing some degree of social isolation or those suffering from economic deprivation (Alexander, 1997).

By the twenty-first century, the online world has come to offer yet another way for modern communications technologies to influence the form and spread of religion. Social scientists have been conducting research on this and are beginning to understand how this cyberworld of religion will likely play out (Larsen, 2004; McKenna and West, 2007). First of all, despite the fears of some, it doesn't appear that online religion will replace, or even supplant in any significant way, physical faith communities. Few people actually engage in worship services online; they seem to reserve this for physical religious communities. What they go online for are things that can only be done, or can be done more efficiently, online, such as search for information about their own or another faith, purchase religious items, or e-mail prayer requests. In addition, some participants in virtual religious groups are not active church-goers, so their online faith activities are not replacing anything. And there is some evidence, although we need to do more research on this, that the "virtual" religious experiences of these non-church-goers are a prelude to their joining a physical faith community. In fact, some of these non-church-going religion surfers are using the Internet explicitly to find a church that they would like to attend. In addition, the cyberworld can be a safe and nonthreatening way for people to expand their exploration of religion by learning about faith communities, such as Paganism or other earth-centered religions, that are stigmatized by some people in the mainstream culture.

Research is also showing that participation in online religion provides many of the same benefits as do traditional religious communities: an increased sense of social support, a strengthening in one's faith and one's sense of connection to others, and a greater propensity to join in volunteer helping activities in real life. In addition, when it comes to matters of religion and faith, face-to-face contact in a physical community (going to a church, synagogue, or mosque) still provides benefits that cannot be fully replicated by online experiences. So, while it may be that all of your banking or bill-paying activities may move online in the near future, this seems unlikely to occur in the area of religious life. In fact, among those who use the Internet for religious purposes, community-building involving primary group contact (such as participating in a religious chat room or a religious service) is far less common than more utilitarian, secondary-group activities (such as downloading religious materials).

The interactive nature of the online religious communities suggests that they can exist more easily than physical communities can without some organizational structure—such as a denomination, priesthood, or sect leader—to provide cohesiveness and authority. Given the ease with which one can create communities online, this opens up the possibility of religious involvement that is less dependent on conventional or mainstream religious authorities and institutions. Unlike the audiences for the televangelists, these technologies tend to be used by younger, better educated, and higher SES people.

GROWTH IN ISLAM Of the world's religions discussed earlier in this chapter, Judaism and Christianity clearly have the most members and longest tradition in the United States. Nevertheless, Islam has shown remarkable growth, especially since the 1960s (Lugo, 2008; Niebuhr, 2001; Smith, 1999). Best estimates are that there are five to seven million Muslims in the United States, and if present trends in birthrates and immigration patterns persist, Muslims will soon outnumber the six million Jews, if they don't already. In 2001, there were more than 1,200 mosques in the United States, 80 percent of which were founded since the mid-1980s.

Some African slaves brought to North America during the colonial period were probably Muslim, and small numbers of Muslims came to the United States in the late 1800s and early 1900s. Developments in the 1960s, however, set the stage for the recent upsurge in Islam in the United States. One development was new laws that permitted more immigration from Muslim nations in the Middle East and Asia. The second development was the conversion of African Americans to Islam, inspired partly by Elijah Muhammad, founder of the Nation of Islam, and Malcolm X. Since Islam is a traditional religion in parts of Africa, it was attractive to African Americans as a link to their homeland. Islam also offered an identity that they believed was stripped from them during slavery and a coherent symbol and belief system that was independent of the dominant white culture. Possibly as many as one-quarter of Muslims in the United States are black.

Most Muslims in the United States have assimilated to a significant degree, adopting lifestyles similar to those of non-Muslim Americans. However, as noted, Islamic beliefs include social prescriptions that diverge from other trends in the United States. For example, Islam emphasizes a sexual modesty and con-servatism that, as noted in Chapter 9, is less widely held today by many people in the United States than in the past. Islam also requires clear distinctions in gender roles, with women having primary responsibility for home and family, which Chapter 8 noted many women in the United States find too limiting. Thus there is tension between some traditional Islamic beliefs and the customs of many Americans. But some Christian and Jewish groups hold equally conservative normative strictures, so Islam is not unique in that regard. Despite any distinctiveness that might cause tension, the Muslim community in the United States today is flourishing, with its own schools, social clubs, marriage services, magazines, and bookstores. Muslims will continue to be a significant part of the religious mosaic in the United States.

NEW RELIGIOUS MOVEMENTS The number of new religious groups in the United States has continued to grow over the past few decades (Robbins, 1988). Some of them are offshoots of the mainline religions, such as the Children of God and Jews for Jesus; others are extensions of traditional religions in other cultures, such as the Krishna Consciousness movement and the cult of Bhagwan Shree Rajneesh, which are of Hindu origin. Still others are hybrids, such as the Reverend Sun Myung Moon's Unification Church.

There are a number of misconceptions about these new religions (Melton, 1993). One is that most of them are a by-product of the counterculture of the 1960s. Some of them did emerge in the 1960s, but that was the result of changes in the laws in 1965 that resulted in a large influx of immigrants from Asia. Some of these immigrants established Hindu or Buddhist temples in their new home, and some U.S.–born young people were drawn to these exotic new religions. Buddhism had already begun to make an impact in the

United States in the 1950s, as soldiers who experienced life in Japan following World War II returned with new ideas about religion. Furthermore, more unconventional religions emerged in the 1970s and 1980s than in the 1960s. All these facts suggest that the 1960s were not terribly special, as far as these unconventional religions are concerned; rather, the emergence of these new religions is the result in part of the increasing multicultural nature of the U.S. populace.

A second misconception regarding these religions is that many of them are ephemeral and short-lived, with no significant, lasting impact on U.S. culture. Whereas that is true of a few, most of these groups survive and become a continuing part of the religious environment in their communities. A few even prosper. After all, the Mormons were an unconventional offshoot at their inception in the early 1800s, and they have become a well-established and highly influential member of the social, political, and religious communities of the United States.

There are many reasons why people join these new religions. First of all, like the fundamentalists and evangelicals, the new religions can offer support and sustenance for people suffering from social isolation or economic deprivation. Their intense commitment and bonds of community are often more appealing to people than the more formal and staid approaches of the mainline religions. Second, the growing bureaucracy and impersonality of modern society leaves many people feeling alienated, and the trend toward secularization has left many people with feelings of uncertainty about moral and personal values. Sects and cults offer an escape from that alienation and uncertainty. They offer an exhilarating feeling of becoming a new person, taking control of one's life, and experiencing deep involvement with accepting, like-minded people. Third, sects and cults offer support to people experiencing the uncertainties often associated with transitions in the life cycle, such as young people coming to adulthood and separating from their family or a person who has just dropped out of college or lost a job. Finally, joining religious movements is one way that people use to adapt to the disruption that often accompanies social change.

These, then, are the structural sources of the development of new religions in the United States: social isolation, economic deprivation, bureaucracy, secularization, and life cycle transitions. Because these conditions are permanent features of modern society, new religious movements are likely to have a continuing appeal.

MILLENARIAN RELIGIONS   New religions sometimes take the form of millenarian religious movements, *religions based on the idea that life on earth will be suddenly and dramatically transformed and that a new and*

utopian existence will begin. In their classic form, millenarian religions are "end of the world" groups, positing that earthly existence is about to end, often in a cataclysmic event (Goode, 1992). The recent Branch Davidian and Heaven's Gate religions were millenarian in nature, and a number of others became popular at the end of the millennium marked by the close of the twentieth century. But such religions are not recent developments; they have risen in various forms throughout U.S. history. Some millenarian religions emerged, for example, among the Comanche Indians (discussed in the opening to Chapter 2) and other Indian tribes as they responded to the shattering effect of the invasion of Euro-Americans and the creation of the reservation system. The Comanches, who roamed the southern Great Plains in small bands chasing buffalo, were used to living in small groups and moving around frequently. By the 1860s, the buffalo herds had been largely destroyed, and the Comanches had been forced into geographically limited reservations. There was no longer reason or opportunity for them to roam and hunt.

With the loss of their way of life and their culture torn asunder, sometimes in one generation, the Comanches and other tribal peoples experienced a wrenching dislocation. Under conditions such as these, religion can offer people an explanation of their sufferings and sorrows that provides some hope for the future. Yet established religions often fail in this regard because they are linked to the way of life that is either gone or undergoing change. So new religions, sometimes millenarian in nature, emerge because they offer people a way out of their misery and degradation. One new religion that developed among the Comanche was the peyote cult (La Barre, 1964; Lanternari, 1963). American Indian users of peyote believed that peyote constituted a sacrament enabling its user to absorb some of the powers of the Great Spirit and that it was a vehicle for learning the will of the Great Spirit. Indians believed that the Great Spirit made peyote available to ease their pain and suffering. While under the influence of peyote, people were to examine their lives to see if they had violated certain cultural norms, such as caring for one's family, self-reliance, and the avoidance of alcohol. In this way, peyote helped its users to find the "road to good."

Divisional gatherings of old (described in Chapter 2) had been a time for thousands of Comanches, who had been traveling around hunting in much smaller divisions, to gather together, renew friendships, perform familiar rituals, and share their common heritage and identity as Comanches. On the reservation, however, the divisional gatherings no longer seemed needed, since the Comanches now lived fairly close together year-round. The peyote rituals came to serve the old functions of the divisional gatherings. Thus, the peyote cult provided some American Indians with a coherent set of cultural guidelines to follow and a sacred legitimation for them. In this way, it helped them cope with the disintegration of their traditional culture.

Another millenarian religion that sprang from the same soil of cultural collapse was the Ghost Dance movements of 1870 and 1890 (Thornton, 1987). Both originated among the Northern Paiutes of western Nevada but spread eventually to tribes throughout the Rocky Mountain and midwestern regions. Central to the Ghost Dance movements was the belief that all whites would be destroyed (some said by fire, others by being swallowed by the earth), that dead Indians would be returned to life, and that all Indians would live on in an earthly paradise filled with game (especially buffalo) and other elements of Indian culture.

The link between cultural collapse and the rise of millenarian religions is documented by the close association between the decline in the buffalo herd and the spread of the Ghost Dance movement to new tribes: Those tribes that had most recently experienced the loss of the buffalo were the most likely to adopt the Ghost Dance (Carroll, 1975). A form of *relative deprivation* seemed to be at work: the perception of how deprived one's situation is, especially compared to the past or to others' situation. Those who had more recently experienced the loss of the buffalo herd felt more deprived because their immediate past had been much better.

Remnants of both the peyote cult and the Ghost Dance persist today. The peyote cult coalesced into a group called the Native American Church, which continues to use peyote as a part of its rituals. The Ghost Dance continues as the Bole-Maru cult among some American Indians (Thornton, 1987). The peyote cult and Ghost Dance illustrate the sociological truism that when people are frightened, vulnerable, or in crisis, a certain number will turn to religion as a means of coping. However, neither movement halted the assault on American Indian culture. They may have provided individuals with a sense of peace or personal efficacy, but the domination of European culture still persevered.

Applying Sociology: Identifying Extremism in Religious Cults examines how sociological research can offer a more objective and accurate view of new religions and millenarian movements. The sociological approach identifies both their positive impacts on people and society as well as any dangers they may entail.

Applying Sociology   Identifying Extremism in Religious Cults

Religious cults sometimes do some horrific things. Consider these three events, which occurred over a period of thirty years:

- Over nine hundred members of the People's Temple were murdered or committed suicide on a single day in 1978 in their isolated community in Guyana at the order of their leader the Reverend Jim Jones. Jones was, by all accounts, both charismatic and tyrannical in his control over the members of the cult (Wooden, 1981).
- In 1993, close to one hundred members of a cult called the Branch Davidians holed up in their heavily armed compound called Ranch Apocalypse outside Waco, Texas, on the orders of their charismatic leader David Koresh. Cult members killed four federal agents and wounded sixteen others who had a warrant to search the property for illegal weapons. After a 51-day standoff, federal agents attacked the compound, which exploded in flames, killing 60 adult members of the cult and 26 children and teenagers inside (Gibbs, 1993).
- In 1997, a grisly scene was discovered in a suburban home outside San Diego: thirty-nine members of the Heaven's Gate cult were found dead throughout the house in a ritualized mass suicide. Their leader, Marshall Herff Applewhite, had convinced them that dying only meant that they were leaving their "earthly vehicles" and moving to a higher level of reality where they would join a giant UFO (Taylor, 1997).

Sociologists have studied hundreds upon hundreds of religious sects and cults over the decades and have learned quite a bit about them. One thing that this sociological investigation has found is that the People's Temple, the Branch Davidians, and Heaven's Gate are the exceptions in that very few religious sects go to such extremes. In fact, most sects and cults are fairly respectable and responsible, have a positive impact on their members' lives, and make a positive contribution to society by encouraging their members to work hard and avoid drugs and crime. By looking at the ways people are attracted to these unconventional religions, we can also catch a glimpse of what can go wrong.

People become involved in such unconventional religions for a variety of reasons (Richardson, 1978; Robbins, 1988). First of all, people who are attracted to these groups tend to be those who, possibly because of early socialization, view the world in a religious light and define problems and their solutions in terms of religious forces. Second, people are attracted to these groups because they are experiencing some personal troubles or difficulties or a life transition that has left them temporarily adrift from social ties. All people, of course,

(continued)

experience troubles and transitions, but for some the accompanying pain or self-doubt is so enormous that they are desperate to find a solution to their problems—or avoid them by immersion in some ecstatic experience.

Sociologists have also learned that a key step in the conversion process occurs when people come to believe that a particular religious group can offer them solace, and this belief is where a group's recruitment efforts are directed. Their members are sent to beaches, college communities, or other places where those whose lives are in transition are likely to congregate. Since young people are the category most likely to have lives in some turmoil, many of these recruitment efforts are directed at them.

The popular image is that people are "programmed" or "brainwashed" when they join these groups. An "anticult" or "deprogramming" movement has emerged to fight against such unconventional religions. Sociological research suggests, however, that although these groups certainly influence their members, the influence is limited. In fact, most people leave these groups after a year or two (Levine, 1986). People entered and left both the People's Temple and the Branch Davidians almost until the end. For many, the groups are temporary retreats where they can find support, think through their problems, and decide what their next steps in life will be. Eventually, they return to a more conventional life, although their moral and spiritual lives are likely to remain permanently affected by their experiences.

Why the tragic end for the People's Temple, the Branch Davidians, and Heaven's Gate? Sociological research points to some of the differences between these and other cults and the things to watch for. One is that the cults came under the sway of a charismatic, highly manipulative, and ultimately psychologically unstable leader. Some of the people attracted to such groups are lonely, isolated, and desperate for some certainty in their lives, which makes them especially vulnerable to such exploitation. In most such groups, the leaders do not take exploitative advantage of the situation; Jones, Koresh, and Applewhite did. A second difference is that the leaders went to extremes to isolate their followers from contact with or influence by others. Jones physically isolated them in the rain forests of Guyana; the Branch Davidians were required to surrender all their money and belongings to Koresh, effectively isolating them from any resources that might have enhanced their personal independence. A third difference is the belief in an apocalyptic confrontation with the larger society. Both Jones and Koresh had the paranoid view that society was out to destroy them. Koresh had stockpiled hundreds of rifles, machine guns, and hand grenades at Ranch Apocalypse.

Although most religious sects and cults are reasonably benign, a group that exhibits these characteristics may take more extreme directions. ■

Sociology on the Internet

One example of what online religion might look like as it becomes more popular is Beliefnet (**www.beliefnet. com**), which doesn't promote a particular religion but enables people to choose from a wide variety of religious possibilities. You can subscribe to a daily e-mail newsletter with your choice of inspiration (Bible reading, Jewish wisdom, Buddhist wisdom, Muslim wisdom, and so on). For mate selection, you can subscribe to Soulmatch where you can enter your spiritual proclivities and get matched with compatible others. You can order audiotapes and ringtones that reflect your chosen spiritual approaches. (Beliefnet is currently a part of Fox Digital Media and the News Corporation, media conglomerates discussed in Chapter 13.)

You can also use the Internet to search for religious information: enter "Buddhism," "Taoism," or the names of other religions into a search engine and see what you come up with. Can you describe the organizational structures of these religions? In what parts of the United States or the world are they most popular? Another interesting direction is to search for "electronic church." This can help you assess further the role of the mass media in modern religions. From what you learn about electronic churches, can you say anything about the social organization of religions in modern societies?

An excellent source of information about religion in the United States is the Association of Religion Data Archives (**www.thearda.com**). It contains a number of data sets on many aspects of religious life, as well as maps that can be generated on topics such as membership in churches over time. To learn more about various new religious movements, take a look at this Web site: **religiousmovements.lib.virginia.edu/**. It is maintained by sociologist Douglas Cowan, and it provides a wealth of information about many different religious groups.

Study & Review
SUMMARY OF LEARNING OBJECTIVES
You should be able to define religion and describe the major forms it can take.

As an empirical discipline, sociology cannot assess the truth or falsity of religious beliefs. Rather, sociologists study religions as social institutions that function in the social world, are transmitted through the socialization process, and are influenced by the social and cultural context in which they exist. Religions distinguish between the sacred and the profane. Religion as an institution is a collectively held set of symbols and rituals that express a basic understanding of the world, especially its sacred dimension, and address the ultimate concerns of the meaning of human existence. Religions come in many forms, such as animism, theism, and religions of the way.

You should be able to describe the basic beliefs, teachings, and holy figures of the six major religions in the world and discuss their similarities and differences.

The six major religions of the world today are Judaism, Christianity, Islam, Hinduism, Buddhism, and Confucianism. Some of these are theistic religions, whereas others are religions of the way. They also differ among themselves in terms of what they consider sacred, who they consider to be central religious figures, which books are considered to be holy, and whether they have some central authority. There has been much diffusion of religions around the world as human societies interact with one another through trade or war.

You should be able to describe the approaches of Durkheim, Marx, and Weber concerning the role of religion in society.

According to Durkheim, religions serve a number of important functions: They enhance social solidarity by reinforcing cultural values, they give a sacred legitimation to cultural values and practices, they provide meaning for human lives, and they assist people in understanding life events. According to Marx, religion can serve as a mechanism of oppression whereby the powerful protect their position by convincing subordinate groups that the existing distribution of resources is ordained by some deity. This practice is possible because people become alienated from religion, forgetting that it is a human creation. Weber argued that religion can play a part in social change. The Protestant ethic, for example, played a role in bringing about capitalism in Europe, and Islam today is a force promoting political change in a number of nations around the world.

You should be able to list the basic characteristics of churches, ecclesia, denominations, sects, and cults.

Some religions have very informal organizations, with little specialization of religious roles. Most modern religions, however, are highly specialized and have full-time clergy. In the United States, most religions are organized as churches, denominations, sects, or cults. Some societies also have ecclesia. These various forms of religious organization have different characteristics.

You should be able to discuss religiosity and its correlates, describe the effect of socioeconomic status and politics on religion, and analyze trends in secularization and religious pluralism in the United States.

People in the United States tend to be fairly religious people, especially in comparison to most other nations. People's religiosity is affected by their socioeconomic status. Religion, in turn, has an effect on political party preferences. Secularization has occurred because societies have become highly differentiated and because science has dispelled some of the mysteries in life. The United States is characterized by religious pluralism. Recent developments in this area have been the ecumenical movement, fundamentalism, evangelicalism, the use of the mass media to transmit religious messages, and the growth of Islam. In addition, new religious sects, including millenarian ones, emerge periodically. Most of these religious sects are respectable, responsible, and make a positive contribution to society. However, a few of these cults, such as those led by psychologically unstable individuals who believe in an apocalyptic confrontation with society, can lead to highly destructive outcomes.

CHRONOLOGICAL PRACTICE TEST
For answers to Key Concepts see the page number in parentheses; for other answers see page 329.

What Is Religion?
Key Concepts

1. Sacred (307)
2. Profane (307)
3. Religion (307)
4. Animism (307)
5. Totemism (308)
6. Theistic religions (308)
7. Polytheistic religions (308)
8. Monotheistic religions (308)
9. Religions of the way (308)

True/False

10. T F Voodoo and *Santería* in the Caribbean and the Americas are outgrowths of African tribal religions.
11. T F Totemism is a variant on animism.

Concept Completion

12. Emile Durkheim argued that the distinctive feature of religion is that it views the world as divided into two realms, the _____ and the _____.
13. Polytheistic religions involve a belief in _____.

Critical Thinking

14. How would a sociologist define religion? Describe the major forms that religion can take.

A Global Perspective: Religions of the World

True/False

15. T F Hinduism is older than Christianity and Islam.
16. T F The founder of Confucianism is Siddhartha Gautama, who is known as the Enlightened One.

Concept Completion

17. The branch of Judaism that follows strictly the divine books and the laws as promulgated by Moses is _____.
18. The basic principles of Buddhism are stated in the _____.

Critical Thinking

19. When and how did Judaism, Christianity, and Islam emerge? Describe the basic beliefs of each religion.
20. When and how did Hinduism, Buddhism, and Confucianism emerge? Describe the basic beliefs of each religion.

Sociological Approaches to the Study of Religion

Key Concept

21. Protestant ethic (313)

True/False

22. T F When Karl Marx referred to religion as "the opiate of the people," he meant that religion helped to reduce their feelings of alienation.
23. T F In his studies on religion, Max Weber found that it was difficult for people to follow the Protestant ethic and engage in capitalist activity at the same time.

Concept Completion

24. When Karl Marx said that people become alienated from religion, he meant that they _____.
25. Max Weber argued that there was a(an) _____ between Protestantism and capitalism.

Critical Thinking

26. Compare and contrast the functionalist and conflict perspectives on religion. Show clearly how they differ from one another.
27. According to Max Weber, what is the relationship between Protestantism and capitalism? Describe all the elements of that relationship.
28. In a number of places in the chapter, the role of religion in the process of political and social change is discussed. Review the examples discussed in the chapter, and describe what they tell us about how religion affects social change.

The Organization of Religion

Key Concepts

29. Church (314)
30. Ecclesia (314)
31. Denominations (314)
32. Sects (314)
33. Cults (316)

True/False

34. T F Religious cults are small, loosely organized sects that are often held together by a charismatic figure.

Concept Completion

35. _____ is an official state religion.

Critical Thinking

36. Define and describe the different levels of religious organization that sociologists use in describing religion in modern societies. Give an example of each.

Religion in the United States

Key Concepts

37. Religiosity (317)
38. Secularization (319)
39. Civil religion (321)
40. Millenarian religious movements (324)

True/False

41. T F Before the American Revolution in 1776, none of the colonies in the New World had official state religions or ecclesia.
42. T F The term "ecumenical movement" refers to a millenarian movement that emerged in the United States in the 1990s and believed that the world would end in the near future.
43. T F Islam had no adherents in the United States until the 1970s when immigration from the Middle East began.

Concept Completion

44. _____ is the process through which the influence of religion is removed from many institutions in society and dispersed into private and personal realms.

45. Those who believe in a literal interpretation of the Bible and the use of biblical teachings as a foundation of faith are called _____.

46. The peyote and Ghost Dance movements among American Indians arose as a response to _____.

Critical Thinking

47. What is the extent of religiosity in the United States? How does the United States compare with other nations?

48. What is the relationship between socioeconomic status and politics in the United States?

49. What reasons were given in the text for why new religions emerge in the United States?

ANSWERS TO CHRONOLOGICAL PRACTICE TEST

10. T; 11. T; 15. T; 16. F; 22. F; 23. F; 34. T; 41. F; 42. F; 43. F

12. sacred, profane
13. many gods
17. orthodox Judaism
18. Four Noble Truths
24. view religion as something separate and independent of human beings
25. elective affinity
35. An ecclesia
44. Secularization
45. fundamentalists
46. cultural collapse, cultural dislocation, or cultural change

CUMULATIVE PRACTICE TEST

See page 482 for answers.

1. According to the text, the earliest evidence of religion among human groups is found
   a. with the development of agriculture.
   b. during their horticultural period.
   c. among Paleolithic peoples of thirty thousand years ago.
   d. in Western societies.
   e. in the Middle East ten thousand years ago.

2. Judaism, Christianity, and Islam are considered to be
   a. polytheistic religions.
   b. religions of "the way."
   c. animistic religions.
   d. monotheistic religions.
   e. Both b and d.

3. Which of the following is true of Buddhism?
   a. It is based on ethical practices and disciplined behavior.
   b. It is a religion of "the way."
   c. People often practice it along with some other religion.
   d. All of the above are true.
   e. Only a and b are true.

4. Which of the following religions is based on the belief that Jesus was the Christ or the Messiah?
   a. Christianity.
   b. Judaism.
   c. Hinduism.
   d. Both a and b.
   e. Both a and c.

5. Which of the following religions is based on the belief in the transmigration of souls?
   a. Christianity.
   b. Hinduism.
   c. Judaism.
   d. Islam.
   e. Confucianism.

6. All of the following were identified by Emile Durkheim as functions performed by religion *except*
   a. it enhances social solidarity.
   b. it offers sacred legitimation of values.
   c. it encourages individualistic behavior.
   d. it provides meaning for people's lives.
   e. All of the above were identified by Durkheim.

7. Karl Marx argued that
   a. religion performs important positive social functions for society.
   b. there was an "elective affinity" between ascetic Protestantism and capitalism in sixteenth-century Europe.
   c. sects are good for society because they encourage their members to work hard and avoid drugs.
   d. religion could help people understand their true class consciousness.
   e. religion is a mechanism through which powerful groups maintain their own positions while oppressing the powerless.

8. Which of the following elements of Calvinism, according to Weber, played a role in the emergence of capitalism in Europe?
   a. The doctrine of predestination.
   b. The emphasis on self-denial and austerity.
   c. The belief in Christ as a personal force.
   d. All of the above.
   e. Only a and b played a role.

9. According to the conflict perspective, people tend to become alienated from religion. One consequence of this alienation is that
   a. people drift away from religion.
   b. people's false class-consciousness is reduced.
   c. the status quo is protected.
   d. religion no longer serves as the opiate Marx described.
   e. civil religion expands.

10. In looking at the link between the emergence of capitalism and certain religious beliefs, Max Weber focused on which religious doctrine?
    a. Hinduism.
    b. Judaism.
    c. Animism.
    d. Calvinism.
    e. Taoism.

11. The Roman Catholic Church in the United States today would be considered by sociologists a/an
    a. sect.
    b. civil religion.
    c. ecclesia.
    d. cult.
    e. church.

12. In comparison to churches, sects tend to
    a. gain new members through birth to current members.
    b. be exclusive in their membership practices.
    c. tolerate other religious groups.
    d. have a professional, full-time clergy.
    e. tolerate diversity of beliefs.
13. Small, loosely organized religious groups that are held together by a charismatic figure are called
    a. cults.
    b. churches.
    c. sects.
    d. ecclesia.
    e. civil religions.
14. Which of the following groups would probably have the highest rate of church membership?
    a. Young single people.
    b. Elderly single people.
    c. Young married people.
    d. Elderly married people.
    e. Young Jewish people.
15. The largest proportion of people in the United States state a preference for which of the following religions?
    a. Protestantism.
    b. Catholicism.
    c. Judaism.
    d. Islam.
    e. A majority states a preference for no religion.
16. The emergence of secularization can be attributed to
    a. the rise of highly differentiated societies with an elaborate division of labor.
    b. the victory of civil religion over existing churches.
    c. the breakdown of family and kinship as the central institutions and social bonds in society.
    d. the rise of new sects and cults in the United States over the past few decades.
    e. declining religious diversity in society.
17. Supporters of the ecumenical movement in the United States have tended to be
    a. members of more affluent Protestant denominations.
    b. members of less affluent, evangelical Protestant groups.
    c. the more conservative Protestant denominations.
    d. those with no religious beliefs or little religious commitment.
    e. mostly Muslims and Hindus.
18. Which of the following statements is true regarding the link between religion and politics?
    a. Religious people are more politically conservative than are nonreligious people.
    b. Nonreligious people are more politically conservative than are religious people.
    c. Jews are more likely to be Democrats than are Protestants.
    d. Protestants are more likely to be Democrats than are Catholics.
    e. Jews are more likely to be Republicans than are Protestants.
19. The Ghost Dance movement among American Indians was most clearly due to
    a. cultural collapse.
    b. alienation.

    c. bureaucratization.
    d. increasing levels of education.
    e. increasing affluence.
20. The ecumenical movement in the United States emphasizes
    a. the literal interpretation of the Bible.
    b. a personal commitment to Jesus Christ and being born again.
    c. the use of television to distribute religious messages.
    d. harmony between and the similarities among the various religions and denominations.
    e. the importance of civil religion and secularization.

FOR FURTHER READING

Bainbridge, William Sims. (2002). *The endtime family: Children of God.* Albany: State University of New York Press. This is an excellent, in-depth study of a cult. It dispels many myths about cults and also highlights the activities of anticult groups.

Bromley, David G., & Melton, J. Gordon (eds.). (2002). *Cults, religion & violence.* New York: Cambridge University Press. The articles in this book present research substantiating which social conditions are likely to produce violence in the relationship between cults and society.

Haddad, Yvonne Yazbeck, & Lummis, Adair T. (1987). *Islamic values in the United States: A comparative study.* New York: Oxford University Press. The authors provide a detailed analysis of the adaptations made by Muslim immigrants to the United States.

Hoover, S. M. (1998). *Religion in the news: Faith and journalism in American public discourse.* Thousand Oaks, CA: Sage. By focusing on how the media present religion, this author is able to describe the role and status of religion in contemporary American society.

Lewis, James R., & Melton, J. Gordon (eds.). (1992). *Perspectives on the new age.* Albany: State University of New York Press. This is an interesting book of readings on such new age spiritual practices as channeling and witchcraft. The book assesses whether they should be considered religions and looks at the response to them of some older religions.

McGuire, Meredith B. (2002). *Religion: The social context* (5th ed.). Belmont, CA: Wadsworth. This readable and thorough review of the field of the sociology of religion shows in detail how religion affects societies and individuals.

Richardson, James T., Best, Joel, & Bromley, David G. (eds.). (1991). *The satanism scare.* New York: Aldine de Gruyter. This is an excellent investigation of satanism and satanic cult activity in the United States. The authors provide a realistic description and assessment of the phenomenon as well as an insightful discussion of why it has aroused so much hysteria. It is a good case study of competition among religious communities.

Saliba, John A. (1995). *Understanding new religious movements.* Grand Rapids, MI: William Eerdmans. This book provides a good overview of many of the new religions that have emerged and offers a sociological perspective on them.

CHAPTER 12

Education and the Mass Media

MYTHS & FACTS: About Education and the Mass Media

A Global Perspective on Education

   Informal Education
   Colonization and Education
   Modernization and Education

Sociological Perspectives on Education

   The Functionalist Perspective
     The Transmission of Culture and Skills
     Custody of the Young
     A Social Network for the Young
     Innovation and Change
     Sorting and Social Mobility
   The Conflict Perspective
     Promoting Existing Political and Economic Arrangements
     The Credentials Race

Education and Social Inequality
The Interactionist Perspective
   Labeling
   Ability Grouping

Education in the United States

   A Historical View
   Schools as Bureaucracies
   Effectiveness of the Educational System
   Reforms and Trends
     Magnet Schools, Charter Schools, and Choice
     APPLYING SOCIOLOGY: Evaluating Educational Innovations
     Back to Basics
     Early Childhood Interventions
     School Integration
     Upgrading Schools and Teachers
     Privatization and Home Schooling

Higher Education
   OTHER WORLDS, OTHER WAYS: Japan: Variations in
   Educational Institutions in Industrial Societies

Education, Communication, and the Mass Media
   Emergence of the Mass Media
   Effects of the Mass Media

SOCIOLOGY OF MEDIA AND TECHNOLOGY: Education in
   the Electronic World
Control of the Mass Media
The Global Mass Media: Neocolonization?
   SOCIOLOGY ON THE INTERNET

Study & Review

The Jesuits are a Roman Catholic religious order founded in 1539 by a Spaniard, Ignatius Loyola. In their early years they were a militant monastic order that stressed education and were considered an intellectual and moral elite among Catholics. Emerging in the midst of the Protestant Reformation, the Jesuits were founded to bring people back to the Catholic faith and were staunch defenders of papal authority. They organized themselves along military lines and undertook to spread Catholicism across international boundaries.

Fourteen years after their founding, the Jesuits arrived in Brazil, suffused with zeal and dedication to convert the indigenous tribal peoples, whom they, like all Europeans, called *heathens* (Hemming, 1978). The Jesuits and the Indians got along fairly well. The Jesuits were free of the intense material greed that fueled virtually all of the behavior of the Portuguese colonists, and the Indians found they could trust the priests. In addition, the Jesuits provided some protection against Portuguese excesses. In fact, the Jesuits set up mission villages, called *aldeias* in Portuguese, to which many Indians fled when defeated by the Portuguese in colonial wars.

In the *aldeias*, the Jesuits set up schools for the Indians, but they concentrated their educational efforts mostly on the young. Adults were more resistant to missionary schooling because the Jesuits were asking them to give up some long-held traditional practices, such as polygyny and cannibalism. Children were more impressionable. In the schools, the young were taught Christianity, of course, but they learned much more than that. As one Jesuit wrote from Bahia state in Brazil in 1558: "Their children are instructed; the innocent ones about to die are all baptised; they are forgetting their customs and exchanging them for good ones" (quoted in Hemming, 1978, p. 101). In other words, the schools aspired to replace traditional ways with the more "civilized" ways of sixteenth-century Europeans. The children learned not only to read and write but also to sing songs and play musical instruments from Europe. Girls were instructed in how to weave cloth so that they could cover themselves rather than go naked as was their custom before the Portuguese came. The missionaries believed that the children could then make further inroads on the Indian way of life by teaching their parents. Some Indian children even used their Eu-

ropean education as an excuse to dominate and patronize their parents. The children were beginning to accept the European view that Indian ways were heathen and backward. The children were discouraged from learning tribal ways, such as animistic religions or the skills of hunters and warriors. As a consequence, according to one historian, the children "would also become accomplices in the emasculation of tribal culture" (Hemming, 1978, p. 111). Not only was the education given the Indians devoid of tribal skills, but also it neglected to train the children in the skills and orientations that would make them competitive in the much harsher colonial world dominated by the Portuguese.

Education is *the systematic, formal process through which specialized teachers transmit skills, knowledge, and values to students.* In the long run, the education that the Jesuits provided to the Indians of Brazil helped to solidify colonial domination by encouraging young Indians to accept European religious and political authority and to reject tribal sources of wisdom, tradition, and authority. The schools also helped to reproduce a stratification system based on European dominance and Indian subordination by making sure the Indians did not receive skills that would give them an equal advantage with the Europeans in colonial trade. The experience of the Brazilian Indians begins to shed light on some of the complex ways in which education as a social institution contributes to the maintenance of society. The following analysis of education begins with a discussion of the emergence of education as a separate social institution.

A Global Perspective on Education

You should be able to describe how education differs in preindustrial and industrial societies and how colonization and modernization have changed education.

Informal Education

In traditional Yoruk society in Turkey, many of the women were highly skilled basket makers who produced sophisticated baskets that were both functional

Myths & Facts

About Education and the Mass Media

Myth:

When British and Portuguese explorers after Columbus found new lands, they set up schools to teach the natives skills that would help them survive better.

Fact:

These explorers typically considered the indigenous inhabitants to be uncivilized and believed that the only way they could become civilized was to learn European ways. The primary result of European schooling of the inhabitants was to protect the interests of the Europeans and in many cases to destroy the inhabitants' culture.

Myth:

The primary purpose of education is to teach the young reading, writing, and other skills that are essential for them to make a contribution to society.

Fact:

Although education does this task, it also performs an array of other functions, some not widely recognized. For example, it instills patriotism and other attitudes that encourage students to accept the social order, and it is a sorting mechanism that enables some people to obtain rewarding positions in society while others receive more lowly positions.

Myth:

People need more education today than in former times because today's jobs are more complicated and the technology more sophisticated, requiring more extensive training.

Fact:

This belief is partly true, but reality is more complicated. Only part of the increase in educational requirements for jobs in the twentieth century can be accounted for by actual increases in the training essential to do the jobs. Educational levels for jobs have risen in part because some groups benefit from this "credentials race."

Myth:

Entertaining television shows and movies that contain violence, such as *NYPD Blue*, *The Sopranos*, or *The Patriot*, do not harm young people who watch them as long as the shows are clearly fictional and fanciful.

Fact:

Most research evidence concludes that young children, especially males, who watch violent television shows or movies are more likely to behave aggressively or violently themselves.

and beautiful. Yet they received no formal training and only small amounts of informal instruction in basket making. Rather, during their childhood, Yoruk girls would watch their mothers, aunts, and older sisters weave baskets and would become skilled weavers themselves merely by observation (O'Neale, 1932). In many preindustrial societies, such as the Yoruk, it is difficult to distinguish education from the general process of socialization (see Chapter 3). The reason is that specialized educational institutions had not yet emerged. Instead, education took place during informal, daily interactions with family members and others. There were no special buildings called schools and no specialized roles for teachers or students. In fact, anyone could serve as a teacher if children learned from that person by watching him or her plow the fields, bake bread, or weave baskets, and practically all adults served, at one time or another, as teachers of children.

In agricultural societies, some specialized educational institutions began to emerge, but they were much more limited than they are today (Fagerlind & Saha, 1989). As much as five thousand years ago, for example, scribes in Mesopotamia and Egypt received institutionalized training in the art of writing. In larger agricultural societies, such as ancient China and Greece, a wealthy elite emerged that could afford to withdraw their children from work and send them to school or hire teachers to educate them at home. Confucius, the founder of one of the world's religious systems discussed in Chapter 11, was a teacher in ancient China. Education for the elite, however, had more to do with philosophical, religious, or moral training for society's future ruling class than with practical skills such as those of a carpenter or doctor. Such education of an elite was in marked contrast to the informal education through socialization or apprenticeship that the masses of people experienced.

Colonization and Education

Long before there was much formal schooling, cultural interchange occurred between societies that came together in war or through economic exchange. In these encounters, ideas, art works, and tools were exchanged and often reshaped to fit the new culture. These cultural items then influenced what people learned through general acculturation and whatever formal schooling there was. For example, Europeans entered the Middle East in the twelfth and thirteenth centuries as part of the Crusades, religious wars to capture the Holy Land from the Muslims, and they brought back to Europe Arabic mathematics and medicine, which then became a part of Western civilization and education.

From the fifteenth to the nineteenth centuries, Western European nations explored and colonized much of Africa, parts of Asia, and all of the Western Hemisphere. In most places, the imperial nations viewed the indigenous cultures in the lands they colonized as uncivilized and inferior to European culture (Brint, 1998). The Europeans usually attempted to replace tribal religions, political systems, and economic arrangements with new ones based on European models. In some places, such as North and South America, this policy meant the virtual destruction of tribal cultures either through neglect or active intent. In India, which had a large and ancient civilization before the British came, including the two great religions of Hinduism and Buddhism, the British did not destroy the culture, but they did choose to live apart from it. They created a system of education in English for the elite in India.

In the eyes of these colonizers, the indigenous peoples could become civilized or developed only by adopting European culture, language, and education. To that end, the colonizers imposed Western models of education. In some cases, as with the Jesuits in South America and Canada (see the discussion of the Hurons in Chapter 8), Christian churches ran mission schools where Indians were taught Christianity and encouraged to drop their "pagan" religion. They were also taught Western political and economic concepts as well as Western ideas about family and gender roles. In other cases, such as in India, the colonizing nations established specialized training schools where a small indigenous elite was taught to run the government and businesses. Needless to say, the political and economic ideologies that they learned in those schools tended to be those that supported the interests of the colonizing nations and helped maintain the status quo.

In the midst of and supported by the bounty of this colonization, the European nations began to industrialize in the 1700s (Gutek, 1993). With industrialization, education came to stress training in scientific and technical knowledge and processes that were needed to operate industrial technology. To be sure, some informal education still occurs in industrial societies, as when a young girl learns how to do carpentry by watching her father build kitchen cabinets. Industrial societies, however, have occasioned a massive shift to specialized educational institutions with educational specialists doing the teaching.

Modernization and Education

With the expansion of industrial capitalism in the nineteenth and twentieth centuries, the industrial nations needed raw materials such as oil from many nations around the world. In addition, they turned to the less developed nations as sources of labor and as receptive markets for their products. According to world-system theory, these needs produced an intense interest on the part of industrial nations regarding social and economic developments in the less developed nations of the world (Feinberg & Avakov, 1991; Najafizadeh & Mennerick, 1990). The Western nations believed that economic underdevelopment and illiteracy would cause social instability, which in turn would threaten the economic environment in these nations. To maintain a receptive economic environment, the industrial nations have encouraged the modernization of the "backward" social, economic, and educational institutions of the less developed nations. Modernization refers to *the social and economic changes that accompany the transition to an industrial economy*. The traditional economy of subsistence, labor-intensive farming with little surplus for sale or investment, is seen as backward. It needs to be replaced with an industrial economy based on mass production, specialization, and surplus for investment. Civilization came to be defined in terms of an industrialized and urbanized society. The success of modernization efforts was defined in mostly economic terms, as increases in the gross national product. So governments and experts in the industrial nations provided the resources and expertise to achieve modernization to the governments and experts of the less developed nations.

Two of the major barriers to modernization were believed to be inefficient traditional institutions, such as the schools, and cultural behavior patterns that inhibited productivity, such as a lack of initiative and a heavy reliance on kinship. So the modernization effort focused on establishing modern educational programs that would produce productive and efficient managers and workers and that would change traditional values and behaviors. To those ends, the modernizing schools trained people in literacy skills, technology, and the engineering and managerial specializations that are needed in such an economy. The schools also taught new attitudes of efficiency, productivity, and obedience that would produce good industrial workers. The schools and the growing national communications media also offered new sources of authority to replace clan elders or village authorities. Traditional education, often done by elders, was much more informal and accomplished on the job. Modernizing education is much more formal and competitive, especially at the secondary and postsecondary levels.

As nations modernize, then, they establish centralized, state-run, mass educational institutions. One of the goals of these schools is *nation building*, or encouraging citizens to shift their allegiance to the nation-state. In traditional societies, people feel more of a connection to a tribe, a clan, a caste, or a village than they do to the nation as a whole, since the nation is often the creation of Western colonizing efforts rather than indigenous. These varying sources of loyalty weaken the central authority of the state. As part of the modernization effort, loyalty needs to be shifted to the national government so that it can maintain social control and political stability. Schools play a role in this process through courses in civic education and national history, involving praise of national heroes and emphasis on national symbols. A standardized curriculum with mass-produced textbooks contributes to this effort. The result is more cultural homogeneity and the erosion of local customs and traditions.

Nations around the world vary in how modernized they have become. One indication of this variation is levels of illiteracy, which can vary substantially, even in the same region of the world. Critics argue, however, that modernization is not simply a matter of improving "backward" nations; it is also a part of the world system of capitalist development (see Chapter 6). Modernization is in part a neocolonial Westernization of these societies to make them receptive areas for investment by multinational, mostly Western, corporations and local elites (Fagerlind & Saha, 1989).

Although modernization brings some benefits, such as economic growth and a reduction in illiteracy, these benefits are not universally distributed to all groups in society. For example, the rates of illiteracy reported for nations hide considerable gender disparity that results because women are far less likely to have literacy skills than are men in many nations. In addition, modernization can become a virtual cultural assault on traditional values and institutions, such as religion and the family, and a promotion of Western social and political values. With the changes have come some severely negative consequences, such as the disintegration of family life and increases in violent crime and drug and alcohol abuse.

Another negative, and largely unexpected, consequence is that modernization may actually *reduce* women's chances for educational advancement. Research shows that increasing multinational investment in less developed nations actually slows the entry of women into higher education (Clark, 1992). The reason may be that this sort of economic development creates low-paying jobs that attract women, who are then more likely to have children rather than pursue higher education. Critics charge that these changes in the world system occur because they benefit the dominant nations, and educational systems play a key role in this process.

This overview of education around the globe suggests that educational institutions play a much more complex role in society than just educating the young. The three theoretical perspectives offer some additional insight into the place of educational institutions in society.

Sociological Perspectives on Education

You should be able to analyze educational institutions using the three sociological perspectives, including an assessment of the functions of education, credentialism, the hidden curriculum, and labeling.

The Functionalist Perspective

From the functionalist perspective, education performs a number of important services that contribute to the operation and maintenance of society (Feinberg & Soltis, 1992).

THE TRANSMISSION OF CULTURE AND SKILLS   Schools supplement the family by passing on to youngsters important elements of their culture, particularly the values, norms, and skills that they will need to function in society. These include not only learning how to read and write but also learning a society's history and values. Through reading about the life of Abraham Lincoln, for example, children come to believe that even people from humble backgrounds can succeed in the United States. In grade school, proper interpersonal behavior is taught to children when they are graded on cooperation, deportment, and personal habits. Brazilian Indian schoolchildren in the 1500s learned from the Jesuits that tribal ways were "heathen" and European ways were "civilized." Schoolchildren also learn about patriotism through history and rituals such as reciting the Pledge of Allegiance. In addition, whether one wants to be a carpenter, lawyer, doctor, or welder, much of the training necessary to perform jobs will be learned in either an academic or vocational school. In transmitting culture, schools provide stability to existing social arrangements. Sometimes, however, the elements of culture intended for transmission to the young can be controversial. The contemporary debate in the United States over school prayer, for example, illustrates how groups can disagree over what elements of culture schools should teach.

CUSTODY OF THE YOUNG   In addition to socialization, schools serve the latent function of providing custodial care for children and young people. Prior to industrialization, children were at home much of the time, and adults were usually around, either members of the extended family or parents working the family farm or business. Today, however, parents are usually away from home during the day, typically at work, and other adults are often not available. Thus schools have come to serve as a kind of extended day care that begins at about age four or five and does not usually end until at least age sixteen.

A SOCIAL NETWORK FOR THE YOUNG   Schools are settings in which young people of about the same age can come together, develop friendships, and participate in group activities. Because children and adolescents in industrial societies are largely barred from the adult work world, schools enable them to develop a peer culture in which they can gain status by being popular, dressing fashionably, or excelling in sports. This youth culture has values that are distinct from and may even clash with the values of the wider culture. (You may recall the discussion of argot in teen subcultures in Chapter 2.) Young people, for example, may value different music, freer expressions of sexuality, and different styles of clothing from the preferences of their parents. Among their peers, these values are supported and reinforced.

INNOVATION AND CHANGE   Educational institutions not only transmit knowledge to the young but also create new knowledge or modify existing knowledge. This process, in turn, can result in new technologies or social practices. Many advances in the field of medicine, for example, have resulted from research conducted at universities in such fields as biochemistry and genetics. Beyond the production of new knowledge, educational institutions function to encourage innovation and change by serving as an open forum for the exchange of ideas and viewpoints.

Colleges and universities in particular encourage students to question and doubt as a means of better understanding human values and social arrangements. In addition, young college students, free from parental surveillance, have a chance to experiment with lifestyles that their parents might not approve of.

SORTING AND SOCIAL MOBILITY   Schools are one of the major mechanisms for sorting people into various occupational and social roles. Most jobs call for some minimal educational attainment. Likewise, to move up the educational ladder, one must successfully complete all of the rungs below. At each step, some people are sorted out, while others seek higher educational degrees. Schools, then, are societal screening mechanisms. Schools also enable people from different social backgrounds to become upwardly mobile if they can obtain the requisite educational degrees. In fact, free public education in the United States was designed, in part, as a means of enabling immigrants to become integrated into U.S. society and to advance in the social hierarchy.

Today, it is virtually impossible to attain high-status positions without considerable education, and increasingly, graduate or professional degrees are required. As Figure 12.1 demonstrates, a strong association exists between people's level of education and their ability to obtain jobs that pay a high income—getting more education enhances the ability to support a family. From the functionalist perspective, this is beneficial because society gains when people pursue the higher levels of education called for by today's important occupations; individuals also benefit because they reap rewards by doing things that benefit society (recall the discussion of the functionalist perspective on stratification in Chapter 6).

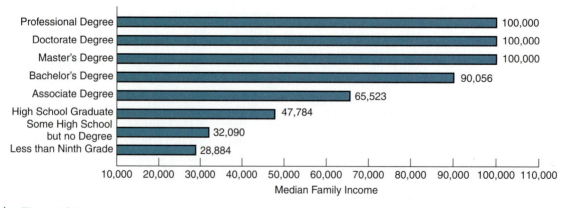

Figure 12.1

Median Income of Family Based on Educational Attainment of the Head of the Household, United States, 2006

Source: U.S. Bureau of the Census, *Current Population Survey*, Annual Social and Economic Supplement (Washington, DC: U.S. Government Printing Office, 2007).

The Conflict Perspective

Although the functionalist view emphasizes the contribution of educational institutions to the maintenance of the whole system, the conflict view stresses the fact that education can be a mechanism that powerful groups use to limit the opportunities of the less powerful in society (Hurn, 1992). The following sections discuss how such limitation can happen.

Promoting Existing Political and Economic Arrangements

According to Marxian conflict theorists, schools in practically all societies tend to promote the existing political and economic structures, which in turn serve the interests of the more powerful groups (Apple, 1982; Carnoy & Levin, 1985). In the United States schools promote the ideology of capitalism—the value of the private ownership of goods, private enterprise, and profit making—and two-party democracy. Although other economic and political arrangements may be discussed, especially at the college level, the overwhelming message is that capitalism and democracy are the preferred systems, verging almost on the sacred.

At a more subtle level, schools support existing economic and social arrangements by teaching a hidden curriculum, *the training of students in values and norms that help to perpetuate the existing system of stratification.* The hidden curriculum exists side by side with the formal curriculum of reading, mathematics, and science. For example, students are trained to be submissive and cooperative in bureaucratic and authoritarian settings. After all, beginning in kindergarten, at least in public schools, children learn to be compliant and cooperative and to adapt to the schedule of the schools as established by educational authorities.

School begins and ends when the authorities say it will, and topics change with a set rhythm that may be totally unrelated to the needs and moods of many of the children. "Good" students sit quietly at their desks, raise their hands and wait to be given permission before speaking, and address teachers and school administrators with respect and deference. Grades reward students who fit best in this system and punish those who create problems by being disruptive. In short, the hidden curriculum produces a cooperative and compliant labor force for work in the corporations and bureaucracies of a capitalist economy. Such behavior helps to maintain a system in which the powerful retain and expand their wealth and authority, although many workers experience alienation and frustration in their jobs.

The Credentials Race

For much of the twentieth century, there was a credentials race in the United States (Collins, 1979; Dore, 1997). In 1940, fewer than 25 percent of adults in the United States had graduated from high school, in comparison with 85 percent today (Figure 12.2). The number of college degrees conferred rose from fewer than 500,000 in 1950 to one and a half million per year today, and the number of doctorates from 6,000 to more than 50,000. Functionalists would argue that this "credentialing" of U.S. society reflects the higher level of skill and education needed for occupations today. Yet, evidence exists that the minimum educational requirements for many jobs today are higher than are actually necessary to do the job. Therefore, only a part of the increase in educational requirements for jobs during the twentieth century can be accounted for by *actual* increases in skills and expertise needed to perform these tasks (Brown, 1995; Collins, 1979; Lowe, 2000).

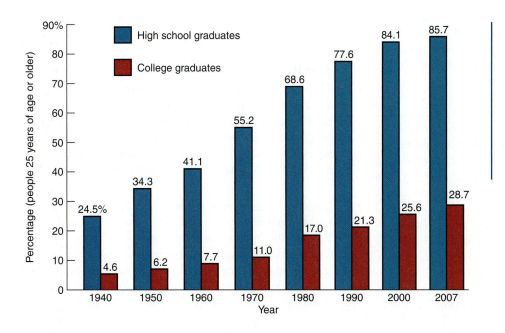

Figure 12.2

Percentage of Adults, Who Are High School and College Graduates in the United States, 1940–2007

Note: From *Statistical Abstract of the United States*, by U.S. Bureau of the Census, Washington, DC: U.S. Government Printing Office, Various years; U.S. Bureau of the Census, *Current Population Survey*, Annual Social and Economic Supplement, 2007.

Furthermore, studies of insurance sellers and clerks show that better educated people in these jobs are not necessarily better or more productive workers than their less educated counterparts (Berg, 1975). Other studies show that although educational credentials are important in getting people jobs in organizations, they do not have much impact on whether these people are promoted (Bills, 1988).

Why, then, is there such a race for higher credentials? Conflict theorists argue that some groups have a vested interest in placing greater emphasis on the importance of educational degrees. For example, raising the educational threshold for particular jobs is an easy out for harried personnel managers who can use educational degrees as a simple sifting device in selecting employees. In addition, educational institutions have a vested interest in this degree inflation because it generates a greater demand for their educational services. In fact, schools help to create this situation by producing more people with degrees than are needed. Students may not need the degrees to *do* the job, but they need the degrees to *get* the job. Most important, however, degree inflation serves as a way of maintaining the privileges of some while controlling the aspirations of others. By elevating degree requirements for particular jobs, people who have earned the degrees, or who are in a position to obtain them, protect their own positions and those of their offspring by restricting competition. Fifty years ago, it was the affluent who were likely to have a high school diploma and thus had access to the better jobs that required a high school education. Today, with high school education increasingly common, the college or graduate degree represents the minimum requirement for many jobs. The less affluent and minority group members have more difficulty obtaining those degrees and thus getting the jobs that require them. Furthermore, argue conflict theorists, because the inequities result from differences in educational levels, they have legitimacy in the eyes of people who believe that educational opportunities are open to everyone. But are there equal educational opportunities in the United States?

EDUCATION AND SOCIAL INEQUALITY   As was explained in Chapter 6, educational attainment in industrial nations is the most critical factor in determining upward social mobility, especially intergenerational mobility. Yet although education makes social mobility possible, according to the conflict perspective, education also makes it much more likely that the offspring of affluent people will succeed than the offspring of the poor. The reason is that affluent youngsters usually attend better schools in which the staff and resources are of higher quality and the atmosphere is more encouraging of academic achievement. In addition, the families of affluent youngsters are supportive of educa-

tional accomplishments and are better able to pay for tutors or tuition for private schools and college. Without such advantages, less-affluent children are more likely to experience failure in school. And failure leads to reduced willingness to put forth the necessary effort to succeed, which increases the likelihood of further failures.

The sociologist James Coleman and his associates (1966), in a report now popularly known as the Coleman Report, documented how these factors affected African Americans in the 1960s. Coleman found that racial segregation in U.S. public schools was extensive. He also discovered that African American students performed more poorly than other racial or ethnic groups. These black students, Coleman and his coauthors argued, suffered from poor facilities and teachers and from school and home environments that provided little motivation to the students to excel. The study also showed that black students who attended desegregated schools with a better motivational atmosphere showed improved academic performance. The motivational atmosphere in the school basically had to do with the proportion of lower-class to middle-class pupils. Blacks attending schools with a middle-class atmosphere did better than blacks attending schools with a lower-class atmosphere.

The overall argument of the conflict perspective, then, is that powerful forces in educational institutions work toward social reproduction, or *passing social and economic inequalities on from one generation to the next and thus perpetuating the existing stratification system.* Just as well-to-do parents can pass their money and property on to their offspring, they also pass along their social and cultural advantages in the form of access to the education that will assist their offspring. Figure 12.1 points to one impact of this social reproduction: the effect of education on a person's economic position in society.

The Interactionist Perspective

The interactionist perspective focuses on face-to-face social interaction between teacher and student in the classroom. It recognizes that social expectations and social meanings are a part of that interaction and play a powerful role in what students learn and accomplish in school as well as how they feel about themselves.

LABELING   Students in school are subjected to constant evaluation between the ages of five and eighteen, because the purpose of schooling, in addition to transmitting skills, is to judge how well students have learned and, by implication, how competent and intelligent they have become. A great deal is at stake for students because their grades and their teachers' written reports about them become an official record—a publicly stamped label—that follows them throughout their lives. According to the interactionist perspective, this labeling can have serious consequences for students (Wilkinson & Marrett, 1985). Chapter 5 noted that labeling a person as a deviant can serve as a self-fulfilling prophecy when people begin to conform to the expectations of the labels attached to them. Likewise, a similar process can occur in the classroom when teachers label students as bright or dull. Once students are so labeled, teachers may treat them a little differently, possibly giving the students who are labeled bright a little more encouragement and assistance. In addition, the students labeled dull may assume that there is some truth in the label and may not try very hard. The result of both the students' and the teachers' reactions may be reinforcement of the label (Dusek, 1985).

ABILITY GROUPING   Another practice common in elementary and secondary schools that has important effects on students is tracking (Hallinan, 1996). *Tracking*, or *ability grouping*, refers to clustering people together into classes or tracks within classes that contain students of comparable abilities or students with similar educational goals (academic versus nonacademic tracks). Tracking is done on the assumption that students will be better able to learn if they are in a classroom with others who have equal ability. The danger in tracking, however, is that the track becomes a label that creates expectations on the part of both the teacher and the students regarding how well individual students will perform. Teachers may tend to encourage performances that are consistent with the track a student is in, and students assume that being placed in a track indicates the performance level of which they are capable (Oakes, 1985). Because of these problems, some schools have discarded formalized ability grouping.

Education in the United States

You should be able to discuss the emergence of educational institutions in the United States, analyze schools as bureaucracies, evaluate how effective schools are, and describe the reforms that have been instituted.

Educational institutions in the United States are as formalized and specialized as those of any other nation. They are also an outgrowth of the country's particular historical and cultural development. This chapter will briefly review that history before moving on to some current controversies and debates about how well U.S. schools work.

A Historical View

During the colonial period, education in the United States was mostly informal, with children learning what they needed to know from family and friends. In fact, the primary purpose of schooling then was to further one's religious training (Mayer, 1961). Literacy was valued because it enabled people to read the Bible, but most of what the average person needed to know in order to make a living was learned from parents and other relatives while growing up. Schools and colleges existed, but extensive formal education was limited to a small elite. It was not until 1864 that the first state compulsory school attendance law was enacted. In 1900, only 6 percent of the seventeen-year-olds in the United States had graduated from high school. With little paperwork and few specialized occupations, a lack of education in a preindustrial United States was not a great hindrance for most people.

As the nation began to industrialize, education underwent drastic changes, and an educational revolution began in the 1870s (Hurn, 1992; Trow, 1961). Increased specialization created thousands of new occupations and generated tremendous amounts of new information. It became more and more necessary for all people to receive a substantial amount of education in order to earn a living in the new industrial nation. The growth of science led to the creation of more technical knowledge, and the expanding size of bureaucratic organizations called for more managers and supervisors to coordinate the activities of other employees. Information became more important in large enterprises with highly specialized workforces, and white-collar workers possessing a mastery of literacy skills controlled this information. The number of white-collar workers in the United States doubled between 1950 and 1975, and the number of technical and professional occupations grew at a rate much faster than the expansion of the workforce as a whole.

Basic educational skills such as the ability to read and write are no longer a privilege of the elite. They have become essential to maintaining even the simplest lifestyle. Consider the things one might do in a normal day that call for such skills: read street signs or textbooks, fill out an online job application form, balance a checkbook, write an e-mail or text message to a friend, or sign one's name on a check.

Schools as Bureaucracies

It has been many years since students in the United States attended one-room schoolhouses where young people of varying ages were clustered together with one teacher to learn the three Rs. Much has changed since those days. As the educational system has become more

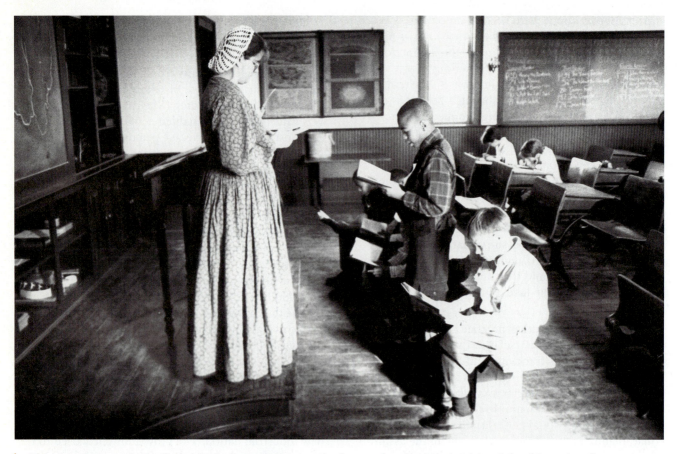

This early classroom in the United States illustrates the growth of mass education in industrial societies. Mass education provided people with the literacy skills they needed in order to work in an industrial, high technology economy and helped to "Americanize" the children of immigrants.

complex and knowledge has become highly specialized, schools have become more bureaucratic. Chapter 4 describes the bureaucratic organization of universities in some detail. Most primary and secondary schools have also become bureaucracies—some would say even more so than many universities—and the consequences continue to be the source of considerable debate. School officials and many sociologists maintain that bureaucracy is necessary in order to deal with the sheer volume of students and the ever-expanding curriculum. Certainly, as we discuss in Chapter 4, bureaucracies can process large numbers of students more efficiently than can other forms of organization. On a more subtle level, sociologist Talcott Parsons (1959) argued that the bureaucratic nature of schools is beneficial in modern societies because it socializes children into the impersonal, competitive adult world with its emphasis on secondary relationships (see Chapter 3). In schools, children learn something that they typically do not learn in families: Bureaucratic schedules operate independently of people's needs and desires. In this way, people learn what to expect in the business and government bureaucracies in which they will probably work as adults.

Critics observe that there is a conflict of interest between the needs of the educational system to process large numbers of students and the individual student's need to be treated as a person rather than a number on a computer printout (Apple, 1982; Giroux, 1985). These observers charge that bureaucratic schools are a classic example of *goal displacement*, where teachers and administrators devote more effort to maintaining the existing system and preserving their jobs than to the traditional goals of the educational process. In addition, modern bureaucratic educational systems tend to stifle creativity, originality, and independent thinking (Katz, 1987). Lesson plans, hall monitors, and rigid class periods promote inflexibility and dependence rather than curiosity and a desire to think independently. By contrast, some critics dispute both the positive and negative views of modern education by calling attention to the rather loosely structured nature of U.S. educational systems, where rules are precariously negotiated by various participants (such as teachers, administrators, and parent groups), with the end result being chaos rather than the kind of efficient organization usually associated with well-functioning bureaucratic institutions (Tyler, 1985).

Effectiveness of the Educational System

For decades, criticism has been directed at the U.S. educational system over whether students are developing adequate competence in the basic skills they will need to make a contribution to society and help the United States retain a competitive edge in the world. In 2007, for example, the Educational Testing Service (Kirsch et al., 2007) released a report indicating that schools are failing to prepare students adequately for work-related positions in an increasingly technological society. Performance on standardized tests, such as the Scholastic Assessment Test (SAT), has fallen substantially since the 1960s, although scores have risen some since 1990 (U.S. Department of Education, 2004). Numerous studies conclude that high school students in Europe and Japan take more demanding science courses than do U.S. students, and that U.S. students do more poorly on science and mathematics tests than do students in many other nations (see Figure 12.3). Most studies on this topic conclude that students in the United States display a disturbing lack of knowledge about science, geography, history, and government; many students, for example, cannot identify Adolph Hitler, do not know who our enemies were in World War II, or know that the Bill of Rights amendment to the Constitution guarantees freedom of speech and religion (Hess, 2008).

Yet, controversy rages over whether and in what realms U.S. schools are failing. Psychologist David Berliner and sociologist Bruce Biddle (1995) argue that much of the criticism is based on a misunderstanding of the data, or in some cases a deliberate attempt to ignore the facts in order to trash the schools. They argue, for example, that SAT scores are no longer falling, that school spending has gone up because we ask so much of the schools in terms of special education programs, and that many standardized tests, such as the SAT, are poor measures of educational quality and achievement. The schools may not be getting any better, Berliner and Biddle argue, but they probably haven't been getting any worse either.

Most researchers agree that, while some students attend good schools and get an excellent education, other students are definitely failed by the educational system. Students who are especially likely to be failed by the schools are those from low-income families, those whose parents have low educational attainment, those from single-parent families, and those who cannot speak English well (Orfield, 2004). The result is an unacceptably high school-dropout rate in the United States, with African American and Hispanic American students especially hurt (see Figure 12.4). The landscape of opportunities for people who drop out of school is bleak. The unemployment rate for dropouts is about twice as high as for those who graduate from high school; the unemployment rate among African Americans who have not completed high school is almost 50 percent; in addition, dropouts earn less when they do work, are more likely to commit crimes, and use more public assistance (U.S. Bureau of the Census, 2007, pp. 146, 172). So, a person without a high school diploma today confronts virtually insurmountable obstacles in terms of finding social and economic opportunities.

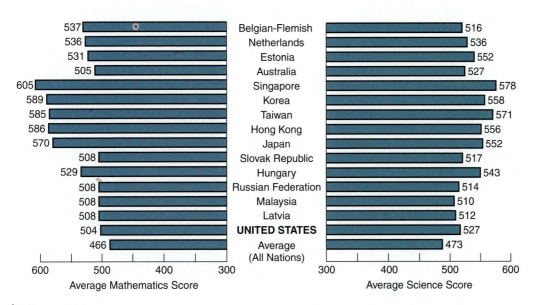

Figure 12.3
Math and Science Test Scores for Eighth Graders, in Various Nations, 2003

Source: Patrick Gonzales et al. *Trends in International Mathematics and Science Study (TIMSS) 2003*. NCES Pub. No. 2005-005. U.S. Department of Education, National Center for Education Statistics. Washington, DC: U.S. Government Printing Office, 2004.

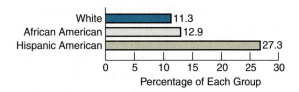

Figure 12.4

High School Dropouts in the United States, 18 to 24 Years Old, by Race and Ethnic Origin, 2005

Note: From *Statistical Abstract of the United States,* 2008 (p. 171) by U.S. Bureau of the Census, 2007, Washington, DC: U.S. Government Printing Office.

Reforms and Trends

A number of reforms have been proposed to help alleviate some of the inadequacies in the schools. This section explores the major innovations, with an eye on evidence regarding their effectiveness.

MAGNET SCHOOLS, CHARTER SCHOOLS, AND CHOICE   Some educators and politicians have suggested that education is like any other consumer market and that schools should compete for students in the same way that other businesses compete for customers—in a free and open competition. If schools have to attract students by convincing them and their parents that they have the best education to offer, then the schools would be motivated to provide the best product: superior teachers, excellent resources, and solid programs. In a competitive market, if schools had a mediocre curriculum or lackluster faculty, their enrollments would decline, and they would either close their doors or improve. This reform is sometimes called *parental choice*; private schools in the United States already operate in such an environment (Coleman, 1992). One way of implementing choice in the public schools would be to permit students to attend any school they please, whether it be in their district or elsewhere in the state. A few years ago, this policy was implemented by developing *magnet schools* that offer special programs in particular areas, such as computer applications or performing arts, in order to attract students. Today, over twenty states allow students some degree of choice in which public school they will attend.

A recent variation on the choice issue is the *charter schools* that have been established in a number of states (U.S. Department of Education, 2004a). Charter schools operate autonomously with a charter directly from the state instead of being under local school district control. They receive state funding but are free from many school district rules and have more freedom than mainstream schools in budgeting, hiring, and curriculum decisions. Charter schools are usually established with some particular curriculum innovation in mind. For example, charter schools have stressed such innovations as experiential learning, team teaching,

and online distance learning using the Internet, to name a few. There are more than 1,600 charter schools in thirty-two states.

Some critics have proposed extending the idea of choice to all of education by having the government give parents a voucher worth enough to pay for a child's education at any public school. Parents would then send their child to the school of their choice, paying for it with the voucher money. Some supporters of voucher plans even propose that parents be able to use the vouchers at private religious schools as partial payment of their tuition, although this may violate the constitutional separation of church and state.

There is both strong support for and opposition to choice, charter schools, and vouchers (Astin, 1992; Smith & Meier, 1995). Proponents argue that these educational innovations offer students more choices and that the competition among schools will enhance the quality. In addition, charter schools encourage parents to become active in their children's school and are more responsive to the needs of the community. Critics of these innovations, however, argue that they may promote more segregation and divisiveness because some parents, both white and nonwhite, would likely choose their children's school on the basis of its racial or ethnic composition. A second criticism is that parents may not always be in the best position to assess the quality of schools. As in other arenas of open competition, desperate schools might sometimes resort to exaggeration, trickery, or downright fraud in their efforts to attract students, and the educations of some children would likely suffer. A third criticism is that some families would be forced to use schools near their homes, especially the poor without access to transportation. These schools would have meager resources and be poorly run because they could not attract students from other communities, but they would survive by getting enough students from poor families in the neighborhood to keep their doors open. Applying Sociology: Evaluating Educational Innovations describes the contributions of applied sociologists in the assessment of educational innovations such as charter schools and vouchers.

BACK TO BASICS   Social science research shows that students in Roman Catholic schools perform better than children in public schools, even when racial and social-class differences between the schools are taken into account (Bryk, Lee, & Holland, 1993; Coleman, Hoffer, & Kilgore, 1982; Marsh, 1991). One reason for this success is that Catholic schools place more emphasis on a strong core curriculum and require students to take more academically demanding course work. Thus, students in Catholic schools are likely to take more academic basics, such as science, math, and history, and fewer nonacademic courses, such as auto mechanics or physical education. Another reason for the better performance in Catholic schools is that they have more effective discipline, with more emphasis on obedience and respect for authority. This emphasis creates a climate that enables teachers to do their job with less disruption or fear of danger and encourages students to learn.

Many educational reformers and parents have pushed for such a back-to-basics approach, with an emphasis on the traditional core curriculum and a return to strong discipline. Many schools have adopted some of these changes, reducing elective courses, having more required courses, and in some cases establishing strict dress codes with punishments for violation. Some states have established standardized examinations that students must pass before receiving a high school diploma.

EARLY CHILDHOOD INTERVENTIONS Virtually all criticism of education in the United States recommends devoting more resources to the early educational experiences of young children, especially low-income children, to create a developmental foundation that will support later learning and achievement. Since the Coleman Report in the 1960s, research has documented that some children come to school educationally handicapped because their home environment does not provide them with the support and assistance that would make learning more effective. Early childhood educational interventions can overcome many of these handicaps (Karoly et al., 1998). In Chapter 6, Applying Sociology: Creating and Evaluating Programs That Assist the Poor discusses one example of such early intervention, the Head Start program. Head Start is a preschool program to help poor children prepare for school. Head Start children are taught reading and language skills that most preschool children learn at home from their parents. Research over the years has provided strong evidence that Head Start gives poor children some significant advantages. Head Start children, when compared to other poor children, are less likely to be assigned to special education classes or to be kept back a grade in school, and they do better on mathematics achievement tests and show more improvement in IQ scores. Head Start children are also

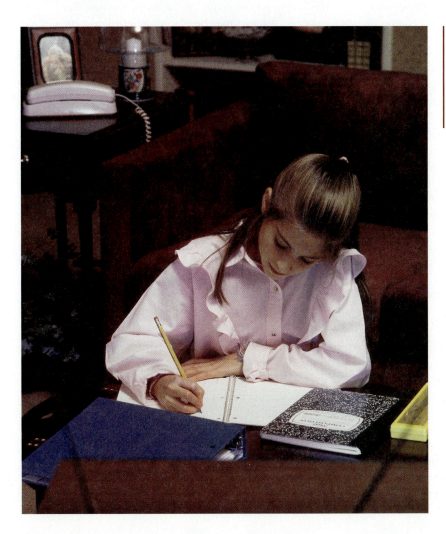

This student is being schooled at home. Home schooling has grown in the United States in part because of a dissatisfaction with traditional public education, which is seen by some as ineffective and by others as promoting values that conflict with the values that parents wish to expose their children to.

Applying Sociology   Evaluating Educational Innovations

One of the major activities of sociologists in the educational realm is the development and evaluation of innovative educational programs for schools. Those who fund education—private foundations, the government, and private citizens—want solid evidence that their money is providing some positive benefit to students. Earlier this chapter discussed the work of sociologist James Coleman in assessing the impact of segregated schools on student achievement. Because of this applied sociological research, new educational policies were developed that focused on desegregating schools and providing compensatory education. Since then, applied sociologists have continued to monitor whether such policies are having positive outcomes, and the results of some of this work were reported in this chapter.

Applied sociologists and other social scientists have also conducted research that is designed to assess the impact of choice, charter schools, and vouchers. Basically, the research involves comparing charter schools and their students with traditional schools and their students (or voucher students with nonvoucher students). The research conducted thus far does not provide much support for the alleged benefits of choice and charter schools (Frankenberg & Lee, 2003; Renzulli & Evans, 2005; Rimer, 2003). Charter schools tend to rely on a much younger, less experienced faculty that is considerably less likely to have a teaching credential and is less well paid than faculty in public schools. This is especially true in schools with low-income and minority students. In addition, choice and charter schools tend to be more highly segregated—much more so than traditional public schools. As for student achievement, studies are now accumulating that show consistently that charter school students do not perform better academically than do public school students, and by many measures they do worse. In addition, these findings have been supported even when comparing students of similar races and socioeconomic backgrounds (Braun, Jenkins, & Grigg, 2006; Nelson, Rosenberg, & Van Meter, 2004; U. S. Department of Education, 2004a). As for vouchers, research doesn't find much difference in academic performance between students who use vouchers to attend private schools and equivalent students who remain in public schools (Dillon, 2007; Metcalf et al., 2002). So, charter schools and vouchers, to this point, do not

appear to provide a panacea for the problems found in public schools. This lack of impact probably reflects the fact that many of the factors that influence school performance (socioeconomic status, family environment, and so on) are not changed just because a student attends a charter school or a private school through vouchers. Nonetheless, policy makers can use this research in deciding whether to continue or change such educational innovations.

Applied sociologists not only work on problems confronting students but also those confronting teachers and school administrators. Schools, after all, are organizations, and the teachers and administrators are influenced by how well or poorly those organizations work. Sociologists with expertise in organizations and organizational behavior can conduct an organizational diagnosis, discussed in Chapter 4, which uses sociological theories and research to assess how well organizations operate and how their performance can be improved (Harrison, 1991). In some schools, the role structure for teachers may be ambiguous or contradictory, and this role strain can cause difficulties for teachers. For example, teachers may be placed under competing and contradictory demands as school boards demand one thing, parents demand another, and students insist on yet a third approach. The teachers' ability to navigate this confusing terrain depends on whether they have clear authority in their classrooms and whether they have consistent direction from principals and other school administrators. In fact, much sociological research shows that teacher performance improves when they have strong leadership in a principal and when the school is organized like a community, with supportive relationships among teachers and a sense of shared values and mission (Lee, Dedrick, & Smith, 1991).

Applied sociologists, then, analyze the role structure and organizational authority in schools and make recommendations for change to enhance teaching effectiveness. Of course, some of these educational problems are not easily resolved because schools are subject to inherently conflicting demands. In these cases, clinical sociologists and other counselors work with teachers on ways to prevent the organizational problems from creating personal stress or depression (Saunders, 1991).

---

less likely to repeat a grade, get in trouble with the law, or become teenage mothers. In addition, they have a better family life and more positive self-concepts. Finally, as young adults, Head Start children are more likely to go to college and hold a steady skilled job.

With benefits such as these, Head Start children should be better equipped to support themselves and their families as adults.

Despite its clear benefits to society, Head Start provides services to only some low-income children.

Many educational reformers argue that the benefits of extending such compensatory education programs to all low-income children would be enormous.

SCHOOL INTEGRATION In part because of the Coleman Report's conclusions about the negative effect of school segregation on student performance, efforts at school integration, sometimes by busing students from one school to another, have been made since the 1960s. Such integration, it was believed, would improve the performance of minority students as well as reduce prejudice and discrimination in the long run.

Busing and integration have been highly controversial policies. Have they worked? In terms of school achievement, some studies have found improvements with integration and others have not (Armor, 1989; Longshore & Prager, 1985; Rist, 1979).

Overall, integration has probably made modest improvements in school achievement by African American students, especially when students are integrated in the early grades. The reason that the impact has not been more uniformly positive is because so many other factors—socioeconomic status, family background, racial tensions in the schools, and the manner in which integration is accomplished—also influence achievement. However, there are signs that school integration may be producing benefits beyond its impact on school achievement. Research in the early 1980s suggested that school integration has helped to reduce racial isolation in the United States and that racial tensions and stereotyping will be reduced in the future as a result (Hawley et al., 1983). Furthermore, recent research suggests that the experience in desegregated schools has an impact on blacks later in life: They are more likely to attend predominantly white colleges, socialize with whites outside of school, and live in integrated neighborhoods as adults (Braddock, 1985; Braddock, Crain, & McPartland, 1984). In addition, concerns about integration and busing have led to creative developments in schools designed to attract both white and minority students such as the magnet schools discussed earlier. So, it may be that the impact of school integration will be more subtle and will surface only after integration has been a reality for a long period, possibly decades.

Nevertheless, despite efforts to integrate the schools, the Civil Rights Project at Harvard's Graduate School of Education reports that schools in the United States have become substantially more segregated over the past few decades, especially for African Americans in the south and Hispanic Americans everywhere (Orfield & Lee, 2004). This situation results from a number of factors: segregated housing patterns, court decisions that have freed school districts from desegregation orders, and a public that is indifferent to the desirability of integrated schools.

UPGRADING SCHOOLS AND TEACHERS In 2004, the Teaching Commission, a panel of leaders in government, business, and education, published a report concluding that many teachers in U.S. schools have not been adequately trained in teaching skills or in the subjects that they teach (Friedman, 2006). Some teachers have neither a college major nor a minor in the main subjects they teach. Given circumstances such as these, most critics of the U.S. educational system recommend devoting more resources to schooling so that teachers have the skills, services, staff, and up-to-date technology they need to be effective. Many critics also argue that society needs to rethink how it prepares and motivates teachers. Teachers should have salaries and opportunities that will make teaching competitive with other professional occupations so that the best people are drawn to teaching. Higher salaries would help, but teachers' pay could also be linked to merit. For example, schools might have a merit hierarchy, with master teachers receiving higher pay and having some responsibility for assisting other teachers to develop their skills and test innovative teaching techniques. In addition, teachers might be subject to standardized testing on a periodic basis in order to assess their continuing competence. Just as many other professions require graduate or professional degrees, some critics suggest that a bachelor's degree be required as a prerequisite for the professional study of teaching and that the minimum degree for being certified as a teacher be a master's degree.

PRIVATIZATION AND HOME SCHOOLING Dissatisfaction with education in the United States, especially public education, has led to two important trends that have grown in prominence in the last two decades. Each, in its own way, represents a rejection of public education. One trend is an effort to privatize education—hire private corporations to run public schools. The primary motivation behind this trend has been the poor performance of some schools. Private education companies have argued that private, competitive companies, confronting the rigors of the marketplace, will be motivated to provide better education for the students in their schools and do it less expensively than the state can. If the private companies don't succeed, states will stop contracting with the companies to provide educational services.

Private education has been around for some time, in the form of private or religious schools where parents pay the tuition of their children. However, this new trend retains the public school system and the government's responsibility to provide education for all, but it achieves this purpose by contracting out to private companies to provide the educational services. Does this approach work? Research does not provide any evidence that these private companies do better at educating children than do traditional public schools

(U.S. General Accounting Office, 2002). They also don't seem to do worse. Opponents of such privatization argue that education of the young is a moral obligation of society, working through government, and that it should not be put into the hands of a private company. In addition, opponents argue that the rigors of the marketplace will inevitably tempt some of the private companies to cut corners in order to enhance profits—to the detriment of the children.

Home schooling has also grown, in part as a rejection of traditional public education (Lines, 2000; Wichers, 2001). As many as two million children are home schooled each year, possibly 4 percent of all school-age children. Some children are taught at home for only a few years, whereas others may go through high school being taught at home. Some school systems provide supports for home-schooled children, such as letting them participate in school athletics or other school programs that would not be available to the children at home. Parents' motivations for home schooling their children are varied: to provide what they believe is a more rigorous education; to provide moral, ethical, or religious training that they see as lacking in the public schools; to provide a safe place free of drugs or violence; or to provide a racial, ethnic, or cultural identity for their children that is lacking in the schools.

Modern technology has assisted the growth of the home-schooling movement. Through computer software and the Internet, parents can now gain access to educational materials and programs that greatly expand the educational activities that parents can provide in the home. And research evidence suggests that home schooling does a pretty good job of educating children. Most research shows that home-schooled students do at least as well, academically and in college, as students who go to traditional public schools.

So, both these trends—privatization and home schooling—are likely to be around for some time and need to be assessed with further research to see how they contribute to the process of education in the United States. There is, needless to say, much controversy over all of the reforms and trends discussed. This is not surprising given the highly pluralistic nature of the United States. The country has many religious, racial, ethnic, and subcultural groups, each expecting the schools to promote, or at least not oppose, its values and lifestyle.

Higher Education

Just as U.S. elementary and secondary schools have been criticized, so have colleges and universities. In the 1980s, for example, philosopher Allan Bloom (1987) published a scathing critique to the effect that college education has become heavily oriented toward narrowly focused, vocationally directed education in fields such as accounting, nursing, and social work. The curriculum has become directed by the students' demands that their education lead to a job and financial success on graduation. The result is a curriculum that downplays or completely ignores areas of literature, philosophy, and the humanities that, Bloom argues, contain the central beliefs and values of Western civilization. Furthermore, Bloom contends, the student, feminist, and Black Power movements of the 1960s and 1970s have led to the emergence of a cultural relativism in college curricula that views all values and cultures as equal and demands little of students in terms of moral decision making or critical thinking. Finally, according to Bloom, efforts to introduce multiculturalism in the curriculum have resulted in the displacement of what he regards as more valuable teachings of the Western heritage. As a consequence of these trends, college students today have a limited appreciation for the roots of the culture of the Western world and the United States.

A very different perspective on higher education was presented by historian Lawrence Levine (1996) in the 1990s. Levine, for example, praises the trend toward multiculturalism as an inevitable and essential response to the racial, ethnic, and cultural diversity that is increasingly characteristic of the United States. Colleges must adapt to these changes. Furthermore, Levine sees a curriculum narrowly focused on Western classics as overly Eurocentric: Students are exposed only to the thoughts of white males of Western European origin and learn little of the literature and art of women or of peoples in Asia, Africa, and the Americas. Instead, colleges should explore the widest range of cultural values and lifestyles in order to most completely enhance an understanding of the human condition. However, Levine is critical of some dimensions of higher education today, especially the tendency for courses to be isolated from one another rather than forming an integrated whole throughout the student's education. He also argues that university faculty tend to become isolated into their own separate, heavily jargonistic disciplines and to give too much weight to research productivity rather than teaching skills in making promotion and tenure decisions.

Other criticisms of today's colleges and universities have surfaced. For example, in 1994, Ernest L. Boyer, president of the Carnegie Foundation for the Advancement of Teaching, criticized colleges and universities in the United States on quite different grounds, arguing that "higher education's historic commitment to service [to society] seems to have diminished" (p. A48). He challenged higher education to put more emphasis on the practical and to tie research to practice in a way that helps people solve problems and improves the human condition.

A final criticism of higher education has been offered by Derek Bok (2003), who was president of

Harvard University for some years. Bok argues that many of the research activities of universities are gradually becoming commercialized and privatized. This is especially true in the fields of medicine and the life sciences where research discoveries, often funded by public money, may have substantial commercial and financial implications. In some cases, universities sell to corporations the right to use scientific discoveries while other corporations fund the positions of faculty members who engage in research relevant to the corporation. Some university researchers commercially exploit their research findings by patenting the results of research or establishing private companies to develop and market products based on their research. Bok believes that this commercialization threatens the open search for knowledge that is at the core of academic values and activities. Science and knowledge develop most fully where openness, sharing, collegiality, and peer review are the predominant motifs. The private exploitation of knowledge leads to secrecy and conflicts of interest and ultimately compromises the development of knowledge. In addition, we are seeing the emergence of for-profit, oftentimes online, institutions of higher education where the fundamental goal

is to turn a profit rather than to produce knowledge or provide the best learning experience for students. Bok believes that this commercialization of higher education will compromise the ability of colleges and universities to fulfill their traditional academic goals of educating students and producing knowledge that is useful to society as a whole.

To appreciate educational institutions in the United States more fully, it is helpful to compare them with those in another advanced industrial nation. Other Worlds, Other Ways: Japan points to some ways in which Japanese education differs from education in the United States.

Education, Communication, and the Mass Media

You should be able to discuss the mass media in terms of when they emerged; how they affect people, schools, and society; who controls them; and whether they constitute neocolonization.

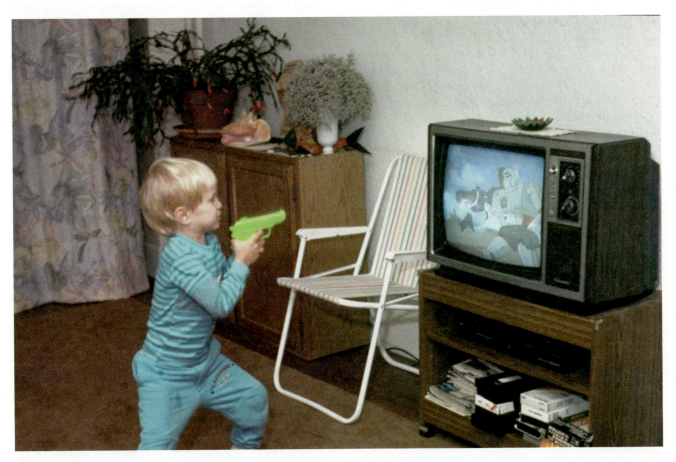

Considerable research has now accumulated to support the conclusion that watching violence on television or in the movies or playing violent video games does increase the likelihood that children and youth will act aggressively or violently themselves.

Other Worlds, Other Ways

JAPAN: VARIATIONS IN EDUCATIONAL INSTITUTIONS IN INDUSTRIAL SOCIETIES

When Japan was defeated in World War II, the United States and its allies imposed demands on their foe that were to change the structure of Japanese society significantly. The changes basically pushed Japan toward a more democratic and egalitarian state in which the hereditary monarchy had less control than formerly over government and society. Included among the changes were giving workers the right to organize and extending complete civil rights to women. In education, the U.S. Occupation sought to eliminate the militarism and extreme nationalism that existed in the schools prior to the war. This involved the dismissal of teachers and administrators who held such views and revising textbooks. The Occupation also gave the Japanese educational system the same basic structure that education has in the United States: six years of elementary school and three years each of junior high school and high school, followed by four years of college.

Japanese education, however, has some features that are quite different from education in the United States (Brint, 1998; Gutek, 1993; Kumagai, 1996). One is that the central government, through the Ministry of Education, controls Japanese educational policy, curriculum design, and even textbook selection. By contrast, the United States decentralizes these matters to the level of state or local school boards. Decentralization provides parents with more control over educational institutions, but it also makes for significant disparities in the resources available to students in schools and in the achievement levels of schools.

Another difference is that Japan treats teachers much better than the United States does. Japanese teachers have a strong national union that assists them with both salary negotiations and having an input into educational policy. They also receive the equivalent of tenure when they are hired, with the assurance of a lifelong job as long as they do not seriously violate expected conduct. Teachers in the United States must earn tenure over a period of three to five years, and they then can be terminated if student enrollments decline. In addition, Japanese teachers are paid better than engineers and some businesspeople, and they are held in high esteem by their fellow citizens (Hayakawa, 1986).

One of the most striking differences between Japanese and U.S. education is the nature of the transitions from one school level to another (Feinberg, 1993; Kumagai, 1996). During the last year in junior high school, Japanese students take a high school entrance examination, which is the key determinant of placement in high school. Students can take the exam for any public, academic high school in their district, but if they flunk the exam, they will probably have to attend a lower-prestige private school or public, vocational high school. The high school entrance exam is so important to Japanese teenagers that a whole industry of private tutors, "cram schools," and magazines and materials has emerged to help them choose the right school and pass the exam.

Entrance into the government-run national universities and the higher-prestige private universities is also determined almost entirely by an entrance examination. Students are allowed to take the exam for only two universities during a given year. Once accepted to a university, students are admitted to a particular department, or major. If they wish to change departments, they must seek entrance to the university again, since each department sets the score on the exam that will be needed for admission to the department.

Because of the stakes involved in the examinations at the end of junior high and high school, Japanese students tend to be much more serious and to study much harder than do students in the United States. Junior high and high school curricula in Japan are also more advanced in science, mathematics, and foreign languages. In some areas, Japanese high school graduates probably have the same knowledge level as college graduates in the United States. The intense pace does not continue at the college level, however, as students seem to ease up after their hard charge through the lower levels. One educational expert concluded: "The Japanese university is notorious as the weakest link in its educational system in terms of the development of academic skills" (Feinberg, 1993, p. 198). ■

This chapter has stated that educational institutions attempt to influence people to adopt new values and acquire new skills. Education is not alone in this effort. Chapter 3 notes that whereas the family is the primary agency of socialization, the mass media are also influential in this regard. The mass media also affect education: Modern mass media have become an important adjunct in the schools' efforts to influence people, while at the same time the media compete with the schools for people's time and attention. The media have become highly controversial because of their power and pervasiveness and because they bring both advantages and disadvantages. This analysis of educational institutions closes with an assessment of the communications and media industries.

Emergence of the Mass Media

The mass media consist of print media, such as books, magazines, and newspapers, and electronic media in the form of television, radio, and the Internet. The print media were the earliest forms of mass media, and their growth depended on a literate population. In any society where most of the population is illiterate, the reach of the print media will be limited. There were high rates of illiteracy in the United States before the twentieth century, a situation that is still true in less developed nations, where 30 percent or more of the people are illiterate. In fact, mass education and the print media tend to expand together, with the former providing a large populace with the skills necessary for the expansion of the latter.

In the fifteenth century, Johannes Gutenberg invented a printing press that used movable type, an invention that opened the door to printing large quantities of text. Single sheets of information and small pamphlets were printed in the eighteenth century. Eventually, the newspaper emerged, which is printed on a regular basis and contains a wide range of information aimed at a whole community. As more people learned to read and newspapers became more widely available, they became a significant source of communication and influence. There were news articles about political and economic events of the day, of course, but there were also advertisements in which businesspeople tried to sell products to consumers. Thus the print media significantly expanded the network of social influence that surrounded people.

In the twentieth century, the print media continued to grow and became more technologically sophisticated, but the real revolution was the electronic media: radio, telephones, television, and computers. All these devices are, of course, products of the twentieth century. In the United States telephones were fairly widely available before World War II and are virtually universal today, but that statement is not true for many parts of the world. Whereas the United States today has almost one telephone for each person, such nations as China, Thailand, and India have much fewer than this. Radios were also widely available before World War II, but there is still a substantial disparity in numbers of radios between the European nations and the less developed nations (U.S. Bureau of the Census, 2007, p. 856).

Although television was invented before World War II, its mass distribution did not begin until the 1950s, and its growth has been phenomenal. As Figure 3.3 shows, virtually every home in the United States has at least one television, and more than half the households have cable television and VCRs, which are indicators of more extensive and sophisticated use of the medium. In addition, television and newspaper usage show contrasting patterns since 1970: a growth in the number of televisions coinciding with a decline in the per capita circulation of daily newspapers. In short, people are watching television more and reading the newspaper, and probably other printed media, less—a trend that is disturbing to some observers. As with the other mass media, the disparity in the distribution of televisions around the globe is substantial. The United States has far more televisions available to its citizens than does any other nation—eight televisions for every ten people. By contrast, Bangladesh and a number of African countries have eleven or fewer televisions for every one thousand people. Going beyond television and newspapers, the growth in the use of computers and the Internet has been phenomenal in recent years (see Figure 12.5). As vehicles for communicating and distributing information, the online world will undoubtedly be a significant supplement to the more traditional vehicles of television and newspapers in the future, and some believe that, over time, it may completely supplant

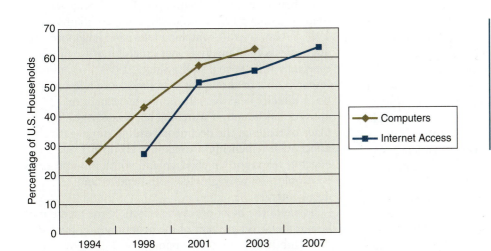

Figure 12.5

U.S. Households with Computers and Internet Access, 1994–2007

Note: From *A Nation Online, 2004: How Americans Are Expanding Their Use of the Internet,* by U.S. Department of Commerce, National Telecommunications and Information Administration 2004, U.S. Bureau of the Census, *Current Population Survey,* Oct. 2007.

them. In addition, media experts expect that the twenty-first century will be witness to the expansion of the mass media and other new communications technologies to all nations around the globe.

Effects of the Mass Media

As the mass media have become a pervasive cultural force, concern has grown about their effects on people's lives. Researchers have been investigating this issue, and some of their research findings are presented in this and other chapters in this book. Some have concluded that the mass media have helped to create a complex popular culture, or *products and activities designed for mass consumption and used for leisure or entertainment* (Brummett, 1991). The media are a part of the popular culture in that the two most common leisure-time activities in the United States are watching television and reading the newspaper. The media also help disseminate information and trends that are a part of the popular culture. Through the media, people can be in touch with such diverse subjects as popular music, professional sports, mud wrestling, and religious services. In a postindustrial economy such as that of the United States, people have free time to devote to these activities and the economic resources to consume the products of popular culture. Sociologists point to the fact that the mass media are not merely vehicles to communicate information; they are also an industry that employs many people and manipulates people's needs and desires through advertising. The explosion of the media is in part a consequence of the expansive nature of a capitalist economy looking for new products to sell and new markets to attract. The intersection of people's desire to be fashionable and to be entertained with capitalism's need to find new markets and enhance profits has made the mass media a major industry in the United States and other affluent nations. When surplus income becomes more available in less developed nations, the mass media are likely to expand there also.

Much of the research on the effects of the mass media has focused on television, because of its pervasiveness, and on the industrial nations where it has been widely available for some time. One focus of concern has been on whether the portrayal of violence in the media can cause people to be more violent in real life. There seems little doubt at this point that television does contribute to the levels of violence in society (Felson, 1996; Huesmann et al., 2003; Potter, 2003). Most research over the past forty years has concluded that when children and youth watch violence on television or in the movies, they are more likely to act aggressively or violently themselves, especially in situations that are conducive to violence. The impact is greater for males than for females and for

children who are more aggressive to begin with (Josephson, 1987). Children between the ages of eight and twelve seem to be especially vulnerable to the effects of watching violence on television. Research has also begun to emerge on the impact on children of playing violent video games. There is much less research on this than on the effects of television and movies, so our conclusions are considerably more tentative. But the research is pointing in the same direction: Playing or watching violent video games leads children to become more aggressive, at least in the short term (Emes, 1997).

Television encourages people toward violence in three ways. First, action dramas can be arousing to viewers and may stimulate them in the direction of physical activity and release. This effect is probably of short duration, from hours to days. Second, television provides viewers with legitimizing models for violence in much the same way that parents or peers can serve as models. In fact, it is difficult to watch television without being exposed to models of violence. Thus, children learn the potential for acting violently in particular situations, and the amount of such violence on television has not declined in the past few decades and may have actually increased. Also, the violence seen on television has some unreal or surrealistic qualities. People bleed little, and the actual pain and agony resulting from a violent attack are rarely portrayed. The consequences of violence often seem antiseptic and rather unimportant. Third, television conveys attitudes and values, and it can teach children to view violence or antisocial behavior as a desirable or "manly" way to behave.

In addition to violence, concern about the effect of watching television has focused on the educational skills and aptitudes of children and youth. A study of three communities in Canada both before and after they had access to television found that children's reading skills declined after the introduction of television, a detrimental effect inasmuch as reading seems to be more beneficial to children's aptitude and achievement than watching television (Gaddy, 1986; Williams, 1986). Also, overall, watching television has more negative effects than positive ones on children's creativity, especially their verbal skills (Singer, 1993). Yet, most research fails to show that watching more television has a directly negative effect on achievement or aptitude (although, if watching television takes the place of reading, the decline in reading can negatively affect achievement) (Gortmaker et al., 1990). So, the effect of television on children and youth in these areas is complex—it may provide both benefits and disadvantages.

One of the most pervasive effects of the media may be not the direct content of the programming but the more subtle and indirect support that it gives to cultural beliefs and stereotypes (Signorielli, 1993).

Sociology of Media and Technology   Effects of the Mass Media

Education in the Electronic World

Modern computer-mediated communications technologies are producing dramatic changes in educational institutions. Some of these changes involve instructional procedures, where the technology enables us to do better the things we did in the past. Other changes involve more fundamental transformations in the social structure of educational institutions made possible by the technology.

As for improvements in instructional procedures, the emerging technologies have produced educational innovations that promise to make the educational process more effective. So, multimedia educational materials combine print, images, and sound into sophisticated and exciting presentations. Software teaches children how to read, write, draw, do math, and design multimedia stories. Some of this software is interactive, which transforms students from passive learners to creative participants in the educational process. In addition, many encyclopedias and other resource materials are now available on CD or online, which means that students with a computer and Internet access can do a substantial amount of research very easily. Such technology will afford teachers many more effective teaching tools to use in the classroom.

These emerging technologies also make it possible to connect teachers, students, and classrooms around the world into networks of educational communities. This is called **distance education** (or *distance learning*) and involves *connecting teachers and educational institutions with students who are physically distant*. It reduces the amount of face-to-face classroom contact or "seat time" and increases the online exposure. It utilizes various technological delivery systems, including broadcast video, Internet chat rooms, videoconferencing, e-mail, instant messaging, and so on. Since modern communications technologies are now interactive, or two-way, communications, students can communicate on a real-time basis with educators and other students at locations around the world. Students in elementary and secondary schools can connect with students in other classes and work together on research and laboratory projects. Such interactive communication can enhance understanding across cultures when the students involved are in classrooms in countries around the world. It may also increase the extent of home schooling as parents and students can tap into a whole host of educational materials from the computer in their home.

These communications technologies reduce or eliminate the constraining factor of geographical distance in the provision of educational services. In its early manifestations, distance education focused on the provision of specific content or individual courses to students. Before long, educators realized that they could provide whole degree programs online, and Internet-based, degree-granting charter schools began to emerge (Dillon, 2008). All of the materials are provided online, and students interact online periodically with a teacher. "Seat time" is eliminated in favor of virtual education. Some Internet-based charter schools purchase the educational materials and even whole degree programs from for-profit corporations. The time may come when much of education will occur in this fashion, and the notion that students must all gather together in a classroom to be taught may become obsolete.

It is this movement of education online that points to the possibility of fundamental transformations in the social structure of education. One change may be the further privatization of education: shifting the responsibility of educating children from the state to private corporations. If online education proves to be convenient and less expensive, more parents may choose this over state-centered educational institutions. As this occurs, it may threaten the integrity of the public school system by diverting control and financial resources from centralized educational authorities to individual schools and educational corporations. In fact, schools could become merely conduits for the provision of educational materials and whole curricula developed, provided, and controlled by for-profit corporations. This would raise the question of who is determining educational policy in the United States: democratically elected state officials, or private educational corporations working with individual schools. The state-centered, centralized, classroom-based education of the past could be replaced by a decentralized system, partially or largely controlled by profit-making corporations, where the "classroom" is an Internet connection (which might be in the student's home, a local library, or a school building). Another consequence of these changes may be a reduction of the power and authority of teachers and their unions as education becomes more decentralized. This could be exacerbated by a tendency for financially pressed schools to see electronic education as a less expensive way of educating children than hiring more teachers or providing teachers with more training. If classrooms can be electronically connected, with teachers and educational materials at remote locations, then school administrators may try to get by with only an Internet connection in the classroom rather than a trained teacher.

Chapter 8 notes that schoolbooks still portray women less frequently overall and also less frequently in jobs outside the home. This practice carries over into newspapers; men appear in newspaper photographs far more often than women, and men are typically photographed doing professional activities whereas women are shown in domestic roles.

Another series of studies found that newspaper and magazine photographs present men's and women's bodies differently: Pictures of men tend to feature the face more prominently, whereas pictures of women show more of the body and treat the face as a less prominent feature (Archer et al., 1983; Nigro, Hill, & Gelbein, 1988). The researchers labeled this gender differentiation *face-ism*, and they studied its impact by having people look at pictures of the same individual that varied only in terms of facial prominence. For the photo where the face was more prominent, the individual was rated as more intelligent, more ambitious, and physically better looking. Thus the extent of face-ism in the photograph influences people's judgments of the person portrayed. When women's faces are less prominently displayed, the stereotype that women are less intelligent, ambitious, and capable may be further perpetuated. The researchers concluded that face-ism may reinforce another cultural stereotype, "that essential aspects of personal identity are thought to be centered in different anatomic locations in men and women. Men are represented by their heads and faces; women are represented using more of their bodies" (Archer et al., 1983, p. 733).

As for television, we saw in Chapter 8 that women are still underrepresented and stereotyped in network shows, children's shows, and news shows. So, the media's greatest impact may be in perpetuating stereotypes that work to the benefit of some groups but to the disadvantage of others. The mass media are also in a position to have great influence in setting the societal agenda—the issues that the public discusses and considers important. National magazines, big-city newspapers, and television networks have this influence because they can reach such large numbers of people. On such topics as what causes crime and whether feminism is losing support, individuals may have strong opinions but relatively little direct knowledge to support them. Those who control the media can communicate their ideas on these topics to millions of people, a capability that affords them enormous influence in defining what topics people will consider important and what solutions to problems will be considered practical.

Much of the impact of the mass media discussed thus far is negative, but an important positive impact should be mentioned: The media considerably expand the channels of communication available to people. Especially with cable television, fiber optics, and electronic networks such as the Internet (see Chapter 4), the number of outlets and vehicles for communication is becoming truly astounding. There are channels devoted to religious programming, MTV offering popular music, community channels that offer community groups a means of getting their message out to a larger audience, and home shopping channels. The Sociology of Media and Technology insert explores some of the ways in which these technologies are making an impact on education. Of course, whether people benefit from these technological developments depends in part on who controls them.

Control of the Mass Media

If all groups had access to the media to present their views, or if television and print journalists worked independently of powerful groups in society, then the media might provide a truly democratic experience. In fact, the press and television do expose various acts of corruption, often motivating different levels of government to prosecute the offenders. Yet the media are themselves private companies and usually corporate in structure. They pursue greater profits and larger amounts of power in the same fashion as other corporations discussed in Chapter 13. And as has occurred in other corporate sectors, there has been concentration of power among the media:

> Sooner or later a handful of corporations [will] control most of what the average American reads, sees, and hears . . . the same few corporations will control all the important mass media not just in the United States but globally. (Bagdikian, 1990, p. x)

Bagdikian's prediction about concentration has largely come true. By the early twenty-first century, fewer than ten corporate giants controlled most of what appears in the global media: Time Warner, Disney, The News Corporation, General Electric, Viacom, and Bertelsmann (Dye, 2002; McChesney, 2004). Together, they own almost all of the fifty most-subscribed-to cable television channels and most of the daily newspapers in the United States. Despite the existence of more than 25,000 media outlets in the United States, a small number of corporations control most of the business in daily newspapers, magazines, television, books, and motion pictures. In many U.S. cities and towns, one newspaper has become a legal monopoly, being the only newspaper in town. And their reach now extends around the globe. At the dawn of the twenty-first century, a race is on, with a few megacorporations trying to control the print, video, and electronic media around the world. With such concentration, it becomes increasingly difficult for new voices to enter the field.

What is the impact of this concentration on the role of the media in society? The simple conclusion is that the media are mere apologists for the power elite and corporate capitalism. Much research shows, however, that the impact is much more subtle (Demers, 2002; Dreier, 1982). As newspapers and other media corporations become larger, form monopolies, and establish links with the power elite, they often develop a viewpoint that has been labeled *corporate liberalism*, which tends to look positively on unions, social welfare programs, and government regulation. However, it is not a socialist position, as discussed in Chapter 13, because corporate liberalism retains the belief that a corporate economy based on private enterprise is the most efficient economic system. In this view, government programs and regulations are intended to protect people against the weaknesses or excesses that can be found in capitalism. In fact, media following this corporate liberal ideology may sometimes be critical of big government and corporate capitalism, but this criticism stems not from an opposition to capitalism but from a desire to promote responsible capitalism. One latent function of such criticism is to protect capitalism from challenges and discourage interest in more radical changes that would significantly threaten corporate control by the power elite.

A more negative criticism of this concentration of the media is that, as we saw in Chapter 1, concentrated media come to have substantial control over people's perceptions of reality, shaping their beliefs and ideas about issues and societal problems. When capitalist corporations control much of the world's communications structure, corporate and capitalist viewpoints on such issues as the causes of crime or the consequences of globalization take an increasingly dominant place in the public discourse and the media. Competing and dissenting voices emanating from less powerful constituencies are less likely to be heard, especially on a global stage (Bagdikian, 2004; McChesney, 2004). The insidious impact of such corporate control can be seen in the gradual erosion of the wall separating news divisions from the advertising and marketing divisions of newspapers, television networks, and other media outlets. When this happens, what is presented as "news" depends in part on what is profitable for the corporate owners. So, instead of a free flow of ideas and information about issues and problems, we have a controlled flow in which problems are defined and solutions assessed on the basis of what benefits a relatively small number of people.

Executives in these corporate media empires, of course, insist that such concentration will *improve* the media. In fact, social scientist David Demers' research (2002) provides some support for this view by showing that concentration in the newspaper industry will enable diversity in newspaper content to survive in a highly competitive media environment. Furthermore, Demers points to the Internet and other emerging telecommunications technologies as developments that may in fact produce a decentralization of the global media and an expansion rather than a concentration of media and communications outlets. Demers' point is that an assessment of modern media developments that is entirely negative distorts a more complex reality.

However, other social scientists would support the concern that concentrated power over public information is potentially antidemocratic. Edward Herman (1993), for example, concludes that, on the important issues, the media "serve mainly as a supportive arm of the state and dominant elites, focusing heavily on themes serviceable to them, and debating and exposing within accepted frames of reference" (p. 25). Media specialist Ben Bagdikian put it this way (2000, pp. x, xv):

> With the countries' widest disseminators of news, commentary, and ideas firmly entrenched among a small number of the world's wealthiest corporations, it may not be surprising that their news and commentary is limited to an unrepresentative narrow spectrum of politics. . . . Politicians hesitate to offend the handful of media operators who control how those politicians will be presented—or not presented—to the voters. . . . Today the combination of the media industry and traditional corporate power has reached dimensions former generations could not match.

The additionally disturbing aspect of such a trend is that, as the dissenting voices are silenced, people become less and less aware that they are being presented a distorted view, because they have fewer guideposts with which to measure the accuracy or completeness of what they see, read, and hear.

The Global Mass Media: Neocolonization?

The United States clearly dominates the global mass media (Turow, 2008). For example, three-quarters of the broadcast and basic cable television revenues and four-fifths of pay-television revenues around the world are generated by mass media materials produced in the United States. Worldwide, more than half of all films rented to theaters or purchased for home video viewing are U.S. products. This overwhelming U.S. presence has produced opposition in many nations that see it as cultural colonialism, *a cultural assault that, if not diminished, will change values, norms, and ways of life.* Indeed, the cultural penetration of the world by U.S. media can be likened to the geographical penetration of other continents by European explorers in earlier centuries. Just as the

Sociology on the Internet

The U.S. Department of Education makes available numerous publications on the Internet and can be a good source of information about educational data, trends, and policies. Go to the home page of the National Center for Education Statistics (nces.ed.gov). At this point, you are free to explore. As a start, click "Search NCES" and type in "Student Outcomes." You will get a list of publications (some available online) reporting research on the factors that influence how well students do in school. Summarize the results of some of this research. Also, search for terms like "social promotion" and "drug-free schools." How does what you find relate to some of the educational issues discussed in this chapter? What other material can you uncover that relates to issues of this chapter?

Among the most influential groups in education policy in the United States are the National Education Association (www.nea.org), the American Federation of Teachers (www.aft.org), and the National Parent Teachers Association (www.pta.org). Explore their Web sites for information on the topics discussed in this chapter.

Use search engines to find information on the topic of home schooling, parents' teaching their children at home rather than sending them to school. Make an assessment about whether the use of home schooling is growing and whether it is a viable alternative to traditional schooling.

For further information and discussion, go to Allyn & Bacon's Social Problems Supersite (see Chapter 1) and explore Problem Area: Problems of Education.

Jesuits brought their schools to the South American Indians, modern media magnates send television serials such as *Friends* or movies such as *Titanic* to nations around the world. The result, many fear, will be the same: Irreversible change in the recipients' cultural values and traditional ways of life. Since the media—television, movies, books, magazines, and music—are key vehicles in the modern world for developing and transmitting a culture, U.S. dominance may make it difficult for other nations to promote their own culture. As U.S. values regarding work, gender relations, religion, violence, and many other things become pervasive, the result could be the transformation of these other cultures. In response, nations as diverse as Canada, France, and China have regulations that control how much of the content of magazines, television shows, and radio music must be indigenous (Riding, 2005).

By the end of the twentieth century, the U.S. media were receiving some fairly stiff competition from the Japanese and European media. Such competition simply means that wealthy industrial nations of the world dominate the media market and are thus in a strong position to communicate their views on capitalism, privatization, commercialization, and civilization. In fact, the United States and other Western nations have worked through the United Nations to encourage freedom of the media in all nations because their well-developed media industries will dominate any open market. Many nations oppose this freedom because they want their indigenous media to have a chance to develop and to preserve aspects of their traditional way of life. Even the notion that the media should be free of government control is a Western cultural value that not all nations around the world agree with. Many nations view the media as a tool of nation building, to be used by the government to encourage patriotism and desired values and behavior.

Study & Review
SUMMARY OF LEARNING OBJECTIVES

You should be able to describe how education differs in preindustrial and industrial societies and how colonization and modernization have changed education.

Education is the systematic, formal process through which specialized teachers transmit skills, knowledge, and values to students. In preindustrial societies much education was informal, being a part of the general process of socialization; with the development of agricultural societies, specialized educational institutions begin to emerge. Colonizing nations have used education to change the cultural values and social practices of the peoples they colonize. In the twentieth century, education was also a key vehicle of modernization, although critics argue that modernization is in part neocolonial westernization of other societies intended to make them receptive to investment. With modernization, education assists in the process of nation building, which means shifting people's allegiances from the clan, village, or other traditional source to the nation as a whole.

You should be able to analyze educational institutions using the three sociological perspectives, including an assessment of the functions of education, credentialism, the hidden curriculum, and labeling.

From the functionalist perspective, education is a social institution that serves a number of important functions, including the transmission of culture, training people for important positions, providing custodial care and a social network for the young, encouraging innovation and social change, sorting people into positions, and enabling social mobility. From the conflict perspective, education is a mechanism for maintaining the existing class structure and protecting the interests of dominant groups. This end is accomplished through the hidden curriculum and the credentials race, where high educational achievements are required in order to get jobs. Such requirements effectively discriminate against people of lower socioeconomic status because they are less able to acquire the necessary education. An overall consequence is social reproduction. The interactionist perspective recognizes that social expectations and social meanings are a part of the interaction between teachers and students. Practices such as grading and tracking students can result in social labels that might produce a self-fulfilling prophecy.

You should be able to discuss the emergence of educational institutions in the United States, analyze schools as bureaucracies, evaluate how effective schools are, and describe the reforms that have been instituted.

Formal education in the United States emerged as religious training and as a way to Americanize immigrants. Mass education developed in the twentieth century because industrialization required a more literate, educated, and skilled workforce. Education in the United States occurs in schools that are highly bureaucratic, a fact which has sparked debate over whether bureaucracies are efficient ways to teach or merely stifle creativity. There has also been severe criticism of U.S. schools in regard to how effectively they teach the young. A number of reforms have been proposed that would improve schools: parental choice, back-to-basics curricula, early childhood education, school integration, and upgrading schools and teachers.

You should be able to discuss the mass media in terms of when they emerged; how they affect people, schools, and society; who controls them; and whether they constitute neocolonization.

The mass media play a key role in educating the young, influencing people, and shaping society. The media affect a number of realms of life: They produce popular culture, they can induce people toward violent behavior, and they give subtle and indirect support for existing cultural beliefs and stereotypes. Control of the mass media is increasingly concentrated in the hands of a few large corporations; this concentration may have detrimental effects on the free flow of information and ideas. Some argue that Western control of the media around the world has produced cultural colonialism.

CHRONOLOGICAL PRACTICE TEST

For answers to Key Concepts see the page number in parentheses; for other answers see page 356.

A Global Perspective on Education
Key Concepts
1. Education (332)
2. Modernization (334)

True/False
3. T F Specialized educational institutions first emerged in hunting-and-gathering societies.
4. T F Even after formal educational institutions have emerged, such as in industrial societies, informal education still occurs.
5. T F In the twentieth century, the Western industrial nations have discouraged more traditional societies from going through the process of modernization.

Concept Completion
6. The social and economic changes that accompany the transition to an industrial economy are called _____.
7. The term *nation building* refers to _____.

Critical Thinking
8. How did the Western European nations use educational institutions as they explored and colonized many nations around the world between the fifteenth and the nineteenth centuries?
9. What role has education played in the processes of modernization and nation building?

Sociological Perspectives on Education
Key Concepts
10. Hidden curriculum (337)
11. Social reproduction (338)

True/False
12. T F The "sorting" function of education has to do with custody of the young.
13. T F The danger of tracking in schools is that the track can become a label that creates expectations for how teachers and students should behave.

Concept Completion
14. The term _____ refers to the training of students in values and norms that help to perpetuate the existing system of stratification.

15. Powerful forces in educational institutions work toward _____, or passing social and economic inequalities on from one generation to the next.
16. According to the interactionist perspective, the grades and other reports that schools accumulate about a student becomes a _____.

Critical Thinking

17. What functions does education perform that contribute to the operation and maintenance of society?
18. According to the conflict perspective, in what ways does education work as a mechanism to limit the opportunities of the less powerful in society?
19. What contribution does the interactionist perspective make to our understanding of education as a social process?

Education in the United States
True/False

20. T F Among those students who are especially at risk for failure in schools in the United States are those whose parents have low educational attainment.
21. T F Overall, integration of schools in the United States has probably resulted in modest improvements in school achievement by African American students.
22. T F In Japan, the central government controls educational policy and curriculum design.

Concept Completion

23. When teachers and administrators in schools devote more attention to maintaining the educational system than to the traditional educational goals, they are engaging in _____.
24. The school reform that is based on the notion that schools should compete for students in an open marketplace is called _____.
25. The _____ approach to education emphasizes the traditional core curriculum and a return to strong discipline.

Critical Thinking

26. Discuss criticisms of the educational system in the United States. Include in your answer an assessment of schools as bureaucracies and of the effectiveness of schools.
27. What reforms are being implemented, or might be implemented, in schools in the United States to overcome some of the problems discussed in the text?
28. How is education in Japan similar to education in the United States? How does it differ?

Education, Communication, and the Mass Media
Key Concepts

29. Popular culture (350)
30. Distance education (352)
31. Cultural colonialism (353)

True/False

32. T F The reach of the print media will be more expansive in societies with a lower rate of literacy.
33. T F Traditional societies in the twenty-first century are no longer threatened by cultural colonialism.

Concept Completion

34. _____ refers to the products and activities designed for mass consumption and used for leisure or entertainment.
35. The overwhelming United States presence in the production and distribution of films and videos around the globe has produced opposition in many nations because it may lead to _____.

Critical Thinking

36. Describe the emergence of the mass media and some of the effects that they have had on society.
37. Both historically and today, who controls the mass media in the United States? What are the advantages and disadvantages of the kinds of control that exists today?

ANSWERS TO CHRONOLOGICAL PRACTICE TEST

3. F; 4. T; 5. F; 12. F; 13. T; 20. T; 21. T; 22. T; 32. F; 33. F
6. modernization
7. encouraging citizens to shift their allegiance to the nation-state
14. hidden curriculum
15. social reproduction
16. publicly stamped label
23. goal displacement
24. parental choice
25. back to basics
34. Popular culture
35. cultural colonialism

CUMULATIVE PRACTICE TEST

See page 482 for answers.
1. When specialized educational institutions emerged in agricultural societies, they were most often intended for
   a. training of the lower classes in practical skills.
   b. a supplement to informal education at home.
   c. religious and moral training of the elite.
   d. training for the middle class in management skills.
   e. nation building among indigenous peoples.
2. Through courses in civic education and national history, schools in traditional societies play a role in
   a. nation building.
   b. informal education.
   c. distance education.
   d. popular culture.
   e. globalization.

3. Which of the following best characterizes the European colonizers as they explored lands around the world from the fifteenth to the nineteenth centuries?
   a. They made efforts to preserve native cultures.
   b. Their schools taught natives in their own language.
   c. They viewed native ways of life as inferior to European culture.
   d. They thought that civilization for the natives meant retaining and enhancing native culture.
   e. They discouraged indigenous people from participating in formal education.

4. To assist the modernization process, schools in less-developed nations were encouraged to train people in all of the following *except*
   a. literacy skills.
   b. indigenous cultural values.
   c. technical training.
   d. engineering and managerial specializations.
   e. schools were encouraged to teach *all* of these.

5. "Educational institutions make a number of contributions that work toward the maintenance of society as a whole." This statement would be most consistent with the
   a. conflict perspective.
   b. functionalist perspective.
   c. interactionist perspective.
   d. evolutionary approach.
   e. modernization perspective.

6. The concept of a "hidden curriculum" in schools is most clearly associated with the
   a. functionalist perspective.
   b. popular culture perspective.
   c. interactionist perspective.
   d. modernization perspective.
   e. conflict perspective.

7. Which of the following is true of the trends in education since 1940?
   a. The percentage of adults who are high school graduates has not changed.
   b. The percentage of adults who are high school graduates has more than doubled.
   c. The percentage of adults who are high school graduates has increased tenfold.
   d. The percentage of adults who are college graduates has increased only slightly.
   e. The percentage of adults who are college graduates has declined slightly.

8. Which of the following is true in regard to the "credentials race" in the United States?
   a. The educational requirements for most jobs today are lower than they need to be.
   b. The educational credentials required for jobs have been going down in the past few decades.
   c. The race actually ended a couple of decades ago.
   d. The educational requirements for many jobs today are higher than they need to be.
   e. It works to discourage social reproduction.

9. The interactionist perspective would give most stress to the importance of
   a. labeling.
   b. the hidden curriculum.

c. the credentials race.
d. sorting and social mobility.
e. social reproduction.

10. During the colonial period in the United States, the primary purpose of schooling was to
    a. encourage social mobility.
    b. discourage social mobility.
    c. incorporate the American Indians into the colonies.
    d. further religious training.
    e. provide opportunities for low-income families.

11. Magnet schools are
    a. schools that centralize all the educational functions in a school district.
    b. the schools that attract the largest number of students in a school district.
    c. schools that offer special programs in particular areas to attract students.
    d. schools that have reduced the extent of bureaucracy in their organization.
    e. schools that have gone "back to the basics."

12. Research has shown that Head Start children, in comparison to other children who do not have such compensatory education,
    a. are more likely to be assigned to special education classes.
    b. are more likely to repeat a grade in school.
    c. do better in sports.
    d. show more improvement in IQ scores.
    e. are more likely to get in trouble with the law.

13. The "back-to-basics" approach to education includes which of the following?
    a. Emphasis on the traditional core curriculum.
    b. Strong discipline.
    c. More freedom for students.
    d. All of the above.
    e. Only a and b.

14. Philosopher Allan Bloom criticizes higher education in the United States for
    a. having narrow, vocationally oriented curricula.
    b. ignoring areas of literature, philosophy, and the humanities.
    c. placing too much emphasis on developing an appreciation for the roots of American culture.
    d. All of the above are true.
    e. Only a and b are Bloom's criticisms.

15. Research on education has shown that
    a. students in Roman Catholic schools perform better than students in public schools.
    b. students in public schools perform better than students in Roman Catholic schools.
    c. students in U.S. schools do better in math and science than students in most other industrial nations.
    d. more highly bureaucratic schools encourage more creativity among their students than less bureaucratic schools.
    e. Both a and d are true.

16. _____ refers to products and activities designed for mass consumption and used for leisure or entertainment.
    a. Mass media
    b. Popular culture
    c. Modernization

d. Merchandising

e. Distance education

17. As the number of televisions in homes in the United States has grown,

a. the number of newspapers in circulation has also grown.

b. the number of newspapers in circulation has declined.

c. the literacy rate has declined.

d. popular culture has declined.

e. Both b and c are correct.

18. The phenomenon of "face-ism" is used in the text to illustrate

a. the impact of distance education.

b. the impact of cultural colonialism on the world.

c. how labeling affects school children.

d. how modernization affects the educational process.

e. how the media help shape cultural stereotypes.

19. Newspapers and other media in the United States criticize government and corporations because

a. the media favor responsible capitalism.

b. the media oppose capitalism.

c. the media are trying to deflect attention from their own inadequacies.

d. the media favor socialism.

e. the media are independent of corporate influence.

20. The group that is most likely to be influenced toward violence by watching violence on television is

a. older adults.

b. teens between 15 and 18 years of age.

c. children between 8 and 12 years of age.

d. children under 5 years of age.

e. young adults in their 20s.

FOR FURTHER READING

Ballantine, Jeanne H., & Hammack, Floyd. (2009). *The sociology of education: A systematic analysis* (6th ed.). Upper Saddle River, NJ: Prentice Hall. This comprehensive textbook on the sociology of education provides a complete overview of the topics, theories, and research that sociologists focus on in the institution of education.

Benjamin, Gail R. (1997). *Japanese lessons: A year in Japanese school through the eyes of an American anthropologist and her children*. New York: New York University Press. An anthropologist uses her expertise at observation to produce an insightful and personal look at education in Japan that serves as a good expansion on the materials discussed in this chapter.

Carnoy, Martin, & Samoff, Joel. (1990). *Education and social transition in the Third World*. Princeton, NJ: Princeton University Press. This volume explores the issue of educational change in less developed nations, especially the extent to which traditional values are preserved or threatened by proposed changes.

Cookson, Peter W., & Persell, Caroline Hodges. (1985). *Preparing for power: America's elite boarding schools*. New York: Basic Books. Based on in-depth interviews at elite boarding schools, these sociologists document how the schools prepare the offspring of the powerful to take over positions of power in American society.

Mazzocco, Dennis W. (1994). *Networks of power: Corporate TV's threat to democracy*. Boston, MA: South End Press. This thought-provoking book describes the extent to which the media, and television in particular, are now concentrated in the hands of a few powerful corporate giants and the consequences this fact may have for democratic institutions.

Mitroff, Ian I., & Bennis, Warren. (1989). *The unreality industry: The deliberate manufacturing of falsehood and what it is doing to our lives*. New York: Oxford University Press. This is a hard-hitting critique of the mass media on the grounds that they invent realities and then encourage people to believe the inventions are true. The authors explore some of the dangerous effects of this behavior.

Molnar, Alex. (1996). *Giving kids the business: The commercialization of America's schools*. Boulder, CO: Westview Press. This educator takes on the trend toward letting market forces and privatization shape what happens in America's classrooms, showing the many ways in which that will make students worse off.

Rothstein, Richard. (2004). *Class and schools: Using social, economic and educational reform to close the black-white achievement gap*. New York: Economic Policy Institute, Teachers College, Columbia University. This author focuses on the reasons for the persistent gap in educational achievement between whites and African Americans in the United States and how it can be narrowed. In doing so, the book tells a lot about how social class influences educational achievement.

Schechter, Danny. (1997). *The more you watch, the less you know: News wars/(sub)merged hopes/media adventures*. New York: Seven Stories Press. This media expert offers a serious criticism of television's inability or unwillingness to truly inform the public on issues.

CHAPTER 13

Political and Economic Institutions

MYTHS & FACTS: About Political and Economic Institutions

Politics, Power, and Authority
Types of Authority
State and Government

Sociological Perspectives on Political and Economic Institutions
The Functionalist Perspective
The Conflict Perspective

Types of Government
Oligarchy and Totalitarianism
Democracy
Social Conditions for Democracy
Political Participation in Democracies

Types of Economic Systems
Capitalism
Socialism
Mixed Economies

Who Rules in the United States?
The Power Elite Model
The Pluralist Model
Assessment of the Models

The U.S. Economy: Concentration and Change
The Corporate Economy
Corporate Growth and Concentration
Multinational and Global Corporations
The Changing Labor Force
Global Competition: Worker Dislocation and Unemployment

The Global Political and Economic System

Concentration and Inequality

The Structure of Globalization

OTHER WORLDS, OTHER WAYS: Nicaragua: Political and Economic Change in a Peripheral Nation

Unemployment, Dislocation, and Resistance

APPLYING SOCIOLOGY: Intervening in the Process of Economic Globalization

Politics, the Economy, the Media, and the Cyberworld

Politics, Persuasion, and Propaganda

SOCIOLOGY OF MEDIA AND TECHNOLOGY: The Media and the Military in Wars

Advertising

SOCIOLOGY ON THE INTERNET

Study & Review

Myths & Facts

About Political and Economic Institutions

Myth:

U.S. citizens are a politically active people, with most of them participating in the democratic process.

Fact:

Actually, most people in the United States are politically acquiescent. Barely one-half of U.S. citizens vote in presidential elections and fewer still in other elections. Most other industrial democracies have much higher rates of political participation among their citizens.

Myth:

States and governments work, especially in democracies, to protect all citizens equally.

Fact:

In all societies, states and governments come to be dominated by particular groups with special interests. Those groups tend to rule in ways that protect and benefit their own interests, although they may believe that they are ruling in the interests of all the people.

Myth:

The U.S. economy represents a pure form of capitalism.

Fact:

There are no pure forms of capitalism in the world today. Even in the United States, the government is involved in controlling and regulating the economy in many different ways.

Myth:

For capitalist economies to be efficient and successful, there should be an atmosphere of freewheeling competition among entrepreneurs, with the government staying out of the picture.

Fact:

Although freewheeling competition has advantages at times, the Japanese economy has been quite strong even though the Japanese see competition as potentially dangerous and disruptive. In fact, the Japanese government works closely with business and industry to keep competition under control.

Before the British colonized parts of Africa, the Tiv were a small tribe in West Africa (Bohannon & Bohannon, 1953). The Tiv had a subsistence economy, producing only enough food and other goods for the needs of their tribe. They did not increase production in order to have a surplus to sell or trade to another tribe. Even though each Tiv family worked their own plot of land, the food produced was considered to be the property of the tribe as a whole rather than the grower. If another family's crop was too small and they needed some extra food, other Tiv families would give it to them, expecting nothing immediate in return but confident that the needy family would come to their assistance at some future time of need.

The Tiv family did not own the plot they worked. The land belonged to the whole tribe, and each family was assigned a plot to work for a period of time. When the soil was exhausted, the plot would be left idle for a while, and the family would be assigned a new plot. The Tiv would actively debate which gardens should be idle each season and where the dispossessed families should start a new garden. The Tiv would have been aghast at the thought of buying and selling land for money. They had a currency, which they used to buy some ceremonial items, but they did not think of purchasing food or land with it because these belonged to the tribe as a whole. The land was considered a resource for the whole tribe to nurture and to use; it

Global corporations have become the most prominent actors on the world scene. Major U. S. corporations, for example, have mounted integrated, worldwide systems of economic production and distribution that impact on nations around the world.

was unimaginable to them that it could be a commodity to be bought and sold.

An economy with some similarities to that of the Tiv existed in New England around the time of the American Revolution in 1776 (Szatmary, 1980). It was a subsistence economy in which yeoman farmers grew just enough food to feed their families. They also produced most of the other things they needed, such as clothing. Some manufactured items, such as glass or gunpowder, had to be bought, and the farmers grew a small surplus of food to barter for these goods. However, they grew much less on their farms than they were capable of. In fact, they typically cultivated only a small portion of their land—as little as 5 or 10 percent, in some cases—because that was sufficient to supply home needs and a small surplus to trade. They increased the amount of land under cultivation only out of necessity, usually because their family had grown larger.

The choice of crops of these New England yeoman farmers also arose from their subsistence approach. One major crop was Indian corn, which had little mar-

ket value and tended to deplete the soil more quickly than crops like hemp or flax for which there was a brisk market. Indian corn was grown because it provided sustenance for both humans and animals on the farm. They also grew small amounts of many crops rather than large amounts of those few crops that had the highest market value; that is, they grew what their forefathers had grown and what would provide the most variety for their families. These subsistence practices stemmed in part from a strong sense of independence. To survive by one's own efforts was seen as indicative of such independence. Independence, however, did not mean competitiveness. These farmers engaged in elaborate cooperative, community-oriented exchanges with other farmers, especially during the busy harvest season. Neighbors would exchange labor, tools, and animals with one another. Like the Tiv, they saw themselves as involved in a communal activity rather than in economic competition with other farmers.

To understand present-day U.S. culture, it is sometimes helpful to look at different cultures. The Tiv and the New England yeoman farmers had an economy largely devoid of some characteristics of modern economies: competition, private property (the Tiv), profit seeking, accumulation of surplus, commercialism, and economic expansion. People often view their own way of life as the natural way to live, seeing competition, for example, or profit seeking as the natural way for human beings to behave. Yet, the Tiv and the New England farmers indicate that such ways are not natural but rather are cultural products— ways of life that people learn as members of a particular culture. As this chapter begins, it is wise to keep in mind that present-day economic and political institutions are also cultural products, outgrowths of centuries-long historical trends.

The term economics refers to *the processes through which goods and services are produced and distributed in societies*. Economic systems are closely linked to political systems. Politics refers to *the use of power to determine whose values will predominate, how rewards and resources will be allocated, and the manner in which conflicting interests in society will be resolved* (Segal, 1974). Both these institutions center on the same key social process in society: the exercise of power in the allocation of scarce resources. In fact, a classic description of politics could aptly be applied to *both* political and economic institutions: They determine "who gets what, when, and how" (Lasswell, 1936). In a small society like that of the Tiv, the two institutions almost blend into one, with the same village leaders playing a part in both realms. In all societies, political decisions influence economic policies and practices, and economic conditions affect what happens in the political realm.

A major bone of contention among social scientists has involved which of these institutions predominates in the exercise of power. Because politicians pass legislation that establishes national economic policy, one might conclude that politics is the main engine allocating resources in society. Yet Frederick Engels (1888/1969) once referred to *economic relations* as "the decisive element" in society while characterizing the political order as "subordinate." This chapter addresses this issue, although not with the goal of resolving it. Rather, the chapter focuses on the role of each institution and the way the institutions work together in exercising power and allocating resources.

Politics, Power, and Authority

You should be able to define power and the different types of authority and explain the differences between state and government.

Power is *the ability of one group to realize its will, even in the face of resistance from other groups* (Weber, 1919/ 1958). Power can arise from many sources: the strength of numbers, efficient organization, access to wealth or status, or control of political and economic institutions. Whatever its source, power enables its possessor to compel others to act in a particular fashion. However, not all power is alike. In some cases, groups have power because they can threaten to use force should others not comply. The U.S. Congress, for example, has the power to require young men to register to be drafted into the military, even though many of them would prefer not to register. Congress's power in this area rests on its ability to levy fines and prison sentences on those who refuse to register.

However, such explicit coercion, although important, is a costly way to exercise power because it ties up resources such as the money necessary to staff police forces and build prisons, and it generates resentment among the governed. For this reason, rulers attempt to make their exercise of power *legitimate*. Legitimacy is *"the capacity of the system to engender and maintain the belief that the existing . . . institutions are the most appropriate ones for the society"* (Lipset, 1959, p. 64). *Legitimate power*, or what sociologists call authority, is *obeyed because people believe it is right and proper that they obey*. Some young people register for the draft, for example, because they believe the government should have the power to create a military force to control internal disorder or protect against external threat. They may still prefer not to enter the military, but they accept the government's right to require them to serve society in this fashion.

Most people in the United States view the existing political and economic arrangements as reasonably legitimate, and this acceptance has been an important source of stability for U.S. society. However, the degree of legitimacy accorded to institutions varies from time to time and group to group in the United States. The antiwar movement of the 1960s and the militia movement of the 1990s are symptomatic that the accordance of legitimacy to political institutions is not universal. Chapter 7 notes that some African Americans, reacting to the enslavement of their ancestors and their own experiences with discrimination, feel some ambivalence toward the legitimacy of U.S. political institutions. Finally, a recent survey found that half of the people expressed no confidence in the U.S. Congress, 58 percent had no confidence in political parties, and 42 percent had no confidence in large corporations (U.S. Bureau of the Census, 2004, p. 254). So, political and economic institutions in the United States have not won the complete support of all citizens.

Types of Authority

Political and economic institutions can rest on one, two, or all three of the following types of authority (Weber, 1925/1947).

Traditional authority is based on historical custom and loyalty to established ways of doing things. Perhaps the best political example is found in societies that have hereditary rule. In such cases, the seat of political power rests with a group leader or chief. In tribal societies, for example, when the ruler dies, leadership is passed to his eldest son, and all of the accumulated power then devolves on that individual. In such societies, the norms surrounding who has authority are often considered sacred. Such traditional leaders not only have great power but also command reverence and sentimental respect from group members.

Charismatic authority is based on the presumed special and extraordinary powers or qualities of some individual. The emphasis here is on the *perception* of unique qualities, whether or not the person actually possesses them. Adolf Hitler and Mao Zedong exemplify charismatic leaders who exercised tremendous political authority in their respective countries, Germany and China. Charismatic authority also exists in democratic societies, and political leaders such as John F. Kennedy, Martin Luther King, Jr., Ronald Reagan, and Jesse Jackson have been acknowledged as having considerable charisma, although their appeal is not universal. Charismatic authority, however, is the most unstable type of authority, because the leader may die or because of illness or injury be unable to remain charismatic. If that happens, the leader's authority may disappear unless it is preserved in traditions or transformed into the third type of authority.

Legal-rational authority depends on laws and rules that define who possesses what type of power over whom. For example, the President of the United States has a great deal of authority, including the ability to recommend that the country go to war, but the President must gain the approval of Congress in order to declare war. Executive privilege gives the President a measure of power that few other political figures in the United States possess. Despite this considerable authority, if Presidents exceed the established boundaries of this privilege, they can be impeached. Because their office is based on legal-rational authority, Presidents cannot pass it on to their offspring. In addition, the rights and obligations of the office remain with the office when a particular President, no matter how charismatic, leaves. This rule affords institutions based on legal-rational authority a high degree of stability.

Authority, of course, can derive from more than one of these sources. The U.S. presidency, for example, gains much of its legitimation from legal-rational authority. However, the Constitution is now more than two centuries old, and this time span has accorded it a degree of traditional authority as well. So, the powers of the presidency, as defined in the Constitution, have also gained legitimation through custom. In addition, some Presidents, such as Ronald Reagan, have used their charisma to gain some support for their presidential actions.

State and Government

Although political authority today rests in specialized offices such as the presidency, that has not always been the case. The emergence of the state as the seat of political authority is linked to societal evolution.

Formal political institutions do not exist in hunting-and-gathering societies. Rather, decisions are made collectively, and somewhat democratically, based on the mutual welfare of the group (see Chapter 2). In horticultural and pastoral societies, separate political leadership emerges in the form of a chieftainship whose authority is passed on through inheritance. However, it is not until agricultural societies arise that the state appears. The state is *a political institution with legitimate control over the use of force within a particular territory* (Weber, 1925/1947). The reasons for the emergence of the state as the supreme political authority are complex (Service, 1975). In general, however, a social hierarchy emerged in agricultural societies that enabled some people to accumulate and control a considerable amount of resources. Control was also extended over a considerable amount of territory. Higher population density, elaborate irrigation systems, the development of trade networks, and increased specialization—these and other factors called for both more centralized and more assured control over a given geographic territory, and the state emerged as the social institution to perform this function. In industrial societies, with larger populations and even greater wealth, the state becomes even more essential to controlling and organizing social and economic life. Increasing levels of military competition in agricultural societies also produced a need for more centralized coordination and control.

The government can be defined as *the operation of the state by a particular group of people who have the authority to make decisions and supervise the allocation of resources.* Today, the legitimacy of the state is usually not questioned. Few people doubt that a single political authority should have the power to rule over a particular geographic territory. However, people often question whether a certain government—meaning the group of people currently in power—should have the legitimate right to rule.

Sociological Perspectives on Political and Economic Institutions

| You should be able to describe the insights of the functionalist and conflict perspectives regarding political and economic institutions.

Before describing the different types of political and economic systems that are found in societies, it is helpful to assess these institutions from both the functionalist and conflict perspectives.

The Functionalist Perspective

From the functionalist perspective, economic institutions accomplish an important task—they produce and distribute the goods and services that are essential to the survival of society. Economic systems provide all the food, clothing, and other material things that people need. Some economic systems do so better than others. Political institutions, such as states and governments, also perform important functions that are beneficial to the societies in which they emerge. First, the state provides a framework in which rules and norms of conduct are created, stability is encouraged, and social order is enhanced. In less complex societies, decision making is based on consensus, and norms are enforced through informal sanctions. More complex societies have far too many people with differing interests for such techniques to be effective. The citizenry grants the state and governmental institutions the authority to make policy choices and to create laws that are binding on everyone. In addition, people recognize the government's authority to apply sanctions against those who disobey established rules and regulations.

A second function of the state is to establish a setting in which individuals and groups can bargain with one another to resolve conflicts. Thus the government makes rules and then serves as a kind of mediator between different parties or interest groups in society, and it also has the power to render decisions that tell each party what it may and may not do. In performing this function, government helps society direct itself and look ahead to the future.

Third, the state has considerable responsibility for maintaining a stable economy. It does so by ensuring that social conditions are conducive to the smooth operation of the economy. Governments, for example, often build railroads and highways to ensure transportation of economic goods. Political policies are also used to control inflation and employment. And the government subsidizes the training of people in certain fields to ensure an adequate supply of labor.

Finally, the state protects society from external threats. A society's government also assists in relationships with other countries. This assistance is sometimes diplomatic, as when the United States acts as mediator for crises in the Middle East, and sometimes economic, as when the United States sends foreign aid to other nations as a way of maintaining friendly relations.

The function of political and economic institutions, then, is to make organized social life possible in societies that are large and complex. Without these institutions, according to the functionalist perspective, life would be chaotic and virtually impossible.

The Conflict Perspective

Unlike the functionalists, who argue that political and economic institutions emerge out of societal need, conflict theorists maintain that these structures are ultimately designed to benefit dominant groups. The French philosopher Jean Jacques Rousseau (1762/1950), writing during the 1700s, provided an early, conflict-oriented explanation of how state and government were born: "The first man who, having enclosed a piece of ground, bethought himself of saying, 'This is mine,' and found people simple enough to believe him, was the real founder of civil society." In other words, the state is merely a *social contract* that is designed to maintain order. But, Rousseau argued, not all citizens benefit equally from this contract; rather, the wealthy gain the most advantage from protecting the status quo.

Later, Karl Marx (1848/1964) argued that economic institutions play a key role in shaping all other institutions. In his view, political institutions, including the state, are created by members of the ruling class in society to protect their economic position. Marx declared, "The history of all hitherto existing societies is the history of class struggle." This class struggle involves two groups, one of which dominates and the other of which is exploited. Political, religious, educational, and other institutions are designed to protect the privileged position of the ruling class by maintaining existing economic institutions.

There is undoubtedly much truth to Marx's argument that the state serves the interests of the powerful. However, we also need to recognize that political and economic institutions are necessary at the same time for other reasons, in particular to fulfill the functions pointed out in the discussion of the functionalist approach. Without some central authority, large and complex societies could not survive. Once these social institutions come into existence to serve these functions, however, they become a prize that benefits any group that can gain control of them. In fact, a major focus of sociological research is the extent to which political and economic institutions in a particular society serve the interests of a small group of people or provide benefits to many groups, both powerful and otherwise. This question will be addressed shortly with regard to U.S. society. First, however, it is necessary to compare some of the different types of political and economic institutions that can be found in various societies.

Types of Government

You should be able to explain the different forms of government and discuss the prerequisites for democracy and the factors influencing political participation in democratic societies.

Governments in modern societies can take a number of different forms. One simple way to distinguish among them is to separate nondemocratic governments, especially oligarchy and totalitarianism, from democratic ones.

Oligarchy and Totalitarianism

In his discussion of the "iron law of oligarchy," Robert Michels (1915/1966) argued that whenever groups reach a size where consensus-oriented decision making is no longer workable, oligarchy is likely to develop. Oligarchy, as noted in Chapter 4, means *rule by a small number of people in which other group members take little part in making decisions.* Power becomes concentrated in the hands of what Michels referred to as *expert leaders.* There are several reasons why oligarchies emerge. First, oligarchy provides a predictable and efficient system of leadership, which could become unruly if too many people were involved. Second, many people are apathetic. They are not really concerned about who rules them and have no particular motivation to take power themselves. Third, most people have neither the time nor the resources to work toward gaining political control. Given these tendencies, it is not surprising that oligarchy is a common form of government. As will be shown, there are even those who argue that the United States is in reality governed by a relatively small, elite group of political and economic leaders who are largely impervious to the wishes of the majority.

A special form of oligarchy is totalitarianism. In this type of government, *all the familiar social institutions, such as the economy, education, and to some extent the family and religion, are under total state control.* Citizens are expected to pay allegiance to only one political regime, which dominates every aspect of social life. Some totalitarian regimes are *dictatorships,* in which a single individual is at the pinnacle of power. The classic example of this type of regime in recent times was Adolf Hitler's Nazi Germany.

Democracy

An absolutely pure democracy has never really existed, for in such a government, every citizen would be able to participate in *every* decision relevant to society. Not only would such a situation be unwieldy, but also people would have time for little else in their lives. The governments that come closest to this democratic ideal are probably those of the early Greek city-states. In fact, the term *democracy* is derived from a Greek term that implies "the people rule." But even there, certain categories of people did not participate in the governmental process, including women and slaves. Taking these practical realities into account, Seymour Martin Lipset (1959) defined democracy as "*a political system which supplies regular constitutional opportunities for changing the governing officials, and a social mechanism which permits the largest possible part of the population to influence major decisions by choosing among contenders for political office*" (p. 27).

In a democracy, political authority is created by the consent of the governed, and this consent serves as a source of legitimacy for the government. Democracies are usually *representative* governments in which citizens choose the rulers through a competitive election process. These representatives need to be sensitive to citizen sentiment, for if they do not represent their constituencies, they will probably fail to be reelected. Certain guaranteed rights, such as freedom of speech, are provided to every citizen in a democracy. Such public liberties are spelled out in documents such as the U.S. Bill of Rights and cannot be arbitrarily removed by the government. Certainly, the rights of some people are violated in a democracy, but checks and balances ensure that these violations are minimized. If people believe that their freedom of speech has been violated, for example, they can file suit against the government.

SOCIAL CONDITIONS FOR DEMOCRACY   Democratic governments do not thrive everywhere. In fact, stable, long-term democracies are relatively rare, being limited largely to advanced industrial societies. Why is this true? There appear to be certain social conditions important to the survival of democracies (Lipset, 1959; Neubauer, 1967; Segal, 1974). First, democracy is closely associated with economic development—more developed economies are more likely to have stable democratic governments. The reason for this connection is probably that developed societies have a well-educated citizenry whose members want to participate in the political process. Such societies also have an entrenched middle class with a stake in maintaining the social order.

Second, stable democracies usually have a system of checks and balances, which keeps the state open to criticism and suggestions for improvements. For example, in the United States, both the President and the Congress have veto power over each other, which ultimately leads to political issues being examined and exposed to considerable scrutiny. Another example is the fact that democratic governments remain open to criticism by the press.

Third, stable democracies are more likely to emerge in societies where people have loyalties to many different groups rather than societies in which there are major social cleavages. These many loyalties prevent society from becoming polarized into a few homogeneous, hostile groups. People may side with a particular group on some issues but oppose that same group on other issues. For example, in the United States, many affluent and well-educated people have favored environmental legislation that was opposed by other affluent, well-educated people in the business community. At the same time, many working class and poor people have sided with the businesspeople in opposing environmental legislation that they viewed as a threat to their jobs.

Fourth, stable democracies are likely to exist when the citizenry is well informed about political practices, and where people share common values about the legitimacy of the governmental system. For example, in the United States, groups tend to believe that their interests will not be ignored even if their political representatives have lost an election. When people know what is going on within their government, a general feeling of trust is promoted. By the same token, when the public learns that their supposedly democratic government is denying them access to information, they may come to distrust government, and the legitimacy accorded it may decline.

Finally, stable democracies are more likely to exist when economic and social systems are viewed as effective. Effectiveness enhances the legitimacy accorded to the political system. When high rates of inflation, high unemployment, or other threatening disruptions exist, people are more likely to question whether the existing political institutions are proper and appropriate.

POLITICAL PARTICIPATION IN DEMOCRACIES   Citizens of the United States have a democratic right to participate in the political process, but how many take advantage of that right? In reality, a relatively small number do. Despite the central importance of voting to a

Proponents of the spread of corporate capitalism around the globe argue that it will spread prosperity to all peoples. Others argue that it hurts some people while benefiting others. The construction of dams, for example, such as this one in India, creates jobs and produces electricity, but it also displaces people from their homes and has negative impacts on the environment.

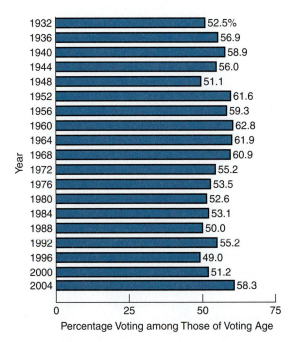

Figure 13.1

Participation in U.S. Presidential Elections, 1932–2004

Note: From *Statistical Abstract of the United States, 2004–2005* (p. 257) by U.S. Bureau of the Census, 2004, Washington, DC: U.S. Government Printing Office; "Voting and Registration in the Election of November 2004," *Current Population Survey*, 2004, by U.S. Bureau of the Census, Washington, DC: U.S. Government Printing Office.

Figure 13.2

Participation in Elections to the U.S. House of Representatives in Years with No Presidential Election, 1934–2006

Note: From *Statistical Abstract of the United States*, 2008 (p. 257) by U.S. Bureau of the Census, 2007, Washington, DC: U.S. Government Printing Office.

democracy, the rate at which people in the United States vote is low—60 percent or less of those of voting age in presidential elections (Figure 13.1). The turnout in 1988 (Bush versus Dukakis) and 1996 (Clinton versus Dole) were the lowest in more than seventy years, although the rate improved a little in 2004.

In years when there is no presidential election, the picture is even more disturbing, as Figure 13.2 shows. In the last three decades of off-year elections for the House of Representatives, only about one-third of the people of voting age voted; since 1934, no off-year election has produced more than a 45 percent voter turnout. Still fewer people vote in most state and local elections. Moreover, the United States ranks last in voter turnout among the world's major democracies, where 70 to 80 percent of the eligible voters participate in national elections (Rimmerman, 2005).

Why do so few people in the United States exercise their democratic right to vote? The reasons vary from one jurisdiction to another (Patterson, 2002). Many barriers to voter registration have been reduced with government requirements for motor-voter and mail-in registrations, along with registration opportunities at various government agencies. However, many people still say they cannot get time off work to vote or that the voting lines are too long after work. In addition, people often have to travel long distances to vote. In some jurisdictions, people avoid voting because of their fear that voting lists are used to select people for jury duty; in other cases, people convicted of felonies lose their right to vote, at least for a time. Voter turnout is also low because many people don't like any of the candidates. Finally, some people lack a sense of political efficacy: the feeling that their actions, including voting, have an impact on what politicians or the government actually do (Southwell & Everest, 1998).

Who votes and who doesn't in the United States? Generally, the well-to-do are most likely to vote, and the dispossessed are least likely to do so. Voting rates increase among those with higher incomes, higher levels of education, and more prestigious occupations (Figure 13.3). The reason for these patterns is that the affluent and well-educated probably think they have more of a stake in who wins an election. They also probably think that their voting will make a difference and thus is worth the time and effort. In addition, the better educated and more affluent are more likely to be informed about the issues in a campaign.

Voting rates also increase as people get older. Considerably less than one-half of the people under twenty-five who are eligible to vote actually do so in presidential elections. Many young people do not feel strong ties to a community, in part because they have yet to establish families and careers. They may not feel that expressing their preferences through voting

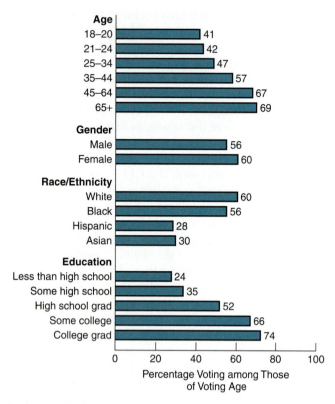

Figure 13.3

Percentage Who Reported That They Voted, 2004, by Age, Gender, Race/Ethnicity, and Education

Note: From "Voting and Registration in the Election of November 2004," *Current Population Survey*, 2004, by U.S. Bureau of the Census, Washington, DC: U.S. Government Printing Office.

is necessary or will gain them anything. As marital and occupational ties are established, people tend to feel more of a stake in their community, and voting rates increase. Political party preference is also affected by social factors, as mentioned in Chapter 11. Those who vote Republican are likely to be affluent, Protestant, and rural, whereas Democratic voters are more likely to be working-class, Catholic, and urban. There are certainly exceptions to this likelihood, but these relationships point to the fact that the Republicans tend to be the party of the privileged, whereas the Democrats represent the "common people."

Gender also influences political participation. Women are slightly more likely to register to vote and to vote than men are. In addition, research documents the existence of a gender gap in voting behavior, with women favoring Democratic candidates and men favoring Republican candidates. Women are more likely to identify themselves as Democrats than men are, and in presidential elections more women vote for the Democratic nominees than men do. This gender gap is probably attributable to the fact that the Democratic party has traditionally been more supportive of

issues that directly affect women, such as the right to an abortion and equal employment and educational opportunities for women.

Types of Economic Systems

You should be able to describe the basic principles of capitalist, socialist, and mixed economies.

To survive, every society must ensure that food, clothing, shelter, and other materials are produced and distributed to the members of society who need them. The rules and social practices that govern this production and distribution make up the economic institutions of a society. Economic institutions can take many different forms. For example, in some societies such as the Tiv, discussed earlier, every member has a right to a share of societal resources, including food, shelter, and clothing. Everyone is expected to work, and those who do not may be ridiculed and even ostracized. In turn, anyone who produces a surplus of food or anything else is under strong normative pressure to share it with others. No money changes hands, and the idea of paying for food and shelter would not occur to anyone. This form of reciprocal exchange is quite different from the economies of modern nations. Most nations today have a *market economy*, which is based on the exchange of money for goods and services in the marketplace. People sell their labor for a certain amount of money, and then the money is used to purchase goods and services. Although modern economies share this market foundation, they differ from one another in significant ways. This chapter looks at three main types of modern economic systems: capitalism, socialism, and mixed economies.

Capitalism

Capitalism contains three features that, taken together, distinguish it from other economic systems: *the means of economic production and distribution are privately held, the profit motive is the primary force guiding people's economic behavior, and there is free competition among both producers and consumers of goods* (Gottlieb, 1988). The proponents of capitalism argue that these features provide for consumer control over the quantity, quality, and price of goods. In its pure form, capitalism works like this. Seeking profits is, in a sense, merely unleashing personal greed. But that is quite appropriate, argue proponents of capitalism, because the possibility of profit gives capitalists the motivation to provide more and better goods and services. If a demand exists for some product, someone will come along and provide it if he or she can profit from doing so. Furthermore, the profit motive encourages innovation and creativity because entrepreneurs will look for novel goods and services—some that the consumer has not even thought of—that they can sell for a profit. Capitalists must be constantly on the lookout for new products lest someone else beat them to the punch and corner a market. Thus, from this profit-seeking motive, consumers benefit from having more and better goods available. Open competition among capitalists also benefits consumers by enabling them to choose among a number of items, comparing price against quality. If the quality of products is too low or the price too high, people will not buy them and the capitalists will be out of business unless they change. Adam Smith referred to the conjunction of profit seeking with competition as the *invisible hand* of market forces that would ensure that the supply of goods is roughly equivalent to the demand for them and that the public has available the goods that it can afford with the highest quality possible.

The role of government in this process, argue those who favor pure capitalism, should be to stand aside and let market forces operate unhindered. The government is necessary to maintain public order and protect against foreign threats, but any effort by the government to regulate the market is regarded as disastrous. Government regulation of prices or wages, for example, would interfere with both the profit motive and the competitive element and thus reduce the incentive to develop new and better products. In short, government policy under capitalism should be one of laissez-faire: The government should leave the market alone.

There are no pure forms of capitalism in the world today. Even in the United States, the government has always been involved to a degree in controlling and regulating the economy. Toward the end of the nineteenth century, for example, the freewheeling economic environment was highly aggressive, with small competitors being eliminated by ever larger ones. Huge monopolies resulted in which one company dominated a given product field. Through legislation such as the Sherman Antitrust Act of 1890 and the Clayton Act of 1914, the government controlled the ability of companies to monopolize a market and ensured that there would be some competition.

The government has also worked to protect people against some of the ravages of open-ended competition. For example, the government provides price supports for many agricultural products, because otherwise a bountiful crop would bring intense competition among farmers, who might be forced to lower their prices below the point at which they could make a profit. The government also legislates minimum wages, establishes unemployment insurance, and arbitrates labor disputes.

Welfare capitalism is the term for *economies* such as the United States *that combine a strongly competitive market and private property with some government regulation for the public good.*

Despite this government involvement in economic activity, the U.S. economy is one of the most capitalistic in the world. There is strong resistance to government interference in the economy and little support for government ownership of utilities, railroads, or other industries that are often government-owned in other capitalist societies.

Socialism

Socialism refers to *economies in which the means of production and distribution are collectively held so that the goods and services that people need are provided and equitably distributed.* In capitalism, production is based on *economic demand*: goods and services are provided if people can afford them. With socialism, production is based on *human need*: Goods and services are produced because people need them, irrespective of whether they can afford them (Harrington, 1989). Pure socialist economies reject the profit motive, recognizing that one person's profit is another's loss. In addition, socialists argue, the profit motive provides a built-in incentive for one person to exploit another, for example, by keeping wages low in order to increase profits. In fact, socialism emerged as a coherent ideology during the early stages of industrialization when workers' wages were exceedingly low, often barely enough to survive. People worked long hours under dangerous conditions with little hope of improving their lot. Although conditions in today's capitalist societies have improved, socialists still argue that capitalism sets one person in competition with another—either capitalist against capitalist or capitalist against consumer—and the inevitable outcome is a highly unjust and inequitable distribution of resources.

In socialist economies, the primary motivation for economic activity is to achieve collective goals, such as a higher standard of living for all citizens. To do so, the economy is highly centralized, with national authorities making decisions for the whole nation about what to produce and how to distribute these products. Because profit and consumer demands are not key elements in these decisions, the decisions can presumably be made with the collective interests of society as a whole in mind. If national leaders decide that the country should strengthen its industrial base, for example, then heavy machinery and equipment are produced, which might result in fewer consumer items, such as clothing or radios, being available. Because collective goals rather than profit govern production, unprofitable businesses might be kept running or prices for products kept lower than production costs in order to ensure their distribution.

As with capitalism, pure socialism is rare. Most socialist economies do allow for the private ownership of some goods, such as personal or household items, and people are allowed to engage in capitalist activity in some economic sectors, such as selling home-grown food in marketplaces. Most means of economic production in socialist economies, however, are still collectively rather than privately owned.

At this point, a word needs to be said about communism, a term that is routinely misused in the United States. *Communism* is the term Karl Marx used to describe the utopian end stage of the struggle over capitalism. In a communist society, all goods would be communally owned; people would not work for wages but rather would give according to their abilities; and there would be no scarcity of goods and services, allowing people to receive whatever they needed. In addition, the state would become less important and its role would dwindle. According to these criteria, the nations that were commonly referred to as communist during the Cold War were actually socialist.

Mixed Economies

The economies discussed thus far tend toward pure capitalism or pure socialism, although each includes some elements of the other. Another type of economy, found in Sweden, Denmark, and a number of other Western European nations, is the mixed or democratic socialist economy, *in which there are strong elements of both capitalism and socialism* (Brus & Laski, 1989). In mixed economies, most industry is privately owned and oriented toward profit making. In addition, despite considerable government regulation, there is a competitive market economy, and consumer demand determines much of what is produced. However, in mixed economies, many important industries, such as banks, railroads, the communications industry, the media, and hospitals, are state owned. Mixed economies provide for strong regulation of the private sector by the state. High taxes and an elaborate welfare system are established in hopes of achieving the national goal of a fair and equitable distribution of resources. Through such mechanisms, proponents of mixed economies hope to avoid the extensive social inequality that can accompany capitalism and the economic inefficiency that sometimes afflicts socialist economies.

With this background on the various types of political and economic institutions found in societies, attention can now turn to sociological research on the workings of these institutions in modern societies. The first topic is the distribution of political and economic power in the United States.

Who Rules in the United States?

You should be able to explain the power elite and pluralist perspectives on power in the United States and assess the evidence for each one.

Two major models of power, the power elite model and the pluralist model, have been developed to describe the exercise of power and authority in the United States.

The Power Elite Model

In the 1950s the sociologist C. Wright Mills (1956) proposed what has come to be called the power elite model to explain the exercise of power in the United States. Deriving his approach from the conflict perspective, Mills argued that *a small group of very powerful people make just about all the important decisions in the United States.* This power elite consists of the people who hold the top positions in the government, the economic realm, and the military. Included in this group are the President and the cabinet, the executives who run the large corporations, and the generals and admirals who run the Pentagon. According to Mills, the government, corporations, and the military dominate people's lives today, and it is from controlling them that power is derived. Other theorists argue that the power elite also includes the major media corporations that control publications such as *Time* and *Newsweek*, the major foundations (such as the Ford and Lilly foundations), and the presidents and trustees of the major private universities (such as Harvard and Yale) (Dye, 2002).

The people who make up the power elite, according to Mills, share certain social characteristics that set them apart from others in the United States. For example, they tend to come from affluent families that have been wealthy for at least two generations, families whose wealth in most cases far exceeds what the average person can ever expect to have. The elite is almost exclusively made up of white males whose parents were born in the United States. They come largely from urban areas and have attended the more prestigious colleges and universities, such as Princeton, Yale, Stanford, Dartmouth, and Harvard. Furthermore, their offspring attend the same private schools and universities, where social contacts are forged that will later prove beneficial in establishing their own positions among the elite. When these young members of the power elite graduate, their careers and lifestyles will be similar and will crisscross throughout their lifetime. Finally, the informal social ties of the power elite, such as what parties they attend or where they go for vacation, tend to reinforce their dominant positions. The

Bohemian Grove, for example, is a vacation retreat in California, but it is also a place where the powerful can develop or nurture acquaintances that will later prove helpful in landing a contract or passing a piece of legislation.

According to Mills, the power elite is a cohesive group, and the interests of its various members in the government, corporate, and military sectors tend to coincide. Below the elite, there is a middle level of diverse interest groups that includes most members of Congress, professional organizations, many lobbyists, and most unions. Members of these groups participate in making decisions about issues of secondary importance that have little effect on the elite. At the bottom is the great mass of citizens who have virtually no power because they do not belong to organizations that wield power. They may vote, but Mills viewed this privilege as meaningless because most elected officials are only in middle-level positions, whereas real decision-making power rests with the elite. In addition, the power elite is highly influential in determining which candidates the political parties will place before the electorate.

The Pluralist Model

Some sociologists argue that Mills's view is distorted and overly conspiratorial because there is actually little concentration of power and coincidence of interests among the elite (Kornhauser, 1966). Instead, the pluralist model views power as *pluralistic*, or *spread over a large number of groups with divergent values, interests, and goals*. According to David Riesman (1961), society contains veto groups with the ability to block decisions that might adversely affect their positions. For example, labor unions can exert considerable influence on issues affecting their members, such as raising unemployment benefits or minimum wage laws. Similarly, farmers may fight to stop the lowering of price supports for farm products. To be sure, pluralists recognize that some groups have far more power and other resources than do other groups, and there is considerable inequity in society. However, they argue that there is no single, cohesive, dominant elite, and power is not centralized in the hands of a few.

Below the elite, according to the pluralists, is the unorganized, but not entirely powerless, public (Rose, 1967). With the vote, the public can exercise some constraint over the behavior of those in power. In addition, the public has other ways to exert influence such as organizing large numbers of people into protests or boycotts that can change corporate or government policies. The environmental movement, for example, has used its ability to organize large numbers of people for public protest as a tool in struggling against corporate power. Especially in the areas of air pollution and the use of pesticides, these groups have organized seemingly powerless people to shape public policy successfully. Given these examples, pluralists dispute the power elite view and argue that the mass of the citizenry can effectively exert an influence, even against what seem to be formidable corporate foes.

Assessment of the Models

Research suggests that the realities of holding power in the United States are more complex than either the power elite or the pluralist models alone suggest. For example, the political scientist Thomas R. Dye (2002) reviewed the corporate and governmental sectors in the United States and located approximately seven thousand positions in corporations, the government, and the military that direct most of the nation's economic and social policy. According to Dye, this very small group of people represent Mills's power elite. The sociologist G. William Domhoff (2006) went a step further by studying the social backgrounds of the people who occupy these elite positions. He discovered that members of the upper class participate in an elaborate network of informal social contacts, just as Mills suggested. However, Domhoff did not find the cohesiveness or coincidence of interests among these people that Mills implied. Nevertheless, there are significant linkages and influence peddling among the various sectors of the power elite. Members of the corporate elite, for example, make sizeable contributions to both the Republican and Democratic parties in hopes of influencing the decisions of the President, congressional representatives, and other politicians. In fact, some would argue that, because of political contributions, corporate lobbying, and other forms of influence, the corporate elite exercises overwhelming control over politicians, government regulatory agencies, and government bureaucrats who are supposed to be controlling the corporations and protecting the rights and interests of the average person. In this view, the average citizen has little influence and is largely at the mercy of corporate goals (Greider, 1992).

Research on the power elite has also focused on links between business and the military. In his final speech before leaving office in 1961, former President Dwight D. Eisenhower, himself a five-star general during World War II, warned of the dangers posed by a military-industrial complex, referring to *the relationship between the military that wants to purchase weapons and the corporations that produce the weapons*. Both the military and the corporations benefit from a large military budget and from policies favoring military solutions to international problems. The potential danger of a powerful military-industrial complex is that defense decisions and the development of weapons systems may be influenced by what is beneficial to the military and defense industries rather than by what is necessary for national security. One way in which the coincidence of interests among members of the military-industrial complex might occur is if there were a periodic interchange of top-level personnel between the military and defense industries. And, as Mills and other researchers have shown, such interchanges do occur and are extensive (Project on Government Oversight, 2004). When corporations hire former government officials, they hope that their contacts and knowledge of government and the policy process will work to the benefit of the corporation.

Although there clearly are important links between the military and corporations suggesting a military-industrial complex, the picture is considerably more complicated. Many corporations actually oppose increases in defense spending, fearing that these will adversely affect the economy and result in higher taxes (Lo, 1982). So the military-industrial complex, although important, does not exist in a vacuum. There are other powerful groups, even among the power elite, with competing interests, and there are less powerful groups that still wield considerable power, especially on domestic issues.

In short, both the power elite and pluralist models offer significant insight into the question of who rules the United States. As the power elite model suggests, a relatively small number of people hold enormous power. They control much of foreign policy and make decisions that shape the direction of economic development. This ruling group, although possibly not conspiratorial or completely cohesive, ranks far above most other citizens in political, economic, and social clout. Yet as the pluralist position suggests, many groups that are not a part of this elite can occasionally wield power, especially on domestic social policy and local and regional issues. This is the realm in which many of the battles over solutions to social problems addressed by sociologists are likely to be fought. And most people in the United States have an opportunity to play a part in these less powerful, but still quite important, groups.

The U.S. Economy: Concentration and Change

You should be able to describe recent trends in the U.S. economy and discuss the problems they have created.

Capitalism in the United States has undergone considerable change in the past two centuries. This chapter focuses on three central issues: the rise of corporations, the changing labor force, and the globalization of the labor force.

The Corporate Economy

Capitalism in the United States once consisted of small, local businesses and many competitors. Consequently, power in the economic sector was decentralized, diffused, and limited to local or regional levels. It was almost impossible for businesses to accumulate substantial power at the national level. Today, the economy is very different: It is highly centralized and international in scope, and a small number of people can gain enormous control over wealth and power.

CORPORATE GROWTH AND CONCENTRATION   Capitalism in the United States is no longer based on the individual ownership of businesses. Rather, the dominant form of business today is the corporation, *a business enterprise that is owned by stockholders, most of whom are not involved in running the daily affairs of the business* (Nace, 2003). Three key characteristics distinguish corporations from individually owned businesses. First, corporations have access to a much broader source of capital than do individuals because the former can sell stock to thousands of stockholders. Second, stockholders, who own the corporation, have only a limited liability should the corporation be sued or go bankrupt. Stockholders lose only the funds they have invested. Third, the ownership of corporations is separate from the control of its policies and daily affairs. The stockholders own a part of the corporation, but most stockholders are not involved in the actual running of the company. It is run by professional managers who are ultimately appointed by a board of directors that is elected by stockholders. These managers may own little or no stock in the company. Legally, the stockholders run the corporation, but for all practical purposes the board and the managers do. Unlike in individually owned businesses, the ownership of corporations is easily transferable, and should a major stockholder die, the corporation continues to function as usual. Because of these characteristics, the corporate economic structure is extremely attractive to investors. Large amounts of capital can be accumulated with minimum risk to individuals.

Because of the advantages that stem from corporate organization, corporations now dominate the economy, with a relatively small number of corporations accounting for most business activity (Nace, 2003). There are more than three million corporations in the United States, but economic resources, and thus influence and power, tend to be concentrated in the larger corporations. As these large corporations have come to dominate the economy, it has become possible for some to control substantial segments of economic life to the point of restricting competition in the marketplace.

One form of restrictive growth is called a *monopoly*—the control of a product or service by one company. For example, in the early 1990s, Nintendo controlled about 80 percent of the $5 billion video-game market in the United States. Related to the monopoly is the *oligopoly*, in which a few corporations control a market. Some sectors of the U.S. economy are highly oligopolistic, in some cases approaching a monopoly. In a 1980s court case, for example, the American Telephone and Telegraph Company was broken up into a number of smaller companies because it had gained almost complete control over local and long-distance telephone service in the United States. In 1998, the government began antitrust proceedings against the Microsoft Corporation because its computer operating system was installed on over 90 percent of computers sold, making it difficult for other software producers to compete in the market.

Another form of corporate growth representing a concentration of economic power is the *conglomerate*, which is a corporation that owns other companies in fields quite different from that of the parent company. By the late 1990s, for example, a number of conglomerates emerged that centered on the media (television, book publishing, motion pictures, magazines, and the Internet) but also expanded into ownership of sports teams, farms, factories, and other corporations (Dye, 2002; McChesney, 2004). On a global level at the beginning of the twenty-first century, six corporate giants control most of what appears in the global media: Time Warner, Disney, the News Corporation, General Electric, Viacom, and Bertelsmann (see Chapter 12). Together, they own almost all of the 50 most-subscribed-to cable television channels. Conglomerates are advantageous in that they provide stability through diversity. Losses in one industry can be counterbalanced by the parent company through profits made in an unrelated business.

MULTINATIONAL AND GLOBAL CORPORATIONS As corporations have grown over the decades, the larger ones have extended their activities into a number of different countries (Barnet & Cavanagh, 1994). By the 1970s, *multinational corporations* had emerged, which made a large commitment of resources to international business and engaged in manufacturing, production, and sales in a number of countries. These overseas corporate activities tended to involve separate operations in the various countries, often tailored to local social and economic conditions. By the 1990s, *global corporations*—a few hundred corporations whose economic activities span the globe, using modern financial, industrial, and telecommunications technology to mount a worldwide, integrated system of production and distribution—had become the prominent actors on the world scene. Corporations have gone multinational, and then global, because

enormous profits can be made with such an organization. There are lucrative markets for their goods outside the United States. In addition, the cost of labor, land, and taxes is considerably lower in places such as Mexico, Vietnam, and Indonesia than in the United States. These factors suggest the extent to which U.S. corporations now participate in a global economy, in which national boundaries have become less important as determinants of or restraints on economic competition. As a result, labor and capital in the United States must compete with labor and capital in many countries around the world.

The concentration of economic power and the growth of global corporations raises the question of whether corporations pursue goals that are broadly beneficial to society or goals that enhance the narrow interests of particular groups. Large corporations control such vast resources that their activities shape in substantial ways the lives of average people in the United States. With their primary goal being to make and increase profits and to ensure corporate growth, corporations may not necessarily act in the best interests of other groups or society as a whole. For example, when a corporation decides to relocate outside a central city area to reduce its taxes, the city loses jobs and tax revenue; these losses can bring about increases in unemployment and poverty in the city. Such job movement illustrates one of the major problems created by multinational and global corporations: Because their primary intent is to maximize profits, their actions can run counter to national political and economic goals. For example, the president of NCR Corporation, when asked about the competitiveness of the United States, responded, "I don't think about it at all. We at NCR think of ourselves as a globally competitive company that happens to be headquartered in the United States" (quoted in Uchitelle, 1989, p. 13). However, others argue that at least some of this drain of U.S. productive dollars is offset by foreign corporations that pump money into their U.S. operations, which creates jobs here.

The Changing Labor Force

Workers have also made efforts to concentrate economic power in their own hands. It was not until the late nineteenth century and the emergence of business firms employing thousands of workers that the labor movement emerged as a significant political force in the U.S. economy. Capitalists, pursuing the profit motive, were inclined to pay workers as little as possible. The capitalists could do so more easily because large numbers of people had immigrated to the United States in the late 1800s, creating a labor surplus in some industries. In response, working people organized to pursue their own interests. Capitalists staunchly opposed the labor movement, believing that higher

An ABC News correspondent reports from Baghdad at the beginning of the Iraq War in 2003. The media and modern communications technologies play an important role in shaping people's perceptions of political and economic institutions, including war. They are "contested territory" that different groups attempt to control in order to benefit themselves.

wages would generate laziness among workers and threaten the American way of life.

The owners' resistance and the workers' determination made U.S. labor history one of the bloodiest and most violent of any industrial nation. However, the workers eventually prevailed, and by the 1930s legislation gave them the right to organize and to bargain collectively with employers. The number of workers belonging to labor unions continued to grow, reaching more than 22 million in the 1970s. With the right to strike firmly established for most workers, unions have been in a strong position to gain even higher wages and larger fringe benefit packages for their members.

Although unions have gained considerable power in the United States, their future is somewhat uncertain. Union membership as a proportion of the workforce has been declining since the 1950s and is presently at its lowest point since 1940 (Figure 13.4). The number of people belonging to unions has declined to fewer than 16 million. One reason for this decline is that occupations traditionally unionized—blue-collar industrial jobs—have been declining in numbers

whereas the number of white-collar employees, who have traditionally not unionized, is growing. In fact, sometimes the United States is called a postindustrial society because a shrinking proportion of the workforce labors in industrial occupations. Because of automation, robotization, and other technology, fewer workers are needed to make the products necessary for the U.S. lifestyle (Chapter 15). The largest growth in the workforce has been in white-collar jobs such as sales, management, teaching, or clerical work (Figure 13.5). A second reason for the decline in unions is that many corporations over the past four decades have relocated in states having weak union organizations or have moved overseas where unions are either weak or nonexistent. A third reason for the decline in unions has been the emergence in the past few decades of active opposition to unionization efforts by corporations and other employers. This opposition is often supported by a phalanx of consulting organizations who specialize in helping employers fight unionization efforts. In their fight to keep unions out of the workplace, employers have sometimes resorted to various forms of intimidation: Union activists are fired,

Figure 13.4

Union Membership in the United States as a Percentage of Total People Employed, 1950–2007

Note: From *Statistical Abstract of the United States,* 1984 (p. 439) by U.S. Bureau of the Census, 1983, Washington, DC: U.S. Government Printing Office; *Employment and Earnings* by U.S. Department of Labor, Bureau of Labor Statistics, January, various years.

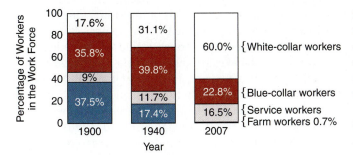

Figure 13.5

Changing Occupational Structure in the United States, 1900–2007

Note: From *Historical Statistics of the United States, Colonial Times to 1970, Bicentennial Edition Part 2* (p. 139) by U.S. Bureau of the Census, 1970, Washington, DC: U.S. Government Printing Office; *Employment and Earnings,* 55(1), p. 208, by U.S. Department of Labor, Bureau of Labor Statistics, 2008.

companies threaten to move jobs overseas, and employers engage in lengthy and expensive litigation to keep unions from organizing.

Global Competition: Worker Dislocation and Unemployment

Over the past forty years, the percentage of people in the United States who have been unemployed has fluctuated considerably. Today, the unemployment rate is lower than at many points during that period, but it is slightly higher than forty years ago. Teenagers, African Americans, and other minority groups are most heavily affected by this problem and exhibit considerably higher unemployment rates than do whites. However, these official unemployment statistics do not include people who are unemployed but have quit looking for a job—so-called discouraged workers. It also does not include those who are underemployed, working part time, or working at a temporary job that does not pay enough to support a family. When these people are counted, the unemployment problem in the United States is even more grave than the government unemployment statistics might suggest.

One of the reasons for this persistent unemployment in the United States has been increased competition for jobs in the world economic system (Baldwin, 2003). This has resulted in what is variously called "downsizing," "outsourcing," "offshoring," or "offshore outsourcing." Businesses in the United States have closed and moved overseas, or they contract out many tasks to low-wage, usually nonunion manufacturers in the United States or other countries. Countries in Latin America and Asia have been especially receptive to U.S. businesses. The minimum wage in the United States is more than $5 per hour, while well-paid workers on automobile assembly lines can earn $24 per hour. By contrast, global sportswear companies headquartered in the United States pay young girls and women in Indonesia $1.35 per day to assemble sports shoes for export to the United States (Barnet & Cavanagh, 1994). Hundreds of U.S. companies have left the United States and opened up shop in *maquiladoras,* factories in northern Mexico that take advantage of the cheap labor, weak unions, and lax environmental regulations to assemble products and export them to the United States. Many thousands of U.S. jobs have been lost to these *maquiladoras,* which have the best of both worlds—cheap labor and easy access to U.S. markets to sell their products (see Other Worlds, Other Ways: Mexico in Chapter 8).

This global competition for jobs is no longer limited to manufacturing or blue-collar jobs. The twenty-first century has seen this offshore outsourcing extend into service and technology jobs, including jobs held by well-paid and highly educated professionals (Lohr, 2003). Computer programmers, computer technicians, and even physician-radiologists find themselves competing with less expensive workers in other countries. After all, writing computer code or interpreting X-rays or MRI scans can be done anywhere, and the results communicated around the globe instantaneously. The Internet and modern communications technologies have eliminated the requirement that jobs must be done in particular geographic locales. Projections are that millions of these jobs will be lost to workers in the United States over the next decade (Lohr, 2003). The only jobs that are safe from this trend are those that require face-to-face contact between worker and boss or customer, and in an information-based economy, fewer jobs will have that characteristic.

Although world competition is probably the major factor in the growth in unemployment in the United States, other factors contribute. There has been considerable growth in the teenage labor market, and the number of women joining the workforce has grown over the decades. Still another dimension of the problem is automation, which replaces human workers with machines.

Workers thrown out of work by foreign competition are called "displaced workers," numbering 4 million people between 2003 and 2005, and their ranks continue to grow as more workers are displaced (Moore, 1996; U.S. Bureau of the Census, 2007, p. 387). Some displaced workers never return to the labor force. Those who do often find themselves unemployed for some time—one and a half years, on average—and almost all experience a permanent decline in family income because of their job loss. Many are forced to accept irregular work at low-paying jobs with few fringe benefits. In addition, African Americans and Hispanic Americans are hit much harder by job displacement than whites: These groups are more likely to be displaced, are jobless longer, and are much less likely to be reemployed (Kletzer, 2001; Uchitelle, 2006).

Unemployment, as tragic as it may be, is not the only form in which difficulties confront workers in the United States. A related problem is that the jobs available to them, especially at the low end of the income scale, may not pay as well as they did in the past (Mishel, Bernstein, & Schmitt, 2001; Rank, 2004; Tonelson, 2000). The proportion of jobs that pay poverty-level wages has been increasing for the past three decades, and the new jobs created in recent decades have tended to be at the low end of the pay scale. In addition, corporations have resorted to hiring more temporary and contract workers because they can save on salaries or fringe benefits and have more flexibility in terminating such employees. Unemployment,

low pay, and temporary work produce feelings of job insecurity that can have widespread and negative ramifications for the economy. When work is unstable, workers are less likely to seek training and skills that will enable them to be more productive and employers are less inclined to invest in such training. So, since advances in employee training promote higher levels of economic productivity and growth, job insecurity thus works against greater economic productivity.

With advanced industrial capitalism and a global economy, then, the situation of workers has changed, and the relative power of workers and employers seems to have shifted toward the latter (Harrison, 1994). Although labor unions still provide some workers with important protections against low wages or job loss, unions have become a less effective counterbalance to the substantial power of corporations.

Whereas predicting the ultimate outcome of these changes is difficult, a number of trends are emerging that may influence labor relations of the future. One is that labor unions may globalize by encouraging union organizing among workers overseas. Unions in the United States, for example, are helping workers organize unions in Mexico, South Africa, and other nations. If pay and working conditions in these other nations rise, then those workers will pose less of a threat to the jobs of workers in the United States (Cavanagh & Broad, 1996).

A second trend has been for workers to protect their interests through *worker empowerment*—workers gaining management authority and responsibility and more control over the operation of corporations (Greider, 2003; Melman, 2001). In some cases, this has involved employee stock ownership plans (ESOPs) where workers gain ownership in a company and have a stake in how it is run and in the consequences of their own work performance. Today, eleven thousand U.S. firms with ten million employees have some form of ESOP (The ESOP Association, 2007). In other cases, worker empowerment has involved changes in the structure of companies so that employees have more of a say in company decision making, more opportunities for advancement, and increased access to powerful people and resources in the organization. Worker empowerment might even involve a fundamental restructuring of corporations so that workers are seen as fundamental stakeholders in the corporations and thus deserving of permanent representation on the boards of directors of the corporations. Such representation in the past, and for most corporations today, is limited to shareholders in the corporation.

Whatever form it takes, worker empowerment has focused on reducing the sense of powerlessness and lack of control that many workers experience. And research shows that worker participation and employee ownership can increase a company's productivity (Rosen & Youngs, 1991).

Although these trends would provide some protection for workers, employees may still be vulnerable without some fundamental changes in economic institutions. True protection of workers would occur, some argue, only if the United States and other nations developed more of a mixed economy, with the government taking more control of some economic realms in order to pursue collective goals. Proponents of an extreme power elite position would argue that inequality and exploitation are inherent elements of capitalism because capitalism is ultimately fueled by personal greed and acquisition. As such, capitalism can only work to benefit the powerful. Some form of mixed economy would balance the avarice inherent in capitalism by injecting an element of the public good into economic activities and decisions. Others, including some pluralists, would argue that capitalism can benefit most citizens through the checks and balances of competing interest groups. This is not to say that capitalism can achieve equality or that everyone will benefit. But if the government encourages the development of diverse interest groups, large numbers of citizens will be able to pursue their goals.

The Global Political and Economic System

> You should be able to discuss the extent of and reasons for economic concentration and inequality among the nations of the world, the problems that this creates, the structures of globalization that have developed, and the forms of resistance that have emerged.

By the end of the twentieth century, political and economic systems had become truly global in nature. Political globalization refers to *the emergence of interconnected and unified structures and organizations that transcend national boundaries and that are used to exercise power, allocate resources, and resolve conflicts of interest on a global scale.* Economic globalization refers to *structures and processes, unified and interconnected on a worldwide basis, for producing and distributing goods and services* (Boli & Thomas, 1997; Halliday & Osinsky, 2006). Part of this globalization is discussed earlier in this chapter in terms of the emergence of multinational and global corporations. But this emerging global structure also includes nation-states and a variety of intergovernmental organizations along with some nongovernmental organizations. The nature of this global system is described in the following sections.

Concentration and Inequality

Some of the trends found in the U.S. economy are reproduced on a global scale. In particular, the trends show a pattern of concentration of wealth and resources in the hands of a few nations—the highly industrialized, capitalist nations of North America, Europe, and Asia, which now dominate the world economy. For example, the world's corporate resources are concentrated in the hands of a very few nations, with most large corporations in the world headquartered in a small number of nations ("Global 500 . . .," 2004). Looking at the 500 largest corporations in the world, 377 of them—75 percent—are headquartered in the United States, Japan, and three European nations. Even more astonishing, 54 percent of those 500 corporations are found in just two of the world's more than 200 nations: the United States and Japan. So, when we talk of global corporations dominating world trade, we really mean that a relatively few nations of the world dominate that trade.

Another way to look at the economic circumstances of the world is by comparing the economic resources that people have available to spend. The gross national income (GNI) represents the total output of goods and services in a nation and is sometimes taken as a rough measure of the wealth of a nation. Naturally, large nations will have a larger GNI, so the key measure of wealth is the GNI per person. Figure 6.2 on page 156 shows the GNI per person for the nations around the world. The industrialized nations of North America, Europe, and Asia, along with a few of the oil-producing nations of the Middle East, do very well, while most other nations lag far behind. To give a sense of the enormous disparities that exist, the United States, Japan, Switzerland, Denmark, and Norway have a GNI of more than $30,000 per person, whereas very poor nations such as Ghana, Nigeria, Vietnam, and Mozambique have a GNP of less than $700 per person (World Bank, 2007).

Many reasons can be found for these disparities, but the three chief explanations are circumstances, cultural theory, and world-system theory. Some of the differences are the result of a particular country's geographic or historical circumstances. Saudi Arabia, Kuwait, and the United Arab Emirates, for example, do quite well because they have large reserves of oil to tap as a source of wealth. The United States is fortunate to have much highly arable land. Some of the nations of sub-Saharan Africa have parched land with unpredictable rainfall and often long periods of drought. In short, some nations are more blessed with good resources, and they tend to be among the "have" nations.

The second explanation, cultural theory, argues that some cultural traditions encourage ways of thinking and behaving that are more conducive to producing wealth and economic growth. Chapter 11 addressed this issue in discussing how the Protestant ethic encouraged people to work hard, be frugal, save, and reinvest.

Max Weber used this cultural orientation to help account for the rise of capitalism in Europe. More recently, analysts have suggested that Confucian traditions in such countries as South Korea, Hong Kong, Singapore, Japan, and Taiwan may have a similar outcome (Huntington & Harrison, 2001). Confucianism places high value on attaining an education as a route toward the highest form of service to society—governing for social reform and advancement (see Chapter 11). In ancient China, Confucian education emphasized merit in the educational process, so that those with the greatest skills and highest virtues would become the governors of society. In these Asian countries, educational administrators and teachers are held in high regard. This combination of education and merit means that social mobility is a part of social and economic life in these nations. Thus, their cultural orientation encourages people to work hard and achieve, behaviors that in turn will increase the likelihood of national economic growth and development.

The third explanation of these worldwide economic disparities focuses on the centuries-long historical process discussed in Chapter 6 as the capitalist world system. *World-system theory* focuses on the expansive nature of capitalism and its emphasis on market forces, profit making, and surplus accumulation. Capitalism's drive to find new markets creates a pressure to seek out new territories in which to invest. Today, corporations' search for new markets has created a global economy with an international stratification system. According to world-system theory, a hierarchy of nations has emerged, divided roughly into *core nations* (capitalist, technologically advanced nations searching for opportunities to expand investment) and *peripheral nations* (less developed nations that provide cheap labor, produce food, and serve as a source of raw materials). There are also *semiperipheral nations* that are large or have some special resources and therefore fall in between; they are less dependent on the core nations and sometimes act as core nations themselves (Apter, 1986; Bornschier & Trezzini, 1997; Chase-Dunn & Grimes, 1995). Figure 6.2 identified the core nations of the world as the high-income economies, the semiperipheral nations are the middle-income economies, and the peripheral nations are the low-income economies.

In this international stratification system, the core nations dominate and exploit the peripheral nations. The key to the system is trade, with some nations exporting goods while others serve primarily as a labor pool and a source of natural resources. Some world-system theorists argue that the nature of capitalism is such that it creates social inequalities through its tendency to distribute resources unequally. This inequality exists within nations, which have both rich and poor people, and at the international level, where

the policies of core nations help keep peripheral nations less developed. The core nations extract natural resources and cheap labor from the peripheral nations in order to produce manufactured goods that are then exported for profit. Through political, economic, and sometimes military intervention, the core nations encourage the emergence of political and economic elites in the peripheral nations who will assist in the economic expansion of the core.

The Structure of Globalization

Political and economic globalization are manifested through various regional and national organizations, treaties, and other structures through which the interconnectedness of the system is maintained and promoted. It is this structure that provides a coherent and unified set of rules and regulations for the effective operation of the system. One element of this structure is the global financial institutions that emerged during the twentieth century, such as the International Bank for Reconstruction and Development (or World Bank) and the International Monetary Fund (IMF) (Danaher, 2001; Stiglitz, 2006). These organizations work to coordinate global economic activity by lending money, guaranteeing private investments, helping stabilize prices and currencies, and encouraging private investment in development. They receive funding from their member nations (most nations belong), but their decision-making and voting power tend to be dominated by the wealthy industrial nations of Europe and North America. In short, they function much like a central bank for the world, lending money and expertise to support economic development in developing nations. However, the support is not free: They demand that nations organize their economies, and sometimes their political systems, in ways that support global capitalism and corporate growth. Often this means reducing domestic spending on things like schools, health, and social services. It can also require that nations stress export industries rather than production for domestic consumption.

Another element of the structure of political and economic globalization is the global trade agreements that encourage free trade among nations and discourage hindrances to trade, such as tariffs, restrictive labor policies, or environmental regulations. The most recent such trade agreements are the North American Free Trade Agreement (NAFTA) of 1994 and the World Trade Organization (WTO) of 1995. There has been much controversy about these trade agreements, especially in terms of who benefits and who loses from them (Stiglitz, 2004; Nace, 2003). In terms of benefits, one of the clear winners has been large, global corporations and their stockholders, who have enjoyed greater profits and more protection from government regulations and other limitations in areas such as environmental, safety, health, and labor policy. These large corporations, after all, have the resources to compete effectively in such a free-for-all trade environment. Also winning are consumers who often pay lower prices for goods because of the freer trade. Clear losers have been industrial workers in the United States, whose jobs have gone to other countries, and workers in all countries who have fewer environmental, labor, health, and safety protections under these agreements. Also losing have been rural farmers in Mexico and other countries who can't compete against the large-scale agribusinesses that have taken over. Beyond this shifting of resources from one group to another, these trade agreements may have had little long-term impact beyond what would have occurred with the previous trade policies. Still, the groups that benefit most from these trade agreements are also in the best position to influence what present and future trade policies will be like.

Political and economic globalization also manifests itself in the form of various treaties, courts, tribunals, arbitration panels, and regulatory bodies to which people, nations, and corporations turn for international regulation of actions and peaceful resolution of disputes (Halliday & Osinsky, 2006). Nations turn to groups such as the International Criminal Court, the Convention for the Regulation of Whaling, or to various United Nations resolutions. These groups provide a worldwide structure of laws and regulations that creates a foundation upon which global economic activity can occur in a way that people will see as fair, trustworthy, and predictable. Now, such treaties and tribunals have been around for centuries, but the difference in the twenty-first century is that this global structure is far more extensive, pervasive, and interconnected. It is not perfect, of course, since nations and organizations sometimes ignore treaties or the rulings of tribunals, but international organizations are better able today to sanction those that do so.

Finally, the structure of globalization is supported by the various regional and global organizations that create many of the treaties, courts, and tribunals just mentioned. The United Nations is probably the most prominent of these, with all nations of the world belonging to it. It plays a very significant part in regulating the relationships between nations. Another example is the European Union (EU), which is a political and economic entity to which most nations of Europe belong. It regulates economic relations, for example, by promoting free trade among member nations and establishing a common currency (the euro). It also promotes common labor and environmental standards, as well as a unitary passport system. It has a parliament elected by all citizens of the EU. The UN and the EU are called *international governmental organizations*, or IGOs, because they are primarily organizations of governments.

Global corporations and their supporting organizations generally subscribe to the ideology that levels of world prosperity are unlimited, that such prosperity can extend to all people, and that economic development and capitalist expansion, largely unfettered by government intervention, is the best means to achieve such global prosperity. In fact, many supporters of these organizations claim that they will eventually eradicate poverty around the world. To support such economic development, world economies have become organized around market-oriented production and continual mass consumption. This has been called the *commodification of the globe*, a system in which everything is a commodity to be sold and market value determines all (Rich, 1994, p. 6). In such a global economic environment, political boundaries and national allegiances are becoming less important determinants of economic activity. In Chapter 2 we discussed the possibility that globalization would lead to some degree of cultural unification around the world. Likewise it is possible that globalization tendencies in political and economic realms will bring about some degree of political and economic convergence among the nations of the world. In particular, nations will move toward more corporate and capitalist forms of economic organization and more democratic forms of government. Other World, Other Ways: Nicaragua looks at how the workings of the world economic system affected the historical development and economic circumstances of the peoples of Nicaragua.

Unemployment, Dislocation, and Resistance

On a global scale, there is considerable controversy over whether the policies of organizations such as the World Bank or the IMF benefit all, or even most, citizens of the nations in which they operate (Rich, 1994; Stiglitz, 2006). Although many people do benefit, the policies have also meant drastic reductions in wages for some; lowered expenditures for health, education, and other social services; and devastating degradation of the environment. Around the world, 120 million people are officially registered as unemployed—a figure that everyone agrees is conservative—and at least another 700 million are underemployed, which means that they do not earn enough to support themselves and their families.

As with unemployment in the United States, the world situation is due in part to the nature of the global economy that is emerging as industrialism and capitalism advance around the world. This world economy is characterized by a relative dearth of entry-level jobs that pay a decent wage. There is also a shortage of jobs for people with low levels of

NICARAGUA: POLITICAL AND ECONOMIC CHANGE IN A PERIPHERAL NATION

Nicaragua is a Central American nation of about 5 million people, the largest nation in the region (World Bank, 2007). It is rich in natural resources, with much open land and soil and a climate that will support a variety of agricultural products. It also has reserves of timber, silver, and gold, as well as coastlines along both the Pacific Ocean and the Caribbean Sea for shipping. Yet, Nicaragua is a poor nation, with a GNI of about $1,000 per person (compared to more than $44,000 in the United States). Over the years, the Nicaraguan economic elites have focused their attention on international trade, viewing poor Nicaraguans as a cheap labor supply to be exploited. In the past few decades, Nicaragua has gone through considerable political instability and has experienced significant changes in its social, economic, and political structures. Nicaragua provides a good illustration of some of the political and economic processes discussed in this chapter.

Nicaragua's problems began with the Spanish conquest in the sixteenth century (Newson, 1987). Before the arrival of the Spanish, the indigenous peoples had an advanced agrarian society that supported them quite well. The *conquistadores* took control and demanded payment in gold from the Indians. They also took Indians for the slave trade and introduced disease for which the Indians had no immunity. Within a matter of decades, the Spanish devastated the Nicaraguan economy and society. The agricultural base of the region was nearly destroyed, and disease and a lack of food produced a high death rate. The Spanish elite accumulated wealth from mining gold and exporting timber, cattle, and some crops to other Spanish colonies. They used the Indians as cheap labor and denied their traditional rights to the land.

With the collapse of Spanish colonial rule in the early 1800s, Nicaragua began to resurrect an internally focused economy that provided more food and other goods to Nicaraguans. A part of this economy involved Indians reclaiming land that was theirs by tradition. Between cattle ranching and peasant farming, the economy of Nicaragua was fairly self-sufficient.

This self-sufficiency ended when the coffee boom hit Central America in the late 1800s (Walker, 1991). Since the elite needed much fertile land to expand coffee production for export, they manipulated the government to pass legislation saying that any land not owned by legal title belonged to the government and could be sold to the highest bidder. Since many Indians were squatters on their land without such title, they were dispossessed and the coffee barons expanded. In addition, these new landless peasants provided a large, unskilled workforce that the coffee growers needed during the few months of harvest season each year.

The peasants revolted over this shabby treatment in the War of the Communeros, but they lost. With no other way to survive, many Nicaraguans who had once been self-sufficient peasant farmers became a rural laboring class dependent on the coffee plantations. This new coffee economy depended on a greater investment in machinery and labor, and so it became dominated by big business, large landholders, and foreigners. Some small peasant farming persisted, along with some cattle ranching, but the Nicaraguan economy had become heavily dependent on one export product.

The profits of coffee production went to the elite and foreigners, while average Nicaraguans were exploited through low wages and few opportunities for improvement. Nicaragua became a nation with a large mass of people living at a desperate subsistence level and a tiny middle and upper class to whom most resources and profits flowed. The country was also drawn into and became dependent on the capitalist world system. According to one expert on Nicaragua, the nation had become a classic example of world-system dependency: "a special situation in which the economy of a weak country is externally oriented and the government is controlled by national and/or international elites … that benefit from this economic relationship" (Walker, 1991, p. 3).

The United States has a long history of involvement in Nicaragua. U.S. troops occupied it from 1927 to 1933, fighting a peasant rebellion led by Augusto Sandino. During its occupation, the United States established and trained the Nicaraguan National Guard. Unable to defeat Sandino, the United States worked out a compromise and withdrew in 1933. Within a few years, the leader of the National Guard, Anastasio Somoza Garcia, arranged to have Sandino killed, overthrew the president of Nicaragua, and arranged for his own election as president. Somoza or one of his sons ruled Nicaragua from 1936 to 1979 (Walker, 1991).

Nicaragua eventually became less dependent on coffee but remained dependent on export. When the world price of cotton increased in the 1950s, for example, cattle ranches and peasant farms were converted to cotton production, resulting in more landless peasants and less agricultural production for domestic consumption. This "development" and "progress" tended to benefit the small elite. For much of the twentieth century, the Somoza family controlled the government and the National Guard and used them to suppress any dissent or rebellion. The elite supported the Somoza family rule, since it provided the political and social stability that permitted them to run their profitable export activities. Political institutions under the Somozas appeared democratic, with elections, constitutionally guaranteed human rights, and a bicameral legislature. In reality, the Somozas were complete dictators, supported by the National Guard. The elections, for example, were a sham, controlled by the Somozas through press censorship, ballot-box stuffing, and multiple voting by their supporters. Other political parties existed, but they had virtually no chance of gaining control of the government through elections. Workers and peasants had no channels of influence to the Somoza government.

The 1970s were a decade of decline for the Somoza regime. It began with a devastating earthquake that killed ten thousand Nicaraguans, but the Somoza family responded by ruthlessly exploiting the tragedy for their own economic benefit. This and other events intensified opposition to the regime, even among the Nicaraguan elite, who resented the way the Somoza family shamelessly took personal advantage of every economic sector in the nation and excluded the elite from even a small role in politics. The Somozas also came under international pressure. President Carter and Amnesty International wanted the Somozas to reduce the political repression and torture by which they maintained their grip on power. The International Monetary Fund wanted Nicaragua to institute economic reforms that would enable its economy to modernize. This decline in support led to the success of a popular revolt, and the Somoza government was overthrown by the Sandanist Front of National Liberation (FSLN) in 1979. Nicaragua is still struggling, however, since the successful revolution was followed by a decade of civil war that further devastated the Nicaraguan economy. In the civil war, the United States supported the counterrevolutionary contras against the ruling FSLN.

---

education or few skills. The modern workplace is increasingly a high-technology environment, calling for considerable education and training. Those who, because of poverty or lack of access, do not receive such training and education find few places where they can earn a living wage. These trends have resulted in a polarization of the world's workforce: An increasing chasm between high-wage and low-wage workers. This means that people who get good jobs do fairly well for themselves and their families, but those without the necessary education and skills live increasingly marginal and precarious lives. Added to this is the increasing use of a geographically mobile labor force—immigrants, both legal and illegal, who are forced to travel to where the jobs (typically low-paying) are. It doesn't matter whether it is Mexican peasants traveling to the United States, Palestinians going to Kuwait, or Turks going to Germany. Corporations depend on this flexible, low-paid pool of labor to help keep costs down and profits up.

In addition to fostering unemployment, the global economy has displaced tens of thousands of poor people from their homes to make way for dams, logging activities, or large-scale agricultural and industrial developments. Often, these people must resettle in less desirable areas. Some critics dispute whether organizations such as the World Bank and the IMF have been successful in their stated goals of promoting development through large loans to governments. Critics of these organizations argue that their practices have dislocated people, exacerbated economic inequality and ethnic tensions, and promoted environmental degradation while benefiting corporations, the elite, and a small segment of the workforce.

The globalization of corporate control in the past century has also created new or enhanced threats to democratic practices and institutions around the world (Stiglitz, 2006). These large corporations are sometimes wealthier than the nations in which they operate, giving the corporations enormous power from which to demand that a country adopt policies that are beneficial to the corporation. Global financial institutions, such as the IMF and the World Bank, also intervene in the democratic process of some nations. Because these world institutions often operate in secret, ordinary citizens and their governments may have little knowledge of or input into what these organizations do. Dispensing large amounts of money and making policies at the international level, these organizations have become almost quasi-governments themselves, whose policies affect people's lives around the world.

Corporations and their world financial institutions are private or semiprivate organizations and as such are largely beyond democratic control. The result is that the important economic and political decisions that shape the lives and opportunities of people around the world are in the hands of these powerful private and semiprivate entities. Their decisions often change traditional cultures and ways of life as they push social and political changes that further economic development.

On a global scale, people have organized to fight against the actions of governments, corporations, and international financial organizations. The term *nongovernmental organizations* (NGOs) is now used to refer to grass-roots citizen organizations that have emerged to fight the intrusive and destructive policies of governments or groups like the World Bank and the IMF. These NGOs use whatever resources they have available, including education, boycotts, and demonstrations, in order to stop or change activities with detrimental social or environmental consequences. The NGOs are usually small and focus on specific problems that a village or a people confront. International networks of NGOs have emerged to provide mutual help through the exchange of information, resources, and personnel. These NGOs have had some success in alleviating the negative impact of the actions of corporations and of organizations such as the World Bank and the IMF.

In recent years, some of the actions of NGOs, along with the actions of other groups, have coalesced into what is sometimes called the *antiglobalization movement*. In places such as Seattle in 1999, Genoa, Italy, in 2001, and New York City in 2002, thousands of people have supported this movement by gathering to protest the trends toward globalization and to exert an influence on the way globalization proceeds. The term "antiglobalization movement" is actually somewhat of a misnomer because many of the participants involved recognize that globalization in some form will likely be a feature of the modern world. For these participants, the focus is to shape the terms of the debate about globalization rather than to derail the process altogether. The primary strategy at this point is to express divergent opinions by massing in large numbers whenever the World Bank, the IMF, the WTO, or other global corporate institutions meet. One of the main demands of the protesters is that the process of

globalization be made more democratic, with citizens around the world having input into the process. Currently, globalization is occurring mostly at the direction of global financial institutions, which, as we have seen in this chapter, have no formal mechanisms for citizen input into their decision-making process. The protesters want labor, environmental, human rights, and other groups to sit at the tables where decisions about the global economy are made. Another demand of the protesters is that globalization promote the reduction of inequalities between the rich and the poor—between the powerful and the powerless—around the world. Applying Sociology: Intervening in the Process of Economic Globalization explores some of the ways in which applied sociologists have worked with both the global institutions and with groups supportive of the antiglobalization movement.

Politics, the Economy, the Media, and the Cyberworld

You should be able to discuss how the media and the cyberworld impact the process of influence and persuasion in political and economic realms.

Applying Sociology   Intervening in the Process of Economic Globalization

Chapter 1 mentions that sociology has long focused its attention on social reform, or making improvements in people's lives. As political and economic changes have occurred on a global scale, sociologists have worked with a variety of interest groups in order to promote reforms that would be as broadly beneficial as possible.

Some applied sociologists have worked with political and economic institutions that are at the forefront of globalization in order to alleviate the negative effects and promote the positive consequences of the actions of these organizations. For example, sociologists and other social scientists work for the World Bank to predict and evaluate the consequences of World Bank policies on all aspects of social and economic life (Cernea, 1997). They look at such consequences as landlessness, homelessness, health problems, and the disintegration of social supports that can occur when the World Bank encourages the involuntary relocation of people in order to pursue policies of economic development. The sociologists collect data on what has occurred in earlier such episodes and use this information to predict what may happen as a result of current and future policies. Then they make recommendations for how to change programs in order to alleviate the negative consequences. They might recommend, for instance, that the people being relocated have

a greater say in how it is done or that the World Bank provide full financing for the resettlement. In some cases, World Bank policies might be changed substantially in order to alleviate the negative consequences projected by the applied research.

Applied sociologists have also worked with groups that find themselves in opposition to some of the ways in which corporations promote globalization. Sociologists have worked, for example, with labor unions, conducting surveys of their members (Greider, Denise-Neinhaus, & Statham, 1992; Shostak, 2001). Such surveys have focused on assessing union members' attitudes on a variety of issues and projecting whether members would honor a strike called by the unions. Other surveys have provided unions with information about the needs of their members as well as assessed the effectiveness of programs to train displaced workers and return them to the workforce. Surveys have also focused on working conditions, the morale of workers, worker health and safety, and other topics related to the workplace. In addition to surveys, sociologists have used data from a variety of sources to conduct long-range forecasts for labor unions to help the unions and their members to adapt to projected changes in their industries as a result of globalization. ▪

The interactionist perspective stresses how people's definitions of reality serve as mechanisms of social control, shaping their thoughts, desires, and behaviors. In both political and economic realms, efforts are made to shape those definitions through persuasion and influence. And today, the mass media and the cyberworld each play a central role in shaping definitions of political and economic reality.

Politics, Persuasion, and Propaganda

Politicians use the resources available to them to gain the support of other politicians, elites, and the citizenry in advancing a particular political agenda that encompasses, among other things, a particular set of values. At the same time, the elites and ordinary citizens make efforts to control and manipulate the actions of politicians. These efforts at persuasion sometimes become propaganda: *the deliberate spread of one-sided information or ideas with the intent of helping or harming particular people, groups, institutions, or societies.* Other terms sometimes used in this context are *misinformation, disinformation,* or *censorship.* The power elite, pluralist, and world-system theories all agree that the ability to persuade and influence is not equally distributed among all groups in society. Access to and control over the modern media and computer-mediated communications technology can be a key determinant of a group's ability to persuade, influence, or propagandize (Croteau & Hoynes, 2002).

A naive view of the media in this process is that they serve as a passive mechanism of communication, enabling various contenders in the process of political persuasion to communicate with the others and to learn what the others are thinking and doing. In reality, the modern mass media have become one of the most powerful forces shaping and controlling the persuasive process. The media play this role by being used by others as well as by being an independent institutional force in society that pursues its own goals. This role can be well illustrated by the contrasting experiences and contributions of the media in the Vietnam, Persian Gulf, and Iraq Wars, as the Sociology of Media and Technology insert describes. This illustrates the "gatekeeping" function of the traditional media: They control the information available to people, and in so doing they influence what issues will be considered important and publicly debated, and they influence what will be seen as reasonable and acceptable solutions to these issues. The nature of the traditional media technology made it possible for a relatively small number of people to control this process. The traditional media consisted of a small, or at least limited, number of outlets and it involved one-way communication with a largely passive audience. This structure meant that direction and control of the persuasive process was in the hands of the media elites.

By the twenty-first century, technological advances have produced a new media environment (Maratea, 2008; Winograd & Hais, 2008). First came the growth in cable and satellite television, which tremendously expanded the number of channels of influence and persuasion available. This increased the volume of information and the number of persuasive communications that people were exposed to. It also transformed this process of communication and persuasion into a continuous, 24-hour process. The next technological development was the cyberworld, including the Internet, e-mail, message boards, text messaging, blogs, social networking sites, and the like. Efforts at persuasion and influence expanded into this electronic world, and the nature of this technology suggests that its impact may be quite different from the traditional media. Cyberworld technology opens up many more channels of possible influence—truly, an infinite number of channels. This destroys the monopoly over influence that a small number of people could claim with traditional media, and, at least potentially, empowers everyone with the ability to influence. And some of these technologies are interactive rather than one-way, which means that audiences can actively shape the debate instead of being only passive recipients of the persuasive efforts of others.

Given these characteristics of cyber technology, the traditional gatekeeping function of the media will probably be significantly weaker, or at least different, in the future. One argument is that the technology will usher in a truly democratic environment because everyone will be able to participate in the process of exchanging information and shaping definitions of reality. As long as they have a computer and an Internet connection (and the time to prepare materials), people can create a blog that others can read, send out e-mails, or share information with thousands of people through social networking sites such as MySpace. A person with a YouTube account, inexpensive video equipment, and cheap editing software can distribute compelling videos that are available around the world and may influence how people view a presidential candidate or a particular corporation. All of these outlets have already become important channels through which information, persuasion, and propaganda about political and economic matters are being disseminated.

A somewhat more complicated view is that the leveling and democratizing effect of cyber technology will be limited because, in reality, relatively few people will have the time, energy, resources, or desire to join in this fray in any major way, especially when they can't earn a living by doing so. In the "blogosphere," for

Sociology of Media and Technology

The Media and the Military in Wars

The Persian Gulf War of 1991 was a short war against Iraq, initiated because Iraq had invaded and occupied neighboring Kuwait (Dorman, 1997; Mowlana, Gerbner, & Schiller, 1992). Kuwait was both an ally of the United States and a significant source of oil for Western nations. The war involved a multinational force of United Nations members but was largely organized and directed by the United States. As a means of controlling potential opposition to the war, political and military leaders decided to strictly control the media's access to information and to the war zone. The policy was to keep the media as far away from the war zone as possible and to place maximum restrictions on their activities. A great deal of information about the war came from political and military press briefings; staged news events such as political speeches; and tapes, graphics, and interviews supplied to the press by the military or government. As a result, the information and images that the media had available were mostly those approved by military and political leaders and those that placed the war in the most positive light.

The outcome was remarkable: For people in the United States watching the war on television, it appeared to be an astonishingly "clean" war, devoid of the bloodshed, terror, pain, and horror that normally accompany war. Almost no one reported from or sent images back directly from the field of battle. People did not see the suffering and death that accompany war. The images available to the media also stressed the role of technology in the form of smart bombs and laser-guided missiles. Battles appeared to be fought by experts and technicians; people saw fuzzy but dramatic pictures taken from planes of buildings blowing up, and organized charts and maps at press briefings showing the progress of the war. Even the images of soldiers going into battle stressed the mastery of technology: They were the pilots of highly sophisticated jet fighters or the monitors of sophisticated radar in AWACS surveillance planes. The image presented was of businesslike and professional experts doing their job.

The media experience during the Gulf War was quite different from what occurred during the Vietnam War when reporters, photographers, and television crews were given fairly free reign to go where they wished. They could ride helicopters into battle and join soldiers on dangerous patrols. The more realistic, and certainly more sobering, media portrayal of that war undoubtedly

helped to turn some public opinion against the war. In fact, the tight controls of the media in the Gulf War were clearly a reaction on the part of the government to what was seen as a loss in the battle to influence the public during the Vietnam War.

In the Iraq War of 2003, individual journalists were "embedded," which means they were permitted to join particular military units and lived and traveled with them for some period of time (Schechter, 2003). While providing more access than during the Persian Gulf War, it also involved less freedom and access than during the Vietnam War. First of all, the military agreed to embed journalists only if the press would agree to restrictions on what would be reported. Embedded journalists could only travel with the unit in which they were officially embedded, and limits were placed on what they could report and how they could do so. Because they lived with the same soldiers for a long period of time and because they were dependent on the soldiers for protection and physical survival, there was a natural tendency for journalists to view the soldiers positively or at least to show some reluctance to portray the soldiers and the war in a negative light. In addition, military press officers worked closely with journalists to encourage positive reporting. Gruesome images of the dead or maimed were minimized. In addition, just as in the Persian Gulf War, the military worked hard to present to the media as sanitized and positive view of the war as possible.

So, without question, politicians and military leaders exploited the media to persuade the public in the United States to support the war and military solutions to international conflicts. Yet, the media also constitute an independent institutional force in society with its own agenda. After all, the media could have chosen not to broadcast any images rather than give the one-sided portrayal that was available to them. However, sociologist David Altheide (1993) points out that, in the modern mass media, "marketing logic, or what the audience approves of or 'buys,' informs message selection or production" (p. 54). A primary motivation of the media, even in the news divisions, is an economic one: to increase audience share, which enhances advertising revenues. In this view, the media were not exploited, but were co-conspirators: They willingly worked with political and military leaders to present a certain image of the war because the media elite believed it would be the most marketable image (MacArthur, 1992).

example, research is already showing that a few blogs are read by large numbers of people while most blogs go largely unnoticed (Maratea, 2008). The blogs that are prominent and influential tend to be those written by media personalities who are known to the general public because of their appearances on television and other traditional media outlets. So, influence and persuasion in the cyberworld may also prove to be hierarchical, although less so than the traditional media of some decades ago.

Whether in its more hierarchical or less hierarchical forms, the media and the cyberworld are not solely the coercive mechanism of one group. Rather, they can be thought of as contested territory that is battled over by various groups. Cyber technology may open that battle up to more groups, but political and economic elites will still have more opportunities and resources with which to shape definitions of reality than does the average person.

Advertising

In the economic realm, advertising is a form of persuasion, with economic interests expending enormous advertising efforts and resources through the media to persuade the public to purchase goods. In fact, modern capitalist economies, which are based on economic growth through the mass production of goods and services, can be sustained only through the mass consumption of all that is produced. So advertising, which is the primary vehicle for persuading people to purchase those goods and services, is an essential element in maintaining modern economies.

While most people complain about the intrusiveness or the insipidness of advertising, sociologists search for its social importance. Chapter 1 discusses the concepts of manifest and latent functions. Certainly the manifest function of advertising is to serve as a vehicle of communication whereby consumers learn what goods and services are available and economic interests try to influence people's purchasing decisions. However, sociologists are never content to focus only on the manifest functions of an activity or institution, since most also serve some latent functions. One of the latent functions of advertising is to provide support, often subtle and indirect, for cultural values, beliefs, and stereotypes. At a basic level, the pervasiveness of advertising itself is an affirmation of and legitimation for capitalism, consumerism, and economic growth. It is an embodiment of the commodification of the world, discussed in Chapter 2, in which the social worth of an object or activity is determined by its economic worth in the marketplace. Through advertising, people come to believe that their social worth as human beings is embodied in their ability to purchase an array of products. In other words, beyond the information about a product contained in an advertisement, there are messages about what is good and proper that may have nothing to do with the product itself but that do influence people's definitions of reality.

Sociology on the Internet

The Internet is such a new technology that it is impossible to discern yet what its role in society will ultimately be: a vehicle to be used by large governments and corporations to further extend the concentration of their power, or a vehicle of empowerment by enabling dispersed populations to communicate and organize electronically. Certainly, the Internet has made possible more direct, immediate, and interactive contact between citizens and government. Both houses of the U.S. Congress have Web sites: **www.senate.gov** and **www.house.gov**. The Senate Web site will give you such options as Senators, Legislation & Records, or Committees. The Legislation & Records link offers you a number of options for finding what business is currently before the Senate. Browse through this and find topics that relate to issues discussed in this text. Do the same at the House's Web site.

At a global level, the two organizations discussed in this chapter also have Web sites: the World Bank (**www.worldbank.org**) and the IMF (**www.imf.org**). Explore those sites and report to the class on any information you find that can expand on issues discussed in this chapter.

The Internet can be a very useful tool for discovering the social movement organizations that have arisen to deal with various issues and problems in the world. Using a search engine, enter keywords, such as "globalization" and "organization" or "environment" and "organization." There are many particular problem areas that could be searched. Another approach is to search for "nongovernmental organization" or "NGO." The Economic and Social Council of the United Nations offers a long list of NGOs at its Web site (**www.un.org/esa/coordination/ngo/**). Report to the class on the NGOs that you have located, the problems they focus on, and their strategies and successes. What conclusions can you draw regarding the effectiveness of these efforts at counterbalancing the concentrated power of corporations and governments?

For further information and discussion, go to Allyn & Bacon's Social Problems Supersite (see Chapter 1) and explore Problem Area: Problems of Economic and Political Inequality.

Study & Review
SUMMARY OF LEARNING OBJECTIVES

You should be able to define power and the different types of authority and explain the differences between state and government.

Economics involves the processes through which goods and services are produced and distributed. Politics is the use of power to determine whose values will predominate, how rewards and resources will be allocated, and the manner in which conflicting interests will be resolved. Legitimacy is the capacity of the system to engender and maintain the belief that the existing institutions are the most appropriate ones for the society. Legitimate power is what sociologists call authority. There are three types of authority: traditional, charismatic, and legal-rational. The state is a political institution with legitimate control over the use of force within a particular territory. Government involves the operation of the state by a particular group of people who have the authority to make decisions and supervise the allocation of resources.

You should be able to describe the insights of the functionalist and conflict perspectives regarding political and economic institutions.

According to the functionalist perspective, political and economic institutions perform certain functions that are beneficial to the societies in which they emerge, and these functions make organized social life possible. Conflict theorists maintain that political and economic institutions emerge as a consequence of the efforts of dominant groups in society, which these structures are ultimately designed to benefit.

You should be able to explain the different forms of government and discuss the prerequisites for democracy and the factors influencing political participation in democratic societies.

There are many different types of governments, including oligarchy, totalitarianism, and democracy. Democratic governments are more likely to survive in economically developed societies that have a system of checks and balances and where people have loyalties to many different groups. Democracies also thrive where citizens are well informed and see the government as legitimate and where economic and social systems are viewed as effective. Political participation is affected by barriers to voting, by low politi-cal efficacy, and by socioeconomic status, age, religion, and gender.

You should be able to describe the basic principles of capitalist, socialist, and mixed economies.

Capitalism involves the private ownership of property, the profit motive, and free competition between producers and consumers of goods. Socialism involves collectively held means of production and distribution where human need rather than economic demand determines what is produced and distributed. Mixed economies include strong elements of both capitalism and socialism.

You should be able to explain the power elite and pluralist perspectives on power in the United States and assess the evidence for each one.

The power elite model, which is based on the conflict perspective, maintains that a small group of very powerful people, drawn from the economic sector, politics, and the military, make all the important decisions in the United States. It is a cohesive group that shares common interests. The pluralist model maintains that power is spread over a large number of groups with divergent values, interests, and goals. There are large inequalities but no cohesiveness of interests among these groups. In reality, the exercise of power in the United States sometimes looks like the power elite description and sometimes like the pluralist description.

You should be able to describe recent trends in the U.S. economy and discuss the problems they have created.

The U.S. economy has undergone considerable change. The dominant form of business organization is now the corporation, a business enterprise that is owned by stockholders who may not be involved in running the daily affairs of the business. Corporations have concentrated power by taking the form of monopolies, oligopolies, conglomerates, multinational corporations, and global corporations. Another development has been the emergence of powerful labor unions. However, in an advanced industrial economy, labor unions find some of their power dwindling as blue-collar workers come to constitute a smaller proportion of the workforce and the labor force becomes global.

You should be able to discuss the extent of and reasons for economic concentration and inequality among the nations of the world, the problems that this creates, the structures of

globalization that have developed, and the forms of resistance that have emerged.

Political and economic systems have become global in nature. The global economy seems to reproduce some of the characteristics of the U.S. economy, especially the concentration of wealth and economic resources in the hands of a few. Three explanations for this situation are circumstances, cultural theory, and world-system theory. The structure of globalization consists of international financial institutions, trade agreements, treaties and courts, and regional and global organizations—all of which give the global system stability and predictability. This economic concentration and inequality produce a variety of problems in various nations (such as unemployment and social dislocation) and generate organized resistance (in the form of nongovernmental organizations and the antiglobalization movement).

You should be able to discuss how the media and the cyberworld impact the process of influence and persuasion in political and economic realms.

The media and the cyberworld are a key resource that groups can use in an effort to influence political and economic life. The cyberworld is probably less hierarchical and more democratic than the traditional media. While the media and the cyberworld are contested territory, with numerous groups attempting to use and control them, elite groups are generally more successful at gaining such control.

CHRONOLOGICAL PRACTICE TEST

For answers to Key Concepts see the page number in parentheses; for other answers see page 388.

Politics, Power, and Authority
Key Concepts

1. Economics (362)
2. Politics (362)
3. Power (362)
4. Legitimacy (362)
5. Authority (362)
6. State (363)
7. Government (363)

True/False

8. T F Politics refers to the processes through which goods and services are produced and distributed in society.
9. T F Today in the United States, the legitimacy of the state is usually not questioned, but people sometimes do question the legitimacy of particular governments.

Concept Completion

10. Authority is referred to by sociologists as _____ power.
11. The three types of authority found in political and economic institutions are _____, _____, and _____.
12. A political institution with legitimate control over the use of force within a particular territory is called _____.

Critical Thinking

13. Define and give examples of the various types of authority on which political and economic institutions can rest. Distinguish between the concepts of *state* and *government*.

Sociological Perspectives on Political and Economic Institutions
Critical Thinking

14. Compare and contrast what the functionalist and conflict perspectives have to say about political and economic institutions.

Types of Government
Key Concepts

15. Oligarchy (365)
16. Totalitarianism (365)
17. Democracy (365)

True/False

18. T F Totalitarianism is a special form of oligarchy.

Critical Thinking

19. What is a democracy? What social conditions seem to be important to the survival and long-term stability of democratic political institutions?

Types of Economic Systems
Key Concepts

20. Capitalism (368)
21. Welfare capitalism (369)
22. Socialism (369)
23. Mixed economy (370)
24. Democratic socialist economy (370)

True/False

25. T F The primary motivation for economic activities in socialist economies is to earn a profit.

Concept Completion

26. In capitalist economic systems, _____ is the primary motive guiding people's economic behavior.
27. Economic systems in which there are strong elements of both capitalism and socialism are called _____.

Critical Thinking

28. Define capitalism, socialism, and mixed economies. Show how each economic system differs from the others in terms of organization and motivation for economic activity.

Who Rules in the United States?

Key Concepts

29. Power elite model (370)
30. Pluralist model (371)
31. Military-industrial complex (371)

True/False

32. T F In assessing the power elite model, the text concludes that a small group of people in the United States hold enormous power, control foreign policy, and shape the direction of economic development.

Concept Completion

33. A sociologist by the name of _____ originally proposed what has come to be called the power elite model of the exercise of power in the United States.

Critical Thinking

34. Assess how well the power elite and pluralist models describe the exercise of power in the United States. What evidence is presented on this issue in the text?

The U.S. Economy: Concentration and Change

Key Concept

35. Corporation (372)

True/False

36. T F In the United States, union membership as a proportion of the workforce has been declining since the 1950s.
37. T F Worker dislocation has affected white workers more severely than black workers in the past few decades.
38. T F In the last few decades in the United States, the relative power of workers and employers seems to have shifted toward employers and away from workers.

Concept Completion

39. A _____ is a corporation that owns other companies in economic spheres quite different from that of the parent company.
40. _____ are workers who have lost their jobs because manufacturing plants in the United States have closed in the face of foreign competition.

Critical Thinking

41. What is a corporation? What are the benefits and disadvantages of corporate organization in the economy?

42. Describe the kinds of corporate concentration and restrictive economic growth that can occur in capitalist economies. Why are these things a problem?
43. How is the labor force in the United States changing? Why are these changes occurring? Include in your answer a discussion of displaced workers.

The Global Political and Economic System

Key Concepts

44. Political globalization (377)
45. Economic globalization (377)

True/False

46. T F Less than half of the world's largest 500 corporations are headquartered in the United States or Japan.
47. T F In the international stratification system, according to world-system theory, the peripheral nations dominate and exploit the core nations.

Concept Completion

48. According to world-system theory, the three types of nations that make up the world economic system are _____, _____, and _____.

Critical Thinking

49. Describe the concentration of economic resources at a global level. How does world-system theory explain this concentration?
50. Describe the political and economic changes that have occurred in Nicaragua historically and in the present. Relate the changes to the world economic system.

Politics, the Economy, the Media, and the Cyberworld

Key Concept

51. Propaganda (383)

Concept Completion

52. The text uses the term _____ to describe the mass media as something that many groups battle to control.

ANSWERS TO CHRONOLOGICAL PRACTICE TEST

8. F; 9. T; 18. T; 25. F; 32. T; 36. T; 37. F; 38. T; 46. F; 47. F
10. legitimate
11. traditional, charismatic, legal-rational
12. a state
26. profit-making
27. mixed economies, democratic socialist economies
33. C. Wright Mills
39. conglomerate
40. Displaced workers
48. core, peripheral, semiperipheral
52. contested territory

CUMULATIVE PRACTICE TEST

See page 482 for answers.

1. Both political and economic institutions center on the same key social process, namely
   a. the exercise of power in the allocation of scarce resources.
   b. the transition from socialist to capitalist economies.
   c. the emergence of market economies in advanced industrial societies.
   d. the globalization of labor.
   e. the emergence of the world economic system.

2. Traditional authority is best defined as based on
   a. the extraordinary powers or qualities of some individual.
   b. laws and rules that define who can do what.
   c. power elite position.
   d. the powers of the state.
   e. loyalty to established ways of doing things.

3. According to the text, separate, formal political leadership first emerged in which type of society?
   a. Hunting and gathering.
   b. Horticultural.
   c. Agricultural.
   d. Industrial.
   e. *Gesellschaft.*

4. Which of the following is true regarding voting behavior in the United States?
   a. Older people are more likely to vote than are younger people.
   b. Those with low incomes are more likely to vote than are those with high incomes.
   c. Men are more likely to vote than are women.
   d. People in the United States vote at higher rates than do people in the other major democracies in the world.
   e. Those with less education are more likely to vote than are those with more education.

5. Gender influences voting behavior in which of the following ways?
   a. Women are less likely than men to register to vote.
   b. Women are more likely than men to vote for Democratic candidates.
   c. Women are more likely than men to vote for Republican candidates.
   d. Men are more likely than women to actually vote.
   e. Women are more likely to identify with the Republicans than with the Democrats.

6. As used by Karl Marx, the term "communism" refers to
   a. socialist economies in advanced industrial societies.
   b. the emergence of democratic socialist economies.
   c. oligarchical political structures such as exist in Russia and China.
   d. the process of bringing corporations under state ownership and control.
   e. the utopian end stage of the struggle with capitalism.

7. According to proponents of a pure capitalist economy, the government should do all of the following *except*
   a. regulate prices and wages.
   b. maintain public order.
   c. protect against foreign threats.
   d. Government should do all of these.
   e. Government should do none of these.

8. The _____ model takes the position that power in the United States is spread over a large number of groups, each with different values and interests.
   a. power elite
   b. oligarchical
   c. functionalist
   d. pluralist
   e. monopolist

9. Which of the following statements is consistent with the power elite model of power distribution in the United States?
   a. A small group of powerful people make most important decisions.
   b. Power is spread over a large number of groups.
   c. There is no significant military-industrial complex in the United States.
   d. There is no cohesive elite with power centralized in its hands in the United States.
   e. The unorganized public can exercise constraint over those in power through use of the vote.

10. Which of the following is *not* one of the reasons for the decline in the proportion of workers in the United States who are unionized?
    a. Traditionally unionized occupations have declined in number.
    b. Multinational corporations have declined in significance.
    c. Corporations have relocated to states with weak union organizations.
    d. The number of white-collar occupations has been growing.
    e. All of the above are such reasons.

11. A major advantage of corporations over individually owned businesses is that
    a. corporations have access to a much broader source of capital.
    b. corporations are more highly bureaucratic.
    c. corporations are more profit oriented.
    d. corporations can function in capitalist, socialist, or mixed economies.
    e. individually owned businesses are less profitable.

12. If the ABC Corporation controlled 96 percent of the sales for breakfast cereal in the United States, the corporation would be called a (an)
    a. oligopoly.
    b. monopoly.
    c. conglomerate.
    d. oligarchy.
    e. bureaucracy.

13. Which of the following is true regarding changes in the occupational structure in the United States since 1900?
    a. The proportion of farm workers has increased.
    b. The proportion of blue-collar workers has increased.
    c. The proportion of service workers has declined.
    d. The proportion of working-class people has declined.
    e. The proportion of white-collar workers has increased.

14. The problem of unemployment in the United States has grown worse over the decades because
    a. the proportion of blue-collar jobs has grown and the proportion of white-collar jobs has declined.

b. the number of women entering the workforce has declined.

c. there is increased competition from foreign workers.

d. U.S. corporations have avoided competing in global markets.

e. the amount of automation has declined.

15. According to the text, the inequalities in wealth and resources found in nations around the world can be explained by all of the following *except*

a. oligarchical tendencies.

b. peculiar natural, geographic, or historical circumstances.

c. cultural theory.

d. world-system theory.

e. All of the above were explanations given.

16. *Maquiladoras* contribute most directly to which of the following problems?

a. The enhancement of oligarchy in organizations.

b. The weaknesses of socialist economies.

c. The loss of jobs in the United States.

d. The abuse of governmental authority.

e. The rise of totalitarianism.

17. "Worker empowerment" refers to programs that attempt to

a. socialize the economy.

b. increase alienation among workers.

c. free workers from the control of labor unions.

d. give workers some management authority and control.

e. move jobs to *maquiladoras*.

18. What was the relationship between the political and economic institutions in Nicaragua for much of the twentieth century?

a. Politicians supported workers' unions against the depredations of economic elites.

b. Political democracy provided social stability for elites to run profitable businesses.

c. A socialist government controlled economic activity so that it benefited the peasants.

d. Political dictators provided social stability for elites to run profitable businesses.

e. Both b and d are true.

19. Which of the following are groups that have emerged to fight against the policies of groups like the World Bank and the International Monetary Fund?

a. Nongovernmental organizations.

b. Military-industrial complexes.

c. Democratic socialism.

d. All of the above fight against those groups.

e. Only a and c fight against those groups.

20. The World Bank and the International Monetary Fund are most correctly identified as

a. global corporations engaging in international trade.

b. agencies of the United Nations working for global peace.

c. nongovernmental organizations working to protect the environment.

d. global financial institutions that promote the spread of capitalism.

e. international organizations that support worker empowerment.

FOR FURTHER READING

Chua, Amy. (2002). *World on fire: How exporting free market democracy breeds ethnic hatred and global instability.* New York: Doubleday. This author provides a strong critique of current trends toward globalization, describes its negative consequences, and presents some ideas about a better route.

Derber, Charles. (2002). *People before profit: The new globalization in an age of terror, big money, and economic crisis.* New York: St. Martin's Press. This book describes a grassroots resistance to corporate-led globalization and proposes a path based on international democracy and social justice.

Gans, Herbert J. (2003). *Democracy and the news.* New York: Oxford University Press. This author argues that corporatization, among other trends, is causing the vital role of the press and the media in democracy to change in ways that could lead to the disempowerment of people from meaningful participation in civic life.

Greider, William. (1998). *Fortress America: The American military and the consequences of peace.* New York: Public Affairs. This book provides an enlightening analysis of how the military-industrial complex has continued to shape defense policy and the distribution of resources in the United States since the end of the Cold War.

Head, Simon. (2003). *The new ruthless economy: Work & power in the digital age.* New York: Oxford University Press. This eye-opening book argues that the new information technology is producing huge social and economic disparities, as well as other serious problems in the workplace.

Mokhiber, Russell, & Weissman, Robert. (1999). *Corporate predators: The hunt for megaprofits and the attack on democracy.* Monroe, ME: Common Courage Press. This is a muckraking book that catalogs the negative, exploitative actions of U.S. corporations. While it is one-sided, it is also eye-opening.

Prestowitz, Clyde. (2003). *Rogue nation: American unilateralism and the failure of good intentions.* New York: Basic Books. This author, who has served in government, argues that the unilateralism of the current foreign policies has caused us to lose the respect and cooperation of nations around the globe. He calls for a foreign policy that puts much more stress on multilateralism.

Wallerstein, Immanuel. (2004). *World-systems analysis: An introduction.* Durham, NC: Duke University Press. This book provides a brief, but readable and informative, presentation of world-systems theory by the sociologist who was one of the original developers of the modern version of the theory.

HUMAN ECOLOGY AND SOCIAL CHANGE

CHAPTER FOURTEEN
Human Ecology: Population, Community, and Environment

CHAPTER FIFTEEN
Collective Behavior, Social Change, and Modernization

The chapters in Part V focus on the processes of social change and the consequences of that change. In particular, they address issues of population growth and distribution, urbanization, collective efforts by people to bring about or resist change, and theories of social change.

CHAPTER 14

Human Ecology: Population, Community, and Environment

MYTHS & FACTS: About Population, Community, and Environment

The Study of Human Populations

Elements of Demographic Change
Fertility
Mortality
Migration
Population Composition: Age and Sex Structure

World Population Growth

The Demographic Transition
The Extent of Overpopulation
The Consequences of Overpopulation
Controlling Population Growth
Family Planning
Economic Development

The Status of Women
Case Study: Population Policy and Family Planning in China

Communities and Urbanization

The Emergence of Cities
Suburbanization
The Postindustrial City
SOCIOLOGY OF MEDIA AND TECHNOLOGY: Technology and the Growth of Cities
A Global Perspective on Urbanization
Growth and Overurbanization
OTHER WORLDS, OTHER WAYS: Mexico: The Social Organization of Slums in Poor Communities
Global Cities

Urbanism as a Way of Life

Urban Consciousness
Urban Communities

Urban Subcultures
Urban Life: An Assessment

Urban Ecology
Urban Processes
Urban Structures

The Future of Cities in the United States
Economic Decline
Government Programs and Urban Renewal
Private Investment
Gentrification

APPLYING SOCIOLOGY: Fear of Crime: Working to Improve the Quality of Urban Life

Population and the Environment
Social Sources of Environmental Problems
Extent of Environmental Problems
Solving Environmental Problems
SOCIOLOGY ON THE INTERNET

Study & Review

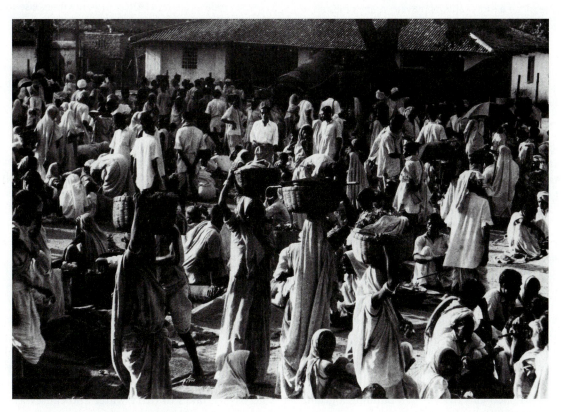

While the rate of population growth in the world has slowed over the decades, the world's population is still growing, and the doubling time is relatively short.

A number of chapters highlight different non-European peoples of the Americas. Chapter 2 discusses the Comanches of the Great Plains in North America, Chapter 4 the Yanomamos of Brazil. Other chapters look at the Natchez, the Hurons, and the tribal peoples of Brazil. One notable fact about all the groups mentioned is that they lived in small villages and survived by a combination of hunting, horticulturalism, and pastoralism. This survey could leave the impression that these tribal peoples of the Americas never organized large civilizations with great cities at their center, such as was common in Europe and Asia. This impression would be quite wrong.

The Aztecs emerged as a distinct hunting society in Mexico in the twelfth century (Farb, 1978). They were few in number and had a difficult time securing a spot in central Mexico, which was crowded with various other tribes. Eventually, they settled in a large plain filled with lakes and surrounded by mountains, the area where Mexico City later emerged. By the early 1400s, the Aztecs had multiplied, successfully battled many rival tribes, and emerged as the mightiest state in Mexico. By terror and by diplomacy, they forced the other peoples of central Mexico to accept their dominion over the region and created a vast agricultural civilization. By the time the Spanish and Portuguese

Myths & Facts

About Population, Community, and Environment

Myth:

The most important factor in controlling world population growth is technology: Modern contraceptive technology is essential if people are to control their fertility.

Fact:

The most crucial ingredient in world population growth is human values and desires. Effective contraceptive procedures have been available for some time, but as long as people place a high value on having many children, world population will continue to grow.

Myth:

The United States achieved Zero Population Growth (ZPG) when the birthrate dropped below replacement level during the 1970s.

Fact:

Although the U.S. birthrate has been dropping steadily and has remained below replacement level for some time, this rate will have to continue for another generation (about seventy years) before the country reaches ZPG.

Myth:

Latin America's cities have grown rapidly in recent decades because young people prefer not to live on farms or in rural communities, and they migrate to the cities.

Fact:

Although preference for urban life certainly plays a part in this migration, other complex social processes are at work. For example, international corporations often purchase large amounts of farmland to grow export products, and this practice throws peasants off the land. These landless peasants often have nowhere else to go but the cities.

Myth:

In the teeming slums of cities in Latin America, family disintegration is a major problem, which exacerbates other problems such as drug use and crime.

Fact:

Although families have their problems in the cities, families often remain together, and kinship helps to define important networks of reciprocal exchange through which people with few material resources help one another survive. Each family in a network contributes what it is able and receives on the basis of what other families have. In these ways, families persist and display innovative responses to adversity.

---

explorers were beginning to head for the Americas in the late 1400s, the Aztecs ruled over much of what today is the nation of Mexico, with a population of possibly six million people.

At the center of their domain, on the site of modern-day Mexico City, they began building a grand city in the mid-1300s. This city, Tenochtitlán, was called by one anthropologist "one of the most magnificent cities ever erected on any continent" (Farb, 1978, p. 157). Built on an island in a chain of lakes, it was easily defensible from attack and centrally located for controlling trade with many surrounding groups. At the center of the city stood the remarkable Great Temple, which was dedicated by the sacrifice of twenty thousand captives. The Aztecs established schools and encouraged people in the crafts and literature. When the Spanish arrived, the Aztecs were ruled by a king named Moctezuma, and they had achieved a high and sophisticated culture.

Tenochtitlán was, by all accounts, magnificent (Hardoy, 1975). Estimates of its size range from 100,000 to 300,000 residents—a good-sized city even by today's standards. It was surrounded by snow-covered peaks and cultivated mountain slopes. Rising majestically above the calm turquoise of the lakes on which it was built and the green of the trees planted in groves around it, it appeared to be part city and part floating garden. The Aztecs built aqueducts across the lakes to carry water and causeways for people to walk to the mainland, where they worked plots of land. Dozens of temples rose above the skyline, which was dominated by the Great Temple. There were broad plazas and exotic gardens, and ornate palaces dotted the city. Bernal Díaz, a Spanish conquistador who first gazed on Tenochtitlán in 1519, described it this way:

> It was like the enchantments they tell of in the legend of Amadis, on account of the great towers and [temples] and buildings rising from the water, and all built of masonry. And some of our soldiers even asked whether the things that we saw were not a dream. . . . I do not know how to describe it. . . . Some of the soldiers among us who had been in many parts of the world, in Constantinople, and all over Italy, and in Rome, said that so large a marketplace and so full of

people and so well regulated and arranged, they had never beheld before. (Díaz, 1638/1956, pp. 218–219)

Tenochtitlán was not the only pre-Columbian city in the Americas. Seven hundred years earlier the Mayans, at the height of their rule of the same region, built the city of Teotihuacán about forty miles north of Mexico City. Farther south the Incas solidified their control over territory covering modern-day Ecuador, Peru, and Bolivia and ruled from the Peruvian city of Cuzco. So, in the Americas, as in other parts of the world, empires arose through diplomacy and military might, and cities emerged because they served as centers of trade and culture and because they could centralize military authority.

This chapter is about *human ecology,* the size and distribution of human populations, including the growth of cities. The term *ecology* is connected in most people's minds with the biological world of plants and animals and their relationships to their environment. Over the past few decades, ecology has become a popular topic primarily because of the growing concern with environmental pollution and degradation. We should remember that human beings are one of the many animals studied by ecologists. Sociologists use the term human ecology to refer to *the study of human populations and communities, including their distribution across and impact on the physical environment they inhabit.* This chapter reviews the basics in the field of human ecology: the growth of human populations, their geographic distribution, and the emergence of communities and cities.

The Study of Human Populations

You should be able to describe the three demographic variables and current trends in the age and sex structure of the United States.

There are many things about each of our lives that we generally consider to be very personal, such as whether we marry, how often and with whom we have sexual relations, whether we use contraceptives, and how many children (if any) we plan to have. There are, however, social scientists, called *demographers,* who are acutely interested in these matters because they help shape the population of the United States and the world. Demography is *the study of the size, composition, and distribution of human populations and how these factors change over time.* Each of us participates in at least two demographic acts that affect human populations—we are born and we will eventually die. Many of us also engage in other demographic acts, such as having children. All of these individual decisions and activities combine into an enormous wave of actions that make the world population what it is today.

Elements of Demographic Change

The term population refers to *the total number of people inhabiting a particular geographic area at a specified time.* The three basic elements that shape the size, composition, and distribution of human populations are fertility, mortality, and migration.

FERTILITY Fertility to *the actual number of children born.* It is distinguished from fecundity, or *the biological maximum number of children that could be born.* Because women rarely have the maximum number of children of which they are capable, the fertility of a society is normally quite a bit lower than its fecundity. The simplest measure of fertility is the *crude birthrate,* the number of live births occurring in a particular population during a given year for each one thousand people in that population. Figure 10.1 (on p. 279) shows the changes in the crude birthrate in the United States since 1910. This method of calculating fertility is crude because it ignores the age and sex structure of populations. A more refined measure is the *general fertility rate,* the number of live births per year for each one thousand women of childbearing age, generally considered to be between fifteen and forty-four. This general fertility rate provides a more accurate view of how fertile a society is because it is calculated using only women who are in the age bracket where they might have children. As can be seen in Figure 10.1, the crude birthrate in the United States dropped to a fairly low level in the 1930s, below nineteen births per one thousand people. This decline was undoubtedly related to the Great Depression, when many people could not afford to have children. By 1940, however, the birthrate was on the rise. The late 1940s was the period of the postwar *baby boom* when couples who had postponed having children during World War II established their families. By the mid-1950s, the birthrate peaked, and after 1957 another decline began. This decline continued fairly steadily until the mid-1970s, when the birthrate reached an all-time low of less than fifteen per one thousand people. Since then, the crude birthrate has stayed at that low level, with slight increases or decreases in some years.

Demographers also use another measure of fertility called the *total fertility rate,* which is the average number of children a woman will have in her lifetime, based on current birthrates. With today's birthrates, for example, women average about 2 children in contrast to 3.5 children in the early 1960s (U.S. Bureau of the Census, 2007, p. 66). For other purposes, demographers use *age-specific birthrates,* which calculate the number of births among women in a particular age category.

MORTALITY Mortality refers to *the number of deaths that occur in a particular population.* As with fertility, mortality in a society can be described in a number of ways. The *crude death rate* refers to the total number of deaths for every 1,000 people (see Figure 10.1). The crude death rate in the United States has declined substantially over the past century, from 17 per 1,000 in 1900 to about eight today. However, as Figure 10.1 illustrates, there has been relatively little change in the past three decades. The crude death rate, although useful for some purposes, is necessarily limited because certain social factors place some people at much greater risk of death than others. The very young and the old, for example, have much higher death rates than other age groups. Thus, *sex-* or *age-specific death rates* are often used to measure the number of people in an age or sex grouping who have died for each 1,000 people in that category. In fact, deaths among infants under one year of age have shown the greatest declines of all age groups, dropping from about 100 per 1,000 births in 1915 to fewer than 7 today. Finally, *life expectancy* refers to the number of years, on the average, that people can expect to live. People in the United States have experienced a substantial increase in life expectancy during this century, as Table 14.1 illustrates. As can be seen, the life expectancy of women has increased more than that of men. The difference in life expectancy between the sexes was only one year in 1920, and it is almost six years today. Some of the reasons for this difference are discussed in Chapter 10.

When we combine the results of the crude birthrate and the crude death rate, we derive an indi-cation of the growth of a population, and the difference between these two figures is referred to as the *rate of natural increase*. For example, today, the crude birthrate of the United States is about 14.2 and the crude death rate is 8.3, yielding a rate of natural increase of 0.59 percent.

MIGRATION   On the most general level migration refers to *a permanent change of residence*. The term *immigration* refers to movement *into* a particular country, whereas *emigration* involves moving *out*. In analyzing migration, demographers look for *push* and *pull* factors. Sometimes, people are pushed out of one country because of poor economic times, unstable political conditions, and the like. Many Southeast Asians migrated to the United States in the 1970s and 1980s, for example, because of the unpredictable political situation in that part of the world. In other cases, there is a pull or attraction that leads people to migrate to a particular place. Many Europeans migrated to the United States in the belief that they would have better economic and social opportunities.

Emigration from the United States has been very low, but immigration has been a significant factor in U.S. population growth. All people in the United States are immigrants or the descendants of immigrants. Even recently, immigrants have made a significant impact on the populace. Since 1980, for example, more than 18 million people immigrated to the United States. Although that is only 6 percent of the current population, most of these people were young and will eventually bear children, thus adding further to the population growth. The composition of these immigrant groups has also changed (see Figure 7.4 on p. 194). Although in the past most came from Europe, the largest group today comes from Asia.

Migration is also an important variable in the population within a particular nation. For example, the population density of the southern and western states in the United States has risen dramatically in recent decades because of in-migration from other states. Likewise, the number of people living in some other states has declined because of out-migration. Since 1980, North Dakota, West Virginia, and the District of Columbia have experienced a net decline in population, and some states, such as Iowa, Maine, and Nebraska, have shown almost no increase (U.S. Bureau of the Census, 2007, p. 17). All other states showed some increase. The population stagnation in some regions can contribute to high rates of unemployment and fewer job opportunities in the states showing little growth. These socioeconomic factors then have a further effect on migration patterns. People have moved out of some states and into others in search of employment or more lucrative career opportunities.

Table 14.1

EXPECTATION OF LIFE AT BIRTH IN THE UNITED STATES, 1920–2010

Year	Male	Female	Total
1920	53.6	54.6	54.1
1930	58.1	61.6	59.7
1940	60.8	65.2	62.9
1950	65.6	71.1	68.2
1960	66.6	73.1	69.7
1970	67.1	74.7	70.8
1980	70.0	77.5	73.7
1990	71.8	78.8	75.4
2000	74.3	79.7	77.0
2010*	75.6	81.4	78.5

*Projection.
Note: From *Statistical Abstract of the United States,* 1978 (p. 69) by U.S. Bureau of the Census, 1978, Washington, DC: U.S. Government Printing Office: *Statistical Abstract of the United States,* 2008 (p. 74) by U.S. Bureau of the Census, 2007 Washington, DC: U.S. Government Printing Office.

Population Composition: Age and Sex Structure

Fertility, mortality, and migration affect not only the size of a population but also its composition. Every population has a wide variety of demographic characteristics, such as sex and age. Demographers use the term *sex ratio* to describe the number of males per 100 females in a given population. If an equal number of males and females exists, the sex ratio is 100. Today, the sex ratio in the United States is 96, meaning there are 96 men for every 100 women (U.S. Bureau of the Census, 2007, pp. 10, 64). This figure varies according to age, however. There are approximately 106 males born for every 100 females. Among those over sixty-five years of age, the ratio drops to around 70, which reflects a higher death rate for males. The sex ratio also varies from one time period to another. It was 106 in 1910, showing a surplus of men over women.

Changes in the composition of a population can have important social ramifications. An unbalanced sex ratio, for example, can affect people's opportunities to marry or have children. Changes in the age composition also have consequences. An aging populace means that there are fewer workers in proportion to retired people. This imbalance creates problems when it comes to supporting retired citizens in the fashion to which they have become accustomed. It has also meant that there are fewer young people enrolled in school, which has resulted in school closings and reduced job opportunities for teachers. During the 1980s, the same problem also began to affect the nation's colleges.

World Population Growth

You should be able to describe current patterns of population growth in the world and explain why such growth occurs, what the consequences of it are, and how to control population growth.

Most of human history has passed on an earth that was only sparsely populated. It has been estimated, for example, that there were fewer people on the Earth seven thousand years ago than there are in larger cities such as New York or Tokyo today. At the time of Christ, approximately two thousand years ago, there were probably not many more people alive than currently live in the United States. In Figure 14.1, it can readily be seen that, prior to 1750, world population was small and

Figure 14.1
World Population Growth through History

Note: From *World Population: Fundamentals of Growth* (3rd ed.) by Population Reference Bureau, 1995.

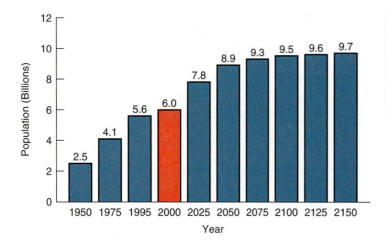

Figure 14.2
World Population, 1950–2150 (based on a medium fertility scenario)

Source: Population Division of the Department of Economic and Social Affairs, United Nations Secretariat, *Long-Range World Population Projections: Based on the 1998 Revision* (New York: United Nations, 2002). www.un.org/esa/population/publications/longrange/longrange.htm

growth was slow. After 1750, world population began to increase at a more rapid rate, and it continues to grow even more rapidly today. Only in the last two centuries has world population exceeded one billion. Currently, world population is about 6.6 billion (Figure 14.2). Current projections are that the world population could come close to doubling again over the next century or just beyond. Demographers caution, however, that such long-range projections are speculative because levels of birthrate and death rate are likely to shift in the interim in ways that are difficult to predict. The largest nation in the world today is China, with 1.3 billion people. With a population of 305 million, the United States is the third largest nation, behind China and India.

The primary reason for the low rate of population growth in the world prior to 1750 was the relatively high death rate in practically every society. For example, until 1600, the average life expectancy in European countries was little more than thirty-five years, in comparison to more than seventy years in industrial societies today. One important factor in the high death rate at that time was the extremely high infant mortality rate. In some societies, as many as 50 percent of the infants born would die within their first year of life (Antonovsky, 1972). The two most important variables producing these high death rates were disease and famine. In fact, disease has accounted for more deaths in the Western world than any other factor throughout history. Famine has at times led to astonishingly high death rates. For example, a severe famine in China in 1877 and 1878 was responsible for the deaths of between nine and thirteen million people (Petersen, 1975). Before the modern era, knowledge and technology related to medicine, sanitation, and agriculture were not sufficiently advanced to lower the death rate and thus increase life expectancy.

The Demographic Transition

One of the earliest attempts to understand population growth began two centuries ago, at the beginning of the Industrial Revolution in Europe, when the English clergyman Thomas Robert Malthus (1798/1960) published his *Essay on the Principle of Population.* Malthus argued that an immutable passion exists between the sexes that leads to reproduction, and that societies have a limited ability to produce food. The consequence of these facts, he believed, is that the human population tends to grow at a faster rate than does the ability to produce food. If these tendencies continue unchecked, then populations will eventually grow larger than the food supply can support. Malthus believed that human beings could intercede in this process and control population growth by postponing marriage or remaining celibate, but he was pessimistic about whether human intervention would completely save the day. He thought populations would continue to grow, ultimately being checked by deaths due to starvation, disease, and war.

Malthus's view of population growth is basically functionalist, because he viewed population size and food supplies as two parts of a system that should be balanced. If either part changes, it will affect the other. Karl Marx disputed Malthus' position and took a more conflict-oriented approach toward population problems. He argued that there are powerful groups, the capitalists, who benefit from restrictions in the food supply. Because capitalism is based on profit making, food and other goods are not produced unless people are willing to pay a profitable price for them. And less food may be produced than people actually need so that the low supply of food will increase the price. With an economy based on producing food for human *need* rather than profit, Marx argued, technology could be harnessed to produce a sufficient amount of food for a growing population. (The foundations of

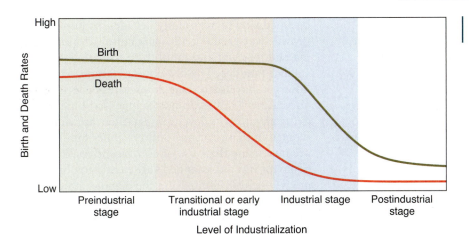

Figure 14.3
The Demographic Transition

capitalist and socialist economies are discussed in Chapter 13.)

Both the Malthusian and Marxian views of population problems have adherents today, and both views are applicable to some elements of the problem of population growth. Rather than debate which approach is more accurate, modern demographers have attempted to understand what underlies the rapid world population growth of the past few centuries. Underlying this growth is a process referred to as the demographic transition, *the changing patterns of birthrates and death rates brought about by industrialization* (Ginn Daugherty & Kammeyer, 1995). The reasons for this transition are complex. It is useful to divide the demographic transition into four stages (Figure 14.3).

The *preindustrial stage* is characterized by high birthrates and death rates, resulting in a population that grows slowly, if at all. Throughout much of human history, societies have been in this preindustrial stage.

For most Western nations, including the United States, the preindustrial stage existed until the onset of industrialization between 1750 and 1850, when the *transitional*, or *early industrial*, *stage* began. This stage is characterized by continuing high birthrates but declining death rates. The falling death rates occur because of improvements in lifestyle resulting from industrial development (see Chapter 10). More and better food was available, for example, which helped people resist infectious diseases and reduced infant mortality. In addition, improvements in transportation, communication, and sanitation contributed to a lowering of the death rate. Cultural values, however, still encouraged people to have large families, so the birthrate stayed high. The *gap between the high birthrates and low death rates*—commonly called a demographic gap—resulted in explosive population growth during the early industrial period. The death rate was too low to keep population size stable when the birthrate remained high.

The third stage, called the *industrial stage*, is characterized by a continued decline in the death rate and a declining birthrate. During this stage medicine became more effective in controlling acute and chronic diseases and thus contributed to additional declines in the death rate. In addition, industrial technology eventually made it possible for people to lead cleaner and healthier lives. The decline in the birthrate was a response to the impact of industrialization on cultural values regarding childbearing. Urbanization and increasing education, for example, led couples to desire smaller families than in the past.

The *postindustrial stage* of the demographic transition, which some demographers prefer to consider a continuation of the industrial stage, is characterized by low birthrates and low death rates, once again a roughly stable population with little growth. The industrialized nations, such as the United States, Japan, and some European countries, may be currently entering this stage, although how low their birthrates and death rates will go and for how long are matters of some speculation.

The Extent of Overpopulation

The fully industrialized nations in the world today, including the United States, have experienced the demographic transition and now exhibit relatively low birthrates and death rates. If these low rates continue, then the populations of these countries will eventually stabilize, with little if any subsequent growth (assuming no migration). However, many nations in the world are considerably less industrialized and have not yet gone through this transition in birthrates and death rates; they are where the largest increases in the world's population can be found today. In these nations, the death rate has dropped considerably, owing in large part to the introduction of modern medicine, sanitation, and public health efforts. Insecticides, better transportation, and improved agricultural practices, for example, have made more and better food available. The impact of these changes on mortality has frequently been dramatic. In Sri Lanka between 1945 and 1949, the crude death rate declined from twenty-two deaths per one thousand people to twelve per one thousand; in 1947 alone, the life expectancy rose from forty-three to fifty-two.

Although the developing nations of the world have not gone through the demographic transition, many of them have experienced a significant decline in their fertility. Nations such as Peru and Mexico, for example, have seen their total fertility rate decline from more than six children per woman in the 1970s to fewer than three today (Robey, Rutstein, & Morris, 1993; U.S. Bureau of the Census, 2007, p. 831). However, these lower fertility rates are still quite high and contribute significantly to world population growth. When these high birthrates are combined with the substantial declines in the death rate that have occurred, the result is a continuing and large demographic gap. Ghana and Bolivia, for example, have rates of natural increase of about 2 percent. This increase compares with the U.S. rate of natural increase of 0.59.

When today's industrialized nations went through the demographic transition, their death rates declined slowly over many decades, so population growth was gradual, allowing cultural values regarding childbearing and family size to change, yielding smaller families. The developing nations of today, however, have seen their death rates drop rapidly, and cultural values do not change that quickly. The cultural values in developing nations are changing—women in these nations desire smaller families and are increasing their use of contraceptives. However, behavior has not changed sufficiently to come anywhere near eliminating the demographic gap that represents world population growth. Thus the developing regions of the world grew at an annual rate of 1.5 to 2 percent during the 1990s, as compared with 0.5 percent in the fully industrialized nations (United Nations, 2004, p. 253). Figure 14.4 shows the impact of these differing rates of natural increase: Europe and North America, where most of the industrial nations are, will contain a dwindling proportion of the world's population, whereas Africa and Latin America, containing mostly developing nations, will see their proportion of the world's population grow significantly.

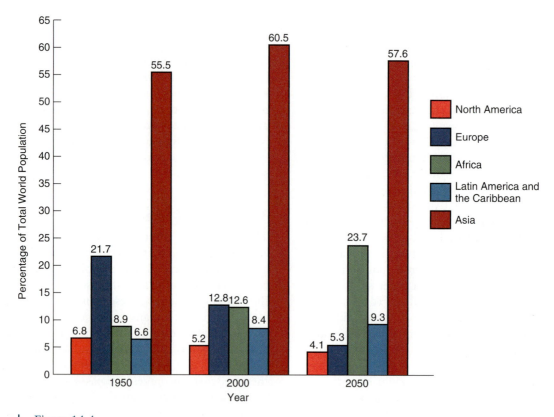

Figure 14.4

Percentage Distribution of the World's Population in Various Geographic Areas, 1950–2050 (based on a medium-fertility scenario)

Source: Population Division of the Department of Economic and Social Affairs, United Nations Secretariat, *Long-Range World Population Projections: Based on the 1998 Revision* (New York: United Nations, 2002). www.un.org/esa/population/publications/longrange/longrange.htm

The impact of these changes can be better understood if we examine the number of years required for the world's population to double in size. Demographers refer to this figure as the *doubling time*. From the beginning of the Christian era, it took 1,650 years for the population to double. By comparison, if current rates of world population growth continue, only 200 years will pass until world population again doubles its size.

Will the developing nations of the world today lower their birthrates before world population grows disastrously out of control? It must be kept in mind that the demographic transition is a description of a long historical trend found in some nations, all of which have experienced occasional changes in birthrates or death rates that go against this trend. We do not know if the developing nations of today will follow the same path. One thing is clear, however. In a preindustrial era, population growth, or the lack of it, was determined primarily by a high death rate, over which people had little control. Today, growth is determined to a large extent by factors, especially fertility, over which people do have some control. Thus, the attention of those concerned about overpopulation today has been focused on issues of fertility control.

The Consequences of Overpopulation

One important consequence of population growth is *crowding*. Studies of animals have shown that extreme crowding can have considerable negative consequences, including elevated aggression levels and erratic behavior. Animal studies, however, are only suggestive of how crowding may affect human beings, because people's reactions would depend on people's past experiences and expectations. In addition, it is possible to design living quarters and work areas in which density is high but people do not have the impression of being crowded, so potentially negative effects could be avoided. The psychologist Jonathan Freedman (1975) has argued that crowding by itself does not have negative consequences. Rather, crowding is usually associated with other social conditions such as poverty that produce increases in crime or aggression (Ehrlich & Ehrlich, 1990; Liddell & Kruger, 1987). Thus, there is considerable controversy over the impact of crowding. Yet if world population doubles in the next 200 years and doubles again after that, we will experience serious overcrowding.

Another consequence of population growth is the potential for food shortages (Brown, 1998). Especially in developing nations, it is difficult to increase agricultural production enough to keep up with population growth. As a consequence, millions of people die each year from starvation and malnutrition. It is a poignant commentary on Marx's view of population problems that farmers in the United States are sometimes paid to keep some of their cropland out of production while other people in the world do not have enough food to eat.

The biotechnology revolution that began in the late twentieth century offers some new possibilities for expanding the food supply (Rifkin, 1998). Through gene splicing and other techniques, it is now possible to produce modified species that grow faster, reproduce quicker, or provide larger quantities of proteins or other nutrients than do naturally occurring species. While these new developments hold considerable promise, it is too early to assess how much they will expand the food supply and whether their negative consequences may not outweigh the benefits in terms of expanding the food supply.

Still another consequence of population growth is the growing *depletion of the world's natural resources*. There is considerable debate over precisely how serious this problem is. A few decades ago, estimates based on world supplies of various resources and the rates of their use forecast a grim future. For example, petroleum, natural gas, and aluminum were all estimated to be exhausted in fifty years or less. More recent assessments are generally more optimistic because they take into account new discoveries of supplies of the resources and changing estimates of rates of use of the resources (Bartsch & Müller, 2000; Cohen, 1995; Goodstein, 2004). For example, some assessments conclude that many minerals can be maintained at desirable levels through judicious use and discoveries of new sources. However, many assessments still warn of serious shortages at some point during the twenty-first century. Oil supplies may begin to decline within the next decade or two, which could result in dramatic shortages in supply and a substantial increase in price. We may begin to run out of fossil fuels completely by the end of this century. On the other hand, coal is plentiful and could replace some of the depleted fuels. But coal has its own problems, in terms of environmental destruction when it is mined and serious pollution when it is burned. Beyond fossil fuels, new technologies based on nuclear fusion, solar power, or wind power may be able to replace fossil fuels as they are depleted. Despite these disagreements about what the future holds, most agree that the most prudent course is to begin to plan for the possibility that some of our most important resources will be in short supply in the not-to-distant future. One of the world's natural resources is *living space*. Wars have been fought over the need for more land. Population growth in the future could result in other wars over land space or other dwindling natural resources.

Population growth also has consequences for environmental degradation, which will be explored in some depth after discussing urbanization.

Controlling Population Growth

Given the problems of overpopulation, intense efforts have been directed toward controlling population growth through the only reasonable means that we have—reducing fertility.

FAMILY PLANNING   Some modern population control efforts have focused on encouraging people to decide consciously how many children they want, with the hope that they will choose to have smaller families. Such family-planning programs encourage couples to have children when and if offspring are desired. Experience with such programs has shown that, when women realize they have a choice of whether to have children, they most often choose to have fewer children than they would have had otherwise. Still, people who desire children will have them, and people's desires arise out of socialization into a particular set of cultural values.

Research on the effectiveness of family-planning services generally shows that they increase contraceptive use, reduce fertility, and result in smaller families (Jacobson, 1988; Mauldin, 1975; Robey, Rutstein, & Morris, 1993). However, the provision of such services is not a total answer to the world's population problem. In many countries with active family-planning efforts, such as China, South Korea, and Costa Rica, social and economic changes—to be discussed in a moment—probably account for much of the lowering of fertility. In other countries, such as Kenya, India, and the Dominican Republic, family-planning programs have had little observable effect. Why? As noted earlier, values are a critical element in reducing fertility—people must want to have fewer children before family-planning efforts will work. In many countries, however, women have large numbers of children because they have been taught to want them, and cultural values are supportive of large families. In addition, in some societies, large families are a central support when people are sick, out of work, or face other misfortunes. In short, children take the place of old-age or unemployment insurance. In such settings, family planning will probably have only a marginal effect.

ECONOMIC DEVELOPMENT   Certain social and economic changes probably account for more of the decline in fertility than family planning. These changes are generally called *economic development* (Bouvier, 1984). Developing nations that are actively involved in programs to control population growth have placed a major emphasis on economic development. Although these countries recognize the need for family planning, they argue that no program of population control can be completely effective unless it is part of a more general program of economic development. A number of changes that accompany economic development—especially urbanization, increasing levels of education, and a rising standard of living—lead people to view large families as less desirable. In urban settings and since the passage of child labor laws in the United States, there is no longer a distinct economic advantage to having many children. In fact, in urban, industrial societies, large families lead to crowded housing and a drain on family finances. Furthermore, when women receive more education, they usually want to pursue a career or develop talents other than domestic ones, and large families make this effort more difficult. Finally, economic development affords people a more affluent lifestyle, and large families are expensive. Many couples decide to spend their resources on consumer goods or leisure activities rather than raise a large family. Even with economic development, most people want to become parents, but they are more likely to opt for a smaller number of children. And as small families become common, they are viewed increasingly as normal, and people feel social pressures not to have large families.

Recent research suggests, however, that economic development may not be as critical to reducing fertility as once thought (Robey, Rutstein, & Morris, 1993). Many of today's developing nations have reduced their fertility significantly even though they have not experienced significant economic development. In fact, some nations have experienced declining fertility even though their economic circumstances have become worse. It appears that some of the elements originally linked with economic development, such as urbanization, also influence fertility in the absence of economic development: Even in less developed nations, people in cities have fewer children because there are fewer advantages to having children in such settings. In addition, the mass media have contributed to the spread of information about contraception and to the propagation of values regarding small families in less developed nations, and this has helped bring down fertility levels. What is uncertain at this point is whether fertility levels can be brought down to the level in industrial nations without significant economic development.

THE STATUS OF WOMEN   Another important element in controlling population growth is the status of women. The United Nations has for decades vigorously promoted programs to improve women's lives by providing them with opportunities in education, employment, and political participation, as well as support in their domestic and maternal roles (see Chapter 8). Research has shown consistently that educational attainment and labor force participation of women are particularly important elements in a population policy: Educated women who work outside the home have fewer children than do less educated women who are not part of the labor force (Houseknecht, 1987; Sen, 1999). So, programs intended to advance gender equality around the world will likely have a positive impact on controlling population growth.

CASE STUDY: POPULATION POLICY AND FAMILY PLANNING IN CHINA

China has a tremendous problem on its hands. Geographically, it is about the same size as the United States, but with more than four times as many people! To further complicate matters, China's population is much younger than the U.S. population; therefore, a larger proportion of the Chinese are still planning to have children. Such a large population puts an enormous strain on China's environment as well as hindering economic development. By the end of the 1970s, the Chinese authorities were sufficiently concerned about controlling population growth to institute a "one-child family" program for all couples who did not already have more than one child. Incentives were created for families that achieved this goal and penalties for families with more than two children, including salary deductions and tax surcharges. Even more controversial was the use of government-employed family-planning workers to consult with, and in some cases cajole, couples about their sexual behavior and use of contraceptives.

The birthrate in China did come down, but by the late 1980s, it looked like the Chinese would not reach the targets they had set for themselves. Alarmed authorities introduced a "responsibility system" in which district and township officials would be held personally responsible if the people under their jurisdiction did not achieve the goals (Kristof, 1993). These officials could lose bonuses or be fined or dismissed. Another part of the program was compulsory, organized sterilizations, in which family-planning cadres would descend on a village and take all women who already had a child to a clinic to be fitted with an IUD or sterilized. A third part of the program focused on women who became pregnant without authorization, with strong social pressure exerted on them to have an abortion. Some overly zealous local officials got carried away, forcing some women to have abortions and smashing the huts of a few women who had unauthorized births (WuDunn, 1993).

This draconian program had an effect. By 2000, the birthrate in China was about the same as in the United States. In addition, the number of sterilizations went way up, and very few births involved third or subsequent children. However, these successes have not been without costs, a major one of which may have been to increase female infanticides. The Chinese, especially in rural areas, want sons so they can extend the male line into the future; some even believe they have dishonored their ancestors if they fail to do so. Female infanticide is a way to try again for a male child when the government strongly encourages one-child families.

Information on the sex ratio in China supports the idea that some female infanticide is occurring. Biologically, in human populations, about 94 females are born for every 100 males. However, in recent years in China, as few as 85 females were reported born for each 100 males, undoubtedly due in part to female infanticide (Secondi, 2002).

By the end of the twentieth century, the one-child policy had begun to lose some of its force (Yardley, 2005). One reason for this trend is that the birthrate has declined substantially. In addition, economic development is enhancing the trend toward smaller families, as it did in the currently developed countries. In fact, economic development may have contributed as much to China's declining birthrate as did the government-promulgated one-child policy. However, the experience of China highlights the importance of cultural values in influencing people's behavior. Even when the government provides benefits for those who lower their fertility and penalties for those who do not cooperate, people will continue to have more children if they value them. So, programs of family planning and population control are likely to be less effective when they fail to gain the backing of the citizenry.

Communities and Urbanization

> You should be able to trace the pattern of urbanization and suburbanization in the United States and cities of less developed countries and describe what is distinct about postindustrial cities.

This chapter has discussed some of the major elements of human ecology—the size and composition of human populations. In the context of migration, it mentioned the geographical distribution of people. This section of this chapter discusses the topic of population distribution in more detail, especially the emergence of communities and urbanization in human societies. A community is more than a gathering of people in a geographic location. A community consists of *a group of people who share a common territory and a sense of identity or belonging, and who interact with one another.*

The Emergence of Cities

The earliest human communities were small hunting-and-gathering bands, usually consisting of between forty and one hundred people. These bands were usually nomadic, roaming the land in search of food and game, and all the people knew one another well. Then, about fifteen thousand years ago, small fishing villages began to appear around the Baltic Sea, surviving off the plentiful fish. Approximately ten thousand years ago, people discovered how to cultivate plants and domesticate animals. These skills afforded them greater control over their food supply and permitted a growing surplus of food. The result was the emergence of agricultural villages, and later cities, in fertile river valleys around the world. A city is *a relatively large, permanent community of people who rely on surrounding agricultural communities for their food supply.* As a consequence of developing agriculture, then, human communities grew enormously in size (Hawley, 1971). At the height of the Roman Empire, Rome is estimated to have had as many as one million residents, and the Aztec city of Tenochtitlán, as noted earlier, may have contained a few hundred thousand inhabitants.

Industrialization ushered in ever-increasing urbanization, with cities growing far larger than their preindustrial predecessors. By the mid-twentieth century, cities such as New York, Paris, and Tokyo had many millions of inhabitants. Two hundred years ago, only 5 percent of all people in the United States lived in urban areas, in contrast to 79 percent today (Figure 14.5). The New York metropolitan area has more than 18 million people, and Mexico City—site of ancient Tenochtitlán—has 24 million. Why has this extensive urbanization occurred? One of the main reasons is that most economic activity in industrial societies is nonagricultural, and such activity benefits from being concentrated geographically. With industry and jobs located in cities, people are drawn to the cities to find work. So *community* for most people in the United States today means a city, whether it be large or small.

Suburbanization

Equally as important as the growth of cities has been the growth of suburbs, *less densely populated areas, primarily residential in nature, on the outskirts of a city.* Mass suburbanization is a relatively recent development. In the United States, it arose out of a complex set of social factors (Banfield, 1990). One factor was the economic and technological developments that made it possible for people to live far from where they worked. Early in the twentieth century, most people were limited in where they could live by the need to find transportation to work. This need meant that most had to live in the cities, near where the jobs and stores were. By the 1940s and 1950s, the increasing affluence of many people, along with the automobile, made it feasible for them to live farther from work and opened up suburban life to the middle class.

In addition to these economic developments, government policy contributed to suburbanization. For example, the federal government paid 80 percent of the cost of developing the interstate highway system. With cars and high-speed highways, people can now live far from where they work and shop. The policies of the Federal Housing Administration (FHA) and the Veterans Administration (VA) also encouraged the development of suburbs (Bullock, Anderson, & Brady, 1983). Beginning in the 1930s, the FHA and the VA made available federally guaranteed mortgage loans for the purchase of new homes. Because land outside the cities was both inexpensive and available, that was where much of the construction took place. The FHA and VA

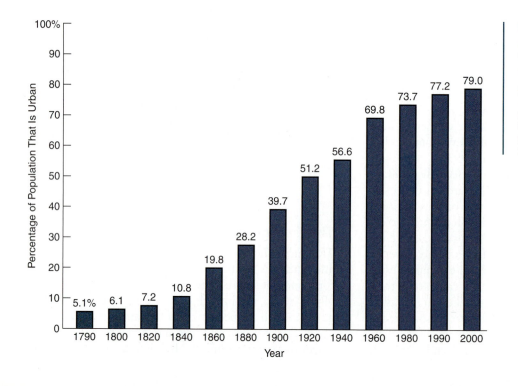

Figure 14.5

Percentage of Urban Population in the United States, 1790–2000

Note: From *Statistical Abstracts of the United States,* 1991 (pp. 17, 27) by U.S. Bureau of the Census, 1991, Washington, DC: U.S. Government Printing Office; and *Statistical Abstract,* 2007, p. 34.

One of the premier problems faced by some U.S. cities has been economic stagnation and decline. As some cities have lost people and jobs because of global competition, they sometimes find whole neighborhoods practically abandoned.

did not provide loans to purchase existing homes or build apartments, policies that would have encouraged people to continue living in the cities. Other social policies have contributed to suburban development, such as a low tax on gasoline, which removes an economic incentive for people to live in more centralized communities, and a tax deduction for the interest on a home mortgage and property taxes. By contrast, most European nations have taxed gasoline heavily and have devoted more resources to maintaining public transportation than to building highways. The European policies have focused more on population concentration as a way to preserve open space.

It should be kept in mind that this suburbanization occurred not simply because people wanted to move to the suburbs. It also depended on the development of new transportation technologies and on federal social policy on taxes, housing, and transportation. That these developments had such wide-ranging effects should not be surprising given the functionalist point about the interdependence among the different elements of social systems. The manifest function of the social policies was to stimulate

economic development. Their latent function was to encourage decentralization of urban areas and to bring about the eventual decline of many cities. Clearly, all the ramifications of these policies were not considered when they were established.

These same developments eventually made it possible for businesses and factories also to move outside cities. Businesses were originally located in cities because workers lived there and transportation was available to ship their products. By the 1950s, cities no longer possessed those exclusive attractions. A labor force and highways were available in the suburbs. In addition, suburban land was typically less expensive, taxes were lower, and affluent suburbs could afford to offer tax breaks to industries to relocate. Increasing crowding and congestion in cities, along with the growth of numerous other problems, also made the suburbs popular as a "rural refuge." In their early development, suburbs were not economically self-supporting, since many residents made their livelihood in the cities. By the 1970s, however, 75 percent of all suburban residents both lived and worked in the suburbs and only about 25 percent commuted to the central city to work. Today, the United States is a nation of suburbanites, with 60 percent of its metropolitan population living in the suburbs.

The Postindustrial City

Although many people and some jobs have left the city, other jobs have remained. Many cities have retained or increased jobs in the financial service industries, those related to the functioning of corporate headquarters, telecommunications and publishing, and those involving nonprofit and governmental activities (Abrahamson, 2004). In other words, the changes in cities reflect the changes in the economy discussed in Chapter 13: the

stagnation in the manufacturing sector and the growth of the service sector.

Recent technological developments, however, may reduce the need for corporations or service industries to concentrate their workers in one locale. The Sociology of Media and Technology insert describes these developments, along with the role of technology in shaping urban development.

A Global Perspective on Urbanization

GROWTH AND OVERURBANIZATION   Nations vary tremendously in how much of their populations live in cities. At one extreme is Rwanda with only 6 percent of its

---

Sociology of Media and Technology

Technology and the Growth of Cities

Technology has played a powerful, but complex, role in shaping the development of cities around the globe. At times, different technologies have produced conflicting tendencies. Industrialization as a technological mode has been one powerful force in the centralization and concentration of both social power and social activity (Volti, 2006). Industrial and factory modes of economic production, for the most part, benefit from concentration of activity. Factories concentrate workers in one locale, and the workers need to live a short distance from their workplace. Factories also find it beneficial to locate near other factories and businesses because these provide them with a ready supply of materials and services as well as access to affordable transportation. All this has meant that the cities of the twentieth century were propelled by industrialization toward the concentration and centralization of populations.

At the same time, other technologies have been forces for the dispersal of populations rather than the concentration of them. In particular, modern forms of transportation, such as automobiles and high-speed trains, have enabled people to live far from where they work. As we have seen, this was an important factor in dispersing people from cities to suburbs and small towns, but still in somewhat close proximity to places of work.

More recently, technological developments in telecommunications and computer-mediated technologies have raised the possibility of even further decentralization of urban areas. The basic idea is that digitalization, instantaneous electronic communication, and computer technologies have smashed the link between geographic location and economic production (Knox & Taylor, 1995; Sassen & Appiah, 1998). Some people can now work in *electronic space,* or *e-space,* that

is global in nature, connecting all geographic points on the globe through instantaneous transmission of data. In this view, the concentration of economic activity in cities or urban areas is no longer necessary, or at least it is less necessary than it once was. With computers, fax machines, fiber-optic networks, high-speed and wireless Internet connections, and e-mail, voices, words, video, and documents can be transmitted from any location to any location (that also has that modern technology). When this is the case, why have everyone work in the same locale?

So, workers can do much of their work at home or other dispersed locations and then connect to their offices and fellow employees or supervisors electronically. Conference calls, with both audio and video, are now more financially feasible; these enable a number of people to "meet" and discuss problems or make decisions when they are widely dispersed geographically. They can transmit documents and other data to one another over fiber-optic cables. These capabilities have already enabled many corporations to move some divisions to suburbs or small towns, because the workers and their work output can be communicated electronically to the headquarters office.

With these technological developments, then, the character and development of urban life is likely to be different in the twenty-first century. These trends mean that populations will be more dispersed into smaller communities rather than concentrated in large cities serving as centers of economic activity. In fact, it may be that e-space will force us to think about economic "centers" in an entirely different way: Instead of being defined geographically, the center will be that location at the nexus of electronic communications and electronic economic transactions.

population in urban areas; at the other is the city-nation of Singapore with all its citizens living within the urban shadow of its sole city, Singapore. Whereas overall levels of urbanization in Asia and Africa are significantly lower than in Europe or the Americas, many cities in those regions are growing rapidly. In addition, many cities in Latin America have experienced explosive growth in the past four decades. Both Mexico City and São Paulo, Brazil, for example, grew from approximately 3 million people to 24 million since 1950. By contrast, Los Angeles, one of the fastest-growing cities in the United States, grew from 2 to 3.8 million during the same period.

The preceding description of the process of urbanization focused mostly on the experiences of industrial nations such as the United States. Urbanization in the developing nations of the world has been influenced by different social and economic forces. Nevertheless, a few generalizations can be made (Kasarda & Crenshaw, 1991). One is that the industrialized nations tend to have higher rates of urbanization than the less industrialized nations. This difference is explained by the fact that, as in the United States, urbanization develops with and is supportive of industrialization.

A second generalization is that the rapidly growing cities in many developing nations today are facing more adverse conditions than did the cities of Europe and North America that matured during the nineteenth and early twentieth centuries. For one thing, today's developing cities are growing much more rapidly and thus experiencing the problems of crowding, crime, and pollution to a much higher degree. In addition, they face much more severe economic competition from the advanced industrial nations with their already modernized cities and substantial economic resources. When the cities of the United States and Europe were developing, they were the advanced cities of their time and thus were attractive to investors and credit markets. Today's developing cities struggle to compete with already mature adversaries in other nations.

A third generalization is that urbanization in developing nations has been driven as much, or possibly more, by the pressures of the capitalist world system as it has been by internal pressures toward industrialization. For example, Other Worlds, Other Ways: Nicaragua in Chapter 13 noted that international investors bought large tracts of land in Nicaragua to grow coffee and cotton for export. This practice forced Nicaraguan peasant farmers off the land and fueled population growth in the cities. In other places, capital-intensive foreign investment in manufacturing for export products has stimulated booming growth in small and medium-size cities, as happened in Mexico with the *maquiladoras* along the U.S. border, as described in Chapters 2 and 8. These plants sprouted in cities such as Juarez and Matamoros, manufacturing goods for export and drawing in thousands of people from surrounding rural areas. So, some of the pressures toward urbanization in these developing nations are external, controlled by international elites rather than national leaders.

A final generalization, which really stems from the previous one, is that some cities in developing nations have experienced *overurbanization*, having populations larger than the city can house, employ, and adequately take care of (D. Smith, 1991). When foreigners invest in agriculture for export and retard industrial development, people are pushed off the land, but there are insufficient jobs and housing for them in the cities. When there are too many people in the cities for the available resources, the result is squatter slums. Other Worlds, Other Ways: Mexico: The Social Organization of Slums in Poor Communities describes how people adapt to city life under these conditions.

GLOBAL CITIES   World urbanization is not characterized solely by the growth of more and larger urban centers around the world; in addition, some cities are performing some new functions in the world economy (Abrahamson, 2004; Smith & Timberlake, 1993). The term global cities has been given to *cities in a postindustrial society that serve as centers of commerce, finance, and political and economic decision making for the global economic system.* It is in these urban centers that economic and political leaders coordinate the activities of global corporations. The design and marketing of products as well as financial activities, accounting, and advertising are performed in these global centers. However, in a postindustrial city, the actual production and manufacturing of goods are often done elsewhere. These cities are also often the centers of cultural production and distribution through the mass media. It is in these cities that the organization and design of movies, television shows, and news production occur. The emergence of these global cities has rested on the revolutions in computers and telecommunications of the past few decades; these advances have meant that geographic distance is no longer a hindrance to communication and control. So, these cities serve not only as the economic centers of their particular region of the world but also as the centers of coordination and control of global economic production, finance, and marketing. In the United States, New York and Los Angeles would certainly be considered global cities; likewise, London, Tokyo, and Hong Kong would be given this designation.

Global cities, like other cities around the world, attract the poor and those dislocated by economic development. As a consequence, global cities often exhibit vast disparities in wealth, with the richest beneficiaries

Other Worlds, Other Ways

MEXICO: THE SOCIAL ORGANIZATION OF SLUMS IN POOR COMMUNITIES

Mexico, along with many other developing nations, has been undergoing rapid urbanization, which has put a strain on the ability of its cities to house and employ all the people living there. In the mid-1960s, half of Mexico's population lived in rural areas; today only one-quarter does (World Bank, 2007). This rural-to-urban migration is typically the result of push–pull factors. People are pushed out of the rural environment because of a lack of jobs or land on which to make a living; they are pulled toward cities by the belief, or hope, that they will have better opportunities there. The result is often massive crowding and poverty in squatter settlements or shantytowns. What is remarkable about these settlements, however, is not just the poverty but the creativity, initiative, and persistence with which the inhabitants adapt to and attempt to overcome the almost insurmountable adversity they face.

One form that this takes is the creative development of networks of exchange that provide people with some economic security when they are chronically underemployed or unemployed. In squatter settlements in Mexico City, for example, the basic unit of social organization is the nuclear family, but each nuclear family develops an elaborate exchange network with other families, often relatives, but not always (Lomnitz, 1988). Sometimes a family, especially a young couple, will temporarily move in with relatives, but couples prefer to live on their own if they can. More often a group of families will inhabit a compound, each family in its own residence but sharing a common outdoor area for cooking, washing, and playing. In this case, geographic proximity helps to define the social network: Each family is a separate economic unit, but all families in the compound provide reciprocal assistance to one another. In other cases, one family will develop reciprocal ties with a family in another compound because they are related through blood or marriage.

These social networks engage in daily, or almost daily, exchanges of goods and services, enabling each impoverished family to tap into a resource base that is substantially larger than its own. The families in a network might pool money for rent or entertainment, use common cooking facilities, help one another on construction projects, or share a television or latrine. Each family contributes what it is able and receives on the basis of what it needs and what resources the network has. Through such networks, the poor in these squatter communities display an innovative response to adversity: With few resources available to each family, they maximize the resource base through social arrangements based on communal sharing. ▪

---

of the global economy living alongside the desperately poor. For example, Los Angeles, as the center of global media production, is home to some fantastically wealthy media stars and moguls; yet in 1995, seventy immigrants from Thailand, mostly women, were found in a prisonlike garment factory where they worked and lived in virtual slavery. The women had migrated from desperate poverty in Thailand in hopes of improving their circumstances; once in the United States, they found themselves toiling long hours for low wages under conditions that violated health and safety laws, and prevented from leaving the factory at any time. So, increasingly these global cities are characterized by powerful and highly profitable global corporations coexisting with masses of poor people and low-wage workers. In fact, as is pointed out in Chapter 13, it is often the actions of the corporations, at least in part, that have created the circumstances of those urban poor. Some of the largest clothing manufacturers in the United States bought their stock from the factories that enslaved the Thai women just mentioned, and some of the toniest department and clothing stores in U.S. global cities sold products from the factories to their wealthy customers.

Urbanism as a Way of Life

> You should be able to discuss the different perspectives on the nature and quality of urban life.

Sociologists have made numerous efforts to characterize the impact of city life on people and their relationships with one another. All these characterizations focus, in some way, on whether city life involves any sense of community. Three approaches are particularly useful in understanding urban life.

Urban Consciousness

The observations of Ferdinand Tönnies (1887/1963) and others lead to the conclusion that urbanization results in more secondary group relations in people's lives and fewer primary group ties (see Chapters 2 and 4). It is the extension of secondary group ties that lends city life its impersonal character, the feeling that most people care little about anyone else as a person. This impersonality can lead to feelings of alienation from others. People who have many secondary ties and few primary ones might even feel a desperate sense of isolation.

Based on the work of Tönnies and others, Louis Wirth (1938) and other urban sociologists at the University of Chicago championed the viewpoint that city life shapes city dwellers by creating an urban consciousness, a distinctive way of thinking about and a unique awareness of their surroundings.

Three elements of city life play a role here: Large numbers of people, high density, and heterogeneity. People protect themselves from the large numbers and the density by interacting with one another in highly impersonal ways, and their lives become segmented, with only specialized roles being relevant in particular settings. Social relations are also highly depersonalized, with kinship bonds weakening and community identity fading. Given the thousands of people and dozens of settings that urban dwellers might face each day, it is not surprising that they respond with impersonality and emotional distance. To devote time and energy to all these people would be draining and impractical. In this mass of humanity, individuals can feel quite insignificant, knowing little about and having few contacts with most people around them. What knowledge one has of other people is often very superficial. Furthermore, relationships that do develop are most often secondary and based on rational calculation of self-interest rather than affection. This calculation can lead city dwellers to feel preyed on by others. What emerges is a distinctive urban consciousness: People are reserved in social relationships, rational, and self-interested.

The heterogeneity of cities also has important effects on the urban consciousness. Neighborhoods are often highly segregated along racial, ethnic, religious, or socioeconomic lines. Yet it is difficult to avoid mingling with many different kinds of people at work, while shopping, or while traveling from place to place. These people not only may be different but also may be viewed as potentially dangerous or threatening. A mentally disturbed person shouting obscenities in the street or some tough-looking teenagers can be frightening and can motivate people to take a cold and aloof attitude toward those around them. Again, a distinctive urban consciousness emerges that says it is probably best to ignore much of what goes on around you lest it bring you trouble. This diversity leads to a greater tolerance of different lifestyles, but often the tolerance is not based on acceptance but on resignation. City dwellers typically have little choice but to mingle with people very different from themselves, no matter how they feel about it.

Urban Communities

The dreary picture of urban life painted by Wirth and others of the early Chicago school may have been due in part to the fact that many of these sociologists were first-generation urbanites themselves, having grown up in small towns or rural villages, and the negative aspects of urbanism deeply impressed them. It may also have resulted from the fact that the Chicago of the 1920s and 1930s that they studied was undergoing a period of considerable growth, in-migration, and social disorder. More recent perspectives on urban life have focused more on the positive elements of urbanism.

In contrast to Tönnies, Wirth, and others, Herbert Gans (1972) argues that cities do retain a sense of community in neighborhoods where people identify with and have a sense of positive regard for one another. In fact, contrary to what Wirth proposed, research shows that family ties remain as strong in urban areas as in rural areas (Wilson, 1993). In some places, strong ethnic or racial bonds may lend a considerable degree of cohesiveness to a neighborhood. In Hispanic communities, for example, ethnic identity may be reflected in stores and restaurants catering to Hispanic tastes or in the routine use of Spanish in shops. There may also be organizations of Hispanic students or businesspeople that emphasize the common heritage and interests of the people in the community. In addition, even in neighborhoods with a number of ethnic or racial groups, ethnic group boundaries often serve as symbols of solidarity and regulate patterns of interaction, with people having close ties to members of their own racial or ethnic group and maintaining distance from others (Suttles, 1968). Furthermore, communities in cities are not limited to particular neighborhoods but may be based on common interests or leisure activities.

Gans's argument, then, is that urban life does not have a uniform impact on people, although the tendencies described by Wirth can certainly be found. Rather, there are many lifestyles in cities, and the impact of the city on particular people depends on the groups to which they belong. Thus social characteristics such as age, education, or racial and ethnic group membership are critical factors affecting people's adaptations to city life.

Urban Subcultures

Claude Fischer (1975) attempted to synthesize Wirth's and Gans's positions. Fischer recognized that the social characteristics considered important by Gans—race, sex, age, income level, and so on—play significant roles in shaping the variety of lifestyles that emerge in cities. Yet he argued that the variables considered central by Wirth—size, density, and heterogeneity—are also important, lending an intensity to the impact of subcultural group membership that is usually absent in small towns and rural areas. One reason for this greater intensity is that there are enough people with particular characteristics in cities that they will learn about one another, establish meeting places such as bars or parks, develop specialized activities, and thus form a subculture (see Chapter 2). Research supports Fischer's basic idea that nontraditional or unconventional subcultures are more likely to emerge and thrive in urban areas (Jang & Alba, 1992). In nonurban areas, such subcultures are considerably less likely to form because there will be fewer people with similar characteristics, and the chance of their forming a subculture is considerably reduced. In addition, because city dwellers are unlikely to know most people they come in contact with each day, they rely on characteristics such as social class, age, or ethnicity to decide whether they have anything in common with a person, how to relate to the person, or whether the person represents a threat. Because these subcultural characteristics are so important in social contacts, urbanites become more skilled at picking up cues, such as styles of dress, that signify subcultural membership, and this skill is often considered sophistication by both urbanites and nonurbanites alike. In short, according to Fischer, urban life is different because it tends to magnify the importance of subcultural differences between people. Within this context, though, many urbanites maintain rich and complex networks of social relationships. Fischer's conclusion is that community size by itself does not lead to alienation or other negative consequences.

Urban Life: An Assessment

It should be clear by now that the impact of urban life cannot be characterized simply as good or bad. Reality is more complex than that. Impersonality, isolation, and anonymity do exist in cities—especially among those with few economic or social resources or no subcultural ties—but there are also many communities and subcultures in cities that are rich sources of personal relationships and identity. Cities also offer leisure, cultural, and economic resources that are usually not available in rural areas. There are, for example, baseball, football, and hockey games; opera and ballet; museums; large shopping centers; and restaurants with many cuisines. In addition, the anonymity of cities can be a source of freedom from the curious eyes of one's neighbors. People are freer to pursue lifestyles that might be frowned on in smaller towns. Finally, cities offer a wider range of occupational opportunities than are found in small communities. This dimension of city life can be especially important to couples pursuing dual careers (see Chapter 9). In small towns with fewer job opportunities, many such couples would either have to break up or settle for only one partner pursuing a career.

Urban Ecology

You should be able to describe the processes of urban change and the three theories of urban structure.

Urban ecology is *the study of the distribution of people and families within urban centers and how cities relate to the surrounding environment.* One of the major concerns of urban ecologists has been to understand how cities change over time and what urban patterns emerge.

Urban Processes

Urban ecologists have identified three core processes that describe how cities change: *segregation, invasion,* and *succession.* **Segregation** refers to *the isolation of certain activities or people in particular areas of a city,* which occurs for a number of reasons. In some cases, one particular use is incompatible with another. Industrial and residential uses tend to be segregated from one another, for example, because people generally prefer that their homes not be located near factories. Segregation can also occur because it is beneficial to a particular activity. Commercial establishments, for example, are often concentrated in particular areas so that shoppers can have ready access to many different business establishments. Finally, segregation occurs because people with particular characteristics or lifestyles either prefer to live in a particular neighborhood or are forced to.

Invasion *occurs when new people or activities move into an already established area.* Invasion can be motivated by many factors. An area with a growing population may cease to meet people's needs and force them to disperse into new areas. Economic decisions can also cause invasion. A business, for instance, may decide to relocate in a residential area because the land is cheaper, the taxes lower, or the clientele closer at hand. Political decisions can also play a role in invasion.

If the invasion of an area is large enough, the previous residents or users may leave, and the new residents may come to dominate the area. This transition is called **succession.** One of the most noticeable examples of invasion and succession has been the changing racial composition of neighborhoods in many cities during the twentieth century. As African Americans migrated from the South to the cities of the Northeast, Midwest, and West, scarce housing forced them to begin to invade previously all-white neighborhoods, although often not without considerable tension and violence. As the African American population in the neighborhood grew, many whites left until eventually the area became predominantly black.

Urban Structures

The urban processes of segregation, invasion, and succession are continual, resulting in constantly changing patterns in the urban quilt. In most cases, this urban structure reflects some combination of three patterns: *concentric zones, sectors,* and *multiple nuclei.*

Early in the twentieth century, sociologists Robert Park, Ernest Burgess, and Roderick McKenzie (1925) detected certain patterns in the way that Chicago was evolving. From their observations, they formulated the concentric-zone theory of urban growth. What they observed was essentially *a succession of zones, each having a particular purpose or use, that radiated out from the center of the city in a pattern of concentric circles* (Figure 14.6). A critical factor determining the use to which a neighborhood was put was its distance from the center of the city. The central business district, for example, contained the major commercial, social, and civic activities—the stores, office buildings, banks, theaters, and so on. This location facilitated transportation to work and other activities, especially prior to the widespread availability of the automobile. The zone in transition surrounding the business district was an area of deteriorating residences with businesses and light manufacturing beginning to invade. It was also characterized by higher rates of crime than the zones farther out. The next zone, of low-class residential housing, contained inexpensive housing that was superior to that available in the transition zone but still within easy access to the places of work in the central business district. Beyond it were the zones of better residences, containing well-to-do single-family dwellings and apartment buildings. Outside the city limits was the commuter's zone, which contained housing for the relatively affluent. People in this zone could afford to take the train or own an automobile to get to work.

The concentric-zone theory suggests a direct link between socioeconomic status and place of residence. This theory is most accurate in describing cities such as New York and Chicago that developed during the nineteenth and early twentieth centuries when public transportation was commonly used and automobiles were either nonexistent or very expensive. It was the affluent who could afford the transportation that enabled them to live far from their workplace in the central business district.

To explain how urban growth can differ from a simple concentric approach, Homer Hoyt (1939) developed sector theory, which argues that *some cities grow in the form of sectors, or slices of land use, that extend outward from the center of the city toward the*

Concentric Zone Theory

Sector Theory

Three generalizations of the internal structure of cities

District

1. Central business district
2. Wholesale light manufacturing
3. Low-class residential
4. Medium-class residential
5. High-class residential
6. Heavy manufacturing
7. Outlying business district
8. Residential suburb
9. Industrial suburb
10. Commuters' zone

Multiple Nuclei

Figure 14.6
Three Descriptions of the Internal Structure of Cities

Note: From "The Nature of Cities" by Chauncy D. Harris and Edward L. Ullman, *The Annals of the American Academy of Political and Social Science, 242.* Copyright 1945 by The American Academy of Political and Social Science.

periphery, much like slices of a pie. The city is still seen as roughly circular, growing out from the center toward the periphery. However, expansion of various types of land use does not occur evenly around the center; rather, it extends out along main lines of transportation (by road, rail, or river) or in directions that offer the least resistance. Thus transportation routes and geographic factors, rather than distance from the center of the city, shape urban development. For example, an industrial area that began on the southern side of the city would continue to develop in a southerly direction along a major highway or some other transportation artery.

Some cities do not fit either the concentric-zone theory or the sector theory. To describe the development of these cities, Chauncy Harris and Edward Ullman (1945) have advanced the multiple-nuclei theory, which holds that *cities develop a number of different areas, or nuclei, that are devoted to particular uses.* A city may begin with a single nucleus—a retail district, for example, or the port facilities of a transportation hub. Over time, other nuclei develop as the city experiences migration or specialization. The rise of separate districts is due to a number of factors. First, some uses require special facilities and resources, and urban nuclei will arise where appropriate facilities are available. Water transportation, for instance, requires access to a river or bay, and manufacturing requires large blocks of land on which to build factories. Second, some activities benefit from concentration. For example, retail districts concentrate businesses to attract large numbers of customers. Third, the history and traditions of a particular area in a city can shape its use. The Boston Common, for example, and New York's Central Park are prime pieces of property in or adjacent to business areas, yet sentiment in both cities would strongly oppose any commercial development in the parks. Thus Harris and Ullman argue that growth will be influenced by numerous factors, and larger cities will have more numerous and specialized nuclei.

Cities grow and change in complex ways, and each of these approaches to urban development offers important insights into the process of urban change. As cities in the United States have evolved, they have come to face serious problems, some of which are discussed in the next section.

The Future of Cities in the United States

> You should be able to discuss the major problems faced by cities in the United States and some of the policies that have been devised to resolve these difficulties.

Problems such as crime, poverty, unemployment, and deteriorating housing can be found in both urban and rural areas, but the magnitude of these problems is generally much more evident in cities. It is the central city in a metropolitan area that suffers most severely from these problems, although some suburban communities in recent years have found themselves beset with similar difficulties. Many problems that have an impact on urban areas have been discussed elsewhere in this book, for example in Chapters 5, 6, and 7. An element common to many of these problems is economic decline.

Economic Decline

One of the premier problems that many U.S. cities confront is that they are in a state of economic stagnation or decline (Caraley, 1992; Feagin, 1998). Indeed, since the 1970s, a number of cities, especially in the Northeast and Midwest, have been on the brink of financial collapse. During the 1980s, Boston and Detroit were so short of funds that their governments had to consider not paying for essential city services such as fire and police protection. In the early 1990s, New York City was in fiscal crisis, cutting services and raising local taxes.

One major cause of these financial problems has been the flight of people and jobs from many cities since World War II, and this flight arises in part from the capitalist nature of the economy of which the cities are a part (Costells, 1977; Feagin, 1998). As is pointed out in Chapter 13, the centralization of economic organization in the United States has meant that a relatively small number of corporations account for an increasingly large share of economic activity. Corporations pursue profits, and if that corporate activity benefits a particular city, then that city does well. If corporate profit-making activities do not benefit a city—if they result in jobs leaving the city—then the city suffers. When one of these large business enterprises leaves a city, the departure has a ripple effect as smaller companies that support it also move. As businesses and affluent residents leave the cities, the tax rolls decline. The poor and elderly who remain pay fewer taxes and use more city services than do the well-to-do who leave.

The plight of cities in the United States and around the world also needs to be placed in the context of the global economic competition discussed in Chapter 13. That chapter discusses the dramatic transition of the United States economy from a goods, production-based system to an information-based service economy. This has meant that, for the urban poor, unskilled manual labor jobs that are more common in a goods-production industrial economy have become less common in a service-oriented economy. This has dramatically reduced the ability of cities to provide jobs that pay sufficiently to support a family at a decent level. The problems created by the shift in the U.S. economy are exacerbated by the global competition among capitalist corporations. Cities in the United States have to compete with cities and nations around the globe for jobs, and the result for many U.S. cities has been fewer jobs, especially well-paying ones.

Government Programs and Urban Renewal

Until the 1980s, urban policy in the United States was based on the assumption that the federal government was in the best position to fund programs to attack urban problems. Cities and states have fewer funds for such efforts and more incentives to underfund such programs. In the last twenty years, however, urban policy has changed dramatically, with a decided shift in the opposite direction—toward less federal government involvement (Caraley, 1992). The Reagan and Bush administrations argued that a strong and healthy economy is a far more promising approach to solving urban problems than direct federal intervention. From their perspective, the key role of the federal government in solving urban problems is to keep the economy healthy,

not to intervene with federal programs and funding. States and cities should be allowed to choose which services they need and want. The result of this shift has been a catastrophic decline in federal support for cities. Federal programs have been turned over to the states and cities, and the states and cities—in poor financial shape themselves—have drastically cut or eliminated the programs.

Despite this shift toward a laissez-faire policy, some significant federal urban programs persist. The many federal programs that provide direct funds or services to the poor are a significant form of assistance to urban areas. These programs include Medicaid, Social Security, welfare, housing assistance, and food stamps. All these programs are key resources used by cities to alleviate the problems their citizens face. The Housing Act of 1949 initiated a program of *urban renewal*, which has been a prominent approach to urban problems over the years (Hawley, 1971). The major purpose of urban renewal has been to rebuild blighted areas of cities, to provide low-cost housing for urban poor, and to stimulate private investment in the inner city through the physical redevelopment of deteriorated areas. Government funds were used to acquire and

When certain chemicals escape into the atmosphere, sometimes because of human activity, they destroy the ozone that surrounds the earth. Ozone protects humans by screening out harmful ultraviolet rays from the sun. This map shows a blue spot over Antarctica, which indicates an area of depleted ozone.

clear land and to relocate people who lost their dwellings on account of this program. Urban renewal was also supposed to attract private investors.

After many years of operation, urban policy makers recognized that urban renewal had probably not produced its intended benefits. Rather than try to renovate existing buildings, planners typically had them torn down, in part because they believed that destroying dilapidated buildings was an essential first step in solving the problems of crime and poverty. Often these buildings were replaced with luxury apartments or office buildings that were more profitable to private-sector developers. The poor, who had originally occupied a neighborhood, were driven into other neighborhoods, which then often began to deteriorate. The original neighborhood entered a chain of invasion, and then succession, from a working-class area to a slum. Because of these problems, urban renewal funds declined over the years, and in the 1980s the programs were combined into the Community Development Block Grant (CDBG) program (Wong & Peterson, 1986). The CDBG program has goals similar to those of urban renewal, but it gives local officials a larger role in developing urban renewal projects and greater flexibility in how federal funds are used. The CDBG program shifted from an emphasis on providing direct assistance to low-income residents to a focus on economic development.

These and other federal programs have channeled significant resources to cities with serious problems. However, the hands-off posture in the United States' urban policy in recent years has meant fewer funds than in the past. Many urban policymakers argue that federal assistance for urban problems is still appropriate because the cities, for the most part, did not create the problems that now ravage them: poverty, drug addiction, homelessness, AIDS, and so on. It is the cities that suffer from these problems most seriously, and these policymakers argue that society as a whole has a responsibility to assist cities with them.

Private Investment

Despite the prominent role of the federal government in attacking urban problems over the years, there has been a trend since the 1970s to turn to private investment as a means of improving the conditions of cities. A major thrust of these efforts is to use private funds to develop shopping centers in cities that can compete with suburban shopping malls and to construct housing that can draw people away from suburban tract homes. In this way, it is hoped, people—and financial resources—can be attracted back into the city. The idea is that if cities can be made into enjoyable places to live and work, then decentralization might be slowed or halted and the financial problems

that are at the core of so many urban difficulties alleviated. Many cities now boast such developments: Water Tower mall in Chicago, Union Station in Cincinnati, Quincy Market in Boston, Renaissance Center in Detroit, and Pier 39 in San Francisco to name a few. Although some of these developments used federal funds, private financing has been central to their completion.

Another approach to encouraging private development in cities through minimal government action is variously called *enterprise zones, urban free-enterprise zones,* or *empowerment zones* (Beck, 2001). The basic idea is to designate a neighborhood as an enterprise zone based on high levels of unemployment or poverty and little economic development. Businesses locating in such zones would be taxed at a lower rate than in other areas of the city and would be subject to less stringent regulation than businesses outside the zone. This approach is based on the assumption that the tax and regulatory systems stifle initiative and self-improvement. Remove these inhibitors, proponents argue, and new businesses will arise to take advantage of the opportunities for economic development that exist even in blighted neighborhoods. These new ventures will then help rebuild the neighborhood economy, providing jobs that will improve the general economic conditions in the city.

Gentrification

Another development in resettling cities in the last few decades has been dubbed gentrification: *The return of relatively affluent households to marginal neighborhoods where run-down housing is being rehabilitated or new housing constructed* (Freeman & Braconi, 2004; Vigdor, 2001). Gentrification is a complicated process that occurs in different ways in different cities. In some cases, it is encouraged by the policies of local, state, or federal governments; in others, it is driven by the actions of private developers looking for a profitable business deal. In some places, private–public partnerships have been the catalyst. Gentrification is more likely to occur in neighborhoods with good-quality housing stock of some historical value and where there is no organized group in the community that resists it. Gentrification is also fueled by the decisions of affluent families who may find suburban life too expensive or who do not feel the need for large houses because they have smaller families than their parents had. For others, especially professional couples with fairly substantial incomes, the city affords easy access to restaurants, cultural events, and the like. For dual-career couples, who are far more common today than in the 1950s when suburbanization surged, the city offers access to many desirable jobs for both partners.

Gentrification has been hailed as the beginning of the rebirth of urban areas in the United States. Although it will probably help to stem the flow of economic resources out of the city, the numbers involved are difficult to calculate but are probably somewhat small. Nevertheless, it should contribute to increasing the tax base of the city, restoring neighborhoods through the rehabilitation of housing, and enhancing neighborhood businesses. Some urban planners argue that these renovated neighborhoods will serve as a magnet that will attract more affluent people into the city.

However, not all the effects of gentrification are beneficial. As affluent people move into and renovate neighborhoods, the value of property increases and both rent and property taxes escalate. As a result, the people who lived in the neighborhood prior to gentrification—often the poor, the elderly, and minorities—can no longer afford it and are forced to move, sometimes from homes they have occupied for decades. The only housing these people can afford may be more dilapidated than their previous residence.

As we review these issues related to cities in the United States and around the world, it is important to recognize that urban conditions are shaped by macrosociological conditions, such as industrialization, modernization, and the world economic system. As these conditions change, cities are affected. Urban sociologists continue to accumulate knowledge about how these structures affect life for people in cities, some of which has been presented in this chapter. Applying Sociology: Fear of Crime gives a concrete example of how sociologists can contribute to making city life better.

Applying Sociology   Fear of Crime: Working to Improve the Quality of Urban Life

One area to which applied sociologists have devoted considerable attention is urban policy and planning: using sociological theories and research to design cities and social patterns that make urban life safer and more enjoyable. Undoubtedly, the quality of life in cities is lowered by crime, fear of crime, and the restrictions that city residents impose on their daily routines as a consequence. Social science research has proved very useful to urban planners by pointing to ways to design cities that make urban life safer, more enjoyable, and more fulfilling.

One focus of attention has been urban residents' relationship to their community, especially people's involvement in their community and the crime-fighting effort in their neighborhood (Adams & Serpe, 2000; Bennett, 1995). Research shows that, at least in some cities, the existence of formally and informally organized neighborhood associations can alleviate the fear of crime, reduce the self-imposed limitations on activities, and even reduce crime rates. Neighborhood watch programs, for example, or programs in which residents can meet the police officers assigned to their neighborhood help to get people involved in their community. In the absence of such formal efforts, some urban dwellers develop informal techniques for dealing with fear and victimization, such as casual gatherings designed to air mutual concerns about crime and discuss possible strategies for protection. Research investigations show that urban residents who are active in these formal and informal community organizations are less fearful of crime and place fewer restrictions on their behavior.

Based on years of study of crime in cities, sociologists and urban planners have also come to recognize that architecture and urban design play a part in the crime problem. These policy analysts have developed a new approach to designing cities that has come to be called the *defensible space* strategy because it focuses on changes in the physical environment that make it easier for neighborhoods and communities to defend themselves against crime (Cisneros, 1995; Donnelly & Kimble, 1997; Newman, 1972). This approach is based on the recognition that many criminals are, to a degree, rational; they calculate how they can obtain the greatest gain for the least risk. As the likelihood of getting caught increases, criminals either commit crimes somewhere else or avoid committing crimes. In addition, many neighborhoods and buildings in cities are designed in such a way that they discourage social interaction and social participation on the part of residents. They isolate people from one another, a fact which tends to increase the opportunities for criminals to operate unobserved. So, the defensible space strategy designs buildings and neighborhoods so that intruders believe that they will be observed, be identified, and have difficulty escaping if they commit a crime. With such ideas in mind, sociologists and urban planners suggest a few design considerations that would make crime less likely:

1. Buildings should have only a small number of units sharing the same entryway off the street. In this way, residents know who lives there, who has a right to be there, and who is a stranger.
2. Windows, lighting, entryways, and paths should be designed so that there is continuous surveillance by the residents. This arrangement reduces the number of isolated spots where crime can occur unobserved.
3. Lobbies should be designed not merely as entryways to buildings but as social centers where people congregate. This might be done by having newsstands or recreation items in or near the lobby.

(continued)

4. Buildings should be low-rise with fewer residents to reduce feelings of anonymity, isolation, and lack of identity with the building. Research shows that the crime rate is higher in taller and more populous buildings.

5. Neighborhoods should be designed as small mini-neighborhoods, with no through streets and a limited number of entryways and exits. Existing neighborhoods can use street closings to accomplish this. In this way, the neighbors know who belongs there and who is an intruder, and criminals will fear being trapped in a neighborhood that has only one exit.

These and other urban design features are important to consider in the fight against crime because, as social scientists have demonstrated, social behaviors such as crime are significantly influenced by the nature of the physical surroundings. This use of urban design to attack crime, while important, is also limited because it may only deflect crime to another neighborhood rather than reduce it. As pointed out in Chapter 5, crime-fighting efforts also need to focus on social reform. ∎

Population and the Environment

> You should be able to describe the social sources of environmental problems, the extent of environmental problems today, and what can be done to alleviate them.

The field of human ecology includes the study of the impact of human populations and communities on the environment they inhabit. At the beginning of the twenty-first century, there is little question that a "perfect storm" of sociological and other forces have been converging that will have profound consequences for the state of that environment. In fact, environmental degradation may be one of the most serious threats that human beings face in today's world, and the actions of human beings are a key factor in bringing such degradation about.

Social Sources of Environmental Problems

Biologists Paul Ehrlich and Anne Ehrlich (1990) developed the following formula that summarizes the major social factors that affect the impact that human beings have on their environment:

$$I = P \times A \times T$$

That is, Impact = Population times Affluence times Technology. These key factors, along with some others, are reviewed in this section.

Without question, the sheer number of people on the earth today is a key factor in environmental damage. If the human population were one-tenth or one-fiftieth of what it is, the same social and economic activities that people engage in today would produce much less damage. The carrying capacity of the environment refers to *an upper size limit imposed on a population by its environmental resources that cannot be permanently exceeded without environmental deterioration.* Exceeding the carrying capacity of an ecosystem means that people are depleting or destroying resources at a more rapid rate than they can be replaced. Forests are being cut down faster than nature can replace them, or air is being polluted at higher levels than the actions of photosynthesis can cleanse it. The carrying capacity can be exceeded for brief periods so long as population drops below that level in time for the environment to regenerate itself. However, exceeding the carrying capacity on a long-term or permanent basis may do sufficient damage to threaten an ecological catastrophe.

Human beings today have achieved levels of affluence and material comfort unimagined by most people in the past. To achieve such high levels of affluence and material comfort, people have to consume the earth's resources and pollute its environment. The list of things that contribute to this lifestyle is almost endless: automobiles, airplanes, computers, cell phones, and on and on. Each of these products consumes natural resources and energy during production, consumes more energy resources when operated, pollutes the air or water as a byproduct of its operation, and then pollutes streams or fills landfills when it is discarded. If few people had these material goods, of course, the environmental problems would be minimal. Today, however, human populations and the goods they consume are so numerous that the problem has become dire.

Any technological development that brings a new product into the world that many people will buy and use is almost inherently polluting, because if it supports the sought-after affluent lifestyle, many millions of these new products will be produced and consumed. Although modern technology does some wonderful things, it can also be very damaging. The wonders of electricity exist all around us, as it lights homes, heats buildings, and runs the laptop computer on which these words are being written. Yet the cost is the gouging of coal out of the earth in strip mines that pollute nearby streams and ultimately results in air pollution as that coal is burned to generate the electricity.

However, technology is a two-edged sword: Advances in technology result in new products that produce additional environmental damage, but at the same time technological developments can also result in less polluting ways of doing things.

Extent of Environmental Problems

The impact of pollution and other factors on the ecosystem is enormous. Significant parts of the earth's water supply are contaminated, sometimes to the point of being dangerous. Solid and toxic wastes are accumulating at a rapid pace, in some places already being health hazards. Forests are being destroyed more rapidly than they are being replaced, and some parts of the earth are turning into parched deserts that can no longer grow food to sustain life. Many different plants and animals are being driven to extinction, thus reducing biodiversity, which is crucial to a thriving ecosystem.

One serious environmental concern is the heavy consumption of energy resources. The affluent industrialized nations of the world consume an inordinate share of the world's energy, and the United States is among the largest consumers, per person, even among the industrial nations (see Figure 14.7). Most traditional energy resources are finite. There is no question that they will eventually be exhausted; the only debate is over when this depletion will occur (Goodstein, 2004). Most nations of the world are dependent on a few particular energy resources, primarily the fossil fuels: coal, petroleum, and natural gas. These fill 95 percent of the United States's energy needs, and the United States and other nations continue to place higher and higher demands on them.

Geologists have calculated that coal will be our longest-lasting nonrenewable resource, with the earliest date of depletion occurring well into the twenty-first century. Although coal is an excellent ongoing energy resource, we must avoid becoming overly optimistic because the costs, both economic and social, of continuing to use it could be prohibitive. Economically, coal will become more costly to mine as nations become more dependent on it; and socially, the costs include the vast wastelands created by strip-mining operations, increased air pollution, and deaths and injuries from the mining process itself. Although alternative sources of energy have been identified, some of these also have detrimental consequences for the environment. For example, the use of wood fuel instead of oil or gas might seem like an excellent alternative because this resource is renewable, but widespread burning of wood also leads to increased air pollution. We may actually be overlooking some alternative sources of energy, however. Various forms of garbage, for example, have been wasted for many years when it could save million of barrels of oil a day as a combustible fuel source (Dunn, 2001). However, burning garbage also produces air pollution. Regarding nuclear energy, there are some very serious risks in using it: illness and death from radiation leakage, possible disaster from nuclear accidents, and the problem of disposing of nuclear waste. While all of these sources of energy will probably have to be used to an extent, a reasonable energy policy would also involve the exploration of new energy sources, utilizing techniques, such as wind, solar, and wave energy, that do not involve as many risks and hazards.

A problem closely related to energy consumption is global warming and climate change (Intergovernmental Panel on Climate Change, 2007). High levels of affluence and modern technology depend on the production and consumption of fossil fuels as a source of energy,

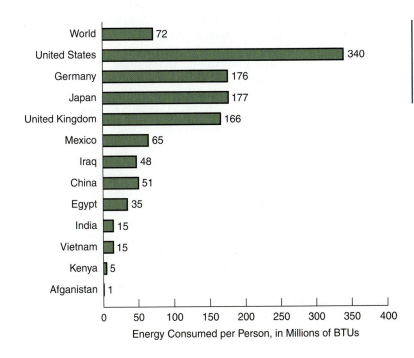

Figure 14.7
Energy Consumption Among Various Nations, 2005

Source: U.S. Department of Energy, Energy Information Administration, *International Energy Annual, 2005*, www.eia.doe.gov/emeu/iea/wecbtu.html

and their consumption releases great quantities of carbon dioxide and methane, among other gases, into the atmosphere. These gases produce a "greenhouse effect": They act like the glass roof of a greenhouse, allowing sunlight to reach the earth's surface but preventing the escape of solar infrared radiation back into space. If these gases continue to accumulate in the atmosphere, as scientists project that they will, the temperature of the earth's atmosphere could rise as much as five degrees over the next one hundred years—a process called "global warming" (Committee on Environment and Natural Resources, 2008). This could substantially alter weather patterns and climate. It could also melt much of the earth's water that is now stored as ice at the poles and in glaciers. This could cause the world's oceans to rise seven feet or more from their current levels, with devastating flooding of low-lying coastal regions. There would be more, and more severe, heatwaves, storms, floods, and droughts. It could cause some of the great food-producing regions of the world to dry up into dust bowls, resulting in disastrous extinctions of many species of plants and animals (Thomas et al., 2004). Some scientists are concerned that this global warming already has, or soon will have, progressed to the point where it will produce a long-term, possibly permanent, change in the earth's climate. If so, human beings will have to live with the negative consequences of this climate change for the foreseeable future.

Many factors contribute to this accumulation of greenhouse gases, some of them natural processes such as the decay of materials in forests. But there is a growing consensus among scientists that human activities of the past few centuries have made a significant and growing contribution to the accumulation of these gases. Among these human activities is the consumption of energy, especially in the form of fossil fuels, deforestation, the burning of forests, the burning and decay of biomass, and others.

There has been lively debate over global warming and climate change. Some economists and scientists even argue that it is not a serious problem, that the fluctuations in temperature and various gases that we see are part of a normal cycle, or that it will produce only mild disruptions to which human societies can adapt. They also argue that some of the consequences will be positive (such as longer growing seasons in some agricultural regions) and that significant efforts to reduce greenhouse gases could stunt economic growth. However, at this point in time, the preponderance of scientific opinion is that global warming has the potential to create serious problems and that it will have many more negative consequences than positive ones (Intergovernmental Panel on Climate Change, 2007).

Solving Environmental Problems

A key notion that many environmentalists use today is sustainability: *A sustainable society is one that satisfies its needs without jeopardizing the prospects of future generations* (Renner, 2004). Attaining sustainability will probably call for modifications in one or more elements of the formula mentioned earlier, $I = P \times A \times T$.

1. Efforts to control population growth, discussed earlier in this chapter, will be essential. The earth's environment simply cannot sustain a continuously growing population.
2. The striving for greater levels of affluence will have to be moderated, or at least occur in ways that are less detrimental to the environment. This may require serious restrictions on people's use of automobiles or limitations on how large people's living dwellings can be. Public transportation and apartment-living in the city may have to replace driving your own car to work or living in a suburban McMansion many miles from your place of work in the city.
3. Modern economies will have to adjust so that they consume fewer resources. More materials will have to be reused and recycled, less packaging used, and more food purchased from local producers rather than being shipped thousands of miles to consumers.
4. Urban areas will need to become more centralized and densely populated rather than less so. This will make mass transportation more feasible and less expensive and reduce the overall carbon footprint. It will also mean less encroachment of human beings on the habitats of other species.

Some of these goals can be accomplished through market mechanisms, such as higher prices for fossil fuels, carbon offsets, and carbon trading. But this will undoubtedly need to be supplemented by government regulation and international agreements if true sustainability is to be approached. For example, most nations of the world approved a treaty in 2001, called the Kyoto Protocol, that requires the industrialized nations to reduce their emissions of greenhouse gases, principally carbon dioxide, to levels below what they were in 1990. If implemented, this treaty will produce a substantial drop in greenhouse gases emitted into the atmosphere in comparison to what would occur without the treaty. The treaty was not approved by the United States and has yet to be ratified and implemented.

Sociology on the Internet

The United Nations is an excellent location to find information about population and immigration problems around the world. Two good Web sites are the UN's Development Programme (**www.undp.org**) and its Population Fund (**www.unfpa.org**). Report to the class about the information that is available at each site. What other UN sites can you find, and what information about population issues do they contain?

Other organizations that play a part in developing policy about population problems are the Population Council (**www.popcouncil.org**), the Population Reference Bureau (**www.prb.org**), and the Population Institute (**www.populationinstitute.org**). Report to the class on the information that is contained at their Web sites. Explore the following Web sites for information and policy discussion of environmental issues: the U.S. Environmental Protection Agency (**www.epa.gov**), the Sierra Club (**www.sierraclub.org**), the Sightline Institute (**www.sightline.org**), and the Global Footprint Network (**www.globalfootprint.org**).

For further information and discussion, go to Allyn & Bacon's Social Problems Supersite (see Chapter 1) and explore Problem Area: Problems of Population, Immigration, and Urbanization.

Study & Review
SUMMARY OF LEARNING OBJECTIVES

You should be able to describe the three demographic variables and current trends in the age and sex structure of the United States.

Human ecology and demography study the growth and distribution of populations through the investigation of fertility (children born), mortality (number of deaths), migration (change of residence), and the rate of natural increase. These factors also have an impact on the age and sex structure of the population and the sex ratio.

You should be able to describe current patterns of population growth in the world and explain why such growth occurs, what the consequences of it are, and how to control population growth.

The theory of the demographic transition is concerned with changing patterns of birth and death rates brought about by industrialization. The demographic gap is the gap between high birthrates and low death rates, which during the early industrial period in different societies' development resulted in explosive population growth. Populations that have experienced the demographic transition have low birthrates and low death rates, resulting in stable population size, but other developing countries are still growing at rapid rates. Some of the consequences of overpopulation are crowding, food shortages, and depletion of the world's natural resources. Family planning, economic development, and improving the status of women are among the programs that have been employed in dealing with overpopulation.

You should be able to trace the pattern of urbanization and suburbanization in the United States and cities of less developed countries and describe what is distinct about postindustrial cities.

A community is a group of people who share a common territory and sense of identity or belonging, and who interact with one another. In industrial societies, cities have grown through a process of urbanization and suburbanization, and a postindustrial city may be emerging that is less centralized than are industrial cities. Technological developments have contributed to the tendencies for cities to both centralize and decentralize. Cities in developing nations have had different experiences, especially in terms of confronting more adverse conditions and being more affected by the capitalist world system, and have actually experienced overurbanization. With a global economy, global cities have emerged that perform some special functions in the world economy.

You should be able to discuss the different perspectives on the nature and quality of urban life.

Tönnies and Wirth viewed urban life as involving a special urban consciousness that is shaped by the numbers of people, the density, and the heterogeneity in cities. Gans argued that cities do retain a sense of community in neighborhoods where people identify with and have a sense of positive regard for one another. Fischer combined elements of both Wirth's and Gans' approaches to describe the character of urban life.

You should be able to describe the processes of urban change and the three theories of urban structure.

Urban ecology is the study of the distribution of people and facilities within urban centers and how cities relate to the surrounding social environment. Urban change involves such processes as segregation, invasion, and succession. Three theories of urban growth have been described: the concentric-zone theory, the sector theory, and the multiple-nuclei theory.

You should be able to discuss the major problems faced by cities in the United States and some of the policies that have been devised to resolve these difficulties.

Among the problems facing cities in the United States are economic decline and crime. Among the programs to deal with these problems are: government programs focused on urban renewal, private investment and enterprise zones, and gentrification.

You should be able to describe the social sources of environmental problems, the extent of environmental problems today, and what can be done to alleviate them.

Among the major sources of environmental problems are population size and overpopulation, high levels of affluence, and growth in technology. The environmental problems created by these conditions include water pollution, waste accumulation, deforestation, declining biodiversity, depletion of energy resources, and global warming and climate change. Environmental problems can be alleviated by controlling population growth, reducing levels of affluence, and changing lifestyles so that people use fewer damaging technologies.

CHRONOLOGICAL PRACTICE TEST

For answers to Key Concepts see the page number in parentheses; for other answers see page 421.

The Study of Human Populations
Key Concepts

1. Human ecology (395)
2. Demography (395)
3. Population (395)
4. Fertility (395)
5. Fecundity (395)
6. Mortality (395)
7. Migration (396)

True/False

8. T F The fertility of a society is usually at about the same level as its fecundity.

Concept Completion

9. The difference between the crude birthrate and the crude death rate is referred to as the _____.
10. The two types of migration discussed in the text are _____ and _____.

Critical Thinking

11. Define the field of demography. What are the elements of demographic change? How have they changed in the United States during the twentieth century?

World Population Growth
Key Concepts

12. Demographic transition (399)
13. Demographic gap (399)

True/False

14. T F The two largest nations in the world in terms of population are China and the United States.
15. T F When the demographic gap gets narrower, societies experience greater population growth.
16. T F The current doubling time for the world's population is approximately 200 years.

Concept Completion

17. The _____ stage of the demographic transition is characterized by high birthrates and high death rates.
18. Two of the consequences of overpopulation that are discussed in the text are _____ and _____.
19. China's one-child family program for reducing population growth appears to have resulted in an increase in _____.

Critical Thinking

20. What is the demographic transition? Describe the stages of the demographic transition, discussing what happens during each one.
21. What consequences of world population growth does the text discuss? Summarize the impacts of those consequences.
22. What efforts does the text discuss for controlling world population growth? Describe each one and assess its effectiveness.

Communities and Urbanization
Key Concepts

23. Community (403)
24. City (404)
25. Suburbs (404)
26. Global cities (407)

True/False

27. T F Cities are communities, but communities are not necessarily cities.
28. T F In the 1930s and 1940s, the United States government, in order to promote racially integrated communities, promoted policies that discouraged people from moving to the suburbs.

Critical Thinking

29. Describe the growth of cities and suburbs in human societies. What policies of the federal government contributed to the growth of the suburbs in the United States? How are the postindustrial cities different from cities in an industrial era?
30. Using Mexico as an example, describe the social organization of slums in developing societies, especially in terms of people's ability to adapt to their adversity.

Urbanism as a Way of Life

True/False

31. T F According to Louis Wirth, the urban consciousness that city dwellers often develop involves a reserve in social relationships and a focus on rational self-interest.

Concept Completion

32. In understanding how living in cities affects people, Claude Fischer stressed the importance of _____.

Critical Thinking

33. Describe the three perspectives that the text presented on the nature and quality of urban life.

Urban Ecology

Key Concepts

34. Urban ecology (410)
35. Segregation (410)
36. Invasion (410)
37. Succession (410)
38. Concentric-zone theory (411)
39. Sector theory (411)
40. Multiple-nuclei theory (412)

True/False

41. T F The changing racial composition of neighborhoods in many cities in the United States provides an example of the urban processes of invasion and succession.

Concept Completion

42. The study of the distribution of people and families within urban areas is called _____.
43. The theory of urban structures that argues that the critical factor in urban usage is the distance of a neighborhood from the center of the city is called _____.

Critical Thinking

44. Describe the three core processes that urban ecologists use in describing how cities change over time. Summarize the three theories that predict the urban structures that result from these processes of change?

The Future of Cities in the United States

Key Concept

45. Gentrification (414)

True/False

46. T F The urban renewal program continues to be the major federal program providing support for urban areas in the United States.
47. T F The poor in cities in the United States are the major beneficiaries of the process of gentrification.

Concept Completion

48. Areas of a city where new businesses are given tax breaks or are subject to less stringent regulation are called _____.
49. _____ refers to the return of relatively affluent households to marginal neighborhoods where run-down housing is rehabilitated.

Critical Thinking

50. What factors have produced the economic decline of cities in the United States?
51. What programs and trends, both public and private, can be currently identified as affecting urban problems in the United States?

Population and the Environment

Key Concepts

52. Carrying Capacity (416)
53. Sustainability (418)

ANSWERS TO CHRONOLOGICAL PRACTICE TEST

8. F; 14. F; 15. F; 16. T; 27. T; 28. F; 31. T; 41. T; 46. F; 47. F
9. rate of natural increase
10. immigration, emigration
17. preindustrial
18. crowding, food shortages, depletion of natural resources
19. female infanticide
32. urban subcultures
42. urban ecology
43. concentric-zone theory
48. urban free enterprise zones, empowerment zones
49. Gentrification

CUMULATIVE PRACTICE TEST

See page 482 for answers.

1. According to the text, the *crude birthrate*
   a. is the simplest measure of fertility.
   b. is the most accurate measure of fertility.
   c. ignores the age and sex structure of populations.
   d. All of the above.
   e. a and c above.

2. In regard to life expectancy in the United States,
   a. men live longer than women.
   b. the life expectancy of men and women is the same.
   c. the gap between the life expectancy of men and women is larger today than eighty years ago.
   d. the life expectancy of men has been declining in the past few decades.
   e. the gap between the life expectancy of men and women is smaller today than eighty years ago.

3. With respect to the effects of migration on the United States population,
   a. immigration has been a significant factor in our population growth.
   b. emigration from this country has been very high over the years.
   c. since 1970, immigration has had very little effect on our population.
   d. All of the above.
   e. None of the above.

4. Until 1600 in European countries, the average life expectancy for human beings was
   a. about 70 years.
   b. approximately 55 years.
   c. about 15 years.
   d. little more than 35 years.
   e. There are no records from which to calculate life expectancy in preindustrial societies

5. The United States is currently entering which stage of the demographic transition?
   a. The preindustrial stage.
   b. The transitional stage.
   c. The early industrial stage.
   d. The industrial stage.
   e. The postindustrial stage.

6. According to Malthus' view of human population growth,
   a. he was optimistic that human intervention would be effective in controlling population growth.
   b. contraception was the ultimate answer to controlling population growth.
   c. populations would continue to grow, and ultimately, be checked by deaths due to starvation, disease, and war.
   d. powerful groups such as the capitalists benefit from restrictions in the food supply.
   e. None of the above.

7. Which region of the world will see its proportion of the world population grow most significantly in the next fifty years?
   a. Asia.
   b. North America.
   c. Europe.
   d. Africa.
   e. The Caribbean.

8. The social and economic changes that probably account for more of the decline in fertility than family planning in nations today are called
   a. urban homesteading.
   b. fecundity.
   c. economic development.
   d. demography.
   e. gentrification.

9. Programs to promote gender equality around the world will probably have which effect?
   a. A negative impact on controlling world population growth.
   b. Little impact on world population growth.
   c. A reduction in fecundity.
   d. A positive impact on controlling world population growth.
   e. An increase in fertility.

10. According to the text, agricultural villages and then cities emerged in human history because of
    a. industrialization.
    b. capitalism.
    c. globalization.
    d. technological developments in transportation.
    e. the cultivation of plants and domestication of animals.

11. Which of the following contributed to the mass suburbanization of the United States in the twentieth century?
    a. The widespread availability of automobiles.
    b. The growth of the interstate highway system.
    c. The expansion of public transportation.
    d. All of the above.
    e. Only a and b.

12. In comparison to cities in industrial nations, cities in less developed nations today
    a. have experienced underurbanization.
    b. have been ignored by the capitalist world economic system.
    c. face more adverse conditions than did cities emerging in Europe and North America a century ago.
    d. have been growing at a slower pace.
    e. have much smaller populations.

13. Which of the following best describes the social networks among poor families in Mexico City?
    a. Most income is from crime and the drug trade.
    b. They maximize the resource base available to each family.
    c. They are mostly dysfunctional, both for the individual families and society as a whole.
    d. The helping networks are limited to the members of each nuclear family.
    e. Married couples prefer to live with their parents.

14. Which of the following statements would *not* be consistent with Gans's "urban community" perspective on city life?
    a. Urban life does not have a uniform impact on people.
    b. Tendencies toward impersonality and emotional distance can be found among people in cities.
    c. The existence of urban subcultures tends to increase feelings of alienation.

d. All of the above are consistent.

e. Both b and c are inconsistent.

15. _____ is a transition that occurs when the invasion of an urban area is large enough that the previous residents or users leave, and the new residents come to dominate the area.

a. Segregation

b. Sectors

c. Concentric zones

d. Succession

e. Gentrification

16. According to the sector theory of urban growth, urban development is shaped most importantly by

a. distance from the center of a city.

b. the capitalist world economic system.

c. transportation routes and geographic factors.

d. the number of specialized nuclei that develop.

e. b and c are both important for this theory.

17. According to the text, the premier problem faced by many cities in the United States today is

a. dilapidated housing.

b. crime.

c. ghettos.

d. educational problems.

e. economic decline.

18. One major cause of the financial problems in cities in the United States has been

a. the growing demographic gap in cities.

b. the flight of people and jobs from cities.

c. the overpopulation of cities.

d. the gentrification of cities.

e. overurbanization.

19. People are least fearful of crime in their neighborhoods in cities when

a. crime is at its highest level.

b. the population in the neighborhood is elderly.

c. the police keep a low profile in the neighborhood.

d. they are active in formal and informal community organizations.

e. they do not participate in community organizations.

20. In the formula summarizing the factors that impact on the environment and cause pollution and degradation, $I = P \times A \times T$, the letter "A" stands for

a. affluence.

b. anomie.

c. assimilation.

d. authority.

e. androgyny.

FOR FURTHER READING

Gans, Herbert J. (1991). *People, plans, and policies: Essays on poverty, racism, and other national urban problems.* New York: Columbia University Press. This is an excellent set of essays by a well-respected specialist in urban affairs. The issues discussed range from problems of architecture to poverty and the underclass.

Garreau, Joel. (1991). *Edge city: Life on the new frontier.* New York: Doubleday. *Edge city* is the author's name for those suburbs that have grown large enough to be considered self-sufficient. He provides an interesting perspective on that part of urban life where many people live, suggesting that edge cities reflect such U.S. values as individualism and homesteading.

Kasarda, John D., & Parnell, Allan M. (eds.). (1993). *Third World cities: Problems, policies, and prospects.* Newbury Park, CA: Sage. These two sociologists have brought together some of the most recent research being done on the problems confronting cities in Third-World nations. This volume views the problems of cities from a global perspective.

Kolbert, Elizabeth. (2006). *Field notes from a catastrophe: Man, nature and climate change.* New York: Bloomsbury. This book provides a readable overview of the causes and consequences of global warming and climate change. Even if only some of Kolbert's projections come true, the consequences will be dire.

Meadows, Donella H., Meadows, Dennis L., & Randers, Jorgen. (1992). *Beyond the limits: Confronting global collapse, envisioning a sustainable future.* Post Mills, VT: Chelsea Green. This is a recent assessment by three of the same scientists who conducted the study for the Club of Rome thirty years ago. Their conclusions are a little more optimistic now, but only assuming that there are changes in both lifestyle and technology.

Portes, Alejandro, & Stepick, Alex. (1993). *City on the edge: The transformation of Miami.* Berkeley: University of California Press. This is an excellent analysis of the development of Miami as its Cuban population has grown. It is a complex story that ties in urban development, ethnicity, and socioeconomic status.

Sale, Kirkpatrick. (1980). *Human scale.* New York: Coward, McCann, & Geohegan. Assessing huge urban developments, Sale contends that going beyond "human scale" causes impersonality and a number of other problems. He argues for small-scale developments in urban planning.

Williams, Terry, and Kornblum, William. (1994). *The uptown kids: Struggle and hope in the projects.* New York: Putnam. This is an intimate portrait of what life is like for youth who grow up in crowded and dangerous urban public housing projects. The authors make suggestions for how things could be improved.

Collective Behavior, Social Change, and Modernization

MYTHS & FACTS: About Collective Behavior and Social Change

The Nature of Collective Behavior

The Preconditions of Collective Behavior

APPLYING SOCIOLOGY: Preventing Urban Riots: The Los Angeles Riot in Retrospect

Rumors

Mass Behavior

Panic

Mass Hysteria

Fads and Fashions

Crowds

Characteristics of Crowds

Types of Crowds

Behavior in Crowds

Social Movements

The Development of Social Movements

OTHER WORLDS, OTHER WAYS: Afghanistan: The Social Roots of Terrorist Violence

Social Change

Theories of Change

Evolutionary Theories

Functionalist Theories

Conflict Theories

Cyclical Theories

The Future: Global Modernization?

Modernization in the Less Developed Nations

SOCIOLOGY OF MEDIA AND TECHNOLOGY: Social Movements and Resistance to Globalization

The United States: A Postindustrial Future?

The Globalization of Labor

SOCIOLOGY ON THE INTERNET

Study & Review

In the sweltering August heat of eastern Pennsylvania in 1897, miners in the anthracite coal fields walked off their jobs. It was a clumsy, haphazard, and disorganized strike. The miners were not unionized—they were simply fed up with low wages and dangerous working conditions. There was little safety equipment in the mines, and cuts, bruises, broken bones, and disfigurement were common. In 1894 alone, 446 men were killed in coal-mining accidents in eastern Pennsylvania.

On top of this volatile situation, intense ethnic hostilities existed among the coal miners. Groups that had migrated to the United States decades earlier—the Welsh, Irish, and Germans—considered themselves "true Americans" and were repelled by the onslaught of more recent immigrants from Italy and Eastern Europe. These "new" immigrants spoke little English, but they worked very hard and saved their money hoping to return to the "old country"—Poland, Hungary, Slovakia, the Ukraine—or bring their families to the United States.

The strike limped along for a few weeks, with initiative fluctuating from the hands of mine owners to the hands of the strikers. Finally, on the hot afternoon of September 10, the strikers confronted a posse in the small, depressing mining town of Lattimer, near Hazleton, Pennsylvania. The sound of gunfire roared across the fields and forests. Nineteen miners—with rich ethnic names such as Broztowski, Chrzeszeski, Rekewicz, and Ziominski—fell mortally wounded. Another thirty-nine were injured (Novak, 1978).

Seventeen years later in Colorado, eight thousand miners went on strike when the Colorado Fuel and Iron Company refused to recognize the right of the United Mine Workers of America to unionize (Taft & Ross, 1969). The strikers moved their families out of company-owned houses and into a tent city at Ludlow. National Guard troops were called in. On April 20, 1914, the troops attacked the tent colony. Five men and a boy were killed by the machine-gun crossfire. Still unsatisfied, the militia burned the tent colony. This

Myths & Facts
About Collective Behavior and Social Change

Myth:

In the race riots that have occurred in U.S. cities over the past forty years, the rioters have come from the ranks of the criminals, the unemployed, and the poor.

Fact:

Although such people certainly played a part, the people arrested for rioting have also included educated, employed, and seemingly law-abiding citizens who were reacting against what they saw as the injustices of racial discrimination and oppression.

Myth:

When people are pushed to the limit in terms of deprivation or oppression, they become susceptible to the appeals of revolutionary demagogues.

Fact:

The origins of revolution are often found in relative rather than absolute deprivation. Severely deprived people tend to respond with apathy or acquiescence. On the contrary, people with some hope that their lives will get better, but who see that hope threatened, are more likely to join a revolution.

Myth:

Now that we have moved into a postindustrial era, automation and computerization will usher in a life of leisure and material comfort for people in the United States.

Fact:

There is little consensus about what technological developments such as automation and computerization will hold for the future. Some argue that there will be fewer jobs and that many of them will be tedious and low-paying with few prospects for advancement. There may be intense competition for the limited number of good jobs, and those who get them will live comfortably while the less fortunate will scrape by.

Myth:

Modernization is a worldwide trend that will result in the less developed nations achieving the economic productivity and standard of living of the United States, Japan, and other fully industrialized nations.

Fact:

This could happen, but reality may be more complex. The developing nations today face much more adverse conditions in their struggle to industrialize than their predecessors did. In addition, there may be economic and social processes at work that will keep the global system stratified into the well-off industrial nations and the less-well-to-do developing nations.

These trolley drivers in Boston had gone out on strike to protest over pay and working conditions. Such collective actions were among the mechanisms that forged power and authority relations between workers and owners as the United States industrialized.

holocaust, which has since come to be known as the Ludlow Massacre, resulted in the suffocation deaths of two women and eleven children. The surviving strikers and their families dispersed into the countryside, and for ten days there were sporadic clashes between the strikers and the militia. By the time the strike had ended, the death toll had risen to seventy-four.

Lattimer and Ludlow are hardly household words today. Yet these two incidents—by themselves seemingly minor events in the sweep of history—were critical parts of a profound revolution that changed the nature of human societies. Those events in the hot, dusty summer of Pennsylvania and the chilly spring of Colorado were links in the vast process of social change that we call the Industrial Revolution. As has been described throughout this book, industrialization led to dramatic changes in all social institutions, including the family, religion, education, politics, and the economy. In the process of industrialization, new power and authority relations were forged between workers and industrial managers. Clashes such as those at Lattimer and Ludlow were examples of the mechanisms through which these social changes were made. One wonders whether the miners in Lattimer and Ludlow were ever able to gain some perspective on

their actions. Did they (or the mine owners) recognize the small but significant part that their actions played in one of the vastest transformations in human history? In all likelihood, their goals were more modest—to end this strike, to gain a little more compensation, and to introduce a few safety devices into the mines. Yet their actions played a part, however small, in modernizing the United States.

Social change is the topic of this chapter. First it discusses what sociologists call collective behavior and social movements, which can play an important part in the process of change, and then it analyzes the major theories of social change.

The Nature of Collective Behavior

You should be able to discuss the various forms of collective behavior and the conditions necessary for their development.

The working people of Lattimer and Ludlow took matters into their own hands. The conventional ways of doing things—looking for a better job or asking their boss for higher wages—seemed unlikely to resolve their

Figure 15.1
The Continuum of Institutionalized and Collective Behavior

plight, so they engaged in what sociologists call collective behavior: *relatively unstructured and spontaneous actions that arise in situations where more conventional behavior seems inappropriate or ineffective* (Goode, 1992). Collective behavior is less enduring than institutionalized behavior based on established social norms, roles, and relationships. In fact, in collective behavior, people's actions often do not appear to be guided by the usual norms governing human conduct. Rather, new and temporary norms emerge as accepted standards. Collective behavior covers a broad range of activities: a rioting mob, a crowd panic, fads and fashions, responses to disaster, a mass migration, the spread of a rumor, or the actions of an audience at a soccer match.

Although collective behavior contrasts sharply with the more institutionalized forms of behavior, the difference is actually a matter of degree. That is, completely institutionalized behavior lies at one end of a continuum and totally spontaneous, unorganized behavior at the other extreme (Figure 15.1). For example, the inauguration of a President falls at the institutionalized end of the scale: It is a rigid, predictable, ritualized performance with little opportunity for spontaneity or creativity. At the other end of the scale, some mass panics involve practically no structure or coordination of behavior. In between those two extremes, we can identify some race riots in which people coordinate their behavior in order to loot stores or attack the police. Protest demonstrations exhibit still more structure, including extensive planning, leadership, monitors, and the like.

The Preconditions of Collective Behavior

Understanding collective behavior is a substantial task in view of its spontaneous nature and the many forms that it can take. What, after all, do a panic, a riot, and a fad have in common? The sociologist Neil Smelser (1963) has provided us with a comprehensive approach to this problem. He argues that, whatever form collective behavior takes, it involves people's efforts to cope with stressful and uncertain social conditions. Smelser suggests that the following six preconditions must all exist for collective behavior to occur:

1. *Structural conduciveness* refers to the social conditions that make it *possible* for a particular kind of collective behavior to occur. A panic, for example, could not occur if people were standing in an open field where there was no possibility of their being trapped. Likewise, a race riot would be impossible in a community where there was only one racial group.

2. *Structural strain* refers to ambiguities, discrepancies, threats, or conflicts in people's lives that place strain on them and generate frustration or anger. This strain can take many forms: poverty, unemployment, racial or sexual discrimination, or any situation in which people's expectations are unfulfilled. College students, for example, experience structural strain when their educational accomplishments do not lead to the jobs they expect to obtain.

3. *Generalized belief* refers to the ideas that people have about the source of the strain they are experiencing and about what can be done to alleviate it. These ideas are not necessarily accurate—they are people's *definition of the situation*, and people act on the basis of these judgments. People on the extreme edge of the patriot movement in the United States, for example, believe in white supremacy and espouse virulent forms of anti–Semitic and anti-African American bigotry. Groups such as Posse Comitatus and American Christian Patriots attribute problems such as crime and unemployment to the power of Jews and racial minorities. Such a generalized belief has motivated some extreme members of the patriot movement to espouse, and even carry out, acts of violence against members of minorities in order to advance their goal of white supremacy (Dees, 1996).

4. *Precipitating factors* are incidents that make strain or frustration immediate and intense and that serve as a trigger or a catalyst to collective outbursts.

Applying Sociology   Preventing Urban Riots: The Los Angeles Riot in Retrospect

The images of the riot in south central Los Angeles in 1992 were very disturbing: towers of smoke from many buildings burning at once, looters emerging from stores with their arms laden with stolen goods, store owners shooting their guns at crowds to keep them at bay, innocent bystanders savagely beaten and helpless. By the time it was over, fifty-three people had died, and there was $1 billion in property damage. Especially disturbing was the realization that we had seen it all before: in Miami in the 1980s and in many U.S. cities in the 1960s. Most people are familiar with the immediate precipitant of the Los Angeles riot (Cannon, 1997; Dentler, 1992). Four police officers were acquitted of the beating of the African American motorist Rodney King. The acquittal of the officers, Smelser's precipitating factor, sparked the riot. The acquittal was seen by African Americans in Los Angeles as convincing proof that the police were free to assault blacks at will and that the criminal justice system would provide blacks with little legal recourse against such violence. This was their generalized belief. Other recent events in Los Angeles provided fuel for such beliefs: African American men were routinely arrested and mistreated by the police, and a store owner who shot and killed a sixteen-year-old African American girl was convicted of a minor charge and spent no time in jail.

The various urban riots that have occurred in the past century have been studied extensively by sociologists and other social scientists. These riots essentially served as field experiments in which sociologists could compare cities that experienced riots with those that did not and compare people who joined in the riots with those who lived in the riot community but did not participate (Bergeson & Herman, 1998; McPhail, 1971; Olzak & Shanahan, 1996). From this research, sociologists and policymakers learned a great deal about why riots happen.

One lesson is that such riots start when a highly volatile event, such as the acquittal of the police officers, enrages an aggrieved group. The same thing happened in the Miami riot in 1980 when the acquittal of four Miami police officers in a murder trial for the death of an African American insurance agent infuriated African Americans. The climate in Miami was the same as in Los Angeles: There had been police killings and assaults of blacks in Florida to fuel beliefs about police racism and disregard for African Americans. Despite these lessons, authorities in Los Angeles apparently did not take seriously enough the potential threat posed as the trial of the officers came to an end.

In addition to discovering the immediate causes of riots, the research on riots also tells us about the structural strain that can play a part. It is almost a cliché to say that economic deprivation and racial discrimination lay at the root of many of these urban riots. Clearly, people who are well-off economically are disinclined to take to the streets, even if provoked. But people who are severely oppressed are also unlikely to engage in such activism. Their feelings of helplessness are more likely to result in resignation or withdrawal. Instead of the total underdog, it is people who have hopes for improvement in their lives but see those hopes threatened who are most inclined to respond to deprivation through rioting. In other words, it is *relative deprivation* that often underlies collective violence. So it is not cities where minorities are the poorest that experience riots but rather those where minorities have made considerable improvements in income and education. Such advances lead people to hope for further improvement and produce deeply felt frustration when the improvements are not forthcoming.

Likewise, research shows that rioters by no means come exclusively from the ranks of the poor, the unemployed, or criminals. Criminals or the unemployed may play a part in starting a riot, but seemingly respectable people provide the numbers that keep it going and contribute to heightening the levels of emotion and destruction. What evidence we have at this point from Los Angeles suggests the same thing: Many looters and arrestees worked or were in school. In addition, economic competition plays an important part. Recent research shows that riots are more likely to occur in cities where job opportunities for African Americans have contracted and where immigration has created tight labor markets (Bergeson & Herman, 1998; Olzak & Shanahan, 1996). The combination of relative deprivation along with stiff competition for jobs makes cities especially susceptible to unrest.

Riots are also more likely to occur when members of minority groups feel left out of society, isolated from sources of political and economic power, and ignored by the powers that be. When there are few channels for resolving grievances or when the system appears unresponsive to expressions of discontent, people are more willing to turn to collective violence. In earlier riots, isolation from the political system was evidenced by such things as few or no African American police officers in a city. Presumably, a city sensitive to the needs of blacks would hire black police officers, and such officers would be more responsive to the needs and problems of the black community. In these earlier riots, cities with fewer black police officers or store owners were more likely to experience a riot.

Once again, Los Angeles in 1992 fit the profile for a riot-prone city fairly well. The city did have a black mayor, but blacks were underrepresented at all levels of the police force. It also had a relatively small number of black store owners and professionals, especially in south central Los Angeles where the riot occurred. In addition, competition for jobs was stiff, and many of the store owners in south central Los Angeles were Asian Americans who seemed to be doing fairly well even though they had immigrated to the United States only recently. Their apparent success contributed to the feelings of resentment and isolation in the African American community.

We learned a great deal about collective violence from the research conducted in earlier decades. Our failure to apply that research by making changes in social policy is one of the reasons for the disastrous riot in Los Angeles in 1992. Social policies could have been established that would have improved the economic circumstances of African Americans and reduced feelings of isolation and disenfranchisement. Many of these policies are discussed in Chapters 6 and 7, and need not be repeated here. What does need reiteration is the understanding that, if society does nothing, it will probably have more such riots in the future. ■

In the 1980 riot in the predominantly African American Liberty City area of Miami, for example, the catalyst was the acquittal of four white police officers in the beating death five months earlier of an African American insurance agent. This acquittal infuriated the African American community because it seemed like yet another instance of whites going unpunished for perpetrating violence against African Americans. Eight white people and nine blacks died before the violence finally subsided.

5. *Mobilization* occurs when people are brought into action and their behaviors are directed toward some specific goals. Such direction might involve, for example, someone standing on a car exhorting a crowd to attack the police or loot a store. Mobilization might also take the form of someone throwing the first rock, thereby serving as a model for others. In other words, mobilization can be spontaneous and unstructured, or it can involve highly structured leadership.

6. *Social control* refers to any mechanisms that prevent, interrupt, or slow down the emergence of collective behavior. It could take the form of police actions to control a crowd, negotiations to stop a riot, or pulling the plug on a loudspeaker to prevent a leader from mobilizing a group. Social control can intervene in any of the other five preconditions. Weak or ineffective social control is necessary for collective behavior to occur.

Smelser's approach to collective behavior is useful because it is sufficiently general to be applicable to all forms of collective behavior. To understand whether collective behavior will occur in a particular situation or what form it will take, we need to assess the character of the six preconditions in that situation. As this chapter discusses some different types of collective behavior, readers should keep Smelser's approach in mind.

Applying Sociology: Preventing Urban Riots (pp. 428–429) discusses sociological research on riots and applies it to the riot in south central Los Angeles in 1992. The role of Smelser's preconditions can be seen in that riot and also the role that sociological research can play in helping people figure out how to prevent such ghastly events from happening again. Riots actually contain within them a number of types of collective behavior, such as rumors and crowd behavior. This chapter will explore more of the process of collective behavior by analyzing three types of such behavior: rumors, mass behavior, and crowd behavior.

Rumors

Rumors are *unauthenticated messages, although they are not necessarily false* (Rosnow & Fine, 1976). Rumor is a form of collective behavior, and it also plays an important role in many other forms of collective behavior, such as mass hysteria and riots. Although people often discount the importance of rumors (as in "It's *only* a rumor"), rumors are important mechanisms of communication and information seeking in many different situations (Rosnow, 1991; Turner, 1994). For example, in ambiguous settings where something unusual or startling has occurred, rumors may be the only source of information that people have. In addition, in stressful or anxious situations, people may pass on and accept rumors as a way of alleviating their anxiety. This was shown to be the case in the study of the willingness of college students to accept and pass on rumors about AIDS: Students experiencing the most anxiety and uncertainty were most willing to believe and transmit misconceptions about AIDS, regardless of whether they had confidence in the truth of the rumors they were passing on (Kimmel & Keefer, 1991).

Tamotsu Shibutani (1966) has referred to rumors as *collective transactions* to emphasize their role as group efforts to develop a shared definition of some situation. "Rumor develops as [people] caught together in an ambiguous situation attempt to construct a meaningful interpretation of it by pooling their intellectual resources" (p. 164). Shibutani's approach to understanding rumor focuses on the concerns of the interactionist perspective regarding the importance of social meanings and their emergence from social interaction. Thus the rumor process is an interchange between people in which new bits of information are weighed and assessed against what is already known or suspected.

Although rumors are often distorted as they are exchanged, such distortion does not always result. There are situations in which people take a *critical set* toward rumors, which means that because of their own knowledge or the characteristics of the situation, people are skeptical about rumors and better able to assess their accuracy (Buckner, 1965). In other situations, however, people have an *uncritical set* and are likely to pass on an untruth or distort a rumor. Another factor that is likely to affect the distortion of a rumor is the group context in which it spreads. If it is spread serially from one person who knows the rumor to another person unfamiliar with it, then distortion is likely to occur because there are few checks on any person distorting it in the process of passing it on. If a rumor comes to a whole group of people at one time, however, the resulting interchange and feedback will reduce the likelihood of distortion.

When rumor distortion does occur, it can happen in three different ways. First, as a rumor is retold, a process of *leveling* occurs in which the rumor is shortened and made more concise by eliminating some details. Second, through a process called *sharpening*, people give selective emphasis to some parts of a rumor, reporting some details and ignoring others. Finally, through what is called *assimilation*, elements of the rumor are changed, so that the overall rumor is consistent and fits in with prejudices or preconceptions of those transmitting the rumor (Koenig, 1985).

Although many rumor situations are characterized by ambiguity or anxiety, people pass on rumors for many reasons. In some cases, they may simply be bored and have nothing better to do. In other cases, individuals may feel that they will gain something from telling others about a rumor.

> One can readily visualize rumormongering as a transaction in which someone passes a rumor for something in return—another rumor, clarifying information, status, power, control, money, or some other resource. When information is scarce, the rumormonger can exact a high price for his tales. When the market for rumors expands, the number of rumors will proliferate. (Rosnow & Fine, 1976, p. 77)

This element in the rumor process can be a significant motivation to pass on rumors—even rumors whose authenticity one might doubt.

Mass Behavior

Mass behavior is *collective behavior in which the actions of people are not coordinated, people have little or no contact with one another, and yet there is still some uniformity of behavior and a general awareness of the others in the group.* Three types of mass behavior will be discussed: panic, mass hysteria, and fads and fashions.

PANIC   On a cold and snowy winter evening in 1913, the Italian Hall in Calumet, Michigan, was gaily decorated for a Christmas party intended to bring some joy into the lives of children whose fathers, copper miners, had been on strike for many months. As the children celebrated, someone shouted "fire." The frightened children rushed for the exits. In a horrifyingly brief period of time, seventy-four people were dead, mostly children. They were crushed to death by the sheer weight of their own small bodies as they rushed to the exits of the building because the exit doors would not open. There was no fire (Thurner, 1984).

The Italian Hall disaster is a classic case of a panic, *an uncoordinated, mass attempt to avoid some immediate, perceived threat.* Panic behavior is sometimes referred to as irrational, but such statements are based on a misunderstanding of panic by people who observe it only from a distance. For people in the situation, mass behavior at the time seems rational, logical, and understandable. In a panic situation, people have relatively little information on which to base their decisions (e.g., the shouted word "fire" and the immediate reactions of others). In addition, there is a sense of urgency—if there is a fire, we must act quickly to save ourselves. This lack of information coupled with the sense of urgency leads people to be very suggestible. If the behavior of others—for example, their tentative movements toward exits—hints that the danger is real, people are likely to accept the suggestion and follow suit.

Although there was no actual fire in the Italian Hall in Calumet, all too often there is real danger, and with horrifying results: 600 people died in the Iroquois Theater fire in 1903; the Coconut Grove Night Club fire in Boston in 1942 resulted in 488 deaths; the Station concert club fire in Rhode Island in 2003 claimed 100 lives. Some of these lives probably would have been saved if there had not been mass panic. But how can panic be avoided in such situations? Studies indicate that people are much more likely to survive such disasters when they are familiar with emergency exits from buildings (Abe, 1976; Johnson, Feinberg, & Johnston, 1994). Thus fire drills, when possible, can build in behavior patterns for people to rely on in panic situations. People also are more likely to survive when they engage in familiar and habitual behavior, such as moving to a known part of buildings. In addition, the survivors are those who act cautiously and avoid following in the footsteps of large numbers of people. A final thing we have learned about panics is that they are rarely the kind of disorganized, individualistic flight that popular imagery often portrays. Instead, people's behavior in such situations is shaped by their social bonds with others present, such as friends or relatives, and by social roles, such as occupational roles. In other words, people coordinate their actions with others with whom they have social ties, and employers or others in leadership roles can exert considerable influence on how people behave.

MASS HYSTERIA In 1938, Orson Welles performed a radio dramatization of H. G. Wells's science fiction novel *The War of the Worlds*, about an invasion of the Earth by creatures from Mars. Welles's hour-long performance was cast as a musical show that was repeatedly interrupted by live "newscasts" of the invasion. As the show progressed, the newscasts reported that U.S. cities were being attacked and destroyed and their residents killed by the "invaders." If one listens to recordings of the broadcast today, it is obvious that it is a fictional account. The events recounted, for example, span many days but the show itself is only an hour long. In addition, the "newscasters" appear to be everywhere: in cities, in farmhouses, even riding with pilots in airplanes attacking the Martians. Yet, despite its clearly fictional nature, a survey found that a quarter of the listeners believed the broadcast was authentic. Many of these people were frightened by the broadcast, and some actually panicked and fled their homes out of fear. Others telephoned relatives or prayed as a means of consolation (Cantril, 1940).

The reaction to this radio broadcast is an example of *mass hysteria*: *an emotionally charged reaction by a large number of people to some anxiety-producing event.* Mass hysteria is similar to panic but spread over a larger area and a longer time period. Despite the name of *mass* hysteria, recent research has shown that most of these episodes are less widespread than the term implies (Marx & McAdam, 1994). Only a small number of the listeners to Welles's broadcast took any substantial action. Nonetheless, how could a reaction such as this happen? One reason was that radio was still a relatively new phenomenon in 1938, and people were not as sophisticated regarding the broadcast medium as they are today. People were just beginning to get much of their daily news from the radio, and interruptions of programs for news—the format used in Welles's program—were quite common. Furthermore, relatively little was known about other planets, and many people assumed that there might be life forms on them. The famous Martian "canals" had been observed, and there was speculation that they might have been constructed by "Martians." Adding to this credulity was the fact that science fiction had only recently acquired a mass audience by 1938. Given all these elements, the stage was set for a mass hysterical reaction to Welles' broadcast. Such a response to the same stimuli would be unlikely today because the preconditions that existed then have changed. This is not to say that people are less susceptible to mass hysteria today—only that the precipitating conditions are likely to be different.

FADS AND FASHIONS A *fad* is a *short-lived behavior engaged in by a large number of people; it is not part of a longer trend.* The list of fads in recent U.S. history is almost endless: meditation, jogging, hot tubs, roller blading, bungee jumping, break dancing, body piercing, and so on. Not everyone, of course, participates in every fad. People are attracted to particular fads for a variety of reasons. In some cases, a fad is a means of asserting one's identity and feeling part of a group. In other cases, people are attracted to particular fads when they see celebrities or other well-known and prestigious people adopting them.

Whereas fads often carry slightly negative connotations—as in the pejorative term faddist—fashions tend to be more socially acceptable. *Fashion* refers to *behavior that is a part of the continuous process of establishing currently acceptable modes of dress, appearance, or behavior.* Fashions are much like fads although more continuous: There is always something that is considered in-style and other things that are considered outmoded. Because of the part they play in establishing normative behavior, fashions can be found in all societies (Kroeber, 1919). Both fads and fashions are considered collective behavior because they are relatively unstructured and spontaneous, with their precise content emerging from the interactions of many people.

Crowds

The most thoroughly investigated form of collective behavior is probably the *crowd*. A *crowd* is *a temporary grouping of people who are in fairly close physical proximity to one another and whose attentions are focused on some common object or event.* Crowds include such things as a mob of looters roaming the streets, a pack of celebrants enjoying their home team's World Series victory, and a hostile group confronting a police squadron.

CHARACTERISTICS OF CROWDS Despite the considerable variety among crowds, many crowds share some or all of the following characteristics (Blumer, 1951; Goode, 1992):

1. *Uncertainty.* Crowds involve a degree of ambiguity or uncertainty: People are not sure what others will do

or how they themselves ought to behave. This is even true among spectators at a sporting event. Although most will watch the game with a degree of decorum, some might shout obscenities, while others might throw objects onto the playing field; a fistfight might even break out between two excited spectators. Professional hockey matches in North America are notorious for this uncertainty regarding the behavior of both spectators and players. In fact, uncertainty is one element of sporting events that makes them so exciting to watch.

2. *Suggestibility.* Because of the lack of structure in crowds, people need to look for guidance for their behavior in places other than the preexisting normative structure. This need makes crowd members much more open and sensitive to the suggestion of others in the crowd than they might normally be. This suggestibility, however, is not totally uncritical. People take suggestions only if the suggestions are consistent with the prevailing mood and conception of appropriate behavior in the crowd.

3. *Anonymity.* Surrounded by a mass of other people, individuals in crowds often feel that they are unrecognized and thus anonymous. They believe they will go unnoticed and so will not be held responsible for their actions. People might shout, throw rocks, or set fire to buildings if their feelings of anonymity offer a sense of protection.

4. *Permissiveness.* The atmosphere of a crowd tends to encourage a broadening of the limits of acceptable behavior, and people are likely to express attitudes or engage in actions that they would refuse to do under other conditions. Permissiveness should not, however, be confused with a total *lack* of limits. In crowds, normative limitations may be extended considerably, but they are never eliminated. In the riot in Los Angeles in 1992, for example, rioters did not loot all businesses—they tended to attack Korean-owned and white-owned shops and spare those owned by African Americans or Latinos.

5. *Emotional Arousal.* Heightened emotional arousal results from the rapid communication that occurs between crowd members. In crowds, a person is bombarded with stimuli: sounds, shouts, large numbers of people, and movement. These stimuli tend to increase one's awareness of others and easily translate into a heightening of one's own emotional arousal.

TYPES OF CROWDS Although crowds have much in common, there are also differences among crowds, especially in terms of goals and the amount of coordination of behavior among members. Using these criteria, we can distinguish among four types of crowds (Blumer, 1951; Goode, 1992).

A **casual crowd** is *a temporary grouping in which there is little structure and the members do not engage in any distinct, coordinated crowd actions.* Crowd members are passive, and there is little sense of crowd unity or involvement. Casual crowds, such as people watching firefighters control a blaze, are very unstable, and people enter and leave them easily. Despite their temporary and unstable nature, casual crowds are important because they can serve as a nucleus for other types of crowds.

Conventional crowds are *one of the more "regularized" forms of crowds because they are planned and socially sanctioned gatherings that are relatively structured.* Audiences at a sporting event, a religious rally, or a rock concert are examples of conventional crowds. Although such gatherings are planned and sanctioned, they nonetheless exhibit the characteristics—uncertainty, suggestibility, permissiveness, and emotional arousal—found in other crowds. At a rock concert, for example, there is often an air of expectancy—almost an electricity—about how things will turn out. How will the audience behave? Will there be any untoward events? Might things even get totally out of control?

An **acting crowd** is *one in which attention and activity are directed toward some goal or objective.* Rioting mobs, looters, and protest demonstrators are examples of acting crowds. Acting crowds are often the most violent and destructive type of crowd, but they are also among the most significant crowds in terms of social change.

Expressive crowds are *crowds that focus on the expression of emotions and the personal gratification of their members.* Their goal is to change the mood, feelings, or behavior of those participating in the crowd. Expressive crowds are often more highly charged with emotion and more frenzied in behavior than are other crowds. For example, people often pour into the streets and engage in ecstatic behavior when a home sports team wins a prized victory, such as the World Series in baseball or the Stanley Cup in hockey. People may drink, smash property, loot stores, and engage in other behaviors that they would normally avoid. Behavior that is normally inhibited can become common.

BEHAVIOR IN CROWDS One of the major concerns in the sociological study of crowds has been to discover the factors that shape the behavior of people in crowds (McPhail, 2001). In the past few decades, sociological understanding of crowd behavior has been revised substantially. We now recognize that people in crowds are not necessarily behaving irrationally, nor do all members of a crowd feel and behave in the same fashion. To understand crowd behavior more fully, it is useful to review the four major processes that can shape human behavior in crowds: contagion, convergence, emergent norms, and decision making. Much of what is discussed here involves Smelser's precondition of mobilization, because it involves the face-to-face social interaction that influences whether people will participate in a crowd action. Even if structural strain, a generalized belief, and a precipitating factor are present, people are not likely to become part of a crowd unless they are mobilized.

Contagion refers to the rapid spread of feelings, attitudes, and behaviors through a crowd. A phenomenon called circular reaction can play an important part in contagion (Blumer, 1951). *Circular reaction* refers to a process of "interstimulation" in which person A's response reflects, possibly to a heightened degree, the emotions that person B has just expressed and then serves as a stimulus for further reaction on the part of person B. Thus A and B repeatedly stimulate each other, thereby increasing their respective intensity and emotion. Person B, for example, shouts, "Let's attack the police." Person A quickly agrees, and this agreement serves as further impetus for B to proceed. The process involves quick reactions without the assessment and consideration that usually occur in less emotionally volatile settings. Another important factor that can affect contagion is *milling*: random, erratic, fluctuating behavior. People in crowds are constantly walking around, talking, looking, moving, or shouting. In terms of the contagion process, milling makes people more sensitive to and responsive to the behavior of others in the crowd. When there is great, agitated movement, we tend to direct our attention toward it. By restricting our focus of attention to the crowd actions, we become more aware of the feelings and attitudes of the crowd members and are more likely to be influenced by them.

A second process that can affect crowd behavior is *convergence*: People may be drawn together in part because they share common qualities, predispositions, or interests (Milgram & Toch, 1968). The nature of these predispositions and interests can be highly variable. For example, some convergence theories focus on such things as frustration and strain as the common predisposition that underlies crowd behavior. The psychologists John Dollard and his colleagues (1939) along with Leonard Berkowitz (1971) have argued that increasing frustration leads to an enhanced tendency toward aggression and that aggression can readily take the form of rioting and other types of crowd behavior. Certainly, for example, the urban riots of the 1960s and the riots in Miami and Los Angeles in the 1980s and 1990s involved people who were reacting to common experiences of discrimination and oppression. We need to be careful, however, and recognize that not all crowd members act on the same motivations. Although some rioters may be responding to discrimination and oppression,

others act out of the possibility of personal gain or are in search of a little excitement.

In addition to contagion and convergence, crowd behavior is often influenced by a third process: normative prescriptions and proscriptions, called *emergent norms*, not unlike the norms that guide behavior in other settings (Turner, 1964). In crowd settings, a new social structure comprised of new norms and social roles emerges to shape and constrain behavior. This new normative structure is unique to the situation in which it evolves, and it changes or disappears as the situation changes. Social pressure develops that encourages crowd members to behave in conformity to the emerging norms—or at least not to violate them. People become aware of the emergent norms by observing what others in the crowd say and do. In a riot, for example, seeing others looting stores—especially if the looters appear otherwise respectable—suggests that some people view looting as appropriate in this situation. And we know from considerable research that people in ambiguous or emotional situations tend to adopt the standards and judgments of those around them. This tendency can give the emergent norms considerable power over people's behavior.

A fourth process affecting crowd behavior is *collective decision making* in which crowd members calculate the benefits and costs of particular actions and choose those with the most desirable outcomes (Berk, 1974). The benefits of participating in a riot, say, might include the ability to vent one's anger or the opportunity to acquire some goods by looting a store. The costs would include the chance of being injured or arrested. If others join the rioting, then the costs are lowered because each person is less likely to be picked out of a large crowd by the police. In fact, there may be a threshold for participating in riot actions, such as a minimum number of people a person would have to see join in before that person would do so (Granovetter, 1978). Thus people in crowds assess alternatives in much the same fashion as people do in more institutionalized settings. However, given the highly emotional and volatile nature of many crowd settings, the decision making occurs much more quickly and with less consideration than in other situations.

To understand crowd behavior, then, we need to consider all four processes of contagion, convergence, emergent norms, and decision making. Other factors contribute to crowd situations, such as Smelser's conduciveness, which was discussed earlier. In addition, if people are to participate in crowd actions, they need to learn, possibly through radio or television, that the crowd exists (McPhail, 2001). After all, despite the existence of factors such as conduciveness and strain, a crowd will not develop unless sufficient people assemble at a common site and direct their attention to some common event. So an important factor in crowd

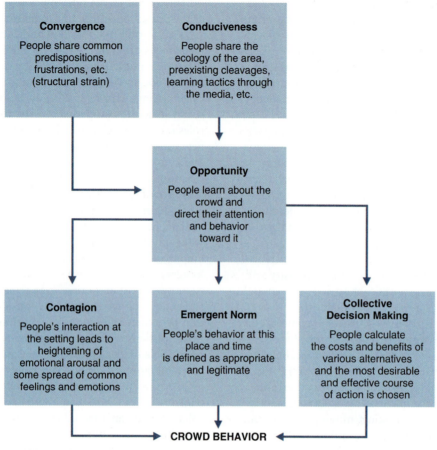

Figure 15.2
A Sociological Explanation of Crowd Behavior

development is the communication process that makes such assembling likely. Thus, crowds are very complex phenomena. The major elements involved are summarized in Figure 15.2.

Social Movements

You should be able to describe what social movements are and trace their development.

A social movement is *an enduring, collective attempt to bring about or resist social change by noninstitutionalized means* (Snow & Oliver, 1995). Examples of social movements are the French Revolution, the American Revolution, the feminist movement, the environmental movement, the gay liberation movement, and the various white supremacist movements. In their early stages, social movements are like other forms of collective behavior, rather unorganized and spontaneous. In fact, social movements sometimes grow out of dissatisfaction that first makes itself felt through other forms of collective behavior such as crowds or riots. Over time,

however, social movements develop more organization, possibly including a formal leadership and decision-making apparatus, rules and regulations, established meeting times, and the like. Some social movements even go through a process of *institutionalization* whereby they become a formal and accepted part of society. For example, when the Mormons (Latter-Day Saints) emerged in the early 1800s, they were an unconventional social movement that was the target of considerable hostility and vituperation. Today, the Mormon Church is an accepted and respectable institution in the United States.

The Development of Social Movements

Smelser's preconditions for collective behavior provide a useful scheme for understanding the way social movements develop. Three of the preconditions will be emphasized: structural strain, generalized belief, and mobilization. In terms of structural strain, social movements tend to arise in situations in which there is some oppression, deprivation, frustration, or contradiction (Wood & Jackson, 1982). The social movement constitutes people's effort to rectify the undesirable social conditions. And the deprivation that produces social movements tends to be relative rather than absolute. *Relative deprivation* occurs when people believe that their situation is worse than it should be when compared to the situations of others. Some people in the United States, for example, might feel deprived if there were no meat or poultry available in the stores because they have become used to these foods as a matter of course. Many people in Bangladesh, by contrast, view those foods as a luxury rather than a necessity. Thus social conditions that would constitute sufficient strain to produce a social movement in one setting would not necessarily do so in another.

A special set of circumstances that can produce relative deprivation is called the *phenomenon of rising expectations*. This phrase refers to a situation in which people have been experiencing some improvements in their lives and come to expect further improvements in the future. This phenomenon is an element of James C. Davies's (1962) J-curve theory of revolutions. This theory posits that support for a social movement or revolution is greatest when a long period of improving conditions, accompanied by expectations that improvement will continue, is followed by a halt or reversal in improvements. It is called the J-curve because the line tracing these economic conditions (Figure 15.3) looks like an inverted J. As the gap between what people expect and what they actually receive widens, it reaches a point at which these circumstances seem intolerable.

The people may still be fairly well-off compared to earlier years or compared to the circumstances of others, but they are comparing their present circumstances to where they expected to be, not to where they were previously or where others are. At this point, says Davies, people are in a revolutionary state of mind in that they would be receptive to joining a social movement should the opportunity arise.

The historian Crane Brinton (1965) argues that the American Revolution of 1776 illustrates the effect of rising expectations on the propensity to revolt. In the half-century before the Revolution, the colonies were growing and prosperous. The balance of trade was improving, and the colonists had gained increasing political independence from England. What, then, triggered the Revolution? England engaged in a few actions that, although posing no major threat to existing economic conditions, cast doubt on whether opportunities would continue to expand in the future. For example, England incorporated some of the lands west of the Allegheny Mountains into Canada. American land speculators, including George Washington, had been hoping to expand their economic fortunes westward, and their hopes were thus threatened. Other British actions limited the rights of colonists to levy their own taxes and tightened the money supply to the colonies. It was these threats to the continuing growth in prosperity in the colonies, rather than extremes in poverty or political oppression, that generated support for the Revolution. (Applying Sociology: Preventing Urban Riots,

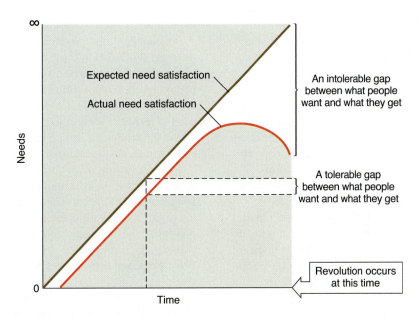

Figure 15.3

The J-Curve Theory of Revolutions

Note: Reprinted from "Toward a Theory of Revolution" by James C. Davies, 1962, *American Sociological Review, 27*, p. 6.

Other Worlds, Other Ways

AFGHANISTAN: THE SOCIAL ROOTS OF TERRORIST VIOLENCE

The date of September 11, 2001, has been seared into the memories of many people. The terrorist attacks on the World Trade Center in New York and the Pentagon in Washington, DC, on that day were horrific, both in their intent and their scale. Three thousand people died. The attacks led to the U.S. military campaign against the Al Qaeda terrorist network in Afghanistan and the Taliban government of Afghanistan that provided support for the terrorists. Terrorism is usually supported by one or more social movements, and sociologists search for the social conditions that tend to lead social movements toward terrorist actions (Calhoun, Price, & Timmer, 2002; White, 2009). Neil Smelser's preconditions for collective behavior provide a good framework with which to analyze terrorism.

In terms of structural strain, terrorism is most likely to be resorted to by people who are desperate and fairly powerless. They see no other way to advance toward their goals. They may be materially bereft or have little in the way of armies or other conventional ways of influencing events. In addition, they lack the political alliances with more powerful groups that might be used to advance goals. Terrorism is a relatively inexpensive way to attack an enemy.

In addition, economic deprivation and social dislocation often provide fertile ground for widespread support for terrorism. While terrorism can occur without economic deprivation or popular support (as evidenced by Timothy McVeigh's killing of hundreds of people in the Oklahoma City bombing in 1995), it is more likely to develop into a persisting social movement and gain recruits among desperate and deprived people. As we have discussed elsewhere in this book, a substantial gap persists in the world between the well-to-do and the poor. Such people can be attracted by groups or ideologies that demonize the rich as the source of their economic distress and that propose destruction of the "enemy" as relief from their problems.

In terms of a generalized belief, terrorists typically have perceived grievances that serve as justification in their minds for their actions. While others may disagree that the grievances are real, or that they justify terrorism, it is important to recognize that the terrorists believe these things. The United States, as the world's predominant superpower, is often a major focal point of these grievances. As for the September 11 terrorists, as best we know, their grievances focused on some U.S. policies toward the Arab world and the Middle East. In particular, they were angered by U.S. support for Israel in the struggle with the Palestinians, the stationing of U.S. troops in Saudi Arabia, which is some of

the holiest land in the Islamic religion, and U.S. bombing and blockading of Iraq. As mentioned in the previous paragraph, this generalized belief also focused on demonizing the affluent Western nations, and particularly the United States, as the source of many of the world's ills.

While many terrorist beliefs are purely secular in nature, religion was a powerful ideological legitimation for the September 11 terrorists (Calhoun, Price, & Timmer, 2002; White 2009). While many Muslims would disagree with them, the terrorists believed that their religion justified the most extreme actions against those they perceived as infidels who were intent on destroying them and their religious values. With religious justifications such as this, terrorists can approach their tasks with certainty, single-mindeness, and ferocity. Their actions are supported by a transcendent justification and are seen as a road to cosmic salvation.

In looking at the social roots of terrorism, it is also important to consider mobilization processes. For example, technological advances have made it easier for relatively small groups to gather together the resources and people to mount substantial terrorist actions. One impact of modern technology is that it can put highly destructive weapons into the hands of anyone willing to invest time, effort, and modest financial resources toward learning how to develop and use them. Some chemical and biological weapons can be acquired by small groups of people. There is also fear that nuclear weapons might become available. The terrorists who attacked the World Trade Center and the Pentagon turned commercial aircraft into powerful and destructive weapons; they only needed to gain some rudimentary knowledge of how to fly such aircraft and sneak simple weapons on board to take over the planes in flight. It was a very inexpensive, but well-organized, operation.

Modern communications technology, especially the Internet, also assists in the mobilization of terrorist groups. It provides an instantaneous, worldwide mechanism of communication that enables terrorist groups to maintain contact and coordinate activities. The Internet also can be used to recruit new members, maintain contact with them, and maintain morale among individuals or groups who must remain isolated in order to carry out a mission.

Reducing the extent of terrorism or eliminating it altogether is no simple task. An important part of this involves police, intelligence, and military activities in numerous locations around the world. These activities focus mostly on disrupting or preventing the mobilization processes. Equally important, however, is focusing on the structural strain: the grievances, dislocations, and deprivations that make some people sympathetic to terrorists. In some cases, these grievances arise from economic disparities, whereas in other cases they emerge from disagreements with policies or actions of the United States or other powerful nations in the world. At numerous places in this book, we have discussed proposals for dealing with such problems. ▪

A casual crowd, such as these people waiting in a line, can serve as a nucleus for the development of other types of crowds, such as an acting crowd or an expressive crowd.

earlier in this chapter, discusses relative deprivation in the context of race riots, a form of crowd behavior rather than a more permanent and enduring social movement.)

Relative deprivation and a threat to rising expectations, although essential in the emergence of social movements, are not sufficient. In addition, people need to develop a *generalized belief* in the form of shared targets of hostility who are held responsible for hardship, suffering, and oppression. People begin to express their concerns and anger, and a sense of identity and common fate emerges. Possibly with the help of political leaders or intellectuals, people refine their concerns and identify those people or social conditions responsible. They also set forth a vision of the future, portraying the changes that are possible or likely if a certain course of action is followed.

Finally, if a sustained social movement is to emerge, there must be a *mobilization of resources* toward that end (Lofland, 1996; Zald, 1992). Leaders must be found, money must be collected, and ways of exercising power must be located. In addition, organization, administration, procedures, and strategies must evolve. If an organization fails to accomplish these things, its survival is threatened. The movement may divide into a number of weak and powerless factions, or its lack of success in accomplishing goals may drive members away. Many incipient social movements—even when the strain was substantial and the generalized belief existed—have floundered because the essential mix of resources was not mobilized. Other Worlds, Other Ways: Afghanistan (p. 436) uses this sociological analysis of the preconditions for social movement development to shed light on the social conditions that give rise to terrorism.

Social Change

You should be able to explain the four different theoretical perspectives on social change.

With an understanding of collective behavior and social movements, one can look back on incidents such as Lattimer and Ludlow with a better sense of why those men and women did what they did and the part that their actions played in changing the United States.

Social change refers to *relatively long-term and permanent alterations in the components of culture, social structure, and social behavior.* These alterations can include changes in cultural values, norms, and roles, as well as changes in social institutions such as the family, religion, or education. This book has discussed many illustrations of social change. At this point a more general understanding of the process of social change is needed.

Theories of Change

Sociologists, anthropologists, and historians have all developed theories of social change. Their investigations have addressed the issue of whether there is any pattern or purpose to the seeming kaleidoscope of change that we observe over the span of human history. Although there is some overlap among the various theories, we can classify them into four distinct groups: evolutionary, functionalist, conflict, and cyclical theories. Each theory makes a unique contribution to the understanding of social change (Lauer, 1991; Vago, 2004).

EVOLUTIONARY THEORIES   Evolutionary theories have had many proponents in both Europe and the United States over the past two centuries (Durkheim, 1893/1947; Morgan, 1877; Parsons, 1951). These theories are based on the assumption that change is natural and that human societies move through a set of predictable, cumulative stages. Much of the evidence for evolutionary theories of change derives from historical and anthropological studies showing that some small and simple societies have become large and complex. This development convinced many observers that such a transition was natural. The approach of early evolutionists was called *unilinear evolution* because all societies were assumed to develop along a single sequence of stages involving "progress." Lewis Henry Morgan (1877), for example, reasoned that "primitive" societies became more "advanced," evolving from savagery to a barbaric state and ultimately to civilization. The transition from one stage to another occurs because of some major invention such as the making of fire, the development of the bow and arrow, or the harnessing of fossil fuels.

As more anthropological and historical evidence accumulated during the twentieth century, social scientists began to recognize some basic flaws in unilinear theories of evolution. First of all, they were too simple. Not all societies moved through the same stages, and some skipped stages by moving from very simple starting points to merging with complex industrial societies. In addition, the early unilinear theories were very ethnocentric, as Morgan's use of the terms *savagery* and *barbarism* illustrates. These observers viewed their own society as preferable and the others as less desirable. It was assumed not only that all societies *would* become like Western industrial society, but also that they *should* do so. They also tended to emphasize one aspect of change, namely technological and economic development, as the key criterion of evolution.

More recently, some sociologists and anthropologists have argued for a *multilinear theory* of evolutionary change (Nolan & Lenski, 2006; Steward, 1955). According to this approach, there is a *tendency* for societies to evolve toward greater complexity and adaptability, although evolution may not be universal. Furthermore, because each society begins from a different starting point and encounters different experiences along the way, the outcome of the evolutionary process is unlikely to be uniform. Rather, it occurs along a number of different paths, and change is no longer equated with progress as it was with many unilinear theorists. There may even be periodic or short-term reversals in the trend. Nevertheless, multilinear evolutionists argue that, over the long run, there is a general direction to social change: from small, simple societies to large, complex ones.

FUNCTIONALIST THEORIES   Functionalist theories of society place considerable emphasis on factors that contribute to social order and stability. Most functionalists, however, also recognize the importance of social change. Robert Nisbet (1969), for example, argues that "the fundamental assumption of the functionalist is . . . that . . . there are sources of change within social systems, more or less natural sources, and that from these there flow patterns of change that are as congruent to the social system as growth is within the living organism" (p. 235).

Functionalists argue that social systems are never fully or completely integrated. There are always strains, contradictions, and inconsistencies. For example, educational institutions are intended to train people to fill occupational roles in the economic sector, yet today many college graduates cannot find jobs that use their college training. Going to college generates expectations on the part of individuals regarding the jobs they will probably hold. For many, these expectations go unfulfilled, a situation of inconsistency that causes one of the strains in contemporary U.S. society. Social change results when the system attempts to adjust to the strains. Minor amounts of malintegration are not terribly disruptive and would probably lead to little, if any, social change. As malintegration increases, however, there is more of a tendency for the system to respond.

Another aspect of the functionalist theory of social change is structural differentiation, or the increasing specialization of roles. Differentiation can arise because of population growth, technological developments, or other factors. For example, as noted in Chapter 9, the many functions that were once performed by the family are now differentiated and performed by other institutions, such as schools, churches, or businesses.

When structural differentiation occurs, other parts of society must change in order to be integrated with the newly emerged structures. In this fashion, functionalists view societies as constantly adapting and evolving as new situations arise. Many functionalists argue that the pattern of this evolution is generally toward more complex and differentiated social structures.

Despite the part accorded to social change by functionalists, the functional approach has still been criticized for deemphasizing change, especially rapid and substantial change. By suggesting that social change normally involves slow and incremental adjustments, functionalists seem to imply that existing social arrangements are the most desirable and that disruptive social change is unusual or abnormal.

CONFLICT THEORIES The conflict view of social change is discussed in Karl Marx's analysis of social stratification described in Chapter 6. Marx characterized society as involving a constant struggle between social classes over scarce resources. The more dominant classes use their resources to coerce and exploit those below them. In some societies, it is the peasants who are dominated by a nobility or landed aristocracy; in other societies, it is the workers who are controlled by factory owners, or it may be a racial or ethnic minority that is subordinated to a dominant racial group. In the long run, however, subordinate groups will push for changes in the distribution of resources. It might take some leadership to get them moving, or it might require the mobilization of some new resources, as discussed earlier regarding the development of social movements. But when the opportunity arises, said Marx, they will push, and the ultimate outcome will be changes in the distribution of resources in society.

Ralf Dahrendorf (1959) criticized Marx on the grounds that Marx had overemphasized the role of economic processes in social change. Dahrendorf argued that we should look more broadly at *authority*, the legitimate power to enforce the norms of a group. For example, parents have authority over their children, teachers over students, and correctional officers over prison inmates. There is typically an unequal distribution of authority, and those with authority find it in their own interests to maintain and protect the status quo, whereas those without authority find that some form of change would be more beneficial to them. Thus for Dahrendorf, like Marx, there is an inherent tendency toward change in society, and the change will occur if the right opportunities arise.

Both Marx and Dahrendorf tend to emphasize the importance of impersonal social forces, and especially economic forces, in social change and to downplay the role of other factors. More recent conflict approaches to understanding social movements and social change have departed from this view by recognizing the part of

factors other than economic change and class conflict (Buechler, 1995). Such theorists as Herbert Marcuse and Jurgen Habermas, for example, argue that people's ideas, awareness, and identity can be important and thus education and consciousness-raising can serve as catalysts for social change. Other research documents that social movements that are focused around issues of ethnicity, gender, or religion can be important sources of social change. Conflict over ideas, beliefs, values, or ways of life can be as important as conflicts over economic or political resources and power. Furthermore, all these factors can serve as catalysts for social change even when the economic or social conditions seen as important by Marx do not exist. According to these new approaches to social movements and social change, then, society is characterized by conflict and struggle, but social change is not solely, or in some cases even primarily, the result of impersonal structural forces; other noneconomic and nonstructural factors can play an important role.

CYCLICAL THEORIES The notion that life is a cycle is a familiar one; we can see it as people age and die or the seasons change. There have also been cyclical theories to explain how societies change. Cyclical theory "essentially argues that all man's experience has happened before—a kind of sense of *déjà vu* on the grand scale, the disturbing sensation that we have been along this way before. . . . [The theory] does not deny change, but it does deny that it is leading anywhere over the long term" (Moore, 1974, p. 44). It can be seen that cyclical theories clearly contrast with evolutionary theories. The best-known cyclical theory in sociology was developed by Pitirim Sorokin (1937), although he never called his theory cyclical.

Sorokin maintained that societies are made up of three primary orientations: the *ideational*, the *sensate*, and the *idealistic*. The ideational system emphasizes faith, spiritual matters, religion, and feelings; the sensate emphasizes sense experiences and tends to be rational, scientific, and materialistic; the idealistic orientation is a combination of the other two, emphasizing human creativity and rationality. Sorokin conceived of societal change as a fluctuation over long historical periods from an emphasis on an ideational orientation through the idealistic to a sensate emphasis, and then back to ideational.

Another cyclical theory of societal change was developed in the early twentieth century by the German historian Oswald Spengler, who argued that societies age like people: They are born, grow to a mature state or *golden age*, and then decline and die. There are, of course, societies that appear to fit the descriptions of change offered by a Sorokin or a Spengler. The Roman Empire, for example, had a golden age and then declined. It also seemed to make the transition from an ideational orientation to an idealistic and then a sensate one. Some have argued that Western civilization is also in a sensate period with a heavy emphasis on materialism and science, and that it is in its decline.

Although it is difficult to discount cyclical theories completely, social scientists and historians have been hesitant to adopt them for one primary reason: It is difficult to prove that a particular theme dominates a given era. One can always find historical proof to document the existence of other themes at the same time. If the contemporary United States, for example, is interpreted as a sensate culture, how does one account for the emergence of fundamentalist Christians and other devoutly religious groups? In other words, depending on where we wish to direct our attention, we can find proof for the existence of all three of Sorokin's cultural trends during a given era. Which trend is dominant becomes a matter of interpretation over which historians will naturally disagree. It is equally difficult to define what constitutes the maturity of a civilization. For these reasons, sociologists have not found cyclical theories of social change to be particularly useful in understanding human history.

The Future: Global Modernization?

You should be able to discuss the different positions on modernization and the development of a postindustrial society in the United States and the less developed nations of the world.

The concept of modernization, introduced in Chapter 12, warrants reemphasis here because it has become one of the more profound influences on human societies. Modernization refers to *the economic, social, and cultural changes `that occur when a preindustrial society makes the transition to an advanced industrial society*. Many nations in the world today, including the United States, Japan, and the other industrial nations, have modernized, and many others are moving in that direction. These issues have been discussed at a number of points in this book, but it is worth returning to that discussion to see what the future might hold.

Modernization in the Less Developed Nations

Many proponents of the evolutionary theories of social change assume that the experience of the advanced industrial nations will be reproduced by the less developed nations of the world today. That is, those nations are destined to change in the direction of the same high levels of industrialization, urbanization, education, income, and lifestyles that now characterize the developed nations. Presumably, these nations will experience improvements in health care, housing, and nutrition and will become consumer societies with a wide array of goods and services available and a generally affluent citizenry to purchase them. In other words, the world will move toward global modernization: The twin engines of capitalism and industrialism will propel all nations into a materially comfortable future.

Sociology Of Media and Technology

Social Movements and Resistance to Globalization

This book has emphasized the centrality of two trends in the modern world: globalization and technological change. We have explored many of the forms that these trends can take and the myriad ramifications they have for social life. We have also seen how these two trends are linked: globalization is fueled by the modern technologies of communication and transportation. What we also need to identify are the many forms of reaction and resistance that these trends generate among various groups.

Social scientists have explored the overall implications of technological change for society, and these explorations can be summarized by three perspectives on the social role of technology (Gendron, 1977; Volti, 2006). The *utopian perspective* views technology as a beneficial force that promotes social progress and makes people's lives better. In this view, technological change will solve social problems, eliminate scarcity, and cure disease. This is not to say that technological change does

not produce some negatives and is not detrimental to some people. But in the long run, the positives far outweigh the negatives.

The *dystopian perspective* sees technological change as a primarily negative force that produces more problems than it solves. In this view, at least as many people are hurt by new technologies as benefit from them. While technology often provides people with more material comfort and wealth and better health, it also often results in alienation, disruptions in family life and religious communities, and degradation of the environment. In the dystopian view, the social ills generated by technological change are, on the whole, far more significant than the benefits.

The *realist perspective* views technology as neither necessarily positive nor negative, but it does view technological change as a subversive force that inevitably modifies and often undermines established cultures and social structures. Referring to concepts introduced in Chapter 2, technology changes values, norms, social roles, groups, and institutions. We have seen in this chapter that social and cultural change can produce structural strain, relative deprivation, and the other social factors that contribute to the emergence of collective behavior and the formation of social movements. So, major social changes often generate crowd actions, riots, and social movement organizations as people react to, and often resist, technological change and globalization. From the realist perspective on technology, this kind of resistance is normal. Many of the people whose culture and social lives are being dramatically changed by globalization in the world today are the indigenous peoples, in countries such as Mexico and Brazil, who trace their heritage to inhabitants from before the colonial occupations (Chase-Dunn, 2002; Thorn, 2007; Vanden, 2007). For example, indigenous farmers in Mexico lose their land to global agricultural corporations while the way of life of indigenous forest peoples in the interior of Brazil is lost because global lumbering corporations clear the forests.

In resistance to these changes, indigenous social movements have formed to protect their traditional way of life. These movements usually demand, among other things, the right to some degree of self-determination and the right to preserve their culture and heritage. They also demand greater participation in the various decision-making bodies that govern economic and political globalization, and they promote more democratic governance over these changes. These indigenous movements have also formed transnational organizations to promote the rights of indigenous peoples everywhere against the overwhelming intrusion of technology, globalization, and industrialization. And they have joined with global labor movements and global environmental movements in challenging the depredations of global capitalism. In the beginning of this chapter, we talked of the collective actions of miners in the United States in the nineteenth and early twentieth century and of how the clashes between these miners and the mining companies were one of the mechanisms through which new power and authority relations were forged as the nation industrialized. Likewise, the clashes between these indigenous movements and global corporations today are the contemporary vehicles out of which the shape and form of a globalized world will emerge.

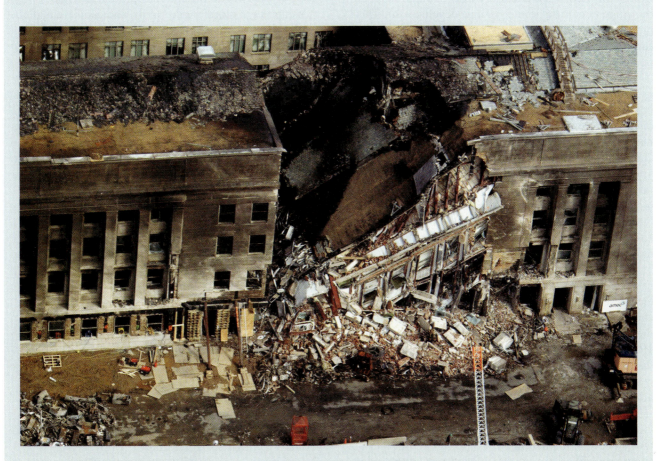

The Pentagon building in Washington, D. C., a few days after it was attacked by terrorists on September 11, 2001. Such terrorism is a form of social movement activity whose causes sociologists try to understand.

Certainly, many nations around the world are moving toward modernization. Levels of urbanization, education, literacy, and standard of living are rising in many places. It may be overly optimistic, however, to conclude that all nations can or should strive for the standards of the currently industrialized nations. One reason why the experiences of today's less developed nations may be different is that most currently industrialized nations modernized under different and much more favorable circumstances. They had a long time to industrialize and no already-industrialized nations to compete for resources and markets. They also had a much more abundant supply of natural resources to support industrialization. The United States, for example, had an ample supply of fertile land, coal, and iron ore and access to cheap foreign oil and other resources.

The currently industrialized nations of the West were also assisted in their industrialization and modernization by centuries of ruthless exploitation of weaker nations and peoples. England, the United States, and others used slavery and colonization in India, the Americas, and many other places around the world as vehicles of economic development. In the Americas, European imperial nations drove the Indians from their land and if necessary exterminated them in the name of cultural and economic development. This plunder of land, resources, and peoples added immeasurably to the economic wealth and development of many currently industrialized nations.

Because of the political, military, and cultural climate in the world in the late twentieth century, most developing nations today do not have access to the same forms of exploitation to assist them in modernizing. They also have access to fewer resources in general, so they must compete for them with other nations in overseas markets at great expense. Many of these nations have had to go heavily into debt by borrowing from the already-industrial nations in order to purchase these materials. Recent research shows that the burden of these debts has had severely negative consequences for developing nations. Brazil and Venezuela, as noted in Chapter 6, have had to cut back on social services in recent decades in order to pay off these mounting debts. Such cutbacks have resulted in higher infant mortality, reduced childhood immunization, less adequate nutrition for children, and lower economic growth (Bradshaw et al., 1993). These are burdens that the currently industrialized nations did not have to face as they industrialized.

World-system theorists argue that we need to look at the entire capitalist world system to grasp the circumstances of the developing nations today (Chase-Dunn & Grimes, 1995). They would agree that the experience of today's developing nations will be different, but they attribute this difference to their dependency on the industrial nations. The currently industrial nations have been core, or dominant, nations for centuries, and in fact it

was their exploitation of the other nations that helped support their industrialization. As noted in Chapter 13, the corporate might in the world resides in a small number of core nations. These corporations invest in other nations and create jobs for some workers, but they also exploit their natural resources and siphon off profits and wealth to the core nations.

The debts mentioned a moment ago contribute to the transfer of wealth from periphery to core nations. The banks of industrial nations earn interest on those debts, interest which comes out of the gross national product of the periphery nations. The agricultural and industrial development in which the core nations invest also tends to be land-intensive and capital-intensive, with the result that it produces relatively few jobs while removing land from the control of peasants who once lived from it. Although some people in less developed nations benefit from these practices, the outcome for many is fewer jobs, low-paying jobs, and inadequate housing in crowded cities.

Modernization brings with it many positive things, such as a higher standard of living, but it is not solely an economic process. It also changes cultural norms, values, and institutions. In the currently industrialized nations, for example, modernization has produced weaker kinship ties, a more fragile family, and gender equality. As has been noted throughout this book, many of the less developed nations are more traditional cultures that place great value on strong kinship ties, large families, and in some cases male dominance, or patriarchy. Not all peoples view cultural change as a result of modernization positively. As more nations modernize, we may learn whether the economic dimensions of modernization can be achieved without all the social and cultural changes that accompanied the process in the West. It may be that unique social and cultural forces will produce a number of versions of modernization.

There is no consensus, then, about what the future holds for the developing nations (Robertson, 1992). Some see *convergence*, with these countries becoming very much like the already-developed nations. Others predict *divergence*, with the developing nations having different experiences, retaining unique social and cultural elements, and possibly remaining subordinate to the core nations in the world stratification system. The Sociology of Media and Technology section explores some final issues about the role of technology in social life and social change and the emergence of resistance movements in response to globalization.

The United States: A Postindustrial Future?

Some sociologists suggest that the United States is becoming a postindustrial society, *one that is dominated by a highly technological form of production and that devotes greater resources to providing services than to industrial production* (Bell, 1973; Esping-Andersen, 1999). There is still some debate over what a postindustrial society will be like. Social scientists who consider themselves futurists attempt to predict developments based on contemporary trends. This discussion illustrates some of the projections that they have made and about which there is some consensus.

The economy of a postindustrial society will probably be quite different, reflecting trends already under way. Although industrial societies emphasize the extraction of natural resources and the manufacturing of goods, there will in the future be a shift: Most workers will manage other workers, process information, or provide services to other people. As noted in Chapter 13, an ever-growing proportion of the workforce is in white-collar and service occupations, and in the future there will probably be even fewer industrial workers. In this kind of economy, access to information and the possession of a specialized knowledge will come to play a greater role in determining a person's position in society. Daniel Bell (1973) coined the term *knowledge class* to refer to people such as teachers, computer programmers, and engineers whose basic stock-in-trade is the knowledge and intellectual skills they have acquired.

Many futurists believe that postindustrial society will be a high-technology society, with computers and advances in electronic engineering opening up vast possibilities for both affluence and leisure. *Automation*, the use of machines to operate the manufacturing process, will free people from many of the laborious and boring jobs and make it possible to produce vast quantities of products inexpensively. Many industries already use robots extensively. In a few cases, factories are run almost entirely by robots, with only a few technicians to ensure that nothing goes awry.

A postindustrial society will also involve a greater extension of secondary groups into people's lives (see Chapter 4). This extension has already occurred through the removal of many activities such as education from the family context. With the recent emergence of day-care centers, even the socialization of the very young sometimes occurs in a secondary context.

Despite the optimistic tone of some futurists, dark clouds are on the horizon. Some people argue that changes in the workforce will actually increase unemployment and poverty. With automation, for example, there may be fewer jobs for people to do. In addition, many people in the rapidly expanding service and white-collar sectors receive low pay, such as maids, bank tellers, waitresses, and clerks. Thus there may be intense competition for the better jobs, and those who get them will live comfortably while others will continue to live a considerably less affluent life.

Others argue that an increasingly sophisticated technology poses many serious problems. For example, energy resources are consumed in vast amounts, which threatens to deplete the resources and degrade the environment; nuclear weapons still pose the threat of calamitous destruction if they are ever used; invasion of personal privacy threatens to become epidemic in proportion as a result of computerization and miniaturization. So, although a postindustrial society will have many benefits, the social processes analyzed in this book—including conflict, exploitation, and oppression—will by no means be eliminated.

The Globalization of Labor

Just as the circumstances of the developing nations can be fully understood only in a global context, the future of the United States is also affected by worldwide trends. Chapter 13 pointed out that the global concentration of power has been enhanced by global trade agreements that encourage free trade among nations and discourage hindrances to trade, such as tariffs or restrictive labor policies. The most recent such trade agreements are the North American Free Trade Agreement (NAFTA) of 1994 and the World Trade Organization (WTO) of 1995. These treaties promote a global free-for-all in trade that benefits large, established corporations because they have the resources with which to compete in this environment. The treaties point to an important world trend: the globalization of labor as labor markets become world phenomena rather than simply national. Such globalization has occurred for centuries, as this book has illustrated at many points (for example, the Europeans' use of indigenous people's labor in the Americas). But today it is much more extensive. More than in the past, corporations roam the globe looking for cheap sources of labor. As a result, every worker is potentially competing with the cheapest workers in the world. Nations often use tariffs against imported goods as a way to protect their own industries and workers. Workers in the United States have definitely benefited from this protectionist policy in the past and are among the best paid in the world. In the case of NAFTA, many fear that elimination of tariffs will mean job migration to Mexico where wages are lower, and that this competition will lower the wages of U.S. workers. Only time will tell if these predictions are correct.

One of the challenges confronting the discipline of sociology is to understand societies and social change in sufficient detail that sociologists can make predictions about the future with some accuracy. There are, of course, always uncertainties because unknown events that have not yet happened will influence future outcomes. This discussion of modernization and a postindustrial United States reflects the current state of

Sociology on the Internet

The Internet can be a useful tool for discovering the social movement organizations formed to deal with various issues and problems in the world. These organizations often make themselves prominently visible on the Internet as a mechanism for attracting new members and support. Search using keywords such as "feminism" with "organization" or "environment" with "organization." There are many particular problem areas that could be searched. Another approach is to search for nongovernmental organizations (NGOs),

since these are often social movements themselves or are parts of larger social movements. Use Smelser's preconditions of collective behavior to help understand what you find. Based on what you locate, can you say anything about such matters as structural conduciveness, structural strains, generalized beliefs, or mobilization?

For further information and discussion, go to Allyn & Bacon's Social Problems Supersite (see Chapter 1) and explore Problem Area: Problems of Social Change.

---

knowledge: Some things we can understand and predict fairly well, but for others we have to wait and see how events play out. Either way, sociologists make available what they know to planners and policymakers who make decisions about the political, economic, and social future of the United States and other nations around the globe.

Study & Review
SUMMARY OF LEARNING OBJECTIVES
You should be able to discuss the various forms of collective behavior and the conditions necessary for their development.

Collective behavior is less enduring than institutionalized behavior and plays an important part in social change. Actually, there is a continuum of behavior that ranges from the highly structured at one end to the very unstructured at the other. Smelser argues that collective behavior arises when the following six preconditions for collective behavior exist: structural conduciveness, structural strain, a generalized belief, precipitating factors, mobilization, and the failure of social control. The chapter analyzes three types of collective behavior: rumors, mass behavior, and crowd behavior. Rumors are unauthenticated messages. They are forms of collective behavior themselves, in addition to serving as a form of communication in other types of collective behavior. Rumors are collective transactions in which a group attempts to develop a shared definition of some situation. Rumors can be distorted through leveling, sharpening, and assimilation. Mass behavior is collective behavior in which the actions of people are not coordinated, people have little or no contact with one another, and yet there is still some uniformity of behavior. The major types are panic, mass hysteria, fads, and fashions. A crowd is a temporary grouping of people who are in fairly close physical proximity to one another and whose attentions are

focused on some common object or event. Crowds are characterized by uncertainty, suggestibility of crowd members, anonymity, permissiveness, and emotional arousal. There are casual, conventional, acting, and expressive crowds. Four major social processes shape behavior in crowds: contagion, convergence, emergent norms, and collective decision making.

You should be able to describe what social movements are and trace their development.

Social movements emerge as ways for people to cope with some deprivation or frustration. Relative deprivation and the phenomenon of rising expectations play an important role here. If social movements are to emerge, there must also be a generalized belief and a mobilization of the necessary resources.

You should be able to explain the four different theoretical perspectives on social change.

Evolutionary theories of social change are based on the assumption that change is natural and societies evolve through a set of predictable, cumulative changes. Functional theories argue that social change is necessary as societies adapt to strains, inconsistencies, or a lack of integration in the social structure. Conflict theories posit that change results when oppressed groups rearrange the patterns of dominance and subordination in society. Cyclical theories are based on the assumption that change occurs in repetitive cycles over long periods of time.

You should be able to discuss the different positions on modernization and the development of a postindustrial society in the United States and the less developed nations of the world.

Modernization is a worldwide trend in social change today, but there is debate as to whether the fate of the developing nations will be convergence or divergence. Some argue that developing nations will not achieve the same level of industrialization as the currently industrialized nations. The United States may be moving toward a postindustrial society, a trend which would have both positive and negative consequences.

CHRONOLOGICAL PRACTICE TEST

For answers to Key Concepts see the page number in parentheses; for other answers see page 000.

The Nature of Collective Behavior

Key Concepts

1. Collective behavior (427)
2. Rumors (429)
3. Mass behavior (430)
4. Panic (430)
5. Mass hysteria (431)
6. Fad (431)
7. Fashion (431)
8. Crowd (431)
9. Casual crowd (432)
10. Conventional crowds (432)
11. Acting crowd (432)
12. Expressive crowds (432)

True/False

13. T F In most cases, collective behavior is less enduring than is institutionalized behavior.
14. T F The acquittal of four police officers in the beating of an African American was the precipitating event of the riot in south central Los Angeles in 1992.
15. T F People who take a more critical set toward rumors will be more likely to pass on untruths or distort rumors.
16. T F Fads are more continuous than are fashions.
17. T F A process called *circular reaction* can play an important part in the spread of feelings and behaviors through a crowd.

Concept Completion

18. _____ is the precondition of collective behavior that refers to the ideas that people have about the source of the strain they are experiencing.
19. Rumors are best referred to as _____.
20. Tamotsu Shibutani has referred to rumors as _____ to emphasize their role as group efforts to develop a shared definition of some situation.
21. Three ways in which rumor distortion can occur are _____, _____, and _____.
22. A _____ is an emotionally charged reaction by a large number of people to some anxiety-producing event.
23. Three of the characteristics that all crowds share are _____, _____, and _____.
24. An audience at a sporting event would most clearly be a (an) _____ crowd.
25. Two ways in which contagion can be spread are through _____ and _____.

Critical Thinking

26. Define and give an example of all of the preconditions for collective behavior.
27. What are the social conditions that helped produce urban riots in the United States, such as the south central Los Angeles riot in 1992?
28. Describe and give an example of the characteristics that crowds often share.
29. Define the different types of crowds and give an example of each.
30. Compare and contrast the contagion, convergence, emergent norms, and collective decision making approaches to understanding people's behavior in crowds.

Social Movements

Key Concept

31. Social movement (434)

True/False

32. T F The American Revolution of 1776 was triggered more by absolute deprivation than by relative deprivation.
33. T F In terms of the emergence of terrorism, modern technological developments, such as the Internet, would be considered important for the precondition of mobilization.

Critical Thinking

34. Describe the J-curve theory of revolutions. Relate it to the American Revolution of 1776.
35. Describe the social conditions that tend to contribute to the emergence of terrorism using Smelser's set of preconditions for collective behavior as a framework.

Social Change

Key Concept

36. Social change (437)

True/False

37. T F One of the flaws of unilinear theories of societal evolution is that they are too simple.

Concept Completion

38. Relatively long-term and permanent alterations in the components of culture, social structure, and social behavior are called _____.
39. According to Pitirim Sorokin's cyclical theory of social change, societies are made up of three primary orientations: _____, _____, and _____.

Critical Thinking

40. Compare and contrast the four theories of social change presented in the text.

The Future: Global Modernization?

Key Concepts

41. Modernization (440)
42. Postindustrial society (442)

True/False

43. T F Most social scientists agree that the modernization of nations in the future will follow the path of divergence rather than convergence.
44. T F A postindustrial society will see a greater extension of secondary groups into people's lives.

Critical Thinking

45. What is the process of modernization? What does modernization hold in the future for the less developed nations of the world as well as for the United States?
46. Describe the three perspectives that summarize the possible role of technology in society.

ANSWERS TO CHRONOLOGICAL PRACTICE TEST

13. T; 14. T; 15. F; 16. F; 17. T; 32. F; 33. T; 37. T; 43. F; 44. T.
18. Generalized belief
19. unauthenticated messages
20. collective transactions
21. leveling, sharpening, assimilation
22. mass hysteria
23. uncertainty, suggestibility, anonymity, permissiveness, emotional arousal
24. conventional
25. circular reaction, milling
38. social change
39. ideational, idealistic, sensate

CUMULATIVE PRACTICE TEST

See page 482 for answers.

1. "Collective behavior" is best defined as
   a. disorganized behavior that arises in situations that are tense and ambiguous.
   b. disorganized behavior that arises in situations where more conventional behavior is inappropriate or ineffective.
   c. unstructured and spontaneous behavior that arises in situations where conventional behavior is ineffective.
   d. a collection of actions that move a group toward its goals.
   e. group behavior that involves some deviation from societal norms.

2. Which of the following would involve the most highly institutionalized behavior?
   a. Mass panic.
   b. Looting in a riot.
   c. A baseball game.
   d. A political protest demonstration.
   e. The ceremony inaugurating a monarch.

3. As a precondition of collective behavior, the term "generalized belief" refers to

a. the ideas that people have about the source of the strain they are experiencing.
b. the rumors that emerge in collective action.
c. the ambiguities, threats, or conflicts in people's lives that place a strain on them and generate frustration or anger.
d. the ideas that people have about how their society is organized.
e. the incident that makes the strain intense and immediate.

4. Which of the following are types of mass behavior?
   a. Panic.
   b. Fads.
   c. Rioting crowd.
   d. All of the above are mass behavior.
   e. Only a and b are mass behavior.

5. In studies of urban riots in the United States over the last four decades, which of the following conclusions were drawn?
   a. Absolute deprivation rather than relative deprivation is the cause of collective violence.
   b. Participants in the riots were mostly the criminals and unemployed.
   c. Relative deprivation rather than absolute deprivation is the cause of collective violence.
   d. The cities that experienced riots were the ones in which African Americans had been most successful at gaining political office.
   e. The cities that experienced riots had a large number of black store owners and professionals.

6. A/an _____ crowd is one in which attention and activity are directed toward some goal or objective.
   a. acting
   b. conventional
   c. casual
   d. expressive
   e. mass

7. Someone standing on a car exhorting a crowd to attack the police most clearly exemplifies which precondition of collective behavior?
   a. Structural conduciveness.
   b. Structural strain.
   c. Mobilization.
   d. Generalized belief.
   e. Critical set.

8. The process of "contagion" in crowd behavior refers to
   a. the rapid spread of feelings, attitudes, and behavior through a crowd.
   b. directing attention and activity toward some objective or goal.
   c. drawing people together who share common qualities, predispositions, or interests.
   d. calculating the benefits and costs of particular actions in a crowd and choosing the most desirable outcome.
   e. the development and spread of emergent norms in a crowd.

9. People become aware of the emergent norms in a crowd by
   a. reading about them in the newspaper.
   b. learning about them in school.
   c. reasoning and intuition.

d. observing what others in the crowd say and do.

e. identifying the generalized belief of the crowd.

10. According to the text, social movements constitute

a. the breakdown of social order.

b. an outgrowth of their members personal problems and instabilities.

c. the expression of absolute deprivation.

d. the victory of acting crowds over expressive crowds.

e. people's efforts to rectify undesirable social conditions.

11. According to the text, the deprivation that produces social movements tends to be

a. relative rather than absolute.

b. absolute rather than relative.

c. sporadic rather than continuous.

d. mild rather than intense.

e. institutionalized rather than emergent.

12. When social movements go through the process of institutionalization, they

a. cease to exist as a part of society.

b. become a formal and accepted part of society.

c. become a part of the process of collective behavior.

d. become more susceptible to rumors.

e. complete the process of modernization.

13. The J-curve theory of revolutions explains the emergence of social movements as being related to

a. the phenomenon of rising expectations.

b. absolute deprivation.

c. an evolutionary theory of change.

d. mass behavior.

e. contagion and convergence processes.

14. The theory of social change that is referred to as "unilinear evolution" posits that

a. only Western societies have evolved from small and simple societies to large and complex ones.

b. all societies develop along a single sequence of stages involving "progress."

c. there is only a *tendency* for societies to evolve toward greater complexity, and such evolution is not universal.

d. change is cyclical with no necessary development in the direction of "progress."

e. change arises out of the struggle between social classes over scarce resources.

15. "Social change occurs when a social system attempts to adjust to the strains or inconsistencies that can be found in any system." This statement would be most consistent with the

a. cyclical theory.

b. conflict theory.

c. functionalist theory.

d. multilinear evolutionary theory.

e. unilinear evolutionary theory.

16. Which of the following statements would be most consistent with the multilinear theory of evolutionary change?

a. There is a tendency for societies to evolve toward greater complexity and adaptability.

b. In the long run, subordinate groups in society will push for changes in the distribution of resources, producing change.

c. Change occurs because social systems are never fully or completely integrated.

d. There are cycles of change in societies, but they do not lead anywhere over the long term.

e. All societies develop along a single sequence of stages involving "progress."

17. Which of the following is a criticism of cyclical theories of social change?

a. They tend to follow too closely the evolutionary theories of change.

b. They tend to deemphasize change, especially rapid and substantial change.

c. It has not been proven that societies tend to progress.

d. They tend to overemphasize the extent of change.

e. It is difficult to prove that a particular theme dominates a given era.

18. Proponents of which of the following theories of social change would be most likely to assume that the less developed nations of the world will go through the same modernization process as did the currently industrialized nations?

a. Conflict theories.

b. Evolutionary theories.

c. Cyclical theories.

d. Emergent norm theories.

e. Relative deprivation theories.

19. Which of the following would be *least* indicative of a transition toward a postindustrial society?

a. A growing emphasis on the manufacture of goods and industrial production.

b. Greater devotion of resources to providing services.

c. Greater emphasis on processing information.

d. Growing white-collar and service occupations.

e. A growth in the importance of the knowledge class.

20. Which of the following perspectives would tend to see technology as a beneficial force that promotes social progress?

a. The cyclical perspective.

b. The realist perspective.

c. The dystopian perspective.

d. The utopian perspective.

e. The social movement perspective.

FOR FURTHER READING

Aronowitz, Stanley, & Cutler, Jonathan. (eds.). (1997). *Postwork: The wages of cybernation.* New York: Routledge. The readings in this book give one vision of what the workplace in a highly technological future will look like. For most workers, it is a rather negative and dreary vision.

Barkan, Steven E., & Snowden, Lynne L. (2001). *Collective violence.* Boston: Allyn and Bacon. This book provides a good exposure to the many interesting topics covered in the sociological study of collective behavior and social movements.

Chirot, Daniel. (1994). *How societies change.* Thousand Oaks, CA: Pine Forge Press. This book stresses the evolutionary approach to social change and provides an excellent synopsis of how societies have changed since early human societies.

Hirsch, James S. (2002). *Riot and remembrance: The Tulsa race war and its legacy.* Boston: Houghton Mifflin. This is an excellent case study of an episode of collective violence in which white citizens of Tulsa, Oklahoma, organized to attack and destroy a good part of the African American community of the city. It documents many of the forms of collective behavior addressed in the chapter.

Levitas, Daniel. (2002). *The terrorist next door: The militia movement and the radical right.* New York: Thomas Dunne Books/St. Martin's Press. This is a sobering analysis of the homegrown terrorist groups that continue to exist in the United States, including the Militia Movement, Christian Identity, and Aryan Nations. It provides a good analysis of the social sources of terrorist groups.

Postman, Neil. (1992). *Technopoly: The surrender of culture to technology.* New York: Knopf. This book contains a strong and controversial criticism of what technology is doing to modern society. The author especially focuses on how technology can change cultural values and even demean the importance we place on human beings.

Richardson, Louise. (2006). *What Terrorists Want: Understanding the Enemy, Containing the Threat.* New York: Random House. This author provides a detailed analysis of the ideology and the strategy of the modern terrorist threat in the world and argues that it can best be contained through effective police work, political and economic development, and counterintelligence.

Rochlin, Gene I. (1997). *Trapped in the Net: The unanticipated consequences of computerization.* Princeton, NJ: Princeton University Press. This insightful book explores the changes that computers have already brought about in our lives and the future changes that are likely—and points to ways in which computers unavoidably bring troubles into people's lives.

Silver, Lee M. (1997). *Remaking Eden: Cloning and beyond in a brave new world.* New York: Avon Books. This book offers a good overview of what we are likely to see as a consequence of emerging biotechnologies. One of the author's points is that the technology to do many of these things is already available.

achieved status   Status or social position based on a person's own accomplishments or activities.

acting crowd   Temporary group of people in which attention and activity are directed toward some goal or object.

acute disease   Disease with a fairly quick, and sometimes dramatic and incapacitating, onset, from which a person either dies or recovers.

affinal kin   People related to one another by virtue of a marriage bond, such as husband and wife or parents-in-law.

agencies of socialization   People, groups, and institutions that play a part in the socialization process; the most important agencies of socialization for children are the family, peer groups, schools, and the media.

androgyny   Condition where male and female characteristics are not rigidly assigned and there is a blending of the traits, attitudes, and roles of both sexes.

animism   Belief that souls, spirits, or spiritual beings inhabit the world and play a significant role for good or ill in human affairs.

anomie   Inconsistencies that arise when people are taught to strive for certain goals but are not provided with the culturally approved means necessary to attain those goals.

anomie theory   View that posits that inconsistencies and contradictions in the social system precipitate many forms of deviance and crime.

anticipatory socialization   Learning the values, beliefs, and behaviors of groups that one does not belong to but that one anticipates joining in the future.

applied sociology   Research and other activities designed to focus sociological knowledge or research tools on a particular problem identified by some client with some practical outcome in mind.

ascribed status   Status that is assigned to a person; people have virtually no control over their ascribed status.

assimilation   Process by which a racial or ethnic minority loses its distinctive identity and way of life and becomes absorbed into the dominant group.

authority   Power that is legitimate such that people obey because they believe it is right and proper to do so.

basic sociology   Sociological research whose purpose is to advance knowledge about human social behavior with little concern for any immediate practical benefits that might result.

beliefs   People's convictions about what is true in the world—what exists, how things work, and how they relate to one another.

bilateral descent system   Descent system in which descent is reckoned more or less equally through the male and female lines.

biological determinism   Belief that human behavior and many elements of social structure are a product of genetic and physiological characteristics.

blended family   *See* Reconstituted family.

bureaucracy   Rational, hierarchical, formal organization based on explicit procedural rules.

capitalism   Economic system in which the means of economic production and distribution are privately held, the profit motive is the primary force guiding people's economic behavior, and there is free competition among both producers and consumers of goods.

career deviance   *See* Secondary deviance.

carrying capacity   An upper size limit imposed on a population by its environmental resources that cannot be permanently exceeded without damaging the environment.

caste system of stratification   Stratification system in which membership in a rank is hereditary, people in different ranks are rigidly segregated from one another, and marriage between ranks is strictly forbidden.

casual crowd   Temporary group with little structure in which members do not engage in any distinct, coordinated crowd actions.

chronic disease   Disease that progresses over a long period of time and often exists long before it is detected.

church   Religious organization that is recognized and socially accepted, tolerates other religions, and exists in harmony with the larger society.

city   Relatively large, permanent community of people who rely on surrounding agricultural communities for their food supply.

civil religion   Set of beliefs and rituals that exists outside of any organized religious body and sanctifies a particular nation and its way of life.

class system of stratification   Stratification system in which the boundaries between classes are somewhat permeable, a person's socioeconomic position depends in good part on achievement, and there are fairly frequent opportunities to change social positions.

closed stratification system   Stratification system having ranks with well-defined and rather rigid boundaries that are difficult or impossible for people to cross.

cohabitation   Relationships in which two people live in the same household and share sexual, emotional, and often economic ties without being legally married.

collective behavior   Relatively unstructured, spontaneous actions that arise in situations in which more conventional behavior seems inappropriate or ineffective.

community   Group of people who share a common territory and a sense of identity or belonging and who interact with one another.

computer-mediated communication   The various forms of communication made possible by modern computer technology.

concentric-zone theory   View that urban growth occurs in a succession of zones that radiate out from the center of the city in a pattern of concentric circles; each zone has a particular purpose or usage.

conflict perspective   Theoretical view that emphasizes the importance of coercion, domination, conflict, and change in society. It is based on the assumption that struggle over scarce valued resources is the fundamental social mechanism.

consanguineal kin People who are biologically related to one another, such as brothers and sisters or parents and their children.

continued subjugation A pattern of intergroup relations in which a dominant group uses a variety of practices to maintain subordination and exploitation of a minority group.

conventional crowd Temporary group that involves planned and socially sanctioned gatherings that are relatively structured.

corporation Business enterprise owned by stockholders, many of whom are not involved in running the daily affairs of the business.

crime Act that violates a criminal code enacted by an officially constituted political authority.

crisis medicine Treating people's illnesses after they become ill.

crowd Temporary group of people who are in fairly close physical proximity to one another and whose attentions are focused on some common object or event.

cult Small, loosely organized religious sect that is typically held together by a charismatic figure.

cultural colonialism A cultural assault by the mass media of one culture on another culture that will change the values, norms, and ways of life of that other culture.

cultural determinism View that cultural influences form the behaviors and personalities of people.

cultural globalization The spread of a set of beliefs, values, norms, language, and meaning systems that are shared by people who participate in the global community.

cultural relativity View that human behavior patterns can be understood only in the context of the culture in which they occur rather than through comparison with other cultures.

cultural transmission theories Theories that view deviance as learned behavior that is culturally transmitted through socialization.

culture Total lifestyle of a people, including all the ideas, knowledge, behaviors, and material objects that they share. Culture is a learned social heritage that accumulates through time and is passed on to succeeding generations.

curative medicine *See* Crisis medicine.

definition of the situation People's perceptions and interpretations of what is important in a situation and what actions are possible or appropriate.

democracy Political system that supplies regular constitutional opportunities for changing the governing officials and a social mechanism that permits the largest possible part of the population to influence major decisions by choosing among contenders for political office.

democratic socialist economy *See* Mixed economy.

demographic gap Gap between high birthrates and low death rates that occurs during the transitional stage of the demographic transition.

demographic transition Changing pattern of birth- and death rates that occurs during industrialization.

demography Study of the size, composition, and distribution of human populations and how these factors change over time.

denominations Organized churches whose members live in harmony with society but have no official relationship with the state; denominations often have a sizeable membership.

dependent variable Variable that is affected or changed over time by some other variable.

deviance Behaviors or characteristics that violate important group norms and as a consequence meet with social disapproval.

differential association theory View that deviant behavior is learned in interaction with other people in a process of communication and that this learning occurs for the most part within intimate primary groups such as families and friendship groups.

discrimination Unequal treatment of people because they are members of a particular group.

distance education The connection of teachers and educational institutions with students who are physically distant (also called distance learning).

ecclesia Sociological term for religion officially sanctioned by the state.

economic globalization Structures and processes, unified and interconnected on a worldwide basis, for producing and distributing goods and services.

economics Processes through which goods and services are produced and distributed.

education Systematic, formal process through which specialized teachers transmit skills, knowledge, and values to students.

egalitarian family Family in which husband and wife share somewhat equally in power and authority.

endogamy Rule requiring marriage within a particular group or community.

estate system of stratification A stratification system in which social position is strongly influenced by heredity, but unlike in the caste system, land ownership or political and military power can also be important.

ethnic group People who share a common historical and cultural heritage and sense of group identity and belongingness.

ethnocentrism Tendency to view one's own culture as the best and only proper way to live and to compare other cultures to one's own as the standard.

exogamy Rule requiring people to choose a mate outside their own social group or community.

experiment Controlled method of observation in which independent variables are manipulated to ascertain their influence on dependent variables.

expressive crowd Crowd that focuses on the expression of emotions and the personal gratification of its members.

expressive roles *See* Socioemotional roles.

extended family Family of three or more generations of people who live together or in close proximity.

fad Behavior engaged in by a large number of people for a short time; fads are not part of longer trends.

family Social institution based on kinship that derives from common ancestry, marriage, or social agreement; it functions to replace and nurture members of society.

fashions   Currently acceptable modes of dress, appearance, or behavior.

fecundity   Biological maximum number of children that could be born in a group or society.

feminist movement   Collective activities of individuals, groups, or organizations whose goal is the fair and equal treatment of women and men around the world.

fertility   Actual number of children born in a group or society.

folkways   Norms such as handshaking that are customary, popular, and widely performed but not required.

formal organizations   Large, special-purpose organizations explicitly established to achieve specific goals.

functionalist perspective   Theoretical view based on the notion that a society is a system made up of a number of interrelated and interdependent elements, each of which performs a function that contributes to the operation of the whole.

gemeinschaft   Type of society in which social life is governed by personal, informal considerations, with tradition and custom prevailing.

gender   Learned behavior involving how we are expected to behave as males and females in society.

generalized other   Organized attitudes, rules, and judgments of an entire group.

genocide   Pattern of intergroup relations in which a dominant group attempts to exterminate a minority group.

gentrification   Return of affluent households to urban neighborhoods where run-down housing is being rehabilitated or new housing constructed.

gesellschaft   Type of society characterized by specialization, individualism, rationality, and impersonality.

global cities   Cities in a postindustrial society that serve as centers of commerce, finance, and political and economic decision making for the global economic system.

globalization   Trends toward increasing interconnectedness between different peoples around the world and the growing unification of social and cultural life.

government   Operation of the state by a particular group of people who have the authority to make decisions and supervise the allocation of resources.

group   Collection of people who have an awareness that they share something in common and who interact with one another on the basis of interrelated statuses and roles.

group cohesion   Degree to which groups stick together and members feel committed to one another and attracted to the group.

group polarization   Tendency for decisions that evolve from group participation to be more extreme than those made by individuals.

groupthink   Tendency in highly cohesive groups to encourage unanimity of opinion and consensus at the expense of critical abilities and the realistic appraisal of alternatives.

health maintenance organization   Organization that agrees to provide for all of a person's health-care needs for a fixed periodic premium.

hidden curriculum   Training of students in school in the values and norms that help to perpetuate the existing system of stratification.

human ecology   Study of human populations and communities, including their distribution across and impact on the physical environment they inhabit.

hypothesis   Tentative statement that can be tested regarding relationships between two or more variables.

ideal culture   Culture that people claim to accept or wish existed.

impression management   Effort to control the meanings that others attach to our performance or to a situation.

independent variable   Variable that brings about changes in other variables.

in-group   Group that one feels positively toward and identifies with, and that produces a "we" feeling.

institutionalized discrimination   Inequitable treatment of a group resulting from practices or policies that are incorporated into social, political, or economic institutions, and that operate independently from the prejudices of individuals.

institutionalized racism   *See* Institutionalized discrimination.

instrumental roles   *See* Task roles.

interactionist perspective   Theoretical view that focuses on everyday social interaction between people rather than on larger societal structures such as politics or education. It emphasizes the importance of the subjective interpretation of reality.

internal colonialism   Situation in which a subordinate group provides cheap labor that benefits the dominant group; the subordinate group is then further exploited by having to purchase expensive goods and services from the dominant group.

internalization   Process of incorporating beliefs, values, and norms into our personal codes of conduct to the point that they seem to come from inside us instead of being dictated from the outside.

invasion   Urban process in which new people or activities move into an already established area of a city.

kin   People who are related to one another through common ancestry, marriage, or social agreement.

labeling theory   Theory of deviance suggesting that whether others label or define a person as deviant is a critical determinant in the development of a pattern of deviant behavior.

laws   Rules that have been formally codified and enacted by a political authority. Laws often reflect mores.

leadership   Exercise of influence over a group such that the group's behavior is directed toward particular outcomes or goals.

legitimacy   Capacity of a social system or institution to engender and maintain the belief that the existing institutions are the most appropriate ones for a society.

life cycle   Succession of statuses and roles that people in a particular society experience in a fairly predictable pattern as they grow older.

life span   *See* Life cycle.

looking-glass self   Process through which we develop a self-concept based on the reactions of other people to ourselves and our behavior.

managed care   A health-care system that focuses on controlling costs by monitoring and controlling the health-care decisions of doctors and patients.

mass behavior   Collective behavior in which the actions of people are not coordinated and people have little or no contact with one another, and yet there is still some uniformity of behavior and general awareness of the others in the group.

mass hysteria   Emotionally charged reaction to an anxiety-producing event by a large number of people.

mass media   Channels of communication in modern societies that can reach large numbers of people, sometimes instantaneously.

master status   Status central to people's views of themselves and to how others respond to them.

material culture   All of the physical objects, or artifacts, made or used by a people.

matriarchal family   Family in which women are dominant in power and authority.

matrilineal descent system   System in which descent is determined through the female line, and children belong to the kin group of their mother.

matrilocal family   Family system in which a couple lives with or near the wife's family.

Medicaid   Joint federal–state program to provide medical care for low-income people of any age.

medical-industrial complex   Coincidence of interests between physicians and other health-care providers and the industries producing health-care goods and services, with both parties profiting from the increased use of these commodities.

Medicare   Government health insurance for those over sixty-five years of age.

migration   Permanent change of residence.

military-industrial complex   Relationship between the military, which needs to purchase weapons, and the corporations that produce the weapons.

millenarian religious movements   Religions based on the idea that life on earth will be suddenly and dramatically transformed and that a new and utopian existence will begin.

minority group   Group whose members share distinct physical and cultural characteristics; who are denied access to power and resources available to other groups; and who are accorded fewer rights, privileges, and opportunities.

mixed economy   Economy in which there are strong elements of both capitalism and socialism.

modernization   Economic, social, and cultural changes that occur when a preindustrial society makes the transition to an advanced industrial society.

modified extended family   Family that retains elaborate networks of visitation and support even though each nuclear unit lives separately.

monogamy   Marriage between one man and one woman at a time.

monotheistic religions   Religions based on a belief in one supreme God who is ultimately responsible for the universe.

mores   Norms that are mandatory and that invoke strong feelings of right and wrong; their violation usually results in punishment.

mortality   Number of deaths that occur in a particular population.

multiple-nuclei theory   Theory that cities develop a number of different areas, or nuclei, that are devoted to particular uses.

national health insurance   Government health insurance covering all citizens.

neolocal family   Family system in which a couple resides separately from the families of either wife or husband.

nonmaterial culture   All of the parts of culture that have no physical existence, such as language, ideas, knowledge, and behaviors.

norms   Expectations or rules of conduct that guide people's behavior.

nuclear family   Family that consists of parents and their offspring.

observational techniques   Direct observation of behavior by sociologists, by either seeing or hearing what people do.

oligarchy   Concentration of power in the hands of a few people at the top of an organization.

open stratification systems   Stratification systems having ranks with less well-defined boundaries that may be crossed more readily.

organizational culture   The ideas, values, knowledge, behaviors, and material objects that are shared by members of a particular organization.

organizational diagnosis   Using the theories, methods, and research findings from sociology and other social sciences to assess the cultures of particular organizations and how those cultures affect organizational operation.

out-group   Group to which one does not belong and toward which one feels neutral or hostile. We view out-groups as "they" who are different from and less desirable than ourselves.

panic   Uncoordinated mass attempt to avoid some immediate perceived threat.

participant observation   Research design in which researchers involve themselves in the daily round of activities of the group being studied and observe group members in their natural environment.

parties   Social strata resulting from differences in power.

patriarchal family   Family in which the males are dominant in making political and economic decisions and women and children are subordinate.

patrilineal descent system   System in which descent is determined by the male line and children belong to the kin group of their father.

patrilocal family   Family system in which the married couple lives with or near the husband's family.

personality   Constellation of attitudes, needs, traits, feelings, and behavior patterns that are relatively stable throughout life.

pluralism   Existence of a number of racial and ethnic groups living side by side, each retaining a distinct identity and lifestyle while still participating in some aspects of the larger culture.

pluralistic family system   Family system in which a number of different types of family exist side by side, each having an attraction for some people.

pluralist model   View that power in U.S. society is spread over a number of groups rather than concentrated in a single group.

political globalization   The emergence of interconnected and unified structures and organizations that transcend national boundaries and that are used to exercise power, allocate resources, and resolve conflicts of interest on a global scale.

politics   Use of power to determine whose values will predominate, how rewards and resources will be allocated, and how conflicting interests will be resolved.

polyandry   Form of polygamy in which a woman can marry more than one man at a time.

polygamy   Form of marriage in which people can have more than one spouse at a time.

polygyny   Form of polygamy in which a man can marry more than one woman at a time.

polytheistic religions   Religions that posit a belief in the existence of a number of gods.

popular culture   Products and activities designed for mass consumption and used for leisure or entertainment.

population   Total number of people inhabiting a particular geographic area at a specified time.

population transfer   Pattern of intergroup relations in which the dominant group moves a minority, either voluntarily or involuntarily, to a particular geographic area.

postindustrial society   Societies that are dominated by a highly technological form of production and devote more attention to service industries, information production, and economic consumption than they do to industrial production.

power   Ability of one group to realize its will even in the face of resistance from other groups.

power elite model   View of power distribution in the United States that characterizes society as having an extremely unequal power structure with a small group of people making all important decisions.

prejudice   Irrational attitude toward certain people based solely on their membership in a particular group.

prestige   Social esteem or honor that is accorded to particular people by others; for Weber, a key dimension of the stratification system.

preventive medicine   Making changes in lifestyle or taking other steps that help avoid the occurrence of disease.

primary deviance   Violation of social norms in which the violator is not caught or is excused rather than labeled as a deviant.

primary group   Small group in which relations between members are personal, intimate, and nonspecialized.

primary socialization   Process that transforms infants into truly social human beings by teaching them basic values, skills, and language.

profane   World of ordinary and routine things that can be easily comprehended, as distinct from sacred.

propaganda   The deliberate spread of one-sided information or ideas with the intent of helping or harming particular people, groups, institutions, or societies.

protestant ethic   Belief that an ascetic life of strict discipline and hard work that results in economic success is a sign of one's worth or that one is among the elect who will go to heaven.

race   Group of people who are believed to be a biological group sharing genetically transmitted traits that are defined as important.

racism   View that certain ethnic or racial groups are biologically inferior to other groups and the practices of domination and exploitation that result from such a view.

real culture   Actual behavior of people in relation to the beliefs, values, and norms of their culture.

reconstituted family   Family based on kinship ties that accumulate as a consequence of divorces and remarriages.

reference group   Group that people use as a standard in evaluating or understanding themselves, their attitudes, and their behavior.

refined divorce rate   Measure of the divorce rate that involves dividing the number of divorces each year by the total number of existing marriages in the year.

relationship-oriented roles   *See* Socioemotional roles.

religion   Collectively held set of symbols, rituals, and beliefs that expresses a basic understanding of the world, especially its sacred dimension, and addresses the ultimate concerns of the meaning of human existence.

religions of the way   Religions based not on the existence of deities but on immutable truths in the minds of believers that reveal the proper way to achieve fulfillment.

religiosity   Importance or degree of commitment accorded religion by a person.

research methods   Detailed plan that specifies how observations will be made in order to test hypotheses.

resocialization   Learning of new sets of values, beliefs, and behaviors that are different from those previously held.

role conflict   Situation in which two or more roles a person must play are incompatible or inconsistent.

roles   Behaviors expected of people who occupy particular statuses.

role set   All the roles that are associated with a particular social status.

role strain   Situation in which people have difficulty performing a role.

role-taking   Rehearsing in imagination how others perceive things and how they are likely to behave.

rumors   Unauthenticated messages that may be true or false.

sacred   Ideas or objects viewed as awesome, mysterious, extraordinary, or absolute that transcend everyday experience.

sanctions   Rewards or punishments people receive for conforming to or violating norms.

science   Method of obtaining objective and systematic knowledge of the world through observation.

secondary deviance   Deviant behavior that a person adopts in response to the reaction of others to that person's primary deviance.

secondary group   Group characterized by limited face-to-face contact, task-oriented and impersonal relationships, and specialized and limited ties.

sector theory   View that cities grow in sectors, slices of land use that extend outward from the center of the city toward the periphery much like slices of a pie.

sects   Religious bodies that are less formally organized than churches, whose members reject some elements of the larger society, and that exist in some degree of tension with society.

secularization   Process through which the influence of religion is removed from many institutions in society and dispersed into private and personal realms.

segregation   Urban process in which certain activities or people are isolated in particular areas of cities; also, a pattern of intergroup relations in which the social lives of dominant and minority groups are kept separate.

self-concept   Conception that we have of who we are—our unique characteristics and attributes—as well as about our nature and worth as human beings.

serial monogamy   Marriage practice in which people are allowed to have more than one spouse, but not at the same time.

sex   Biological role that each of us plays, such as in reproduction or nursing.

sexism   Belief that one sex is superior to and should dominate the other sex.

sick role   Set of expectations intended to guide the behavior of people who are ill.

significant others   Specific people, such as a parent or sibling, whose opinions children care about.

significant symbol   Symbol based on shared meanings that people understand and recognize in the same way.

social change   Relatively long-term and permanent alterations in the components of culture, social structure, and social behavior.

social class   Social stratum based on wealth or economic position; people in the same social class share similar life chances or opportunities.

social control   Social mechanisms used to encourage people to conform to the norms of society.

social epidemiology   Branch of sociology that deals with how social factors influence the distribution of disease within a population.

social institution   Relatively stable cluster of statuses, roles, and groups that work together to fulfill some needs that all societies must satisfy.

socialism   Economic system in which the means of production and distribution are collectively held so that the goods and services that people need are produced and equitably distributed.

socialization   Process by which people develop their personal identities and learn the ways of a particular group or society.

social mobility   Movement of people from one social position to another in the stratification hierarchy.

social movement   An enduring collective attempt to bring about or resist social change through noninstitutionalized means.

social reproduction   Passing on social and economic inequalities from one generation to the next and thus perpetuating the existing stratification system.

social stratification   Ranking of people into a hierarchy in which the resources considered valuable by society are unequally distributed.

social structure   Organized patterns of social interaction and social relationships that exist in a group or society.

society   Group of people who are relatively self-sufficient and who share a common territory and culture.

sociobiology   Field based on the idea that the genetic makeup of humans and other animals plays a powerful role in shaping their social behavior.

socioeconomic status (SES)   A person's social location on the basis of three dimensions of stratification: wealth, power, and prestige.

socioemotional roles   Roles in which leaders work to produce harmony, enjoyment, relaxation, and high morale among group members.

sociological imagination   Ability to understand the relationship between what is happening in people's personal lives and the social forces that surround them.

sociological perspective   View that emphasizes the powerful role that group membership and social forces play in shaping human behavior.

sociology   Scientific study of society and human social behavior.

split labor market   Competitive situation in which two groups of workers are willing to do the same work but for different wages.

state   Political institution with legitimate control over the use of force within a particular territory.

status   Designated position in a group or society.

status group   People who occupy similar prestige levels and thus share a common lifestyle.

status inconsistency   Situation in which a person ranks high on one dimension of stratification but low on another.

subculture   Group within a culture that has some values, beliefs, and norms that are different from those of the larger culture.

suburbs   Less densely populated areas, primarily residential, on the outskirts of a city.

succession   Urban process in which previous residents or users of a neighborhood leave and new residents come to predominate.

survey   Research design in which data are collected from a large group of people by asking them questions about their behavior or attitudes.

sustainability   Designing a society such that it satisfies its needs without jeopardizing the prospects of future generations.

task roles   Actions of leaders that move a group toward achieving its goals.

theistic religion   Religion that posits the existence of one or more gods, not of human origin, that are believed to play a role in the creation and maintenance of the universe and take an interest in human affairs.

theoretical perspective   Set of fundamental assumptions about the nature and operation of society that serves as a source of more specific theories.

theory Set of statements that explains the relationship among phenomena.

third-party medicine Medical payment system in which the patient pays premiums into a fund and the doctor or hospital is paid from this fund for each treatment provided to the patient.

total institutions Organizations that tightly regiment the lives of their members or inmates, who are isolated from the rest of society for part of their lives.

totalitarianism Type of government in which all the familiar social institutions, such as the economy, education, and to some extent the family and religion, are under total state control.

totemism Belief system in which a plant, animal, or object is considered to have some sacred power or spirit.

urban ecology Study of the distributions of people and facilities within urban centers and how cities relate to the surrounding environment.

values Conceptions of what is right and desirable that serve as criteria for choosing goals or behaviors.

variable Property or characteristic that can take differing values.

wealth Person's total economic assets; for Weber, one important dimension of the stratification system.

welfare capitalism Economies that combine a strongly competitive market and private property with some government regulation for the public good.

women's movement *See* Feminist movement.

world-system theory Proposition that the world's nations have become increasingly interdependent, both economically and politically, and are now linked in a worldwide stratification system, with some nations having more power and resources than other nations.

Abadinsky, H. (2007). *Organized crime* (8th ed.). Belmont, CA: Wadsworth.

Abe, K. (1976). The behavior of survivors and victims in a Japanese nightclub fire: A descriptive research note. *Mass Emergencies, 1,* 119–124.

Abrahamson, M. (2004). *Global cities.* New York: Oxford University Press.

Acuna, R. (1987). *Occupied America: A history of Chicanos* (3rd ed.). New York: Harper & Row.

Adam, H., & Moodley, K. (1986). *South Africa without apartheid: Dismantling racial domination.* Berkeley: University of California Press.

Adams, R. E., & Serpe, R. T. (2000). Social integration, fear of crime, and life satisfaction. *Sociological Perspectives, 43,* 605–629.

Adelman, C. (1991). *Women at thirtysomething: Paradoxes of attainment.* Washington, DC: U.S. Department of Education.

Adler, F., Mueller, G. O. W., & Laufer, W. S. (2004). *Criminology* (5th ed.) New York: McGraw-Hill.

Agnew, R. (1991). A longitudinal test of social control theory and delinquency. *Journal of Research in Crime and Delinquency, 28,* 126–156.

Alba, R. D. (1995). Assimilation's quiet tide. *Public Interest, 119,* 3–18.

Alexander, B. C. (1997). Televangelism: Redressive ritual within a larger social drama. In S. M. Hoover & K. Lundby (Eds.), *Rethinking media, religion, and culture.* Thousand Oaks, CA: Sage.

Alex-Assensoh, Y. (1995). Myths about race and the underclass: Concentrated poverty and "underclass" behaviors. *Urban Affairs Review, 31,* 3–19.

Allan, E. A., & Steffensmeier, D. J. (1989). Youth underemployment and property crime: Differential effects of job availability and job quality on juvenile and young adult arrest rates. *American Sociological Review, 54,* 107–123.

Alperovitz, G. (2004). *America beyond capitalism: Reclaiming our wealth, our liberty, and our democracy.* New York: Wiley.

Alsop, R. (2001, July 25). Business schools struggle to add more female students to bottom line. *Wall Street Journal,* B1–B4.

Altheide, D. L. (1993). Electronic media and state control: The case of Azscam. *Sociological Quarterly, 34,* 53–69.

Altman, L. K. (2002, July 3). U.N. forecasts big increase in AIDS death toll. *New York Times,* p. A1.

Alwin, D. F., Cohen, R. L., & Newcomb, T. M. (1991). *Political attitudes over the life span: The Bennington women after fifty years.* Madison: University of Wisconsin Press.

Amato, P. R. (1987). Family processes in one parent, stepparent, and intact families: The child's point of view. *Journal of Marriage and the Family, 49,* 327–337.

Amato, P. R. (1993). Children's adjustment to divorce: Theories, hypotheses, and empirical support. *Journal of Marriage and the Family, 55,* 23–38.

Amato, P. R., & Booth, A. (1997). *A generation at risk: Growing up in an era of family upheaval.* Cambridge, MA: Harvard University Press.

Amato, P. R., & Rezac, S. J. (1994). Contact with nonresident parents, interparental conflict, and children's behavior. *Journal of Family Issues, 15,* 191–207.

Amichai-Hamburger, Y., (Ed.). (2005). *The social net: Understanding human behavior in cyberspace.* New York: Oxford University Press.

Andersen, R. M. (1995). Revisiting the behavioral model and access to medical care: Does it matter? *Journal of Health and Social Behavior, 36,* 1–10.

Andersen, R., & Anderson, O. W. (1979). Trends in the use of health services. In H. E. Freeman, S. Levine, & L. G. Reeder (Eds.), *Handbook of medical sociology* (3rd ed.). Englewood Cliffs, NJ: Prentice Hall.

Anderson, K. (1991). *Chain her by one foot: The subjugation of women in seventeenth century New France.* New York: Routledge.

Antonovsky, A. (1972). Social class, life expectancy, and overall mortality. In E. G. Jaco (Ed.), *Patients, physicians, and illness* (2nd ed.). New York: Free Press.

Apple, M. W. (1982). *Education and power.* London: Routledge & Kegan Paul.

Apter, D. E. (1986). *Rethinking development, modernization, dependency, and post-modern politics.* Beverly Hills, CA: Sage.

Archer, D., Iritiani, B., Kimes, D. D., & Barrios, M. (1983). Face-ism: Five studies of sex differences in facial prominence. *Journal of Personality and Social Psychology, 45,* 725–735.

Ardrey, R. (1967). *The territorial imperative.* New York: Atheneum.

Argyris, C. (1964). *Integrating the individual and the organization.* New York: Wiley & Sons.

Aries, E. (1996). *Men and women in interaction.* New York: Oxford University Press.

Ariès, P. (1962). *Centuries of childhood* (R. Baldick, Trans.). New York: Random House.

Arizpe, L., & Aranda, J. (1981). The comparative advantages of women's disadvantages: Women workers in the strawberry export agribusiness in Mexico. *Signs, 7,* 453–473.

Armor, D. J. (1989). After busing: Education and choice. *Public Interest, 95,* 24–37.

Armor, D. J. (1995). *Forced justice: School desegregation and the law.* New York: Oxford University Press.

Aronson, E., & Gonzalez, A. (1988). Desegregation, jigsaw, and the Mexican-American experience. In P. Katz & D. Taylor (Eds.), *Eliminating racism: Profiles in controversy.* New York: Plenum.

Ashton, H. (1967). *The Basuto* (2nd ed.). London: Oxford University Press.

Astin, A. W. (1992). Educational "Choice": Its appeal may be illusory. *Sociology of Education, 65,* 255–260.

Atchley, R. C., & Barusch, A. S. (2004). *Social forces and aging: An introduction to social gerontology* (10th ed.). Belmont, CA: Wadsworth.

Aviezer, O., van Ijzendoorn, M. H., Sagi, A., & Schuengel, C. (1994). "Children of the dream" revisited: 70 years of collective early child care in Israeli kibbutzim. *Psychological Bulletin, 116,* 99–116.

Axinn, W. G., & Thornton, A. (1996). The influence of parents' marital dissolutions on children's attitudes toward family formation. *Demography, 33,* 66–81.

Axinn, W. G., & Thornton, A. (2000). The transformation in the meaning of marriage. In L. J. Waite (Ed.), *The ties that bind: Perspectives on marriage and cohabitation*. New York: Aldine de Gruyter.

Bagdikian, B. H. (1990). *The media monopoly* (3rd ed.). Boston: Beacon Press.

Bagdikian, B. H. (2000). *The media monopoly* (6th ed.). Boston: Beacon Press.

Bagdikian, B. H. (2004). *The new media monopoly*. Boston: Beacon Press.

Baker, T. L., & Vélez, W. (1996). Access to and opportunity in postsecondary education in the United States: A review. *Sociology of Education* [Special issue], 82–101.

Bales, R. F. (1953). The equilibrium problem in small groups. In T. Parsons, R. F. Bales, & E. A. Shils (Eds.), *Working papers in the theory of action*. Glencoe, IL: Free Press.

Baldwin, R. E. (2003). *The decline of US labor unions and the role of trade*. Washington, DC: Institute for International Economics.

Ball-Rokeach, S. J. (1973). From pervasive ambiguity to a definition of the situation. *Sociometry, 36*, 378–389.

Banfield, E. C. (1990). *The unheavenly city revisited*. Prospect Heights, IL: Waveland Press.

Bankston, C. L., III. (1995). Gender roles and scholastic performance among adolescent Vietnamese women: The paradox of ethnic patriarchy. *Sociological Focus, 28*, 161–176.

Barakat, H. (1993). *The Arab world: Society, culture, and state*. Berkeley: University of California Press.

Barnet, R. J., & Cavanagh, J. (1994). *Global dreams: Imperial corporations and the new world order*. New York: Simon & Schuster.

Barnett, R. C., & Rivers, C. (1996). *She works/he works: How two-income families are happier, healthier, and better off*. San Francisco: HarperSanFrancisco.

Barnlund, D. C. (1989). *Communicative styles of Japanese and Americans: Images and realities*. Belmont, CA: Wadsworth.

Baron, J. M., & Newman, A. E. (1990). For what it's worth: Organizations, occupations, and the value of work done by women and nonwhites. *American Sociological Review, 55*, 155–175.

Baron, R. A., & Richardson, D. R. (1994). *Human aggression* (2nd ed.). New York: Plenum.

Barongan, C., & Hall, G. C. N. (1995). The influence of misogynous rap music on sexual aggression against women. *Psychology of Women Quarterly, 19*, 195–207.

Barringer, H. R., Takeuchi, D. T., & Xenos, P. (1990). Education, occupational prestige, and income of Asian Americans. *Sociology of Education, 63*, 27–43.

Bartos, O. J. (1996). Postmodernism, postindustrialism, and the future. *The Sociological Quarterly, 37*, 307–325.

Bartsch, U., & Müller, B. (2000). *Fossil fuels in a changing climate: Impacts of the Kyoto Protocol and developing country participation*. Oxford, UK: Oxford University Press.

Basow, S. A. (1992). *Gender: Stereotypes and roles* (2nd ed.). Pacific Grove, CA: Brooks/Cole.

Beck, F. D. (2001). Do state-designated enterprise zones promote economic growth? *Sociological Inquiry, 71*, 508–532.

Beeghley, L. (2008). *The structure of social stratification in the United States* (5th ed.). Boston: Allyn & Bacon.

Bell, D. (1973). *The coming of post-industrial society*. New York: Basic Books.

Bellaby, P., & Oribabor, P. (1980). The history of the present—contradiction and struggle in nursing. In C. Davies (Ed.), *Rewriting nursing history*. Totowa, NJ: Barnes & Noble.

Bellah, R. N. (1964). Religious evolution. *American Sociological Review, 29*, 358–374.

Bellah, R. N. (1988). Civil religion in America. *Daedalus, 117*, 97–118.

Bellah, R. N., Madsen, R., Sullivan, W. M., Swidler, A., & Tipton, S. M. (1985). *Habits of the heart: Individualism and commitment in American life*. Berkeley: University of California Press.

Belsky, J. (2006). Early child care and early child development: Major findings of the NICHD study of early child care. *European Journal of Developmental Psychology, 3*.

Bennett, A., & Adams, O. (1993). *Looking north for health: What we can learn from Canada's health care system*. San Francisco: Jossey-Bass.

Bennett, S. F. (1995). Community organizations and crime. *Annals of the American Academy of Political and Social Science, 539*, 72–84.

Benokraitis, N. V., & Feagin, J. R. (1995). *Modern sexism: Blatant, subtle, and covert discrimination* (2nd ed.). Englewood Cliffs, NJ: Prentice Hall.

Berg, B. L. (2007). *Qualitative research methods for the social sciences* (6th ed.). Boston: Allyn and Bacon.

Berg, I. (1975). Rich man's qualifications for poor man's jobs. In I. L. Horowitz & C. Nanry (Eds.), *Sociological realities II*. New York: Harper & Row.

Bergen, R. K. (1999). *Marital rape*. VAWnet Applied Research Forum, National Resource Center on Domestic Violence, www.vaw.umn.edu/Vawnet/mrape.pdf.

Berger, P. L. (1963). *Invitation to sociology: A humanistic perspective*. Garden City, NY: Anchor Press.

Bergeson, A., & Herman, M. (1998). Immigration, race, and riot: The 1992 Los Angeles uprising. *American Sociological Review, 63*, 39–54.

Berk, R. A. (1974). *Collective behavior*. Dubuque, IA: W. C. Brown.

Berkowitz, L. (1971). The study of urban violence: Some implications of laboratory studies of frustration and aggression. In J. C. Davies (Ed.), *When men revolt and why*. New York: Free Press.

Berliner, D. (1988). Math teaching may favor boys over girls. *Education Digest, 53*, 29.

Berliner, D. C., & Biddle, B. J. (1995). *The manufactured crisis: Myths, fraud, and the attack on America's public schools*. Reading, MA: Addison-Wesley.

Bernstein, D. S. (1996). Expanding the split labor market theory: Between and within sectors of the split labor market of mandatory Palestine. *Comparative Studies in Society and History, 38*, 243–266.

Bernstein, D. S. (1998). Strategies of equalization, a neglected aspect of the split labour market theory: Jews and Arabs in the split labour market of mandatory Palestine. *Ethnic and Racial Studies, 21*, 449–475.

Berreman, G. D. (1987). Caste in India and the United States. In C. S. Heller (Ed.), *Structured social inequality: A reader in comparative social stratification* (2nd ed.). New York: Macmillan.

Best, R. (1983). *We've all got scars: What boys and girls learn in elementary school*. Bloomington: Indiana University Press.

Betz, M., Davis, K., & Miller, P. (1978). Scarcity, income advantage, and mobility: More evidence on the functional theory of stratification. *Sociological Quarterly, 19,* 399–413.

Biagi, S., & Kern-Foxworth, M. (Eds.). (1997). *Facing difference: Race, gender and mass media.* Thousand Oaks, CA: Pine Forge Press.

Biblarz, T. J., & Raftery, A. E. (1993). The effects of family disruption on social mobility. *American Sociological Review, 58,* 97–109.

Bieber, I., et al. (1962). *Homosexuality.* New York: Basic Books.

Billingsley, A. (1992). *Climbing Jacob's ladder: The enduring legacy of African-American families.* New York: Simon & Schuster.

Bills, D. B. (1988). Educational credentials and promotions: Does schooling do more than get you in the door? *Sociology of Education, 61,* 52–60.

Billson, J. M., & Disch, E. (1991). Empowering women: A clinical sociology model for working with women in groups. In H. M. Rebach & J. G. Bruhn (Eds.), *Handbook of clinical sociology.* New York: Plenum Press.

Billy, J. O. G., Tanfer, K., Grady, W. R., & Keplinger, D. H. (1993). The sexual behavior of men in the United States. *Family Planning Perspectives, 25,* 52–60.

Bird, C. E., & Rieker, P. P. (1999). Gender matters: An integrated model for understanding men's and women's health. *Social Science & Medicine, 48,* 745–755.

Black, D. (1993). *The social structure of right and wrong.* San Diego: Academic Press.

Black, F. L. (1978). Infectious diseases in primitive societies. In M. H. Logan & E. E. Hunt, Jr. (Eds.), *Health and the human condition.* North Scituate, MA: Duxbury Press.

Blalock, H. M., Jr. (1982). *Race and ethnic relations.* Englewood Cliffs, NJ: Prentice Hall.

Blasi, J. (1986). *The communal experience of the kibbutz.* New Brunswick, NJ: Transaction Books.

Blau, F. D., Ferber, M. A., & Winkler, A. E. (1998). *The economics of women, men, and work* (3rd ed.). Upper Saddle River, NJ: Prentice Hall.

Blau, P. M., & Duncan, O. D. (1967). *The American occupational structure.* New York: Wiley & Sons.

Bloom, A. (1987). *The closing of the American mind.* New York: Simon & Schuster.

Bloom, J. (1987). *Class, race, and the civil rights movement.* Bloomington: Indiana University Press.

Blumer, H. (1951). Collective behavior. In A. M. Lee (Ed.), *New outline of the principles of sociology.* New York: Barnes & Noble Books.

Blumstein, P., & Schwartz, P. (1983). *American couples.* New York: Morrow.

Boccuti, C., & Moon, M. (2003). Comparing Medicare and private insurers: Growth rates in spending over three decades. *Health Affairs, 22,* 230–237.

Bodley, J. H. (1994). *Cultural anthropology: Tribes, states, and the global system.* Mountain View, CA: Mayfield.

Bohannon, L., & Bohannon, P. (1953). *The Tiv of Central Nigeria.* London: International African Institute.

Bok, D. (2003). *Universities in the marketplace: The commercialization of higher education.* Princeton, NJ: Princeton University Press.

Boli, J., and Thomas, G. M. (1997). World culture in the world polity: A century of international non-governmental organization. *American Sociological Review, 62,* 171–190.

Bonacich, E. (1972). A theory of ethnic antagonism: The split-labor market. *American Sociological Review, 37,* 547–559.

Bornschier, V., & Trezzini, B. (1997). Social stratification and mobility in the world system. *International Sociology, 12,* 429–455.

Bornstein, M. H., Maital, S. L., & Tal, J. (1997). Contexts of collaboration in caregiving: Infant interactions with Israeli kibbutz mothers and caregivers. *Early Child Development and Care, 135,* 145–171.

Bourgois, P., Lettiere, M., & Quesada, J. (1997). Social misery and the sanction of substance abuse: Confronting HIV risk among homeless heroin addicts in San Francisco. *Social Problems, 44,* 155–173.

Bouvier, L. F. (1984). Planet Earth 1984–2034: A demographic vision. *Population Bulletin, 39*(1).

Bowen, W. G., & Bok, D. (1998). *The shape of the river: Long-term consequences of considering race in college and university admissions.* Princeton, NJ: Princeton University Press.

Boyer, E. L. (1994, March 9). Creating the new American college. *The Chronicle of Higher Education,* p. A48.

Braddock, J. H. (1985). School desegregation and black assimilation. *Journal of Social Issues, 41,* 9–22.

Braddock, J. H., Crain, R. L., & McPartland, J. M. (1984). A long-term view of desegregation: Some recent studies of graduates as adults. *Phi Delta Kappan, 66,* 259–264.

Bradshaw, Y. W., Noonan, R., Gash, L., & Sershen, C. B. (1993). Borrowing against the future: Children and Third World indebtedness. *Social Forces, 71,* 629–656.

Brandon, G. (1990). Sacrificial practices in Santeria, an African-Cuban religion in the United States. In J. E. Holloway (Ed.), *Africanisms in American culture.* Bloomington: Indiana University Press.

Branegan, J. (1993, January 18). Is Singapore a model for the West? *Time,* pp. 36–37.

Braun, D. (1997). *The rich get richer: The rise of income inequality in the United States and the world* (2nd ed.). Chicago: Nelson-Hall.

Braun, H., Jenkins, F., & Grigg, W. (2006). *A closer look at charter schools using hierarchical linear modeling.* U. S. Department of Education, National Center for Education Statistics, Institute of Education Sciences, Pub. No. NCES 2006-460. Washington, DC: U. S. Government Printing Office.

Brehm, S. S. (1985). *Intimate relationships.* New York: Random House.

The brethren's first sister (1981, July 20). *Time,* pp. 8–19.

Brewer, M. B., & Miller, N. (1996). *Intergroup relations.* Pacific Grove, CA: Brooks/Cole.

Brint, S. (1998). *Schools and society.* Thousand Oaks, CA: Pine Forge Press.

Brinton, C. (1965). *The anatomy of revolution* (rev. ed.). New York: Vintage.

Broch, H. B. (1990). *Growing up agreeably: Bonerate childhood observed.* Honolulu: University of Hawaii Press.

Broder, M. S., Kanouse, D. E., Mittman, B. S., & Bernstein, S. J. (2000). The appropriateness of recommendations for hysterectomy. *Obstetrics and Gynecology, 95,* 199–205.

Brown, J. K. (1969). Female initiation rites: A review of the current literature. In D. Rogers (Ed.), *Issues in adolescent psychology.* New York: Appleton-Century-Crofts.

Brown, J. (1970). A note on the division of labor by sex. *American Anthropologist, 72,* 1073–1078.

Brown, L. R. (1998). Struggling to raise cropland productivity. In L. R. Brown et al. (Eds.), *State of the world, 1998: A Worldwatch Institute report on progress toward a sustainable society.* New York: W. W. Norton.

Brown, M. K., Carnoy, M., Currie, E., Duster, T., Oppenheimer, D. B., Shultz, M. M., & Wellman, D. (2003). *Whitewashing race: The myth of a color-blind society.* Berkeley: University of California Press.

Brown, P. (1995). Cultural capital and social exclusion: Some observations on recent trends in education, employment and the labour market. *Work, Employment and Society, 9,* 29–51.

Brown, R. S., Clement, D. G., Hill, J. W., Retchin, S. M., & Bergeron, J. W. (1993). Do health maintenance organizations work for Medicare? *Health Care Financing Review, 15,* 7–23.

Brownlee, S. (2008). *Overtreated: Why too much medicine is making us sicker and poorer.* New York: Bloomsbury Publishing.

Brownmiller, S. (1975). *Against our will: Men, women and rape.* New York: Simon & Schuster.

Bruhn, J. G., & Rebach, H. M. (1996). *Clinical sociology: An agenda for action.* New York: Plenum.

Brummett, B. (1991). *Rhetorical dimensions of popular culture.* Tuscaloosa: University of Alabama Press.

Brus, W., & Laski, K. (1989). *From Marx to the market: Socialism in search of an economic system.* Oxford: Clarendon Press.

Brydon, L., & Chant, S. (1989). *Women in the Third World: Gender issues in rural and urban areas.* New Brunswick, NJ: Rutgers University Press.

Bryk, A. S., Lee, V. E., & Holland, P. B. (1993). *Catholic schools and the common good.* Cambridge, MA: Harvard University Press.

Buckner, H. T. (1965). A theory of rumor transmission. *Public Opinion Quarterly, 29,* 54–70.

Buechler, S. M. (1995). New social movement theories. *The Sociological Quarterly, 36,* 441–464.

Bullock, C. S., III, Anderson, J. E., & Brady, D. W. (1983). *Public policy in the eighties.* Monterey, CA: Brooks-Cole.

Bullock, H. E., Wyche, K. F., & Williams, W. R. (2001). Media images of the poor. *Journal of Social Issues, 57,* 229–246.

Bullough, V. L. (1976). *Sexual variance in society and history.* New York: Wiley & Sons.

Bunzel, J. H. (1991). Black and white at Stanford. *Public Interest, 105,* 61–77.

Burchinal, M. R. (1999). Child care experiences and developmental outcomes. *Annals of the American Academy of Political and Social Science, 563,* 73–97.

Burkett, E. (1996). *The gravest show on Earth: America in the age of AIDS.* New York: Houghton Mifflin.

Burks, A. (1984). *Japan: Profile of a post industrial power.* Boulder, CO: Westview Press.

Burn, S. M., O'Neil, A. K., & Nederend, S. (1996). Childhood tomboyism and adult androgyny. *Sex Roles, 34,* 419–428.

Cabaj, R. P., & Stein, T. S. (Eds.). (1996). *Textbook of Homosexuality and Mental Health.* Washington, DC: American Psychiatric Press.

Calhoun, C., Price, P., & Timmer, A. (Eds.). (2002). *Understanding September 11.* New York: New Press.

Campbell, F. A., Pungello, E. P., Miller-Johnson, S., Burchinal, M. R., & Ramey, C. T. (2001). The development of cognitive and academic abilities: Growth curves from an early childhood educational experiment. *Developmental Psychology, 37,* 231–242.

Cancian, M., & Reed, D. (2001). Changes in family structure: Implications for poverty and related policy. In S. H. Danziger & R. H. Haveman (Eds.), *Understanding poverty.* New York: Russell Sage Foundation and Cambridge, MA: Harvard University Press.

Cannon, L. (1997). *Official negligence: How Rodney King and the riots changed Los Angeles and the LAPD.* New York: Times Books.

Cantril, H. (1940). *The invasion from Mars.* Princeton, NJ: Princeton University Press.

Caraley, D. (1992). Washington abandons the cities. *Political Science Quarterly, 107,* 1–30.

Carey, A. (1967). The Hawthorne studies: A radical criticism. *American Sociological Review, 32,* 403–416.

Carlson, D. K. (2005, June 14). Do Americans give women a fighting chance? *The Gallup Poll.* Princeton, NJ: The Gallup Organization, www.gallup.com.

Carnoy, M., & Levin, H. M. (1985). *Schooling and work in the democratic state.* Stanford, CA: Stanford University Press.

Carroll, M. P. (1975). Revitalization movements and social structure: Some quantitative tests. *American Sociological Review, 40,* 389–401.

Cavanagh, J., & Broad, R. (1996, March 18). Global reach: Workers fight the multinationals. *The Nation,* pp. 21–24.

Cavender, G. (1991). Alternative theory: Labeling and critical perspectives. In J. F. Sheley (Ed.), *Criminology: A contemporary handbook.* Belmont, CA: Wadsworth.

Center for American Women and Politics. (2008). *Women Officeholders: Fact Sheets and Summaries.* Rutgers, The State University of New Jersey. www.cawp.rutgers.edu.

Centers for Disease Control and Prevention. (2006, June 2). Twenty-five years of HIV/AIDS—United States, 1981-2006. *Morbidity and Mortality Weekly Report, 55,* 585–592.

Cernea, M. M. (1997). Sociological practice and action-research on population resettlement: Part II. *Journal of Applied Sociology, 14,* 105–123.

Chagnon, N. A. (1992). *Yanomamo* (4th ed.). Fort Worth, TX: Harcourt Brace Jovanovich.

Chalfant, H. P., Beckley, R. E., & Palmer, C. E. (1994). *Religion in contemporary society* (3rd ed.). Itasca, IL: Peacock.

Chambliss, W. J. (1975). Toward a political economy of crime. *Theory and Society, 2,* 149–170.

Chambliss, W. J. (1991). Biology and crime. In J. F. Sheley (Ed.), *Criminology: A contemporary handbook.* Belmont, CA: Wadsworth.

Chase-Dunn, C. (2002). Globalization from below: Toward a collectively rational and democratic global commonwealth. *Annals of the American Academy of Political and Social Science, 581,* 48–61.

Chase-Dunn, C., & Grimes, P. (1995). World-systems analysis. *Annual Review of Sociology, 21,* 387–417.

Chase-Lansdale, P. L., Brooks-Gunn, J., & Paikoff, R. L. (1991). Research and programs for adolescent mothers: Missing links and future promises. *Family Relations, 40,* 396–403.

Cherlin, A. J. (1992). *Marriage, divorce, and remarriage.* Cambridge, MA: Harvard University Press.

Cherlin, A. J., & Furstenberg, F. F., Jr. (1994). Stepfamilies in the United States: A reconsideration. In J. Hagen & K. S. Cook (Eds.), *Annual review of sociology: Vol. 20.* Palo Alto, CA: Annual Reviews Inc.

Children Now. (2004). *Fall colors 2003–04: Prime time diversity report.* Oakland, CA: Children Now, www.childrennow.org.

Chirot, D. (1986). *Social change in the modern era.* San Diego: Harcourt Brace Jovanovich.

Church, N. (1991). The effects of social change on clinical practice. In H. M. Rebach & J. G. Bruhn (Eds.), *Handbook of clinical sociology.* New York: Plenum.

Cisneros, H. G. (1995). *Defensible space: Deterring crime and building community.* Washington, DC: U.S. Department of Housing and Urban Development.

Clancy, P. M. (1986). The acquisition of communicative style in Japanese. In B. B. Schieffelin & E. Ochs (Eds.), *Language socialization across cultures.* Cambridge: Cambridge University Press.

Clark, R. (1992). Multinational corporate investment and women's participation in higher education in noncore nations. *Sociology of Education, 65,* 37–47.

Clark, R., Lennon, R., & Morris, L. (1993). Of Caldecotts and kings: Gendered images in recent children's books by black and non-black illustrators. *Gender and Society, 7,* 227–245.

Clement, U. (1989). Profile analysis as a method of comparing intergenerational differences in sexual behavior. *Archives of Sexual Behavior, 18,* 229–237.

Clore, G. L., Bray, R. M., Itkin, S. M., & Murphy, P. (1978). Interracial attitudes and behavior at a summer camp. *Journal of Personality and Social Psychology, 36,* 107–116.

Clymer, A. (1987, March 31). Survey finds many skeptics among evangelists' viewers. *New York Times,* p. 1.

Cockerham, W. C. (2006). *Sociology of mental disorder* (7th ed.). Englewood Cliffs, NJ: Prentice Hall.

Cockerham, W. C. (2007). *Medical sociology* (10th ed.). Englewood Cliffs, NJ: Prentice Hall.

Codrington, R. H. (1965). Mana. In W. A. Lessa & E. Z. Vogt (Eds.), *Reader in comparative religion* (2nd ed.). New York: Harper & Row.

Cohen, J. (2002). *Protestantism and capitalism: The mechanisms of influence.* New York: Aldine de Gruyter.

Cohen, J. E. (1995). *How many people can the Earth support?* New York: W. W. Norton.

Cohen, L. E., Broschak, J. P., & Haveman, H. A. (1998). And then there were more? The effect of organizational sex composition on the hiring and promotion of managers. *American Sociological Review, 63,* 711–727.

Cohen, L. E., & Felson, M. (1979). Social change and crime rate trends. *American Sociological Review, 44,* 588–609.

Cohen, L. E., Felson, M., & Land, K. C. (1980). Property crime rates in the United States: A macrodynamic analysis, 1947–1977; with ex ante forecasts for the mid-1980s. *American Journal of Sociology, 86,* 90–118.

Cohen, T. F. (1987). Remaking men: Men's experiences becoming and being husbands and fathers and their implications for reconceptualizing men's lives. *Journal of Family Issues, 8*(1), 57–77.

Coleman, J. S. (1992). Some points on choice in education. *Sociology of Education, 65,* 260–262.

Coleman, J. S., Campbell, J. E., Hobson, L., McPartland, J., Mood, A., Weinfield, F., & York, R. (1966). *Equality of educational opportunity.* Washington, DC: U.S. Government Printing Office.

Coleman, J. S., Hoffer, T., & Kilgore, S. (1982). *Public and private high schools: An analysis of high schools and beyond.* Washington, DC: National Council for Education Statistics.

Coleman, J. W. (2006). *The criminal elite: Understanding white-collar crime* (6th ed.). New York: Worth.

Collins, R. (1971). A conflict theory of sexual stratification. *Social Problems, 19,* 3–21.

Collins, R. (1975). *Conflict sociology: Toward an explanatory science.* New York: Academic Press.

Collins, R. (1979). *The credential society.* New York: Academic Press.

Coltrane, S., & Collins, R. (2001). *Sociology of marriage and the family* (5th ed.). Chicago: Nelson-Hall.

Colvin, M. (1991). Crime and social reproduction: A response to the call for "outrageous" proposals. *Crime and Delinquency, 73,* 436–448.

Comer, D. R. (1995). A model of social loafing in real work groups. *Human Relations, 48,* 647–667.

Committee on Environment and Natural Resources. (May 2008). *Scientific assessment of the effects of global change on the United States.* Washington, DC: National Science and Technology Council, Executive Office of the President of the United Sates.

Conlin, M. (2002, November 25). Mommy is really home from work. *Business Week,* 101–102.

Cooley, C. H. (1902). *Human nature and the social order.* New York: Scribner's.

Costells, M. (1977). *The urban question: A Marxist approach.* (Ann Sheridan, Trans.). Cambridge, MA: MIT Press.

Côté, J. E., & Allahar, A. L. (1996). *Generation on hold: Coming of age in the late twentieth century.* New York: New York University Press.

Coult, A. D., & Habenstein, R. W. (1965). *Cross tabulations of Murdock's "world ethnographic sample."* Columbia: University of Missouri Press.

Crabb, P. B., & Bielawski, D. (1994). The social representation of material culture and gender in children's books. *Sex Roles, 30,* 69–79.

Craig, H. K., Thompson, C. A., Washington, J. A., & Potter, S. L. (2003). Phonological features of child African American English. *Journal of Speech, Language, and Hearing Research, 46,* 623–635.

Cravey, A. J. (1998). *Women and work in Mexico's maquiladoras.* Lanham, MD: Rowman & Littlefield.

Cromwell, P. F., Marks, A., Olson, J. N., & Avary, D. W. (1991). Group effects on decision-making by burglars. *Psychological Reports, 69,* 579–588.

Crossman, R. K., Stith, S. M., & Bender, M. M. (1990). Sex role egalitarianism and marital violence. *Sex Roles, 22*(5/6), 293–304.

Croteau, D., & Hoynes, W. (2002). *Media/society: Industries, images, and audiences* (3rd ed.). Thousand Oaks, CA: Pine Forge Press.

Cuklanz, L. M. (1996). *Rape on trial: How the mass media construct legal reform and social change.* Philadelphia: University of Pennsylvania Press.

Cullen, F. T., Link, B. G., & Polanzi, C. W. (1982). The seriousness of crime revisited: Have attitudes toward white-collar crime changed? *Criminology, 20,* 83–102.

Cullen, J. B., & Novick, S. M. (1979). The Davis-Moore theory of stratification: A further examination and extension. *American Journal of Sociology, 84,* 1414–1437.

Currie, E. (1985). *Confronting crime: An American challenge.* New York: Pantheon Books.

Curtiss, S. (1977). *Genie: A psycholinguistic study of a modern-day "wild child."* New York: Academic Press.

Dahrendorf, R. (1959). *Class and class conflict in industrial society.* Stanford, CA: Stanford University Press.

Danaher, K. (2001). *Democratizing the global economy: The battle against the World Bank and the IMF.* Monroe, ME: Common Courage Press.

Daniels, R. (1988). *Asian America: Chinese and Japanese in the United States since 1850.* Seattle: University of Washington Press.

Darrow, W. W., et al. (1987). *Multicenter study of human immunodeficiency virus antibody in U.S. prostitutes.* Paper presented at the Third International Conference on AIDS, Washington, DC.

Davenport, W. H. (1977). Sex in cross-cultural perspective. In F. A. Beach (Ed.), *Human sexuality in four perspectives.* Baltimore: Johns Hopkins University Press.

Davies, J. C. (1962). Toward a theory of revolution. *American Sociological Review, 27,* 5–19.

Davis, J. A., & Smith, T. W. (2007). *General social surveys, 1972–2006.* Chicago: National Opinion Research Center, producer; Storrs: University of Connecticut, Roper Center for Public Opinion Research, distributor.

Davis K. (1940). Extreme social isolation of a child. *American Journal of Sociology, 45,* 554–564.

Davis, K. (1947). Final note on a case of extreme isolation. *American Journal of Sociology, 52,* 432–437.

Davis, K., & Moore, W. (1945). Some principles of stratification. *American Sociological Review, 10,* 242–249.

Day, R. A., & Day, J. V. (1977). A review of the current state of negotiated order theory: An appreciation and a critique. *Sociological Quarterly, 18,* 126–142.

Decker, S. H., & Van Winkle, B. (1996). *Life in the gang: Family, friends, and violence.* Cambridge: University of Cambridge Press.

Deckhard, B. (1979). *The women's movement.* New York: Harper & Row.

Deegan, M. J. (1988). *Jane Addams and the men of the Chicago school.* New Brunswick, NJ: Transaction Books.

Dees, M. (1996). *Gathering storm: America's militia threat.* New York: HarperCollins.

DeLaat, J. (2007). *Gender in the workplace* (2nd ed.). Thousand Oaks, CA: Sage.

Demers, D. (2002). *Global media: Menace or Messiah?,* rev. ed. Cresskill, NJ: Hampton Press.

Demo, D. H., & Hughes, M. (1990). Socialization and racial identity among black Americans. *Social Psychology Quarterly, 53,* 364–374.

Dentler, R. A. (1992). The Los Angeles riots of spring 1992: Events, causes, and future policy. *Sociological Practice Review, 3,* 229–244.

Devine, J. A., Sheley, J. F., & Smith, M. D. (1988). Macroeconomic and social-control policy influences on crime rate changes, 1948–1985. *American Sociological Review, 53,* 407–420.

Devine, J. A., & Wright, J. D. (1993). *The greatest of evils: Urban poverty and the American underclass.* Hawthorne, NY: Aldine de Gruyter.

Díaz, B. (1956). *The discovery and conquest of Mexico.* New York: Farrar, Straus, & Cudahy. (Original work published 1638)

Dillon, S. (2007, June 22). Voucher use in Washington wins praise of parents. *New York Times,* p. A13.

Dillon, S. (2008, Feb. 1). Online schooling grows, setting off a debate. *New York Times,* p. A1.

DiPrete, T. A. (1993). Industrial restructuring and the mobility response of American workers in the 1980s.

American Sociological Review, 58, 74–96.

Dobrzynski, J. H. (1996, November 6). Somber news for women on corporate ladder. *New York Times,* p. C1.

Dollard, J., Miller, N. E., Doob, L. W., Mowrer, O. H., & Seers, R. R. (1939). *Frustration and aggression.* New Haven, CT: Yale University Press.

Domhoff, G. W. (2006). *Who rules America? Power, politics, and social change* (5th ed.). New York: McGraw-Hill.

Donnelly, P. G., & Kimble, C. E. (1997). Community organizing, environmental change, and neighborhood crime. *Crime & Delinquency, 43,* 493–511.

Doob, C. B. (1999). *Racism: An American cauldron* (3d ed.). Boston: Allyn & Bacon.

Dore, R. (1997). *The diploma disease: Education, qualification and development* (2nd ed.). London: Institute of Education.

Dorman, W. A. (1997). Press theory and journalistic practice: The case of the Gulf War. In S. Iyengar & R. Reeves (Eds.), *Do the media govern? Politicians, voters, and reporters in America.* Thousand Oaks, CA: Sage.

Dorr, A., Kovaric, P., & Doubleday, C. (1990). Age and content influences on children's perceptions of the realism of television families. *Journal of Broadcasting and Electronic Media, 34,* 377–397.

Dowd, N. E. (1997). *In defense of single-parent families.* New York: New York University Press.

Draper, D. A., Hurley, R. E., Lesser, C. S., & Strunk, B. C. (2002). The changing face of managed care. *Health Affairs, 21,* 11–23.

Dreier, P. (1982). The position of the press in the U.S. power structure. *Social Problems, 29,* 298–310.

Driskell, R. B, & Lyon, L. (2002) Are virtual communities true communities? Examining the environments and elements of community. *City & Community, 1,* 1–18.

Duke, J. T. (1976). *Conflict and power in social life.* Provo, UT: Brigham Young University Press.

Dukes, R. L., Martinez, R. O., & Stein, J. A. (1997). Precursors and consequences of membership in youth gangs. *Youth and Society, 29,* 139–165.

Dunn, F. L. (1978). Epidemiological factors: Health and disease in hunter-gatherers. In M. H. Logan & E. E. Hunt, Jr. (Eds.), *Health and the human condition*. North Scituate, MA: Duxbury Press.

Dunn, S. (2001). Decarbonizing the energy economy. In L. R. Brown et al. (Eds.), *State of the world, 2001: A Worldwatch Institute report on progress toward a sustainable society*. New York: W. W. Norton.

Dunphy, D. C. (1972). *The primary group: A handbook for analysis and field research*. New York: Appleton-Century-Crofts.

Durfee, A., & Rosenberg, K. (2004). Domestic violence in the United States: Current research, new directions. In R. Perrucci, K. Ferraro, J. Miller, & P. C. Rodriguez Rust (Eds.), *Agenda for social justice, 2004*. Knoxville, TN: Society for the Study of Social Problems.

Durkheim, E. (1947). *The division of labor in society* (G. Simpson, Trans.). New York: Free Press. (Original work published 1893)

Durkheim, E. (1965). *The elementary forms of religious life*. (J. W. Swain, Trans.). New York: Free Press. (Original work published 1915)

Dusek, J. B. (Ed.). (1985). *Teacher expectancies*. Hillsdale, NJ: Erlbaum.

Dye, T. R. (2002). *Who's running America: The Bush restoration* (7th ed.). Upper Saddle River, NJ: Prentice Hall.

Eagly, A. H., & Johannesen-Schmidt, M. C. (2001). The leadership styles of women and men. *Journal of Social Issues, 57*, 781–798.

Earley, P. C. (1989). Social loafing and collectivism: A comparison of the United States and the People's Republic of China. *Administrative Science Quarterly, 34*, 565–581.

Early, J. D., & Peters, J. F. (1990). *The population dynamics of the Mucajai Yanomama*. San Diego: Academic Press.

Eck, D. L. (2001). *A new religious America: How a "Christian country" has become the world's most religiously diverse nation*. San Francisco: HarperSanFrancisco.

Eckholm, E. (2002, September 13). U.S. labeling of group in China as terrorist is criticized. *New York Times*, p. A6.

Edwards, W. F., & Winford, D. (Eds.). (1991). *Verb phrase patterns in black English and Creole*. Detroit: Wayne State University Press.

Ehrlich, P. R., & Ehrlich, A. H. (1990). *The population explosion*. New York: Simon & Schuster.

Eisenberg, D. M., Kessler, R. C., Foster, C., Norlock, F. E., Calkins, D. R., & Delbanco, T. L. (1993). Unconventional medicine in the United States: Prevalence, costs, and patterns of use. *New England Journal of Medicine, 328*, 246–252.

Ellis, G. J., & Petersen, L. R. (1992). Socialization values and parental control techniques: A cross-cultural analysis of child-rearing. *Journal of Comparative Family Studies, 23*, 39–54.

Emes, C. E. (1997). Is Mr Pac Man eating our children? A review of the effect of video games on children. *Canadian Journal of Psychiatry, 42*, 409–414.

Engels, F. (1969). Ludwig Feuerbach and the end of classical German philosophy. In *Karl Marx and Frederick Engels: Selected works*. New York: International. (Original work published 1888)

Engerman, S. L. (1977). Black fertility and family structure in the United States: 1880–1940. *Journal of Family History, 2*.

England, P. (1992). *Comparable worth: Theories and Evidence*. New York: Aldine de Gruyter.

Entman, R. M. (1997). Modern racism and images of blacks on local television news. In S. Iyengar and R. Reeves (Eds.), *Do the media govern? Politicians, voters, and reporters in America*. Thousand Oaks, CA: Sage.

Entwisle, D. R., & Alexander, K. L. (1994). Winter setback: The racial composition of schools and learning to read. *American Sociological Review, 59*, 446–460.

Ergil, K. V. (1996). China's traditional medicine. In M. S. Micozzi (Ed.), *Fundamentals of complementary and alternative medicine*. New York: Churchill Livingstone.

Erikson, E. H. (1950). *Childhood and society*. New York: Norton.

Erikson, E. H. (1982). *The life cycle completed: A review*. New York: Norton.

Erikson, K. T. (1966). *Wayward puritans*. New York: Wiley & Sons.

Eshleman, J. R., & Bulcroft, R. A. (2006). *The family* (11th ed.). Boston: Allyn and Bacon.

The ESOP Association. (2007). *ESOP statistics*. Washington, DC: The

ESOP Association, www.esopassociation.org.

Esping-Andersen, G. (1999). *Social foundations of postindustrial economies*. New York: Oxford University Press.

Evans, E. D., Rutberg, J., Sather, C., & Turner, C. (1991). Context analysis of contemporary teen magazines for adolescent females. *Youth and Society, 23*, 99–120.

Fagerlind, I., & Saha, L. J. (1989). *Education and national development: A comparative perspective* (2nd ed.). Oxford: Pergamon Press.

Farb, P. (1978). *Man's rise to civilization: The cultural ascent of the Indians of North America* (2nd ed.). New York: E. P. Dutton.

Farkas, G., Lleras, C., & Maczuga, S. (2002). Does oppositional culture exist in minority and poverty peer groups? *American Sociological Review, 67*, 148–155.

Farley, J. E. (1991). Combatting racial polarization: A sociologist's contribution. *Sociological Practice Review, 2*, 287–297.

Farrag, A. (1971). Social control among the Mzabite women of Beni-Isguen. *Middle Eastern Studies, 7*, 317–327.

Fausto-Sterling, A. (1992). *Myths of gender: Biological theories about women and men*. New York: Basic Books.

Fay, B. (1987). *Critical social science: Liberation and its limits*. Ithaca, NY: Cornell University Press.

Feagin, J. R. (1998). *The new urban paradigm: Critical perspectives on the city*. Lanham, MD: Rowman and Littlefield.

Feagin, J. R., & Sykes, M. P. (1994). *Living with racism: The black middle-class experience*. Boston: Beacon Press.

Feagin, J. R., Vera, H., & Batur-VanderLippe, P. (2000). *White racism*. New York: Routledge.

Featherman, D. L., & Hauser, R. M. (1978). *Opportunity and change*. New York: Academic Press.

Federal Bureau of Investigation. (2007). *Uniform crime reports: Crime in the United States, 2006*. Washington, DC: U.S. Government Printing Office, www.fbi.gov/ucr.

Feinberg, R. E., & Avakov, R. M. (1991). *U.S. and Soviet aid to developing countries*. New Brunswick, NJ: Transaction Books.

Feinberg, W. (1993). *Japan and the pursuit of a new American identity: Work and education in a multicultural age.* New York: Routledge.

Feinberg, W., & Soltis, J. F. (1992). *School and society* (2nd ed.). New York: Columbia University, Teachers College Press.

Feldman, R., Wholey, D., & Christianson, J. (1996). Effect of mergers on health maintenance organization premiums. *Health Care Financing Review, 17,* 171–190.

Felson, R. B. (1996). Mass media effects on violent behavior. In J. Hagan & K. S. Cook (Eds.), *Annual review of sociology: Vol. 22.* Palo Alto, CA: Annual Reviews, Inc.

Fernald, A., & Morikawa, H. (1993). Common themes and cultural variations in Japanese and American mothers' speech to infants. *Child Development, 64,* 637–656.

Fernandez-Kelly, M. P. (1983a). *For we are sold, I and my people: Women and industry in Mexico's frontier.* Albany: State University of New York Press.

Fernandez-Kelly, M. P. (1983b). Mexican border industrialization, female labor force participation, and migration. In J. Nash & M. P. Fernandez-Kelly (Eds.), *Women, men, and the international division of labor.* Albany: State University of New York Press.

Ferree, M. M. (1991). The gender division of labor in two-earner marriages: Dimensions of variability and change. *Journal of Family Issues, 12,* 158–180.

Ferree, M. M., & Hall, E. J. (1990). Visual images of American society: Gender and race in introductory sociology textbooks. *Gender and Society, 4,* 500–533.

Fiedler, F. E. (1967). *A theory of leadership effectiveness.* New York: McGraw-Hill.

Fiedler, F. E. (1981). Leadership effectiveness. *American Behavioral Scientist, 24,* 619–632.

Fijnaut, C. (1990). Organized crime: A comparison between the United States of America and Western Europe. *British Journal of Criminology, 30,* 321–340.

Fine, G. A. (1984). Negotiated orders and organizational cultures. *Annual Review of Sociology, 10,* 239–262.

Fine, G. A., & Kleinman, S. (1979). Rethinking subculture: An interactionist analysis. *American Journal of Sociology, 85,* 1–20.

Fiorentine, R. (1988). Increasing similarities in the values and life plans of male and female college students? Evidence and implications. *Sex Roles, 18,* 143–158.

Fischer, C. (1975). Toward a subcultural theory of urbanism. *American Journal of Sociology, 80,* 1319–1341.

Fishbein, D. H. (1990). Biological perspectives in criminology. *Criminology, 28,* 27–66.

Fishman, M. (1978). Crime waves as ideology. *Social Problems, 25,* 531–543.

Fitzpatrick, J. P. (1987). *Puerto Rican Americans: The meaning of migration to the mainland* (2nd ed.). Englewood Cliffs, NJ: Prentice Hall.

Flacks, R. (1971). *Youth and social change.* Chicago: Markham.

Flowers, R. B. (2000). *Domestic crimes, family violence and child abuse.* Jefferson, NC: McFarland.

Foner, A., & Kertzer, D. (1978). Transitions over the life course: Lessons from age-set societies. *American Journal of Sociology, 83,* 1081–1104.

Ford, C. S. (1970). Some primitive societies. In G. H. Seward & R. C. Williamson (Eds.), *Sex roles in society.* New York: Random House.

Foster, G. M., & Anderson, B. G. (1978). *Medical Anthropology.* New York: Wiley & Sons.

Foster, M. W. (1991). *Being Comanche: A social history of an American Indian community.* Tucson: University of Arizona Press.

Fowler-Salamini, H., & Vaughan, M. K. (Eds.). (1994). *Women of the Mexican countryside, 1850–1990.* Tucson: University of Arizona Press.

Fox, T. G., & Miller, S. M. (1965). Intercountry variations: Occupational stratification and mobility. *Studies in Comparative International Development, 1,* 3–10.

Frankenberg, E., & Lee, C. (2003). *Charter schools and race: A lost opportunity for integrated education.* Cambridge, MA: Civil Rights Project, Harvard University.

Frankl, R. (1998). Transformation of televangelism: Repackaging Christian family values. In L. Kintz and J. Lesage (Eds.), *Media, culture, and the religious right.* Minneapolis: University of Minnesota Press.

Freedman, J. L. (1975). *Crowding and behavior.* San Francisco: Freeman.

Freeman, D. (1983). *Margaret Mead and Samoa: The making and unmaking of an anthropological myth.* Cambridge, MA: Harvard University Press.

Freeman, L., & Braconi, F. (2004). Gentrification and displacement. *Journal of the American Planning Association, 70,* 39–52.

Freeman, R. B., & Holzer, H. J. (Eds.). (1986). *The black youth employment crisis.* Chicago: University of Chicago Press.

Freidson, E. (1970). *The profession of medicine.* New York: Dodd, Mead.

Friedkin, N. E. (1999). Choice shift and group polarization. *American Sociological Review, 64,* 856–875.

Friedman, T. L. (2006, March 29). Facts and folly. *New York Times,* p. A27.

Fritz, J. M. (1991). The contributions of clinical sociology in health care settings. *Sociological Practice, 9,* 15–29.

Furstenberg, F. F., & Cherlin, A. J. (1991). *Divided families: What happens to children when parents part.* Cambridge: Harvard University Press.

Furstenberg, F. F., Jr., & Teitler, J. O. (1994). Reconsidering the effects of marital disruption: What happens to children in early adulthood? *Journal of Family Issues, 15,* 173–190.

Gaddy, G. D. (1986). Television's impact on high school achievement. *Public Opinion Quarterly, 50,* 340–359.

Gaede, S. (1977). Religious participation, socioeconomic status, and belief-orthodoxy. *Journal for the Scientific Study of Religion, 16,* 245–253.

Gage, M. G., & Christensen, D. H. (1991). Parental role socialization and the transition to parenthood. *Family Relations, 40,* 332–337.

Gallagher, T. J., Johnson, E. O., Van Valey, T. L., & Malaret, D. R. (1992). *Job-seeking and academic success among sociologists: The effects of departmental prestige and gender.* Paper presented at the annual meeting of the American Sociological Association, Pittsburgh.

Gallup, Jr., G. H. (2003, June 24). Current views on premarital, extramarital sex. *The Gallup Poll Tuesday Briefing.* Princeton, NJ: Gallup Organization, www.gallup.com.

The Gallup Poll. (2007, April 10). *Poll topics A to Z: Homosexual relations.* Princeton, NJ: Gallup News Service, www.gallup.com/content/default.aspx?ci=11755

The Gallup Poll. (2008, June 10). *Religion*. Princeton, NJ: Gallup News Service, www.gallup.com/poll/1690/religion.aspx.

Gans, H. J. (1972). Urbanism and suburbanism as ways of life: A re-evaluation of definitions. In J. J. Palen & K. Flaming (Eds.), *Urban America*. New York: Holt.

Gastil, J. (1990). Generic pronouns and sexist language: The oxymoronic character of masculine generics. *Sex Roles, 23* (11/12), 629–643.

Geertz, C. (1966). Religion as a cultural system. In M. Banton (Ed.), *Anthropological approaches to the study of religion*. New York: Praeger.

Geertz, C. (1973). *The interpretation of cultures*. New York: Basic Books.

Gelles, R. J. (1992). Poverty and violence toward children. *American Behavioral Scientist, 35,* 258–274.

Gelles, R. J., & Conte, J. R. (1990). Domestic violence and sexual abuse of children: A review of research in the eighties. *Journal of Marriage and the Family, 52,* 1045–1058.

Gelles, R. J. (1997). *Intimate violence in families* (3rd ed.). Newbury Park, CA: Sage.

Gendron, B. (1977). Technology and the Human Condition. New York: St. Martin's Press.

Gibbs, N. (1993, May 3). Oh, my god, they're killing themselves. *Time,* pp. 26–43.

Giele, J. Z. (1978). *Women and the future*. New York: Free Press.

Gilbert, D. (1998). *The American class structure in an age of growing inequality* (5th ed.). Belmont, CA: Wadsworth.

Gilens, M. (1996). Race and poverty in America: Public misperceptions and the American news media. *Public Opinion Quarterly, 60,* 515–541.

Gilliam, Jr., F. D., Iyengar, S., Simon, A., & Wright, O. (1997). Crime in black and white: The violent scary world of local news. In S. Iyengar and R. Reeves (Eds.), *Do the media govern? Politicians, voters, and reporters in America*. Thousand Oaks, CA: Sage.

Gilligan, C. (1983, May). *Challenging existing theories: Conclusions*. Paper presented at the Eighth Annual Conference for Helpers of Adults, University of Maryland, College Park.

Gilmore, S., & Crissman, A. (1997). Video games: Analyzing gender iden-tity and violence in this new virtual reality. *Studies in Symbolic Interaction, 21,* 181–199.

Ginn Daugherty, H., & Kammeyer, K. C. W. (1995). *An introduction to population* (2nd ed.) New York: Guilford Press.

Giroux, H. A. (1985). Theories of reproduction and resistance in the new sociology of education: A critical analysis. *Harvard Educational Review, 53*(3), 257–293.

Gladney, D. C. (1991). *Muslim Chinese: Ethnic nationalism in the People's Republic*. Cambridge, MA: Harvard University, Council on East Asian Studies, and Harvard University Press.

The Glass Ceiling Commission. (1995). *Good for business: Making full use of the nation's human capital, a fact-finding report of the federal Glass Ceiling Commission*. Washington, DC: U.S. Government Printing Office.

Glass, S. P., & Wright, T. L. (1992). Justifications for extramarital relationships: The association between attitudes, behavior, and gender. *Journal of Sex Research, 29,* 361–387.

"Global 500: World's Largest Corporations." (2004, July 26) *Fortune,* 163–180.

Godley, M. D., & Velasquez, R. (1998). Effectiveness of the Logan Square Prevention Project: Interim results. *Drugs & Society, 12,* 87–103.

Goduka, I. N. (1990). Ethics and politics of field research in South Africa. *Social Problems, 37,* 329–340.

Goff, C., & Nason-Clark, N. (1989). The seriousness of crime in Fredericton, New Brunswick: Perceptions toward white-collar crime. *Canadian Journal of Criminology, 31*(1), 19–34.

Goffman, E. (1959). *The presentation of self in everyday life*. New York: Doubleday.

Goffman, E. (1961). *Asylums: Essays on the social situation of mental patients and other inmates*. Chicago: Aldine Press.

Goffman, E. (1963). *Stigma: Notes on the management of spoiled identity*. Englewood Cliffs, NJ: Prentice Hall.

Gold, M. (2003). Can managed care and competition control Medicare costs? *Health Affairs, 22,* 176–188.

Gold, S. J. (1992). *Refugee communities: A comparative field study*. Newbury Park, CA: Sage.

Goldberg, M. (2006). *Kingdom coming: The rise of Christian nationalism*. New York: W. W. Norton.

Goldstein, M. C. (1971). Stratification, polyandry, and family structure in Central Tibet. *Southwest Journal of Anthropology, 27,* 65–74.

Golombok, S., & Tasker, F. (1996). Do parents influence the sexual orientation of their children? Findings from a longitudinal study of lesbian families. *Developmental Psychology, 32,* 3–11.

Gonzalez, J. (2000). *Harvest of empire: A history of Latinos in America*. New York: Viking.

Goode, E. (1992). *Collective behavior*. Fort Worth, TX: Harcourt Brace Jovanovich.

Goode, W. J. (1960). A theory of role strain. *American Sociological Review, 25,* 483–495.

Goodman, M. E. (1967). *The individual and culture*. Homewood, IL: Dorsey.

Goodstein, D. (2004). *Out of gas: The end of the age of oil*. New York: W. W. Norton & Company.

Gordon, J. S. (1984). Holistic health centers in the United States. In J. W. Salmon (Ed.), *Alternative medicines: Popular and policy perspectives*. New York: Tavistock.

Gordon, M. (1978). *The American family: Past, present, and future*. New York: Random House.

Gordon, M. M. (1964). *Assimilation in American life*. New York: Oxford University Press.

Gordon, M. M. (1978). *Human nature, class and ethnicity*. New York: Oxford University Press.

Gordon, M. M. (1988). *The scope of sociology*. New York: Oxford University Press.

Gornick, M. E., Eggers, P. W., Reilly, T. W., Mentnech, R. M., Fitterman, L. K., Kucken, L. E., & Vladeck, B. C. (1996). Effects of race and income on mortality and use of services among Medicare beneficiaries. *New England Journal of Medicine, 335,* 791–799.

Gortmaker, S. L., Salter, C. A., Walker, D. K., & Dietz, W. H., Jr. (1990). The impact of television viewing on mental aptitude and achievement: A longitudinal study. *Public Opinion Quarterly, 54,* 594–604.

Gottfredson, M. R., & Hirschi, T. (1990). *A general theory of crime*. Stanford, CA: Stanford University Press.

Gottlieb, M. (1988). *Comparative economic systems: Preindustrial and modern case studies*. Ames: Iowa State University Press.

Gouldner, A. W. (1976). The dark side of the dialectic: Toward a new objectivity. *Sociological Inquiry, 46,* 3–16.

Granovetter, M. (1978). Threshold models of collective behavior. *American Journal of Sociology, 83,* 1420–1443.

Grant, J. W. (1984). *Moon of wintertime: Missionaries and the Indians of Canada in encounter since 1534.* Toronto: University of Toronto Press.

Grant, P. R. (1991). Ethnocentrism between groups of unequal power under threat in intergroup competition. *Journal of Social Psychology, 13,* 21–28.

Greeley, A. M. (1989). *Religious change in America.* Cambridge, MA: Harvard University Press.

Green, G. D., & Bozett, F. W. (1991). Lesbian mothers and gay fathers. In J. C. Gonsiorek & J. D. Weinrich (Eds.), *Homosexuality: Research implications for public policy.* Newbury Park, CA: Sage.

Greenberg, J. R., McKibben, M., & Raymond, J. A. (1990). Dependent adult children and elder abuse. *Journal of Elder Abuse and Neglect, 2*(1/2), 73–86.

Greenfield, S., Rogers, W., Mangotich, M., Carney, M. F., & Tarlov, A. R. (1995). Outcomes of patients with hypertension and non-insulin dependent diabetes mellitus treated by different systems and specialties: Results from the medical outcomes study. *Journal of the American Medical Association, 274,* 1436–1444.

Gregg, S. A. (Ed.). (1991). *Between bands and states.* Carbondale: Southern Illinois University, Center for Archaeological Investigations.

Gregory, R. F. (2003). *Women and workplace discrimination: Overcoming barriers to gender equality.* New Brunswick, NJ: Rutgers University Press.

Greider, P., Jr., Denise-Neinhaus, S., & Statham, A. (1992). Education and training as facilitating reemployment after a plant shutdown. *Sociological Practice Review, 3,* 220–228.

Greider, W. (1992). *Who will tell the people: The betrayal of American democracy.* New York: Simon & Schuster.

Greider, W. (2003). *The soul of capitalism: Opening paths to a moral economy.* New York: Simon & Schuster.

Gross, E., & Etzioni, A. (1985). *Organizations in society.* Englewood Cliffs, NJ: Prentice Hall.

Gross, G. R., Cross, T. M., & Smith, J. E. (1991). *The Michigan corrections officers' stress survey: Organizational versus individual stressors.* Paper presented at the annual meeting of the Academy of Criminal Justice Sciences, Nashville, TN.

Gumperz, J. J., & Levinson, S. C. (1996). *Rethinking linguistic relativity.* Cambridge: Cambridge University Press.

Gutek, G. L. (1993). *American education in a global society.* New York: Longman.

Gutman, B. (1976). *The black family in slavery and freedom: 1750–1925.* New York: Pantheon.

Hadaway, C. K., Marler, P. L., & Chaves, M. (1993). What the polls don't show: A closer look at U.S. church attendance. *American Sociological Review, 58,* 741–752.

Hadden, J. K. (1993). The rise and fall of American televangelism. *Annals of the American Academy of Political and Social Science, 527,* 113–130.

Hafferty, F. W., & Light, D. W. (1995). Professional dynamics and the changing nature of medical work. *Journal of Health and Social Behavior* [Special issue], 132–153.

Haines, D., Rutherford, D., & Thomas, P. (1981). Family and community among Vietnamese refugees. *International Migration Review, 15,* 310–319.

Hall, E. T. (1966). *The hidden dimension.* Garden City, NY: Doubleday.

Hall, R. H., & Tolbert, P. S. (2005). *Organizations: Structures, processes, and outcomes* (9th ed.). Englewood Cliffs, NJ: Prentice Hall.

Halliday, T. C, & Osinsky, P. (2006). Globalization of law. *Annual Review of Sociology, 32,* 447–470.

Hallinan, M. T. (1996). Track mobility in secondary school. *Social Forces, 74,* 983–1002.

Halloran, R. (1969). *Japan: Images and realities.* New York: Knopf.

Hamer, D., & Copeland, P. (1994). *The science of desire: The search for the gay gene and the biology of behavior.* New York: Simon & Schuster.

Handel, M. J. (2002). *The sociology of organizations: Classic, contemporary, and critical readings.* Thousand Oaks, CA: Sage.

Hardoy, J. E. (Ed.). (1975). *Urbanization in Latin America.* Garden City, NY: Anchor Press.

Hare, A. P., Blumberg, H. H., & Davies, M. F. (1996). *Small groups: An introduction.* Westport, CT: Praeger.

Harley, G. W. (1941). *Native African medicine: With special reference to its practice in the Mano tribe of Liberia.* Cambridge, MA: Harvard University Press.

Harrington, C., Woolhandler, S., Mullan, J., Carrillo, H., & Himmelstein, D. U. (2001). Does investor ownership of nursing homes compromise the quality of care? *American Journal of Public Health, 91,* 1452–1455.

Harrington, M. (1989). *Socialism: Past and future.* New York: Arcade Publishing.

Harris, C. D., & Ullman, E. L. (1945). The nature of cities. *Annals of the American Academy of Political and Social Science, 242,* 7–17.

Harris, M. (1977). *Cannibals and kings: The origins of cultures.* New York: Random House.

Harrison, B. (1994). *Lean and mean: The changing landscape of corporate power in the age of flexibility.* New York: Basic Books.

Harrison, M. I. (1991). Invitation to organizational diagnosis. *Sociological Practice Review, 2,* 169–179.

Hauser, R. M., & Featherman, D. L. (1973). Trends in the occupational mobility of U.S. men, 1962–1970. *American Sociological Review, 38,* 302–310.

Hawley, A. H. (1971). *Urban society: An ecological approach.* New York: Ronald Press.

Hawley, W. D., et al. (1983). *Strategies for effective desegregation.* Lexington, MA: Lexington Books.

Hayakawa, M. (1986). *The quality and socioeconomic status of teachers in Japan: Final report.* Aichi, Japan: Japanese National Institute of Education.

Headley, B. D. (1991). Race, class, and powerlessness in world economy. *Black Scholar, 21,* 14–21.

Hechter, M. (1987). *Principles of group solidarity.* Berkeley: University of California Press.

Heimer, K., & Matsueda, R. L. (1994). Role-taking, role commitment, and delinquency: A theory of differential social control. *American Sociological Review, 59,* 365–390.

Hemming, J. (1978). *Red gold: The conquest of the Brazilian Indians.* Cambridge: Harvard University Press.

Hemming, J. (1987). *Amazon frontier: The defeat of the Brazilian Indians.* London: Macmillan.

Hendry, J. (1995). *Understanding Japanese society* (2nd ed.). London: Routledge.

Henkin, A. B., & Nguyen, L. T. (1981). *Between two cultures: The Vietnamese in America.* Saratoga, CA: Century Twenty One Publishing.

Herman, E. S. (1993). The media's role in U.S. foreign policy. *Journal of International Affairs, 47,* 23–45.

Hero, R. E. (1992). *Latinos and the U.S. political system.* Philadelphia: Temple University Press.

Hersch, S. M. (1970). *My Lai 4.* New York: Random House.

Hertz, R. (1986). *More equal than others: Women and men in dual-career marriages.* Berkeley: University of California Press.

Hess, F. M. (2008). *Still at risk: What students don't know, even now.* Washington, DC: Common Core, www.commoncore.org.

Hewitt, J. P. (2007). *Self and society: A symbolic interactionist social psychology* (10th ed.). Boston: Allyn and Bacon.

Heydebrand, W. (1977). Organizational contradictions in public bureaucracies: Toward a Marxian theory of organizations. *Sociological Quarterly, 18,* 83–107.

Hickey, G. C. (1964). *Village in Vietnam.* New Haven, CT: Yale University Press.

Higher Education Research Institute. (2004). *Cooperative Institutional Research Program Freshman Survey.* Los Angeles: University of California at Los Angeles, www.gseis.ucla.edu/heri/heri.html.

Himmelstein, D., Woolhandler, S., & Hellander, I. (2001). *Bleeding the patient: The consequences of corporate health care.* Monroe, ME: Common Courage Press.

Hirschel, J., Hutchison, I., III, & Dean, C. (1992). The failure of arrest to deter spouse abuse. *Journal of Research in Crime and Delinquency, 29,* 7–33.

Hirschi, T. (1969). *Causes of delinquency.* Berkeley: University of California Press.

Hirschman, C., & Wong, M. G. (1986). The extraordinary educational achievement of Asian-Americans: A search for historical evidence and explanations. *Social Forces, 65,* 1–27.

Hirst, L. F. (1953). *The conquest of plague: A study of the evolution of epidemiology.* Oxford: Clarendon Press.

Hoebel, E. A. (1972). *Anthropology: The study of man* (4th ed.). New York: McGraw-Hill.

Hoecker-Drysdale, S. (1992). *Harriet Martineau: First woman sociologist.* Oxford: Berg.

Hoffman, C., Lau, I., & Johnson, D. R. (1986). The linguistic relativity of person cognition: An English-Chinese comparison. *Journal of Personality and Social Psychology, 51,* 1097–1105.

Hofstede, G. (1980). *Culture's consequences: International differences in work related values.* Beverly Hills, CA: Sage.

Hoge, D. R., & Carroll, J. W. (1978). Determinants of commitment and participation in suburban protestant churches. *Journal for the Scientific Study of Religion, 17,* 107–127.

Holden, K. C., & Smock, P. J. (1991). The economic costs of marital dissolution: Why do women bear a disproportionate cost? In W. R. Scott & J. Blake (Eds.), *Annual review of sociology: Vol. 17.* Palo Alto, CA: Annual Reviews.

Honey, M. (1984). *Creating Rosie the Riveter: Class, gender, and propaganda.* Amherst: University of Massachusetts Press.

Hong, L. K. (1978). Risky shift and cautious shift: Some direct evidence on the culture-value theory. *Social Psychology, 41,* 342–346.

Horn, C. L., & Flores, S. M. (2003). *Percent plans in college admissions: A comparative analysis of three states' experience.* Cambridge, MA: Civil Rights Project at Harvard University.

Hornung, C. A., McCullough, B. C., & Sugimoto, T. (1981). Status relationships in marriage: Risk factors in spouse abuse. *Journal of Marriage and the Family, 43,* 675–692.

Horowitz, R. (1987). Community tolerance of gang violence. *Social Problems, 34,* 437–450.

Horsfield, P. G. (1984). *Religious television: The American experience.* New York: Longman.

Horton, H. D., Allen, B. L., Herring, C., & Thomas, M. E. (2000). Lost in the storm: The sociology of the black working class: 1850 to 1990. *American Sociological Review, 65,* 128–137.

Hostetler, J. A. (1993). *Amish society* (4th ed.). Baltimore: Johns Hopkins University Press.

Hourani, A. (1991). *A history of the Arab peoples.* Cambridge, MA: Harvard University Press, Belknap Press.

Houseknecht, S. (1987). Voluntary childlessness. In M. B. Sussman & S. K. Steinmetz (Eds.), *Handbook of marriage and the family.* New York: Plenum Press.

Houseknecht, S. K., Vaughan, S., & Macke, A. S. (1984). Marital disruption among professional women: The timing of career and family events. *Social Problems, 31,* 273–284.

Hout, M. (1988). More universalism, less structural mobility: The American occupational structure in the 1980s. *American Journal of Sociology, 93,* 1358–1400.

Howard, I. (2002). Power sources: On party, gender, race, and class, TV news looks to the most powerful groups. *Extra!,* May/June.

Howard, P. E. N. & Jones, S., Eds. (2004). *Society online: The Internet in context.* Thousand Oaks, CA: Sage.

Hoyt, H. (1939). *The structure and growth of residential neighborhoods in American cities.* Washington, DC: U.S. Government Printing Office.

Hudson, F. M. (1991). *The adult years: Mastering the art of self-renewal.* San Francisco: Jossey-Bass.

Huesmann, L. R., Moise-Titus, J., Podolski, C., & Eron, L. D. (2003). Longitudinal relations between children's exposure to TV violence and their aggressive and violent behavior in young adulthood: 1977–1992. *Developmental Psychology, 39,* 201–221.

Hugick, L., & Leonard, J. (1991, October). Sex in America. *Gallup Poll Monthly,* pp. 60–73.

Humphreys, L. (1970). *Tearoom trade.* Chicago: Aldine Publishing.

Huntington, S. P., & Harrison, L. E. (2001). *Culture matters: How values shape human progress.* New York: Basic Books.

Hurn, C. J. (1992). *The limits and possibilities of schooling* (3rd ed.). Boston: Allyn and Bacon.

Hurst, C. E. (1992). *Social inequality: Forms, causes, and consequences.* Boston: Allyn and Bacon.

Huston, A. C., et al. (1992). *Big world, small screen: The role of television in*

American society. Lincoln: University of Nebraska Press.

Illich, I. (1976). *Medical nemesis.* New York: Bantam Books.

Ima, K. (1982). Japanese Americans: The making of "good people." In A. G. Dworkin & R. J. Dworkin (Eds.), *The minority report* (2nd ed.). New York: Holt.

Intergovernmental Panel on Climate Change. (2007). *Climate change 2007: Mitigation of climate change.* Cambridge, UK: Cambridge University Press.

Jacobsen, J. P., & Levin, L. M. (1992). *The effects of intermittent labor force attachment on female earnings.* Paper presented at the meetings of the American Economic Association, New Orleans.

Jacobson, J. (1988). Planning the global family. In L. R. Brown et al. (Eds.), *State of the world 1988: A Worldwatch report on progress toward a sustainable society.* New York: Norton.

Jaffe, H. W., et al. (1983). National case-control study of Kaposi's sarcoma and *pneumocystis carinii* pneumonia in homosexual men: 1. Epidemiological results. *Annals of Internal Medicine, 99,* 145–151.

Jamieson, N. L. (1993). *Understanding Vietnam.* Berkeley: University of California Press.

Jang, S. J., & Alba, R. D. (1992). Urbanism and nontraditional opinion: A test of Fischer's subcultural theory. *Social Science Quarterly, 73,* 596–609.

Janis, I. L. (1982). *Victims of groupthink* (2nd ed.). Boston: Houghton Mifflin.

Jankowski, M. S. (1991). *Islands in the street: Gangs and American urban society.* Berkeley: University of California Press.

Jayakody, R., Chatters, L. M., & Taylor, R. J. (1993). Family support to single and married African American mothers: The provision of financial, emotional, and child care assistance. *Journal of Marriage and the Family, 55,* 261–276.

Jekielek, S. M. (1998). Parental conflict, marital disruption and children's emotional well-being. *Social Forces, 76,* 905–935.

Jencks, C. (1992). *Rethinking social policy: Race, poverty, and the underclass.* Cambridge, MA: Harvard University Press.

Jencks, C., Smith, M., Acland, H., Bane, M. J., Cohen, D., Gintis, H., Heyns, B., & Michelson, S. (1972). *Inequality: A reassessment of the effect of family and schooling in America.* New York: Basic Books.

Jesilow, P., Pontell, H. N., & Geis, G. (1993). *Prescription for profit: How doctors defraud Medicaid.* Berkeley: University of California Press.

Johnson, A. W., & Earle, T. (1987). *The evolution of human societies: From foraging group to agrarian state.* Stanford, CA: Stanford University Press.

Johnson, C. L., Klee, L., & Schmidt, C. (1988). Conceptions of parentage and kinship among children of divorce. *American Anthropologist, 90,* 136–144.

Johnson, J. D., Adams, M. S., Ashburn, L., & Reed, W. (1995). Differential gender effects of exposure to rap music on African American adolescents' acceptance of teen dating violence. *Sex Roles, 33,* 597–605.

Johnson, N. R., Feinberg, W. E., & Johnston, D. M. (1994). Microstructure and panic: The impact of social bonds on individual action in collective flight from the Beverly Hills Supper Club fire. In R. R. Dynes & K. J. Tierney (Eds.), *Disasters, collective behavior, and social organization.* Newark: University of Delaware Press.

Johnson, S. M., & O'Connor, E. (2002). *The gay baby boom: The psychology of gay parenthood.* New York: New York University Press.

Johnston, L. D., et al. (2007). *Monitoring the future national survey results on drug use, 1975–2006. Vol. 1: Secondary school students.* NIH Publication No. 07-6205. Bethesda, MD: National Institute on Drug Abuse, www.monitoringthefuture.org.

Jones, E. E., Farina, A., Hastorf, A. H., Markus, H., Miller, D. T., & Scott, R. A. (1984). *Social stigma: The psychology of marked relationships.* New York: Freeman.

Jones, S. R. G. (1990). Worker interdependence and output: The Hawthorne studies reevaluated. *American Sociological Review, 55,* 176–190.

Josephson, W. L. (1987). Television violence and children's aggression: Testing the priming, social script, and disinhibition predictions. *Journal of Personality and Social Psychology, 53*(5), 882–890.

Joyner, C. (1978). Crabgrass and bureaucrats. *Midwest Quarterly, 20,* 18–31.

Kalinich, D. B., & Pitcher, T. (1987). *Surviving in corrections: A guide for corrections professionals* (2nd ed.). Springfield, IL: Chas. C Thomas.

Kalmuss, S., & Straus, M. A. (1982). Wife's marital dependency and wife abuse. *Journal of Marriage and the Family, 44,* 277–286.

Kanter, R. M. (1989). *When giants learn to dance.* New York: Simon & Schuster.

Kanter, R. M. (1993). *Men and women of the corporation.* New York: Basic Books.

Kaplan, H. B. (1989). Health, disease, and the social structure. In H. P. Freeman & S. Levine (Eds.), *Handbook of medical sociology* (4th ed.). Englewood Cliffs, NJ: Prentice Hall.

Karau, S. J., & Hart, J. W. (1998). Group cohesiveness and social loafing: Effects of a social interaction manipulation on individual motivation within groups. *Group Dynamics, 2,* 185–191.

Karnow, S. (1981). *Vietnam: A history.* New York: Penguin Books.

Karoly, L. A., et al. (1998). *Investing in our children: What we know and don't know about the costs and benefits of early childhood interventions.* Santa Monica, CA: Rand.

Kasarda, J. D., & Crenshaw, E. M. (1991). Third World urbanization: Dimensions, theories, and determinants. In W. R. Scott & J. Blake (Eds.), *Annual review of sociology: Vol. 17.* Palo Alto, CA: Annual Reviews.

Katz, D., & Ryan, R. A. (1992, May 10). Symbols of success, targets of rage. *Detroit News,* Sec. B, p. 1.

Katz, M. B. (1987). *Reconstructing American education.* Cambridge, MA: Harvard University Press.

Kaufman, D. R., & Richardson, B. L. (1982). *Achievement and women: Challenging the assumptions.* New York: Free Press.

Kay, F. M., & Hagan, J. (1998). Raising the bar: The gender stratification of law-firm capital. *American Sociological Review, 63,* 728–743.

Kelling, G. W. (1975). *Language: Mirror, tool, and weapon.* Chicago: Nelson-Hall.

Kennedy, L. W. (1990). *On the borders of crime: Conflict management and criminology.* New York: Longman.

Kepel, G. (2002). *Jihad: The trail of political Islam.* Cambridge, MA: Belknap Press/Harvard University Press.

Kerbo, H. R., & McKinstry, J. A. (1995). *Who rules Japan? The inner circles of economic and political power.* Westport, CT: Praeger.

Kersten, J. (1993). Street youths, *bosozoku,* and *yakuza:* Subculture formation and societal reactions in Japan. *Crime and Delinquency, 39,* 277–295.

Kessler, R. C., House, J. S., & Turner, J. B. (1987). Unemployment and health in a community sample. *Journal of Health and Social Behavior, 28,* 51–59.

Kett, J. F. (1977). *Rites of passage: Adolescents in America, 1970 to the present.* New York: Basic Books.

Kibria, N. (1993). *Family tightrope: The changing lives of Vietnamese Americans.* Princeton, NJ: Princeton University Press.

Kiecolt-Glaser, J. K., et al. (1987). Marital quality, marital disruption, and immune function. *Psychosomatic Medicine, 49,* 13–34.

Kimmel, A. J., & Keefer, R. (1991). Psychological correlates of the transmission and acceptance of rumors about AIDS. *Journal of Applied Social Psychology, 21,* 1608–1628.

Kimmel, M. (1996). *Manhood in America: A cultural history.* New York: Free Press.

Kirby, D. (2001). *Emerging answers: Research findings on programs to reduce teen pregnancy (summary).* Washington, DC: National Campaign to Prevent Teen Pregnancy.

Kirsh, B. (1983). Sex roles and language use: Implications for mental health. In V. Franks & E. D. Rothblum (Eds.), *The stereotyping of women: Its effects on mental health.* New York: Springer.

Kirsch, I., Braun, H., Yamamoto, K., & Sum, A. (2007). *America's perfect storm: Three forces changing our nation's future.* Princeton, NJ: Policy Information Center, Educational Testing Service.

Kitano, H. H. L. (1976). *Japanese Americans* (2nd ed.). Englewood Cliffs, NJ: Prentice Hall.

Klein, M. (1995). *The American street gang: Its nature, prevalence, and control.* New York: Oxford University Press.

Kleinknecht, W. (1996). *The new ethnic mobs: The changing face of organized crime in America.* New York: Simon and Schuster.

Kletzer, L. G. (2001). *Job loss from imports: Measuring the costs.* Washington, DC: Institute for International Economics.

Knottnerus, J. D. (1987). Status attainment research and its image of society. *American Sociological Review, 52,* 113–121.

Knox, P., & Taylor, P. J. (Eds.). (1995). *World cities in a world-system.* Cambridge, U.K.: Cambridge University Press.

Koenig, F. (1985). *Rumor in the market-place: The social psychology of commercial hearsay.* Dover, MA: Auburn House.

Koentjaraningrat. (1988). The Indonesian mentality and development. *Sojourn, 3*(2), 107–133.

Kohlberg, L. (1981). *The philosophy of moral development.* New York: Harper & Row.

Kohn, M. L., & Slomczynski, K. M. (1990). *Social structure and self-direction: A comparative analysis of the United States and Poland.* Cambridge, MA: Basil Blackwell.

Kooistra, P. G., Mahoney, J. S., & Westervelt, S. D. (1998). The world of crime according to "Cops." In M. Fishman and G. Cavender (Eds.), *Entertaining crime: Television reality programs.* New York: Aldine de Gruyter.

Kornhauser, W. (1966). "Power elite" or "veto groups." In R. Bendix & S. M. Lipset (Eds.), *Class, status, and power* (2nd ed.). New York: Free Press.

Kosberg, J. I. (Ed.). (1992). *Family care of the elderly: Social and cultural changes.* Newbury Park, CA: Sage.

Krantz, D. S., Grunberg, N. E., & Baum, A. (1985). Health psychology. *Annual Review of Psychology, 36,* 349–384.

Kressel, N. J. (1996). *Mass hate: The global rise of genocide and terror.* New York: Plenum.

Kristof, N. D. (1993, April 25). China's crackdown on births: A stunning and harsh success. *New York Times,* p. 1.

Kroeber, A. L. (1919). On the principle of order in civilization as exemplified by changes of fashion. *American Anthropologist, 21,* 235–263.

Kroeber, A. L., & Kluckhohn, C. (1952). *Culture: A critical review of concepts and definitions.* New York: Random House.

Krymkowski, D. H., & Krauze, T. K. (1992). Occupational mobility in the year 2000: Projections for American men and women. *Social Forces, 71,* 145–157.

Kumagai, F. (1996). *Unmasking Japan today: The impact of traditional values on modern Japanese society.* Westport, CT: Praeger.

Kuper, H. (1963). *A South African kingdom: The Swazi.* New York: Holt.

La Barre, W. (1964). *The peyote cult* (enlarged ed.). New York: Schocken.

Lafree, G., Drass, K. A., & O'Day, P. (1992). Race and crime in postwar America: Determinants of African-American and white rates, 1957–1988. *Criminology, 30,* 157–185.

Lanternari, V. (1963). *The religions of the oppressed.* New York: Mentor.

Larsen, E. (2004). Deeper understanding, deeper ties: Taking faith online. In P. E. N. Howard & S. Jones (Eds.). (2004). *Society online: The Internet in context.* Thousand Oaks, CA: Sage.

Larson, C. J. (1995). Theory and applied sociology. *Journal of Applied Sociology, 12*(2), 13–29.

Lasswell, H. D. (1936). *Politics: Who gets what, when, and how.* New York: McGraw-Hill.

Latane, B., Williams, K. D., & Harkins, S. (1979). Many hands make light the work: The causes and consequences of social loafing. *Journal of Personality and Social Psychology, 37,* 822–832.

Latha, K. S., & Narendra, R. (1998). Dowry deaths: Implications of law. *Medicine, Science and Law, 38,* 153–156.

Lattimore, P. K., Trudeau, J., Riley, K. J., Leiter, J., & Edwards, S. (1997). *Homicide in eight U.S. cities: Trends, context, and policy implications.* Washington, DC: National Institute of Justice, Office of Justice Programs.

Lauer, R. H. (1991). *Perspectives on social change* (4th ed.). Boston: Allyn and Bacon.

Lazarsfeld, P. F., & Reitz, J. G. (1989). History of applied sociology. *Sociological Practice, 7,* 43–52.

Leacock, E. (1980). Montagnais women and the Jesuit programme for colonization. In M. Etienne & E. Leacock (Eds.), *Women and colonization.* New York: Praeger.

Leavitt, G. C. (1992). General evolution and Durkheim's hypothesis of crime frequency: A cross-cultural test. *Sociological Quarterly, 33,* 241–263.

Lee, J. (2002). From civil relations to racial conflict: Merchant-customer interactions in urban America. *American Sociological Review, 67,* 77–98.

Lee, V. E., Dedrick, R. F., & Smith, J. B. (1991). The effect of the social organization of schools on teachers' efficacy and satisfaction. *Sociology of Education, 64,* 190–208.

Lenski, G. (1966). *Power and privilege: A theory of social stratification.* New York: McGraw-Hill.

Levin, J., & Levin, W. C. (1994). *The functions of discrimination and prejudice* (2nd ed.). New York: Harper & Row.

Levin, J., & McDevitt, J. (1993). *Hate crimes: The rising tide of bigotry and bloodshed.* New York: Plenum Press.

Levine, L. (1996). *The opening of the American mind.* Boston: Beacon Press.

Levine, L. (2001). *The gender wage gap and pay equity: Is comparable worth the next step?* Washington, DC: Congressional Research Service Report for Congress, Library of Congress.

LeVine, R. A. (1969). Culture, personality, and socialization: An evolutionary view. In D. A. Goslin (Ed.), *Handbook of socialization theory and research.* Chicago: Rand McNally.

Levine, S. (1986). *Radical departures: Desperate detours to growing up.* San Diego: Harcourt Brace Jovanovich.

LeVine, S. (1993). *Dolor y alegria: Women and social change in urban Mexico.* Madison: University of Wisconsin Press.

Levinger, G., & Moles, O. C. (Eds.). (1979). *Divorce and separation: Context, causes and consequences.* New York: Basic Books.

Levinson, D. J. (1978). *The seasons of a man's life.* New York: Knopf.

Levinson, D. J. (1996). *The seasons of a woman's life.* New York: Knopf.

Levy, F. (1998). *The new dollars and dreams: American incomes and economic change.* New York: Russell Sage Foundation.

Lewin, E. (1993). *Lesbian mothers: Accounts of gender in American culture.* Ithaca, NY: Cornell University Press.

Lewin, K., Lippitt, R., & White, R. K. (1939). Patterns of aggressive behavior in experimentally created "social climates." *Journal of Social Psychology, 10,* 271–299.

Lewin, T. (1998, April 15). Men assuming bigger share at home, new survey shows. *New York Times,* p. A16.

Lewis, R. A. (1984). Some changes in men's values, meanings, roles, and attitudes toward marriage and family in the U.S.A. In *Social change and family policies: Part 1.* Melbourne: Australian Institute of Family Studies.

Li, D. J. (1978). *The ageless Chinese.* New York: Scribner's.

Liddell, C., & Kruger, P. (1987). Activity and social behavior in a South African township nursery: Some effects of crowding. *Merrill-Palmer Quarterly, 33*(2), 195–211.

Likert, R. (1967). *The human organization.* New York: McGraw-Hill.

Lindorff, D. (1992). *Marketplace medicine: The rise of the for-profit hospital chains.* New York: Bantam Books.

Lindsey, L. L. (2005). *Gender roles: A sociological perspective* (4th ed.). Upper Saddle River, NJ: Prentice Hall.

Lines, P. M. (2000). Homeschooling comes of age. *Public Interest, 140,* 74–85.

Lipset, S. M. (1959). *Political man: The social bases of politics.* Garden City, NY: Anchor.

Lipset, S. M., & Bendix, R. (1959). *Social mobility in industrial society.* Berkeley: University of California Press.

Little, R. W. (1970). Buddy relations and combat performance. In O. S. Grusky & G. A. Miller (Eds.), *The sociology of organizations.* New York: Free Press.

Lo, C. Y. H. (1982). Theories of the state and business opposition to increased military spending. *Social Problems, 29,* 424–438.

Loeb, S., et al. (2004). Child care in poor communities: Early learning effects of type, quality, and stability. *Child Development, 75,* 47–65.

Loeb, S., et al. (2007). How much is too much? The influence of preschool centers on children's social and cognitive development. *Economics of Education Review, 26,* 52–66.

Lofland, J. (1996). *Social movement organizations: Guide to research on insurgent realities.* Hawthorne, NY: Aldine de Gruyter.

Lofland, J., Snow, D., Anderson, L., & Lofland, L. H. (2006). *Analyzing social settings* (4th ed.). Belmont, CA: Wadsworth.

Lohr, S. (2003, December 22). Offshore jobs in technology: Opportunity or a threat? *New York Times,* p. C1.

Lombroso, C. (1911). *Crime: Its causes and remedies.* Boston: Little, Brown.

Lomnitz, L. (1988). The social and economic organization of a Mexican shantytown. In J. Gugler (Ed.), *The urbanization of the Third World.* New York: Oxford University Press.

Longshore, D., & Prager, J. (1985). The impact of school desegregation: A situational analysis. *Annual Review of Sociology, 11,* 75–91.

Loomis, L. S., & Landale, N. S. (1994). Nonmarital cohabitation and childbearing among black and white American women. *Journal of Marriage and the Family, 56,* 949–962.

Love, J. M., et al. (2002). *Making a difference in the lives of infants and toddlers and their families: The impacts of Early Head Start.* Washington, DC: Administration of Children and Families, Department of Health and Human Services, and Mathematica Policy Research, Inc., www.acf.hhs.gov/programs/core/ongoing_research/ehs/ehs_reports.html.

Lowe, J. (2000). International examinations: The new credentialism and reproduction of advantage in a globalising world. *Assessment in Education, 7,* 363–377.

Luckmann, T. (1967). *The invisible religion.* New York: Macmillan.

Lucy, J. A., & Shweder, R. A. (1979). Whorf and his critics: Linguistic and nonlinguistic influences on color memory. *American Anthropologist, 81,* 581–615.

Lugo, L., et al. (2008). *U. S. religious landscape survey.* Washington, DC: The Pew Forum on Religious and Public Life, religions.pewforum.org.

Luker, K. (1996). *Dubious conceptions: The politics of teenage pregnancy.* Cambridge, MA: Harvard University Press.

Lynch, F. R., & Beer, W. R. (1990). You ain't the right color, pal: White resentment of affirmative action. *Policy Review, 51,* 64–67.

Lynch, J. W., Kaplan, G. A., & Shema, S. J. (1997, December 25).

Cumulative impact of sustained economic hardship on physical, cognitive, psychological, and social functioning. *New England Journal of Medicine, 337,* 1889–1895.

MacArthur, J. R. (1992). *Second front: Censorship and propaganda in the Gulf War.* New York: Hill & Wang.

MacDonald, K., & Parke, R. (1986). Parent-child physical play: The effects of sex and age of children and parents. *Sex Roles, 15,* 367–378.

Mackie, D., & Cooper, J. (1984). Attitude polarization: Effects of group membership. *Journal of Personality and Social Psychology, 46,* 575–585.

Macklin, E. (1987). Non-traditional family forms. In M. Sussman & S. Steinmetz (Eds.), *Handbook of marriage and the family.* New York: Plenum Press.

MacLeod, J. (2008). *Ain't no makin' it: Aspiration and attainment in a low-income neighborhood* (3rd ed.). Boulder, CO: Westview Press.

Maddison, A., et al. (1992). *The political economy of poverty, equity, and growth: Brazil and Mexico.* New York: Oxford University Press and World Bank.

Mageo, J. M. (1991). Samoan moral discourse and the *Loto. American Anthropologist, 93,* 405–420.

Maguire, K., & Pastore, A. L. (Eds.). (2004). *Sourcebook of criminal justice statistics: 2002.* Washington, DC: U.S. Department of Justice, Bureau of Justice Statistics. Available online at www.albany.edu/ sourcebook.

Malinowski, B. (1929). *The sexual life of savages in North-Western Melanesia.* New York: Harcourt.

Malinowski, B. (1954). *Magic, science, and religion and other essays.* New York: Anchor Press.

Malthus, T. R. (1960). *On population.* (G. Himmelfarb, ed.). New York: Modern Library. (Original work published 1798)

Mansfield, P. K., Koch, P. B., Henderson, J., Vicary, J. R., Cohn, M., & Young, E. W. (1991). The job climate for women in traditionally male blue-collar occupations. *Sex Roles, 25*(1/2), 63–79.

Maratea, R. (2008). The e-rise and fall of social problems: The blogosphere as a public arena. *Social Problems, 55,* 139–159.

Marden, C. F., Meyer, G., & Engel, M. H. (1992). *Minorities in American society* (6th ed.). New York: HarperCollins.

Marks, C. (1981). Split-labor markets and black-white relations, 1865–1920. *Phylon, 42,* 293–308.

Marks, C. (1991). The urban underclass. *Annual Review of Sociology, 17,* 445–466.

Marsh, H. W. (1991). Public, Catholic single-sex, and Catholic coeducational high schools: Their effects on achievement, affect, and behaviors. *American Journal of Education, 99,* 320–356.

Marshall, D. S. (1974). Too much sex in Mangaia. In E. Goode & R. Troiden (Eds.), *Sexual deviance and sexual deviants.* New York: Morrow.

Martin, C. L. (1990). Attitudes and expectations about children with nontraditional and traditional gender roles. *Sex Roles, 22*(3–4), 151–165.

Martindale, M. (1991). Sexual harassment in the military: 1988. *Sociological Practice Review, 2,* 200–216.

Martinez, R., & Dukes, R. L. (1991). Ethnic and gender differences in self-esteem. *Youth and Society, 22,* 318–338.

Martinez, T. A. (1997). Popular culture as oppositional culture: Rap as resistance. *Sociological Perspectives, 40,* 265–286.

Marty, M. (1984). *Pilgrims in their own land: 500 years of religion in America.* Boston: Little, Brown.

Marx, G. T., & McAdam, D. (1994). *Collective behavior and social movements: Process and structure.* Englewood Cliffs, NJ: Prentice Hall.

Marx, K. (1964). *Selected writings in sociology and social philosophy.* (T. B. Bottomore & M. Rubel, eds.). Baltimore: Penguin. (Original work published 1848)

Marx, K. (1967). *Das kapital.* New York: International. (Original work published 1867–1895)

Maryanski, A., & Turner, J. H. (1992). *The social cage: Human nature and the evolution of society.* Stanford, CA: Stanford University Press.

Massey, D. S. (1987). Understanding Mexican migration to the United States. *American Journal of Sociology, 92,* 1372–1403.

Massey, D. S. (1990). American apartheid: Segregation and the

making of the underclass. *American Journal of Sociology, 96,* 329–357.

Massey, D. S. (2001). Residential segregation and neighborhood conditions in U.S. metropolitan areas. In N. J. Smelser, W. J. Wilson, & F. Mitchell (Eds.), *America becoming: Racial trends and their consequences,* vol. 1. Washington, DC: National Research Council, National Academy Press.

Massey, D. S., & Denton, N. A. (1992). Residential segregation of Asian-origin groups in U.S. metropolitan areas. *Sociology and Social Research, 76,* 170–177.

Matras, J. (1984). *Social inequality, stratification, and mobility* (2nd ed.). Englewood Cliffs, NJ: Prentice Hall.

Matsueda, R. L. (1992). Reflected appraisals, parental labeling, and delinquency: Specifying a symbolic interactionist theory. *American Journal of Sociology, 97,* 1577–1611.

Mauldin, W. P. (1975). Assessment of national family planning programs in developing countries. *Studies in Family Planning, 6,* 30–36.

Maume, D. J., Jr. (1991). Child-care expenditures and women's employment turnover. *Social Forces, 70,* 495–508.

Maume, D. J., Jr. (1998). Occupational constraints on women's entry into management. In D. Vannoy & P. J. Dubeck (Eds.), *Challenges for work and family in the twenty-first century.* New York: Aldine de Gruyter.

Maxwell, C. D., Garner, J. H., & Fagan, J. A. (2001, July). The effects of arrest on intimate partner violence: New evidence from the spousal assault replication program. *Research in Brief.* Washington. DC: National Institute of Justice, U.S. Department of Justice.

Mayer, M. (1961). *The schools.* New York: Harper & Brothers.

Mayo, E. (1933). *The human problems of an industrial civilization.* New York: Macmillan.

McCall, R. B. (1988). Real men do change diapers. *Parents, 63,* 202.

McChesney, R. W. (2004). *The problem of the media: U.S. communication politics in the 21st century.* New York: Monthly Review Press.

McClendon, M. J. (1976). The occupational status attainment process in males and females. *American Sociological Review, 41,* 52–64.

McCoy, N. L. (1985). Innate factors in sex differences. In A. G. Sergent (Ed.),

Beyond sex roles (2nd ed.). St. Paul, MN: West Publishing.

McCue, J. D. (1989). *The medical cost-containment crisis: Fears, opinions, and facts.* Ann Arbor, MI: Health Administration Press.

McKenna, K. Y. A., & West, K. J. (2007). Give me that online-time religion: The role of the Internet in spiritual life. *Computers in Human Behavior, 23,* 942–954.

McKeown, T., Brown, R. G., & Record, R. G. (1972). An interpretation of the modern rise of population in Europe. *Population Studies, 26,* 345–382.

McKeown, T., Record, R. G., & Turner, R. D. (1975). An interpretation of the decline of mortality in England and Wales during the twentieth century. *Population Studies, 29,* 391–422.

McKinlay, J. B. (1986). A case for refocusing upstream: The political economy of illness. In P. Conrad & R. Kern (Eds.), *The sociology of health and illness: Critical perspectives* (2nd ed.). New York: St. Martin's Press.

McKinlay, J. B., & McKinlay, S. M. (1977). The questionable contribution of medical measures to the decline of mortality in the United States in the twentieth century. *Milbank Memorial Fund Quarterly/Health and Society, 55,* 405–428.

McLanahan, S., & Sandefur, G. (1994). *Growing up with a single parent: What hurts, what helps.* Cambridge, MA: Harvard University Press.

McManus, P. A., & DiPrete, T. A. (2001). Losers and winners: The financial consequences of separation and divorce for men. *American Sociological Review, 66,* 246–268.

McPhail, C. (1971). Civil disorder participation: A critical examination of recent research. *American Sociological Review, 36,* 1058–1073.

McPhail C. (2001). *Acting together: Purposive individual and collective action in crowds.* New York: Aldine de Gruyter.

McPherson, J. M., Popielarz, P. A., & Drobnic, S. (1992). Social networks and organizational dynamics. *American Sociological Review, 57,* 153–170.

McQuade, S. (2006). *Understanding and managing cybercrime.* Boston: Allyn & Bacon.

McRoberts, O. M. (1999). Understanding the "new" black Pentecostal activism: Lessons from ecumenical urban ministries in Boston. *Sociology of Religion, 60,* 47–70.

Mead, G. H. (1934). *Mind, self, and society.* (C. W. Morris, ed.). Chicago: University of Chicago Press.

Mead, M. (1961). *Coming of age in Samoa: A psychological study of primitive youth for Western civilization.* New York: Morrow Quill.

Melman, S. (2001). *After capitalism: From managerialism to workplace democracy.* New York: Knopf.

Melton, J. G. (1993). Another look at new religions. *Annals of the American Academy of Political and Social Science, 527,* 97–112.

Merton, R. K. (1949). Discrimination and the American creed. In R. M. MacIver (Ed.), *Discrimination and national welfare.* New York: Harper & Brothers.

Merton, R. K. (1968). *Social theory and social structure* (2nd ed.). New York: Free Press.

Mertus, J. A. (1999). *Kosovo: How myths and truths started a war.* Berkeley: University of California Press.

Metcalf, K. K., West, S. D., Legan, N., Paul, K., & Boone, W. J. (2002). *Evaluation of the Cleveland Scholarship and Tutoring Program, 1998–2001.* Bloomington: Indiana Center for Evaluation, Indiana University.

Michels, R. (1966). *Political parties.* New York: Free Press. (Original work published 1915)

Micozzi, M. S. (Ed.). (1996). *Fundamentals of complementary and alternative medicine.* New York: Churchill Livingstone.

Middleton, R. (1962). Brother-sister and father-daughter marriage in ancient Egypt. *American Sociological Review, 27,* 603–611.

Middleton, R. (1976). Regional differences in prejudice. *American Sociological Review, 41,* 94–117.

Milgram, S. (1973). *Obedience to authority: An experimental view.* New York: Harper & Row.

Milgram, S., & Toch, H. (1968). Collective behavior: Crowds and social movements. In G. Lindzey & E. Aronson (Eds.), *The handbook of social psychology: Vol. 4* (2nd ed.). Reading, MA: Addison Wesley.

Miller, A. D., & Ohlin, L. E. (1985). *Delinquency and community: Creating opportunities and controls.* Beverly Hills, CA: Sage.

Miller, D. E. (1997). *Reinventing American Protestantism.* Berkeley: University of California Press.

Miller, G. A. (1963). *Language and communication.* New York: McGraw-Hill.

Miller, J. S. (1991). Clinical sociology and mediation. In H. M. Rebach & J. G. Bruhn (Eds.), *Handbook of clinical sociology.* New York: Plenum Press.

Miller, S. C. (1969). *The unwelcome immigrant.* Berkeley: University of California Press.

Mills, C. W. (1956). *The power elite.* New York: Oxford University Press.

Mills, C. W. (1959). *The sociological imagination.* New York: Oxford University Press.

Milne, R. S., & Mauzy, D. K. (1990). *Singapore: The legacy of Lee Kuan Yew.* Boulder, CO: Westview Press.

Min, P. G. (Ed.). (1994). *Asian Americans: Contemporary trends and issues.* Thousand Oaks, CA: Sage.

Mishel, L., Bernstein, J., & Schmitt, J. (2001). *The state of working America: 2000/2001.* Ithaca, NY, and London: ILR Press and Cornell University Press.

Moghadam, V. M. (Ed.). (1996). *Patriarchy and economic development: Women's positions at the end of the twentieth century.* Oxford, U.K.: Clarendon Press.

Mol, H. (1979). The origin and function of religion: A critique of, and alternative to, Durkheim's interpretation of the religions of Australian aborigines. *Journal for the Scientific Study of Religion, 18,* 379–389.

Montagu, A. (1998). *Man's most dangerous myth: The fallacy of race* (6th ed.). Thousand Oaks, CA: Altamira Press.

Monti, D. J. (1991). The practice of gang research. *Sociological Practice Review, 2,* 29–39.

Monti, D. J. (1993). Origins and problems of gang research in the United States. In S. Cummings & D. J. Monti (Eds.), *Gangs: The origins and impact of contemporary youth gangs in the United States.* New York: State University of New York Press.

Moore, K. A., & Stief, T. M. (1991). Changes in marriage and fertility behavior: Behavior versus attitudes in young adults. *Youth and Society, 22,* 362–386.

Moore, T. S. (1996). *The disposable work force: Worker displacement and employment instability in America.* New York: Aldine de Gruyter.

Moore, W. E. (1974). *Social change* (2nd ed.). Englewood Cliffs, NJ: Prentice Hall.

Moorhead, G., Ference, R., & Neck, C. P. (1991). Group decision fiascoes continue: Space shuttle *Challenger* and a revised groupthink framework. *Human Relations, 44,* 539–550.

Morgan, L. H. (1877). *Ancient society.* Chicago: H. Kerr.

Moskos, C. C. (1970). *The American enlisted man.* New York: Russell Sage Foundation.

Mowlana, H., Gerbner, G., & Schiller, H. I. (Eds.). (1992). *Triumph of the image: The media's war in the Persian Gulf—A global perspective.* Boulder, CO: Westview Press.

Mufwene, S. S., Rickford, J. R., Bailey, G., & Baugh, J., (eds.) (1998). *African American English: Structure, history, and use.* London: Routledge.

Mukerji, C., & Simon, B. (1998). Out of the limelight: Discredited communities and informal communication on the Internet. *Sociological Inquiry, 68,* 258–273.

Mulira, J. G. (1990). The case of voodoo in New Orleans. In J. E. Holloway (Ed.), *Africanisms in American culture.* Bloomington: Indiana University Press.

Munnell, A. H., Tootell, G. M. B., Browne, L. E., & McEneaney, J. (1996). Mortgage lending in Boston: Interpreting HMDA data. *American Economic Review, 28,* 25–53.

Murdock, G. P. (1934). *Our primitive contemporaries.* New York: Macmillan.

Murdock, G. P. (1967). *World ethnographic atlas.* Pittsburgh: University of Pittsburgh Press.

Murphy, R. F. (1968). Social distance and the veil. In M. H. Fried (Ed.), *Readings in anthropology: Cultural anthropology* (2nd ed.). New York: Thomas Y. Crowell.

Myers, D. G., & Lamm, H. (1976). The group polarization phenomenon. *Psychological Bulletin, 83,* 602–627.

Nace, T. (2003). *Gangs of America: The rise of corporate power and the disabling of democracy.* San Francisco, CA: Berrett-Koehler Publishers.

Najafizadeh, M., & Mennerick, L. A. (1990). Educational ideologies and technical development in the Third World. In M. Mtewa (Ed.), *International science and technology.* New York: St. Martin's Press.

Najjar, O. A. (1992). Between nationalism and feminism: The Palestinian answer. In J. M. Bystydzienski (Ed.), *Women transforming politics: Worldwide strategies for empowerment.* Bloomington: Indiana University Press.

National Center for Health Statistics. (1997). *Vital statistics of the United States, 1993* (Vol. 2, Sec. 6, Life Tables). (DHHS Pub. No. [PHS] 97-1104). Hyattsville, MD: Public Health Service.

National Council of La Raza. (1997). Don't blink: Hispanics in television entertainment. In S. Biagi & M. Kern-Foxworth (Eds.), *Facing difference: Race, gender and mass media.* Thousand Oaks, CA: Pine Forge Press.

National Institute of Child Health and Human Development Early Child Care Research Network. (2003). Does amount of time spent in child care predict socioemotional adjustment during the transition to kindergarten? *Child Development, 74,* 976–1005.

National Telecommunications and Information Administration. (2008). *Networked nation: Broadband in America, 2007.* Washington. DC: U. S. Department of Commerce.

Neckerman, K. M., & Kirschenman, J. (1991). Hiring strategies, racial bias, and inner-city workers. *Social Problems, 38,* 433–447.

Neier, A. (1998). *War crimes: Brutality, genocide, terror, and the struggle for justice.* New York: Times Books.

Nelson, F. H., Rosenberg, B., & Van Meter, N. (2004). *Charter school achievement in the 2003 National Assessment of Educational Progress.* Washington, DC: American Federation of Teachers, www.aft.org.

Neubauer, D. E. (1967). Some conditions of democracy. *American Political Science Review, 61,* 1002–1009.

Newcomb, T. M. (1943). *Personality and social change.* New York: Dryden Press.

Newcomb, T. M. (1958). Attitude development as a function of reference groups: The Bennington study. In E. E. Maccoby, T. M. Newcomb, & E. L. Hartley (Eds.), *Readings in social psychology* (3rd ed.). New York: Holt.

Newman, K. S. (1999). *No shame in my game: The working poor in the inner city.* New York: Knopf and the Russell Sage Foundation.

Newman, O. (1972). *Defensible space.* New York: Macmillan.

Newson, L. A. (1987). *Indian survival in colonial Nicaragua.* Norman: University of Oklahoma Press.

Nie, N. H., et al. (2004). *Ten years after the birth of the Internet, how do Americans use the Internet in their daily lives?* Palo Alto, CA: Stanford University Center for the Quantitative Study of Society.

Niebuhr, G. (1999, August 7). Lutherans to vote again on link to Episcopalians. *New York Times,* p. A9.

Niebuhr, G. (2001, April 27). Study finds number of mosques up 25% in 6 years. *New York Times,* p. A12.

Nielson, F. (1994). Sociobiology and sociology. *Annual Review of Sociology, 20,* 267–303.

Nigro, G. W., Hill, D. E., & Gelbein, M. E. (1988). Changes in the facial prominence of women and men over the last decade. *Psychology of Women Quarterly, 12,* 225–235.

Nimkoff, M. F. (Ed.). (1965). *Comparative family systems.* Boston: Houghton Mifflin.

Nisbet, R. A. (1969). *Social change and history.* New York: Oxford University Press.

Nolan, P., & Lenski, G. (2006). *Human societies: An introduction to macrosociology* (10th ed.). Herndon, PA: Paradigm Publishers.

Novak, M. (1978). *The guns of Lattimer: The true story of a massacre and a trial, August 1897–March 1898.* New York: Basic Books.

Oakes, J. (1985). *Keeping track: How schools structure inequality.* New Haven, CT: Yale University Press.

O'Brien, D. J., & Fugita, S. S. (1991). *The Japanese American experience.* Bloomington: Indiana University Press.

Ogburn, W. F. (1938). The changing family. *Family, 19,* 139–143.

O'Kelly, C. S., & Carney, L. S. (1986). *Women and men in society: Cross-cultural perspectives on gender stratification.* Belmont, CA: Wadsworth.

Oliver, D. (1955). *A Solomon Island society.* Cambridge, MA: Harvard University Press.

Oliver, M. B., & Armstrong, G. B. (1998). The color of crime: Perceptions of Caucasians and African-Americans' involvement in crime. In M. Fishman and G. Cavender (Eds.), *Entertaining crime: Television reality programs.* New York: Aldine de Gruyter.

Oliver, M. I., & Shapiro, T. M. (1990). Wealth of a nation: A reassessment of asset inequality in America shows at least one third of households are asset-poor. *American Journal of Economics and Sociology, 49,* 129–151.

Oliver, S. C. (1968). Ecology and cultural continuity as contributing factors in the social organization of the Plains Indians. In Y. A. Cohen (Ed.), *Man in adaptation: The cultural present.* Chicago: Aldine-Atherton.

Olmos, M. F., & Paravisini-Gebert, L. (Eds.). (1997). *Sacred possessions: Vodou, santeria, obeah, and the Caribbean.* New Brunswick, NJ: Rutgers University Press.

Olsen, M. E. (1978). *The process of social organization: Power in social systems* (2nd ed.). New York: Holt.

Olzak, S. (1992). *The dynamics of ethnic competition and conflict.* Stanford, CA: Stanford University Press.

Olzak, S., & Shanahan, S. (1996). Deprivation and race riots: An extension of Spilerman's analysis. *Social Forces, 74,* 931–961.

O'Neale, L. M. (1932). *Yurok-Karok: Basket weavers.* Berkeley: University of California Press.

Orcutt, J. D., & Turner, J. B. (1993). Shocking numbers and graphic accounts: Quantified images of drug problems in the print media. *Social Problems, 40,* 190–206.

Orfield, G. (2004). *Dropouts in America: Confronting the graduation rate crisis.* Cambridge, MA: Harvard Education Press.

Orfield, G., & Lee, C. (2004, January 17). *Brown at 50: King's dream or Plessy's nightmare.* Cambridge, MA: Civil Rights Project, Harvard University.

Ozaki, R. (1978). *The Japanese: A cultural portrait.* Tokyo: Tuttle.

Packard, R. M., & Epstein, P. (1992). Medical research on AIDS in Africa: A historical perspective. In E. Fee & D. M. Fox (Eds.), *AIDS: The making of a chronic disease.* Berkeley: University of California Press.

Padilla, F. M. (1985). *Latino ethnic consciousness: The case of Mexican Americans and Puerto Ricans in Chicago.* Notre Dame, IN: University of Notre Dame Press.

Pallas, A. M., Entwisle, D. R., Alexander, K. L., & Weinstein, P. (1990). Social structure and the development of self-esteem in young children. *Social Psychology Quarterly, 53,* 302–315.

Park, R. E., Burgess, E. W., & McKenzie, R. D. (1925). *The city.* Chicago: University of Chicago Press.

Parkinson, C. N. (1962). *Parkinson's law* (2nd ed.). Boston: Houghton Mifflin.

Parsons, T. (1951). *The social system.* New York: Free Press.

Parsons, T. (1956). Suggestions for a sociological approach to the theory of organizations. *Administrative Science Quarterly, 1,* 63–85.

Parsons, T. (1959). The school class as a social system. *Harvard Educational Review, 29,* 297–318.

Parsons, T. (1971). *The system of modern societies.* Englewood Cliffs, NJ: Prentice Hall.

Pate, A. M., & Hamilton, E. E. (1992). Formal and informal deterrents to domestic violence: The Dade County spouse assault experiment. *American Sociological Review, 57,* 691–697.

Patterson, O. (1999). *Rituals of blood: Consequences of slavery in two American centuries.* Washington, DC: Counterpoint Press.

Patterson, T. E. (2002). *The vanishing voter: Public involvement in an age of uncertainty.* New York: Knopf.

Pattillo, M. E. (1998). Sweet mothers and gangbangers: Managing crime in a black middle-class neighborhood. *Social Forces, 76,* 747–774.

Paul, J. R. (1966). *Clinical epidemiology.* Chicago: University of Chicago Press.

Peña, D. G. (1997). *The terror of the machine: Technology, work, gender, and ecology on the U.S.–Mexico border.* Austin: Center for Mexican American Studies, University of Texas.

Perrucci, R., & Wysong, E. (2002). *The new class society: Goodbye American Dream.* Lanham, MD: Rowman & Littlefield.

Perry, M., Kong, L., & Yeoh, B. (1997). *Singapore: A developmental city state.* Chichester, England: John Wiley & Sons.

Pessen, E. (1971). The egalitarian myth and the American social reality: Wealth, mobility, and equality in the "era of the common man." *American Historical Review, 76,* 989–1034.

Peter, L. J., & Hull, J. (1969). *The Peter principle.* New York: Morrow.

Petersen, W. (1975). *Population* (3rd ed.). New York: Macmillan.

Peterson, J. (1990). The challenge of comparable worth: An institutionalist view. *Journal of Economic Issues, 24,* 605–612.

Peterson, S. B., & Kroner, T. (1992). Gender biases in textbooks for introductory psychology and human development. *Psychology of Women Quarterly, 16,* 17–36.

Peterson, S. B., & Lach, M. A. (1990). Gender stereotypes in children's books: Their prevalence and influence on cognitive and affective development. *Gender and Education, 2*(2), 185–197.

Petrocelli, W., & Repa, B. K. (1992). *Sexual harassment on the job.* Berkeley, CA: Nolo Press.

Pettigrew, T. F. (1988). Integration and pluralism. In P. A. Katz & D. A. Taylor (Eds.), *Eliminating racism: Profiles in controversy.* New York: Plenum.

Pettigrew, T. F. (1998). Intergroup contact theory. *Annual Review of Psychology, 49,* 65–85.

Phelps, E. S. (1997). *Rewarding work: How to restore participation and self-support to free enterprise.* Cambridge, MA: Harvard University Press.

Phillips, G. M., & Wood, J. T. (Eds.). (1984). *Emergent issues in human decision making.* Carbondale: Southern Illinois University Press.

Phillips, U. B. (1963). *Life and labor in the old South.* Boston: Little, Brown.

Pillemer, K., & Finkelhor, D. (1988). The prevalence of elder abuse: A random sample survey. *Gerontologist, 28*(1), 51–57.

Pillemer, K., & Finkelhor, D. (1989). Causes of elder abuse: Caregiver stress versus problem relatives. *American Journal of Orthopsychiatry, 59,* 179–187.

Platt, A. M. (1991). *E. Franklin Frazier reconsidered.* New Brunswick, NJ: Rutgers University Press.

Popenoe, D., & Whitehead, B. D. (2003). *The state of our unions, 2003: The social health of marriage in America.* Piscataway, NJ: National Marriage Project, Rutgers, The State University of New Jersey.

Portes, A., & Stepick, A. (1993). *City on the edge: The transformation of Miami.* Berkeley: University of California Press.

Pospisil, L. J. (1958). *Kapauku Papuans and their law.* New Haven, CT: Yale University Publications in Anthropology.

Pospisil, L. J. (1963). *The Kapauku Papuans of New Guinea.* New York: Holt.

Potter, W. J. (2003). *The 11 myths of media violence.* Thousand Oaks, CA: Sage.

Proctor, R. N. (1995). *Cancer wars: How politics shapes what we know and don't know about cancer.* New York: Basic Books.

Project on Government Oversight. (2004). *The politics of contracting.* Washington, DC: Project on Government Oversight, www.pogo.org.

Prucha, F. P. (1985). *The Indians in American society: From the Revolutionary War to the present.* Berkeley: University of California Press.

Purcell, P., & Stewart, L. (1990). Dick and Jane in 1989. *Sex Roles, 22*(3–4), 177–185.

Putnam, R. D. (2000). *Bowling alone: The collapse and revival of American community.* New York: Touchstone/Simon & Schuster.

Quadagno, J. (2005). *One nation, uninsured: Why the U. S. has no national health insurance.* New York: Oxford University Press.

Quinney, R., & Shelden, R. G. (2001). *Critique of the legal order: Crime control in capitalist society.* Princeton, NJ: Transaction Books.

Rabin, A. I., & Beit-Hallahmi, B. (1982). *Twenty years later: Kibbutz children grown up.* New York: Springer.

Rahman, Q., & Wilson, G. D. (2003). Born gay? The psychobiology of human sexual orientation. *Personality and Individual Differences, 34,* 1337–1382.

Ramey, S. L., & Ramey, C. T. (2000). Early childhood experiences and developmental competence. In S. Danziger & J. Waldfogel (Eds.), *Securing the future: Investing in children from birth to college.* New York: Russell Sage Foundation.

Rank, M. R. (2004). *One nation, underprivileged: Why American poverty affects us all.* New York: Oxford University Press.

Raudenbush, S. W., & Kasim, R. M. (1998). Cognitive skill and economic inequality: Findings from the National Adult Literacy Survey. *Harvard Educational Review, 68,* 33–68.

Read, J. G. (2004). *Culture, class, and work among Arab-American women.* New York: LFB Scholarly Publishing LLC.

Reiman, J. (2007). *The rich get richer and the poor get prison: Ideology, class, and criminal justice* (8th ed.). Boston: Allyn and Bacon.

Reischauer, E. O. (1988). *The Japanese today.* Cambridge, MA: Harvard University Press.

Relman, A. S. (1980). The new medical-industrial complex. *New England Journal of Medicine, 303,* 963–970.

Renner, M. (2004). Moving toward a less consumptive economy. In L. Starke et al. (eds.), *State of the world, 2004: A Worldwatch Institute report on progress toward a sustainable society.* New York: W. W. Norton.

Rennison, C. M. (2003). Intimate partner violence, 1993–2001. *Crime Data Brief,* NCJ 197838. Washington. DC: U.S. Department of Justice, Bureau of Justice Statistics.

Renzulli, L. A., & Evans, L. (2005). School choice, charter schools, and white flight. *Social Problems, 52,* 398–418.

Reynolds, A. J., Temple, J. A., Robertson, D. L., & Mann, E. A. (2001, May 9). Long-term effects of an early childhood intervention on educational achievement and juvenile arrest. *Journal of the American Medical Association, 285,* 2339–2346.

Rhode, D. L. (2001). *The unfinished agenda: Women and the legal profession,* Chicago: American Bar Association.

Rice, B. (1982). The Hawthorne defect: Persistence of a flawed theory. *Psychology Today, 16,* 71–74.

Rich, B. (1994). *Mortgaging the Earth: The World Bank, environmental impoverishment, and the crisis of development.* Boston: Beacon Press.

Richardson, J. T. (Ed.). (1978). *Conversion careers: In and out of the new religions.* Beverly Hills, CA: Sage.

Richmond-Abbott, M. (1992). *Masculine and feminine: Gender roles over the life cycle* (2nd ed.). New York: McGraw-Hill.

Rickford, J. R. (1999). *African American vernacular English: Features, evolution, educational implications.* Oxford: Blackwell.

Ridgeway, C. L. (2001). Gender, status, and leadership. *Journal of Social Issues, 57,* 637–656.

Riding, A. (1989). *Distant neighbors: A portrait of the Mexicans.* New York: Vintage Books.

Riding, A. (2005, February 5). A global culture war pits protectionists against free traders. *New York Times,* p. A19.

Riesman, D. (1961). *The lonely crowd.* New Haven, CT: Yale University Press.

Rifkin, J. (1998). *The biotech century: Harnessing the gene and remaking the world.* New York: Jeremy P. Tarcher/Putnam.

Rimer, S. (2003, April 8). Study finds charter schools lack experienced teachers. *New York Times,* p. A12.

Rimmerman, C. A. (2005). *The new citizenship: Unconventional politics, activism, and service* (3rd ed.). Boulder, CO: Westview Press.

Rist, R. C. (1979). *Desegregated schools: Appraisals of an American experiment.* New York: Academic Press.

Ritchie, J., & Ritchie, J. (1989). Socialization and character development. In A. Howard & R. Borofsky (Eds.), *Developments in Polynesian ethnology.* Honolulu: University Press of Hawaii.

Rivkin, S. G. (1994). Residential segregation and school integration. *Sociology of Education, 67,* 279–292.

Rizzini, I. (1996). Street children: An excluded generation in Latin America. *Childhood, 3,* 215–233.

Robbins, T. (1988). *Cults, converts and charisma: The sociology of new religious movements.* Newbury Park, CA: Sage.

Roberts, L. W. (1991). Clinical sociology with individuals and families. In H. M. Rebach & J. G. Bruhn (Eds.), *Handbook of clinical sociology.* New York: Plenum Press.

Robertson, R. (1992). *Globalization: Social theory and global culture.* London: Sage.

Robey, B., Rutstein, S. O., & Morris, L. (1993). The fertility decline in developing countries. *Scientific American, 269,* 60–67.

Robinson, B. E., Skeen, P., Hobson, C. F., & Herrman, M. (1982). Gay men's and women's perceptions of early family life and their relationships with parents. *Family Relations, 31,* 79–83.

Robinson, J. D., & Skill, T. (2001). Five decades of families on television: From the 1950s through the 1990s. In J. Bryant & J. A. Bryant (Eds.), *Television and the American family,* (2nd ed.) Mahwah, NJ: Lawrence Erlbaum Associates.

Roche, J. P., & Ramsbey, T. W. (1993). Premarital sexuality: A five-year follow-up study of attitudes and behavior by dating stage. *Adolescence, 28,* 67–80.

Rodriguez Rust, P. C. (2004). Civil unions, domestic partnerships, and the extension of marital rights to same-sex partners. In R. Perrucci, K. Ferraro, J. Miller, & P. C. Rodriguez Rust (Eds.), *Agenda for social justice, 2004.* Knoxville, TN: Society for the Study of Social Problems.

Roethlisberger, F. J., & Dickson, W. J. (1939). *Management and the worker.* Cambridge, MA: Harvard University Press.

Roof, W. C., & McKinney, W. (1987). *American mainline religion: Its changing shape and future.* New Brunswick, NJ: Rutgers University Press.

Rose, A. M. (1967). *The power structure: Political process in American society.* New York: Oxford University Press.

Rose, R. (1990). Northern Ireland: The irreducible conflict. In J. V. Montville (Ed.), *Conflict and peacemaking in multiethnic societies.* Lexington, MA: Lexington Books.

Rosen, C., & Youngs, K. M. (Eds.). (1991). *Understanding employee ownership.* Ithaca, NY: ILR Press.

Rosenberg, M., & Pearlin, L. I. (1978). Social class and self-esteem among children and adults. *American Journal of Sociology, 84*(1), 53–77.

Rosenhan, D. L. (1973). On being sane in insane places. *Science, 179,* 250–258.

Rosnow, R. L. (1991). Inside rumor: A personal journey. *American Psychologist, 46,* 484–496.

Rosnow, R. L., & Fine, G. A. (1976). *Rumor and gossip.* New York: Elsevier.

Ross, C. E., & Mirowsky, J. (1988). Child care and emotional adjustment to wives' employment. *Journal of Health and Social Behavior, 29,* 127–138.

Ross, M. W., Paulsen, J. A., & Stalstrom, O. W. (1988). Homosexuality and mental health: A cross-cultural review. *Journal of Homosexuality, 15,* 131–152.

Rossi, A. (1984). Gender and parenthood. *American Sociological Review, 49,* 1–19.

Rossi, P. H., Berk, R. A., & Lenihan, K. J. (1980). *Money, work, and crime: Experimental evidence.* New York: Academic Press.

Rossides, D. W. (1990). *Social stratification: The American class system in comparative perspective.* Englewood Cliffs, NJ: Prentice Hall.

Rousseau, J. J. (1950). *The social contract.* New York: Dutton. (Original work published 1762)

Ruggles, P. (1990). *Drawing the line: Alternative poverty measures and their implications for public policy.* Washington, DC: Urban Institute Press.

Sacco, V. F. (1995). Media constructions of crime. *Annals of the American Academy of Political and Social Science, 539,* 141–154.

Sadker, M., & Sadker, D. (1994). *Failing at fairness: How America's schools cheat girls.* New York: Charles Scribner's.

Salmon, J. W. (1984). Introduction. In J. W. Salmon (Ed.), *Alternative medicines: Popular and policy perspectives.* New York: Tavistock.

Samuelsson, K. (1961). *Religion and economic action: A critique of Max Weber* (E. G. French, Trans.). New York: Harper Torchbooks.

Sanders, W. B. (1974). *The sociologist as detective: An introduction to research methods.* New York: Praeger.

Sapir, E. (1929). The status of linguistics as a science. *Language, 5,* 207–214.

Sassen, S., & Appiah, K. A. (1998). *Globalization and its discontents.* New York: New Press.

Saunders, B. (1991). Clinical educational sociology: Interventions for school staff. In H. M. Rebach & J. G. Bruhn (Eds.), *Handbook of clinical sociology.* New York: Plenum Press.

Saxton, L. (1980). *The individual, marriage, and the family* (4th ed.). Belmont, CA: Wadsworth.

Scarce, R. (1994). (No) Trial (But) Tribulations: When Courts and Ethnography Conflict. *Journal of Contemporary Ethnography, 23,* 123–149.

Schaefer, R. T. (2008). *Racial and ethnic groups* (11th ed.). Upper Saddle River, NJ: Prentice Hall.

Schaefer, R. T., & Zellner, W. W. (2007). *Extraordinary groups: An examination of unconventional lifestyles* (8th ed.). New York: Worth.

Schafer, M., & Crichlow, S. (1996). Antecedents of groupthink. *Journal of Conflict Resolution, 40,* 415–435.

Schechter, D. (2003). *Embedded: Weapons of mass deception: How the media failed to cover the war on Iraq.* Amherst, NY: Prometheus Books.

Scheff, T. (1999). *Being mentally ill* (3rd ed.). New York: Aldine de Gruyter.

Schein, E. H. (1992). *Organizational culture and leadership* (2nd ed.). San Francisco: Jossey-Bass.

Schein, V. E. (2001). A global look at psychological barriers to women's progress in management. *Journal of Social Issues, 57,* 675–688.

Scheper-Hughes, N. (1993). *Death without weeping: The violence of everyday life in Brazil.* Berkeley: University of California Press.

Schlegel, A., & Eloul, R. (1988). Marriage transactions: Labor, property, status. *American Anthropologist, 90,* 291–309.

Schlossberg, N. K. (1985). The adult experience. In A. G. Sargent (Ed.), *Beyond sex roles* (2nd ed.). St. Paul, MN: West.

Schmid, C. L. (1981). *Conflict and consensus in Switzerland.* Berkeley: University of California Press.

Schnall, P. L., & Kern, R. (1986). Hypertension in American society: An introduction to historical materialist epidemiology. In P. Conrad & R. Kern (Eds.), *The sociology of health and illness* (2nd ed.). New York: St. Martin's Press.

Schor, J. B. (2004). *Born to buy: The commercialized child and the new consumer culture.* New York: Scribner.

Schusky, E. L., & Culbert, T. P. (1967). *Introducing culture.* Englewood Cliffs, NJ: Prentice Hall.

Scott, J., & Leonhardt, D. (2005, May 15). Class in America: Shadowy lines that still divide. *New York Times,* p. 1.

Scott, W. R. (2003). *Organizations: Rational, natural, and open systems* (5th ed.). Upper Saddle River, NJ: Prentice Hall.

Scully, D. (1994). *Men who control women's health: The miseducation of obstetrician-gynecologists*. New York: Teachers College Press.

Seccombe, K., & Amey, C. (1995). Playing by the rules and losing: Health insurance and the working poor. *Journal of Health and Social Behavior, 36,* 168–181.

Secondi, G. S. (2002). Biased childhood sex ratios and the economic status of the family in rural China. *Journal of Comparative Family Studies, 33,* 215–234.

Segal, D. R. (1974). *Society and politics.* Glenview, IL: Scott, Foresman.

Segal, D. R., Schubert, J. D., & Li, X. (1991). Establishing unit cohesion in the U.S. Army: A half-century of applied research. *Sociological Practice Review, 2,* 9–14.

Sen, A. (1999). *Development as freedom.* New York: Knopf.

Service, E. R. (1975). *Origins of the state and civilization.* New York: Norton.

Sewell, W. H. (1971). Inequality of opportunity for higher education. *American Sociological Review, 36,* 793–808.

Shaw, M. E. (1976). *Group dynamics* (2nd ed.). New York: McGraw-Hill.

Shaw, M. E., & Costanzo, P. R. (1982). *Theories of social psychology* (2nd ed.). New York: McGraw-Hill.

Sheehy, G. (1998). *Understanding men's passages: Discovering the new map of men's lives.* New York: Random House.

Sherif, M. (1936). *The psychology of social norms.* New York: Harper & Brothers.

Sherman, L. W., & Berk, R. A. (1984). The specific deterrent effects of arrest for domestic violence. *American Sociological Review, 49,* 261–271.

Sherrill, R. (1995, January 9/16). Dangerous to your health: The madness of the market. *The Nation,* p. 45–72.

Shibutani, T. (1966). *Improvised news: A sociological study of rumor.* Indianapolis: Bobbs-Merrill.

Shils, E. A., & Janowitz, M. (1948). Cohesion and disintegration in the Wehrmacht in World War II. *Public Opinion Quarterly, 12,* 280–315.

Shilts, R. (1987). *And the band played on: Politics, people, and the AIDS epidemic.* New York: St. Martin's Press.

Shipler, D. K. (2004). *The working poor: Invisible in America.* New York: Alfred A. Knopf.

Shostak, A. (2001). Applied sociology and organized labor: On going better together. In W. Du Bois & R. D. Wright (Eds.), *Applying sociology: Making a better world.* Boston: Allyn and Bacon.

Shupe, A. D., Jr., & Bromley, D. G. (1980). Walking a tightrope: Dilemmas of participant observation of groups in conflict. *Qualitative Sociology, 2,* 3–21.

Sigelman, L., Bledsoe, T., Welch, S., & Combs, M. W. (1996). Making contact? Black-white social interaction in an urban setting. *American Journal of Sociology, 101,* 1306–1332.

Sigerist, H. E. (1977). The special position of the sick. In D. Landy (Ed.), *Culture, disease, and healing: Studies in medical anthropology.* New York: Macmillan.

Signorielli, N. (1993). Television, the portrayal of women, and children's attitudes. In G. L. Berry & J. K. Asamen (Eds.), *Children and television: Images in a changing sociocultural world.* Newbury Park, CA: Sage.

Silverstein, K. (1993, June 28). The miracle runs out in Venezuela. *The Nation,* pp. 904–906.

Simmons, J. L. (1969). *Deviants.* Berkeley, CA: Glendessary.

Simons, R. L., & Gray, P. A. (1989). Perceived blocked opportunity as an explanation of delinquency among lower-class black males: A research note. *Journal of Research in Crime and Delinquency, 26,* 90–101.

Simpson, G. E., & Yinger, J. M. (1985). *Racial and cultural minorities: An analysis of prejudice and discrimination* (5th ed.). New York: Plenum Press.

Simpson, J. C. (1995). Pluralism: The evolution of a nebulous concept. *American Behavioral Scientist, 38,* 459–477.

Singer, D. G. (1993). Creativity of children in a television world. In G. L. Berry & J. K. Asamen (Eds.), *Children and television: Images in a changing sociocultural world.* Newbury Park, CA: Sage.

Skocpol, T. (1996). *Boomerang: Clinton's health security effort and the turn against government in U.S. politics.* New York: W. W. Norton.

Slavin, R. E. (1985). Cooperative learning: Applying contact theory in desegregated schools. *Journal of Social Issues, 41,* 45–62.

Slonim, M. B. (1991). *Children, culture, and ethnicity: Evaluating and understanding the impact.* New York: Garland.

Smedley, B. D., Stith, A. Y., & Nelson, A. R. (2002). *Unequal treatment: Confronting racial and ethnic disparities in health care.* Washington, DC: National Academy Press, Institute of Medicine.

Smeeding, T. M. (1997). American income inequality in a cross-national perspective: Why are we so different? Luxembourg Income Study Working Paper No. 157, Center for Policy Research, The Maxwell School. Syracuse, NY: Syracuse University.

Smelser, N. J. (1963). *Theory of collective behavior.* Glencoe, IL: Free Press.

Smith, D. (1997, May 1). Study looks at portrayal of women in media. *New York Times,* p. A17.

Smith, D. A. (1991). Method and theory in comparative urban studies. *International Journal of Comparative Sociology, 32,* 39–58.

Smith, D. A., & Timberlake, M. (1993). World cities: A political economy/global network approach. In R. Hutchison (Ed.), *Research in urban sociology, Vol. 3.* Greenwich, CT: JAI Press.

Smith, H. (1991). *The world's religions.* San Francisco: HarperSanFrancisco.

Smith, J. I. (1999). *Islam in America.* New York: Columbia University Press.

Smith, K. B., & Meier, K. J. (1995). *The case against school choice: Politics, markets, and fools.* Armonk NY: M. E. Sharpe.

Smitherman, G. (1997). "The chain remain the same": Communicative practices in the Hip Hop nation. *Journal of Black Studies, 28,* 3–25.

Smock, P. J., & Wilson, F. D. (1991). Desegregation and the stability of white enrollments: A school-level analysis. *Sociology of Education, 64,* 278–292.

Smole, W. J. (1976). *The Yanoama Indians: A cultural geography.* Austin: University of Texas Press.

Snipp, C. M. (1989). *American Indians: The first of this land.* New York: Russell Sage Foundation.

Snow, D. A., & Oliver, P. E. (1995). Social movements and collective behavior: Social psychological dimensions and considerations. In K. S. Cook, G. A. Fine, & J. S. House

(Eds.), *Sociological perspectives on social psychology*. Boston: Allyn and Bacon.

Solorzano, D. G. (1991). Mobility aspirations among racial minorities, controlling for SES. *Sociology and Social Research, 75,* 182–188.

Sommers-Flanagan, R., Sommers-Flanagan, J., & Davis, B. (1993). What's happening in music television? A gender role content analysis. *Sex Roles, 28,* 745–753.

Sorokin, P. A. (1937). *Social and cultural dynamics.* New York: American Book.

Soule, S. A. (1992). Populism and black lynching in Georgia, 1890–1900. *Social Forces, 71,* 431–449.

Southwell, P. L., & Everest, M. J. (1998). The electoral consequences of alienation: Nonvoting and protest voting in the 1992 presidential race. *The Social Science Journal, 35,* 43–51.

Sowell, T. (1981). *Ethnic America: A history.* New York: Basic Books.

Sowell, T. (1996). *Migrations and cultures: A world view.* New York: Basic Books.

Spears, R., Postmes, T., Lea, M., & Wolbert, A. (2002). When are net effects gross products? The power of influence and the influence of power in computer-mediated communication. *Journal of Social Issues, 58,* 91–107.

Spencer, J. W., & Drass, K. A. (1989). The transformation of gender into conversational advantage: A symbolic interactionist approach. *Sociological Quarterly, 30,* 363–383.

Stacey, J. (1998). Gay and lesbian families: Queer like us. In M. A. Mason, A. Skolnick, & S. D. Sugarman (Eds.), *All our families: New policies for a new century.* New York: Oxford University Press.

Stacey, J., & Biblarz, T. J. (2001). (How) does the sexual orientation of the parents matter? *American Sociological Review, 66,* 159–183.

Stamps, P. L. & Piedmonte, E. B. (1986). *Nurses and work satisfaction.* Ann Arbor, MI: Health Administration Press.

Stanko, E. A. (1995). Women, crime, and fear. *Annals of the American Academy of Political and Social Science, 539,* 46–58.

Stark, R. (1972). The economics of piety: Religious commitment and social class. In G. Thielbar & A. Feldman

(Eds.), *Issues in Social Inequality.* Boston: Little, Brown.

Stark, R., & Bainbridge, W. S. (1979). Of churches, sects, and cults: Preliminary concepts for a theory of religious movements. *Journal for the Scientific Study of Religion, 18,* 117–131.

Steeh, C., & Schuman, H. (1992). Young white adults: Did racial attitudes change in the 1980s? *American Journal of Sociology, 98,* 340–367.

Steiner, J. (1990). Power-sharing: Another Swiss "export product"? In J. V. Montville (Ed.), *Conflict and peacemaking in multiethnic societies.* Lexington, MA: Lexington Books.

Stets, J. E. (1991). Cohabiting and marital aggression: The role of social isolation. *Journal of Marriage and the Family, 53,* 669–680.

Stevens, R., & Slavin, R. E. (1995). The cooperative elementary school: Effects on students' achievement, attitudes, and social relations. *American Educational Research Journal, 32,* 321–351.

Stevenson, R. W. (1993, September 19). Racial tensions in London as neo-Nazi wins election. *New York Times,* p. 8.

Steward, J. H. (1955). *Theory of culture change.* Urbana: University of Illinois Press.

Stiglitz, J. E. (2004, January 6). The broken promise of Nafta. *New York Times,* p. A27.

Stiglitz, J. E. (2006). *Making globalization work.* New York: W. W. Norton.

Stolberg, S. G. (1999, June 27). Internet prescriptions boom in the "wild West" of the Web. *New York Times,* p. A1.

Stolberg, S. G. (2001, April 19). Researchers find a link between behavioral problems and time in child care. *New York Times,* p. A18.

Stolberg, S. G. (2002, August 8). Patient deaths tied to lack of nurses. *New York Times,* p. A14.

Stone, P. (2007). *Opting out? Why women really quit careers and head home.* Berkeley, CA: University of California Press.

Stouffer, S. A., et al. (1949). *The American soldier: Combat and its aftermath.* Princeton, NJ: Princeton University Press.

Straus, M. A. (1991). Physical violence in American families: Incidence rates, causes, and trends. In D. D. Knudsen & J. L. Miller (Eds.), *Abused and*

battered: Social and legal responses to family violence. New York: Aldine de Gruyter.

Straus, R. A. (Ed.) (2002). *Using sociology: An introduction from the applied and clinical perspectives* (3rd ed.). Lanham, MD: Rowman & Littlefield.

Strauss, A., Denzin, N. K., & Lindesmith, A. R. (1999). *Social psychology* (8th ed.). Thousand Oaks, CA: Sage.

Strauss, A., Fagerhaugh, S., Suczek, B., & Wiener, C. (1985). *The social organization of medical work.* Chicago: University of Chicago Press.

Street, M. D. (1997). Groupthink: An examination of theoretical issues, implications, and future research suggestions. *Small Group Research, 28,* 72–93.

Strong, B., DeVault, C., & Cohen, T. F. (2008). *The marriage and family experience,* (10th ed.). Belmont, CA: Wadsworth/Cengage Learning.

Strouse, J. S., Buerkel Rothfuss, N., & Long, E. C. J. (1995). Gender and family as moderators of the relationship between music video exposure and adolescent sexual permissiveness. *Adolescence, 30,* 505–521.

Stryker, S. (1990). Symbolic interactionism: Themes and variations. In M. Rosenberg & R. H. Turner (Eds.), *Social psychology: Sociological perspectives.* New Brunswick, NJ: Transaction Books.

Substance Abuse and Mental Health Services Administration. (2007). *Results from the 2006 national survey on drug abuse and health.* Rockville, MD: Office of Applied Studies, Department of Health and Human Services, www.oas.samsa.gov/NHSDA.htm.

Sullivan, T. J. (2001). *Methods of social research.* Belmont, CA: Wadsworth.

Sumner, W. G. (1906). *Folkways.* Boston: Ginn.

Suro, R. (1998). *Strangers among us: How Latino immigration is transforming America.* New York: Knopf.

Sutherland, E. H., & Cressey, D. R. (1978). *Criminology* (10th ed.). Philadelphia: Lippincott.

Suttles, G. D. (1968). *The social order of the slum.* Chicago: University of Chicago Press.

Suzuki, B. H. (1985). Asian-American families. In J. M. Henslin (Ed.), *Marriage and family in a changing society* (2nd ed.). New York: Free Press.

Swain, C. M. (2001). Affirmative action: Legislative history, judicial interpretations, public consensus. In N. J. Smelser, W. J. Wilson, & F. Mitchell (Eds.), *America becoming: Racial trends and their consequences,* Volume I. Washington, DC: National Academy Press.

Swanton, J. R. (1911). Indian tribes of the lower Mississippi valley and adjacent coast of the Gulf of Mexico. *Bureau of American Ethnology Bulletin.*

Switzer, J. Y. (1990). The impact of generic word choices: An empirical investigation of age- and sex-related differences. *Sex Roles, 22,* 69–82.

Sykes, G. M., & Cullen, F. T. (1992). *Criminology* (2nd ed.). Forth Worth, TX: Harcourt Brace Jovanovich.

Szatmary, D. P. (1980). *Shays' rebellion: The making of an agrarian insurrection.* Amherst: University of Massachusetts Press.

Taft, P., & Ross, P. (1969). American labor violence: Its causes, character, and outcome. In H. D. Graham & T. R. Gurr (Eds.), *Violence in America.* New York: Bantam Books.

Tanfer, K., & Cubbins, L. A. (1992). Coital frequency among single women: Normative constraints and situational opportunities. *Journal of Sex Research, 29,* 221–250.

Tanfer, K., & Schoorl, J. J. (1992). Premarital sexual careers and partner change. *Archives of Sexual Behavior, 21,* 41–68.

Tannen, D. (1994a). *Gender and discourse.* New York: Oxford University Press.

Tannen, D. (1994b). *Talking from 9 to 5.* London: Virago.

Tavris, C. (1992). *The mismeasure of woman.* New York: Simon & Schuster.

Taylor, C. S. (1993). *Girls, gangs, women and drugs.* East Lansing: Michigan State University Press.

Taylor, J. (1997, June). Heaven couldn't wait. *Esquire, 127,* 40.

Thio, A. (2007). *Deviant behavior* (9th ed.). Boston: Allyn and Bacon.

Thistlewaite, A., Wooldredge, J., & Gibbs, D. (1998). Severity of dispositions and domestic violence recidivism. *Crime & Delinquency, 44,* 388–398.

Thoits, P. A. (1995). Stress, coping, and social support processes: Where are we? What next? *Journal of Health and Social Behavior* [Special issue], 53–79.

Thomas, C. D., et al. (2004). Extinction risk from climate change. *Nature, 427,* 145–148.

Thomas, W. I., & Thomas, D. S. (1928). *The child in America.* New York: Knopf.

Thörn, H. (2007). Social movements, the media and the emergence of a global public sphere: From anti-apartheid to global justice. *Current Sociology, 55,* 896–918.

Thorne, B. (1993). *Gender play: Girls and boys in school.* New Brunswick, NJ: Rutgers University Press.

Thornton, A. (1985). Changing attitudes toward separation and divorce: Causes and consequences. *American Journal of Sociology, 90,* 856–872.

Thornton, R. (1987). *American Indian holocaust and survival: A population history since 1492.* Norman: University of Oklahoma Press.

Thornton, R. Y., & Endo, K. (1992). *Preventing crime in America and Japan: A comparative study.* Armonk, NY: M. E. Sharpe.

Thurman, M. D. (1982). A new interpretation of Comanche social organization. *Current Anthropology, 23,* 578–579.

Thurner, A. W. (1984). *Rebels on the range: The Michigan copper miners' strike of 1913–1914.* Lake Linden, MI: Forster.

Tienda, M. (1989). Puerto Ricans and the underclass debate. *Annals of the American Academy of Political and Social Science, 501,* 105–119.

Tinbergen, N. (1955). The curious behavior of the Stickleback. In *Twentieth century bestiary.* New York: Simon & Schuster.

Tjaden, P., & Thoennes, N. (2000). *Full report of the prevalence, incidence, and consequences of violence against women: Findings from the National Violence against Women Survey.* Washington, DC: National Institute of Justice, U.S. Department of Justice.

Tjosvold, D., Andrews, I. R., & Struthers, J. T. (1992). Leadership influence: Goal interdependence and power. *Journal of Social Psychology, 132,* 39–50.

Tobias, S. (1997). *Faces of feminism: An activist's reflections on the women's movement.* Boulder, CO: Westview Press.

Tobin, J. N., et al. (1987). Sex bias in considering coronary bypass surgery. *Annals of Internal Medicine, 107,* 19–25.

Toffler, A. (1980). *The third wave.* New York: Morrow.

Tonelson, A. (2000). *The race to the bottom: Why a worldwide worker surplus and uncontrolled free trade are sinking American living standards.* Boulder, CO: Westview Press.

Tönnies, F. (1963). *Community and society.* East Lansing: Michigan State University Press. (Original work published 1887)

Totti, X. F. (1987). The making of a Latino ethnic identity. *Dissent, 34,* 537–543.

Treiman, D. J., & Terrell, K. (1975). The process of status attainment in the United States and Great Britain. *American Journal of Sociology, 81,* 563–583.

Triandis, H. C. (1988). The future of pluralism revisited. In P. A. Katz & D. A. Taylor (Eds.), *Eliminating racism: Profiles in controversy.* New York: Plenum Press.

Troiden, R. R. (1989). The formation of homosexual identities. *Journal of Homosexuality, 17,* 43–73.

Trow, M. (1961). The second transformation of American secondary education. *International Journal of Comparative Sociology, 2,* 144–166.

Tuchman, B. W. (1978). *A distant mirror: The calamitous 14th century.* New York: Random House.

Tumin, M. M. (1953). Some principles of stratification: A critical review. *American Sociological Review, 18,* 387–394.

Turnbull, C. M. (1961). *The forest people.* New York: Simon & Schuster.

Turner, J., & Maryanski, A. (1979). *Functionalism.* Menlo Park, CA: Benjamin/Cummings.

Turner, M. A., et al. (2002–2003). *Discrimination in metropolitan housing markets.* Washington, DC: U.S. Department of Housing and Urban Development and The Urban Institute.

Turner, R. H. (1964). Collective behavior. In R. E. L. Faris (Ed.), *Handbook of modern sociology.* Chicago: Rand McNally.

Turner, R. H. (1994). Rumor as intensified information seeking: Earthquake rumors in China and the United States. In R. R. Dynes and K. J. Tierney (Eds.), *Disasters, collective behavior, and social organization.* Newark: University of Delaware Press.

Turow, J. (2008). *Media today: An introduction to mass communications* (3rd ed.). New York: Taylor & Francis.

Tyler, P. E. (1997, February 28). Ethnic strain in China's far west flares with bombs and rioting. *New York Times,* p. A1.

Tyler, W. B. (1985). The organizational structure of the school. *Annual Review of Sociology, 11,* 49–73.

Tylor, E. B. (1958). *Primitive culture: Vol. 1.* New York: Harper Torchbooks. (Original work published 1871)

Uchitelle, L. (1989, March 26). Trade barriers and dollar swings raise appeal of factories abroad. *New York Times,* pp. 1, 13.

Uchitelle, L. (2006). *The disposable American: Layoffs and their consequences.* New York: Knopf.

United Nations. (1991). *The world's women, 1970–1990: Trends and statistics.* (United Nations Publication No. E. 90.XVII. 3). New York: United Nations.

United Nations. (2000). *The world's women, 2000: Trends and statistics.* (United Nations Publication No. E.00.XVII.3). New York: United Nations, Department of Economic and Social Affairs.

United Nations. (2001). *Human development report, 2000.* New York: Oxford University Press.

United Nations. (2004). *Human development report, 2003: Millenial development goals: A compact among nations to end human poverty.* New York: Oxford University Press.

United Nations. (2006). *Human development report, 2006: Beyond scarcity: Power, poverty and the global water crisis.* Gordonsville, VA: Palgrave Macmillan.

United Nations Development Fund for Women. (2002). *Progress of the world's women: Gender equality and the millennium development goals.* New York: United Nations, www.unifem.undp.org.

U.S. Bureau of Indian Affairs. (2008). *Mission Statement.* Washington, DC: U.S. Department of the Interior, mits.doi.gov/quickfacts/bia2.cfm.

U.S. Bureau of the Census. (2001). *Profile of the foreign-born population in the United States: 2000* (Current Population Reports, Series P23-206). Washington, DC: U.S. Government Printing Office.

U.S. Bureau of the Census. (2004). *Statistical abstract of the United States, 2004–2005.* Washington, DC: U.S. Government Printing Office.

U.S. Bureau of the Census. (2005). *We the people of Arab ancestry in the United States: Census 2000 special reports.* Washington, DC: U.S. Government Printing Office.

U.S. Bureau of the Census. (2007). *Statistical abstract of the United States, 2008.* Washington, DC: U.S. Government Printing Office.

U.S. Department of Commerce. (2001). *Survey of women-owned business enterprises, 1997.* Washington, DC: U.S. Government Printing Office.

U.S. Department of Education, National Center for Education Statistics. (1997). *The condition of education, 1997,* NCES 97-388. Washington, DC: U.S. Government Printing Office.

U.S. Department of Education, National Center for Education Statistics. (2004). *The condition of education, 2004,* NCES 2004077. Washington, DC: U.S. Government Printing Office.

U.S. Department of Education, National Center for Education Statistics. (2004). *Digest of education statistics, 2003.* Washington, DC: U.S. Government Printing Office, nces.ed.gov/program/digest/.

U. S. Department of Education. (2004a). *The nation's report card: America's charter school report,* NCES 2005-456. Washington, DC: National Center for Education Statistics.

U.S. Department of Health and Human Services, Office of the Assistant Secretary for Planning and Evaluation. (2002). *Trends in the well-being of America's children and youth: 2002.* Washington, DC: U.S. Government Printing Office.

U. S. Department of Health and Human Services. (2005, December). Fertility, family planning, and reproductive health of U. S. Women: Data from the 2002 national survey of family growth. *Vital Health and Statistics,* Series 23, No. 25. Hyattsville, MD: Centers for Disease Control.

U.S. Department of Homeland Security. (2007). *Yearbook of immigration statistics: 2006.* Washington, DC: U.S. Government Printing Office, www.dhs.gov/ximgtn/statistics/publications/yearbook.shtm.

U.S. General Accounting Office. (2001). *Women in management: Analysis of selected data from the Current Population Survey,* report no. GAO-02-156. Washington, DC: U.S. Government Printing Office.

U.S. General Accounting Office. (2002). *Public schools: Insufficient research to determine effectiveness of selected private education companies,* report no. GAO-03-11. Washington, DC: U.S. Government Printing Office.

Vago, S. (2004). *Social change* (5th ed.). Englewood Cliffs, NJ: Prentice-Hall.

Vanden, H. E. (2007). Social movements, hegemony, and new forms of resistance. *Latin American Perspectives, 34,* 17–30.

van der Dennen, J., & Falger, V. (Eds.). (1990). *Sociobiology and conflict: Evolutionary perspectives on competition, cooperation, violence, and warfare.* London: Chapman & Hall.

Van der Geest, H. (1993). Homosexuality and marriage. *Journal of Homosexuality, 24,* 115–123.

Van Gennep, A. (1960). *The rites of passage.* Chicago: University of Chicago Press.

Van Horn, S. H. (1988). *Women, work, and fertility, 1900–1986.* New York: New York University Press.

Vannoy-Hiller, D., & Philliber, W. W. (1989). *Equal partners: Successful women in marriage.* Newbury Park, CA: Sage.

Veblen, T. (1912). *The theory of the leisure class.* New York: Macmillan.

Vega, M. M. (2000). *The altar of my soul: The living traditions of Santería.* New York: Ballantine/One World.

Vega, W. A. (1990). Hispanic families in the 1980s: A decade of research. *Journal of Marriage and the Family, 52,* 1015–1024.

Verbrugge, L. M. (1979). Marital status and health. *Journal of Marriage and the Family, 41,* 267–285.

Verbrugge, L. M. (1983). Multiple roles and physical health of women and men. *Journal of Health and Social Behavior, 24,* 16–30.

Vigdor, J. L. (2001). *Does gentrification harm the poor?* (Terry Sanford Institute of Public Policy, Duke University).

Vinovskis, M. A. (1978). Angel's heads and weeping willows: Death in early

America. In M. Gordon (Ed.), *The American family in social-historical perspective*. New York: Random House.

Volti, R. (1995). *Society and technological change* (3rd ed.). New York: St. Martin's Press.

Volti, R. (2006). *Society and technological change* (5th ed.). New York: Worth.

Waitzkin, H. (1991). *The politics of medical encounters: How patients and doctors deal with social problems*. New Haven, CT: Yale University Press.

Waldman, P. (1987, July 24). Motivate or alienate? Firms hire gurus to change their "cultures." *Wall Street Journal*, p. 1.

Waldron, I. (1986). Why do women live longer than men? In P. Conrad & R. Kern (Eds.), *The sociology of health and illness: Critical perspectives* (2nd ed.). New York: St. Martin's Press.

Walker, T. A. (1991). *Nicaragua: The land of Sandino*. Boulder, CO: Westview Press.

Wall, D. S. (2007). *Cybercrime: The transformation of crime in the information age*. Cambridge, UK: Polity Press.

Wallace, A. F. C. (1966). *Religion: An anthropological view*. New York: Random House.

Wallace, E., & Hoebel, E. A. (1952). *The Comanches: Lords of the southern plains*. Norman: University of Oklahoma Press.

Wallerstein, I. (1979). *The capitalist world-economy*. New York: Cambridge University Press.

Wallerstein, I. (1984). *The politics of the world-economy: The states, the movements, and the civilizations*. London: Cambridge University Press.

Wallerstein, J. S., Lewis, J. M., & Blakeslee, S. (2000). *The unexpected legacy of divorce: A 25-year landmark study*. New York: Hyperion.

Wanner, R. A., & Lewis, L. S. (1978). The functional theory of stratification: A test of some structural hypotheses. *Sociological Quarterly, 19*, 414–428.

Ware, J. E., Jr., Bayliss, M. S., Rogers, W. H., Kosinski, M., & Tarlov, A. R. (1996). Differences in 4-year health outcomes for elderly and poor, chronically ill patients treated in HMO and fee-for-service systems. *Journal of the American Medical Association, 276,* 1039–1047.

Watson, W., Michaelsen, L. K., & Sharp, W. (1991). Member competence, group interaction, and group decision making: A longitudinal study. *Journal of Applied Psychology, 76,* 803–809.

Weber, M. (1947). *Theory of social and economic organization* (A. M. Henderson & T. Parsons, Trans.). New York: Free Press. (Original work published 1925)

Weber, M. (1958). *The Protestant ethic and the spirit of capitalism* (Talcott Parsons, Trans.). New York: Scribner's. (Original work published 1905)

Weber, M. (1958). *From Max Weber: Essays in sociology* (H. H. Gerth & C. Wright Mills, eds., trans.). New York: Oxford University Press. (Original work published 1919)

Weinrich, J. D., & Williams, W. L. (1990). Strange customs, familiar lives: Homosexualities in other cultures. In J. C. Gonsiorek & J. D. Weinrich (Eds.), *Homosexuality: Research implications for public policy.* Newbury Park, CA: Sage.

Weisner, T. S., Garnier, H., & Loucky, J. (1994). Domestic tasks, gender egalitarian values, and children's gender typing in conventional and nonconventional families. *Sex Roles, 30,* 23–54.

Wellman, B. (2001). Physical place and cyberplace: The Rise of personalized networking. *International Journal of Urban and Regional Research, 22,* 227–252.

Wellman, B., Salaff, J., Dimitrova, D., Garton, L., Gulia, M., & Haythornthwaite, C. (1996). Computer networks as social networks: Collaborative work, telework, and virtual community. In J. Hagan & K. S. Cook (Eds.), *Annual review of sociology, Vol. 22.* Palo Alto, CA: Annual Reviews Inc.

Wells, L. E., & Rankin, J. H. (1991). Families and delinquency: A meta-analysis of the impact of broken homes. *Social Problems, 38,* 71–93.

Westermann, W. L. (1955). *The slave systems of Greek and Roman antiquity*. Philadelphia: American Philosophical Society.

Whitbourne, S. K., Zuschlag, M. K., Elliot, L. B., & Waterman, A. S. (1992). Psychosocial development in adulthood: A 22-year sequential study. *Journal of Personality and Social Psychology, 63,* 260–271.

Whitcomb, G. R., & Williams, E. G. (1978). Leadership and productivity in planning organizations: A case study. *Administration in Social Work, 2,* 85–94.

White, D. R., Murdock, G. P., & Scaglion, R. (1971). Natchez class and rank reconsidered. *Ethnology, 10,* 369–388.

White, J. R. (2009). *Terrorism and homeland security: An introduction,* (6th ed.). Belmont, CA: Wadsworth/Cengage Learning.

White, R. K., & Lippitt, R. O. (1960). *Autocracy and democracy.* New York: Harper & Brothers.

White, S. (1989). Backchannels across cultures: A study of Americans and Japanese. *Language in Society, 18,* 59–76.

Whorf, B. (1956). *Language, thought, and reality.* New York: Wiley & Sons.

Whyte, W. F. (1965). *Street corner society.* Chicago: University of Chicago Press.

Wichers, M. (2001). Homeschooling: Adventitious or detrimental for proficiency in higher education. *Education, 122,* 145–151.

Widdicombe, S., & Wooffitt, R. (1995). *The language of youth subcultures: Social identity in action.* New York: Harvester Wheatsheaf.

Wilkinson, B. (1988). Social engineering in Singapore. *Journal of Contemporary Asia, 18,* 165–188.

Wilkinson, L. C., & Marrett, C. B. (Eds.). (1985). *Gender influences in classroom interaction.* Orlando, FL: Academic Press.

Williams D. R., & Collins, C. (1995). U.S. socioeconomic and racial differences in health: Patterns and explanations. *Annual Review of Sociology, 21,* 349–386.

Williams, R., Jr. (1970). *American society: A sociological interpretation.* New York: Knopf.

Williams, S., & Taormina, R. J. (1992). Group polarization in business decisions in Singapore. *Journal of Social Psychology, 132,* 265–267.

Williams, T. (1989). *The cocaine kids: The inside story of a teenage drug ring.* Reading, MA: Addison-Wesley.

Williams, T. M. (Ed.). (1986). *The impact of television: A natural experiment in three communities.* Orlando, FL: Academic Press.

Willie, C. V. (1981). *A new look at black families.* Bayside, NY: General Hall.

Wilson, B. (1982). *Religion in sociological perspective.* Oxford: Oxford University Press.

Wilson, C. C., II, Gutiérrez, F., & Chao, L. (2004). *Racism, sexism, and the media: The rise of class communication in multicultural America.* Thousand Oaks, CA: Pine Forge Press.

Wilson, K. L., & Zurcher, L. A. (1976). Status inconsistency and participation in social movements: An application of Goodman's hierarchical model. *Sociological Quarterly, 17,* 520–533.

Wilson, R. W. (1977). Perceptions of group structure and leadership position as an aspect of deviance and social control. In A. A. Wilson, S. L. Greenblatt, & R. W. Wilson (Eds.), *Deviance and social control in Chinese society.* New York: Praeger.

Wilson, T. C. (1993). Urbanism and kinship bonds: A test of four generalizations. *Social Forces, 71,* 703–712.

Wilson, W. J. (1987). *The truly disadvantaged: The inner city, the underclass, and public policy.* Chicago: University of Chicago Press.

Wilson, W. J. (1996). *When work disappears: The world of the new urban poor.* New York: Alfred A. Knopf.

Wilson, W. J. (1999). *The bridge over the racial divide: Rising inequality and coalition politics.* Berkeley and New York: University of California Press/Russell Sage Foundation.

Wiltfang, G. L., & Scarbecz, M. (1990). Social class and adolescents' self-esteem: Another look. *Social Psychology Quarterly, 53,* 174–183.

Winograd, M., & Hais, M. D. (2008). *Millennial makeover: MySpace, YouTube, and the future of American politics.* New Brunswick, NJ: Rutgers University Press.

Winter, J. A. (1977). *Continuities in the sociology of religion.* New York: Harper & Row.

Wirth, L. (1938). Urbanism as a way of life. *American Journal of Sociology, 44,* 8–20.

Wolfe, A. (1993). *The human difference: Animals, computers, and the necessity of social science.* Berkeley: University of California Press.

Wolff, E. N. (1995). *Top heavy: A study of the increasing inequality of wealth in America.* New York: Twentieth Century Fund.

Wong, K. K., & Peterson, P. E. (1986). Urban response to federal program flexibility: Politics of community development block grant. *Urban Affairs Quarterly, 21,* 293–310.

Wong, S-K. (1990). Understanding cross-national variations in occupational mobility. *American Sociological Review, 55,* 560–573.

Wood, J. L., & Jackson, M. (1982). *Social movements: Development, participation and dynamics.* Belmont, CA: Wadsworth.

Wooden, K. (1981). *The children of Jonestown.* New York: McGraw-Hill.

Worchel, S., & Shackelford, S. L. (1991). Groups under stress: The influence of group structure and environment on process and performance. *Personality and Social Psychology Bulletin, 17,* 640–647.

World Bank. (2003). *World development report 2004: Making services work for poor people.* New York: Oxford University Press.

World Bank. (2004). *World development report 2005: A better investment climate for everyone.* New York: Oxford University Press.

World Bank. (2007). *World development report 2008: Agriculture for development.* Washington, DC: The World Bank.

World Health Organization. (1998). *AIDS epidemic update: December 1998.* UNAIDS Joint United Nations Programme on HIV/AIDS. Online at www.who.int/emc-hiv/december1998/wadr98e.pdf. Accessed July 8, 1999.

Wright, E. O., & Martin, B. (1987). The transformation of American class structure. *American Journal of Sociology, 93,* 1–29.

WuDunn, S. (1993, April 25). Births punished by fine, beating, or ruined home. *New York Times,* p. 6.

Wuthnow, R. (2005). *America and the challenges of religious diversity.* Princeton, NJ: Princeton University Press.

Yardley, J. (2005, January 31). Fearing future, China starts to give girls their due. *New York Times,* p. A3.

Yinger, J. (1995). *Closed doors, opportunities lost: The continuing costs of housing discrimination.* New York: Russell Sage Foundation.

Young, G. (1993). Gender inequality and industrial development: The household connection. *Journal of Comparative Family Studies, 24,* 1–20.

Young, T. K. (1994). *The health of Native Americans: Toward a biocultural epidemiology.* New York: Oxford University Press.

Youniss, J. (1985). *Adolescent relations with mothers, fathers, and friends.* Chicago: University of Chicago Press.

Zablocki, B. D., & Kanter, R. M. (1976). The differentiation of lifestyles. In A. Inkeles (Ed.), *Annual review of sociology: Vol. 2.* Palo Alto, CA: Annual Reviews, Inc.

Zald, M. N. (1992). Looking back to look forward: Reflections on the past and future of the resource mobilization research program. In A. D. Morris & C. M. Mueller (Eds.), *Frontiers in social movement theory.* New Haven, CT: Yale University Press.

Zane, J. P. (1991, December 8). In some cities, women still battle barriers to membership in all-male clubs. *New York Times,* p. 35.

Zebrowitz, L. A., Tenenbaum, D. R., & Goldstein, L. H. (1991). The impact of job applicants' facial maturity, gender, and academic achievement on hiring recommendations. *Journal of Applied Social Psychology, 21,* 525–548.

Zey-Ferrell, M. (1981). Criticisms of the dominant perspective on organizations. *Sociological Quarterly, 22,* 181–205.

Zigler, E., & Muenchow, S. (1992). *Head Start: The inside story of America's most successful educational experiment.* New York: Basic Books.

Zimbardo, P. G. (1973). A field experiment in auto shaping. In C. Ward (Ed.), *Vandalism.* New York: Van Nostrand Reinhold.

Zinn, M. B., & Eitzen, D. S. (1990). *Diversity in families* (2nd ed.). New York: HarperCollins.

ANSWERS TO CUMULATIVE PRACTICE TESTS

Chapter 1

1. d
2. b
3. b
4. c
5. e
6. d
7. d
8. e
9. b
10. e
11. e
12. d
13. d
14. e
15. e
16. e
17. d
18. c
19. d
20. b

Chapter 2

1. c
2. b
3. e
4. a
5. e
6. a
7. d
8. d
9. b
10. b
11. c
12. b
13. e
14. e
15. a
16. c
17. b
18. e
19. b
20. a

Chapter 3

1. d
2. d
3. b
4. c
5. d
6. a
7. d
8. e
9. e
10. d
11. c
12. c

13. e
14. e
15. a
16. e
17. a
18. c
19. e
20. e

Chapter 4

1. c
2. c
3. a
4. b
5. a
6. d
7. d
8. b
9. e
10. b
11. e
12. d
13. c
14. e
15. c
16. c
17. e
18. e
19. e
20. b

Chapter 5

1. e
2. a
3. b
4. a
5. e
6. b
7. d
8. b
9. e
10. e
11. e
12. b
13. d
14. b
15. e
16. a
17. b
18. a
19. e
20. e

Chapter 6

1. b
2. b
3. d

4. d
5. e
6. e
7. a
8. a
9. d
10. c
11. b
12. b
13. e
14. c
15. d
16. a
17. a
18. d
19. d
20. c

Chapter 7

1. a
2. d
3. e
4. a
5. c
6. d
7. c
8. e
9. d
10. b
11. c
12. c
13. c
14. b
15. e
16. d
17. a
18. b
19. b
20. e

Chapter 8

1. b
2. e
3. c
4. e
5. e
6. d
7. a
8. e
9. a
10. d
11. e
12. c
13. d
14. b
15. a
16. b

17. b
18. e
19. e
20. a

Chapter 9

1. a
2. e
3. a
4. a
5. c
6. e
7. b
8. d
9. b
10. b
11. c
12. a
13. e
14. e
15. d
16. e
17. d
18. b
19. c
20. a

Chapter 10

1. b
2. d
3. c
4. b
5. d
6. b
7. a
8. e
9. a
10. e
11. d
12. d
13. e
14. d
15. e
16. d
17. e
18. a
19. b
20. c

Chapter 11

1. c
2. d
3. d

4. a
5. b
6. c
7. e
8. e
9. c
10. d
11. e
12. b
13. a
14. d
15. a
16. a
17. a
18. c
19. a
20. d

Chapter 12

1. c
2. a
3. c
4. b
5. b
6. e
7. b
8. d
9. a
10. d
11. c
12. d
13. e
14. e
15. a
16. b
17. b
18. e
19. a
20. c

Chapter 13

1. a
2. e
3. b
4. a
5. b
6. e
7. a
8. d
9. a
10. b
11. a
12. b

13. e
14. c
15. a
16. c
17. d
18. d
19. a
20. d

Chapter 14

1. e
2. c
3. a
4. d
5. e
6. c
7. d
8. c
9. d
10. e
11. e
12. c
13. b
14. c
15. d
16. c
17. e
18. b
19. d
20. a

Chapter 15

1. c
2. e
3. a
4. e
5. c
6. a
7. c
8. a
9. d
10. e
11. a
12. b
13. a
14. b
15. c
16. a
17. e
18. b
19. a
20. d

A

Abadinsky, H., 130, 144
Abe, K., 430
Abrahamson, M., 406, 407
Acuna, R., 190
Adam, H., 179
Adams, M. S., 265, 266
Adams, O., 298
Adams, R. E., 415
Addams, J., 25
Adelman, C., 220
Adler, F., 87, 120, 122
Adler, P., 87
Agnew, R., 11, 121
Alba, R. D., 185, 410
Alexander, B. C., 322
Alexander, K. L., 182, 202
Alex-Assensoh, Y., 199
Allahar, A. L., 82
Allan, E. A., 122
Alperovitz, G., 160
Alsop, R., 228
Altheide, D. L., 384
Altman, L. K., 284
Alwin, D. F., 7, 93
Amato, P. R., 250
Amey, C., 293
Amichai-Hamburger, Y., 111
Amin, Q., 226
Andersen, R., 170, 187
Anderson, B. G., 285
Anderson, J. E., 404
Anderson, K., 210
Anderson, O. W., 170
Andrews, I. R., 95
Angell, M., 303
Anthony, S. B., 226
Antonovsky, A., 279, 398
Appiah, K. A., 406
Apple, M., 337, 340
Applewhite, M. H., 325, 326
Apter, D. E., 155, 378
Aranda, J., 225
Archer, D., 351
Ardrey, R., 66
Argyris, C., 103
Aries, E., 214
Ariès, P., 82, 87
Arizpe, L., 225
Armor, D. J., 202, 345
Armstrong, G. B., 125
Armstrong, J. D., 61
Aronowitz, S., 447
Aronson, E., 201
Ashburn, L., 265, 266
Ashton, H., 5
Astin, A. W., 342
Atchley, R. C., 79
Avakov, R. M., 334
Avary, D. W., 96
Aviezer, O., 73
Axinn, W. G., 246, 251

B

Bagdikian, B. H., 351, 353
Bailey, G., 43
Bainbridge, W. S., 314, 330
Baker, T. L., 168
Bakker, J., 322
Baldwin, R. E., 375
Bales, R. F., 95
Ballantine, J. H., 358
Ball-Rokeach, S. J., 18
Banfield, E. C., 404
Bankston, C. L., III, 254
Barakat, H., 226
Barkan, S. E., 447
Barnet, R. J., 373, 375
Barnett, R. C., 257
Barnlund, D. C., 91
Baron, J. M., 228
Baron, R. A., 182
Barongan, C., 216, 265, 266
Barringer, H. R., 192, 193
Bartos, O. J., 109
Bartsch, U., 401
Barusch, A. S., 79
Basow, S. A., 52
Batur-VanderLippe, P., 196
Baugh, J., 43
Baum, A., 51
Beck, F. D., 414
Beckley, R. E., 314, 317, 321
Beeghley, L., 159
Beer, W. R., 200
Beit-Hallahmi, B., 73
Bell, D., 56, 442
Bellaby, P., 290
Bellah, R. N., 4, 37, 38, 39, 314, 321
Belsky, J., 74
Bender, M. M., 262
Bendix, R., 167
Benjamin, G. R., 358
Bennett, A., 298
Bennett, S. F., 415
Bennis, W., 358
Benokraitis, N. V., 215
Berg, B. L., 19
Berg, I., 338
Bergen, R. K., 130, 223
Berger, A. A., 61
Berger, B., 116
Berger, B. M., 31
Berger, P. L., 8, 65, 116, 134
Bergeson, A., 428,
Berk, R. A., 20, 263, 264, 433
Berkowitz, L., 182, 433
Berliner, D. C., 215, 341
Bernstein, D. S., 181
Bernstein, J., 160, 376
Berreman, G. D., 151
Best, J., 330
Best, R., 215
Betz, M., 152
Biagi, S., 197

Biblarz, T. J., 167, 261
Biddle, B. J., 341
Bieber, I., 20
Bielawski, D., 215
Billingsley, A., 251
Bills, D. B., 338
Billson, J. M., 229, 235
Billy, J. O. G., 255
Bird, C. E., 283
Black, D., 134
Black, F. L., 279
Blakeslee, S., 250, 271
Blalock, H. M., 181
Blasi, J., 73
Blau, F. D., 219
Blau, P. M., 99, 167
Bledsoe, T., 185
Bloom, A., 346
Bloom, J., 188
Blum, D., 235
Blumberg, H. H., 94
Blumer, H., 431, 432, 433
Blumstein, P., 80
Boccuti, C., 291
Bodley, J. H., 82
Bohannon, L., 360
Bohannon, P., 360
Bok, D., 200, 346, 347
Boli, J., 377
Bonacich, E., 181
Bonvillain, N., 235
Booth, A., 250
Bornschier, V., 155, 157, 378
Bornstein, M. H., 73
Bourgois, P., 19, 278
Bouvier, L. F., 402
Bowen, W. G., 200
Boyer, E. L., 346
Bozett, F. W., 260
Braconi, F., 414
Braddock, J. H., 345
Bradshaw, Y. W., 442
Brady, D. W., 404
Brandon, G., 306
Branegan, J., 118
Braun, D., 157
Braun, H., 344
Bray, R. M., 201
Brehm, S. S., 248
Brewer, M. B., 201
Brint, S., 334, 348
Brinton, C., 435
Broad, R., 376
Broch, H. B., 3, 4
Broder, M. S., 296
Bromley, D. G., 19, 330
Brooks-Gunn, J., 87, 260
Broschak, J. P., 228
Brown, J., 212
Brown, J. K., 82
Brown, L. R., 401
Brown, M. K., 196
Brown, P., 337

Brown, R. G., 280
Brown, R. S., 297
Browne, L. E., 196
Brownlee, S.,293
Brownmiller, S., 130
Bruhn, J. G., 26, 31
Brummett, B., 350
Brus, W., 370
Brydon, L., 45
Bryk, A. S., 342
Buckner, H. T., 430
Budrys, G., 303
Buechler, S. M., 439
Buerkel-Rothfuss, N., 265
Bulcroft, R. A., 243
Bullock, C. S. III, 169, 404
Bullough, V. L., 127
Bunzel, J. H., 200
Burchinal, M. R., 74
Burgess, E. W., 411
Burkett, E., 277
Burks, A., 38
Burn, S. M., 215
Burtless, G., 164

C

Cabaj, R. P., 20
Calhoun, C., 436
Callaghan, K. A., 61
Callahan, D., 304
Calvin, J., 313
Campbell, F. A., 74
Cancian, M., 260
Cannon, L., 428
Cantril, H., 431
Caraley, D., 412, 413
Carey, A., 106
Carlson, D. K., 222
Carnegie, A., 166
Carney, L. S., 212, 226, 247
Carnoy, M., 337, 358
Carroll, J. W., 317
Carroll, M. P., 325
Cavanagh, J., 373, 375, 376
Cavender, G., 124
Cernea, M. M., 382
Chagnon, N. A., 89, 245
Chalfant, H. P., 314, 317, 321
Chambliss, W. J., 120, 123
Chant, S., 45
Chao, L., 197
Chase-Dunn, C., 155, 378, 441, 442
Chase-Lansdale, P. L., 260
Chatters, L. M., 251
Chaves, M., 317
Chavez, C., 190
Cherlin, A. J., 242, 250, 258
Chirot, D., 155, 447
Christensen, D. H., 79
Christianson, J., 298
Chua, A., 390
Church, N., 54
Cisneros, H. G., 415
Clancy, P. M., 78
Clark, R., 215, 335
Clement, U., 255
Clinton, B., 159

Clore, G. L., 201
Clymer, A., 322
Coakley, J., 61
Cockerham, W. C., 120, 128, 168, 287, 297, 298
Codrington, R. H., 308
Cohen, J., 314
Cohen, J. E., 401
Cohen, L. E., 122, 228
Cohen, R. L., 7, 93
Cohen, T. F., 223, 246, 247, 249, 255
Cole, D., 144
Coleman, J. S., 338, 342, 344
Coleman, J. W., 131
Collins, C., 283
Collins, R., 13, 31, 213, 241, 246, 247, 254, 337
Coltrane, S., 241, 246, 247, 254
Colvin, M., 136
Combs, M. W., 185
Comer, D. R., 107
Comte, A., 25
Conley, D., 207
Conlin, M., 228
Conte, J. R., 263
Cookson, P. W., 358
Cooley, C. H., 68, 69, 70, 82, 83
Coontz, S., 271
Cooper, J., 96
Copeland, P., 255
Cosby, B., 197
Costanzo, P. R., 96
Costells, M., 412
Côté, J. E., 82
Coult, A. D., 241
Crabb, P. B., 215
Craig, H. K., 43
Crain, R. L., 345
Cravey, A. J., 225
Crenshaw, E. M., 407
Cressey, D. R., 123
Crichlow, S., 98
Crissman, A., 216
Cromwell, P. F., 96
Crossman, R. K., 262
Croteau, D., 17, 383
Cubbins, L. A., 254
Cuklanz, L. M., 125
Culbert, T. P., 44
Cullen, F. T., 120, 131
Cullen, J. B., 152
Currie, E., 122, 136, 139
Curtiss, S., 67
Cutler, J., 447

D

Dahrendorf, R., 153, 154, 439
Danaher, K., 378
Daniels, R., 192
Danziger, S. H.,164
Darrow, W., 278
Davenport, W. H., 127
Davies, J. C., 435
Davies, M. F., 94
Davis, B., 216
Davis, J. A., 158, 254, 255, 318
Davis, K., 67, 152, 154

Day, J. V., 108
Day, R. A., 108
Dean, C., 264
Decker, S. H., 94
Deckhard, B., 227
Dedrick, R. F., 344
Deegan, M. J., 25
Dees, M., 427
DeLaat, J., 104, 105, 218
Demers, D. P., 353
Demo, D. H., 78
DeMott, B., 175
DeNavas-Walt, C., 294
Denise-Neinhaus, S., 382
Dentler, R. A., 428
Denton, N. A., 185
Denzin, N. K., 42, 70
DeParle, J., 175
Derber, C., 390
DeVault, C., 246, 247, 249, 255
Devine, J. A., 122, 164
DeVita, P. R., 61
Díaz, B., 394, 395
Dickson, W. J., 23, 102
Dillon, S., 344, 352
DiPrete, T. A., 167, 250
Disch, E., 229
Dobrzynski, J. H., 228
Dollard, J., 433
Domhoff, G. W., 371
Donnelly, P. G., 415
Doob, C. B., 181
Dore, R., 337
Dorman, W. A., 384
Dorr, A., 266
Doubleday, C., 266
Dowd, N. E., 250
Draper, D. A., 297
Drass, K. A., 122, 214
Dreier, P., 353
Driskell, R. B., 110
Drobnic, S., 94
Du Bois, W. E. B., 25, 26
Duke, J. T., 13
Dukes, R. L., 128, 182, 216
Duncan, G. J., 87
Duncan, O. D., 167
Dunn, F. L., 279
Dunn, S., 417
Dunphy, D. C., 91
Durfee, A., 245, 262
Durkheim, E., 121, 134, 307, 312, 313, 438
Dusek, J. B., 339
Dye, T. R., 370, 371, 373
Dyer, J., 144, 351

E

Eagly, A. H., 96
Earle, T., 54
Earley, P. C., 107
Early, J. D., 90
Eck, D. L., 321
Eckholm, E., 315
Edwards, W. F., 43
Ehrenreich, B., 175
Ehrlich, A. H., 401, 416
Ehrlich, P. R., 401, 416

Eisenberg, D. M., 287
Eisenhower, D. D., 371
Eitzen, D. S., 251
Elliot, L. B., 71
Ellis, G. J., 73
Eloul, R., 243
Emes, C. E., 77, 350
Endo, K., 139
Engel, M. H., 179
Engels, F., 362
Engerman, S. L., 251
England, P., 228
Entman, R. M., 197
Entwisle, D. R., 182, 202
Epstein, P., 284
Ergil, K. V., 286
Erikson, E. H., 70, 71, 80, 82
Erikson, K. T., 133, 144
Eshleman, J. R., 243
Esping-Andersen, G., 56, 442
Etzioni, A., 99, 101,
Evans, E. D., 52
Evans, L., 344
Everest, M. J., 367

F

Fagan, J. A., 264
Fagerhaugh, S., 108
Fagerlind, I., 333, 335
Falger, V., 66
Farb, P., 147, 185, 242, 393, 394
Farkas, G., 196
Farley, J. E., 201, 202
Farrag, A., 135
Fausto-Sterling, A., 211
Fay, B., 23
Feagin, J. R., 196, 200, 207, 215, 412
Featherman, D. L., 167
Feinberg, R. E., 334
Feinberg, W., 335, 348
Feinberg, W. E., 430
Feldman, R., 298
Felson, M., 122
Felson, R. B., 350
Ferber, M. A., 219
Ference, R., 98
Fernald, A., 78
Fernandez-Kelly, M. P., 45, 226
Ferree, M. M., 215, 219
Fiedler, F. E., 95
Fine, G. A., 47, 108, 429, 430
Finkelhor, D., 263
Fiorentine, R., 230
Fischer, C., 409, 410
Fishbein, D. H., 120
Fisher, C. R., 293
Fishman, M., 125
Fitzpatrick, J. P., 190
Flacks, R., 82
Flores, S. M., 202
Flowers, R. B., 263
Foner, A., 79
Ford, C. S., 212
Foster, G. M., 285
Foster, M. W., 34
Fowler-Salamini, H., 45
Fox, T. G., 167

Frankenberg, E., 344
Frankl, R., 322
Frazier, E. F., 25
Freedman, J. L., 401
Freeman, D., 65
Freeman, R. B., 163
Freidson, E., 288
Friedan, B., 226
Friedkin, N. E., 96
Friedman, T. L., 345
Fritz, J. M., 26
Fugita, S. S., 193
Furstenberg, F. F., Jr., 242, 250, 258

G

Gaddy, G. D., 350
Gacdc, S., 318
Gage, M. G., 79
Gallagher, M., 271
Gallagher, T. J., 81
Gallup, Jr., G. H., 254
Gans, H. J., 175, 390, 409, 423
Garner, J. H., 264
Garnier, H., 215
Garreau, J., 423
Gastil, J., 214
Gates, B., 159
Geertz, C., 36, 307
Geis, G., 296
Gelbein, M. E., 351
Gelles, R. J., 245, 262, 263
Gendron, B., 440
Gerbner, G., 384
Gibbs, D., 264
Gibbs, J., 325
Gibson, R. M., 293
Giele, J. Z., 212
Gilbert, D. A., 159
Gilens, M., 169
Gilliam, Jr., F. D., 197
Gilligan, C., 81
Gilmore, S., 216
Ginn Daugherty, H., 399
Giroux, H. A., 340
Gladney, D. C., 315
Glass, S. P., 255
Godley, M. D., 128
Goduka, I. N., 24
Goff, C., 132
Goffman, E., 50, 61, 83, 116, 120
Gold, M., 291
Gold, S. J., 253
Goldberg, M., 315
Goldstein, L. H., 218
Goldstein, M. C., 241
Golombok, S., 261
Gonzales, P., 341
Gonzalez, A., 201
Gonzalez, J., 190
Goode, E., 51, 324, 427, 431, 432
Goodman, M. E., 37
Goodstein, D., 401, 417
Gordon, J. S., 287
Gordon, M., 196, 243
Gordon, M. M., 23, 185
Gordon, S., 304
Gornick, M. E., 283

Gortmaker, S. L., 350
Gottfredson, M. R., 120
Gottlieb, M., 368
Gouldner, A. W., 23
Grady, W. R., 255
Granovetter, M., 433
Grant, J. W., 209
Grant, P. R., 45
Gray, P. A., 122
Greeley, A. M., 318
Green, G. D., 260
Greenberg, J. R., 263
Greenfield, S., 297
Gregg, S. A., 54
Gregory, R. F., 229
Greider, P. Jr., 382
Greider, W., 371, 376, 390
Grigg, W., 344
Grimes, P., 155, 378, 442
Gross, E., 101
Gross, G. R., 51, 54
Grunberg, N. E., 51
Gumperz, J. J., 42
Gutek, G. L., 334, 348
Gutenberg, J., 349
Gutiérrez, F., 197
Gutman, B., 251

H

Habenstein, R. W., 241
Habermas, J., 439
Hadaway, C. K., 317
Haddad, Y. Y., 330
Hadden, J. K., 322
Hafferty, F. W., 288
Hagan, J., 219
Haines, D., 253
Hais, M. D., 383
Hall, E. J., 215
Hall, E. T., 39
Hall, G. C. N., 216, 265, 266
Hall, R. H., 95, 99, 102, 103
Halliday, T. C., 377, 379
Hallinan, M. T., 339
Halloran, R., 91
Hamer, D., 255
Hamilton, E. E., 264
Hammack, F., 358
Handel, M. J., 101, 109
Hardoy, J. E., 394
Hare, A. P., 94
Harkins, S., 107
Harley, G. W., 285
Harrington, C., 291
Harrington, M., 369
Harris, C. D., 411, 412
Harris, M., 61, 119
Harrison, B., 376
Harrison, L. E., 378
Harrison, M. I., 105, 344
Hart, J. W., 107
Hauser, R. M., 167
Haveman, H. A., 228
Haveman, R. H., 164
Hawley, A. H., 404, 413
Hawley, W. D., 202, 345
Hayakawa, M., 348

Head, S., 390
Headley, B. D., 123
Hechter, M., 97
Heimer, K., 124
Heiner, R., 31
Hellander, I., 291, 297
Hemming, J., 177, 178, 332
Hendry, J., 139
Henkin, A. B., 253
Herman, E. S., 353
Hero, R. E., 190
Herrman, M., 256, 428
Hersch, S. M., 97
Hertz, R., 257, 271
Hess, F. M., 341
Hewitt, J. P., 14
Heydebrand, W., 106
Hickey, G. C., 253
Hill, D. E., 351
Hill, R. B., 271
Himmelstein, D. U., 291, 297
Hirsch, J. S., 447
Hirschel, J., 264
Hirschi, T., 11, 120, 121
Hirschman, C., 192
Hirst, L. F., 274
Hitler, A., 180, 341, 363, 365
Hobson, C. F., 256
Hoebel, E. A., 34, 42
Hoecker-Drysdale, S., 25
Hoffer, T., 342
Hoffman, C., 42
Hofstede, G., 107
Hoge, D. R., 317
Holden, K. C., 250
Holland, P. B., 342
Holzer, H. J., 163
Honey, M., 213
Hong, L. K., 96
Hoover, S. M., 330
Horn, C. L., 202
Hornung, C. A.,170
Horowitz, R., 19
Horsfield, P. G., 322
Horton, H. D., 167
Hostetler, J. A., 40
Hourani, A., 226
House, J. S., 283
Houseknecht, S., 248, 257, 402
Hout, M., 168
Howard, I., 216
Howard, P. E. N., 17, 52
Hoynes, W., 17, 383
Hoyt, H., 411
Hudson, F. M., 80, 81
Huesmann, L. R., 350
Hughes, M., 78
Hugick, L., 254
Hull, R., 101
Humphreys, L., 23, 25
Hunt, H. L., 166
Huntington, S. P., 378
Hurn, C. J., 337, 339
Hurst, C. E., 151
Huston, A. C., 265
Hutchison, I., III, 264

I

Illich, I., 292
Ima, K., 193
Itkin, S. M., 201
Iyengar, S., 197

J

Jackson, J., 363
Jackson, M., 464
Jacobsen, J. P., 228
Jacobson, J., 402
Jaffe, H. W., 278
Jamieson, N. L., 253
Jang, S. J., 410
Janis, I. L., 98
Jankowski, M. S., 94, 116
Janowitz, M., 97
Jayakody, R., 251
Jekielek, S. M., 250
Jencks, C., 164, 168, 195, 200
Jenkins, F., 344
Jesilow, P., 296
Johannesen-Schmidt, M. C., 96
Johnson, A. W., 54
Johnson, C. L., 242, 260
Johnson, D. R., 42
Johnson, D. W., 116
Johnson, E. O., 81
Johnson, F. P., 116
Johnson, J. D., 265, 266
Johnson, N. R., 430
Johnson, S. M., 261
Johnston, D. M., 127, 430
Jones, E. E., 120
Jones, J., 325, 326
Jones, S., 17, 52
Jones, S. R. G., 22
Josephson, W. L., 350
Joyner, C., 101

K

Kalinich, D. B., 47
Kalmuss, S., 262
Kammeyer, K. C. W., 399
Kane, J., 116
Kanter, R. M., 104, 109, 150,
Kaplan, G. A., 283
Kaplan, H. B., 287
Karau, S. J., 107
Karnow, S., 253
Karoly, L. A., 343
Kasarda, J. D., 407, 423
Kasim, R. M., 219
Katz, M. B., 195, 340
Kaufman, D. R., 81
Kay, F. M., 219
Keefer, R., 429
Kelling, G. W., 42
Kellner, H., 116
Kennedy, J. F., 363
Kennedy, L. W., 122
Kepel, G., 315
Keplinger, D. H., 255
Kerbo, H. R., 38, 175
Kern, R., 283
Kern-Foxworth, M., 197

Kersten, J., 139
Kertzer, D., 79
Kessler, R. C., 283
Kett, J. F., 82
Kibria, N., 254
Kiecolt-Glaser, J. K., 250
Kilgore, S., 342
Kimble, C. E., 415
Kimmel, A. J., 429
Kimmel, M., 223, 235
King, M. L., 363
King, R., 428
Kirby, D., 260
Kirsch, I., 341
Kirschenman, J., 164
Kirsh, B., 214
Kitano, H. H. L., 193, 195
Kitson, G. C., 271
Klee, L., 242, 260
Klein, M., 128
Kleinknecht, W., 130
Kleinman, S., 47
Kletzer, L. G., 376
Kluckhohn, C., 36
Knottnerus, J. D., 84
Knox, P., 406
Koch, E., 277
Koenig, F., 430
Koentjaraningrat, 4
Kohlberg, L., 73
Kohn, M. L., 73
Kolbert, E., 423
Kong, L., 118
Kooistra, P. G., 125
Koresh, D., 316, 325, 326
Kornblum, W., 423
Kornhauser, W., 371
Kosberg, J. I., 265
Kosmin, B. A., 319
Kotlowitz, A., 175
Kovaric, P., 266
Krantz, D. S., 51
Krauze, T. K., 168
Kressel, N. J., 184
Kristof, N. D., 403
Kroeber, A. L., 36, 431
Kroner, T., 215
Kruger, P., 401
Krymkowski, D. H., 168
Kumagai, F., 348
Kuper, H., 148

L

La Barre, W., 324
Lach, M. A., 215
Lachman, S. P., 319
Lafree, G., 122
Lamm, H., 96
Land, K. C., 122
Landale, N. S., 258
Lanternari, V., 324
Larsen, E., 322
Larson, C. J., 26
Laski, K., 370
Lasswell, H. D., 362
Latane, B., 107
Latha, K. S., 243

Lattimore, P. K., 130
Lau, I., 42
Lauer, R. H., 438
Laufer, W. S., 120, 122
Lazarsfeld, P. F., 25
Lea, M., 110
Leacock, E., 210
Leavitt, G. C., 121
Lee, C., 344, 345
Lee, J., 193
Lee, S., 197
Lee, V. E., 342, 344
Lenihan, K. J., 20
Lennon, R., 215
Lenski, G., 54, 153, 154, 438
Leonard, J., 254
Leonhardt, D., 163, 167
Lettiere, M., 19, 278
Levin, H. M., 337
Levin, J., 180, 184
Levin, L. M., 228
Levin, W. C., 180
Levine, H. G., 144
Levine, L., 228, 346
LeVine, R. A., 82
LeVine, S., 45
Levine, S., 326
Levinger, G., 349
Levinson, D. J., 80, 81
Levinson, S. C., 42
Levitas, D., 448
Levy, F., 163, 168
Lewin, E., 260
Lewin, K., 95
Lewin, T., 219
Lewis, J., 271
Lewis, J. M., 250
Lewis, J. R., 330
Lewis, L. S., 152
Lewis, R. A., 223
Lewontin, R. C., 87
Li, D. J., 107
Li, X., 97
Liddell, C., 401
Liebow, E., 175
Light, D. W., 288
Likert, R., 103
Lincoln, A., 166
Lindesmith, A. R., 42, 70
Lindorff, D., 291, 297
Lindsey, L. L., 52, 216
Lines, P. M., 346
Link, B. G., 131
Lippitt, R., 95
Lipset, S. M., 167, 362, 365
Little, R. W., 104
Lleras, C., 196
Lo, C. Y. H., 372
Locke, J., 66,
Loeb, S., 74
Lofland, J., 19, 437
Lohr, S., 376
Lombroso, C., 9, 120
Lomnitz, L., 408
Long, E. C. J., 265
Longshore, D., 202, 345
Loomis, L. S., 258

Lopez, J., 197
Lorber, J., 304
Loucky, J., 215
Loue, S., 271
Love, J. M., 165
Lowe, J., 337
Luckmann, T., 319
Lucy, J. A., 42
Lugo, L., 323
Luker, K., 260
Lummis, A. T.330,
Luther, M., 313
Lynch, F. R., 200
Lynch, J. W., 283
Lyon, L., 110

M

MacArthur, J. R., 384
MacDonald, K., 215
Macke, A. S., 248
Mackie, D., 96
MacKinnon, C. A., 235
Macklin, E., 257
MacLeod, J., 84
Maczuga, S., 196
Maddison, A., 157
Mageo, J. M., 65
Maguire, K., 136
Mahoney, J. S., 125
Maital, S. L., 73
Malaret, D. R., 81
Malinowski, B., 47, 239, 254
Malthus, T. R., 398
Mann, E. A., 165
Mansfield, P. K., 218
Mao Zedong, 363
Maratea, R., 383, 385
Marcuse, H., 439
Marden, C. F., 179
Marks, A., 96
Marks, C., 164, 188
Marks, P. M., 207
Marler, P. L., 317
Marrett, C. B., 339
Marsh, H., W., 342
Marshall, D. S., 127
Martin, B., 167
Martin, C. L., 215
Martin, J., 116
Martindale, M., 229
Martineau, H., 25, 26
Martinez, R., 182, 216
Martinez, R. O., 128
Martinez, T. A., 77, 266
Marty, M., 321
Marx, G. T., 431
Marx, K., 13, 23, 123, 153, 154, 155, 312, 313, 318, 364, 370, 398, 401, 439
Maryanski, A., 12, 67
Massey, D. S., 45, 164, 185
Matras, J., 167
Matsueda, R. L., 124
Mauldin, W. P., 402
Maume, D. J., Jr., 219, 228
Mauzy, D. K., 118
Maxwell, C. D., 264
Mayer, M., 339

Mayo, E., 102
Mazzocco, D. W., 358
McAdam, D., 431
McCall, R. B., 223
McChesney, R. W., 351, 353, 373
McClendon, M. J., 168
McCoy, N. L., 211
McCue, J. D., 292
McCullough, B. C., 170
McDevitt, J., 184
McEneaney, J., 196
McGuire, M. B., 330
McKenna, K. Y. A., 332
McKenzie, R. D., 411
McKeown, T., 280
McKibben, M., 263
McKinlay, J. B., 280
McKinlay, S. M., 280
McKinney, K. D., 2-7
McKinney, W., 318
McKinstry, J. A., 38
McLanahan, S., 260
McManus, P. A., 250
McPartland, J. M., 345
McPhail, C., 428, 432, 433
McPherson, J. M., 94
McQuade, S., 130
McRoberts, O. M., 321
McVeigh, T., 436
Mead, G. H., 69, 70, 71, 82, 83
Mead, M., 64, 65, 87
Meadows, D. H., 423
Meadows, D. L., 423
Meier, K. J., 342
Melman, S., 376
Melton, J. G., 323, 330
Mennerick, L. A., 334
Merton, R. K., 12, 13, 49, 79, 101, 121, 122, 180
Mertus, J. A., 184
Messner, M. A., 235
Metcalf, K. K., 344
Meyer, G., 179
Michaelsen, L. K., 96
Michels, R., 108, 365
Micozzi, M. S., 287
Middleton, R., 181, 241
Milgram, S., 21, 433
Miller, A. D., 122
Miller, D. E., 316, 321, 322
Miller, G. A., 42
Miller, J. S., 229
Miller, N., 201
Miller, P., 152
Miller, S. C., 192
Miller, S. M., 167
Mills, C. W., 7, 8, 31, 101, 153, 154, 370, 371, 372
Milne, R. S., 118
Min, P. G., 193
Mirowsky, J., 51, 304
Mishel, L., 160, 376
Mitroff, I. I., 358
Moen, P., 271
Moghadam, V. M., 225
Mokhiber, R., 144, 390
Mol, H., 312

Moles, O. C., 349
Molnar, A., 358
Montagu, A., 179
Monti, D. J., 128
Moodley, K., 179
Moon, M., 291
Moore, K. A., 246
Moore, L. J., 304
Moore, T. S., 376
Moore, W., 152, 154
Moore, W. E., 439
Moorhead, G., 98
Morgan, L. H., 438
Morikawa, H., 78
Morris, L., 215, 400, 402
Moskos, C. C., 97
Mowlana, H., 384
Mueller, G. O. W., 120, 122
Muenchow, S., 165
Mufwene, S. S., 43
Muhammad, E., 323
Mukerji, C., 111
Mulira, J. G., 306
Müller, B., 401
Munnell, A. H., 196
Murdock, G. P., 147, 213, 239, 254
Murphy, P., 201
Murphy, R. F., 5
Myers, D. G., 96

N

Nace, T., 372, 378
Najafizadeh, M., 334
Najjar, O. A., 226
Narendra, R., 243
Nason-Clark, N., 132
Nathan, R. P., 32
Neck, C. P., 98
Neckerman, K. M., 164
Nederend, S., 215
Neier, A., 184
Nelson, A. R., 283
Nelson, F. H., 344
Neubauer, D. E., 365
Newcomb, T. M., 7, 93
Newman, A. E., 228
Newman, K. S., 163, 175
Newman, O., 415
Newson, L. A., 380
Nguyen, L. T., 253
Nie, N. H., 111
Niebuhr, G., 321, 323
Nielson, F., 66
Nigro, G. W., 351
Nimkoff, M. F., 242
Nisbet, R. A., 438
Nolan, P., 54, 438
Novak, M., 425
Novick, S. M., 152

O

Oakes, J., 339
O'Brien, D. J., 193
O'Connor, E., 261
O'Day, P., 122
Ogburn, W. F., 243

Ohlin, L. E., 122
O'Kelly, C. S., 212, 226, 247
Oliver, D., 241
Oliver, M. B., 125
Oliver, M. I., 157
Oliver, P. E., 434
Oliver, S. C., 149
Olmos, M. F., 306
Olsen, M. E., 108
Olson, J. N., 96
Olzak, S., 181, 182, 428
O'Neale, L. M., 333
O'Neil, A. K., 215
Orcutt, J. D., 125
Orenstein, P., 236
Orfield, G., 341, 345
Oribabor, P., 290
Osinsky, P., 377, 379
Osteen, J., 322
Ozaki, R., 91

P

Packard, R. M., 284
Padavic, I., 236
Padilla, F. M., 191
Paikoff, R. L., 260
Pallas, A. M., 182
Palmer, C. E., 314, 317, 321
Paravisini-Gebert, L., 306
Park, R., 411
Parke, R., 215
Parkinson, C. N., 101
Parnell, A. M., 423
Parsons, T., 37, 106, 152, 154, 275, 340, 438
Pastore, A. L., 136
Pate, A. M., 264
Patterson, O., 252
Patterson, T. E., 367
Pattillo, M., 144
Pattillo, M. E., 128
Paul, J. R., 274
Paulsen, J. A., 20, 256
Pearlin, L. I., 170
Peña, D. G., 225
Perrucci, R., 164
Perry, M., 118
Persell, C. H., 358
Pessen, E., 160
Peter, L. J., 101
Peters, J. F., 90
Petersen, L. R., 73
Petersen, W., 398
Peterson, J., 219
Peterson, P. E., 414
Peterson, S. B., 215,
Petrocelli, W., 229
Pettigrew, T. F., 198, 201
Phelps, E. S., 164
Philliber, W. W., 257
Phillips, G. M., 96
Phillips, K., 175
Phillips, U. B., 187
Piedmonte, E. B., 51
Pillemer, K., 263
Pitcher, T., 47
Platt, A. M., 25
Polanzi, C. W., 131

Pontell, H. N., 296
Popenoe, D., 246
Popielarz, P. A., 94
Portes, A., 195, 423
Pospisil, L. J., 44, 135
Postman, N., 448
Postmes, T., 110
Potter, S. L., 43
Potter, W. J., 350
Prager, J., 202, 345
Prestowitz, C., 390
Price, P., 436
Proctor, B. D., 294
Proctor, R. N., 283
Prucha, F. P., 192
Purcell, P., 215
Putnam, R. D., 111

Q

Quadagno, J., 293
Quart, A., 87
Quesada, J., 19, 278
Quinney, R., 122

R

Rabin, A. I., 73
Raftery, A. E., 167
Rahman, Q., 255
Rainwater, L., 164
Ramey, C. T., 165
Ramey, S. L., 165
Ramsbey, T. W., 254
Randers, J., 423
Rank, M. R., 376
Rankin, J. H., 250
Raudenbush, S. W., 219
Rawlins, W. K., 116
Raymond, J. A., 263
Read, J. G., 194
Reagan, R., 159, 166, 363
Rebach, H. M., 26, 31
Record, R. G., 280
Reed, D., 260
Reed, W., 265, 266
Reiman, J., 131
Reinarman, C., 144
Reischauer, E. O., 38
Reitz, J. G., 25
Relman, A. S., 291
Renner, M., 418
Rennison, C. M., 262
Renzulli, L. A., 344
Repa, B. K., 229
Reskin, B. F., 236
Reynolds, A. J., 165
Rezac, S. J., 250
Rhode, D. L., 219
Rice, B., 106
Rich, B., 379
Richardson, B. L., 81
Richardson, D. R., 182
Richardson, J. T., 325, 330
Richardson, L., 448
Richmond-Abbott, M., 215, 216, 227
Rickford, J. R., 43
Ridgeway, C. L., 96

Riding, A., 45, 354
Rieker, P. P., 283
Riesman, D., 371
Rifkin, J., 401
Rimer, S., 344
Rimmerman, C. A., 367
Rist, R. C., 345
Ritchie, J., 65
Ritzer, G., 116
Rivera, G., 197
Rivers, C., 257
Rivkin, S. G., 202
Rizzini, I., 157
Robbins, T., 323, 325
Roberts, L. W., 26
Robertson, D. L., 165
Robertson, P., 322
Robertson, R., 442
Robey, B., 400, 402
Robinson, B. E., 256
Robinson, J. D., 265
Robinson, R., 207,
Roche, J. P., 254
Rochlin, G. I., 448
Rockefeller, J. D., 166
Rodriguez Rust, P. C., 261
Roethlisberger, F. J., 23, 102
Roof, W. C., 318
Rose, A. M., 371
Rose, R., 186
Rosen, C., 376
Rosenberg, B., 344
Rosenberg, K., 245, 262
Rosenberg, M., 170
Rosenhan, D. L., 129
Rosnow, R. L., 429, 430
Ross, C. E., 51, 304
Ross, M. W., 20, 256
Ross, P., 425
Rossi, A., 215
Rossi, P. H., 20
Rossides, D. W., 159
Rothstein, R., 358
Rousseau, J. J., 364
Ruggles, P., 160
Rushing, W. A.,304
Rutberg, J., 52
Rutherford, D., 253
Rutstein, S. O., 400, 402
Ryan, R. A., 195
Rymer, R., 87

S

Sacco, V. F., 125, 126
Sadker, D., 216
Sadker, M., 216
Sagi, A., 73
Saha, L. J., 333, 335
Sale, K., 423
Saliba, J. A., 330
Salmon, J. W., 286
Samoff, J., 358
Samuelsson, K., 314
Sandefur, G. D., 260
Sanders, W. B., 11
Sandino, A., 380
Sapir, E., 42

Sassen, S., 406
Sather, C., 52
Saunders, B., 344
Saxton, L., 247
Scaglion, R., 147
Scarbecz, M., 170
Scarce, R., 25
Schaefer, R. T., 40, 191, 195
Schafer, M., 98
Schechter, D., 358, 384
Scheff, T. J., 128, 129
Schein, E. H., 105
Schein, V. E., 96
Scheper-Hughes, N., 157
Schiller, H. I., 384
Schlegel, A., 243
Schlossberg, N. K., 80
Schmid, C. L., 186, 187
Schmidt, C., 242, 260
Schmitt, J., 160, 376
Schnall, P. L., 283
Schoorl, J. J., 254
Schor, J. B., 77
Schubert, J. D., 97
Schuengel, C., 73
Schuman, H., 200
Schusky, E. L., 44
Schwartz, P., 80
Scott, J., 163, 167
Scott, W. R., 99, 103, 106
Scully, D., 295
Seccombe, K., 293
Secondi, G. S., 403
Segal, D. R., 97, 362, 365
Sen, A., 402
Serpe, R. T., 415
Service, E. R., 363
Sewell, W. H., 168
Shackelford, S. L., 96
Shaiken, H., 107
Shanahan, S., 428
Shapiro, T. M., 157
Sharp, W., 96
Shaw, M. E., 95, 96
Sheehy, G., 81
Sheen, F. J., 322
Shelden, R. G., 122
Sheley, J. F., 122
Shema, S. J., 283
Sherif, M., 97
Sherman, L. W., 263, 264
Sherrill, R., 292
Shibutani, T., 429
Shils, E. A., 97
Shilts, R., 277, 278
Shipler, D. K., 162
Shorris, E., 207
Shostak, A., 23, 382
Shupe, A., 19
Shweder, R. A., 42
Sigelman, L., 185
Sigerist, H. E., 277
Signorielli, N., 350
Sikes, G., 144
Silver, L. M., 448
Silverstein, K., 157
Simmons, J. L., 119

Simon, A., 197
Simon, B., 111
Simon, D. R., 144
Simons, R. L., 122
Simpson, G. E., 183
Simpson, J. C., 186
Singer, D. G., 350
Skeen, P., 256
Skill, T., 265
Skocpol, T., 297
Slavin, R. E., 201
Slomczynski, K. M., 73
Slonim, M. B., 241, 252
Small, A., 25, 26
Smedley, B. D., 283
Smeeding, T. M., 162, 164
Smelser, N. J., 427, 428, 429, 433, 434, 436
Smith, D., 216, 407
Smith, D. A., 407
Smith, H., 308
Smith, J., 294
Smith, J. B., 344
Smith, J. I., 323
Smith, K. B., 342
Smith, M. D., 122
Smith, T. W., 158, 254, 255, 318
Smitherman, G., 77, 216
Smock, P. J., 202, 250
Smole, W. J., 89
Snipp, C. M., 191, 192
Snow, D. A., 434
Snowden, L. L., 447
Solorzano, D. G., 189
Soltis, J. F., 353
Sommers-Flanagan, J., 216
Sommers-Flanagan, R., 216
Somoza, A., 380, 381
Sorokin, P., 439
Soule, S. A., 182
Southwell, P. L., 367
Sowell, T., 187, 195
Spears, R., 110
Spencer, J. W., 214
Spengler, O., 439
Spradley, J. P., 144
Stacey, J., 260, 261, 271
Stalstrom, O. W., 20, 256
Stamps, P. L., 51
Stanko, E. A., 130
Stanton, E. C., 226
Stark, R., 314, 318
Starr, P., 304
Statham, A., 382
Steeh, C., 200
Steffensmeier, D. J., 122
Stein, J. A., 128
Stein, T. S., 20
Steiner, J., 186, 187
Stepick, A., 195, 423
Stets, J. E., 262
Stevens, R., 201
Stevenson, R. W., 184
Steward, J. H., 438
Stewart, L., 215
Stief, T. M., 246
Stiglitz, J. E., 378, 379, 381
Stith, A. Y., 283

Stith, S. M., 262
Stolberg, S. G., 74, 289, 294
Stone, P., 228
Stouffer, S. A., 97
Straus, M. A., 262
Straus, R. A., 26, 32
Strauss, A., 42, 70, 108
Street, M. D., 98
Strong, B., 246, 247, 249, 255
Strouse, J. S., 265
Struthers, J. T., 95
Stryker, S., 14
Suczek, B., 108
Sugimoto, T., 170
Sullivan, T. J., 8, 26, 32, 202
Sumner, W. G., 41, 92
Suro, R., 190
Sutherland, E. H., 123
Suttles, G. D., 409
Suzuki, B. H., 252
Swaggert, J., 322
Swain, C. M., 200
Swanton, J. R., 147
Switzer, J. Y., 214
Sykes, G. M., 120
Sykes, M. P., 200
Szatmary, D. P., 361

T

Taft, P., 425
Takeuchi, D. T., 192, 193
Tal, J., 73
Tanfer, K., 254, 255
Tannen, D., 105, 214
Taormina, R. J., 96
Tasker, F., 261
Taub, R. P., 207
Tavris, C., 211
Taylor, C. S., 46
Taylor, J., 325
Taylor, P. J., 406
Taylor, R. J., 251
Teitler, J. O., 250
Temple, J. A., 165
Tenenbaum, D. R., 218
Terrell, K., 168
Thio, A., 122, 127
Thistlewaite, A., 264
Thoennes, N., 262
Thoits, P. A., 283
Thomas, C. D., 418
Thomas, D. S., 14
Thomas, G. M., 377
Thomas, P., 253
Thomas, W. I., 14
Thompson, C. A., 43
Thörn, H., 441
Thorne, B., 215
Thornton, A., 246, 249, 251
Thornton, R., 325
Thornton, R. Y., 139
Thrasher, F., 128
Thurman, M. D., 34
Thurner, A., 430
Tienda, M., 199

Tijerina, R. L., 190
Timberlake, M., 407
Timmer, A., 436
Tinbergen, N., 66
Tjaden, P., 262
Tjosvold, D., 95
Tobias, S., 224
Tobin, G. A., 207
Tobin, J. N., 288
Toch, H., 433
Toffler, A., 109
Tolbert, P. S., 95, 99, 102, 103
Tonelson, A., 376
Tönnies, F., 55, 91, 408, 409
Tootell, G. M. B., 196
Totti, X. F., 191
Treiman, D. J., 168
Trezzini, B., 155, 157, 378
Triandis, H. C., 198
Troiden, R. R., 256
Trow, M., 339
Tuchman, B. W., 273, 274
Tumin, M., 153
Turkle, S., 87
Turnbull, C. M., 36
Turner, C., 52
Turner, J., 12, 67
Turner, J. B., 125, 283
Turner, M. A., 196
Turner, R. D., 280
Turner, R. H., 429, 433
Turow, J., 353
Tyler, P. E., 315
Tyler, W. B., 340
Tylor, E. B., 36

U

Uchitelle, L., 373, 376
Ullman, E. L., 411, 412

V

Vago, S., 438
Van Ausdale, D., 207
Vanden, H. E., 441
van der Dennen, J., 66
van der Geest, H., 256
Van Gennep, A., 82
Van Horn, S. H., 213
van Ijzendoorn, M. H., 73
Van Meter, N., 344
Vannoy-Hiller, D., 257
Van Valey, T. L., 81
Van Winkle, B., 94
Vaughan, M. K., 45
Vaughan, S., 248
Veblen, T., 101
Vega, M. M., 306
Vega, W. A., 252
Velasquez, R., 128
Vélez, W., 168
Vera, H., 196
Verbrugge, L., 250, 285
Vigdor, J. L., 414
Vinovskis, M. A., 280
Volti, R., 109, 111, 406, 440

W

Waite, L., 271
Waitzkin, H., 276, 288, 304
Waldman, P., 106, 107
Waldron, I., 283
Walker, T. A., 380
Wall, D. S., 130
Wallace, A. F. C., 308
Wallace, E., 34
Wallerstein, I., 155, 390
Wallerstein, J. S., 250, 271
Wanner, R. A., 152
Washington, G., 435
Washington, J. A., 43
Waterman, A. S., 71
Watson, W., 96
Weber, M., 23, 99, 102, 103, 112, 148, 149, 150, 153, 158, 168, 312, 313, 314, 316, 362, 363, 378
Weiman, D., 144
Weinrich, J. D., 255
Weinstein, P., 182
Weisner, T. S., 215
Weissman, R., 390
Welch, S., 185
Welles, O., 431
Wellman, B., 109, 110
Wells, H. G., 431
Wells, L. E., 250
West, K. J., 322
Westermann, W. L., 187
Western, B., 144
Westervelt, S. D., 125
Whitbourne, S. K., 71
Whitcomb, G. R., 95
White, D. R., 147
White, J. R., 436
White, R. K., 95
White, S., 78
Whitehead, B. D., 246
Wholey, D., 298
Whorf, B., 42
Whyte, W. F., 94
Wichers, M., 346
Widdicombe, S., 46, 47
Wiener, C., 108
Wilkinson, B., 118
Wilkinson, L. C., 339
Williams, D. R., 283
Williams, E. G., 95
Williams, K. D., 107
Williams, R., Jr., 37
Williams, S., 96
Williams, T., 19, 423
Williams, W. L., 255
Williams, W. R., 169
Willie, C. V., 251
Wilson, B., 316
Wilson, II, C. C., 197
Wilson, F. D., 202
Wilson, G. D., 255
Wilson, G. L., 116
Wilson, K. L., 170
Wilson, R. W., 107
Wilson, T. C., 409

Wilson, W. J., 164, 182, 198, 207
Wiltfang, G. L., 170
Winford, D., 43
Winfrey, O., 197
Winkler, A. E., 219
Winograd, M., 383
Winter, J. A., 314
Wirth, L., 409
Wolbert, A., 110
Wolf, D. R., 61
Wolf, N., 236
Wolfe, A., 67
Wolff, E. N., 160, 162
Wong, K. K., 414
Wong, M. G., 192
Wong, S-K., 167
Wood, J. L., 434
Wood, J. T., 96, 236
Wooden, K., 325
Wooffitt, R., 46, 47

Wooldredge, J., 264
Woolhandler, S., 291, 297
Worchel, S., 96
Wright, E. O., 167
Wright, J. D., 164
Wright, O., 197
Wright, T. L., 255
WuDunn, S., 403
Wuthnow, R., 321
Wyche, K. F., 169
Wysong, E., 164

X

Xenos, P., 192, 193

Y

Yardley, J., 403
Yeoh, B., 118
Yinger, J. M., 183, 196

Young, G., 225
Young, T. K., 192, 283
Youngs, K. M., 376
Youniss, J., 73

Z

Zablocki, B. D., 150
Zald, M. N., 437
Zane, J. P., 230
Zebrowitz, L. A., 218
Zellner, W. W., 40, 61
Zey-Ferrell, M., 106
Zigler, E., 165
Zimbardo, P. G., 118
Zinn, M. B., 251
Zurcher, L. A., 170
Zuschlag, M. K., 71

A

Ability grouping, 339
Absolutist view of deviance, 119
Acquired Immune Deficiency Syndrome
  (AIDS), 19, 254, 277–278, 284–285
  414, 429
Adolescence, 7, 46–47, 53, 71, 82, 259–260,
  335–336
Advertising, 17–18, 52–53, 385
Affinal kin, 240
Affirmative action, 200–202, 228
Afghanistan, 315–316, 436
Africa, 284–285, 306, 360–362
African Americans,
  discrimination and prejudice against, 179,
    182, 185–189, 195–196, 200–202,
    251–252, 428–429
  drug use and, 127
  education and, 187–189, 217–218, 338,
    341–342, 345
  family and, 195–196, 251–252, 259–260
  health and, 283
  income and, 187–189, 221–222
  language and, 43
  media and, 197–198
  politics and, 267–268
  poverty and, 159–164, 188
  religion and, 323
  segregation of, 185, 200–201, 410
  socialization of, 77–78
  socioeconomic status and, 195–196
  work and, 187–188, 376
  See also Minority groups
Age, 159–164, 246, 250–251, 317, 322,
  367–368, 397
  See also Elderly
Aggregates, 93
Aggression, 66–67, 182, 211, 350, 401, 433
Agricultural societies, 7, 55–56, 91, 153–154,
  212, 279, 332–334, 360–362, 363,
  403–404
AIDS. See Acquired Immune Deficiency Syndrome
Alcohol and alcoholism, 41, 120, 127
Alianza Federal de Mercedes, 190
Alienation, 312–313, 323–324, 408–409
Altruism, 66–67
American Indian Movement, 192
American Indians,
  discrimination against, 177–178, 180, 185
  genocide of, 177–178, 185, 442
  health and, 44, 191–192, 283
  language and, 42
  media and, 197–198
  religion and, 324–325
  social structure of, 34–35, 89–90, 147,
    209–211
  stratification and, 147, 191–192,
American Medical Association, 276, 288,
  289, 291
American Revolution, 435
American Sociological Association, 24–25

Amish, 40–41
Androgyny, 231
Anglo conformity, 196, 198
Animism, 285, 307–308, 332
Anomie theory, 121–122, 124
Anticipatory socialization, 79
Apartheid, 179
Applied sociological research, 9–10
  on AIDS, 278
  on crime, 128, 263–264, 415–416
  on day care, 74
  on drugs, 128
  on economic globalization, 382
  on education, 201–202, 344
  on family issues, 74, 263–264
  on gangs, 128
  on gender, 229
  on health and health care, 278
  on language, 46–47
  on organizations, 105
  on poverty, 165
  on prejudice and discrimination,
    201–202, 229
  on religious cults, 325–326
  on riots, 428–429
  on sexual assault and harassment, 229
  on soldiers in war, 97
  on spouse abuse, 263–264
  on unemployment, 382
  on urban life, 415–416
  on workers and the workplace, 382
Applied sociology, 25–27
Arab Americans, 193–194
Argot, 46–47, 73
Asian Americans, 181, 188–189, 192–193,
  197–198, 218, 222, 252–254, 287
  See also Minority groups
Assault, 129–130
Assimilation, 185–186, 195–198
Association for Applied and Clinical
  Sociology, 25
Attitudes, 93, 180, 246
Authority,
  definition of, 150, 362
  in family, 241–242
  in organizations, 21, 97, 100–103,
    108–109, 201–202, 344
  relationships, 38–39, 426, 439
  types of, 363
Automation, 123, 373–376, 443
Aztecs, 42, 393–394, 404

B

Babylonians, 277
Banaro of New Guinea, 37
Basic sociology, 25–27
Basuto of Southern Africa, 5
Beauty, 52–53
Beliefs, 37, 350–351, 427–428,
  434–437
Bilateral descent system, 241, 243
Biological determinism, 66–67

Biological perspective, 9, 66–67, 120, 211,
  255–256
Birthrate, 257–260, 279, 395–400, 403
Black Americans. See African Americans
Black English, 43
Blended family. See Reconstituted family
Bonerate, 3–5
Bourgeoisie, 153
Branch Davidians, 316, 325–326
Brazil, 157, 177–178, 185, 332, 335
Brideservice, 243
Bridewealth, 243
Britain, 184–185
Bubonic plague, 273–274
Buddhism, 39, 253, 308, 310, 312,
  315, 323, 334
Bureaucracy, 90, 99–102, 106–109, 324,
  339–340
Burnout, 51–52
Busing, school, 202, 345

C

Calvinism, 210–211, 313–314
Canada, 198, 298–299
Capitalism, 368–369
  cities and, 412–414
  corporate, 337–338, 372–373, 376–377
  crime and, 153
  education and, 334–338
  the family and, 245
  the health field and, 289–292, 297–299
  mass media and, 350–354, 385
  popular culture and, 350
  population and, 398–399
  poverty and, 153
  religion and, 313–314
  stratification and, 153–158
  welfare, 369
  women and, 225–226, 334–335
  the world system and, 155–158, 184–185,
    334–335, 440–444
Capitalist world system, 184–185, 210–211,
  225–226, 306, 377–382, 407, 412–414
  See also World system theory
Career deviance. See Secondary deviance
Carrying capacity, 416
Caste stratification system, 151, 211, 310, 313
Causality, 8–9
Cell phones, 77
Cesarean births, 296
Charisma, 316, 324–326, 363
Charter schools, 342
Chicano movement, 190
Child abuse, 262–263
Child care. See Day care
Childlessness, 256–257
Children,
  child rearing, 67–77, 443
  divorce and, 250–251
  education and, 201–202, 332, 335–339,
    342–346
  and the family, 53, 71–77, 260–261

mass media and, 350–351
poverty, 157, 161–165
in single-parent families, 74
China, 107, 310–311, 315–316, 403
Chinese Americans, 192–194
Chinese medicine, 252, 286
Christianity, 39, 210, 309, 311–314,
317–319, 325–326, 332
Christian Reconstructionism, 315–316
Church, 314
Circular reaction, 433
Cities,
crime and, 411, 415–416
decentralization of, 404–406, 411–415
the economy and, 412–415
global perspective on, 406–408, 412
growth of, 404–406, 411–415
health in, 274
mass media and technology and, 406
in postindustrial societies, 404–408
poverty and, 407–408, 412–414
in preindustrial societies, 393–395,
403–404, 406–408
socioeconomic status and, 411–412
sociological perspectives on, 408–412
Civic involvement, 108–111
Civil Rights Act of 1964, 185, 188, 227
Civil rights movement, 186, 188, 200
Class conflict, 13, 106, 153, 364, 439
Class consciousness, 153, 313
Class stratification systems, 152
Clayton Act of 1914, 369
Climate change, 417–418
Clinical sociology, 26–27
Closed stratification systems, 150–151
Cocaine, 19, 127
Cohabitation, 134, 254–255, 258
Cohesion, 97, 102–103, 371
Collective behavior, 426–427
Collectivism, 38, 107, 253–254,
360–361, 369–370
Colleges. See Universities and colleges
Colonialism, 333–335, 353–354,
380–381, 442
Comanche Indians, 34–35, 324–325
Commodification, 39, 77, 346–347, 379, 385
Common sense, 9–10
Communication, 42–43, 52–53, 78, 110–111,
351, 429–430, 433–434, 436
Communism, 153, 184–185, 370
Community, 3–5, 35, 38, 40–41, 89–90,
110–111, 360–361, 395, 403, 408–409,
322–323
Compadrazgo, 241
Comparable worth, 228
Competition,
economic, 213, 360–361, 368–369,
375–377, 407, 428–429
education and, 342, 345–346
gender and, 213
in the health field, 289–292, 297–299
prejudice and discrimination and, 180–181
and social unrest, 428–429
Computer-mediated communication, 17–18,
52–53, 110–111, 169–170, 289, 322–323,
406, 436, 352, 383
See also Mass media

Computers, 52–53, 110–111, 130–131,
346, 349
Concentric-zone theory, 411–412
Confidentiality, 23–25
Conflict, 91, 106, 180–181, 196–198
Conflict perspective, 13–14, 17–18
on concentration of power, 370–372
on crime and deviance, 122–123
on discrimination and prejudice, 180–181
on education, 337–338
on the family, 245–246
on gender, 213–214
on health and health care, 275–276
on the mass media, 17–18
on organizations, 106–107
on politics and the economy, 364, 370–372
on population, 398–399
on poverty, 153
on religion, 312–313
on social change, 14–16, 439
on socialization, 82–83, 337–338
on social stratification, 153, 439
Conformity, 94–95, 97–98, 103–105, 121,
134–135, 181, 312, 432–434
Confucianism, 39, 139, 253, 308, 310–311,
315, 378
Conglomerates, 373
Congo, 284–285
Consanguineal kin, 240–241
Consumerism, 39
Contact, 201–202
Contagion, 433–434
Contraception, 254–255
Control group, 20–21
Control theory of delinquency, 11
Convergence, 433–434, 442–443
Conversational styles, 214
Corporate crime, 125
Corporations, 290–293, 297–299, 337–338,
345–346, 351–354, 372–373, 375–377,
412–413,
Correctional officers, 51, 54
Credentials race, 337–338
Crime,
biological perspective on, 9, 67, 120
cities and, 411, 415–416
costs of, 132–134
crowding and, 401
culture and, 120–122, 139
cyber, 130–131
definition of, 126
economic conditions and, 20–21,
120–122, 139
extent of, 126–132, 135–138
fear of, 129–130, 133
global perspective on, 118–119, 122–123,
130, 139
industrialization and, 121–122
in Japan, 139
mass media and, 125–126
measurement of, 122–123, 135–138
psychological approaches on, 120
social constructionist approach,
125–126
sociological perspectives on, 121–124
solutions to, 20–21, 130–131, 136–139,
415–416

types of, 126–131, 135–136, 263–264
victims of, 125–126
See also Deviance, Delinquency
Criminal justice system, 125–126, 136–139,
252, 263–264
Crisis medicine, 280–282
Cross-cultural perspective, 6–7, 240–243,
285–287
Crowding, 401
Crowds, 429, 431–434
Cuban Americans, 189–190, 195, 252
See also Hispanic Americans; Minority
groups
Cults, 316, 323–326
Cultural change, 44, 324–325, 332–335,
440–441
Cultural colonialism, 332–335, 353–354
Cultural determinism, 64–66
Cultural diversity, 5–8, 24, 37–39, 43–47,
56–57, 91, 308–312, 321–326, 346
Cultural globalization, 56–57
Cultural integration, 43–44
Cultural relativity, 45, 47, 346
Cultural transmission theories, 123–125
Culture,
components of, 36–43, 72–73, 350–351
crime and, 120–122, 139
definition of, 36
deviance and crime and, 120–122
family and, 240–243
global, 56–57
ideal versus real, 44–45
Internet and, 110–111
language and, 42–43, 46–47
mass media and, 52–53, 349–351
material versus nonmaterial, 36, 57
online, 110–111
in organizations, 105
popular, 350–351
transmission of, 52–53, 72–73, 335
values and, 4–5, 37–39, 52–53, 64–66, 78,
104–106, 119, 139, 152, 154, 195,
353–354, 377–378, 385, 398–399,
402–403
Curanderas, 287
Curative medicine. See Crisis medicine
Cybercrime, 130–131
Cyber world. See Online world
Cyclical theories of social change,
439–440

D

Dahomeans of western Africa, 308
Day care, 51–53, 74, 443
Death. See Infant mortality; Mortality
Decision making, 96–97, 433–434
Defensible space, 415–416
Definition of the situation, 14–15, 17–18,
429–430
Delinquency, 11, 128, 250
Democracy, 108–109, 337, 365–368,
379–381, 383, 385
Democratic socialist economies, 370
Demographic gap, 399
Demographic processes, 395–396
Demographic transition, 398–401
Demography, 395

Denominations, 314, 316
Dependency theory, 155
See also World-system theory
Dependent variable, 11, 20–21
Deprivation, 324–326, 434–437
See also Poverty; Relative deprivation
Descent, rules of, 240–241
Desegregation, school, 345
Developing nations, 157–158, 333–335,
406–408, 440–442
Deviance,
consequences for society, 132–134
definition of, 119, 126–127
extent of, 126–132
functions versus dysfunctions of, 132–134
illness as, 275
industrialization and, 121–122
mass media and, 125–126
nonsociological perspectives on, 120
relative nature of, 119
social control and, 134–135
sociological perspectives on, 121–124
types of, 121–124, 126–131
See also Crime; Violence
Dictatorship, 365
Differential association theory, 123–124
Diffusion, 44, 311–312
Disasters, 430–431
Discrimination,
consequences of, 182–183, 428–429, 433
definition of, 180
forms of, 183–186
institutionalized, 181–182, 200
against men, 223
programs to combat, 200–202
race-based, 163–165, 177–178, 184–185,
198–200, 251–252
reverse, 200
sources of, 180–182
against women, 217–222, 294–296
Disease, 274–278, 279–283
See also Mental illness
Diversity, 5–8, 24, 38–41, 43–47, 56–57,
308–311, 321–326
Division of labor, 100–103, 212–213, 314,
319–320, 438–439
Divorce, 246–249, 250–251, 258–260,
264–266
Doctors. *See* Physicians
Domestic violence. *See* Child abuse;
Spouse abuse
Dowries, 243
Dramaturgical analogy of social
interaction, 50
Drugs and drug abuse, 6, 19, 41, 127–128,
130, 139, 252, 277–278, 414
Dual-earner family, 256–257

E

Ebonics, 43
Ecclesia, 314, 321
Ecology. *See* Human ecology; Urban ecology
Economic development, 332–335, 365, 378,
402–403
See also Modernization
Economic discrimination, 217–221
Economic globalization, 377–379

Economics, 152–153, 362
See also Capitalism; Mixed economies;
Socialism
Economy, 362
cities and, 412–415
crime and, 121–123, 136–139
in developing nations, 406–408
discrimination and, 180–181, 184–185,
192–193, 200
global perspective on, 373, 375–382,
406–408
in industrial societies, 109, 379–382
mass media and, 385
of Mexico, 45, 408
in postindustrial society, 109, 167–168,
442–443
poverty and, 163–165, 406–408
in preindustrial societies, 360–362
religion and, 313–314
social mobility and, 167–168
sociological perspectives on,
12–13, 364
types of, 360–361, 368–370
in the United States, 372–377
women and, 45, 251–253
Ecosystem, 416–418
Ecumenical movement, 321
Education,
bureaucracies in, 339–340
children and, 165, 332, 335–336,
342–346, 442
colonialism and, 332–335
crime and, 136–139
definition of, 332
distance, 352
family and, 243–244, 260, 402–403
gender and, 294–295, 335
global perspective on, 224, 332–335, 348
income and, 336–338
mass media and, 169–170, 350–352
medical, 280–282, 294–295
minorities and, 187–196, 200–202,
217–218, 338, 345
modernization and industrialization and,
333–335, 339, 402–403, 440, 442
online, 352
politics and, 367–368
in preindustrial societies, 332–334
religion and, 318–319, 322, 332–333, 339,
377–378
social inequality and, 165, 294–295,
337–338
socialization and, 78–80, 332–334,
335–339
social stratification and, 165, 168–170, 332,
336–338
sociological perspectives on, 12–13,
335–339
technology and, 345–346, 352
in the United States, 339–347
and women, 79–81, 215–218, 224,
294–295, 335, 402–403
Egalitarian family, 224–226
Elderly,
abuse of, 263
health and health care and, 293, 296–297
politics and, 367–368

poverty and, 161–164, 222
religion and, 317, 322
in Samoa, 64–65
treatment of, 82–83
Electronic world. *See* Online world
Emergent norms, 433–434
Employment, 217–219, 224–226
See also Work; Unemployment
Empowerment, 8, 229, 376, 414
Endogamy, 241
Energy consumption, 417
Enron Corporation, 131
Environmental movement, 371, 434
Environmental problems,
extent of, 417–418
population and, 416, 418
social sources of, 416
solutions to, 418
technology and, 416
Equality, 38, 44–45
Equal Rights Amendment (ERA), 227
Eskimos. *See* Inuit
Estate stratification systems, 151
Ethics in research, 23–25
Ethnic conflict, 184–187, 196–200, 315,
425–426
Ethnicity, 128, 130, 179, 184–185, 197–198,
287, 367–368, 409, 439
Ethnocentrism, 45–47, 179–180, 182,
184–185
European Union (EU), 379
Evangelicalism, 321–322
Evolutionary theories, 153–154, 438,
442–443
Exchange relationship, 246, 368
Exogamy, 241
Experience, 9–10
Experimental group, 20–21
Experimenter effects, 21
Experiments, 20–21, 263–264, 428
Expressive roles. *See* Socioemotional roles
Extended family, 242–244, 253–254

F

Fads, 430–431
Family,
crime and deviance and, 120–122, 139
definition of, 240
in developing nations, 225–226, 408
education and, 243–244, 260
female headed, 72–74, 162–164, 221, 239,
251–253
future of, 264–266
gay, 260–261
gender and, 45, 80–81, 215, 218–219,
225–226, 252–253
global perspective on, 225–226, 253–254,
262, 408
health and, 51–54, 283–285
industrialization and, 45, 212–213,
242–244, 440–443
in Israel, 73
in Japan, 38–39, 139, 195
mass media and, 17–18, 265–266
minority groups and, 195, 251–254,
259–260
poverty and, 220–221, 406–408

in preindustrial societies, 64–65, 209–211, 239, 243–244
religion and, 252–254, 309, 317, 323
size of, 242–245, 402–403
socialization and, 72–78, 243–244, 260–261, 265–266
sociological perspectives on, 12–13, 243–246
types of, 36–37, 45, 240–243, 256–261
Vietnamese, 253–254
violence in, 262–264
Family planning, 402–403
Fashions, 430–431
Fecundity, 395
Federal Housing Administration (FHA), 404–405
Feminist movement, 255, 434
Fertility, 167–168, 395–398
Field experiments, 20–21, 428
Folkways, 39–41
Food shortages, 401
Formal organizations,
applied sociological research on, 105
bureaucracy and, 90, 99–101
culture in, 105, 107
definition of, 99
in education, 339–340, 344
gender in, 104
human relations approach to, 102–103
informal structure in, 103–104, 108
mass media and, 110–111
oligarchy in, 108–109
in religion, 314, 316
social loafing in, 107
sociological perspectives on, 106–108
types of, 99, 109
Free enterprise zones. See Urban free enterprise zones
Friendship, 91
Frustration, 182, 433–435
Functionalist perspective, 12–13, 16–18
of crime and deviance, 121–122, 132–134
of discrimination and prejudice, 180, 183
of education, 12–13, 335–336
of family, 12–13, 243–244, 248
of gender, 212–213
of health and health care, 274–275
on mass media, 17–18, 76–77
of organizations, 106
of politics and the economy, 12–13, 364, 385
of population, 398–399
of poverty, 163–164
of religion, 312
of social change, 12–13, 16, 438–439
of socialization, 82
of stratification, 152
of technology, 17–18
of urban growth, 405
Fundamentalism, 321–322

G

Game stage of socialization, 70
Gangs, 19, 94, 127–128, 130
Gay family, 260–261, 266
Gemeinschaft, 55–56
Gender,

biological perspective on, 211
definition of, 214, 231
education and, 215–219, 335
employment and, 217–221
family and, 218–219, 225–226, 253–254, 402–403
group leadership and, 96
in groups and organizations, 96–97, 104
health and health care and, 283, 288–290, 294–296
income and, 219–222
industrialization and, 212–213, 440, 442–443
the mass media and, 216–217, 350–351
politics and, 230–231, 367–368
in preindustrial societies, 209–210
religion and, 309, 313, 322
sexual behavior and, 254–256
socialization and, 69, 80–81, 214–217, 229, 288–290
sociological perspectives on, 212–214
stereotypes of, 223
See also Gender inequality; Women
Gender identity, 215–217
Gender inequality,
extent of, 151, 217–223
family violence and, 262–264
global perspective on, 209–210, 224–227
in the health care system, 288–290, 294–296
in the legal system, 223, 227–228
against males, 223
programs to reduce, 227–231
religion and, 210, 313
sources of, 211–214
Generalized other, 70
Genocide, 183–184
Gentrification, 414–415
Germany, 97, 179, 184–185
Geronticide, 119
Gesellschaft, 56
Ghost Dance Movement, 325
Globalization, 7, 56–57, 289, 377–379, 440–441
See also Global perspective
Globalized crime, 130
Global perspective, 6–8
on cities, 406–408, 412–413
on crime, 118–119, 123, 130–131, 139
on culture, 56–57, 440–441
on the economy, 56–57, 373, 375–382, 440–444
on education, 332–335, 348
on the family, 209–210, 224–227, 262
on gender stratification, 224–227
on health and health care, 273–274, 280–282, 284–285, 298–299
on the mass media, 349, 353–354, 440
on modernization, 56–57, 440–444
on politics, 375–382
on postindustrial society, 56–57
on poverty, 162–164
on racial discrimination and conflict, 184–185
on religion, 306–312, 315–316
on social stratification, 155–158, 167–168, 375–382

on work and labor, 107, 225–226, 375–377, 442–444
Global warming, 417–418
Government, 363–368, 370–372, 412–414
See also Democracy; Oligarchy; Totalitarianism
Greenhouse effect, 418
Group polarization, 96
Groups,
boundary maintenance in, 46–47, 92, 151–152
cohesion in, 97, 102–103
conformity in, 39–41, 94–95, 97–98, 103–105
cultural variation in, 91, 107
decision making in, 96–97, 105, 433–434
definition of, 54, 90
functions of, 90–93
gender in, 96, 97
leadership in, 95–98, 104, 107
productivity in, 95, 101–102
structure and process, 93–98
technology and, 110–111
types of, 90–93
Groupthink, 98, 105
Gulf War. See Persian Gulf War

H

Hawthorne effect, 22–23
Head Start, 165, 202, 343–345
Health,
divorce and, 250
family and, 283–285
gender and, 51–54, 283
global perspective on, 273–274, 280–282, 284–285, 298–299
lifestyle and, 273–274, 277–282, 283–285
race and, 190, 283
religion and, 274, 276–277, 285
social structure and, 51–54, 287–292
societal development and, 274, 279–282
socioeconomic status and, 168–170, 282–283
sociological perspectives on, 274–277
Health care,
access to, 293–294, 298–299
corporatization of, 290–292, 297–298
cost of, 290–293, 296–298
crosscultural perspective on, 285–287, 298–299
financing, 292–293, 296–298
gender in, 288–289, 294–296
global perspective on, 289, 298–299
media and technology and, 289
minorities and, 283
quality of, 290–291, 294, 298–299
right vs. privilege, 298
seeking, 287
social structure of, 287–292
socioeconomic status and, 275, 282–283, 287
sociological perspectives on, 274–277
Health insurance, 291–293, 296–298
Health maintenance organizations (HMOs), 297–298
Heaven's Gate religion, 316, 325–326
Heredity and the environment, 66–68
Heroin, 127

Hidden curriculum, 337
Hinduism, 151, 310–312, 313, 323
Hispanic Americans, 189–191
  crime and, 130, 193
  education and, 189–191, 217–218,
    341–342, 345
  family and, 252
  health and, 190
  income and, 189–191, 221–222
  media and, 197–198
  politics and, 367–368
  poverty and, 161–164, 189–191
  work and, 376
  See also Minority groups
Holistic medicine, 286–287
Homelessness, 169-
Homicide, 129–130, 136–139
Homogamy, 246
Homosexuality,
  AIDS and, 277–278
  causes of, 67, 255–256
  as deviance, 119
  families and, 260–261
  incidence of, 255–256
  life span of, 81
  mass media and, 266
  research on, 20, 23, 25
Hopi Indians, 42
Horticultural societies, 55–56, 89–90, 91,
  153–154, 209–210, 363, 393–395
Hospitals, 290–291
Human ecology, 395, 403, 416
Human relations approach, 102–103, 106
Hunting and gathering societies, 54–55,
  89–91, 147, 153–154, 212–213, 247,
  279, 285, 363, 403–404
Huron Indians, 209–210, 242, 275
Hypotheses, 11–12
Hysterectomies, 296

I

Ideal type, 100
Illiteracy, 224, 334–335, 339, 349
Illness. See Disease; Health; Mental illness
Immigrants, 187, 194–198, 253–254
Immigration, 184–185, 192–196, 323, 396
Impression management, 50–51
Incas, 395
Incest, 241
Income, 148–149
  distribution of, 136, 139, 160–164, 288,
    290, 375–377
  education and, 336–338,
  gender and, 219–222
  Internet access and, 169
  politics and, 367–368
  by race and ethnicity, 188–194, 198
  religion and, 318–319, 322
Independent variable, 11, 20–21
India, 151, 310, 313, 334
Indian Citizenship Act, 191
Indian Civil Rights Act, 191
Indians of the Americas, 177–178, 209–210,
  332, 335
  See also American Indians
Individualism, 4–5, 24, 34–35, 37–41,
  52–53, 71–73, 91, 107, 118–119, 139

Industrialization,
  cities and, 403–408
  crime and, 121–123
  democracy and, 365–366
  education and, 333–335, 339
  the family and, 45, 242–244
  gender and, 212–213
  health and, 279–283
  population growth and, 397–401
  preindustrialized society compared with,
    54–56, 82, 91, 121–123, 212–213,
    332–335, 397–401, 403–408
  social change and, 44–45, 425–426,
    440–444
  social stratification and, 79–83, 153–155,
    377–382
  social structure and, 7, 39, 55–57
Inequality. See Social inequality
Infanticide, 279, 403
Infant mortality, 279–282, 396
Informed consent, 23–25
In-group, 92
Innovation, 44, 121
Instincts, 66–67
Institutionalized racism, 181–182, 200
Instrumental roles. See Task roles
Integration, 43–44, 200–202, 345
Interactionist perspective, 14–18
  on collective behavior, 429–430
  on crime and deviance, 123–126
  on education, 338–339
  on gender, 214
  on groups and organizations, 91, 108
  on health and health care, 276–277
  on mass media, 17–18, 383–385
  on political and economic institutions,
    383–385
  on social change, 13–16
  on socialization, 68–71, 79–80
  on technology, 18
Interest groups, 13
Internal colonialism, 181
Internalization, 41
International Governmental Organization
  (IGO), 379
International Monetary Fund (IMF), 157,
  378–382
Internet, 17–18, 52–53, 110–111, 130–131,
  169–170, 216–217, 289, 322–323, 346,
  349, 352, 436
Interviews, 19–20
Inuit, 42, 119, 185, 192
Invasion, 410
Iran, 315–316
Iraq, 436
Iraq War, 222, 384
Irish Republican Army, 186
Islam, 185, 186, 194, 226, 309, 314,
  315–316, 323, 436
Isolation, 67–68, 322–324, 325–326,
  408–410, 428–429
Israel, 73, 181, 436

J

Japan,
  child rearing in, 78
  crime in, 139

  education in, 348
  family in, 38–39, 78, 139
  friendship in, 91
  values in, 38–39, 78
  wealth in, 377
Japanese Americans, 192–193, 195, 252
  See also Minority groups
Java, 42–43
Jesuit missionaries, 178, 210, 332–334
Judaism, 39, 308–309, 311, 313, 314,
  318–319, 323

K

Kapauku Papuans of New Guinea, 44, 135
Kibbutz, 73
Kinship, 209–210, 240–242, 251–254,
  334–335, 440, 442–443
  See also Family
Knowledge, 9–10, 443
Korean Americans, 193, 195
Korean War, 104
Ku Klux Klan, 179
Kyoto Protocol, 418

L

Labeling, 15, 123–124, 128–129, 255–256,
  338–339
Labor. See Unions; Work
Labor force, 373–377, 402, 443–444
Laboratory experiment, 21
Language,
  Black English, 43
  culture and, 36–37, 42–43, 46–47, 57
  gender and, 214
  group identity and, 46–47, 198
  learning in childhood, 78
  subcultures and, 46–47
Latinismo, 191
Latinos. See Hispanic Americans
Latuka of Sudan, 79
Law, 41, 227–228, 363
Leadership, 95–96, 97, 107, 214, 344, 365,
  428, 434–436
League of United Latin American
  Citizens, 191
Legitimacy, 183, 196, 312, 362–363,
  365–366, 438–439
Lesbians. See Homosexuality
Life cycle, 79–81, 312
Life expectancy, 212–213, 279–284, 396–397
Lifespan. See Life cycle
Lifestyles, 279–282, 283–285
Linquistic relativity hypothesis, 42
Literacy. See Illiteracy
Looking-glass self, 69–70, 123–124, 256
Lynchings, 182

M

Machismo, 19, 45
Macrosociology, 12, 415
Mafia, 130
Magnet schools, 342
Managed care. See Health maintenance
  organizations
Mangaia, sexuality in, 126–127
Maquiladoras, 225, 375, 407

Marijuana, 41, 127
Market economic systems, 368
Marriage, 151, 229–230, 241–245, 246–250, 317
    See also Family
Masculinity, 223, 231
Mass behavior, 430–431
Mass media, 17–18
    cities and, 406
    control of, 169–170, 351–353, 383–386
    crime and deviance and, 125–126
    culture and, 52–53, 353–354
    education and, 347–350, 352
    effects of, 350–351
    emergence of, 349
    family and, 265–266
    gays and, 266
    gender and, 216–217, 350–351
    global perspective on, 349, 353–354
    and groups and organizations, 110–111
    health and health care and, 289
    minorities and, 197–198
    modernization and, 440–441
    and political and economic institutions, 17–18, 351–354, 373, 383–385
    population control and, 402
    religion and, 322–322
    social change and, 351–354
    socialization and, 76–77, 216–217
    social stratification and, 169–170
    sociological perspectives on, 17–18
    violence and, 52, 76–77
Materialism, 37–41, 52–53, 152
Mate selection, 242–243, 246
Matriarchal family, 242
Matrilineal descent system, 210, 239, 241, 260
Matrilocal family, 210, 239, 242, 243
Maya Indians, 395
Media. See Mass media
Medicaid, 283, 291, 293, 296–297, 413
Medical care. See Health care
Medical-industrial complex, 291
Medicare, 283, 291, 293, 296–297
Melting pot, 196–197
Men, 223
    See also Gender inequality; Women
Mental illness, 120, 126, 128–129, 168
Mexican American Political Alliance, 190–191
Mexican Americans, 287
    See also Hispanic Americans; Minority groups
Mexico, 45, 225–226, 393–395, 408
Microsociology, 12
Migration, 396
Military, 222–223, 370–372, 384
Military-industrial complex, 291, 371–372
Millenarian religion, 324–325
Milling, 433
Minority groups,
    definition of, 178–179
    discrimination against, 198–200
    domination of, 183–186
    education and, 338, 341–342, 345
    family and, 251–254, 259–260
    health and, 283

income and, 219–222
    mass media and, 197–198, 216–217
    politics and, 428–429
    reactions to domination, 186, 428–429, 440–441
    religion and, 253–254
    self concept and, 182
    socioeconomic status and, 376
    in the United States, 34–35, 187–194
    women as, 217
    See also Race; Racism; and specific minority group
Mixed economies, 370, 377
Mobility. See Social mobility
Mobilization. See Resource mobilization
Modernization, 334–335, 415, 440–444
    See also Industrialization
Modified extended family, 242–244
Monogamy, 241, 243–244, 247–249, 260–261
Monopoly, 351, 352, 369, 371–373
Mores, 41
Mortality, 278–283, 395–396, 398–400
    See also Infant mortality
Multinational corporations, 225–226, 373
Multiple-nuclei theory, 411–412
Murder. See Homicide
Murngin of Australia, 119
Music, 52–53, 76–77, 216, 265–266
Muslims. See Islam
Mzab of Algeria, 135

N

Natchez Indians, 147, 185
National Council of La Raza, 191
National Organization for Women (NOW), 227
Nation building, 334–335, 353–354
Nation of Islam, 323
Native Americans. See American Indians; Minority groups
Naturalistic health-care systems, 285–286
Natural resources, 401, 417
Natural sciences, 10
Nazis, 97, 179, 180, 183, 184, 201
Negotiated order, 108
Neolocal family, 242–243
Newspapers, 349, 351
Nicaragua, 380–381, 407
Nongovernmental organizations (NGOs), 227, 377, 381–382
Norms, 14–16, 39–41, 72, 78, 126–129, 134–135, 181, 433–434
    See also Deviance
North American Free Trade Agreement (NAFTA), 378, 443
Nuclear family, 73, 242–245, 256
Nurses and nurse practitioners, 51–52, 290, 294–296
Nurture vs. nature issue, 66–68

O

Objectivity. See Scientific objectivity
Observation, 8–9
Observational techniques, 16, 18–19, 23–25

Occupation, 148–149, 158–159, 318, 337–338
    See also Employment; Socioeconomic status
Occupational structure, 167–168, 373–375
Oligarchy, 108–109, 365
Oligopoly, 373
One-parent families. See Single-parent families
Online world, 17–18, 46–47, 52–53, 76–77, 110–111, 130–131, 169–170, 216–217, 289, 322–323, 349, 352, 382–385
Open stratification systems, 150–152
Organizational culture, 105
Organizational diagnosis, 105, 344
Organizations. See Formal organizations
Organized crime, 130, 139
Out-group, 92

P

Palimony, 258
Panics, 427, 430–431
Parkinson's Law, 101
Participant observation research, 19, 23–25, 94
Parties, 150
Pastoral societies, 55, 363, 393
Patriarchal family, 45, 225–226, 241–245, 253–254, 309, 442
Patrilineal descent system, 241, 309
Patrilocal family, 242–243
Peer group, 73
People's Temple, 325–326
Persian Gulf War, 222, 384
Personalistic health-care systems, 285–
Personality, 49–50, 64–65, 67–68, 77–78, 91, 120, 211
    See also Self-concept
Peter Principle, 101
Peyote Cult, 324–325
Physicians and physician's assistants, 282, 286, 288–290, 292–293, 298
Play stage of socialization, 70
Plessey v. Ferguson, 187–188
Pluralism, 186, 196–198, 321–326
Pluralistic family, 264–265
Pluralist model of power, 371–372
Police, 125–126, 181, 263–264, 428–429
Political attitudes, 93
Political globalization, 377–379
Political participation, 366–368
    See also Voting
Political systems. See Democracy; Oligarchy; Politics; Totalitarianism
Politics,
    defined, 362
    democracy and, 365–368
    gender and, 224, 230–231
    global perspective on, 377–382
    health care and, 277
    mass media and, 382–385
    minorities and, 367–368, 428–429
    religion and, 318–319, 322, 368
    socioeconomic status and, 367–368
    sociological perspectives on, 364, 383
    See also Power
Polyandry, 241
Polygamy, 241, 309

Polygyny, 44, 241
Popular culture, 350
Population,
    age and sex composition of, 397
    controlling growth of, 402–403
    definition of, 395
    environmental problems and, 416–418
    gender and, 402–403
    global perspective on, 403
    growth of, 397–403
    mass media and, 402
    overpopulation, 399–401
    sociological perspectives on, 398–399
    See also Demography
Population change. See Birth rate; Fertility;
        Migration; Mortality
Postindustrial society, 56–57, 109–111,
        164–165, 349, 373–376, 406–408,
        442–444
Poverty,
    causes of, 163–165
    crime and, 121–123, 136–139, 401
    in developing nations, 408
    the economy and, 408
    extent of, 159–163
    family violence and, 262–263
    feminization of, 221
    global perspective on, 157, 162–164,
        406–408
    health and health care and, 168, 170, 296
    media portrayal of, 169
    minorities and, 161–165, 188–193,
        195–196
    sociological perspectives on, 152–155
Power,
    concentration of, 153–154, 351–353, 365,
        370–372, 377–382
    defined, 150, 362
    in family, 210–211, 241–242, 262–263
    in health care, 275
    sharing, 186–187
Power elite model, 351–353, 370–371,
        383–385
Preindustrial societies, 54–56, 210, 212–213,
        279–282, 332–335, 397–401, 406–408
Prejudice, 179–181, 201–202
    See also Discrimination
Prestige, 149–150, 158–159, 288
Preventive medicine, 280–282
Primary deviance, 125
Primary groups, 90–92, 97, 102–103, 124,
        323, 408–409
Primary socialization, 77–79
Prisons and prisoners, 20–21, 46–47, 51–52,
        54, 83
Privacy, 23–25
Privatization of services, 111, 290–291,
        345–347, 352–354, 414
Profane, 307
Professional organization, 109
Professions, 288
Profit making, 125, 155, 275, 290–291,
        313–314, 361–362, 368–369, 373,
        398–399
Program evaluation, 165
Progress, 37–38, 438
Proletariat, 153

Propaganda, 383–385
Property crimes, 135–136
Prostitution, 127, 130, 278, 284
Protest. See Social protest
Protestant ethic, 313–314, 377–378
Protestantism, 274, 309, 313–314, 321
Psychological approaches, 120, 255–256
Puberty rites, 82
Puerto Rican Americans, 189–190, 260
    See also Hispanic Americans; Minority
        groups
Puerto Rican Organization for Political
        Action, 191

Q
Qaeda, Al, 315–316, 436
Questionnaires, 19–20

R
Race,
    crime and, 139
    definition of, 179
    discrimination and, 151, 177–178,
        180–181, 183–187
    health and, 283, 287
    income and, 160–164, 188–193
    marriage and, 151, 241, 246, 249, 251–253
    media and, 197–198
    mobility and, 167
    politics and, 367–368
    See also Minority groups
Race-class controversy, 198–200
Racism, 24, 164–165, 179–182, 192–193,
        198–200, 251–253, 428–429
Rape, 127, 129–130, 135–136, 223, 229
Rationalization, 100
Reactivity, 22–23
Rebellion, 121–122, 186, 315
Recidivism, 20–21
Reconstituted family, 242–243
Reference groups, 93, 171
Relationship-oriented roles. See
        Socioemotional roles
Relative deprivation, 325, 428–429, 434–435
Relativity of deviance, 119, 124
Religion,
    Amish, 40–41
    civil, 321
    and collective violence, 436
    crime and deviance and, 120–122, 139
    definition of, 307
    education and, 332–334, 339, 342–343
    family and, 253–254, 309, 323
    gender and, 309, 313, 323
    global view of, 306–312, 315–316
    health and, 274, 276–277, 285
    in India, 151, 310, 313
    marriage and, 246, 249, 317
    mass media and, 322–323
    organization of, 314, 316, 323–326
    politics and, 318–319, 322, 368
    science and technology and, 319–321,
        322–323
    and sexual behavior, 254–255
    social and cultural change and, 313–314,
        315–316, 323–326

    and social stratification, 151, 312–313
    socioeconomic status and, 318–319, 322
    sociological perspectives on, 312–314
    types of, 307–312, 323–326
    values and, 38–41
    in Vietnam, 253–254
Religions of the way, 308, 310–311
Religiosity, 317–318
Replication, 8
Research, 11, 16–25
    See also Science
Research methods, 16–22
Resocialization, 79, 83
Resource mobilization, 429, 433, 432–433,
        434–437
Retirement, 223
Retreatism, 121–122
Revolution, 315–316, 380–381
Riots, 193, 202, 427–429
Rising expectations, 434–437
Risky shift in groups, 96
Rites of passage, 82, 312
Ritualism, 121–122
Robbery, 129–130
Role, 49–54, 94–95, 128–129, 275, 344,
        433–434
Role conflict, 51–54
Role expectations, 49–51
Role performance, 49–51
Role set, 49–50
Role strain, 51–54, 81, 344
Role-taking, 50–51, 70
Rumor, 429–430

S
Sacred, 307
Samoa, 64–65
Sampling, 20
Sanctions, 39–41, 134–135
Sandinist Front of National Liberation
        (FSLN), 381
Santeria, 306,
Sapir-Whorf hypothesis, 42
Scapegoating, 182
Schizophrenia, 119, 128–129
School busing, 202
Schooling, Home, 345–346, 352
School integration. See Desegregation
Schools,
    as bureaucracies, 339–340
    drop outs, 250, 341–342
    effectiveness of, 341–346, 348
    gender and, 215–216
    integration of, 202, 345
    privatization of, 345–347, 352–354
    reforms in, 342–346
    social inequality and, 152–153, 337–338
    socialization in, 73–75, 215–216,
        335–339
    See also Education
Science, 8–11, 16–22, 319–321
Scientific health care system, 286
Scientific objectivity, 8–9, 23–24
Secondary deviance, 124, 128–129
Secondary groups, 91–92, 323, 408–410, 443
Sect, 314, 316, 323–325
Sector theory, 411–412

Secularization, 319–321, 324

Segregation, 185–187, 200–202, 338, 344–345, 410

Self-concept, 68–71, 77, 91, 124, 134–135, 182, 255–256

Self-esteem, 170–171, 182, 214, 216

Self-fulfilling prophecy, 96, 124, 128–129, 339

Separatism, 186, 198, 315

Sex, definition of, 214
See also Gender; Men; Women

Sexism, 211–214

Sex ratio, 397, 403

Sexual assault. See Rape

Sexual behavior, 126–127, 209–211, 239, 243, 251, 254–256, 277–278

Sexual deviance, 126–127

Sexual harassment, 229

Sexual identity. See Gender identity

Sexual inequality. See Gender inequality; Women

Sherman Antitrust Act of 1890, 369

Shintoism, 39, 312

Sick role, 275, 287

Significant others, 70

Significant symbol, 70

Singapore, 118–119

Singlehood, 257

Single-parent families, 162–164, 221, 224–226, 250–251, 258–260, 265–266, 341

Skinheads, 179, 184

Slang. See Argot

Slavery, 178, 180–181, 185, 186, 187, 195–196, 251–252, 306, 323, 442

Social category, 93

Social change,
culture and, 44–45, 332–335
definition of, 437–438
deviance and, 134
media and, 350–354
modernization and, 334–335, 425–426, 440–444
religion and, 313–314, 315–316, 323–326
schools and, 333–338
social movements and, 434–437
sociological perspectives on, 13–16, 438–440
technology and, 44–45, 352–354

Social class, 83–84, 148–149, 153, 158–165
See also Social stratification; Socioeconomic status

Social collectivity, 93

Social construction, 125–126

Social control, 11, 17–18, 39–41, 54–56, 118–119, 134–135, 136–139

Social control theory, 121

Social engineer, 26

Social epidemiology, 278

Social group. See Groups

Social inequality,
in developing nations, 157–158
economy and, 369–370
education and, 152–153, 336–338
family and, 245–246
global view of, 155–158, 162–164
industrialization and, 153–155, 167–168, 406–408

mass media and, 169–170, 352
among racial and ethnic minorities, 177–182
religion and, 312–313
stratification and, 152–153, 155–157, 169–170
in the United States, 159–165
See also Minority groups; Social stratification

Social institutions, 54–56, 239, 362

Social integration, 17–18, 40–41, 43–44

Social interaction, 14–15, 49–53, 90–91, 110–111, 123–124, 214, 429–430, 432–434

Socialism, 353, 369–370
See also Economic systems

Socialization,
agencies of, 72–77
biological perspective on, 66–68
as cause of prejudice and discrimination, 181
crime and, 121–124
definition of, 65
in the family, 72–75, 215, 243–245, 260–261
gender and, 69–70, 80–81, 214–217, 287
in Israel, 73
in preindustrial and industrial societies, 82–
life span perspective on, 68–71, 79–81
mass media and, 76–77, 216–217, 265–266
religion and, 323–324
in Samoa, 64–65
in the schools, 73–75, 215–216, 335–339
social class and, 83–84
sociological perspectives on, 68–70, 81–84
stages of, 69–71, 79–81
types of, 77–79
See also Education; Family; Self-concept

Socialized medicine, 299

Social loafing, 107

Social mobility, 147, 150–152, 166–169, 188–189, 336–338, 377–381

Social movements, 323–326, 382, 434–437, 440–441

Social networking websites, 216–217, 383, 385

Social protest, 186

Social reform, 25–27, 165, 377–382

Social reproduction, 338

Social role. See Role

Social science, 10

Social status. See Prestige; Status

Social stratification,
American Indians and, 147
consequences of, 168–171
definition of, 147
dimensions of, 148–152
education and, 168, 332, 336–338
gender and, 151, 209–211, 214–215, 217–222
global perspective on, 155–158, 162–164, 377–381
health and health care and, 168–170, 275, 287–291
in India, 151, 313
industrialization and, 153–155, 379–382
media and technology and, 169–170
race and ethnicity and, 151, 160–164, 177–182

sociological perspectives on, 152–157, 439
types of, 150–152
in the United States, 151, 158–166
See also Power; Prestige; Social class; Socioeconomic status

Social structure,
comparative view of, 54–56, 89–91
components of, 39–41, 48–52, 72, 94
of education, 352
of groups, 94–98, 433–434
of health and health care, 287–291
language and, 42–43, 46–47
religion and, 313–315

Society, 35–36, 54–56

Sociobiology, 66–67

Socioeconomic status (SES),
definition of, 150
divorce and, 249–250
education and, 168
gender and, 151, 217–222
health and, 168–170, 282–284, 287–290
marriage and, 246
measurement of, 158–159
politics and, 367–368
religion and, 318–319, 322
self-esteem and, 170–171
urban structures and, 411–412
See also Social class; Social stratification

Socioemotional roles, 95, 212–213

Sociological consultant, 26–27

Sociological imagination, 8

Sociological perspectives, 12–18
See also Conflict perspective; Functionalist perspective; Interactionist perspective

Sociological practice, 26–27

Sociology,
applied versus basic, 26
and common sense, 9–10
definition of, 5–8
history of, 25–26
research in, 16–25
science of, 8–10
theoretical perspectives of, 12–18

Solidarity, 312

South Africa, 24, 179

Soviet Union, 184

Split labor market, 181, 213–214

Spouse abuse, 170, 245, 262–264

State, 363

Status, 48–50, 94, 149–150
achieved, 48–50, 150–152, 211
ascribed, 48–50, 150–152, 178, 211
master, 48–50, 124, 211
structure in groups, 94, 201–202

Status groups, 149–150

Status inconsistency, 170

Stereotypes, 96, 164, 182, 192–193, 201–202, 223, 294–296

Stigma, 119–120, 128, 182–183, 249, 258, 276–277

Strain, social, 425–426, 427–429, 431–432, 434–435, 436–437

Stress, 52–54

Strikes. See Unions

Students. See Universities and colleges

Subcultures, 46–48, 52–53, 186, 216–217, 409–410

Subjugation, 185
Submission, 186
Suburbs, 404–406
    See also Cities
Success, 37, 121–122
Succession, 410–411, 414–415
Survey research, 19–20
Sustainability, 418
Sweden, 298–299
Switzerland, 186–187
Symbolic interactionism. *See* Interactionist
    perspective
Symbols, 14–18, 42, 69–70, 214, 276–277,
    307–308
Syndicates, 130

T

Taliban in Afghanistan, 51, 315
Taoism, 253, 308, 312
Task roles, 95, 212–213
Teachers, 344, 345, 348
Technology,
    bureaucracy and, 110–111
    cities and, 404–406
    crime and, 125–126
    culture and, 52–53, 352–354
    education and, 345–346, 352–354
    and environmental problems, 416
    and family, 265–266
    gender and, 216–217
    health and health care and, 289, 293
    media and, 349, 352–354, 384
    minorities and, 197–198
    politics and the economy and, 379–385
    population growth and, 398–399, 401
    religion and, 319–321, 322–323
    and sexual behavior, 254–255
    and socialization, 76–77
    and social change, 44, 52–53, 379–382,
        440–441
    social interaction and, 110–111
    social movements and, 440–441
    social stratification and, 169–170, 379–382
    sociological perspectives on, 17–18,
        440–441
    work and, 109–111, 373–377
Teenagers. *See* Adolescence
Televangelists, 322
Television, 76–77, 216–217, 265–266,
    349–351
    See also Mass Media
Territorial imperative, 66
Terrorism, 436
Theistic religion, 308–310
Theoretical perspectives in sociology, 12–18
    See also Conflict perspective; Functionalist
        perspective; Interactionist perspective
Theory, 12–19, 26
Third-party medicine, 293, 296–297
Total institutions, 83
Totalitarianism, 365
Totemism, 308
Tracking, 339
Tradition, 8–10, 38–39, 363
Treaty of Guadalupe Hidalgo, 190
Trobriand Islanders, 47, 239
Tuareg, of Saharan Africa, 5

U

Underclass, 164, 198–200
Unemployment, 139, 184–185, 191–192,
    283, 375–377, 379–382, 396,
    412–413, 443
Unions, labor, 225–226, 348, 373–377, 382,
    425–426, 443–444
United Farm Workers, 190
United Nations Commission on the Status of
    Women, 227
Universities and colleges, 19–20, 346–347
Urban ecology, 410–412
Urban free enterprise zones, 414
Urbanism, perspectives on, 408–410
    See also Cities
Urbanization, 399, 402–408, 410–414, 442
    See also Cities
Urban planning, 412–416
Urban renewal policies, 413–414
Urban subcultures, 409–410

V

Values, 37–41
    Amish, 40–41
    change in, 332–335
    Chinese, 107, 118–119
    crime and, 139
    Japanese, 38–39, 78, 139, 195
    mass media and, 52–53, 197–198,
        352–354, 385
    in organizations, 105–107
    population and, 398–403
    religion and, 39–41, 253, 312
    Samoan, 64–65
    in scientific research, 23–25
    socialization and, 72–73, 92–93, 181,
        332–335
    United States mainstream, 4–5, 37–38,
        52–53, 152, 183
    of University students, 19–20
Variables, 11–12, 20–21
Venezuela, 157–158
Verification of theories, 11
Veterans Administration, 404–405
Video games, 76–77, 216–217, 350
Vietnamese, 253–254
Vietnam War, 97–98, 384
Violence,
    collective, 428–429, 436
    in the family, 262–264
    gang, 19, 128
    mass media and, 52–53, 76–77, 265–266, 350
    mental illness and, 128–129
    race and, 178–179, 184–185, 193
    sources of, 211
    women and, 216–217
Violent crime, 129–130, 136–140. *See also*
    Crime
Voodoo, 285, 306
Voting, 366–368, 371
Voting Rights Act of 1965, 188
Vouchers, for school choice, 342

W

War, 44, 66–67, 97–98, 147, 384
    See also Violence

War on drugs, 252
Wealth, 147–149, 155–157, 377–379
White-collar crime, 131–132
White flight, 202
Women,
    adult life stages of, 79–81
    in business, 104, 228–230
    in developing nations, 225–226, 402–403
    discrimination against, 181, 217–223
    divorce and, 249–251
    education and, 217–218, 335, 402–403
    employment of, 212–213, 217–223,
        225–226, 228–230, 256–257, 294–296,
        375–377, 402–403
    empowerment of, 229
    in the family, 45, 225–226, 228, 245–246,
        256–257, 402–403
    global perspective on, 224–227
    in health care, 51–54, 283–285, 294–296
    income and, 219–222
    mass media and, 52–53, 216–217, 265–266
    in the military, 222–223
    as minority group, 178–179, 217
    in organizations, 104
    politics and, 224, 230–231
    population growth and, 402–403
    poverty and, 162–164, 219–222
    in preindustrial societies, 44, 209–211
    rape and, 127, 129–130, 135–136
    religion and, 209–211
    role strain and, 51–52
    violence and, 52–53, 127, 129–130,
        135–136, 216–217
    See also Gender; Gender inequality
Women's Movement. *See* Feminist movement
Women's Suffrage Amendment, 227
Work,
    ethic, 37, 40–41, 195
    industrialization and, 212–213, 373–377
    in postindustrial societies, 108–109,
        373–377, 443–444
    research on, 22–23, 382
    technology and, 108–109
    women and, 79–81, 104–105, 212–213,
        217–219, 228–230, 256–257
    See also Employment
Worker empowerment, 376
Worker productivity, 22–23
World Bank, 157, 378–382
World-system theory, 155–158, 334,
    377–380, 442
World Trade Organization (WTO),
    378–382, 443
World War II, 97, 213, 348

Y

Yakuza, 139
Yanomamo, 89–90, 178
Yoruba, of Nigeria, 306
Youth, 52–53, 76–77, 128, 335–336
Yugoslavia, 184–185

Z

Zuni Indians, 42